AFIPS
CONFERENCE PROCEEDINGS

DENNIS J. FRAILEY
Editor and Program Chairman

RUSSELL K. BROWN
Conference Chairman

1984
NATIONAL COMPUTER CONFERENCE

AFIPS PRESS

1899 PRESTON WHITE DRIVE
RESTON, VIRGINIA 22091

July 9–12, 1984
Las Vegas, Nevada

The ideas and opinions expressed herein are solely those of the authors and are not necessarily representative of or endorsed by the 1984 National Computer Conference or the American Federation of Information Processing Societies, Inc.

Library of Congress Catalog Card Number 80-649583
ISSN 0095-6880
ISBN 0-88283-043-0

AFIPS PRESS
1899 Preston White Drive
Reston, Virginia 22091

Printed in the United States of America

Preface

RUSSELL K. BROWN
1984 NCC Chairman

The purpose of the National Computer Conference is to provide an atmosphere in which designers, suppliers, users, managers, educators, and representatives of government and society at large can meet and interact. Discussions of new technical developments, as well as national and international issues and challenges facing the information processing community, are encouraged.

This year's discussions and developments are included, for the most part, in this anniversary Volume 53 of the *Proceedings* of the National Computer Conference, completing 12 years as the world's premier computer exposition.

The decision to chair a second National Computer Conference may well be one of the more major choices one makes in even a complicated lifetime. Certainly this choice was compounded by the change in site from Houston to Las Vegas, made only 15 months before the Conference date. Perhaps a few words on that move are in order.

In Fall 1982 the NCC Committee and Board were again faced with a dilemma of great magnitude. After the move of the 1982 NCC from New York to Houston—because of space (3,200 booth units) and facility considerations—and the plan to use Houston in 1984, the plan for 1984 was also scrapped because of the same considerations. With a need to expand yet another 600 booth units, only Las Vegas and Chicago could house the show. And since Chicago is the site of NCC '85, the decision seemed obvious.

Compounding the decision, however, was the fact all NCCs of the past were presented in a major population center. Over the past four years, local and nearby interest added as much as 50,000 to the total attendance. It was obvious that a total nationalization of the NCC, with massive publicity, would be needed to turn out crowds approaching those of recent years. This week, we hope, you will be able to observe our success.

A major show in Las Vegas in July presents its own special challenges. Thirty thousand hotel rooms guarantee close-in housing for those attending. And certainly no one can fault Las Vegas' ability to entertain its guests. In addition, you will see *no* shortcuts or shortcomings in the presentation of this NCC.

What you will see is a display of 650 companies filling 3,800 booth units for a new NCC record. You will be exposed to a high-quality program, high-quality Professional Development Seminars, a major keynote address, a special Pioneer Day program, and numerous other attractions that we feel will make this a noteworthy week. It is the intention of the CSC to give attending registrants all the positive values of moving to a new city and to make any negatives as invisible as possible.

An example of this is the largest busing expenditure in Las Vegas history for the various round trips between hotels and the Conference during the warm summer days.

If I may return to our program, I may be able to elicit in you a feeling of satisfaction to match the pride I feel. The program is made permanent by the archival record of the *Proceedings*. Here we capture for posterity the most current reports on recent achievements and new applications, on advances at the frontiers of computer science and technology.

Dr. Dennis Frailey of the Texas Instruments corporation was buffeted in mid-preparation of this program and these *Proceedings* by the move. Through all the personnel shuffling and turmoil, he managed to steer a straight course toward a superior presentation.

Dennis recognized, early on, that the registrant has only three days, on the average, to assimilate all aspects of an NCC. His first decision was to direct that—with a superior Professional Development Program and 12 football fields of exhibits—the program as defined in the past be intensely screened for shortcomings. His Committee introduced a much finer mesh in their screen than has ever been used before. The number of papers and sessions are down slightly from what you have seen in previous NCCs, but we are confident that their value to you will be high.

Volunteers, for a conference of this magnitude, number in the hundreds. They are members of the NCC Sponsoring Societies and the other AFIPS Constituent Societies. To these groups and their participating members I would like to give my heartiest thanks, particularly in view of the truncated schedules on which we were all operating.

To the Las Vegas Convention Bureau, which greatly eased our move into a new city, my thanks for the myriad arrangements and assistance you provided.

To the NCC Board and Committee, who well knew the danger to NCC '84 if plans were not well organized, my thanks for your confidence and support.

To the AFIPS Headquarters Staff and all the members of our CSC, thank you for your dedication, time, and effort you have contributed to an ongoing tradition of excellence.

To my wife, who in 1981 asked, "Why?" in 1982 asked, "How can I help?" and in 1983 said, "Let me be a part of this," you know my thoughts.

And finally, to ten of the previous NCC Chairmen, thank you for your assistance, guidance, and inventiveness. Much of what you created is embodied here.

Introduction

DENNIS J. FRAILEY
1984 NCC Program Chairman

1984! Orwell's year is here! Have events happened as Orwell predicted in *1984?* Have computers become the tool of those who would suppress our individual freedoms? These were the obvious questions when the program committee first sat down in fall 1982 to develop a theme for the 1984 NCC. Each of us reread Orwell's classic. We discussed ideas for a conference theme that would truly represent the current state of computing. And we were struck by a simple fact: computers are being used today in many ways that were totally unexpected. The choreographer whose computer provides a breakthrough in explaining his ideas to dancers; the businessman whose spread sheet program turned his company around financially; the physically handicapped whose voice-activated personal computers give them control over their environment—these and others whose uses of computers were only recently the stuff of science fiction serve to point out what is really important and unique about computing today—creative use of computers by individuals.

The availability of computers to individuals has evolved from timeshared mainframe systems to minicomputers to personal computers. Each step has provided a significant increase in availability and power through dramatic cost reduction. Data communication technology has kept pace in recent years, enabling a truly worldwide system of information exchange to be developed. What is important about this technology, and indeed what is anti-Orwellian about it, is that control is migrating away from the center—toward the individual. This is what's different about computers today. This is what promises to continue the computer revolution. And this creative use by individuals—in the office, the factory, and the home—is the theme that ties together the diverse topics addressed by the NCC program.

The program consists of over 90 sessions, presented over a four-day period. Ten topic areas or tracks represent the committee's way of dividing a broad set of subjects into manageable components. In addition to a wide range of sessions on such topics as hardware and architecture, software, management, automation of office and factory, databases, data communications, personal computers and societal issues, we've augmented the program in the areas of artificial intelligence and computer graphics and entertainment—areas where those attending recent NCCs have shown particularly high interest. We've also oriented the focus toward the questions we believe are uppermost in the minds of NCC attendees: "What's new?" and "How will it affect me?"

Although this *Proceedings* volume contains more than 80 papers, they represent less than a third of the total NCC program. Panel discussions occupy more than half of the program, and some of the sessions include presentations on topics too recent to meet the publication deadline for the *Proceedings,* such as the very latest microprocessors and networks. The *Proceedings* are organized by track, and each section begins with an overview of the whole track—panel sessions as well as papers. For those attending, this serves as a guide to the program as a whole. For those unable to attend, it serves to give the flavor of the program and helps to put the papers into perspective. Because of the frequent overlap of topics, readers are likely to find sessions and papers of interest in several of the tracks.

The 1984 NCC program is the combined effort of almost 1,000 people, most of whom are unpaid volunteers. This includes 12 program committee members; more than 90 session organizers and chairs; almost 300 presenters, panelists, and authors of technical papers; and nearly 500 referees who helped us select the technical papers. (There were also several hundred people whose high-quality papers and session proposals could not be accommodated.) In addition, recognition must go to at least a dozen AFIPS staff members; the program committee staff, headed by Jean Presnell; and the spouses and employers of all of the above, whose forbearance and assistance made their contributions possible. All of us sincerely hope that each person attending NCC will find the program stimulating, helpful, and educational.

CONTENTS

The automated office

Michael Alsup, Track Chair

The Office Automation track at this year's NCC includes 12 sessions rich with ideas and information. The contributions that office systems can make to productivity and managerial effectiveness are reviewed from functional, technical, strategic, and end-user perspectives; and the depth and breadth of office automation is presented by a number of industry experts.

The current state of the art in office automation is outlined in the first session, entitled "Office Automation: State of the Art." Noted consultants summarize current trends in the marketplace and analyze vendor offerings.

The key to the implementation of successful office systems is to identify user requirements and select equipment that satisfies those requirements. Two sessions outline approaches that have been successful in the definition of user requirements. In "Analyzing Managers'/Professionals' needs for OA," a consultant will discuss how to evaluate user requirements for office systems, and representatives from two organizations that have recently evaluated these requirements and implemented advanced office systems will share their experiences. In a second session, "Office Automation in Large Organizations," two organizations that have implemented very large and integrated office systems summarize their experiences and outline their successes and failures. Organizations that are considering their requirements for office automation have a valuable opportunity in these sessions to learn from others who have pioneered in this area.

As microcomputers and word processors have become more powerful, additional attention is being focused on design and functionality in office systems. Vendors are integrating the delivery of a number of functions and application systems into a single work station with powerful communications capabilities and a standard user interface to all applications. Four sessions explore the changing role of work stations in the office. "Design and Functionality in Office Systems" examines how the user aspects of office systems are evolving. A consultant summarizes the trends and likely market direction and evaluates several well-known products. A second session, "Management Work Stations and Integrated Information Systems," examines three new work stations that include powerful capabilities for data, voice, and video; and it evaluates the issues involved in the successful implementation of these systems. "The Micro-Mainframe Connection" explores benefits and pitfalls in the connection of microcomputers and mainframe computers from software, communications, and end user points of view. Finally, the role and potential of voice in office systems will be explored in "Voice Technology in the Office." These sessions are especially useful to organizations considering the role and fast-evolving capabilities of work stations in their organizations.

The strategic and managerial implications of office automation are explored in two sessions. "Strategic Systems Planning: Art, Science, or Nonsense?" explores whether it is possible to develop a strategic plan for office automation in the face of rapid and profound technological change. "Office Automation Selection Criteria: A Q&A Session" explores and defines appropriate selection criteria for office automation systems from a management point of view.

Communications networks are becoming the nervous systems of large organizations. Three office automation sessions examine the impact of developments in communication technology for the office environment. The advantages and disadvantages of three different approaches for integrating office systems equipment are presented in "Integration Alternatives and Strategies." Representatives of a well-known mainframe vendor, a PBX vendor, and a local area network vendor outline the short- and longer-term advantages of their systems architectures in the office.

One of the principal advantages of a local area network is the attachment of devices whose capabilities are shared among the work stations on the network. These devices include intelligent copiers, electronic file cabinets, communications gateways, and mainframe computers. "Shared Network Resources" summarizes the advantages and capabilities of these resources, and two leading vendors summarize their offerings.

Electronic mail is an important and practical way to improve productivity and reduce costs. It can be broadly defined as the transmission of messages by electronic means. "Electronic Mail: Current Developments" summarizes the alternatives available in electronic mail, and three vendors with leading-edge products summarize their offerings.

Implementing a large office automation system—how to make it work

by JACK GOLDEN and STUART BELL
The MITRE Corporation
McLean, Virginia

ABSTRACT

This paper discusses the implementation of a large office automation system to be used by nondata processing as well as data processing staff, i.e., the knowledge worker. At its completion the system will encompass more than 1,000 terminals (one terminal per office). The paper covers the nature of the basic system, IBM's Professional Office System (PROFS), what it does, how it functions, the extent of use, and how to encourage potential users to use it. The paper reviews training procedures from one-on-one to higher ratios and the reasoning behind them, and goes over in detail the nature of the "innovation" curve. Also reviewed are the computer performance and the Local Area Network (broadband with Sytek bus interface units). We currently serve more than 500 users with around 300 terminals already distributed.

INTRODUCTION

We discuss here the implementation of a large office automation (OA) system and how we made it work. By and large, we're talking about one terminal per office, or a total of 1,000 terminals, covering nine buildings within a two-mile radius.

Our discussion will go over the nature of the corporation, a nonprofit organization that does business primarily with the federal government. We will review our office automation architecture and design goals, our implementation strategy in terms of our basic system, the pilot group used in developing the system, and how we controlled additions to the group.

And most importantly, we'll cover what actually happened in terms of acceptance of OA concepts by the pilot group, communications problems, and wide-implementation problems.

Corporation Background

The MITRE Corporation is a not-for-profit systems engineering company chartered in the public interest. MITRE was established in 1958 to assist the Air Force, but today assists most federal civilian agencies, as well as other DoD agencies in the areas of command and control systems, information systems, as well as the energy/environmental area. The major product of the corporation is information, utilizing the media of reports, specifications, memos, briefings, etc.—paper in general.

We cover here office automation activities supporting the 1,500 or so staff at the Washington center. We will allude to other systems used throughout the rest of the corporation and how we interface with them. Additionally, we wish to stress the implementation problems and solutions, not the specific hardware or software components of the system.

OA at MITRE

MITRE entered the office automation area in 1972 when we developed a centralized word processing support facility with an administration support center. During this period we had two shifts (eight operators each shift, working six days per week at its high point). In 1976 we migrated to the decentralized word processing concept (approximately 40 word processing terminals off cluster controllers). From 1976 until 1980, word processing and computer useage was growing at a rapid rate.

In 1981, the Corporate management decided it was time to develop an integrated plan for the spread of information services to our professionals, secretaries, and administrative staff. An internal study group, consisting of four senior managers, was chartered to review the computer and telecommunication support needs of the company. The committee's work was completed in the fall of 1981 with corporate management's acceptance of a "target system," a four-phase implementation plan, and authorization and funding for the plan's first two phases.

The system was designed to account for the heterogeneous user population in terms of data processing skills, typing skills, the nature of work being performed, and the level of each person in the company. The design encompassed hundreds of terminals and tens of computers with multiple vendors making up the system.

The target system networked computer resources, allowing the users to share data, programs, and special-purpose peripherals. We also strongly wanted to have a local area network that would support video in terms of both security (e.g., badge readers from remote buildings) and instructional TV (e.g., the lunch-time seminars).

Based on the 1981 recommendations of the committee, our 1983 architecture evolved to a fully connected system. We are basically utilizing a Sytek LocalNet 20 bus interface unit in our broadband data distribution system. We now have connectivity and information transfer among all of our major segments, internally in the Washington Center and with the outside world.

Implementing a Large-Scale OA System

We would now like to discuss how our implementation strategy obtained a workable office automation system.

There are four major components that make the system work:

- the computer system
- the local area network
- user acceptance
- applications software

Our implementation strategy was as follows. In late 1981 we evaluated the available software options in the office automation area. Our primary concern, beyond the normal OA functions, was that the software reside on our IBM mainframe. The Professional Office System (PROFS) was chosen because of cost, maturity of the product, breadth of applications, and relative ease of use. 1982 was spent debugging, customizing, testing the product, and implementing a prototype system. By mid-1983 we were ready for corporate-wide implementation.

PROFS is a menu-driven system; that is, the capabilities are accessed through menus (or lists). There are three main menus and numerous submenus. The display terminal's Program Function Keys (PF Keys) are used to move between menus and to invoke specific functions. The system was customized over time to offer the various user segments different levels of information. These included (what we deemed important) management needs, and staff needs.

As was stated, the PROFs architecture allows for the ready access of information not provided by the basic software. The basic software offers general OA tools such as electronic mail, calendar functions, electronic filing/retrieving, reminder functions, and document preparation.

From March to August 1983 we undertook several studies. These included a system evaluation, communication options between buildings (statistical multiplexing, microwave option, etc.), a definition of our FY84 configuration, a definition of an adequate support structure, a finalized training mechanism, and, of course, a study of the role of the personal computer in our environment.

Starting in August 1983 and extending to August 1984, we have been installing an additional 180 terminals (which translates to an additional 270 or so users to the system). This is Phase 1 of across-the-company implementation. FY85 will be an additional 180 terminals, and so on until there will be one terminal per office.

The Local Area Network

For our local area network we used a broadband CATV system utilizing Sytek LocalNet 20 system. LocalNet is a packet-switched local area data communications network providing communication functions and standard broadband CATV coaxial cables. The properties of a broadband system permit LocalNet to construct independent subnetworks—terminal channels. Each of those subnetworks provides data communications for hundreds of users. In the summer of 1982, we initiated a limited test of the system within one building to ensure functional compatibility of all components. In 1983 we extended the network to cover our five remote buildings, all within a two-mile radius. Our problems arose when we could not physically connect the buildings with a cable. We experimented with a host of alternatives; these included telephone lines at 9,600 bits per second, microwave transmission at a very high effective data rate, laser transmission, and the use of statistical multiplexors. We are currently utilizing all of these for one reason or another.

The LocalNet medium provides the high band with 300 to 400 MHZ proven reliability and multidrop capability required for growing data communications requirements. Analog video or voice applications can share the same cable using dedicated frequency channels. A single channel can accommodate approximately 100 simultaneous virtual circuits.

Getting The System "Used"

We would now like to discuss how one goes about generating productive use of the system. Nothing is more important than having senior management commitment; however, 100% commitment is really not needed to have successful implementation. Management should not be negative. Once this commitment is in place, the road to success can then be followed.

Aside from the typical notes and messages on any office automation system, it is important to have tools on the system that would be helpful to the knowledge worker or the professional. We chose to have project financial information as the first application on the system for management use. This financial planning and analysis tool proved to be most useful inasmuch as the system was used immediately (in other words, users took the time to become familiar with the system because they were getting something useful out of it). People will not take the time to learn a system that does not have useful information: if all they have are the note and message functions, its utility is small, (although these functions are important and some OA systems are designed just around notes).

We suggest that the system population be enriched as soon as possible. We added approximately 15 terminals per month (25 users per month), but doubling this number would have been more productive. Additionally, the service divisions or entities of the corporation should be made part of the system as soon as possible. This allows the support people to become productive almost instantaneously. The message here is to not be discouraged by the lack of enthusiasm among the users. At the beginning, having a sparse population is like having a telephone with no one to call.

In an early, sparse system, the financial systems and other individual productivity aids predominate. As the system becomes richer and the conductivity fuller, mail and documents become the most popular features.

We would now like to discuss the implications of having a "rich" vs. "sparse" network in terms of individual use of the system. From observation, the typical nondata processing user can be thought of as going through five phases. We call the first phase *tinkering* or learning. Depending on the number of people on the system, this can last anywhere from one to six months, with the average around three months. During this time the unsophisticated user (not data processing oriented) learns how to use the machine, not that it actually takes three months to learn, but rather that the user is "too busy" to read the manual or ask questions. After the initial tinkering stage, there is a two- to three-month *getting acquainted* period. The user starts to generate mail, type a few documents, and use some of the applications on the system. No (real) productivity is gained during this time, just an awareness of what can be done. We call the next phase the *suggestions* phase. During this phase the user realizes the potential of the computer and becomes an instant expert on how to do things better. Suggestions come pouring in on what to put on the system and how to make it more productive. Overlapping this suggestion phase is the *commitment* phase. At this point in the user profile, he will not move to another office when office moving time comes around unless there is a terminal in his office (similar to a telephone). The next phase is the most important, the *synergistic* phase. It is at this time that individual users help and compliment one another on the system, and we finally see corporate productivity increases rather than just individual productivity gains. From beginning to end this cycle can take anywhere from 6 to 18 months depending on the background of the individuals involved. This is why we previously stated, "Don't get discouraged during the early life of the system or when suggestions come pouring in."

Initially, we spent about three months (one person) in developing the training manual and procedures. For the first 50 users, we trained on a one-to-one basis; for the next 100 users, we trained on a one-to-three ratio, with one-to-seven for the remainder of the early population, (the first 250 users). Our philosophy was that we should build a strong foundation during the first 50 users, so that they could be called upon to answer questions from their coworkers (the next generation of users). This philosophy works out very well.

Concurrent with training, we established a user services group (three staff); one telephone number was established by which all questions could be handled. We also instituted monthly user meetings where innovations and particular questions could be discussed and guest lecturers presented. We are now starting to use computer-aided instruction.

Although we feel that our initial training mode worked out well, we recommend a slightly different approach. More effort should be spent in the development of training material, and several skill-level/position-level materials should definitely be prepared. A training ratio of one-to-five with a large-screen terminal projection, followed by a 30-minute one-to-one follow-up is recommended.

Once the network is enriched, users tend to help each other; so, the task of training should actually decrease as users are added to the system. Although there are more individuals to train, there are more training aides around.

We keep an accurate record of *all* questions and comments that come into our user services group as an example of the problems and questions that arise. The format is as follows:

- General PROFS (five categories)
- General "other" software
- Hardware (when system is down)
- Administrative (training requests (other than PROFS); documentation)
- software
- Word Processing (Wang or NBI questions)
- UNIX
- Cable Plant
- Personal Computer
- Miscellaneous
- Consulting (more than 15 minutes on the phone)

Once a significant number of users have been added to the network, system reliability is a major issue. Therefore, it is prudent to have accurate records of why the system, or any component, is down and what the "fix" or resolution is. This is important, since you will often hear, "the system is always down," when actually it may have been down for only five minutes during a given week.

In regard to our local area network (LAN), we found that there is plenty to choose from. But remember, a LAN may not be for you. In our installation the cost for the backbone cable ran from $5 to $10 per liner foot, depending on the building layout size (e.g., needing amplifiers). This averages $300 to $1,000 per drop or tap, depending on the building configuration. For comparison, point-to-point averages $500 per terminal.

One important item is new skills; the type of person needed to run this type of activity is usually not within the organization. And, of course, the LAN facilitates office moves.

One is always asked, What are your productivity gains? How many people have you let go?, etc. The answer to the first is, "don't know and probably won't," and the answer to the second is, "none. . .but you can be sure, things get done faster, more efficient, and with better results." We usually don't get rid of people, but redefine their roles.

We make *no* attempt to get a productivity figure, but we do make an attempt to evaluate the system. This is done in several ways): first, we get user feedback on a daily basis; then meetings and our PROFS Answer Line (PAL) provide additional feedback. We also investigate the usefulness of the system by means of questionnaires, telephone interviews, and usage data.

Most importantly, we get feedback on how the system has changed the way we do business, both as individuals and as a group. As individuals, we see uses other than OA functions being used, e.g., spreadsheet. As a group, we see reports going electronically to our sponsors, remote sites sending their documents for review back to the main office, and more dialog among and between groups. We see the service organizations modernizing in large ways.

Health Effects

When the potential health effects of using VDTs came up, we performed a literature review in the area of terminal effect on operator fatigue. The study covered optical, musculoskeletal, morale, and radiation issues. The medical literature revealed little risk in all areas. We realize that the specific area of radiation is not satisfactorily documented and is still an area of volatile discussion. Additionally, VDT use and eye strain are still being investigated.

The Computer

In this section, we describe the facilities we employ to deliver the office automation service to our customers.

The overriding goal in an office automation environment is excellent response. The most important aspect of excellent response is choosing the correct definition of excellent. At the MITRE Washington Computer Center (MWCC), we aim for a general consensus that our response is excellent. Customers are encouraged to send notes or mail to the computing center management whenever they see a response problem. Regular presentations are made to the community describing our response measurement techniques, and as a consulting company, we have an internal interest in both the techniques and the results.

Office automation makes everyone neighbors and removes (at least in its initial phases) the traditional management lines of filtering. Everyone becomes a performance expert, everyone wants a hand in running the computing center; and everyone has instant access to everyone else. Thus, the systems team must be selected and trained to be customer-oriented; and although we have a user services section, each member of the systems team and operations staff must always be aware, and willing, to work with any user or customer who is having a problem with the delivered system.

Our present configuration is an IBM 4341 with 16 million characters of main storage. Please note that this is a historical accident and not an endorsement of either IBM or the 4341 product line. While this device serves our needs very well, MITRE is in no way suggesting this as a recommended device, nor are we in the position to comment on the strength of this compared with other, similar configurations proposed by other vendors.

The local area network has substantial performance impact since it presents each terminal image to the central computer as though it were locally attached to the CPU, thus yielding substantial (over one second) performance improvements. The customer on the remote end of the local network sees these performance improvements directly.

The path between the central computer and the remote terminal is operated at 9,600 bits per second, roughly 1,000 characters per second. In a normal IBM remote terminal environment, the screen of a remote terminal remains blank until the full image is transmitted (1,920 characters plus overhead). Thus, in a normal multibuilding campus environment such as MITRE, the fastest response that can be delivered is a woeful two seconds per screen (assuming zero CPU).

Performance in a growth environment requires an understanding of both the growth effects and the prediction of added load to be placed on the system. As we described earlier, we have a clear understanding of our expected load growth. We are adding 15 terminals per month for the next three years (approximately). The main effect is in the increase in logged-on-users. We are growing at the rate of approximately five users per month (about one peak logged-on user per each three new terminals).

The number of active users is a better indication of the load on the central facility. It is well known that a CPU will support a large number of terminals if they are not used. In our office automation environment, logged-on terminals tend to be active because of a strange anomaly of our office automation software: it keeps a clock on the screen up to date by refreshing the screen once each minute. Thus, the active user count is also growing by about one user for each three terminals added to the network.

Capacity comes in chunks; a machine is typically either upgraded or replaced whenever there is insufficient capacity to support the required workload. Given this fact, we can expect response to degrade slowly as the user load grows until the response goals are no longer being met consistently. At that point (or ideally, just before), a capacity upgrade is required. This, in turn, causes an improvement in response and the cycle starts again.

There are many elaborate tools for capacity planning on the market. Each attempts to predict, based on past performance, when the present hardware will become saturated and require upgrade. If you are fortunate to locate a measure of performance that correlates well with response, you may save a lot of money and time. In our case, interactive response time is reported by the system. The reported figure is the inboard response and does not include communication software, line, and terminal delay. The time the user sees is not as good as this number, but it is a constant ratio.

We have determined from previous experiments that interactive response time below 200 milliseconds is excellent. We are not claiming that the end user sees response within 200 milliseconds of the pressing of a function key. While we believe it is close, we have not measured this number and can make no such claims. We prefer, however, to state that the response delivered is well correlated to the number presented, and the majority of our users feel that response is excellent when numbers below 200 milliseconds are reported by the system reporting software.

During a typical day, six to seven seconds per minute are devoted automatically by the computer scheduling software to the interactive OA users. This low percentage of the CPU resource (10%–12%) is sufficient to provide a repeatedly measured response time of less than two-tenths of a second for all interactive transactions of a short duration. Those interactive functions of a longer duration, such as database queries and massive report generations, are detected by the computer scheduler and scheduled over a one- or two-second period by the remaining 80% to 90% of the CPU resource.

Modern disk subsystems provide a large amount of data per disk. We have found that our disk access mechanism will serve between 15 and 30 simultaneous office automation users, providing for their storage and systems support needs in an efficient and timely manner. Currently disks yield about 10 million characters of storage per user by just providing sufficient disk drives to meet the needs of system responsiveness.

This leads to a very well balanced condition in a modern operating system environment that permits the mixing of system and user data. Each increment of user growth requires more storage for private data and more access arms to ensure excellent system response time. Both are delivered in a balanced package with modern disk subsystems.

Real memory is the critical factor in delivering excellent performance in a central support office automation configuration. Each vendor's scheme for mapping virtual storage into real memory differs in its implementation detail; however, all must be provided with sufficient real storage to ensure that most of a user's program is in real storage whenever required.

In our environment, we feel that a program portion, or page, once referenced should remain in real memory for a minimum of 10 seconds before being replaced by another user's pages. Our current 16 million bytes of real memory constantly better this goal for a peak of 180 simultaneous users.

Bottlenecks always exist in meeting the stated performance goals for any computing center. In an office automation environment, they extend beyond the traditional CPU and DISK SPACE numbers normally considered in a batch environment. The nontraditional bottlenecks extend to printers, communication ports, and terminals. High-quality printers are a must in an office automation environment. It is a myth that electronic mail replaces paper. Try to read a 500-line message on a video terminal. A hundred or so lines into it, you automatically reach for a magic marker and circle something to go back to for further study. The result, in our case, is needing a cloth and a spray bottle to clean the screen several times per day.

Our customers depend on the timeliness of the printing facility to meet their production schedules. Several very high quality printers must be utilized to ensure sufficient capacity and redundancy for any expected action. For example, this briefing was prepared electronically on an IBM 6670 LASER printer using software developed at the MWCC. The final charts were previewed on the terminal and only a single, camera-ready copy was produced on the printer.

You might think this would reduce the printing demands. Actually, the opposite has proven to be true. Our customers were expecting several-day turnaround for the production of high-quality VUGRAPHs by the reprographics department. We have shortened that time to 15 minutes. Unfortunately, the customer has also shortened the time before the briefing to work on the presentation by a like amount. Thus, the computing center must be able to deliver very rapid turnaround with extreme reliability whenever the VUGRAPH software is invoked.

CPU BUSY is the first number everyone wants to know when looking at response. It is not an important number in an OA environment since BUSY is normally a measure of batch rather than interactive workload. A better number is the number of seconds per minute the CPU spends servicing the interactive workload.

A channel is a path from memory to a direct access device, tape, or communications controller. In our environment, no more than six disk drives share a single channel. You may be able to support more or fewer disks per channel depending on the speed of the pack and the size of the disks.

There is no single value that can be determined for all hardware and software configurations; however, any one configuration should work for a balanced configuration, acquiring hardware and relocating data to meet this need.

In the environment shown, we began an aggressive balancing program in January and are now running a balanced I/O configuration.

Real memory is the critical determination of response in office automation or any other environment employing IBM equipment. We suspect real memory is the critical response factor in any environment. Real memory usage is a difficult item to measure precisely. We have examined many different reports to try and identify a single number of sets of numbers that characterize the utilization of real storage in our environment.

In doing this, we examined the dynamics of paging in our computing center. Our system operates in a demand paging environment. This means that a user's program does not require storage sufficient to hold the entire program before it can begin operating. The result, in a memory-constrained environment, is frequent suspension of the program while additional portions of the code or data are brought into memory from a backing storage device such as a disk.

When a user's program finishes executing, the code and data remain in storage for some time until that area of memory must be reused by other users for their code or data. Ideally, an active user will always have all code and data in storage for each execution of a program. Since OA customers tend to perform the same functions over and over, there is generally little or no paging or other I/O activity required; thus, excellent response is possible without exotic system tuning.

In our environment there is a table, called the CORETABLE (historical interest in core memory), that is scanned to find free pages. The system reports the rate of scanning of this table (SCAN RATE) in one of its regular performance charts. The change in SCAN RATE took place when we added an additional eight million characters of real memory to our overloaded computer.

SCAN TIME, the reciprocal of the SCAN RATE, is a derived number that IBM does not directly report in their performance software. A portion of a user program will remain in real memory for 10 seconds if it is not utilized. For example, if an OA customer uses a program section more often than once per 10 seconds, no I/O will result when the SCAN TIME is longer than 10 seconds.

There is a tendency to understate the costs of implementing an OA program throughout the company. Management is prone to forget the second-order costs and focus on the cost of the terminal and the terminal support cable plant.

Often there is a CPU replacement or upgrade required. There is always more printout, and printout of a more urgent nature. In our environment, much of the new printout can be of a sensitive nature (performance reviews, interview reports) and must be specially handled and retained for the users in a dispatch area.

The training demands jump. Prior to OA, our systems programmers conducted classes informally, as our user community was small and stable. Now, we have a very large percentage of nondata processing users with urgent training demands. Frequently, these training demands are placed on us by high executives who are satisfied only with, "Yes" or "Yes, sir," as answers to our schedule conflicts.

Documentation must often be written (or rewritten) to address customers who have never used a central computer before. Have you ever pondered how many different ways to spell ENTER as you survey the range of terminals that use RETURN or various graphic symbols rather than one consistent symbol?

Everyone wants to manage the computing staff. Systems team members suddenly get messages from vice presidents and are expected to be at their beck and call. Substantial interpersonnel training is required of the systems team. Members who were accustomed to hiding are suddenly connected electronically with everyone in the company.

Operations and system members must become diplomats! We have replaced nearly our entire systems team since the office automation project began. New systems programmers are selected as much for tact as for technical skills—it is a myth that systems people are hard to deal with and each systems programmer tries to cultivate that myth. There is a large group of professional systems programmers who understand they are responsible for many millions of dollars and long for the respect and responsibility that such investments demand. Our staff has an excellent attitude toward our customers and recognizes that each of them directly contributes to support our mortgage, hobbies, growth, and professional aspirations.

One of the good (and bad) side effects of a centralized office automation configuration is that everyone in the company becomes a performance expert. Terms such as Q1TIME, SRM, RMF, PAGE RATE, and such are not the measure of excellence in performance. Use terms such as excellent, good, fair, and poor; and encourage complaints when response is other than excellent.

Measure everything easily available in your environment and look for items that correlate well. Hunt for those numbers that change sharply with a small change in response. Consider yourself, or your performance expert, as a detective. Request regular reports and expect presentations on trends and bottlenecks on a frequent basis.

Excellent performance is mandatory for office automation. Our software performance measurement tools report the introduce response time, excluding network delays, as 200 milliseconds maximum. This number is not an absolute measurement, but an indication of excellence. Users are consistently satisfied when the number is two-tenths of a second or below and begin to grumble when it rises above three-tenths of a second.

You must rethink and understand your goals in a large OA environment. Batch production must take second place on the machine dedicated to supporting the office automation customer.

The growth of the computing terminal network will be a byproduct of OA. The decision to introduce OA carries the decision to provide a very large number of terminals for use by professionals and support staff. It is MITRE's goal to install a terminal in every office occupied by professional or support staff. You cannot expect people to walk down the hall to use the telephone or read their morning mail.

User support is absolutely required in an OA environment. We select a portion of our user support team from the secretarial staff to ensure a minimum of jargon and ensure a goo relationship between the customers and the support peopl

Computer hardware and architectures

Fayé Briggs, Track Chair

Achieving high performance in computer systems depends not only on using faster and more reliable hardware devices but also on major improvements in computer architecture and processing techniques. The Computer Hardware and Architecture track focuses on these issues. The track is composed of nine sessions that address the new generation of high-performance computers. The topics of these sessions are

1. Trends in Supercomputer Systems
2. The Fifth Generation
3. VLSI Design
4. 32-Bit Microprocessors
5. Attached Numerical Processors
6. New Microprocessor-Based Computer Architectures
7. Multiprocessor Systems
8. Distributed Processors
9. System Reliability

"Trends in Supercomputer Systems: Design and Use," a panel session, discusses five major issues: new system organizations, design trends, application software, the implications in operating systems and languages, and the Japanese effort in these areas. Another panel, "The Fifth Generation Revisited," follows the very successful panel on the same subject last year. The objective of this year's panel is to present an updated report on the status of the various worldwide programs that are fifth-generation computer research and development efforts.

"VLSI Systems" is a paper session investigating the impact of VLSI designs and structures on computer architecture and hardware. The session starts with a tutorial paper on the status of VLSI. A design automation system and a sample design and application of a VLSI co-processor will be presented.

The new generation of "32-Bit Microprocessors" and microcomputers is organized as a paper session. This session looks at the organization of these new high-performance microprocessors and the new challenge for integrating them into systems. They display advanced architectural features often found in minicomputers and mainframes. Examples of features presented are pipelining, prefetching schemes, larger virtual and physical address spaces, and data buffering schemes. "New Microprocessor-Based Computer Architectures" takes a look at complete computer systems based on these newer microprocessors.

The next paper session, "Attached Numerical Processors," looks at the software and hardware approaches to implementing floating- and fixed-point arithmetics for use in the new generation of powerful microprocessors. The goals and design tradeoffs for one specific system are presented, and a new approach to designing a fast numerical workbench is also discussed. The latter scheme uses a set of replicated functional processors for fine and coarse granules of numerical processing.

Two sessions are devoted to multiprocessing systems. The previously mentioned session, "New Microprocessor-Based Computer Architectures," focuses on how to exploit these new microprocessors in multiprocessing and other distributed applications. A paper session on multiprocessing investigates general multiprocessing concepts. The first paper illustrates the design of a high-performance multiprocessor using off-the-shelf microprocessors. The other two papers discuss new data-sharing techniques and models to estimate the throughput of multiprocessor systems.

The "Distributed Processors" session consists of papers looking at new techniques for network control. The first paper investigates a new bus arbitration scheme when VLSI functional units are destributed on the network. An innovative concurrency control mechanism and a practical implementation of a network operating system are also presented.

Finally, we have a paper session, "System Reliability." This session investigates innovative methods for diagnosing a multiprocessor system and methods for incorporating fault tolerance in system-level designs.

In summary, the Computer Architecture and Hardware track presents exciting continuity in the quest for reliable high-performance computing structures that are needed for the exploding computing needs of the late eighties and nineties.

A multiaccess bus arbitration scheme for VLSI-densed distributed systems

by JIE-YONG JUANG
and BENJAMIN W. WAH
Purdue University
West Lafayette, Indiana

ABSTRACT

A VLSI-densed shared-bus distributed system is a computer system consisting of a large number of VLSI processing units (VPUs) connected to one another by a high-speed bus. Data traffic in such a system is characterized by three distinct features: large population, bursty transmission, and task-dependent accesses with priority. A bus arbitration scheme is required to resolve contentions when several VPUs generate requests simultaneously. Conventional schemes such as daisy chaining, polling, and independent requests are shown to be inadequate. In this paper, a multiaccess code-deciphering (MACD) scheme is proposed. Two versions of the scheme are studied. The first version is a load-dependent scheme that can resolve contentions of N VPUs in an average time of $O(\log_{K/2} N)$ steps where K is equal to the bus width. The second version estimates the number of contending VPUs and resolves contention in a constant average time independent of load. The proposed schemes can support task-dependent accesses with priority.

INTRODUCTION

Recent advances in very large scale integrated logic (VLSI) and communication technology, coupled with the explosion in size and complexity of new applications, have led to the development of distributed computing systems. These systems possess a large number of general- and special-purpose processing units joined by an interconnection network. Notable examples are the PUMPS architecture,[1] the systolic-array architecture,[2] the recently announced Cyberplus computer,[3] and specialized systems, such as the processors at the joints of robot arms. PUMPS is a pattern analysis and image database machine that incorporates pools of special-purpose VLSI processing units. In a systolic-array architecture, sets of VLSI systolic processors, which perform functions such as matrix inversion, fast Fourier transform, and sorting, are connected to a host. The Cyberplus computer has a maximum configuration of 64 processors and a speed of 16 billion calculations per second. We call this kind of system a VLSI-densed system, and the processing unit, a VPU.

In a VLSI-densed system, one of the most important issues is the connection of the VPUs. A shared bus is widely used because of its simplicity in connection, flexibility in expansion, and efficiency in communication. Figure 1 depicts a typical configuration of such a system. Wah has shown that a shared bus provides enough bandwidth for a large class of VLSI-densed systems.[4] Large computer systems usually implement a number of relatively independent shared buses. The Cyberplus Computer has four independent "rings" that can partition the processors for four different applications.

In this paper, we propose a bus arbitration scheme for resolving contentions when several VPUs try to access the bus simultaneously. Characteristics of data traffic in a VLSI-densed system are discussed in the next section. Three conventional bus arbitration schemes, namely daisy chaining, polling, and independent requests are compared.[5–7] These schemes are found to be inadequate for VLSI-densed systems. A load-dependent Multiaccess Code-Deciphering (MACD) bus arbitration scheme is proposed, and this scheme is extended so that an estimate of the number of contending VPUs is taken into account. The enhanced scheme can resolve contentions in a constant average time, independent of the number of contending stations.

CONVENTIONAL BUS ARBITRATION SCHEMES

The operations of a VPU alternate between computations and data communications. We assume that when a VPU requests bus access, it has a large volume of data to transmit and requires a rapid response. That is, there is a large peak-to-average ratio of bus use. This type of data traffic is called *bursty* traffic.[8] Another characteristic of data traffic is that messages may have different priorities. Priority, in turn, depends on the urgency with which the bus is needed by a certain VPU for executing a task. The bus should be granted to the message with the highest priority.

On the other hand, a bus shared by autonomous VPUs alternates between bus contentions and data transmissions (Figure 2). A VPU with data ready to transmit is allowed to contend for the bus during a contention period. In order to resolve the contentions in the minimum amount of time, a good bus arbitration scheme should be used. Three bus arbitration schemes have been proposed for conventional computer systems. They were identified by Thurber as daisy chaining, polling, and independent requests.[7]

In daisy chaining, all input–output devices are connected serially along a common control line. During the bus-granting process, a bus grant signal propagates sequentially, device by device, until a requesting device is encountered. This device blocks further propagation of the signal and gains control of the bus by setting the bus busy line. This scheme involves the

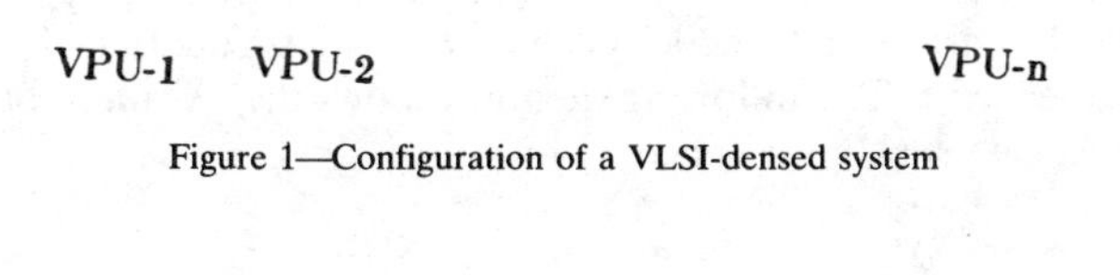

Figure 1—Configuration of a VLSI-densed system

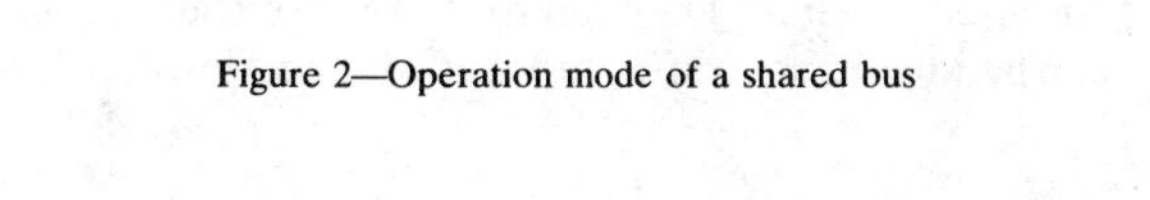

Figure 2—Operation mode of a shared bus

use of at least three control lines: bus grant, bus request, and bus busy.

In a bus system with polling, a set of poll count lines is connected directly to all the devices on the bus. In response to bus requests, a sequence of numbers, each of which corresponds to the address of a device, is generated on the poll count lines. When a requesting device finds that its address matches the number on the poll count lines, the bus is granted to this device, and the bus busy line is set. This scheme requires $\lceil \log_2 M \rceil$ poll count lines, where M is the number of devices on the bus, and two additional control lines are for bus request and bus busy.

In an independent-request scheme, each device has a separate pair of bus request and bus grant control lines connected to the arbitrator. When a device requests bus access, it sends a request signal on its bus request line. Bus control will be granted to one of the requesting devices based on predetermined priorities assigned to the devices. For M devices on a system implementing this scheme, more than 2M control lines are necessary. This scheme is the most costly as far as the number of control lines is concerned.

As VLSI-densed systems bear distinctions in the operating environment from that of conventional systems, the above bus arbitration schemes are found to be inadequate. We examined these schemes with respect to the control line complexity, the time complexity and the capability of task-dependent priority accesses.

1. Control-line complexity. The polling scheme is impractical when the number of VPUs is large because the number of poll count lines must be large enough so that each VPU can be identified by a unique address. A pair of control lines is needed for each VPU in the independent-request scheme. This is impractical even when the number of devices is moderately large.
2. Time complexity. Daisy chaining and polling are basically sequential schemes. They are inadequate for handling bursty traffic, which is characterized by a high ratio of peak-to-average data transmission rate and the fact that only a few VPUs are requesting bus access at any time. Suppose there are N out of M independent requesting devices, the average time to identify a requesting device is M/N. When N is small and the data transmission time is short, the overhead for bus arbitration is large.
3. Capability of task-dependent priority accesses. Priority of a device connected in a daisy chain is determined by its physical position in the chain. In a polling scheme, it is determined by the device's order in the sequence of polling counts. The priorities of the bus request lines in an independent-request scheme are usually fixed at design time. Since the priority of devices cannot be changed easily, the three existing schemes are incapable of handling task-dependent priority accesses.

The above observations reveal that none of the three conventional bus-arbitration schemes is sufficient for the needs of VLSI-densed systems. They call for a new arbitration scheme that can handle bursty traffic and that will access with priority.

LOAD-DEPENDENT MULTIACCESS ARBITRATION SCHEME FOR VLSI-DENSED SYSTEMS

In this section, a deterministic MACD scheme is presented. The scheme is discussed with respect to access without and with priority.

MACD Bus Arbitration for Access without Priority

We have previously studied a window search scheme to resolve contentions in a local multiaccess network.[9,10] In that scheme, a global window is maintained by all the stations, and each contender generates a contending parameter. A contender is eliminated from contention if its parameter is outside the window. A distributed control rule is applied to expand or to shrink the window in each contention step. As the contending process proceeds, the window size becomes smaller and smaller. Eventually, a unique contender is isolated in the window.

We can adapt the above scheme for resolving bus contentions. To support the scheme, two mechanisms are needed: a collision detection mechanism and a window control mechanism. The collision detection mechanism can be implemented by using the Wired-OR property of the bus. When two or more VPUs write simultaneously on the bus, the result is simply the bitwise logical OR of these numbers. By interpreting the result after a write, each VPU can determine whether a collision has occurred. The window control scheme described in References 9 and 10 is based on information of previous contentions and an estimate of the channel load. It is too complicated to be useful in the bus environment. The MACD technique, however, is a fast and effective scheme that combines window control and collision detection in a simple manner.

To describe the scheme formally, let us assume that there are N requesting VPUs, and each VPU writes a binary number X_i ($i = 1, 2, \ldots, N$) to the bus. The X_is are chosen from a structured code space S with the following properties:

$$X_i, X_j \in S, \quad i \neq j, \text{ are related, i.e., } X_i > X_j \text{ or } X_i < X_j \tag{1}$$

$$f(X_1 \oplus X_2 \oplus \cdots \oplus X_N) \leq \max\{X_1, X_2, \ldots, X_N\} \; X_i \in S, N \geq 1 \tag{2}$$

where $\oplus$ is the bitwise logical OR operator. By reading data on the bus and applying the code-deciphering function, f, a VPU knows the maximum number written on the bus. This information provides a basis for the window search mechanism to set the window. If the initial window is set so that the maximum value is included in the window, then an optimal detection procedure can be designed so that exactly one VPU will be isolated finally.

In order for the MACD technique to work properly, we need to prove that a code space that satisfies Equations 1 and 2 does exist. The following theorem shows the existence of at least one such code space.

Theorem: There exists a code space S of n-bit binary numbers and a deciphering function f which satisfy the constraints in Equations 1 and 2.

Proof: Let $S = \{0^a 10^b \mid a + b = n - 1, \quad a \geq 0, \quad b \geq 0\}$ where 0^k represents a consecutive sequence of k zeroes. Then for any two different elements u and v in S, it is easy to verify the relatedness property. For any n-bit binary number, $X = (x_1 x_2 \cdots x_n)$, we define a deciphering function f on X such that:

$$f(X) = 0^p 10^{n-p-1}, \quad \text{if } x_{p+1} = 1,\ x_j = 0 \text{ for all } 1 \leq j \leq p.$$

We claim that S and f as defined above satisfy Equations 1 and 2. To verify this, we can define N codes such that:

$$c_i = 0^{a(1)} 10^{n-a(i)-1}, \quad i = 1, \ldots, N$$

By definition of S,

$$c_i \in S,$$

and

$$\max(c_1, c_2, \ldots, c_N) = 0^m 10^{n-m-1}$$

where $m = \min\{a(i) \mid i = 1, 2, \ldots, N\}$. An overlapped variable $Y = (y_1 y_2 \cdots y_n)$ is defined to be the bitwise logical OR of the c_is; that is,

$$(y_1 y_2 \cdots y_n) = c_1 \oplus c_2 \oplus \cdots \oplus c_N.$$

Y as defined retains the following properties:

$$y_{m+1} = 1,$$

and

$$y_k = 0 \quad \text{for all } k \leq m.$$

By definition of the deciphering function f,

$$f(Y) = 0^m 10^{n-m-1}$$

or

$$f(c_1 \oplus c_2 \cdots \oplus c_N) = \max(c_1, c_2, \ldots, c_N).$$

Using code deciphering, a bus arbitration protocol can be designed. The network supporting the protocol should have the following components: a synchronous parallel bus for transmitting data and codes, a bus status control line for indicating the busy status of the bus, and an intelligent VPU-bus interface for each VPU that is capable of (1) sensing the bus-status control line, (2) reading data from the bus, (3) writing data to the bus, (4) generating random codes, and (5) deciphering codes read from the bus. The time interval for generating a random number, writing the number to the bus, and deciphering the code read from the bus is called a *slot*.

Whenever a VPU has data ready to transmit, it checks the bus status first. If the bus is in use, it waits until the bus becomes idle. To contend for the bus, a VPU chooses a code randomly from the code space S and writes it to the bus. The resulting code written on the bus is the bitwise logical OR of all the codes written by the contending VPUs. Each contending VPU reads the resulting code written and computes the deciphered code using the code-deciphering function. It compares the deciphered code with the code generated locally. Three results are possible:

1. the locally generated code is equal to the code read
2. the locally generated code is not equal to the code read but is equal to the deciphered code
3. the locally generated code is equal to neither the code read nor the deciphered code.

The last outcome implies that this VPU has not generated the maximum code and has to wait until the next contention period. The first and second outcomes imply that this VPU has generated the maximum code and should be allowed to transmit. However, there may be other VPUs that have generated the same code. If there are more than one VPU in this set *(hidden collision),* the contention resolution process has to be repeated. There are two ways to detect hidden collision. First, each VPU in this set generates an n-bit random number and writes it to the bus. To prevent the possibility of two VPUs generating the same random number, each VPU can use a distinct n-bit station identification code as the random number. If the number read from the bus matches the number written, then hidden collision has been resolved. If collision is detected, the MACD scheme is repeated. Second, we can assume that hidden collision is not resolved, and the collision-detection process is repeated. The process has to be repeated a number of times until there is high confidence that exactly one VPU is isolated.

When the probability is high that a large number of stations have generated the maximum code, the second method of resolving hidden collision is better because it is very likely that the MACD process has to be repeated, and the time for propagating the random number in the first method is lost. On the other hand, if the probability is high that exactly one station has generated the maximum code, the first method is better because hidden collision can be detected efficiently. In the second method, the code space S is much smaller (the size is n for an n-bit number). As a result, a few additional steps are necessary in order to achieve a high enough confidence that there is no hidden collision. In this paper, we have used the first method of resolving hidden collisions because the number of contending VPUs is usually relatively small compared to the bus width. Even when this is not true, we propose in the next section a method of using a variable-sized code space so that the number of VPUs contending in a slot is small.

It is important to note that the code space discussed in Theorem 1 (unary representation) is not unique. If binary codes are used, Equation 1 is still satisfied. A new code-deciphering function has to be designed so that Equation 2 is satisfied. By detecting the most significant bit that is mismatched among the codes generated by the contending VPUs, half of the stations, on the average, can be eliminated in each contention. This is not as efficient as unary-code representations because 1/W stations remain (W is the bus width) after each contention, if unary codes are used.

MACD Bus Arbitration for Priority Access

In a system with priority accesses, a VPU is assigned a *priority level* by the task that invokes its execution. The set of

VPUs with the same priority level constitutes a *priority class*. The *global priority class* is the class of contending VPUs with the highest priority level in the system. In a contention period, bus control is granted to a VPU that belongs to the global priority class.

To support accesses with priority, the system should be able to identify the global priority. One way to do so is to add a set of control lines to the system, each of which corresponds to a priority level. A requesting VPU is responsible for setting the corresponding priority line. The global priority level can then be identified by finding the control line with the highest priority level that is being set. This scheme works well when there are a limited number of priority levels.

On the other hand, the MACD scheme proposed earlier can be adapted to priority accesses in two ways: First is MACD by code space partitioning. The code space of the original MACD scheme is partitioned into subspaces so that each subspace corresponds to a priority level. The partition should satisfy the following condition:

$$\text{If } X \in S_i,\ Y \in S_j \text{ and } i > j, \text{ then } X > Y$$

where S_i and S_j are subspaces corresponding to priority levels i and j respectively. Using this partitioning, priority levels are encoded into the contending codes, and the deciphering function proposed in Theorem 1 can identify the global priority level and the largest code in this level.

The other method of adaptation is MACD by two-phase identification. The partitioning of code space is practical when the number of priority levels is relatively small as compared to the size of the code space. When the number of priority levels is large, a contention period can be divided into two phases: a priority resolution phase followed by an intraclass contention phase. In the priority resolution phase, a strictly increasing function, which maps a set of priority levels onto a code space, is defined in each contention slot. The mapping is done so that the minimum number of priority levels is assigned to the same code. In a contention slot, every contending VPU writes its code to the bus and deciphers the number read from the bus. A set of VPUs with the highest priority levels (corresponding to the deciphered code) is identified. The process is repeated until the set of VPUs with the highest priority level is identified. When the bus width is larger than or equal to the number of priority levels, this phase can be completed in one contention slot.

Evaluation of Load-dependent MACD Bus Arbitration Scheme

Bus arbitration schemes can be evaluated with respect to the following attributes: complexity of implementation, complexity of contention time, flexibility, reliability, and priority access capability. The MACD scheme requires one control line (bus busy). The control logic for the bus interface is relatively simple. A VPU can be added to or removed from the bus without disturbing other components of the system. This system is, therefore, flexible for expansion and convenient for the removal of faulty units. The MACD scheme can support accesses with priority. Moreover, the scheme is efficient as far as contention time is concerned. The analysis and simulation results are shown in the remaining part of this section.

The time complexity of contention resolution can be measured by the mean number of contention slots in each contention period. To analyze this complexity, let N be the number of contending VPUs at the beginning of a contention period and K be the size of the code space equal to the bus width W. Assuming that codes are chosen randomly, a VPU generates a given code c_i $(i = 1, 2, \ldots, N)$ with probability 1/W. Designate the maximum of N such c_is as c_m, the m-th code in the code space, i.e., $c_m = \max\{c_i \mid i = 1, 2, \ldots, N\}$. If exactly one VPU generates code c_m and other VPUs generate codes less than c_m, then the contention is resolved. The probability for this event to occur is:

$$q(m \mid N, K = W) = N\left(\frac{1}{W}\right)\left(\frac{m-1}{W}\right)^{N-1} \tag{3}$$

Since m ranges from 1 to W and these W events are mutually exclusive, the probability that contention is resolved in one step is $P_{K,W,N}$ where $K = W$ is:

$$\begin{aligned} P_{K,W,N} &= \sum_{m=1}^{W} q(m \mid N, K = W) \\ &= \sum_{m=1}^{W} N\left(\frac{1}{W}\right)\left(\frac{m-1}{W}\right)^{N-1} \\ &= \frac{N}{W^N} \sum_{u=1}^{W-1} u^{N-1} \end{aligned} \tag{4}$$

In Figure 3, $P_{K,W,N}$ is plotted against N/W. It is observed that the probability of success in one attempt is higher if the code space (equal to bus width) is larger and the number of contending VPUs is kept constant. It is observed that $P_{K,W,N}$ is a strictly decreasing function of N and decreases to zero when N is large. This means that the MACD technique is unable to resolve contention in one step when the load is extremely heavy. However, most of the contending VPUs are eliminated in one attempt. The number of survivors is reduced significantly as contention proceeds, and the probability of success is increased consequently. The following analysis demonstrates this phenomenon.

Given that the maximum of codes generated by the contending VPUs is c_m, the m-th code in the code space. Define indicator variables X_i, $i = 1, \ldots, N$,

$$X_i = \begin{cases} 1 & \text{with probability } 1/m \\ 0 & \text{with probability } 1 - 1/m \end{cases}$$

Let

$$Z = \sum_{i=1}^{N} X_i.$$

The random variable Z indicates the number of VPUs that generate c_m in the contention. These VPUs are allowed to contend in the following steps. The expected value of Z given m, N, and W, $E(Z \mid m, N, W)$, represents the average number of surviving VPUs. It is easy to show that:

$$E(Z \mid m, N, W=K) = \frac{N}{m}. \quad (5)$$

Furthermore, the probability that the current maximum code with N contending stations and a bus width of W is c_m can be expressed as:

$$p(m \mid N, W=K) = \left(\frac{m}{W}\right)^N - \left(\frac{m-1}{W}\right)^N \quad (6)$$

The expected number of VPUs that would survive a contention is:

$$\begin{aligned} E(Z \mid N, W=K) &= \sum_{m=1}^{W} E(Z \mid m, N, W=K)\, p(m \mid N, W=K) \\ &= \sum_{m=1}^{W} \left(\frac{N}{m}\right)\left[\left(\frac{m}{W}\right)^N - \left(\frac{m-1}{W}\right)^N\right] \\ &= \left[\left(\frac{N}{1} - \frac{N}{2}\right)\left(\frac{1}{W}\right)^N\right] + \left[\left(\frac{N}{2} - \frac{N}{3}\right)\left(\frac{2}{W}\right)^N\right] \\ &\quad + \cdots + \left[\left(\frac{N}{W-1} - \frac{N}{W}\right)\left(\frac{W-1}{W}\right)^N\right] + \left[\frac{N}{W}\left(\frac{W}{W}\right)^N\right] \\ &= \frac{N}{W^N}\left\{\frac{1^{N-1}}{2} + \frac{2^{N-1}}{3} + \cdots + \frac{(W-1)^{N-1}}{W}\right\} + \frac{N}{W} \\ &\leq \frac{N}{W^N}\left\{W \cdot \frac{(W-1)^{N-1}}{W}\right\} + \frac{N}{W} \\ &\leq \frac{N}{W} \cdot \left(\frac{W^{-1}}{W}\right)^{N-1} + \frac{N}{W} \\ &\leq \frac{2N}{W} \end{aligned} \quad (7)$$

The ratio $\gamma = \frac{E(Z \mid N, W=K)}{N} \leq \frac{2}{W}$ is a measure of the average fraction of contending VPUs that can survive a contention. Let $N_t(t = 0, 1, \ldots)$ be the expected number of contending VPUs in step t. By Equation 7, we have

$$N_t \leq \left(\frac{2}{W}\right)^t N_0 \qquad t \geq 0.$$

Therefore,

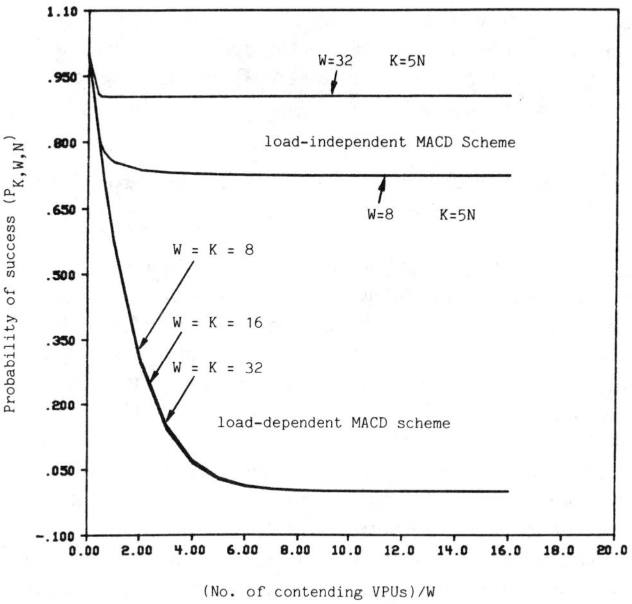

Figure 3—Probability of success in one contention using multiaccess code-deciphering bus arbitration scheme (*K* is the size of code space; *W* is the bus width, *N* is the number of contending VPUs)

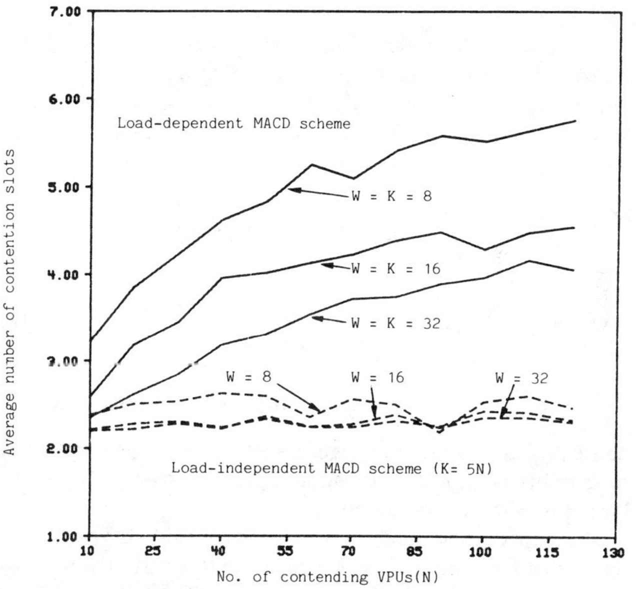

Figure 4—Average number of contention slots for resolving conflicts of bus requests using multiaccess code-deciphering scheme (*K* is the size of code space; *W* is the bus width, *N* is the number of contending VPUs)

$$N_t \to 1 \quad \text{as} \quad t \to \log_{k/2} N_0. \quad (8)$$

As shown in Figure 3, we can see that $P_{K,W,N} \to 1$ as $N < W$, and $P_{K,W,N} \to 0$ as $N \gg W$. This fact reveals that the contention process of MACD can approximately be divided into two phases. The effect of the first phase, that is, when $N_t > W$, is in reducing the number of contending VPUs. When the process enters the second phase, $N_t \leq W$, contention can be resolved in about one step. The overall contention process will stop within an average of $\log_{W/2} N_0$ steps. Figure 4 shows the simulation results that confirm our analysis. The number of contention slots shown includes the additional slots required for resolving hidden collisions. MACD performs better when the bus width is large.

LOAD-INDEPENDENT MACD BUS ARBITRATION SCHEME

As shown in Equation 8 and Figure 4, the scheme proposed in the last section is load-dependent and performs well when the bus width is large and the number of contending VPUs is small. Since the number of contention slots grows logarithmically with the number of contending VPUs, the scheme is inefficient when the number of contending VPUs is large or the bus width is small.

The cause for the load dependency is the fixed code space. In order to reduce the number of VPUs contending in a slot, th code space can be designed so that it is a function of the number of contending VPUs and the bus width. By choosing the size of the code space so that the number of VPUs contending in a slot is a relatively small constant as compared to the bus width, contention can be resolved in a time that is load-independent. We have studied a similar scheme for contention resolution on carrier-sense-multiple-access bus networks.[9, 10]

The solution depends on choosing the size of the code space and estimating the number of contending VPUs. Suppose N can be estimated accurately, and a code is chosen so that $K/N = r$. The probability that contention is resolved in one step (refer to Equation 4) is:

$$P_{K,N,W} = \sum_{m=K-w+1}^{K} q(m \mid N = K/r, K, W)$$

$$= N\left(\frac{r}{N}\right)^{N} \sum_{u=K-W}^{K-1} u^{N-1} \qquad (9)$$

where $q(m \mid N = K/r, K, W)$ is defined in Equation 3. The value of $P_{K,N,W}$ is plotted in Figure 3. It is seen that the success probability is higher and load independent as a result of the increase in the code space size.

The expected number of VPUs that would survive a contention can also be derived similarly. In this case, the number of surviving VPUs is N if no station contends in the slot. That is, Equation 5 is changed to:

$$E(Z \mid m, N = K/r, W) = \begin{cases} \frac{N}{m} & K \le m \le K - W + 1 \\ N & 1 \le m \le K - W \end{cases} \qquad (10)$$

The definition of $p(m \mid N, W)$ in Equation 6 remains true. The expected number of surviving VPUs in one contention is:

$$E(Z \mid N = K/r, W) = \sum_{m=1}^{K} E(Z \mid m, N = K/r, W)\, p(m \mid N = K/r, W)$$

$$= \sum_{m=K-W+1}^{K} \frac{N}{m} \cdot p(m \mid N = K/r, W) + \sum_{m=1}^{K-W} N \cdot p(m \mid N = K/r, W)$$

$$\le \frac{2N}{K} + \left[\left(\frac{K-W}{K}\right)^{N} - \left(\frac{K-W-1}{K}\right)^{N}\right](K-W)N \qquad (11)$$

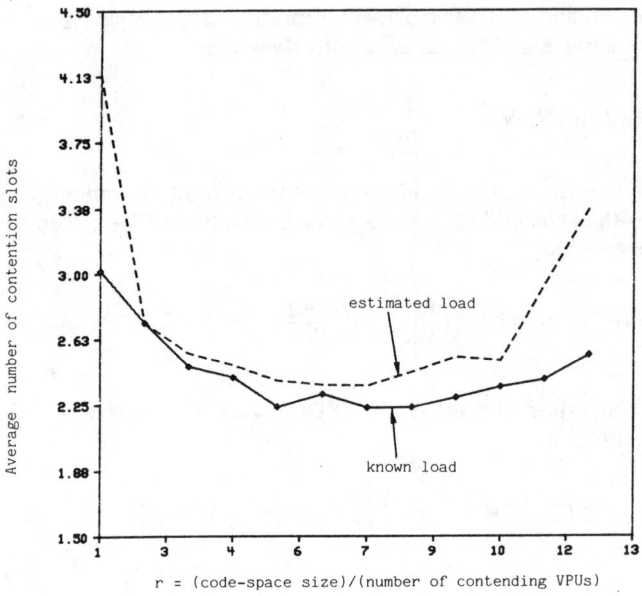

Figure 5—The optimal choice of the code-space size ($W = 16$, $N = 60$)

Since $K/N = r$ is a constant, $E(Z \mid N = K/r, W)$ is a constant independent of load (= N) if K is large as compared to W.

The correct choice of r is shown in Figure 5. There is an optimal choice of r so that the number of contention slots is minimum. The optimal value depends on the value of W and is load independent (assuming that N is known). The value is approximately five for the combinations of W and N tested. Using the optimal value of r, the performance of the load-independent MACD scheme is plotted in Figure 4. In generating these results, the size of the code space, K, is chosen to be W if $r \times N$ is smaller than W; that is, the scheme proposed earlier is used when the load is light. It is observed that the proposed scheme requires a small constant number of slots when the load is heavy.

The proposed scheme requires N to be known. In general, this is not possible due to the distributed control. One way is to estimate N based on information collected during the contentions. However, this information can indicate that one or more contending VPUs have generated the same code, but cannot reveal the exact number of contending VPUs. If the number of VPUs contending in a contention slot is small, a reasonable estimate of N can be obtained by using the number

Table I—Comparison of MACD with conventional bus arbitration schemes. (M = number of VPUs connected to the bus)

Comparison of MACD with Conventional Bus-Arbitration Schemes							
Attributes	Hardware Complexity		Contention Time		Reliability	Flexibility	Priority
Schemes	Control Logic	Control Line	light Load	Heavy Load	Failure Tolerance	Easy Reconfig.	Task Dependence
MACD	O(M)	1	~ 1	~ 1	Yes	Yes	Yes
Daisy-Chaining	O(M)	3	O(M)	~ 1	No	No	No
Polling	O(M)	$2+\log_2 M$	O(M)	~ 1	Yes	No	No
Independent Requests	O(M)	2M	$O(\log_2 M)$	$O(\log_2 M)$	Yes	No	No

of bits that are ones in a contention slot, B, as the number of VPUs contending in this slot. That is,

$$\hat{N} = \frac{B \times K}{W} \tag{12}$$

This will systematically underestimate the actual value of N, and some correction to the value of r used should be introduced. In Figure 5, the optimal value of r that should be used is slightly different when the estimate in Equation 12 is used. The number of contention slots required is slightly increased when N is estimated.

A maximum-likelihood estimate of N also can be derived. However, the complexity of such a scheme is high and cannot be used in real-time applications.

CONCLUSION

In this paper, we have studied the problem of bus contentions in VLSI-densed shared-bus systems. Data traffic generated by VPUs in such systems are characterized by three distinct features: large population, bursty transmissions, and task-dependent priority accesses. A bus arbitration protocol is necessary to resolve access conflicts when several VPUs are trying to access the bus simultaneously. Conventional schemes such as daisy chaining, polling, and independent requests are shown to be inadequate because of the large overhead or the high complexity of implementation.

The load-dependent MACD scheme presented in this paper can resolve contention of N VPUs in an average time of $O(\log_{W/2} N)$ steps where W is the width of the bus. For bursty traffic in a system with a parallel bus, N is usually relatively small as compared to W. Nearly perfect bus scheduling is achievable. An extended scheme is proposed that estimates the value of N and uses a code space of variable size depending on N. It is found that contentions can be resolved in a time that is load-independent.

The proposed MACD scheme can support task-dependent priority accesses that cannot be supported by conventional bus arbitration schemes. Comparisons between the MACD and the conventional bus arbitration schemes are summarized in Table I. These comparisons clearly indicate that the MACD scheme is superior in almost every respect.

ACKNOWLEDGMENT

This research was partially supported by National Science Foundation Grant ECS80-16580 and by CIDMAC, a research unit of Purdue University, sponsored by Purdue, Cincinnati Milicron Corporation, Control Data Corporation, Cummins Engine Company, Ransburg Corporation, and TRW.

REFERENCES

1. Briggs, F. A., K. S. Fu, K. Hwang, and B. W. Wah. "PUMPS Architecture for Pattern Analysis and Image Database Management." *IEEE Transactions on Computers,* C-31 (1982), pp. 969–983.
2. Kung, H. T. et al. *VLSI Systems and Computations.* Rockville, Md.: Computer Science Press, 1981.
3. Control Data Corporation. "Technical Information: Control Data Cyberplus." News Release and Fact Sheet, Oct. 1983.
4. Wah, B. W., "A Comparative Study of Distributed Resource Sharing on Multiprocessors." *Proceedings of 10th Annual International Symposium on Computer Architecture.* Stockholm, Sweden: ACM, 1983, pp. 300–308c.
5. Baer, J. *Computer Systems Architecture,* Rockville, Md.: Computer Science Press, 1980.
6. Hayes, J. P. *Computer Architecture and Organization.* New York: McGraw-Hill, 1978.
7. Thurber, K. J. et al. "A Systematic Approach to the Design of Digital Bussing Structures." *AFIPS, Proceedings of the National Computer Conference* (Vol. 41), 1972, pp. 719–740.
8. Tobagi, F. A. "Multiaccess Protocols in Packet Communication Systems." *IEEE Transactions on Communications,* COM-28 (1980), pp. 468–488.
9. Wah, B. W. and Y. Y. Juang, "Load Balancing on Local Multiaccess Networks." *Proceedings of 8th Conference on Local Computer Networks,* Minneapolis, Minn.: IEEE, 1983, pp. 55–61.
10. Juang, J. Y., and B. W. Wah. "Unified Window Protocol for Local Multiaccess Networks." *Proceedings of Third Annual Joint Conference of the IEEE Computer and Communications Societies.* San Francisco, California: IEEE, 1984, pp. 97–104.
11. Metcalf, R. M., and D. R. Boggs. "Ethernet: Distributed Packet Switching for Local Computer Networks." *Communications of the ACM,* 19 (1976), pp. 395–404.

DMERT—An operating system for telecommunications systems

by S. F. HO, C. J. RICHARDSON, W. C. SCHWARTZ
AT&T Bell Telephone Laboratories
Naperville, Illinois

ABSTRACT

The duplex multi-environment real-time (DMERT) operating system is a process-oriented, fault-tolerant operating system designed to provide a versatile software base for telecommunication systems. DMERT provides general fault recovery capabilities, virtual machine layers to meet application needs, a UNIX environment, and I/O interfaces to peripheral devices. This paper gives a detailed description of the DMERT architecture and its capabilities.

This paper is a revision of the paper presented in the 1983 National Communications Forum.

INTRODUCTION

A major goal of the duplex multi-environment real-time (DMERT) operating system is to provide a versatile software base to fulfill the varied processing needs of telecommunication applications. While the needs of these applications are different, they have several common characteristics. First, a major component of these applications is software. Second, the major mission of this software is real-time oriented with response times as short as several milliseconds. Third, each application has a need for continuous operation and hence stringent processor availability requirements. Fourth and finally, each application is to be operated over a long period of time, which requires extensive software for monitoring and reporting on system status as well as changing and upgrading the system while it is in operation. To satisfy these needs, DMERT is designed to:

1. Support multiple real-time applications. It is necessary for the DMERT operating system to support many applications, each with different real-time demands. Some applications include databases that need many disk jobs serviced quickly. Others control telecommunication equipment requiring rapid response to an event such as an interrupt and dedicated processing capacity for an interval thereafter. To satisfy these diverse needs, a design objective was established to provide modularity in the operating system that allows a high degree of application tailoring.
2. Improve application development productivity. Software for telecommunication applications is usually implemented in assembly language. To increase productivity of the developers, an objective of efficiently supporting the C programming language[1] was established. Telecommunications systems often have major software components that are not time critical. Hence a design objective of DMERT was to support a UNIX interface as a familiar operating system environment for the non-time-critical software.
3. Be fault tolerant. To meet the reliability objectives of the applications, it is necessary to support software packages for error checking and recovery. In order to reduce the complexity of both the operational and recovery components of the system, a design objective was established to separate recovery software from the core of the system. An objective of incorporating extensive internal consistency and integrity checks within all software components was established to ensure that critical software modules protected themselves from errors in other parts of the system.

In summary, DMERT is a process-oriented operating system designed to support both real-time and time-shared operations, with an emphasis on high reliability and availability. This paper outlines the DMERT capabilities and describes how these design objectives are achieved. The second section gives an architectural overview of DMERT. The process types, process communication primitives, and the time-sharing and real-time scheduling policies are described. The last section highlights DMERT features for achieving the high reliability and availability goals.

DMERT ARCHITECTURE

The architecture of DMERT is based on an earlier system, MERT,[2] a real time operating system derived from the UNIX operating system.[3] The "D" in DMERT reflects one of the characteristics that distinguishes it from the previous two operating systems, namely DMERT is designed to execute on a fault-tolerant 3B20D duplex processor.[4] Thus, the DMERT architecture is dependent on proven concepts from UNIX and MERT, which are extended to support highly reliable telecommunication applications.

One of the basic goals for DMERT was to build modular and independent processes, each having localized data known only to itself. Hence, the notion of a process is fundamental to the DMERT architecture, which is essentially composed of a kernel and a collection of cooperating, concurrent processes. The following sections define what a process is and how processes communicate with each other.

Definition of a Process

A process is a collection of related, logical segments (programs and data) that can be brought into memory to form an executable entity. A segment is the basic memory entity in DMERT. A segment is composed of 1 to 64 pages, each 512 32-bit words in length. Segments can grow dynamically in increments of a page. A process typically consists of four segments: code or text, a stack used for temporary data, a data segment containing global data, and a special type of data segment called a process control block (PCB). The PCB segment contains unique information that identifies the process to the operating system. This information includes the process number, type of process, priority, and address space qualifiers that define the virtual address for a process. Each process has its own virtual address space of up to 128 segments. These virtual addresses are mapped to physical addresses by 3B20D hardware under the control of the DMERT operating system.

Besides the regular process entries for handling process

events and interrupts, any process may have a fault entry. A process is entered at its fault entry when another process sends a fault to this process, or a hardware/software fault is detected by the system when the process is running. The purpose of the fault entry is to give the faulted process an opportunity to perform some recovery action based on where the process was faulted and why. Every faulted process has a fault code that indicates the nature of the fault and state information that indicates the state of the process at the time the fault occurred.

A process can be dynamically created to perform a set of functions and then terminated when the task is completed. Processes that continually perform work remain "alive" at all times, however, they may sleep or be inactive until an event, message, or interrupt occurs. An inactive process may be swapped out to the disk, i.e., the process memory image is copied to the disk and the memory occupied by the process is released. This keeps main memory to be loaded with the working set of processes at a given point in time.

Process Types

DMERT has four basic types of processes: kernel, kernel process, supervisor process, and UNIX process. DMERT may be viewed as a hierarchy of virtual machines, where successive levels put additional restrictions on access right and further remove the programmer from details of the physical machine. However, the high level may take advantage of services provided by the lower levels. In general, the higher the level, the more services are available to the application programmer; the lower the level, the more real-time efficient is the program execution. This level structuring of virtual machines permits DMERT to manage real-time applications, while at the same time providing the flexibility of a time-sharing system. This approach avoids contention for system resources with priority tasks and simplifies the implementation effort for lower priority tasks.

Kernel

The DMERT kernel provides the most primitive virtual machine. The kernel handles hardware interrupts, timer interrupts, and operating system traps. In all cases, the kernel saves the state of an interrupted process, provides whatever service is requested, and restores the state of the interrupted process. The kernel services are basic and they execute efficiently.

Also part of the DMERT kernel are special processes that provide scheduling, memory management, and other services. Special processes behave as kernel processes, except that they do not have their own virtual address space, but rather reside in the kernel's address space. These special processes communicate with the kernel through function calls instead of operating system traps, and they have access to global system data. For example, the memory manager and the scheduler are two special processes in DMERT. The memory manager loads processes into memory, selects segments to be swapped out to disk when additional main memory is required, and provides routines that may be called by the kernel. The scheduler controls the execution of time-shared processes, i.e., supervisor and UNIX processes.

Kernel processes

Kernel processes comprise the next virtual machine layer in DMERT. They are completely interrupt driven and are designed to provide time-critical processing in a real-time environment. Kernel processes have their own virtual address space. However, they share the kernel's stack and the kernel's message buffer segment to provide quick access to arguments of operating system traps and fast message communications between processes. Kernel process segments are always memory resident to ensure rapid response to events such as interrupts. The various peripheral device drivers and the file manager are examples of kernel processes.

Supervisor and UNIX processes

Supervisor and UNIX processes form the third layer of virtual machine. These processes can use all the services provided by the kernel and kernel processes. Supervisor and UNIX processes provide time-sharing services that can be considered background tasks. They share the real time of the processor with each other according to priorities administered by the scheduler. In general, these processes are not locked in memory and can be swapped out. Thus, supervisor and UNIX processes may take longer to dispatch than special and kernel processes.

UNIX processes are actually supervisor processes, but a shared library hides the supervisor interface and replaces it with a UNIX environment. Conceptually, supervisor and UNIX processes are different, but they are the same from the operating system's point of view.

Inter-process Communication

DMERT provides a rich set of inter-process communication and synchronization mechanisms including messages, events, inter-process traps, and shared memory. These inter-process communication primitives are fundamental to the DMERT structure. Most of the system services are requested by an exchange of events and messages between a requesting process and either a system process or the kernel.

Messages and ports

Processes are in general independent and distinct entities. Two processes working together on a task must be able to exchange information. To satisfy this need, messages may be sent from any level process to any other level process. The sender needs only to know the target process number and a pre-agreed format of the message. An optional acknowledgement message is provided so the sender can synchronize actions with the receiver.

Process ports permit processes to communicate with each

other without knowing each other's process number. A process port is a globally known "device" to which a process may attach itself for receiving messages. Other processes may communicate with a process connected to a port by sending messages to that port. Thus process ports permit unrelated processes to communicate with each other.

Events

Communications between processes may occur using an event mechanism. An event is a one-bit *message* that can be sent from one process and be interrogated by the receiving process. Presently, 32 events are available, of which the DMERT operating system reserves 16 for its use. Application processes communicating using events can define the usages of the remaining 16 events. Thus, two or more processes can communicate internal states using events.

Inter-process traps

Trapping implies a transfer of control from one process to another with the passing of input parameters to the target process. The trapped process returns status and control back to the trapping process after if has completed the requested service. Any process may trap to another process, as long as the argument-passing protocol is mutually agreed upon.

Shared memory

Processes are built with a view of their own virtual address space and in general cannot access any other process's address space. This affords protection. However, sharing of large amounts of data is difficult with messages or events. Cooperating processes that must exchange information at higher rates than those supported by message or events can share segments. A shared segment is a part of the virtual address space of several processes simultaneously.

Process Scheduling

The DMERT operating system simultaneously supports both a real-time and a time-sharing philosophy. Kernel processes operate in the real-time environment. The remaining processor time is shared among supervisor and UNIX processes.

Real-time

DMERT's real-time allocation strategy is based on execution levels and preemptive scheduling. DMERT maintains a process hierarchy based on 16 execution levels. A kernel process can belong to levels 3 through 15 (levels 0 through 2 are reserved for the time-sharing environment). Kernel processes are used to implement tasks with stringent real-time requirements. DMERT dispatches processes at the highest execution level first. Generally, once a kernel process is dispatched, it is allowed to run to completion, i.e., until the kernel process relinquishes its control of the processor. However, if another kernel process at a higher execution level is awakened, DMERT preempts the executing process. Upon completion of the preempting process, if no other higher level processes were also awakened, DMERT resumes the suspended process.

DMERT applications are allowed to assign their own processes' execution levels, thus allowing applications to control and distribute the real time. This approach is flexible and supports a variety of applications.

Time sharing

The portion of real time not utilized by the kernel and kernel processes is time shared among supervisor and UNIX processes. Processes supporting the time-shared environment, such as the scheduler and memory manager, reside at execution level 2. These processes are at the bottom of the real-time hierarchy and gain control of the processor only after all other real-time work is completed.

Supervisor and UNIX processes execute at levels 0 and 1. The scheduling hierarchy of supervisor processes is based on software priority. The major difference between priority in the time-sharing environment and execution levels in the real-time environment is that DMERT adjusts software priorities dynamically depending on the I/O characteristics of the process and the system load, whereas execution levels are fixed.

RELIABILITY AND AVAILABILITY

The DMERT operating system must be able to support the stringent electronic switching system's reliability requirements. To minimize the number of system failures and the associated down-time per failure, DMERT supports audits and overload control, progressive initialization, reconfiguration, preventive and corrective maintenance, field updates, and system updates. These features are described in the following sections.

Audit and Overload Control

The DMERT audit package verifies the validity of critical system data. Audit strategies are based on the inherent properties of the data structures and redundancies that are built into the structures. Audits are distributed throughout the system within processes that control the data to be audited. Audits can be issued by manual requests or the audit control structure. The DMERT system integrity monitor (SIM) is responsible for scheduling and dispatching all audits, and for handling all overload conditions. SIM receives overload conditions from DMERT operating system processes. The application and the craft are then notified that these conditions exist.

DMERT overload controls handle conditions in which critical system resources (e.g., message buffers, swap space, etc.) are in short supply or the system's real-time performance falls below a predetermined limit. These conditions occur when the system is overloaded with input requests, or sufficient resources are lost due to software errors over a long period of system operation. Most overload strategies involve changing the policy of assigning resources to processes and running audits to recover system resources. The combination of audits and overload control is a powerful mechanism to maintain system integrity.

Progressive Initialization

The DMERT recovery strategy attempts to minimize the service disruption caused by an initialization in response to hardware and software faults. Several levels of recovery actions are provided to match the level of initialization to the severity of the fault. Although DMERT attempts to recover at the lowest possible level, the recovery level is automatically escalated if the current level fails.

The initialization of application processes only is the least disruptive or the lowest level of initialization. Applications determine their own recovery strategies. This level of initialization can be requested by a craftperson or by an application process. DMERT administers the initialization counts and timers, but a DMERT operating system initialization is not taken.

The next level of recovery involves initializing DMERT processes as well as application processes. This level is the primary recovery mechanism in DMERT and uses a rollback strategy. The goal of this initialization level is to restore the system to a sane and operational state with minimal effect on service. Each process in the system is notified by its fault entry that a system initialization has been taken. Using state information that is maintained during normal operation, each process cleans up any transactions in progress and then returns. This strategy is effective because only a few processes are actually active at any given time.

If the rollback strategy fails, DMERT is rebooted from disk. Even when such a bootstrap occurs, several regions of memory are protected to maintain some continuity. The successively more severe levels of initialization involve reinitializing these protected regions. However, one protected memory region is preserved for applications, and is initialized only by manual request or a power up.

Reconfiguration

DMERT takes full advantage of the redundancy provided by the 3B20D processor. The equipment configuration database maintains information concerning the hardware configuration and hardware error rates. This provides a basis for automatic reconfiguration and allows the recovery strategy to be tuned to meet the needs of the individual applications.

In processing a hardware error interrupt, the unit causing the error is determined. The error count for that unit is then incremented and compared with its error threshold. If the threshold has not been exceeded, the unit remains in service. If the threshold has been exceeded, the configuration management routines decide on the corrective action. This decision is based on the availability and status of a replacement unit. Configuration options include removing the unit, switching in a replacement unit, or continuing operation on the faulty unit.

Preventive and Corrective Maintenance

DMERT provides a comprehensive set of diagnostics that can be invoked directly by the craftperson or under program control. Diagnostics ensure the operational capabilities of hardware units.

A routine exercise is performed daily to verify the operation of all units in the system. These units are diagnosed and a status report is generated indicating their conditions.

In addition to the routine exercise, if a unit is removed from service because of a fault condition, diagnostics are scheduled. If the unit fails diagnostics, a report is generated indicating the failure cause. If the unit passes diagnostics, it remains in service. However, to prevent a unit remaining in service that passes diagnostics, but fails repeatedly during actual operation, a count is kept of the number of times operational failure occurs. Any unit that exceeds a predetermined limit may be removed from service, pending some corrective action (e.g., more exhaustive diagnostics and unit replacement).

Field Update

Field update, which is typically called overwriting in traditional electronic switching systems, is the problem correction mechanism for DMERT. Field update may be used to modify data and programs on the 3B20D disk or in main memory. Field updates must be performed without disturbing system operations (e.g., call processing, critical system functions, etc.). The features of field update are the ability to change a file both instantaneously and in a temporary way, the ability to update a function in a running process, the ability to coordinate changes to functions within a process, and the ability to change data contents or the structure of data in a running process. Changes made to the running process update the disk image of the process as well as the main memory image.

System Update

DMERT system update provides a safe, reliable mechanism to introduce new versions of DMERT and application software into the 3B20D/DMERT systems, while minimizing service disruption. System update differs from field update in the magnitude of the program and data changes being installed. Normally, a system update will replace all the software in the system, which is a complete reissue of DMERT, application software, and/or data. For this reason, system updates always include a memory reinitialization of all processes and data from disk. Only the protected memory areas are not reinitialized.

SUMMARY

The DMERT system has achieved its objective of providing a cost- and real-time-effective base for a wide variety of telecommunication systems. The concepts of multiple levels of functional support, reliability and availability features, and versatile I/O interfaces provide an adaptable base that can be tailored to many differing needs. More than one hundred DMERT systems have been installed in the field. These systems include electronic switching applications, database applications, as well as add-on extensions to existing switching machines to enhance processing power. The DMERT system is also the basis of a number of telecommunication system designs currently under way. This widespread use of 3B20D/DMERT marks it as a processor/operating system combination of significance in telecommunication systems.

REFERENCES

1. Kerninghan, B. W., and D. M. Ritchie. "The C Programming Language," Englewood Cliffs, N. J.: Prentice-Hall, 1978.
2. Lycklama, H., and D. L. Bayer. "The MERT Operating System." *The Bell System Technical Journal,* 57 (1978), pp. 1905–1929.
3. Ritchie, D., and K. Thompson. "The UNIX Time Sharing System." *The Bell System Technical Journal,* 57 (1978).
4. Toy, W. N., and L. E. Gallaher. "Overview and Architecture of The 3B20D Processor." *The Bell System Technical Journal,* 62 (1983).

Global concurrency control mechanisms for a local network consisting of systems without concurrency control capability

by YAHIKO KAMBAYASHI

*Kyushu University**
Fukuoka, Japan

and

SEI-ICHI KONDOH

Mitsubishi Electric Co.
Kamakura, Japan

ABSTRACT

A powerful and expandable system can be economically realized by a local computer network consisting of various kinds of microprocessor-based systems. The following three problems must be solved to organize a distributed processing system using nonidentical elements: (1) communication, (2) query conversion, and (3) global concurrency control. Except in the case when all transactions are read-only ones, (3) must be handled. Since each system in a network does not usually have concurrency control capability or may not use the identical mechanism, it is necessary to develop a global concurrency control mechanism for a local network consisting of systems without such capability. In this paper two such mechanisms are presented. By assigning ordered numbers to the component systems, a consistent and deadlock-free global mechanism is realized for a semijoin-based query procedure. To improve efficiency, a mechanism permitting dynamic modification capability of ordering is also presented.

*This paper was written when the authors were at Kyoto University.

INTRODUCTION

The top-down and the bottom-up approaches are those that can be used to organize a distributed system. Through the former approach, which takes a global view of the whole system, consistent and efficient systems can be easily designed. This paper, however, will discuss the latter approach, since it is a practical solution to the problem of constructing a distributed system using already existing systems, such as work stations with database capability, database machines, and picture file systems using laser discs. For this approach the following problems must be solved: (1) communication procedures among systems, (2) conversion of user requests, and (3) global concurrency control. Except for the case when all transactions are read-only ones, Problem 3 must be solved. Since Problems 1 and 2 are handled by various authors, this paper will focus on Problem 3.

As described below (see Figure 1(a)), Problem 3 must be considered even when there exists no global write transaction. That is, considering only query processing procedures is not enough to handle global read-only transactions when local write transactions at each site are permitted. Although this problem is very important when constructing a network using various different subsystems, the authors believe that it has not been discussed before. To simplify the problem, we will use the following three restrictions, which are considered to be reasonable:

1. To avoid Problems 1 and 2, we assume that the component systems realize relational databases with an identical query language.
2. For a network we only consider an Ether-type local network with broadcasting capability.
3. We decompose a global transaction into a global read-only transaction and local read-write transactions so that global read-write transactions can be avoided. Since handling of such a global read-write transaction makes discussion complicated, it is excluded in order to present basic ideas.

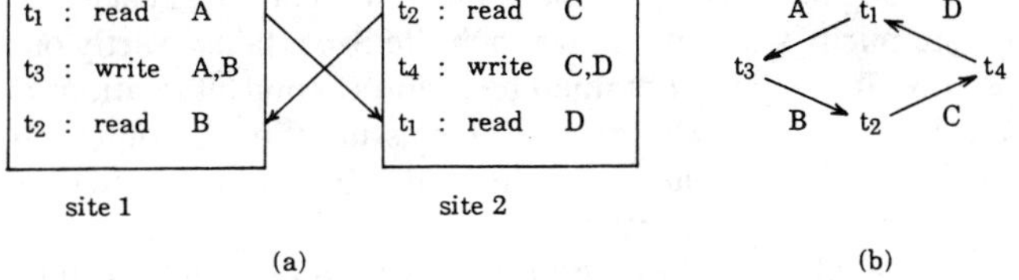

Figure 1—Necessity of the global concurrency control mechanism even if there are no global write transactions

For the global concurrency control problem, the following three cases must be considered:

1. There may be a system that does not have any concurrency control mechanisms. All transactions are proposed serially at this system, and local locking mechanisms are not available to global control mechanisms.
2. Even if a system has a concurrency control mechanism, it may not be usable for global control. That is, there may be a system with an independent concurrency control mechanism in order to improve efficiency at its own site, which is not suitable for distributed control.
3. Even if all the systems have global concurrency control mechanisms, they may not be identical. For example, some systems use time-stamp-based mechanisms, whereas other systems employ two-phase lock mechanisms. We cannot combine these different global concurrency control mechanisms.

Since Case 1 is the most restrictive, this paper will discuss that case. Since the locking mechanism is not available for global concurrency control, a query modification approach is used to realize such control.

Figure 1(a) shows that we need a global concurrency control mechanism when all global transactions are read-only. We will consider the following four transactions where t_1 and t_2 are global read-only ones and t_3 and t_4 are local write transactions:

t_1: After reading value A at site 1, read value D at site 2.
t_2: After reading value C at site 2, read value B at site 1.
t_3: Modify values A and B at site 1.
t_4: Modify values C and D at site 2.

The order of the transaction processing at sites 1 and 2, by the schedule shown in Figure 1(a), is as follows:

site 1: $t_1 \rightarrow t_3 \rightarrow t_2$
site 2: $t_2 \rightarrow t_4 \rightarrow t_1$

Since these two orderings are not compatible, we have to restart either t_1 or t_2. This example shows that we need a global concurrency control mechanism even if all global transactions are read-only.

In order to avoid such a problem, the order of transaction processing at each site should be controlled by a global concurrency control mechanism. We will present a global concurrency control mechanism that uses ordering numbers assigned to the sites. A semijoin-based query-processing procedure is combined with the mechanism. Another mechanism is also presented, which improves efficiency by modifying the site ordering numbers adaptively.

BASIC CONCEPTS

Concurrency Control

For efficient processing, it is important to execute many transactions concurrently. In this case a semantically correct schedule must be generated. Here a schedule consists of a sequence of read and write operations (see Figure 1(a)). Generally we shall assume that the schedule is consistent if and only if its effect is equivalent to that obtained by executing the same transactions serially in some order, called serializable.[1] We say that two schedules are equivalent if and only if the value that one transaction reads was written by the same transaction in both schedules. For example, in Figure 1(a), t_2 reads the value that t_3 wrote at site 1, so t_2 must be before t_3 in an equivalent serial schedule. The graph in Figure 1(b) shows this kind of precedence relationship among transactions. Since it has a cycle, there is no equivalent serial schedule; that is, this schedule is not serializable. To guarantee serializability, many methods have been introduced. In centralized database systems, concurrency control mechanisms are not essential, since transactions can be executed serially. In distributed database systems, however, since transactions are executed in parallel at several sites, a global concurrency control mechanism is necessary even if each site has a local concurrency control mechanism. When many transactions are executed concurrently, deadlock may occur; so a deadlock-free mechanism is also required.

One of the methods used to ensure that schedules are serializable and deadlock-free is the tree protocol.[3] If each transaction obeys the tree protocol, no global scheduler is required. The relationship among data is assumed to be represented by a tree, which is true for hierarchical database systems.

The basic operations to be considered are LOCK and UNLOCK. Only one transaction is permitted to lock a datum at a time. We use L(A) and U(A) to represent LOCK A and UNLOCK A, respectively. A tree protocol is satisfied by a transaction with respect to T, a tree whose nodes corresponds to data if

1. Any datum can be locked for the first time.
2. A datum can be locked if its parent is currently locked.
3. Any datum can be unlocked at any time.
4. No datum is ever locked twice by one transaction.
5. Transactions requiring access to data at different levels of the tree structure must lock each record connecting the different levels.

Example 1: We will consider the four transactions used in Figure 1. We assume that the tree showing the relationships among data is shown as Figure 2. In order to obey the tree protocol, transactions are modified as follows:

t_1: L(A)L(C)U(A)L(D)U(C)U(D)
t_2: L(C)L(B)U(C)U(B)
t_3: L(A)L(C)U(A)L(B)U(C)U(B)
t_4: L(C)L(D)U(C)U(D)

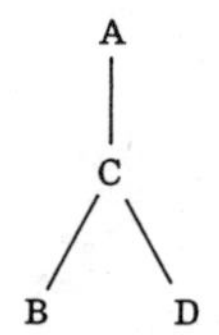

Figure 2—Ordering on data for the tree protocol

Although t_1 requires A and D only, it has to lock C because of the requirement 2 of the tree protocol. Since the first lock of a transaction is not restricted, t_2 and t_4 start by locking C.

Query Processing

Let R be a relation on a set $\{A_1, \ldots, A_n\}$ of attributes, where the set is denoted by *R*, the relation schema of R. Let u be a tuple of a relation and u[X] be the part of u corresponding to the attribute set X. In this paper the following notations of relational algebra will be used:

Projection: $R[X] = \{u[X] \mid u \in R\}$
Natural equijoin $R_i \bowtie R_j = \{u \mid u \in R,\ u[R_i] \in R_i,\ u[R_j] \in R_j,\ R = R_i \cup R_j\}$

A query graph $G_q = (V,E,L)$ corresponding to a natural join query q is a labeled undirected graph. V is a set of vertices, where v_i in V corresponds to relation R_i referred to in q. Two vertices v_i and v_j corresponding to R_i and R_j are connected by an edge if and only if there is $R_i \bowtie R_j$. The label of the edge is a subset of $R_i \cap R_j$. E is the set of edges, and L is the set of labels for E.

A query is called a tree query if there exists a query graph that corresponds to it and it is circuit-free; otherwise it is cyclic.

A semijoin of R_i by R_j is denoted by $R_i \ltimes R_j$ and defined as

$$\begin{aligned} R_i \ltimes R_j &= (R_i \bowtie R_j)[R_i] \\ &= R_i \bowtie R_j[R_i \cap R_j] \end{aligned}$$

In distributed database systems semijoins are used in order to reduce the cost of communications. For tree queries there exists an efficient procedure to calculate partial results for all relations using semijoins only. Here a partial result for R_i is the result of the join projected on R_i. Since conversion methods exist which can transform cyclic queries into tree queries,[4,5] we consider tree queries only in this paper.

Although there may be more than one relation at each site, for simplicity we assume that each site S_i contains exactly one relation R_i, which is obtained by preprocessing all relations at site S_i involved in the query. This assumption is commonly used, and the scheme shown here may be easily extended to handle more general cases.

A general semijoin-based tree query-processing procedure is as follows (because of space limitations, we have simplified the description):

Procedure 1: Query-processing procedure for a tree query using semijoins.

1. In the tree graph representing the given query, select an arbitrary relaton as a root of the tree.
2. Phase 1: Starting from the leaf relations, perform semijoins by sending values of join attributes.
3. At the root relation, a partial result is obtained.
4. Phase 2: Starting from the root relation, perform semijoins by sending values of join attributes. At each site partial results are then obtained.

Example 2: Let us consider the tree query in Figure 3. The attributes of the relations are as follows:

$R_1(AD)$ $R_2(ABCE)$ $R_3(BF)$ $R_4(CG)$

We assume that each R_i is stored at site S_i (i = 1,2,3,4). The following R is required as the result:

$$R = R_1 \bowtie R_2 \bowtie R_3 \bowtie R_4$$

Partial results for these relations are as follows:

R[AD] R[ABCE] R[BF] R[CG]

If only partial results are required, the semijoin-based algorithm is sufficient. If this is not the case (i.e., if R is required at some site), the algorithm can be used as a preprocess.

1. We can select any relation as a root. Let R_1 be the root.
2. Phase 1:
   (2-1) Send B values of R_3 from site S_3 to site S_2. Perform a semijoin with R_2.
   (2-2) Send C values of R_4 from site S_4 to site S_3. Perform a semijoin with the result of (2-1).
   (2-3) Send A values of the result of the above two operations from site S_2 to site S_1. Perform a semijoin with R_1.
3. At site S_1 the partial result R[AD] is obtained.
4. Phase 2:
   (4-1) Send A values of the above result to site S_2. Perform a semijoin and the partial result R[ABCE] is obtained at site S_2.
   (4-2) Send B (and C) values of R[ABCE] to site S_3 (and site S_4, respectively). By performing a semijoin the partial result R[BF] (and R[CG]) can be obtained at site S_3 (and site S_4, respectively).

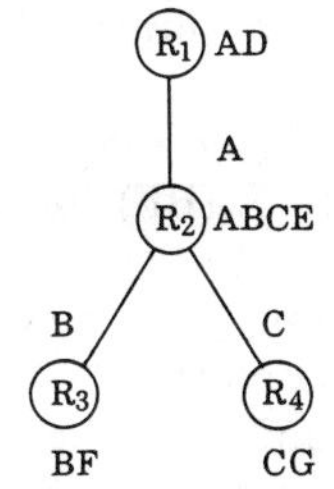

Figure 3—A tree query

THE PROBLEM

Although an overview of some of the problems involved with global concurrency control, as well as the assumptions made, were discussed in the introduction, we will give specific details here.

Consider the case when systems without concurrency control mechanisms are connected by an Ether-type bus line. This network satisfies the following properties: (1) a message can be broadcast to all the sites, and (2) it is not possible to transmit messages simultaneously from more than one site.

All global transactions are assumed to be read-only. Modification of relations is assumed to be realized by local transactions. This is similar to a relational database system that realizes views. Usually, however, modification operations are permitted to be applied to the base relations only (read-only views), because the general view update problem is known to be very difficult.

Since semijoin-based query-processing procedures are very efficient, we will use them in this paper. We have to modify the procedure, however, because of the following problem.

If the data are modified between Phase 1 and Phase 2 in Procedure 1, we may not get the correct result. If we organize a distributed database system by the top-down approach, we usually use a locking mechanism to prevent such a modification. Since the assumption that the subtransaction at Phase 1 and one at Phase 2 are considered to be different at the processing site, data may be modified before the second subtransaction. To handle the problem caused by such a local write transaction, one simple method is to store the values at Phase 1 that will be used at Phase 2. This approach, however, may require many duplicated data, and there still exists a global consistency problem (Introduction); so we will discuss methods to prevent this problem in following sections.

We will consider query-processing procedures together with concurrency control mechanisms. Usually read-only transactions are called queries. In the following sections we use the term *query* instead of *transaction* when a transaction performs only read requests.

A QUERY-PROCESSING PROCEDURE AND A BASIC GLOBAL CONCURRENCY CONTROL MECHANISM

As shown in the previous section, it is necessary to modify the semijoin-based query-processing procedure when local write transactions are permitted. In this section we will present a query-processing procedure having the following properties.

1. Instead of visiting the same site twice at Phases 1 and 2, it requires that each site be visited only once.
2. Relations in a query tree can be processed in an arbitrary order.

We need the first property because of the problem pointed out in the previous section. The second property is used to combine the query-processing procedure with a tree-protocol–based global concurrency control mechanism.

First we modify the basic semijoin-based procedure to satisfy Property 1 above.

Example 3: Let us consider the same query as Example 2. We assume that the target relation R[ABG] is required at site S_1. By sending values contained in ABG together with the join attributes, the result can be obtained at site S_1 by performing Phase 1 only.

1. Let R_1 be the root.
2. (2-1) Same as Example 2.
   (2-2) Send R_4(CG) to site S_2, since C is the join attribute and G is contained in the target. Perform a join.
   (2-3) Send combined values of ABG to site S_1 and perform a join.
3. At site S_1 R[ABG] is obtained.

We assume that projection R[X] of the join of all relations in the query is required at one site. In such a case we only need Phase 1 of Procedure 1 by transmitting attributes in X together with join attributes.

A tree query is usually processed from leaf sites by Procedure 1; but by using the broadcast capability of Ether-type networks, we can change the order of processing.

Procedure 2: Query-processing procedure using the broadcast capability.

1. Let T be the tree representing the given query.
2. Select one arbitrary relation R_i in T. Let X be the attribute set of the target relation (i.e., R[X] is required at site S_t, where R is the join of all relations involved in the query). Let Y be the union of attributes satisfying

$$Y = R_i \cap (X \cup_{\substack{j \\ j \neq i}} R_j)$$

   where $\bigcup_{\substack{j \\ j\neq i}} R_j$ denotes the union of all the join attributes of R_i. Broadcast $R_i[Y]$ to all sites.
3. Let $R_{j1}, \ldots, R_{jm}$ be all relations satisfying $R_i \cap R_j \neq \emptyset$. Let R_k be one of the relations.
   (3-1) Except R_k, perform the following semijoin at the site of R_j $(j = j_1, \ldots, j_m)$.

$$R_j \bowtie R_i[R_i \cap R_j]$$

   (3-2) At the site of R_k perform the following join:

$$R_k \bowtie R_i[Y]$$

   Note that attribute set of R_k may change if R_i contains attributes in X that were not originally contained in R_k.
4. Let T′ be the new tree obtained from T by eliminating R_i. T′ can be obtained by the following steps:
   (4-1) Remove all edges connecting between R_i and R_j $(j = j_1, \ldots, j_m)$ directly. Remove R_i.
   (4-2) Connect R_k and R_j's $(j = j_1, \ldots, j_m, j \neq k)$ directly.

The conversion of (4-1) and (4-2) is shown in Figure 4(a) and (b). Let T′ be the new T and goto step (2).

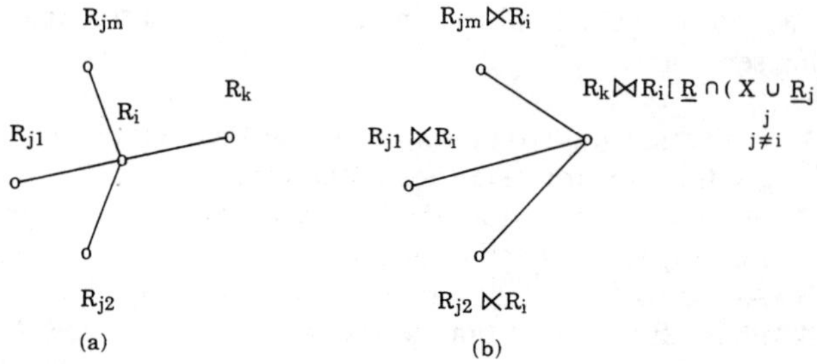

Figure 4—Conversion of a tree

5. Repeat the above process until only the relation at the target site remains. At that time the result R[X] is obtained at the site.

Theorem 1: Procedure 2 is correct.

Proof: We only need to prove that the transformation shown in Figure 4(a) and (b) is correct. It is easily shown by the following equation.

$$\begin{aligned} R_i \bowtie R_{j1} \bowtie \cdots \bowtie R_{jm} = & (R_{j1} \ltimes R_i) \\ & \bowtie (R_{j2} \ltimes R_i) \\ & \bowtie \cdots \bowtie (R_{jm} \ltimes R_i) \\ & \bowtie (R_k \bowtie R_i[Y]) \end{aligned}$$

QED

One possible problem of Procedure 2 is to find a method to determine R_k in Step 3.

Procedure 3: Select of R_k at Step 3 of Procedure 2.

1. Let S_0 be the site where it is required to obtain the target relation.
2. Among R_j's select R_k which is close to R_0. Here distance on the tree is determined by the number of edges between the two nodes.

Example 4: Let us consider the tree query shown in Figure 3. We assume that the target relation R[ABG] is required at site S_1. X = ABG.

1. Let $R_2 \rightarrow R_3 \rightarrow R_4 \rightarrow R_1$ be the linear order of the relations; we assume that relations are processed in this order.
2. R_2:
   (2-1) Select R_1 as the relation to apply to the join.
   (2-2) Broadcast R_2[ABC] (A, B, and C are join attributes) and perform a join at S_1 and semijoins at S_3 and S_4. The resulting relation at each site is as follows:

   R_1(ABCD) R_2(BF) R_4(CG)

   (2-3) By eliminating R_2, a new query graph, shown in Figure 5, is obtained.
   (2-4) Process R_3 and R_4 by the conventional tree-query-processing procedure.
3. At site S_1 R[ABG] is obtained.

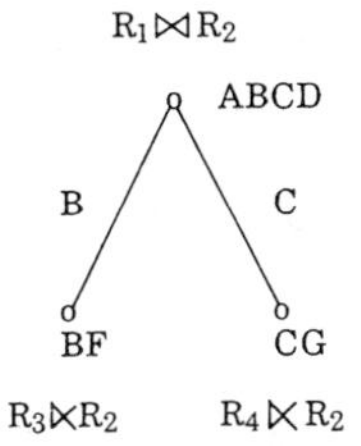

Figure 5—A new query graph

Since for any query we can use the same order to process relations, the following concurrency control mechanism can be used:

Procedure 4: Query-processing procedure for a tree query preserving global consistency.

1. There is a fixed ordering of the sites. Let $S_1, S_2, \ldots, S_n$ be the sequence of the sites in this order. Since we assume that each site does not process queries concurrently, at any moment each site processes at most one query.
2. For each query we use the ordering $(S_1, S_2, \ldots, S_n)$ to select sites by Procedure 2. We must consider the following two cases in order to apply Procedure 2.
   (2-1) After processing R_i, we must proceed to R_{i+1}, but there are cases when R_{i+1} is not contained in the query. In such cases we need put dummy processing of R_{i+1} in the query.
   (2-2) The target site R_t may not be R_n, which is the last relation to be processed. In such a case we apply Procedure 2 as if S_n is the target site. After obtaining the result at the site it is transmitted to the target site.

3. After processing R_i, if S_{i+1} is occupied by another query, wait until it completes. When R_i is assigned to process query q_i, it starts to perform joins received from R_j $(j < i)$ for q_i (see Example 4).

The pipeline processing is achieved by (1) serial processing at each site and (2) the serial processing property of the communication bus line.

Theorem 2: Procedure 4 is correct, and it ensures serializability and deadlock freedom.

Proof: In the method shown in Procedure 4, a mechanism similar to a special case of the tree protocol is used. Data items are replaced by sites, and the chain showing the ordering $(S_1, \ldots, S_n)$ is a special tree structure. Thus, serializability and deadlock freedom result from the fact that the tree protocol satisfies these conditions.

QED

Example 5: Let us consider the tree query shown in Figure 6(a). Here attributes of relations are as follows.

$R_1(AD)$ $R_2(ABCE)$ $R_3(BF)$ $R_5(CG)$

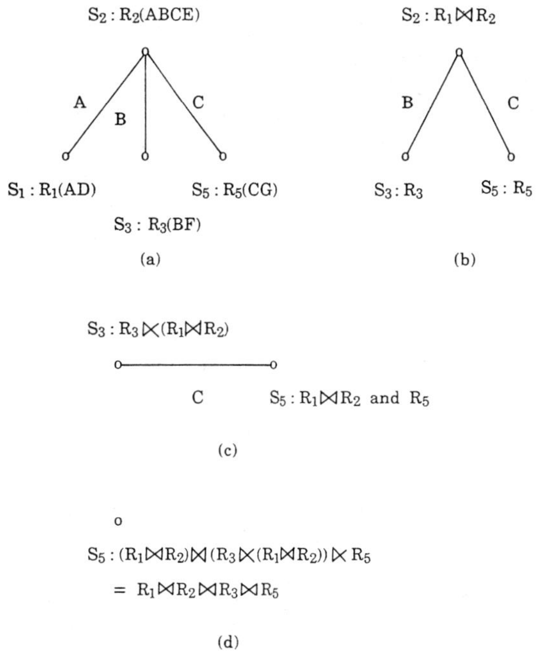

Figure 6—An example of Procedure 4

We assume that each R_i is stored at site S_i $(i = 1,2,3,5)$ and that the joins of all relations is R. R is required to be calculated at site S_2. We give a fixed linear order as follows:

$$S_1 \rightarrow S_2 \rightarrow S_3 \rightarrow S_4 \rightarrow S_5$$

S_1: Send R_1 to S_2. The resulting query graph is shown in Figure 6(b).

S_2: Perform a join. Select R_5 as R_k and broadcast $R_1 \bowtie R_2$. At site S_5, $R_1 \bowtie R_2$ is stored. The computation starts when S_5 becomes the site to process the query.

S_3: Perform a semijoin and $R_3 \ltimes (R_1 \bowtie R_2)$ is obtained. Broadcast $R_3 \ltimes (R_1 \bowtie R_2)$.

S_4: Since R_4 is not contained in the query, it is used to synchronize with other queries. No computation is made at S_4.

S_5: Perform a join ($R_1 \bowtie R_2$ from S_2, $R_3 \ltimes (R_1 \bowtie R_2)$ from S_3, and R_5 at S_5) and R is obtained. Send its result to the S_2.

A GLOBAL CONCURRENCY CONTROL MECHANISM USING ADAPTIVE ORDERING OF SITES

In the previous section we discussed a basic global concurrency control mechanism. Since every query has to visit all sites in a fixed order between the first site and the last site required, it has the following disadvantages: (1) for each query the optimal ordering is usually different, so the cost for processing may become high; and (2) there are queries that need to visit only a few sites. The base mechanism may require that several sites be visited which are not used. This produces unnecessary overhead.

In this section we will develop a mechanism that changes

ordering adaptively according to the query set. As the network has broadcasting capability, each site can know the status of processing at other sites as well as queries in the queue. By the new mechanism, the ordering of the sites is modified according to the queries in the queueing list.

We will define a graph showing the order of the sites.

Definition 1: An order graph $G_0(V,E)$ is a directed graph. V is a set of vertices, where v_i in V corresponds to site S_i. E is a set of all directed edges. If there exists an edge e_{ij} from v_i to v_j, site S_i precedes S_j in order. Let V_0 be vertices in V that have an incoming edge and/or an outgoing edge.

For the first query for the system we can determine an arbitrary order of sites. For the second query, sites that are not used by the first query can be processed in an arbitrary order. The order determined by the queries currently processed is shown by the order graph in Definition 1. When a new query is added or a query is completed, we can change the graph to improve the efficiency as compared to the fixed-order approach. We assume that the order graph is kept by all the sites.

Procedure 5: Procedure for the order graph modification.

Let V_0 be a set of vertices corresponding to the sites currently involved in the query processing. A subset V_m of V_0 determined by Case 2 is called a set of vertices whose orders are modifiable. Initially $V_0 = \emptyset$ and $V_m = \emptyset$.

Case 1: When a new query Q is added.

Let S be the set of sites used by Q. We can determine the ordering of sites as follows:

(1-1) For sites in $S \cap (V_0 - V_m)$ the order does not conflict with the current order graph.

(1-2) For the sites $S \cap V_m$ the following graph modification process can be applied:

(1-2-1) Let a vertex in $S \cap V_m$ be v_i. We assume that there are edges e_{ki} and e_{ih}. By the condition implied when generating a vertex in V_m, each vertex in V_m has an outgoing edge. Add edge e_{kh}.

(1-2-2) Remove e_{ki} and e_{ih}. If v_i does not have incoming edges, Step 1-2-1 is not necessary.

(1-2-3) The position of v_i is arbitrary if the new position is the successor of the old v_i.

(1-3) For sites in S but not in V_0, an arbitrary order can be assigned. Since Q is assumed to be a tree query, we can determine the ordering necessary to obey the ordering determined by the query graph as much as possible. $V_0 \cup S$ becomes new V_0, and $V_m - S$ becomes the new V_m.

Case 2: When a query Q terminates, sites used by Q only may be eliminated from the graph. There are the following two cases.

(2-1) The site used by Q only has an outgoing edge. We cannot eliminate the vertex corresponding to the site, but the position of the vertex can be moved. We put the vertex to V_m.

(2-2) The site used by Q only does not have an outgoing edge. In such a case we can eliminate the vertex corresponding to the site from V_0. This process is applied recursively until no further elimination is possible.

Example 4: We assume that the following queries Q_1 and Q_2 are currently processed in the system:

Q_1: It uses S_1 and S_2 in the order $S_1 \rightarrow S_2$

Q_2: It uses S_3, S_4, and S_5 in the order $S_3 \rightarrow S_4 \rightarrow S_5$

We assume that Q_3 which uses S_1, S_2, S_4, and S_6 is added to the system.

$$V_0 = \{S_1, S_2, S_3, S_4, S_5\}$$
$$V_m = \emptyset$$
$$S = \{S_1, S_2, S_4, S_6\}$$

For $S \cap V_0 = \{S_1, S_2, S_4\}$, we must follow the orders determined by the queries Q_1 and Q_2, that is $S_1 \rightarrow S_2$. The order for Q_3 must not conflict with $S_1 \rightarrow S_2$. Let the order for Q_3 be

$$S_1 \rightarrow S_2 \rightarrow S_6 \rightarrow S_4$$

By merging these orders we get the following order:

$$S_3 \rightarrow S_1 \rightarrow S_2 \rightarrow S_6 \rightarrow S_4 \rightarrow S_5$$

Now we assume that Q_2 terminates. Sites used by Q_2 only are S_3 and S_5. Since S_5 does not have outgoing edges, it can be eliminated from V_0. Since S_3 has an outgoing edge, $V_m = \{S_3\}$.

An outline of the proof of the correctness of Procedure 5 is as follows. For any currently executing queries the visitation order is the same, so the process is the same as that in Procedure 4. The problem is caused by queries that have already terminated when query Q is added. We assume that the last site of Q is S_1. If such a query terminates at S_1's descendant, it is obvious that it is before Q in the equivalent serial schedule, so there is no contradiction. If it terminates at S_1's ancestor, the sites that it used cannot become the descendant of sites used by Q, so no contradicton occurred.

SUMMARY

In this paper we have shown global concurrency control mechanisms for a local network consisting of systems that do not have concurrency control capability. Because of this assumption we do not use a locking mechanism at each site. The whole query is decomposed into subqueries at the site where the query is produced. Since the data flow control can be expressed in a query, the whole mechanism can be realized by a so-called query modification approach. The major reasons why we do not need locking or timestamp mechanisms are that (1) at each site queries are serially processed and (2) by observing the data transmitted on the bus line, the status of the processing can be determined.

ACKNOWLEDGMENT

The authors are grateful to Professor Shuzo Yajima and members of Yajima Laboratory for helpful discussions.

REFERENCES

1. Bernstein, P. A., and N. Goodman. "Concurrency Control in Distributed Database Systems." *ACM Computing Surveys,* 13 (1981).
2. Eswaran, K. P., J. N. Gray, R. A. Lorie,and I. L. Traiger. "The Notions of Consistency and Predicate Locks in a Database System." CACM 19 (1976).
3. Silberschatz, A., and Z. Kedem. "Consistency in Hierarchical Database Systems." JACM, (1980).
4. Kambayashi, Y., M. Yoshikawa, and S. Yajima. "Query Processing for Distributed Databases Using Generalized Semi-Joins." I *Proceedings of the* ACM SIGMOD, June 1982.
5. Kambayashi, Y., and M. Yoshikawa. "Query Processing Using Dependencies and Horizontal Decomposition." I *Proceedings of the* ACM SIGMOD, June 1983.
6. Bernstein, P. A., and D. M. Chiu. "Using Semi-Joins to Solve Relational Queries." JACM, 28 (1981), pp. 25–40.

Synapse tightly coupled multiprocessors: A new approach to solve old problems

by STEVE FRANK
and ARMOND INSELBERG
Synapse Computer Corporation
Milpitas, California

ABSTRACT

The theoretical merits of a tightly coupled multiple-processor/shared-memory architecture have long been recognized. Two major problems in designing such an architecture are the performance limitations imposed by shared-memory bus contention in cached processors and multiple-processor data coherency. In the Synapse system, memory contention was significantly reduced by designing a processor cache employing a non-write-through algorithm, which minimized bandwidth between cache and shared memory. The multicache coherency problem was solved by a new bussing scheme, the Synapse Expansion Bus, which includes an ownership level protocol between processor caches. Using a non-write-through cache and the Synapse Expansion Bus, Synapse has designed a symmetric, tightly coupled multiprocessor system, capable of being expanded on line and under power from two through twenty-eight processors with a linear improvement in system performance.

INTRODUCTION

Imagine being able to plug dozens of processors together, and have them become a single, logical, transaction-processing entity. The significant tasks of load balancing and system tuning would be an impossibility in current efforts to use multiple, loosely coupled microprocessors in on-line transaction processing.

With the new Synapse mainframe system,[1,2] designed for high-performance database transaction processing, as many as 28 processors can share a common, fault-tolerant memory system. The more processors there are, the faster a common transaction job queue is handled. Measured results with many processors have shown that incremental processing power has increased additively with more processors. In other words, four processors linked together produce the same computing power as four independent processors, a ten-processor Synapse system has the power of ten processors, and so on. The key to the Synapse Expansion Architecture approach is a focus on the nature of on-line transaction processing, and a new look at bus arbitration and caching in tightly coupled systems.

HISTORICAL ASPECTS OF CACHING

Memory hierarchies in the form of cache memories are used in most current computer systems to improve processor performance. Cache memory temporarily holds the in-use contents of main memory. Data present in cache memory can be accessed by the processor in much less time than if located in main memory. Thus, processor performance is increased, since less time is spent waiting for instructions and for data to be fetched. Typically, cache memory can be accessed 5–10 times faster than main memory.

Increases in performance due to cache memories are explained by the properties of temporal and spatial locality. Temporal locality, or locality by time, means that data referenced in the near future are likely to be in use already. Temporal locality is exhibited by program loops in which instructions and data are reused. Spatial locality, or locality by space, means there is a high probability of making references in the near future that are close to the locations of the current reference. This behavior is influenced by some common characteristics of programs: Instructions are mostly executed sequentially, and related data items, such as arrays, are stored together.

Optimizing the design of cache memories has four aspects.[3] They are (1) maximizing the hit ratio, (2) minimizing the access time to cache data, (3) minimizing delay due to a cache miss, and (4) minimizing the overhead of updating main memory and maintaining cache coherency. Optimizing these aspects maximizes single processor performance by minimizing the average processor memory access time. Bandwidth between the cache and backing store (memory) is often larger than would be necessary without a cache.

MULTIPLE-PROCESSOR CONSIDERATIONS

When designing a system where more than one processor share common memory (Figure 1), a major limiting factor on system performance is the number of processors that can share memory effectively. The limiting factor on the number of processors is the bus bandwidth and, in turn, memory contention. As memory contention increases, the average memory access time increases, and the performance of each processor decreases.[4–6] It became clear that the design goals required to maximize the performance of the Synapse multiprocessor system were to maximize bus and shared-memory bandwidth, and to minimize the bus bandwidth required per processor. More specifically, in order to meet these goals, the most critical aspect of the Synapse multiprocessor, shared-memory cache design, was to minimize bus bandwidth use between cache and shared memory.

Techniques for maximizing bus and shared-memory bandwidth are straightforward. A description of how the Synapse Expansion Bus (XBUS) meets these goals is described later in this article. A more significant problem is that of designing a cache that minimizes bus bandwidth use per processor.

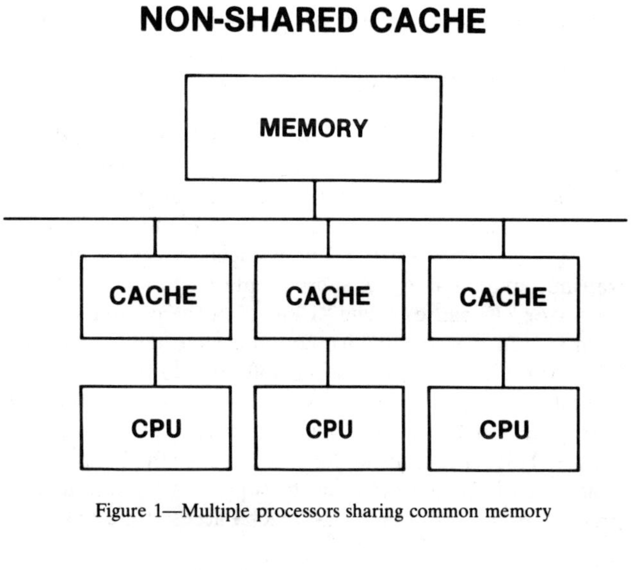

Figure 1—Multiple processors sharing common memory

WRITE-THROUGH VS. NON-WRITE-THROUGH

Extensive studies have been conducted on the effects of standard cache design parameters (such as cache size, block size, set associativity, prefetch and fetch algorithms, and replacement algorithms) on the bandwidth between cache and memory.[3,7,8] Two different techniques for processing write operations have significantly different effects on bus bandwidth between cache and memory.

In the write-through method of write operations, a processor write to cache is immediately written through to shared memory. This method is used in systems such as the IBM 3033 and the VAX 11/780.

In the non-write-through method,[3,4,9] processor reads and writes are treated alike: If the block to be written is currently not present in the cache, it is copied from shared memory. All subsequent read or write accesses to this block are processed by the cache until such time as selected by the replacement algorithm. At this time the data are written back to shared memory. Data need not be written back to shared memory if they were not modified. A single cache access by the processor can potentially cause zero, one (read), or two (purge old block, read new block) accesses to shared memory.

The advantage of the non-write-through algorithm is that the access rate between the cache and shared memory can be reduced to any value by a sufficient increase in cache size. In contrast, in the write-through method, the access rate between cache and shared memory can only be reduced to the write access rate of the processor. Instruction mix analyses show that write accesses vary from 10% to 30%, depending on processor architecture and application. Therefore, when write-through is used, a minimum 10–30% of processor accesses also generate accesses to shared memory. The non-write-through approach results in a three- to tenfold reduction in the transfers between cache and shared memory.

THE MULTICACHE COHERENCE PROBLEM

Unfortunately, in a multiple-cache/multiple-processor system, both methods of cache write operation run into difficulties with memory coherence (Figure 2). A shared-memory scheme is coherent if the data returned on a read are always the data last written to the same address.[3,4,10]

As a specific example, assume that in a two-processor system, two caches use the non-write-through method and share memory connected by a common bus. Let "A" be the memory address of a block of data which is read and modified by both processors. A modification of the contents of address "A" is done by processor "0" in its cache, but the result is not transmitted to memory. A subsequent read of address "A" by processor "1" causes cache "1" to read the contents of "A" from shared memory, which contains stale data for address "A." There are several possible solutions to this:

First, all processors in the system can use a *shared cache* (e.g., the Univac 1100/80 has two processors sharing one cache). This solution is not feasible because the bandwidth of a single cache is not sufficient to support a large number of processors. In addition, longer cache access time delays are incurred, because the shared cache cannot be physically close to all processors.

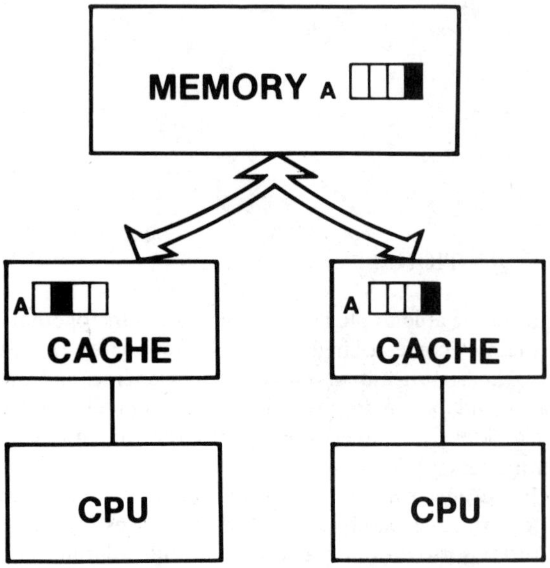

Figure 2—Multicache coherency

Second, each time a processor performs a write to the cache, it broadcasts the write to all other caches in the system. If the address is found in another cache, it can be invalidated. The IBM 3033 processors use invalidation. The major drawback to broadcasting all writes is that an increase in bus bandwidth is required (write-through method).

Finally, software control can be used to guarantee coherency. Certain addresses containing such items as semaphores or a job queue can be designated noncacheable and can be accessed only from shared memory. The drawback of noncacheable data is that the access time between the processor and shared memory is substantially increased. Thus, for efficiency, some shared data must be cached. The processor must then be equipped with commands that allow it to purge any address from its cache. An additional disadvantage of this technique is that the caching mechanism is no longer software-transparent. The Honeywell Series 66 and Elxsi 6400 system use similar techniques.

THE SYNAPSECACHE

The Synapse System uses a fourth method, *ownership*, to solve the multicache coherence problem. The processors (general-purpose—GPP, and input/output—IOP) and the XBUS implement a distributed ownership protocol to ensure that no data are write-shared. In addition, GPP caches use the non-write-through method to minimize required bandwidth between cache and shared memory. The protocol allows data to shift dynamically from multiple-cached copies in a read-only mode, to a single copy, which can be modified. System performance is optimized by allowing efficient sharing of data while minimizing the overheads of multicache coherence.

Figure 3 is a block diagram of the Synapse N + 1 system.

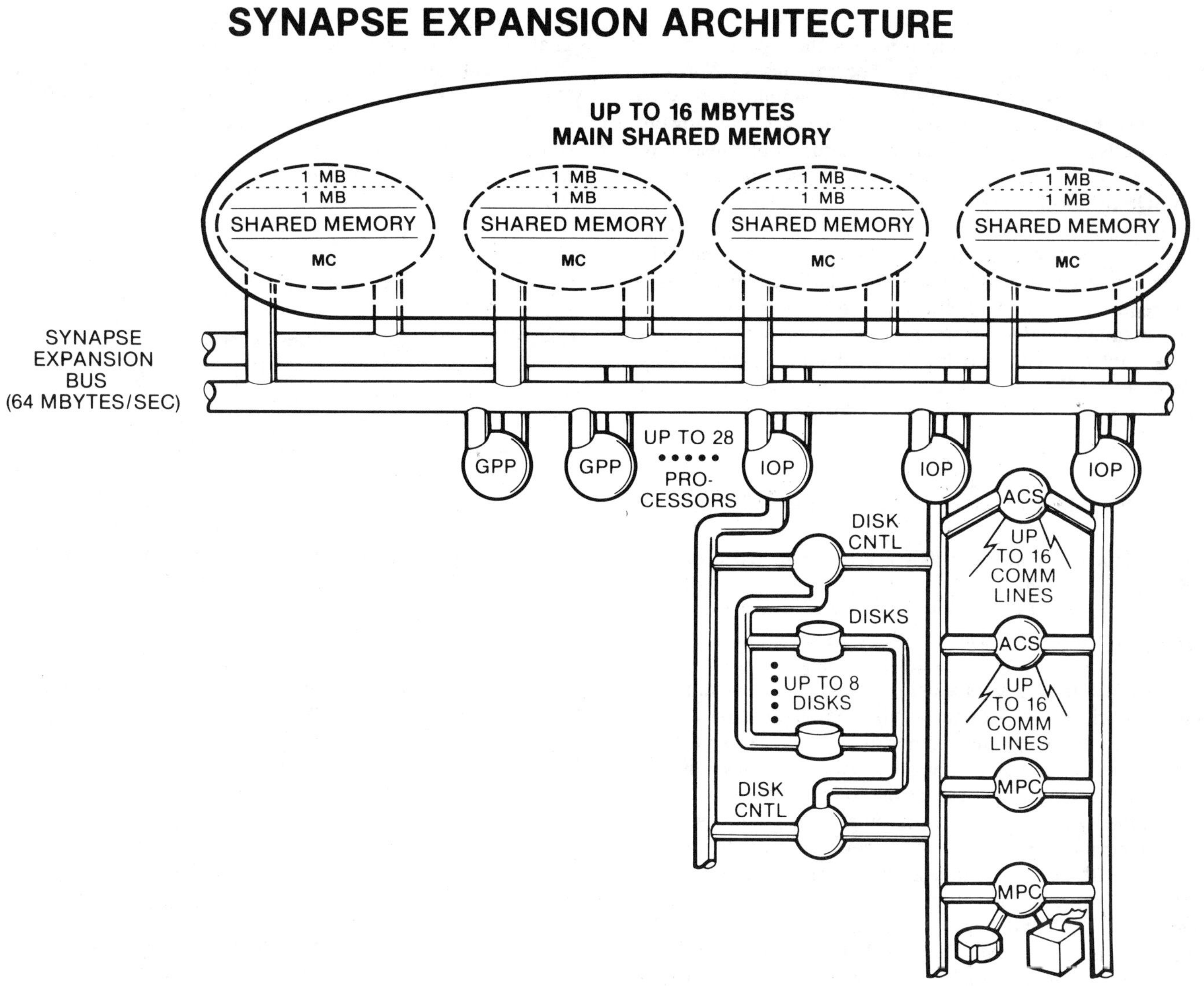

Figure 3—The Synapse N + 1 system

Two types of processor module, GPP and IOP, access shared memory via the XBUS. Each processor type uses the Motorola 68000 microprocessor as its instruction engine. Shared memory is the repository for the operating software, application programs, control structures, and lists used by several processors to schedule system activities. Shared memory can be expanded in 1-mbyte increments for a total of 16 mbytes distributed over as many as four main memory controllers (MMCs). Each MMC contains a 15-entry job queue to handle multiple requests and to pipeline requests with responses.

The GPP is the instruction processor that executes user programs and the majority of the operating software from shared memory. Each GPP includes a 16-kbyte non-write-through cache, which increases processor performance while minimizing XBUS use. Each cache participates in the bus ownership protocol to ensure data coherency. Other functions include a paged-address translation and protection scheme implemented with an address translation cache.

The IOP also interfaces to the XBUS and accesses shared memory. Each IOP has a private, 512-kbyte local memory in which a portion of the operating system software resides. Each IOP manages up to 16 device controllers including Advanced Communication Subsystems (ACSs), Disk Controllers, and Multiple Purpose Controllers (MPCs). Even though the IOP does not contain a cache, it also participates with GPPs and MMCs in XBUS ownership protocol.

SYNAPSE EXPANSION BUS: UNIQUE FOUR-LEVEL PROTOCOL

The XBUS consists of two independent buses, which ensure the highest possible system availability. The buses are identical, allowing accesses to be interleaved on both buses, but can be used singularly when one bus fails. The XBUS provides checked parallel information transfer, synchronous with a common system clock (in actuality, dual clocks for fault-tolerance reasons), but asynchronous with respect to device read and write cycle times (deferred response). Words of 32-bits are transferred at a 10-MHz rate simultaneously on each bus, with bus transactions consisting of one quadword (four words, or 16 bytes). Total bandwidth of both buses is 64 Mbytes/second when address overhead is accounted for.

XBUS protocol can be broken down into four levels: electrical, signal, transaction, and ownership. Most single-processor bus protocols consist of the first three levels. The ownership level protocol supplies the additional logical interface required to allow several processors to share memory, while maintaining data coherency. The ownership level protocol is implemented in a distributed manner among GPPs, IOPs, and MMCs, to allow incremental on-line system expansion.

ELECTRICAL AND SIGNAL LEVEL PROTOCOL

XBUS data and control signals are implemented using the Schottky TTL logic family. System clocks are distributed using differential ECL technology. Each bus consists of 61 signals, which are divided into three signal groups: arbitration, information transfer, and acknowledge.

XBUS arbitration uses a unique binary tree technique to allow one-clock synchronous arbitration of up to 64 devices using only nine signal lines, rather than one signal per device. Arbitration policy has two priority levels, with responses at the higher level and requests at the lower level. Within each level, priority is by device slot number with round-robin enforcement allowing all requesting devices access to the bus before any device can gain a second access.

The information transfer group consists of a four-bit command field, a 32-bit address and data field, and a six-bit requestor–number field. Each field is protected by at least byte parity. The requestor–number field contains the card slot number of the transmitter for requests and the requestor card slot number for responses.

The acknowledge group allows the receiver to communicate to the transmitter that the data or addresses have been transferred correctly and accepted. The acknowledge group is always valid two timeslots (clock periods) after the data are transferred. The receiver signals a negative acknowledge code to the transmitter if parity or protocol errors are detected. If the receiver is unable to execute the transmitted command, it signals a busy acknowledge, which causes the transmitter to retry the command after a retry interval. For example, if the MMC job queue is full, a read request from a GPP would be busied. Ownership protocol uses the busy acknowledge to serialize simultaneous requests for the same quadword address. Busy acknowledges are infrequent in normal system operation.

TRANSACTION LEVEL PROTOCOL

There is a fixed, pipelined, timeslot relationship between arbitration, information, and acknowledge groups. For the information group transmitted during timeslot "n," arbitration takes place during timeslot "n − 1," and acknowledge takes place during timeslot "n + 2." All bus transactions are broken into unidirectional transfers, called exchanges. The six types of exchanges are read-request-public, read-request-private, read response, write-modified, write-unmodified, and write new data. The unidirectional nature of XBUS exchanges maximizes the efficiency of bus and shared-memory use by allowing up to 64 pending interleaved requests.

A read transaction consists of a read request followed by a deferred read response. Figures 4a and 4b show the timing relationship between the three signal groups. The request consists of one timeslot of address and the response consists of four timeslots of data (16 bytes). Note that the timeslots between the read request and deferred response are variable and are available for additional exchanges initiated by other processors.

Bus timing for write exchanges is shown in Figures 5a and 5b. Write-modified and write new data consist of one timeslot of address and four timeslots of data. The write-unmodified consists of one timeslot address only. The pipelined nature of arbitration, data transfer, and acknowledgement is illustrated by multiple read and write exchanges in Figure 6.

OWNERSHIP PROTOCOL

The key to Synapse's ability to allow a large number of tightly coupled processors to execute in a linear, performance-additive manner is the XBUS ownership protocol and its implementation in the GPP, IOP, and MMC. This protocol is

Relative Timeslot	1	2	3	4	5	6	7	8
Arbitration Group	arb							
Information Group		read addr						
Acknowledge Group				ack addr				

Relative Timeslot	1	2	3	4	5	6	7	8
Arbitration Group	arb	hold	hold	hold				
Information Group		data word0	data word1	data word2	data word3			
Acknowledge Group				ack word0	ack word1	ack word2	ack word3	

Figure 4—A read request (a) followed by a deferred read response (b)

Relative Timeslot	1	2	3	4	5	6	7	8
Arbitration Group	arb	hold	hold	hold	hold			
Information Group		write addr	data word0	data word1	data word2	data word3		
Acknowledge Group				ack addr	ack word0	ack word1	ack word2	ack word3

Relative Timeslot	1	2	3	4	5	6	7	8
Arbitration Group	arb							
Information Group		write addr						
Acknowledge Group				ack addr				

Figure 5—The write transaction (a) includes four words of data; the write-unmodified transaction (b) does not include data

Relative Timeslot	1	2	3	4	5	6	7	8	9	10
Arbitration Group	arb	arb	arb	hold	hold	hold	hold			
Information Group		read addr	read addr	write mod	data word0	data word1	data word2	data word3		
Acknowledge Group				ack addr	ack addr	ack write	ack data0	ack data1	ack data2	ack data3

Figure 6—Multiple read and write exchanges

made up of a basic set of general concepts that can be implemented in a straightforward manner on all XBUS devices.

The physical shared-memory system is partitioned into *quadwords* of 16 bytes each. Each quadword is identified by a unique physical quadword address. All data transfers involve one complete quadword. Partial transfers (bytes, halfwords, or words) are not supported on the bus, although cache–processor transfers of these types are, of course, provided. For each physical quadword address in the system, there is one XBUS device that is said to be the current *owner* of that quadword address. By definition, the owner of a quadword address always has the correct value of the quadword data for that address.

Each quadword address in the system also has a usage mode of *public* or *private* associated with it. The usage mode of a quadword address applies to any and all copies of the quadword data for that address. If the usage mode of a quadword address is public, then the shared memory is the owner of the quadword address and has the correct data for that address; other XBUS devices may have copies of the quadword data for the quadword address, and these copies are guaranteed to be correct; and the value of the quadword data for the quadword address cannot be modified by anyone.

If the usage mode of a quadword address is private, then the owner of the quadword address has the correct quadword data for that address and can modify it in any way, and there are no other valid copies of the quadword data for that address in the system.

The current owner and usage mode of a quadword address will change dynamically as the system executes. The ownership and usage modes of a quadword address can always be determined from the last bus transactions that occurred for the given quadword address.

EXAMPLES OF SYNAPSECACHE QUADWORD OWNERSHIP

The following set of examples illustrates the ownership level protocol using three GPPs and one MMC. At the start of this sequence, the memory is the owner of quadword address "A." The GPP0 cache issues a read request public, and the shared memory responses with quadword data for address "A" (Figure 7). Quadword address "A" is still owned by shared memory with a public usage mode. The GPP0 cache has a copy of quadword "A," which cannot be modified. In Figure 8, a second read request public is issued by GPP1 cache with the owner, shared memory, responding with quadword

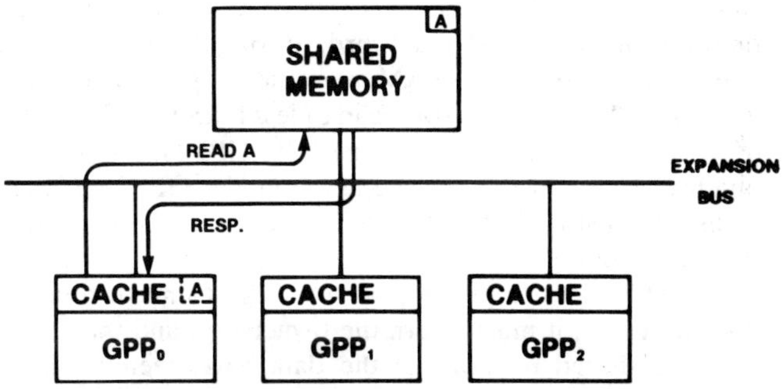

Figure 7—The read-request-public exchange

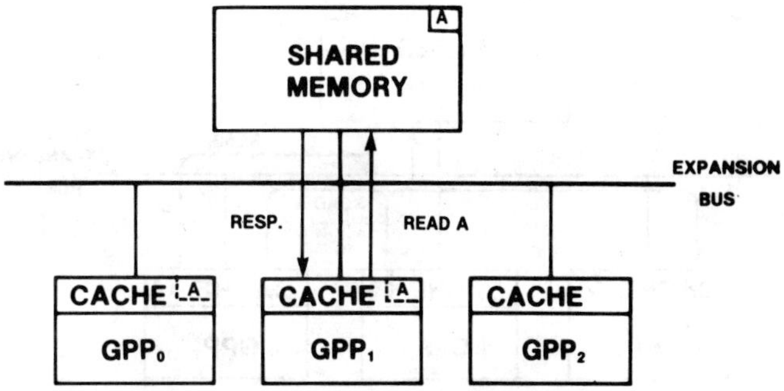

Figure 8—A second read-request-public exchange

data for "A." At the end of the second read public transaction, both caches (GPP0 and GPP1) contain read-only copies of quadword "A" with a public usage mode. Shared memory is still the owner. Most requests in the system are public (70–80%) for such items as processor instructions and read-only data. In general, the public usage mode allows data that are not being modified to be shared by all processors with no interference. Since shared memory owns quadword "A," the cache just invalidates the entry corresponding to quadword address "A" when it must be purged.

GPP2 next decides it must modify quadword address "A." The GPP2 cache issues a read private to transfer ownership of quadword "A" from shared memory, with shared memory responding with quadword "A" data. GPP0 and GPP1 caches monitor the XBUS for all exchanges corresponding to cached quadwords. When GPP0 and GPP1 detect the read private "A," public copies of quadword "A" are invalidated in real time. Figure 9 shows the result of GPP2's read private exchange: GPP2 owns quadword "A," with a private usage mode, and has the only correct value of quadword "A" data; shared memory no longer owns quadword "A," and the GPP0 and GPP1 public copies are invalidated.

GPP0 next requires that it modify quadword address "A." The GPP0 cache issues a read private to transfer ownership of quadword "A." The GPP2 cache bus monitor detects a read private to quadword "A," which it owns with a private usage mode, and so issues a cache acknowledge to GPP0. The GPP2 cache then responds directly to GPP0 while also transferring ownership. This is a direct cache-to-cache transfer. Shared memory has ignored the read request for quadword "A" because it is not the owner. This is accomplished by an additional mode bit for each quadword. Storing the mode bit adds one 64-kbyte dynamic RAM per one megabyte memory, which implies a memory overhead of less than 1%. The results of this exchange are shown in Figure 10. GPP0 is the owner of quadword "A," with a private usage mode; GPP2 no longer owns quadword "A"; and shared memory is not involved in the transaction.

If GPP0 needs to purge quadword "A" to make room for another entry, it must return the ownership, and the correct data, to shared memory. If the data have been modified, GPP0 issues a write-modified exchange, which returns both ownership and data to shared memory. If the data have not

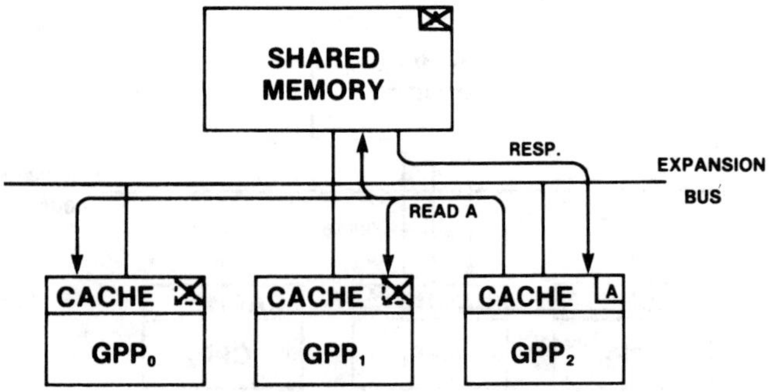

Figure 9—Public-to-private transition

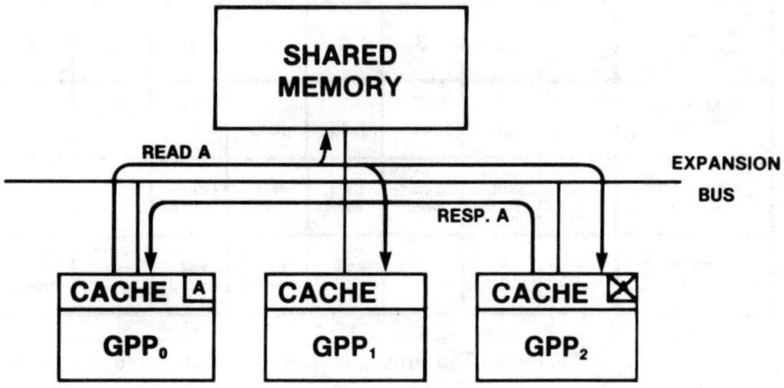

Figure 10—Cache-to-cache response

been modified, GPP0 issues a write-unmodified command, which returns ownership to shared memory and uses the last value of the data in shared memory as the current correct data.

If GPP2 cache issues a read public request (Figure 11a), GPP0's bus monitor detects a public request for quadword "A" with private usage mode and issues a busy acknowledge to GPP2. The GPP0 cache then passes quadword "A" ownership and data back to memory using a write-modified or a write-unmodified exchange. GPP2 then reissues (Figure 11b) the read public request (since it was previously busied) and memory responds with quadword "A" data. At the end of this sequence, shared memory owns quadword "A," the GPP2 cache contains a public copy of quadword "A," GPP0 no longer owns quadword "A," and its copy has been invalidated. Transitions of the usage mode from public to private or private to public between GPP caches occur very infrequently.

Several requests for the same quadword address are automatically handled, since the current owner of the quadword is responsible for acknowledging each request it owns. If a request is received for a quadword address for which a response is already pending, the current owner (who is waiting for the response) is responsible for issuing a busy acknowledge to the requestor. The requestor will reissue the read request after a retry period.

The IOP reference characteristics are markedly different from the GPP's. The nature of IOP accesses is to move large contiguous blocks of data, to or from shared memory, which exhibit little temporal locality. For example, disk data are transferred in multiples of disk sectors which are 2 kbytes long. One strategy in order to modify a quadword in shared memory would be to have the quadword read privately first and then written with the write-modified command. This is inefficient because the quadword data read are immediately replaced with new data and will not be referenced again by the IOP. A solution to this problem is to create a command to allow the quadword data to be written directly to memory without requiring a read request private to gain ownership and still maintain memory coherency. The *write new data* command steals ownership of the quadword address from the current owner and transfers ownership to shared memory. All public or private cache entries corresponding to the quadword address of the write new data are invalidated.

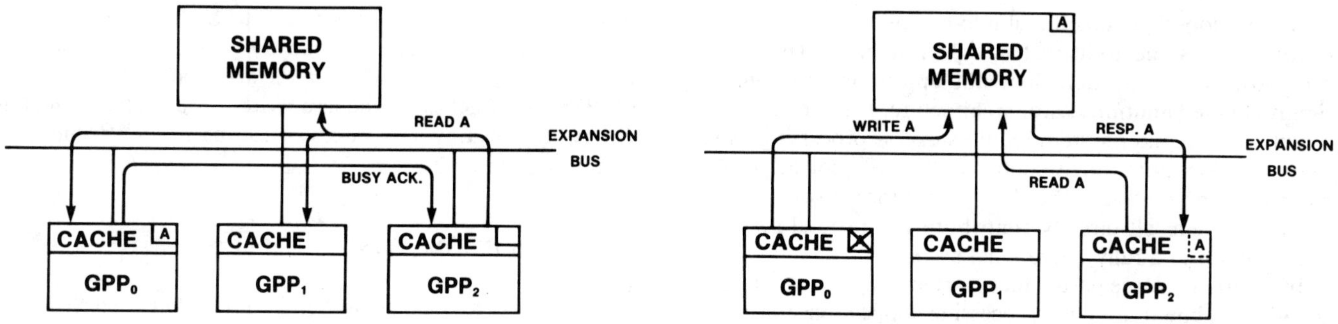

Figure 11—Read public request (a) causes the owner to busy the request; (b) shared memory responds to subsequent request

GPP IMPLEMENTATION

The GPP is a single-board, Motorola 68000-based processor, which serves as the execution unit for system software and application programs. The major GPP subsystems are shown in Figure 12. The 68000 subsystem includes a 10-MHz 68000, 32-KB EPROM for selftest, timers, and two serial ports that can be used for a system debugger and local console.

The remainder of the GPP is controlled by a microengine, which includes a 1-kbyte-by-72-bit-wide microinstruction word and special-purpose data paths. The microengine controls all GPP datapaths, implements the address translation mechanism, controls the address translation cache, controls the data cache (including algorithms), and controls the XBUS interfaces and monitors.

The GPP cache permits reads and writes by the 68000 with no wait states for cache hits. It is physically separated into quadword address tag RAM, including address comparitors and quadword data RAM. Figure 13 illustrates the GPP cache organization. Three mode bits included with the cache address tags are the valid bit (which indicates that the corresponding cache entry is allocated), the usage mode (private or public) bit, and the data-modified bit. The generation of address tags, cache replacement algorithms, and transfer of data between the quadword data RAM and the XBUS is controlled by the microengine.

Cache size is 16 kbytes divided into blocks of one quadword (16 bytes). The cache is two-set associative and uses the non-write-through method in conjunction with XBUS ownership protocol. The replacement algorithm is random between sets.[3,8]

Dual *XBUS interfaces* allow data to be transferred between the shared memory or another processor and the GPP data cache. Each XBUS interface contains bus monitor logic, which monitors all exchanges on each bus. Data cache tags are replicated (for a total of three copies of the cache tags) in each bus monitor, to allow the tags to be accessed and updated in parallel with 68000 execution. The bus monitor provides two types of functions. A real time function includes invalidation–validation or acknowledgment of read requests based on exchanges with quadword addresses corresponding to cache entries. When a response is required, the bus monitor queues the address and issues an interrupt to the microengine. The microengine then initiates the response by controlling transfer of the data from the data cache to the XBUS interface.

CONCLUSIONS

Why did Synapse go to the trouble of tying multiple processors—tightly coupling them—to a shared-memory system? One reason is that the interprocessor communication that

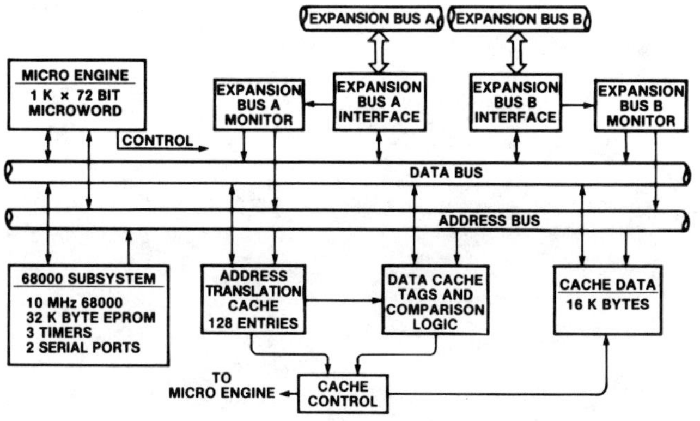

Figure 12—Synapse general-purpose processor

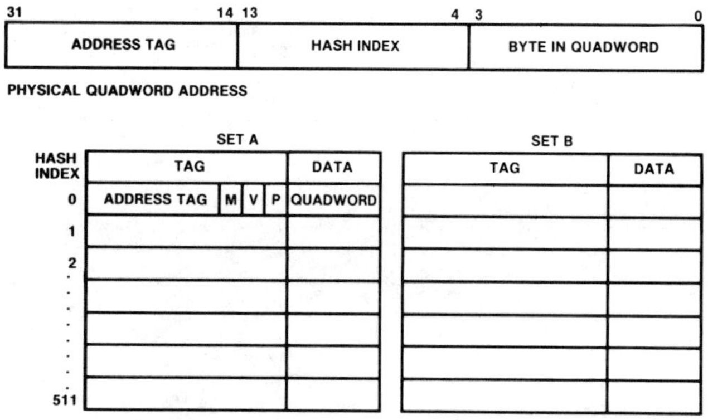

Figure 13—Synapse GPP cache organization

arises in a loosely coupled multiple-computer system significantly reduces the total system's performance. This interprocessor communication does not appear in the Synapse tightly coupled multiprocessor architecture. Fault tolerance in a multiple-computer system requires excess processing capability that does not directly contribute to the production environment. In contrast, the N + 1 multiprocessors of the Synapse system all directly contribute to the total system's performance in a fully operational system.

In addition, a large part of the effort in designing and implementing on-line transaction processing applications for loosely coupled systems is in the areas of system growth, tuning and load balancing, and file distribution. A tightly coupled architecture automates these areas, thereby accelerating project development and reducing project costs. The system can grow on line because distributed ownership protocols allow modules to be added or deleted under power; it requires no load balancing or tuning because all processes are dispatched from a common list in shared memory; and it requires no file distribution because all files are equally available to all processors.

The Synapse XBUS ownership protocol is designed to minimize bus bandwidth required per processor (GPP or IOP), while maintaining memory coherency. The non-write-through algorithm always produces less bus traffic than does the write-through algorithm for caches larger than 1–2 kbytes and block sizes that are not too large. The 16-byte quadword block size is a tradeoff between minimizing bus traffic (small block size is better) and maximizing cache hit rate. Cache allocation algorithms are optimized such that most quadwords are fetched with a public usage mode that has two positive performance effects. First, since public quadwords are read-only, they need not be written to memory when purged from cache. Second, several GPPs can have public copies in their individual caches, without interfering with each other. Single-processor modification of quadword data is handled efficiently. Concurrent write access to a quadword has been infrequent in operating the Synapse system.

Measurements during system operation have verified that bus bandwidth use per processor is very low. The percentage of Synapse XBUS bandwidth used per GPP has been measured at 2% of the total bus bandwidth. Performance has increased linearly with each processor added. During that time, the cache hit rate was found to be in excess of 95%.

A final advantage of the Synapse bus ownership protocol is that it allows future flexibility in the actual algorithms used by GPP caches. Because of the non-write-through algorithm, bus bandwidth used by any processor can be further reduced by increasing the cache size.

ACKNOWLEDGMENTS

We would like to thank Scott Merritt for his help in developing the ownership protocol and Mark Francis, George Franzen, John Galloway, and Joe Hull of the OS Group for their input and extreme patience during the debugging of the multiprocessor system. We are also grateful for the support and assistance given by many members of the Hardware and Software Development Groups.

REFERENCES

1. Inselberg, A. "Multiprocessor Architecture Ensures Fault-Tolerant Transaction Processing." *Mini-Micro Systems,* 16 (1983), pp. 165–172.
2. Jones, S. "High Application Availability." In *Proceedings of Compcon83.* New York: IEEE, pp. 12–17.
3. Smith, A. J. "Cache Memories." *ACM Computing Surveys,* 14 (1982), pp. 473–530.
4. Goodman, J. R. "Using Cache Memory to Reduce Processor Memory Traffic." *SIGARCH Newsletter,* 11 (1983), pp. 124–131.
5. Pohm, A. V., and O. P. Agrawal. "A Cache Technique for Bus Oriented Multiprocessor Systems." In *Proceedings of Compcon82.* New York: IEEE, pp. 62–66.
6. Ravishankar, C. V. and J. R. Goodman. "Cache Implementation for Multiple Microprocessors." In *Proceedings of Comcon83.* New York: IEEE, pp. 346–350.
7. Smith, J. E., and J. R. Goodman. "A Study of Instruction Cache Organizations and Replacement Policies." *SIGARCH Newsletter,* 11 (1983), pp. 132–140.
8. Strecker, W. D. "Cache Memories for the PDP-11 Family Computers." In *Proceedings of the 3rd Annual Symposium Computer Architecture.* New York: ACM, pp. 155–158.
9. Briggs, F. A. and M. Dubois. "Effectiveness of Private Caches in Multiprocessor Systems with Parallel-Pipelined Memories." *IEEE Transactions on Computers,* C-32 (1983), pp. 48–59.
10. Dubois, M. and F. A. Briggs. "Effects of Cache Coherency in Multiprocessors." *IEEE Transactions on Computers,* 3–32 (1982), pp. 1083–1099.

Throughput of multiprocessors with replicated shared memories

by SIGURD L. LILLEVIK
Oregon State University
Corvallis, Oregon
and
JOHN L. EASTERDAY
Tektronix, Incorporated
Beaverton, Oregon

ABSTRACT

Multiprocessors with replicated shared memory use a memory structure consisting of a set of memories, one for each processor, with identical contents. This minimizes read interference since each processor simply accesses its own private copy of the shared memory. To ensure shared-memory integrity, write requests transfer data to all copies in parallel. Compared to traditional shared memories, multiprocessors with replicated shared memories may achieve a speed-up which approaches O(N), with N equal to the number of processors. This speed-up occurs for systems with large N, a small number of shared memories, and large shared-memory use and fractions of read requests.

INTRODUCTION

Multiprocessor computers provide the potential for increased performance through concurrent computation, and for increased fault tolerance through hardware redundancy. Theoretically, a multiprocessor computer with N processors should achieve an O(N) speed-up compared to a uniprocessor computer. Of the several factors limiting multiprocessor speed-up, the interprocessor interference of shared memory significantly degrades performance. One method to minimize memory interference involves use of replicated shared-memory structures. Rather than a single memory, replicated shared memory consists of a set of memories, one for each processor, with identical contents. Reads may occur concurrently since each processor accesses its own copy. To maintain shared memory consistency, writes update all copies in parallel, and require arbitration and synchronization. Replicated shared memory structures increase multiprocessor throughput because of decreased interprocessor interference. In addition, these shared-memory structures may provide for increased fault tolerance because of multiple copies. Still, given a multiprocessor computer with replicated shared-memory structures, which application characteristics affect the increase in throughput, and to what extent? These questions will be studied in this paper.

A following section of this paper reviews previous work in replicated shared-memory structures and outlines a throughput model used to determine the speed-up of such memories compared to single memories. Next, some definitions and an example are provided to describe the parameters of an application. Using these definitions, the last section discusses the speed-up of generalized, symmetrical multiprocessors with replicated shared memories.

BACKGROUND

Experience with multiprocessor computers has shown designers that minimizing interprocessor interference is one of the keys to exploiting parallelism. To minimize interference, several techniques have been investigated including crossbar switches, reconfigurable busses,[1] and multiport memory. The latter, multiport memory, requires several sets of address, data, and control busses, one for each port. Both Covo[2] and Pearce and Majithia[3] have suggested that memory replication, a copy for each port, may be used as a multiport memory structure. More recently, Lillevik et al.[4] have presented guidelines for the design of multiport memory using replication techniques.

One specific example of the decrease in bus interference provided by replicated shared memory is in implementing global data such as semaphores. Usually, semaphore "busy waits" require consecutive accesses of the system bus. But with replicated shared memory, processors first read their local copy of the semaphore until released (which does not use the system bus), and then perform a "locked" read–modify–write cycle (which does use the system bus). This feature has led Borrill[5] and the IEEE P896 Future Bus Committee to consider supporting replicated shared memory in their standard.

Replicated Shared Memory Example

At Oregon State University, a five-processor computer has been developed and is in operation to investigate replicated shared memory structures.[6] From the PMS diagram in Figure 1, the system contains five 8086/8087 microprocessors inter-

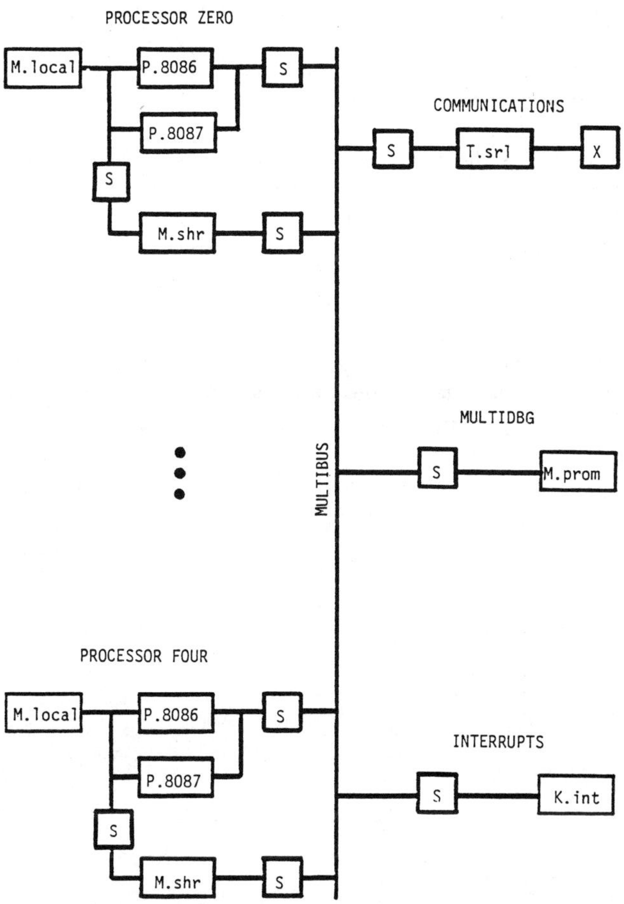

Figure 1—PMS diagram of a multiprocessor with replicated shared memory

connected with Intel's MULTIBUS. Each of the five processors contains 256 Kbytes of dynamic random access memory (RAM) of which 128 Kbytes is shared. The multiprocessor functions as follows: For reads from shared memory, each processor accesses its own copy of RAM using a resident bus, but for writes to the shared memory, the MULTIBUS provides an arbitration protocol and data path for broadcasts. In this case, all of the shared RAMs become slave resources and data are transferred on the bus to all slaves in parallel. In Reference 6, the authors point out that each processor, memory copy, and set of switches could be integrated on a single chip as a versatile building-block for multiprocessor computers.

Multiprocessor Throughput Model

To assess the performance of multiprocessors, Lillevik et al.[7] have developed a model of throughput under conditions of interprocessor interference. The model assumes a hardware environment of N processors connected to M shared resources (memory, coprocessor, input–output, etc.) as shown in Figure 2. In this figure, notice that each processor also connects to local or resident resources, and that an N × M conflict-free interconnection network links the processors to the shared resources. Besides N and M, the model considers the bandwidth ratios of processors to shared and resident resources, the priority assignment of processors, and the use of shared and resident resources by processors. This stochastic model combines the above information, considers interference conditions, and generates individual processor and total system throughput.

Basically, the model functions as follows: For each possible combination of requests for shared and resident resources (which describes one of many possible system states), some processors will experience a delay because another processor has higher priority. The sum or union of the probabilities of occurrence of those states causing processor delay then equals the total probability of delay for the time interval of interest. And one minus this delay indicates the probability of no delay or the average throughput for a specific processor. To determine the probability of occurrence of a specific state, the model considers the intersection event that all of the processors are accessing the resource as defined by that state. Since the individual processor requests are assumed independent, the probability of occurrence of a state equals the product of individual processor occurrences. These individual probabilities of occurrence may be determined from the use of shared and resident resources by processors. Using the experimental multiprocessor described above, Easterday has collected laboratory data to verify the model.[8] For total shared resource use of 60–70%, the error is less than 3%, and at saturation (100%) it increases to 10%. This results from the assumption on independence, which begins to fail at higher use because the hardware queues requests. The model has been programmed on an HP-1000, which requires, for example, approximately 20 seconds for an N = 16 and M = 16 multiprocessor.

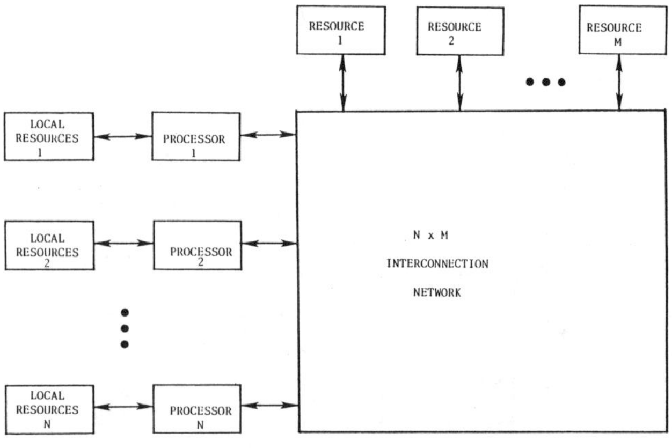

Figure 2—A multiprocessor computer block diagram

DEFINITIONS

Algorithms intended for execution on multiprocessor computers seek to exploit the inherent parallelism of the application. Typically, programmers separate the problem into several tasks, which may either execute concurrently or which may require a strict sequential order. The operating system must manage the tasks and resolve such dilemmas as mutual exclusion of shared resources, intertask communication, and task synchronization and scheduling. Although the interaction of the hardware and software changes dynamically, an approximate description may consider it constant over an interval of time. Fundamentally, one may characterize a multiprocessor system in terms of the hardware involved and its extent in solving a problem. To represent this involvement, consider the following:

Definition 1

A *multiprocessor algorithm* $A(N, M, U)$ describes over an interval of time the interaction of N processors connected to M shared memories, where the use of each memory by each processor may be found from an $N \times M$ matrix U defined as follows:

$$U = \begin{bmatrix} u_{11} \cdots u_{1M} \\ u_{N1} \cdots u_{NM} \end{bmatrix}$$

with $u_{nm} =$ probability that processor n accesses shared memory m. As probabilities, the sum over m of the u_{nm} must be less than or equal to one. In fact, processors access resident resources with probability one minus this sum. Notice that the definition of U exactly parallels the role of processor use as described for the model of the previous section. Since access to a shared memory may contain both read and write requests, as defined by the instruction mix, each u_{nm} actually consists of two factors as follows:

Definition 2

Each element u_{nm} of utilization matrix U contains a *read utilization* r_{nm} and a *write utilization* w_{nm} such that

$$u_{nm} = r_{nm} + w_{nm} \tag{1}$$

where r_{nm} = probability that processor n requests a read from shared memory m, and w_{nm} = probability that processor n requests a write to shared memory m. Furthermore, let α_{nm} represent the *fraction of read requests* compared to total requests,

$$\alpha_{nm} = \frac{r_{nm}}{r_{nm} + w_{nm}} = \frac{r_{nm}}{u_{nm}} \tag{2}$$

The above definitions provide a method to determine the speed-up of multiprocessor computers with replicated shared memories compared to single or conventional shared memories. Since replicated shared memories provide nearly conflict-free read requests, the read fractions α_{nm} may be used to determine a modified utilization matrix U', which depends on a given application. Specifically, consider the next definition.

Definition 3

A *modified* $N \times M$ *utilization matrix* U' represents the effect of replicated shared memories as follows,

$$U' = \begin{bmatrix} u'_{11} \cdots u'_{1M} \\ u'_{N1} \cdots u'_{NM} \end{bmatrix}$$

where u'_{nm} = probability that processor n requests a write to replicated shared memory m.

Using Definition 2 and Equations 1 and 2,

$$\begin{aligned} u'_{nm} &= w_{nm} \\ &= u_{nm}(1 - \alpha_{nm}) \end{aligned} \tag{3}$$

In Equation 3, the u'_{nm} represents reduced values of the u_{nm} because some fraction α_{nm} of the total requests for a replicated shared memory are nearly conflict-free—the reads—and essentially accesses to a resident memory.

From Definitions 1 and 3, an expression may be developed for the speedup of a multiprocessor with replicated shared memories compared to single, conventional shared memories.

Definition 4

Let $T(a)$ represent the *throughput* of a multiprocessor executing algorithm "a." The *speedup* S of a multiprocessor with replicated shared memories compared to conventional, single memories may be found from

$$S = \frac{T(A')}{T(A)} \tag{4}$$

where A' = an algorithm defined with modified utilization matrix U', and A = an algorithm with utilization matrix U. In Equation 4, the throughput $T(A')$ will be greater than throughput $T(A)$ because fewer memory accesses will result in interference. To determine numeric values for Equation 4, the model presented in the previous section may be used.

FFT Example

To solidify the definitions and methodology of the previous sections, consider a multiprocessor implementation of an eight-point fast Fourier transform (FFT) as shown in Figure 3. Each output value will be found by a specific processor, so the assumed hardware consists of $N = 8$ processors. Also, it will be assumed that a single shared memory ($M = 1$) holds the initial, intermediate, and final data of all processors. At each node in the figure, a processor must complete a computation of the form:

$$y(l,m) = y(l-1,m_1) + W^r y(l-1,m_2) \tag{5}$$

where l = node row, m = node column, and m_1, m_2, r, W are constants.

If in Equation 5, each operation requires one instruction fetch, two argument reads, and one resultant write to memory, then the total number of memory accesses for 3 nodes equals:

$$\begin{aligned} R &= \text{total number memory requests for one processor} \\ &= (2 \text{ ops})(1 \text{ fetch} + 2 \text{ reads} + 1 \text{ write})(3 \text{ nodes}) \\ &= 24 \end{aligned}$$

Next, assume the 6 instruction fetches are from resident memory. Thus, from Definition 1

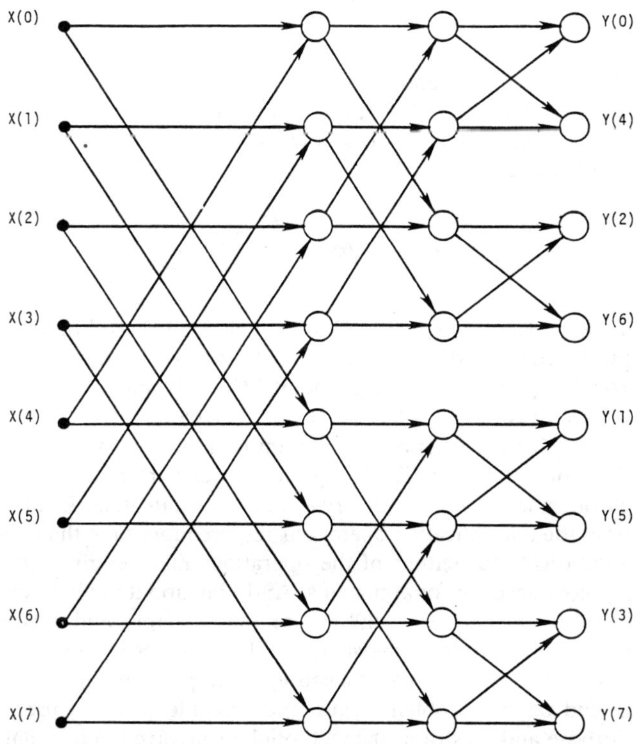

Figure 3—Signal flow graph for an eight-point FFT

$$u_{nm} = \frac{24-6}{R} = 0.75; \quad 1 \leq n \leq N,\ M = 1$$

$$U = \begin{bmatrix} 0.75 \\ 0.75 \\ \cdot \\ \cdot \\ \cdot \\ 0.75 \end{bmatrix} \tag{6}$$

Of the 18 accesses to shared memory, 12 involve read requests and 6 involve writes; hence, from Definition 2

$$\alpha_{nm} = \frac{6}{18} = 0.33$$

and from Equations 2 and 1

$$r_{nm} = \alpha_{nm} u_{nm} = 0.25, \text{ with}$$

$$w_{nm} = u_{nm} - r_{nm} = 0.50; \quad \text{for } 1 \leq n \leq N,\ M = 1$$

From Equation 3, the modified utilization matrix U' may be determined as:

$$U' = \begin{bmatrix} 0.5 \\ 0.5 \\ \cdot \\ \cdot \\ \cdot \\ 0.5 \end{bmatrix} \tag{7}$$

From Equations 6 and 7, the eight-point FFT application may be characterized as $A(N, M, U)$ and $A'(N, M, U')$. Using the two utilization matrices U and U' in the model produced the following result,

$$S = \frac{T(A')}{T(A)} = \frac{4.99}{2.99} = 1.66 \tag{8}$$

Thus, in Equation 8, the use of a replicated shared memory produced a speed-up of 1.66, or a 66% increase in throughput. For this example of an eight-point FFT, this implies that the hardware could sample data at a 66% greater rate.

The obvious question at this point is "How realistic a result does this represent?" Clearly, the processors require synchronization to share memory and intermediate data. In addition, the multiplication operations require more time than the additions, and neither of the operations may require three memory accesses for arguments. And what about the inherent error of the model itself? All of these factors and others modify the results somewhat, but Equation 8 represents a first-order, approximate speed-up and possibly an upper bound on the problem. Thus, the example serves a useful purpose and illustrates the methodology involved in the analysis of multiprocessors with replicated shared memories.

SPEEDUP OF SYMMETRICAL MULTIPROCESSORS

From the results of the previous example, clearly the use of replicated shared-memory structures with multiprocessor computers provides the potential for significant speed-up. This section will discuss several unanswered questions: Was the eight-point FFT example an isolated case? More precisely, can speed-up be determined for the more general case? What are the key application characteristics that influence speed-up, and how much speed-up can be expected? To answer these and other questions, one must begin with a set of assumptions about the hardware and software of the multiprocessor computer.

Rather than consider an unlimited number of combinations of N processors, M shared memories, and various utilizations and read fractions, we will analyze symmetric multiprocessors. Here, each processor divides its memory accesses equally between the M shared memories. In addition, we will vary the read fraction α_{nm} over the range $0.1 \leq \alpha_{nm} \leq 0.9$. Also, we will let the number of processors and shared memories be less than or equal to five. Using the above assumptions, utilizations for various numbers of shared memories and read fractions may be found in Table I. The first column in this table corresponds to processor use of conventional memories, and the remaining columns correspond to processor use of replicated shared memories (which change with the read fraction). For example, an $N = 3$ and $M = 2$ system with read fraction $\alpha_{nm} = 0.7$ would correspond to the following utilization and modified utilization matrices:

$$U = \begin{bmatrix} 0.5 & 0.5 \\ 0.5 & 0.5 \\ 0.5 & 0.5 \end{bmatrix}$$

$$U' = \begin{bmatrix} 0.15 & 0.15 \\ 0.15 & 0.15 \\ 0.15 & 0.15 \end{bmatrix}$$

By using Equation 4 and the model discussed in the previous section, a table of speed-ups may be developed to provide a database for the following discussions (see Table II).

The speed-up as a function of read fraction for several values of the number of processors (and constant number of shared memories, $M = 2$) is shown in Figure 4. In all cases, the speed-up begins at zero percent for read fraction zero, and

Table I—Use factors for various numbers of memories and read fractions

M Memories	α_{nm}, Read Fraction 0.0	0.1	0.3	0.5	0.7	0.9
1	1.00	0.90	0.70	0.50	0.30	0.10
2	0.50	0.45	0.35	0.25	0.15	0.05
3	0.33	0.30	0.23	0.16	0.10	0.03
4	0.25	0.22	0.17	0.12	0.07	0.02
5	0.20	0.18	0.14	0.10	0.06	0.01

Table II—Percent speed-up for various numbers of processors, memories, and read fractions

N Processors	M Memories	α_{nm}, Read Fraction 0.1	0.3	0.5	0.7	0.9
2	1	19	51	75	91	99
	2	6	17	25	30	33
	3	4	11	16	19	20
	4	3	7	11	13	14
	5	2	6	8	10	11
3	1	30	87	138	176	197
	2	12	34	52	64	71
	3	8	21	32	39	42
	4	5	14	22	27	29
	5	4	12	17	21	23
4	1	40	119	194	256	294
	2	18	52	80	100	111
	3	12	32	48	60	66
	4	8	22	34	42	46
	5	6	17	26	32	35
5	1	50	150	247	333	391
	2	24	69	108	138	156
	3	15	42	65	85	90
	4	10	30	46	57	63
	5	9	23	35	44	48

as the read fraction increases the speed-up increases. Moreover, the greater the number of processors, the greater the speed-up. One would expect speed-up to increase with read fraction because fewer write requests (which require arbitration) imply reduced shared memory interference. Yet as the number of processors increases, the speed-up increases. This occurs because for a fixed number of shared memories, a greater number of processors results in increased interference, and replicated shared memories reduce interference to a greater extent.

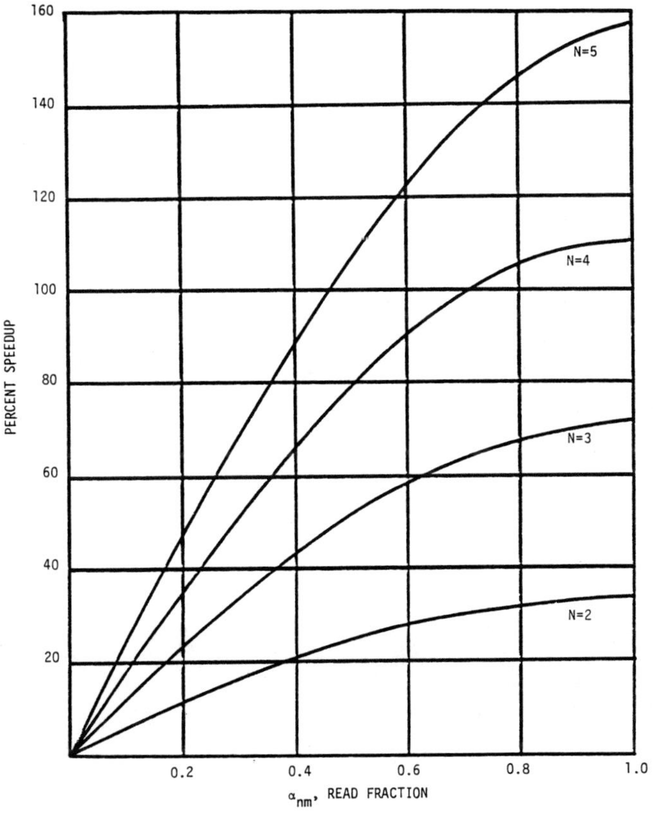

Figure 4—Speed-up as a function of read fraction for M = 2 shared memories

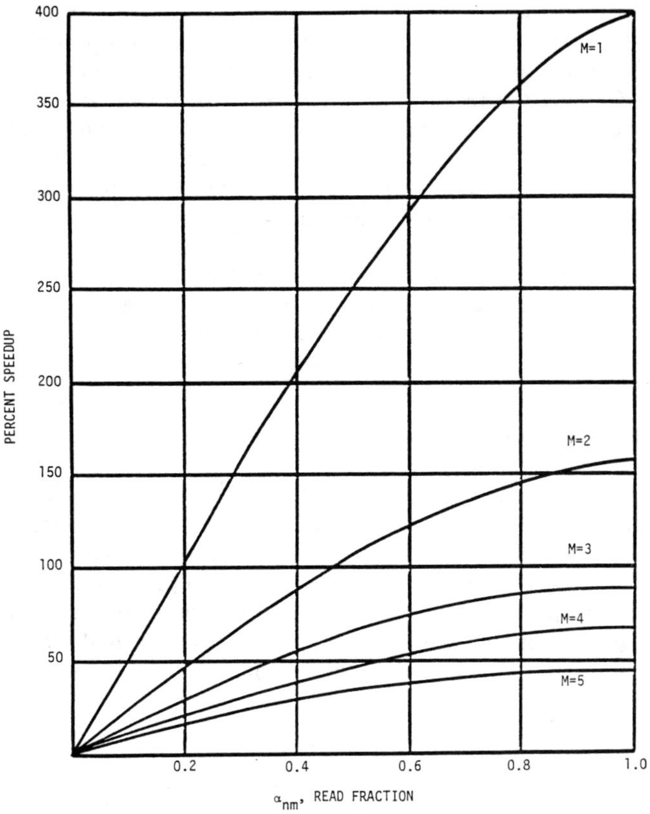

Figure 5—Speed-up as a function of read fraction for N = 5 processors

Next, how does the number of shared memories affect the speed-up? Figure 5 illustrates the speed-up as a function of read fraction for several values of the number of shared memories (and constant number of processors, $N = 5$). As before, the speedup begins at zero percent for read fraction zero, and increases with read fraction for the same reasons (fewer writes and interference). But now the speed-up decreases with increasing number of shared memories. For a fixed number of processors, individual memory use and interference decrease as the number of shared memories increases. Replicated shared memories produce less of an effect with a greater number of shared memories because processor interference is less to begin with. Thus, the speed-up decreases with an increased number of shared memories for fixed number of processors.

In both Figures 4 and 5, the speed-up flattens as the read fraction approaches one, or 100% reads and no writes. This occurs because the processors have now become essentially independent of each other, which results in no interference and maximum possible throughput $0(N)$.

Summarizing Table II, maximum speed-up occurs for a single replicated shared memory with all N processors performing reads only. In fact, the maximum speedup equals $0(N)$. To generalize this result, a multiprocessor with replicated shared memories will increase the throughput of a multiprocessor with conventional shared memories to the greatest extent, when the multiprocessor contains a large number of processors, all accessing a single replicated shared memory, with all accesses reads. Under such ideal conditions, the processors experience no shared memory interference and achieve maximum theoretical throughput $0(N)$. So the net effect of replicated shared memories is to decrease interprocessor interference and increase system throughput.

CONCLUSIONS

A multiprocessor with replicated shared memory uses several copies of the memory, one for each processor, to decrease interference. Each multiprocessor application may be described over an interval of time using a utilization matrix U, which specifies the interaction of the N processors and M shared memories. For multiprocessors with replicated shared memories, a modified utilization matrix U' may be used, which also considers the fraction of read requests α_{nm}. Speed-up of a multiprocessor with replicated shared memories compared to a multiprocessor with conventional shared memories approaches $0(N)$. This maximum occurs for a large number of processors, a small number of shared memories, large shared-memory use, and a large fraction of reads.

REFERENCES

1. Arden, B. W., and R. Ginosar. "MP/C: A Multiprocessor/Computer Architecture." *IEEE Trans. Comput.* C-31 (1982), pp. 455–473.
2. Covo, A. A. "Analysis of Multiprocessor Control Organizations with Partial Program Replication." *IEEE Trans. Comput.* C-23 (1974), pp. 113–120.
3. Pearce, R. C., and J. C. Majithia. "Analysis of a Shared Resource MIMD Computer Organization." *IEEE Trans. Comput.* C-27 (1978), pp. 64–67.
4. Lillevik, S. L., H. T. Voorheis, and M. L. Skinner. "Multiport Memory Design." *Proceedings 14th International Symposium Mini and Micro.* Anaheim, Calif.: ACTA Press, 1981, pp. 2–6.
5. Borrill, P. L. "Multiprocessor Synchronisation Primitives on Backplane Busses." Report to IEEE P896 Committee, University College (London, U.K.) Mullard Space Science Laboratory, September 1982.
6. Lillevik, S. L., and J. L. Easterday. "A Multiprocessor with Replicated Shared Memory." *AFIPS, Proceedings of the National Computer Conference* (Vol. 52), 1983, pp. 557–564.
7. Lillevik, S. L., J. L. Easterday, and M. L. Skinner. "Multiprocessor Throughput with Shared Resource Interference," *Proceedings 16th Asilomar Conference on Cir., Sys., and Comput.* November 1982, pp. 524–530.
8. Easterday, J. L. "Design and Analysis of Multiprocessors with Replicated Shared Memory." M.S. thesis, Oregon State University, May 1983.

The DCS—A new approach to multisystem data-sharing

by AKIRA SEKINO, KEIZO MORITANI, TERUAKI MASAI, TOSHIAKI TASAKI, and KAZUO GOTO
NEC Corporation
Tokyo, Japan

ABSTRACT

This paper describes a special purpose computer, the Data-sharing Control System (DCS), which was developed for multisystem data-sharing. This computer enables efficient block-level data sharing among several loosely coupled computer systems. Major architectural features incorporated into the design of the DCS are discussed in some detail, in the light of general requirements for such systems. The DCS-based loosely coupled multiprocessor architecture, together with the traditional tightly coupled multiprocessing, provides a new framework for the design of reliable large-scale database systems.

INTRODUCTION

With the cost of computer hardware falling steadily and the need for processing power and high availability ever-rising, the demand is growing for a new kind of multiprocessing computer architecture that allows efficient data processing, smooth and extensive system growth, and a high degree of overall reliability. Mainframe computer manufacturers traditionally have offered tightly coupled and loosely coupled multiprocessor architectures,[1] and minicomputer manufacturers offer new fault-tolerant architectures,[2] in order to satisfy this kind of demand. The traditional tightly coupled multiprocessor architecture allows connection between several processors under the control of a single operating system at a main storage level, while the loosely coupled multiprocessor architecture allows connection of several computer systems under the control of multiple operating systems at a channel connection level. Each of these multiple computer systems may well be a tightly coupled multiprocessor.

Large-scale commercial computers can usually include up to four central processing units (CPUs) to improve their performance, as well as their availability in tightly coupled multiprocessor (TCMP) configurations, as seen in IBM 3080 series or NEC ACOS 1000 computers.[3] To build a larger, more reliable system, one needs to introduce a loosely coupled multiprocessor (LCMP) capability, which connects independent computer systems by a shared secondary storage and optional direct channel-to-channel intersystem adapters. This capability often becomes essential in the design of large-scale on-line database systems. Japanese banking systems, for example, are expected within the next few years to execute 300 to 500 transactions per second.[4]

Today's LCMP architecture, however, has some difficulties in achieving effective data-sharing among multiple loosely coupled computer systems. Multisystem data-sharing requires that the data-sharing control information necessary for data-access serialization be accessible commonly from all the computer systems. In one LCMP implementation, this is done by storing the control information at commonly accessible disk controllers.[4] In another implementation, the same effect is produced by passing data-locking request information all around the computer systems, using a ring of channel-to-channel intersystem adapters spanned between these systems.[5] Low intelligence of the disk controllers will limit the number of lockable data entities in the first implementation, while the communication overhead between loosely coupled computer systems will become a serious performance bottleneck in the second implementation, thereby limiting the performance of the entire computer complex. It is therefore difficult in these implementations to achieve effective multisystem data-sharing for a high transaction environment.

This paper presents still another approach that attempts to solve the above problem of multisystem data-sharing, by describing the architecture of NEC's newly developed Data-sharing Control System (DCS). The DCS-based LCMP architecture and the traditional TCMP architecture combine to provide a new framework for the practical design of reliable large-scale database systems.

DESIGN REQUIREMENTS

Given a general background of the demand for a new kind of multiprocessing computer framework, the following describes a set of design requirements that were postulated in determining the DCS-based LCMP system architecture:

1. Flexible structure to allow cost-effective large-scale system designs—Both TCMP and LCMP architectures must be usable in configuring an optimized computer complex to satisfy various application needs. Large-scale computer complexes, involving up to eight computer systems, each of which may be a TCMP system, should be configurable in this architectural framework, with low incremental cost.
2. Efficient data-sharing in high transaction environments —Efficient data-sharing among large-scale computer systems must be achievable in order to facilitate cost-effective high-transaction system designs. For this purpose, the DCS must have sufficient performance capability for processing up to several thousand data lock–unlock requests per second, for data access serialization. It must be possible to choose granularity of locks at a data-block level.
3. Reliable system operation—The resulting computer complex must be fault-tolerant at various levels and have extensive serviceability and data recovery considerations to improve system availability. The DCS, being a critical component of the computer complex, should be extremely reliable.
4. Smooth field migration and upgrade capability—The new architectural framework must allow smooth field migration from a single-system environment to a loosely coupled, multisystem environment. It also must allow smooth field upgrades involving additions of various system components, preferably with minimal or no stoppage of system operation.
5. System operation with minimal human intervention— The resulting computer complex must have considerations to reduce human intervention in operating the computer complex.

SYSTEM ARCHITECTURE

The approach chosen by the DCS is to design a reliable new high-performance control system, which is specialized in multisystem data-sharing management and does not require significant hardware changes to existing host computers or their secondary storage systems.

Overall System Organization

The overall organization of a lage-scale DCS-based LCMP computer complex is shown in Figure 1. It specifically includes eight host computers (NEC's ACOS computers), a secondary storage system (disks), and the DCS.

Each of the host computers may have up to four CPUs organized as tightly coupled multiprocessors. Therefore, the entire computer complex may include 32 CPUs. The secondary storage system contains ordinary disk controllers and disk units, which may store sharable data. In order that sharable data be accessible from a host computer, there must be at least one channel path between the host computer and the disk controller, which controls access to the sharable data stored on a disk unit. It is not necessary to modify the secondary storage system, the stored data itself, or application programs that run on host computers when an installation migrates from a single-system environment to a multisystem environment. Thus, users' investment in purchased hardware and developed software are protected from undesirable system changes. The DCS is a new stand-alone special-purpose computer designed to control data-sharing among the loosely-coupled host computers. It is a sophisticated processor complex by itself, as will be described later, which makes it a very reliable high-performance control system. There must be at least one channel path between each host computer and the DCS.

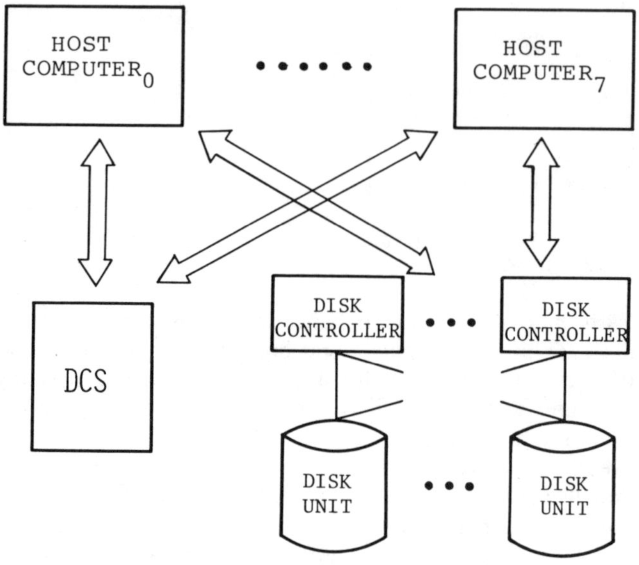

Figure 1—Overall system organization

Division of Functions

The major functions offered by the DCS include block-level and file-level serialization of conflicting host task accesses made to sharable data in the secondary storage system; interhost message communication; graceful degradation of the DCS configuration, upon detection of unrecoverable failures; functions related to data recovery, such as multisystem journal serialization, bad block freezes, etc., and statistical data collection.

The multisystem data-sharing requires a functional cooperation of host computers and the DCS in the following way. Serialization of conflicting data accesses made by host tasks are conducted either by host computers or the DCS, in order to control data integrity efficiently. If a host task accesses global data, that is, data that potentially can be accessed by tasks of multiple host computers, the operating system of the host computer issues a LOCK command to the DCS before it issues a data access command to the secondary storage system. The DCS then attempts to execute this command for the host task, but if it detects a deadlock situation, it notifies the host task that the command would cause a deadlock. If a host task accesses local data, that is, data accessed only locally within a particular host, the operating system similarly issues a LOCK command to itself and attempts to process the request within that particular host. If the command cannot be immediately executed because of conflicting data accesses, the operating system must notify the DCS of this situation for a deadlock examination, as described in more detail later. This kind of arrangement is called a hierarchical deadlock detection protocol.[6]

Another example of host–DCS cooperation is data recovery needed in the event of data damage due to malfunction of the secondary storage system. The operating system for each host computer normally keeps its own journal in the secondary storage system. When damaged data must be recovered, several journals created by the host computers must be merged by using a journal serialization function of the DCS. In addition, the DCS normally freezes the damaged data area upon detection of data damage, to prevent further host access to the damaged data.

Diversity in Serialization Commands

The DCS command repertoire has a variety of control commands to make efficient and reliable multisystem data-sharing possible. However, most distinctive commands are data-access serialization commands, which include a set of LOCK-UNLOCK commands and a WAIT STATUS NOTIFICATION command.

LOCK and UNLOCK commands

A LOCK command is used by a host operating system to obtain exclusive control of a particular data entity, such as a physical file or block of data, on behalf of a specified application task; the use of the data entity can thus be serialized properly. Without this kind of serialization control, sharable data might lose its integrity in various ways because of uncon-

Task 1	time	Task 2
READ RECORD A (=100)	t_1	
	t_2	READ RECORD A (=100)
ADD 10	t_3	
REWRITE RECORD A (=110)	t_4	
	t_5	ADD 100
	t_6	REWRITE RECORD A (=200)

(a) Task 1's update is lost

Task 1	time	Task 2
LOCK RECORD A (→ grant)	t_1	
WRITE RECORD A	t_2	
	t_3	LOCK RECORD B (→ grant)
	t_4	WRITE RECORD B
LOCK RECORD B (→ wait)	t_5	
	t_6	LOCK RECORD A (→ wait)

(b) Deadlock occurs at time t_6

Figure 2—Inconveniences caused by multiple data accesses

trolled simultaneous updating of the same data.[7] In a situation shown in Figure 2(a), for example, a record update operation in Task 1 will be lost, because of a conflicting update operation in Task 2. This inconvenience, however, can be avoided by delaying the read operation in Task 2 until the completion of the rewrite operation in Task 1, in order to serialize the use of this record.

A lock request using a LOCK command may or may not be granted by the DCS, depending on the status of data in question and the nature of the request. Once a lock request is granted, this situation continues until an unlock request concerning the same data is received from the *same* task. There are two kinds of locks; exclusive locks, which are generally used for data updates and shared locks, used for data retrievals. An exclusive lock request is granted only to a single task at a time, whereas a shared lock may be simultaneously granted to several independent tasks, each requesting shared data access using a shared lock. If a lock request cannot be granted, the DCS advises the task to wait until that data are released.

At this point, care must be taken to avoid a deadlock, by advising the task to wait. This requires that the DCS determine whether or not a new wait would cause a deadlock and to advise the task to wait only when deadlock will not be caused. If it does cause a deadlock, as shown in Figure 2(b), for example, the DCS informs the host operating system of the resulting deadlock, instead of asking the task to wait. Then, the operating system rolls back the task and releases all the data entities held by it. The detailed information on the deadlock is available to the operating system for later analysis. If the task is advised to wait, it will be notified by the DCS when the data becomes available, that the wait is over.

Data entities held by a task are normally released by the task's release request using either an UNLOCK or an UNLOCK ALL command. The former unlocks a set of specified data entities, while the latter unlocks all data entities held by the task. When several tasks share the same buffer area in the main storage, the use of an UNLOCK AND LOCK command allows a complete transfer of all data entities held by one task to another, thus saving the cost of executing another set of data input commands.

WAIT STATUS NOTIFICATION command

A WAIT STATUS NOTIFICATION command is used by a host operating system to notify the DCS of a wait status for a local sharable data. When this command is used to notify the DCS of an occurrence of a new local wait, the DCS determines whether or not this new wait will cause a deadlock involving both local and global data. If it finds a deadlock, the DCS informs the host of this situation; otherwise, it records the new wait-status concerning the local sharable data. The DCS keeps this information for other deadlock examination involving local and global data, until it receives another WAIT STATUS NOTIFICATION command notifying it of the termination of the local wait.

DCS ARCHITECTURE

It is important that a DCS have architecture that is suitable to its design requirements. In particular, special considerations are necessary to satisfy requirements in regard to performance and reliability. The following describes the architectural aspect of the DCS hardware and software, which is crucial to the DCS design.

DCS Hardware

The DCS hardware organization is shown in Figure 3. The major components are host interface controls (HICs), data-sharing control processors (DCPs), common storage units (CSUs), and the associated interconnection buses. This organization allows highly parallel DCS operations, which are important in achieving high processing throughput, as well as dynamic reconfiguration based on component redundancy, which is important to attaining high availability.

Host interface control

The DCS has a maximum of eight HICs, each of which provides up to four channel paths. These channel paths oper-

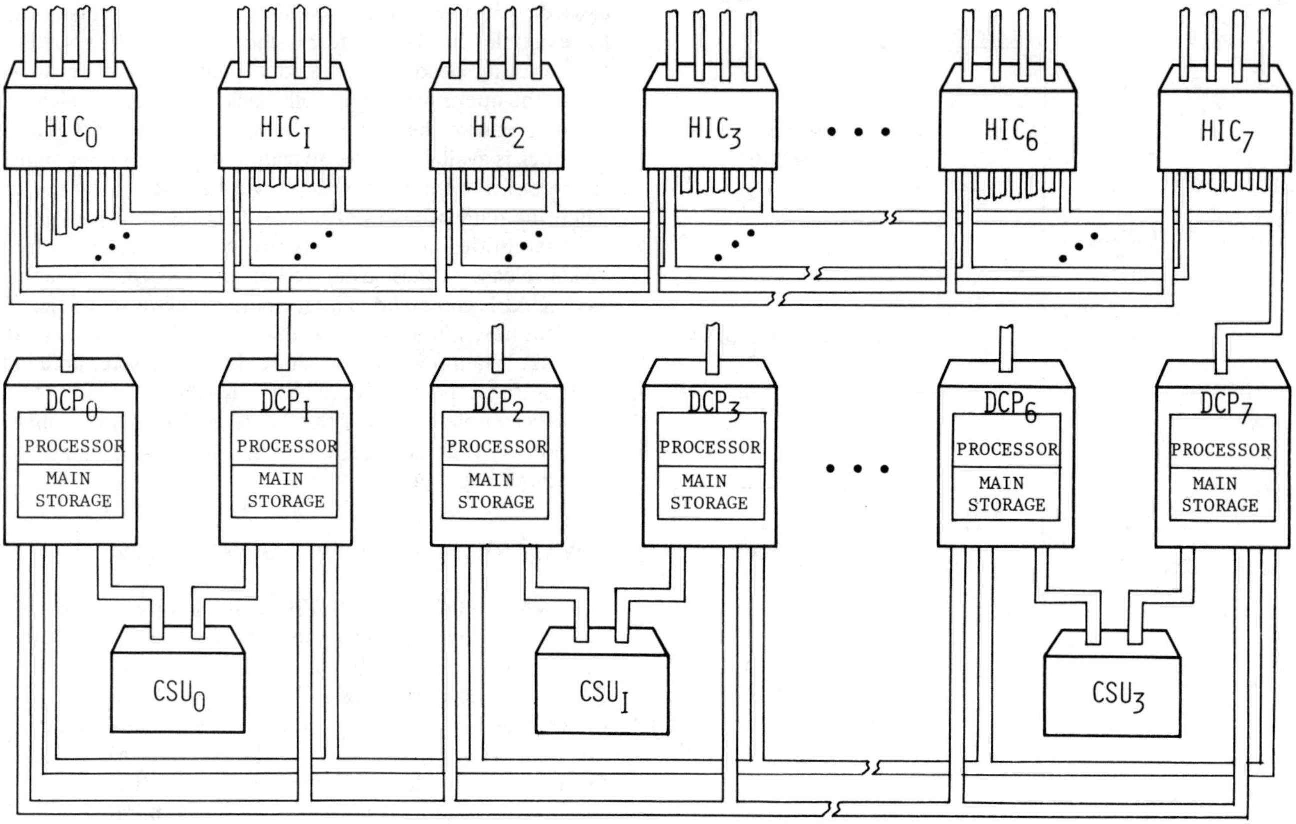

Figure 3—DCS hardware organization

ate in parallel, receiving the DCS commands from multiple host computers and returning the corresponding final responses to these computers. The DCS can receive these commands at any HIC and pass them to any DCP for command execution. However, which DCP will execute a given data-access serialization command is decided upon by hashing based on the identifier of the data entity under consideration, because DCPs are designed in such a way that each individual data entity can be controlled only by a certain DCP. A minimum of one channel path is required for a host–DCS connection.

Data-sharing control processor

A maximum of eight DCPs, which are responsible for command execution, exist in the DCS. The DCPs are organized as DCP-pairs for reasons of availability, as shown in Figure 3, but normally work as independent processors—each executing a separate stream of DCS commands. Each DCP has a three-million-instructions-per-second (MIPS) processor and its own main storage. The control program and data-sharing control tables reside in this main storage. Therefore, data-access serialization commands are executed in parallel by the DCPs. However, if a wait situation results from a LOCK command execution by a DCP, the DCP reports to one of the DCPs specifically designated as the deadlock examiner, using one of the inter-DCP buses. The deadlock examiner then looks for the possibility of a deadlock—using its deadlock detection tables—and returns the answer to the previous DCP. The results will be given to the original HIC, through which the LOCK command was received. DCPs organized as DCP-pairs can back each other up in the event of an unrecoverable DCP failure, including that of the deadlock-examiner DCP.

Common storage unit

A common storage unit (CSU) is used to keep duplicate copies of the DCP control program, data-sharing control tables, and so on. This information is not necessary for normal DCP operation, but it is essential to the DCP recovery functions described later. The DCS contains a maximum of four CSUs.

Power supply

Various components of the DCS have their own power supplies, so that independent maintenance of failed components may be possible without stopping the DCS operation.

DCP Control Software

The DCP control software includes various program modules, in addition to data-sharing control tables, as outlined in

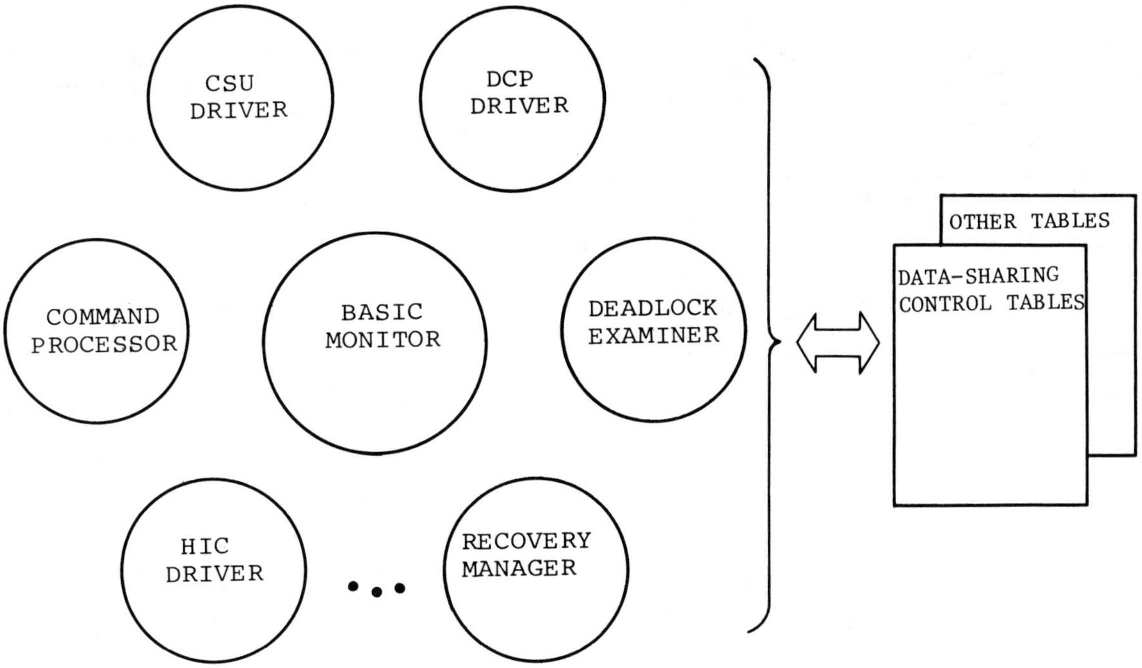

Figure 4—DCP control software

Figure 4. Major components are as follows.

The basic monitor is the nucleus of the DCP control program. This module controls task switching, main storage management, configuration management, exception handling, etc. The HIC driver is responsible for receiving DCS commands from HICs. The command processor consists of a collection of program modules capable of executing DCS commands. The CSU driver is responsible for CSU data read–write operations. The DCP driver is responsible for inter-DCP communication using the inter-DCP buses. The recovery manager manages DCS recovery functions. These are described in the next section. Finally, the deadlock examiner is responsible for examining the possibility of a deadlock. It resides with other program modules mentioned above only on a DCP designated as the deadlock examiner.

The general flow of control within the DCP control program that is needed to execute a LOCK command is depicted in Figure 5. Though this figure is almost self-explanatory, brief comments are in order.

The path most frequently taken is 1–2–10–11–12. It represents the case where a lock request can be granted immediately. This path is the shortest one. On the other hand, paths 1–2–3–4–5–8–9–10–11–12 and 1–2–3–4–5–6–7–8–9–10–11–12 represent cases where the same request results in a wait, respectively involving and not involving a deadlock. Boxes 6 and 10 represent duplicate table-update operations. The length of the most frequently taken path, 1–2–10–11–12, is about 1500 steps, requiring about a 500-microsecond processing time on a three-MIPS DCP. In other words, a single DCP is capable of executing roughly a thousand typical DCS commands, with 50% DCP utilization. This implies that the maximum DCS configuration, including eight DCPs, has performance capa-

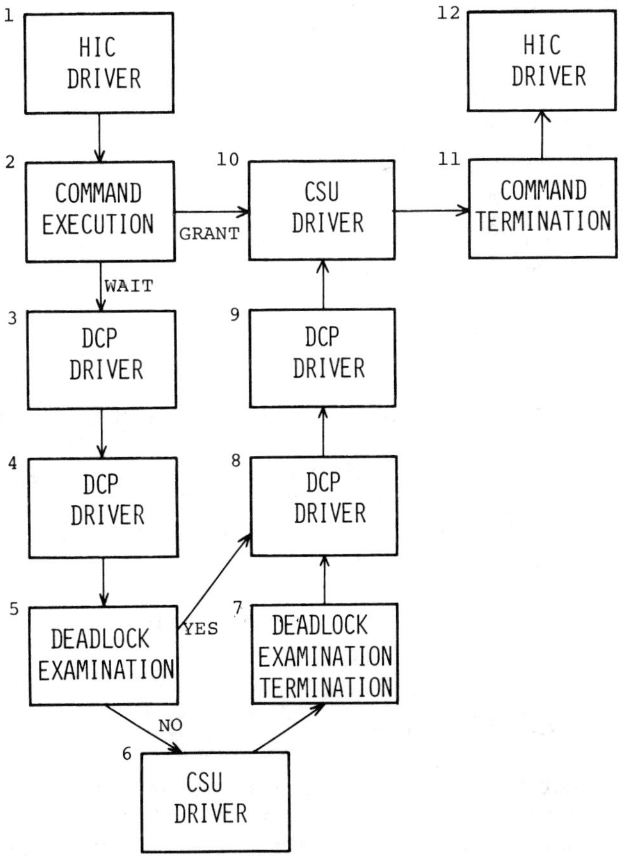

Figure 5—General control flow representing a "LOCK" command execution

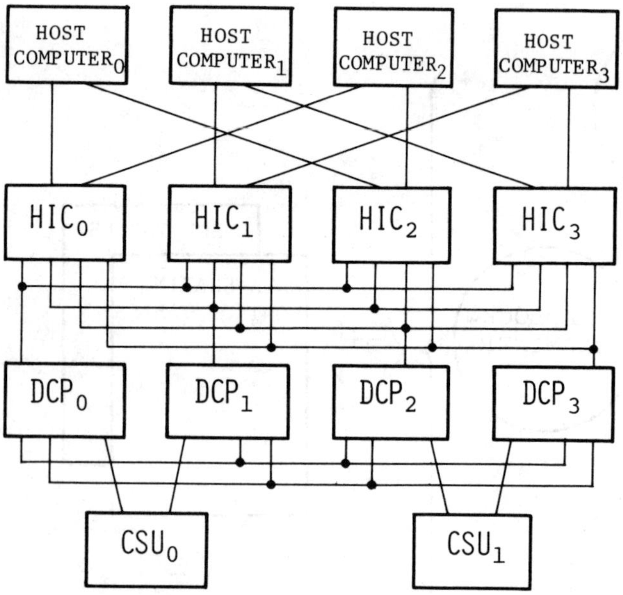

Figure 6—System redundancy in a four-host DCS configuration

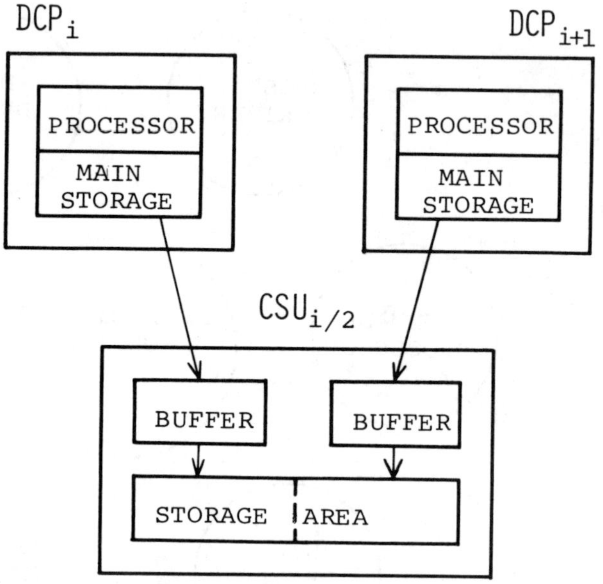

Figure 7—CSU internal organization

ble of processing as many as 8000 simple DCS commands per second.

RELIABILITY, AVAILABILITY, AND SERVICEABILITY CONSIDERATIONS

Satisfactory operation of loosely coupled multiple computers requires various reliability-related considerations on the DCS, in addition to locking and recovery considerations on multisystem sharable data. In fact, high availability of the DCS is most essential to the overall system operation. The DCS offers several reliability, availability, and serviceability considerations, which are discussed in the following sections.

1. System-wide hardware and software redundancy to allow dynamic system reconfiguration upon various unrecoverable failures
2. Automatic rebooting of the DCP software as a means of recovery from DCP software troubles
3. Continuous bookkeeping of a set of duplicate data-sharing control tables in CSUs
4. DCP-pair mutual backup capability to improve system availability
5. Faulty component maintenance simultaneous with the DCS operation, and on-line addition of recovered components

Redundant Organization

Figure 6 explains system redundancy by showing a DCS-based multisystem computer complex involving four host computers. A number of redundancy types exist in this configuration, making graceful degradation possible, based on dynamic reconfiguration. Each host computer has two channel connections with the DCS. Although failure of a channel or an HIC might occur, the host computer can still issue DCS commands using the remaining host–DCS channel connection. DCPs organized as a DCP-pair (e.g., DCP 0 and DCP 1) can back each other up in the event of an unrecoverable DCP failure. Data-sharing control tables exist in duplicate, one in a DCP main storage and the other in the associated CSU. Failure of a CSU, however, will not cause stoppage of the associated DCPs. Two inter-DCP buses exist for message communication. Failure of an inter-DCP bus will not separate DCPs.

Automatic DCP Software Rebooting

This is useful for straightening out a situation where some unknown portion of the DCP software is suspected of damage caused by a possibly undetected intermittent DCP failure. The DCP software, including the control programs and data-sharing control tables, is reloaded from its CSU, and the DCP operation is then automatically restarted. Automatic DCP software rebooting decreases the probability of unrecoverable DCP failures.

Bookkeeping of Duplicate Control Tables

Each DCP keeps an up-to-date duplicate copy of the data-sharing control tables it maintains in main storage. This duplicate copy is held in the associated CSU and is updated every time its counterpart in the main storage is dynamically updated by each DCP. It exists only as a backup copy of the data-sharing control tables and, as such, is normally not read by the associated DCP for the purpose of data-sharing control. As a matter of fact, each DCP occasionally reads out the content of the duplicate data-sharing control tables from its

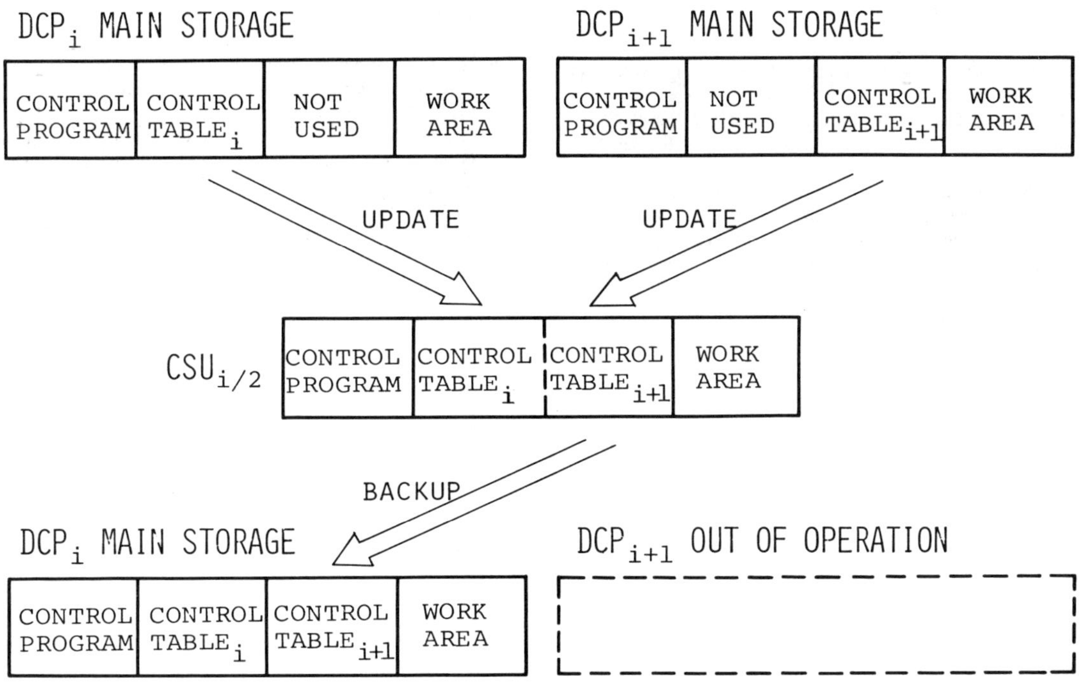

Figure 8—Storage area allocation maps

CSU, just to make sure that the contents of both tables are consistent.

Special consideration is needed in updating the content of duplicate control tables in a CSU. It must be assured that a set of specified table entries is always updated as an atomic action;[8] a set of table updates must either be all done or not be done at all, in order to maintain system integrity. For this purpose, a CSU has two independent 4000-byte buffers, through each of which the CSU receives a set of specified table-update requests from the associated DCP, as shown in Figure 7. If a set of table-update requests is fully received, the CSU proceeds to update actual table entries in the storage area. However, if only a partial set of requests is received because of a DCP failure, this partial request is simply discarded by the CSU. Thus, it is possible for each DCP to keep an up-to-date copy of duplicate control tables in the associated CSU, without losing integrity of table data.

DCP-Pair Mutual Backup Capability

A rough sketch of storage area allocation maps for DCP main storage and the associated CSU is shown in Figure 8. This allocation makes it possible for one DCP to back up its mate-DCP by receiving a copy of the mate's data-sharing control tables from the associated CSU, whenever the mate-DCP suffers from an unrecoverable DCP failure. This kind of DCP-pair reconfiguration is automatically carried out in the DCS.

All of these reliability-related functions must be implemented very carefully; if erroneously implemented, they can introduce additional problems. False failure techniques are being used for system debugging.

CONCLUSION

This paper describes a special purpose computer approach to multisystem data-sharing, as taken by the DCS. In particular, major architectural features incorporated into the design of the DCS have been discussed to show their implications for large-scale loosely coupled computer systems. These features include support of various access serialization commands, a hierarchical deadlock-detection mechanism involving host computers and the DCS, a modular computer-complex DCS organization based on DCP-pairs, a CSU design with an atomic data-update capability, DCP-pair mutual backup capability, and so on. All of these considerations significantly contribute to satisfying the overall system design requirements stated at the beginning of this paper.

It is now possible to envision a very reliable special purpose computer, the DCS, capable of processing several thousand block-level access serialization commands per second, for realization of cost-effective multisystem data-sharing. Finally, it should be stressed that the DCS-based LCMP and traditional TCMP architectures blend naturally to form a new framework for the design of reliable large-scale database systems.

ACKNOWLEDGMENT

The authors would like to thank the many people who participated in the design and development of the DCS. We are especially grateful to the management of NEC for continuous encouragement concerning the DCS project, and to K. Ohtsuka, T. Torii, M, Araki, A. Tashiro, T. Terayama, Y. Ebino, T. Takahashi, S. Nomiyama, and M. Terao for stimulating discussions on the DCS architecture.

REFERENCES

1. Enslow, P. H. (ed.), *Multiprocessors and Parallel Processing*. New York: John Wiley and Sons, 1974.
2. Katzman, J. A. "A Fault-Tolerant Computing System," *11th Hawaii Conference on System Sciences,* (Vol, 3). Honolulu: University of Hawaii Press, 1978, pp. 85–102.
3. Tashiro, S. and K. Tomita. "A Fault-Tolerant Computer with Processor Relief," *Transactions of the Institute of Electronics and Communication Engineers of Japan,* J65-D (1982), pp. 1065–1072 (in Japanese).
4. Abe, Y., "A Japanese On-line Banking System," *Datamation,* 23 (1977), pp. 89–97.
5. IBM Corporation, *OS/VS2 MVS Planning: Global Resource Serialization,* IBM Manual GC28-1062. Poughkeepsie, N.Y.: IBM, 1981.
6. Ho, G. S. and C. V. Ramamoorthy, "Protocols for Deadlock Detection in Distributed Database Systems" *IEEE Transactions on Software Engineering,* SE-8, (1982), pp. 554–562.
7. Gray, J. N. "Notes on Data Base Operating Systems," in R. Bayer, R. M. Graham, and G. Seegmüller, (eds.), *Operating Systems*. Berlin: Springer-Verlag, 1978, pp. 393–481.
8. Randell, B., P. A. Lee and P. C. Treleaven, "Reliability Issues in Computing System Design," *Computing Surveys,* 10 (1978), pp. 123–165.

Reduced-instruction set multi-microcomputer system

by LEWIS FOTI, DAVID ENGLISH, RICHARD P. HOPKINS, DAVID J. KINNIMENT, PHILIP C. TRELEAVEN, and WANG LONG WANG
University of Newcastle upon Tyne
Newcastle upon Tyne, England

ABSTRACT

This paper presents the initial design and implementation of a simple microcomputer with a reduced instruction set, which forms a building block for a parallel multi-microcomputer system. The microcomputer has a 16-bit word size, with each register and data element being 16 bits. It has less than 20 operators. Each microcomputer in the multi-microcomputer system is addressable, and behaves as a combined memory cell and processor that is able to service the LOAD, STORE, and EXECUTE operations. The multi-microcomputer system centers on a 16-bit global address space. An address consists of two parts: the high eight bits define a specific microcomputer, and the low eight bits define a word in that microcomputer. When the top eight bits are zero the address is considered local to the microcomputer. Although a microcomputer can load or store any word in the global address space, an attempt to execute code at an alien address causes execution to transfer to the specified microcomputer. Although the microcomputer design is based on 16-bit units, we ultimately wish to design the simplest microcomputer that is able to handle variable length information.[1,2]

DESIGN PHILOSOPHY

Traditionally, the trend in designing microprocessors and mainframe computers has been toward increasingly complex instruction sets and associated architectures.[3,4] In contrast, designs based on the so-called reduced-instruction set philosophy have a simple set of instructions, and a correspondingly simple machine organization tailored to their efficient execution.[3] In very large scale integration (VLSI) scaled to submicron dimensions, the traditional approach of attempting to make larger single microprocessors becomes self-defeating because of communications problems and the escalating costs of designing and testing such complex processors. One obvious solution is miniature (reduced-instruction set) microcomputers that can be replicated like memory cells and operate as multiprocessor systems. In such systems the potential performance benefits of VLSI are exploited by parallelism, rather than by attempting to improve the performance of a single processor. Provided that appropriate means for programming can be found, this is a more general solution. The aim of the ongoing reduced-instruction set multi-microprocessor system (RIMMS) project is to design the simplest conventional microcomputer—with primitive communications mechanisms—able to form a component of a tightly coupled multi-microcomputer system.

The initial design and implementation of a RIMMS microcomputer is presented below. This microcomputer has a 16-bit word size, with each register, data element, and address being 16 bits. Instructions, however, are 2×16 bits and use a three-address format. There are less than 20 operators. Each microcomputer in the multi-microcomputer system is addressable, and behaves as a combined memory and processor that is able to service the LOAD, STORE, and EXECUTE operations. Design of the multi-microcomputer system centers on the 16-bit global address space. An address consists of two parts: the high eight bits define a specific microcomputer, while the low eight bits define a word in that microcomputer's memory. Although a microcomputer can access any word in the global address space, an attempt to execute alien code causes execution to transfer to the specified microcomputer.

This design contains a number of important concepts. First, although a microcomputer can make a data access to any word in the global address space, code is always executed by the local microcomputer. Second, a microcomputer has the minimal basis for parallelism, namely a FORK instruction, which creates a parallel flow of control. Third, a microcomputer executes a process to completion, thus providing a primitive form of synchronized access to the contents of its local memory. Finally, to facilitate simple process migration, the amount of state information held in the processor's registers is minimized.

In this paper we present the architecture and implementation of an initial RIMMS microcomputer. We follow this with a discussion of problems with the current design and of future work of the RIMMS project.

ARCHITECTURE

The architecture and programming of RIMMS is described in terms of two levels of machine: the multi-microcomputer level handles interprocess and interprocessor communication supporting nonlocal LOAD, STORE, and EXECUTE operations; and the microcomputer level services these operations and handles the atomic execution of a single process.

Multi-microcomputer System

RIMMS consists of a linear array of up to 255 microcomputers that communicate via a shared bus, as shown in Figure 1. Each microcomputer has a simple processor and 256 words of local memory.

The system has a 16-bit address space: (see Figure 2). The top eight bits are a global address (in the range 1–255) defining a microcomputer, while the bottom eight bits are a local address (in the range 0–255) defining a word in its memory. Global address zero is the default for specifying the current local address space and is therefore not recognized at the multi-microcomputer level.

When one microcomputer wishes to communicate with another, for example to access its local memory, the microcomputer generates a "packet." The format of a packet, as shown in Figure 3, consists of a two-bit operation field, a 2×8-bit destination address, and a 16-bit operand. The four

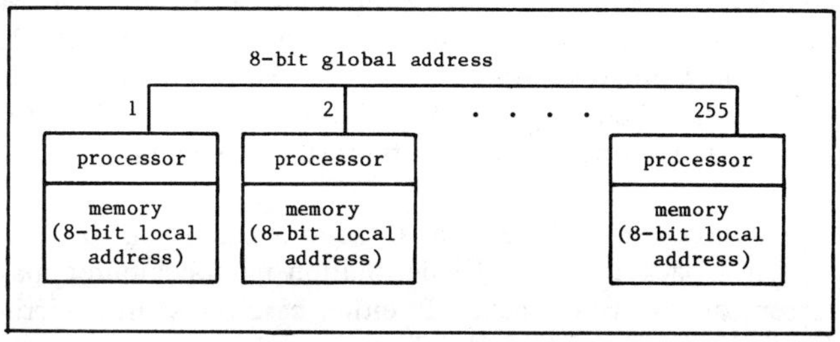

Figure 1—Multi-microcomputer system

microcomputer | memory cell

Figure 2—RIMMS address

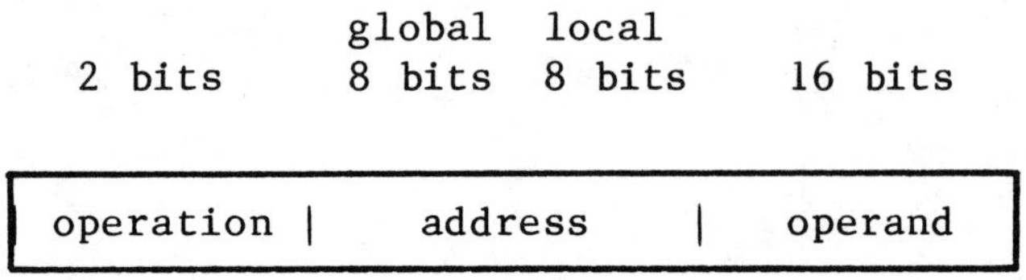

Figure 3—Multi-microcomputer packet format

	Packet Received			
	LOAD	STORE_REG	STORE_MEM	EXECUTE
Processor Status				
BUSY				
. EXECUTING	-	error	-	reject
. WAITING	-	accept	-	reject
IDLE	-	error	-	accept
Memory Status				
BUSY	reject	reject	reject	reject
IDLE	accept	accept	accept	accept

Figure 4—Microcomputer status versus packet received

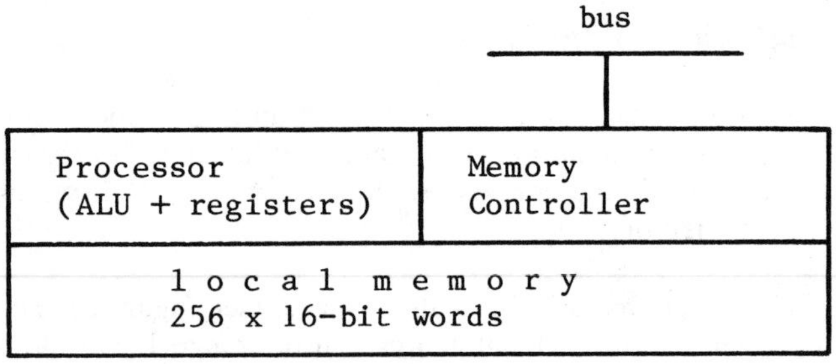

Figure 5—Microcomputer

operations are: load from memory (LOAD), store into register (STORE_REG), store into memory (STORE_MEM), and execute instruction (EXECUTE).

The packet operations are defined as follows: LOAD copies the contents of MEMORY [address] to the microcomputer's register defined by the 16-bit operand. This is implemented by the destination microcomputer generating a STORE_REG packet. STORE_REG places the operand in the microcomputer's register defined by the address. STORE_MEM places the operand into the MEMORY[address]. EXECUTE starts a new process whose code is at MEMORY[address] and data environment is at MEMORY[operand]. For all these packets the global address defines the destination microcomputer.

Microcomputers take turns to send a packet on the bus. When a packet is sent the destination microcomputer may accept or reject the packet. In either case the source microcomputer relinquishes the bus. If rejected, the source microcomputer will attempt to send the packet again at its next turn to use the bus. Whether a packet is accepted or rejected depends on the status of the processor and memory of the destination microcomputer. In simple terms, LOAD and STORE operations may be serviced by the memory concurrently with the operation of the processor. However an EXECUTE packet may be accepted only when the processor is idle, having completed the execution of its previous process. Figure 4 lists the complete rules for processing packets.

memory operation register	MOP	(2 bits)
memory address register	MAR	(16 bits)
memory data register	MDR	" "

Figure 6—Memory controller registers

In Figure 4, BUSY EXECUTING specifies that the processor is executing instructions, and BUSY WAITING specifies that the processor is executing but temporarily waiting for an operand to be loaded from a memory. Next we examine the architecture of a microcomputer.

Microcomputer

The microcomputer-level machine consists of three basic components: the local memory of up to 256 × 16-bit words, the memory controller, and the 16-bit processor for arithmetic, as illustrated by Figure 5. The memory controller is connected to the global bus, and to the local processor and memory. It supports communication—in the form of packets—between these three units. To hold a packet, the memory controller has three registers: a 2-bit memory operation register, a 16-bit memory address register, and a 16-bit memory data register (Figure 6). These registers correspond to the operation, address, and operand fields, respectively, of a packet.

When a memory controller is idle it can receive a packet either from the local processor or from some other microcomputer. A packet from the processor can be destined for the local memory or for another microcomputer, whereas a packet from the bus can be destined for the local processor or memory. A packet's destination is specified by the top eight bits of the address in the memory address register (MAR).

The processor, the last component of the microcomputer, consists of an arithmetic logical unit (ALU) and seven registers supporting a 16-bit word size. Each register, data element, and address is 16 bits. Instructions, however, are 2 × 16 bits and use a three-address format. Figure 7 shows the seven registers of which only the first two are addressable. The program counter, C, points to the local code currently being executed. The data register, D, points to the current data environment, which may be anywhere in the global address space. I1, I2 holds the current 2 × 16-bit instruction. A1, A2, and A3 are the input registers to the ALU, holding the current instruction's operands. Their contents have no meaning from one instruction to the next.

program counter	C	(16 bits)
data register	D	(16 bits)
instruction registers	I1,I2	(2x16 bits)
ALU register 1	A1	(16 bits)
ALU register 2	A2	" "
ALU register 3	A3	" "

Figure 7—Processor registers

```
             M1  M2  M3        01              02              03
5 bits        1   1   1      8 bits          8 bits          8 bits

|operator|mode bits|literal/address|literal/address|literal/address|
            0  -  literal
            1  -  address (memory [D+ signed literal])
```

Figure 8—Microcomputer instruction format (2 × 16 bits)

Operation	Mnemonic	Description
arithmetic	ADD	-
	SUB	-
logical	AND	-
	OR	-
	NOT	-
shift	LSHIFT	logical shift
	ASHIFT	arithmetic shift
compare	EQ	equals
	GT	greater than
control	IF	if TRUE jump
	FORK	fork flow of control
	HALT	halt processor
movement	MOVE	move argument to address
	STORE C	store program counter
	LOAD D	load data register
	STORE D	store data register

Figure 9—Processor instruction set

An instructions format, as illustrated by Figure 8, consists of a five-bit operator field, 3 × 1-bit mode (Mi) fields, and 3 × 8-bit operand (0i) fields. Modes and arguments are interpreted as follows. If the value of mode bit Mi = 0, then the corresponding eight-bit operand 0i is treated as a literal. 0i is sign-extended to 16 bits and the resulting argument is placed in the corresponding ALU register Ai. If the mode bit Mi = 1, then the eight-bit operand 0i is treated as a signed displacement relative to the data register D. The resulting address, D + 0i, is dereferenced (via the multi-microcomputer level if necessary) and the memory content is placed in the ALU register Ai. Notice that the modes and operands are interpreted independently both of the operator and of whether they are to be used for input and output by the ALU. However, the operator does determine how many of the three arguments are used by the ALU.

The ALU supports only two information types: 16-bit integers (2's complement) and booleans (TRUE = FFFF, FALSE < > FFFF), and following the reduced instruction set philosophy only a minimal set of operators are provided. These operators are listed in Figure 9. Finally, note that the reason we have chosen a three-address instruction format and only two addressable registers is to minimize the state information that needs to be moved from one microcomputer to another, when control is transferred.

Programming

In briefly examining the programming of RIMMS we will continue to discern two levels of machine. At the multi-microcomputer level, because of the shared 16-bit address space, the system can be programmed as a single, sequential computer with up to 255 × 256 words of memory or, more interestingly, as a parallel computer with up to 255 processors each with 256 words of memory. For instance, if allocated consecutive memory locations, a large sequential program will span a number of microcomputers. As control reaches the boundary of a microcomputer (Figure 10) its program counter will contain a nonlocal address, causing the contents of the program counter C and the data register D to migrate to the next processor.

Time	Micro 1 C	Micro 1 D	Micro 2 C	Micro 2 D
↓	0100	9999	-	-
	...	...	...	...
	01FF	9999	-	-
	0200	9999	-	-
	-	-	0200	9999
	...	...	...	...

Figure 10—Sequential execution

For parallel execution a separate process must be placed in each processor. These processes are started by the use of FORK instructions; a FORK may be thought of as a GOTO that not only transfers control but also continues execution. Normally in a parallel-control-flow computer additional operators are necessary to synchronize access to shared memory locations. With RIMMS, the programmer has a choice of causing unsynchronized LOAD and STORE operations, which compete for memory access, or of executing code in the target microcomputer, which accesses its local memory. Since code is executed atomically by a processor, such an access is treated as a critical region. Figure 11 illustrates the RIMMS parallelism. In this example, a series of FORK instructions in Microcomputer 1 are executed to create parallelism. A FORK specifies new C and D values, and causes the generation of an EXECUTE packet. Having created the parallelism, Microcomputer 1 executes a HALT instruction. Then as each processor finishes, it returns controls "GOTO 1040" to Microcomputer 1. For each processor, Microcomputer 1 subtracts one from the count of processors, executing "SUB p 1 p," and

```
         Micro 1                  Micro 2              Micro 3

Create
 parallelism    C'   D'
   0100: FORK 0200 02E0  | 
   0102: FORK 0300 03E0  | 0200:                |
   0104: FORK 0400 04E0  | 0202:   . . .        | 0300:
                         |                      |
Halt processor           |Return                |
   0130: HALT            | 0260: GOTO 0140      |Return
                         |                      | 0360: GOTO 0140
Count terminating        |                      |
 processors              |                      |
   0140: SUB p 1 p       |                      |
   0142: GT  p 0 c       |                      |
   0144: IF c 0148 0146  |                      |
   0146: HALT            |                      |
   0148:                 |                      |
```

Figure 11—Parallelism and synchronization in RIMMS

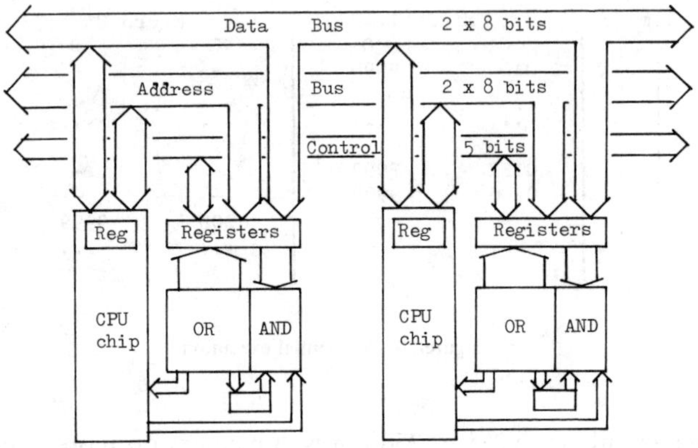

Figure 12—Bus and memory controllers

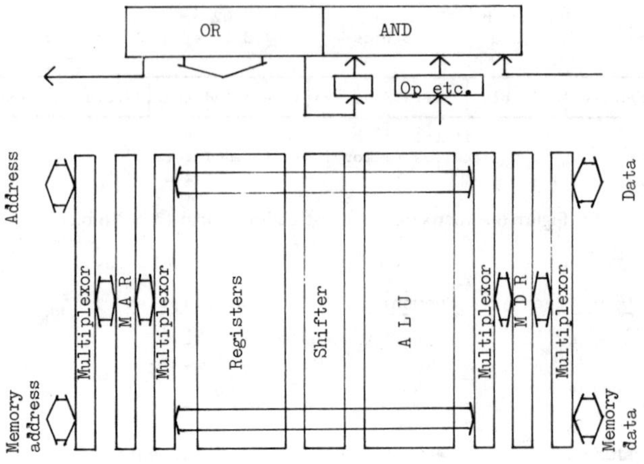

Figure 13—CPU chip

then tests to see if the count "p" is still greater than zero "GT p 0 c." If greater, "c" then control-goes to instruction "0146" which HALTs the processor, otherwise it control-continues at instruction "0148."

At the microcomputer level, as the reader will see from Figure 9, CALL, GOTO, LOAD C operators, and so forth, are not included in the instruction set as might have been expected. This is for two reasons: First we have attempted to minimize the operators, therefore CALL, etc., must be programmed, and second, because of the 2×16-bit, three-address instruction format, operators such as GOTO and LOAD C can be specified as "IF TRUE address null." Having examined the architecture and programming of RIMMS, in the next section we examine its actual implementation.

IMPLEMENTATION

In the initial implementation of RIMMS our aim has been to keep the structures as simple and conventional as possible in order to concentrate on a realization that would highlight any design difficulties relevant to the system rather than the implementation. At the multi-microcomputer level, this consists of a passive bus connected to an array of microcomputers. At the microcomputer level, because of present limitations in available level of integration and in order to ease testing, the computer itself is implemented as three components: a CPU chip, a programmable logic array (PLA) chip for the memory controller, and commercially available parts for the memory.

Multi-microcomputer System

The multi-microcomputer system centers on a bus, as illustrated by Figure 12. The bus carries a 16-bit address made up of an 8-bit micro address, an 8-bit memory address, 16 bits of data, and three memory operation bits to cover a fifth "no operation" memory access. In order to reduce the total pin count on the CPU and memory controller chips, both data and address are sent as two bytes on two parallel eight-bit busses between communicating microcomputers and between CPU and memory.

Access to the bus by the microcomputers is controlled by an additional wire loop, which is daisy-chained through the micros. This wire conveys a single "token" successively from one microcomputer to the next. When the token is received, the microcomputer may attempt to transmit a packet of data and address bits. When a packet is accepted, the packet is transmitted between the memory controller registers of the source and destination microcomputers. When the microcomputer finishes with the bus, the token is passed to the next microcomputer.

Microcomputer

Implementation of a microcomputer centers on the design of two custom chips for the memory controller and the processor. The memory controller, as illustrated by Figure 12, is a PLA; for simplicity its registers are part of the CPU chip (Figure 13). The task of this PLA is to control the movement of packets between the processor, the local memory, and the bus.

The processor, as shown in Figure 13, is a simple, conventional two-bus data path[5] consisting of a register file, shifter, ALU MAR/MDR registers, and a control PLA to implement the instruction set. The register file contains the 7×16-bit registers shown in Figure 7. Next comes the shifter. Then the ALU with two 16-bit input and two output registers. Lastly, there are the memory address and memory data registers, whose contents are moved between the processor-local memory-bus, under control of the memory controller PLA.

Both the memory controller PLA and the CPU chip are in the final stages of design, and an estimate of the CPU chip size indicates that it will occupy approximately 8×8 mm in an NMOS process with $\lambda = 3\mu$. The floor plan of the CPU chip is shown in Figure 14. Within this overall floor plan the system is partitioned into three distinct sections, a data path, microprogram control unit, and I/O ports.

The data path "DATAPA" contains a set of registers, a shifter and an ALU. The microprogram control unit contains a PLA "CNTROL," buffer drivers "CTLDRV," and decoders "UPDECD" and "LRDECD." The micro-instruc-

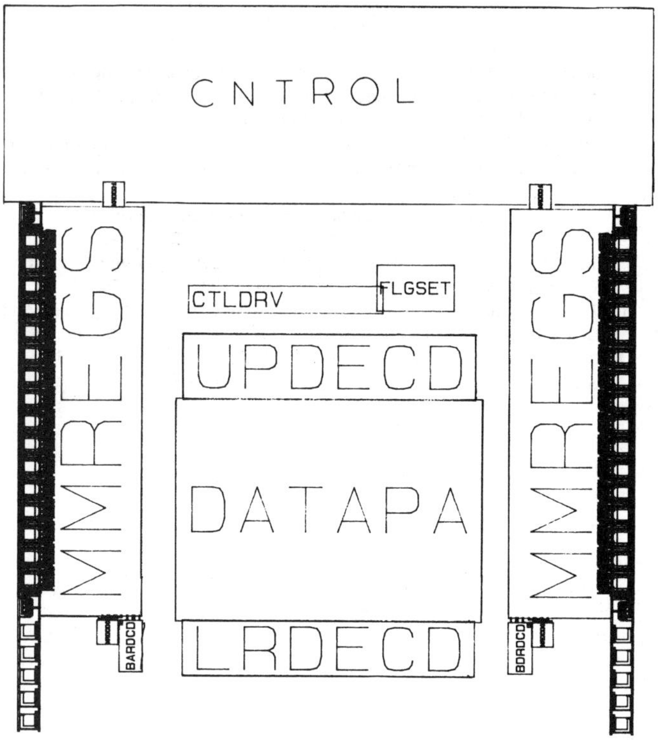

Figure 14—Floor plan of CPU chip

tions are partially encoded in the PLA, and the control inputs from the PLA to the data path determine which operations occur in the data path during a given clock cycle. Decoding is done by upper and lower decoders, which drive the data path directly. Control sequences not only depend on the data stored in the registers but also on external signals from the memory control chip to the control unit.

Data communication between the data path and the other chips in the set is through I/O ports "MMREGS," i.e., MDR and MAR. The communication itself is achieved using packet operation instructions. The ports are tristate and can be used as inputs or outputs.

DISCUSSION

For a multi-microcomputer system the most fundamental problem to be solved is how to orchestrate a single computation so that it can be distributed across an ensemble of processors.[6,7] One good example of special-purpose multiprocessors is Kung's Systolic Arrays.[8,9] Examples of general-purpose multi-processors are the INMOS Transputer and the OCCAM programming language.[10]

The RIMMS design is a more conventional solution, which achieves the programming and distribution of a single computation across multiple processors by minimal extensions to conventional microprocessors. To achieve this distribution, the RIMMS design is based on a number of important concepts. First, each microcomputer has its own local memory, thereby encouraging locality of reference and reducing system-wide communication. Second, each microcomputer forms part of a global address space and is able to access the contents of any other microcomputer's memory. Finally, each component microcomputer may be viewed as a single component able to service LOAD, STORE, and EXECUTE operations on its contents.

Architecture

To conclude the presentation of RIMMS, in this section we discuss problems with the current design and future work of the project. In designing architecture for RIMMS, three areas require optimization: the handling of *parallelism,* the *programmability* of the instruction set, and the *layout* of the microcomputer chip. For parallelism, we believe, the initial architecture has a number of important properties. These include the two-component address, FORK instructions, the minimal state information held in registers (C and D registers and three-address instructions), and the local (and atomic) execution of code.

In contrast, the programmability of the microcomputers is poor. The three-address format leads to large instructions and redundant fields for certain operators. The decision to process the modes and operands of an instruction before examining the operator leads to dissimilar input and output arguments. And the choice of modes (i.e., literal, MEMORY[D + Oi]) makes programming difficult. A choice of MEMORY [C + Oi] and MEMORY[D + Oi] would have been an improvement.

Architectural improvements to assist layout also are necessary. Implicit in the architecture is that registers A1, A2, and A3 are the input registers of the ALU. In fact, during implementation it was necessary to use extra input and output registers for the ALU. In addition, the choice of eight-bit instruction operands requires all operands to be sign-extended before use.

Implementation

Because the initial RIMMS architecture is not intended to be optimum and the development is continuing, detailed criticism of its implementation is best deferred. In a new implementation the common bus will be replaced by bidirectional, point-to-point connections between microcomputers, allowing greater parallelism in data transfers between each unit. We intend to make the local memory part of the CPU by increasing the number of registers in the data path. Finally, we expect to be able to implement the whole of a microcomputer on one chip, as a step towards the aim of an integrated VLSI multi-microcomputer system.

ACKNOWLEDGMENTS

Numerous people have contributed to the multi-microcomputer design presented in this paper. In particular, as part of special computer architecture courses, P.C. Treleaven led group designs of RIMMS microcomputers at Vrije University in Brussels, Belgium in 1981 and at the Federal University of Rio Grande do Sul in Porto Alegre, Brasil in 1983. We also thank the United Kingdom Science and Engineering Research Council for funding and encouraging this research.

REFERENCES

1. Treleaven P. C. and R. P. Hopkins. "A Recursive Computer Architecture for VLSI." *Proceedings of the Ninth International Symposium on Computer Architecture,* April 1982, pp. 229–238.
2. Wilner W. T. "Recursive Machines." Xerox Palo Alto (Calif.) Research Center, Internal Report 1980.
3. Patterson D. and D. Ditzel. "The Case for the Reduced Instruction Set Computer," *Computer Architecture News,* 8 (1980), pp. 25–32.
4. Treleaven P. C. "VLSI Processor Architectures." *COMPUTER,* 15 (1982), pp. 33–45.
5. Mead C. A. and L. Conway. *Introduction to VLSI Systems.* Reading, Mass.: Addison-Wesley, 1980.
6. Seitz C. "Ensemble Architectures for VLSI—A Survey and Taxonomy." In P. Penfield (ed.), *Proceedings of the 1982 Conference on Advanced Research in VLSI,* MIT, January 1982, pp. 33–45.
7. Treleaven P. C., D. R. Brownbridge, and R. P. Hopkins. "Data Driven and Demand Driven Computer Architecture." *ACM Computing Surveys,* 14 (1982), pp. 93–143.
8. Kung H. T., "Why Systolic Arrays." *COMPUTER.* 15 (1982), pp. 37–46.
9. Fisher, A. L., H. T. Kung, L. M. Monier, and Y. Dohi, "Architecture of the PSC: A Programmable Systolic Chip." *Proceedings Tenth International Symposium on Computer Architecture.* June 1983 pp. 48–53.
10. Taylor R. and P. Wilson. "OCCAM Process-oriented Language Meets Demands of Distributed Processing." *Electronics,* 55 (1982), pp. 89–95.
11. Patterson D. and D. Sequin. "A VLSI RISC." *COMPUTER,* 15 (1982), pp. 8–21.

System considerations in the NS32032 design

by RICHARD MATEOSIAN
National Semiconductor
Santa Clara, California

ABSTRACT

The key element in the high-performance systems toward which the 32-bit microprocessors are targeted is the memory and its buses. Viewing memory rather than the CPU as the key system element leads to an important rule for CPU designers: *don't hog the bus*. The NS32032 avoids *hogging the bus* by increasing the information content of memory transactions, and by keeping key data where it's needed rather than moving it across the bus each time it's used. The information content of transactions is increased through the use of a wide bus and a compact instruction encoding. Key data is kept in registers and in an MMU translation lookaside buffer.

INTRODUCTION

The high-performance 16-bit microprocessors introduced over the last five years have broken ground in a new market for microprocessors: high-performance systems such as engineering and CAD workstations, and even general-purpose mainframe-level computers. The 16-bit microprocessors generally have plenty of computing power, but suffer in these applications from an inefficient use of memory. The principal purpose of the 32-bit microprocessors now reaching the market is to overcome this difficulty and to provide efficient engines for high-performance systems.

Designing high-performance microprocessor-based systems requires viewing the memory and its buses as the critical elements. DMA, graphics, and multiple CPUs must all contend for this resource, and the key design criterion for CPUs intended for this environment is that they provide high levels of computing power without *hogging the bus*. In this paper we shall see how the NS32032 was designed to meet that criterion.

HOW NOT TO *HOG THE BUS*

If the memory bus is seen as the critical resource in a system, then there are two main ways to optimize its use. The first is to convey more information per transaction, and the second is to keep key data where it is to be used, without passing it across the bus each time it is needed. The NS32032 design makes use of both of these techniques.

Conveying as much information as possible in each transaction is made possible in the NS32032 in several ways. First is the 32-bit width of the bus. Since many of the entities dealt with in workstation applications are 32 bits in size, a 32-bit bus represents a substantial increase in the efficiency of accessing such items, when compared with a 16-bit bus.

The second way that the NS32032 maximizes the information content of bus transactions is to use a compactly encoded instruction set. Variable sized instructions and displacements, special addressing modes, complete orthogonality, and unrestricted instruction alignment all contribute to program compactness. To further improve the bus efficiency of instruction fetching, accesses to instruction memory are made asynchronously to execution. An 8-byte instruction prefetch queue (FIFO) allows transfers to be made on 32-bit boundaries and at low priority. Instruction alignment is handled automatically inside the CPU, and under normal circumstances instructions are presented to the execution unit as fast as it can handle them, but without placing undue demands on the memory.

Keeping data where it is to be used is facilitated in the NS32032 design in several ways. Most importantly, general-purpose registers in the CPU and in the floating point unit allow frequently accessed variables to be used without an argument transfer over the memory bus. Similarly, in the MMU, a cache of recently used translations allows address translation to proceed with infrequent access to the large memory-based translation tables required for demand paged virtual memory.

NS32032 DETAILS

The architecture of the NS16000 Family has been described elsewhere. In brief, the main processing chips of an NS16000 system are a CPU, Memory Management Unit (MMU), and Floating Point Unit (FPU). All CPUs of the NS16000 Family have the same 32-bit architecture and 32-bit internal implementation. They differ only in the width of the bus to memory. The NS32032 has a 32-bit bus.

Instruction Encoding

The compact instruction encoding of the NS32032 arises from a number of interrelated factors:

1. Orthogonality of operation, data type, addressing mode
2. No instruction alignment restriction
3. No instruction size restriction
4. Variable sized displacements
5. A variety of register-relative addressing modes

Orthogonality serves to reduce the number of instructions required to perform typical high-level language functions. For example, the statement

$$A = A + B$$

normally translates into a single NS32032 instruction, regardless of whether A and B are local, global, or external and whether they are variables, array elements, or record fields. Furthermore, this instruction rarely occupies more than 4 bytes of instruction memory.

Instructions for the NS32032 can be any number of bytes in size and can begin at any byte of memory. This requires special circuitry in the CPU (see Figure 1), which could be avoided if size and alignment restrictions like those of older microprocessor families were enforced. The resolution of the tradeoff in favor of special circuitry is easily understood when the memory and its buses, rather than the CPU, are regarded as the critical system resource.

NS32032 CPU Block Diagram

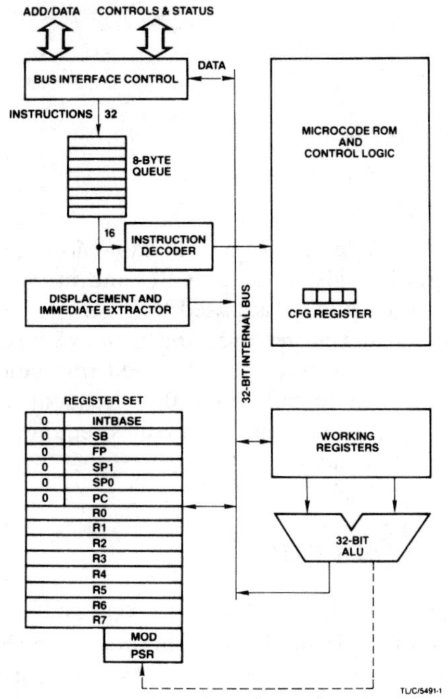

Figure 1—Special NS32032 circuitry avoids alignment restrictions

Variable sized displacements and the register-relative addressing modes that use displacements contribute to the compactness of NS32032 programs. Figure 2 shows the NS32032 addressing modes. Note that many involve the use of a base register to contain a memory address, and a displacement encoded in the instruction. The first two bits of a displacement are used to encode its size in bytes. The encoding allows displacements ranging between −64 and 63, by far the most common case, to be encoded in a single byte, while displacements up to 4 bytes in size allow the entire addressing range

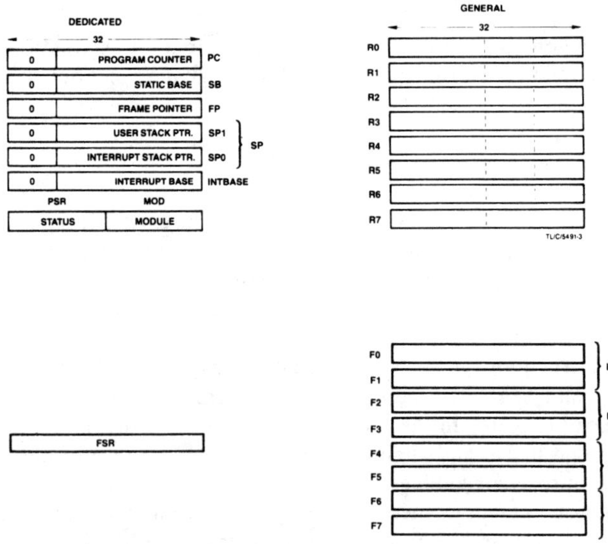

Figure 2—Many NS32032 addressing modes use displacements

ENCODING	MODE	ASSEMBLER SYNTAX	EFFECTIVE ADDRESS
Register Relative			
01000	Register 0 relative	disp(R0)	Disp + Register.
01001	Register 1 relative	disp(R1)	
01010	Register 2 relative	disp(R2)	
01011	Register 3 relative	disp(R3)	
01100	Register 4 relative	disp(R4)	
01101	Register 5 relative	disp(R5)	
01110	Register 6 relative	disp(R6)	
01111	Register 7 relative	disp(R7)	
Memory Relative			
10000	Frame memory relative	disp2(disp1(FP))	Disp2 + Pointer; Pointer found at address Disp1 + Register. "SP" is either SP0 or SP1, as selected in PSR.
10001	Stack memory relative	disp2(disp1(SP))	
10010	Static memory relative	disp2(disp1(SB))	
Absolute			
10101	Absolute	@disp	Disp.
External			
10110	External	EXT (disp1) + disp2	Disp2 + Pointer; Pointer is found at Link Table Entry number Disp1.
Memory Space			
11000	Frame memory	disp(FP)	Disp + Register; "SP" is either SP0 or SP1, as selected in PSR.
11001	Stack memory	disp(SP)	
11010	Static memory	disp(SB)	
11011	Program memory	* + disp	

Figure 3—Registers reduce bus traffic

to be spanned. The base register can be either a general-purpose register or one of several registers designed to support directly the data structures most frequently used by compiled code.

General Registers

The general-purpose registers of the NS32032 CPU and its associated floating point unit (the NS16081 FPU) reduce bus traffic by eliminating memory transactions for operand accesses. The use of compiler techniques like data flow analysis, which optimize the use of general-purpose registers by high-level language programs is further facilitated in the NS32032 architecture by orthogonality, which allows all variables to be treated uniformly.

Figure 3 shows the register set of the NS32032, which contains eight general purpose registers and eight floating point registers. Even though floating point operations are handled by a separate chip, the floating point operations and registers are integrated with the NS32032 architecture so that floating point variables can be handled exactly like integer variables by compilers.

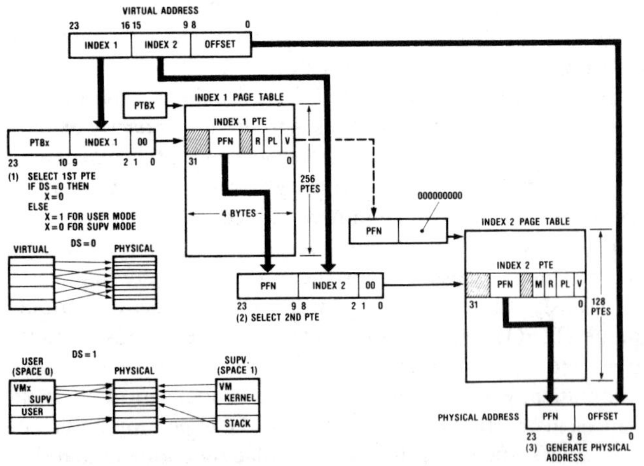

Figure 4—NS32032/NS16082 memory management uses memory-based tables

Memory Management

Demand paged virtual memory for the NS32032 is achieved with the NS16082 MMU, which uses extensive memory-based tables to define three-level address translation and access protection for user and supervisor address spaces. (See Figure 4.) Memory management for the NS32032 avoids burdening the memory bus in two ways. First, memory accesses with or without address translation look identical to the memory. The MMU automatically inserts an additional cycle into translated transactions, but does so invisibly to the memory.

The second feature of the MMU that avoids burdening the memory bus is a 32-entry cache of recently used page translations, automatically updated with a clocked FIFO algorithm. In typical applications this cache allows translation to proceed without access to the memory-based tables better than 98% of the time. Without this feature, each memory access would incur an address translation overhead of between two and four memory accesses.

SUMMARY

The key element in the high-performance systems toward which the 32-bit microprocessors are targeted is the memory and its buses. Viewing memory rather than the CPU as the key system element leads to an important rule for CPU designers: don't *hog the bus.* The NS32032 avoids hogging the bus by increasing the information content of memory transactions and by keeping key data where it's needed, rather than moving it across the bus each time it's used.

An inside look at the Z80,000 CPU: Zilog's new 32-bit microprocessor

by ANIL PATEL
Zilog Corporation
Campbell, California

ABSTRACT

With recent advances in very large scale integrated circuit (VLSI) design, the once-distinct boundaries of micro-, mini-, and mainframe computer architectures are eroding. For example, the Motorola 68000, the Z8000 CPU, and the Intel 8086 have broken the once-distinct boundary between micro- and minicomputers. Now the Z80,000 CPU, Zilog's new 32-bit processor chip, has broken the distinct boundary between mini- and mainframe computers by featuring a mainframe power on an integrated-circuit chip. The distinguishing features of the Z80,000 CPU—such as on-chip virtual memory management, on-chip cache memory, six-stage pipeline architecture, burst memory transfer, and multiprocessing support—put it ahead of any CPU in its class.

The CPU supports linear and segmented addressing. The regular instruction set and rich and powerful addressing modes are well suited to compilers and operating systems. The flexibility and simplicity of the Z80,000 provide an easy solution to hardware and software system design.

ARCHITECTURE

The Z80,000 CPU is a register-oriented machine that provides sixteen 32-bit general purpose registers (Figure 1). The registers are truly general purpose, with no restrictions on their use as accumulators, addressing registers, Stack Pointers, or data registers. Therefore, bottlenecks encountered with register organizations that dedicate specific registers for accumulators (or data) and addressing are eliminated. In addition, because any register can be used as a Stack Pointer, the registers lend themselves to high-level language support by providing the multiple Stack Pointers required for parsing operations.

The organization of the registers also provides for efficient handling of mixed data types. Registers can be used for 8- or 16-bit arithmetic and logical operations without loss of the high-order 24 and 16 bits, respectively, giving the effect of a much larger register space. In addition, 32-bit registers can be paired for 64-bit data.

The Z80,000 CPU uses 32-bit logical addresses to directly access up to 4 gigabytes of memory in each of 4 address spaces. Separate address spaces are provided for system and normal modes and for instructions and data. The programmer has available four different address representations in accessing the memory space (Figure 2), providing maximum flexibility in applying the processor to the specific requirements of the application environment. Two bits in the flag and control word (FCW) select compact, segmented, or linear address representation.

Compact mode uses a 16 bit address, which gets concatenated to the upper 16 bits of the Program Counter to form a 32-bit address. Programs operating within a 64K workspace can take advantage of the compact mode's dense code and efficient use of base registers.

RQ0	RR0	7 RH0 0	7 RL0 0	7 RH1 0	7 RL1 0	R0, R1
	RR2	7 RH2 0	7 RL2 0	7 RH3 0	7 RL3 0	R2, R3
RQ4	RR4	7 RH4 0	7 RL4 0	7 RH5 0	7 RL5 0	R4, R5
	RR6	7 RH6 0	7 RL6 0	7 RH7 0	7 RL7 0	R6, R7
RQ8	RR8	15 R8 0		15 R9 0		
	RR10	15 R10 0		15 R11 0		
RQ12	RR12	15 R12 0		15 R13 0		
	RR14	15 R14 0		15 R15 0		
RQ16	RR16	31			0	
	RR18	31			0	
RQ20	RR20	31			0	
	RR22	31			0	
RQ24	RR24	31			0	
	RR26	31			0	
RQ28	RR28	31			0	
	RR30	31			0	

Figure 1—General purpose registers

Many applications lend themselves to the use of segmented mode, where individual objects are allocated to separate protected segments. The segment remains unchanged during address calculations; only the offset is affected. There are two segment sizes available with the Z80,000 CPU, controlled by the most significant bit of the address field. Thus, the programmer has the flexibility of having 128 segments of up to 16 megabytes, and 32K segments of up to 64K in size.

Applications requiring a large linear address space without the formal structure of segmentation include graphics and the processing of large arrays. Additionally, with the availability of 32 bits of addressing, certain application-specific implementations use address lines creatively and would otherwise be hampered by the structure imposed by segmentation. The Z80,000 CPU supports 32-bit linear addressing, as well as segmented and compact addressing, to provide maximum flexibility to the system designer.

Nine general addressing modes provide efficient access to the many types of data structures. A rich instruction set combines with the address modes to operate on a variety of data types, including 8-, 16-, and 32-bit integer and logical values, as well as bits, bit fields, packed decimal, and dynamic length strings. Additionally, high-level language support is enhanced by instructions for procedure linkage, array indexing, and integer conversion, as well as the more common operations.

A separate system mode, with its own Stack Pointer and protected address space, supports operating systems. Because some instructions are privileged, executing only in system mode, the operating system and system resources are protected from programs operating in normal mode. The System Call instruction is used by the normal mode program to communicate with the operating system through the Z80,000 CPU trap facility. The processor also includes an extensive trap mechanism for run-time error detection and software debugging.

MEMORY MANAGEMENT

The Z80,000 CPU memory management mechanism has been integrated with the CPU on-chip, offering two primary advantages to the system designer: a parts count reduction and faster access to memory. Memory access is faster because the CPU generates physical addresses, thus eliminating the delay of an external memory mapping device.

The CPU's Paged Memory Management Unit (PMMU) provides translation of logical addresses to physical addresses,

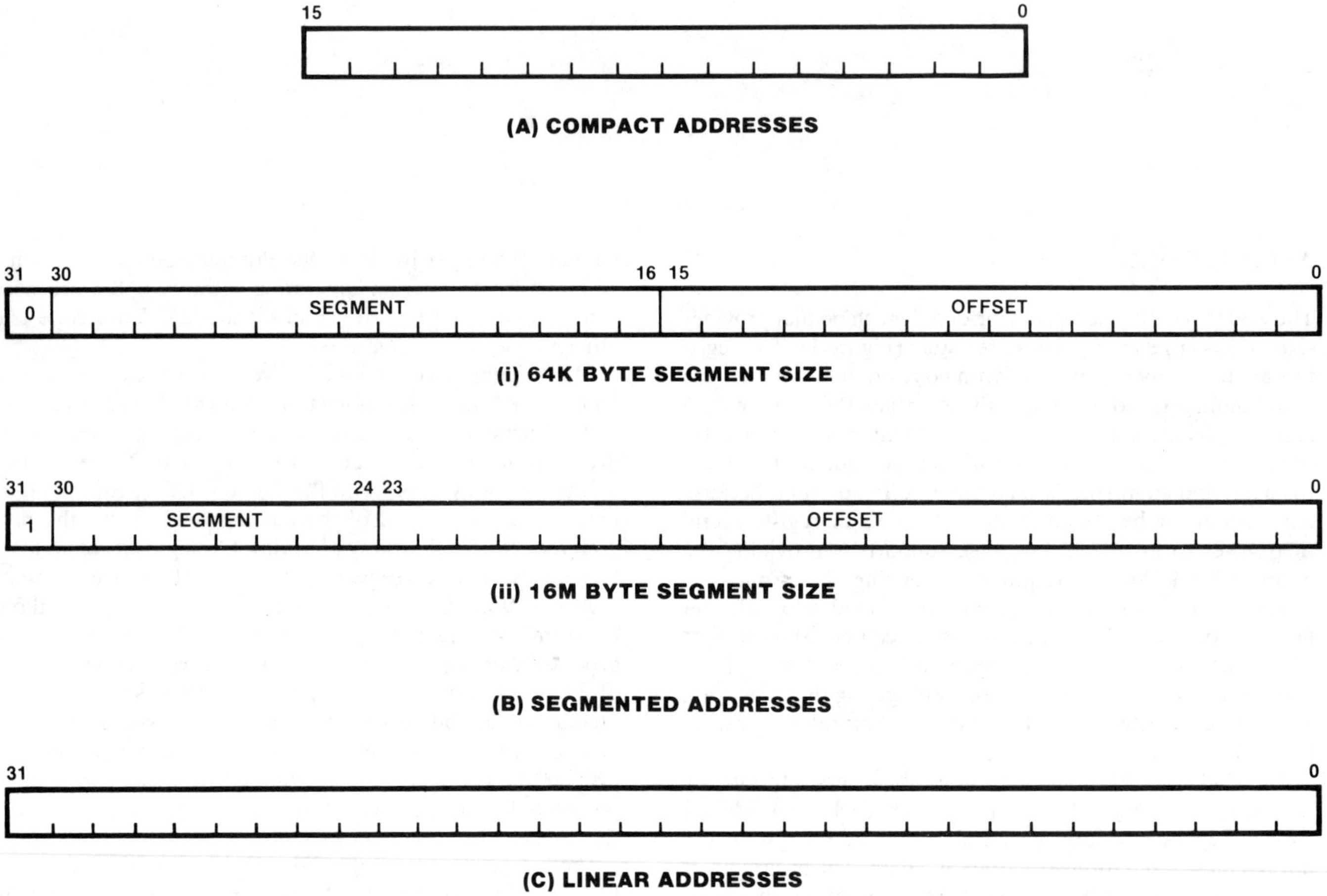

Figure 2—Address representation

memory access protection, and protected access to memory mapped I/O devices. Demand-paged virtual memory is easily implemented without special software recovery routines or storage of the internal state following address translation faults. The implementation is accomplished through early detection of translation faults, resulting in the ability to restart all instructions efficiently. Besides providing access protection, the page attribute mechanism also contains referenced and modified bits that aid the operating system in determining which page in physical memory should be swapped with the required page from mass storage.

To manage the Z80,000 CPU's 4G-byte logical address space, the translation scheme divides it into fixed-size, 1K-byte pages. The logical address's 22 high-order bits select a page in the address space, while the 10 least significant bits select a byte within the page. Similarly, physical memory is divided into 1K-byte units, called frames. The memory management unit maps a logical page to a frame. Having both logical and physical units of the same size simplifies the operating system's memory allocation problem.

The CPU and operating system cooperate to translate a program's logical addresses into physical addresses that are used to access memory. The CPU's paging scheme is similar to that of most mainframes and super-minicomputers. First, the operating system creates translation tables in memory, then initializes pointers to the tables in control registers. The CPU automatically references the tables to perform the address translation and access protection for each memory access. Delays that would be associated with referencing the translation tables are minimized by using an additional on-chip cache associated with the Memory Management Unit, the Translation Lookaside Buffer (TLB). Logical addresses, their corresponding physical addresses, and access attributes are stored in the TLB (Figure 3) as they are translated through

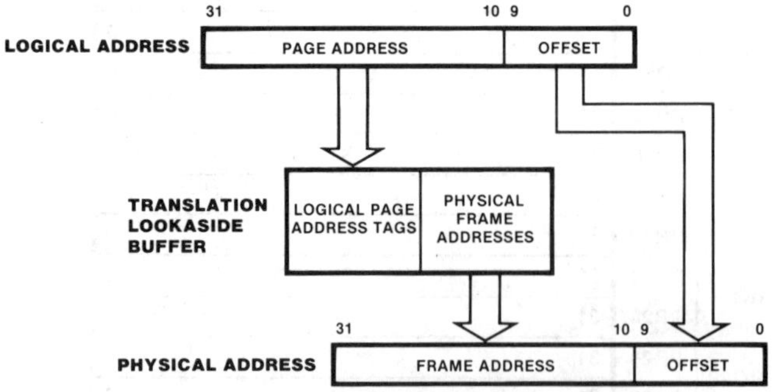

Figure 3—Address translation using the TLB

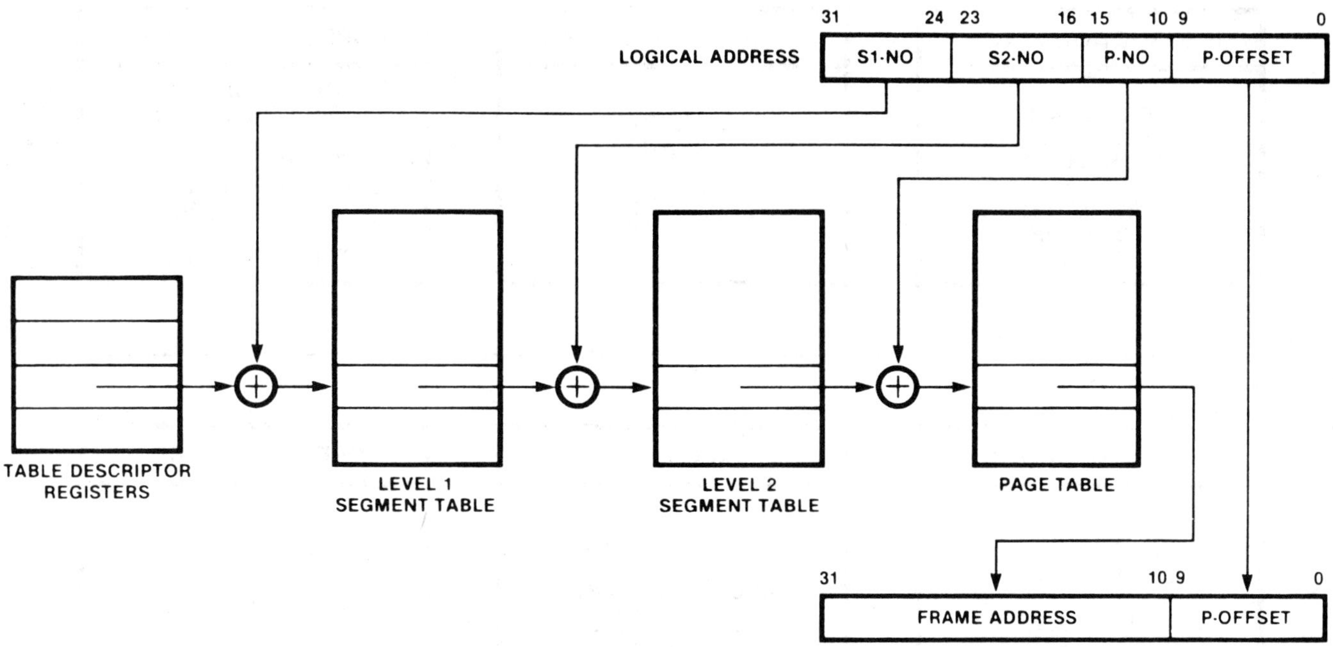

Figure 4—Address translation

the translation tables. Subsequent accesses to the same page do not require access to the translation tables stored in memory; they are simply retrieved from the TLB. The tables are accessed only when an entry does not exist in the TLB, a TLB "miss." The least recently used entry is then replaced with the new address translation and access information. The TLB can hold the 16 most recently referenced pages, providing a TLB hit ratio that is typically over 96%.

The Z80,000 CPU implements a three-level address translation process. Once the operating system creates the translation tables and initializes the control registers, the CPU automatically references the level-1, level-2, and page tables to perform address translation and access protection (Figure 4). Access protection is encoded in a 4-bit field at any level of the translation process. This allows access protection to be accomplished at the page level, level-1, level-2, or a mixture of the 3. The use of 3 levels of translation is dictated by the 32-bit logical address of the Z80,000 CPU, whereas a 2-level translation mechanism would be appropriate for 24-bit logical addresses.

It is possible to reduce the number of levels of translation by specifying in the table descriptor registers (the control registers containing pointers to the translation tables) that either or both the level-1 and level-2 tables should be omitted during the translation process. Skipping level-1 tables is useful when only a 24-bit address space is required. Both tables can be skipped when 16-bit addressing is sufficient for the needs of the application. Additionally, the tables can be reduced in size by specifying in the table entries the size of the next level table in increments of 256 bytes. Thus, maximum flexibility in translation, access protection, and table organization is maintained by the Z80,000 CPU memory management implementation.

PERFORMANCE BOOSTERS: CACHE, SIX-STAGE PIPELINE, BURST MEMORY TRANSFER

The Z80,000 CPU implementation includes a six-stage pipeline (Figure 5) supported by two 32-bit ALUs, one assigned to address calculation and the other associated with the execution stage. The pipeline allows concurrent operation of up to six instructions.

All pipeline stages can operate in a single processor cycle, which is composed of two clock cycles. The pipeline allows simple instructions, such as register-to-register Load and memory-to-register Add, to be executed at a rate of one instruction for each processor cycle, leading to a peak performance of 12.5 million instructions per second with a 25-MHz clock. In practice, the actual instruction rate is about one-third of the peak rate because of certain delays.

Because the pipeline may require two memory fetches during each processor cycle—one to fetch the instruction and the other for the operand fetch stage—it is necessary to buffer the high execution rate of the pipeline from the relatively slow memory access rate. Because memory fetches typically take three or more bus cycles, the pipeline would be idle most of the time if all references had to access main memory. By including an on-chip cache that can be accessed in one processor cycle, most memory references can be made without external bus transactions, allowing the pipeline to function at an extremely high level of performance.

The cache holds copies of the most recently accessed memory locations. On each memory fetch, the CPU examines the cache to determine if the data at that address is available on chip, in other words, a cache "hit." If available, the data is read from the cache rather than from external memory. If it is not available, a cache "miss," the CPU generates an

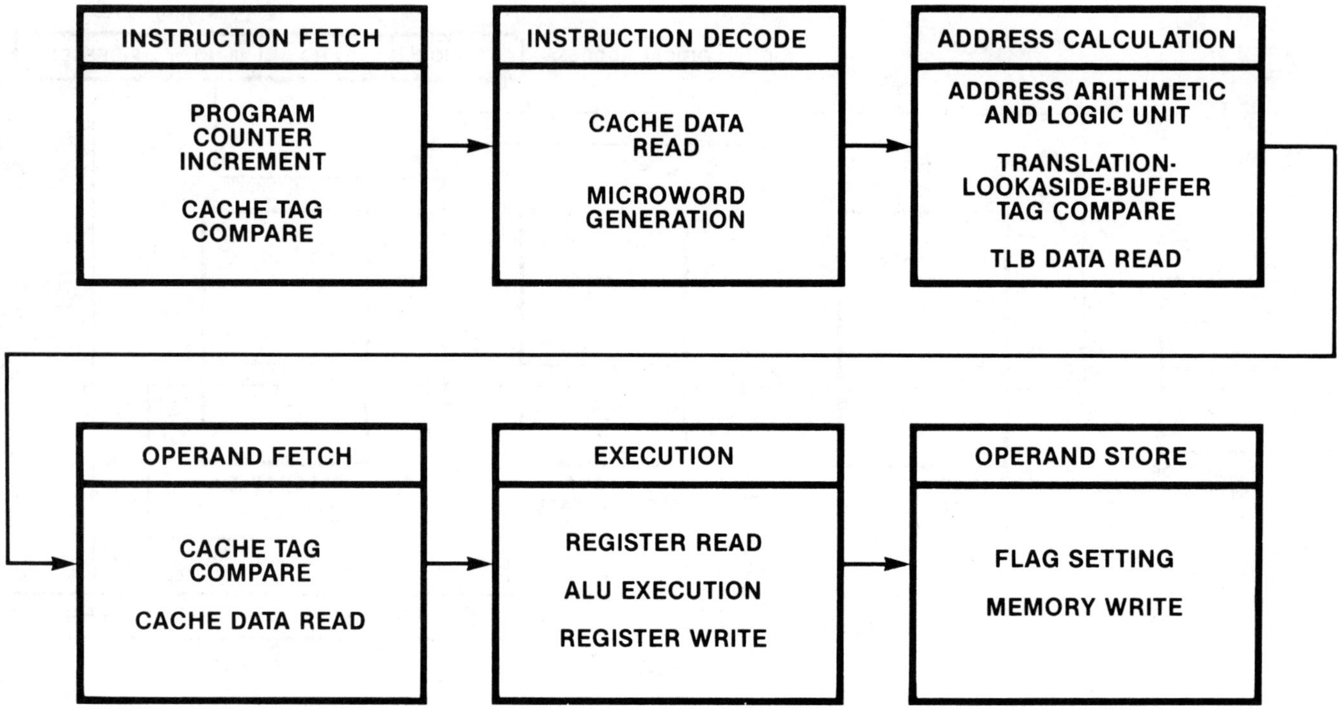

Figure 5—Six-stage pipeline

external memory transaction to fetch the data and then stores the fetched information in the cache. The Z80,000 CPU cache is organized as 16 lines, or blocks, of 16 bytes, for a total of 256 bytes of data (Figure 6). Each block is associated with a 28-bit tag that represents the most significant bits of the address of the block. The lower 4 bits of the address select the appropriate byte, word, or longword within the block. There are eight validity bits, each corresponding to a word within the block. This structure represents an optimum tradeoff between performance and silicon area (cost).

The Z80,000 CPU cache is mode programmable to best fit the requirements of the application. Modes include instruction only, data only, instruction/data (all mainframes implement instruction/data), and local memory. Whereas particular applications for the Z80,000 CPU may require instructions only to be cached, caching data along with instructions will typically increase cache performance by 20%. Local memory allows a specific address to be assigned to each block; thus, the cache takes on the form of an extremely fast 256-byte memory. For example, in a highly intensive interrupt driven environment, the interrupt service routines (ISR) may be allocated to the on-chip local memory to maximize ISR throughput.

For references requiring operand stores, the data is always written to main memory. The cache is also updated if it contains the addressed location; otherwise it is unaffected. This mechanism, called write-through, ensures that main memory represents the most recent value stored at any address. Without the ability to write through cache to main memory, the CPU would be required to update memory whenever the least recently used cache line is flushed to allow space for new code or data during a cache miss operation. The write-through mechanism allows processing to continue, concurrent with the bus activity associated with the write. The pipeline allows concurrent operation because the next instruction is most likely to be present in the CPU. Additionally, burst transfers into cache further increase the probability that instructions are present on-chip, minimizing the potential of write-through operations conflicting with bus read transactions.

Increased bus bandwidth can be achieved by taking advantage of the optional burst transfer capability of the Z80,000 CPU bus interface. Burst memory transactions use multiple data strobes following each address strobe to transfer consecutive memory locations. The CPU uses burst transactions to prefetch a cache block on an instruction fetch cache miss. A read transaction with a single data strobe and one wait state

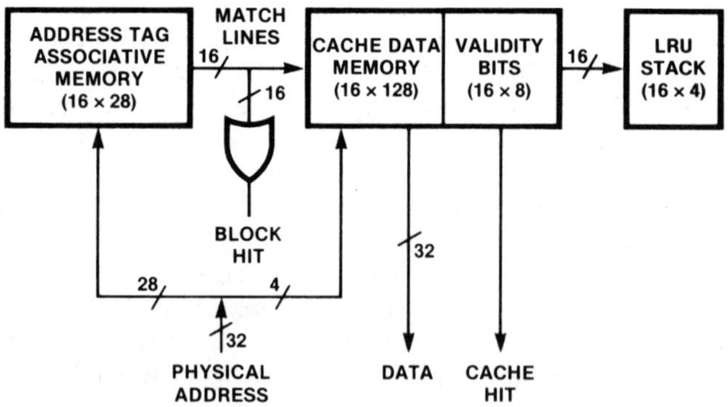

Figure 6—Cache organization

requires three bus clocks. However, with burst transfers, a transaction with four data strobes and one wait state requires six bus clocks, resulting in twice the bus bandwidth of the single transfer transaction. With a 12.5-MHz bus clock (25-MHz CPU clock), 32-bit data path, and 4 data transfer per transaction, with no wait state, the bus bandwidth is 40 megabytes a second. Burst transactions are also used for fetching and storing operands when multiple transfers are necessary, such as string operations, Load Multiple instructions, and loading of program status, and when unaligned accesses occur.

MULTIPROCESSING

The CPU provides support for interconnection in four types of multiprocessor configurations (Figure 7): coprocessor, slave processor, tightly coupled multiple CPUs, and loosely coupled multiple CPUs. Coprocessors work concurrently with the CPU to execute a single instruction stream using the Extended Processing Architecture (EPA) facility. This allows extension of the Z80,000 CPU architecture to include floating point operations and other specialized functions. Additionally, the processing speeds offered by extended processing units (EPUs) optimized for particular operations, such as the Z8070 Arithmetic Processing Unit, can provide significant performance improvements.

When the CPU encounters an EPU instruction (and the EPA bit in the FCW is set to 1), it begins a CPU-to-EPU instruction transaction that broadcasts the first two words of the EPU instruction to all (as many as four) EPUs in the system. If a data transfer is required, the CPU and the selected EPU conduct the appropriate data transfer transaction. The CPU is the bus master, handling address translations and bus transactions. The $\overline{\text{EPUBSY}}$ signal is used by the CPU and EPUs to synchronize transfers. EPU operations are efficient because the CPU is not required to wait for completion of the EPU operation, and no elaborate handshaking is necessary. In fact, up to four EPUs can be actively processing data while the CPU handles other chores. In systems supporting the functionality of an extended processing unit without the actual EPU present (the EPA bit in the FCW is cleared to 0), the EPU instructions are trapped and emulated in software.

Slave processors, such as the Z8016 DMA Transfer Controller, perform dedicated functions asynchronously to the CPU. The CPU and slave processor share a local bus, of which the CPU is the default master. When the slave wishes to use the bus, it requests the bus using the $\overline{\text{BUSREQ}}$ line. The CPU responds by asserting $\overline{\text{BUSACK}}$ and placing all other output signals in 3-state. The slave then gains control of the bus (and in the case of the Z8016, it provides DMA capabilities). When the slave no longer needs the bus, it relinquishes the control back to the CPU.

Tightly coupled, multiple CPUs execute independent instruction streams and generally communicate through shared memory located on a common (global) bus using the CPU's $\overline{\text{GREQ}}$ and $\overline{\text{GACK}}$ lines. Each CPU is default master only of its local bus; an external arbiter chooses the global bus master. The CPU also provides status information about interlocked memory references so that bus control is not relinquished

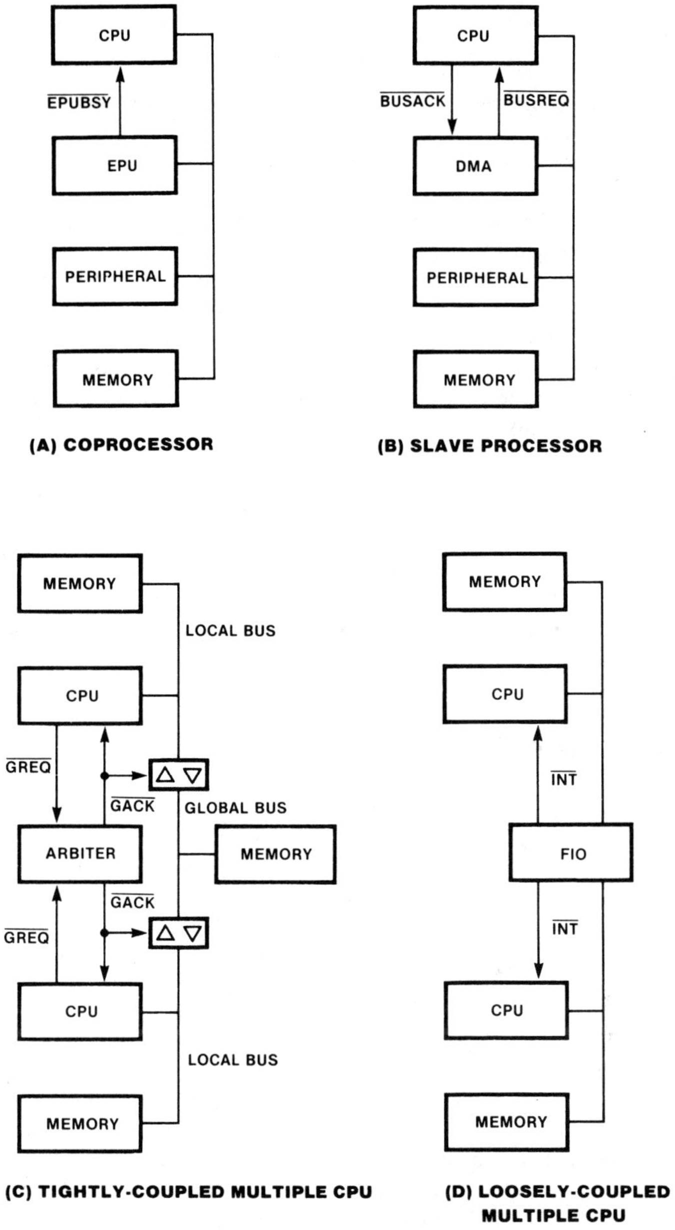

Figure 7—Multiprocessing support

during an indivisible operation such as Test and Set or Increment Interlocked.

The Z80,000 CPU's I/O and interrupt facilities support loosely coupled multiple CPUs, which generally communicate through a multi-ported peripheral, such as the Z8038 FIFO I/O Controller.

EXCEPTION PROCESSING

The Z80,000 CPU supports four types of exceptions: reset, bus error, interrupts, and traps. A reset exception occurs when the reset line is activated. In responding to a reset exception, the CPU fetches the program status (FCW and PC) from physical address 2 and resets itself into the initialized state.

When external hardware indicates a bus error exception on the memory response lines RSP_0-RSP_1, the CPU terminates the transaction in progress. The CPU also terminates the instruction in execution. In processing bus error exception, the CPU saves the program status, the physical address for the transaction, and a word identifying the status and control signals used for the transaction.

Three types of interrupts are supported: vectored, nonvectored, and nonmaskable. The vectored and nonvectored interrupts have mask bits in the FCW. All interrupts read an identifier word from the bus during an interrupt acknowledge transaction and save the word on the system stack. Vectored interrupts use the lower byte of this word to select a unique PC value from the program status area.

The CPU supports 12 trap conditions: extended instruction, privileged instruction, system call, address translation, reserved instruction, odd PC, trace, breakpoint, conditional, integer overflow, bounds check, and subscript error.

In descending order, the priority of exceptions is: reset, bus error, trap, nonmaskable interrupt, vectored interrupt, and nonvectored interrupt.

Z80,000 CPU PERFORMANCE

Cache memory and the pipelined structure cause the performance evaluation of the Z80,000 CPU to be complex. The best approach is separation of instruction processing time into a sum of three components: execution time, pipeline delays, and memory delays. Performance was evaluated by statistically measuring activities of 10 C language programs and then performing a computer simulation of the cache, Translation Lookaside Buffer, and pipeline mechanisms.

The execution time for an instruction is the number of cycles required to execute the instruction if there are no other delays such as cache miss or register interlock. Common instructions, such as loading a register with a word operand specified by a base-register-plus-displacement addressing mode, execute in 1 processor cycle (2 clock cycles), but the average instruction execution time is 1.3 processor cycles.

Pipeline delays are caused by branch instructions, register interlocks, and other miscellaneous delays. The most significant of these is delay due to branch instructions. When a branch is taken, instructions in the pipe behind the branch instruction are flushed. Unconditional branches introduce a delay of two processor cycles. Conditional branches cause a three processor cycles delay if the condition is met and no delay if the condition is not met. The average delay due to branches is 0.5 processor cycles per instruction.

Another significant pipeline delay is register interlock. Whenever the execution stage modifies a register that is to be used in a subsequent instruction as an address register, the address calculation must be held up (interlocked) until the execution is complete. The interlock ensures that the proper register value is used in the address calculation. The average register interlock delay is 0.2 processor cycles per instruction. All the other miscellaneous delays add up to 0.2 processor cycles. Therefore, the total average pipeline delay is 0.9 processor cycles per instruction.

Memory delays are caused by cache misses and TLB misses. When the processor fetches an instruction or operand for which a corresponding entry in the cache or TLB does not exist, a reference to main memory is generated. The average delay due to these memory transfers is 1.2 cycles per instruction. This delay calculation is based on a 32-bit data path, a memory cycle time of 3 processor cycles, and support of burst transfers.

Instruction processing time, Ti =
Execution delay + Pipeline delay + Memory delay.
Therefore $Ti = 1.3 + 0.9 + 1.2 = 3.4$ processor cycles.

The total processing time is an average of 3.4 processor cycles per instruction. At 10 MHz, this corresponds to 1.5 MIPS; at 25 MHz, the instruction execution rate is 3.7 MIPS.

EASE OF SYSTEM DESIGN

The Z80,000 CPU allows particular cost and performance objectives to be met by allowing designers to balance memory access and bus bandwidth appropriately and to incorporate burst transfers into designs. The Hardware Interface Control register (HICR) defines the characteristics of the hardware configuration surrounding the CPU. By setting appropriate bits in the HICR, the system designer can specify bus speed, memory data path, and the number of wait states to be automatically inserted for different types of bus accesses.

The bus speed can be one-half or one-fourth the CPU's clock frequency. Because the cache effectively decouples the CPU from the external bus, high processing rates can be achieved on-chip supported by an external bus that is not only easier to design but also less costly than one operating at the high clock frequencies of the Z80,000 CPU. A performance of 1.5 MIPS can be achieved at 10 MHz, using slow and inexpensive memory of 600-nanosecond memory cycle time. Using 240-nanosecond memory cycle time, a performance of 3.7 MIPS can be achieved at 25 MHz. In addition, because the bus can operate at two frequencies relative to the processor's clock, design migration to faster versions of the CPU will not incur major redevelopment. For instance, a 10 MHz Z80,000 design using a 5 MHz bus can be increased to 20 MHz while maintaining the same external bus speed.

The memory data path width can be specified separately for the upper and lower portions of the memory space as either 16 or 32 bits. The number of wait states to be automatically inserted during bus accessses can be specific to the upper and lower portions of the memory and I/O spaces. Thus, a system can accommodate a slow, 16-bit-side ROM and a fast 32-bit-wide RAM.

CONCLUSION

The Z80,000 provides the following benefits:

1. High performance
   a. On-chip Memory Management Unit (MMU)

   b. On-chip cache—instruction/data
   c. Six-stage pipeline architecture with two 32-bit ALUs
   d. Burst memory transfers
   e. EPU overlap (CPU is able to run while coprocessor is running)
2. Flexible architecture
   a. Available linear, segmented, and compact addressing
   b. Programmable hardware configuration (e.g., bus speed, wait states)
   c. Support for multiprocessing: tightly coupled, loosely coupled, slave processor, coprocessor
3. Simple and regular architecture
   a. Regular use of operations, addressing modes, and data types in instruction set
   b. Rich and powerful addressing modes
4. Miscellaneous benefits
   a. Instruction set well suited for high-level, structured languages like C, PASCAL
   b. Architecture well suited for operating systems
   c. On-chip MMU for easy and cost-effective hardware design
   d. Simple memory management and task switching for operating system
   e. Largest virtual memory available per task
   f. Largest register set
   g. Execution rate of up to 12.5 MIPS
   h. Memory mapped I/O
   i. Single phase clock

The Z80,000 CPU addresses a wide range of system applications including high-performance, desk-top general purpose computing, graphics, and array processing, wherever mainframe performance is at low cost.

An interleaved array-processing architecture

by J. R. JUMP,
J. D. WISE,
and D. T. HARPER III
Rice University
Houston, Texas

ABSTRACT

This paper describes an array-processing architecture capable of executing high-level vector operations. There are two distinguishing features of this architecture: First, the user can define for later use complex vector operations that involve several arithmetic operations and branching. Once defined, they appear as built-in vector instructions to the user. Second, the algorithms for accessing and aligning vectors are implemented in hardware, eliminating the need for user programs to deal with memory addresses.

INTRODUCTION

This paper presents a bus-organized array processor designed to execute high-level vector operations. Unlike conventional array processors that can only execute basic arithmetic vector operations, such as addition and multiplication, and that rely heavily on pipelined arithmetic units, the system proposed here uses programmable processing units that can execute complex vector operations involving several arithmetic operations as well as conditional branching within the body of the operation. One of the primary motivations for this work is to provide an experimental research system for investigating different methods for implementing vector algorithms. It is felt that by organizing vector calculations so that the basic operations on the vector components are more complex than simple arithmetic operations, a higher degree of parallelism can be realized.

The next section provides a discussion of the considerations that have motivated this high-level approach to array processing. The third section presents the array processor architecture we have developed to support this approach. The final section summarizes some of the research projects planned for and motivated by the array processor presented in section three.

BACKGROUND AND MOTIVATIONS

A major problem encountered in the design and use of high performance parallel systems involves the movement of data between functional units. As the speed and number of processor and memory units are increased, the capacity of the data transfer paths between these units becomes the critical bottleneck to overall system performance. There are two general solutions to the problem: (1) increase the number and bandwidth of the data transfer paths in the system, or (2) organize computations to decrease the amount of data that must be transferred between the different units. While the first solution is more general—it does not place additional restrictions on how the system is used—it is usually the most expensive. An implied objective of the second solution is to reduce the need for expensive, high-speed data transfer paths by reducing the amount of data that must be passed between functional units. This is usually possible only if the class of computations to be performed is restricted in some way.

The simplest scheme for connecting several functional units is a bus shared by all of the units (Figure 1a). The problem with this interconnection structure is that only one item of data at a time can be transferred between functional units. Several techniques for increasing the capacity of data transfer paths in a computer system have been developed. Most of these use multiple data paths to reduce the number of functional units that must share a common data path. For example, if the number of functional units is relatively small (less than 16–20), a crossbar switch (Figure 1b) can be used to provide a direct connection between any two units.[1,2] While the cost of such a switch is proportional to the square of the number of functional units, any two or more different pairs of units can transfer data simultaneously. If the number of functional units is large (more than 16–20), a multistage interconnection network (Figure 1c) can provide a more cost-effective interconnection structure than the crossbar.[3,4] These are networks that provide the capability for any unit to transfer data to any other unit, but they cannot support as many simultaneous transfers as a crossbar. However, for n functional units, the cost of a multistage interconnection network is only on the order of $n(\log n)$ instead of n^2 for the crossbar.[5,6]

This paper is concerned with the second approach to relieving the data transfer bottleneck, namely, restricting the amount of necessary data movement between functional units so that a simple bus can be used for all data transfers between functional units. While this will not work for all types of computations, it will usually be successful for algorithms that can be decomposed into a large number of independent sub-algorithms. One source of algorithms with this property is the class of vector calculations where the same operation is applied to all elements of one or more vectors. Since the operations on different components of a vector are usually independent, these calculations can involve a large number of independent operations with little if any sharing of data. Therefore, the architecture proposed in this paper will be bus-organized and optimized to execute vector calculations with a minimum of data movement between processors and memories. It is intended to be used as a back-end processor that adds vector-processing capability to a general-purpose processor.

The key to using a bus effectively in vector calculations is to organize the system and the algorithms so that the time required to perform a component operation is large relative to the time required to transfer the operands and results on the bus. In this way the bus can be time shared among several functional units without significant loss of performance. To do this, the processing units should be capable of performing operations that are more complex than simple arithmetic operations. In fact, they should be capable of executing algorithms composed of several arithmetic operations and simple branching instructions. Then, the execution of several operations on several vector components can be executed simultaneously in different processors and overlapped with the transfer of operands and results.

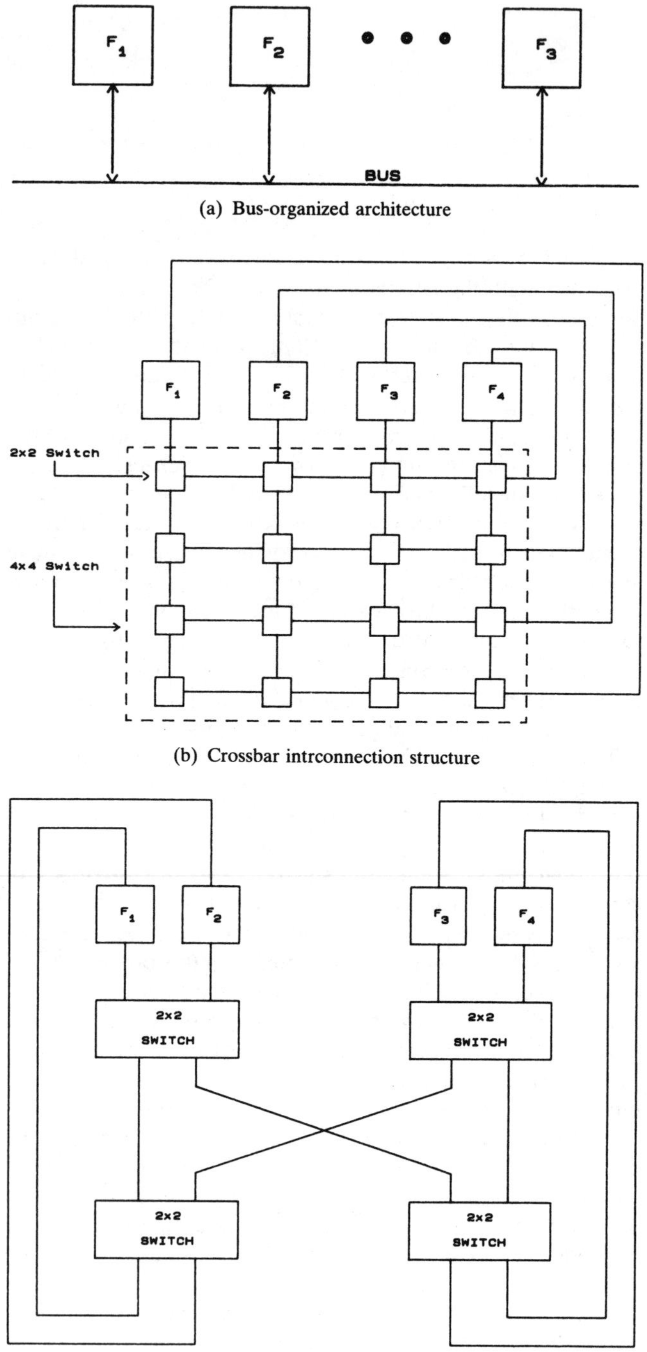

(a) Bus-organized architecture

(b) Crossbar intrconnection structure

(c) Multistage interconnection structure

Figure 1—Intermodule communication

Let N denote the maximum number of processing units that can be kept busy, each performing an operation on different components of a vector, in a bus-organized system. Then N is equal to $\lceil t_p/t_t \rceil + 1$, where t_p is the processing time of the operation, t_t is the bus transfer time for its operands and results, and $\lceil x \rceil$ denotes the smallest integer greater than or equal to x. To see this, note that an operation can be initiated in a processor each t_t time units. After $t_t + t_p$ time units, the operation in the first processor is complete so that it can be assigned another. The number of processors that can be assigned an operation before the first one is free is just $\lceil t_p/t_t \rceil$. Hence, $\lceil t_p/t_t \rceil + 1$ processors can be kept busy. If more processing units were available, they would not increase the performance of the system, since the bus would be saturated and unable to supply data fast enough to keep all of the processors busy. Therefore, by organizing a vector algorithm so that the time to execute operations on vector elements is large relative to the time to transfer data between memory units and processors, the performance limitations inherent in a bus-organized system can be alleviated. Again, this argues for general-purpose functional units that can be programmed to perform complex operations.

If $\lceil t_p/t_t \rceil + 1$ processors are used to perform an operation on vectors of length k in a bus-organized system, then the total time required to perform the operation is given by

$$T = k \cdot t_t + t_p$$

This follows from the fact that the bus is saturated so that all processing time is overlapped with bus transfers. Therefore, the total time to perform the vector operation is approximately equal to $k \cdot t_t$, the time required to transfer the operands and results for the k component operations. The extra t_p term is for the time to complete the last component operation during which no bus transfers are taking place.

To illustrate the concepts outlined above, consider performing the operation $Z \leftarrow X^2 + Y^2$, where X, Y, and Z are vectors of length 100. Figure 2 shows two ways this calculation could be organized for a system in which all data transfers between memory and processing units take place via a common time-shared bus. The 200 multiplications and 100 additions that must be executed to perform the vector operation are shown in Figure 2a. For the purpose of illustration assume that the multiply and add instructions each require two time units, and one time unit is required to transfer a single component of a vector between a memory unit and a processing unit. Figure 2b shows the instructions that must be executed if the instructions in Figure 2a are executed horizontally (i.e., row 0, then row 1, then row 2).

Figure 2c shows the other possibility where the instructions are executed vertically (i.e., column 0, then column 1, . . . , then column 99). Four time units are needed to execute each of the first 200 rows in Figure 2b and five time units are needed for each of the last 100 rows. In both cases only two processors can be used giving a total execution time of approximately 700 time units for the complete calculation of $X^2 + Y^2$ using two processors. If the instructions are organized as shown in Figure 2c, then the instructions in each row of that figure require nine time units, but three processors can be kept busy. This gives a total computation time of 300 time units using three processors. The improvement of more than a factor of two for the algorithm in Figure 2c, over the one in Figure 2b, is due to two factors:

1. 400 of the 700 data transfers in Figure 2b have been eliminated

$$P_0 \leftarrow X_0*X_0;\ P_1 \leftarrow X_1*X_1;\ \ldots\ P_{99} \leftarrow X_{99}*X_{99}$$
$$Q_0 \leftarrow Y_0*Y_0;\ Q_1 \leftarrow Y_1*Y_1;\ \ldots\ Q_{99} \leftarrow Y_{99}*Y_{99}$$
$$Z_0 \leftarrow P_0+Q_0;\ Z_1 \leftarrow P_1+Q_1;\ \ldots\ Z_{99} \leftarrow P_{99}+Q_{99}$$

(a) Arithmetic instructions involved in computing $X^2 + Y^2$

$$\text{fetch } X_0;\ P_0 \leftarrow X_0*X_0;\ \text{store } P_0;$$
$$\text{fetch } X_1;\ P_1 \leftarrow X_1*X_1;\ \text{store } P_1;$$
$$\ldots$$
$$\text{fetch } X_{99};\ P_{99} \leftarrow X_{99}*X_{99};\ \text{store } P_{99};$$
$$\text{fetch } Y_0;\ Q_0 \leftarrow Y_0*Y_0;\ \text{store } Q_0;$$
$$\text{fetch } Y_1;\ Q_1 \leftarrow Y_1*Y_1;\ \text{store } Q_1;$$
$$\ldots$$
$$\text{fetch } Y_{99};\ Q_{99} \leftarrow Y_{99}*Y_{99};\ \text{store } Q_{99};$$
$$\text{fetch } P_0;\ \text{fetch } Q_0;\ Z_0 \leftarrow P_0*Q_0;\ \text{store } Z_0;$$
$$\text{fetch } P_1;\ \text{fetch } Q_1;\ Z_1 \leftarrow P_1*Q_1;\ \text{store } Z_1;$$
$$\ldots$$
$$\text{fetch } P_{99};\ \text{fetch } Q_{99};\ Z_{99} \leftarrow P_{99}*Q_{99};\ \text{store } Z_{99};$$

(b) Horizontally organized computation

$$\text{fetch } X_0;\ \text{fetch } Y_0;\ P \leftarrow X_0*X_0;\ Q \leftarrow Y_0*Y_0;\ Z_0 \leftarrow P+Q;\ \text{store } Z_0$$
$$\text{fetch } X_1;\ \text{fetch } Y_1;\ P \leftarrow X_1*X_1;\ Q \leftarrow Y_1*Y_1;\ Z_1 \leftarrow P+Q;\ \text{store } Z_1$$
$$\ldots$$
$$\text{fetch } X_{99};\ \text{fetch } Y_{99};\ P \leftarrow X_{99}*X_{99};\ Q \leftarrow Y_{99}*Y_{99};\ Z_{99} \leftarrow P+Q;\ \text{store } Z_{99}$$

(c) Vertically organized computation

Figure 2—Computation of $X^2 + Y^2$

2. three processors can be effectively used (kept busy) executing the algorithm in Figure 2c, while only two can be used effectively for the algorithm in Figure 2b

As another example of this approach, consider the following FOR loop, which might be part of a larger program.

```
FOR I = 1 TO 100 DO
  T ← X[I] + Y[I];
  IF (X[I] > Y[I])
    THEN U ← X[I] − Y[I];
    ELSE U ← Y[I] − X[I];
  Z[I] ← T² + 4*U
END
```

If the body of this loop is considered as an operation performed on the vectors X and Y to produce the result vector Z, then the type of advantages illustrated by the previous example can also be realized for this example. In particular, the components of X and Y only need to be transferred from memory to a processing unit once, and only the result Z must be stored. Moreover, because several arithmetic operations are performed during each execution of the loop, the ratio of processing time to data transfer time should be large enough to enable the concurrent use of several processing units. If the processors were unable to execute programs involving branches and several arithmetic operations, these advantages would not be realized.

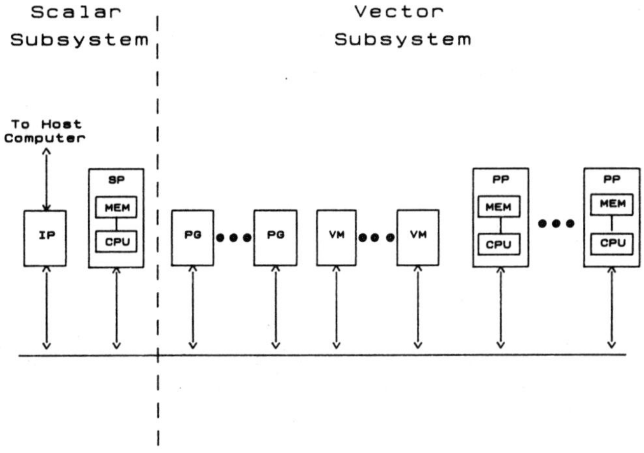

Figure 3—Array processor block diagram

OVERVIEW OF THE ARRAY PROCESSOR

The general organization of the array processor is shown by the block diagram in Figure 3. It is composed of two major subsystems, the *vector subsystem* consisting of the PG, VM, and PP modules, and the *scalar subsystem* consisting of the IP and SP modules. The system functions by passing packets of information between the modules along a high-speed bus. A general description of the operation of each of the five types of modules is given below.

The Interface Processor

This module provides an interface between the array processor and a host computer. Programs and data for the array processor are downloaded from the host processor, and results are uploaded through the interface processor module. Since the array processor is used as a back-end processor for a general-purpose computer, it has no I/O capability. All access to large-capacity storage devices (e.g., disk and tape drives) is provided by the host computer through the interface processor module. A consequence of this is that the array processor does not support virtual memory, and all data for a computation must be present in the array processor's memories during the computation.

The Scalar Processor

The scalar processor is a general-purpose processor in that it contains both a CPU and local memory, and it interprets programs by fetching and executing instructions from its local memory. It is the module that is in overall control of a computation performed in the array processor. Such a computation is specified by a main program containing instructions executed by the scalar processor as well as special vector instructions. These are instructions that initiate vector operations to be performed in the vector subsystem using vectors stored in the vector memory (VM) modules. The main program is executed by the scalar processor until a vector instruction is encountered. At that point, the vector subsystem is instructed to perform the vector operation and inform the scalar processor when it is finished. Thus the vector subsystem can be viewed as a powerful slave processor for the scalar processor that provides storage space for vectors and performs all vector operations.

The Packet Processor

The normal operation of the vector subsystem is for each packet processor to be performing the same operation, but on different components of the operand vectors. In the previous section, it was argued that if this is to be most effective, the processors should be capable of executing relatively complex operations. For these reasons, the packet processors are small and fast general-purpose computers with local memory. Prior to initiating a computation on the array processor, copies of programs defining all of the vector operations to be performed must be downloaded to all of the packet processors. Programs for frequently used operations could also be stored permanently in the packet processors using ROMs. A packet processor is idle until it receives a packet containing components of the operand vectors, an op-code specifying which operation is to be performed, and addresses in vector memory for the results. Then, the processor proceeds to execute the program for the specified operation. When that program terminates, the packet processor forms a new packet consisting of the results and their vector memory addresses and sends it to the vector memory modules. It then returns to the idle state and waits for another packet of operands.

The Vector Memories

These modules are used to hold all vector operands and results during a computation performed by the array processor. All vector operands must be downloaded from the host computer to these modules before the computation can be initiated. Similarly, all result vectors must be uploaded to the host computer when the computation is complete. When a vector operation is performed, the components of the vector operands are sequentially fetched from the memory modules and passed to the packet processors. When a component operation completes execution in a packet processor, the resulting components are passed back to the memory modules and stored in the result vectors. It was observed in section two that the highest performance is achieved when the bus is saturated. For that reason, multiple interleaved vector memory modules can be used to increase the memory bandwidth and match it to the bandwidth of the bus.

The Packet Generator

Once a vector operation is initiated by the scalar processor, it is under the control of one of the packet generator modules. These modules also control downloading and uploading of data between the vector memory modules and the host computer. Multiple packet generators are allowed so that several vector operations and data transfers can be active simultaneously. If this capability is not needed, only one packet generator module is required.

To explain the operation of the packet generators, consider the vector operation $Z \leftarrow X^2 + Y^2$. To initiate this operation a packet generator would be passed a command packet from the scalar processor that specified the number of operand and result vectors, their lengths, their starting locations in vector memory, and an op-code specifying the operation $X^2 + Y^2$. Recall that the program defining this operation would have been preloaded into the packet processors. The packet generator would then proceed to generate a sequence of packets for the packet processors. The i-th packet would contain the operands X_i and Y_i, the op-code, and the address of Z_i. Therefore, the packet generator must be capable of generating a sequence of addresses for each vector involved in the operation. To form the i-th packet, the packet generator first sends fetch requests to the vector memory modules for components X_i and Y_i. When these operands are available, it combines them with the op-code and the address of Z_i to form the packet. The packet generator also must monitor the bus to know when all of the generated packets have been executed and their results stored in vector memory. When this occurs, the packet generator notifies the scalar processor that the vector operation is complete.

Since the packet generator must be capable of generating the sequence of addresses for the components of a vector, it is the logical choice for controlling the transfer of data between the host computer and the vector memory modules. This process is similar to the generation of operand packets. To upload a vector the IP generates a sequence of packets where each one contains one component of the vector and sends these packets to the interface processor instead of the packet processors. To download a vector, a sequence of store addresses is generated and paired with vector components requested from the interface processor instead of the vector memory modules. These packets are then sent to the vector memories instead of the packet processors.

The array processor is used by the host to perform computations that contain a number of vector operations. The programs for these computations are compiled in the host computer and then downloaded to the array processor for execution. The identification and definition of the vector instructions are done by the compiler or the user before the programs are downloaded. The operation of the array processor as it performs one of these computations is summarized as follows:

Phase 1—Initialization

1. The main program defining the computation is downloaded from the host computer to the scalar processor.
2. Programs defining each of the vector instructions are broadcast from the host computer to the packet processors. Identical copies of each are loaded into every packet processor.
3. Data vectors needed during the computation are downloaded from the host computer to the vector memory modules under the control of a packet generator.

Phase 2—Execution

1. The scalar processor executes the main program. All instructions except vector instructions are executed sequentially in the scalar processor.
2. When a vector instruction is encountered by the scalar processor, it sends a command packet to one of the packet generators. This is a packet that contains all of the information needed by the packet generator to control the execution of the vector instruction.
3. Once it receives a command, a packet generator controls the execution of the vector instruction corresponding to that command by generating and sending packets to the packet processor modules. Each packet corresponds to the operation performed on one component of the operand vectors and contains an op-code for the operation, addresses for the results, and the vector components fetched by the packet generator from the vector memory modules.
4. When a packet is received at a packet processor, it executes the operation specified by the op-code and forms a packet containing the results and their vector memory addresses. This packet is then sent to the vector memory, and the packet processor enters an idle state waiting for another packet.
5. When all of the components of the operand vectors have been processed, the packet generator notifies the scalar processor of the completion of the vector instruction.

Phase 3—Termination

1. Once the main program terminates, the scalar processor initiates a transfer of result vectors to the host computer.
2. When all results are transferred to the host computer, the computation is complete and the array processor waits for the host to initiate another one.

We note two distinguishing features of the proposed architecture. First, the generation of addresses, the memory accesses, and the execution of operations are all decoupled and implemented by independent functional units. Second, the functional units are data driven. That is, there is no central control unit that synchronizes the different units. Instead, their operations are initiated by the arrival of packets from other units. Similar features can be found in several other architectures.[7–9] However, most of these systems have applied the concepts at a relatively low level (e.g., the machine instruction level), and many have used complex parallel interconnection networks. An important goal of our research is to explore the possibility of improving the effectiveness of a bus-organized system by applying these two concepts at a higher level.

An early version of the proposed architecture and the concept of interleaving both memory and processor modules was studied by S. Ahuja in his doctoral dissertation.[10] His technique of interleaving the processors was also reported in Reference 11. A method for using queues to match the performance of interleaved memory modules and interleaved processor modules can be found in Reference 12.

CONCLUSION

A prototype of the array processor described in this paper is currently under construction at Rice University. We expect to produce a system capable of sustaining from one- to five-megaflop performance over a wide range of vector operations. While this will provide a powerful tool for numerical computation, our main goal is to develop a testbed for research into the best way to organize computations for this type of architecture and to compare it with other types of array processors. To this end, the following three research projects have been identified.

Project 1—Data Skewing in Vector Memory

In order to sustain a high rate of data transfer to and from the vector memories, it will be necessary to use several interleaved modules. However, when vectors are fetched with a stride that is a multiple or divisor of the number of memory modules, the memory requests will not be equally distributed among the modules, negating the effect of interleaving. To alleviate this problem, different algorithms for skewing vectors across memory modules can be used. Both the vector memory modules and the packet generators are being designed to support the implementation of different skewing algorithms. The goal of this project is to use this ability to investigate the effects of different skewing algorithms on overall system performance.

Project 2—Numerical Algorithms

The purpose of this project is to develop new algorithms that take advantage of the unique properties of the array processor. The initial effort will concentrate on numerical algorithms that can be formulated naturally using vector instructions. Here, the goal is to find ways to partition and vectorize the algorithms to use the ability of the packet processors to execute complex operations.

Project 3—Compiler Design

This is a long-range project with the goal of producing a FORTRAN compiler for the array processor. This compiler will be capable of recognizing vector operations and producing programs that realize them on the packet processors. It is expected that with the ability of the packet processors to execute complex operations, the compiler will be able to vectorize complex data-dependent FOR loops.

ACKNOWLEDGMENT

This work was supported by National Science Foundation Grants MCS-8001661-01 and MCS-8121884.

REFERENCES

1. Kuck, D. J., and R. Stokes. "The Burroughs Scientific Processor (BSP)." *IEEE Transactions on Computers,* C-31 (1982), pp. 363–376.

2. Wulf, W. A., R. Levin, and S. P. Harbison. *HYDRA/C.mmp*. New York: McGraw-Hill, 1981.
3. Barnes, G. H., and S. F. Lundstrom. "Design and Validation of a Connection Network for Many-Processor Multiprocessor Systems." *Computer,* 14 (1981), pp. 31–41.
4. Batcher, K. E. "The Multidimensional Access Memory in STARAN." *IEEE Transactions on Computers,* C-26 (1977), pp. 174–177.
5. Patil, J. H. "Performance of Processor-Memory Interconnections for Multiprocessors," *IEEE Transactions on Computers,* C-30 (1981), pp. 771–780.
6. Dias, D. M., and J. R. Jump. "Packet Switching Interconnection Networks for Modular Systems." *Computer,* 14 (1981), pp. 43–53.
7. Cohler, E. U., and J. E. Storer. "Functionally Parallel Architecture for Array Processors," *Computer,* 14 (1981), pp. 28–36.
8. Smith, J. E. "Decoupled Access/Execute Computer Architectures." In *Proceedings of the 9th Annual Symposium on Computer Architecture.* New York: IEEE, April 1982, pp. 112–119.
9. Treleaven, P. C., D. R. Brownbridge, and R. P. Hopkins. "Data-Driven and Demand-Driven Computer Architecture," *ACM Computer Surveys,* 14 (1982), pp. 93–143.
10. Ahuja, S. R. "A Modular Multiprocessor Architecture for Array Processing." Ph.D. Dissertation, Electrical Engineering Department, Rice University, Houston, Tex., May 1977.
11. Ahuja, S. R., and J. R. Jump. "A Modular Vector Processing Unit." In *Proceedings of the 1976 International Conference on Parallel Processing.* New York: IEEE, August 1976.
12. Ahuja, S. R., and J. R. Jump. "A Modular Memory Scheme for Array Processing." In *Proceedings of the 4th Annual Symposium on Computer Architecture.* New York: IEEE, March 1977.

Compatible software and hardware implementations permitted by IEEE standards for binary floating-point arithmetic

by HARRY W. LOOK
Zilog Corporation
Campbell, California

ABSTRACT

Zilog's* System 8000, a UNIX*-based system using the Z8000 microprocessor family, incorporates the vision held by the authors of the IEEE 754 Standard for binary floating-point arithmetic. Floating-point implementation can be realized entirely in software with Zilog's Z8070 Software Emulator, or entirely in hardware with the FFP-8/01 processor board or the Z8070 chip. Each of these implementations is examined separately. Because the IEEE standard specifies numerical precision and exception handling, the user can choose either the software or the hardware implementation without any sacrifice in the accuracy of the results. And as the hardware availability increases and the cost decreases, floating-point operations can be easily transported from software to hardware for increased performance.

*UNIX is a trademark of Bell Laboratories; Zilog is licensed by AT&T.

Z8070 SOFTWARE EMULATION PACKAGE

The Software Emulator provides floating-point arithmetic capability for Zilog's 16-bit microprocessors, the Z8000 CPU family. The Emulator deals with a range of integers from -9×10^{18} to 9×10^{18} and with a range of real numbers from 3.4×10^{-4932} to 1.2×10^{4932}. Like the Z8070 chip, the Emulator can operate on single precision (32-bit), double precision (64-bit), or double extended (80-bit) data types. Integer formats supported are long (32 bits), quad (64 bits) and decimal (80 bits), which can include up to 19 binary-coded decimal digits and a sign bit. All computations and all values are automatically converted to the 80-bit double extended format when they are loaded into the Emulator.

The Z8000 trap structure permits floating-point operations to be performed with either the Software Emulator or a hardware device. Bit 13 of the Z8000's Flag and Control Word register (FCW) is set by the user to indicate the presence of the Extended Processor Unit (e.g., Z8070 chip). The EPU instruction set serves as an extension of the Z8000 instruction set and has a unique set of opcodes to distinguish it from Z8000 instructions. If an EPU instruction is encountered and Bit 13 of the FCW is reset to indicate that the EPU is not present, an extended instruction trap will occur, and the Emulator will be invoked. If the EPU hardware is present and Bit 13 is set, no trap is generated, and the hardware captures and processes the instruction.

The Emulator itself consists of a system dependent module and a system independent module. The system independent module, which contains the floating-point routines used for computations, is about 5,000 bytes of code and requires fewer than 30 words of stack space for operation. The system dependent module, which is used to call the independent module, is a small set of assembly language interface routines that can be tailored to the host system. Functionally, the Emulator, which is a software trap handler for floating-point instructions, is responsible for the following functions:

1. Decoding the floating-point Instruction that was not "recognized" by the Z8000 (Bit 13 of FCW reset)
2. Performing the floating-point computation with a format in conformance to the IEEE standard
3. Handling exceptions either by a trap to a service routine or by default (the user selects the approach by setting a bit)
4. Saving the required status information prior to the trap and restoring the information (the computational engine is the Z8000 rather than the Z8070 EPU chip)

Most floating-point operations with the Emulator finish in about 1 ms, using a 6 Mhz Z8000, which includes the trapping and operating system overhead.

ZILOG'S FPP-8/01 FLOATING-POINT PROCESSOR BOARD

Zilog's FPP-8/01 is a two-board hardware implementation of the full IEEE standard. Like the Software Emulator, it performs all internal operations in double extended format. Designed for the 32-bit Z-Bus Backplane Interconnect (ZBI bus) used in Zilog's System 8000, it greatly increases the speed of floating-point operations. Typically performing 125K floating-point Operations per second (KFLOP), performance is over 100 × that of the Software Emulator. The performance figures were obtained by finding the dot product of two 1,000-element vectors. The FPP-8/01 board set contains 400 equivalent integrated circuits, which includes 4K-by-4-bit static RAMS, 16-bit-by-16-bit multipliers, and 4-bit microprocessor slices.

Functionally, the FPP-8/01 (Figure 1) consists of five units:

1. The ZBI interface
2. A microcode sequencer and control store
3. A sign engine
4. An exponent engine
5. A fraction engine

The ZBI interface serves as the communication path between the FPP-8/01 and the rest of the System 8000. Floating-point microcode is loaded into the control store through the ZBI bus when power is applied to the system.

Once loaded, the FPP-8/01 monitors the ZBI bus for floating-point instructions. When the CPU encounters an FPP-8/01 instruction, it performs the address calculation and provides the address and data timing signals for data transfer. The microcode control sequencer then captures the instruction and data and begins processing. Unlike the Software Emulator, which uses the CPU trap structure, the FPP-8/01 operates as a coprocessor, and no CPU trap is generated. While the FPP-8/01 is performing number crunching, the CPU continues its normal functions. But if the CPU detects a second FPP-8/01 instruction while the first is being executed, the CPU stops until the first floating-point instruction finishes. When finished, the CPU completes the instruction fetch, and operation resumes. The sign, exponent, and fraction engines perform the actual floating-point operations with sixteen 4-bit slices. The fraction engine also uses 16 × 16 multipliers.

The FPP-8/01 is a hardware emulation of the Z8070 chip. There are a few minor exceptions, which, of course, have no effect on the precision of the calculations or the handling of exceptions. With the FPP-8/01, the CPU stops if sequential floating-point instructions are encountered. Processing of the first floating-point instruction must be complete before the instruction fetch of the second instruction is completed. The

Z8070, on the other hand, has a one-deep queue. The CPU may not need to stop at all for sequential floating-point instructions. The CPU stops only if the subsequent floating-point instruction is one of the following:

1. A Load or Store operation where a value from the first operation is needed by the second instruction.
2. A Load or Store operation where conversion of data types is involved.
3. Waiting because the instruction queue is full.

In addition, the User and Flags registers, which are present in both the FPP-8/01 and Z8070, cannot be bit-set. The FPP-8/01, unlike the Z8070, required that the entire register be reloaded to change bit information.

Z8070 EXTENDED PROCESSING UNIT

With the Z8070 Floating-Point Processor, floating-point operations can be performed significantly faster (100 × to 500 ×) than if done through software emulation. Applications like graphics, engineering workstations, C and PASCAL programs declaring floating-point variables, and FORTRAN programs can benefit from the addition of a floating-point coprocessor to a system. Because of the Z8000's trap structure, software does not need to be rewritten if the Z8070 is added. One simply sets Bit 13 of the FCW register to indicate that the Z8070 is present, and the Z8070 processes the floating-point instructions; this is in contrast to trapping to floating-point subroutines for Z8000 processing if the Z8070 is not present.

Execution times for the Z8070 chip are listed below in clock cycles.

	32-bit (Single)	64-bit (Double)	80-bit (Double Extended)
Addition/subtraction	18	18	18
Multiplication	28	42	48
Division	29	43	49

(Execution time in microseconds is obtained by dividing clock cycles by the clock speed in Mhz. For example, a 32-bit Multiply will take 2.8 microseconds using the standard 10-Mhz Z8070.) This performance level is 1.7 × to 7 × that of other announced floating-point chips at their standard clock rate.

Z8070 Architecture

The Z8070 is functionally organized as two processors: an Interface processor and a Data processor. These two processors, which are integrated onto the same chip, have separate clocks (Figure 2). This allows a slower speed microprocessor to operate with a faster Z8070 (or vice versa) by matching the interface processor clock to that of the system microprocessor and still operate the data processor at a faster clock speed. The interface and data processor operate independently. The interface processor fetches and aligns floating-point instructions and data, manages the internal queue, and executes certain control and data instructions. The internal queue can store one instruction with associated data while another separated instruction is being executed. The data processor contains eight 80-bit data registers and performs the actual floating-point processing. Like the Software Emulator and the FPP-8/01, all computations done internally are in the double extended format. All floating-point operations fully comply

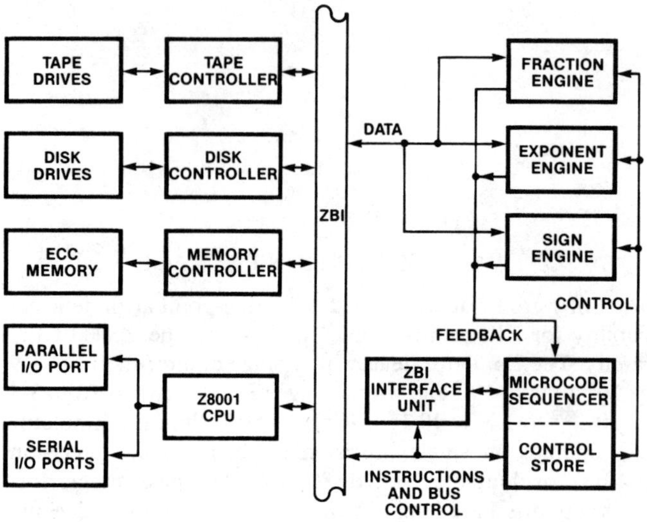

Figure 1—The FPP-8/01 Floating-Point Processor

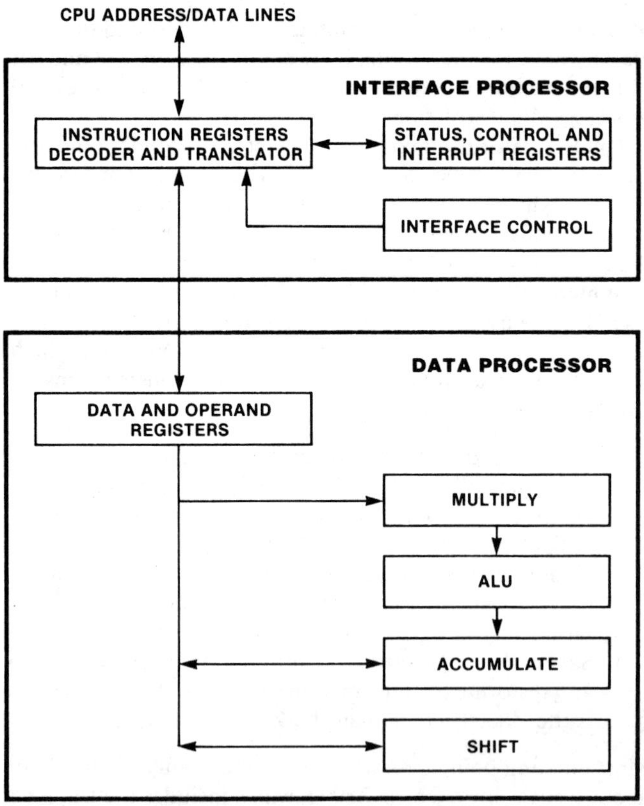

Figure 2—Z8070 Block Diagram

with the IEEE standard, including exception handling, manipulation of denormal numbers, infinities, and NaNs.

Z8070 Interface

Unlike the FPP-8/01, which monitors the ZBI bus, the Z8070 monitors the CPU bus for floating-point instructions. The Z8070 supports interfaces to the Z800™ 16-bit CPU, which is code-compatible with the Z80® CPU, the Z8000 CPU, the Z80,000™ 32-bit CPU with on-chip cache and MMU, and a Universal Interface. The interface is selected by configuring two pins as high or low in the 68-pin Leadless Chip Carrier package. Interface selection using this approach provides a universal device without the problem of balancing the production and inventory mix. With the Universal Interface, the Chip Select line, rather than the microprocessor's bus signals, is monitored. An active signal on this line indicates that the instruction on the bus is meant for the Floating-Point Processor. The Z8070 then reads data from the bus during each processor cycle until it collects the full instruction and data. Data bus widths of 8, 16, and 32 bits are supported with the Universal Interface.

With the Z8070's Coprocessor Interface, the CPU always remains a bus master. This eliminates the overhead that results if the Bus request/Bus acknowledge approach is used. For a transfer of data between the Z8070's internal registers and main memory, the CPU calculates the memory address, places it on the address/data bus, and generates the appropriate timing signals. The data are then placed on the address/data bus by the Z8070 and written into memory. This bus efficiency contrasts with alternative approaches, which require a transfer of data from the Floating-Point Processor to the CPU and then to memory.

IEEE 754 STANDARD FOR BINARY FLOATING-POINT ARITHMETIC

The IEEE standard assists in accuracy of results, independent of the particular hardware or software implementation. The Z8070 Software Emulator, the FPP-8/01, and the Z8070 fully comply with the standard. The standard specifies the following:

1. The minimum number of bits to represent exponents and mantissas in the single, double, and double-extended formats
2. The set of floating-point operations that must be supported (Add, Subtract, Multiply, Divide, Square Root, Remainder, Rounding integer to floating-point, Data Type Conversion, and Compare)
3. Bit representations for plus and minus infinity, zero, denormalized numbers, and NaNs
4. Acceptable rounding methods
5. Default handling of exceptions caused by overflow, underflow, division by zero, square root of negative number, and operation on an NaN

SUMMARY

For floating-point intensive applications where computational speed is critical, hardware solutions such as the Z8070 and FPP-8/01 are more suitable than software solutions. For other applications which may require occasional floating-point computations, a Software Emulator is more cost effective. Whatever method is used, a microprocessor like the Z8000 provides a convenient trap structure that supports both software and hardware solutions without software redesign. And, because of compliance with the IEEE standard, accuracy of results is ensured.

Goals and tradeoffs in the design of the MC68881 floating point coprocessor

by JOEL BONEY
Motorola Inc.
Austin, Texas

ABSTRACT

This paper describes the goals and tradeoffs in the design of the MC68881 Floating Point Coprocessor. The Motorola MC68881 is a complete implementation of the proposed IEEE floating point standard on a single VLSI chip. It is a coprocessor for the MC68020 microprocessor and is a peripheral processor for other M68000 family processors.

The design of the MC68881 was guided by a set of goals. This paper discusses the major goals of the MC68881 project and their impact on the design. During the definition of the architecture of the MC68881 many engineering tradeoffs were made by the design team. This paper also documents how some of these tradeoffs affected our decisions. Lastly, the paper gives enough of an overview of the MC68881 to make the discussions of the goals and tradeoffs meaningful.

INTRODUCTION

No design project should be undertaken without a good set of clear goals that are the guiding information allowing the designers to make the necessary tradeoffs during the design process. This paper documents the design goals and some of the architectural tradeoffs of the MC68881 design project. This VLSI design project will take about 4 years from the first preliminary specification to first silicon (which is expected about the time this paper is published).

The Motorola MC68881 is a complete implementation of the proposed IEEE floating point standard on a single VLSI chip.[1] It is a coprocessor for the MC68020 microprocessor and is a peripheral processor for other M68000 family processors. Since it will be necessary to have some knowledge of the MC68881 in order to understand the goals and tradeoffs, this paper also includes an overview of the MC68881. More specific detail about the MC68881 can be obtained from other papers and articles published by the design team.[2,3,4]

AN OVERVIEW OF THE MC68881

The MC68881 is a high performance floating point unit designed to interface with the 32-bit MC68020 as a coprocessor. It can also be used as a peripheral processor with some performance degradation, in systems where the MC68020 is not the main processor (e.g. MC68000, MC68008, MC68010). The configuration of the MC68881 as a coprocessor or a peripheral processor can be completely transparent to user software.

The MC68881 utilizes the general purpose M68000 family coprocessor interface to provide a logical extension of the CPU's instruction set and register set such that it is transparent to the programmer. The programmer is *never* aware that the coprocessor and main processor are implemented on two separate chips.

Internally the MC68881 is divided into two processing elements, the Bus Interface Processor (BIP) which handles the coprocessor interface and the Arithmetic Processor (AP). All interaction with the main processor is handled by the BIP while the AP executes all MC68881 instructions.[4]

Bus Interface Processor

All interprocessor transfers are initiated by the MC68020. During the processing of an MC68881 instruction, the MC68020 transfers instruction information and data to the coprocessor via standard M68000 write bus cycles using a unique CPU function code and receives data, requests for service, and status information from the coprocessor via standard M68000 read bus cycles.

The MC68881 contains a number of coprocessor interface registers which are addressed like memory by the MC68020's micro-machine. These registers are not part of the programmer visible register set.

Reserved opcodes in the M68000 instruction map that formerly trapped out to an exception routine (Line 1111 Emulator Trap) are now defined as coprocessor instructions. Only the MC68020 tracks the instruction stream. When it detects a coprocessor instruction, it writes the next word in the instruction stream to the coprocessor and reads the coprocessor's response. The BIP encodes in the response any additional action required of the main processor on behalf of the coprocessor. A typical request for service is "evaluate the effective address and transfer N bytes of data to the coprocessor interface operand register."

The coprocessor interface permits the MC68881 to execute most floating point instructions concurrent with the MC68020's execution of non-floating point instructions.

The MC68881 is designed to operate over 8-, 16-, or 32-bit data buses. The part is packaged in a 64-pin DIP or 68-pin Pin-Grid-Array package.

The coprocessor interface is fully compatible with the MC68020's on-chip instruction cache and virtual memory architecture. The interface insures that *all* coprocessor execution time exceptions, including instruction single-step, are handled identically to main processor execution time exceptions. Both the MC68020 and the MC68881 are designed for 16.67-Mhz operation. Since the interface is based solely on standard M68000 *asynchronous* bus cycles, the MC68881 need not run at the same clock speed as the main processor.

Arithmetic Processor

Once the BIP has decoded an instruction and requested any operands it needs, the microcode in the Arithmetic Processor is started to acquire the operands and to perform the requested operation. The AP is implemented as a pseudo two-level micro-machine much like the MC68000.[7]

Architecture Overview

The architecture of the MC68881 appears to the user as a logical extension of the M68000 family architecture. It is a register oriented, one-and-a-half-address processor similar to the MC68000 and its derivatives.[6]

Programmer's model

The MC68881 adds the following registers to the programmer's model of the M68000 family:

1. Eight 80-bit floating point data registers analogous to the M68000 integer data registers.
2. A 32-bit control register contains enable bits for each class of exception trap, and mode bits to select rounding mode and rounding precision.
3. A 32-bit status register contains the floating point condition codes, quotient bits set by remainder and modulo, and exception status information.
4. A 32-bit instruction address register contains the address in memory of the last floating point instruction. This address is used in exception trap handling.

Data formats

The MC68881 supports the following data formats:

1. Byte, word, and long word integers,
2. Single, double, and extended precision binary real,
3. Decimal real string (packed BCD).

The three integer data formats are identical to those supported by M68000 family processors. The floating point data formats, single precision (32-bits), and double precision (64-bits) are as defined by the IEEE standard.[2]

The extended precision data format is also in conformance with the IEEE standard, but the standard does not specify this format to the bit level as it does for single and double. The format on the MC68881 consists of 96 bits, 3 long words, with an explicit most significant mantissa bit. Only 80 bits are actually used, the other 16 bits are left for future expandability.

The decimal real string format consists of a signed 3-digit base 10 exponent and a signed 17-digit base 10 mantissa. All digits are packed BCD so that a whole string fits in 96 bits.

Integer, single precision, double precision, and decimal real string format operands are always converted to an extended precision floating point number prior to participating in an MC68881 operation. The floating point data registers always contain extended precision values, and all internal computations are performed to extended precision.

Instruction set

The instruction set of the MC68881 can be subdivided as follows:

1. Moves; register to register, external operand to register, and register to external operand forms are provided. The external operand may be any of the 7 data formats supported, and may be specified by any MC68020 addressing mode.
2. Arithmetic and Transcendental Operations; register to register and external operand to register forms are provided. The external operand may be any of the 7 data formats supported, and may be specified by any MC68020 addressing mode. The result is always placed in the specified floating point data register.
3. Miscellaneous; move multiples (in and out) branches, set on condition, trap on condition, save context, restore context, etc.

The arithmetic and transcendental operations are listed in Figure 1. Dyadic operations (those requiring two operands) are listed first followed by the monadic operations.

Add	IEEE Remainder
Compare	Scale Exponent
Divide	Single Precision Divide
Modulo	Single Precision Multiply
Multiply	Subtract
Absolute Value	Log Base 2
Arc Cosine	Log Base e
Arc Sine	Log Base e of x + 1
Arc Tangent	Negate
Hyperbolic Arc Tangent	Sine
Cosine	Sine and Cosine
Hyperbolic Cosine	Hyperbolic Sine
e to the x Power	Square Root
e to the x Power − 1	Tangent
Get Exponent	Hyperbolic Tangent
Get Mantissa	10 to the x Power
Integer Part	Test
Log Base 10	2 to the x Power

Figure 1—Supported operations

All operations required by the IEEE standard are provided on the MC68881 plus many more. All instructions support all IEEE defined special values (normalized, zeroes, infinities, denormalized numbers, and 'not-a-numbers'), and return the IEEE specified results with accuracy as specified in the standard.

Following the precedent set by the orthogonal instruction set in the M68000 family of processors, MC68881 instructions are provided for move, arithmetic, and transcendental operations using any data format and any addressing mode. The domain of an operand in a given data format is unrestricted for all operations. *No* operations require software envelopes to conform to the standard. Similarly, for the transcendentals, all argument reduction is performed *on-chip*.

The MC68881's conditional instructions utilize 32 floating point conditional predicates encoded in five bits. The four possible relations between two floating point numbers, greater than, equal, less than, or unordered, are encoded into four bits. The fifth bit, as required by the proposed standard, indicates whether an exception should be raised if the predicate evaluation yields an unordered relationship.

GOALS AND TRADEOFFS

Goals

There were five major goals for the MC68881 project given in the following priority:

1. The MC68881 should have the same style of architecture as the other members of the M68000 family
2. Performance
3. Functionality and user friendliness
4. Reduce design time and long term design costs
5. Producibility

M68000 Family Style of Architecture

Since we felt that the functionality of the MC68881 would eventually be moved onto the same die as the main CPU, an important goal was to insure that the architecture of the MC68881 fit in with the rest of the family. The MC68881 should expand the instruction set of the main CPU in an orthogonal manner that was transparent to the programmer (i.e., the user should not be aware that the MC68020/MC68881 consisted of two devices).

The coprocessor interface scheme is crucial to achieving this goal. The philosophy was to split the work done by the coprocessor interface between the main CPU and the coprocessor such that each element does what it can do best. For example, the MC68020 decodes the original instruction and determines that it is a coprocessor instruction. It then informs the coprocessor by writing a coprocessor defined operation word to the coprocessor. The coprocessor decodes this word and requests that the main CPU do the effective address calculation and transfer operands of 'n' bytes to the coprocessor. Or if a floating point exception occurred, the coprocessor might ask the main CPU to commence exception processing. Thus it can be seen that the MC68020 does what it already knows how to do: decide basic instructions, calculate effective addresses, and take exceptions. The coprocessor knows about its defined operation and knows what kind and size of data it wants from the main CPU or if an exception occurred.

A tradeoff was made in the coprocessor interface scheme to use standard asynchronous M68000 bus cycles for communication between the main CPU and the coprocessor. There was a minor speed penalty for this method when the MC68881 was used as a coprocessor for the MC68020, but it allowed the MC68881 to be used by all other M68000 family members as a peripheral.

This decision, along with the decision to *not* make the MC68881 a bus master (i.e., the MC68881 does not fetch its own operands; they are fetched by the main CPU and passed to the MC68881) greatly simplifies the system hardware interface to the MC68881 and allows flexibility.

Another tradeoff/decision made by the MC68881 design team was the selection of a register based one-and-a-half address architecture. In this type of architecture one of the operands typically comes from memory while the other operand comes from a register with the result going to the register or memory. This architecture is consistent with the architecture of the other M68000 family members. Further, since the M68000 processors have 8 integer data registers, the decision was made to have 8 additional floating point data registers. Studies have indicated that 8 registers are optimal for expression evaluation, etc.; and by having the same number of integer and floating point data registers compiler writers should be able to use the same register allocation algorithms for integers and floating point.

Orthogonality across the instruction set and addressing modes is a feature of the M68000 family that was preserved by the MC68881. All the addressing modes of the MC68020 are available for accessing floating point operands. Further, the safety features supported by the M68000 processor such as illegal instruction and illegal addressing mode traps are also supported by the MC68020/MC68881 pair.

Performance

Within the constraints of M68000 family architectural consistency, performance was the next most important design goal for the MC68881. Both the MC68020 and the MC68881 were designed for a clock speed of 16.67 Mhz. Even though the HCMOS process results in a slightly larger die, it was selected for both projects because of speed and low power consumption.

Performance of the basic functions, add, subtract, multiply, and divide, was emphasized. Special hardware was added to the execution unit to speed up these basic operations. Table I gives the execution times for the register to register forms of these operations on a MC68020/MC68881 pair. These times do not reflect the potential throughput increase from concurrency.

The single multiply and single divide operations assume that their operands are single precision, and produce a single precision result (while maintaining the range of extended). These operations are provided for special applications where multiply and divide performance is more important than loss of significance.

Even though we wanted the operations to be very fast on the average, one tradeoff we made was to insure that the worst case execution times would not be significantly different from the best case times. In some applications the only important item would be the average execution time, but in real-time applications the whole system usually has to be designed using the worst case time. Floating point units that depend on slow *software envelopes* to handle special cases will be very hard to use in real-time applications.

All calculations in the MC68881 are done internally to full IEEE extended precision. Even though we might have achieved marginally faster single and/or double precision times by including special hardware for single and double precision, we decided to concentrate our efforts in making extended precision very fast. This gives us very competitive times for all operand size not just single or double.

The last major performance-related tradeoff was the deci-

TABLE I—Execution times

Operation (reg-reg)	Clock Cycles	Time (μsec) @ 16.67 Mhz
Add	40	2.4
Subtract	40	2.4
Multiply	60	3.6
Divide	92	5.5
Single Mul	46	2.8
Single Div	58	3.5

sion to support concurrent operation. Concurrency means that once an instruction is started in the MC68881 the MC68020 is free to continue executing other non-MC68881 instructions. Thus the two processors overlap their execution, which increases the overall throughput of the pair. The support of concurrency did cost some silicon area and added some complexity, but we felt that the potential benefits outweighed the silicon costs.

Functionality and User Friendliness

Probably the biggest tradeoff we made toward functionality and user friendliness was the decision to support the proposed IEEE standard in its entirety in silicon.[1] As participants in the standardization process we felt the accuracy and safety provided by the standard greatly outweighed the minor impact it had on die size and hence, cost. Many people seem needlessly frightened by the complexity of the standard. If all the defaults of the standard are selected, the user is hardly aware of it except that he gets better results and has fewer problems with his algorithms blowing up than with conventional floating point implementations.[5] Most of the special modes are included for the expert numerical analysts and can be ignored by the average user.

Conformance to the standard involves much more than just conformance to the specified data formats. The standard specifies what operations must be supplied in a conforming implementation, and what accuracy is required for the operations. Further, it defines exceptions, specifies their detection, and specifies the results of exceptional operations in both trapping and non-trapping environments. The standard specifies *special* data types within each format (signed zeroes and infinities, not-a-numbers, denormalized numbers) and specifies the results of operations involving these special data types. It also specifies user selectable modes for rounding mode and precision. Any floating point hardware element that does not support all these requirements does *not* conform to the IEEE standard.

In addition to the functions required by the standard we decided to support many additional functions including a complete set of transcendental functions. As with the IEEE required functions, no software envelope is required to make the functions work correctly. The transcendentals even do the argument reduction on chip.

A slightly more efficient use of silicon would have been made if we had just implemented a set of primitive transcendentals on the chip. All the functions we support can be derived from a subset of primitives. There are perhaps a few hundred people in the world who know how to derive these correctly. It took us several years to figure it out. We didn't want our customers to have to go through what we did to become numerical experts in order to use our part, nor did we want to ship a large, slow software envelope with every part. The silicon impact was minimal, so we just put everything on the chip.

Another major tradeoff we made was whether to support all of the data types supported by the M68000 family in addition to the floating point data types and conversions required by the standard. We decided to support all data types including a decimal real string type. This feature along with the fact that all internal operations are done to full extended precision makes the MC68881 very easy to use and very accurate. The old FORTRAN problem of mixed modes goes away when an MC68881 is used since all sizes and types of data can take part in a floating point calculation with maximum accuracy.

As mentioned previously, we decided to support concurrency for performance reasons; however, we made a lot of minor design tradeoffs to insure that the concurrency is completely transparent to the programmer.

Reduce Design Time and Long Term Design Cost

As VLSI chips have gotten bigger, the time it takes to do the architectural design, the circuit design, and the layout has increased dramatically. We therefore made many tradeoffs in the design to reduce the design complexity. The MC68881 is implemented as a pseudo two-level microcode machine. It has a very wide control word with very little residual control.[7] Several PLAs are used for microcode address generation and for the coprocessor responses.[4]

Nearly all the cost of implementing the IEEE standard is contained in several PLAs and a small amount of microcode. There is almost no random logic used to implement the IEEE standard or for that matter any of the other functionality improvements of the MC68881. The only time we used random logic was in the performance paths in the execution unit for the basic four functions and in parts of the BIP. The MC68881 is the most regular non-memory VLSI microprocessor device we have ever produced.

As for long term design cost, we felt that no manufacturer could afford to make a whole family of floating point coprocessors—the market just isn't big enough to justify the cost. Because we felt this way, we were more likely to include extra functionality on the MC68881 so that we don't have to do an enhanced version later. Further, the general purpose coprocessor interface insures us that we won't have to do a new version of the MC68881 for each existing M68000 family member nor will we have to do a new version for any new family members. Therefore, we may have put more design effort and cost into the original MC68881 design, but we feel we greatly reduced the long term design cost to Motorola.

Producibility

The best paper design in the world is useless unless it can be produced cheaply in volume. Although at times we did tradeoff die size for regularity and functionality, the final die size is producible in the HCMOS process. And if processing improvements continue at the pace they have in the past, in a few years the MC68881 will seem like a tiny die.

In fact, testing and package costs will dominate the device cost over time. To this end we will package the MC68881 in a 64-pin DIP or 68-pin Pin-Grid-Array package. Both of these packages will be high volume packages. For testing, the MC68881 has extensive on-chip test logic to reduce test costs that I am not free to discuss in this paper.

SUMMARY

This paper has attempted to provide a glimpse into the thought processes of the designers of the MC68881. The project had more goals than the 5 mentioned and there were an endless number of tradeoffs made daily with only the major ones mentioned here. Of course, dozens of people participate in the design of any VLSI device from the initial marketers who gave us customer input to the final layout draftsmen who put it on silicon. Rarely were any of the decisions mentioned in this paper made by one or two people, but rather by groups.

REFERENCES

1. IEEE Computer Society Microprocessor Standards Committee Task P754. "A Proposed Standard for Binary, Floating Point Arithmetic, Draft 10.0." January 1983. A copy may be obtained now from Richard Karpinski, UCSF U-76, San Francisco, Calif. 94143, and ultimately from IEEE, 345 East 47th St., New York, NY. Draft 10.0 is a substantial revision of Draft 8.0 published in *Computer,* March, 1981.
2. Boney, J., P. Harvey, and V. Shahan. "Floating Point Power for the M68000 Family." *Proceedings of 1983 Mini/Micro West,* November 1983, Session 16, paper #5.
3. Cawthron, D. and C. Huntsman. "The MC68881: Motorola's Floating-Point Solution." *IEEE Micro,* December 1983.
4. Shahan, V. "The MC68881: The IEEE Floating Point Standard Reduced to One VLSI Chip." *Proceedings of COMPCON, Spring 84.*
5. Kahan, W. "The Proposed IEEE Standard p754 for Floating Point Arithmetic: What Good Is It?" *Proceedings of 1983 Mini/Micro West,* November 1983, Session 16, paper #1.
6. Zolnowsky, J. and N. Tredennick. "Design and Implementation of System Features for the MC68000." *Proceedings of COMPCON, Fall 79,* September 1979,
pp. 2–9.
7. Stritter, E. and N. Tredennick. "Microprogrammed Implementation of a Single-Chip Microprocessor." *Proceedings of the 11th Annual Workshop on Microprogramming* (Micro-11), November 1978, pp. 8–16.

An extended-precision operand computer for integer factoring

by
JEFFREY W. SMITH
University of Georgia
Athens, Georgia
and
SAMUEL S. WAGSTAFF, JR
Purdue University
West Lafayette, Indiana

ABSTRACT

We describe an extended-precision operand computer (EPOC). The single-precision word length is 128 bits. This makes possible calculations with large integers without resort to multiprecision techniques in software. Since this is a special-purpose machine, the hardware and software have been developed from scratch to implement it. The application toward which the EPOC is directed is the factoring of large integers using the continued fraction algorithm. This application presents interesting mathematical and architectural problems to solve and has implications in cryptography.

INTRODUCTION

We have built a special-purpose computer with properties that facilitate the calculations for a class of mathematical problems. These are problems in number theory, specifically the factoring of large (50- to 80-digit) integer numbers. We present some features of this computer, an Extended-Precision Operand Computer (EPOC), which differs from conventional architectures in several ways.

The most prominent feature of the computer is the extended precision of the operands. In most computer architectures, large numbers must be handled by multiprecision software routines. This is time-consuming (8+5n operations per multiprecise operation in one package on the S/370, where n is the degree of extra precision). Quadruple precision addition, for instance, requires 28 operations rather than one. To make calculations with large numbers faster, EPOC provides 128-bit operands in memory and registers that the programmer can fetch, store, and manipulate with single operations. This degree of precision accommodates up to 38-digit decimal numbers. The operand length of the EPOC is extendible within the architecture by linking additional hardware and adjusting the timing.

One measure of a computer system is its speed. In compute-bound applications, the speed of the processor directly limits performance. Traditional architectures expend processor time in the instruction fetch portion of the instruction cycle. This expenditure is avoided if the instructions are fetched in parallel with their execution as pipelined processors do. In microcoded processors, the next microinstruction is fetched while the present microoperation is executed. Microcoded procedures run up to ten times faster than those coded in software. EPOC is microcoded in a user-defined language, making use of a family of system programs developed specifically for this project.

The factoring problem to which EPOC is directed must operate on candidate numbers by calculating their residues modulo a set of prime numbers. EPOC includes an array of remainder elements which will figure the residues of a candidate by all members of a set of primes at once. This has some aspects of parallel processing, some aspects of vector or array processing. The dividers are a set of separate (but not autonomous) arithmetic elements which are hard-wired to perform the specific remainder operation required.

Many of the problems to which EPOC will be applied have long running times (on the order of months). To assure correct operation, we have built sanity checks into the operational software, can run diagnostics quickly between program segments, and have segmented the algorithm so that it can be checkpointed periodically. Checkpoint and restart procedures are necessary when problems must run for an extended period of time in an exposed environment.

EPOC HARDWARE

EPOC is a prototype. It has been constructed with simplicity and ease of maintenance in mind. A multibus backplane holds multibus prototype cards on which sockets and integrated circuits are mounted. The circuit interconnection technique is wirewrap, chosen for its simplicity, flexibility, and reliability. The circuits used in EPOC are from the Schottky TTL and Advanced Schottky TTL families.[1,2] These technologies are fast at the circuit level, rugged, and straightforward as a design medium. EPOC consists of 18 cards, but only 4 card types. There are 12 dividers, 4 ALUs, and one each sequencer and IOTE. (See Figure 1).

Input/Output Terminal Emulator (IOTE)

The IOTE is an input/output terminal emulator. This device is the channel between EPOC and the external world (host computer and operator). EPOC's channel need not have a high data rate, since the EPOC application is processor-

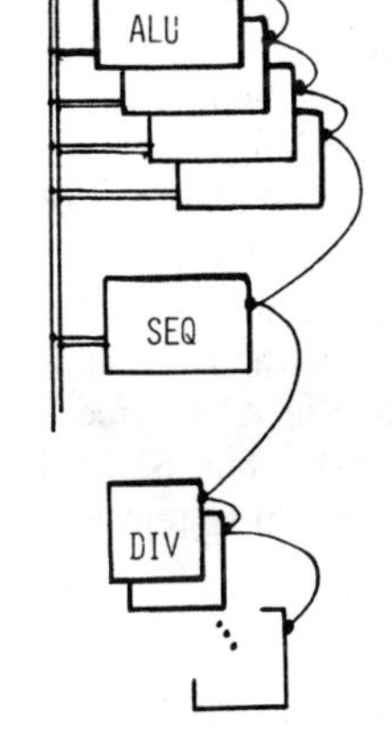

Figure 1—EPOC hardware connections

bound. This fact has been exploited in the EPOC system by providing all input/output via terminal emulation. This means that when EPOC wishes to communicate with the host system, it appears to the host to be a user typing on a terminal keyboard. When the host system is sending, EPOC must be able to 'read' the data off the emulated terminal screen. Doing input/output via terminal emulation has the benefits of simplicity and inherent portability, since any system to which a terminal can be attached could serve as host to EPOC in operation.

The IOTE is a microcomputer subsystem that provides synchronous control of EPOC in addition to buffering and I/O functions. The hardware is based on a Z80A processor and has minimum circuitry to support the required activities, most functional capability and operational logic resident in the program. The IOTE handles communications connections to the host and operator's console on one side. It buffers and decodes or encodes messages, and inserts or removes protocol information. On the other side, the IOTE has access to the EPOC control register, can respond to EPOC service requests, and can request the processor to stop. When EPOC is stopped, the IOTE acts as a DMA channel to/from the EPOC data store. One of the purposes to which this capability is put is the loading of the microcode store on the sequencer and the initialization of the data store on the ALU. Another is the unloading of results from EPOC to the host computer. In this case, the transfer is requested from the EPOC side of the interface. To report these results, the IOTE will sign on to the host computer system, transfer the required data, then sign off.

Sequencer

The microprogram of the EPOC processor resides on the sequencer (SEQ), which assures that operations are performed in the correct order. The function of SEQ is to produce the address of the next microinstruction, given the present instruction and the status of the machine. The EPOC sequencer is based upon the AMD2910 microprogram sequencer[1]. This device has the ability to handle up to 12-bit addresses (implying a 4K microinstruction space), a 5-deep call/return stack, a counter, and 16 instructions (most of them conditional). Conditions are fed into the sequencer from around the EPOC dataflow by the P2 bus on the backplane, and selected by fields in the microword. SEQ configures the ALU slices, holds the microprogram store (4K × 64bits), and controls the operation of the divider bank. The microinstruction store is loaded over the EPOC backplane bus by the IOTE. SEQ controls and monitors ALU operation by means of the conditions bus on the backplane, and a command bus which is broadcast to the ALU slices and other parts of the processor on the top cable bus. SEQ also controls the divider bus, and provides the main system 8MHz clock to the rest of the hardware.

Arithmetic and Logic Unit (ALU)

Central to the calculations done by EPOC is the 128-bit arithmetic and logical unit (ALU). The AMD2903A register and arithmetic and logic unit (RALU) 4-bit slice[1] is the central component in the ALU. 25 operations can be performed among the accessible operands, with sources and destinations selectable. The ALU gives the progammer 16 gpr's and a Q register, each 128 bits in length. The ALU board also contains a 128-bit 65MHz shift register which is used to provide a general shifting capability and to communicate with the dividers. The ALU board contains the operand store, a 4k × 128bit static RAM with 100nsec access (MOSTEK 4804).

Packaging an ALU of this size is challenging, especially when performance contraints are considered. EPOC is built on multibus prototype boards; the 128 bit ALU is made up of 4 such boards, each with 32 bits of ALU, GPRs, store, and shifter. The partitioned ALU communicates with more significant and less significant neighbors via top-card cables in such a way that the hardware of each slice is identical to the others and no positional dependency is built in. The ALU has carry look-ahead so that the cycle time will be limited as little as possible by the length of the operands.

Divider

The factoring algorithm to be used on EPOC relies on the identification of possible factor components as survivors of a trial division process. 128-bit candidate numbers are divided by small primes from a factor base. All the numbers are positive and the quotients are not of interest, only the remainders. This means that trial dividers can be made from a simple 16-bit ALU and shift register. Division then consists of shifting and conditional substraction. An EPOC with 10 dividers attached will perform 6–8 times better at the factoring algorithm than EPOC without the dividers. Since the dividers are simple and inexpensive, they are a cost-effective way to accelerate this algorithm. The dividers are clocked at 16MHz, so they process one bit of the input value every 62.5 nsec. A remainder will be produced after 8 usec. With 10 dividers in operation, allowing for overhead in startup and termination of the operation, the divider bank can produce a remainder on the average of every microsecond.

The dividers are packaged separately from the main EPOC logic and controlled over a dedicated bus and cable. The separation in the package makes it possible to expend the divider subsystem independently to meet future needs. This flexibility may prove useful in adjusting EPOC performance, since the best mix of dividers to main processors for the CFRAC factoring algorithm (see below) is not known.

EPOC SYSTEM SOFTWARE

EPOC is a hardware implementation of the inner loops of a specific algorithm. It is a special-purpose processor. The components however, have some generality and can serve as the basis for other special-purpose devices. The source of this generality is the programmability of the devices. Programmability also permits modification of the operational algorithm (tuning) as the EPOC application evolves. (See Figure 2.)

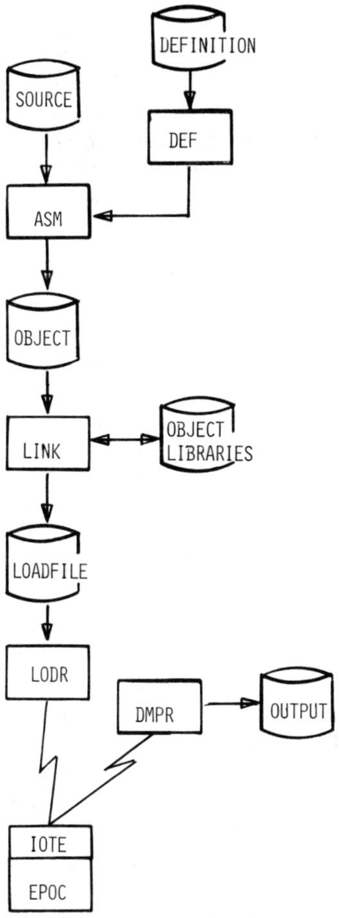

Figure 2—EPOC system software

Definition Program

To allow the maximum flexibility to the programmer in the language in which he will program EPOC (and because the machine specification was not complete when the assembler project was begun) there is a definition program. Using this program, the programmer can define to the assembler the target machine and source language of the program. This is functionally equivalent to the definition statements included in the AMDASM microcode assembler[3] but the details differ.

Input to this program is a machine definition file, while output is a set of internal-format tables suitable for insertion into the assembler. These are passed to the assembler along with the user's symbolic source code as primary inputs. The definition program serves as a 'shock absorber' in the processor-to-assembler interface. Two programmers can be programming the same machine in two different languages by the use of different definition files. One programmer or team of programmers can program two different machines in the same language by adjustments to the definition of the machines.

Microcode Assembler

To program EPOC in a reasonable format, we have developed a symbols-to-binary translator in the form of a symbolic assembler[4]. This assembler is a nontraditional two-pass assembler. Mnemonics are not built in, but are read from the definition program output described above. The assembler is a cross-assembler which is portable from one host system to another to the extent that RATFOR programs are portable[8]. Generality in the target machine is attainable by providing parametric mnemonics, word lengths, and other semantic attributes of the assembler. Only the syntax must be preserved to use this one assembler for two entirely different machines. With a preprocessor to absorb syntax differences, this assembler can assemble code for many assembler-level languages. Generality arises by treating the assembler as the most general possible translator—from symbols to bit fields. The generality is purchased at the expense of efficiency, in this case of speed of assembly and complexity in the definition file.

Linker

Assembler output is in the form of an object module which is not directly executable. In addition to the binary microwords that are the object of the assembly, there is relocation information (RLD) pointing to the location in the object code where the relocatable values are located, and library subprogram linkages (ESD) asking for code from the system libraries. The linker will convert the object file into a load file with all addresses which require it to be properly modified for relocation and all external references to be resolved in the linkage process. The linker also maintains the subprogram libraries, allowing additions and deletions and entering new object files into the library if the user requests it.

Portability is a characteristic of the linker as of all EPOC systems programs. The library format is also portable, since library files are text files. Files in text (ASCII hex) are at least double the size of the same information in binary. Assuming that the EPOC microcode files will be small makes the use of text files reasonable and convenient.

Loader and Unloader

The structure of the EPOC system files and the host connection method makes the process of loading data or a program to be executed into EPOC store more than a simple copy from the disk to memory. The host system, upon which the linker-output load file exists, is connected to EPOC over a (terminal) communication line. The loader must account for buffer size in the IOTE, a communications protocol from the host to the IOTE, and a code conversion from ASCII-hex to binary. The loader consists of two programs, one written in RATFOR and resident on the host system, the other written in 8080 assembler and controlling the IOTE. The loading process is accomplished by cooperation between these two programs. Since there is a communication line involved, messages are checked for correct transmission and retransmitted if necessary. There is a communications protocol embedded inside the loader programs.

When EPOC reports the results of a calculation, those results must be unloaded from EPOC and placed into a file on the host disk. The unloader program and IOTE accomplish this task in cooperation similar to the loader process described above. The results file will be processed by a subsequent program on the host to produce the answer to the mathematical problem. EPOC has completed its subtask once the intermediate result has been transmitted to the host.

Microcode Simulator

EPOC is programmed directly in horizontal microcode. This means that each bus in the machine data flow is controlled by the programmer during each instruction cycle. This level of programming is difficult to master, but it can yield the best possible machine performance. Debugging microprograms is challenging, since the code is so close to the hardware that nonstandard debugging techniques are required. Even when a microcode compiler becomes available, the debugging of both compiled and assembled programs is a necessary facility.

The IOTE allows operator-interactive support for program debugging. This, however, is expensive in both programmer and machine time and provides a limited window on operation. The microcode can provide a test driver that permits the display of interesting values at breakpoints during operation. The microcode simulator, though, is the best facility for the functional checking of microprogams.

The microcode simulator has the same transfer function that the EPOC itself has. It is a program written in RATFOR that will process data exactly as EPOC would. Since it is a simulator, any internal state that the programmer may wish to access can be made available. Using the simulator, the programmer can run the same load modules that will be sent to EPOC and see that they are operating correctly or where a malfunction has occured.

EPOC OPERATIONAL SOFTWARE

Diagnostic Programs

In the course of system development, many small microprograms have been developed that test the SEQ, ALU, and divider dataflows for expected results. These diagnostic programs exercise the logic and flush the data paths of the machine. When the diagnostic set works properly, the user can be confident of the operational readiness of the EPOC hardware. This capability is useful in operation as well as in development. For reasons of speed and cost, there is little error-checking circuitry built into EPOC. In order to assure that the device is producing good results, the diagnostic set is run periodically. Since EPOC is not involved in real-time or life-critical processing, this periodic diagnosis is the most cost-effective way of ensuring proper operation. Calculated results are compared with expected values and agreement indicates correct operation.

Console and Host Connection

To allow the operator to communicate with the machine while it is in operation, a simple console interface for alter/display has been provided. This facility accomodates the desire of the operator to monitor and affect the progress of the calculation. The class of problem upon which EPOC will work may require many (hundreds or thousands) hours of calculation. During this time, the operator can check the progress of the algorithm. The host can compile reports as described above, but, actual hands-on contact with the machine is useful in both development and operation.

Continued FRACtion Algorithm

The continued fraction (CFRAC) algorithm[6] is a useful method in the factoring of large integers. Large (100-digit) integers and the difficulty in factoring them are the fundamental reason why RSA public key cryptosystems[5] are considered secure. CFRAC was discovered about 1970, and has since been extensively use by investigators factoring numbers of mathematical interest. Pomerance and Wagstaff at the University of Georgia have recently improved the performance of the CFRAC algorithm by the use of early exit heuristics to cut short a calculation when its continuance does not appear promising[10].

CFRAC is an algorithm for the factoring of large numbers, and EPOC is a processor tailored to the accomplishment of certain portions of the CFRAC algorithm. CFRAC deals with numbers in the range of the square root of the number to be factored. These numbers are generated by the algorithm, then divided by a set of small prime numbers called the factor base. When a candidate number divides completely over this factor base, this intermediate result is noted. When enough such numbers have been found, a factorization of the original number is possible. EPOC performs only one part of the CFRAC algorithm, the generation of candidate numbers and their trial division by the factor base. This part requires much computation but small memory. The final result is produced by the second phase of the algorithm which requires less computation but much store. This phase runs on the host system. The combined system, EPOC and host, solves the CFRAC problem—the capability of each processor is complementary to the other in this calculation.

EPOC DEVELOPMENT ENVIRONMENT

Portable Systems

A system can be said to be portable to the extent that its operation does not depend on the specific hardware upon which it runs. Various degrees of portability can be provided by different techniques in systems. The method which has been employed in the case of the EPOC development system is the use of the RATFOR[7,8] preprocessor for FORTRAN. This allows the code in which the development system is written to be ported to any system with a FORTRAN compiler and SOFTWARE TOOLS support[8].

Software Tools

With the adoption of RATFOR as the system programming language, the development aids which come with the software tools[7] system are also available. We have made extensive use of these—some of the utility programs (cat, rev, tsort, sort) are integral parts of the procedures which are executed in the systems programming process.

A good set of development tools that are mature and free from significant flaws, and available in source form so that they can be adapted the specifics of a project, is priceless. For the EPOC project, this role was taken by the SOFTWARE TOOLS environment[8] provided by SA Barman and his staff on the departmental Cyber computer, and at a greater remove by Kernighan and Plauger et.al. to the computing community[7,8].

Computer-aided Design

The hardware design task for EPOC has been performed using a computer-aided design (CAD) system of programs to keep track of pin numbers in networks, signal names, fanin/out levels, etc[9]. This CAD system of programs was developed for prototype digital system fabrication, and has served the EPOC case well.

EPOC is a prototype; interconnection is done by wire wrapping. The CAD system bridges the gap between a computer-readable wire list that can be used to fabricate wrapped boards by automatic wire-wrapping machine and a user-readable representation of the design that can be used to document, communicate, and update the design.

CAD is notable for its simple hardware description language (HDL). The language has only two statement types: a declarative statement denoted by the keyword DEFINE which tells the symbolic (designer-assigned) name of a device(s), its type (index into a technology table), and its location. The other is a connective statement denoted by the keyword WIRE and takes the form:

WIRE list1 TO list2

where list1 and list2 denote pins which are to be connected.

While simplicity has advantages, this language is verbose in description. Computer-readable hardware descriptions are a valuable form of design documentation and the more readable a HDL, the better. CAD has served to make the hardware portion of the EPOC project possible. It is a significant step toward the capability of programming hardware design with computer development aids as is done with software.

In any hardware project, a CAD system, even a primitive one, is vital to success. The CAD software used for EPOC has delivered up much useful information which has helped to avoid problems or repair them quickly when they arise. Designing hardware without a CAD system is like developing programs in binary—it is not productive, though it is possible if the problem is small enough. If the problem is of reasonable size, it is possible in theory, but not in practice.

SYSTEM SUMMARY

EPOC is an extended-precision operand computer. The single-precision word length is 128 bits, making it possible to process large integers without resort to multiprecise software routines. Since this is a special-purpose device, the hardware and software have been invented from scratch to realize it.

The hardware consists of an IOTE, ALU, SEQ, and a bank of divider elements that are specifically for a factoring problem EPOC can solve. The IOTE is a microcomputer system which handles the host and console interfaces to EPOC as a buffered DMA channel. It handles the interface to the host system by emulating a terminal for communications. The SEQ holds the microstore and executes the microinstructions in a sequence dictated by the program and the conditions that arise in the dataflow. The ALU can perform 128-bit operations in a single cycle (some cycles which produce carries are lengthened in time). With the exception of the dividers, EPOC is a general-purpose, fast, small-store, microprogrammable, 128-bit processor data flow.

The software consists of a family of system programs for producing and testing EPOC microprograms: assembler, linker, loader, and a definition program, and a microcode simulator to check the function of the produced code. To make the programs portable, they are all written in RATFOR. To make them as general as possible, they are heavily parameterized.

One point in summary, a system of things is more difficult to develop and operate than a collection of things. A significant fraction of the EPOC design and debugging effort has been spent on the interconnection of the components rather than on the components themselves. The bus layouts, protocols, interfacing conventions and other design considerations of components interconnection and packaging are a lot of work to generate without errors. This significant effort was consistently neglected and underestimated, and this may be in general a cause of systems integration problems.

ACKNOWLEDGMENT

This research was funded in part by the National Science Foundation, MCS – 8302877.

REFERENCES

1. Advanced Micro Devices. *Bipolar Microprocessor Logic and Interface Data Book.* Sunnyvale, Calif.: AMD, 1983.
2. Mick, J., and J. Brick. *Bit-Slice Microprocessor Design.* New York: McGraw-Hill, 1980.
3. Advanced Micro Devices. *AMDASM Reference Manual.* Sunnyvale, Calif.: AMD, 1978.
4. Egan, R. C., and J. W. Smith. "A General Assembler for Horizontal Microcode." *Proceedings of Southeastern Regional Conference of ACM.* New York: ACM, 1983.
5. Rivest, R. L., A. Shimar, and L. Adelman. "A Method for Obtaining Digital Signatures and Public-Key Cryptosystems," *Communications of the ACM,* 21 (1978), pp. 120–126.
6. Morrison, M. A., and J. Brillhart. "A Method of Factoring and the Factorization of F7," *Mathematics of Computation,* 29 (1975), pp. 183–205.
7. Kernighan, B. W. and P. J. Plauger. *Software Tools.* Reading, Mass.: Addison-Wesley, 1976.
8. Hall, D. E., D. K. Scherrer, and J. S. Sventek. "A Virtual Operating System," *Communications of the ACM,* 23 (1980), pp. 495–502.
9. Raymond, I. C. "LSI/VLSI Design Automation," Computer, 14 (1981), pp. 89–101.
10. Pomerance, C. B. "Analysis and Comparison of Some Integer Factoring Algorithms," *Computational Methods in Number Theory.* Amsterdam: North Holland 1983.

New microprocessor-based computer architectures

by OMRI SERLIN
ITOM International Company
Los Altos, California

ABSTRACT

The maturing 16/32 bit microprocessor technology is making possible a variety of multiprocessor architectures, which are either new, or have not been economically feasible heretofore. Such architectures are now being commercially applied to both extremes of the computing spectrum: in multi-user, transaction processing systems, as well as in personal office and engineering workstations. This paper outlines the key architectural features of several notable microprocessor-based, multiprocessor designs.

INTRODUCTION

In addition to *software standardization,* two other unexpected developments are arising out of the maturing microprocessor technology. On the one hand, the proliferation of microprocessor-based, desk-top computers is casting doubt on the validity of the notion that the computer is an expensive resource which must be shared and centrally-controlled. The technical capabilities and price/performance of personal, desk-top workstations, coupled with advances in local area networks, lend plausibility to future scenarios in which the role of central computers (including today's superminis) will no longer be to supply computing power, but will be limited to the control of shared data bases.

On the other hand, the same powerful, low-cost, off-the-shelf microprocessors are making possible a variety of new, multiprocessor architectures, which are especially suitable for handling on-line transaction processing and other multi-user missions. Because of the sensitivity of the data they control, and because many employees and/or customers will be heavily dependent on their availability, these systems often offer fault-tolerant (FT) features.

Microprocessor-based architectures are thus destined to play a significant role at both ends of the computing environs: on the user's desk, and at the "central" facility, where the latter can range from a departmental file server to the central corporate data depository.

This paper examines some of the new microprocessor-based architectures now becoming commercially available for service at these extremes of the spectrum.

FAULT-TOLERANT SYSTEMS

Perhaps the most interesting microprocessor-based architectures are evolving in the field of fault-tolerant (FT) systems. The goal of a fault-tolerant computer system is to protect the applications processes and the data base from being adversely impacted by hardware faults. The system's ability to do this is measured by its *depth,* which is the number of faults of a particular type that can be tolerated concurrently (typically just one), and *coverage,* which is the range of fault types with which the system is equipped to deal.

Demand for FT systems, originally limited to such fields as process control and telephone switching, is now driven mainly by the exploding popularity of on-line transaction processing (OLTP) applications, of which the airline reservations systems were early harbingers in the mid-1960s. Tandem Computers (Cupertino, CA) has been the premier supplier of FT systems for OLTP applications since it shipped its first system in 1976.

It is of value to review the key features of the Tandem system (Figure 1) to provide a perspective on the newer architectures. Each Tandem system is a network of up to 16 minicomputer-class processors, implemented in ad-hoc TTL logic. Inter-processor communications is carried by a duplexed, 16-bit-parallel, 6.7-MHz bus system. All peripheral controllers are dual ported, so each is accessible from two processors. Disk drives are accessible from two controllers. *Disk mirroring* can be invoked, under which the operating system automatically maintains identical copies of the data base on two separate disk drives.

The *message based* operating system, a copy of which resides in each processor, isolates the user processes from configuration details. A user process needing disk service, for example, addresses a "message" to the disk server process; the operating system determines the location of the requested resource, and routes the message accordingly. Thus the user process need not know which two processors are connected to the disk in question, or which of the two currently runs the "primary" disk server process.

Fault-recovery in the Tandem system is achieved by maintaining, for each process, a semi-active *backup* copy in an-

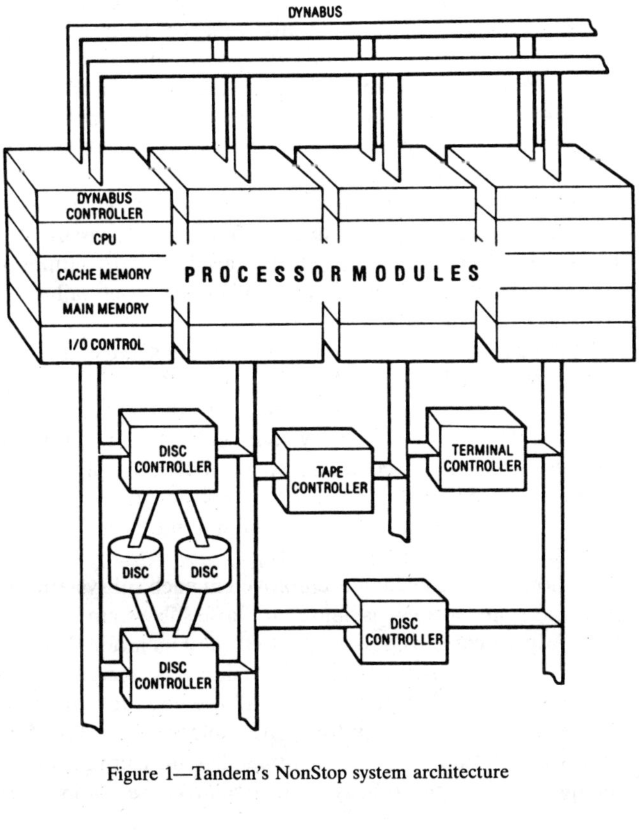

Figure 1—Tandem's NonStop system architecture

other processor. The primary process keeps its backup informed through a series of *checkpoints,* each of which defines the state of the process at some strategic point in the computation. Should the processor running the primary become disabled, (detected by the absence of the I'M ALIVE message it is expected to broadcast every second), the backup resumes from the last good checkpoint. Applications programmers originally had to explicitly implant checkpoint calls in their processes; new software elements have now largely isolated the end-user from the checkpointing details.

The duality in the Tandem architecture eliminates single-points-of-failure, while the message-based software architecture facilitates on-line repair, graceful (modular) growth, and geographically-dispersed networking.

"Pair and Spare" and Related Strategies

Stratus Computer (Natick, MA) is a 1980 start-up that became public in 1983. Stratus addresses the same OLTP markets as Tandem, but offers a drastically different, microprocessor-based FT architecture.

The key architectural concept in the Stratus system, informally known as the "pair and spare" philosophy, involves quadruplication of all major internal functions. First, each internal subsystem has a duplicate counterpart, its "spare." Both such subsystems are *self-checking*; each consists of a "pair" of identical functions which are given identical inputs, and whose outputs are compared on each clock pulse. A mismatch in the outputs of its internal halves creates an error signal in the given subsystem.

In normal operation, a subsystem and its spare run in tight lockstep; both get identical inputs from the duplexed system bus and produce identical outputs to the bus. Once a subsystem discovers an internal mismatch through the "self-checking" comparison process, it immediately "pulls out," letting the spare subsystem carry on with the task at hand, without missing a beat.

Until the faulty subsystem is detected and repaired, the system will operate at a reduced FT depth. To assure that failed subsystems are promptly replaced, Stratus equips its systems with dialers that automatically report such failures to a service center.

When a repaired subsystem is returned to service, an interrupt is generated to the CPU (the spare CPU if the repaired subsystem is the other CPU). The CPU then undertakes to "re-educate" the fresh subsystem and bring it into synchronism with its functioning spare. For example, a new memory board is brought to mirror-image condition by copying into it the contents of the functioning memory. This process may use up to a few seconds.

Although self-checking is employed in each subsystem, the pair-and-spare strategy is limited to those subsystems that can be tightly synchronized, e.g., the CPU and memory. The disk controllers are self-checking through duplicate read and write sections (Figure 2). Signals are not allowed on the system bus (on read) or onto the disk (on write) unless both parts of the relevant section agree. Conventional disk mirroring is implemented by the operating system. Similarly, the communications controllers are self-checking but are not in lockstep; instead, each normally handles half the load, but both have access to all terminals. Should one controller fail, the other picks up the entire load.

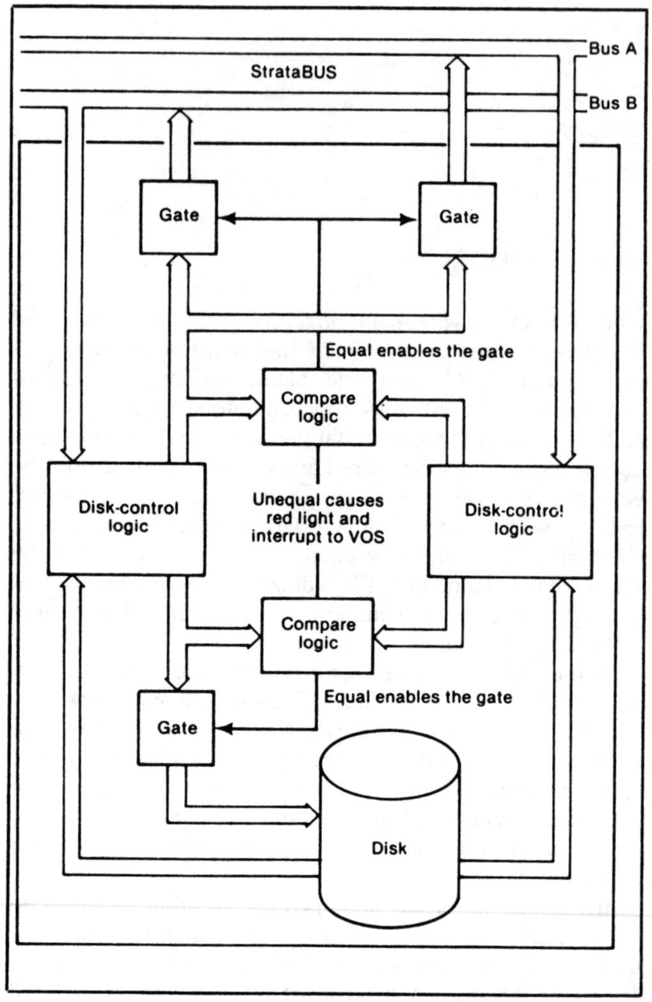

Figure 2—A stratus self-checking disk controller

The modularization into self-checking subsystems is at the printed circuit board level. Each of these large (16″ × 20″) boards contains a self-checking implementation of one of the following functions: CPU; memory control; 1-MB memory; disk controller; tape controller; and communications controller. A fully-duplexed, basic Processing Module (PM) contains 11 boards (the tape controller is not usually duplicated).

This basic PM contains 18 microprocessors. Each CPU board carries 4 Motorola 68000 MPUs: two to implement a basic demand-paging CPU (a pecularity of the original 68000 prevented this from being accomplished with one MPU), and two more to create the duplicate function for on-board self-checking. The disk, tape, and communications controllers are each based on a Zilog Z80A MPU, again duplicated for the self-checking implementation.

While the "pair and spare" strategy is not new, the implementation of the required function quadruplication could not be achieved economically before the advent of low-cost, off-the-shelf microprocessors. A fully-duplexed Stratus system is comparable in price to non-FT superminis, and is well below a similarly configured Tandem system.

Each of Intel Corp.'s 432 microprocessor chip family members contains *Functional Redundancy Checking* (FRC), a feature which facilitates the construction of pair-and-spare systems. With FRC, the comparison circuits needed to perform self-checking in a subsystem are built into the chips. Two chips can be configured in a self-checking pair by merely feeding them identical inputs, and connecting all corresponding output pins together. An external signal determines which chip in a self-checking pair is the "checker" by enabling the comparison circuits on that chip.

A related architecture, dubbed "n-modular-redundancy," replicates each function an odd number of times. Special voting circuits compare the outputs and "vote out" wrong results. Thus in a triple-modular-redundant system, the two functions that agree will suppress the deviant result produced by a presumably malfunctioning third.

August Systems (Tigard, OR) is building FT systems based on a variation of this principle, for service in industrial automation and process control applications. In the August system, the three Intel 8086-based processors perform the voting in software. This is possible because of the repetitive nature of the computation involved in these applications. Voting occurs just prior to launching the next iteration of the control algorithm. (This control algorithm is usually implemented in PROMs rather than RAMs). Through a set of read-only links, the processors can read, but never write each other's memory; thus they can read the values to be voted on, but erroneous results are isolated within the malfunctioning processor. Again, the availability of off-the-shelf microprocessors has made the high degree of duplication involved in such schemes economically feasible.

The "pair-and-spare" scheme is in one sense more robust than the backup/checkpointing strategy, since a single fault cannot "crash" a function, but merely results in the temporary loss of FT depth. This in turn means that the system need not employ backup processes, thereby dispensing with the checkpointing traffic and related programming complexity. Also unnecessary are the I'M ALIVE broadcasts. All applications software, and most system software, can treat the system as a conventional computer.

The principal disadvantage of the "pair-and-spare" and n-modular-redundant strategies is that system growth can only be achieved in large steps, if at all. In the Stratus system, for example, processing capacity is increased by interconnecting additional Processing Modules, each accompanied by its own memory, controllers, and peripherals, over an 11.2-Mbit/sec ring-type local area network. Each PM is essentially an independent system; load sharing, if any, is achieved by explicit user programming.

Tightly-coupled, "Pool" Systems

Synapse Computer (Milpitas, CA), a well-funded 1980 start-up, has developed a load-sharing, tightly-coupled multiprocessor architecture that is more flexible in its ability to accommodate growth. Synapse, too, focuses on the OLTP field.

The strategic concept in the Synapse N + 1 system is to treat the multiple processors as a pool, from which the system draws idle resources to service the next pending transaction. By configuring just one more than the N processors needed to service a given load, the system attains essentially the same resiliency as a 2N system, where each processor is backed by another.

The key architectural element is a shared memory system, which holds the only copy of the operating system, and is accessible to up to 28 processors via a duplexed, 8-MHz, 32-bit-parallel bus system (Figure 3). The processors, all of which are based on the Motorola 68000 MPU, are of two types: general-purpose processors (GPPs), and I/O processors (IOPs). Dual ported controllers for disk/tape and communications allow access from two IOPs to each peripheral. Thus the "pool" concept does not strictly apply beyond the applications processors; the IOPs and disk controllers use the 2N strategy. Disk mirroring may be optionally invoked to protect against disk drive failures.

In normal operation, the GPPs and IOP schedule work for each other by making dispatching requests against queues in shared memory. When idle, the processors look up these queues for work to do. An elegant "memory data ownership" scheme is used to prevent two processors from assigning themselves to the same task. IOPs have 128 KB of local storage, while the GPPs have 16 KB of high-speed cache to minimize memory bus loading and permit operation at an optimum speed.

The cache employs a non-write-through policy, so requests for memory "owned" by a given cache are satisfied by interprocessor communications. The 16-MB address space of the 68000 is divided into domains of 1 MB code and 1 MB data

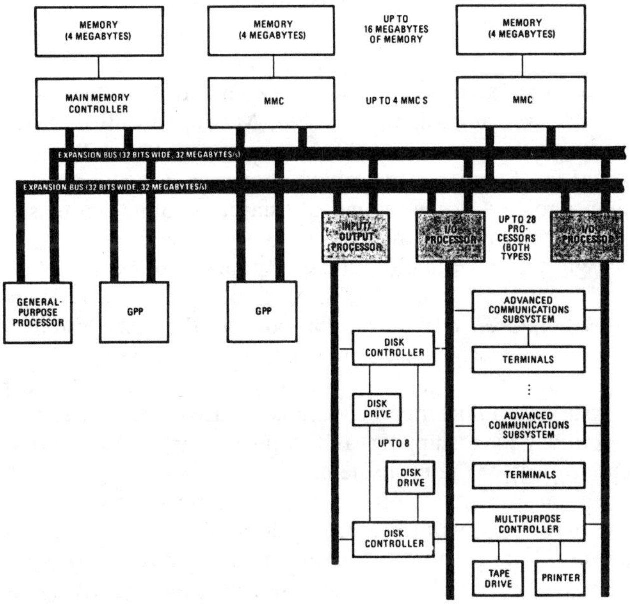

Figure 3—The Synapse system architecture

each. This was done in order to facilitate rapid context switch: a process domain calling on a system service, for example, is switched in about 100 microseconds by merely switching the address space. Since the system requires small program modules in any case (see below), this limitation on the address space size was deemed acceptable.

Process and processor failures can be easily handled by merely reassigning the incomplete tasks to the "work to do" queues. A semi-transparent checkpointing system is maintained. The users need not implant explicit checkpoint calls; however, they must build their applications from small modules, called "Program Units," according to specific design rules. The system automatically invokes checkpoints between Program Units (this feature can be optionally disabled). Crashed processes are restarted in a functioning processor from the last good checkpoint. Checkpoints are saved on disk.

The related data base system, which is integrated with the operating system rather than imposed on it at a higher level, implements a COMMIT strategy that assures the effects of incomplete transactions can be completely removed. This is achieved by the "write-ahead log" technique.

A ROM-based bootstrap program allows a freshly-installed processor to load the needed code into its buffer (IOP case), or begin execution at the right point (GPP case).

A memory failure is the most severe problem that can occur in the Synapse system, since such a failure can wipe out the work queues, data base buffer pool, and pieces of the operating system. Rather than maintain a duplicate, mirror-image memory system, the Synapse system deals with this situation by automatically rebooting the system. The memory controller detecting this failure raises an interrupt signal that tells all processors to reset. Then the mass-storage controller in the first I/O slot attempts to reboot the operating system into shared memory, bypassing the bad module. Should it fail to do so within a given time interval, the second mass-storage controllers will attempt the boot. A data base recovery process then uses the mirrored log file to undo all uncommitted transactions, and implement pending committed transactions. End users are guaranteed to sustain no more than the loss of the screen they were manipulating at the time of the crash since such screens are not yet checkpointed.

Each system component (CPU, Memory Control, 1-MB memory, IOPs and controllers) occupies one 15″ × 17″ board. There are 64 slots in the cabinet; however, not all are interchangeable. A triple-redundant, majority-voting power system protects against the loss of a power supply.

Tightly-coupled multiprocessor "pool" systems are not entirely new. In the mid-1960s, using mainframe technology, IBM employed elements of the idea in the 9020 system, a three-processor arrangement used in air traffic control centers. A few years ago, BTI (Mt. View, CA) implemented such a system in minicomputer technology. Elxsi (San Jose, CA) recently began shipping a high-performance, ECL-based, multiprocessor "pool" system.

The availability of off-the-shelf 16/32 bit microprocessors has made this architecture considerably more appealing in terms of both economics and implementation time. To assure some degree of independence in selecting the underlying microprocessor, Synapse coded most of its operating system in PASCAL.

The Auragen Synchronized Cluster Scheme

Auragen (Ft. Lee, NJ) is another 1980 start-up that is targeting the OLTP market with a multiprocessor, 68000-based FT system. Conceptually, the Auragen system is rather similar to Tandem's, but includes several interesting improvements in hardware and software capabilities, and in price/performance.

The system consists of up to 32 clusters, interconnected over a duplexed, 32-bit-parallel, 4-MHz bus system. Each cluster is a self-contained multiprocessor system using the VERSAbus to interconnect a number of specialized processors with a shared-memory subsystem of up to 8 MB. The 68000-based Executive Processor interfaces to the duplexed system bus and has 128 KB of private memory. It executes the local operating system, which is based on UNIX System III. The system is modified and augmented to provide interprocess communications in the multi-cluster environment, synchronization functions (see below), and crash recovery. The Exec Processor generally does not need access to the cluster's shared memory.

The Work Processor consists of two 68010 MPUs, each of which can work on an independent process, while interleaving their memory requests to obtain the maximum benefit from the shared-memory bandwidth. The Work Processor executes user tasks, as well as such "global" system tasks as the page server, file server, TTY (terminal) server, and "root server" or process scheduler.

Other processors which may be part of the cluster include the 68000-based Communications Processor with its own 128-KB memory, and a disk/tape controller implemented with 2901 bit slices. The disks and communications interfaces are dual ported, to be accessible to two controllers residing in two separate clusters. Although the AUROS operating system presents the user with UNIX-compatible interfaces, internally it is implemented as a message-based system. All inter-process communications is via system-controlled messages.

Fault-tolerance in the Auragen system is based on *synchronization*. This is a variation of the checkpointing scheme, which is user-transparent and more efficient. Each primary process has an inactive backup in another cluster. The backup has access to all the input messages sent to its primary, and keeps track of the number of messages sent by its primary. At either periodic intervals, or when the number of input messages read by the primary exceeds an installation-defined limit, the backup is automatically synchronized with its primary; at that point, input messages and output counts may be discarded.

Should the primary process fail when detected by the usual local mechanisms, plus I'M ALIVE broadcasts, the backup restarts from the state defined in the last synchronization. It reprocesses the input messages accumulated since the last synchronization, taking care to suppress output messages already issued by the primary (indicated by the output message count). By keeping the backup only approximately in step with the primary, the scheme conserves system resources, at the expense of some additional processing steps that are invoked only when recovering from a (presumably rare) fault.

More details on the systems described above may be found in References 7–17.

APOLLO DOMAIN: DISTRIBUTED VIRTUAL MEMORY

A testimony to the attraction of the "one man, one computer" concept is the dazzling success of Apollo (Chelmsford, MA), a 1980 start-up that was well on its way to becoming a $100-million company in 1983. Apollo was one of the first to recognize the potential market for personal engineering workstations, made possible by the technological advances in microprocessors, Winchester disks, and local networking.

The Apollo product philosophy is to combine the best features of time-sharing systems (resource sharing) with those of dedicated minicomputers (interactiveness and quick response). To achieve these goals, the Apollo DOMAIN system consists of locally-networked, 68000-based, personal workstations, running under control of a multi-tasking operating system, driving a multi-window, high-resolution graphics display.

The powerful local processing capabilities of these workstations are augmented by a resource sharing scheme, promoted by a network-wide object name space. Programs, data files, and some system structures are accessible as addressable objects across the entire network. Users may identify desired objects with a UNIX-like path name, which is translated by the system into a 96-bit object address. The object address consists of a 64-bit unique object identification (UID) and a 32-bit, byte-within-object address. UID uniqueness is assured by encoding into it the serial number of the workstation that created it, and the time of its creation.

Within the workstation, processes have a 24-bit virtual address space, defined by the hardware addressing capability of the 68000. Objects requested by user commands are mapped into the 16-MB virtual process address space in segments. Thus the user process need not do explicit I/O. No data movement takes place until a page fault actually occurs. The 1-KB pages are retrieved as needed from either local storage, if any, or from a remote disk structure, across the network.

The network is a coaxial ring, operating at a 12-Mbits/sec signaling rate. Access arbitration is implemented by a token-passing scheme: stations may transmit only after receiving a unique bit pattern, the token, from the station immediately upstream, and must regenerate this pattern at the end of the transmission and send it to the next downstream station. Bit stuffing is used to distinguish several flag characters, including the token, from random data.

Several models of the Apollo workstations have evolved, but the internal architecture is largely invariable across the line. It consists of a proprietary 32-bit bus connecting the 68000-based CPU, two-level memory management unit, display subsystem, disk subsystem, and network interface. In addition, a Multibus controller is available on some models, to allow attachment of additional peripherals. The display subsystem consists of a large, high-resolution display (typically 1024×800) driven from a separate, dual-ported display memory. Special high-speed, bit-moving hardware facilitates scrolling and window moves.

CONVERGENT TECHNOLOGIES' MEGAFRAME

A 1979 start-up, Convergent Technologies (Santa Clara, CA) has been notably successful with its AWS and IWS lines of personal office workstations. These workstations, now both based on the Intel 8086 MPU, are optionally configurable into a resource-sharing cluster. The proprietary operating system, CTOS, supports multi-tasking and real-time capabilities.

In mid-1983, Convergent introduced the MegaFrame, a microprocessor-based multiprocessor system. Full fault-tolerance had been considered at the start of the project, but due to various constraints, the designers settled on less ambitious goals. The system was designed to accommodate modular growth while shielding existing applications from its impact. In particular, one or more Applications Processors, running a version of UNIX, are supported by several specialized support (e.g., file and terminal) processors, whose number can also be increased in the field. The support processors run specialized software based on CTOS. A 2.7-MHz, 32-bit-parallel bus system interconnects all processors.

The Applications Processors (APs) are based on Motorola 68010, which improves on the original 68000 by allowing the processor to recover from, rather than crash on, page faults. A full two-level, demand-paging, 4-MB virtual memory system is supported. Up to 4 MB of real memory can be associated with each AP, using a private bus. Up to 16 APs can be accommodated.

The File Processor (FP) uses the Intel 80186 MPU, which is upward compatible from the 8086 employed in Convergent's previous products. The File Processor executes the UNIX file system portion, which has been removed from the kernel in the AP. In addition, the FP can execute more sophisticated file systems (e.g., ISAM) or even a relational DBMS. The FP directly controls up to three 50-MB disk drives. Up to five additional FPs may be present, each with its own set of up to three drives. One FP is designated as the "master": it is responsible for system initialization, and for coordinating the other FPs.

Other specialized processors include the 186-based Cluster Controller, which interfaces to a network of existing Convergent workstations and the new, 8088-based Personal Terminal (PT); the 186-based Terminal Controller, which allows "dumb terminals" to access the UNIX-running APs; and the Signetics 8X300-based SMD controller, supporting SMD-type disk drives.

Processors communicate over the bus via a message-based communications software system, supported by "hardware mailboxes" and a "doorbell interrupt" that alerts a given processor to look into its mailbox for a message. A system-wide address space is defined by 40-bit addresses. Each consists of an 8-bit "slot number," which specifies a processor, and a 32-bit address, allowing a larger address space than is currently supported by either the 186 or the 68000.

The Master File Processor, in addition to its duties in initializing the entire system and in coordinating the other FPs (e.g., by initiating parallel path name searches through the individual UNIX file trees on each FP), also maintains a multiple "watchdog timer" system: every second it sets a value in a designated memory location of every processor in the system. Should any processor fail to clear that location, the MFP assumes that processor is crashed or stalled, and initiates diagnostic and recovery procedures. Each processor occupies one large PCB, which also hosts 256–512 KB of local memory. Up to six 6-slot "low boy" cabinets may be configured on the system bus.

SUMMARY

The term "new computer architectures" tends to be associated today with such long-range undertakings as Japan's AI-based "Fifth Generation" project, or Columbia University's "Non-Von" program. In contrast, the innovative multiprocessor architectures made possible by the maturing 16/32 bit microprocessor technology, illustrated by the examples cited above, are currently available. Microprocessor-based designs are rapidly claiming large stakes not only in desk-top, personal workstations, but also in multi-user and transaction processing systems.

How smart the computer: Status and future on building its brain

by DAVID J. ELLIOTT
Shipley Company
Newton, Massachusetts

ABSTRACT

Silicon "intelligence" is explored from the viewpoint of integrated circuit manufacturing technology. The capabilities of future computers are largely predicated on its brain function, or integrated-circuit-based intelligence. The major technologies that comprise integrated circuit fabrication are explored. The current status and likely future direction of each is presented. The major areas are integrated circuit design, silicon crystal manufacturing, wafer preparation, imaging, etching, doping, and deposition.

Microelectronics technology, the science of microstructure formation, is explored, and various imaging strategies necessary to extend the resolution limits of VLSI devices are summarized. The various device manufacturing technologies are presented on a time scale, showing current mature technologies (1983), emerging technology (1984–1987), and future technology (1987–1990). Finally, VLSI device functions are compared to human brain functions, with projections made to the year 2000.

INTRODUCTION

The intelligence we increasingly ascribe to computers is derived form the integrated circuit (IC) "brains," or chips residing in their cores. ICs are the source of the increasing power embodied in the disciplines of microelectronic device fabrication. The "suborders" of this technology are IC pattern design, silicon crystal manufacturing, wafer preparation, imaging, etching, doping, and deposition.

In this paper, we will examine each of these areas, considering the current and future state of technology and its relative ability to meet the demands of future IC device fabrication. The overall challenge in producing a VLSI chip is one of transferring a computer-generated series of patterns into a silicon or gallium arsenide crystal slice, along with a specified level of dopant to provide conductive paths for electron movement. This must be done at submicron resolution levels in volume production on semi-automated equipment and in super-clean environments. Last but not least, the process must produce economic chip yield. Figure 1 summarizes the decrease in IC geometries.

	1983	1986
1. Die Size	150 mils	100-350 mils
2. Cell Size	45μm^2	11μm^2
3. Mask levels (total)	10	12
4. Mask levels (critical)	3	5
5. Line space size	2.5μm	1.5μm
6. Alignment tolerance	1.5μm	0.1μm
7. Critical dimension tolerance	0.4μm	0.15μm
8. Total dimensional tolerance	0.5μm	$\pm$0.3μm
9. Diffusion widths	5.0μm	1.5μm
10. Metallization line widths	3.0μm	2.0μm
11. Contact size	2.0μm	0.8μm
12. Resolution	2.0μm	0.8μm
13. Metallization thickness	1.2μm	1.0μm
14. Oxide thicknesses (minimum)	800 angstroms	200 angstroms
15. Junction depths	1.5μm	200 angstroms
16. Etch selectivity ratio (Si)	8:1	20:1

Figure 1—Integrated circuit feature size and registration control trends

IC PATTERN DESIGN

The design, layout, and data preparation for integrated circuit patterns have evolved from a laborious task done almost entirely by hand to a highly automated process with very little human intervention. Computers have invaded the IC design and layout process to a considerable extent, first as electronic drafting boards and recently as highly interactive systems requiring only simplistic circuit stick drawings, or even concepts, in order to completely implement a set of finished VLSI masks. All computer-aided design (CAD) information is fed into a digitizer, which converts information into digital data for the photo or e-beam master reticle generator.

Increased computer assistance in mask pattern design has resulted in almost fully automated processing. This is accomplished by first selecting a type of pre-established or optimized software that approximates or has built-in algorithms coinciding with the type of device being built. When overall design parameters for chip architecture are set, the designer's role is reduced to one of placing individual sections of the chip in different places within the chip, and even then the computer optimizes these decisions. The number of circuit elements per section must be specified, and again tested electronically (in the computer) for violation of design rules.

Highly automated chip design software is used for arrays, microprocessors, logic chips, and other device types with predictable elements. Automatic placement and routing software routines are also used to reduce circuit layout time. The designer may place various elements within the chip area and the computer is used to place the circuit pathways and find interconnections. Figure 2 shows the stick-diagram input and computer-generated pattern output, automatically compensating for preprogrammed design rules.

A major benefit of computer design, layout routing, and interconnection is freeing the creative talents of a designer from monotonous and time consuming essential mechanical tasks. Advanced software, such as silicon compilers, uses high-level abstract language that will take a very simple sketch or statement from a designer and automatically determine the macro- and microelements of the chip; creating first a diagram, then an actual pattern. Placement and routing functions are performed by a silicon assembler. These approaches minimize human intervention into areas where time consumption would be high, thereby freeing designers to think about more important aspects of design.

In the future, even higher levels of abstraction will be used for design and artwork production. Symbolic logic, device modeling by the computer, and silicon compilers are examples of the reduced role of the human in these functions. A printout of a computerized three-dimensional model of a device is

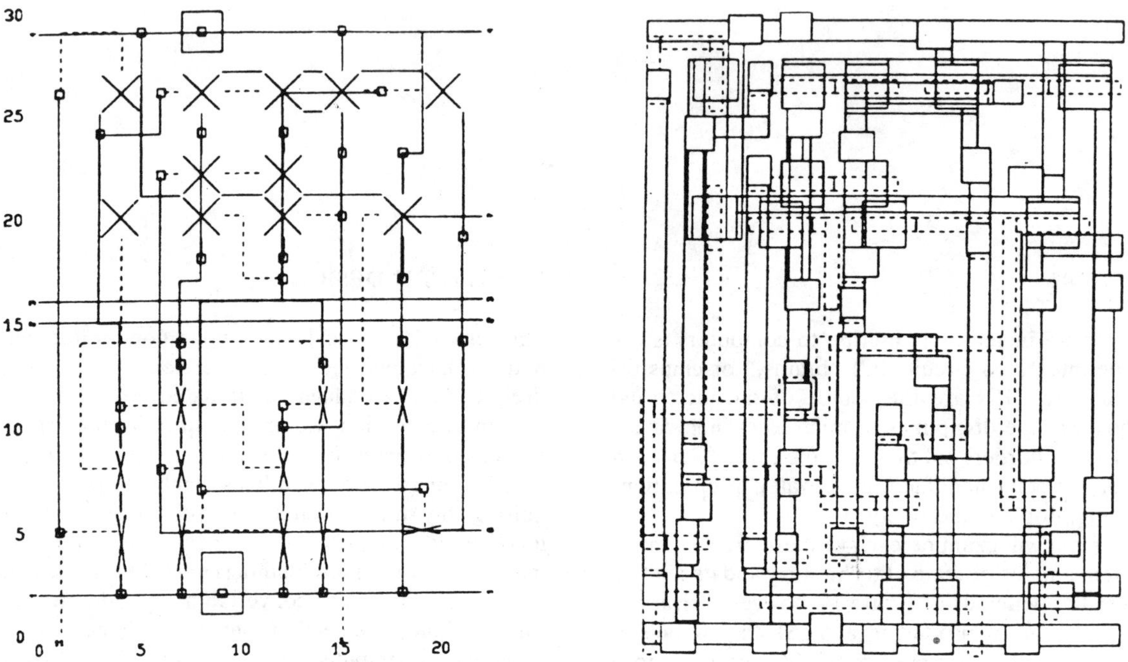

Figure 2—Stick-diagram input and computer output

shown in Figure 3. More complex designs are produced faster and at much lower cost.

SILICON CRYSTAL MANUFACTURING

A large part of the success of future VLSI devices rests on the quality of silicon and other crystals from which wafers are made. In order to meet current demands for high-quality silicon ingots, computer-controlled manufacturing is essential. The challenge of supplying a nearly perfect, defect-free crystal is complicated by the rapid increase in wafer diameter, as shown in Figure 4.

In the past two years, four-inch wafers have become the dominant production size, yet five- and six-inch wafers are already used in limited quantities, and plans for eight-inch crystals are being made. The primary problem in crystal-pulling technology is the removal of internal impurities and defects. Increasing crystal diameter by 50% per year magnifies this problem many times. For example, carbon and oxygen impurities occur in silicon and act as unwanted dopants by modifying the charge-carrying properties of the crystal. While ambient helium or argon is used as the gas during crystal growth, these impurities enter in ppm levels as contaminants from surrounding equipment and gases. The carbon content affects the electrical properties, and oxygen may weaken the structure of the crystal, as well as forming complexes with carbon to alter electrical properties. Heat treatments, such as annealing, are used to keep defects and impurities at a minimum level. Defects in the as-grown ingot are called intrinsic, and include stacking faults, point defects, oxygen, carbon and other impurities, crystal dislocations, interstitial vacancy clusters, and swirls.

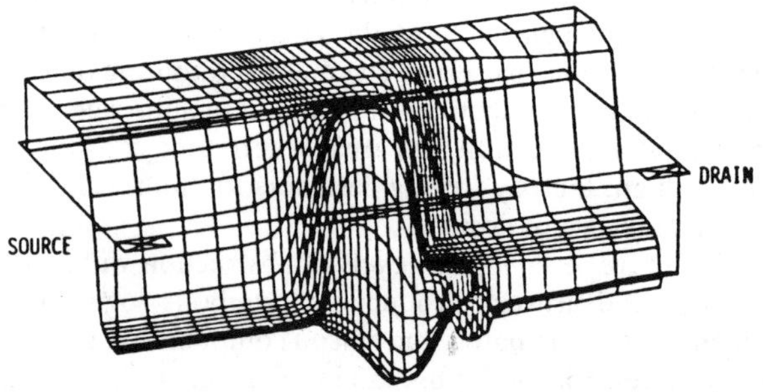

Figure 3—Example of computerized device modeling

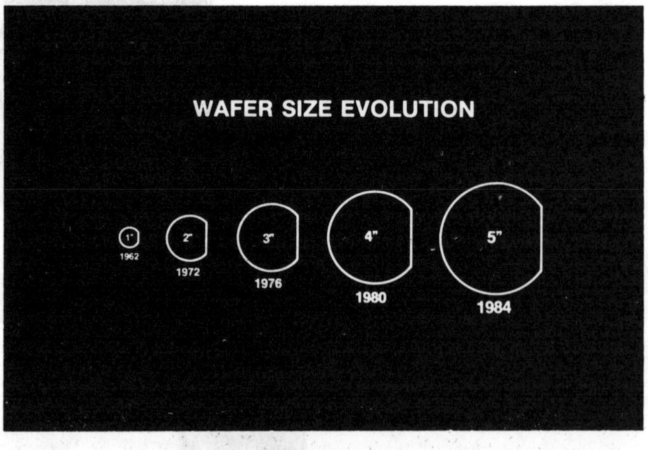

Figure 4—Crystal diameter trends

Computer control of all major crystal growth parameters is essential to producing dislocation-free crystals. These parameters include melt temperature, crystal and crucible rotation speed, lift speed, heater temperature, and other variables. The most promising location for producing perfect crystals is a space lab, where a zero-gravity environment is available. The Sony development of a high-magnetic field (MCA—magnetic field CA) greatly improved crystal quality by suppressing thermal convection in the melt, and thereby reducing oxygen content and growth defects. Figure 5 compares CZ with MCZ crystal growth environments. The MCZ process also reduces distortion and warpage in wafers sliced from MCZ ingots.

In the future, new crystal material, including gallium arsenide, which is now used for special high-speed IC applications, will be put into production for higher speed devices. Future crystal production in a zero-gravity space lab will most likely provide the ultimate in crystal quality.

WAFER PREPARATION

The physical dimensions of silicon wafers, and specifically flatness and surface uniformity, have become critical in advanced IC fabrication processes. Many additional steps are now taken to classify these important wafer parameters. For example, wafers are identified by the ingot from which they came, since nonuniformities in wafer batches are often traceable to a crystal growth problem.

Surface flatness across the water diameter is critical because it acts essentially as an optical plane. After resist is coated onto the wafer surface, it becomes an optical medium for microstructure formation. Energy of various wavelengths will be reflected off the water surface, and thus the degree of surface "polish," a chemical process, is important. If either the overall flatness or individual area nonuniformity vary, microimaging variations will occur.

Wafer preparation involves making one side of the silicon wafer surface as optically perfect as possible. The availability of software-driven, laser-based analytical equipment for mapping the contour of the wafer surface allows for careful screening of all substrates. Figure 6 shows a typical wafer surface "map."

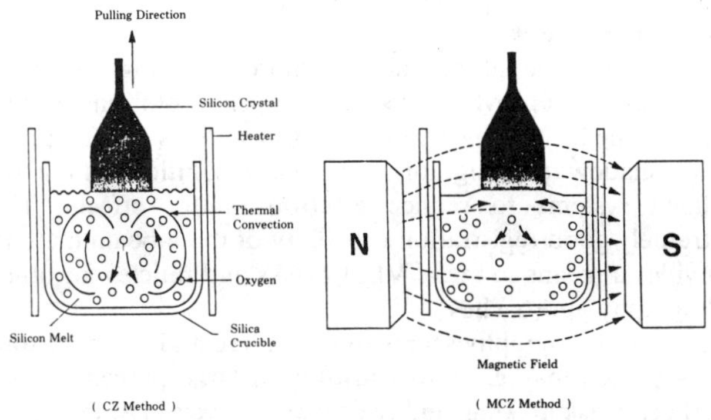

Figure 5—CZ and MCZ crystal types

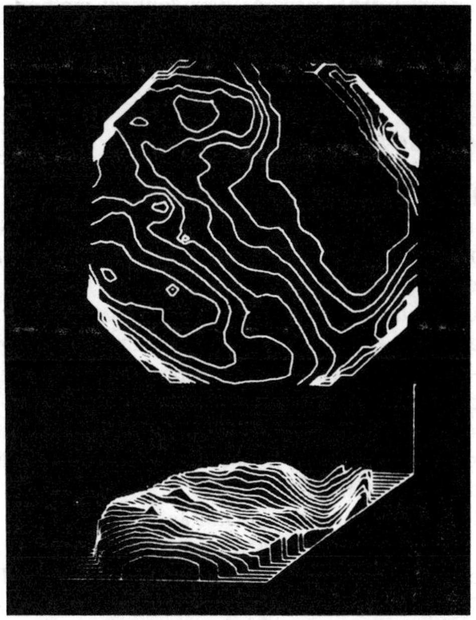
Figure 6—Wafer surface map

An ultra-flat wafer that enters the wafer fabrication process must be checked continually because the wafer process steps involve high-temperature operations. Thermal stress induced in ion implantation or etching causes warpage, and future processes will strive for temperature reduction at *all* steps. Since wafers are continually reimaged during fabrication, surfaces should be defect free (zero particulates above 0.5-μm diameter) and flat to one-half wave.

IMAGING

The technology that drives IC fabrication is microlithography, the process of forming microstructures on semiconductor surfaces. When resist-patterning technology proves its capability for a record level of resolution, pressure is exerted on etching and other fabrication processes to at least equal the new level of resolution. Current microimaging for IC production is accomplished primarily with a mix (die-by-die) exposure and scanning-slit imaging. These methods are being used for 246K RAM production, but may not be capable of the submicron imaging needed for one-megabit and denser devices. Current resolution levels (minimum geometries) are ~1.5 μm, and minimum geometries needed for devices by 1985 or 1986 will be 0.9–0.7 μm. Current printing technologies can image the level of resolution, but not with sufficient control to deliver acceptable device yield.

On the immediate horizon are several patterning technologies that all promise to deliver the submicron geometries needed to produce one-megabit and denser memories in production. These technologies are either extensions or optical methods now in use, or fall into the category of "beam" techniques. Extending current technology will certainly place a strain on optical stepping capabilities, perhaps requiring multilevel resist processes. At best, optical methods will be working near their practical resolution limit to pattern lines and spaces that are 0.5 μm wide.

Optical Lithography (Nonbeam)

Multilevel structures are one method used to obtain higher resolution, and are produced by using a three-level structure consisting of a thick (2 μm) planarizing layer, a thin (1000 Å) middle oxide (deposited) layer, and a thin (7000 Å) "top" coating of positive resist. The top layer is patterned with high resolution geometries, and the oxide etched, followed by reactive-ion etching through the planarizing layer with the etched oxide as the mask. Many variations on this central multilevel theme are possible, but conceptually and practically are very much alike in both degree of process difficulty and resolution potential (Figure 7).

Multilevel lithography has advantages in that it uses existing imaging equipment, provides resolution possible down to 0.5 μm, and retains existing process experience (same learning curve). The disadvantages include the addition of extra processing steps, increases in potential defects due to handling, and the requirement of a higher level of process control.

Optical lithography with nonbeam exposure sources has as its limit the exposing wavelength. This translates into a resolution of between 0.21 μm and 0.44 μm. Current technology limits the practical resolution of optical (nonbeam) imaging at 0.5–0.7 μm. This figure will undoubtedly be reduced with time, as shorter wavelength steppers and shorter wavelength-sensitive resists become available.

Optical Beam Lithography

Laser beams are the logical extension of optical lithography for advanced IC fabrication. Ultraviolet laser beams from a 308-nanometer wavelength eximer laser have carved 0.5-μm images in resist as thick as 1.0 μm. The super-bright (10 W) emission of the UV eximer laser will permit exposure throughput above that of conventional UV mask aligners. The chlorine and fluorine gases associated with these tools, and their size, are a concern, but the results shown in Figure 8 are very impressive. Computer-directed laser imaging will certainly become a key lithography technique.

Figure 7—SEM of Multilevel resist image

Lasers also are used in holographic lithography, where holograms of the various masks are made. In resist exposure, a laser "reads out" the hologram, projecting the mask images onto the wafer. The projected image is spatially filtered to remove defects.

Optical beam lithography can be summarized as follows:

Pros	*Cons*
—Extends resolution limit to sub-half-micron range	—Requires new process technology
—Potential cost is below e-beam and X-ray for equivalent throughput	—Production equipment not available
—Technology remains "optical"	

Figure 8—Laser-generated resist image

Electron Beam Lithography

A complete modulated beam of electrons is the primary method for electron lithography. The flexibility of pattern placement makes electron beams ideal for custom mask and "small-run" prototype devices. The principle of operation is shown in Figure 9.

Electron beam lithography is limited by slow exposure throughput, but provides excellent 0.5-μm resolutions as indicated in the SEM shown below. Advancements include proximity shadow printing for improved resolution and high-voltage systems to reduce electron scatter effects. The extremely good registration capability of the e-beam method provides a means to make VLSI masks and reticles for other lithography approaches.

E-beam lithography seems to be finding a niche in custom chips (which may grow to constitute a large percent of the market), mask making, and critical mask levels in wafers. Pros and cons are as follows:

Pros	*Cons*
—Rapid turnaround on mask sets for protoevaluations	—Relatively small wafer exposure throughput
—High level of alignment tolerance	—Electron scattering in resist detracts from resolution
—Excellent chip customization tool	—Relatively high capital equipment costs as a beam-writing technique

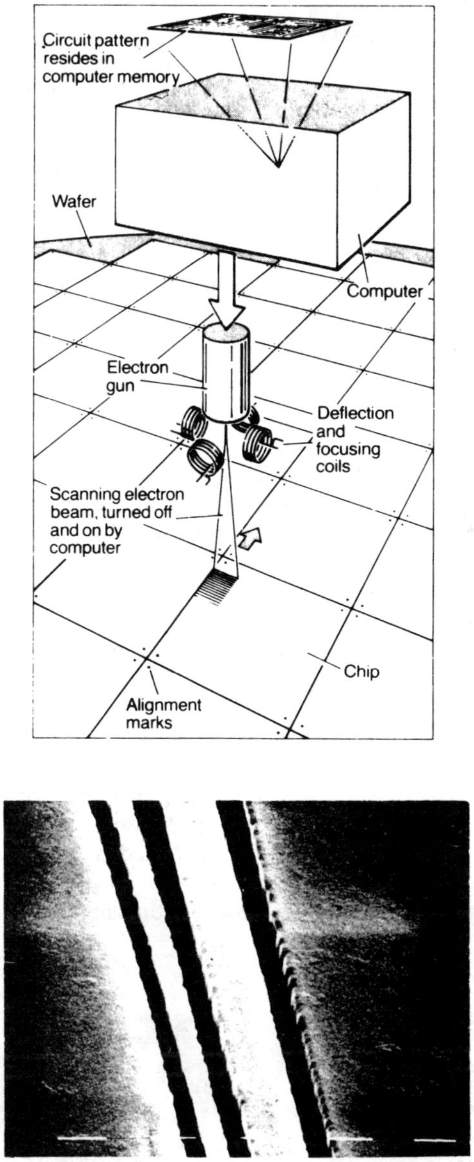

Figure 9—E-beam exposure principle and resulting resist image

X-ray Lithography

X-rays promise the highest resolution and throughput product of all existing lithography techniques. Wavelengths are optimized around 7Å, and conventional X-ray sources to emit this energy are well understood. The operating principle is shown in Figure 10.

Sharp point sources are needed to cast a sharp shadow through the mask and into the resist. Plasma gas discharge X-ray sources are more powerful than the 1–2 W electron-beam-generated X-ray sources, but are unreliable. Plasmas are equivalent to electron-gun-generated X-rays as point sources, but both lack the power needed for good production rates.

Electron storage rings promise power, highly collimated X-rays and tunable wavelengths, but cost about $5 million. Even though X-ray storage rings offer several exposure stations, companies are still reluctant to plunge into a relatively new technology with such high initial investment. Lithographers are left to choose between low-power X-ray sources and a multilevel resist with only a thin top layer to expose, or a more powerful source and a simpler one-level resist process. An example of the high resolution attainable with X-rays is shown here along with a summary of this technology.

Pros	*Cons*
—Extremely high resolution	—High-quality masks difficult to produce
—Not dust sensitive	—Sources not powerful enough for good throughput
—Blanket exposure favors high throughput	—Alignment for sub-half-micron geometries critical

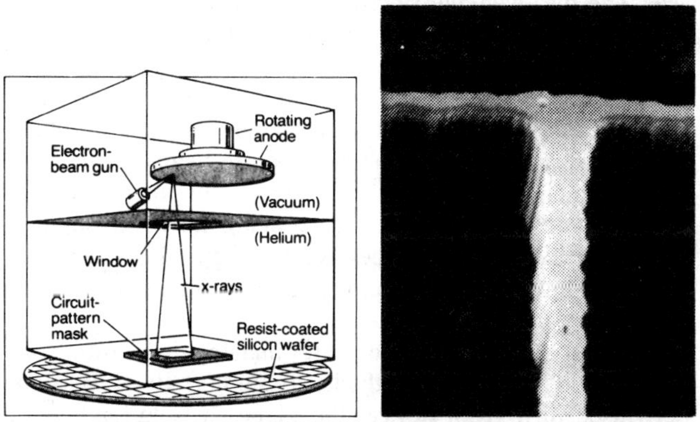

Figure 10—X-ray exposure principle and resist image

Ion Beam Exposure

Collimated beams of protons (hydrogen ions) are the basis for ion beam imaging, and resists (positive optical) have greater sensitivity to ions than they do to electrons, X-rays, or UV light. Production throughput is further enhanced by the behavior of ions, since protons do not have high-energy electrons that scatter into unwanted areas. All ion energy resides in the desired area during resist exposure. The mechanism used for ion beam lithography is shown in Figure 11.

Ion scatter in a mask material is a problem, and good masks are difficult to produce, especially when made from 0.4-μm thick, single-crystal silicon. Ion beam exposure does have very

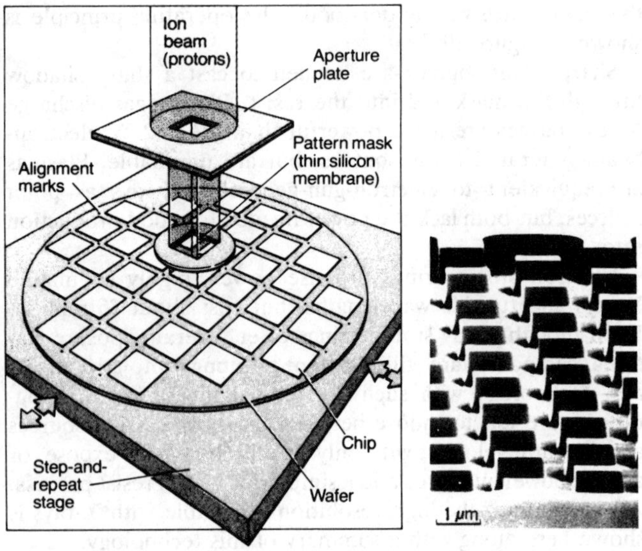

Figure 11—Ion beam exposure principle and resist image

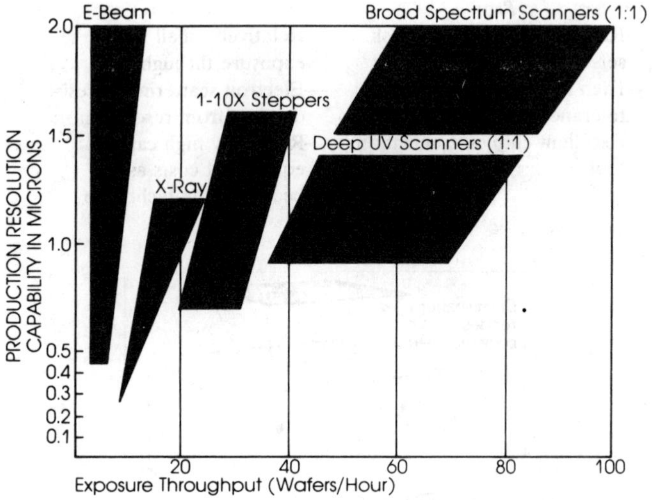

Figure 12—IC lithography strategy vs. image resolution and wafer throughput

high resolution potential, as indicated by the ion-imaged photo below. Throughput is currently pegged at 40 wafers per hour. The advantages of this lithography include the sub-micron (0.5-μm) resolution in single-level resist, that good resists are available, and the high exposure sensitivity of resists. The disadvantages include masks that are hard to produce, alignment that is semi-critical, and that commercial systems are not available.

In summary, both optical and nonoptical imaging technologies are available for submicron imaging in the near future. The higher resolution devices will require beam-writing strategies. Which one is chosen depends on equipment throughput, cost, and resolution, the winner being most efficient in all areas. The likely result of these various emerging techniques will be the integration of several imaging strategies for a single chip.

The most likely scenario for wafer imaging in the future will be a hybrid of several methods. Assuming 10–12 masking steps used in a given device, the highest resolution–central imaging method will be used for the two or three most critical mask levels. In descending order of resolution, subsequent imaging methods will be used for various mask levels. A mixture of the methods shown below is likely (Figure 12).

ETCHING

The etching process in IC fabrication involves selective removal of several different types of films. Films typically etched include silicon dioxide, silicon nitride, polysilicon, aluminum alloys, tungsten, and metal silicides. Etching is used to open windows for dopant ions, to form areas for ohmic contract, to create the interconnection patterns, or to form bonding pads.

Etching technology has moved rapidly from wet acid immersion processes to dry reactive ion removal. The driving force in this change is the need to conserve silicon area by eliminating lateral etching. Both wet and dry plasma etches act isotropically (etch equally in all directions) in films being etched. Reactive-ion etch technology is anisotropic, etching only in the vertical plane, keeping etched structures narrow and deep, as shown in Figure 13.

The advantages of reactive-ion etching (RIE) include the elimination of toxic chemicals posing waste disposal and safety problems. A typical RIE etcher schematic is shown in Figure 14.

The challenge of future etch technology is to provide very precise control of the etch process as films approach 200–300 thickness and less. Etching of a given film must be complete without attacking the underlying layer or "chewing up" or pinholing the mask, above the etched layer. The removal rate of etched films vs. films not to be etched is called the selectivity ratio. This ratio is kept high (10:1 to 20:1) by carefully blending active etch specie gasses, optimizing power levels in

Figure 13—Reactive-ion etched structure

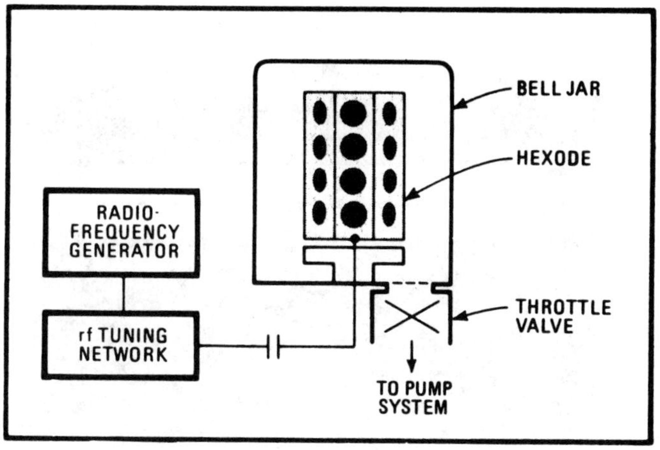

Figure 14—Reactive-ion etched schematic

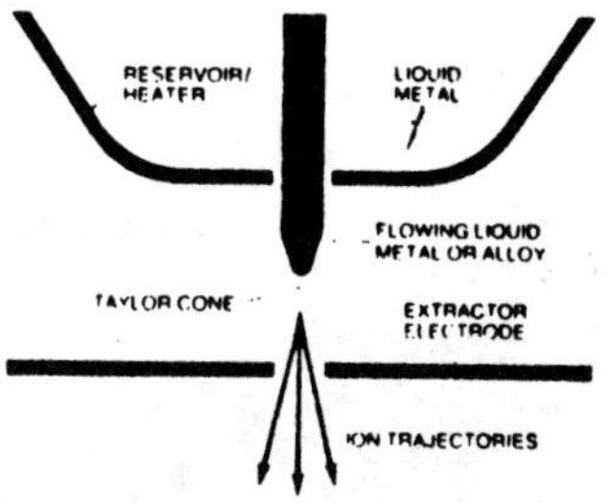

Ion source

Figure 15—Direct ion implant technique

the etcher, and treating etch masks—such as deep-UV curing of resist etch masks. laser end-point detection has been added to the etch process to prevent overetching.

DOPING

Doping is the IC fabrication step that differentiates the silicon wafer's electrical properties, giving rise to the conductive electron pathways that form the actual circuit. Doping is placing "impurity" ions of phosphorus, boron, or arsenic within the silicon crystal lattice. The higher the level of impurity ions, the greater the conductivity of the silicon. Areas of the wafer left undoped become the insulating areas of the circuit. The steps prior to doping are imaging and etching of a mask, which is usually a silicon dioxide film, to open up areas directly to the base silicon.

Traditional doping processes, where predeposition of the dopant is followed by thermal "drive-in" or diffusion, are quickly being replaced by ion implantation. The reasons for this change are the same as for the move into anisotrophic dry etching from isotropic wet etching. The lateral diffusion of ions in standard doping processes results in a consumption of silicon area that is no longer tolerable with current high-density VLSI chips. Ion implantation provides a more anisotropic dopant ion profile, keeping the concentration shallow and deep. The damage to the silicon crystal caused by smashing a highly accelerated ion into the silicon is removed by laser annealing, also a relatively low-temperature operation. Ion implantation is still a blanket process where the wafer is scanned by a stream of ions, and a resist or oxide mask delineates the dopant profile.

The future for doping processes in IC fabrication may be direct doping, where the ion implant mask steps are completely eliminated. This would greatly simplify the process by removing two steps (imaging and etching), and probably result in a yield increase. A new tool for maskless ion doping is depicted in Figure 15. Announced in 1983, the submicron probe, which uses a liquid metal source, represents a major advancement in chip fabrication capability. The computer programmed ion probe permits precise delivery of ions to coordinate with accuracies of less than 0.1 μm. A high degree of control is made possible by using digitally controlled ion optics and beam-monitoring electronics.

DEPOSITION

A primary technology in IC fabrication is the application of high-quality semiconductor films. Deposition of a wide range of materials is required, and many new metals silicides and refractory metals are now used along with conventional oxides (doped and undoped), polysilicon, silicon nitride, aluminum alloys, and even special polymeric films. Deposited layers must be extremely uniform, cover wafer topography well, and be relatively free of contaminants or defects that arise in the manufacturing process.

Deposition technology has kept pace with the other processes in IC fabrication by supplying lower temperature environments, suitable reactant gases, and high film uniformity. Advances in chemical vapor deposition (CVD) have led to plasma-enhanced CVD (PECVD), a very promising technology for low-temperature deposition of a wide variety of materials. DECVD also has a high deposition rate, but needs improvements yet in the areas of film stress and particulate level. PECVD reactors need to be designed for high throughput as well. The two reactors shown in Figure 16, one single-plate and there other multiple-plate, illustrate approaches currently used.

Film uniformity is more easily achieved in the larger but lower throughput parallel plate system, while the multiple-plate reactor may result in uneven film thickness at the edges of wafers. The factors that must be monitored to achieve good film properties include load size, process cycle time, gas depletion rates, deposition rate, system pressure and temperature, "radiation" energy flux to the substrate (determines stress); and system cleanliness. The need for lower temperatures in all aspects of IC fabrication makes PECVD attractive for future applications.

A primary concern in the area of deposition is the materials used. The material used for interconnection patterns has traditionally been aluminum alloyed with copper and silicon. Advanced deposition methods, including magnetron sputtering, have satisfied the physical requirements for thin, uniform

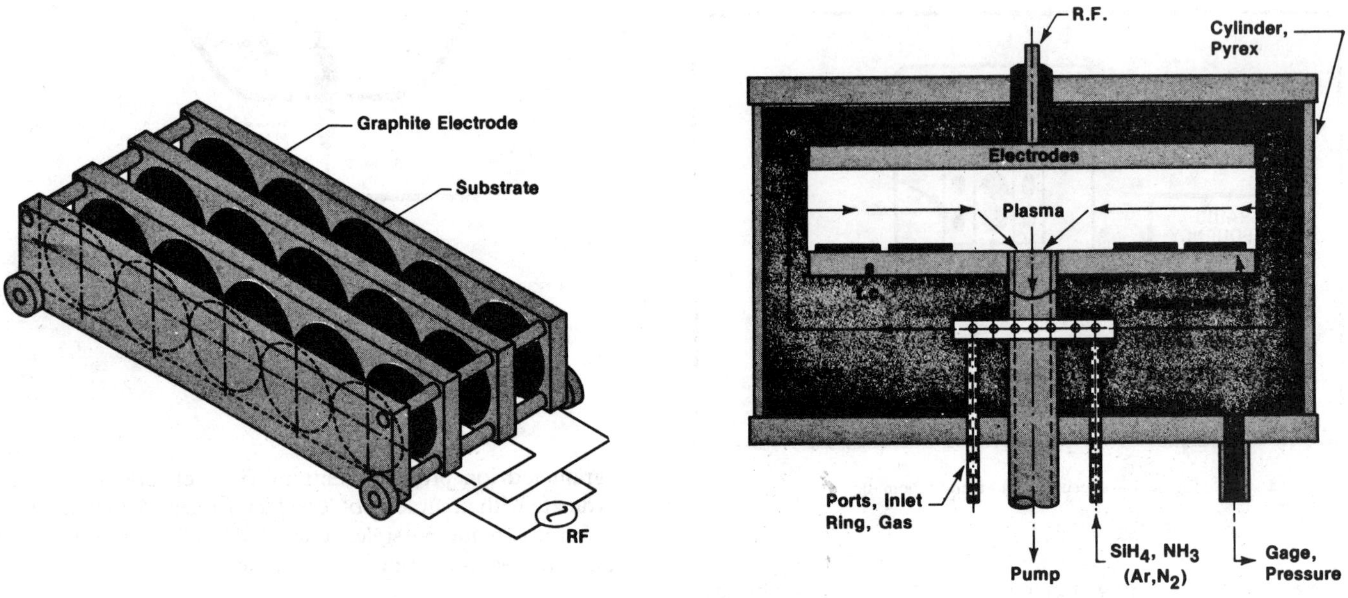

Figure 16—Two types of PECVD reactors

films. However, aluminum is subject to electromigration, has a low melting point, and interacts with silicon. Gate materials likewise suffer from limitations due to rapid advances in IC technology. Polycrystalline silicon has been the material of choice in MOS circuits, but suffers from high sheet resistance, which reduces circuit speed. At elevated temperatures, polysilicon undergoes grain growth, a factor that interferes with fine-line imaging.

The new replacements for aluminum alloys and polysilicon are refractory metals and their silicides. While electron beam evaporation, sputtering, and CVD can be used to apply these materials, PECVD is very desirable. Tungsten, molybdenum, and tungsten silicide films have been successfully applied with PECVD, as shown in Figure 17.

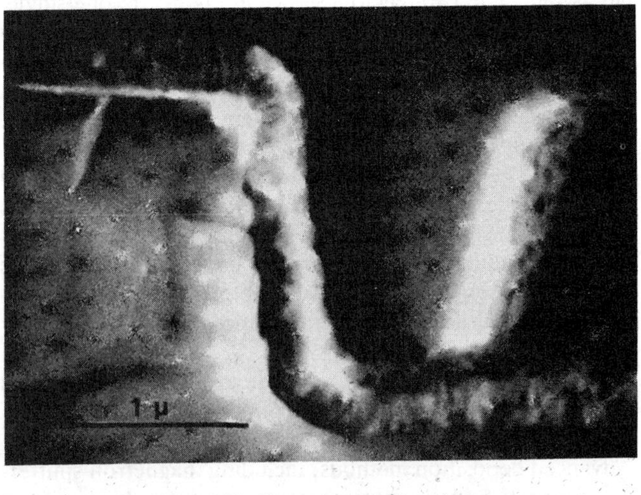

Figure 17—Step coverage of tungsten

Transition metal and metal silicide films represent the future direction for high-density and high-speed integrated circuits. Smooth, pinhole-free films of new materials deposited in high-purity environments with low stress and good step coverage are moving from the laboratory to the production line to meet future chip specifications for many applications.

IC FABRICATION PROCESS TRENDS

A comparison of the current and projected technological level of key IC process parameters is shown in Figure 18. The areas cited represent critical areas of change needed to implement the high-density chips of the future. In general, all films using IC manufacturing will need to be thinner, and produced with more exact control. All key IC dimensions that regulate IC electrical behavior are being reduced, such as gate thickness and width. All dimensional tolerances are necessarily smaller, bringing the degree of control of some dimensions to ± 0.1 μm.

The necessity for all of these changes will bring considerable pressure in equipment and material supplies alike. For example, reducing the thickness of an oxide layer from 800Å to 200Å affects several aspects of IC process technology, including deposition, imaging, etching, doping, and design. The incentive that drives all of these disciplines within IC fabrication technology is the production of chips with greater application capabilities at lower cost.

The "more-for-less" improvement has been an earmark of semiconductor technology since ICs first went into production more than 20 years ago. The continuance of this unique economic value, in a world where inflation causes a a more typical "less-for-more" relationship in products, has made IC-based

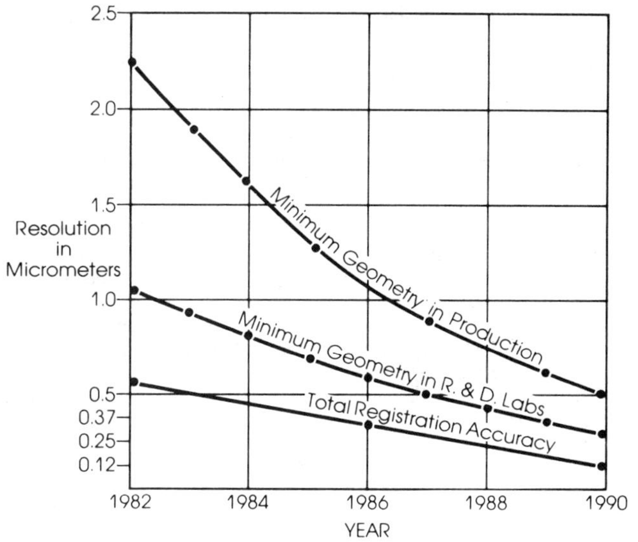

Figure 18—Pattern transfer technology trends

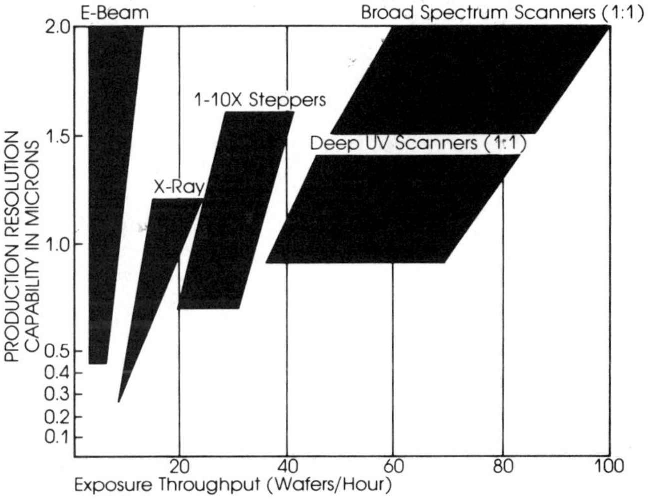

Figure 19—Lithography strategy vs. resolution vs. throughput

products pervasive. The incentive for all IC industry participants is the opening up of new, large markets.

SUMMARY

The major disciplines that make up integrated circuit fabrication technology have been examined with respect to current technology status and likely future developments to meet VLSI device trends. At the end of 1983, current technology considered mature for IC device manufacturing is summarized along with emerging and future technology. Time frames indicate technology used for the bulk of IC devices worldwide.

IC Device Fabrication: Technology Used Vs. Time

1983—Mature Technology
—Scanning projection printing
—Proximity and contact printing
—Optical resists
—E-beam masking
—Barrel plasma etching
—Diffusion doping
—Track-type wafer handling
—Wet etching
—LPCVD deposition
—Semiautomated process

1984–1987—Emerging Technology
—Mid-UV wavelength imaging
—Deep UV wavelength imaging
—Reactive ion etching
—MOCVD and PECVD deposition
—Optical stepping
—E-beam wafer writing
—Ion implantation
—Planar plasma etching
—Ion milling
—Galium arsenide crystals
—Multilevel resists and e-beam resists
—Fully automated process segments

1987–1990—Emerging Technology
—X-ray storage ring energy for imaging
—Ion beam imaging
—Laser doping and imaging
—Resist-less imaging (ion beam and laser)
—Holographic imaging
—All-dry resist developing and etching
—Novel IC structures (3-D, superlattices, etc.)
—Robotic interface with automatic equipment
—Software-controlled processing

Finally, a comparison of semiconductor device operating parameters with the human brain is made as a benchmark for technological progress. Indeed, the "silicon brain" is beginning to rival ours in certain areas of comparison. In terms of total density, however, the human brain is likely to stay ahead of silicon chips well into the 21st Century.

		Semiconductor Technology		
Area of Comparison	Human Brain	1960	1980	2000
Memory Density (bits/cm^3)	10^{16}	10^3	10^5	10^9
Computing Power (switches/second)	10^{12}	10^{12}	10^{13}	10^{15}
Speed (cycles per second)	10^2	10^6	10^8	10^{10}
Total Density (circuits/cm^2)	10^7	10	10^2	10^5

ACKNOWLEDGMENT

The author wishes to acknowledge Ms. Lynn Glusco for her work in preparing the manuscript.

SUGGESTED READINGS

1. *Integrated Circuit Microlithography—Market and Technology Report.* Woburn, Mass.: Semiconductor Information Services, Jan. (1983), pp. 5–21, 6–14.
2. *IEEE Proceedings on Electron Devices, Special Issue on Device Design,* Aug. (1983).
3. Moody, J. W., and R. A. Frederick. "Developments in Czochralski Silicon Crystal Growth." *Solid State Technology,* Aug. (1983), pp. 221–225.
4. Huff, H. R. "Chemical Impurities and Structural Imperfections in Semiconductor Silicon." *Solid State Technology,* May (1983), pp. 211–212.
5. Sony Corporation Newsletter. "High Quality Silicon Crystals with MCZ Technology. Aug. (1980), pp. 1–4.
6. Tell, W. C., and J. T. Luxon. *Integrated Circuits: Materials, Devices and Fabrication,* Englewood Cliffs, N.J.: Prentice Hall, 1982.
7. Einspruch, N. G., Ed. *VLSI Electronics Microstructure Science,* New York: Academic Pres, 1981.
8. Elliott, D. J. *Integrated Circuit Fabrication Technology.* New York: McGraw Hill, 1982.
9. *Proceedings, International Conference on Microlithography,* Sept. 26–29, 1983, Cambridge, England. (Copyright Dept. of Engineering, Cambridge University, England).
10. Special Issue on Multilayer Resist Lithography, *Semiconductor International,* June (1983).
11. Harrell, S. "X-Ray Source Technology for Microlithography," *Semiconductor International,* Sept. (1983), pp. 74–77.
12. Sain, R. J., and B. Gorowitz. "High Rate Aluminum Etching in a Batch Loaded Reactive Ion Etcher." *Solid State Technology,* April (1983), pp. 247–252.
13. Ion Beam Technologies, Beverly, Mass. Technical Data Sheet on ion implant, September, 1983
14. Johnson, W. L. "Design of Plasma Deposition Reactors. *Solid State Technology,* April (1983), pp. 191–195.
15. Tong, C. C., J. K. Chu, and D. W. Hess. "Plasma-Enhanced Deposition of Tungsten, Molybdenum, and Tungsten Silicide Films," *Solid State Technology,* (March 1983), pp. 125–128.
16. Editor, Semiconductor International. "MOCVD Technology," October, 1983, p. 34.
17. *Status 1983: A Report on the Integrated Circuit Industry,* Phoenix, Ariz.: Integrated Circuit Engineering, 1983.

IDAS—An integrated design automation system

by STEPHEN Y. H. SU
State University of New York
Binghamton, New York

ABSTRACT

Computer-aided design tools are vital to the design of VLSI (very-large-scale integration). This paper presents a new integrated design automation system for describing, documenting, simulating, and synthesizing digital systems. The system consists of a new hardware description language, LALSD II; a translator; a simulator; and a logic synthesizer. The language allows the designer to describe a digital system at various levels of detail, to define modules for implementation, and to describe the system at the behavior level, the structure level, or both. The language can accurately describe the timing for various operations. It can precisely describe multilevel, parallel operations. LALSD II can describe synchronous, asynchronous, or mixed systems.

The translator converts the language into a database for simulation and logic synthesis. It can translate each module of the system independently. This means that a designer can modify any module without retranslating other modules.

The multilevel hierarchical simulator is a six-valued, table-driven, significant event simulator with selective trace capabilities. Synchronous, asynchronous, or mixed systems and concurrent events can also be simulated. It can simulate intricate timing relations among different components.

The logic synthesizer accepts the database, the library of logic modules, the key modules, and the clock period specified by the user and produces the logic design in terms of logic modules and their interconnections.

INTRODUCTION

With the advances in very-large-scale integration (VLSI) and the increasing complexity of digital systems, computer-aided design is no longer optional; instead, it is vital for designing modern VLSI digital networks. The gap to be bridged in the design automation area is the automated logic/system design, simulation, and testing of digital systems.[1-5]

Under the direction of this author, the research work has been performed and the implementation of an integrated design automation system has been carried out by the Research Group on Design Automation and Fault-tolerant Computing at SUNY—Binghamton.

Our goal is to develop a design automation (DA) system that will reduce the design effort and make complex system design possible. It will allow the designer to experiment with various design configurations. The system should greatly reduce the time and effort required to implement, test, and refine the design. A powerful hardware description language (HDL) should be the basis of this design automation system. With it, a single hierarchical simulator will be used to check the performance and the operations of a digital system from the behavior level to the gate level. A logic synthesizer will allow systematic transformation of the behavior description into the connections of hardware modules under the user's directions. Even a functional test generator can be used to generate tests automatically from behavior description.

The DA system is shown in Figure 1. The designer uses the new language,[6,7] called Language for Automated Logic and System Design (LALSD II), to express his design. The translator checks the syntax of the language and reports errors for the designer to modify the description.[8] When the language statements are free from syntax errors, the translator produces a common database to be used by the simulator, the logic synthesizer, and the test generator. The simulator[9] verifies the design and evaluates the performance at various levels of detail. The logic synthesizer produces logic design containing two parts: the structure part and the control part (implemented in microcode).[2,7] The translator, simulator, and logic synthesizer have been implemented. Some research results on hardware description language-driven test generation have been reported by our Research Group.[10-13] The test generator, when implemented, will generate test sequences for detecting faults in hardware modules at different levels.

In the next section, the features of the new language, LALSD II, will be discussed. An example will be given to show that the same language can be used for describing the same module at various levels. The third section outlines the key features of the translator. The LALSD-driven simulator is described in the fourth section, with examples of simulation runs. In the final section, the key features of the logic synthesizer are pointed out, and computer time for translation and synthesis of several digital systems (effective address computation, blackjack machine, PDP-8, and Chu's computer) are given.

THE NEW LANGUAGE—LALSD II

For a hardware description language to cover the broad design spectrum—i.e., to achieve the purposes of describing, simulating, synthesizing, and testing digital systems—it should contain the following features:

1. Hierarchical structure with user-definable modules. The hierarchical structure permits the functional decomposition of large systems. It allows the descriptions of subsystems at various levels. Breaking up the description into subsystems can also make the design easier. A hierarchical system allows either top-down or bottom-up design procedure, which will provide smooth transitions from one level to another. The modular construct is the basis for the hierarchical structure. The modules will bear a close resemblance to the actual hardware components. The interaction between a module and the out-

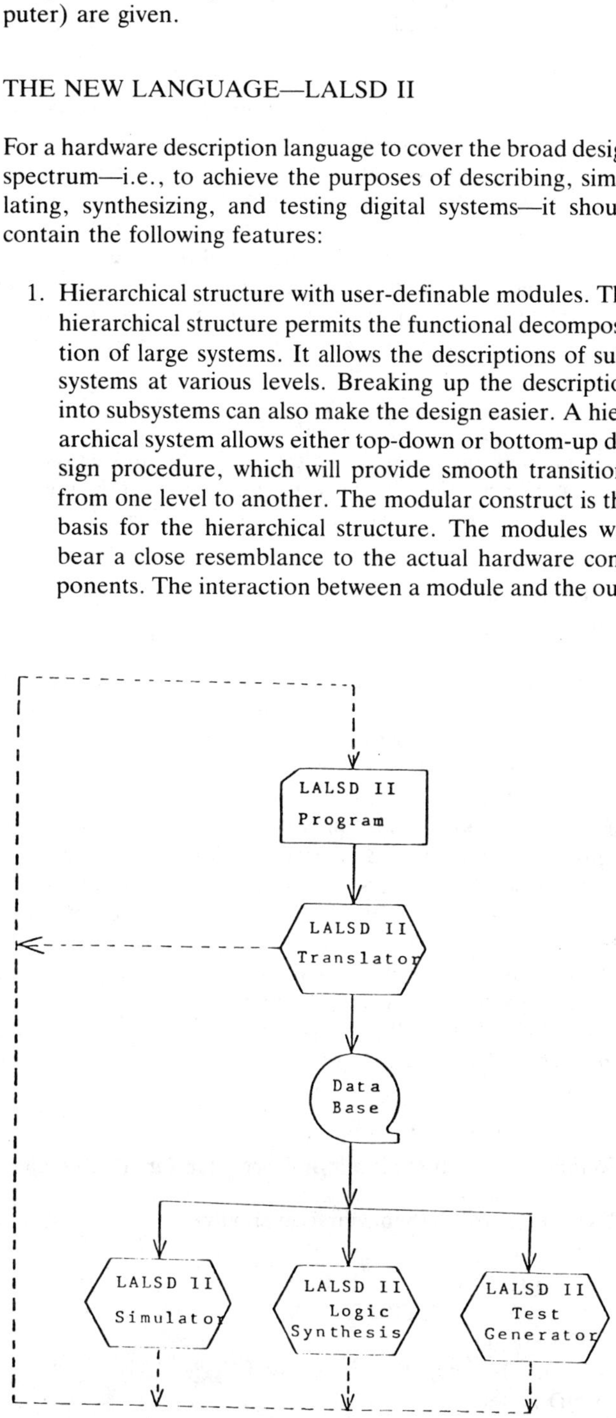

Figure 1—LALSD-II-driven design automation system

side should go through its input/output ports, and the design language should allow the user to define his/her own modules.
2. Multilevel description. The design of digital systems is usually an iterative process. In the early stage of the design process, emphasis is placed on the behavior of the system. More and more structural implementations are added to the design until the final implementation, composed of hardware primitives only. Besides that, in design or simulation, only a part of the system is under close investigation at one time. The language should allow the detailed description of this part and high-level descriptions of the others. This will substantially reduce both design effort and simulation time.
3. Behavior-level control description. The language should provide the capability of specifying the system's behavior in a concise, systematic, structured, readable form. No implementation detail should be required for the high-level description.
4. Detail-level accurate timing facility. The language should provide the facility of accurately describing the digital system operations without requiring gate-level implementation. In the lower level, not only the operations but also the timing of a module must be defined. The race, hazard, etc., should be detected by simulating the description of a digital system.
5. Parallel operation description. In hardware systems many activities occur concurrently. Hence the language should provide a simple way of describing parallelism.

The new language, LALSD II, possesses all five of these features.[6,7]

The following example shows the flexibility of LALSD II in describing the same system at the behavior or structure level or a mixture of both. First, only behavior description is given. Second, only the structure is given to describe it as a connection of 8 full-adders with ripple carries. It is assumed that a UNIT-TYPE called full-adder has been defined. The statement "USE add (0..7): full-adder;" instantiates (activates) eight 1-bit full adders. In the last part, it is described as composed of two 4-bit adders, with the behavior specified in the last CONTROL part. The WAIT procedure is required before the reading of the bit 4-add's output. Note that the UNIT adder contains a subunit which is a 4-bit adder that can further be decomposed into four subunits; each is a one-bit full-adder. Note that in all examples, capital characters are used for system keywords. Lowercase words are user-defined entities.

Example 1. The three levels of description for an 8-bit adder

Description No. 1: behavioral level only

```
UNIT adder;
    b(0..7), c(0..7): INPUT;
    a(0..8): OUTPUT;
CONTROL
    a: = b + c;
END adder;
```

Description No. 2: structural level only

```
UNIT adder;
    b(0..7), c(0..7): INPUT;
    a(0..8): OUTPUT
STRUCTURE
    USE add (0..7): full-adder;
        CONNECTION
            add (*).in1 = b(*); add (*).in2 = c(*);
            FOR i:0 to 6 DO add(i).cin =
              add(i + 1).cout;
            add(7).cin = 0; a(*) = add(0).cout
              @ add(*).out;
END adder;
```

Description No. 3: mixed-level description

```
UNIT adder;
    b(0..7), c(0..7): INPUT;
    a(0..8): OUTPUT;
STRUCTURE
    USE add4(0..1): bit4-add;
    CONNECTION add4(0).cin = add4(1).cout;
                   add4(1).cin = 0;
    UNIT-TYPE bit4-add;
        in1(0..3), in2(0..3), cin: INPUT;
        out(0..3),cout: OUTPUT;
    CONTROL
        add4(0).in1 @ add4(1).in1: = b;
        add4(0).in2 @ add4(1).in2: = c;
        wait (20);
        a:=add4(0).cout @ add4(0).out @ add4(1).out;
END adder;
```

Examples describing the timing facility of LALSD II and an LALSD II description of the PDP-8 computer can be found in References 6 and 7. Readers are encouraged to read these references for detail. The syntax and lexicon of LALSD II are available from the author.

TRANSLATOR

The block diagram for the LALSD II translator is given in Figure 2. The translator consists of three components: lexical analyzer, parser, and semantic routines. The lexical analyzer takes the text program as input and separates it into proper tokens. A source listing is provided during the process. A proper token can be a keyword, an operator, or a delimiter. If an improper token is found, an error message is generated, and the lexical analyzer neglects this token and goes on to find the next one.

The parser calls the lexical analyzer to get the next token of the input text. It also drives the translation process to accept the proper syntax and perform the corresponding semantic actions. The translator uses a syntax-directed translation scheme. The syntax of LALSD II is defined in nonambiguous, context-free productions. These productions are fed into a parser generator to produce a lookahead left-to-right (LALR) parsing table. The parsing process starts at the initial state. If the lexical analyzer provides a token that the parser does not

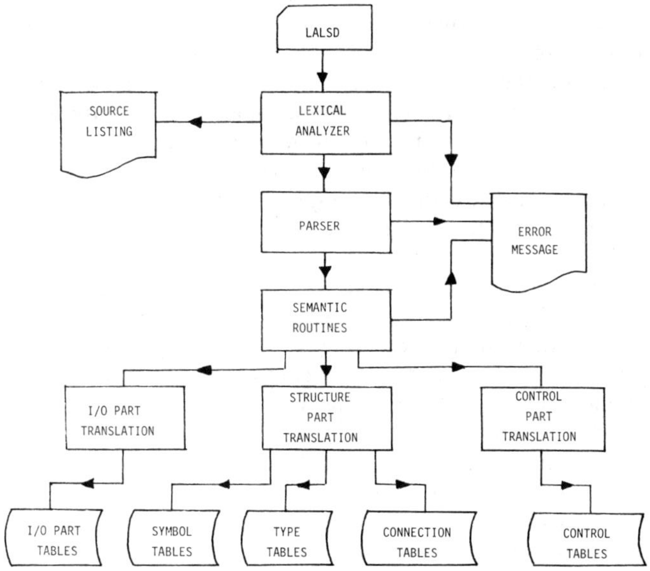

Figure 2—Block diagram for translator

expect to see, the parser is in an error state. An error message is then issued.

The semantic routines are for the sole purpose of generating all tables as a database output of the input digital system description. The language hierarchy of LALSD II is a block-oriented language. There are four types of blocks: UNIT, UNIT-TYPE, FUNCTION, and PROCEDURE. Each block corresponds to a module table, and the table contains pointers to all other tables necessary for describing the information of a block. Within each block there are three sections: INPUT/OUTPUT (I/O) PART, STRUCTURE PART, and CONTROL PART. However, not all these sections are mandatory; it depends on the level of description desired. For example, a digital system described in functional level will probably disregard the interconnections as well as detail timings.

The I/O part translation will produce the I/O part table through which we can obtain the number and the type of I/O pins (input, output, tristate, bidirection, open collector) of a module. The structure part translation will produce tables conveying all structural information. All physical components (corresponding to a symbol in the language description) are stored in the symbol table. All physical boundaries and attributes are stored in the type table. The interconnection between modules is shown by the connection table and the I/O identification table together. Finally, the control part of the translation records all behavior descriptions of a module in the control table and the condition table of the database.

SIMULATOR

The LALSD-II-driven simulator uses the database produced by the translator. It is a six-valued, significant event simulator with selective trace capabilities. The six values are 0, 1, Positive edge P, Negative edge N, Unknown U, and High-impedance Z. Inclusion of P and N is to represent signal rise

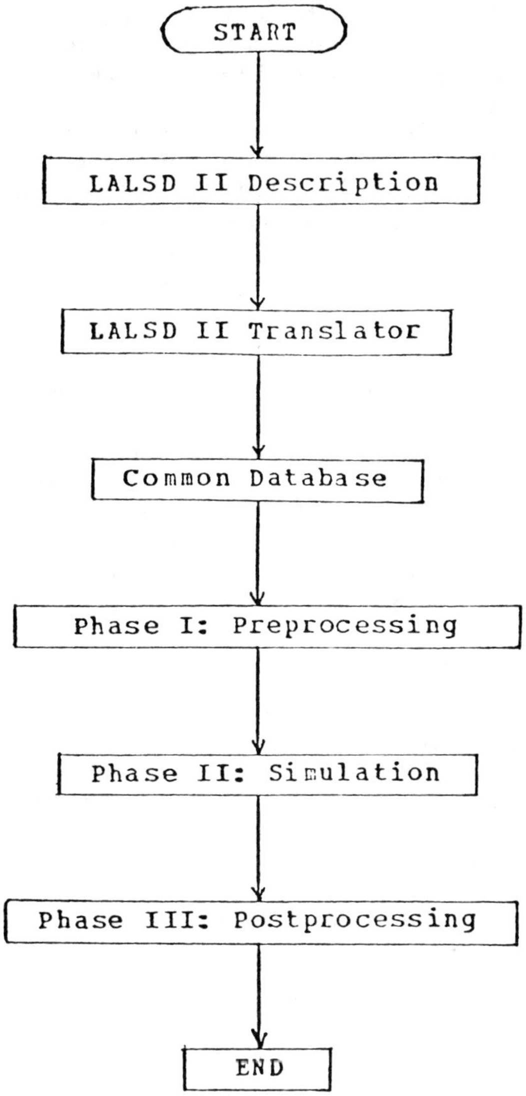

Figure 3—Overall structure of LALSD-II-driven simulator

(transition from 0 to 1) and fall (transition from 1 to 0). In initializing the system, certain signal values are not known; they are represented by U. Any signal at the high-impedance state is represented by the Z value. The choice of significant event and selective trace is for reducing simulation execution time. This is done by simulating only units whose input(s) have changed. Furthermore, if after the change of an element's input(s) its output does not change, then the fanout of that element is not simulated. The simulator can simulate a digital system at various levels. It can simulate synchronous, asynchronous, or mixed systems as well as concurrent events. The LALSD II simulator is capable of simulating intricate timing relations among different components of a system.

The simulator has been implemented in PL/I for ITEL AS/6 (similar to IBM 370/158). Several examples, such as the PDP-8 computer, blackjack machines, Chu's computer, and Su and DuCasse's reconfiguration fault-tolerant system, have been run by the simulator to show its salient features. The entire simulator consists of 71 subroutines. The source code contains approximately 10,000 lines. The simulator consists of three phases, as shown in Figure 3.

Phase 1: Preprocessing Phase—In this phase, all necessary processing of the common database is done to prepare it for the simulation phase. This includes database inputting, event queue creation, space allocation and initiation, and the processing of simulation command language such as RUN, INIT (for initialization), DISPLAY, TRACE, ACTIVATE, and END.

Phase 2: Simulation Phase—In this phase, the simulation of the behavior of the system takes place. This includes unit activation, the processing of connection and control parts, and expression evaluation.

Phase 3: Postprocessing Phase—In this phase, the HISTORY file generated during the simulation phase will be processed to print the desired value of I/O parts or variables of the system under simulation. The HISTORY file contains all the changes to the I/O parts and variables of the system and the corresponding time of their changes.

The overall flow of the simulation process is given in Figure 4, starting from the top block. The common database, generated by the LALSD II translator from the LALSD II description of the digital system, is one of the simulator's input files. The other input file is the user-specified simulation command file, shown on the left side of Figure 4. The function of the main routine is to control the entire operation of the simulator. All other blocks in the next level are subservient to this main program. Each routine at each level invokes one or more of the next level subroutines to carry out appropriate processing. The preprocessing routine's task is to allocate space

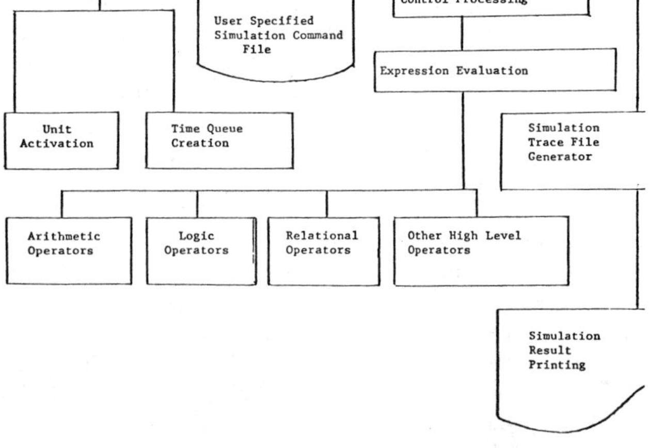

Figure 4—Overall flow of the simulation process

for all the data structures in the database, transform the common database to a form more readily usable by the next phase of the simulator, and initialize all the required variables into either unknown or user-specified values. The preprocessing program invokes the time queue creation and unit activation.

The time queue creation is responsible for setting up the required data structures to implement the event queue and event scheduling mechanism. The unit activation activates either all units in the system—in the absence of a user-specified activate command—or only units specified by the designer in the activate command.

The main program calls upon the control-processing routine. This routine serves as the control statement recognizer. It indentifies the type of the control statement, and, depending on this recognition, takes the appropriate action to implement that control statement properly. The control processing routine in turn, in cases where it is required to evaluate an expression or a conditional statement, calls upon the expression evaluation program. This evaluation program, depending on the type of the expression to be evaluated, either evaluates the final value of the expression or returns a TRUE or FALSE value for the condition to be tested. This routine also returns a delay value equal either to zero or to the amount of delay associated with the expression to be evaluated. The expression evaluation routine in turn calls upon one of its subordinate routines, shown in Figure 4. The operation of each block in this level is self-explanatory, except the last one, which contains subroutines for implementing all the primitive operations in the LALSD II not included in the other categories. For the list of these operations the reader may see Reference 9.

The final block in the second level is the simulation trace file generator, which produces the trace of all the changes during simulation. This file includes all the changes in the system variables with the corresponding time for the changes. It can be processed either off line to print it in different formats, or by the simulation result printing routine to print the designer-specified variables' states for the entire simulation run.

Table I shows the results of simulation runs for six examples: Adder, Address Generation, Multiplier, Chu's computer,[14] Su and DuCasse's reconfiguration scheme for fault-tolerance,[15] and the PDP-8 computer.

LOGIC SYNTHESIZER

Although almost all manufacturers have a design automation system for the physical design, very few have included an automated logic design system. This system will expedite the design process, shorten design time, and reduce design cost. The system should allow the designer to experiment with various design configurations as easily as possible. The system should also greatly reduce the time and effort required to implement, test, and refine the design.

With the user-specified key components, the library of other components, and the period for clock, the logic synthesizer transforms the common database produced by the translator into the integrated circuit chips and their interconnections instead of producing a logic diagram in terms of gates and flip-flops and going through the tedious process of partitioning and assignment.

The essential features of our logic synthesis approach are given below:

1. Modular primitive binding. The synthesis output is given in terms of the integrated circuit chips (functional primitives, such as registers, adders, multiplexers, etc.) and their interconnections. It is more suitable for contemporary hardware design than gate-level implementations. Since the synthesizer output is of the same format as the original program, it can be directly used as simulation input.
2. Inherent parallelism exploitation. Since LALSD II description does not require operations to be specified clock cycle by clock cycle, the synthesizer tries to arrange operations to be executed as fast as possible under the given configuration. In this instance, a hardware module may be shared by several operations at different times.
3. User-directed configuration. Unlike some HDLs, which require the data part to be specified exactly, the synthesizer needs only user's directions on key components. By changing key component specification, the user can try several different configurations to pursue the optimum design.
4. Iterative design procedure. The output of the synthesizer is compatible with the LALSD II program. Hence, the user can even change part of the output, then rerun the synthesizer to get results.
5. Behavior-level redundancy elimination. One drawback of a high-level language is that many redundancies exist in the description, though they may not be needed in the actual implementation. These kinds of redundancies are eliminated by the synthesizer.

Several examples have been run using the logic synthesizer to produce the implementation in terms of ICs and interconnections. Four of them will be included here: the address translation, the blackjack machine, the PDP-8 computer, and Chu's computer.[5] A brief summary of computer runs is given in Table II.

By changing the key components, two designs for the address translation and three implementations of the blackjack machines are generated by the computer, using the logic synthesizer program. The third column shows the CPU time in terms of the number of seconds for translating the LALSD II description. The next column gives the time for logic synthesis. Note that it only took a little over two and one-half minutes of CPU time on the ITEL AS-6 computer to design (translation and synthesis) the PDP-8 automatically. The last column gives the number of clock cycles needed in the controller for activating the structure part of each implementation. The above results for this logic design automation are very encouraging.

TABLE I—Statistics of simulator example runs

Example No.	Name of Circuit	No. of Stmts. in LALSD II Description	Simulation Time (Secs)	Virtual Storage
1	ADDER	61	9.17	760K
2	ADDGEN	24	6.73	710K
	ADDGEN	24	6.82	710K
3	MULTIPLY	29	7.83	708K
4	CHUCOMP	65	10.72	710K
5	NMR	106	12.84	730K
6	PDP-8	143	19.50	712K

CONCLUSION

This paper has introduced the various parts of this integrated logic design automation system—the new design language, logic synthesis, and simulation. This system will greatly reduce design effort and make complex system design possible. Furthermore, new research problems can be solved by using the system as the basis.

Using LALSD II, a user can describe the function of the system to be designed in a systematic way. In the beginning, the description is procedure-oriented, with no explicit timing relations. The LALSD II simulator can be invoked to check its operation. When the description is correct, the logic synthesizer is applied to transform the sequential procedural description into parallel nonprocedural modular interconnections. By changing variables such as technology to be used and quantity and types of key modules used, the user may try tens or hundreds of different design configurations. This greatly aids the user in finding a very good, if not an optimum, design configuration. The same simulator can be invoked again, this time to check the detailed timing relations. After the user is satisfied with the design configuration, he/she may choose the actual integrated circuits for each module used by the synthesizer. Then the logic design is completed.

Even with our prototype logic synthesizer, the reduction of design time is very promising. The user usually spends an hour to describe a digital system, such as the PDP-8 computer. The synthesizer needs only 89 seconds to generate an implementation consisting of the interconnections of modules and the control signal chart. If the user is not satisfied with the designed configuration, he/she can try again by specifying different key modules. Usually three or four runs can generate a satisfactory design configuration.

TABLE II—Summary of computer runs

Computer Run	No. of Source Statements	Trans. Time	Synth. Time	No. of Clock Cycles
ADDGEN1	22	7	4	2
ADDGEN2	22	7	5	5
BLACK1	52	13	13	18
BLACK2	52	13	13	17
BLACK3	52	13	13	16
PDP-8	140	68	89	87
Chu's Computer	50	27	33	35

Of course more work needs to be done on this approach in order to facilitate really automated design. An automated module selector for choosing the actual integrated circuits will be very useful. Some criteria need to be established to help the user to choose key modules. Alternatively, these criteria can be combined with the logic synthesizer to generate a near-optimum design without the user's directions.

One problem for future research is to establish some criteria for the automatic logic synthesis. Instead of using components selected by the user, algorithms may be investigated to pursue the optimum design under the established criteria. Another problem is the design for testability. Extra components and test points may be incorporated to enchance testability. The third problem deals with the combination of logic design and physical design—i.e., instead of partition, placement, and routing being performed at the final gate level, they may be applied at the hardware modular level. We speculate that in the future the difference between hardware and software will become smaller and smaller, and a digital system may be designed using one algorithmic language. When the actual implementation is performed, cost, performance, and reliability will be taken into consideration so that part of a digital system is implemented in hardware and the others in software.

ACKNOWLEDGMENTS

The author expresses his sincere appreciation to Dr. Chi-Lai Huang for revising the original LALSD[16] and implementing the logic synthesizer, to Patrick Y. K. Fu for implementing the translator, and to Dr. Bahram Amini for implementing the simulator.

REFERENCES

1. Huang, Chi-Lai, and S.Y.H. Su. "Approaches for Computer-Aided Logic/System Design Using Hardware Description Language." *Proceedings of International Computer Symposium 1980,* Taipei, Taiwan, December 1980, pp. 772–790.
2. Huang, C.L., and S.Y.H. Su. "Logic Design Automation Based on LALSD II (Language for Automated Logic and System Design)." *Proceedings of the Sixth International Symposium on Computer Hardware Description Languages and Their Applications,* Pittsburgh, May 23–25, 1983. Amsterdam: North-Holland, 1983, pp. 165–178.
3. Su, S.Y.H., and T. Lin. "Functional Testing Techniques of Digital LSI/VLSI Systems." *Proceedings of the 21st Design Automation Workshop.* New York: IEEE and ACM, 1984.
4. Zimmerman, G. "The Minola Design System: A Computer-Aided Digital Processor Design Method." *Proceedings of 16th Design Automation Conference.* New York: IEEE and ACM, 1979, pp. 53–58.
5. Siewiorek, D. P., and M. R. Barbacci. "The CMU RT-CAD System—An Innovative Approach to Computer-Aided Design." *AFIPS, Proceedings of the National Computer Conference* (Vol. 45), 1976.
6. Su, S.Y.H., C.L. Huang, and P.Y.K. Fu. "A New Multi-Level Hardware Design Language (LALSD II) and Translator." *Proceedings of 5th International Symposium on Computer Hardware Description Languages and Their Applications,* Kaiserlautern, W. Germany, Sept. 8–9, 1981. Amsterdam: North-Holland, pp. 155–169.
7. Huang, Chi-Lai. *Computer-Aided Logic Synthesis Based on a New Multi-Level Hardware Design Language—LALSD II.* Ph.D. dissertation, Computer Science Department, State University of New York—Binghamton, 1981.
8. Su, S.Y.H., and P.Y.K. Fu. "*LALSD II Translator.*" Technical Report, Research Group in Design Automation and Fault-tolerant Computing, State University of New York—Binghamton, December 1981.
9. Amini, B. "*LALSD II Simulator.*" Ph.D. thesis, Computer Science Department, State University of New York—Binghamton, 1984.
10. Su, S.Y.H., and Y. I. Hsieh. "Testing Functional Faults in Digital Systems Described by Register Transfer Languages." *Digest of Papers, 1981 Test Conference,* pp. 447–457. Also *J. of Digital Systems,* Summer/Fall, 1982.
11. Min, Y., and S.Y.H. Su, "Functional Testing of VLSI." *Proceedings of the 19th Design Automation Conference,* pp. 384–392, 1982.
12. Shen, L., and S.Y.H. Su. "VLSI Functional Test Generation Using Critical Path Traces at a Hardware Description Language Level." Paper presented at the IEEE VLSI Test Workshop, Atlantic City, N.J. March 21–22, 1984.
13. Shen, L., and S.Y.H. Su. "A Functional Testing Method for Microprocessors." *Proceedings of 14th International Symposium on Fault-tolerant Computing,* June 1984.
14. Chu, Y. *Digital Computer Design Fundamentals.* New York: McGraw-Hill, 1962, Chapter 11.
15. Su, S.Y.H., and E. DuCasse. "A Hardware Redundancy Reconfiguration Scheme for Tolerating Multiple Module Failures." *IEEE Transactions on Computers,* C-29, (1980), pp. 254–258.
16. Su, S.Y.H., and M.B. Baray. "LALSD—A Language for Automated Logic and System Design." *Proceedings of the International Computer Symposium,* Vol. 1, Taipei, Taiwan, August 1975, pp. 31–42.

A versatile VLSI fast Fourier transform processor

by KUANG-CHENG TING and CHUAN-LIN WU
University of Texas at Austin
Austin, Texas

ABSTRACT

A versatile special-purpose VLSI fast Fourier transform (FFT) processor is presented. It can process variant data sizes of FFT and cooperate with other identical FFT processors to accomplish cascade and parallel FFT processing schemes. The operations of the single processor FFT processing scheme, the multiprocessor cascade FFT processing scheme, and the multiprocessor parallel FFT processing scheme are described. The results of performance analysis show that the combination of adaptive architecture capability and VLSI technology can provide a practical solution for meeting the goal of advanced real-time FFT processing.

INTRODUCTION

The fast Fourier transform (FFT) algorithm[2] is one of the most widely used tools in digital signal processing systems. A large body of knowledge has been generated on the subject of the FFT algorithm, and its parallelism has been studied extensively.[3,4,5,6,7,8] Recently, the VLSI FFT computational networks were proposed[9,10,11] for constructing the special-purpose FFT processor. However, these studies of VLSI FFT computational networks do not consider the flexibility of processing different data sizes. The VLSI technology is constrained by the chip density, packaging area, and pins number. These constraints also cause the problem of I/O bound and computation bound. If one processes a user's FFT task in a special-purpose hardware FFT processor, the I/O operations of the source and result data may easily impose the performance limitation. In addition, for the distributed processing system, the distrubuted source data might be stored in a computer unit with several I/O ports or be arranged (or mapped) in multiple-port memories. Processing a user's FFT task with the arrangement of source data and available resources can improve the resource utilization and can prevent the performance limitation imposed by the I/O operations.

This paper presents a versatile VLSI FFT processor for the Star local network,[1] which not only can process variant data sizes of FFT but also can cooperate with other identical FFT processors to accomplish the cascade and parallel FFT processing schemes. Star is a local computer network designed to integrate image database management and image analysis into a system. It consists of a reconfigurable communication subnet (Starnet), heterogeneous resource units, and distributed-control software entities. The fault-tolerant, reconfigurable communication subnet interconnects multiple host computers, special VLSI units, and various memory units for real-time management of the image. Figure 1 is the block diagram of the Star communication subnet. The system components are attached to the interface unit,[1] which in turn connects to multiple ports of the interconnection network. The communication path is established via the destination tag-routing technique, and a path establishment is less than one microsecond. Star is flexible and can be configured into various topology to provide better peformance level than other rigid special architecture.

In Section 2, the various parts of the versatile VLSI FFT processor are described. A detailed description of the processing user's FFT task on Star is given in Section 3. The operations of the single processor FFT processing scheme, the multiprocessor cascade FFT processing scheme, and the multiprocessor parallel FFT processing scheme are discussed separately. The performance analysis is done in Section 4. Section 5 is the conclusion.

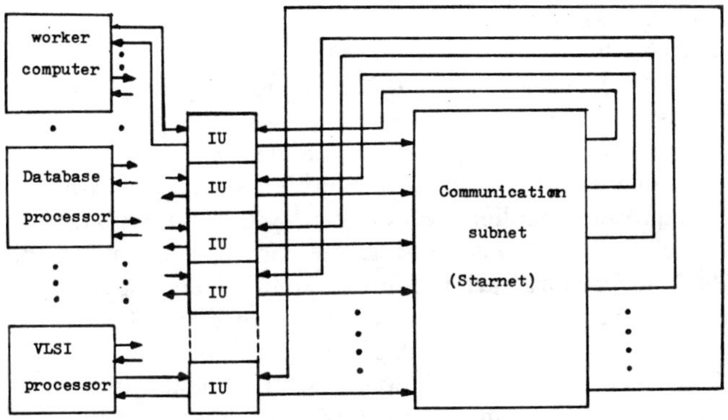

Figure 1—The block diagram of the Star communication subnet.

A VERSATILE VLSI FFT PROCESSOR

Figure 2 is the block diagram of a versatile VLSI FFT processor. The processor communicates with other processors and data units through four interface units (IUs), denoted as IU_{00}, IU_{01}, IU_{10}, and IU_{11}, that connect to the Starnet. The processor control unit (PCU) accepts the FFT task description from the user (or other processor) and decides the sequence of actions to be taken; it coordinates and controls the activities of the whole processor. The MCSW switches between the memory bank unit and the computation unit (CU) serve the function of switching the input and output ports of the CU with two memory bank units MB_0 and MB_1. Such config-

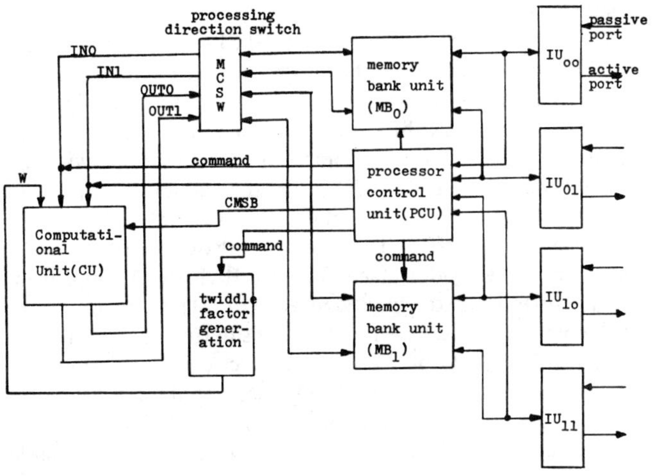

Figure 2—The block diagram of a versatile VLSI FFT processor

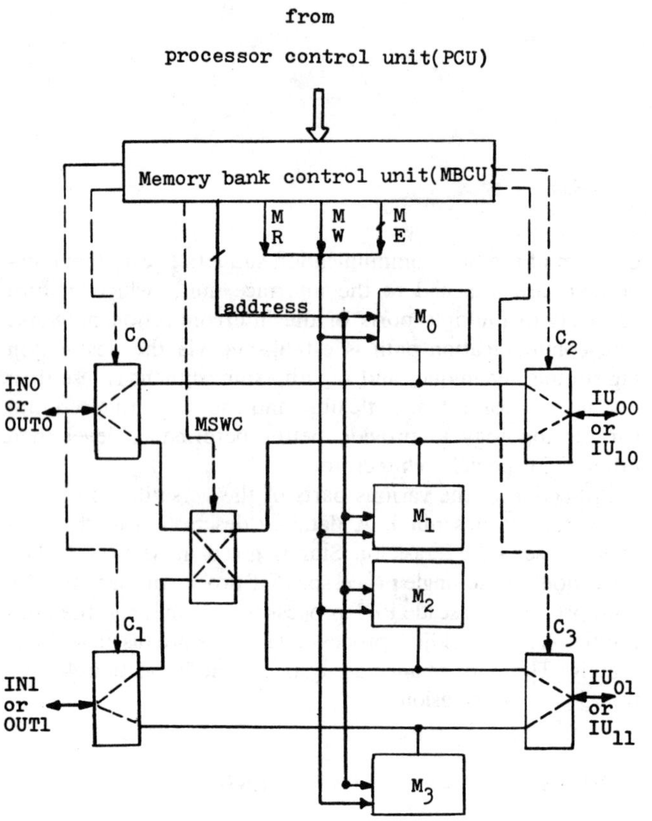

Figure 3—The circuit diagram of memory bank unit

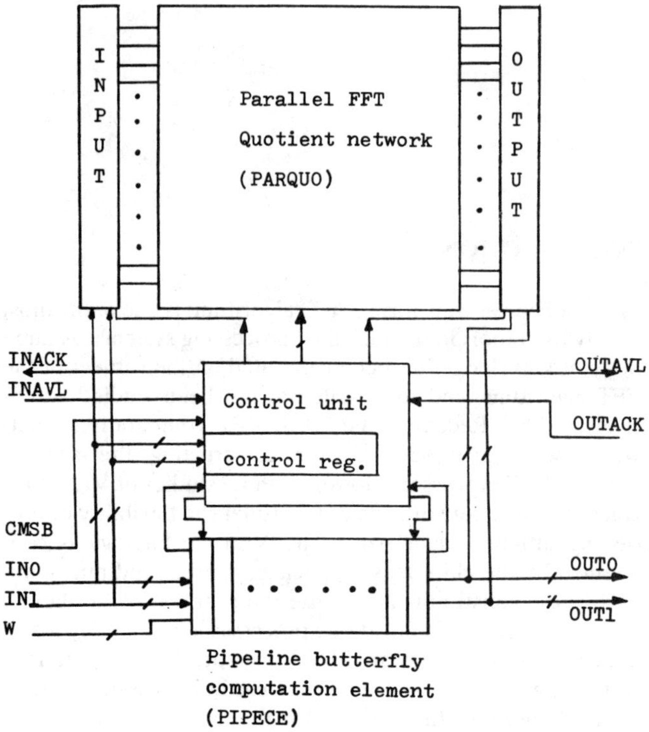

Figure 4—The block diagram of a VLSI FFT circuit

uration and bidirectional IUs eliminate the restriction of fixed I/O ports and allow the FFT processor to act as a bidirectional FFT processing processor. The memory bank control unit (MBCU) generates the memory address sequences and controls the read/write operation of four data storages M_{0-3} in the memory bank unit. The switch control signals MSWC and C_{0-3} set up the paths among data storages, IUs, and CU. The memory enable (ME), memory read (MR), and memory write (MW) signals control the operation of individual data storage. The circuit diagram of one of the memory bank units, is shown in Figure 3.

The computation unit is an FFT VLSI chip that contains a pipeline butterfly computation element (PIPECE) and a parallel FFT quotient network (PARQUO) as shown in Figure 4. The PIPECE offers the capabilities of a fast butterfly computation rate and the overlapping of I/O operations with the computation. The PARQUO offers the capability of parallel processing the FFT within certain data size ranges. The twiddle factors of the PIPECE come from the outside of the VLSI chip, while the twiddle factors of the PARQUO come from the presorted Read Only Memory (ROM) associated with each computation element (CE). Considering the pins limitation, the I/O ports of the VLSI FFT circuit are denoted as IN0, IN1, OUT0, and OUT1. The hand-shaking mechanism of the VLSI FFT circuit with the external world is done by the control unit with four hand-shaking signals: input available (INAVL), input acknowledge (INACK), OUTPUT available (OUTAVL), and output acknowledge (OUTACK). The control unit performs the function of accepting the operation command from the external world, coordinating the data input/output operations, and controlling the operations of CEs. The external world issue command to the control unit by activating the Command Strob (CMSB) signal and putting the command work into the IN0 and/or IN1 ports. The command word contains parameters to specify the active PIPECE or the active PARQUO operation mode.

The construction of the PIPECE is straightforward. With three pipeline real adders, three pipeline real subtracters, four pipeline real multipliers, and delays, one can form a pipeline butterfly computation element as shown in Figure 5. Considering the PIPECE as L concatenated computation stations, each station performs a portion of the butterfly computation. For computation station i, $1 < i < L$, it can accept data from station $i - 1$ only if its intermediate result was accepted by station $i + 1$. Therefore, the last computation station accepts data from its previous station only after the external world has received its output. The hand-shaking mechanism can be incorporated between computation stations and implemented by means of simple hand-shaking protocol.[12,13]

The transformation from the complete parallel FFT computational network such as the Shuffle-Exchange network[4] to the equivalent quotient network can be found in Fishburn and Finkel's paper.[14] Figure 6 is the circuit diagram of the PARQUO. Since each CE in the quotient network emulates the actions for several CEs in the large network, buffers are required to hold data, and this is accomplished by two parallel double queues (DEQs) denoted as DEQ0 and DEQ1. Two DEQs share two common pointers and an INQUE signal that controls one of the DEQs in accessing data from the IN0 or

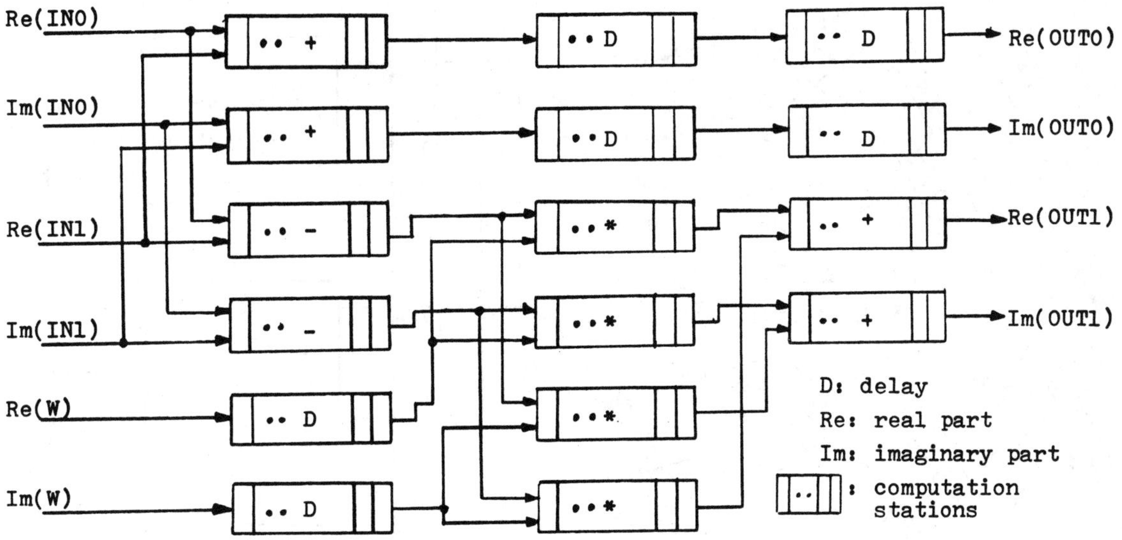

Figure 5—A pipeline butterfly computation element

IN1 port. Assume that the PARQUO is designed with 2^a CEs, which are addressed as $C_{a-1} \ldots C_0$, and its maximum processing capability is 2^q-point FFT, where $a < q$. The input sequence of source data A(k), where $k = 0$ to $2^b - 1$ and $a < b \leq q$, is defined as

$$IN0 := A(0i_{b-2} \ldots i_0);$$
$$IN1 := A(1i_{b-2} \ldots i_0); \quad i_{b-2} \ldots i_0 = 0 \text{ to } 2^{b-1} - 1.$$

The control unit enables the $CE(0C_{a-2} \ldots C_0)$ and $CE(1C_{a-2} \ldots C_0)$ to access 2^{b-a} data points from the IN0 and IN1 ports, respectively, by activating the INQUE signal and the CE addressing signals. After completing the external data input operation, each $CE(C_{a-1} \ldots C_0)$ holds the source data $A(C_{a-1} \ldots C_0 0 i_{b-a-1} \ldots i_0)$ in DEQO and $A(C_{a-1} \ldots C_0 1 i_{b-a-1} \ldots i_0)$ in DEQ1. The control unit starts activating all CEs to process the FFT. At the end of FFT computation, each $CE(C_{a-1} \ldots C_0)$ holds the final Fourier coefficients $X(0 i_1 \ldots i_{b-a-1} C_0 \ldots C_{a-1})$ in DEQ0 and $X(1 i_1 \ldots i_{b-a-1} C_0 \ldots C_{a-1})$ in DEQ1 according to the bit-reversal output order of the DIF isogeometry algorithm with perfect shuffle permutation. The output operation is then accomplished by sequentially accessing 2^{b-a-1} pairs of data from the DEQs of each CE, and it is expressed as

$$X(0i_1 \ldots i_{b-1}) := OUT0;$$
$$X(1i_1 \ldots i_{b-1}) := OUT1; \quad i_1 \ldots i_{b-1} = 0 \text{ to } 2^{b-1} - 1.$$

The PARQUO accepts the next group of data only if its DEQs are empty. This nonpipeline restriction simplifies the design of the control unit, but a price is paid for increasing the processing time.

PROCESSING THE FFT WITH VERSATILE VLSI FFT PROCESSORS

From a careful observation of Gentleman and Sande Decimation-In-Frequency (DIF) FFT algorithm[15] as shown in

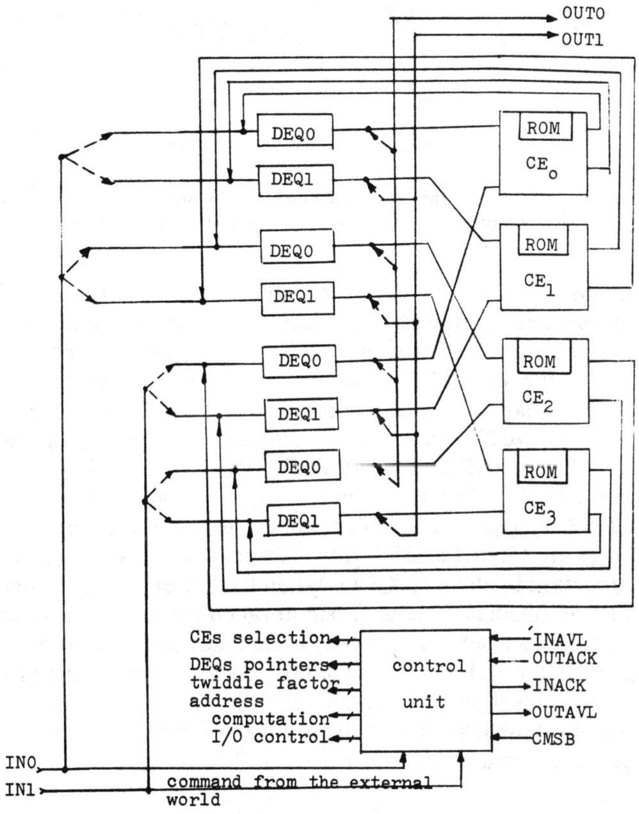

Figure 6—The circuit diagram of the parallel FFT quotient network (PARQUO) with four computation elements

Figure 7, one can see that a 2^m-point FFT can be processed as s stages of butterfly computation and then 2^s groups 2^{m-s}-point FFT, where $0 \leq s \leq m-1$. Since the PARQUO has the maximum processing capability of 2^q-point FFT and the minimum processing capability of 2^{a+1}-point FFT without zero padding, the decision in decomposition is based on the

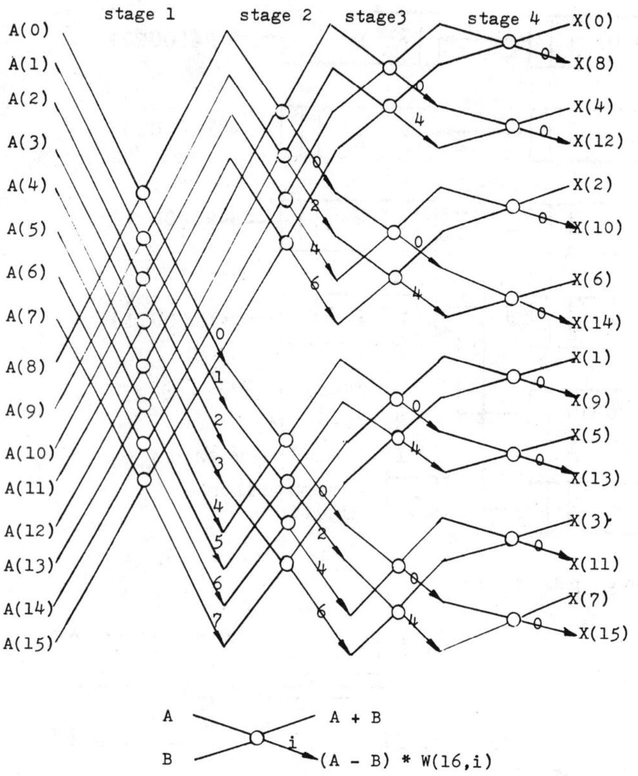

Figure 7—The signal flowgraph of a 16-point radix-2 Decimation-In-Frequency FFT algorithm with the in-place property

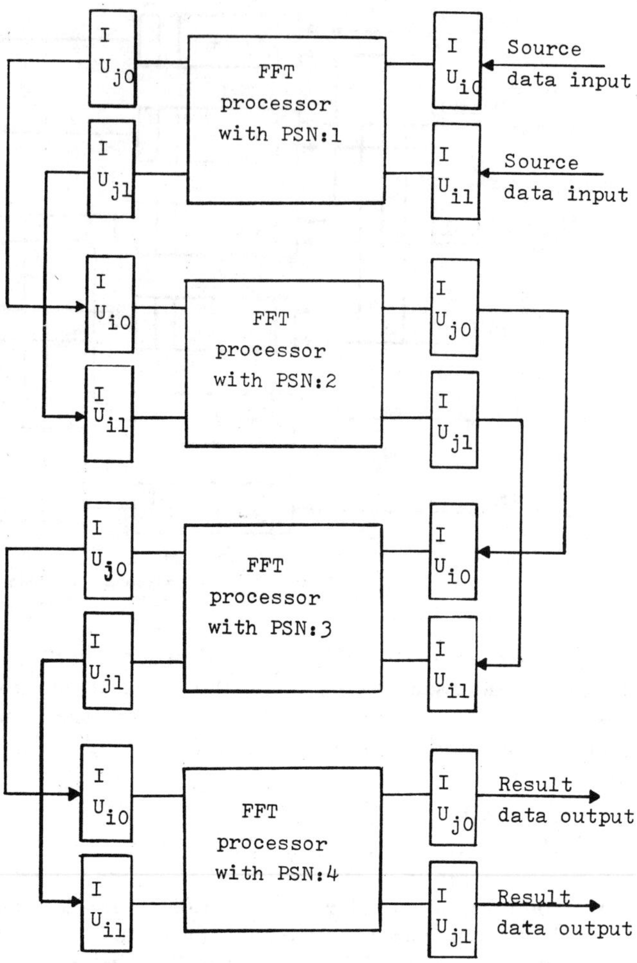

Figure 8—The topology and connection pattern of the linearly connected FFT processors

data size and the processing capability of the PARQUO. To avoid the side effect of zero padding, when the data size is smaller than 2^{a+1}, the given FFT task is processed by activating the PIPECE. If the data size is larger than 2^a and smaller than 2^{q+1}, then it is processed by the PARQUO. As the data size 2^m exceeds the the maximum processing capability of the PARQUO, the FFT computation will first be performed by processing $m-q$ stages of butterflies in the PIPECE, and then the intermediate results of the $(m-q)$th stage are treated as 2^{m-q} groups 2^q-point FFT, which can be processed by the PARQUO. When the PIPECE is activated, the intermediate results of one iteration are arranged in the internal data storages properly to be ready for the next iteration. After each iteration, the processor will change the processing direction by controlling the MCSW switches. Following the above decomposition rules, variant sizes of FFT can be processed in a single FFT processor.[16]

Multiprocessor Cascade FFT Processing Scheme

In Figure 7, after the first half of the butterflies in stage 1 are done, the successive output of stage 1 can be processed in stage 2, and so on. Hence, for a given FFT task with G groups of 2^m data points, one can linearly connect an m number of FFT processors, and according to the sequence order of the linear connection, each processor is then assigned a Pseudo Number (PSN) to charge one stage of butterfly computation. The Linear(P,j,i) defines the linear connection pattern such that the IU_{j0} and IU_{j1} of the FFT processor with PSN = k connect to the IU_{i0} and IU_{i1} of the FFT processor with PSN = k + 1, where P is the number of processors and $1 \le k \le P$ and i,j represent the two IU groups. The FFT processor with PSN = 1 accepts pairs of source data from its IU_{10} and IU_{i1}, whereas the processor with PSN = P produces the Fourier coefficients from its IU_{j0} and IU_{j1}, which are connected to the destination unit through the Starnet. Figure 8 shows the connection pattern of Linear(4,1,0).

The data movement operation is divided into three phases and is shown in Figure 9. Suppose a 2^4-point 1-D FFT task, as shown in Figure 7, is processed by four linearly connected processors. At phase 1, the first processor queues the OUT1 data of the first four butterflies in M_1 and sends the OUT0 data through the IU_{j0} to the next processor, which will queue the received data in M_0. At phase 2, the first processor queues the OUT1 data of the next four butterflies in M_3 and send the OUT0 and queued M_1 data through the IU_{j1} and IU_{j0} to the next processor. The second processor stores the incoming data from the IU_{i0} and M_1 data storage and processes the queues M_0 data and the incoming data from the IU_{i1} as a pair of IN0 and IN1 data. Finally, at phase 3, the first processor

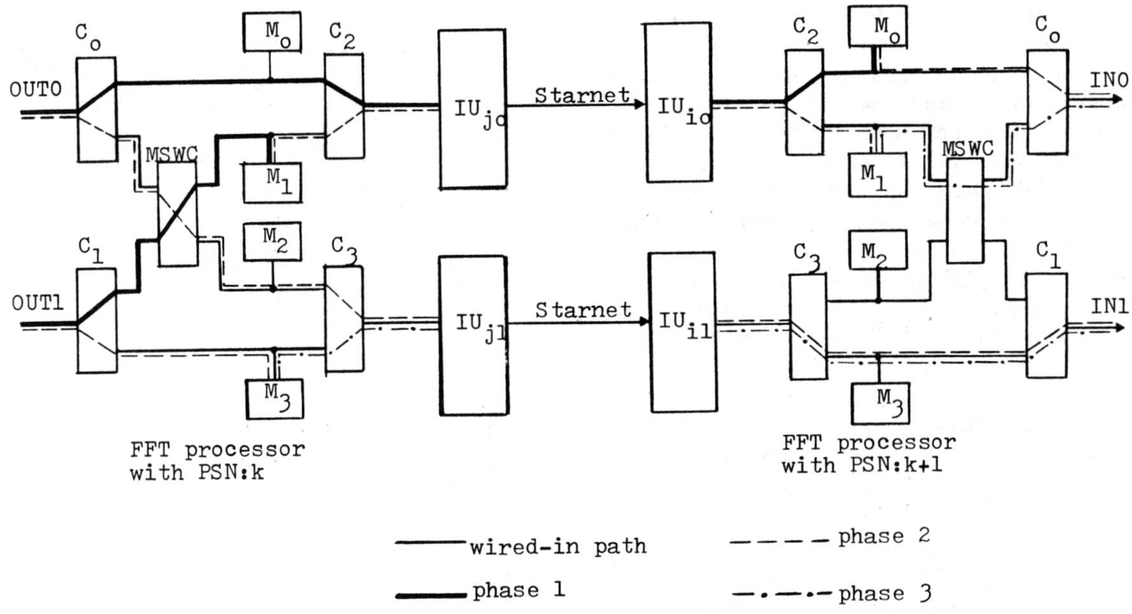

Figure 9—The data movement of cascade 1-D FFT processing scheme

```
(*COMMENT:
TASK TYPE:    CAScade Multiple One Dimensional FFTs.
TOPOLOGY:     Linear.
DATA SIZE:    G groups of M-point data, M = 2^m,
REQUEST:      log2M processors.
ASSIGN:       Pseudo number PSN, v = 0 and u = 1, where PSN is an
              integer and 1 ≤ PSN ≤ m.
SOURCE:       Source data are sent to the processor with PSN = 1
              as the sequence of

                   For I = 0 to G − 1
                   IU_i0 ← A(I, k);
                   IU_i1 ← A(I, k + M/2);
              where 0 ≤ k ≤ M/2 − 1 and i = v.
*)
Begin
   Linear(m, 1, 0); (* establish linear connection*)
   MCSW: = pass; i: = v; j: = u; (* set direction *)
   s: = PSN; (* specify computation stage*)
   (* performing the FFT computation *)
   For I: = 0 to G − 1 do
      For c: = 0 to 2^(s−1) − 1 do
         For k: = 0 to 2^(m−s) − 1 do
            Begin
               [INPUT DATA FEEDING PROCESS]
                  Case of s
                  s = 1:  MB_i(C0↑, C1↓, C2↑, C3↓);
                          IN0 ← IU_i0;
                          IN1 ← IU_i1;
                  s > 1:  If k < 2^(m−s−1)
                          Then
                             If I = 0 and c = 0
            (phase 1)        Then MB_i(C1↑);
                                M0(k) ← IU_i0;
            (phase 2)        Else MB_i(C0↑, C1↓, C2↓);
                                MB_i(C3↓, MSWC = pass);
                                INO ← M0(k);
                                IN1 ← IU_i1;
                                M1(k) ← IU_i0;
                          Else MB_i(C0↓, C1↓, C2↑);
                             MB_i(C3↓, MSWC = pass);
                             If I = G − 1 and c = 2^(s−1) − 1
                             Then IN0 ← M1(k − 2^(m−s−1));
                                IN1 ← IU_i1;
            (phase 1 & 3)    Else IN0 ← M1(k − 2^(m−s−1));
                                IN1 ← IU_i1;
                                M0(k − 2^(m−s−1)) ← IU_i0;
               End of Case;
               [COMPUTATION PROCESS]
                  (* active PIPECE *)
                  OUT0 ← IN0 + IN1;
                  OUT1 ← (IN0 − IN1) * W(M, k * 2^(s−1));
               [OUTPUT DATA HANDLING PROCESS]
                  Case of s
                  s = m: MB_j(C0↑, C1↓, C2↑, C3↓);
                         IU_j0 ← OUT0;
                         IU_j1 ← OUT1;
                  s < m: If k < 2^(m−s−1)
                         Then MB_j(C0↑, C1↑, C2↑);
                            MB_j(C3↓, MSWC = cross);
                            If I = 0 and c = 0
            (phase 1)       Then IU_j0 ← OUT0;
                               M1(k) ← OUT1;
            (phases 1 & 3)  Else IU_j0 ← OUT0;
                               M1(k) ← OUT1;
                               IU_j1 ← M3(k);
            (phase 2)    Else MB_j(C0↓, C1↓);
                            MB_j(C2↑, C3↑, MSWC = cross);
                            IU_j0 ← M2(k − 2^(m−s−1));
                            IU_j1 ← OUT0;
                            M3(k − 2^(m−s−1)) ← OUT1;
                  End of Case;
            End;
   If s < m
   Then MB_j(C3↓);
      For k: = 0 to 2^(m−s−1) do
         IU_j1 ← M3(k);
End.
```

Figure 10—CASMOD algorithm

sends its M_3 data through the IU_{j1} to the next processor, which processes the queued M_1 data and the incoming data from the IU_{i1} and a pair of IN0 and IN1 data. Similarly, the data movement operation is available for the second and third processor, and so on. In general, the processor with PSN = k, $1 \leq k \leq m$, repeats 2^{k-1} times of phase 1, 2, and 3 operations, and each processor overlaps the phase 3 operation with the next repetitive phase 1 operation. In the case of processing G groups of 1-D FFT, the first processor (i.e., PSN = 1) overlaps the phase 3 operation with the next group's phase 1 operation, and the rest of the processors (except the last processor) repeat $G*2^{k-1}$ times of phase 1 to 3 operations. Note that the cascade FFT processing scheme only involves the active PIPECE operation mode.

The algorithm CASMOD (Figure 10) describing the cascade FFT processing scheme is given as follows. The notation "destination $\leftarrow$ source" stands for the data transfer operation, and the transfer operations in each PROCESS occur concurrently except when they are separated by the conditional statement If-Then-Else. The INPUT DATA FEEDING PROCESS, COMPUTATION PROCESS, and OUTPUT DATA HANDLING PROCESS are pipelined. The states of switch control signals C_{0-3} are represented with " $\uparrow$ " or " $\downarrow$ " to stand for the upper or lower link. The data path set by the MCSW or MSWC is either "pass" or "cross."

The multiprocessor cascade FFT processing scheme becomes attractive when the G value is greatern than one, because it reduces the external data transferring time by overlapping the receiving of source data and the transmitting of the results with the butterfly computation.

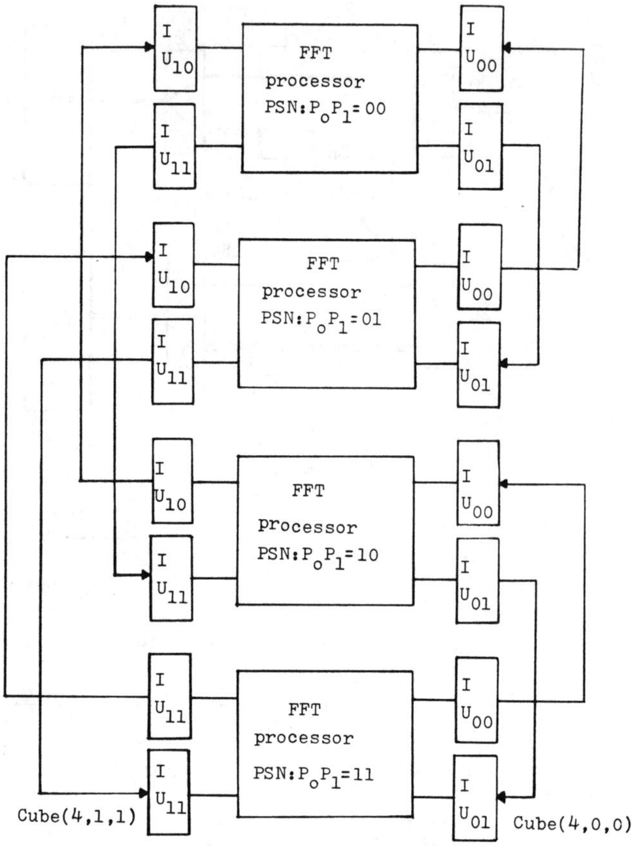

Figure 11—The topology and connection pattern of Cube(4,1,1) and Cube(4,0,0)

Parallel Processing Multiple One-Dimensional FFTs

Representing 2^x FFT processors in binary form as PSN = $P_{x-1} \ldots P_0$, the Cube(P,c,i) defines the connection pattern of the IU_{i1} of processor $P_{x-1} \ldots P_c \ldots P_0$ connecting to the IU_{i1} of processor $P_{x-1} \ldots \bar{P}_c \ldots P_0$, and the IU_{i0} of processor $P_{x-1} \ldots P_c \ldots P_0$ connecting to the IU_{i0} of processor $P_{x-1} \ldots \bar{P}_c \ldots P_0$, where $P = 2^x$, and $0 \leq c \leq x-1$ and i represent one of two IU groups. Figure 11 shows the connection pattern of Cube(4,1,1) and Cube(4,0,0). Suppose one requests four FFT processors with PSN = P_1P_0 to process a 16-point 1-D FFT task as shown in Figure 7, then each processor will charge two-butterfly computations in each stage according to the order of PSN. Assume that the source data input ports will the IU_{00} and IU_{01}, before starting the computation, and that each processor establishes Cube(4,1,1) as shown in Figure 11. Those processors with $P_1 = 0$ queue the OUT0 data and send the OUT1 data through IU_{10}, and processors with $P_1 = 1$ queue the OUT1 data and send OUT0 data through IU_{11}. This data exchange operation is shown in Figure 12. When the last pair of incoming source data arrive, each processor establishes Cube(4,0,0) as shown in Figure 11 and stage 2 computation can start after finishing the exchange of intermediate results and switching the processing direction. It allows each processor to have two-butterfly computation time to establish the next connection pattern Cube(4,0,0). In Starnet, a path establishment time is less than one microsecond. This procedure is then continued until there is no need to exchange data; i.e., c = 0. In general, processing 2^m-point FFT with 2^x processors, where $0 < x < m$, requires x times of exchange steps and each step takes 2^{m-x-1} data transfer operations. After the xth data exchange step, each processor processes 2^{m-x}-point FFT independently. The operation of parallel-processing multiple one-dimensional FFT is described in the PARMOD algorithm (Figure 13).

When x = 0, the above parallel processing scheme becomes a single processor FFT processing scheme. If x = m-1, i.e., each processor executes only one butterfly computation in each stage, one obtains the maximum parallelism in processing one-dimensional FFT.

PERFORMANCE ANALYSIS

The following parameters are defined.

1. T_s = one data item transfer operation time between the source/result data unit and the FFT processor.
2. T_e = one data item transfer operation time between FFT processors.
3. T_i = the input or output operation time of the PASQUO for one pair of data.
4. T_b = one butterfly operation time.

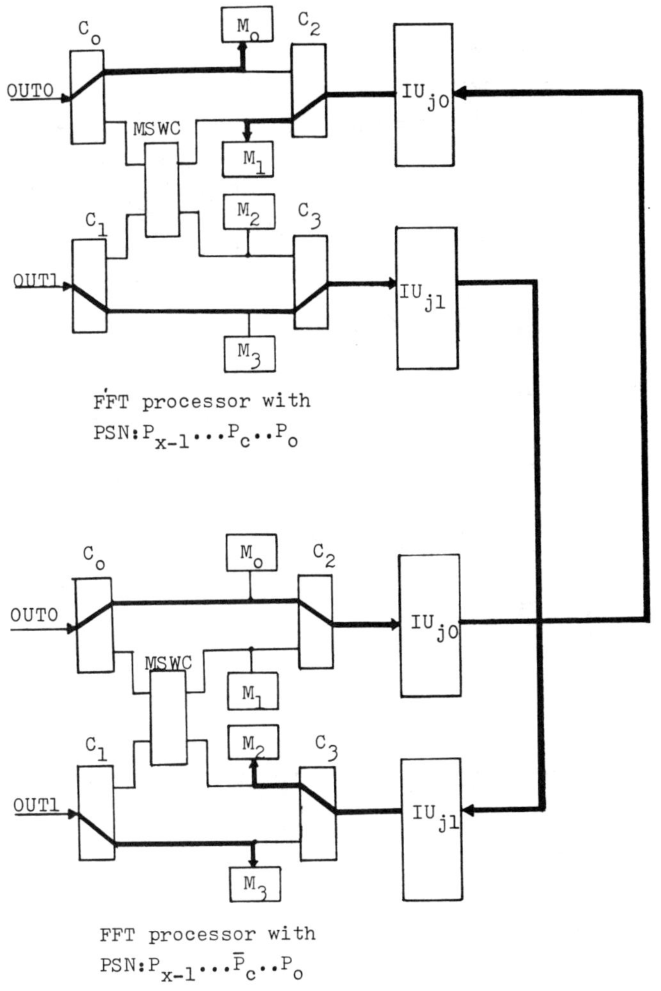

Figure 12—The data exchange of parallel 1-D FFT processing scheme

5. L = the number of computation stations in the pipeline butterfly computation element (PIPECE).
6. The number of CEs in the PARQUO is 2^a and its maximum processing capability is 2^q-point FFT, where $a < q$.

Suppose the PIPECE and the CEs of the PARQUO are designed with the same kind of real adder/subtracter/mutiplier; then the input-output time of the PIPECE is also denoted as T_b and the time to start the successive butterfly computation in the PIPECE is T_b/L. In addition, according to the defined parameters, assume that $T_s \geq T_e \geq T_b/L \geq T_i$. The FFT processing time will be calculated from the receiving of source data to the end of transmitting results and without concern for the output sequence of the final Fourier coefficients. Also, the overhead time spent in the processor control unit after accepting the user's FFT task description is neglected.

The Performance Measures of the Single FFT Processor

The total FFT processing time of G groups 2^m-point FFT is the single versatile FFT processor is formulated as follows:

(* COMMENT:
TASK TYPE: PARallel Multiple One Dimensional FFTs.
TOPOLOGY: Cube.
DATA SIZE: G groups of M data pointss, $M = 2^m$.
REQUEST: 2^x processors, where $0 \leq x < m$.
ASSIGN: $v = 0$, $u = 1$ and $PSN = P_{x-1} \cdots P_0$,
SOURCE: For processor $PSN = P_{x-1} \cdots P_0$, the incoming source data follows the sequence of
$IU_{i0} \leftarrow A(I, 0P_{x-1} \cdots P_0 j_{m-x-2} \cdots j_0)$;
$IU_{i1} \leftarrow A(I, 1P_{x-1} \cdots P_0 j_{m-x-2} \cdots j_0)$;
where $j_{m-x-2} \cdots j_0 = 0$ to $2^{m-x-1} - 1$, $i = v$.
*)
Begin
For s: = 1 to x do
(* setting the processing direction *)
If s = even
Then MCSW: = cross; i: = v; j: = u;
Else MCSW: = pass; i: = u; j: = v;
(* path establishment *)
Cube(2^x, x − s, j);
(* performing the FFT computation *)
For I: = 0 to G − 1 do
For k: = 0 to $2^{m-x-1} - 1$ do
[INPUT DATA FEEDING PROCESS]
If s = 1
Then (* access the source data *)
$MB_i (C_0 \uparrow, C_1 \downarrow, C_2 \uparrow, C_3 \downarrow)$;
$IN0 \leftarrow IU_{00}$;
$IN1 \leftarrow IU_{01}$;
Else (* access internal data *)
If $P_{x-s} = 0$
Then MB_i(MSWC = cross, $C_0 \uparrow, C_1 \uparrow$);
$IN0 \leftarrow M_0 (I, k)$;
$IN1 \leftarrow M_2 (I, k)$;
Else MB_i(MSWC = cross, $C_0 \downarrow, C_1 \downarrow$);
$IN0 \leftarrow M_1 (I, k)$;
$IN1 \leftarrow M_3 (I, k)$;
[COMPUTATION PROCESS]
(* active PIPECE *)
$t = :k + PSN * 2^{m-x-1}$;
$OUT0 \leftarrow IN0 + IN1$;
$OUT1 \leftarrow (IN0 - IN1) * W(M, t * 2^{s-1})$;
[OUTPUT DATA HANDLING PROCESS]
(* including the data exchangement *)
If $P_{x-s} = 0$
Then $MB_j (C_0 \uparrow, C_1 \downarrow, C_2 \uparrow, C_3 \downarrow)$;
$M_0 (I, k) \leftarrow OUT0$;
$IU_{j1} \leftarrow OUT1$;
$M_2 (I, k) \leftarrow IU_{j0}$;
Else $MB_j (C_0 \uparrow, C_1 \downarrow, C_2 \uparrow, C_3 \downarrow)$;
$IU_{j0} \leftarrow OUT0$;
$M_3 (I, k) \leftarrow OUT1$;
$M_2 (I, k) \leftarrow IU_{j1}$;
End;
m: = m = x; v: = j; u: = i;
Single processor Multiple 1 − D FFT (Section 3.1);
End.

Figure 13—PARMOD algorithm

Case 1. $m \leq a$, active PIPECE.

$$T_{FFT} = T_s * G * 2^m + T_b * [m + G * (m-2)/L * 2^{m-1}]. \quad (1)$$

Case 2. $a < m \leq q$, active PARQUO.

$$T_{FFT} = G * T_s * 2^m + G * T_b * m * 2^{m-a-1}. \quad (2)$$

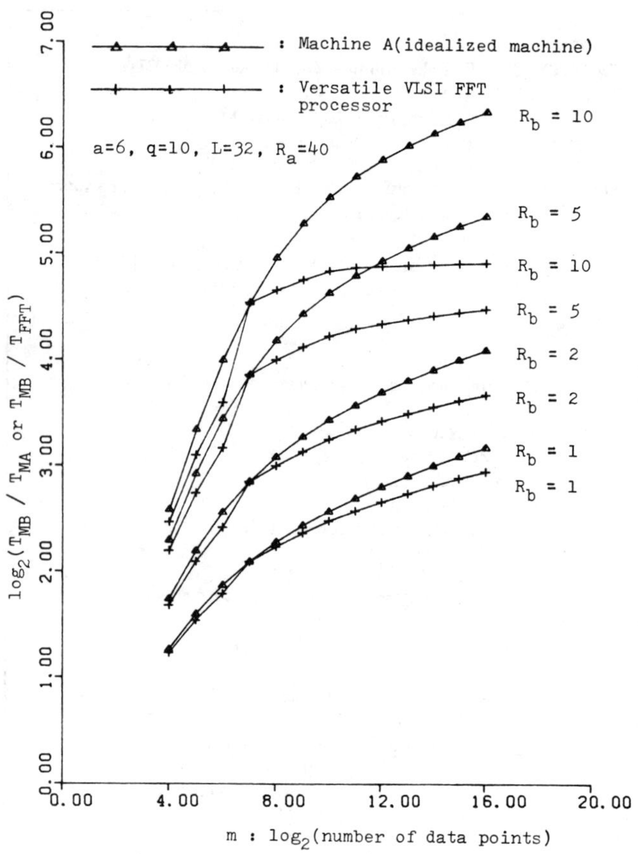

Figure 14—The $\log_2$ speed-up of the machine A and versatile FFT processor in 1-D FFT processing scheme as a function of m and R_b

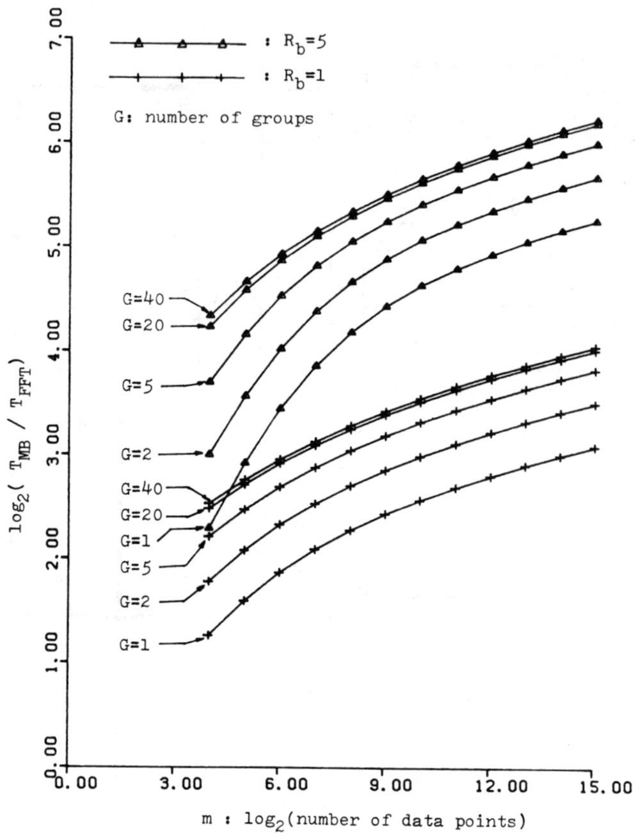

Figure 15—The $\log_2$ speed-up of the cascade 1-D FFT processing scheme, as a function of m and G

Case 3. $q < m$, active PIPECE and PARQUO.

$$T_{FFT} = G*T_s*2^m + G*T_i*2^{m-1} + T_b*[m - q + G*(m-q-1)/L*2^{m-1} + G*q*2^{m-a-1}]. \quad (3)$$

To evaluate the speed performance of the designed versatile FFT processor, two conceptual machines are defined. The first one, named machine A, can always process any given size of FFT in maximum parallelism. The second machine, named machine B, is the sequential-type hardware FFT processor that sequentially executes the butterflies. If machine A and B each have two input ports and two output ports, then the processing time of 2^m-point FFT in machine A is expressed as

$$T_{MA} = T_s*2^m + m*T_b, \quad (4)$$

and in machine B it is expressed as

$$T_{MB} = T_s*2^m + m*2^{m-1}*T_b. \quad (5)$$

One might note that the speed-up ratio of machine A is about $0(m/2*T_b/T_s)$ over machine B.

Denote R_b as T_b/T_s, R_a as T_b/T_i, and let $a=6$, $q=10$, $L=32$, and $R_a=40$. Figure 14 shows the $\log_2$ speed-up of machine A and a versatile VLSI FFT processor, compared with machine B, as a function of m and R_b. As R_b decreases, the I/O operation becomes a dominate term in evaluting the FFT processing time. In some applications, the source/result data might be stored in the medium-speed storage, which may cause the R_b value to be small. In such a case, further improvement of the speed performance should be done by using either the multiprocessor cascade FFT processing scheme or the multiprocessor parallel FFT processing scheme. As semiconductor technology progresses, the increasing speed of hardware circuits reduces the T_b value and results in the importance of the I/O consideration.

The Performance Measures of the Cascade Processing Scheme

Since the cascade FFT processing scheme only activates the PIPECEs and each processor overlaps its butterfly computation with the incoming data from the previous processor, its output handling rate is determined by the next processor. For easy illustration, assuming that $T_e = T_s$ and counting from the time the first pair of source data arrive at the first processor, the second processor can start its butterfly computation after $M/4*T_e + T_b$ time units and the third processor can start its butterfly computation after $(M/4 + M/8)*T_e + 2*T_b$ time units, and so on. This means that it takes about $M/2*T_e + m*T_b$ time units to produce the first pair of Fourier coefficients. The total processing time of G groups 2^m-point FFT with m linearly connected versatile VLSI FFT processors is then formulated as

$$T_{FFT} = 2^{m-1}*(G+1)*T_s + m*T_b. \quad (6)$$

Figure 15 shows the $\log_2$ speed-up ratio of the cascade FFT processing scheme, relative to machine B, as a function of m and G with $R_b = 5$ and $R_b = 1$ respectively. As G increases, the CASMOD FFT processing scheme gets better performance, and its throughput is twice as high as that of machine A for large G value. In applications where the source/result data storages only have several input/output ports, the designed cascade FFT processing scheme can achieve both high performance and high throughput.

The Performance Measures of the Parallel Processing Scheme

The total processing time of 2^x processors, $0 < x < m$, parallel-processing G groups 2^m-point FFT is formulated as

Case 1. $m - x \leq a$.

$$T_{FFT} = G*T_s*2^{m-x} + G*T_e*[1 + (x-1)*2^{m-x-1}] + T_b*[m + G*(m-x-1)/L*2^{m-x-1}]. \quad (7)$$

Case 2. $a < m - x \leq q$.

$$T_{FFT} = G*T_s*2^{m-x} + G*T_e[1 + (x-1)*2^{m-x-1}] + G*T_i*2^{m-x-1} + T_b*[G*(m-x)*2^{m-x-a-1} + x]. \quad (8)$$

Case 3. $q < m - x$.

$$T_{FFT} = G*T_s*2^{m-x} + G*T_e*[1 + (x-1)*2^{m-x-1}] + G*T_i*2^{m-x-1} + T_b*[m - q + G*(m-x-q)/L*2^{m-x-1} + G*q*2^{m-x-a-1}]. \quad (9)$$

Because the data exchange of the first stage is overlapped with the butterfly computation and the incoming source data, its actual data exchange operation time is the last produced intermediate result. Siegel[6] has presented a parallel processing 1-D FFT algorithm for the SIMD machine. Performing 2^m-point FFT in an SIMD machine with 2^x processing elements, $0 < x < m$, takes $m*2^{m-x-1}$ butterfly operations and $x*2^{m-x-1}$ external data transfer operations. Due to the lack of information about the internal data transfer operations in the processing elements of an SIMD machine, which depends on the detail hardware circuit design, the processing time of 2^m-point 1-D FFT in an SIMD machine is approximately and optimistically expressed as

$$T_{SIMD} = T_s*2^{m-x} + T_b*m*2^{m-x-1} + T_e*x*2^{m-x-1}. \quad (10)$$

Assuming that $T_e = T_s$, Figure 16 is the $\log_2$ speed-up of an SIMD machine and designed FFT processors in the parallel 1-D FFT processing scheme, relative to machine B, as a function of x and R_b. The result shows that the parallel FFT

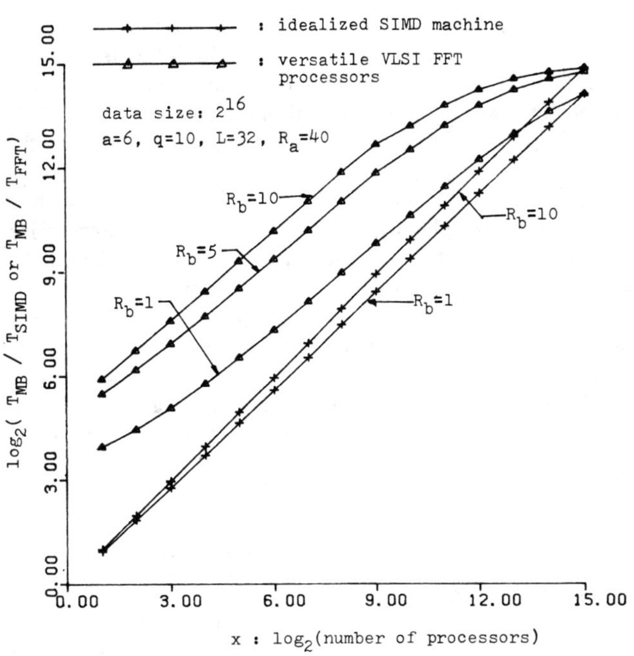

Figure 16—The $\log_2$ speed-up of an idealized SIMD machine and versatile FFT processors in parallel 1-D FFT processing scheme as a function of x and R_b

processing scheme of designed versatile FFT processors gains higher speed performance. Note that in Figure 16, with $R_b = 10$, 32 designed FFT processors can have the same performance as an SIMD machine with 1,024 processing elements. Such comparison gives only the approximation; in fact, the processing elements of an SIMD machine are usually not designed to process the FFT algorithm only. Hence, the T_b value of an SIMD machine will be larger than that of a special-purpose FFT processor.

CONCLUSION

As semiconductor techology progresses parallel FFT computing architecture becomes more and more attractive in real-time applications. However, the associated communication problem and the related I/O problem also become more and more important. Performance of a theoretical special-purpose hardware FFT processor that can process any given size of FFT with maximum parallelism can easily be limited by the I/O operation.

The versatile special-purpose VLSI FFT processor described in this paper facilitates single and multiple processors using cascade and parallel FFT processing schemes for various applications and source data arrangements. The design of the FFT VLSI computation unit takes a more practical approach by considering the pins limitation and the progress of VLSI technology. The flexible memory organization and bidirectional processing capability allow the processor to deal with a variety of source input and result output sequences. Furthermore, the flexibility of processing variant sizes of FFT in single FFT and multiple FFT processors will be suitable for a multiuser real-time processing environment.

The results of the performance analysis show that the combination of Star architecture capability with VLSI technology and related technology developments can provide a practical approach toward meeting the goal of advanced real-time FFT processing. The cascade FFT processing scheme offers the capability of meeting both the high performance and high throughput requirements with limited I/O ports. Such a scheme appears to be attractive for collecting and processing large amounts of data in real-time. It is concluded that the parallel FFT processing scheme with multiple versatile VLSI FFT processors in Star can achieve higher performance than can the SIMD machine. In addition, the achievement of high performance through an exploitation of parallelism using a distributed computing approach not only significantly improves fault tolerance but also allows maximum flexibility.

REFERENCES

1. Wu, C., Feng, T., and Lin, M. "Star: A Local Network System for Real-Time Management of Imagery Data. *IEEE Trans. on Computers* (Vol. C-31), 1982, pp. 923–932.
2. Cooley, J. W., and Turkey, J. W. "An Algorithm for the Machine Calculation of the Complex Fourier Series." *Math. Comp.*, 19 (1965), pp. 297–301.
3. Pease, M. C. "An Adaption of the Fast Fourier Transform for Parallel Processing." *J. ACM,* 15 (1968), pp. 252–264.
4. Stone, H. S. "Parallel Processing with Perfect Shuffle." *IEEE Trans. Computers* (Vol. C-20), 1971, pp. 153–161.
5. Parker Jr., D. S. "Notes on Shuffle/Exchange-type Switching Networks." *IEEE Trans. Computers* (Vol. C-29), 1980, pp. 213–222.
6. Siegel, L. J., Mueller, P. T., and Siegel, H. J. "FFT Algorithms for SIMD Machines." *Proc. 17th Allerton Conf. Commun., Contr., Comput.*, October 1979, pp. 1006–1015.
7. Gold, B. and Bially, T. "Parallelism in Fast Fourier Transform Hardware." *IEEE Trans. Audio Electroacoustic* (Vol. AU-21), 1973, pp. 5–16.
8. Groginsky, H. L., and Works, G. A. "A Pipeline Fast Fourier Transform," *IEEE Trans. Computers,* (Vol. C-19), 1971, pp. 1015–1019.
9. Thompson, C. D. "Fourier Transform in VLSI." *International Conf. on Circuits and Computers,* 1980, pp. 1046–1051.
10. Preparata, F., and Vuillemin, J. "The Cube-Connected-Cycles: A Versatile Network for Parallel Computation." *20th Annual Symp. on Foundations of Computer Science, IEEE Computer Society,* 1979, pp. 140–147.
11. Kung, H. T. "Why Systolic Architecture?" *IEEE Computer Magazine,* January 1982, pp. 37–46.
12. Kung, D., et al. "Wavefront Array Processor: Language, Architecture and Applications." *IEEE Trans. Computers* (Vol. C-31), 1982, pp. 1054–1065.
13. Kung, S. Y., and Galezer, R. J. "Synchronous vs Asynchronous Computation in VLSI Array Processors." *SPIE Conf. Arlington,* May 1982,
14. Fishburn, J. P., and Finkel, R. A. "Quotient Network." *IEEE Trans. Computers,* (Vol. C-31), 1982, pp. 288–295.
15. Gentleman, W. M., and Sande, G. "Fast Fourier Transform for Fun and Profit." *AFIPS, Proceedings of the National Computer Conference* (Vol. 29), 1966, pp. 563–578.
16. Ting, K. "A Versatile VLSI Fast Fourier Transform Processor Star Local Network." Master's thesis, University of Texas at Austin, August 1983.

Design diversity: An approach to fault tolerance of design faults

by ALGIRDAS AVIZIENIS
University of California, Los Angeles
Los Angeles, California

ABSTRACT

Diversity of design is discussed as a means to attain fault tolerance with respect to latent design faults in software and hardware. Some potential advantages of this approach in software versus a single design protected by fault avoidance (verification, validation, and proofs) are presented. An extension to design fault tolerance in VLSI circuits is identified. The results of earlier experimental studies are reviewed, and new results of a specification-oriented multiversion software experiment are summarized.

INTRODUCTION: THE DESIGN DIVERSITY APPROACH

Over the past two decades, several successful fault-tolerant systems (tolerating faults of physical origin, to be called "physical faults" in this paper) have been designed, built, and used in important applications.[6,7] Major examples are the JPL-STAR (Self-Testing And Repairing) computer for multi-year interplanetary space missions,[3,4] the Bell Laboratories duplexed ESS central processors,[33] and the advanced SIFT[20] and FTMP[21] designs intended to serve as real-time control computers for commercial airliners of the future. THE SIFT and FTMP designs use a minimum of three complete and separate computing channels with majority voting (by software in SIFT; by hardware in FTMP) to assure system survival after the first physical fault. Reconfiguration and sparing are then used to lower the probability of system failure to the desired value of 10^{-9} for a 10-hour flight.

In contrast to the successful systems that exercise tolerance of physical faults, there are no examples of operational systems that tolerate design faults either in software or in hardware. The fault-avoidance approach is exclusively used to eliminate design faults. The inevitable left-over design faults are removed by maintenance procedures applied off-line, i.e., after a system crash has occurred. The question whether design faults can be successfully tolerated by extensions and generalizations of fault tolerance techniques has remained unanswered. The question can be addressed in two parts:

1. Is it possible to implement design fault tolerance regardless of cost?
2. Can this approach compete, with respect to cost, with the currently prevalent design fault-avoidance approaches that use verification, validation, and correctness proofs?

In setting out to investigate the potential of fault tolerance techniques in the domain of design faults, we note that a strong analogy exists between physical and design faults, as show in Figure 1.

The existence of systems with strong tolerance of physical faults attained through multiple-channel computing is an encouraging fact. However, it is evident that the channels are identical and therefore do not possess the critically important property of *design diversity* that is needed to tolerate the manifestation of a latent design defect. Clearly, the multiple computing channels will have the potential for design fault tolerance only if there is a very high probability that the left-over design faults do not evoke the same forms of undesirable behavior in a majority of channels; that is, if their symptoms are not isomorphic at the points of observation.

Consequently, *design diversity* is the new key requirement for design fault tolerance that needs to be added to a multi-channel system that tolerates physical faults. Design diversity in this context means the independent generation of two or more software or hardware elements (e.g., program modules, VLSI circuit masks, etc.) to satisfy a given requirement. It must be noted that the discussion of diversity applies not only to the initial generation of programs and designs but also to subsequent modifications or redesigns that are made in order to improve performance or to correct discovered defects and inadequacies.

CONDITIONS FOR THE INDEPENDENCE OF DESIGN FAULTS

Independence of the design and implementation efforts is the mechanism that is employed to minimize the probability of identical design-fault symptoms in a majority of computing channels. It is approached first by the use of different algorithms, programming languages, translators, design automation tools, implementation techniques, machine languages, and so on. The second condition for independence is the employment of independent programmers or designers, preferably with diversity in their training and experience.

The third and most critical condition for independence of design faults is the existence of a complete and correct *initial statement* of the requirements to be met by the diverse designs. This is the hard core of the fault-tolerance approach. Latent defects, such as inconsistencies, ambiguities, and omissions in the initial statement, are likely to bias otherwise en-

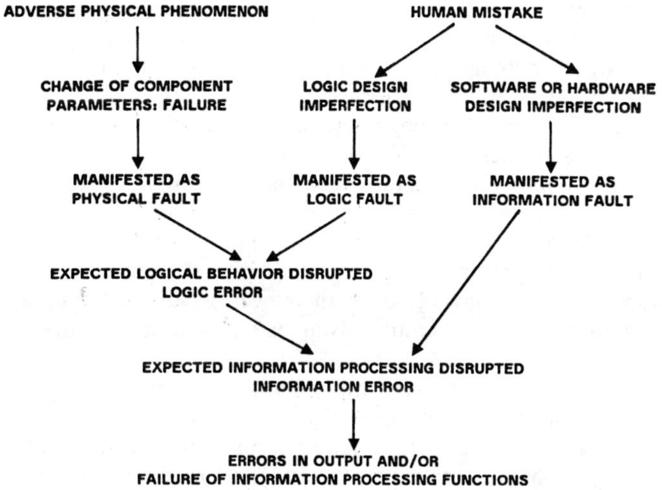

Figure 1—An analogy between physical and design faults

tirely independent programming or logic design efforts so that they produce isomorphic design faults.

The most promising approach to create the initial statement is the use of formal, very-high-level specifications that themselves can be automatically tested for latent defects, or even proven to be defect-free. Here perfection is required only at the highest level of specification; the rest of the design and implementation process and its tools are not required to be perfect, but only as good as possible within existing constraints on resources and time.

POTENTIAL ADVANTAGES OF DESIGN DIVERSITY

The most immediate and direct application of design fault tolerance through design diversity exists in the multichannel systems with very complete tolerance of physical faults (e.g., SIFT[20]) that are employed in life-critical applications. The hardware resources and architectural features to support design diversity are already present, and implementation of design diversity is a logical extension of the existing physical fault tolerance mechanisms. Furthermore, design faults in the hardware of a channel can be tolerated by choosing for each channel functionally compatible hardware building blocks from different suppliers.

A more speculative, but also much more general application of design diversity is its use as a partial replacement for current software verification and validation (V&V) procedures. Instead of a thorough V&V of a single program, two independent versions are to be executed in an operational environment, completing V&V concurrently with productive operation. The doubled cost of producing the software is compensated by a reduction of the V&V time and a decrease in the cost of manpower and special tools needed for the very thorough V&V effort. The second (backup) version can be taken off line when adequate reliability of operation is reached, and then returned for special operating conditions that require greater reliability assurance, especially after modifications or after maintenance. A potential system lifetime cost reduction exists because such a system can support continued operation after latent design faults are uncovered, providing near 100% availability. The cost of fault analysis and elimination should be reduced because of the lesser urgency of the repair actions, since operation is not interrupted as long as the majority of channels are not affected.

A very intriguing long-range implication of the design diversity approach in software is the possibility of using a "mail-order" approach to the production of two or more versions of software modules. Given a precise formal specification that includes a set of fundamental tests, the software can be generated by programmers working at their own preferred times and locations, possibly using their own personal computing equipment. Two potential advantages have been identified:

1. The overhead cost of programming that accrues in highly controlled professional programming environments would be drastically reduced through this approach, which allows free play to individual initiative and uses low-cost home facilities.
2. The potential of the rapidly growing number of computer hobbyists to serve as productive programmers would be tapped through this approach. For various reasons, many individuals with programming talents cannot fill the role of a professional programmer as defined by today's rigorous approaches to quality control and use of centralized sites during the programming process.

Finally, an important reliability and cost advantage through design diversity may be expected for VLSI circuit design. The growing complexity of VLSI circuits, with 400,000 gates/chip available today and 1 million gates/chip predicted for 1986, raises the probability of latent design faults, since a complete verification of the design becomes very difficult to attain. Furthermore, the design automation and verification tools themselves are subject to latent design faults. Even with multichannel fault-tolerant system designs, a single latent design fault would require the replacement of all chips of the class, since on-chip modifications are impractical. Such a replacement would be a costly and time-consuming process. On the contrary, use of design diversity of VLSI circuits does allow the continued use of chips with design faults, as long as their symptoms are not isomorphic at the circuit boundaries. Reliable operation throughout the lifetime of a system may be obtained by means of design diversity without having a single chip with a perfect design and without any modification of the basic structure of the VLSI circuits.

INITIAL STUDIES OF MULTIVERSION SOFTWARE: AN EXPERIMENTAL APPROACH

The potential advantages that were identified in the preceding section have provided the motivation for study of design diversity and design fault tolerance as alternatives to the generally used verification, validation, and proof methodology that aims to deliver perfect software products and hardware circuits.

An increasing awareness of the need for design fault tolerance led to the initiation of a research effort at UCLA in 1975.[5] The work was founded on a 14-year background of continuous investigations in tolerance of physical faults,[3,8] and its goal was to study the feasibility of adapting to software design fault tolerance the technique of N-fold modular redundancy (NMR) with majority voting, which is effective in the tolerance of physical faults. The approach was called N-version programming (NVP), and the first experimental study of its feasibility was completed in 1978.[11] A literature search in 1975 revealed few other efforts in this area. Suggestions that this approach might be a viable method of software fault tolerance had been published recently.[14,15,17,25] However, quite arguably, the first suggestion on record has been made by Dr. Dionysius Lardner, who wrote in his article "Babbage's Calculating Engine," published in the *Edinburgh Review*, No. CXX, July 1834, as follows:

> The most certain and effectual check upon errors which arise in the process of computation, is to cause the same computations to be made by separate and independent computers; and this

check is rendered still more decisive if they make their computations by different methods.[28]

A second approach already under investigation in 1975 was the recovery block (RB) technique, in which alternate software routines are organized in a manner similar to the dynamic-redundancy (standby-sparing) technique in hardware.[30] The prime objective is to perform run-time software design fault detection by an acceptance test and to implement recovery by taking an alternate path of execution. This technique is also being continuously investigated at several locations. Some comparisons of RB with NVP have been made.[11,16] Several related research activities have been reported more recently.[18,24,27,34]

N-version programming is defined as the independent generation of $N \geq 2$ software modules, called versions, from the same initial specification.[2] Independent generation here means that programming efforts are carried out by individuals or groups that do not interact in the programming process. Wherever possible, different algorithms and programming languages or translators are used in each effort.

The goal of the initial specification is to state the functional requirements completely and unambiguously, while leaving the widest possible choice of implementations to the N programming efforts. The initial specification also states all the special features that are needed in order to execute the set of N versions in a fault-tolerant manner.[11] An initial specification defines (1) the function to be implemented by an N-version software unit; (2) data formats for the special mechanisms: comparison vectors (c-vectors), comparison status indicators (cs-indicators), and synchronization mechanisms; (3) the cross-check points (cc-points) for c-vector generation; (4) the comparison (matching or voting) algorithm; and (5) the response to the possible outcomes of matching or voting. We note that comparison is used as a general term, while matching refers to the $N = 2$ case, and voting to a majority decision with $N > 2$. The comparison algorithm explicitly states the allowable range of discrepancy in numerical results, if such a range exists.

It is a fundamental conjecture of the N-version approach that the independence of programming efforts will greatly reduce the probability of identical software design faults occurring in two or more versions. Together with a reasonable choice of c-vectors and cc-points, this is expected to turn N-version programming into an effective method to achieve tolerance of software design faults. The effectiveness of the entire approach depends on the validity of this conjecture, so an experimental investigation was deemed to be the essential next step of the study. The initial research effort at UCLA addressed two questions:

1. Which constraints (e.g., need for formal specifications, suitable types of problems, nature of algorithms, timing constraints, inexact voting algorithms, etc.) have to be satisfied to make N-version programming feasible at all regardless of the cost?
2. How does the cost effectiveness of the N-version programming approach compare to the two alternatives: nonredundant programming and the recovery block[30] approach?

The scarcity of previous results and an absence of formal theories on N-version programming led to the choice of an experimental approach: to choose some conveniently accessible programming problems, to assess the applicability of N-version programming, and then to proceed to generate a set of programs. Once generated, the programs were executed in a simulated multiple-hardware system, and the resulting observations were applied to refine the methodology and to build up theoretical concepts of N-version programming. A more detailed discussion of the research approach and goals is available,[6] as are detailed discussions of two sets of experimental results, using 27 and 16 independently written programs.[12,11]

THE SPECIFICATION-ORIENTED MULTIVERSION SOFTWARE EXPERIMENT

The preceding experimental work demonstrated the practicality of experimental investigations and confirmed the need for high-quality software specifications. As a consequence, the first aim of the subsequent research was the investigation of software specification techniques. Other aims were to investigate the types and causes of common software errors, to propose improvements to software specification techniques and to the use of these techniques, and to propose future experiments in the investigation of design fault-tolerance in software and in hardware.[22,23]

The following software specification languages were examined as candidates for use in the experiment: OBJ,[19] SPECIAL,[32] DREAM,[31] SEMANOL,[1] UDSS,[9] and PDL.[10] Key attributes required for selection were comprehensibility, testability, maintainability, explicit handling of error conditions, and availability for immediate use.

To examine the effect of specification techniques on multiversion software an experiment was designed in which three different specifications were used. The first was the formal specification language OBJ.[19] The second specification language used was the nonformal PDL[10] that was characteristic of current industry practice. English language was used as the third, or control, specification language, since English had been used in the previous studies.[11]

A specification is formal if it is written in a language with explicitly and precisely defined syntax and semantics.[26] This leads to some very advantageous properties: the specification can be studied mathematically; it can be mechanized and tested to gather empirical evidence of its correctness; it can be computer processed to remove ambiguities, to remove inconsistencies, and to be made complete enough (at least) for empirical testing; the interpretation by implementors and customers in an unambiguous way is easier; and writing rigorous specifications is easier with a formal methodology. OBJ was chosen as the formal specification language because the mechanism necessary to construct and test specifications using OBJ was available at UCLA along with local expertise. This proved to be important since, like all other formal specification languages examined, it had quite inadequate existing documentation. OBJ did, however, promote modularity and explicit handling of error conditions.

The nonformal specification language PDL lacks the power

and sophistication of OBJ, but it does have adequate documentation, is reasonably well known, and has been in use in industry for several years. Writing specifications in PDL is straightforward, the ease of understanding depending largely on the amount of care taken by the writer. PDL provides extensive cross referencing and indexing—a feature that would be very useful in OBJ. Specifications written in PDL do tend to be rather long, however.

The problem chosen for the experiment was an "airport scheduler" exercise. This database problem concerns the operation of an airport in which flights are scheduled to depart for other airports and seats are reserved on those flights. The problem was discussed originally by Ehrig, Kreowski, and Weber[13] and later used to illustrate OBJ by Goguen and Tardo.[19] Because the problem is transaction oriented, the natural choice of N-version cross-check points was at the end of each transaction. With the OBJ specification as a reference point, a specification was written in PDL and another one in English.

EXECUTION OF THE EXPERIMENT

Programmers with reasonable proficiency in PL/1 were recruited among the Computer Science students at UCLA. They were assigned to work with one of the three specifications; no specification was tackled by a group whose overall range of abilities was not representative of the total range. The programmers were given a realistic deadline and a monetary incentive to produce programs of at least minimal quality by the deadline. The experiment proceeded in several steps: (1) recruiting, (2) teaching OBJ and PDL, (3) examining and ranking, (4) Assigning the problem, and (5) evaluating programs.

A seminar was held at the UCLA Computer Science Department to announce the need for programmers; and over the next four weeks 30 programmers were recruited, whose abilities ranged from good to excellent, who were senior or graduate students, and who had anywhere from no professional experience at all up to several years of experience. The next stage was the presentation of a one-day course on OBJ and PDL, which was necessary because of the total lack of familiarity with OBJ and very little familiarity with PDL. Study material was distributed and an examination was held two days later, at which the 30 participants were ranked as good, average, or poor. The members of each ranking were then assigned in roughly equal numbers to use the OBJ, PDL, and English specifications. The purpose of the examination was to avoid loading any of the specifications with either predominantly good or predominantly bad programmers.

At a subsequent meeting each programmer was given a packet containing the specification, a notebook to record programmer effort, bugs encountered, and other problems, and a questionnaire on the specification and its use. It was also made clear that the programmers would not be paid for their work unless their programs passed a straightforward acceptance test. While an example of a typical acceptance test was given, the actual test to be used was not revealed. They were strongly requested to avoid working with other participants, and the goal of the experiment was once again carefully explained to support this request.

At the end of the four-week interval 18 of the 30 programmers returned working program versions of the airport scheduler written in PL/1. Of the 18 program versions seven were written from the OBJ specification, five from the PDL specification, and six from English. All 18 programs were run with the standard acceptance test data. After minor modifications were made to two programs by the original programmers, all 18 were judged satisfactory and were prepared for more detailed testing.

To conduct the more extensive testing, a very demanding set of 100 input transactions was developed in an attempt to exercise as many features of the programs as possible. The immediate consequence of running the programs with this input data was the discovery that 11 of the 18 programs aborted on invalid input. This is, of course, a very dangerous situation to encounter in N-version programming, as Chen had found out.[11] In this case, one aborting bad version usually causes operating system intervention for all versions, effectively allowing the bad version to outvote two otherwise healthy versions. To fix this situation all programs were instrumented using PL/1 language capabilities to detect and to attempt recovery from these otherwise catastrophic errors. After such instrumentation, all programs survived the test case input, with 10 of the 11 previously abortable programs making reasonable recoveries.

Program size and time requirements varied considerably. Table I shows, for each program version, the number of PL/1 statements used in the program (PL/1 Stmts), the number of procedures used (Procs), the compile time (PL/1 MUS*), the

TABLE I—Characteristics of all 18 versions

Version	PL/1 Stmts	Procs	PL/1 MUS	GO MUS	Size
OBJ1	423	22	15.14	3.89	37600
OBJ2	400	28	11.35	3.96	28048
OBJ3	398	17	7.42	4.33	30904
OBJ4	328	14	8.62	4.77	29920
OBJ5	455	14	14.79	3.10	32304
OBJ6	243	16	4.71	2.70	20960
OBJ7	336	23	8.30	4.92	34808
PDL1	455	27	16.96	3.16	24928
PDL2	501	33	19.58	19.58	29656
PDL3	242	19	4.31	4.09	27360
PDL4	437	39	16.31	2.84	30896
PDL5	217	11	4.26	4.30	26440
ENG1	260	21	4.75	3.33	27552
ENG2	372	19	12.41	3.89	37792
ENG3	385	30	8.12	2.41	20648
ENG4	689	25	28.23	2.94	26864
ENG5	481	15	8.76	2.42	24056
ENG6	387	12	19.23	3.99	24656

TABLE II—Test results for individual versions

Version	OK Points	Cosmetic Errors	Good OK+Cos	Detected Errors	Undet. Errors
OBJ1	73	0	73	2	25
OBJ2	71	18	89	8	3
OBJ3	67	11	78	4	18
OBJ4	69	3	72	8	20
OBJ5	67	12	79	0	21
OBJ6	46	0	46	0	54
OBJ7	52	17	69	7	24
PDL1	59	2	61	1	38
PDL2	54	2	56	32	12
PDL3	95	0	95	4	1
PDL4	45	28	73	0	27
PDL5	94	0	94	5	1
ENG1	74	12	86	0	14
ENG2	67	27	94	0	6
ENG3	97	1	98	0	2
ENG4	30	5	35	25	40
ENG5	55	6	61	0	39
ENG6	53	3	56	9	35

execution time for the 100-point test case (GO MUS), and the program size in bytes (Size).

The output produced for each of the 100 input data points was classified as "good" if the output was completely correct or was logically correct with "cosmetic" errors. The numerous cosmetic errors were due mainly to misspelling and bad output formatting. Other data points were classified as either detected or undetected error points. A point was considered to be a detected error if the program version caused execution of the instrumented code that had been added to detect and attempt recovery from abort conditions. In the far more serious case that the output looked legal but was in fact wrong, the point was considered an undetected error detectable only by external means. Table II shows the results of this classification.

Next, all possible triple combinations of the 18 versions were executed as an N-version module. Table III lists the breakdown of these 816 combinations. There were now three output points to consider for each input point, with the output

TABLE III—Three-version triplets

Triplet Composition	Number of Triplets
O O O	35
P P P	10
E E E	20
O P E	210
O O P	105
O O E	126
O P P	70
O E E	105
P P E	60
P E E	75
All	816

TABLE IV—Outputs of members of a triplet

Code	Meaning
G	Good: error free or cosmetic error
D	Detected error in single version
U	Undetected error: distinct
U*	Undetected error: common

TABLE V—The three-version decision function

Type	No. of Errors	Function	Result	Decision	Confidence Level
V1	0	V(G,G,G)	G	Triplex	3
V2	1	V(G,G,D)	G	Duplex	2
V3	1	V(G,G,U)	G	Triplex	2
V4	2	V(G,D,D)	G	Simplex	1
V5	2	V(G,D,U)	D	Duplex	0
V6	2	V(G,U,U)	D	Triplex	0
V7	2	V(G,U*,U*)	U*	Triplex	2
V8	3	V(D,D,D)	D	Null	0
V9	3	V(D,D,U)	U	Simplex	1
V10	3	V(D,U,U)	D	Duplex	0
V11	3	V(D,U*,U*)	U*	Duplex	2
V12	3	V(U,U,U)	D	Triplex	0
V13	3	V(U,U*,U*)	U*	Triplex	2
V14	3	V(U*,U*,U*)	U*	Triplex	3

points coded as in Table IV. Note that U is an undetected error that is not duplicated in one of the other two versions, U* an undetected error that is common to both or all three of the versions. The 14 meaningful combinations of these codes are shown with the corresponding voting function output in Table V. The distribution of the experimental results over the 14 voting categories is shown in Table VI.

All common errors were tabulated and traced to their causes. It was found that there were 21 different cases of common errors. Five of these were caused by specification limitations or errors, seven by logic errors made by the programmers, and nine by implementation errors. These common errors were tabulated in Tables VII–IX.

WORK IN PROGRESS AND GOALS FOR LONG-RANGE RESEARCH

One major goal of the experiments described in the preceding sections is to apply the accumulated experience to the design of the next experiment. It has become evident that the general UCLA campus computing facility is an unsupportive and often hostile environment for multiversion software experiments. With a view to establishing a long-term research facility for such investigations, an effort is in progress to create a multichannel fault-tolerant system as an integral part of the

*Machine unit second (MUS) is actually a measure of time and other resources such as I/O needs.

TABLE VI—Decision function results

Type	3-Version Group					
	All	OOO	PPP	EEE	OPE	Other
V1	36665 44.9%	1703 48.7%	448 44.8%	820 41.0%	9354 44.5%	24340 45.0%
V2	5292 6.5%	129 3.7%	128 12.8%	166 8.3%	1341 6.4%	3528 6.5%
V3	22105 27.1%	842 24.1%	274 27.4%	554 27.7%	5939 28.3%	14496 26.8%
V4	1283 1.6%	48 1.4%	8 0.8%	32 1.6%	347 1.7%	848 1.6%
V5	3986 4.9%	141 4.0%	88 8.8%	80 4.0%	1046 5.0%	2631 4.9%
V6	6838 8.4%	264 7.5%	18 1.8%	206 10.3%	1747 8.3%	4603 8.5%
V7	1944 2.4%	86 2.5%	12 1.2%	82 4.1%	386 1.8%	1378 2.5%
V8	176 0.2%	4 0.1%	0 0.0%	0 0.0%	65 0.3%	107 0.2%
V9	477 0.6%	20 0.6%	7 0.7%	4 0.2%	123 0.6%	323 0.6%
V10	867 1.1%	11 0.3%	6 0.6%	22 1.1%	274 1.3%	554 1.0%
V11	87 0.1%	6 0.2%	0 0.0%	0 0.0%	28 0.1%	53 0.1%
V12	1415 1.7%	173 4.9%	1 0.1%	20 1.0%	275 1.3%	946 1.7%
V13	353 0.4%	48 1.4%	0 0.0%	8 0.4%	62 0.3%	235 0.4%
V14	112 0.1%	25 0.7%	10 1.0%	6 0.3%	13 0.1%	58 0.1%
Total	81600 100.0%	3500 100.0%	1000 100.0%	2000 100.0%	21000 100.0%	54100 100.0%

TABLE VII—Common specification errors

Error	Appears In			Description
	OBJ	PDL	ENG	
S1	1,4,5,7			Only defines four destinations
S2			4,5,6	Time shown as 09:45 in example
S3			4,5,6	Error message order ambiguity
S4			2,4	Duplicate error message ambiguity
S5			6	Parameter checking ambiguity

TABLE VIII—Common logic errors

Error	Appears In			Description
	OBJ	PDL	ENG	
L1	1			CANCEL does not work on last entry
L2	3		5	CANCEL works only on partial database
L3	7			CANCEL unknown cancels last entry
L4		1		Cannot retrieve record
L5		1		Allows duplicate record
L6			4	CANCEL, RESERVE-SEAT ignored
L7			4	Bad input leads to chaos

TABLE IX—Common implementation errors

Error	Appears In			Description
	OBJ	PDL	ENG	
I1	2	1,2,3,4,5		Did not check input parameters first
I2		1,4		Expects time as 09:45
I3	1,2,5	4	1	Wrong error message on illegal input
I4	4	4	1	CREATE does not work the second time
I5		2,4	5	Error message output on legal input
I6	3	1	6	Allows null parameters
I7		1	4	Allows invalid parameters
I8	6			No output after first list produced
I9		2		Cannot handle invalid input

UCLA Computer Science Department advanced local network facility, which uses the LOCUS distributed operating system.[29] The projected six-year effort consists of four phases.

The first phase is the implementation of a multichannel fault-tolerant subset NIFTS, composed of at least three identical computing nodes (DEC VAX 11/750 computers) of the UCLA local network. It is to serve as an experimental vehicle for subsequent design fault tolerance studies. The SIFT[20] concept is being adapted at UCLA to serve as the foundation of NIFTS. In the second phase NIFTS will be used as the means to continue and expand the ongoing experimental research on the tolerance of software design faults that has been described in this paper. In the third phase we will investigate and implement a generalization of NIFTS to encompass N computing nodes with nonidentical hardware. Such an "N-fold diverse hardware" form of NIFTS is intended to tolerate faults due to left-over design errors and to errors introduced during modification and maintenance. In the fourth phase we plan to conduct extensive fault tolerance experiments with NIFTS as developed in the first three phases. The main goal is to evaluate the effectiveness and to refine the methodology of using N-version software and N-version hardware as mechanisms of design fault tolerance.

A second planned extension of our research is to employ the mail order concept of obtaining multiversion software. We are working to secure the cooperation of fault tolerance research groups at several universities in the USA and in Europe. Members of these groups will participate in writing the programs for a larger experiment that will be evaluated on our new experimental facility, NIFTS.

The practicality and generality of the design diversity approach as an alternative to fault avoidance remain to be established or disproved; however, the design fault problem in both software and VLSI circuits remains quite serious, and we consider our research results to be sufficiently encouraging to warrant further and more intensive efforts.

ACKNOWLEDGMENT

The research for this article was supported by NSF Grant No. MCS-78-18918 and by a research grant from The Battelle Institute. (Drs. Liming Chen and John P. J. Kelly have been major contributors to the research effort at UCLA.)

REFERENCES

1. Anderson, E. R., F. C. Belz, and E. K. Blum. "SEMANOL(73), A Metalanguage for Programming the Semantics of Programming Languages." *Acta Informatica 6*, 109–131.

2. Avizienis, A., and L. Chen. "On the Implementation of N-version Programming for Software Fault-Tolerance During Execution." *Proceedings of COMPSAC 77,* (First IEEE-CS International Computer Software and Application Conference), 1977, 1949–155.
3. Avizienis, A. "An Experimental Self-Repairing Computer," Information Processing 1968, (Proceedings of the 1968 Congress of the International Federation for Information Processing, Edinburgh, Scotland). Amsterdam: North Holland Publishing Co., 1969, pp. 872–877.
4. Avizienis, A., et al., "The STAR (Self-Testing-And Repairing) Computer: An Investigation of the Theory and Practice of Fault-Tolerant Computer Design," *IEEE Transactions on Computers,* C-20, (1971), pp. 1312–1321.
5. Avizienis, A., "Fault-Tolerance and Fault-Intolerance: Complementary Approaches to Reliable Computing." Proceedings of the 1975 International Conference on Reliable Software, pp. 458–464.
6. Avizienis, A., "Fault-Tolerant Computing: Progress, Problems, and Prospects." *Information Processing 77, Proceedings of the IFIP Congress 1977.* Toronto, August 8–12, 1977, p. 405–420.
7. Avizienis, A., "Fault-Tolerance: The Survival Attribute of Digital Systems." Proceedings of the IEEE, 66, (1978), pp. 1109–1125.
8. Avizienis, A. "The Four-Universe Information System Model for Fault-Tolerance." *Digest FTCS-12: The 1982 International Symposium on Fault-Tolerant Computing,* Santa Monica, CA, June 1982.
9. Biggerstaff, T. J., "The Unified Design Specification System (UDSS)." *Proceedings on Specifications for Reliable Software,* April 79, 104–118.
10. Caine, S. H., and E. K. Gordon. "PDL—A Tool for Software Design." *AFIPS, Proceedings of the National Computer Conference, 1975* (Vol.), pp.
11. Chen, L., and A. Avizienis. "N-Version Programming: A Fault-tolerance Approach to Reliability of Software Operation," Digest FTCS-8, Toulouse, France, June 1978, pp. 3–9.
12. Chen, L. "Improving Software Reliability by N-version Programming." *UCLA Computer Science Department Technical Report,* UCLA-ENG-7843, University of California, Los Angeles, 1978.
13. Ehrig, H., H. Kreowski, and H. Weber. "Algebraic Specification Schemes for Data Base Systems." *Proc. VLDB,* 1978, 427–440.
14. Elmendorf, W. R. "Fault-Tolerant Programming." *Proceedings of the 1972 International Symposium on Fault-Tolerant Computing,* June 1972, 79–83.
15. Fischler, M. A., et.al., "Distinct Software: An Approach to Reliable Computing" *Proc. 2nd USA-Japan Computer Conference,* Tokyo, Japn, 1975, 1–7.
16. Granarov, A., J. Arlat, and A. Avizienis. "On the Performance of Software Fault-Tolerance Stategies." *Digest of the 1980 International Symposium on Fault-Tolerant Computing,* Kyoto, Japan, October 1–3, 1980, pp. 251–253.
17. Girard, E. and J. C. Rault. "A Programming Technique for Software Reliability." *Proceedings of the 1973 IEEE Symposium on Computer Software Reliability,* 44–50.
18. Gmeiner, L., and U. Voges. "Software Diversity in Reactor Protection Systems: An Experiment." *IFAC Workshop SAFECOMP 1979,* Stuttgart, May 16–18, 1979.
19. Goguen, J. A., and J. J. Tardo, "An introduction to OBJ", *Proc. Specifications for Reliable Software,* April 1979, 170–189.
20. Goldberg, J., "SIFT: A Provable Fault-Tolerant Computer for Aircraft Flight Control", *Information Processing 80* (Proceedings of the IFIP Congress 1980, Tokyo, Japan), pp. 151–156.
21. Hopkins, A. L., Jr. et. al., "FTMP—A Highly Reliable Fault-Tolerant Multiprocessor for Aircraft", *Proc. IEEE,* vol. 66, no. 10, Oct. 1978, pp. 1221–1239.
22. Kelly, J. P. J., "Specification of Fault-Tolerant Multi-Version Software: Experimental Studies of a Design Diversity Approach," *Ph.D. Thesis,* UCLA Computer Science Department, June 1982; also *UCLA CSD Technical Report No. CSD-820927,* September 1982.
23. Kelly, J. P. J., and A. Avizienis, "A Specification-Oriented Multi-Version Software Experiment" IEEE 1983 FTCS 13th Annual International Symposium Fault-Tolerant Computing, pp. 120–126.
24. Kim, K.H., and C.V. Ramamorthy. "Failure-Tolerance Parallel Programming and Its Supporting System Architecture," *AFIPS, Proceedings of the National Computer Conference, 1976* (Vol. 45), pp. 413–423.
25. Kopetz, H., "Software Redundancy in Real Time Systems." *Proc. IFIP Congress 1974,* 182–186.
26. Wegner, P., (ed.), B. H. Liskov, and V. Berzins. "An Appraisal of Program Specifications," *In Research Directions in Software Technology.* Cambridge, Mass.: MIT Press, 1979.
27. Long, A. B., C. V. Ramamoorthy, et al. "A Methodology for Development and Validation of Critical Software for Nuclear Power Plants." *Proc. COMPSAC 77* (IEEE-CS Int. Computer Software & Applications Conf.), 620–626.
28. Morrison, P., and E. Morrison, (eds.) *Charles Babbage and His Calculating Engines,* New York: Dover, 1961, p. 177.
29. Popek, G. et al., "LOCUS—A Network Transparent, High Reliability Distributed System," *The UCLA Computer Science Department Quarterly,* 9, (1981), pp. 75–88.
30. Randell, B. "System Structure for Software Fault-Tolerance." *IEEE Transactions on Software Engineering,* SE-1, (1975), pp. 220-232.
31. Riddle, W. E. et al., "Abstract Monitor Types." *Proceedings on Specifications for Reliable Software,* April 1979, pp. 126–138.
32. Robinson, L., and O. Roubine. "SPECIAL—A Specification and Assertion Language." *SRI Technical Report,* CSL-46, January 1977.
33. Toy, W. N. "Fault-Tolerant Design of Local ESS Processors." *Proceedings of the IEEE, 66,* (1978), pp. 1126–1145.
34. Voges, U. "Aspects of Design, Test and Validation of the Software for a Computerized Reactor Protection System," *Proceedings of the 2nd International Conference on Software Engineering,* San Francisco, 1976, pp. 606–610.

Tradeoffs in system level diagnosis of multiprocessor systems

by A. KAVIANPOUR
Sharif University of Technology
Tehran, Iran
and
A.D. FRIEDMAN
The George Washington University
Washington D.C.

ABSTRACT

The development of LSI technology makes it possible to partition a system into replaceable modules, and the advent of low-cost microprocessors makes possible networks of hundreds (or more) of interconnected modules. The problem of repairing such a system is becoming a matter of major importance in digital systems.

In this paper a new procedure for defining an optimal design with respect to cost of repair for a system consisting of replaceable modules (processors) is introduced. Also the tradeoff between the number of repetitions of the diagnostic test (speed of diagnosis), the number of testing links in the system (complexity), and the number of replaced fault-free modules (accuracy) is considered.

In an early paper, Preparata, Metze, and Chien[4] formulated a model of system level diagnosis and defined two types of diagnosability measures, i.e. one-step t-fault diagnosability, and sequential t-fault diagnosability. They proved that $D_{\delta t}$ is one-step t-fault diagnosable and single loop connection is sequentially t-fault diagnosable. Friedman[12] later generalized this measure to one-step t-out-of-S (t/S) diagnosability, in which t faults are diagnosed to within $S \geq t$ modules. This introduces the possibility of inexact diagnosis—i.e. such that some fault-free modules may have to be replaced in order to repair a system in one step.

So far most of the results that are available are only for single-loop or $D_{\delta t}$ design, and the results for a system in between these two extreme cases are not available. A $D_{\delta t}$ system needs more testing links and a single-loop system needs more steps in order to be repaired. In this paper we have defined a design in between $D_{\delta t}$ and single-loop systems; also the tradeoff between the number of repetitions of the diagnostic test (speed of diagnosis), the number of testing links (complexity), and the number of replaced fault-free modules (accuracy) is considered, and the optimal design with respect to cost of repair is defined.

INTRODUCTION AND BACKGROUND

Several papers considering various aspects of self-diagnosable systems have appeared in the literature,[1–15] and it appears that a graph-theoretic model can be effectively used in the area of system diagnosis. A system is partitioned into a number of modules $m_0, m_1, m_2, \ldots, m_{n-1}$ that can correspond to the processors in a multiprocessor system, and it is assumed that each module can test or be tested by some other modules. The outcome of a test in which m_i tests m_j is denoted by a_{ij}. The variable a_{ij} is binary; $a_{ij} = 1$ indicates "m_i finds module m_j faulty," $a_{ij} = 0$ indicates "m_i finds module m_j fault-free." If m_i is faulty, then the outcome a_{ij} is unpredictable.

Preparata et al.[4] originally considered this graph-theoretic model for the purpose of diagnosis of multiple faults. They defined two types of diagnosability, namely one-step t-fault diagnosability and sequential t-fault diagnosability.

Definition 1. A system of n units is *one-step t-fault diagnosable* if all faulty units within the system can be identified without replacement provided the number of faulty units present does not exceed t.

Definition 2. A system of n units is *sequentially t-fault diagnosable* if at least one faulty unit can be identified without replacement provided the number of faulty units present does not exceed t.

In a sequentially diagnosable system, at each step at least one faulty module can be diagnosed. This module can be replaced by a module that is assumed to be fault-free and the test can be applied again. This is equivalent to identifying one fault-free module. This procedure is repeated until the system is completely fault-free. Preparata et al. proved that it is possible to design a system which has n modules and is one-step t-fault diagnosable if and only if $n \geq 2t + 1$ and each module is tested by at least t other modules (when no two modules test each other). They defined the following canonical system.

Definition 3. A system S is a $D_{\delta t}$ system if there exists a testing link from m_i to m_j if and only if $(j - i) = \delta m$ (modulo n) where δ, m are integers and m assumes the values $1, 2, \ldots, t$.

Figure 1 shows a D_{12} design. Preparata et al. showed that $D_{\delta t}$ systems are one-step t-fault diagnosable. They also considered a single-loop design that is sequentially t-fault diagnosable (a special case of $D_{\delta t}$, D_{11}). Such a system is obtained by connecting the n elements in a cycle. They gave a lower bound on the value of n; Preparata[5] proved that a single loop is sequentially t-fault diagnosable if and only if $n \geq (m + 1)^2 + \lambda(m + 1) + 1$, with $t = 2m + \lambda$, m an integer, and $\lambda = 0,1$.

Friedman[12] later generalized this measure to one-step t-out-of-S(t/S) diagnosability, in which t faults are diagnosed to within $S \geq t$ modules. This introduces the possibility of inexact diagnosis and replacement of the faulty modules plus some modules that may not be faulty. Friedman introduced the following measure.

Definition 4. A system V is k-step t/S-fault diagnosable if by k applications of the diagnostic test sequence any set of $\leq t$ faulty modules can be diagnosed and repaired by replacing at most S modules.

Obviously $S \geq t$ and $n \geq S$ (if $n = S$ repair is trivial since the entire system is replaced). Friedman also considered a one-step repair of a single-loop system with $n \gg t$, which requires the replacement of at most S modules, where $S = \max f(t - f + 2) - 1$ and $f \leq t$ is the actual number of faults in the system.

TRADEOFFS IN SYSTEM LEVEL DIAGNOSIS

In this paper we will develop a procedure for defining an optimal design with respect to cost of repair in a system con-

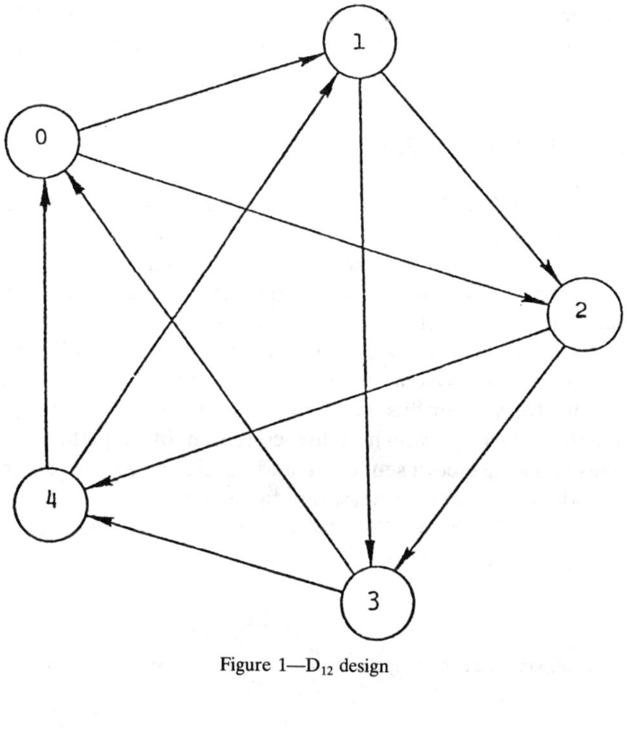

Figure 1—D_{12} design

sisting of replaceable modules, and we will consider the tradeoff between (1) the number of steps (i.e. test iterations) for repairing a system (speed of diagnosis), (2) the number of replaced fault-free modules (accuracy), (3) the number of testing links in the system (complexity). The following general problem will be solved: Given n (the number of modules of the system), and t (upper bound on the number of faults), in order to minimize the total repair cost,

1. In how many steps should the system be diagnosed?
2. What bound on the number of fault-free modules to be replaced should be used?
3. How many testing links should be used?

In order to design a minimum-cost design we must define the parameters that affect the cost. A single-loop system ($n \gg t$) is sequentially t-fault diagnosable and the number of testing links is equal to n. A $D_{\delta t}$ design is one-step t-fault diagnosable and the number of testing links is equal to nt; however, a single loop design needs more steps, k, in order to be diagnosed (in a worst case the diagnostic test may have to be repeated t times) but needs fewer testing links, L, in comparison to $D_{\delta t}$ design; thus there is a tradeoff between the number of steps for repairing a system and the number of testing links. Another factor that affects the minimum-cost design is the number of replaced fault-free modules, S_g. Consider a system with a single-loop connection. This system can be repaired sequentially in at most t steps ($k \leq t$) if no fault-free module may be replaced ($S_g = 0$). However, we can repair this system in one step ($k = 1$) if some of the modules that are possibly faulty may be replaced ($S_g \geq 0$). Thus there is a tradeoff between the number of steps for repeating a diagnostic test (k) and the number of replaced fault-free modules (S_g). In general, by considering $D_{\delta t}$ and single loop designs one sees that there is a tradeoff between the number of repetitions of a test, k (speed of diagnosis), the number of replaced fault-free modules, S_g (accuracy), and the number of testing links/module, L (complexity). Tables I and II illustrate this tradeoff.

k-STEP DIAGNOSABILITY

As was explained, a single-loop system is sequentially t-fault diagnosable, and a $D_{\delta t}$ system is one-step t-fault diagnosable. However, a design in between these two extreme cases was not defined. For example, a design that can be repaired (without replacement of fault-free modules) in two steps, three steps, or in general in k steps is not available. In the following we will define a system that can be repaired in at most k steps for arbitrary k. In this paper by $n \gg t$ we mean $n \geq (\lfloor t/2 \rfloor + 1)(\lceil t/2 \rceil + 1) + 1$,* which is the condition of sequentiality.[4] This is because both sequential and t/S diagnosability require the identification of at least one fault-free module.

In the following we define a system that is k-step t-fault or k-step t/S fault diagnosable.

* $\lfloor\ \rfloor$ indicate the greatest integer $\leq t/2$. $\lceil\ \rceil$ indicate the smallest integer $\geq t/2$.

TABLE I—Tradeoff with no fault-free modules replaced ($S_g = 0$)

Design	k	L
single-loop	t	1
$D_{\delta t}$	1	t

TABLE II—Tradeoff with one testing link ($L = 1$), single-loop design

k	S_g
t	0
1	$t^2/4$

NOTE: See equation (5) and following for definition of $t^2/4$.

Definition 5. A system S is said to belong to a design D_{1L} when a testing link from m_i to m_j exists if and only if $j - i = m$ (modulo n) where $m = 1, 2, \ldots, L$ (special case of $D_{\delta L}$ with $\delta = 1$).

Lemma 1. If a system S with $n \gg t$ modules employs design D_{1L} with $L = \lceil t/k \rceil$, then S is k-step t-fault diagnosable.

Proof. Since each module of the system *S* is tested by $\lceil t/k \rceil$ other modules and $n \gg t$ this implies that at least one fault-free module can be identified. Thus at each step the status of at least $\lceil t/k \rceil$ faulty modules can be diagnosed, and in at most k steps $k \lceil t/k \rceil = t$ faulty modules will be diagnosed.

From Lemma 1 it is seen that when $k = 1$ then $L = \lceil t/k \rceil = t$ and the system can be repaired in one step. If $k = t$, then $L = \lceil t/k \rceil = 1$, and the system can be repaired in at most t steps. Using Lemma 1 the following corollary is immediate.

Corollary 1. If a system S with $n \gg t$ employs design D_{1L} with $L = \lceil t/\alpha \rceil$ then S is k-step t/S-fault diagnosable. Where $\alpha > k$ and $1 < \alpha < t$.

In design D_{1L} with $L = \lceil t/\alpha \rceil$ each module is tested by $\lceil t/\alpha \rceil$ other modules. As will be seen later, the value of α affects the number of replaced fault-free modules S_g for a fixed k; in Corollary 1, the value of S_g is explicitly considered. That $\alpha = k$ implies k-step t-fault diagnosability; if $k < \alpha$, in order to repair a system in k steps some fault-free modules may have to be replaced. The value of k/α also affects the number of replaced modules. When $k = \alpha = 1$ the total number of testing links is $nk\lceil t/\alpha \rceil = nt$ and no fault-free module will be replaced. When $k/\alpha < 1$, that is, in k-step t/S-fault diagnosability, each module is tested by fewer than $\lceil t/k \rceil$ other modules and we have to repair the system in at most k steps. Thus some of the fault-free modules may have to be replaced.

MINIMUM COST DESIGN OF DIGITAL SYSTEM

For cost evaluation we define the following parameters:

C_r = cost of repeating a test/module.
C_L = cost of testing link/module, i.e. nC_L = cost of a single loop connnection.

C_g = cost of replacing a fault-free module. (We assume that all modules have identical costs and that all tests must be repeated.)

First we will find the minimum cost design for k-step t/S-fault diagnosability. Then by using $\alpha = k$ and $C_g \rightarrow \infty$ we can find the minimum cost design for k-step t-fault diagnosability. $C_g \rightarrow \infty$ means that in k-step t-fault diagnosability the cost of replacing a fault-free module is very high and we are not allowed to replace fault-free modules. One factor that affects the number of replaced fault-free modules in the strategy for repair, i.e. which module to replace, and when, for minimum S_g. We must define a strategy for repair that is constrained; that is, a strategy in which we can decide in how many steps we wish to repair a system (the value of k will be specified by the designer, which can be found by the procedure of this paper).

Constraint Strategy

We define the following constraint strategy, which we call $A(k-1,1)$. In this strategy, in the first $(k-1)$ iterations we replace those modules that are definitely faulty and at the kth step we replace all modules that may be faulty, i.e. all modules that cannot be definitely determined to be fault-free. The following example illustrates how strategy $A(k-1,1)$ can be used for repairing a system.

Example 1. Consider a single-loop connection with $n = 17$ and $t = 6$. Let modules m_1, m_3, m_6, m_8, and m_9 $(f = 5)$ be faulty. We wish to repair the system by using strategy $A(k-1,1)$ with $k = 3$. In this strategy, at the first and second applications of the diagnostic test we replace those modules that are definitely faulty and at the third step we replace those modules that are definitely faulty plus those modules that are possibly faulty. The fault pattern in the first iteration is assumed to be as follows:

		*		*			*		*	*							
m_i	0	1	2	3	4	5	6	7	8	9	10	11	12	13	14	15	16
$a_{(i-1)i}$	0	1	0	1	1	0	1	1	1	0	0	0	0	0	0	0	0

Module m_1 (and only m_1) is definitely faulty. Therefore we replace module m_1 and reapply the test. The fault pattern in the second iteration is then as follows:

				*			*		*	*							
m_i	0	1	2	3	4	5	6	7	8	9	10	11	12	13	14	15	16
$a_{(i-1)i}$	0	0	0	1	1	0	1	1	1	0	0	0	0	0	0	0	0

Module m_3 (and only m_3) is definitely faulty. We replace module m_3 we reapply the test. The fault pattern in the third iteration is as follows:

							*		*	*							
m_i	0	1	2	3	4	5	6	7	8	9	10	11	12	13	14	15	16
$a_{(i-1)i}$	0	0	0	0	0	0	1	1	1	0	0	0	0	0	0	0	0

Since we wish to repair the system in 3 steps, we have to replace modules $m_6, m_7, m_8, m_9, m_{10}$ (of which m_6 is definitely faulty and the others possibly faulty). The total number of replaced modules is equal to 7. In this example $7 - f = 7 - 5 = 2$ fault-free modules are replaced; $S_g = 2$. If we want to repair the system with $S_g = 0$, we have to apply the test 6 times.

Minimum-Cost Design

In order to find a minimum-cost design for the constraint strategy we proceed as follows: We restrict ourselves to system D_{1L}, in which each module is tested by $L = \lceil t/\alpha \rceil$ other modules. For minimum-cost design of k-step t-fault diagnosability, $\alpha = k$ and the total number of testing links is equal to $\lceil nt/k \rceil$. In order to calculate the number of replaced modules we will use stategy $A(k-1,1)$. The value of S can be calculated as follows: since each module is tested by $L = \lceil t/\alpha \rceil$ other modules and $n \gg t$, in k iterations we can detect at least $\lceil tk/\alpha \rceil$ definitely faulty modules. However, since t is the upper bound on the number of faults, there may possibly be $t' = t - [tk/\alpha]$ more faulty modules.

The maximum number of modules that may have to be replaced in a worst case for t' faulty modules is $S = f^*(t' - f^* + 2) - 1$, where $f^* = \max$ [number of (01)'s, $\lceil \frac{1}{2}$ number of one's$\rceil$].[13] Thus the total number of replaced modules is

$$S = \lceil tk/\alpha + f^*(t' - f^* + 2) - 1 \rceil \tag{1}$$

where $t' = t - \lceil tk/\alpha \rceil$. Thus we have

$$S = \lceil tk/\alpha + f^*(t - tk/\alpha - f^* + 2) - 1 \rceil. \tag{2}$$

The maximum value of S occurs when $\dfrac{ds}{df^*} = 0$. Equation (2) implies

$$t - \frac{tk}{\alpha} - f^* + 2 - f^* = 0 \rightarrow f^* = \frac{t - tk/\alpha + 2}{2}.$$

Hence

$$f^* = \left\lfloor \frac{t - tk/\alpha}{2} \right\rfloor + 1 = \left\lfloor \left(\frac{t}{2} - \frac{tk}{2\alpha}\right) \right\rfloor + 1.$$

Substituting the value of f^* into equation (2) results in the following:

$$S = \left\lceil \frac{tk}{\alpha} + \left(\frac{t}{2} - \frac{tk}{2\alpha} + 1\right)^2 - 1 \right\rceil \tag{3}$$

where $1 \le \alpha \le t$; $1 \le k \le t$; $k \le \alpha$. Thus the number of replaced fault-free modules is at most

$$S_g = \left\lceil \left(\frac{t}{2} - \frac{tk}{2\alpha}\right)^2 \right\rceil. \tag{4}$$

* It is possible to consider a diagnostic model in which some of the modules are performing computation while others are doing testing. In this case the term knC_r will decrease but the control unit will be more complex, because it has to decide which module must be in the computation or testing phase.

Hence the parameters for minimum-cost design are as follows:

1. k = Number of test iterations; $1 \le k \le t$.
2. $L = \lceil nt/\alpha \rceil$ = Total number of testing links; $1 \le \alpha \le t$; $k \le \alpha$.
3. $S_g = \lceil (t/2 - kt/2\alpha)^2 \rceil$ = Number of replaced fault-free modules.

When k = 1 (i.e. for repairing a system in one step) from equation (4) $S_g = [(t/2 - tk/2\alpha)^2] = 0$. Thus if each module is tested by t other modules, we will not replace any fault-free modules. From equation (4) it is seen that for minimum-cost design of a system two cases can be considered: Case 1 when S_g is not constrained and its value can be obtained from other parameters (α, k); and Case 2 when S_g is constrained and the optimal-cost design will be obtained with respect to it. In this case, since one of the parameters (S_g) is fixed the optimal cost may higher than in Case 1, when all three parameters can vary.

Case 1: Optimal-cost design when S_g is not constrained

The total cost in terms of k,L, S_g is as follows: Total cost = cost of testing links + cost of repeating a test + cost of replacing fault-free modules,

$$C = \left\lceil \frac{nt}{\alpha} \right\rceil C_L + knC_r + [(t/2 - tk/2\alpha)^2]C_g \quad (5)$$

Where $1 \le \alpha \le t$; $1 \le k \le t$; $\alpha \ge k$. In equation (5) the term knc_r* means that all of the modules are taking part in testing during k steps repair. In order to find an optimal-cost design the total derivative must be equal to zero:

$$\frac{\partial C}{\partial \alpha} d\alpha + \frac{\partial C}{\partial k} dk = 0.$$

$$\frac{-nt}{\alpha^2} C_L + \frac{tk}{2}\left(\frac{t}{2} - \frac{tk}{2\alpha}\right) C_g = 0. \quad (6)$$

$$nC_r - \frac{t}{\alpha}\left(\frac{t}{2} - \frac{tk}{2\alpha}\right) C_g = 0. \quad (7)$$

Thus we have

$$\frac{C_L}{C_r} = \frac{k}{t/\alpha} \rightarrow t/\alpha = \left\lceil \frac{kC_r}{C_L} \right\rceil. \quad (8)$$

Substituting equation (8) into equation (6) and simplifying we have

$$\frac{k^3}{2}\frac{C_r}{C_L} - \frac{kt}{2} + \frac{nC_L}{C_g} = 0. \quad (9)$$

From equation (9) the optimal-cost design for k-step t-fault diagnosability can be obtained by substituting $C_g \rightarrow \infty$. Thus we have

$$\frac{k^3}{2}\frac{C_r}{C_L} - \frac{kt}{2} + \frac{nC_L}{C_g} = 0 \rightarrow \frac{k^3}{2}\frac{C_r}{C_L} - \frac{kt}{2} = 0 \rightarrow k = \left\lceil \sqrt{tC_L/C_r} \right\rceil. \quad (10a)$$

Or from equation (8) by substituting $\alpha = k$ the same result can be obtained as follows:

$$C = \left\lceil \frac{t}{k} \right\rceil nC_L + knC_r$$

$$\frac{dC}{dk} = 0 \rightarrow k = \left\lceil \sqrt{tC_L/C_r} \right\rceil. \quad (10b)$$

From equation (10) it is seen that when $C_L/C_r \ge t$, then $k \ge t$ and a single-loop design is optimal with respect to cost of repair for t-fault diagnosability. When $C_L/C_r \le 1/t$ then $k \le 1$ and one-step repair should be used in t-fault diagnosability. This is a consequence of the fact that when C_L, the cost of a testing link, is very high a single-loop design is the obvious choice, and when C_r is very high one-step design must be considered. Figure 2* shows cost versus k for $C_r/C_L = 2$ and it

* The actual forms of the graphs are in the form of step function, but in order to illustrate the actual value of cost between two integer values of k or L, we will draw all graphs in a continuous form.

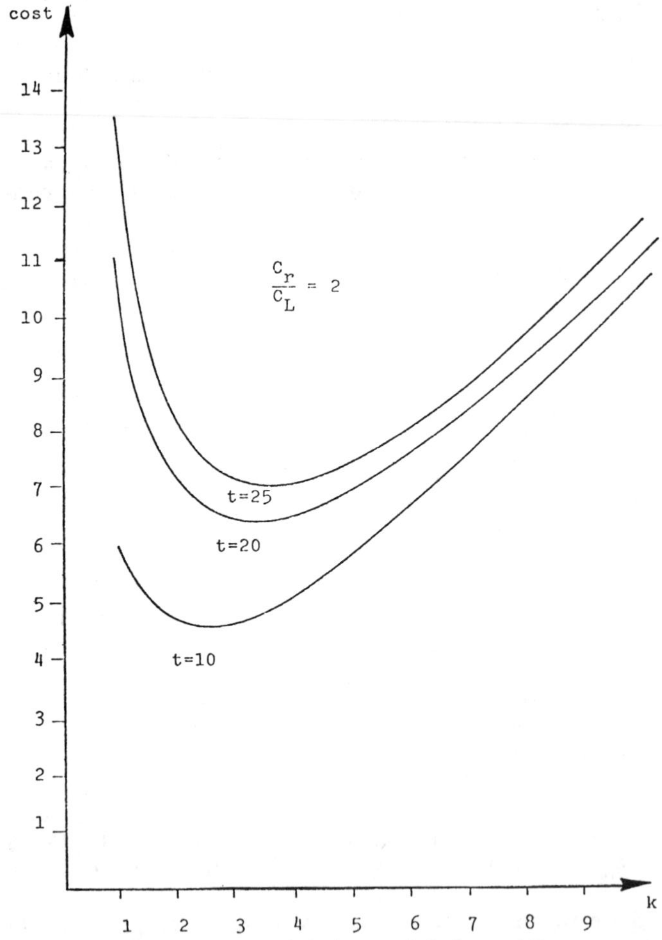

Figure 2—Cost versus k for k-step t-fault diagnosability

TABLE III—Tradeoffs of C_r, C_L, nC_L, and C_g for t-fault diagnosability, t = 20

	k	t/α	S_g	Cost
$\frac{C_r}{C_L}=\frac{1}{4}, \frac{nC_L}{C_g}=16$	8	2	4	4.25 nC_L
$\frac{C_r}{C_L}=\frac{1}{2}, \frac{nC_L}{C_g}=6$	6	3	1	6.16 nC_L

is seen that when testing links are relatively less expensive than repeating a test, then more testing links and fewer test repetitions must be used.

Example 2. Let t = 20 and

$$\frac{C_r}{C_L} = \frac{\text{cost of repeating a test}}{\text{cost of a single loop}} = \frac{1}{4}$$

$$\frac{nC_L}{C_g} = \frac{\text{cost of a single loop}}{\text{cost of replacing a fault-free module}} = 16.$$

The values of k, t/α, S_g, and cost can be calculated as follows:

$$\frac{k^3C_r}{2C_L} - \frac{kt}{2} + \frac{nC_L}{C_g} = 0 \rightarrow \frac{k^3}{8} - 10k + 16 = 0 \rightarrow k = 8.$$

$$\frac{t}{\alpha} = \left[k\,\frac{C_r}{C}\right] = 8.\,\frac{1}{4} = 2$$

$$S_g = \left[\left(\frac{t}{2} - \frac{tk}{2\alpha}\right)^2\right] = (10-8)^2 = 4$$

$$\text{Cost} = \left[\frac{nt}{\alpha}\right] C_L + nkC_r + \left[\left(\frac{t}{2} - \frac{tk}{2\alpha}\right)^2\right] C_g = 4.25\ nC_L.$$

Thus the optimal cost design is as follows:

1. Procedure = t/S-fault diagnosability
2. Maximum number of test applications = 8
3. Number of testing links/module = 2
4. Maximum number of fault-free modules which may have to be replaced = 4
5. Cost = 4.25 (cost of a single loop)

Now if we consider the case that the cost of replacing a fault-free module is relatively high in comparison with the above example, then we have the following: Let $C_r/C_L = 1/2$, $nC_L/C_g = 6$. From equations (8) and (9) we obtain

$$\frac{k^3C_r}{2C_L} - \frac{kt}{2} + \frac{nC_L}{C_g} = 0 \rightarrow \frac{k^3}{4} - 10k + 6 = 0 \rightarrow k = 6.$$

TABLE IV—Cost for t/S = Fault and t-fault diagnosability, t = 20, $C_r/C_L = 1/4$, $nC_L/C_g = 16$

	k	t/α	S_g	Cost
t/S fault diagnosability	8	2	4	4.25 nC_L
t-fault diagnosability	9	3	0	5.5 nC_L

TABLE V—Cost for t/S-fault and t-fault diagnosability, t = 20, $C_r/C_L = 1/2$, $nC_L/C_g = 6$

	k	t/α	S_g	Cost
t/S-fault diagnosability	6	3	1	6.16 n C_L
t-fault diagnosability	7	3	0	6.5 n C_L

From equation (8) we have

$$t/\alpha = \left[k\,\frac{C_r}{C_L}\right] = \frac{6}{2} = 3$$

$$S_g = \left[\left(\frac{t}{2} - \frac{tk}{2\alpha}\right)^2\right] = (10-9)^2 = 1$$

$$\text{Cost} = \left[\frac{nt}{\alpha}\right] C_L + nkC_r + \left[\left(\frac{t}{2} - \frac{tk}{2\alpha}\right)^2\right] C_g = 6.16\,nC_L.$$

Table 3 shows the comparison of these two cases. From Table III it is seen that the value of k decreases as C_r becomes expensive. The number of testing links increases since C_L becomes cheaper, and the value of S_g decreases since C_g becomes expensive.

If we wish to use k-step t-fault diagnosability (i.e. $S_g = 0$), then from equation (10) we have $k = [\sqrt{tC_L/C_r}]$ which results

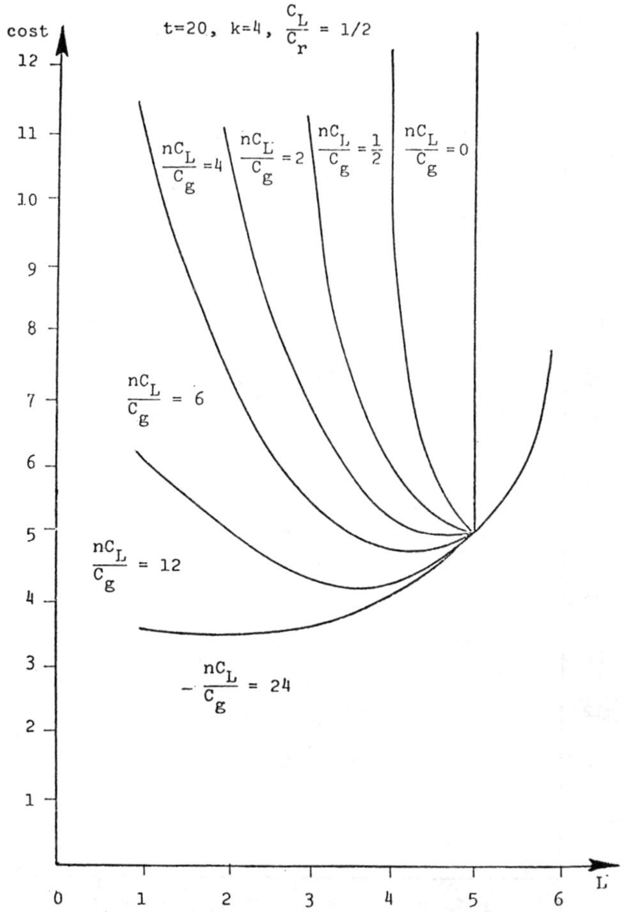

Figure 3—Cost versus L for k-step t/S-fault diagnosability

in $k = 9$, $[t/k] = 3$, and cost $= 5.5\ nC_L$ if $nC_r/C_L = 1/4$. Also, $k = 7$, $[t/k] = 3$, and Cost $= 6.5\ nC_L$ if $nC_r/nC_L = 1/2$. Thus we have the results shown in Tables IV and V. Comparing the cost of repair for these two cases, we see that in both cases the cost of t/S-fault diagnosability is lower than the cost of t-fault diagnosability if $nC_L/C_g > 0$.

Figure 3 shows the graph of cost versus L for $t = 20$, $C_L/C_r = 1/2$, $k = 4$, and $nC_L/C_g = 24,12,6,4,2,1/2$. From Figure 3 it is seen that all curves intersect at point $L = [t/\alpha] = 5$. This is because $k = 4$, and $L = [t/\alpha] = 5 \rightarrow \alpha = 4 \rightarrow k = \alpha = 4$. Thus at point $k = \alpha$ we can use the design for t-fault diagnosability and the cost associated with this design is independent of the cost of replacing good modules. Therefore all curves meet at $L = 5$ and they have the same value. Figure 4 illustrates the effect of the value of t on the cost of repair.

Case 2: Optimal-cost design when s_g is constrained

In Case 1 we have considered the optimal cost design for a case in which S_g is not constrained and determined its value so that the total cost is minimum. We will now consider the case that S_g is constrained, i.e. its maximum value is fixed, and the optimal-cost design is required subject to this constraint. Since in this case we already have fixed one of the parameters, the total cost will always be at least as great as and may be higher than in the previous case.

From equation (4) we have the following:

$$S_g = \left\lceil \left(\frac{t}{2} - \frac{tk}{2\alpha}\right)^2 \right\rceil.$$

Solving for t/α we obtain

$$t/\alpha = \lceil (t - 2\sqrt{S_g})/k \rceil \qquad (11)$$

Equation (11) shows that as the number of testing links decreases, the number of replaced fault-free modules increases. Using equation (5) we have the following result:

$$C = \lceil (t - 2\sqrt{S_g})/k \rceil nC_L + nkC_r + S_gC_g \qquad (12)$$

For the optimal cost design we have $dC/dk = 0$,

$$k^2 = (t - 2\sqrt{S_g})\,\frac{C_L}{C_r} \qquad (13)$$

$$t/\alpha = \left\lceil k\,\frac{C_r}{C_L} \right\rceil \qquad (8)$$

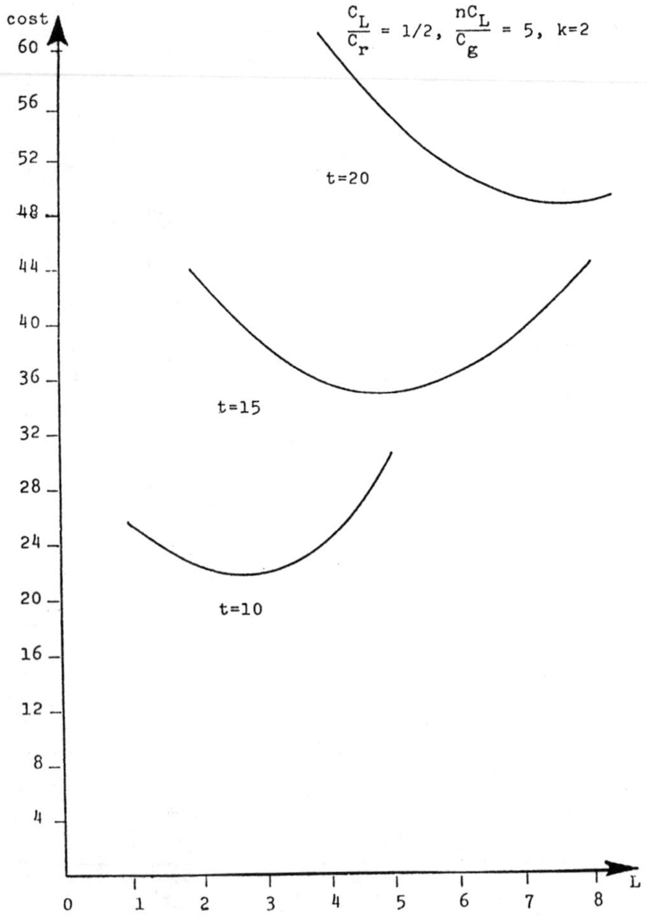

Figure 4—Cost versus L for k-step t/S-fault diagnosability

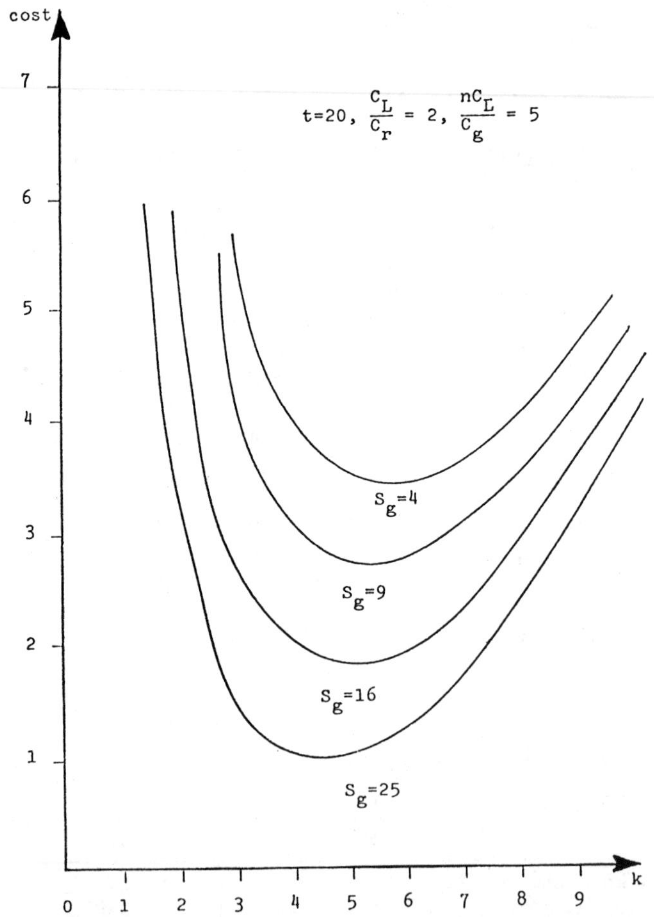

Figure 5—Cost versus k for k-step t/S-fault diagnosability (S_g is constrained)

Figure 5 illustrates cost versus k for k-step t/S-fault diagnosability when S_g is given.

COMPARISON OF k-STEP t/S-FAULT DIAGNOSABILITY WITH k-STEP t-FAULT DIAGNOSABILITY

From the preceding results we can conclude that since the cost of repeating a test divided by the cost of replacing a fault-free module is always greater than zero, i.e. in practice $C_g \neq \infty$, and that even in a worst case that C_r/C_g or nC_L/C_g is very small, k-step t/S-fault diagnosability results in lower costs than k-step t-fault diagnosability. (See Figure 3.) Before constructing an optimal cost design we may wish to know the difference in cost between the optimal-cost designs of a k-step t/S-fault diagnosability and of a k-step t-fault diagnosability. In order to find the difference in cost we proceed as follows.

1. k-step t-fault diagnosability
   a. Find value of k from $k = [\sqrt{tC_L/C_r}]$.
   b. Find cost from $C = [nt/k]C_L + nkC_r$.
2. k-step t/S-fault diagnosability (S_g is not constrained)
   a. Find value of k from $k^3C_r/2C_L - kt/2 + nC_L/C_g = 0$.
   b. Find value of t/α from $t/\alpha = [kC_r/C_L]$.
   c. Find cost from $C = [nt/\alpha]C_L + nkC_r + S_gC_g$.
3. k-step t/S-fault diagnosability (S_g is constrained)
   a. Find value of k from $k^2 = (t - 2\sqrt{S_g})(C_L/C_r)$.
   b. Find value of t/α from $t/\alpha = [(t - 2\sqrt{S_g})/k]$.
   c. Find cost from $C = [(t - 2\sqrt{S_g}/k]nC_L + nkC_r + S_gC_g$.

Now we can compare the costs for each design option. If we wish to use only k-step t-fault diagnosability (although the cost of t/S procedure is lower), then by using the values of C_r and C_L we can find whether to use one-step or k-step t-fault diagnosability immediately;

1. If $C_L/C_r \geq t$ then we use single loop design for t-fault diagnosability.
2. If $C_L/C_r \leq 1/t$ then we use one-step repair for t-fault diagnosability.
3. If $1/t < C/C_r < t$ then we use design D_{1L}.

DISCUSSION OF THE RESULTS

In this paper the design of a digital system that is k-step t/S-fault diagnosable or k-step t-fault diagnosable was considered. The tradeoff of the number of iterations of the diagnostic test for repairing a system (speed of diagnosis), the number of testing links (complexity), and the number of replaced fault-free modules (accuracy) was presented. The procedure for finding an optimal-cost design in terms of cost parameters C_g, C_L, C_r for repairing a digital system was explained, and the comparison between k-step t-fault and k-step t/S-fault diagnosability was considered. Our results show that the cost of k-step t/S-fault design may be less than k-step t-fault design and that the selection of parameters k, L, S_g is very important.

REFERENCES

1. Forbes, R. E., D. H. Rutherford, C. B. Stieglitz, and L. H. Tong. "A Self-Diagnosable Computer." *AFIPS, Proceedings of the Fall Joint Computer Conference,* (vol. 27), 1965, pp. 1073–1086.
2. Agnew, P. W., D. H. Rutherford, R. J. Suhocki, C. M. Yen, and D. E. Muller. "An Architectural Study for a Self-Repairing Computer." U.S. Space Systems Division, Final Tech. Doc. Rept. SSD-TR-65-159, AD47976, November 1965.
3. Ramamoorthy, C. V. "A Structural Theory of Machine Diagnosis." *AFIPS, Proceedings of the Spring Joint Computer Conference,* (vol. 30), 1967, pp. 743–756.
4. Preparata, F. P., G. Metze, and R. T. Chien. "On the Connection Assignment Problem of Diagnosable System." *IEEE Transactions on Electronic Computers,* EC-16, (1967), pp. 848–854.
5. Preparata, F. P. "Some Results on Sequentially Diagnosable Systems." *Proceedings Hawaii International Conference System Science,* University of Hawaii Press, 1968, pp. 623–626.
6. Seshagiri, N. "Completely Self-Diagnosable Digital System." *International Journal of Systems Science,* 1 (1971), pp. 235–246.
7. Hakimi, S. L., and A. T. Amin. "Characterization of Connection Assignment of Diagnosable System." *IEEE Transactions on Computers,* C-23 (1974), pp. 86–88.
8. Kime, C. R. "An Analysis Model for Digital System Diagnosis." *IEEE Transactions on Computers,* C-19 (1970), pp. 1063–1073.
9. Russell, J. D., and C. R. Kime. "System Fault Diagnosis: Masking, Exposure, an Diagnosability Without Repair." *IEEE Transactions on Computers,* C-24 (1975), pp. 1155–1167.
10. Russell, J. D., and C. R. Kime. "System Fault Diagnosis: Closure and Diagnosability with Repair." *IEEE Transactions on Computers,* C-24, (1975), pp. 1078–1089.
11. Adham, M., and A. D. Friedman. "Digital System Fault Diagnosis." *Journal of Design Automation and Fault-Tolerant Computing,* 1 (1977), pp. 115-132.
12. Friedman, A. D. "A New Measure of Digital System Fault Diagnosis." *Digest 1975 International Symposium Fault-Tolerant Computing.* IEEE Computer Society Publications, 1975, pp. 167–170.
13. Karunanithi, S., and A. D. Friedman. "System Diagnosis with t/S Diagnosability." *Digest 1977 International Symposium Fault-Tolerant Computing.* IEEE Computer Society Publications, 1977, pp. 65–71.
14. Kavianpour, A., and A. D. Friedman. "Design of Easily Diagnosable System." *Third USA-JAPAN Computer Conference,* 1978, San Francisco.
15. Kavianpour, A. "Diagnosis of Digital System using t/S Measure." Doctoral dissertation, University of Southern California, Los Angeles, June 1978.
16. Kavianpour, A., and A. D. Friedman. "Different Diagnostic Models for Multiprocessor System." *8th World Computer Congress, IFIP,* October 1980.

Software

A. Winsor Brown, Track Chair

A track on software presents an interesting challenge. All the tracks (except "Hardware and Architecture") have a great deal to do with software. So what should the focus of the software track be? This problem was solved by a proposed description for the track from an archetypical hardware person's view of software: "The problem is just a simple matter of programming." As those of us in software know, the problem is more than just a simple matter of programming. This slight change in wording makes the focus clear. The track explores various aspects of the software life cycle: specification, design, implementation, integration, test, delivery, and maintenance.

The sessions from the Software track have more to do with the why, how, and wherefore of the development process than they do with the what of any particular application or area. Therefore, in the program booklet they are listed in Information Processing Management as well. Despite this listing, all software sessions are described in the present overview.

Using a combination of comparisons, case studies, panel discussions, and formal papers, the Software track attempts to bring to the fore useful information on maintenance, development processes and methods, practical tools and techniques, integrated software, UNIX, delivery, and programming languages. Having maintenance at the top of the list may seem backwards, but its importance is justified by the number of dollars being spent on it. This year also marked a first for maintenance: the Data Processing Management Association now has a special interest group just for maintenance—SIGMA. It assisted in organizing the two sessions on maintenance, which address the subject from two different perspectives.

A session addressing the creative ways being found for doing and managing the enhancement and correction of existing application software, "Software Maintenance: New Synergy," presents some practical methods. Systems information databases, redocumentation, maintaining user satisfaction, and factoring maintenance into the requirements and design of a system are the four specific areas covered. The session thus looks at both what is being done and what can be done now.

"Maintenance: The Future of Present Systems," on the other hand, focuses on how to ensure that present software systems can be made to serve the needs of the future. Concepts like technology transfer, contracted maintenance, prolonging life, and fourth-generation language environments are covered in the papers in this session. All of these come out of a realization that past software systems have survived longer than was expected.

The huge sums of money being spent in data processing system development are probably second only to the costs of maintenance. These large outlays attract the interest and concern of management, practitioners, and providers of services. Not surprisingly, then, the three sessions covering software development processes and methods seem to focus on the traditional data processing software environment and cover the areas of structured tools and methods, development productivity management, and information management methodologies.

"A Battle Royal: Structured Tools and Methods" compares and contrasts the Warnier and Data Flow structured systems development approaches. Panelists represent both training organizations' and users' perspectives. Perhaps hints of the future of systems development tools and methods will be glimpsed in these presentations on productivity improvement techniques.

"Software Development Productivity Strategies" will concentrate on the processes by which costs can be reduced and yields increases in systems development. It will address the topics of conditioning the organization for restructuring the development environment, phased production and implementation of corporate data models, and resolving the conflicts presented by integrating differing schools of development techniques and methodologies.

"New Information Management Methodologies" will discuss how the traditional methodology life cycle must change in order to support corporate information resource management environments. New methods for using the new productivity tools, such as prototyping and fourth-generation languages, will be covered. These new tools allow trial implementation to begin after only the planning or specification phase is complete, and mean that the database cannot wait until after the design phase is complete.

The results of software engineering are seldom directly visible (unlike some of the results of computer hardware engineering). One of the few ways for practitioners to find out about the successes and failures of others is at conference sessions. Focusing on the development process from more a software engineering perspective (and from less a management and data processing perspective) are six sessions presenting results of the use of practical tools and techniques: prototyping, software engineering work stations, software engineering techniques, software automation, software engineering management, and test and validation.

Three different perspectives will be used in the examination of the concept of rapid applications prototyping in the panel session titled "Applications Prototyping." Congruence with general design theory, experiences within a large aerospace firm, and the use of knowledge-based systems are all discussed as they relate to rapid prototyping. As a result, the prerequisites, tools, techniques, and experiences with applications prototyping will be addressed.

Are the cobbler's children finally going to get shoes? Will there be "Software Engineering Work Stations" in our future, as indicated by the title of this session? A lot of effort has gone into work stations for other branches of engineering, so why not software too? In fact, this session discusses issues in the evolution of computer-aided software engineering, using the lessons learned in existing computer-aided engineering systems. Work has been on going in university environments; and information on Plexsys, a workbench environment for information system design (an enhancement of the PSL/PSA system), is presented by one of the panelists. In addition, a paper is presented that shows the possibilities of the personal computer as the basis for software engineering work stations.

"Software Engineering Techniques" reports on specific methods that are all covered by papers in this session: simulation, software manufacturing (code generation), and prototyping. The objectives of the techniques are software transferability, affecting maintenance, and quick implementation or real-time graphics, respectively. The session thus provides an excellent opportunity for software engineers to find out about techniques that others have used.

New aspects of the development process will be addressed in the panel "Software Automation—An International Perspective." The international perspective broadens the topic to include issues of societal/cultural impacts, what the "advanced" nations must do to keep their lead, and how the developing nations might get ahead by avoiding the mistakes that have already been made. Two other questions the panel will attempt to address include whether there is a software revolution in the making and what fifth-generation software will be like.

The first of the three papers in the "Software Engineering Management" session is concerned with the interplay of an integrated methodology and the tools that support it. The second addresses the software management challenges raised by new computer system designs: networks, distributed systems, multi/coprocessors, fault tolerant systems, etc. The third paper presents the results of the application of software engineering principles to real-time projects.

"Software Test and Validation" presents practical results from the application of various techniques to the problems of testing and validating software. Test case selection based on the cost of errors, dynamic assertions for interactive program validation, and tool-based approaches to testing are reported on in three papers.

Two of the hottest topics in software lately have been the UNIX operating system and integrated software. There is a lot of talk about UNIX, but not many end users are actually using it. On the integrated software front, the industry has heard announcements from some of the major software houses, but third-party integrated applications built around those announced products are not yet available.

The existing and proposed integrated systems do have widely varying characteristics—in the core about which they are integrated, in their user interfaces, and in the way the various pieces communicate, among others. "Emerging Trends in Integrated Software" explores the major approaches being used to realize integration and presents two examples of existing integrated software, of which one is icon-based and the other uses a more traditional user interface. The session thus promises to provide some insight into the kinds and forms of integration.

The panel "UNIX: State of the Art" will report on the current status of UNIX technically and commercially. It should thus provide a status report on UNIX, which has been steadily evolving and growing in market importance over the last three years. The panel will then prognosticate the future directions of UNIX from both the market and the technical points of view. What they say about the future of UNIX will actually provide some interesting insight into the realities of the present.

Despite all the ballyhoo about integrated software and icons, users can seldom survive without documentation, the paperware that is often sorely lacking. While concentrating on mini-computer and embedded systems, the comparison of military and commercial documentation requirements in "Military vs. Commercial Documentation" should present factors that also apply to mainframe and microcomputers. Writers must meet not only technical but marketplace requirements, and this session should help them adapt to the differences between military and commercial documentation.

It seems that every Tom, Dick, and Harry is writing micro software, or would like to write it. As book publishers enter the production and distribution channel, it should be easier for budding authors to get their products to market. "Writing Microcomputer Software that Sells" provides three perspectives: publishers', wholesalers', and authors'. The publishers' software editorial philosophy, the wholesalers' evaluation process and services provided to the retailer and consumer, and the authors' viewpoint when working for a publisher should give an interesting glimpse into this new channel of distribution.

Where would the software industry be without programming languages? Three sessions on programming languages complete the software track. The language debates go on much like political ones—seldom with clear winners or losers. The sessions that cover programming languages will address a relatively new language (Modula-2), a new version of an old language (COBOL), and large versus small languages. "Modula-2 and Its Applications" will show this new language in use through case study presentations. The uses cover operating system implementation, computer-aided design, and integrated programming (development) environments. During the presentations, examples of Modula-2 in use as a portable systems implementation language and as a computational applications development tool will be discussed.

Believe it or not, good old COBOL has been back in the news recently. "COBOL-8X—The New Standard" discusses the features of this new version of the language, presents a cost/benefit analysis of the effects of COBOL-8X, and discusses criticisms of potential incompatibilities. The session promises to provide a quick update on the happenings in the COBOL language world.

The panel session "Large vs. Small Programming Languages: Pros & Cons" will provide a forum for a discussion of the merits and demerits of large and small languages. The terms *large* and *small* may be poorly defined, but they are intuitively clear to many. The size of a language is determined by the number of its syntactic and semantic elements and the complexity of their interaction. Specific languages will be used as illustrations, but the session is not a debate about them. For example, the original BASIC represents a small language, whereas PL/I is obviously a large language. Panelists with experience in both large and small languages present their views on the relative advantages and disadvantages of each size.

The Software track obviously covers a great deal more than just programming. Is software just a simple matter of programming? You be the judge.

Maintenance as a function of design

by JAMES R. McKEE
International Monetary Fund
Washington, D.C.

ABSTRACT

Changing one's point of view on the maintenance function can lead to a better understanding of the relationship between maintenance and other aspects of software products. This can lead to an improved allocation of effort when building software products.

INTRODUCTION

The maintenance requirements of software products are generally given insufficient consideration by software product designers because they miscalculate the importance of the maintenance function as a cost component in the life of a software product. One aspect of the problem may be attributable to an inappropriate point of view. The life cycle model most commonly used to portray software development misrepresents the activity it is intended to explain and gives insufficient emphasis to maintenance.

Corrections to these problems may lead to more optimal solutions in the process of software development. This is likely because the trade-off between maintainability and other components of a software product will become more properly balanced. Correspondingly, the analysis and design documents associated with software products will include items of greater value to the maintenance function.

POINTS OF VIEW

When practitioners first started trying to bring some order to the process of software development, they developed the concept of a "life cycle" for new software. The cycle generally began with problem recognition or goals. It then stepped through analysis, design, coding, installation, testing, and operation. The last step of the cycle was maintenance. The problems with this model are numerous. As Zvegintzov has pointed out, this model does not accurately describe a system's life. Moreover, the model is generally portrayed as a linear concept, not as a cycle.[1] In reality the life cycle model mixes a linear concept with a cyclical concept. It ties the concept of the process by which good operational product is generated to the operation of a system that uses the product.

Perhaps the most egregious error in the traditional life cycle model is the mishandling of the concept of maintenance. Maintenance is generally shown as a single step at the end of the cycle; in fact, it is better portrayed as second- (or 3rd-, 4th-, . . . , nth-) round development. The life cycle then becomes develop, operate, develop, operate, develop, and so forth. The model now looks more like a cycle, but has become less useful. This is because the relationship between product building and operations is not so tightly coupled. Much as an airframe manufacturer typically does not operate an airline (and vice versa), the operations of most software products are separated from their manufacture. As an aside, one can make the argument that the failure to isolate software development from operations is a fundamental error that results in a product of extremely poor quality.

What we have left when we dispense with the life cycle model is a view of software development as a process. There is one other effect of the wide acceptance of the life cycle model with which we must deal. When maintenance (dealing with old products) is included at the end of the cycle, then it is presumed that the beginning sections of the cycle are to be applied to new products. This leads not only to a rather wrong-headed view of how the efforts of the analyst–programmer are distributed, but also fosters the impression that structured techniques are best applied only to new projects. As shown in Figure 1, if we are to divide analyst–programmer activity between existing and new applications, at least two thirds of the activity will be attributable to existing applications.[2,3]

Although the analysis to prove the point has not been developed here, it is perfectly clear that the application of structured techniques is equally valid for all analyst–programmer activity. It then follows that the greatest absolute benefit will occur when the analyst–programmer is engaged in maintenance. While this conclusion has been recognized, the process by which we obtained it here has not.

COSTS AND ALLOCATION OF EFFORT

In software development, the validity of a project should be determined by traditional cost–benefit analysis.[4] This approach uses a model in which costs are seen to be rising and benefits falling as the scope of a project expands. The discus-

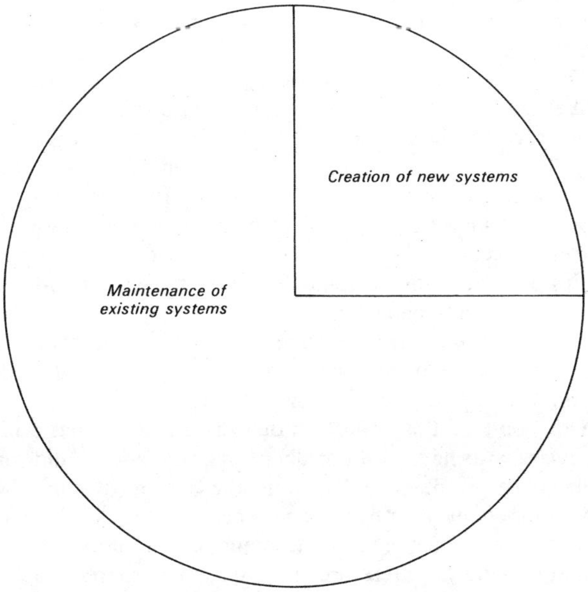

Figure 1—What analyst-programmers do

sion here will be limited to the cost side of the model with the operating assumption that minimization of the total cost of a software product over its entire useful life is a reasonable objective function for the software engineer. This assumption is held to be valid whether the product is an addition, correction, or modification to an already existing product, or a completely new product.

For our discussion the total cost to be minimized consists of three fundamental components: maintenance cost, operating cost, and original development cost. This schema includes all costs of fixing problems or errors, all enhancements, and all changes required by alterations in the operating environment of a product—that is, the costs of any and all changes to a product after it is first delivered—within the definition of maintenance. Operating costs include hardware costs, consumables, and any labor and management costs associated directly with the running of the product. Development costs include all the original analysis, design, coding, and testing costs of a new product. The behavior of these cost components is of considerable interest to the software engineer, as they should be a major determinant of the structure of his product.

The historical trends of these cost components are worthy of review. Operations costs per unit of work are declining largely because the hardware component of these costs is rapidly declining—this overwhelms other operations cost components. However, as the cost of a unit of work has declined, the demand for additional units has expanded in greater proportion. Thus, the overall trend of this expenditure is up, not down. (This behavior can be explained by a concept well known to economists, that of elastic demand. The demand for computer hardware has been highly price elastic throughout the history of the industry and is expected to remain so for the foreseeable future.) Development costs and maintenance costs are both labor intensive and thus are increasing. Maintenance costs may also be increasing because the useful life of software products is increasing. Certainly, our realization of the enormity of maintenance costs is increasing.

The distribution of costs between these major components is likely to vary widely depending on the nature of the work, the maturity of the system, and the work style of the organization. Figure 2 shows the implied distribution between maintenance activity, hardware operations activity, and all other activity within fifteen federal installations surveyed by the General Accounting Office (GAO).[3] The other category includes personnel costs attributable to operations, administrative support, and management, as well as new-product development. The figure is interesting because it demonstrates the great importance of the maintenance function as well as the continuing importance of hardware cost.

The point of this aspect of our discussion is that while hardware costs have traditionally been given, and should continue to be given, great attention, the next most important cost component is software maintenance. Original development costs, which receive tremendous attention in the structured-analysis literature, are a distant third in the actual cost of most systems.

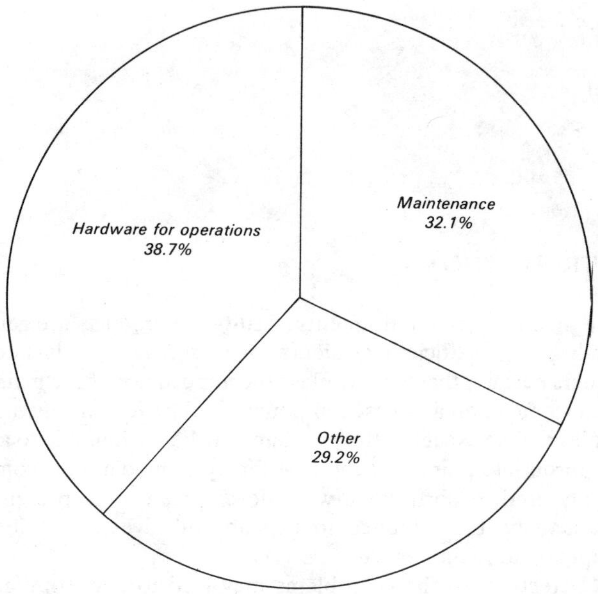

Figure 2—Implied distribution of costs in GAO study

TRADE-OFFS

In all development projects there are many trade-offs. For our purposes, the trade-off between maintenance and other cost components is of interest.

The strong relationship between a well-structured development process and the maintainability of a system is well recognized in the software-engineering literature. In almost every treatise on structured analysis or structured design, long arguments are made about the efficacy of these structured techniques. The arguments always include testimony to the fact that structured development produces systems that have fewer errors, are much easier to understand, and thus much easier to maintain. However, they tend to view maintainability as a fallout of good structured techniques. A better point of view would be to view maintainability as a quantifiable characteristic of software. Maintainability could then be included more usefully in the objective function for a product, and more or less of this quality could be included in the delivered product as a result of design decisions.

Using this view, one can trade additional product development effort for reduced maintenance costs. The technical optimum is when the last added-development costs are just covered by the reduced-maintenance costs, the assumption being that any further development efforts generate insufficient benefits. On a practical basis very few people have hard numbers to cover this issue. Nevertheless, it is probably safe to assert that in most cases the trade-off between development and maintenance costs can be pushed much further in terms of increased development costs. It is also most likely to be the case that this development effort should be pushed beyond the amount of maintainability that falls out of good structured techniques. This additional maintainability is designed in the product.

The same optimality presumptions apply with respect to the trade-off between maintenance and operations costs. However, one should take great care in making any assumptions about operations costs. In all probability the sum of all operations costs for a product over its useful life is not declining. Nevertheless, operations costs have always been given considerable attention, while maintenance costs have not. Thus, on this latter basis alone one could presume that some trade-off in favor of increased operations costs and lowered maintenance costs would be reasonable.

PLANNING FOR MAINTENANCE

As Reutter points out (see Figure 3), most of the activity in maintenance is directed toward product capabilities or characteristics not included in the original product design.[5] Moreover, most of the remaining maintenance activity is directed toward changes in the environment in which the software product operates. Only a small portion of maintenance is directed toward correction of errors. While this may not reflect the experience with all software, it probably does represent what one should expect from fairly well-designed and well-written software products. In high-quality software the error rate may approach zero; this should be an attainable objective. On the other hand, we expect the environment to be changing. We also expect demands for enhancement. Moreover, we expect both of these to occur on a regular basis. What needs to be done is to develop software that is very amenable to these expected changes.

Many areas of expectation for change are identified at the analysis and design stages of product development. In these stages decisions are made that determine the scope of the project. Characteristics to be included in the product are then given the detailed attention necessary to complete the development process and characteristics to be excluded are frequently forgotten. While it is true that many specification documents have a brief statement about avenues of possible extension for the product—and a few even have sentences scattered throughout about points of expandability—these statements are usually treated as asides to the process of building the specified product.

There is another side to the coin of features not included in a product design. This has to do with features or technical solutions that were rejected as being in some way unsuitable for the product. These include all those dead ends encountered during the anaysis and design stages. Also to be considered are those features that once looked so promising, only to be found fundamentally inconsistent with the accepted development of the product. The information and knowledge associated with these considered but rejected features are almost never found in any specification document.

A major set of additions to the specification document is necessary to capture the analysis of features excluded from a product. These additions may be of some value to the builders of the currently specified product, but their objective is specifically to aid the maintenance analyst–programmer. In a sense, these additions will be a resource library that the maintenance programmer can explore to see if his problem has already been addressed. It will also serve another important purpose. It will stand as the justification for the design decisions in the current product that are related to potential extensions of the product. Finally, these additions will be spread throughout the specification and design documents. They will serve as a continuing reminder to all those involved in the development process to include maintenance-related issues in every decision process.

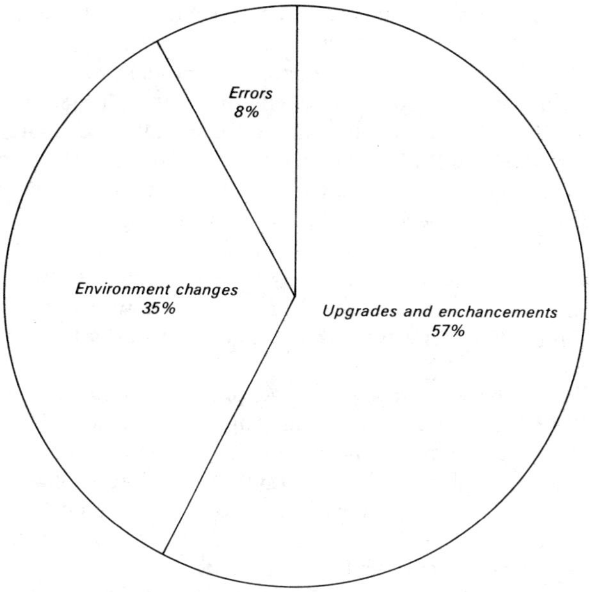

Figure 3—Reutter's distribution of maintenance costs

Case Study—The Economic Information System

The Economic Information System (EIS) is a large (15 gigabyte) database system for the time series data describing the economies of all countries in the world. The system is currently under development at the International Monetary Fund and is scheduled to begin operation in June 1985. The EIS serves well to illustrate some of the points that have been made in this paper. It is a moderately large software project (budget in excess of $3.5 million) that in some aspects is a conversion of a current system and in other aspects a major extension of that system. Thus, it is typical of most of the software projects found in the commercial world. Both components of the project fall within the realm of maintenance.

The current database system consists of a set of ISAM files and home-grown database programs resident on a Burroughs mainframe. In addition, a large set of operations programs have been developed to generate a number of major publications that are run from the database. Most of the code for both the database and the operations are in COBOL. All of the operations code and a subset of the original database code (152,000 lines) will be converted directly to the IBM environment. This will be the batch production part of the new system. An on-line access and update system is also being constructed as an addition to the previous system.

The original charge to the development team was to move the current system to an IBM environment with the on-line extensions, use a commercially available database management system (DBMS), and be up in 18 months. In the initial justification for the project it was stated that "productivity aids would become available in the form of programming tools and software packages which will significantly reduce staff resources required for future systems development and ongoing systems maintenance."[6] Thus, the continuing cost of maintaining systems was given primary focus prior to project initiation.

The first major decision in this project was the choice of DBMS. The question was formed around the type of DBMS (hierarchical, network, inverted file, and relational) as much as the particular vendor. Hierarchical- and relational-type DBMSs were dropped early in the decision process, the former because of its inflexibility to change and large up-front design requirements, and the latter because of known performance problems and the absence of any product with performance experience in large database applications. In the evaluation of the remaining two types of DBMSs, three critical areas—DBMS data structures, database implementation and maintenance, and user access and manipulation capabilities—were identified. Critical requirements were developed within each of these areas. Candidate systems were then evaluated against these requirements.

This DBMS choice provides an excellent example of tradeoff. Because of the mix between batch and on-line activity in this application, neither the network- nor the inverted-file-type of DBMS was found to have an advantage with respect to hardware resources. However, with respect to implementation and maintenance, the inverted-file-type DBMS had an overwhelming advantage. The database design process is much simpler in an inverted-file database. Moreover, inverted-file structures are much more amenable to extension and change than network structures. This became the basis of our choice.

Another example of the maintenance concept entering into a major decision in this project arose in the database design process. In the batch operations process on the current system large data records (10 Kbyte) are read into a buffer. The applications then use a central utility to obtain the sections of the records that they need. This works well in the current batch system; however, the approach is completely inappropriate for on-line update and inquiry activities. The on-line requirements of the project have led to the development of much smaller records in the target database. The question is then whether to build up the large buffer the entire batch stream expects, or to make some major changes in the data-gathering procedures of the batch application code. From the design and development effort point of view, building the buffer would be the best choice. From an operations point of view, building the buffer would be more expensive. However, overnight batch costs are 10% of daytime costs in our environment and there is a succession of use of various parts of the large buffer in our current operations. Thus, the operations costs are not an overriding issue. What is clear is that the large buffer structure is not likely to be suitable for the extensions of this application that will be forthcoming after it is put in place. Moreover, the structure that is chosen now will be cast, if not in steel, at least in bronze for some years to come.

It was decided to change the data presentation procedures. This decision will raise development costs for the project. The decision will also have a negative effect on our ability to produce a product on a timely basis. However, the ability to enhance the product after its initial delivery will be significantly increasd.

CONCLUSION

There is still substantial room for improvement in our understanding of the process by which software products are constructed. A more carefully constructed life cycle model will improve this understanding. In addition, a clear analysis of the cost trade-off between maintenance and other cost components of a software product is likely to lead to a better resource allocation. However, these suggestions are limited to creating the setting in which improved maintainability may be developed. The many techniques that may be employed for improving maintainability have not been explored. This remains the task of future explorers in this field of endeavor. The growing cost of software maintenance suggests such efforts be given high priority.

ACKNOWLEDGMENTS

I would like to thank my colleagues, Soon Choi, Thomas L. Williams, Kathleen X. Nelick, and S. Stuart Morrison, and my wife, Mary Jane McKee, for the many suggestions and improvements they have provided in the production of this paper, and the Graphics Section of the IMF, for providing the charts. The errors and omissions remain my own.

The ideas and opinions expressed herein are solely those of the author and are not necessarily representative of, or endorsed by, the International Monetary Fund.

REFERENCES

1. Belady, L. A. "Software Complexity." In *Tutorial on Models and Metrics for Software Management and Engineering.* Los Alamitos, Calif.: IEEE, 1980.
2. Belady, L. A., and Lehman, M. M. "A Model of Large Program Development." *IBM Systems Journal,* 15 (1976), pp. 225–252.
3. Boehm, B. W. *Software Engineering.* Redondo Beach, Calif.: TRW, 1976.
4. Boehm, B. W., Lipow, M., and White, B. B. *Software Quality Assurance: An Acquisition Guidebook.* Redondo Beach, Calif.: TRW, 1977.
5. Chapin, Ned. "Productivity in Software Maintenance." *AFIPS, Proceedings of the National Computer Conference* (Vol. 50), 1981, pp. 349–352.
6. IMF. *IMF Economic Information System Planning Document.* Internal (mimeographed) document, International Monetary Fund, Washington, D.C.

SUGGESTED READINGS

1. DeMarco, T. *Structured Analysis and System Specification.* Englewood Cliffs, N.J.: Prentice-Hall, 1979.

2. Elshoff, J. L., and M. Marcotly. "Improving Computer Program Readability to Aid Modification." *Communications of the ACM,* 21 (1982), pp. 512–521.
3. Harrison, W., K. Magel, R. Kluczny, and A. DeKrock, "Applying Software Complexity Matrice to Program Maintenance." *Computer,* 15 (1982), pp. 65–79.
4. Hester, S. D., D. L. Parnas, and D. F. Utter. "Using Documentation as a Software Design Medium." *The Bell System Technical Journal,* 60 (1981), pp. 1941–1977.
5. Linger, R. C., H. D. Mills, and B. I. Witt. *Structured Programming: Theory and Practice.* Reading, Mass.: Addison-Wesley, 1979.
6. Myers, G. J. *Software Reliability: Principles and Practices.* New York: John Wiley & Sons, 1976.
7. Page-Jones, M. *The Practical Guide to Structured Systems Design.* New York: Yourdon Press, 1980.
8. Reutter, J. III. "Maintenance is a Management Problem and a Programmer's Opportunity." *AFIPS, Proceedings of the National Computer Conference* (Vol. 50), 1981, pp. 343–347.
9. Schwartz, B. "Eight Myths About Software Maintenance." *Datamation,* 28, (1982), pp. 124–128.
10. U.S. General Accounting Office. *Federal Agencies' Maintenance of Computer Programs: Expensive and Undermanaged.* Report AFMD-81-25, February 26, 1981.
11. Yau, S. S., and J. S. Collopello. "Some Stability Measures for Software Maintenance," *IEEE Transactions on Software Engineering,* SE-6, (1980), pp. 545–552.
12. Yourdon, E. *Techniques of Program Structure and Design.* Englewood Cliffs, N.J.: Prentice-Hall, 1975.
13. Zvegintzov, N. "What life? What cycle?" *AFIPS, Proceedings of the National Computer Conference* (Vol. 51), 1982, pp. 561–568.

Maintaining user satisfaction with performance of an online system

by A. MARTIN SELLERS
OCLC, Online Computer Library Center, Inc.
Dublin, Ohio

ABSTRACT

This paper discusses the experience of OCLC, Online Computer Library Center, Inc., with maintaining user satisfaction with performance of its online system. OCLC is an innovator in the field of automated library services. Because it is a service organization, user satisfaction with its online services of cataloging, interlibrary loan, serials control, and acquisitions is a major concern. An important component of that satisfaction is online system performance, primarily measured by response time and system availability.

This paper also discusses the considerable effort that has been devoted to system support activities to address response time and availability improvement. Among the system support activities discussed are creation of an internal problem reporting and monitoring system, organizing to more clearly delineate responsibility and authority, and communication of system support activities to the user. These activities have had a positive effect on user satisfaction with OCLC's online system.

INTRODUCTION

OCLC, Online Computer Library Center Inc., a privately funded, not-for-profit corporation, was founded in 1967 to help libraries improve patron access to the ever expanding body of worldwide knowledge and information. The first online service in support of that corporate purpose was the OCLC Shared Cataloging subsystem originally designed for 54 academic libraries in the state of Ohio. As libraries' recognition of cost savings and service enhancement possible with with this system grew, the OCLC computer system, the complexity of software, and the need for corrective, adaptive, and perfective maintenance also grew. OCLC's current system of custom manufactured terminals, dedicated telecommunications lines, front end minicomputers, network supervisor, host computers, and back-end database processors provides cataloging, serials control, acquisitions, and interlibrary loan services to approximately 3,500 member instituions serving over 6,000 libraries internationally via more than 5,000 terminals.

Our physical facility, located in Dublin, Ohio, contains over 44,000 square feet of secure, environmentally controlled computer floor space, a dramatic change from the space rented from Ohio State University little more than a decade before. More dramatic, however, is the change in the people who support and use the system.

OCLC was founded by the Ohio College Association, a group of university presidents, to increase availability of library resources and reduce costs among the academic institutions in the state. That founding resulted in an initial computer-based system that was designed, developed, and modified almost experimentally by a few dedicated people committed to making dramatic—at the time, revolutionary—changes in the library community. From that foundation evolved the current OCLC organization of over 670 staff and a customer base of over 6,000 libraries of all types—not just college libraries, but public, governmental, school, medical, law, and corporate libraries, serviced through a multiple-tier distribution channel.

Associated with the internal change of OCLC is a change in user expectations. System performance expectations continue to grow with increased user sophistication regarding online systems use. Additionally, as the OCLC system becomes the backbone of operations in a growing number of customers' libraries, high expectations of maintaining adequate online system performance are not unreasonable.

THE PROBLEM

The problem of maintaining user satisfaction with performance in an online system entails a complex system of external and internal perceptions and constraints that vary over time. Key factors of perceptions and constraints are interrelated and seem to be part of a zero-sum game in informal systems such as ours; if one area of performance is satisfactory, another area is perceived less so by some measure. Therefore, one element of a solution is more formal measures of acceptable performance for each component that affects user perceived system performance.

Users' perceptions of performance areas for interactive systems include response time, system availability, and reliability measures as well as expectations of database integrity, completeness, currency, and high expectations of new systems development and responsive maintenance. As is only proper, failure to meet formal performance standards results in unacceptable performance from the users' perspective. However, if performance is measured informally, even what at one time was satisfactory performance may no longer be so; change takes place in the level of user expectations of adequate performance to target the lowest area of performance as unacceptable. This change in level of expectation seems to be natural; and systems performance expectations seem to vary with user sophistication, which in the OCLC system has grown substantially during the last decade.

The key aspects of this increasing demand for maintaining user satisfaction with performance in an online system are understood measures of performance consistent over time;[1] development of new systems; and adequate system maintenance in terms of its adaptive, perfective, and corrective aspects. It is because of the universality and typical symptomatic treatment of those needs that OCLC's approach may be appropriate to other interactive environments.

SYMPTOMATIC TREATMENT

Using internally defined measures of response time and availability and using informal, individually conceptualized measures of other performance factors mentioned above, OCLC staff have had their hands full chasing the illusion of satisfactory performance; users continued to be dissatisfied. The effects of this lack of measurability have materially affected system support activities where patchwork maintenance and damage control have been consuming activities to keep the system available in the short term to the exclusion of addressing other user-perceived performance criteria for a longer term. Attaining the right mix of performance levels in an informal system may be harder than finding the pot of gold at the end of the rainbow, but it has the same allure.

To help understand the shifting nature of priorities and the long-term effects of looking only at short-term system performance, we must understand our online environment. OCLC online is a dynamic system that accommodates growth of accessibility for added terminals and new functions. Barbara Taute calls this type of environment unstable, and that is certainly the case.[2] Users and OCLC staff agree that growth has typically been followed by periods of unacceptable reliability, availability, and response time. Growth demands have taken their toll on maintainability. The environment is not a desirable one, because induced periods of instability have caused wholesale shifts of staff for support at the expense of new development. The result of these shifts is conflicting performance criteria: new development vs. current system stability.[3] This unacceptable trade of performance issues highlighted our need to address internal problems requiring immediate remedy as longer-term remedies were formulated.

INTERNAL PROBLEM

The OCLC online system is growing: over 600 user terminals and over a million new records are added per year. The result of this growth is a continuing imbalance of staff need and availability. Reactive approaches to this imbalance included cutbacks in training, increases in Band-Aid problem fixing, and redirecting staff from other areas to help. We did all of these things we knew were harmful in the long term but that we could easily justify in the short term. The result was a temporary increase in system stability, but at a heavy cost, akin to running faster to keep from falling; it only works for awhile.

As if things weren't bad enough, there were role perception difficulties regarding software maintenance. What is it? Who does it? When and how is it done? How is it regarded in the company? The diversity of answers to these questions adversely affected even short-term maintenance activities. Meanwhile, users were demanding that we do something to improve performance.

DOING SOMETHING

We isolated four areas to address: user expectations, system problems, procedures, and the organization. As we were thinking about how to manage our problems, we focused on *time to repair* as a critical element in user-perceived performance in an online system.

Doing Something About User Expectations

Although user expectations have always been considered by OCLC staff, it is increasingly important to address those expectations formally in the development and operation of a system,[1] and it is acutely important in interactive systems.

Developing understood measures of system performance, improving communications about system aberration and expected resumption of normal service, improving problem-call handling, and increasing availability of problem-call staff, in addition to the Herculean task of improving system performance, are the activities we felt most important to bring user expectations and actual performance closer together.

Developing commonly understood measures of performance that relate well to user experience at a terminal, and yet can be monitored and controlled at a central site, is a nontrivial task in an online environment. In addition, user-perceived measures of performance in an online system of transaction response time, system availability, and system reliability are made even more complex by potential misinterpretation of the statistics necessary to describe these performance measures.

To explore the complexity of communicating online system performance characteristics, let's look at response time. Certainly we should be able to agree that user-perceived system response time can be measured as the interval of time between the SEND/DO IT key stroke of the terminal user and the full screen display of the system's response. Figure 1 shows the components of our system a transaction may exercise; however, not all components are used for every transaction. Add human-related variables, and it should be obvious that a statement of an average response time of 8 seconds can mean many different things to many people.

Other complicating factors are the nonhomogeneous resource requirements for different ways of requesting the same information, cyclical use of the system by season, week within season, day within week, and hour within day, continuing

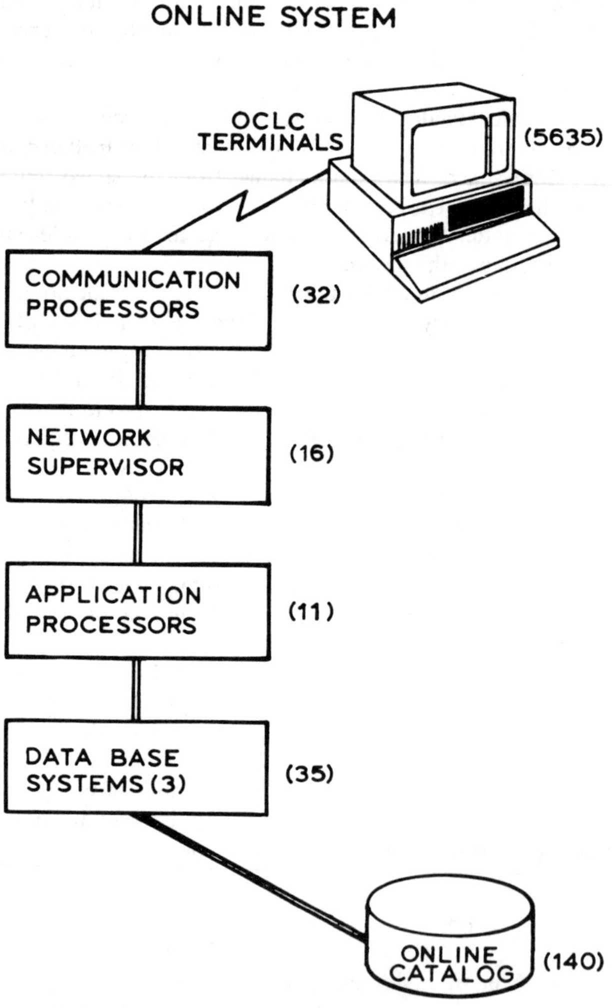

Figure 1—Online system

change in system environment, and lack of monitoring tools for understanding those changes better. A system person's approach is to make various assumptions concerning unmeasured activities and add that to monitored activities to calculate an average over time. A user's approach is to time activities at the terminal, whether with a clock or not. Our experience indicates that the system person and the user have difficulty communicating performance measurements with such disparate baselines of measurement. Therefore, developing common measures is precisely what must be done for effective communication.

OCLC is currently conducting investigations to determine how best to characterize user-perceived online system performance in order to relate it to our characterization of performance; the first step is to come to a common definition. The first investigation consisted of 14 user institutions that manually timed specific transactions at a predetermined time of day and reported their observed response times and system availability to OCLC for summarization. This manual approach was meant only to give us a feeling of users' experience. The other study involves a hardware device attached to a user's terminal to directly measure and calculate response time statistics over a period of terminal use. The user reported statistics are then correlated to OCLC-measured computer system response times. Figure 2 shows user vs. OCLC measures for response times and system availability over a 41-week period. This has dramatically improved our ability to communicate response time and availability performance measures with the user.

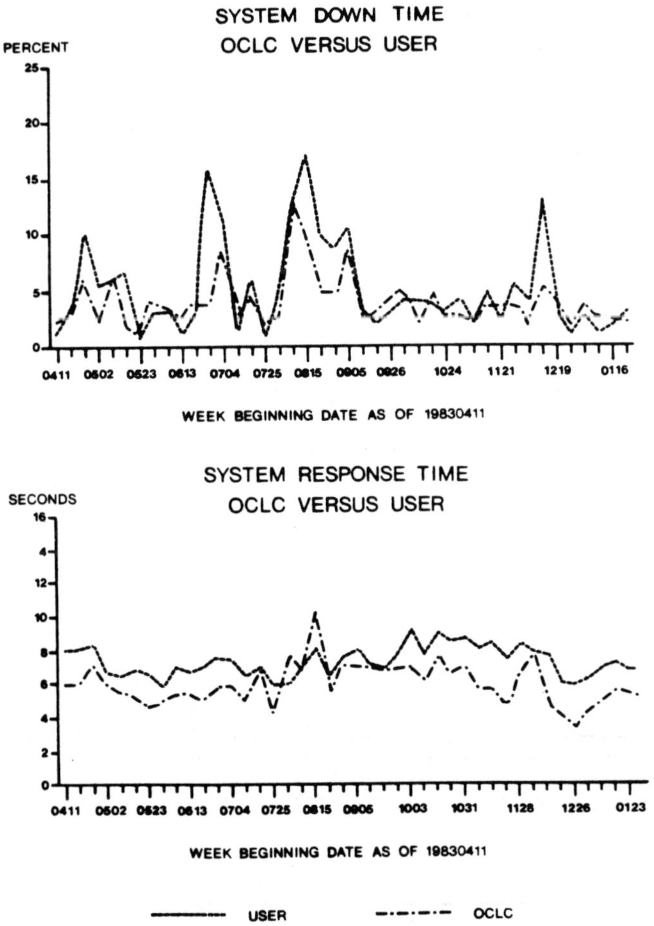

Figure 2—System performance

Other activities to promote user satisfaction with system performance are to increase communication about system activity, increase the use of meaningful broadcast messages via the users' terminals, and increase responsiveness to trouble calls by providing a hierarchy of user-call handling.

The entry level of our hierarchy of problem-call handling is the OCLC reception staff, which discriminates between informational and assistance calls and transfers calls that require more attention to a second level. At the second level, the Marketing and User Services Division of OCLC staffs a trouble call function where further discrimination among user-, application-, and system-caused problems is made. Only computer system problems are then passed on to network operation technicians for further diagnosis and resolution. Network operation technicians dispatch field service aid for terminal and modem problems and deal with the telephone companies for telecommunications problems; computer hardware and software problems are passed to system support personnel for resolution, the final level of the problem resolution hierarchy. The severity of the problem coupled with the estimated time to repair determines the mechanics of problem resolution.

Doing Something About the System

Although terminal and telecommunications are components of our online system, it is our computer environment that is the subject of this section. Our computer hardware is stable at over 99% availability for each major component on a regular basis. Although 99% component availability seems more than adequate, the number of components and the number of terminals can produce over 5,000 terminal hours outage per week. That much outage translates into user dissatisfaction and lost revenue for the period. OCLC from the beginning adopted a philosophy of self-reliance. It currently has 24-hour-a-day, seven-day-a-week computer maintenance support to provide immediate reaction to any hardware malfunction to try to reduce the mean time to repair and hence increase system availability. A substantial investment in spares inventory, test equipment, staff, and staff training help keep our computer hardware running at that relatively high availability. The software component is not as stable as the hardware, nor is the environment as straightforward.

Dealing with software has resulted in major changes to our existing environment. Some of those changes are further identified in the following sections on procedures and organization. The main change to be identified here is a recognition by the corporation of the primary importance of user perception of performance and a recognition that maintenance of adequate performance had failed. As part of an overall effort, OCLC temporarily redirected the work of our development staff from installing additional software to an already unstable system to attending to medium-term-problem resolution. The support group, which has primary responsibility for restoring the system after a failure, necessarily operates in the short term, often allowing only symptomatic treatment and leaving the real problem unresolved. Recovery vs. resolution is a resource problem intensified by online systems. OCLC recognized the unmet need for problem resolution as an activity simultaneous with the requirement to recover on a day-to-day basis.

The significance of this recognition of time between recovery and medium-term resolution resulted in new procedures for problem solving. It also allowed system support staff's significant expertise to be more productively employed in resolving problems rather than continuing symptomatic treatment, a result of sufficient resources to use innovative methods to combat long-neglected problems.[4] We call the system support activities of resolving maintenance hot spots *systems manageability*.

Doing Something About Procedures

The most significant result of dealing with procedures was the creation of a problem reporting and monitoring system that is itself an online application. Previous attempts at prob-

OCLC

PROBLEM REPORT

TO RECOVERY COORDINATOR
SYSTEM SUPPORT DEPT., M.C.373

REPORT DATE

REPORT ☐ NEW ☐ UPDATE

PROBLEM NUMBER (Assigned by SSD)

REPORTER NAME

PHONE EXT.

MAIL CODE

PROBLEM TITLE (Use 24 characters or less--for Corporate Problem List)

SYSTEM AFFECTED (e.g., ACQ, ADT, MS, etc.)

CLASS NUMBER (1-4)

DATE AND TIME OF PROBLEM OCCURRENCE

FOR MUSD PROBLEM REPORTING

USER/NETWORK CONTACT (Person reporting problem)

TELEPHONE NUMBER ( )

ORGANIZATION NAME

OCLC SYMBOL

NETWORK

AUTHORIZATION NUMBER

TERMINAL LOGICAL NUMBER(S)

AUTHOS SUBSYSTEM

MUSD REPORT MANAGER

PHONE EXT.

MAIL CODE

PROBLEM DESCRIPTION

Describe completely the conditions/circumstances at the time of the problem, what happened and how often, commands entered, error messages, etc. Attach any related reports or listings.

PROBLEM RESOLUTION

RESOLVER (Dept. Manager Responsible)

ASSIGNED TO

DATE ASSIGNED

NOTES (Record changes in status below. Describe results of investigation and any action taken on the back of this report.)

PROREP-820617

Figure 3—Problem report

lem reporting and monitoring systems had not been effective. This time success is directly attributable to the managers, who regard this process as their communications tool.

The problem resolution process is a result of analyzing what was needed to identify and resolve significant problems. It required line managers to take an active role in refining the process as well as to accept responsibility for managing problem resolution as they would a development project. It requires their commitment to be effective.

The essence of the problem resolution process is its use as a common mechanism for problem reporting, responsibility assignment, status communication, priority reassignment, and reference for similar problems. This process is recognized across the company as the way to bring problems of significance to light and to ensure appropriate recognition and resolution of those problems. The element of time is used in this process to identify the type of effort and responsibility for problem resolution: short, primarily recovery and patches; medium, planned problem fixes and small rewrites; and long, inclusion of fix in redesign and new development projects. All problems of any significance are entered into this process. A problem report form is shown as Figure 3. Biweekly problem report process meetings have a specific purpose, have well prepared attendees sharing a common problem solving attitude, and enable continuing refinement of the resolution process to take place.

Doing Something About the Organization

The organization is the framework within which staff perform activities. Intuitively, the better the definition of organization within the context of desired goals, the more likely it is that there will be congruence of activities and goals. Obversely, the fuzzier the organization is in terms of definition, the more likely it is that conflict will appear as a result of overlapping responsibilities and accountabilities.

In software maintenance, OCLC's experience displayed the characteristics of a fuzzy organization. Improved organizational definition was required to set the stage for assigning goal-congruent responsibilities. Our definition of support organizations embodied the attributes of adaptive, perfective, and corrective maintenance as defined in current software maintenance documents.[5] Additionally, we used maintenance response time as a qualifier of organizational definition, since it is a critical factor in availability as a component of performance of online systems.

Maintenance response time is defined and measured as the elapsed time between problem recognition and problem recovery, where recovery may mean patch or repair. We identified three intervals of maintenance response time to help emphasize organizational maintenance responsibilities: short-term, medium-term, and long-term. Immediate problem recovery is a special case of short-term maintenance response time. These may seem trivial; however, simplicity has an elegance of its own, and the addition of response time to the definitions of maintenance helped us identify solutions to our responsibility problems.

Each of the operations organizations, shown as the lower four boxes in Figure 4, have some system maintenance responsibilities. Time helps identify specific responsibilities. For immediate maintenance, Computer Operation recovers and Systems Support provides corrective and perfective maintenance. Short-term maintenance is the responsibility of Systems Support. Medium- and long-term maintenance involving system software is the responsibility of Computer Systems Engineering; medium- and long-term maintenance for application software is handled in the Product Development Division.

Other universal software maintenance issues were also treated after a combined look at procedures and organization. Maintenance adhocracy is giving way to increased planning, and motivational improvements have resulted from recognition of maintenance staff expertise and their accomplishments.[6]

An additional motivational boost has resulted from effective use of support staff in more than short-term corrective maintenance. Although not eradicated, artificial status barriers between development and maintenance within OCLC have been reduced. However, our experience with recruiting indicates that the term *maintenance* still has negative connotations in the data processing world, something we'll all have to continue to campaign against. User recognition of accomplishments of improving the performance of the OCLC online system has also been a great help in solidifying the importance of support staff.

The improved procedures and organizational responsibility described above are providing more effective online system maintenance, which has a direct positive effect on systems performance and on users' perception of system performance.

SUMMARY

Positive effects of this integrated program to improve OCLC online system performance have been measured by its users

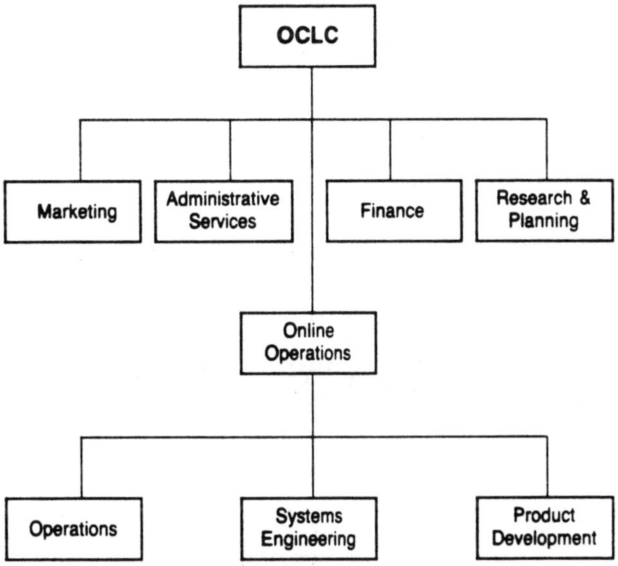

Figure 4—OCLC organization

and providers. System performance measures of response time, availability, and reliability have improved significantly since these activities have started. This improvement has allowed us to resume scheduling system enhancements to increase users' satisfaction with online system performance in the area of system enhancements.

Although not as amenable to measurement as external ones, internal effects such as staff morale and productivity have improved also.

A program of systems manageability is under way to ensure maintaining user satisfaction with the OCLC Online System by improving response time and availability. It includes refinement of the above activities of formalizing and communicating system performance measures, increasing the quality of software maintenance, and improving the systems environment, as well as showing progress in new feature development with engineered maintainability improvements.

REFERENCES

1. Stevens, Barry A., and Phillip C. Howard. "Management Control of EDP Performance." *Applied Computer Research.* Phoenix, Ariz.: Applied Computer Research, 1980.
2. Taute, Barbara J. "Quality Assurance and Maintenance Application Systems." *AFIPS, Proceedings of the National Computer Conference* (Vol. 52), 1983, pp. 122–129.
3. Parnas, D. L. "Designing Software for Ease of Extension and Contraction." *IEEE Transactions on Software Engineering, SE-5* (1979), pp. 128–137.
4. Kapur, Gopal. "Software Maintenance." *Computer World, 17* (1983), "In-depth" section, pp. 13–22.
5. Glass, Robert L., and Ronald A. Noiseux. *Software Maintenance Guidebook.* Englewood Cliffs, N.J.: Prentice-Hall, 1981.
6. Marselos, Nicholas L. "Human Investment Techniques for Effective Software Maintenance." *AFIPS, Proceedings of the National Computer Conference* (Vol. 52), 1983, pp. 131–136.

Redocumentation: Addressing the maintenance legacy

by GARY RICHARDSON and EARL D. HODIL
Texaco Inc.
Houston, Texas

ABSTRACT

Over the past decade or so there has been much attention paid to techniques and methodologies to produce high-quality systems. A concurrent development has been the emergence of software tools that aid in the production and maintenance of software systems; yet the maintenance environment continues to be littered with poorly written and poorly documented programs.

The focus of this paper is to outline a conceptual approach to the allocation of software maintenance resources and the role of automated tools in this process. It is contended that software maintenance tools cannot be simply purchased or built and then used indiscriminately. Rather, it takes an administrative activity to quantitatively decide which code units are best for resource allocation. Finally, to demonstrate the utility of this approach, a case study based on the author's experience is presented.

THE MAINTENANCE LEGACY

Over the past decade or so much attention has been paid to techniques and methodologies to produce high-quality, maintainable systems. Yet DP management still finds itself left with a swelling production library containing a hodgepodge of code that shows little resemblance to what we now define as good.

In the late seventies Dr. Gerry Tompkins of UCLA surveyed 120 DP organizations.[1] This survey found the mean age of installed systems to be nearly five years and the average size of these systems to be approximately 23,000 lines of source code. A review of the typical production library often reveals high levels of poorly written code with inadequate documentation, a statistic that is not surprising when one considers the time-consuming, laborious nature of manually producing high-quality code that is also well documented. This impetus has stimulated the recent proliferation of software maintenance tools.

The author believes that structured code, clear mechanical format, and other such forms of architectural definition are positive when produced at reasonable cost. Studies indicate somewhat conclusively that structured programming can lower maintenance costs. One point, however, is becoming increasingly clear. That is, methodologies and tools in and of themselves will not automatically correct all the errors of the past. Indeed, the new techniques can become costly and ineffectual if they are used randomly. Our challenge here is to describe a rational approach to correcting this maintenance legacy by proper allocation of resources, including a growing set of software tools designed to aid in this process.

PROBLEM DEFINITION

The road to reduced maintenance effort begins with the answers to two questions:

1. Which programs abend most frequently?
2. Which programs, though they may run perfectly, are so poorly written and/or documented that they cannot be easily changed?

The significance of these two questions is considerable when one considers that two of the essential activities associated with software maintenance are correcting program errors and implementing user-requested changes to software. Even though many firms have recognized the need to answer these questions, most large DP shops have found the quest arduous.

Surprisingly, many organizations find the first question difficult to answer. They can neither locate nor statistically quantify their production source code, much less begin to describe quantitatively which code units could be classified as good, average, or poor. This situation must be resolved before subsequent steps, outlined below, can be undertaken. The three administrative systems following can aid in this process.

Library Control

An automated control package to insure that all production source code is located in approved libraries and that production load modules contain only these source modules. Though there are many reasons for installing such a system, its purpose is to bind the execution errors associated with executing a load module to the source code responsible for them.

Operations Logging

A tracking system that traps all production jobs and records completion status (e.g., good completion, space abort, JCL error, bad completion code). This tool should provide execution information at least down to the load module level.

System Profile

A text-oriented system, summarizing basic system metrics such as

1. age,
2. language,
3. total lines of source code,
4. user evaluations of the current system,
5. future enhancement plans at the aggregate level.

By using these three techniques it is possible to identify the target code population accurately, then array the code units according to abort frequency.

Phase 2 of the problem definition activity begins once operational statistics are available regarding code performance. It is then necessary to divide code units into three broad categories:

1. Good Code—low abort frequency
2. Bad Code—high abort frequency
3. Marginal Code—borderline abort frequency

Here we are left with both a philosophical and a technological problem. Philosophically, we may believe that well-written code has a low abort history and vice versa. Alternatively, some believe that abort history is independent of code structure. It is observed that some systems require highly skilled operational support personnel and code modifications; are complex, owing to a lack of a coherent design architecture; yet are stable, judging by abort statistics. It is the authors' opinion that the subject of good versus bad code is multidimensional, involving both mechanical and operational factors. The maintenance function involves both aspects of operation and enhancement; therefore goodness of code must involve more than one view. A second philosophical issue surrounds the idea of documentation value. When one looks at the millennia of existing production code without supporting documentation, some doubt must exist about whether it is of value to be concerned about such things. In attempting to rationalize such behavior there is at least the obvious conclusion that the cost of documentation production outweighs its value. The authors believe that an automated approach to producing documentation improves both software accuracy and cost effectiveness.

Now for the technical problem: It is theoretically possible to quantify abort frequency and arbitrarily divide code units into good, marginal, and bad categories; however, we have already said that this is not enough. There are at least two other code grading technical issues that should be addressed. First, code complexity needs to be evaluated. McCabe[2] and others have defined quantitative measures of code complexity, although once again there is no broad agreement about when a code unit is too complex. Indeed, some productive code requires complexity; and in some cases it is rationally added to the code architecture for efficiency or other reasons. In any case, high-complexity index values could be warnings to review an existing code unit and decide whether it is feasible to simplify it in some way. A third aspect of the technical problem is the architecture of the code unit itself. This is manifested by unstructured or large modules. Within this realm one might attempt to review style, language, structure, size, and existing documentation of the unit in order to supply a qualitative grade. The final aspect of code review requires judgment about whether the code should be a candidate, based on strategic objectives. For example, if an old batch system is being replaced in less than one year with a new online system, then it makes sense not to give that code any extra support. Alternatively, an old system with no upgrade planned would be a candidate. This activity is designed with a view to future evaluation.

We have indicated that in order to effectively allocate maintenance resources it is necessary to quantify where current operational problems now exist through formalized abort history statistics. In addition to this we should provide some type of grading scheme at the code unit level to identify potential modules for which resources can be profitably allocated to repair. It is feasible to use automated tools to do much of the scanning work for items such as size (lines of code), complexity, adherence to code standards, and other related functions. After all the automated statistics are summarized it should be possible to select high-priority targets for closer manual examination. From this aggregation of data it is then necessary to select and rank code units to be given special consideration for rework. Some day this process can be highly automated; however, it currently will involve a high degree of subjective judgment.

THE PURIFICATION PROCESS

We have outlined an analytical process designed to identify systems and code units (i.e., programs) that are candidates for rework. The key question now is, "What do we do with the subset of problem code defined?" Figure 1 shows schematically the process described above. Note that two new items show up at the bottom of the figure, rewrite and redocumentation. Each of these deserves more discussion here. Rewrite represents code units in such shape that manual rearchitecture of the system is required to resolve the indicated problem. Typically this means that new functionality is required or that the basic database design approach is flawed. Obviously placement of code in this category should be done only as a last resort because of inherent cost and time to accomplish.

The second form of code repair is automated redocumentation, which is defined as the software-driven process of producing documentation for existing code directly from the syntax itself. Elshoff and Marcotty from General Motors have documented their company's approach to the use of similar automated techniques to improve code readability and modification.[3] We feel that these tools are most useful when used as an aid to the maintenance programmer who is trying to draw understanding from a block of unyielding (and usually undocumented) source code. These tools may be categorized as follows:

1. Dynamic analyzers
2. Static analyzers
3. Restructure/recoding tools

Dynamic analyzers have long been accepted as a part of the maintenance programmer's workbench. Debugging compilers and interpreters compose this group of tools. Usually, the dynamic analyzer is used in conjunction with test data during an interactive session. Features commonly associated with dynamic analyzers are (1) fast syntax checking, (2) one step

```
+------------------------------------------------------------+
:                    PRODUCTION LIBRARY                      :
:             ::::::::::::::::::::::::::::::::::             :
:             :             Type I             :             :
:             :          (leave alone)         :             :
:             ::::::::::::::::::::::::::::::::::             :
:             :                                :             :
:             :           Good Code            :             :
:             :                                :             :
:             ::::::::::::::::::::::::::::::::::             :
:             ::::::::::::::::::::::::::::::::::             :
:             :             Type II            :             :
:             :          (leave alone)         :             :
:             ::::::::::::::::::::::::::::::::::             :
:             :                                :             :
:             :         Marginal Code          :             :
:             :                                :             :
:             ::::::::::::::::::::::::::::::::::             :
:             ::::::::::::::::::::::::::::::::::             :
:             :            Type III            :             :
:             :           (retrofit)           :             :
:             ::::::::::::::::::::::::::::::::::             :
:             :    Rewrite     :   Redocument  :             :
:             : manual effort  :  auto. tools  :             :
:             :                :               :             :
:             : $5 to $50/LOC  : $.2 to $2/LOC :             :
:             :                :               :             :
:             ::::::::::::::::::::::::::::::::::             :
:                                                            :
:                                                            :
+------------------------------------------------------------+
```

Figure 1—Decision schematic for production code

compile and run, (3) program path tracing, (4) execution suspension and restart, and (5) variable dump and modification.

The difficulty with this method of analysis is that it considers only the paths traveled by the selected test data. Dynamic analysis is, therefore, analysis by trial and error. It is best suited for the investigation of a particular test case or a limited set of test cases, not for gaining an all-path understanding of a program.

Static analyzers are more of a newcomer to the maintenance environment. To be sure, flowcharting programs have existed for some time. Yet the flowcharting program merely provides a rehashed version of program logic in graphic form. In the output of a typical static analyzer, we see the beginnings of an attempt to unravel program logic. Moreover, static analysis can provide useful information regarding program style and complexity.

Yet of all the tools now available to maintenance programming, the *restructuring/recoding tools* are surely the most exciting. They combine the intelligence of the static analyzer with the ability to generate code. Unstructured code (i.e., code with GOTO statements) is the input to this tool. The tool analyzes the unstructured code and produces a structured version. Collectively, this family of tools represents our central focus here.

THE ECONOMICS OF REDOCUMENTATION

We believe that automated redocumentation is the preferred alternative for code repair. For some justification of this let us first look at the resource economics involved in the code repair decisions.

Type I and II code (see Figure 1) represent the code library that is to be essentially left alone. For this segment of the library it is generally possible to allocate resources at the rate of one maintenance programmer per 40,000 to 70,000 lines of source code (independent of the language). This allows for a small amount of enhancement but generally provides for very little extra resources for more than daily operational requirements. Obviously, numerical guidelines such as this need to be validated locally before extensive reliance is placed on them. For the Type III subset, it is a truly complex job to specify an appropriate level of resource allocation. In many DP organizations, the aggregate resources dedicated to the maintenance function can range from almost 90% to as low as 30%. A proper number lies only in management's eyes and is closely tied to a general philosophy of maintenance. We are suggesting that at least 10% of the maintenance library has been neglected. Various studies, reported by Jones[4] at IBM and Hermann[5] at Shell Oil and others, document the development cost of systems at values ranging from \$5 to \$50 or more per line of code produced. Our experience, however, is that automated documentation can be produced at a cost of between 20¢ and \$2.00 per line. This represents a cost ratio of 25:1! In stable database situations the redocumenation strategy is often viable and cost effective. A small allocation of resources can produce dramatic results for properly chosen code units. It is true that even more dramatic improvements can be made through the rewrite process. However, the allocation of resources is concomitantly much higher; and the benefit often occurs much later, after an extended development cycle.

Having now examined how to identify targets for profitable use of redocumentation tools and the economic rationale for using automated redocumentation, let us turn to a case study, drawn from the authors' own experience, to demonstrate the utility of this approach.

A CASE STUDY

Texaco Inc. is typical of many large DP operations and recently faced the problem of rising maintenance costs. There were a large number of diverse applications, each with its own maintenance staff and procedures. Also, like many DP organizations, Texaco had invested a considerable amount of money and staff time in learning to use new design technologies and tools. These efforts notwithstanding, many staff members felt that the level of effort expended on maintenance was still too high, primarily because of the large volume of old, poorly written code that had existed before the new methodologies were implemented.

To quantify the actual maintenance effort, functional applications were manually inventoried. This inventory confirmed the previously held suspicion that approximately half of the professional programming staff worked on maintenance. Because of the increasing backlog of new applications and enhancements to existing systems, and because of the omnipresent goal of holding costs to a minimum, this situation was deemed unacceptable. Early schemes to reduce this effort called for the mass redocumentation of all the production libraries via automated tools. Despite the relative cheapness of these tools, cost-benefit estimates precluded the use of this tactic. Hence it was decided that particular systems and subsystems would be targeted for rewrite or redocumentation.

First, manual methods were used to identify the relevant applications. Two points become apparent as this process was carried out: (1) manual code reviews were too time consuming, and (2) manual records of abends were difficult to organize.

It was decided to expand the use of automated tools to address these problems more effectively. In addition to the previously stated features, an automated library management system was required to improve control of source and load libraries across multiple sites. Having unsucessfully searched the outside software market for an integrated tool that would meet these requirements, it was decided to create a custom library management system, LIBMAN. LIBMAN is a control system using the services of several existing software tools (SPF, VTAM, PANVALET, ACF2, etc.) to provide control over both the repair and enhancement of production programs. The operational logging system used for the actual identification of problem programs was the MVS Integrated Control System (MICS) from Morino Associates, Inc., which gathers information from diverse sources such as SMF and TSO/MON. This information was then collected on a SAS database from which reports on code unit performance were derived. Finally, profiles were created to assist in the process of describing current systems. Originally a manual effort, this system has now been converted into an online one, using DATAMANAGER as a repository.

After the administrative-level systems were in place and the code universe was well defined, it was possible to identify code that was structurally poor. This subset of the code population became the target code, which would be examined in more depth. Through the process outlined earlier, some of these code units were amenable to automated redocumentation. At this point several automated tools were applied to the selected programs. First, for the COBOL systems an outside product, SCAN/370 from Group Operations, Inc., was selected. SCAN/370 produces a report that traces all the logic paths of a given program. This program also provides a source listing containing imbedded path data, complete with identification of dead code.

Later a restructuring/recoding tool for COBOL source programs became available. This program, called SUPERSTRUCTURE (also by Group Operations, Inc.), creates a *scorecard* that identifies unacceptable program flaws such as (1) interparagraph GOTO statements, (2) run away paths, and (3) fall-through execution of paragraphs. Having created the scorecard and identified the paths of a program, SUPERSTRUCTURE rewrites the program paths using only structured constructs (sequence, iteration, and selection). The resultant source code contains essentially none of the flaws of the original source program.

Most of the company's developmental programming is produced in PL/I. Though the language itself contains elements that may encourage good programming style, a number of older systems were found to abend with regularity and were difficult to modify. A significant review was undertaken to find analyzers and documentors that fit a PL/I development environment. Unfortunately, no vendor-supplied tool was found that would be compatible with the current methodologies, so an in-house tool was developed. The tool, TEXJAX, conducts static analyses of program paths via code scanning and renders several forms of documentation:

1. Complexity measures
2. Jackson style structure charts
3. Module hierarchy charts
4. Annotated source code

The next documentation tool selected was a system redocumentation tool linked to JCL. This tool, DOCU/TEXT from Diversified Software Systems, Inc., was tested on a few selected applications; and it appeared that it could be used on all the JCL libraries. This was in marked contrast to the way the other tools were used, but in this case it seemed to be feasible. Our evaluation is that system-level tools of this type cause one of two events to occur. Either you modify the tool to fit the prevailing customs, or prevailing customs have to change. In this case, the traditional system documentation, manually produced, was so widely used that output from the purchased version of DOCU/TEXT required extensive modification to fit desired formats. Consequently, work is ongoing to implement a JCL scanning process that will use DOCU/TEXT as a nucleus. Its output will be used to duplicate and replace the current manual run books used by the operations group.

All the tools and techniques outlined in this paper continue to evolve. As with most management-oriented concepts, it is difficult to quantify the relationship of improved productivity to the use of automated tools. We have, however, recorded a decline in resource requirements in the period during which these tools have been installed. Part of this is due to management's increased interest in this subject, as well as improved procedures and tools.

CONCLUSION

There are many disjointed software tools on the market today, and more are emerging daily. Various combinations of these tools will fit unique organizations. We have attempted to outline an approach to the selection of target code units and general types of tools that collectively aid in the maintenance function. A most important conclusion resulting from our experience is that tools cannot be purchased or built and then used indiscriminately. Rather, it takes an administrative activity to identify which code units are best for resource allocation. Then, management has to support these efforts with rational levels of resources designed to "purify" production libraries. Even more pertinently, it requires a high level of management focus to cause the process to occur in an orderly manner. Within the software tools marketplace we anticipate more innovation in the area of automatic restructuring/recoding. It seems inevitable that artificial intelligence (expert systems) may lead the way in this area. One possible way to implement such a scheme would be to create an expert system that is well versed in one of the popular design methodologies (Jackson, Yourdon, etc.), give it access to the path information provided by static analysis tools, then restructure accordingly. Once this can be successfully done, the family of redocumentation tools will become more coherent.

Whatever the case may be, it is probable that tools will continue to play an increasingly visible role in the maintenance of software systems and will require continued management effort to keep them cost effective.

REFERENCES

1. Lientz, B. P., and E. B. Swanson. *Software Maintenance Management.* Reading, Mass.: Addison-Wesley, 1980.
2. McCabe, Thomas J. "A Complexity Measure." *IEEE Transactions on Software Engineering,* SE-2 (1976), pp. 308–320.
3. Elshoff, James L., and Michael Marcotty. "Improving Computer Readability to Aid Modification." *Communications of the ACM,* 25 (1982), pp. 512–521.
4. Jones, T. C. "Measuring Programming Quality and Productivity." *IBM Systems Journal,* 17 (1978), pp. 39–63.
5. Hermann, L. T. "Productivity and Performance Measurement." Paper presented to the American Petroleum Institute (API) Subcommittee on Systems and Programmer Productivity, December 1983, Houston.

System information database: An automated maintenance aid

by LINDA BRICE
and JOHN CONNELL
Los Alamos National Laboratory
Los Alamos, New Mexico

ABSTRACT

Documenting application systems has long been considered a necessary evil. Necessary because documentation provides a map to present systems, serves as a maintenance aid, and is required by the auditors; evil because it is an activity generally dreaded by those who develop the systems. Since normal behavior regarding unpleasant chores is avoidance, application systems documentation is sometimes absent and often incomplete.

Documenting may be unpopular for a number of reasons, including psychological ones. One very obvious problem is that, except for a few automated tools at the program level, documentation is a manual process used in an automated environment. Automating the process is a way to reduce the laboriousness of the task.

This paper is a case study of how one data processing organization applied student labor and a relational database management system in a prototype to automate much of their applications systems documentation function. The capabilities, fringe benefits, and future enhancements of the tool are discussed.

INTRODUCTION

Why should maintenance aids be automated? In many installations system documentation is still a cumbersome manual process. There are automated data dictionaries and program documentors on the market, but few link to other aspects of an organization's functions, and most take several years to populate with data. Some organizations commit to five or ten years' worth of data gathering and data entry, unassured of the results. Others accept as a fact of life that manual documentation is not an effective maintenance aid, but continue to set up frameworks with strict requirements and standards.

This paper shows how a relational data base management system was used to develop an in-house automated documentation system for the Administrative Data Processing (ADP) Division of the Los Alamos National Laboratory. The database has been given the acronym SID, system information database. It contains much of the documentation pertaining to production application systems. This documentation has historically been maintained manually in Central File folders. At the time of this writing, SID has proven to be very effective for entering, updating, and retrieving documentation data rapidly and accurately.

WHY THE NEED TO DOCUMENT

Documentation is considered the "map" of present systems, and a valuable aid to maintenance programmers. Accurate documentation is also a reliable guide to relationships within and between systems. It provides a means for reducing the risk of introducing errors during maintenance work. If an error does occur, a visual picture of control flow is available to help locate the source of the error. In the normal course of events, clear documentation makes staff turnover less disruptive by providing a useful training aid. Finally, adequate documentation will satisfy auditors' requirements for information about how systems work.

Data processing professionals have long been admonished to document in certain standard ways. Most shops were led to believe, by the literature of the 1970s, that visual tables of contents (VTOCs), IBM's hierarchical input process output (HIPO), and flow charts, for example, were the best tools for documentation and were necessary. Now, we are told to produce data flow diagrams, structure charts, Chapin charts, data models, Jackson diagrams, and Warnier–Orr diagrams, as well as myriad forms supplied by structured methodologies.

Many installations simply have not sorted out which old tools to discard, which new ones to adopt, what to make retroactive, or whether or not all tools need to be applied at the system, task, and program level. Most organizations have viewed documentation as a program level activity, with recent emphasis on the data element level. There is much more than a program in the makeup of most application systems. They are also composed of operating system procedures, database interfaces, data files, and other elements. Documentation must not only be present, it must be flexible. Few DP organizations can bear the expense of throwing a system away and rewriting it from scratch. When "the intent is to modify functionality or capability or even performance, the trend is to add code, a front end, or a box... 'Add on, not replace' is the trend in software."[1] Documentation must be enhanced easily, just like software. Martin and McClure state that "what is needed is succinct, high-quality documentation that is easily accessible and easily updatable. To be maintainable, programs and their associated documentation must be flexible and extensible."[2] To that statement we could add that all documentation pertaining to an applications system must fit the same description as that for a program.

BASIC ELEMENTS OF DOCUMENTATION GENERALLY NEEDED FOR EACH APPLICATION

Regardless of the tool used or the level at which it is applied, the basic elements of documentation needed for a typical business application include:

1. The basic purpose of the system
2. Identification of the customer
3. How the system runs (tasks, procedures, call files, jobs, operating system commands)
4. How execution begins and proceeds
5. Which groups of higher level languages or fourth-generation language instructions exist
6. How the groups of languages (or programs) are invoked
7. Which functions are performed
8. Which files exist
9. How is the data processed—and by which tasks or programs
10. What the output (input) looks like (files, screens, reports, etc)
11. Who is responsible for the system maintenance

Whatever the capacity of the hardware, the size of the application, the programming language employed, the number of staff members, or whether a database management system is used or not, these types of basic elements need to exist for maintainers and auditors of the system.

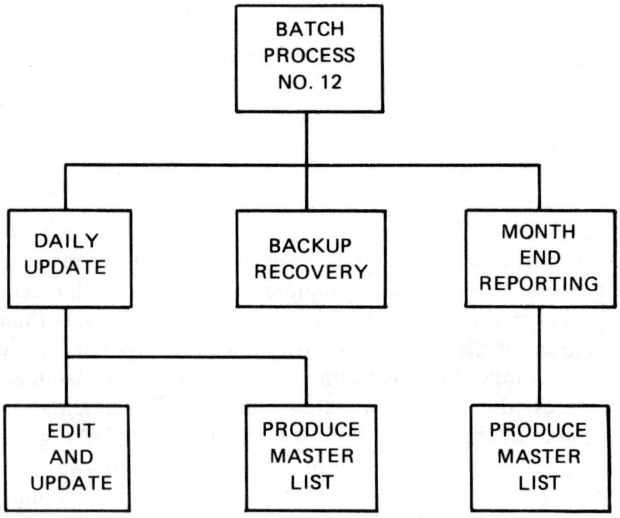

Figure 1—Visual table of contents (VTOC)

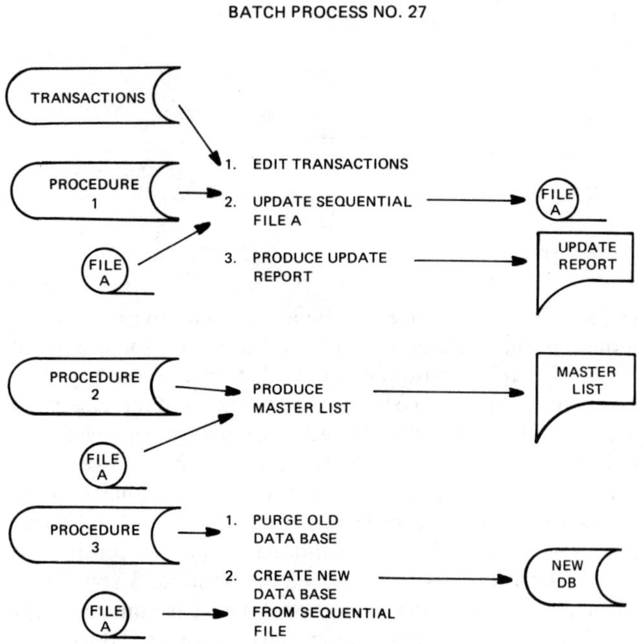

Figure 2—Hierarchial input process output (HIPO)

WHY DOCUMENTING IS SO UNPOPULAR

Documentation, useful if not absolutely necessary, is often the least favorite part of most DP professionals' duties. This is so because documentation is seldom scheduled as part of the job. When schedules slip, system implementation is a more important feature; there must be a system. The documentation portion of the schedule, often inadequately allotted at the start, is diminished because it is often performed after the fact and because it is usually a clumsy, manual system. Sometimes documentation begins when maintenance begins.[3]

Documentation in ADP was completely manual prior to the development of SID and included several elements: First was a visual table of contents (VTOC) describing the hierarchy of tasks. This is a manually drawn set of boxes within a strict format. The major functions of the system appear as text within the boxes of this system schematic (Figure 1). The VTOC was initiated during system design and maintained during the life of the system. It was normally produced after system implementation, to merely fulfill a documentation requirement, and often was not maintained because of the necessity to manually redraw and retype the chart.

The next item was a hierarchical input process output (HIPO) describing the flow of input and output with respect to the functions of a program or task. Special symbols to represent files, output listings, and direction of flow (arrows) were drawn by hand with the aid of a template, and a narrative was typed (Figure 2). HIPOs were intended to be design aids, but were usually produced post-implementation and then only because of standards requirements. Obviously, due to the nature of the format, changes of any consequence required redrawing of one or more pages, or a manual cut-and-paste procedure. Such inconvenience discouraged the maintenance of the charts to accurately reflect the state of the system as it changed character over time because of maintenance and enhancement.

Next were the indices of programs and files, which provided simple lists, usually alphabetized. Other information, such as what task invoked the listed program, or what files were referenced by the program was usually included (although some of the data existed in other forms in the HIPO). The frustration in manually maintaining such lists is that the data must be recorded at least twice (the I/O files are listed on the program index; the referencing programs are listed on the file index).

Also included was information about file and data elements. Data elements were typically described by a record layout form (Figure 3). The record layouts often were hand-drawn.

Finally, there were program listings, which were maintained in hard-copy form in folders arranged in an order meaningful to the organization (by section, by function, and so on). The listings were checked out to maintenance programmers in a library-type arrangement.

FILE NAME: A RECORD NAME: EMPLOYEE					
FIELD NAME:	EMPLOYEE NUMBER	EMPLOYEE NAME	DATE OF BIRTH	SEX	. . .
CHARACTERISTICS:	X(6)	X(14)	X(6)	9	. . .
RELATIVE POSITION:	1–6	7–20	21–26	27	. . .

Figure 3—Record layout

AUTOMATION CAN MAKE DOCUMENTATION MORE PALATABLE

Streamlining of documentation procedures may improve the product to the point that it becomes a true maintenance aid instead of a mere fulfillment of standards requirements. There are psychological reasons that programmers are more comfortable with automated tools than with manual ones. Data processing professionals, like the shoemaker with his barefoot children, automate the lives of others, but often have no time to automate their own business. Naturally, programmers become frustrated at being forced to deal with internal paper work when they are accustomed to automation in every other aspect of their work.

If manual processes are clumsy, they also tend to produce incomplete and inaccurate results. Although management makes rules in the form of standards, having an understandable incentive for profit, they reinforce the message to their staff that the most important part of a job is to get the system up and running. Of course, the message is well received by programmers, who often view documentation as a nuisance.

Automated documentation has all of the advantages of any other automated system, including interactive retrievals, simultaneous access by several parties, and easy aggregates. One particular advantage of automated documentation is the retrieval of information across systems. For example, manual documentation shows program and file relationships within a particular system, but if one wanted to list every program that reads File XXX because the format must change to increase the field length of a data item, then all manual documentation for systems suspected to relate to the file must be searched, or all machine-readable files across those systems must be searched to complete the list; an easy retrieval for a properly formatted system information database. Size considerations, an aid in estimation of the effort required for a job, are also available, e.g., the number of files within the number of systems that reference Purchase Order Number or one of its aliases. As Brown writes, "the most common error in documentation is to provide masses of detail . . . but little on overall organization . . . and on the relationship between parts."[4]

AUTOMATING DOCUMENTATION: A CASE STUDY

At Los Alamos National Laboratory, management and staff agreed that an automated documentation process should be attempted. A relational database system was already licensed in-house, had proved to be an excellent tool for other applications, and was chosen to inventory and manage parts of our documentation function. There existed, however, a resource problem. All available analysts, designers, and programmers were committed to other projects. Given the work load facing the entire division, there was little justification in hiring staff for the documentation project, which was considered overhead. It was not a development of an application desired by the customers who pay the bills. There also was a little skepticism on the part of management. There had been no official cost–benefit study performed for the project and management could not be certain it would be worth the effort to disturb the status quo to implement a new documentation system when the staff was in the throes of a great deal of new development.

By a fortunate circumstance, the ADP Division was host for the summer to four young men from the service academies.* The Service Academy Research Associates (SARAs) came to us from the Air Force and the Naval academies; three of them were in their senior year, one was a computer science major, and none had practical data processing experience. They were enthusiastic about learning a state-of-the-art tool, so it was decided to assign them the documentation project, even though they could not work as a true team since their four- to six-week tenures overlapped very little. Armed with a name, SID, and a database management tool, they produced a prototype that proved to be quite successful in convincing management and staff that the documentation procedures could indeed change for the better.

While the first SARA was en route to Los Alamos, a systems requirements definition was produced as a guide to the current manual system and what we wanted to accomplish with SID. Normally, a systems design document follows the requirements definition in the development of any new project. In this case, however, the detailed design was replaced with the prototype version of the system.

A pilot system was rapidly available for management to evaluate in terms of cost and benefit and for the staff to evaluate in terms of usability. The pilot project had small-scale actual data; data were entered for small but complete systems.

The system was refined by submitting the prototype version to selected members of the programming staff for critique. Tables were easily restructured to add and delete data elements or to modify attributes, without the loss or troublesome reloading of any of the real data. Additional live data were loaded from a hierarchical database on a separate computer via magnetic tape. Live data also were loaded from files that programmers had set up to keep track of various systems for which they were responsible. It was interesting to note that many programmers had already discovered that the manually maintained central files were inadequate for maintenance purposes and that several members of the staff had taken steps to record applications data in a more usable state.

A recent survey of programmer opinion indicated that the current ADP staff was 100% in favor of maintaining an automated system to map the state of present systems and the evolution of future systems. When a representative task force of the programming staff viewed demonstrations of the retrievals, they responded favorably.

Some of the automated retrievals that replaced manual documentation elements include the VTOC (Figure 4), HIPO (Figure 5), index of programs, index of files, index of tasks, and catalog of systems (Figure 6). The VTOC is somewhat different in format from the original. To allow for an unrestricted number of high level functions, the information is spread down the page instead of across. The informational

*Midshipman Christian N. Haugen, U.S. Naval Academy; Cadet Edwin O. Heierman, U.S. Air Force Academy; Midshipman Matthew J. McKelvey, U.S. Naval Academy; Midshipman Gard J. Clark, U.S. Naval Academy.

VISUAL TABLE OF CONTENTS
FOR SYSTEM 23
CAPITAL EQUIPMENT BUDGET SYSTEM
(CEBS)
PROCEDURE NO. 10

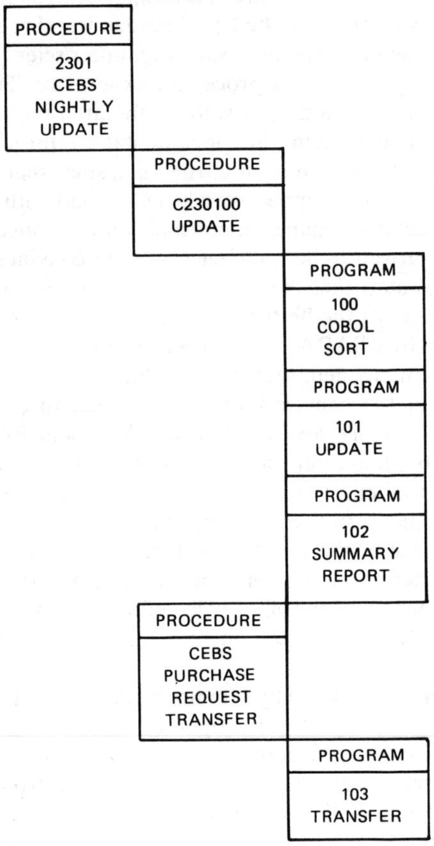

Figure 4—VTOC

HIERARCHICAL INPUT PROCESS OUTPUT
FOR SYSTEM 23
CAPITAL EQUIPMENT BUDGET SYSTEM
BATCH PROCESS NO. 27
PROCEDURE NO. 2301

INPUT FILES	PROGRAM	OUTPUT FILES
• TRANSACTIONS	230501	• FILEA
• FILE A	• EDIT TRANSACTIONS	• REPORT
	• UPDATE FILE A	
	• PRODUCE UPDATE REPORT	
• FILE A	230605	
	• PRODUCE MASTER LIST	• MASTER
• FILE A	230625	• NEW DB
• OLD DB	• PURGE OLD DB	.
	• CREATE NEW DB	.
.	.	.
.	.	
.	.	

Figure 5—HIPO

CATALOG OF SYSTEM,
TASK, PROGRAM, FILE

SYSTEM ID	TASK (PROCEDURE) ID	PROGRAM NAME	FILE(S) USED
23-CEBS	2301	230601 EDIT/UPDATE	FILE A REPORT
		230605 MASTER LIST	FILE A MASTER
		230625 NEW DB	FILEA OLD DB NEW DB
.	.	.	.
.	.	.	.
.	.	.	.

Figure 6—System catalog

elements are retained, however, and both hierarchical and sequencing attributes are preserved. A catalog of systems relates files to programs, programs to tasks, and tasks to systems. In the example in Figure 6, the capital equipment budget system (CEBS) is documented. CEBS is identified as system 23. Task 2301 is a procedure file that executes three programs—230601, 230605, and 230625. Each program is also identified by its generic name. Files appearing as I/O within the programs are documented in the rightmost column. Source data is input to the database using the input screen tools supplied by the database management system (Figure 7). Updates to documentation of the present system are accomplished using the same screens.

FRINGE BENEFITS

SID was devised with the intent of helping programmers to map present and future systems. However, once in place, it provided several other benefits. A matrix describing system identifiers and associated responsible programmers had been maintained on word processing equipment. A similar matrix detailing application system, organizational section where the functional responsibility for that application resides, and programmers identified in order by level of responsibility (primary responsibility, back-up to primary responsibility, and secondary back-up responsibility) can now be made by a fairly simple merge of relations. The query language commands are collected into an executable procedure so that the matrix can be produced with one operating system level command. The

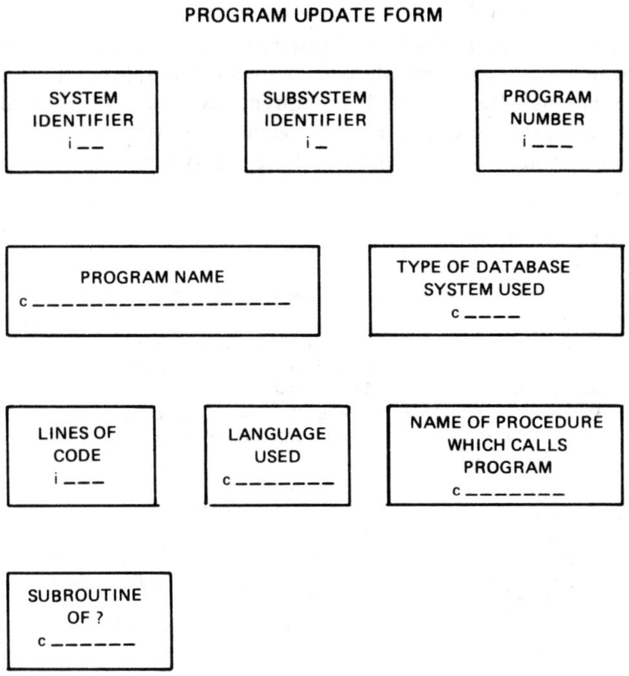

Figure 7—SID data entry screen

word processing files have been deleted and the clerical staff updates employee information as it relates to system responsibility directly on the database. Section leaders (first-line management to whom the responsible programmers report) likewise record responsibility changes directly on the database. Figure 8 is an example of the responsibility matrix. Of course, responsibility information can be retrieved by name of staff member as well as by application system. It is sometimes useful for management to know—by employee—for which systems each employee maintains responsibility, and what constitutes the level of responsibility. Once system responsibility data are captured, it is a simple step to report organizational entity, telephone number, and location for members of staff, either as a complete organizational report or as retrievals for single individuals or groups of individuals.

Another fringe benefit of storing gross system data in one place is the ability to estimate system size. Many installations can list the modules present in a system, but few can report much about actual system size, because expansion and contraction take place continuously with modification. There is an occasional need to give at least approximate-figure answers to questions about how long it will take to convert completely to a new hardware vendor or what the estimate is for converting to a new language version or a different control language. These questions frequently are not just academic; entire installations can change hardware vendors, and it is not unusual for vendors of software to cease support of earlier versions. Approximate figures for lines of code per language, languages per system, programs per system, tasks (operating procedure level commands) per system, and other sums can provide the basis for estimating conversion effort, and therefore, monetary cost. Such queries can be processed easily by the count and sum features of most databases.

FUTURE ENHANCEMENTS

While the primary intent of the database is to serve the programming staff who maintain present systems and develop new ones, the functions can be expanded to include the operations side of systems production. Run and recovery instruc-

RESPONSIBILITY TABLE

SYSTEM ID	SYSTEM NAME	ORGANIZATIONAL SECTION	PRIMARY	1st BACKUP	2nd BACKUP
12	PAYROLL	EMPLOYEE INFORMATION	HAWKINS	RICH	McCALISTER
20	COMMITMENTS	ACCOUNTING AND OPERATIONS	TOMLINSON	HUDGINS	ARMSTRONG
23	CAPITAL EQUIPMENT	BUDGET AND PLANNING	ROYBAL		HILL
70	GENERAL LEDGER	ACCOUNTING AND OPERATIONS	HUDGINS	OSBORN	
85	PROPERTY MANAGEMENT	MATERIALS	ARMSTRONG		
⋮	⋮	⋮	⋮	⋮	⋮

Figure 8—SID retrieval

tions, file access and permits, account restrictions, job setups, file retentions, expected outputs, and other operations data can be appended to system, task, program, file, or data element relations as appropriate. Operations information is a natural addition because operators and production controllers are also interested in employee system responsibilities and system functional descriptions, which have already been described in the database.

Information about system functions, responsibilities, and operations can form a useful link to controlling resources and measuring activities associated with a system. The level of activity against a system is a guide to future staffing in an organization. Activity in the form of customer requests for service (maintenance, enhancements) on a particular system can be married to the system information database to get a complete picture of current system activity levels. For example, it can be noted that system #98 is general ledger, that task #107 account update executes 12 programs and 7 files (from SID), that the task is executed approximately 30 times per month (from SID), that program #203 aborted seven times last month (from SID with operations data), and that program #203 had five service requests logged against it in the past six weeks (from the resource control or metrics database). Other data, such as the effort required to complete the requests for service on the program and history of the program, can be used in assessing staffing levels for the system as well as for considerations in the program's redesign.

CONCLUDING REMARKS

No database, even a modern relational database, is magic. The organization considering support of a SID must commit to some amount of overhead. As in the case of the automated systems we deliver to our customers, data must be entered, the database tool must be understood, and more likely than not, programs will have to be designed and maintained to perform sophisticated retrievals and to provide links from one database to another.

When SID was developed by ADP at Los Alamos, the prototype was brought up almost entirely by the SARAs, a real tribute to the ease of use of the relational database management system. Yet several programs were required, adding to the overhead of maintenance and documentation for those remaining after the student apprentices have left. Like all systems, data processing's management information systems must be staffed to watch for and prevent system degradation.

REFERENCES

1. Zvegintzov, N. "Nanotrends." *Datamation,* 29, (1983), pp. 105–116.
2. Martin, J., and C. McClure. *Software Maintenance: The Problem and Its Solutions.* Englewood Cliffs, N.J.: Prentice-Hall, 1983. p. 174.
3. Schneider, E. "Structured Software Maintenance." *AFIPS, Proceedings of the National Computer Conference* (Vol. 52), 1983, pp. 137–144.
4. Brown, P. J. "Why Does Software Die?" In G. Parikh and N. Zvegintzov (eds.), *Tutorial on Software Maintenance.* Silver Spring, Md.: IEEE Computer Society Press, 1983.
5. Parikh, G. "Structured Maintenance the Warnier/Orr Way." In G. Parikh and N. Zvegintzov (eds.), *Tutorial on Software Maintenance.* Silver Spring, Md.: IEEE Computer Society Press, 1983.
6. Yourdon, E., and L. L. Constantine. *Structured Design: Fundamentals of a Discipline of Computer Program and Systems Design* (2nd ed.). New York: Yourdon Press, 1978.
7. De Marco, T. *Structured Analysis and System Specification.* New York: Yourdon, 1978.
8. Chapin, N. "New Format for Flowcharts." *Software Practice and Experiences,* 4 (1974), pp. 341–357.
9. Rigo, J. T., and J. R. Rudikoff. "HIPO: Structured System Design Documentation." *Auerbach Information Management Series.* Philadelphia, Pa.: Auerbach Publishers, 1975.
10. Hunter, B. "Documentation—Management Problems and Solutions." *Auerbach Information Management Series.* Philadelphia, Pa.: Auerbach Publishers, 1977.
11. Page-Jones, M. *The Practical Guide to Structured Systems Design.* New York: Yourdon Press, 1980.
12. Yoder, C. M., and M. L. Schrag. "Nassi–Shneiderman Charts—An Alternative to Flowcharts for Design." *Software Engineering Notes of the ACM,* 5 (1978), pp. 79–86.
13. Nassi, I., and B. Shneiderman. "Flowchart Techniques for Structured Programming." *Sigplan Notices of the ACM,* 8 (1973), pp. 12–26.
14. Allen, F. W., M.E.S. Loomis, and M. V. Mannino. "The Integrated Dictionary/Directory System." *ACM Computing Surveys,* 14 (1982), pp. 245–286.
15. Center for Programming Science and Technology. "Functional Specifications for a Federal Information Processing Standard Data Dictionary System." National Bureau of Standards Publication 82-2619, Washington, D.C., 1983.

COBOL-80: The new structured language

by JEROME GARFUNKEL
Jerome Garfunkel Associates, Inc.
Litchfield, Connecticut

ABSTRACT

This paper includes a presentation of the most important new features of COBOL-80, with examples for each. In addition, an analysis of the potential costs and benefits of this new language is presented. Finally, criticism of potential incompatibilities is discussed.

The features discussed in this paper are among the more significant new features of the draft proposed revised X3.23 American National Standard Programming Language COBOL (COBOL-80). The features presented here represent only a sample of all the new features of the revised COBOL standard. Many other more subtle features of COBOL-80 are included as well.

Based on my own analysis as well as on a government analysis conducted on a sizable sample of its own program inventory, I expect a significant increase in productivity will be derived from using COBOL-80 in program development and maintenance. Particularly in the area of program maintenance, although the cost savings will be deferred as programs go through their normal life cycle, the productivity gains derived from the maintenance of well-structured COBOL-80 programs will be a significant factor in systems maintenance operating costs.

This revision of the COBOL standard has, in addition to the new features, numerous clarifications of poorly defined (ambiguous and undefined) rules that existed in the previous COBOL-74 and COBOL-68 standards. These clarifications, although constructively serving the COBOL user community at large, may inadvertently conflict with a specific implementor's COBOL compiler. This occurs when a specific implementor-defined interpretation of an ambiguous rule occasionally differs from the newly defined standard interpretation. Much attention has been paid to this group of features over the past few years.

Many of the new features of COBOL-80 will greatly ease the use of COBOL in structured programming environments. Some of the new features specifically useful in structured programs are included in the following sections.

EVALUATE

The EVALUATE verb provides a means of testing multiple conditions and specifying multiple control branches (see Figure 1).

PERFORM

An in-line version of the PERFORM statement is now permitted. In addition "DO-while" and "DO-until" constructs can now be written with the addition of the WITH TEST BEFORE and WITH TEST AFTER clauses.

```
PERFORM   WITH TEST AFTER UNTIL X > =  100
      ADD 1 TO X
      MOVE TABLE-ITEM (X) TO TABLE-ITEM ( X + 1)
END-PERFORM
```

Note the new relational operator GREATER THAN OR EQUAL, and the new relative subscript (X + 1).

STRUCTURED CONDITIONAL STATEMENTS

With the inclusion of 19 scope terminators (i.e., END-IF, END-READ, END-ADD, etc.), constructs of nested conditional statements may be written with clarity.

```
IF      FINAL-RECORD-PROCESSED
THEN    PERFORM  LAST-TRANSACTIONAL-PROC.
        READ         BATCH-KEY-FILE
          AT END     EXIT PROGRAM
        END-READ
        IF           BATCH-KEY = "D"
          THEN       PERFORM DELETION-PROC.
          ELSE       PERFORM   MODIFY-PROCEDURE
        END-IF
ELSE    PERFORM NORMAL-RECORD-PROCEDURE
        CONTINUE
END-IF
```

```
EVALUATE       AGE-OF-DEBT    ALSO    CREDIT-RATING
  WHEN           0 THRU 30    ALSO    "A" THRU "B"     PERFORM NO-NOTICE
  WHEN           0 THRU 30    ALSO        "C"          PERFORM MILD-NOTICE
  WHEN          31 THRU 60    ALSO        "A"          PERFORM MILD-NOTICE
  WHEN          31 THRU 60    ALSO        "B"          PERFORM NORMAL-NOTICE
  WHEN          31 THRU 60    ALSO        "C"          PERFORM FIRM-NOTICE
  WHEN          61 THRU 90    ALSO        "A"          PERFORM NORMAL-NOTICE
  WHEN          61 THRU 90    ALSO        "B"          PERFORM FIRM-NOTICE
  WHEN          61 THRU 90    ALSO        "C"          PERFORM COLLECTIONS
  WHEN          91 THRU 999   ALSO        "A"          PERFORM FIRM-NOTICE
  WHEN          91 THRU 999   ALSO    "B" THRU "C"     PERFORM COLLECTIONS
END-EVALUATE
```

Figure 1—The EVALUATE Statement

FALSE CONDITION BRANCH

To add structured symmetry to all conditional clauses (AT END, ON SIZE ERROR, etc.) a negative version of the clause is also allowed as in:

```
READ            MASTER-FILE
  AT END        EXIT PROGRAM
  NOT AT END    PERFORM PROCESS-RECORD
END-READ
```

NESTED PROGRAMS

Complete programs may be wholly contained within other programs. This permits, among other things, the outside program to specify GLOBAL data items, which may be shared by any of the contained (inside) programs; as in this example:

```
01 SHARED-DATA IS GLOBAL PIC X(20).
```

Additionally, GLOBAL USE procedures may be specified in the DECLARATIVE section of the outer program that allows for file error processing in the contained programs to be centralized and controlled by the outer (Master) program:

```
USE GLOBAL AFTER STANDARD ERROR
PROCEDURE ON INPUT.
```

CALL

Data items that are passed to "sub-programs" may protect their contents from being modified by the addition of the BY CONTENT phrase of the CALL statement.

```
CALL PAYROLL USING BY CONTENT WEEKLY-PAY,
YTD-PAY.
```

INITIALIZING SUB-PROGRAMS

When the PROGRAM-ID of a subprogram contains the phrase IS INITIAL after its program name, the programmer can be assured that all data values will be initialized before it starts executing.

```
PROGRAM-ID. ACCOUNTS-PAYABLE IS INITIAL.
```

OCCURS-VALUES AND SUBSCRIPTS

Seven dimensions (seven levels of subscripting) may now be specified (previously only three levels were provided). Also, initial values may now be specified for table elements without the need to REDEFINE the table.

```
01.
  03  TABLE-ELEMENT PIC 999V99 OCCURS 100
      TIMES VALUE ZERO.
```

SYMBOLIC CHARACTERS

The symbolic character clause in the SPECIAL-NAMES paragraphs provides a means for a programmer to specify a user-defined name for nonprintable characters in the ASCII (or other) character sets.

```
SYMBOLIC CHARACTER BELL IS 8 IN ASCII
```

In this example 8 refers to the eighth ordered character in the ASCII character set, and BELL is a user-defined figurative constant.

FILLER

The word FILLER is optional and is no longer restricted to elementary data items.

```
01.
     02    COUNTER-1    PIC    999V99.
     02                 PIC    X.
     02    COUNTER-2    PIC    999V99.
```

DE-EDITING

Numeric-edited data items (PIC $$$,$$$) may be moved to a purely numeric data item (PIC 9(6)V99). This results, for example, in moving a data item that contains $1,234 to a data item containing 00123400.

SORT

Multiple output files are permitted. In addition, the WITH DUPLICATES IN ORDER clause now allows the programmer to specify that duplicate sort keys appearing on the input file will be in the same sequence on the output file.

```
SORT                       SORT-WORK FILE
  ON ASCENDING KEY         WORK-ORDER-NUMBER
  WITH DUPLICATES IN       ORDER
  INPUT PROCEDURE IS       EDIT-INPUT-PROCESS
  GIVING                   DAILY-WORK-SEQ
                           DAILY-WORK-REL
                           DAILY-WORK-INDX.
```

Note also that the SORT input procedure (EDIT-INPUT-PROCESS) may reference procedures outside of the SORT section. Likewise, procedures within the SORT may be referenced by procedures in the main program.

REFERENCE MODIFICATION

Programmers may now reference a portion of a data item without needing to REDEFINE that portion previously in the DATA DIVISION.

```
MOVE TELEPHONE (4:3) TO EXCHANGE
```

In the above example only the fourth, fifth, and sixth position of the data item TELEPHONE are moved (starting in position 4: for a length of 3). I suggest that programmers be careful when using this feature because its misuse can lead to poorly documented programs.

INITIALIZE

A series of subordinate elementary data items may be initialized all at once using the INITIALIZE verb. Given the following group data item:

```
01 SCREEN-PAGE.
   03 NAME          PIC     X(20).
   03 TELEPHONE     PIC     999B999B9999.
   03 BALANCE-DUE   PIC     9999V99.
   03 CUST-STATUS   PIC     A.
```

if a programmer writes INITIALIZE SCREEN-PAGE, all numeric data items will be cleared to zero and all nonnumeric data items will be cleared to spaces. There are facilities to restrict the initializing process to certain classes of data (numeric only, alphanumeric-edited only, etc.) as well as to initialize fields to values other than zero and spaces.

INSPECT. . .CONVERTING

The CONVERTING clause of the INSPECT statement permits a shorthand way of writing multiple character replacement clauses.

```
01    BOTTLE PIC X(5) VALUE "WATER".

INSPECT BOTTLE CONVERTING "ATR" TO "IN"
```

This INSPECT statement results in three character replacements ("A" to "I", "T" to "N", and "R" to space). It is a cheap way to PERFORM miracles in COBOL-80 by converting WATER to WINE.

REPLACE

To aid the programmer in dealing with possible conflicts in new reserved words with COBOL-74/68 programs, the REPLACE statement operates on source text and converts the source program before it is compiled.

```
REPLACE
==END-READ==     BY  ==END-READ-PROCEDURE==
==CLASS==        BY  ==DATA-CLASS==
==ALPHABETIC==   BY  ==ALPHABETIC-UPPER==.
```

I expect that this will be most useful where COBOL installations create standard conversion library routines that can be copied into individual programs.

RECORD DELIMITER

A means of specifying Variable Length Record conventions is provided in the FILE-CONTROL paragraph.

```
SELECT                       INDEXED-FILE A
  ASSIGN TO                  DISC
  ORGANIZATION IS            INDEXED
  RECORD DELIMITER IS        STANDARD-1.
```

DAY-OF-WEEK

This reserved word DAY-OF-WEEK represents a one digit character: 1 = Monday, 2 = Tuesday, 3 = Wednesday, etc. It is used as follows:

```
ACCEPT DAY-CODE FROM DAY-OF-WEEK
```

CLASS

A new CLASS clause in the SPECIAL-NAMES paragraph allows a programmer to name his own class of characters.

```
CLASS FIRST-HALF-ALPHA-UPPER IS "A" THRU "M"
```

These new features, along with some other more subtle additions and changes, contribute to an up-to-date application language complementing current trends in structured programming methodologies.*

* Those with questions regarding the revised COBOL 80 standard are invited to contact the author at Jerome Garfunkel Associates, Inc., Cobble Court, Litchfield, Connecticut 06759.

Is COBOL-8x cost effective?

by MARCO FIORELLO
Titan Systems
Vienna, Virginia
and
JOHN CUGINI
National Bureau of Standards
Washington, D.C.

ABSTRACT

The purpose of the study is to assess the estimated costs and benefits to the federal government that would result from adoption of the proposed revision of American National Standard COBOL as a Federal Information Processing Standard (FIPS). Potential benefits of $90.2 million have been identified, stemming primarily from improved productivity in both the development and maintenance of COBOL programs. Estimated costs of $17.9 million have been identified, arising principally from the effort needed to convert old COBOL programs to the new specification, which is incompatible in some respects with the current one. In support of the study, we conducted interviews with federal ADP managers and officials, and also analyzed more than one thousand federal COBOL programs for various syntactic characteristics.

Extracted from National Bureau of Standards Internal Report 83-2639; not subject to copyright in the U.S.

STUDY SCOPE AND QUALIFICATIONS

The scope of this study is limited to COBOL-related effects on the federal ADP community. Of course similar effects may be expected in the private sector insofar as the characteristics of its COBOL usage resemble those of the federal government.

In this analysis, we are concerned with effects that may result if the proposed changes to ANSI COBOL-74 are also adopted in the Federal Information Processing Standard (FIPS) for COBOL. Data available on applications software development and maintenance in the federal government are general and approximate in nature, and are particularly limited regarding any one specific programming language such as COBOL (although COBOL is by far the most commonly used language within the government, and therefore can hardly be regarded as atypical). We augmented the available general data with staff interviews at nine federal agencies and with a detailed analysis of a sample of 1068 COBOL programs from eleven federal agencies.

BASE CASE STATISTICS

The base case statistics are derived from various reference materials, cited in this document, and the study survey and program sample.

Programmer Pool

For the past 10 years the number of federal agency staff programmers has remained fairly steady—in the range of 118,000–120,000 staff-years.[1] Of those work-years, roughly 60% were primarily for COBOL-related activities in 1980, with a growth to 65% projected for 1985.[2] Depending upon the federal agency, the annual programmer turnover rate will vary from a low of 10% to a high of 30%. A reasonable average appears to be 20%. In most installations, more than half of the staff are devoted to maintenance (corrective, adaptive, and perfective) activities, which reflect the life cycle distribution of application software costs.[3–5] Based on very limited data, it appears that on the average a programmer spends 15% to 25% of available time performing coding functions.

COBOL Program Inventory

There are roughly 500,000 application software programs in the federal inventory. Of these, 50% to 60% are in some form of COBOL. Very few, 5–10%, of these 250,000–300,000 COBOL programs are in full conformance with the current COBOL FIPS 21-1. The average COBOL program in our sample contains about 1270 lines of source code and was developed about six years ago. This latter figure compares reasonably well with the 5.4-year estimate given in Reference 4.

In our sample of 1068 COBOL programs, with more than 1.3 million lines of code from 11 federal agencies, we learned that 80% use one or more of the 50 proposed incompatible changes analyzed in this study. If we discount the somewhat special case of the incompatibility concerning the DISPLAY verb (see below), this figure drops to about 40%.

An important point about interpretation of the statistics is that the detection of incompatibilities was done by a syntactic scan of the source code. Where the incompatibility involves a syntactic change (e.g., the deletion of ENTER), this is a reliable procedure. In those cases where the semantics are being changed or clarified (EXIT PROGRAM closing out PERFORMs, for example), however, the best that can be done is to look for source code where such a change might make a difference. This analysis represents, therefore, only a worst-case estimate. The DISPLAY incompatibility is an especially striking example of this. Syntactically, we counted every occurrence of DISPLAY as an incompatibility, even though the great majority of vendors currently implement this verb as described in the revision.

The age of programs was determined simply by the contents (if any) of the DATE-WRITTEN paragraph. This is, of course, not a foolproof metric. Nonetheless, we feel the data are worth presenting, and they do agree with a previous General Accounting Office estimate. We were able to find a DATE-WRITTEN entry in 58% of the sample programs.

Application Program Conversion and Maintenance

In the current setting, the source code for application programs is updated for a variety of reasons:

1. Conversion to a new or modified host system (hardware or software)
2. Accommodation of modified functional requirements
3. Correction of errors detected in the code
4. Reprogramming to reduce the number of compilers used or to improve processing efficiency

The interviews with federal ADP managers revealed that COBOL programs are recompiled at least once a year because of maintenance activities, and sometimes as often as six times annually. A reasonable average is two or three times per year.

COSTS AND BENEFITS

Program Development

The proposed revised standard COBOL features that have the potential to enhance programmer productivity include the following:

1. Nested programs provide a facility for segmenting large programs into smaller logical units
2. Scope delimiters assist in the generation of structured code
3. Reference modification allows the programmer to access any part (substring) of a character field without having to redefine the item
4. EVALUATE statements incorporate a well-known construct from structured programming practices, the multi-way conditional
5. Other constructs that should prove useful in clearing up previously awkward aspects of COBOL are the ability to PERFORM routines in-line, set up tables with more than three dimensions, accept as well as generate numbers in edited form, and INITIALIZE the values in tables.

Of the above, we were able to search the sample programs for programming practices in which features 3 and 4 could have been used and would have saved time for the programmer. For feature 3, we searched for data items defined as PIC X (one character only) with an OCCURS clause. For feature 4, we searched for GO TO . . . DEPENDING ON. In our sample, roughly 22% of the programs could have employed feature 3, and 5% could have used feature 4.

Feature 1 will be especially useful for organizing large programs. In our sample, programs with more than 1500 lines of source code account for approximately 65% of all the lines of code (even though they constitute only 25% of all programs). We note that all COBOL programs can make use of feature 2. Moreover, in the interviews conducted with representatives of various federal agencies, this enhancement was the one most often cited as potentially improving programming practice. Thus, we anticipate that the enhancements to COBOL will apply to some degree to virtually all programs in the federal inventory. For a considerable percentage of the code, the effect will be quite significant.

We make the following conservative assumptions: First that COBOL-8x will be adopted by federal agencies at the rate of approximately 10% per year, and second, that the use of the advantageous features will result in a 5% increase in productivity during the coding phase of development. These assumptions generate a savings of $36.1 million over the next ten years.

Program Maintenance

Program maintenance concerns those activities involving correcting, perfecting, and adapting existing application software, and currently represents 50–70% of the program life cycle costs.[3–5]

The principal ways in which the proposed changes to standard COBOL would affect the maintenance function are by increasing the understandability of COBOL programs and by reducing the error-prone features of COBOL-74. The enhancements to the language cited above under program development apply strongly to program maintenance as well, since they make it easier to read and write code. Many of the proposed 50 incompatibility changes are intended to eliminate or clarify certain error-prone or ambiguous features of the current COBOL standard.

Again, assuming that federal agencies adopt COBOL-8x at the rate of 10% per year, and that the advantages of COBOL-8x generate a 1% savings in maintenance activities, the resulting savings will be $54.1 million over the next 10 years.

Program Conversion

Software conversion is the transformation, without functional change, of computer programs and data elements to new hardware or software processing environments. The greater the degree of incompatibility between the source and target systems and the setting, the more difficult the conversion.

Clearly, there will be an extra cost associated with moving programs from a COBOL-74 compiler to a COBOL-8x (this is the name sometimes used to refer to the proposed new standard) compiler insofar as there are incompatibilities between the two. This cost is the object of the quantitative analysis. It is also true, however, that in those cases involving the definition by the proposed revision of features that had been ambiguous or implementation-defined, there will be an associated benefit. This is because future conversions within the COBOL-8x standard will not be vulnerable to different implementation of these features.

Programs may be brought into conformance with COBOL-8x in the following ways:

1. Recoding for the sole purpose of conforming to the new standard
2. Recoding in conjunction with a system conversion to a new host system
3. Recoding in conjunction with normal software maintenance requiring recompilation
4. Reprogramming to meet new functional requirements of the application

In assessing the effect of the incompatibilities, it is useful to consider the federal COBOL inventory as a whole, and to ask how many of these programs will eventually be converted to COBOL-8x (as opposed simply to being left as-is until no longer needed), and in which of the four ways listed above this will occur. The list is ordered from greatest to least effect per program. At one extreme, if a program is converted purely for the sake of conformance, then the entire cost of conversion is attributable to the adoption of the new standard. At the other extreme, if a program is completely redesigned anyway, there is no measurable additional cost in seeing that it conforms to the standard. Midway between these cases would be bringing a program into conformance in conjunction with some other form of updating, be that conversion or maintenance. While there is some extra effort involved, much of the conversion overhead (e.g., recompilation, retesting) is "free," in that it would be done even if the two versions of the standard were completely compatible. It is worth recalling that programs are recompiled rather frequently (at least once a year) for routine maintenance, and so there is plenty of opportunity for re-coding in category 3.

The cost effect is the additional effort expended in each of the above categories. Based on interviews with federal agencies, and also on a review of the transition process from COBOL-68 to COBOL-74, we conclude that very few, if any, conversions will be done merely for the sake of conformance.

Also, the previous experience in making the transition from COBOL-68 to COBOL-74 indicates that installations will continue to maintain the compiler for the previous version of the standard for a considerable time after introduction of the new version. We conclude, then, that the cost of achieving conformance in categories 1 and 4 is negligible, because virtually no conversion will be done in category 1 and there is no effect on conversion in category 4.

Measurable costs, then, are confined to categories 2 and 3, which we will treat together. The key questions are how many conversions will be done this way (as opposed to category 4 or not being done at all), and how much extra effort will be introduced by the incompatibilities.

The first question, about the percentage of programs to be converted, may be approached by noting some of the characteristics of the age of programs. The statistics on age allow us to formulate only a rough idea about the pattern of longevity for the current federal inventory. Note that the statistics are for the age of existing programs. This age distribution would directly reflect longevity only if we assumed that COBOL programs were being created at a constant rate over the past 15 years or so—clearly not the case. Nonetheless, almost any reasonable model one can develop that assumes an average age of six years for federal COBOL programs will yield a result no greater than 70–75% for the share of programs that will be converted to COBOL-8x over the next 10 years.

Next, we must consider the degree of extra effort entailed by the incompatibilities. For this analysis, we decided to use various parts of the Federal Conversion Software Center model.[6] Its formulation is exclusively oriented to and based on federal ADP systems. Also it provides reasonable definitions of the conversion complexity classes and of average conversion cost per line of code by class. Through the use of this model, we can express in a precise way the intuitively natural notion that the costliness of a given incompatibility will depend strongly on how often the incompatibility is used (as measured by the sample) and how complex is the conversion that it entails. Based on this model, the cost of converting to COBOL-8x over the next 10 years is $17.9 million.

Sensitivity Analysis

The principal objective of a sensitivity analysis is to assess the degree of variation in the cost–benefit effect estimates generated by changes in the study assumptions, and to provide insight about the validity of the study findings (see Table I for a summary). Therefore, we will discuss in greater depth those assumptions that are most subject to doubt and that affect the outcome most strongly.

Benefits

The benefits, as is typically the case for standards, are broad but shallow. Estimating the breadth (i.e., scope) of the benefit is relatively simple: Clearly, the effect extends throughout the use of COBOL in the federal government. The difficulty is in arriving at a reasonable estimate for the depth: How much good will the new standard do in an "average" federal agency? We have tried to be cautious in our estimates of the programming savings factor (PSF = 5%) and maintenance savings factor (MSF = 1%). The less precise of these is probably MSF. If we assume that MSF is 2%, instead of 1%, the maintenance benefit increases by $54 million. Such value is well within reason, but cannot be demonstrated with the available data.

Cost

We now examine those assumptions upon which depend the most likely cost estimate of $17.9 million. Clearly, the bulk of the cost stems from those incompatibilities that both occur frequently and force a more severe modification. There are four of these that deserve some individual comment:

1. Deleting MEMORY SIZE from the standard
2. Deleting ENTER from the standard
3. Defining the effect of EXIT PROGRAM on PERFORMs
4. Defining the order of evaluation of subscripts within PERFORMs

TABLE I—Sensitivity analysis (figures in $ millions)

		Assume MSF = 1%	Assume MSF = 2%
most likely assumptions	Benefit:	90.2	144.3
	Cost:	-17.9	-17.9
	Net:	72.3	126.4
assume ENTER unchanged, 10% benefit loss	Benefit:	81.2	129.9
	Cost:	-11.3	-11.3
	Net:	69.9	118.6
Conversion of 50% of Program Inventory	Benefit:	90.2	144.3
	Cost:	-12.8	-12.8
	Net:	77.4	131.5

Items 3 and 4 cannot reasonably be changed back to the original specification of COBOL-74. They simply define the semantics of two cases that were not described in COBOL-74.

For item number 1, the effect was completely dependent on the implementation in any event; almost all modern systems accept such information as part of their system control language. For item 2, it is technically feasible to keep the specifications of COBOL-74. If this were done, the cost estimate would shrink to $11.3 million. There would also be, however, an adverse effect on the benefit side. ENTER was deleted precisely because it encourages the development of the code that is error-prone and difficult to maintain. It would take only a 7% reduction of the benefits to cancel out the $6.6 million cost savings.

It is worth noting that in all four cases above, programs depending on the COBOL-74 specification were not guaranteed to be portable by that specification; all four changes are examples of taking aspects of the COBOL-74 standard that were ill-defined (purposely or not) to begin with, and either deleting the feature outright, or simply defining its effect. In none of these cases is a truly well-defined portable feature being affected.

The final issue is which policy federal agencies will adopt governing coding practices in the years leading up to the actual transition to a COBOL-8x implementation. We have somewhat pessimistically assumed that as new code replaces discarded programs, it will have the same degree of incompatibility. If, on the other hand, new code under development were monitored for conformance to COBOL-8x, then the effective percentage of code actually needing to undergo conversion would shrink from 70% to 50% within a few years. A figure of 50% implies conversion costs of $12.8 million.

FINDINGS AND RECOMMENDATIONS

This study shows that the effect of revising the COBOL standard as proposed should not be dramatic, either for good or ill. There is a real opportunity to improve certain features of the language, which should not be ignored, but the changes will hardly revolutionize COBOL programming in the federal sector. At the same time, there will be some problems created by incompatibility. These are not unusual, either in kind or in degree. Nor should it be surprising that the effect is relatively small; the proposed revision is just that: a revision of an existing standard—and not that markedly different from it.

It is important to put the projected costs and benefits into perspective. An effect of $100 million, spread out over 10 years, represents 0.3% of the salaries (unadjusted) of federal programmers over that same period. Concerning incompatibility, there was virtual consensus among the ADP personnel we interviewed that modifying source code was among the easier aspects of conversion. They had experienced far more difficulty with conversion of data and of job control code. Some agencies actually had to write their own input–output routines, rather than use those of the new system, because of data incompatibility. When asked what their biggest problem was, most answered, "the lack of documentation." One interviewee characterized this as the problem of "portability of programs between programmers."

There is no need to improve compatibility between the current and proposed versions of COBOL. While there are theoretical problems, the way in which COBOL is actually used in the federal government renders them relatively minor. The introduction of any further incompatibilities, however, should be subject to careful evaluation to ensure that their effects are no more adverse than those considered in this study.

The benefits of revising the COBOL standard are largely associated with the COBOL programs yet to be written. The costs are associated with those that already exist and depend on features unique to COBOL-74. Therefore, the sooner the standard becomes known and adopted, the better. The problems of incompatibility, real as they are, do not justify delaying the ongoing maintenance and improvement of the COBOL language.

REFERENCES

1. *The Effects of Future Information Processing Technology on the Federal Government ADP Situation,* A. D. Little, Inc., General Systems Group, Inc., Aurora Associates, Inc., NBS GCR 81-342, National Bureau of Standards, September 1981.
2. Gray, M. G. *An Assessment and Forecast of ADP in the Federal Government,* NBS Special Publication 500-79, Institute for Computer Sciences and Technology, Washington, D.C.: National Bureau of Standards, 1981.
3. Boehm, B. W. *Software Engineering Economics,* Englewood Cliffs, N.J.: Prentice Hall, 1981.
4. Comptroller General. *Federal Agencies' Maintenance of Computer Programs: Expensive and Undermanaged.* GAO, AFMD-81-25, Washington, D.C.: General Accounting Office, February 1981.
5. Lientz, B., and E. Swanson. "Problems in Application Software Maintenance," *Communications of the ACM,* 24 (1981),
6. FCSC. *Federal Conversion Support Center Conversion Cost Model* (Version 2), Office of Software Development, Report No. GSA/FCSC-82/001, Falls Church, Va.: General Services Administration, June 1, 1982.

SUGGESTED READINGS

0. Cugini, J. V. "Assessing the Impact of Revisions to Standards: the COBOL Example." *Computers & Standards,* 1 (1982),
0. Fiorello, M., and J. Cugini. *Cost-Benefit Impact Study on the Adoption of the Draft Proposed Revised X3.23 American National Standard Programming Language COBOL,* NBSIR 83-2639, Washington, D.C.: National Bureau of Standards, March 1983.

Technology transfer in the maintenance environment

by FLORENCE J. BELL
The Equitable Life Assurance Society
of the United States
New York, New York

ABSTRACT

In 1982 The Equitable Life Assurance Society of the United States recognized that software maintenance requires major management attention, and established a maintenance producivity project (MPP). Maintenance was defined as any programming effort that requires at least 25% of a programmer's time to be spent understanding an existing system. Three potential areas were identified for technology transfer: the maintenance function, the maintenance environment, and maintenance metrics. Ongoing programs include cooperation with vendors in developing an integrated environment for the maintenance programmer and manager, a maintenance management handbook, and a maintenance managers' round table. Maintenance is becoming an established and recognized area of specialization for systems professionals at The Equitable.

INTRODUCTION

The Equitable Life Assurance Society of the United States is the third largest mutual life insurance company in the U.S., with assets of more than $45 billion and about $230 billion of life insurance in force. The company installed its first mainframe, an IBM 650, in 1956, and at that time established its systems development department, with a total complement of three people. Twenty-seven years later The Equitable had a total of eight mainframes with over 60 mips capacity, 750 systems professionals, an annual systems budget of $100 million, and an inventory of approximately 350 major systems with 7000 program modules.

In 1974, in keeping with a general decentralization of the company's management, the systems development department was divided into five independent units, whose heads reported to line management. By 1983 there were nine autonomous systems departments. When the systems development department was decentralized, an EDP coordinating committee was formed, composed of the officers who headed each of the systems departments, the head of the data processing department, and the technology officer. The committee was responsible for ensuring that the systems needs of the corporation as a whole were met; specifically that hardware support was available, that well-qualified systems professionals were recruited, trained, and developed, that advances in hardware and software technology and in systems development management were introduced into the company, and that the economies of scale of an EDP installation as large as The Equitable's were not lost through the decentralization.

In 1980 the EDP coordinating committee established an application productivity group (APG) with the charter of technology transfer, specifically to increase the productivity of The Equitable's systems effort by a factor of ten within a period of five years. Within its first two years, the APG introduced interactive computing throughout all systems areas, selected and installed the hardware and operating systems for the interactive testing environment, and established a special interactive testing support organization. The group also introduced the concept of end-user systems development, brought the FOCUS language and database management into the company, and conducted extensive user training.

In 1982, the EDP coordinating committee conducted an off-site planning session to set the direction for future efforts of the APG. At this time, maintenance, methodology, and prototyping were identified as primary areas of concern. Of these, maintenance—which at the beginning of the session had little support—emerged as the top priority, primarily because of an awareness that although maintenance used over half of the systems resources, it had been disregarded in the systems development methodology installed 10 years earlier.

INITIAL SURVEY

Between September and December of 1982, the APG conducted its initial survey of the maintenance effort throughout the company. The purpose of this survey was to define the specific goals of a maintenance productivity project (MPP), to estimate the realizable benefits, and to establish a level of effort and a timetable.

As a first step, the group contracted for the services of Julien Green, a senior consultant with wide systems experience and a thorough knowledge of The Equitable's systems environment. With him, we reviewed current literature and interviewed managers in most of the systems areas to identify the specific needs of The Equitable's maintenance managers and programmers.

The results of this investigation were published in December 1982, and can be summarized under the following headings:

1. Definition of the maintenance function
2. Definition of the maintenance environment
3. Definition of maintenance metrics
4. Project deliverables

Definition of the Maintenance Function

The industry has developed what is now a generally agreed upon terminology in describing maintenance, based upon Swanson's original classification: corrective, adaptive, and perfective maintenance.[1] Corrective maintenance is fixing errors. Adaptive maintenance is changing software to accommodate changes in the computing or business environments without affecting the software's function. Perfective maintenance is enhancing function.

These three quite dissimilar activities have in common the requirement that the programmer spend a considerable portion of time (estimated by Fjeldstad and Hamlen at 50%) in understanding existing materials (code, documentation and procedures).[2] It is this requirement that distinguishes systems maintenance from systems development.

For the purposes of our MPP we define maintenance as any programming effort that requires at least 25% of the programmer's time to be spent understanding an existing system. We believe this is the point at which programmers begin to benefit from maintenance-specific tools, which facilitate the analysis of systems as opposed to their synthesis. If we were to set this cut-off at a lower percentage, we would include some clearly development-type programming, which in a mature EDP environment such as ours usually requires interfacing with, and therefore understanding, existing systems.

We had reviewed other operational definitions used by systems managers; some distinguish small jobs (maintenance) vs. large ones (development); others distinguish modification of existing code (maintenance) vs. the creation of new modules (development); still others, following Barry Boehm,[3] include redesign of less than 50% of existing code (maintenance) vs. redesign of more than 50% (development). We noted however that some small jobs are free-standing, while some large jobs are large precisely because they involve manipulation (i.e., maintenance) of a large existing system; that some projects that require little or no modification of existing systems nevertheless require a major effort in understanding them; and that the redesign of a larger percentage of an existing system requires a greater maintenance effort than the redesign of a smaller percentage.

Accordingly, we concluded that the level of effort required by a technician to understand an existing system is a more fundamental criterion than others that have been proposed. Furthermore, it appears that an operational definition of maintenance from the systems manager's point of view must factor in the cost of understanding code. From this viewpoint, defining maintenance in terms of the effort required to understand existing code makes sense.

Definition of the Maintenance Environment

Our initial survey also identified three components of the maintenance environment, each with its own needs. The first component is the programmers' environment. We found that many tools used in development work were used by maintenance programmers, but that there was a need for tools that addressed the maintenance-specific function of understanding existing code. We also found that, although there were useful maintenance tools, no single product purported to provide an integrated environment—a situation quite different from that on the development side of the house, where it has long been recognized that the greatest productivity gains come not from the sum of the tools, but from the integration of the tools into a structured environment.

The second component of the maintenance environment is the managers' environment. Here we found a need for management tools—packages to assist in estimating programming effort, scheduling and controlling maintenance work, budgeting, and reporting. Again some tools used for development were useful, but some, such as an effort estimator for maintenance work, were not available. In addition there was a need for a description of the sequential steps in maintenance work, and for a checklist with which to determine the accomplishment of each step.

The third component of the maintenance environment is the institutional environment, which encompasses the issues of the image of maintenance, selection and training of maintenance personnel, and career paths for maintenance professionals.

Definition of Maintenance Metrics

Finally, the initial survey identified the need for a good set of maintenance metrics upon which to base rational maintenance decisions. Two types of metrics are needed: First are macro-metrics—used to provide a multidimensional profile of our software inventory. These metrics will allow us to estimate the size, complexity and state of deterioration (or health) of our existing software portfolio, predict the resources needed to maintain our inventory, estimate the cost of maintenance, and identify areas of largest payoff. An example of a macro-metric is the number of man-months required to maintain the "average" program module.

Second are the micro-metrics—used to provide information needed for decisions concerning the maintenance of individual systems. These metrics will serve as a basis for determining when to retire, restructure, or retrofit a system, for measuring productivity trends, for estimating the time and cost of specific maintenance jobs, for preparing an annual maintenance budget, and for evaluating proposed new software tools. An example of a micro-metric is an algorithm to estimate the man-months required to implement a specific program enhancement.

Project Deliverables

Maintenance improvement is an unusually difficult environment for technology transfer. Installed systems cannot be easily adjusted to use a predefined tool or component; nor can an abrupt change of method be implemented by a staff carrying a full load of projects already in progress. A maintenance productivity project does not consist of installing tools, or adopting a methodology, or establishing management policies. Instead, it requires continuing of action on several levels.

Therefore, the initial survey defined our objective as introducing technology transfer into an integrated maintenance environment upon a foundation of sound maintenance metrics. A set of project deliverables for each component of the environment was developed.

These included, for the programmers' environment, a maintenance workbench, i.e., a set of software tools integrated through a common gateway or front end.

Project deliverables specified for the managers' environment were a handbook containing an inventory of the tools in the maintenance workbench, with guidelines for their appropriate use, costs, and expected benefits, a description of the maintenance process, and a milestone checklist; and a set of software tools, probably resident on a personal computer, for estimating, scheduling, controlling, and budgeting maintenance work.

Finally, for the institutional environment, a maintenance managers' round table was recommended. This is a periodic meeting of systems managers to define common maintenance concerns, exchange successful solutions, and channel technical advance. The round table is designed to build a community of interest and to be the main line of communication for technology transfer, for evaluating and integrating tools, for drafting the handbook, and for originating new avenues of investigation.

Strategy

In November 1982, the Application Productivity Group began to address the programmer's environment. There were many reasons why we chose to begin our maintenance project with this activity.

Evaluating and installing software tools is the easiest task for us to work at. Tools pre-exist our efforts, are concrete, and demonstrate measurable results. The APG has had considerable experience in finding, piloting, and evaluating software. Good results are readily realizable through the installation of these tools. Therefore, although we believe that in the long run activities other than the installation and even the integration of tools will prove more important, we started our implementation effort by identifying and evaluating maintenance tools.

Seven types of software tools for the Maintenance Workbench were identified for further investigation. They were retrofitters, restructurers, static code analyzers, interactive debuggers, test data generators, automated documentors, and specialized editors. From among these, we selected a new interactive code analyzer to evaluate and pilot.

INTERACTIVE STATIC ANALYZER BETA TEST

James Martin and Carma McClure had written that "the tool the maintainer most needs is an interactive code analyzer that will help him to understand how the code works, and to predict the side-effects of modification."[4] At the time we completed our initial survey, a vendor was preparing to beta-test an interactive analyzer.

The APG's preliminary evaluations at the vendor's site indicated that the product had powerful functionality. On the basis of this evaluation, The Equitable agreed in February 1983 to be a beta site.

The product loaded COBOL source code to an on-line database, which a maintenance programmer could then access interactively. It presented three views of the program: the structure chart view, which gave the programmer an overview of the design of the program; a source code view, which allowed a programmer to look at selected units of code; and a source code difference view, which presented different versions of the program. In each of these views the programmer could select and trace data flows and control logic. It was at the time the only interactive static analyzer that we were able to find.

Objectives of the Beta Test

The objectives of the beta test were to:

1. Confirm the functionality of the product. Would it effectively trace the logic and data flows of actual production systems, provide accurate flow charts, and compare differences in source code?
2. Determine the quality of the product. How many bugs would be encountered during the beta test, and how seriously would they affect the product's functionality?
3. Evaluate the usefulness of the product in a production environment. Would it provide answers to real maintenance questions, and information actually needed to modify programs?
4. Ascertain training requirements. How long would it take programmers to learn to use the product?
5. Determine the practicality of using the product with programs written for the non-IBM-compatible systems. Could minicomputer programs be analyzed?
6. Evaluate the acceptance of the product by The Equitable's maintenance professionals. If installed, would the product become the systems community's Edsel?
7. Evaluate the support given by the vendor during the beta test. What level of support might we expect when the product was released?
8. Evaluate the system resources required by the product. What effect would its use have on our data centers?
9. Estimate the transfer charges that systems areas would incur for the use of the product. What would it cost to analyze code with it?
10. Estimate the actual productivity gains that could be expected. Would benefits outweigh costs?

Results of the Beta Test

The beta test ran from Feb. 2 through April 15, 1983. During the course of the beta test 100 program modules were analyzed, and approximately 250 hours of interactive testing were logged.

At its conclusion, the functionality of the static analyzer was confirmed. On all other factors, except quality, the product received an acceptable or better rating (Figure 1). However, the vendor withdrew the package.

We learned three major lessons from this experience: First, an interactive static analyzer is a valuable tool, and will be well received by programmers. Since the beta test, whenever programmers evaluate a software tool, they invariably compare it to the analyzer and begin their evaluations, "Well, it isn't a *(product)*, but . . . " We found that a static analyzer can reduce the time a programmer spends understanding code by 20–50%. In our environment a 23% reduction in programmer time for this function would have offset the machine charges. We look forward to the day when a viable interactive static analyzer is on the market.

```
FACTOR                      RATING

                                     1        2        3        4        5

Functionality               XXXXXXXXXXXXXXXXXXXXXXXXXXXXXXXXXXXXXXXXXXXXXX
Quality                     XXXXXXXXXX
Usefulness                  XXXXXXXXXXXXXXXXXXXXXXXXXXXXXXXXXXXXX
Training Requirements       XXXXXXXXXXXXXXXXXXXXXXXXXXXX
Mini-computer programs      XXXXXXXXXXXXXXXXXXX
Programmer Acceptance       XXXXXXXXXXXXXXXXXXXXXXXXXXXXXXXXXXXXX
Vendor Support              XXXXXXXXXXXXXXXXXXXXXXXXXXXXXXXXXXXXX
Resource Requirements       XXXXXXXXXXXXXXXXXXXXXXXXXXXX
Running Costs               XXXXXXXXXXXXXXXXXXXXXXXXXXXX
Productivity Gains          XXXXXXXXXXXXXXXXXXXXXXXXXXXXXXXXXXXXX

Legend: 1. Poor;  2. Acceptable;  3. Satisfactory;  4. Very Good;  5. Excellent
```

Figure 1—Evaluation of interactive static analyzer

Second, we learned more about evaluating maintenance tools. Although most of our criteria had been defined before the test, others emerged during the weekly review meetings we held with the programmers. It was at these meetings that the distinction between functionality, quality, and usefulness was hammered out. We will evaluate other tools against these criteria, as well as against additional criteria that may apply. We expect other maintenance products to appear on the market in the near future, and we intend to integrate the best of them into our environment.

Third, we conclude that the maintenance workbench is a facility whose time has come. The productivity improvement realized by having static analysis functions available in an interactive harness demonstrated the potential benefits of putting many other maintenance functions in such a harness.

CONTINUING ACTIVITIES

At the time of this writing, The Equitable's maintenance productivity improvement program is progressing along the lines laid out in the initial survey. For the programmers' environment, maintenance tools continue to be evaluated. We are particularly looking at packages that restructure and redocument existing code.

For the managers' environment, a maintenance effort estimator has been developed by another consultant to the project, Howard Rubin, as a component of the ESTIMACS package.[5] The maintenance management handbook is being outlined by Julien Green. For the institutional environment, Nicholas Zvegintzov[6] is working with us as a consultant to coordinate the initial meetings of the maintenance managers' round table.

A new software metrics project has been established. Its team will develop the metrics for maintenance specified by the maintenance productivity project, as well as software development measurements.

CONCLUSION

Software maintenance has been a major systems function at The Equitable for many years. It is now recognized as a function whose contribution to the systems and corporate effort deserves the serious attention of upper management. A maintenance productivity improvement program has been developed, approved, and funded. Maintenance is becoming an established and recognized area of specialization for systems professionals at The Equitable.

REFERENCES

1. Swanson, E. B. "The Dimensions of Maintenance." *IEEE Computer Society, 2nd International Conference on Software Engineering.* Los Angeles, California: IEEE Computer Society, 1976, pp. 492–497.
2. Fjeldstad, R. K., and W. T. Hamlen. "Application program maintenance study—report to our respondents." IBM Corporation, DP Marketing Group, January 23, 1979. Reprinted in: G. Parikh, and N. Zvegintzov. *Tutorial on Software Maintenance.* Silver Spring, Md.: IEEE Computer Society, 1983.
3. Boehm, B. W. *Software Engineering Economics.* Englewood Cliffs, N.J.: Prentice-Hall, 1981.
4. Martin, J., and C. L. McClure. *Maintenance of Computer Programming.* Carnforth, England: Savant Institute, 1982. Reprinted as: *Software Maintenance—The Problem and its Solutions.* Englewood Cliffs, N.J.: Prentice-Hall, 1983.
5. Rubin, H. "Macro and Micro-estimation of Maintenance Effort: the ESTIMACS Maintenance Models." *IEEE Computer Society, Software Maintenance Workshop Record,* Los Angeles, Calif.: IEEE CS, 1984.
6. Zvegintzov, N. "What life? What cycle?" *AFIPS, Proceedings of the National Computer Conference* (Vol. 51), 1982, pp. 561–568.

Two perceptions of software maintenance performed by an on-site contractor

by BERNARD NARROW
NASA Goddard Space Flight Center
Greenbelt, Maryland
and
JOHN KELLY
Lockheed, EMSCO
Greenbelt, Maryland

ABSTRACT

Software maintenance is a difficult task under the best of circumstances. Having work performed by an on-site contractor adds an additional layer of complexity to the customer's task. This type of relationship places greater emphasis on formal work procedures and detailed reports of the work in progress. It also promotes the use of performance norms for evaluating contractor performance. These factors are all on the positive side. However, such a relationship also calls for a special awareness of contractor ploys calculated to increase their performance evaluation.

From the contractor's point of view, being on-site imposes a more disciplined environment and places special importance on the manner and means of dealing with the customer. Another special feature is that the contractor receives formal feedback from the users, through periodic performance evaluations, indicating how well the software maintenance group measures up to expectations.

This paper describes the lessons learned by one customer and one on-site contractor.

THE CUSTOMER'S VIEW

On-site contracting is likely to become more pervasive due to its emphasis in the federal government[1] (à la the Office of Management and Budget Circular A-76) as well as in state governments and municipalities. An account is given here of how a large data processing facility with extensive experience in contracting out software maintenance has learned to cope.

Our data processing installation is a large, multisystem government facility, comprised of a mix of manufacturers and types. Included are on-line systems, database systems, batch systems and intercomputer systems. Types of hardware include IBM (370, 4341), UNIVAC (1100, Varian), SEL (32), and Honeywell (Sigma). Altogether, there are 20 stand-alone systems that require software maintenance support. A large measure of the applications run on these systems deal with scientific data; however the operational mode is akin to a large, multistep production process. Other applications relate to production control, cost accounting, inventory control, and database maintenance.

Centralized vs. Decentralized Support

Initially, our technical control over the work performed by the contractor was split along application and functional lines. This led to several independently run units, both on our side and on the contractor's side. However, we exercised overall technical stewardship over the contractor's activities for evaluating performance.

This arrangement, while providing us with a close working relationship and a strong grasp of the technical details, naturally led to parochial viewpoints on both sides. If a key systems person in one area resigned, contractor personnel could not easily call upon another area for temporary assistance because of reluctance by the latter to dilute their level of support. Support problems, resulting from poor management, inexperienced or inadequate numbers of personnel, and the like, tended to be prolonged and not pursued aggressively.

In early 1982, we reorganized to centralize all software maintenance within a single unit. The contractor's organization also was reconstituted on a centralized basis. A number of benefits—some obvious and some not so obvious—were achieved, including

1. uniform reporting of maintenance activities
2. uniform and tighter configuration control
3. more effective communications channels
4. improved response in correcting or resolving problems
5. separation and independence of programming and testing groups
6. improved documentation (due to configuration control oversight)
7. more effective control within the program library
8. more effective establishment of priorities and better allocation of resources
9. more consistent manner evaluation of contractor performance and determination of award fees
10. more availability of the information to build a centralized database for deriving work performance metrics

Establishing an Effective Working Relationship

Because software maintenance cannot easily or readily be translated into a set of well-defined products, the connection between customer and contractor needs special emphasis. This is a critical factor in determining the quality and cost effectiveness of the support provided by the contractor. The key elements characterizing the customer–contractor relationship can be labeled as the three Cs: credibility, coverage, and clout. Credibility hinges largely on the competence of customer personnel. The level of competence should be such as to convince the contractor personnel that the customer is fully aware of work factors—do's and don'ts—and that expectations of the contractor's performance are reasonable. Customers need to be candid in their dealings with contractors and to view them as co-workers rather than as subordinates or in a potentially adversarial position. Unfortunately, this can easily lead to a "chummy" relationship, which can be harmful. Customer personnel should not forget that, basically, this is a business relationship that calls for critical assessment of the contractor's performance. In particular, customer personnel need to distinguish between legitimate extenuating circumstances and groundless excuses. Otherwise, the contractor will not make a concerted effort to correct deficiencies.

Coverage, as used here, refers to the organizational or functional level at which the customer–contractor connection takes place, as well as the depth of reporting detail. Good starting points are the systems and methods for selecting and controlling the jobs to be performed. These come under the general heading of configuration control. In our case, a formal system was agreed upon that would govern the submission, review, disposition, and reporting of change requests. These include system and application software errors, deficiencies, enhancements, and new system releases. Also included are special tasks that compete for the programming group's resources.

At least weekly status meetings should be held and should include contractor line managers (the heads of system software, applications software, and testing), along with the customer technical monitors. Coverage is really a corollary of credibility in that it is meant to ensure that the technical discussions are substantive and are more likely to flush out causes, rather than treat symptoms.

Clout is a two-edged sword. It can be and should be used both to reward the contractor for better-than-expected performance and to penalize for below-expected performance. One way to accomplish this is by way of a cost-plus-award-fee contract, with the award ranging from 0% to 10% of the cost. Expected performance results in a fee in the 4% to 6% range, thereby leaving ample allowance for award level variations based either on positive or negative factors. Another important consideration is the level of management—both sides—that is involved in or is made aware of the fee determination. On the customer side, this should mean the top person in charge of the data processing facility; on the contractor's side, it should mean at least one level above the on-site manager, depending on whether software maintenance represents part or all of the contract. If the latter, the involvement should be at least two levels above the contract manager.

What You Need to Know

What do customers need to know about the contractor's activities in order to monitor and evaluate the contractor's performance effectively? In our case, we have stipulated that reporting should be at the functional (or third) level with system and project reporting being the higher levels.

For our purposes functional reporting was broken down as follows: validation and assessment of the effects of a proposed change (prior to approval by the configuration control board); programming (analysis, coding, and unit testing); acceptance testing; and implementation. This breakdown is predicated on the objective of closely monitoring the work in progress so as to be conversant with current problems and to assess effectively whether proper and timely actions are being taken to resolve them.

Some might argue that on a routine basis it is only necessary to monitor the contractor's activities at either the system or project levels and thereby reduce the cost of monitoring. It is further argued that either periodic or unannounced audits can be made to determine the contractor's performance at the functional level. The problem with this argument is, assuming that substantive deficiencies are uncovered by an audit, the customer monitors are not in a position to assess independently whether the contractor is taking the proper corrective measures—and doing so in a timely manner. Waiting until the next audit takes place to make such a determination is not an effective way to deal with such problems.

It should not be inferred that effective monitoring calls for an item-by-item review. One suggestion is to have an asterisk placed in the margin of a report to highlight those items for which actual hours exceeded estimated hours or for which a data change was made since the last report period. This directs the monitor's attention to the items that require close observation and that should be accompanied by a written explanation. A complementary tactic is to specify the ten most important items in a separate report, which is distributed to a higher level of management than is the full detailed report.

Specifying the detailed items to be reported on is only half the battle. The reports must be reviewed carefully for accuracy, completeness, and currency. Contractor personnel are prone to adopt a casual attitude toward reporting if they are not held closely and consistently accountable for the report contents. Figures 1 and 2 are sample formats of monthly summary reports by system, showing, respectively, the change in status of all work in progress and the actual hours expended by type of job.

Games Contractors Play

Wherever there are performance-type contracts, there is an inclination to "shade" the reporting of activities and events in a way that is advantageous to the contractor. Although shading can, in reality, be a euphemism for fraudulent practices, it is more likely to manifest itself in more subtle and less odious forms. Also, on-site contractors are less likely to engage in these practices than off-site contractors, because of the more personal relationship in the former case.

Noted here are both known and suspected tactics that contractors have used. These tactics represent an overall compilation drawn from a number of different contractors.

	OPERATING SYSTEMS			APPLICATIONS PROGRAMS			SPECIAL
NUMBER OF JOBS	FIXES	ENHANCE.	OTHER	FIXES	ENHANCE.	OTHER	JOBS
Open - Beginning of Month							
Added During Month							
Closed During Month							
Open - End of Month							

Figure 1—Monthly change in work status

TOTAL HOURS EXPENDED FOR		OPERATING SYSTEMS FIXES	OPERATING SYSTEMS ENHANCE.	OPERATING SYSTEMS OTHER	APPLICATIONS PROGRAMS FIXES	APPLICATIONS PROGRAMS ENHANCE.	APPLICATIONS PROGRAMS OTHER	SPECIAL JOBS
Analysis								
Code and Unit Test								
Implementation								
FOR CLOSED JOBS								
Analysis Hours -	Est.							
	Act.							
Code & UT Hours -	Est.							
	Act.							
Implementation Hours-	Est.							
	Act.							
Total Hours -	Est.							
	Act.							

Figure 2—Manhours expended during month

Creative bookkeeping

To prevent actual hours from exceeding estimated hours on a given job, time is charged to "miscellaneous." A variation of creative bookkeeping is where the contractor in the process of trying to correct an error takes a shortcut, e.g., bypassing testing, in order to stay on schedule. Should this in turn cause additional errors, these are reported as new errors and are disposed of expeditiously. This, of course, leads to "favorable" measured performance.

Technical obfuscation

When analysis or diagnosis of a persistent problem does not turn up anything definite, or when an embarrassing event occurs, the contractor might try to talk his way around it. Jargon and vague but technically imposing reasons might be offered to convince customer monitors that the problem is not due to any fault of the contractor.

All in the family

Here, contractors try to be particularly responsive to the customer monitor's pet projects. This is coupled with ego-boosting tactics, which together are an attempt to foster the impression that "we are all family" and we ought to be protective of the other party's interests. A variation of this game is to seek the company monitor's advice and suggestions about how to handle a given problem. This tends to compromise the company monitor's objectivity in assessing the contractor's performance.

End-around play

Should the customer monitors prove rather astute in dealing with the contractor's games, or if the customer monitors are frequently critical of the contractor's performance, a play can be made to a higher level of management. An attempt is made first to establish a close liaison with higher management and then to convince them that the monitors are biased and unreasonable.

Old standbys

Briefly noted here are the more familiar excuses and tactics used by software personnel.

1. overly generous padding of estimates to perform jobs

2. blame it on the vendor's documentation
3. blame it on the operating system
4. blame it on the hardware
5. blame it on the person no longer employed by the contractor

Performance Measurement

Under an incentive-type contract, it is necessary to face the issue of performance measurement squarely. First to be addressed is the formulation of which elements and factors are to be evaluated and measured. The candidate elements are those from which one can derive the desired factors. Examples of such factors include management, productivity, responsiveness, timeliness, communication, planning, and initiative. Factors such as management, communication, and planning are highly subjective in nature and are evaluated in an indirect or on an event basis. Others, such as productivity, responsiveness, and timeliness, are adaptable to objective measurement, and these are the ones discussed herein.

Before qualifying a set of metrics for performance evaluation, it is necessary to define and establish a database. In our case, pertinent information is collected from all jobs including application software changes, operating systems maintenance, and special software tasks. Information about these jobs is collected from the individual programmers, and entered into a database. Weekly reports compiled from this information are carefully reviewed both by the contractor supervisors and the monitors to assure complete reporting and overall accountability. A list of the metrics that we observe is shown in Table I.

Each of the metrics in the table can be further categorized by computer system, language, type (i.e., systems or application software), and so forth. Such breakdowns enable comparisons to be made within the given category; e.g., how does the average time per fix for system A compare with that for system B?

After a sufficient amount of time has elapsed to compile a substantial database and to analyze and interpret the derived metrics, the final step can begin. This is to establish the norms for each of the selected metrics. Here again, contractor personnel should participate in this determination in order to arrive at a set of norms that is deemed to be fair and reasonable to both parties.

Such objective performance measures can be weighed and coupled with the subjective factors referred to earlier so as to arrive at the contractor's overall technical performance assessment.

TABLE I—Performance Metrics

Metric	Derivation
Average time to make a fix or enhancement	Total hours for analysis, coding, unit testing divided by total number of fixes and enhancements
Average elapsed time to make a fix or enhancement	No. of days from start to implementation divided by total number of fixes and enhancements
Actual vs. estimated time per fix or enhancement	Total actual hours divided by total estimated hours for fixes and enhancements
Elapsed time of highest priority fixes vs. others	Average elapsed time to make highest priority fixes divided by average of elapsed time to make all other fixes
Trend analysis of reported software failures	Comparison of distributions of failure occurrences for different systems
Correlation of number of fixes with size of program	Dependent variable is the number of fixes for each program; independent variable is the size of each program
Standard deviation of estimates of large vs. small programs	Standard error of actual vs. estimated hours for each fix, grouped by program size
Ratio of analysis time per fix to coding and unit testing	Total hours for analysis of all fixes divided by total hours for coding and unit testing

THE CONTRACTOR'S VIEW

Interfacing with Customer Personnel

The role of the software professional within a company that performs facility management services is somewhat different from that of a programmer nestled comfortably in a corporate structured arena. Being on-site readily exposes a casual or sloppily managed working group and calls for an awareness or presence that should be calculated to command the respect of the customer. Sloppy personal demeanor, unoccupied desks, persons reading newspapers, and so on, are perceived by the customer as indicators that the contractor is unreliable, unprofessional, or underworked. In effect, the contractor has two "bosses"—the on-site customer as well as company management. This presents a unique dilemma—how to please both factions and maintain proper professional perspective (and sanity) in successfully fulfilling job requirements.

Acquiring the confidence of customer-monitoring personnel is an important goal that must be achieved quickly if successful performance ratings are to be attained. The ability to grasp the technical jargon and the complexities of the customer's subject matter makes customer communication a natural extension of the monitor's working environment.

When special requirements are addressed, the contractor should obtain customer concurrence on how the workload should be adjusted to satisfy all affected users. Too often, additional task requirements are accepted by the contractor without informing the customer of current manpower constraints and the effects of new tasks on current completion schedules. The contractor must not be afraid to oppose additional customer requests and should be prepared to convey to customer management that in reality there is no free lunch. When possible, suitable alternatives should be recommended.

Effective communication of task performance appraisals is an area that requires special contractor attention. The customer needs appropriate status information to provide a sufficient base for pointing out shortcomings, giving plaudits for tasks well done, and recommending an appropriate award fee. Formats for contractually required reports should be determined mutually, at the beginning of the contract, and should be reviewed periodically for possible alteration to respond to changing customer management reporting requirements. In addition to these reports, regularly scheduled status meetings between software management and key customer-management–technical-monitoring personnel should be established. These meetings, which are by design less formal and in the nature of committee sessions, are multipurpose. They not only provide a forum for presenting firsthand status information, but also are an excellent opportunity for discussing customer priorities and perceived deficiencies prior to their being written into the customer's evaluation report. Another helpful measure is to provide a self evaluation—representing the software management's view of task performance—to the customer for consideration in determining periodic award fees.

How Work is Divided and Allocated

As noted in the first part of this paper, we are a centralized software organization, responsible for maintaining more than 50 software systems functioning on more than 20 mainframes, and for all developmental work. Major functions are separated into applications programming, systems programming, and software acceptance testing. By definition, applications programmers are responsible for maintaining the production software (primarily FORTRAN coding, with some assembly language) and the systems programmers are the caretakers of all operating system software. Systems analysts, however, provide the necessary expertise for assuring the validity of both new and modified software through the development and execution of detailed acceptance test plans.

Because of the size of this organization—approximately 85 software professionals—the numerous specially developed computer systems, and the frequency of software changes attributable to data-related and user requirement variances, it is difficult to impose conventional software management techniques. An internal task-tracking system has been developed to monitor several hundred tasks ranging from discrepancy reports (something doesn't look right) to change requests (modifications to accommodate specific problems or requirements). Included within this range are customer-initiated tasks (often new requirements) and tasks generated internally by software management (usually related to normal maintenance activities, such as evaluating release tapes for existing operating systems). Due to the high volume of tasks, complexities of interorganizational interface, and management requirements for up-to-date status reporting, a full-time administrator is employed to maintain and coordinate all transactions and report generation attributed to this tracking system.

Assignment of programmers to support each system can often be a difficult process. Software management must be prepared to evaluate the overall complexity of the system, be familiar with the intricacies of various program components, and be knowledgeable about the stability or volatility of the software. These variables are then matched against individual programmer experience profiles to determine the most appropriate manpower allocation.

Acquiring and Retaining Technical Personnel

Our typical maintenance programmer has almost five years of college training and more than six years of technical experience. Turnover, however, is surprisingly low in our case, because of an unusual phenomenon known as incumbency. Many of our software professionals have selected this area because of the nature of the work—it is highly scientific and very interesting; the physical plant is conveniently located and easily accessible; there is no charge for parking; etc. Even though the contract is bound by a prenegotiated amount of time, the technically oriented employee has little fear of losing a position due to contract expiration. Obviously, even under a new contractor, the job must continue to be performed. Who else, other than those currently doing the job, could satisfy customer requirements with no untoward effect on daily operations? Of course, if there is a new contract awarded, management must be sensitive to the apprehension programmers are likely to exhibit during the recompetion and, if necessary, the changeover periods.

Programmers, like many other skilled professionals, consider themselves creative and take special pride in developing "eternal" systems. There exists, then, an innate stigma attached to the label of "maintenance programmer." This is a difficult but not insurmountable hurdle for software management to overcome. One of the ways to maintain good personnel morale is by offering diversification in mainframes, operating systems, and programming languages. For example, in our case the opportunity to use FORTRAN, assembly language, or PL/I may be found on IBM (370/145 and 4341) using VS1, VM, or MVS; IBM (Series-1) using EDX; UNIVAC (1100/82) using EXEC-8 38R2; SEL (32/77 and 32/75) using RTM and MPX-32; VARIAN 77 using VORTEX; SIGMA 5/9 using BPM and CP-V; and various other special purpose image-processing systems.

Although the term maintenance is used to describe the main functions, many tasks require such extensive systems analysis prior to making appropriate changes that the programmer receives as much challenge and satisfaction as if the program was actually being developed. Another factor is training. In order to keep the staff abreast with state-of-the-art developments, management encourages formal vendor-supplied training classes. Specific analytical and systems-oriented techniques and skills are addressed in these courses. Attendance at user and general conferences is also an added incentive provided to the programming professional for acquiring and dispensing information.

Dealing with Newly Developed Software

Almost all software maintenance groups encounter the problem of assuming responsibility for new software developed by another organization. In our case, this problem is compounded by the fact that the new programs are developed by another contractor. To deal effectively with this situation requires getting involved well before the software is delivered. Plans and interface definitions should be mutually agreed upon and include acceptance testing, documentation, and formal sessions for acquainting the maintenance personnel with the inner workings of each program.

The development of the acceptance test plan requires extensive communication between the maintenance and the development groups. Program design walk-throughs are highly recommended for this purpose, as well as for familiarizing the maintenance personnel with the software. This should be done prior to the turn-over of the program since afterwards development personnel are reassigned to other tasks and often are not easily accessible.

As on-site contractors, we need to be particularly concerned with the way information concerning our dealings with development personnel is presented to the customer. Group interaction problems, such as competing for computer time, should if possible be transparent to the customer. When these problems need to be brought to the customer's attention, it is best to avoid a finger-pointing session. Such sensitivity and awareness contribute measurably to harmonious relations with the customer.

CONCLUSION

Overall, the use of on-site contractors can be a viable and effective means for accomplishing software maintenance in a large data processing facility. To achieve these ends, however, calls for a proper appreciation by both the customer monitors and the contractor management personnel of the factors and considerations described herein.

REFERENCE

1. Office of Management and Budget Circular A-76. This circular has been incorporated into the Federal Acquisition Regulation as Subpart 7.3, effective April 1, 1984.

Prolonging the life of software

by JOHN CONNELL and LINDA BRICE
Los Alamos National Laboratory
Los Alamos, New Mexico

ABSTRACT

Presented here are methods for successfully controlling software maintenance activity so that present systems will be more useful and less expensive to support. While it is based on experience at Los Alamos National Laboratory, it is not based on solutions developed and implemented there. Los Alamos is presently struggling with the problems identified in this paper and is impacted by them to the same extent as the rest of industry. An idea has emerged from this struggle: The deterioration of production software is basically a quality control problem the rate of which can and should be minimized. Many data processing shops currently have two options concerning old (over five years), marginally useful systems; pay the high cost of supporting them or undertake a rewrite. If the principles presented in this paper are applied, a third option may become available; prolonging the useful life of software by making it more cost-effective to support.

INTRODUCTION

The Administrative Data Processing Division of the Los Alamos National Laboratory supports over 70 production software systems for various users within the laboratory. Each system represents a particular financial, personnel, or inventory application consisting of a related set of software modules. Altogether there are about 900 computer programs in production, most of them written in COBOL. The systems reside on both minicomputers and mainframes. There are 50 programmer/analysts involved in developing, implementing, and maintaining the systems.

When new systems are developed or old ones rewritten, a cost/benefit analysis is required prior to design. Assumptions must be made about the expected economic life of a proposed new system in order to estimate future operating costs and determine the payback period. The current standard is to design for a minimum five year economic life. Extrapolating to a ten-year goal for keeping software alive, return on investment is doubled and slack is built in for unanticipated changing requirements that can necessitate premature rewrites.

To prolong the life of software, it is necessary to maximize the continuing maintainability, operability, and usability of current systems. This paper contains suggestions, based on experience at Los Alamos, for that maximization. No new software engineering concepts are introduced. Instead an extant body of knowledge is drawn upon and related to managing the maintenance of current systems in a cost-effective manner.

THE EFFECT OF UNSTRUCTURED MAINTENANCE

Entropy of Structure

Programmer productivity aids such as structured techniques, introduced in the last few years, are now in use in many DP installations and are expected to ease the future maintenance burden. However, many installations have been slow in adopting such techniques and those that have still experience the entropy problem. One of the worst effects that maintenance work can have on production software systems is the deterioration of the original structure of the system. Dozens to hundreds of small, seemingly insignificant patches applied during the life of a system can cause degeneration of even the most structured, modular, top-down original code. The author of an old program is rarely able to tell the current maintenance programmer what the code is doing, primarily because the author cannot remember. Many times the author cannot be located, or even identified. A little-considered factor in the general maintenance dilemma is that the program is really co-authored by all of the programmers who have ever worked on it. Given that many different styles and design philosophies have been incorporated, there is little chance that the current code bears much resemblance to the original.

Introduction of Defects

Many good maintenance programmers might take offense at the suggestion that defects are inserted into systems as they perform their valuable work. They might argue that they always conduct thorough tests before putting changes into production. It should be pointed out that the term thorough, when applied to testing of maintenance changes, is probably a contradiction in terms. As an example, suppose three lines of code in one program of a sixty-program system are changed. Should the entire system be tested as thoroughly as it was during the development phase of the life cycle? If not, is there some chance that although the modified program will work fine, other unsuspected parts of the system will be negatively impacted? Might the system work perfectly for the first several production runs after the changes are put in place, only to have the inserted defect surface and cause trouble months later? Problems involving the worth of regression testing and phenomena such as the ripple effect are well-documented.[1]

The above questions are difficult if not impossible to answer. In many cases, the maintenance programmer has no time to do complete, thorough testing for the same reason that there is no time for elegant coding; the fix is made in a crisis mode. It is not even clear that rigorous, extensive testing is cost-effective for minor changes. On the other hand, it should be assumed that the lack of such testing will guarantee the insertion of defects into the system in at least some cases. It is not pessimism but the logical conclusion that, over time, a system will become increasingly bug-ridden.

Introduction of Psychological Complexity

Psychological complexity can be defined as elements of programming style which make programs difficult to understand. Complexity increases the effort required to make successful maintenance changes and thus increases maintenance costs. An example well documented and measured mathematically is use of the GO TO statement. Use of GO TO's is a violation of structured programming concepts and has been discouraged for some time. At the same time, a GO TO is the easiest, quickest way to modify the control flow of a program and is frequently done, on the fly, to correct a logic flaw. In some cases to do otherwise would involve extensive rewriting of major portions of the program.

Again, a good programmer would be offended at the suggestion that some maintenance changes introduce psychological complexity into the system. Nevertheless, it must be true that at some point in our career all of us have been guilty of making a quick fix with a GO TO, neglecting to thoroughly document a midnight maintenance change, or adding another level of nesting to an already complicated IF statement to incorporate a new requirement. Several years of this type of activity will make the simplest program almost impossible to follow.

Increase in Future Maintenance Costs

As an old application system begins to deteriorate due to entropy of structure and the insertion of defects and psychological complexity, the cost of maintaining that system will begin to rise. At first the increase will be very slight, but as the factors mentioned above are compounded the rate of increase for maintenance cost will become geometric. The level of pain experienced in maintaining a production system can and should be measured; at some point it will become cheaper to scrap the old system and build a new one from scratch. This theory is suggested graphically in Figure 1.

In most data processing organizations, it is politically advantageous and more satisfying to the users to devote development resources to desired new applications than to the rewrite of existing systems, even when it can be demonstrated that there would be a cost/benefit payoff derived from a rewrite. After all, it is somewhat embarrassing to confess to the user that his system has been damaged such that it is no longer maintainable and will have to be frozen for a period of time while it is being rewritten. Therefore, considerable benefits could be derived from putting into place goals, objectives and procedures that would help to delay the necessity for a rewrite by minimizing the rate of deterioration of applications systems. Zvegintzov[2] has stated the desirability of this succinctly in a recent article in *Datamation,* where he says, "Replacement of functions incurs a development cost that more DP organizations will not bear. 'Add on, not replace' is the trend in software." (p. 110)

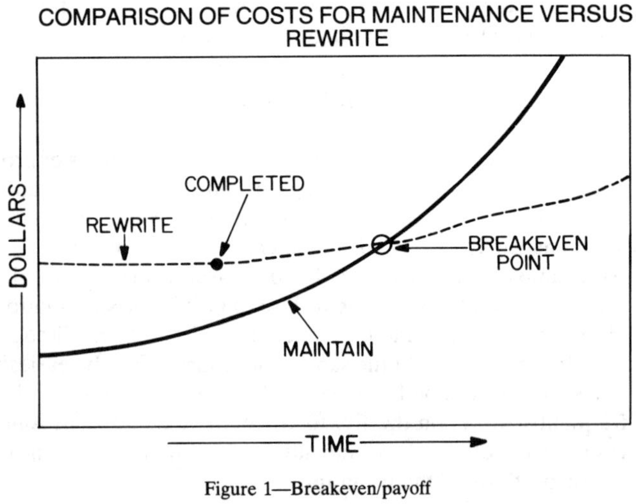

Figure 1—Breakeven/payoff

A BRIEF METHODOLOGY FOR MAINTENANCE WORK

Impact of Changes on Previous Analysis

Analysis documents, if they are accurate, can serve as valuable maintenance aids. If the maintenance programmer understands what the system is supposed to do and what the significance of the implemented functions is to the user, then s/he will have a good basis for knowing how to respond to emergencies that might arise. A document such as an essential requirements definition will also help the maintenance programmer know when the system is or is not successfully performing its required functions.

There are three direct implications of the above assertion. First, it implies that analysis documents such as a System Requirements Definition should become part of the retained system documentation for implemented systems. Second, the portions of this documentation which map the current system, such as Data Flow Diagrams, should be accurately revised when the user's changing requirements result in maintenance changes that modify the functions of the system. Third, to understand and be able to modify an analysis document correctly, a maintenance programmer must also be somewhat of an analyst.

External documentation such as control flows and run procedures also helps to identify the impact of changes to one program on other parts of the system. Such documentation is helpful in testing systems and in returning them to production upon successful test. Like requirements specifications, if the external documentation is to be useful and reliable, it must be revised accurately when maintenance changes affect its correctness.

Structured Maintenance Walkthroughs

Actually coding changes to production source code files can be a frightening activity. Statistics indicate that a line of maintenance code costs 10 to 100 times what a line of development code costs.[1] For the reasons given above, each new line of maintenance code contributes to destroying the viability of a system that cost thousands, maybe millions of dollars to develop. A worthy goal is to minimize mistakes made during this activity.

Walkthroughs are becoming more common in the data processing profession. Managers have been accepting the fact that walkthroughs save time and money by discovering errors more efficiently than any known testing method. Unfortunately, current opinion seems to be that this is a process applicable only to the development phase of the system life cycle. It is true that walkthroughs are critically important during the early phases of development because errors are much less expensive to correct at that time than they are later. This does not constitute proof that walkthroughs would not be effective during the maintenance phase. If walkthroughs are to be successful, they should contain the following elements: checklists, criteria, objectives, trained coordinators, established roles, feedback and feed-forward. The reader is referred to other works[3,4,5] for more information on the walkthrough concept.

Applying Maintenance Walkthroughs

The following explains how maintenance is organized at the Los Alamos National Laboratory. Each system is identified with a unique two-digit number, e.g. General Ledger = 70. The table shown in Figure 2 shows how maintenance responsibility is allocated between these systems where primary responsibility is in the center column, secondary responsibility is in the column labeled backup1, and the person responsible for the system in the event that the first two are unavailable is shown in the rightmost column labeled backup2. In actual operation, systems are not maintained in a fashion as clean as the table suggests. In many cases the secondary backup knows nothing about the system and simply hopes it will never break at a time when neither the primary nor the backup are present. The backup often only has a passing acquaintence with the system, gained when the primary was sick or on vacation and a problem occurred. Even the primary's knowledge may be limited because staff shortages and large service request backlogs mean assigning too much maintenance responsibility to too few programmers.

A suggested format for walkthroughs of maintenance changes under the above circumstances is: the programmer making the change assumes the role of presentor/implementor; the other two programmers are responsible for the review and critique; and a fourth person with appropriate training becomes the coordinator/moderator/scribe. Such walkthroughs do not always have to be as comprehensive as a walkthrough for a major development project. A 15-minute walkthrough for a change that took 8 hours to make would seem sufficient. Such a process would simultaneously accomplish three objectives: insertions of defects and psychological complexity and deterioration of structure would be minimized, maintenance of external documentation would be maintained; and the members of the walkthrough team would be educated through the preparation and attendance necessary for the walkthrough. If such walkthroughs were always required, systems would (we hope) live longer, break less often, and be easier to maintain. In addition, the terms *backup* and *secondary backup* would come to have a more reliable meaning.

system_id	system_name	primary	backupl	backup2
12	payroll	hastings	smith	mcdonald
20	commitments	tompkins	johnson	zeindt
25	materials dist.	benjamin	garfunkle	conners
30	employee info.	hastings	temple	roberts
36	travel	hunker	lowe	stamp
40	stores	halpert	garfunkle	albertson
70	general ledger	lowe	davis	hunker
71	accounts payable	zeindt	schutz	tompkins
75	operating plans	marks	wacker	lake
79	operating budget	schmidt	lake	wacker

Figure 2—System responsibility

Summarizing the Top-Down Approach to Maintenance

Good maintenance work requires a maintenance analyst who is just as professional in terms of software engineering know-how as a good senior programmer/analyst in the development area. The same basic activities are involved: analyze the program, develop a solution, test the solution, implement the solution. The ideas presented in the preceding sections suggest a miniature life cycle approach to making maintenance changes as follows:

1. Do a thorough analysis of the change request to determine needed modifications to system functionality.
2. Study the old functional analysis to determine the impact of the proposed changes on the total system.
3. Revise functional analysis as appropriate.
4. Revise design and internal specification documents as appropriate.
5. Make the changes according to the new analysis and design.
6. Test the changes using both dynamic (standard test beds) and static (walkthroughs) procedures.
7. Implement the changes when they pass all tests.

CONTROLLING THE QUALITY OF MAINTENANCE WORK

Given the above means for doing quality maintenance work, what controls should be put in place to assure that quality will improve? It is recommended that controls consist of workable mechanisms for measurement, evaluation, and feedback. A non-workable mechanism is micro-management, whereby the line manager watches the maintenance programmer carefully and constantly to ensure that mistakes are avoided. If, instead, meaningful measurement of the quality of maintenance work is taking place, it can provide the basis for effective performance evaluations and feedback that should produce the desired results. Ways of evaluating quality include: user surveys; tracking of maintenance costs via measurement of reliability; and counting defects.

User Surveys

Since most data processing professionals belong to organizations whose budget or income is derived by providing a service perceived to be useful by users outside of their organization, user satisfaction surveys should be one of the most important means of measuring quality. Figure 3 shows a portion of such a survey that was taken of users of administrative applications software systems at Los Alamos. Users were asked to give their degree of satisfaction for different classes of services on a numeric scale, providing a means for measuring the degree of user satisfaction quantitatively.

Because users have different personality profiles, some are easier to please than others. Ideally, user personnel would be held constant while the surveys were taken in a time-series fashion, allowing for measurement of change in degree of satisfaction over time. The program of personnel turn-over in

The following systems are supported by ADP for your organization. Please fill in the blanks rating ADP services using: 1 = poor, 2 = below average, 3 = average, 4 = above average, 5 = excellent. You need only rate those systems with which you have personal knowledge and experience.

ID	SYSTEM NAME	DEVELOPMENT QUALITY	MAINTENANCE QUALITY	PRODUCTIVITY
71	ACCTS PAYABLE	3	3	4
12	PAYROLL	5	4	4
30	EIS	4	4	3
20	COMMITMENTS	1	4	3
70	GENERAL LEDGER	1	4	3
36	TRAVEL	4	4	4

Figure 3—User satisfaction survey

the user organization can be circumvented if a profile for the entire organization can be developed. Data relating to quality of maintenance work should come from feedback on the useability, operability, and usefulness of the user's system.

The Importance of Measuring Maintenance Costs

Accurate measurement of maintenance effort in programmer hours is critically important for several reasons. Our goal is to control the quality and the expense of software maintenance, and it has been pointed out that you can't control what you can't measure.[6] Maintenance effort measurement can be used for cost/benefit analysis of proposed rewrites.[7] If maintenance effort is decreasing dramatically on a particular system, the decrease may be an indication that high quality maintenance work is being performed. Useful measurement should differentiate between bug-fixing and making changes necessitated by changing user requirements. This would provide a means for knowing when the quality of a production system was deteriorating if bug-fixing effort begins to rise significantly.

Measuring Software Reliability

Aborts, reruns, and user trouble calls are costly. They can also be reduced by the performance of high quality maintenance work, although recognition of quality can sometimes be difficult. It is possible to force a program to execute successfully under almost any circumstance, but if the output is not correct this will usually be caught either by production control or the user, resulting in a rerun or a trouble call. Careful records of aborts, reruns, and user trouble calls in production logs must be kept and published. The objective of this measurement is to evaluate the quality of maintenance with respect to software reliability.

Measuring Insertion of Defects

We should be very concerned about the rate of insertion of defects into a production system. The walkthrough procedures discussed above should help reduce the insertion of defects, but it provides no guarantee that zero defects will be inserted. Furthermore, it provides no measurement of the insertion of defects since the walkthrough team must stipulate that they are unable to find any defects before a change will be put into production. A measure of defects is the count of fix-a-bug requests from users. Defects reported by users must be differentiated according to the sources of the problem; original code or a maintenance change. The important measure here is the actual number of such requests, not the amount of effort spent on them. Increases in the receiving rate of these requests should be an indictment of the walkthrough team as well as the responsible programmer. Decreases in the receiving rate would indicate that high quality maintenance work is being performed.

Evaluating Maintenance Performance

To effectively implement the controls suggested above, criteria for acceptable performance of maintenance work should be published and distributed among the maintenance programmers. In order to do high quality maintenance work, the staff needs to know what the goals are, how goal achievement will be measured, what constitutes a satisfactory level of performance and how his/her level of performance compares to the rest of the group. Figure 4 shows suggested performance evaluation guidelines for maintenance programmers.

CAREER PATHS FOR MAINTENANCE PROGRAMMERS

Who should do maintenance work? How long should they do it? What should appropriate rewards be for successful maintenance programmers? What should the organizational goal be for maintenance activity as a whole? These topics could serve as the basis for further research, but they deserve at least brief attention within the scope of this paper.

Criteria Description	Measurement	Satisfactory Level
1. Encourages a free exchange of ideas. Gives and accepts criticism and comments.	Walkthru reports.	Effectively participates in structured walkthrus.
2. Contributes in a positive manner to user satisfaction with production systems.	User Survey.	User satisfaction does not deteriorate over time.
3. Makes changes which do not cause systems to be more difficult to maintain.	Maintenance effort statistics.	Effort required to make changes does not increase.
4. Makes changes in a manner which tends to increase the reliability, operability and usability of systems.	Aborts, reruns and trouble calls.	Problem incidents decrease over time.
5. Makes changes in a manner which tends to preserve the functionality of the system.	Number of user requests for enhancement changes.*	Receiving rate of incoming enhancement service requests does not increase.

*Note that a burst of changes may indicate a need for a new system.

Figure 4—Acceptable performance criteria for maintenance work

Maintenance As a Training Experience

In many organizations, maintenance work serves as an initiation period for programmer trainees. This is not an entirely bad idea. Recent graduates have been schooled in the latest structured programming techniques and may have an inclination to keep the code they are responsible for as clean as possible. Also, it provides a series of little problems for the trainee to solve before being faced with a big problem. It becomes a bad idea when an organization has only green recruits supporting its production systems. This situation usually signifies an organizational attitude that maintenance work is not as important or technically demanding as development work. It has been pointed out recently[2] that this attitude is not appropriate since it is software maintenance that keeps the business running smoothly by supporting critical applications.

Maintenance Trouble-Shooters

In most medium- to large-size organizations, it is possible to find several maintenance experts. These software "doctors" are proficient at quickly identifying and solving very complex problems. They usually derive a great deal of enjoyment from it. This is not hard to understand since people usually enjoy doing things at which they excell. These people should be provided with career paths and monetary rewards which encourage them to keep doing what they enjoy and do well. They should not be "promoted" to development projects, which among other negative results, starve them of the pleasure of immediate feedback present in problem-fixing. These seasoned professionals can provide excellent supervision and guidance for the trainees mentioned above.

Maintenance Groups as a Separate Entity

If it makes sense to have different types of employees doing the maintenance work, then it may follow that it is also sensible to have a separate maintenance group in the data processing organization chart. This group would have a different set of talents and/or interests than those doing development work and would be evaluated on a somewhat different basis. Trainees could work on teams with more experienced maintenance analysts supporting production systems. Very successful maintenance analysts could be promoted to team leaders. Those who are very successful and have valuable management talent (proven as team leaders) become likely candidates for line manager of the maintenance group.

Performance Rewards and Appropriate Goal Setting

A suggested goal for the organization is to minimize required maintenance effort and the occurrence of problems with production software on a per-system basis over all production systems. Hopefully, some of the ideas detailed above will prove useful in accomplishing this goal. If all these ideas are implemented, how should a successful maintenance analyst be rewarded? This person has improved the degree of user satisfaction with data processing service, reduced the amount of effort required to maintain systems, extended the useful life of critical applications, and provided excellent guidance and training for new hires. It doesn't take much imagination to see that this is one of the most valuable people in the entire organization, who should receive monetary rewards and career opportunities accordingly. If, for example, most data processing organizations are spending the largest portion of their budget on software maintenance, then an effective data processing manager is one who has demonstrated that s/he can control this activity successfully.

CONCLUSION

Each modification made to a software system carries a risk of weakening it through the introduction of defects or the compounding of psychological complexity or both. As systems become more complex and defect-ridden, they become more costly to maintain. A data processing organization will accomplish its mission more effectively if it is able to prolong the life of the software it supports.

Solutions to the application systems maintenance dilemma include: the retention and maintenance of design documents; the conducting of dynamic system tests; and the conducting of static tests in the form of team walkthroughs. Via walkthroughs the maintenance programmer can share responsibility, maintain external documentation, educate others in the functioning of the system, and minimize entropy.

The methods of controlling the solution include: conducting user surveys; measurement of the maintenance effort; measurement of insertion of defects; measurement of system reliability; establishment of proper criteria by which to evaluate maintenance performance; and creation of a separate maintenance group where motivation and incentives are consistent with talents and interest.

REFERENCES

1. Martin, James, and Carma McClure. *Software Maintenance: The Problem and Its Solutions*. Englewood Cliffs, New Jersey: Prentice-Hall, 1983.
2. Zvegintzov, Nicholas. "Nanotrends." *Datamation,* August 1983, pp. 105–116.
3. Fagan, M. "Design and Code Inspections to Reduce Errors in Program Development." *Writings of the Revolution.* New York: Yourdon Press, 1982.
4. McCabe, T. *Software Quality Assurance: A Survey.* Columbia, Md.: McCabe & Associates, 1980.
5. Yourdon, E. *Structured Walkthrus.* New York: Yourdon Press, 1978.
6. DeMarco, T. *Controlling Software Projects.* New York: Yourdon Press, 1982.
7. Brice, L., J. Connell, and J. Taylor. "Deriving Metrics for Relating Complexity Measures to Software Maintenance Costs." *Proceedings of the 1982 Computer Measurement Group International Conference,* CMG, Inc., Phoenix, Arizona, pp. 134–141.

Software maintenance in fourth-generation language environments

by PAUL C. TINNIRELLO
AT&T Communications
Piscataway, New Jersey

ABSTRACT

It is often asserted that fourth-generation languages will resolve the problems associated with software development in traditional languages, and in particular the technical and morale problems of software maintenance. The analysis of this paper suggests that fourth-generation languages do not solve all of the present problems of maintenance, and indeed they can introduce problems of their own. The successful user of fourth-generation languages will be the organization that takes appropriate countermeasures.

INTRODUCTION

The evolution of software technology coupled with the demand for more productivity from data processing organizations has prompted a widespread appeal for fourth-generation languages (4GL). The term *fourth-generation language* is applied to a class of DP languages developed in the mid-1970s that offer simplified expressions for common DP tasks. These languages allow for system development in significantly less time than third-generation languages such as COBOL, FORTRAN, and PL/I. Advocates of these new languages are confident that they will lessen many of the problems that have burdened traditional language environments.[1,2] Such problems include a heavy backlog of requests, lack of maintainability, lack of adaptability, and human resource issues. High expectations, however, especially in the area of software maintenance, could lead to disappointment for many professionals who are seeking to escape the frustrations encountered in third-generation systems.[3] The overconfidence in a fourth-generation language's ability to eliminate most of the software maintenance issues could seriously jeopardize the recent efforts to improve software maintenance attitudes. An untimely eagerness to abandon concern for software maintenance could also compound maintenance problems in current systems as well as initiate maintenance problems in systems using fourth-generation software.

This paper focuses on several fundamental issues of software maintenance that will continue to exist in many fourth-generation language environments. It is not the intention of this paper to critique the overall effectiveness of fourth-generation languages or to evaluate the necessity of their use, but rather to discuss the impact of these new languages on the software maintenance process.

FACTORS INFLUENCING THE USE OF FOURTH-GENERATION LANGUAGES

Before examining maintenance issues in fourth-generation language environments, it would be advantageous to review the following factors that are promoting the spread of these new language systems:

1. System development problems
2. Maintenance problems and request backlogs
3. Increased DP knowledge by users
4. Pressure for productivity/accountability

System Development Problems

Apportioning of monetary resources and time has been an inherent consideration in traditional system development. Software costs may account for as much as 80% of the total cost of system development.[4] Much of this cost is attributed to escalating programmer salaries; further, many user groups resent department budget cuts because of the high expenses incurred by data processing.[3] Often the time required to replace and/or develop a system is much longer than is acceptable to end users. Fourth-generation languages offer system development with less effort than traditional development techniques, thus offering a savings in time and cost.

Maintenance Problems and Request Backlogs

Software maintenance problems have been a well-known stumbling block for years. Negative attitudes about maintenance work are held by DP managers, programmers, and end users.[5] These attitudes inhibit the necessary effort needed to perform maintenance work successfully. Maintenance problems also include unmaintainable, unadaptable programs and systems. Some systems do not fulfill user requirements and specifications. Numerous corrective measures within these systems have left them in an unmaintainable state. Other systems have been poorly designed, and modifying or enhancing their capability is only possible through rewriting large portions of the system. Software maintenance accounts for as much as 50%–80% of the software activities performed by programmers.[6]

System maintenance problems have created a flood of user requests. Often users submit requests for replacement systems even though there are already numerous outstanding requests for maintenance work on these systems. Request backlogs in some companies may be as high as 2½ years.[3,7,8] Vendor advertising of fourth-generation systems emphasizes the vast improvement in application development over traditional programming methods. These advertising claims support the premise that maintenance problems and lengthy request backlogs, which are attributed to traditional programming, will be reduced.

Increased DP Knowledge by Users

With new technological applications in industry, many end-user professionals have sought to become more computer literate. Much of this need for literacy is due to an increased number of automated business functions that require data processing knowledge to use with them. In other instances, professionals have educated themselves in preparation for the new technology of the personal computer. With this increased knowledge of computing technology, end users are becoming less dependent on data processing professionals and computing resources.[3] Many users want to apply their new found computing knowledge at the workplace in an attempt to make their jobs easier. Numerous vendors claim that their fourth-generation language allows writing a program to be a simple and uncomplicated task. This simplicity gives the non-data-processing professional the ability to use computing resources advantageously.[9]

Pressure for Productivity/Accountability

The problems of development, maintenance, and request backlogs have been apparent to many non-data-processing professionals in the computer-based organization. User groups are expressing dissatisfaction with budgetary spending as more funds are being allocated to data processing departments rather than to user departments. The reaction from upper management in response to this dissatisfaction has been to allow end users to write their own application programs. Upper management would ultimately be making end-user departments more accountable and productive in relation to data processing activities. It has already been recognized that end users have a tremendous optimism toward the use of fourth-generation software products.[7] Vendors of these products propose that the simplicity and ease associated with programming will allow the end user the time to write more programs and thus increase productivity.

EXAMINING THE MAINTENANCE ISSUES

In a previous paper, the author suggested that the software maintenance process could be segmented into the three following areas: maintenance management, maintenance programming, and maintenance attitudes.[5] Maintenance management is defined as the management process necessary when performing maintenance tasks. Maintenance programming is defined as the technical methodology in which a correction, modification, or enhancement takes place. Finally, the maintenance attitude is defined as the position that programmers, managers, and users take toward maintenance tasks.

The fourth-generation language environment will not solve all the problems associated with the three areas of the maintenance process. More specifically, the remaining problem areas of the fourth-generation language environment with respect to the three maintenance segments are the following:

1. software ownership responsibility
2. documentation
3. software selection and quality assurance
4. product releases and software warranty
5. software standards

Software Ownership and Responsibility

Software ownership/responsibility is defined as a policy for maintaining the programs and systems written in fourth-generation languages.[3] The need for such a policy becomes evident when consideration is given to several facts that will be present in the fourth-generation language environment. First, there will be a diverse population of potential language users that include data processing and non-data-processing professionals with varied technical skills. Second, there will be a need to make changes to fourth-generation application programs for product release changes, for business changes, and for ensuring hardware efficiency. Although the last issue was present in third-generation systems, it was usually resolved by a narrower population of language users—programmers. With a broader population of fourth-generation language users, there is concern as to how capable end users are in making the changes to application programs described above.[3,8]

Software ownership/responsibility can be categorized as part of maintenance management. It will require the cooperation and coordination of upper management, data processing, and end-user departments. Without formal agreement on software ownership/responsibility, the maintenance management function would be ineffective and more complex. In addition, required changes to fourth-generation language programs might be circumvented by the data processing and end-user departments as a result of the conflict over which group is better prepared to perform maintenance tasks. Numerous companies who have already implemented fourth-generation language systems may still be in the process of developing ownership/responsibility policy.[10]

One of the more popular ownership/responsibility methods is found in the information center concept that numerous companies are implementing.[10] In this method, the information center serves both as a product support group for vendor changes and as a consulting group for end-user applications. While this approach has merit, there is still a need to manage the end-user application system more carefully. A suggested method of ownership/responsibility that will help the maintenance management function is the designation of end-user department specialists. These individuals will manage the use of the software product or group of software products at the department level. Operating within an established set of company standards for a given product, these specialists will help ensure the quality of code, documentation, and standards in end-user systems. The end-user department specialists will need to have skills in both the department business function and the application software product.

A potential danger of such a position is the reliance of the ownership/responsibility process on one individual. These highly specialized end users could find their combination of business and data processing skills very marketable. It is possible that they would begin the migratory habits that have long been associated with data processing professionals. This might create a kind of maintenance problem similar to the one that exists with programmers in traditional language systems. Perhaps assigning several people as end-user specialists could alleviate this problem.

Another alternative for software ownership/responsibility is the formation of an end-user product group. This group would serve all end users of a specific software product in the computer-based organization. The end-user product group would oversee all development and maintenance work performed with a particular language system. The group would also be responsible for reviewing documentation, release levels, and standards in end-user application systems. This method is similar to the information center concept, with the exception of its decentralized role. The end-user product group could be accountable to the information center department in a company's organizational hierarchy.

Documentation

Documentation problems are not unique to data processing departments. Many end-user departments, which also require retained written information specific to their business functions, suffer from poor or too little documentation. Documentation activities are often the last phase of a business development project, and frequently this phase is hastily completed in an effort to meet project deadlines. In traditional data processing systems, maintenance programmers found that documentation problems accounted for much of the difficulty in maintaining a system.[11] Poor documentation has caused programmers to spend hours tracking errors that could have taken minutes to locate. Inadequate documentation has also made it difficult to locate key system areas where modifications and/or enhancements are required. Although the fourth-generation language concept deemphasizes the need for elaborate documentation, there are still several issues about these new languages that make documentation vital to the software maintenance process.[3]

The first issue is that some fourth-genertion languages are not as self-documenting as the software vendor would have end users believe. In fact, some end users find that many new languages are complex and not so user friendly.[7,10,12] This complex command structure, combined with potential use of complicated end-user logic, could make the maintenance process in new language systems as difficult as it is in third-generation systems.

Another issue concerning documentation is evident when considering the life expectancy of systems developed with fourth-generation software. In several companies, new language systems have been running in a production mode for as long as five years.[8] It would seem unlikely that the applications developed with fourth-generation software would immediately be replaced when the next software evolution occurs. Such is the case for many third-generation systems, which will probably continue to run for the next decade.[13] Given this anticipated longevity of new language systems, it is only practical to document them.

Still another documentation issue is changes in the business environment that will probably occur during the life cycle of an end-user application system. End-user professionals are subject to promotions, career changes, and relocation changes. Without documentation, systems written by these individuals become extremely difficult to maintain from the viewpoints of both business function and programming function.

Finally, the ad hoc development technique that many envision as commonplace in the fourth-generation language environment may create an ad hoc attitude about documentation needs. Thus, end users may become lax in their creation of meaningful program and system documentation.

Several documentation practices can be implemented by the computer-based organization to help minimize software maintenance problems. One practice would be for the end user to document an application system on a business level. Included in this business application description is a section that identifies special algorithms or formulas that are used within the end user program. A business application description is similar to the high-level functional overview found in traditional documentation, except that it reflects more of the business functions than technical functions. This may encourage end users to document more thoroughly, since the style of documentation is in business terminology. Another documentation technique is the establishment of standards that require documentation to be written on the basis of the length of the end-user program or the number of executable commands. This may vary from one software language to another, depending upon the clairty of the command language. Each technique, of course, will require the review of either the end-user departmental specialist or the end-user product group. Whichever documentation plan is chosen, it is important that the issue of documentation be recognized as an integral part of both the software maintenance process and the successful use of the end-user application system.

Software Selection and Quality Assurance

Selecting a fourth-generation language system that will serve the broad needs of the computer-based organization warrants careful consideration.[10] Besides finding agreement among end users on application needs, the advertising strategy used by software vendors makes the selection process difficult even for data processing professionals. An important aspect in software selection is acquiring a language system that will fit the needs of end-user applications. Without a close matching of application needs and language capabilities, end users will struggle with programming logic in an effort to achieve the desired result. Usually the struggle in language usage results in the use of trick code techniques. Often found in third-generation programs, trick code is extremely difficult to correct, modify, or enhance, because the logic does not follow the intended vendor system design. Therefore, the fourth-generation software selected should be readily adaptable to the present business environment.

A variety of techniques can be used to survey the list of potential software products; however, the best method for deciding on the final end-user product is to pilot the system within a typical application environment. The software piloting phase can best determine the true application capabilities, as well as help establish a set of language standards to be followed by end users when the language system is finally installed. The software selection process will affect both the maintenance management and maintenance programming segments of the software maintenance process.

Quality assurance is as vital a process in fourth-generation language environments as it is in third-generation systems. The quality assurance function should certify that the final end-user system performs all the functions for which it was designed. Quality assurance should also review the efficiency of the end-user application programs, since fourth-generation languages can make a heavy demand on hardware.[14]

Quality assurance affects the software maintenance process in several ways. First, poorly designed systems will eventually require corrective action if the system is to remain functional to the end user. As with traditional systems, corrective maintenance can be an ongoing process. Second, inefficient programming techniques and poor program design will complicate modifications and enhancements made to a system. Though modifications and enhancements may be accomplished with greater ease in fourth-generation language systems, the possibility of producing unmaintainable systems can still exist if intended structured procedures are not followed. Finally, the potential problems of trick code from either poor product selection or unique application requirements can make system maintainability poor. This can be even more critical in fourth-generation language systems, because vendors may not be providing diagnostic tools.[8]

The quality assurance function should be addressed within the software ownership/responsibility phase of the new language implementation process. A central quality assurance group could be formed with both data processing and end-user professionals. Aside from exercising their normal function, the quality assurance group would educate end-user specialists who are unfamiliar with programming logic and design. It would be unfair to expect all end users to possess the design and logic expertise acquired by data processing professionals. The end result of this education process would help prevent maintenance problems that are created as a result of poorly designed programs and systems.

Product Releases and Software Warranty

The appeal of new software language systems has created a very competitive environment for software vendors of fourth-generation languages. Many data processing professionals recognize that the software marketplace is flooded with products claiming to have fourth-generation technology. This highly competitive environment has created two important issues that will affect the software maintenance process.

The first issue is that of vendor product releases. When traditional languages systems such as COBOL and FORTRAN underwent release changes, certain difficulties were encountered. In numerous companies, conversions from one release level to another took months and perhaps years to complete, even when vendors provided conversion tools and aids.[15] Although the release changes were supposed to provide upward compatibility, there were countless programs that required line-by-line examination for conversion conflicts.

Release changes have been infrequent in traditional languages when consideration is given to the length of time these languages have been used. There exists a strong possibility, however, that product release changes for fourth-generation language systems will be much more frequent than with traditional languages. The primary reason for these potential release changes, in the author's opinion, is the competitive environment in which software vendors must survive. When a software vendor issues a product with capabilities not found in current fourth-generation systems, there is a tendency for other software vendors to match product capabilities in order to preserve their share of the software marketplace. As mentioned previously, language releases can wreak havoc on the software maintenance process, even though a promise of upward compatibility is given by the vendor.

The second maintenance issue derived from the competitive software marketplace is that of software warranty. When vendors upgrade language capabilities as a result of competition, what guarantees are extended to the computer-based organization concerning the reliability of the new product? The traditional languages of COBOL and FORTRAN have national committees that carefully evaluate language release changes, and even then there are upgrading problems. In the competitive software marketplace, vendors may not have the time that is required to test a new release level thoroughly; the consequences to the software maintenance process and to the computer-based organization are severe. Warranty problems also occur when a software vendor quits the marketplace, leaving the product, and therefore the end users, unsupported.

Product releases and warranty issues affect all segments of the software maintenance process. Maintenance management is affected whenever product release conversions are required. Maintenance programming is required when release conversions fail as a result of special language and logic uses. Maintenance attitudes are affected by the frequency of release changes and the frustration associated with them.

An important consideration in selecting a fourth-generation language system is the reliability of the software vendor. It is beneficial to examine the business history of a prospective vendor and also to inquire about the software warranty. The time invested in selecting a competent software vendor will minimize the problems the computer-based organization will encounter through frequent and unwarranted release changes.

Software Standards

A deficiency in many fourth-generation languages is the absence of a standard set of language commands.[10,11] Considering the variety of specialized software products available on the marketplace, it is probable that numerous companies will use more than one fourth-generation language system. End users, who interact with these systems, will find that a lack of standardized commands among products can be confusing and frustrating. This will be especially true when users write applications with commands that are familiar to them from one language and expect similar results when using other language systems. Nonstandard language commands can yield functional errors that will require correction, either at the time of design or through a maintenance request.

Until language standards are established, it will be important for users to gain an awareness and understanding of the possible differences that exist between new language systems. This information can be imparted by the end-user department specialist or the end-user product group. Without this awareness, much confusion will probably develop among users who work in a multiple-software-product environment.

Another important issue of standardization is the incompleteness of external language interfaces found in numerous fourth-generation languages.[7] This problem can be subdivided into two areas. First, there are few, if any, standard interfaces among fourth-generation products from different vendors. Second, there are poor interface standards for the traditional languages of COBOL, FORTRAN, and PL/I. With the bulk of information stored within traditional systems, there will be a definite need for application programs written in fourth-generation software to interface with many of the existing systems.

For many companies that have implemented fourth-generation software, interfacing problems may have been circumvented by using data transfer programs written in traditional software languages. These data transfer programs are highly specialized and frequently require modifications whenever the data input requirements of an end-user application program change. Data transfer programs may also need modification whenever changes are made to either the new software language, through release upgrades, or to the old software system, through normal maintenance. The data transfer method used to solve the interface problems of fourth-generation software will require both maintenance management and maintenance programming activities. The maintenance management process will be further complicated by the possibility of highly dynamic data interfacing between new language systems and the existing traditional systems. Unless data interfacing requirements between systems are controlled, maintenance personnel could be spending most of their time modifying the data transfer programs.

One technique that can be used to control frequent modifications to data transfer programs is to establish a selection criterion for data items from the corporate database that will be available for end-user application programs. The criterion for selecting transferable data should consider the data items that are most often used in company business functions. Once established, this selection criterion would prohibit end users from making frequent and special requests for transferable data that are infrequently used by the majority of end-user departments. An extension of this technique might be to develop a group of data transfer programs based on different criteria, as prescribed by end-user departments. In this manner, end-user departments can access data unique to their business function and still remain within a controlled process.

CONCLUSION

The movement toward using fourth-generation languages in the computer-based organization is understandable. However, the software maintenance process, as shown in this paper, is an area that will continue to exist in the fourth-generation language environment. This critical fact should be recognized by organizations that are planning to use these new language systems. Forgoing the recognition of maintenance issues will generate unrealistic expectations in the end-user community that will eventually lead to disappointment and frustration. In addition, the efforts to improve the current maintenance process will suffer as a result of increased complexity.

As important as the recognition of the continued maintenance process is the selection of an implementation strategy that reflects the limitations and capabilities of fourth-generation languages. This strategy should include techniques, like those suggested in this paper, that help reduce the impact of fourth-generation languages on the software maintenance process. Finally, the organizations that successfully use fourth-generation software will be those that have not been deceived into thinking that technical advancements that have solved some problems have solved all problems.

REFERENCES

1. Cochran, Henry T. "Fourth Generation Languages." *Computerworld, 17* (1983), pp. 47–49.
2. Goetz, Martin A., Richard L. Kaufman, and Adam N. Rin. "Integrated Fourth Generation Software Languages." *Computerworld Extra, 16* (1982), pp. 37–41.
3. Coble, D. F. "Fourth Generation Languages Will Impact Productivity If . . ." *Data Management, 20* (1982), pp. 29–32.
4. Gutz, Steven, and Anthony I. Wasserman. "The Future of Programming." *Communications of the ACM, 25* (1982), pp. 196–206.
5. Tinnirello, Paul C. "Improving Software Maintenance Attitudes." *AFIPS, Proceedings of the National Computer Conference* (Vol. 52), 1983, pp. 107–112.
6. Kapur, Gopal. "Software Maintenance." *Computerworld, 17* (1983), pp. 13–22.
7. Batt, Robert, "Fourth Generation Tools Get Mixed Reviews." *Computerworld, 16* (1982), p. 15.
8. Stamps, David. "Hail 4th Generation Languages." *MIS Week, 4* (1983), pp. 18–19.
9. Martin, James. "Software Application Development Without Conventional Programming." *Software World, 14* (1983), pp. 14–21.
10. Rifkin, Glenn. "The Information Center: Oasis or Mirage." *Computerworld, OA 17* (1983), pp. 12–15.
11. Lientz, B. P., and E. B. Swanson. "Software Maintenance Management." Reading, Mass.: 1980, Addison-Wesley.
12. Paul, Lois. "Info Center Has Its Drawbacks, Study Warns." *Computerworld, 17* (1983), p. 11.
13. Zvegintzov, Nicholas. "Nanotrends." *Datamation, 29* (1983), pp. 106–108.
14. Read, Nigel S., and Douglas L. Harmon. "Assuring MIS Success." *Datamation, 27* (1981), pp. 109–120.
15. Shoor, Rita. "Travelers Says COBOL Conversion Could Cost a Cool $20 Million." *Computerworld, 15* (1981).

Specification and implementations of interactive information systems

by ANTHONY I. WASSERMAN
University of California
San Francisco, California

ABSTRACT

User Software Engineering is a methodology supported by automated tools for the development of interactive information systems. The specification process decomposes the system into user–program dialogue, database definition, and formal and informal description of system operations. Evolution of the specification is supported by tools for rapid construction of prototype versions of the system, and the resulting specification is easily transformed into the programming language PLAIN. This paper gives an overview of the USE development process, illustrating it with a development dictionary example.

INTRODUCTION

The process of developing a software system may be divided into two steps: producing an accurate specification of what the system is to do, and implementing a system that meets that specification. Other activities typically associated with the software development life cycle may be viewed as supporting one or both of these steps. For example, analysis of system requirements makes it possible to write a better specification, and architectural design leads to program structure.

In practice, these activities are affected by time and resource limitations, organizational structures, inadequate tools, poor analysis, incomplete testing, and communication difficulties, leading to many of the well-known problems of software development and evolution.

The User Software Engineering (USE) project is concerned with the process of developing an interactive information system (IIS), a particular class of software system characterized by conversational access to data. Frequently, the users of an IIS are not experts in computing, and are given a predefined set of operations to use. Examples of such systems include airline reservation systems, bibliographic searching systems, decision support systems, and text editors.

METHODOLOGY OVERVIEW

The USE methodology combines the systematic approach to software development inherent to the life cycle approach, with effective user involvement in the specification process. We view creation of an accurate specification as being more difficult than implementation of a system from the specification. This situation is especially true with an IIS, where users may have a poor concept of their needs and a limited idea of the potential capabilities of a computer system. Thus, production of a functional specification requires extensive analysis and communication.

The USE methodology combines traditional activity- and data-modeling techniques with efforts to design the user–program interface. It creates a preliminary version of the dialogue at the earliest possible stage.

The specification of an IIS is seen to consist of three parts: the user–program dialogue, the database design, and the operations (transactions) associated with various user inputs. The interaction is described in a set of augmented state transition diagrams, each of which is termed a conversation. Various user inputs may cause state transitions, including the invocation of a "subconversation" (another diagram). Actions may be associated with a transition, so that all of the operations may be attached to transitions. The database is described as a set of normalized relations.[1]

The operations are described both formally and informally in the USE methodology to satisfy the different audiences for the specification. The informal approach is simply a short paragraph (two or three sentences at most) of narrative text, whereas the formal approach uses a formal notation employing preconditions and postconditions in conjunction with a description of the behavior of operations similar to that developed for Alphard.[2] For those operations involving database access or modification, the database operations are shown in a data manipulation language.

The following list of steps for the USE methodology shows the emphasis on development of the specification:

1. Preliminary analysis—activity and data modeling, leading to preliminary informal specifications and identification of user characteristics
2. External design—user–program dialogue
3. Creation of a prototype of the user–program dialogue with revisions as needed
4. Completion of the informal functional specification of the system operations using narrative text
5. Preliminary relational database design
6. Creation of a functional prototype system, providing at least some, and possibly all, of the system's functions
7. Formal specification of the system operations using behavioral abstraction[3]
8. Software design at the architectural and module levels
9. Implementation in PLAIN
10. Testing and verification

There is considerable flexibility in the application of these steps, and the methodology supports variations in which some of the steps are emphasized or omitted.

In the remainder of this paper, we first describe the specification process. We then show the RAPID/USE application development tool for the rapid construction of user program dialogues and interactive systems. We then discuss the structured programming language PLAIN, which can also be used for implementation of a system. We use a simple development dictionary system as an example.

DEVELOPING THE SPECIFICATION

A major hindrance to the analysis and specification of interactive information systems is that the user and developer must reach agreement on system capabilities and operation at a very early stage, often with little understanding on the user's part. The resulting system is then, at best, only partly satisfactory, necessitating an expensive process of evolution. Many engineering disciplines build preliminary models of proposed products or systems. A similar approach of prototyping a system is taken in USE. If a prototype system can assist in reaching better user understanding, then there can be significant improvements in system quality and reductions in maintenance costs. The rapid construction and modification of prototype versions of the system are important aspects of the USE methodology.

We perform an initial analysis to identify the principal data objects and the operations upon them. This information is used to define a set of "structured operations" (transactions) visible to each user class, aiding both the formal definition of system properties, which are defined as abstract operations on objects, and the design of the user–program interface.

Analysis also includes the identification of user characteristics, such as user skills, user motivation and intelligence, and physical workplace constraints. These characteristics, when combined with information about output needs (volume; hard copy vs. "soft" copy), are essential to the system design process in general and to the dialogue design process in particular.

DESIGN AND MODIFICATION OF USER–PROGRAM DIALOGUE

In many respects, the user–program dialogue is the most critical aspect of an IIS, since that is what the user sees. Elegant and efficient implementations are useless if the IIS is difficult to use or does not meet the user's needs. Accordingly, our next step is to define the user interface to the system for each identified user class.

The interface can take many forms, including multiple choice (menu selection), a command language, a database query language, or natural-language-like input. In all cases, however, the normal action of the program is determined by user input, and the program may respond in a variety of ways, including results, requests for additional input, error messages, or assistance in the use of the IIS.

At this early stage, the dialogue design is far from complete. Typically, only the major operations are identified, and the options for different operations may not be fully defined. Also, the first design effort may omit some needed operations, and rarely includes more than rudimentary error handling and help facilities.

In short, the initial dialogue design is seen as a starting point for a process of gradual refinement that is achieved through partnership between the developer and the user. The dialogue is represented with USE transition diagrams, an augmented form of state transition diagrams.[4] Initially, we used the diagrams as the sole basis for communication between the developer and user community.[5] While that worked successfully and we were able to show the nature of the interactive interface, we sensed that the users did not really have a very good idea of how the interface would actually behave. (We observed that few people would purchase an automobile without first taking a test drive.)

Accordingly, we sought to automate the USE transition diagrams. The primary intent of such automation was to be able to encode the diagrams quickly and to generate the interface so that the prospective user could use it. Another advantage would be the ability to encode the error-handling and on-line assistance parts of the more detailed diagrams so that users could gain experience with those aspects of the dialogue. In this way, the set of diagrams can be encoded, and a running prototype produced.

There are several other reasons for building such a prototype:

1. It enables the user to evaluate the interface in practice and to suggest changes
2. It enables the developer to evaluate user performance with the interface and to modify it to minimize user errors and improve user satisfaction
3. It facilitates experimentation with alternative interfaces and modification of interfaces
4. It gives the user a more immediate sense of the proposed system and thereby encourages users to think more carefully about needed and desirable characteristics

The prototype gradually evolves into a model of a usable interface, thus yielding a formal description of one aspect of the system specification: the user–program dialogue. Since the database aspect is specified by the data-modeling activity, and by subsequent refinement into normalized relations, the only remaining aspect is the set of operations.

EXAMPLE: DEVELOPMENT DICTIONARY

Some of the concepts of the USE methodology can be seen in the effort to design a static development dictionary to support the methodology, an activity presently underway. The idea of the tool is to support definitions of data elements, data stores, data flow, and processes that are identified during the modeling of USE. In addition to the insertion, deletion, and modification of entries of these different types, the development dictionary system should support the following user queries:

1. List all the data elements contained in a given data flow or data store
2. List all the data flows that contain a given data element or lower-level data flow
3. List all the data stores containing a given data element or data flow
4. List all the processes that input or output a given data element or data flow
5. Display in alphabetic order all entries of a given type
6. Display all entries whose names contain a given input string (partial match)
7. Display all undefined entries

Finally, the system should perform certain consistency checks, such as prevention of duplicate names, and restricted deletion of entries that are part of other entries.

Part of the user–program dialogue, encoded in RAPID/USE, is shown in Figure 1. This segment shows the "main" dialogue in which the user initiates the dialogue, the subconversation dealing with the required retrievals, and the retrieval subconversation for listing the data elements contained in a given data flow or data store. (This figure comprises about 30% of the entire dialogue, but only one action.)

```
        r19,t_0,'7: Display undefined list.', r23,c0,'$'
node Help_Queries
        cs,r3,c0,'Development Dictionary Retrieval.',
        r+2,'For information about a selected query, enter',
        r+1,'command number and ask for help.',
        r+1,'To quit, type "q" or "Q".'
node More?
        cs,r21,c0,'Another retrieval?', r23,c0,'$'
node X
arc S skip to Queries
arc Queries on 'h','H','?' to Help_Queries
            on '1' to <DISPLAY_MODIFY>
            on '2' to <E_IN_FS>
            on '3' to <F_WITH_C>
            on '4' to <S_WITH_C>
            on '5' to <P_INOUT>
            on '6' to <SCAN>
            on '7' to <UNDEFINED>
            else to X
arc Help_Queries else to Queries
arc <DISPLAY_MODIFY> skip to More?
arc <E_IN_FS> skip to More?
arc <F_WITH_C> skip to More?
arc <S_WITH_C> skip to More?
arc <P_INOUT> skip to More?
arc <SCAN> skip to More?
arc <UNDEFINED> skip to More?
arc More? on 'n','no,'N' to X else to S

diagram E_IN_FS entry S exit X
alpha itemname [1:20]
node S
        cs
node Name
        r12,c0,'Please enter flow or store name.', r23,c0,'$'
node Help
        cs,r6,c0,'List all the elements in a given data flow or data store.',
        r+1,'All flow components in the list will',
        r+1,'be broken into the elements which comprise them.'
node Display
        cs,r20,c0,'Above is a list of all the elements which are',
        nl,'contained in ', itemname,
        nl,'Press ', rv, 'RETURN', sv, 'to continue.',
        nl,'$'
node X
arc S skip to Name
arc Name on 'h','H','?' to Help
         on 'q','Q' to X
         on itemname do 1 to Display
% Troll/USE implementation of action is shown in Figure 3
arc Display else to X
arc Help else to Name
```

```
diagram MAIN entry S exit X
tab t_0 4
node S
        cs,r5,c0,'USE Development Dictionary'
node Select
        r21,c0,cl,r22,c0,cl,
        r12,c0,'Please enter command number or first letter of command',
        r+2,t_0,'1: Add a dictionary entry.',
        r+1,t_0,'2: Delete a dictionary entry.',
        r+1,t_0,'3: Modify a dictionary entry',
        r+1,t_0,'4: Retrieve information from development dictionary',
        r+1,t_0,'5: Help', r+1,t_0,'6: Quit', r$-1,c0,'$'
node Help
        cs,r6,c0,'Type "q" or "Q" to quit.',
        r7,'For more information about a command, enter',
        r8,'command number, press return and ask for help',
        r9,'by typing "h","H", or "?"'
node More?
        cs,r21,c0,'Another command?',r23,c0,'$'
node GOOF
        r21,rv,'Unrecognized command. Please try again.',sv,
        r22,'Press ',rv,'RETURN',sv,' to continue'
node X
arc S skip to Select
arc Select
          on '1','a','A' to <ADD>
          on '2','D','d' to <DELETE>
          on '3','M','m' to <MODIFY>
          on '4','r','R' to <RETRIEVAL>
          on '5','h','H','?' to Help
          on '6','q','Q' to X
          else to GOOF
arc <ADD> skip to More?
arc <DELETE> skip to More?
arc <MODIFY> skip to More?
arc <RETRIEVAL> skip to More?
arc GOOF else to Select
arc Help else to Select
arc More? on 'no','n','N' to X else to S

diagram RETRIEVAL entry S exit X
tab t_0 3
node S
        cs
node Queries
        r9,c14,'USE Development Dictionary Retrieval Options',
        r11,c0,'Please enter the number of the desired retrieval type.',
        r13,t_0,'1: Display or modify entry with a given name.',
        r14,t_0,'2: List elements in a given flow or store.',
        r15,t_0,'3: List flows which contain a given element or flow.',
        r16,t_0,'4: List stores which contain a given element or flow.',
        r17,t_0,'5: List processes which input or output a given element or flow',
        r18,t_0,'6: Scan entries of a given type.',
```

Figure 1—Portion of dialogue specification in RAPID/USE for USE development dictionary

Recall that each transition in the diagrams may have an associated action. Thus one may describe, informally at first, all of the actions of the system and the point at which they are performed. The entire IIS may be specified in this manner, showing the dialogue and associated actions as a set of transition diagrams, accompanied by specifications of the actions and the database design. The user may review these diagrams and see the valid inputs and the actions that occur as a result of those inputs. This activity yields an informal specification of the system, along with the prototype of the user–program dialogue previously developed.

ADDING FUNCTIONALITY TO PROTOTYPES

The informal specification and the executable interface gives the user a good sense of what the system will be like. However, with only dialogue management in the prototype tool, it is difficult to provide realistic output messages and impossible to program the IIS functions. From a system construction standpoint, the goal is to have a tool that permits the *rapid* construction of an IIS that performs many of the IIS functions.

A key observation was that many of the operations involve database access and modification, so the desired functionality could be provided by combining dialogue management with a database management system. One of the tools used for several purposes in the methodology is the Troll/USE relational database management system.[6] By linking the dialogue management tool with Troll/USE, one can then store actual data in the database, so that user input can cause actual operations to be performed. In practice, it is necessary to provide some additional operations beyond those of the database management system, so the linkage mechanism is designed to include routines written in the Troll/USE data manipulation language or in any one of a variety of programming languages (PASCAL, C, FORTRAN, or PLAIN).

This tool, called RAPID/USE, permits a rapid implementation of the IIS specification with a notation that provides a close match to the specification method itself.[7] Output mes-

```
relation data_element [key el_name] of
        el_name, el_description, el_code : string;
        el_counter : integer; {reference counter}
end;

relation data_store [key store_name] of
        store_name,
        store_components,        {elements & data flows}
        store_notes : string;
end;

relation data_flow [key flow_name] of
        flow_name,
        flow_components,         {elements & lower level flows}
        flow_notes : string;
        flow_count : integer;    {reference counter}
end relation;

relation process [key pros_name] of
        pros_name, pros_number,
        pros_inflow, pros_outflow,
        pros_module, pros_notes : string;
end;
```

Figure 2—Preliminary relational database design for development dictionary

```
{Troll script for finding components of data flows and data stores}
if exists (data_flow [$0]) | exists (data_store [$0]) then
  begin
    if exists (data_flow [$0]) then
    begin
      $1 := 0; print data_flow [$0].flow_components;
    end else
    begin
      $1 := 1; print data_store [$0].store_components;
    end;
  end else
  begin
    $1 := -1; print 'No data flow or data store named ', $0;
  end;
```

Figure 3—Troll/USE script for action invoked by RAPID/USE

sages are associated with nodes, and actions may be associated with arcs. The message facility is screen-oriented, so that full cursor control is available along with output.

As with the dialogue portion, the prototype can be continuously modified, gradually providing the essential functions of the system. The features desired by users in the prototype affect the specification. In short, the prototype system is used to develop a more accurate specification. User experience with the prototype yields a specification that is a closer fit to the user's perceived requirements, so that less effort will be required for evolution of the system, thereby reducing the overall life cycle costs while increasing user satisfaction.

Turning to the USE development dictionary example, the preliminary relational database design to support the dictionary is shown in Figure 2. In Figure 1, in diagram E_IN_FS, observe that one of the paths from arc Name, reads itemname and invokes an action ('do 1'). Figure 3 shows the Troll/USE data manipulation language for performing that action, using the database structure of Figure 2.

RAPID/USE links all of the necessary action routines, including the invocation of Troll/USE scripts. Thus, one could write Troll/USE scripts for the other development dictionary actions and thereby create a working system.

IMPLEMENTATION IN PLAIN

The specification, of course, is used to design and implement a production version of the IIS, should the system created with RAPID/USE be insufficient. A production implementation frequently is necessary to provide a complete set of IIS functions, along with needed error handling, in a well-structured program. An important goal, though, is to make the interface of the production version identical to that previously developed so that the user will not have to learn a different system. While this implementation proceeds, however, the prototype system can be put to good use, both for productive work and for user training.

The methodology proceeds with architectural design, mapping the highest level transition diagram (main conversation) into the transaction model of structured design.[8] A program design language is used for detailed design of each module, associating an operation (action) in the transition diagram with a module in the detailed design. The preconditions and postconditions derived during the specification phase are similarly carried over into the modules.

The production programming language is PLAIN, a language derived from PASCAL to support both the concepts of systematic programming[9] and the needs of interactive information systems.[10] PLAIN provides excellent support for abstraction and modularity through an abstract data-type mechanism, parameter passing by input and output, and control over access to global and external data objects.

Most of the innovations in PLAIN support the needs of interactive information systems. PLAIN provides strings and relations as built-in data types, along with appropriate facilities for data definition and manipulation. In addition to string manipulation, strings may be compared to patterns and sets of patterns, with the ability to take action based on the result of pattern-matching and comparison operations. PLAIN provides a relational algebralike set of operations on relations, as well as the ability to do tuple processing and to assign the result of database operations to temporary structures (markings).[11,12] Finally, PLAIN provides a powerful exception-handling facility to enhance the reliability of interactive programs.

As a result, implementation of the specified IIS is straightforward in PLAIN, since the primitives of the specification method, including strings, patterns, relational databases, transactions, and pre- and postconditions, have corresponding primitives in PLAIN. Furthermore, the encoding of pre- and postconditions as assertions makes it easier to verify the correctness of the implemented system.

While one could implement the system in another programming language, the USE tools were designed to be used together, so that PLAIN provides the best possible language for transforming the specification into a running system. It can be seen that the string-handling and pattern-matching features support the construction of the user–program dialogue directly from the transition diagrams, and that the relational database design similarly can be programmed directly.

The portion of the development dictionary system shown in Figure 1 has been written in PLAIN and is shown in Figure 4. (Access to the relations is omitted, but the four relations defined in Figure 2 must be declared in an external

```
program usedd;
external

  {declare all relations shown in Figure 2 here to make them accessible
   in PLAIN program}

end external;

const prompt = '$';

var
  command : string;

  procedure main_menu;
  begin
      cursor.pos (21,0); cursor.lineclear;
      cursor.pos (22,0); cursor.lineclear; cursor.pos (12,0);
      write 'Please enter command number or first letter of command.\n';
      cursor.pos (14,0);
      write '   1: Add a dictionary entry\n';
      write '   2: Delete a dictionary entry\n';
      write '   3: Modify a dictionary entry\n';
      write '   4: Retrieve information from development dictionary\n';
      write '   5: Help\n'; write '    6: Quit';
      cursor.pos (23,0);
      write prompt;
  end main_menu;

  procedure retrieve_info;
  imports data_element, data_store, data_flow, process: modified;
  var command: string;
  begin
    loop <retrieve>
      cursor.screenclr; cursor.pos (9,14);
      write 'USE Development Dictionary Retrieval Options\n';
      write '\n';
      write 'Please enter the number of the desired retrieval type.\n';
      write '   1: List elements in a given flow or store.\n';
      write '   2: List flows which contain a given element or flow.\n';
      write '   3: List stores which contain a given element or flow.\n';
      write '   4: List processes which input or output a given element or flow\n';
      write '   5: Scan entries of a given type.\n';
      write '   6: Display undefined list.\n';
      cursor.pos (23,0); write prompt;
      read command;
      if command in ['1'..'6'] then
        case command of
          when '1': entry_in_flow_or_store;
          when '2': flows_which_contain;  {not shown}
          when '3': stores_which_contain; {not shown}
          when '4': process_input_output_entry; {not shown}
          when '5': scan;  {not shown}
          when '6': undefined_list  {not shown}
        end case;
        cursor.screenclr; cursor.pos (21,0);
        write 'Another command?\n';
        read command;
        if substring (command,1,1) = 'n' then exit <retrieve> end if;
      end if;
      cursor.screenclr; cursor.pos (3,0);
      if command in ['h','H','?'] then {provide help}
      else
        write 'Invalid option (', command, ')\n';
        write 'Press'; cursor.rv; write ' RETURN'; cursor.sv;
        write ' to continue.'; read command; {reads return}
      end if;
    repeat <retrieve>
  end retrieve_info;

  procedure entry_in_flow_or_store;
  imports data_flow, data_store: readonly;
  type entries = (none, flow, store);
  var entry_type : entries;
      entry : string;

  begin
    cursor.screenclr; cursor.pos (12,0);
    write 'Please enter flow or store name.\n'; write prompt;
    entry_type := none;
    read entry;
    if entry in ['h','H','?'] then {provide help} read entry; end if;
    if exists (data_flow [entry]) then
      entry_type := flow;
      write data_flow [entry].flow_components;
    end if;
    if exists (data_store [entry]) then
      entry_type := store;
      write data_store [entry].store_components;
    end if;
    case entry_type of
      none: write 'No data flow or data store named ', entry,'\n';
      flow, store:
          cursor.screenclr; cursor.pos (20,0);
          write 'Above is a list of all the elements which are\n';
          write 'contained in data_', entry_type,' ', entry,'\n';
          write 'Press '; cursor.rv; write 'RETURN'; cursor.sv;
          write 'to continue.'; read entry;
    end case;
  end entry_in_flow_or_store;

begin {usedd}
  cursor.screenclr; cursor.pos (5,0);
  write 'USE Development Dictionary\n';
  loop <select>
      main_menu;
      read command;
      command := substring(command,1,1); {get 1st character of input}
      case command of
        when '1', 'A', 'a': add_element;  {not shown}
        when '2', 'D', 'd': delete_element;  {not shown}
        when '3', 'M', 'm': modify_element;  {not shown}
        when '4', 'R', 'r': retrieve_info;
        when '5', 'h', 'H', '?' :
              {provide help}
              read command; {accepts RETURN}
        when '6', 'q', 'Q': exit <select>
        when others :
              cursor.pos (21,0); cursor.rv;
              write 'Unrecognized command (',command,')';
              write 'Please try again.\n'; cursor.sv;
              write 'Press ', cursor.rv; write 'RETURN'; cursor.sv;
              write ' to continue.\n'
              read command;  {accepts RETURN}
      end case;

    cursor.screenclr; cursor.pos (21,0);
    write 'Another command?';
    read command;
    if substring (command,1,1) = 'n' then exit <select> end if;

  repeat <select>;

end usedd.
```

Figure 4—PLAIN code for portion of USE development dictionary

statement.) The resemblance between the two versions is apparent.

Indeed, this program structure is characteristic of many interactive information systems written in PLAIN. The main program consists of a loop in which an input string is read and compared to a set of patterns, causing a multiway dispatch to the appropriate procedure for the input. The procedure corresponds to a "structured operation" or transaction. One possible input terminates the program, causing exit from the loop. The declarations in the main program include an external section, in which all relations of the supporting database are named and brought into the environment of the program.

CONCLUSION

The USE methodology provides a series of steps to support the process of creating an IIS, from its original conception through implementation, verification, and evolution. The methodology is supported by a unified support environment, including RAPID/USE, Troll/USE, and PLAIN. In addition, other tools exist to assist with project management, including TBE, a relation editing and browsing tool, and the Integrated Development Environment, a version control and configuration management tool that guides the developer in the use of the other tools. All of these tools have been designed and developed to be used in the UNIX environment, taking advantage of many of the underlying UNIX tools. Most of the USE tools are available for a handling charge through the UCSF User Software Engineering distribution. (Commercial versions and support for the USE are provided by Interactive Development Environments, Inc., of San Francisco.) Future work will make these tools available on personal development systems, leading to a User Software Engineering machine.

REFERENCES

1. Codd, E. F. "A Relational Model of Data for Large Shared Data Banks." *Communications of the ACM,* 13 (1970), pp. 377–387.
2. Shaw, M. (ed.). *ALPHARD: Form and Content.* New York: Springer Verlag, 1981.
3. Leveson, N. G., A. I. Wasserman, and D. M. Berry. "BASIS: a Behavioral Approach to the Specification of Information Systems." *Information Systems,* 8 (1983), pp. 15–23.
4. Conway, M. E. "Design of a Separable Transition—Diagram Compiler," *Communications of the ACM,* 6 (1963), pp. 396–408.
5. Wasserman, A. I., and S. K. Stinson. "A Specification Method for Interactive Information Systems." *Proceedings of the IEEE Computer Society Conference on Specification of Reliable Software,* Cambridge, Mass., 1979, pp. 68–79.
6. Kersten, M. L., and A. I. Wasserman. "The Architecture of the PLAIN Data Base Handler." *Software—Practice and Experience,* 11 (1981), p. 175–186.
7. Wasserman, A. I., and D. T. Shewmake. "Rapid Prototyping of Interactive Information Systems." *ACM Software Engineering Notes,* 7 (1982), 5.
8. Yourdon, E., and L. L. Constantine. *Structured Design.* Englewood Cliffs, N.J.: Prentice-Hall, 1979.
9. Wasserman, A. I. "The Design of PLAIN—Support for Systematic Programming," *AFIPS, Proceedings of the National Computer Conference,* (Vol. 49), 1980, pp. 731–740.
10. Wasserman, A. I., R. P. van de Riet, and M. L. Kersten. "PLAIN: An Algorithmic Language for Interactive Information Systems," In J.W. deBakker and J. C. van Vliet (eds.), *Algorithmic Languages.* Amsterdam: North-Holland, 1981, pp. 29–47.
11. Wasserman, A. I. "The Data Management Facilities of PLAIN." *Proceedings of the ACM 1979 SIGMOD Conference,* (May, 1979). New York: ACM, 1979, pp. 60–70.
12. van de Riet, R. P., A. I. Wasserman, M. L. Kersten, and W. de Jonge. "High-Level Programming Features for Improving the Efficiency of a Relational Database System." *Transactions on Database Systems,* 6 (1981), pp. 464–485.

Software management issues for new system designs

by ROBERT E. LOESH
Jet Propulsion Laboratory
Pasadena, California
and
DONALD J. REIFER
Reifer Consultants, Inc.
Torrance, California
and
STEVEN M. JACOBS
TRW Defense Systems Group
Redondo Beach, California

ABSTRACT

The management of software development for single and dual processor system designs is making progress towards becoming a mature discipline. A good part of the progress can be attributed to the development and use of standard system and software engineering methods and design principles.

However, new computer system designs (networking, distributed systems, embedded systems, multi- and coprocessors, fault tolerant systems, etc.) will create new challenges for managers of software development. The reason for this effect on management is that some of the system and software engineering methods and design principles developed for single and dual processor system designs are not valid for these newer designs.

Some of the issues that software development project managers will need to cope with are:

1. Life cycle model adjustments
2. Rapid prototyping activities
3. Different hardware and software phasing
4. Increased tool development
5. New trade-offs and hybrid developments of off-the-shelf software and newly developed software
6. Development of concurrent design principles
7. New software design principles to support fault tolerance and the use of new memory technologies

The above items are just now being recognized as problems, and solutions for them either do not exist, or are not widely known.

These problems create a series of new challenges that managers must deal with for software development based on the new architectures and requirements. The purposes of this paper are to discuss these issues and to identify some solutions that can serve in the interim as the technology changes to meet these new challenges.

INTRODUCTION

For the past 30 years, there has been one system design approach used to develop computer-based systems; that is, single or dual processors based on a sequential machine, which had limited main memory and similar instruction sets. Processor technology evolved during this time to become faster, bigger, and cheaper. However, there have not been as many improvements to software design and engineering as there have been for hardware design and engineering. Over the past decade, software engineering methods and design principles have been developed that are suitable for the single–dual processor system design approach. As applications became more demanding, single–dual processor system design and special-purpose hardware with only minimal software support were used. The management of software development for single and dual processor system designs has become a mature discipline. A good part of the progress is due to the development and use of standard system and software engineering methods and design principles, as is described in References 1–6. Even so, software engineering project management is far from being currently recognized as a "discipline,"[7] and is looked upon more as art than science.

Shared-resource designs were accomplished through multiuser interfacing and using hardware front-end and rear-end multiplexers and demultiplexers. The same engineering design that was appropriate for multilevel, priority handling of interrupts was used almost exclusively. There has been little or no effect on development methods or design principles. If an application was too large or the time required for processing too long, designers used some variant of the same engineering methods and design principles that were used in the early days of computing. These methods and principles extrapolated concepts taken from automata theory, which preserved the notion of a sequential, centralized database machine.

Whenever an application did not execute as efficiently as desired on a given class of processor, designers would select a very special high frequency function and would then build a special hardware device to perform that function, using, for instance, convolvers, frame synchronization detectors, and character converters. The special-purpose function was removed from software, and mechanized in hardware such as array processors.

Embedded systems were generally built around miniclass, fully integrated computers that interfaced across point-to-point serial communications, or auxiliary storage devices such as tape, removable disk, or in some cases, a disk and drum, through shared controllers. Existing engineering methods and design principles were used with no changes because they could cope with limited distribution of function.

In the not-too-distant past, failure protection and recovery management were handled in similar ways. Fault tolerance was either designed into the hardware at the integrated circuit level, dealt with by checkpointing, or handled by the use of mirror image backup.

Our evolving engineering methods and design principles were applicable. Based on a build-up of experience using these engineering methods and design principles, management of single–dual processor system design developments is becoming more successful. However, in the past five years, progress in the hardware technologies has allowed the development of applications that previously were not technically feasible or were not acceptable from a cost-effectiveness standpoint. Unfortunately, the hardware capabilities and system designs available are radically different from the single–dual processor design that represents today's state of the art. Following are some new hardware system designs and the attributes they have that affect new software designs:

1. Microprocessor-based embedded systems
2. Multiple processor resource sharing systems
3. Distributed data processing (DDP) systems
4. Coprocessor designs
5. Fault-tolerant systems
6. System architectures
7. New memory and processor designs (e.g., EPROM)
8. VLSI or VHSIC systems

These new design approaches require considerable software support and new software designs. The development of the software for these systems is not supported well by the current software engineering methods and design principles, which exist for single–dual processor system designs. In some cases, the software engineering methods and design principles are not suitable and must be modified. In others, there are voids that require new methods to be developed, understood, and used before a standard evolves.

The result of not having appropriate engineering methods or design principles will be missed schedules, poor performance, unachieved capabilities, cost overruns, and in some cases, failure to deliver a responsive system. These deficiencies will manifest as a software design that does not work, (is either poorly mapped onto the hardware or fails to use available capability) or a hardware and software design integration that cannot be tested or modified easily.

Until the proper engineering approach is known and well understood (adopted as a standard), an interim solution is needed. If we are aware of the problems from initiation of these developments, they can effectively be alleviated or averted. The interim solution recommended combines those approaches that limit the application of such new designs used, emphasize some special advanced, front-end engineering work to make up for the engineering standards deficiencies, and manage projects with special attention.

EXISTING STATE OF AFFAIRS

Software project management is demonstrating that many developments can be accomplished successfully. Some of the criteria for determining a successful software project are being on schedule and within budget, providing agreed-upon and reliable capability, and that the software fulfills its requirements and works. Although a long way from perfect, the following factors are contributing to increased successes in software development:[9]

1. Projects are estimated and supported more realistically
2. Project management capabilities and techniques are improving and becoming more standard
3. Software engineering standards are evolving, and being more widely accepted and employed

The first two of these items seem to be continuously improving, and are generally unrelated to the system design issues. They are nonetheless affected by the technical adequacy, maturity, and wide use of proven system and software engineering standards.

For single–dual processor designs, a software development life cycle (SDLC) has been defined that incorporates phases and delineated products that support good software management practices. Additionally, standard software engineering methods and design principles are evolving that can be applied to the various SDLC phases. These standards contribute to the development of a good product, and establish an ability for software project managers to estimate and control cost, resources, and time. As these engineering standards receive wider use, they will continue to improve, as well as enhance management's ability to qualify and calibrate their effects. By virtue of a continued and increased use, and an increase in resultant knowledge of effectiveness and cost, software management methodology will improve continually.

Following are some of the software engineering methods and design principles that are becoming industry standards that contribute to improved software project management capability:

1. Problem analysis and requirements generation methodologies
   a. Operational concepts formulation, system interface definition
   b. Man–machine interface definition and prototyping
   c. Data flow diagrams[10]
   d. Structured analysis[11]
2. Requirements generation tools
   a. SREM,[12] PSL/PSA,[13] CADSAT, MEDL-R, DARTS
3. Program design methods and tools
   a. Structured design,[14,15] HIPO charts,[16] Jackson methodology[17]
   b. PDL,[18] SDDL,[19] MEDL-D, USE.IT, DBMS
4. Program construction methods and tools
   a. Structured code, data structure definition tools (COMPOOLS)
   b. Languages, word processors, SPF,[20] library functions, checkers
5. Program testing methods and tools[21]
   a. White-box testing, black-box testing, module signature
   b. Test coverage analyzers, automatic test program
6. Resource management awareness and control
7. Performance tuning as part of final stages of testing

All of the above contribute to an increased predictability of the technical and software management task, and therefore to increased success.

There is still need for improvement. Additional methods and design principles must be developed to cope with our entry into the age of distributed computer systems. However, there exists a good technology base from which to work, and considerable attention and effort is being directed to its improvement and use. Clearly, over the next three to five years, the situation will continue to improve. Both engineering methods and design principles, and the software project management discipline based on them, will result in a successful, highly consistent level of software development for single–dual processor designs.

SOFTWARE ENGINEERING STATUS FOR NEW DESIGNS

The prognosis for new system designs, however, is not in the same healthy state. Early experience with distributed systems indicates that the management of software designs is facing considerable difficulty. It is plagued with, for example, poor system performance, unreliable system operations, high cost overruns, missed schedule commitments, and disappointing capability. While the total problem does not lie with the software engineering and associated management technology base, a significant part is due to the following issues:

- Some of the existing methods and design principles do not apply or do not work
- There are real voids where no methods or design principles exist

Following are a number of areas that have significant deficiencies:

1. Existing engineering principles, methods, and tools for concurrent technology are only partially applicable
2. Engineering methodologies are deficient
3. Requirements tools are deficient
4. Program design methods and tools are deficient
5. Program construction methods and tools lag but will mature in the next five years
6. Testing methods and tools are deficient
7. Performance tuning still must be learned
8. Resource management will require additional development of methods and tools

9. System architecture tools are deficient (1) for specifying system configurations for applications, (2) for performing hardware-software tradeoffs, and (3) for comparing candidate system architectures.

Finding solutions to the above deficiencies, for most software development, tends to rely on trial and error. Attempts to use methods and best-guess designs proliferate. Some consequences of this approach to engineering are increased costs, wasted time (delayed schedules), poor performance, and a lack of reliability. In some cases the deficiencies have resulted in total project failure, that is, in nonexecutable systems; of course, the software project manager is held accountable for this.

The situation will improve as problem areas are defined and publicized. Energy and funding will be devoted to finding solutions. Additionally, the random approaches will crystalize methodologies and design techniques that work successfully. From these principles will emerge a new generation of defined, tried and proven, publicized, and readily usable engineering tools and standards.

It has taken nearly 30 years to achieve a significant threshold of software engineering standards applicable to single–dual processor system design. The difficulty of the engineering problem for new system designs is mitigated by new methods using prototyping, simulation, requirements tools, etc. Yet there is a greater focus of interest by many organizations willing to support the research of viable solutions. Industrial interest, communication, and concern about system and software engineering have increased considerably.

The result should be that we will make rapid progress in developing and identifying appropriate engineering standards within these areas in the next seven to ten years. By 1990, there should exist a reasonably capable system for engineering such new designs, with a high probability for success in the management of such software developments.

WHAT TO DO NOW

It is clear that implementation of these new system designs is an urgent matter. Managers of current systems do not have the luxury of waiting a decade to find solutions. Also, if the engineering methods and design principles derived by trial and error, or discovered through research, are not used for actual software developments, they cannot be qualified or accepted as standards. Without application, newly developed methods and design principles will never fully emerge. Therefore, interim solutions are needed now.

Experimentation and published results about what works and what does not are required. There currently exists a set of management and engineering techniques that can be employed to help prevent software development failures and contribute to the emergence of new engineering standards. The following suggestions, based on the authors' experiences, may prevent major problems in software developments resulting from these new system designs:

1. Unless an argument is good, stay with the current design technology (single–dual processor system designs)
2. Go to only a part of new system designs; do not try too much at once
3. Allow for more budget and schedule
4. Do more prototyping
5. Do more in-house research and tool development
6. Watch others
7. Document your experiences
8. As the engineering methods and design principles emerge and become standard, incorporate them

The bottom line is use caution and preserve resources. The key is to control the risk. If indeed we move into these new system designs carefully and meet our professional responsibilities to share our methods, design principles, experiences, and results (both good and bad), we can take advantage of the new technology and still not suffer major setbacks in development and system execution and support. The management of software development for such new system designs can be applied successfully, both during the interim while standards are being developed, and of course after such standards exist.

ACKNOWLEDGEMENT

The authors wish to acknowledge the following people for their review of and contributions to this paper: Herman A. Regusters, Senior Consultant, Ground Data Systems Group, Jet Propulsion Laboratory, as well as William B. Allendoerfer, Imed Bitar, William B. Howard, Odette Knedr, L. David Lutton, Steven P. Munt, and Maria H. Penedo of TRW.

REFERENCES

1. Loesh, R. E. *Software Project Management.* New York: Wadsworth, 1983.
2. Royce, W. W. "Managing the Development of Large Software Systems: Concepts and Techniques." *TRW Software Series* Publication No. TRW-JS-70-01, August 1970.
3. Distaso, J. R. "Software Management—A Survey of the Practice in 1980." *TRW Software Series* No. TRW-SS-80-10, September 1980.
4. Tausworthe, R. *Standardized Development of Computer Software,* Part I, Methods, Jet Propulsion Laboratory Publication #SP 43-29, July 1976.
5. Tausworthe, R. *Standardized Development of Computer Software,* Part II, Methods, Jet Propulsion Laboratory Publication #SP 43-29, August 1978.
6. Jensen, R., and C. Tonies. *Software Engineering,* Englewood Cliffs, N.J.: Prentice-Hall, 1979.
7. Thayer, R. H., A. B. Pyster, and R. C. Ubod. "Major Issues in Software Engineering Project Management." *IEEE Transactions on Software Engineering,* SE-7 (1981), pp. 333–342.
8. Reifer, D. J. *Tutorial: Software Management,* IEEE Computer Society Catalog No. EHO 146-1, 1979.
9. Jacobs, S. M. "Software Management for the 80s." Panel Session, 1983 National Computer Conference, Anaheim, Calif., May 1983.
10. De Marco, T. *Structured Analysis and System Specification.* New York: Yourdon, 1979.
11. Ross, D. T., and K. E. Scherman, Jr. "Structured Analysis for Requirements Definition." *IEEE Transactions on Software Engineering,* SE-3 (1977), pp. 2–15.
12. Alford, M. W. "Requirements Engineering Methodology for Real-Time Processing Requirements." *IEEE Transactions on Software Engineering,* SE-3 (1977), pp. 34–40.
13. Teichrow, D., and E. A. Hershey III. "PSL/PSA: A Computer-Aided Technique for Structured Documentation and Analysis of Information Processing Systems." *IEEE Transactions on Software Engineering,* SE-3 (1977), 34–40.

14. Yourdon, E., and L. Constantine. *Structured Design.* Englewood Cliffs, N.J.: Prentice-Hall, 1979.
15. Yourdon, E. *Managing the Structured Techniques.* New York: Yourdon, 1979.
16. HIPO (Hierarchial Input Process Output). Design Aid and Documentation Technique, GX20-1851. White Plains, N.Y.; IBM, 1974.
17. Jackson, M. A. *Principles of Program Design,* New York: Academic Press, 1979.
18. Caine, S. H., and E. K. Gordon. "PDL: A Tool for Software Design."*AFIPS, Proceedings of the National Computer Conference* (Vol. 00), 1975, pp. 271–276.
19. Kleine, H. *Software Design and Documentation Language,* Jet Propulsion Laboratory Publication #77-24, July 1977.
20. SPF (Structured Programming Facility). White Plains, N.Y.: IBM, 1978.
21. Myers, G. *The Art of Software Testing,* New York: John Wiley and Sons, 1979.

Results of modern software engineering principles applied to small and large projects

by PETER R. H. McCONNELL and WOLFGANG B. STRIGEL
MacDonald, Dettwiler, and Associates
Richmond, British Columbia, Canada

ABSTRACT

This paper discusses the software development environment, tools, techniques, and methodology as applied in two mediums to large real-time software projects. Both quantitative and qualitative measures of success obtained in these projects are discussed. The quantitative measures are statistics representing the size of produced code, the manpower over the project life cycle, and other data relevant to software engineering management. The qualitative evaluation is more concerned with results obtained from walkthroughs and various aspects of the applied methodology. Results are compared with those reported in the literature. Recommendations and suggestions for further improvements are presented.

INTRODUCTION

The literature abounds with details of the increasing demand for software and the limited increases in productivity that have been obtained.[1,5,6] Current predictions hold little hope for major breakthroughs in the future. The results of a recent report by Musa et. al[5] indicate that data processing expenditure has doubled every five years, but with only minimal increases in programmer productivity. These authors' figures indicate that software productivity doubles every 25 years. It is through the better understanding of the software development process and the application of new tools and techniques to this process that industry will improve this productivity factor and meet the increasing demand for software in the future.

The results of a recent survey[2] indicate that a large number of companies are familiar with the modern software techniques but have not applied them in their work environment for various reasons. This same survey indicates that a large number of companies had moderate to excellent results with some of the techniques. One of the problems facing many companies that wish to adopt these techniques to improve their software quality and productivity is deciding which techniques to adopt. The next problem is finding the results of applications of these various techniques in a commercial environment as opposed to a university or an experimental environment. This paper reports on the experiences in applying some of the modern tools and techniques to two medium-sized software development projects in a commercial environment. The tools and techniques which were applied have been reported in the literature[7] and are easily transportable to other environments.

The two projects differed substantially in size, duration, operating environment, and several other ways. What was important, however, was that they shared some of the same tools, techniques, and features of the development environment. Table I summarizes the important characteristics of the two projects.

TABLE I—Characteristics of Projects A and B

Characteristic	Project A	Project B
Effort (programmer-months)	274	37
Duration (months)	36	9
Maximum staff loading	17	7
Principal language	PASCAL	PASCAL
Lines of source code, made up of:[a]	283,000	67,000
Executable source	49%	31%
Header	32%	53%
Commented PDL	N/A	11%
Comments	19%	5%

[a]The percentages for Project B relate only to the PASCAL and PL/M components.

PROJECT DESCRIPTIONS AND RESULTS

In this section the two projects are discussed in some detail. Subjects such as productivity, languages used, and methodologies applied are highlighted.

Project A

Project A is a real-time data acquisition system for the reception and processing of meteorological satellite imagery. The system is intended as a tool for weather observation and forecasting. It provides the capability to receive, process, and store meteorological data transmitted by geostationary as well as orbiting satellites. A VAX 11/750 performed most of the operator dialogue and all image-processing and display functions. The VAX computer was linked via dual ported disks to a multi-microprocessor system, based on Intel 8086 CPUs, which was designed and built by MacDonald, Dettwiler, and Associates (MDA). The software consisted of an MDA operating system and software for real-time image reception and storage.

First, the system as a whole is broken down into two subsystems, one hosted on the VAX, the other consisting of the multi-microprocessor system. The second step was software oriented and defined how the subsystems were to be implemented in software components. The resulting 100 components are almost evenly distributed between the two subsystems. A software component was sized so that it could be handled by one intermediate-level software engineer, the *key designer*. Key designers defined components during the design phase and supervised up to three junior programmers during the coding phase. The largest component had 3,700 lines of code, the smallest only 50. In general, however, an average of 1,280 lines was observed as the typical component size.

During the detailed design phase, each component was subdivided into about 20 modules. Each module was defined as one self-contained subroutine with one entry and one exit point. The average module contained 64 executable instructions.

Using strict coding standards, we were able to compile all code for the microprocessors on the corporate VAX computing facilities by using standard DEC compilers. After module testing the code was recompiled with a cross-compiler and loaded into microprocessors. Software quality assurance was implemented by adapting IEEE Software Quality Assurance

Standard 730. Integration was done bottom-up. This incremental integration necessitated some higher level test drivers, which were developed and maintained by the integration team. During the coding phase a total of 128,000 statements were produced. Not all of the 128,000 source lines were new code. Some modules were ported from a predecessor system. Although reusable, this code still had to be modified and adapted to the new system. Therefore one-half of the ported code is counted to determine the code production rate below. Roughly a quarter of the VAX code could be reused on the microprocessors, since it covered identical functions. Again, some modifications were necessary to use different system calls, etc., and approximately one-half of the original effort can be related to this porting effort. As a result, the total new lines of executable code are now reduced to 98,470 lines. It will be shown later that the total effort of technical staff through all phases of the life cycle amounted to 5,479 person-days. This yields a software productivity of 18 lines per person-day. Note that for both subsystems more than half of the total source lines are in the form of comments and headers. The system was integrated from the bottom up. The key designer and his programmers were responsible for compiling and testing for error-free module interfaces. Once a component was operational in an isolated and simulated environment, it was handed over to the integration team. At this point a component was integrated into a test bed along with the previously integrated components. Test drivers were built by the integration team to exercise the lower level components. The next step was covered by the system test, during which compliance with the high-level design document was verified. At this level the functionality of the system and the interaction of the two subsystems was under scrutiny. The final product, a functional system, underwent the customer acceptance test to prove contractual compliance.

The distribution of total effort for Project A is shown in Figure 1. The area under the curve amounts to 5,479 person-days. Only the effort of technical personnel is included in the graph. It is not possible to indicate a strict separation between the requirement specification phase and the subsequent high-level design. The line was drawn at the point at which the customer had accepted the specification document. The peak in September 1981 coincides with the first major system design review. A significant increase in staff can be noted at the beginning of detailed design. This is because the first small components were ready for coding and junior staff were added to the team for the actual coding. The system test phase includes the customer-witnessed acceptance test, which ends with customer acceptance. The installation phase was not included in this presentation, since it does not contribute to the development effort.

During all life cycle phases each functional entity went through a thorough review process. Software components as defined during high level design formed the basic entities for review sessions. Aside from the widely published benefits of

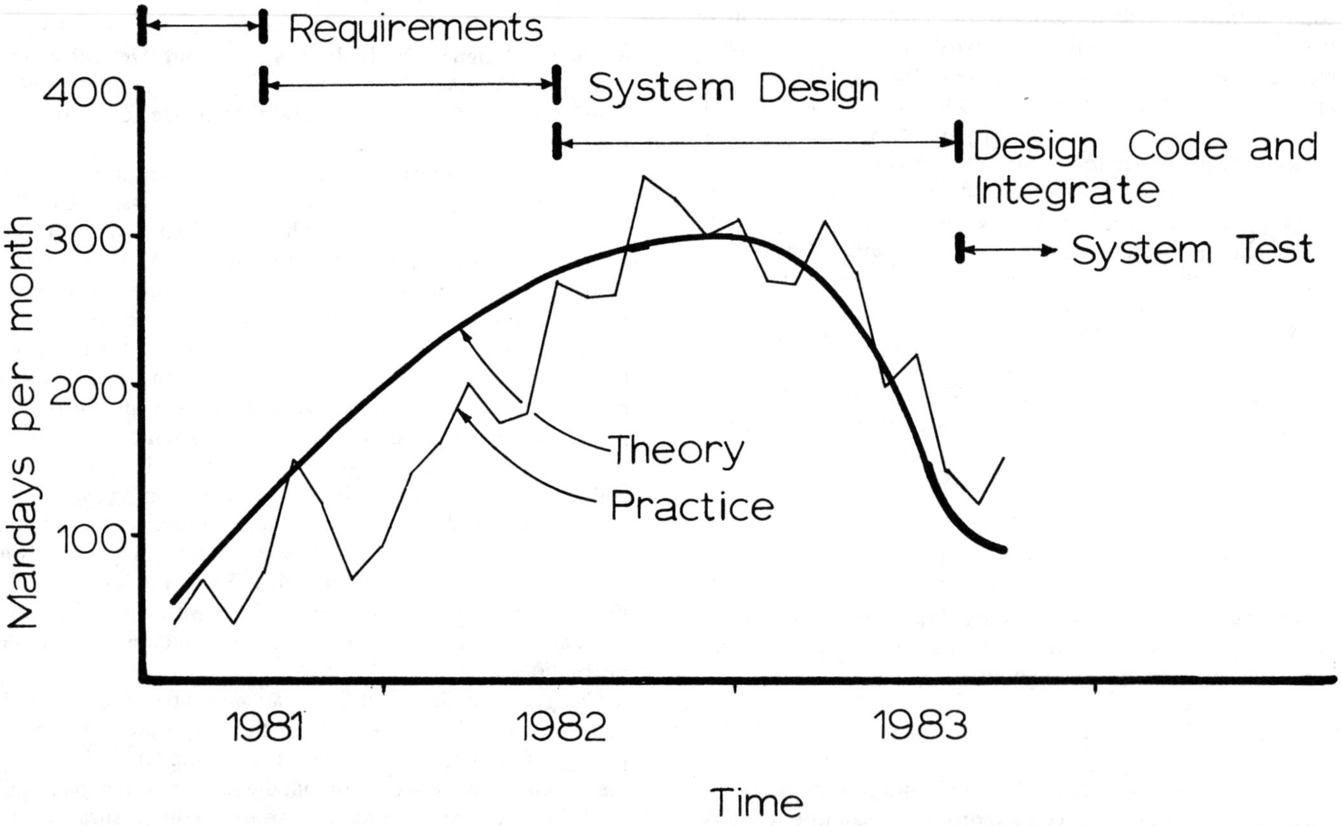

Figure 1—Effort curve for Project A

the review process, each team member gained and maintained a high level of confidence in the whole development process as well as in the expected quality of the resulting system. During the coding phase the walkthroughs assured strict adherence to our quality assurance standards.

The software integration team started up shortly after the beginning of the detailed design phase. Initially it consisted of an integration leader, an integrator, and the librarian. Key designers submitted software components to the integration team as soon as they had completed the module level testing. The integrator then ran the component test plan, which exercised the new component in the environment of previously submitted components. If this test was successful, the key designer was discharged of any further responsibility for the components, and the integration team maintained the component from then on. As a result of this approach, the key designer was freed to concentrate on another component and was not further disturbed with problems that might show up in previously submitted components. On the other hand, the problem-solving effort was not always the most efficient, since the problem solver had to familiarize himself with a component before efficiently attacking a problem.

The data gathered throughout the project invites the application of some of the existing mathematical models in order to determine the extent to which practical experience meets theoretical expectations. In Figure 1 the Second Level Build-up curve, as used in the Aron model,[4] is shown with the data of Project A.

In attempts to improve software productivity, one recurring question is the optimal software component size. A plot of productivity—non-comment source lines per person-day (NCSL/PD)—versus NCSL per component indicated a maximum performance for components of 1,000 to 2,000 source lines. This result was consistent for both the microcomputer-based real-time software and the more application-oriented VAX software. In this calculation the ratio of NCSL/PD did not include the problem-solving effort for a given component, since this effort was booked against the integration team. With an average of 1,280 source instructions per component, Project A has taken full advantage of the optimal component size.

During the implementation and system test phase, close to 1,000 software problem reports (PRs) were filed. The PR reporting mechanism was automated and maintained by the integration team. Once a PR was filed, the integration leader evaluated its importance and assigned it to a problem solver. The PR solver updated the PR to describe the solution approach and the changes applied to the component. This report was again verified by the integration leader, and the integration team took care of regression testing and reintegration of the component. Figure 2 shows the incidence of PRs during the implementation and testing phases. It also shows the time

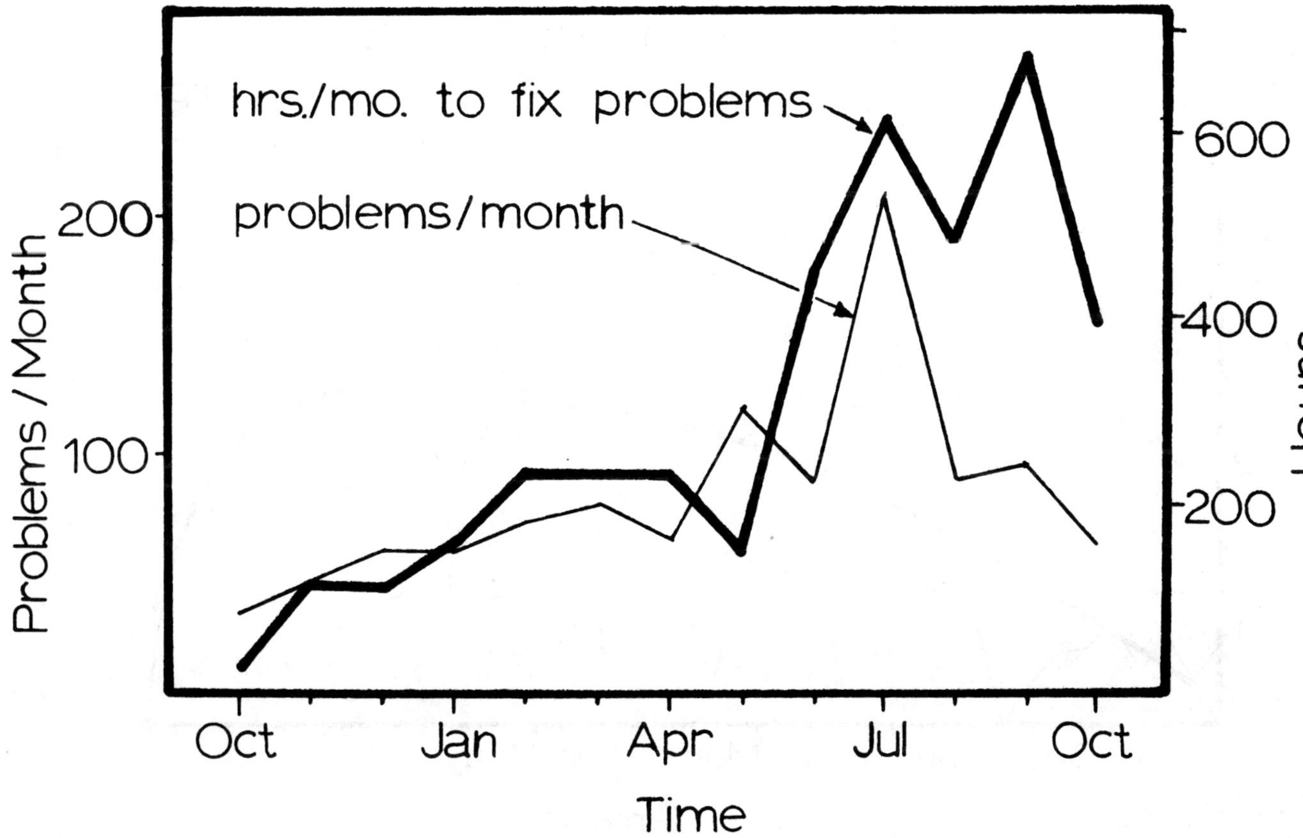

Figure 2—Number of problems found per month and the time to fix them

spent in solving the problems. It can be seen that during the earlier months problems were quite easy to solve, whereas toward the end of the reported period the time to solve a PR increased significantly. This confirms the well-known principle that the later a software problem is discovered, the greater the cost to repair the problem. The problems reported in the beginning were mostly trivial. They were easy to analyze and took an average of only a few hours each to be fixed. Most of those problems were categorized as being related to implementation. As soon as system test started in July 1983, the amount of reported PRs increased remarkably. At about the same time the complexity of problems increased significantly. A high proportion of those PRs was related to design faults, which meant that the detailed design documentation also required some updates.

Project B

The second project consisted of real-time software to control an airborne synthetic-aperture radar system. This software was required to provide all operator interface to the radar system, as well as to respond to and service several different hardware-generated interrupts. The particular system being discussed was a first-time development effort with concurrent hardware and software development. The complete system was developed over a period of two years and the software over a period of nine months.

One of the problems with this type of environment is that the development team has only limited access to the hardware for the software development, and it cannot always be ensured that the hardware is fully operational. In this case this problem required that all of the software be developed on multiuser development facility and ported to the target system, providing maximum system access for the development team.

Many of the software development techniques used on this project had been applied successfully on projects operating in a different environment, and several new techniques were applied.

The actual implementation plan for the entire project is shown in Figure 3. This plan was divided into four distinct activities, which could be associated with various software staff. These were as follows:

1. Requirements analysis and system specification, which were carried out by the senior software engineer with assistance from intermediate software staff.
2. Software system design, which was carried out by the senior software engineer with assistance from an intermediate software engineer.
3. Unit detailed design, code, and test, which were carried

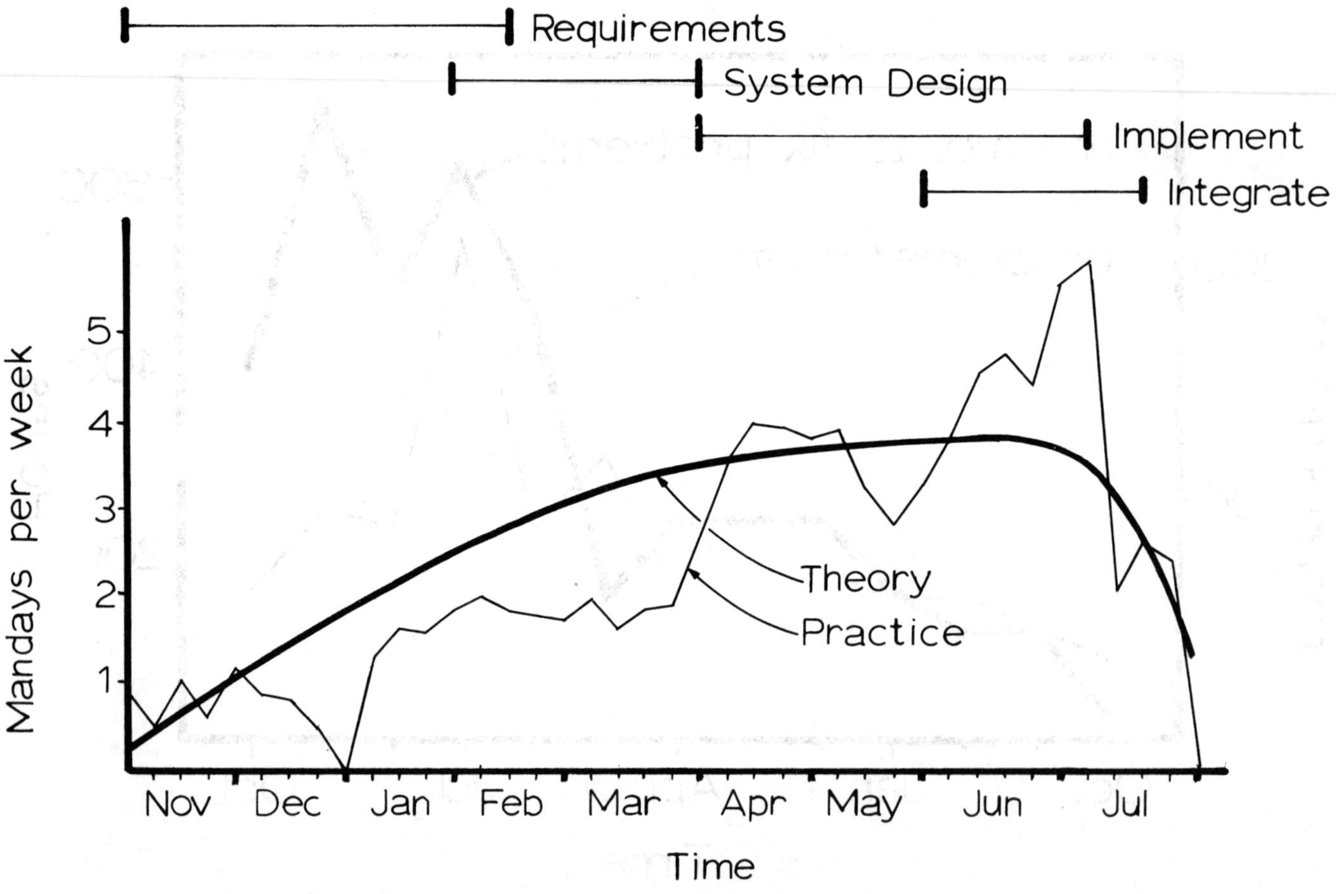

Figure 3—Effort curve for Project B

out by a number of junior and intermediate software engineers.

4. System integration, which was carried out by an intermediate software engineer.

Tools applied at the various steps consisted mainly of methodologies and techniques that have appeared in the literature. A survey was done prior to the start of the work to identify tools that could be best applied to the various phases of the development life cycles. (The term *tools* is used here because these methodologies and techniques serve to aid the software engineering process and make the overall effort more productive.)

The software development life cycle of this project is characteristic of most small- to medium-sized software projects that use modern software development methodologies. This type of project has been referred to by Aron[4] as "First Level." What distinguishes this from a second- or higher-level project, which is typically a larger size project with a labor expenditure curve described by the Rayleigh-Norden curve, is the amount of effort and duration required for the project. The results for this project are compared in Figure 3 with the labor expenditure curve for a second-level project. This curve shows good qualitative agreement with the curve presented by Aron[4] for a second-level project buildup. The shape of this curve results from the software development life cycle adopted and the tools applied at these various steps. These steps were requirements analysis and system specification, system detailed design, system design review, unit detailed design, unit detailed design review, unit code, unit test, unit code and test review, system integration, system test, and system delivery.

The extensive reviews, which required about 10% of the overall effort, ensured that reasonable errors could be removed early in the development of the software. There is extensive information in the literature to support the fact that it is much costlier to remove errors discovered late in the development cycle.[3]

During the initial phases of the project there was some overlap in the requirements analysis and system design phases. The reason for this was that the use of the Petri nets in describing the operator interaction with the system caused us to consider a different approach, which accomplished the same operational goals but resulted in considerable simplification of a major software component. The system design was then completed by means of SADT-like activity diagrams and Petri nets. Following the system design phase, an extensive implementation phase was begun. In this phase each individual software engineer was responsible for the detailed design, coding, and testing of his assigned component. This component consisted of an average of 379 lines of executable source code and 840 lines of header, PDL (program design language), and comments. These components were further broken down into procedures or modules, which averaged about 50 lines of executable code each.

As part of the detailed design process the component designer was expected to perform the design process on the development VAX and deliver the design material in machine-readable form for the design review process. This material consisted of component headers and a PDL that described the design. Each module header in the component provided information on all module inputs, all module outputs, an example of the module usage, an English language description of the procedure, a revision history for that procedure, and a list of all required procedures and included files external to that component. Following the procedure header was the PDL, or pseudocode, for that procedure. This PDL served the purpose of providing a structured-English description of how the procedure processed the inputs and generated the outputs. This material was reviewed during the detailed design review process to examine the headers and the PDL for adherence to the project standards and to check that the module interface and the PDL were correctly specified. The tool used in creating and judging the detailed design was the Myers composite/structured design.[1]

Upon acceptance of the design, the component designer was responsible for implementing that component in the specified language. Most of the components were implemented in PASCAL or PL/M with some of the code being done in assembler. In the case of PASCAL, it was possible to use a subset of the VAX PASCAL that was compatible with the cross-compiler for the target computer. In this way the software engineer could create code and test it on the company development machine. In the case of the PL/M and assembly code components, testing had to be done on the target system. The use of the multiuser development computer allowed the software engineer to use the tools available on that system, such as source code control and a symbolic debugger. The tools available for the target hardware were very limited, basically consisting of a monitor/debugger and task image transfer utility. When it was desired to test a component or subset of the final system, the executable image was created on the VAX and transferred via a serial link to RAM memory in the target system for testing.

Upon completion of the coding and unit testing, the component was submitted for the code and test review. The items of interest here were the adherence to the project standards, a one-to-one correspondence between the PDL and the code, and any weaknesses in the coding.

At the completion of the unit design, code, and test, the component was submitted to the integration directory, where it was available to the integration engineer. This person was responsible for incorporating the components into the total system. In terms of integration, a crude skeleton system was created early in the development, and all missing components were implemented as *stubs*. As the finished components became available, they replaced these stubs and were tested as a functioning part of the entire system. This process continued until a complete system was available for systems testing according to an internal acceptance test. The purpose of this test was to expose the system to a rigorous set of tests which would verify the correct functioning of the software. Any problems that were encountered were corrected and the tests performed again.

Throughout the software development process, quantitative measures were obtained of the effort expended in each of the life cycle steps. These results showed that coding of the software occupies a rather small portion (20%) of the total effort required to develop the final system product. About

42% of the actual effort expended was dedicated to requirements specification, system design, analysis, and detailed design.

Over the duration of the project, about 30,000 lines of executable code and 37,000 lines of nonexecutable code were developed. The required effort was 744 person-days, providing an average productivity figure of 40 non-comment source lines (NCSL) per programmer-day. About 60% of this consisted of PASCAL and PL/M; the remaining 40% was done in assembly language. An interesting number obtained during the implementation phase of the project was the number of terminal connect hours per programmer day. This is the average number of hours per day that a programmer is signed on to a terminal. These results indicated an average of three hours per day at the start of the detailed design and an average of seven hours per day at the peak of the integration. It is readily apparent that a software engineer makes significant use of the computer system available, especially in the later stages of the project, when intensive integration and testing efforts are under way. This fact lends support to the belief that a programmer's work station forms an important part of the software development environment.

CONCLUSIONS

Project A was considered a successful project. The results obtained confirm most commonly found theories on software development. Perhaps one of the weakest points in Project A was the lack of automated tools. For each of the life cycle phases more design and implementation tools should be made available. Enforcing standards on software engineering methodology is extremely difficult without computerized assistance. The few tools available in Project A were mainly geared to integration mechanisms and configuration control. This proved to be highly beneficial, even though only a minimal amount of time was spent to develop those tools specifically for Project A.

The area of problem solving still seems to leave room for improvement. If the problem solvers are not the original developers, high demands are put upon them to familiarize themselves with each new component. Our experiment in incremental integration seems to have been at least as successful as the top-down approach for integration. Low-level modules were the ones exercised for the longest period during integration. This is highly desirable, since an error in low-level routines is not only harder to find at later stages of the project but also has a more detrimental effect on system uptime and stability.

The basic conclusions derived from Project B are that even simple modern software engineering techniques can be successfully applied to a project and can offer positive benefits. This has been evidenced by the reasonably high productivity figure obtained—40 NCSL/PD—compared to averages in the literature of 10 to 20. Although only qualitative statements can be made about the resulting software quality, the very rapid fall-off of effort after the system integration phase indicates that the tools and techniques applied resulted in a very low occurrence of errors. The software developed for this project is being used as foundation software for a more complex system, and preliminary indications are that it is easily adapted to the new environment. Tools to be singled out as the most positive contributors to the success of the project would have to be the walkthroughs and inspections following design, code, and test. It is felt that the following positive benefits resulted from reviews:

1. Impending reviews caused engineers to put more thought into their work. In addition, most errors were caught early, and little rework was required.
2. They served as a learning forum for other engineers on the team.
3. They provided the opportunity to define exact end points for the design and code/test phases of the development. This is very useful for tracking a project's actual status against that planned prior to the implementation phase.
4. They provided convenient checkpoints to ensure that the products complied with the project standards.

The application of simple but effective design tools to the project cannot be overlooked. These tools enabled the software engineer to achieve correct designs. The dedication of effort to up-front design is also a must. Any decrease in this effort would only show up as problems in the later phases of the project.

SUMMARY

The application of modern software development techniques to a software project requires a commitment of both time and money by a company that wishes to benefit from these techniques. Although the two projects discussed in this paper did not implement state-of-the-art tools, they both benefited from the application of simple tools and techniques. The results of the application of these tools and techniques can be summarized as follows:

1. Modern tools and techniques contribute significantly to increased software productivity and quality.
2. Metrics must be developed that can be applied at every step of the software development life cycle. These can then be used to judge the quality of the results at each stage.
3. Results of the application of new tools and techniques must be reported in the literature to allow comparison of the various tools and techniques.
4. Industry must be involved in the evaluation and development of new tools and techniques for software development, since this is where the greatest benefits can be realized.
5. Research must continue to define the software process better and to develop tools and techniques that better serve the user in the design and development process.

REFERENCES

1. Myers, Glenford J. *Composite/Structured Design,* New York: Van Nostrand Reinhold, 1978.
2. Freedman, D. P., and G. M. Weinberg. *Walkthroughs, Inspections, and Technical Reviews.* Boston: Little, Brown, 1982.
3. Fagan, M. E. "Design and Code Inspections to Reduce Errors in Program Development." *IBM Systems Journal, 15* (1976), pp. 182–211.
4. Aron, J. D. *The Program Development Process: The Programming Team.* Reading, Mass.: Addison-Wesley, 1983.
5. Musa, John B., et. al., "Stimulating Software Engineering Progress: A Report of the Software Engineering Planning Group." *IEEE Software Engineering Technical Committee Newsletter* 7 (4), May 1983.
6. Beck, L. L., and Thomas E. Perkins. *Transactions on Software Engineering,* Vol. SE-9, No. 5 (1983), 541–561.
7. Peters, Lawerance J. *Software Design: Methods and Techniques,* New York: Yourdon, 1981.

A portable Modula-2 operating system: SAM2S

by LARRY D. WITTIE and ARIEL J. FRANK
State University of New York at Stony Brook
Stony Brook, New York

ABSTRACT

The Stand-Alone Modula-2 System (SAM2S) is a portable, concurrent operating system and Modula-2 programming support environment. It is based on a highly modular kernel task running on single process-multiplexed microcomputers. SAM2S offers extensive network communication facilities. It provides the foundation for the locally resident portions of the MICROS distributed operating system for large netcomputers. SAM2S now supports a five-pass Modula-2 compiler, a task linker, link and load file decoders, a static symbolic debugger, a filer, and other utility tasks. SAM2S is currently running on each node of a network of DEC LSI-11/23 and Heurikon/Motorola 68000 workstations connected by an Ethernet. This paper reviews features of Modula-2 for operating system development and outlines the design of SAM2S with special emphasis on its modularity and communication flexibility. The two SAM2S implementations differ mainly in their peripheral drivers and in the large amount of memory available on the 68000 systems. Modula-2 has proved highly suitable for writing large, portable, concurrent and distributed operating systems.

INTRODUCTION

The MICROS project is exploring ways to organize networks of thousands of computers (netcomputers) to solve large problems. Its main goals are to develop a portable distributed operating system (MICROS) that can efficiently control many different netcomputers and to produce cost-effective netcomputers that provide high throughput for large classes of applications, that extend easily to form more powerful systems, and that are always available to users at acceptable processing rates even after component failures.

A netcomputer consists of many computer nodes, each with its own primary memory, physical clock, and attached peripherals. Nodes are embedded in a network of communication links over which messages are exchanged to share data from the separate memories. A global decentralized operating system, with some code resident in every node, unifies the nodes into a single computer system. The global operating system strives to provide netcomputer users with a powerful computing facility that can be accessed as a single virtual multiprocessor without regard to physical locations within the network.

Modula-2[1] is a high-level, general programming language that facilitates the building of simple and practical programming support systems. The Stand-Alone Modula-2 System (SAM2S) is a portable, highly modular concurrent operating system. SAM2S was developed initially to assess Modula-2 as a language for writing large systems and to provide portable software for Modula-2 programming support work stations. SAM2S was first developed for DEC LSI-11 work stations and later ported to Heurikon/Motorola 68000 work stations. When replicated in every node of a netcomputer, SAM2S forms the locally resident portions of the MICROS distributed operating system.

The next section of this paper discusses features of Modula-2 systems that are important for writing operating systems. The main section describes the design principles for SAM2S and the organization of both SAM2S implementations. The last three sections give the current status of SAM2S and MICROS, future research plans for MICROS, and conclusions reached in using Modula-2 to develop and port SAM2S.

MODULA-2 SYSTEMS

Modula-2 is a concurrent programming language convenient for both system and user applications. It is an improvement on Pascal, based on the best features of Modula[2] and MESA.[3] It was designed to be suitable both for high-level programming in an architecture-independent manner and for low-level programming of architecture-dependent aspects such as machine access and input/output (I/O) device handling.

Modula-2 shares most of its conceptual goals and programming language features with Ada,[4] but is much simpler and more comprehensible.[5,6] Modula-2 systems are simple but practical. They require only a small underlying run-time kernel, typically including fewer than 1,000 lines of assembly code. The module concept is central to Modula-2, as reflected by its name (MODUlar programming LAnguage). Most system facilities, including I/O operations, are provided by standard library modules. The modularization facilities, extensible high-level language interfaces, low-level machine access capabilities, and coroutine-based concurrency mechanisms all provide an effective environment for modern software systems.

Modularization Facilities

For true modularity, it is essential to be able to refer to another module knowing only the abstract properties contained in its specification. Using modular design, several programmers can develop different modules independently. True isolation of module design decisions can hide implementation details and aid in program readability, verification, and maintenance. Modules can be compiled, tested, debugged, and updated without unpredictable effects on other modules. Having separate modules is especially important for large research projects using many, and often inexperienced, programmers. For example, in three years more than 30 students have together contributed more than 70,000 lines of working Modula-2 code to the MICROS project.

Modularization facilities are strongly supported in Modula-2. A *module* is a program component, normally represented syntactically by a pair of definition and implementation modules. Each module pair provides a separate reference scope for a collection of logically related declarations, procedures, and data. All references across module boundaries involve a matching pair of explicit export and import declarations. All public declarations in the definition module define the *module interface* to module users. An implementation module provides the body of code implementing the defined interface. Each syntactic module can reside in an independent file and can be separately compiled. However, separate compilation does not mean independent compilation, since strong type checking is enforced between modules. Separate modules can be managed in libraries to enhance software reusability and to encourage software growth through accretion.

Extensible Language Interfaces

A common problem of high-level languages is restrictive linguistic constructs. Modula-2 avoids language inflexibility by excluding all process control, storage allocation, exception handling, and I/O facilities from the language definition. Instead, these facilities are easily provided by extensible language interfaces using standard library modules. The burden of supporting extensions thus shifts from the language to the library, allowing the language, compiler, and language runtime support system to remain small. Users of machines with small memories can configure Modula-2 systems with only the interfaces required by their applications. Modula-2 also supports procedure-valued parameters and variables. Procedure-valued variables are useful for process control and for passing functions to generic procedures. The extensible handling of concurrency in Modula-2 provides an example of these benefits.

Low-Level Machine Access

Since it was designed as a systems programming language, Modula-2 provides facilities for low-level machine access. The SYSTEM pseudo-module embedded in the compiler provides the main machine-dependent interface by encapsulating hardware data sizes and address formats. Machine-dependent operations include pointer and address arithmetic, relaxed type checking, explicit type transfer, and manipulations of bit sets. For I/O interfacing, Modula-2 allows access to peripheral device registers residing at fixed memory locations, specification of hardware priorities, and I/O transfers to support interrupt triggered context switching.

Concurrency

Concurrency provides for logically parallel threads of execution that can cooperate synchronously or asynchronously. The *process* is the fundamental unit of sequential execution that is combined for concurrent execution. Modern programming languages distinguish the logical process from the physical processor, allowing various mechanisms for allocating processors to processes. All concurrent programming languages provide some mechanism(s) for process interaction.[7]

There are two contrasting trends in concurrent programming languages. Some languages include many high-level linguistic constructs for process interaction, directly providing a user-oriented interface. However, these languages tend to be large and complex, to embed fixed constructs and rigid interaction mechanisms, and to require an elaborate runtime system. Examples include Ada,[4] Argus,[8] and MESA.[3] In contrast, some languages provide only a few lower-level constructs for process interaction, from which flexible higher-level mechanisms can be built. These languages tend to be simple and comprehensible, to support various types of process interaction, and to require only a modest runtime system. Examples include Edison,[9] Modula-2,[1] and SR.[10]

Modula-2 provides only a low-level coroutine mechanism to support concurrent execution. However, coroutines can be used to model the multiprocess scheduling and execution facilities of any single processor system. In Modula-2, any parameterless procedure can be executed as a process. At the lowest system level, processes are declared by a NEWPROCESS system call and activated with TRANSFER and IOTRANSFER calls. Via this coroutine mechanism, control switching can be explicit for transfer and I/O transfer calls or implicit as a result of I/O interrupts. The conceptual unification of planned process switches and forced interrupt transfers provides a clean mechanism on which to base higher-level mechanisms for process concurrency and synchronization. Users directly interact with higher-level concurrency models, such as a time-slicing mechanism for a uniprocessor.

STAND-ALONE MODULA-2 SYSTEM (SAM2S)

The originally released Modula-2 system (M2RT11)[11] is a Modula-2 programming support environment targeted for DEC PDP-11 and LSI-11 systems and dependent on DEC's RT-11 operating system for services such as file access, editing, and I/O handling. During the summer and fall of 1981, the MICROS research group developed the Stand-Alone Modula-2 System (SAM2S) for the LSI-11 by writing standard Modula-2 library modules for all the RT-11 services used by M2RT11. SAM2S was first developed mainly to find out whether Modula-2 was adequate for producing entire operating systems for programming support work stations. It has proved more than adequate. The original version of SAM2S actually runs slightly faster than M2RT11, primarily because all service routines are kept resident by SAM2S and not paged from disk as for RT-11.

The small memory (60 Kb) addressable by the LSI-11 limits the size of tasks run under the LSI-11 version of SAM2S to about 30 Kb. In practice, this means that we can edit and compile simple modules under SAM2S, but must rely on M2RT11 to change large modules such as the passes of the compiler itself. Since the two systems run on the same processor with exactly the same file format, switching from one to the other requires only a single "boot" command. It was the lack of memory space on the LSI-11, especially as we began to write and test communication software, that led us in 1983 to port SAM2S to work stations based on Motorola 68000 processors.

SAM2S has been designed to provide both a stand-alone programming support environment and a module library that can be the basis for the locally resident portions of the decentralized MICROS operating system. SAM2S is a concurrent system, but not a distributed one. However, it emphasizes flexibility in communications, whether on one machine or many, and includes Ethernet drivers and Xerox communication protocols.[12]

SAM2S Design Principles

SAM2S is a highly portable, independent Modula-2 programming support environment based on a modularized kernel task running on a process-multiplexed microcomputer.

The design for SAM2S uses many advanced features of Modula-2. SAM2S benefits heavily from high-level device drivers and from modularization facilities that allow definition of hidden and hierarchical type managers as well as layered tasks for both system and users.

Hidden type managers

The existence of a module facility does not automatically ensure software modularity. Some programming standards are needed. For example, SAM2S code avoids both exported variables and nested modules. Module structuring in SAM2S is based on abstract data types, encapsulation concepts, and information-hiding principles.[13,14]

A module should be designed to encapsulate one abstract data *type,* which imposes modular structure on data and characterizes all allowed operations and values. Each instance of a type is referred to as an *object.* The procedures in a module that define all operations on an object collectively form the *type manager.* Basic operations include creation, manipulation, and destruction of objects.

Hidden types in Modula-2 are declared only by name in the type definition module. The component substructure for the type is fully declared only in the implementation module. Hidden type objects are completely encapsulated. Only operations defined by their type manager can access or change them. Other modules do not know their structures and cannot directly manipulate their components. That hidden objects must contain all their own state information also allows their type manager to synchronize accesses efficiently. Process blocking is reduced by enforcing synchronization on individual shared objects only, rather than on the shared manager itself, as is done using monitors.

Hierarchical type managers

Two goals of type manager design are simplicity and generality. Simplicity demands a small module with a clean and readable structure. Generality means that each type manager should support an elaborate type with widely useful operations. These two goals usually are in conflict. Both goals can be achieved using policy/mechanism separation[15] and hierarchical type managers.

With policy/mechanism separation, lower levels of the system focus on providing general mechanisms that are as devoid as possible of embedded control decisions, so higher levels have maximum flexibility in choosing policies. Type managers should be designed to adhere to the *type policy* determined by indicators within the object state. Their mechanisms must accommodate all allowed type policies.

With hierarchical type managers, a first-level manager handles the basic version of a general type. A second-level type manager uses the facilities of the first-level manager to offer more advanced operations and to support an extended type. Even higher-level managers may be defined. An example is a process type manager, which provides basic operations like create, suspend, and resume. A more advanced manager uses additional information in each process object for synchronization.

High-level message-oriented device drivers

Physical and logical devices can be regarded as hidden types requiring storage access, data transfer, and synchronization facilities. Physical device drivers manage the details for peripheral devices. Logical device modules support available I/O formats for character and block-oriented devices and interact with physical device drivers. Each device module is an active type manager, since it contains one or more processes for device handling and user interactions. In SAM2S, the only processes that are genuinely concurrent are physical device processes that do real I/O by using the IOTRANSFER mechanism. All other processes are preemptively multiplexed by a time-slicing scheduler.

Device modules are written in high-level Modula-2 code, instead of assembly language, greatly easing system maintenance. Each device driver requires about 500 lines of Modula-2 code. Device drivers use low-level machine access facilities to manipulate device registers. Depending on the exact configuration of SAM2S, I/O service requests may be made directly through procedure calls, locally by interprocess messages using simple queue interfaces, or remotely through socket interfaces by messages from processes on other computers. Although the message interfaces for I/O are slower than direct-entry procedures, they are extremely flexible and make it easy to reconfigure SAM2S for differing devices.

Layered tasks

A *task,* or *concurrent program,* is a software structural unit built from one or more modules. Each task is a separate loading unit. Processes within a task are scheduling units that execute on a single host. Processes communicate and synchronize by passing messages and sharing objects. Linkers, editors, filers, and debuggers are common library tasks.

In Modula-2 systems, a task is specified by the hierarchy of module import dependencies that start from the main module. The modules forming a task are linked together as an overlay onto a host. Normally, the operating system kernel forms the basis for all other task overlays. Other tasks are loaded in layers above it and access its modules by imported procedures. Where there is a system configuration choice of different implementation modules for the same type manager, one has to be specified. Linking the chosen modules automatically selects any library modules that they import. Modules that are needed by higher-level tasks, but have already been provided for lower-level tasks, are not linked again.

The main program module, base task, and selected module choices are presented to the SAM2S task linker to produce a relocatable load unit. The linker manages the module and task libraries, type-checks intermodule interfaces, and places the resulting load file in the task library. The file contains information for controlling task loading.

SAM2S supports the open system concept,[16] which blurs distinctions between system and user tasks to enhance system

```
User Tasks - Compiler, Linker, Filer, Debugger, Decoder, ...

Node Control Modules
  Executive control - ResidentMonitor
  Task Loading - Loader, CommandInterpreter

I/O Service Modules
  Virtual I/O services - Files, Lines, Times
  Logical formats - RT11Files, UnixFiles, ADM3Lines, VT101Lines
  Physical devices - PRIAM, SCCZ8530, Z8536CIO, ME3C400, DMA

Process Interaction Modules
  Communication facilities - Carriers, Messages, Ports,
                             Sockets, Routes, Transport
  Name services - Names, Groups, DeviceTypes, NetTypes
  Process management - Processes, Signals, Gates, Semaphores

Kernel Support Modules
  Structured data types - Lists, Queues, Rings, Maps,
                          Caches, AddressSets
  Basic modules - SystemTypes, Memory
  Low-level modules - SYSTEM, MC68000, Exceptions
```

Figure 1—Structure of the SAM2S/68000 Kernel task

flexibility. The operating system is viewed as a collection of possible facilities that users can selectively include. Unneeded facilities cause no run-time overhead. All module interfaces are available to users. Hierarchical type managers allow users to select interfaces suitable for their application. Code for modules that are heavily shared among tasks is not repeated, reducing task sizes and increasing memory utilization.

SAM2S Organization

Currently, SAM2S runs on development systems based both on the DEC LSI-11/23 (SAM2S/LSI11) and the Heurikon HK-68K board version of the Motorola 68000 (SAM2S/68000). The LSI-11/23 work stations contain only 60 Kb of memory, severely limiting task sizes for SAM2S/LSI11. However, there is no similar constraint on the Heurikon HK-68K work stations. Each currently has 256 Kb to 768 Kb of memory.

The overlay base for the SAM2S system is the highly modularized Kernel task. Most of its modules are hidden type managers. They are available to user tasks also. For SAM2S/LSI11, the Kernel task is generated by merging it with a language support subkernel of 1,000 assembly instructions that provide run-time trap handling and coroutine process primitives. For SAM2S/68000, the Kernel task contains the MC68000 module, written mainly in Modula-2. This module provides run-time facilities similar to those of the LSI-11 assembly subkernel. The Modula-2 CODE procedure is used to generate about 800 lines of assembly code at specific points in the MC68000 module.

The following sections describe kernel modules in functional groups. Figure 1 shows the groups of modules in the SAM2S/68000 kernel task. Differences between the two SAM2S implementations occur only in the low-level kernel support modules and in the physical device drivers.

Kernel support modules

Low-level kernel modules are machine-dependent. In SAM2S/LSI11, the LSI11 module encapsulates the architecture of the LSI-11/23 microprocessor. It defines machine-specific trap and peripheral addresses that are also used by the assembly subkernel. The MC68000 module in SAM2S/68000 provides similar trap and peripheral access services. On each system, the Exceptions trap handling module is closely coupled to the basic trap facilities in the low-level machine module.

The SystemTypes module exports basic constant and type declarations used throughout the system. Grouping common declarations into a single module lessens the number of interfaces that have to be imported by most modules. Memory management, including compaction, is provided in the kernel by the Memory module. Available memory is managed as a dynamic heap, using a circular first-fit algorithm.

The structured data type modules are hidden type managers for abstract data structures needed by the kernel and by user tasks. For example, the Lists module can efficiently manage LIST objects created as a regular list, a descending or ascending priority list, a circular list, or a stack. The Maps module manages MAP objects, which are dynamically varying lists that associate an index for a hidden object with a unique identifier. Sets and caches of network communication addresses are maintained by the AddressSets and Caches modules. Other structured data types include queues and character buffer rings.

Process interaction modules

Process interaction facilities are provided by a hierarchy of type managers. The Processes module provides the basic PROCESS type and standard operations, including process creation, blocking, resumption, suspension, and termination. Priority lists are used for process scheduling. Spawning of processes forms tree hierarchies used for process control and termination. Processes can be synchronized by use of the Signals, Gates, and Semaphores modules. Signals are events or conditions on which processes can wait and about which they can be notified. A SIGNAL object manages a list of processes queued on the associated event. A GATE object is used as a binary semaphore to support mutually exclusive access to shared objects or code sections. It can be used to implement monitors. More elaborate synchronization can be achieved with the general SEMAPHORE type that provides conditional blocking of processes. Other synchronization types include event counts and sequencers.

The Names and Groups managers provide services for registration and lookup of symbolic names. The NAME type associates the name string for an object with its attributes, access capabilities, and unique identifier. A capability contains addressing information and possibly object access rights. To provide for hierarchical name spaces, groups of names are managed in tree directories. The GROUP type supports none, one, or more associated NAMEs. Symbolic names can be searched for on the top level of any specified subtree or recursively throughout the subtree.

Communication facilities are provided by another hierarchy of managers. The Ports module uses Queues to support either First-In-First-Out (FIFO) or priority ports for sending and receiving local messages. It controls port access rights, message forwarding, and conditional passing of messages. For network communication, the NetTypes module declares common addresses and services. The Sockets type manager provides location-independent general message transfer services either locally, within the same host computer, or remotely, between processes on different hosts. A SOCKET is a bidirectional port used as an end-address for sending and receiving messages between processes. The Transport and Routes modules provide for forwarding of packets over the communication subsystem.

To provide type uniformity for messages, Ports and Sockets directly manage carriers, which are standard headers for messages. Information in each carrier includes source and destination addresses, a unique message identifier, the message type, and a pointer to the message itself, if it exists. Empty carriers can be posted in ports for incoming messages. The Messages module provides packaging facilities for marshaling and unmarshaling data into and from packets used for remote procedure calls.

I/O service modules

I/O services are provided on three levels of abstraction: physical, logical, and virtual. There are user interfaces at the virtual level for file and terminal services. The virtual level passes user requests as procedure calls or messages to the appropriate I/O format module on the logical level. The logical level interfaces with the appropriate physical I/O driver by messages using either communication or queue services.

The DeviceTypes module declares constants and types used by the physical and logical device modules. At initialization, device drivers configured in the Kernel task register their existence with the name manager to give users dynamic access to I/O services. Device modules request I/O services and post results by using the IOREQUEST type as a standard message.

In timing experiments, we have found that serving local I/O requests through communication sockets takes about twice as long as through queue interfaces. As a compromise between speed and flexibility, we ordinarily use sockets for higher, logical-level I/O interfaces and faster queues for the lowest, physical-level interfaces. We have not yet found need for remote calls to low-level physical I/O drivers.

Examples of physical drivers for SAM2S/LSI11 QBUS-based devices include a DEC DLV11J serial driver, RX02 and RP02 disk controllers, and a QE3C400 Ethernet controller. The DLV11J driver manages up to four serial lines and provides type-ahead terminal handling, using a RING object for a character buffer. The RX02 floppy disk controller handles two diskette drives. The RP02 module handles eight logical partitions of a 169-Mb Fujitsu Winchester disk. QE3C400 interfaces to one or two 3COM Ethernet boards used for netcomputer communication.

Functionally similar physical drivers exist for MULTIBUS-based devices in SAM2S/68000. The SCCZ8530 module drives the Zilog serial communications chip on the Heurikon HK-68K board. It also handles up to four serial lines. Currently, SAM2S/68000 has a controller for a Priam 70-Mb Winchester disk. Controllers for several other disks (Vertex, Micropolis) and the four direct memory access (DMA) ports on the Heurikon board are under development. The DMA module will support efficient copying of blocks of data for both disk and Ethernet facilities. ME3C400 provides a dual Ethernet interface for SAM2S/68000.

Logical device modules include handlers for serial terminals and disk formats. The logical devices are independent of actual physical interfaces. The RT11Files module handles RT11 directory and file formats. A UnixFiles module for Unix format files is currently being written. ADM31Lines and VT101Lines control ADM31 and VT101 terminals.

The virtual-level modules provide abstract services to their clients. The Times module provides time and timeout facilities, using the KW11L and Z8536CIO physical clock drivers in SAM2S/LSI11 and SAM2S/68000, respectively. The Files and Lines modules provide an abstract file and serial line interface for users. These modules direct user requests to the proper logical device modules.

Node control modules

The ResidentMonitor executive module receives control after kernel initialization and monitors the execution of user tasks. It interacts with the command interpreter and kernel loader to load, execute, and terminate relocatable user tasks on SAM2S. At present, a single user code file at a time may be run. The file name serves as a load command.

SAM2S user-level tasks

Additional library modules are available for tasks run at the system user level. Some allow changes to file names and options. File I/O can be abstracted into character I/O by using Streams. The Strings module supports standard operations, such as extract and concatenate, on strings represented as character arrays. InOut provides transparent access to characters on either files or terminals. SAM2S currently supports a five-pass Modula-2 compiler, a task linker, link and load file decoders, a mini-core debugger, a static symbolic debugger, a filer, an import dependency charter, and other utility tasks.

SAM2S/MICROS STATUS

SAM2S has recently been ported from DEC LSI-11/23 computers to the Heurikon version of Motorola 68000 single-board systems. Both LSI-11s and 68000s are combined in a heterogeneous network of nodes connected by ten million bit-per-second Ethernet links. Between nodes, SAM2S uses flexible communication techniques including location-independent sockets, remote-procedure-call interfaces for file services, and standard Xerox Network System (XNS) packet transport protocols.[12]

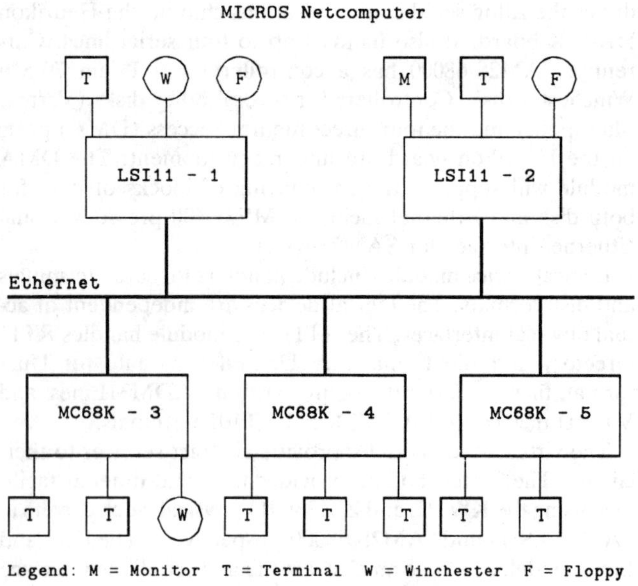

Figure 2—Initial network configuration used by SAM2S

The five existing network nodes, shown in Figure 2, are used as programming support work stations controlling one to three terminals (T) each. One LSI-11 (node 2) controls a color monitor (M) that shows Ethernet traffic among network nodes. Packet glyphs move nearly in real time, with just enough slowing for humans to see. Both LSI-11 systems (nodes 1 and 2) have dual floppy disk drives (F), but two 6800 work stations (nodes 4 and 5) have no attached disks. The flexibility of interfaces in SAM2S allows both diskless 68000 systems to be booted remotely with files supplied either by the other 68000 (node 3) from its Priam Winchester disk (W) or by one LSI-11 (node 1), from its Fujitsu disk (W) or its floppy disk (F). Individual application programs also are remotely loaded into any of the 68000 systems.

Besides the original LSI-11 compiler from Wirth at ETH-Zurich and a VAX/VMS Modula-2 system from the University of Hamburg, there are several locally developed Modula-2 compilers that are being used to port SAM2S to other machines. The most heavily used is a VAX/UNIX cross-compiler that produces 68000 machine code. A recent translation of this compiler from Pascal into Modula-2 allows compilation directly on SAM2S/68000 systems. A Modula-2 cross-compiler system running on VAX/UNIX systems and generating code for the Intel 8086 and 80186 processors has recently been finished. Partial compilers for both Vax/Unix and National 16000/Genix systems generate executable code for simple programs, but need much more work to be fully functional.

The original version of MICROS[17,18] was a modular, distributed operating system written in Concurrent Pascal[19] and assembly code. It ran on a network of DEC LSI-11 systems. With the addition of network communication modules and remote services between nodes, SAM2S has become the local operating system portion of MICROS. This new version of MICROS will be written completely in Modula-2 except for a few hundred lines of assembly code. Modula-2 MICROS will be a highly modular, decentralized operating system that supports transparent execution of distributed applications on netcomputers. Its design emphasizes portable, transparent control structures. Control in MICROS is decentralized and distributed[20,21] throughout the system as groups of cooperating tasks.

The new MICROS system contains more than 100,000 lines of local code. Except for the cross-compilers, almost all is written in Modula-2. The local operating system kernel, support, and communications modules for SAM2S/LSI11 consist of 23,000 lines of code; similar modules for SAM2S/68000 take 27,000 lines. About 18,000 lines are identical in the two systems. The common but different 5,000 lines handle low-level system features and drivers for the almost disjoint sets of peripherals. The extra 4,000 lines in SAM2S/68000 are mainly a hardware-level debugging monitor for the 68000 processor and the more extensive network communication modules that the larger 68000 memory allows. The working cross-compiler for the 68000 and its translation into Modula-2 together take about 40,000 lines. The linker, loader, filer, editor, and other user-level system programs require about 9,000 lines. Each SAM2S system has about 7,000 lines of machine-dependent modules in its compiler, linker, and loader. There are another 20,000 lines in the code-generation passes of the compilers for the 80186, VAX-11, and 16000 processors. In addition, there are about 30,000 lines in LSI-11 compiler, linker/loader, and debugging utilities obtained from Wirth. More than 50,000 lines of high-level code have been added to MICROS in the last year.

RESEARCH PLANS FOR MICROS

The major recent theoretical work[22] in the MICROS project has been in analyzing ways in which to implement and to use multicast communication within dynamic groups of computers in large networks, especially ones linked by grids of horizontal and vertical Ethernets. Group communication techniques developed for Ethernet systems should be applicable to many distributed system environments, even those using dedicated links. The research has included analysis of efficient netcomputer mechanisms to maintain distributed lists characterizing dynamically changing groups and to multicast packets within groups. Efficient communication in large groups can require spanning trees of multicast routing information. Single messages multicast to processes scattered over a network can follow tree branches and be copied at each fork.

A modular, integrated group communication subsystem is being implemented within MICROS to provide a basis for construction of a complete netcomputer system. In the coming year, the subsystem will be used to evaluate proposed group communication techniques. The subsystem will include support mechanisms for planned distributed applications such as the *in/out* medium-level distributed language system[23] and the BugNet[24] parallel debugging system.

The MICROS system must work well both on different types of computers and on networks that are connected in different ways — ways not known while the MICROS soft-

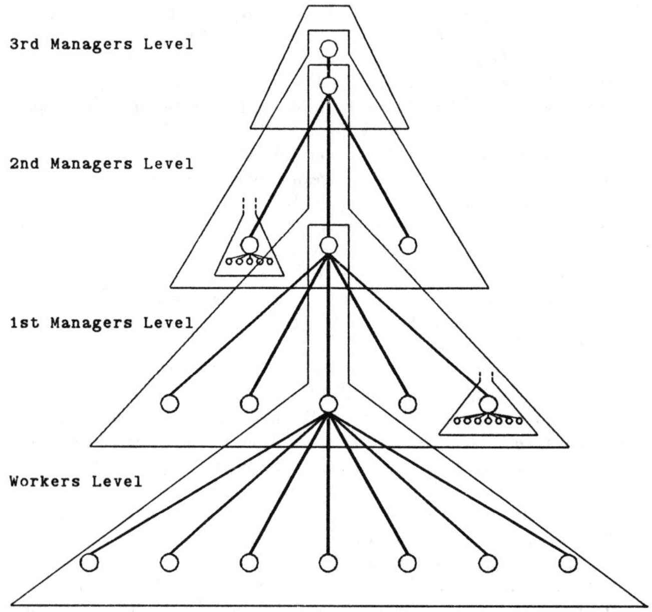

Figure 3—Hierarchical tree based on dynamic communication groups

ware is being written. Distributed control algorithms already designed for MICROS have included a Focus[25] initializer that transparently forms a networkwide hierarchical control structure and a distributed Wave Scheduler[26,27] that assigns idle nodes to task forces. The wave scheduling technique relies on a control hierarchy, includes mechanisms for avoiding static deadlocks, and can extend to any size network. Research in distributed task force scheduling schemes[18] and netcomputer load-balancing mechanisms[28] is planned. We also will evaluate other decentralized algorithms for management of globally shared system resources in large netcomputers with thousands of nodes.

Figure 3 shows one use of overlapping communication groups within a decentralized control hierarchy. Each triangular boundary encloses two groups. The working group consists of a number of sibling nodes plus their common parent. The recovery group adds the grandparent to the parent and siblings. The siblings execute user and management tasks as requested by the parent. To avoid overloading the parent during normal working conditions, the siblings pass to their parent only task results and summaries of management information about lower-level groups. If one of the nodes fails, the remaining members of the recovery group all communicate to redistribute the tasks of a failed sibling or to elect a replacement for a failed parent. Management information in a failed parent can be regenerated from the combined states of the siblings and grandparent. A failed grandparent is replaced as a parent by the next higher group in the hierarchy.

The MICROS network currently consists of three Heurikon 68000s and two DEC LSI-11/23s connected by a single Ethernet. An expanded network including two DEC LSI-11/23 nodes, at least seven Heurikon 68000 nodes, some Intel 80186 nodes, and several DEC MICROVAX nodes is planned for future research. Each node will have two Ethernet ports, probably connected to the nearest two busses in a horizontal/vertical grid of Ethernets. Ethernet links to several SUN work stations and VAX 750/780 computers running Berkeley 4.2 UNIX are planned. We have started developing a fully compatible UNIX file system written in Modula-2 that will allow MICROS users to share files and whole disks with UNIX system users. MICROS will unify local operating systems to present a networkwide UNIX environment to users.

CONCLUSIONS

We have found Modula-2 much better for writing system code than the combination of Concurrent Pascal[19] and assembly code that we used for MICROS during 1978–81. The Modula-2 system, running on the same LSI-11 processor, is faster by a factor of 4 to 10 in several modalities. The 68000 version is even faster. Compiler and system code run faster because native machine code, not interpreted P-code, is produced. Flexible, selective synchronization operations defined by library modules allow faster execution of highly concurrent systems than do Concurrent Pascal monitors, which block processes too indiscriminately. System errors can be located much faster using the post-mortem symbolic debugging system that is part of the Modula-2 task library. System corrections are faster because only a few modules, not the entire system, must be recompiled for each set of corrections, since there is type-checked, separate compilation of Modula-2 modules. System development by a group is faster, because only the definition modules providing the interfaces between modules need to be approved before all programmers can start producing and compiling code.

The tiny run-time system, small compiler, and use of device interfaces written in high-level code all greatly simplify the porting of Modula-2 systems. We did not encounter major problems in porting SAM2S to 68000 systems. A few high-level modules have been changed slightly to make them truly machine-independent. Almost all the changes have involved the consistent use of long and short variants of integers and cardinals on the two systems. Communication between heterogeneous computers requires an external standard for the order of byte transmission. We have chosen the Xerox Ethernet standard of high-byte-first order, which is also the standard for the 68000 microprocessor. Bytes are reversed in order as they enter or leave any of the LSI-11 systems. Porting SAM2S to a new computer requires rewriting of about 7,000 lines for code generation and loader modules, 1,000 lines for low-level kernel modules, and 1,000 to 4,000 lines for new device drivers.

Use of Modula-2 has allowed us to port SAM2S from LSI-11 to 68000 systems in six months. It has allowed us to combine the efforts of dozens of student programmers into a working operating system. The flexibility and portability of Modula-2 systems will allow us to continue to explore ways to control networks of thousands of computers.

ACKNOWLEDGMENTS

Many members of the MICROS research group helped to develop SAM2S. Especially important contributions have been made by Shridhar Acharya, Divyakant Agrawal, Bill Earl, Miguel Garcia, Arun Garg, Mike Palumbo, Yanick Pouffary, Soumitra Sengupta, Rick Spanbauer, Shidan Tavana, and Kok Sun Wong.

This research has been supported in part by National Aeronautics and Space Administration Grant NAG-1-249, Army Research Office Contract DAAG-29-82-K-0103, an external research grant from Digital Equipment Corporation, and National Science Foundation Equipment Grants MCS80-06925 and MCS82-03955.

REFERENCES

1. Wirth, N. *Programming in Modula-2* (2nd ed.). New York: Springer-Verlag, 1983.
2. Wirth, N. "Modula: A Language for Modula Multiprogramming." *Software—Practice & Experience, 7* (1977), pp. 3–35.
3. Mitchell, J. G., W. Maybury, and R. Sweet. "MESA Language Manual." Xerox CLS-79-3, Version 5.0, Xerox Palo Alto Research Center, April 1979.
4. Ichbiah, J. D. "Rationale for the Design of the Ada Programming Language." *ACM SIGPLAN Notices, 14* (1979), Part B.
5. Sumner, R. T., and R. E. Gleaves. "Modula-2—A Solution to Pascal's Problems." *ACM SIGPLAN Notices, 17* (1982), pp. 28–33.
6. Spector D. "Ambiguities and Insecurities in Modula-2." *ACM SIGPLAN Notices, 17* (1982), pp. 43–51.
7. Andrews, G. R., and F. B. Schneider. "Concepts and Notations for Concurrent Programming." Technical Report 82-520, Cornell University, September 1982.
8. Liskov, B. H., and R. W. Scheifler. "Guardians and Actions: Linguistic Support for Robust, Distributed Programs." *9th Conference on Prinicples of Programming Languages*. New York: ACM, 1982, pp. 7–19.
9. Brinch Hansen, P. *Programming a Personal Computer.* Englewood Cliffs, N. J.: Prentice-Hall, 1982.
10. Andrews, G. R. "SR: A Language for Distributed Programming." Technical Report 81-14, University of Arizona, October 1981.
11. Wirth, N. "Modula-2." Technical Report 36, Institut für Informatik, ETH, Zurich, 1980.
12. Xerox Corp. "Internet Transport Protocols," XSIS 028112, Xerox System Integration Standard, December 1981.
13. Parnas, D. "On the Criteria to Be Used in Decomposing Systems Into Modules." *Communications of the ACM, 15* (1972), pp. 1053–1058.
14. Parnas, D. "Designing Software for Ease of Extension and Contraction." *IEEE Transactions on Software Engineering, SE-5* (1979), pp. 128–137.
15. Wulf, W. A., R. Levin, and S. P. Harbison. *HYDRA/C.mmp: An Experimental Computer System*. New York: McGraw-Hill, 1981.
16. Lampson, B. W., and R. F. Sproull. "An Open Operating System for a Single-User Machine." *ACM Proceedings of the 7th Symposium on Operating System Principles,* 1979, pp. 98–105.
17. Wittie, L. D., and A. van Tilborg. "MICROS, A Distributed Operating System for MICRONET, A Reconfigurable Network Computer." *IEEE Transactions on Computers, C-29* (1980), pp. 1133–1144.
18. Van Tilborg, A. "Network Computer Operating Systems and Task Force Scheduling," Ph.D. thesis, State University of New York at Buffalo, September 1982.
19. Brinch Hansen, P. *The Architecture of Concurrent Programs*. Englewood Cliffs, New Jersey: Prentice-Hall, 1977.
20. Abraham, S. M., and Y. K. Dalal. "Techniques for Decentralized Management of Distributed Systems." *Proceedings of the IEEE COMPCON Spring 80.* Piscataway, N. J.: IEEE, 1980, pp. 430–437.
21. Jensen, E. D. "Decentralized Executive Control of Computers." *Proceedings of the 3rd International Conference on Distributed Computing Systems,* Piscataway, N. J.: IEEE, 1982, pp. 31–35.
22. Frank, A. J., L. D. Wittie, and A. J. Bernstein. "Group Communication on Netcomputers." Technical Report #83/057, State University of New York at Stony Brook, September 1983. Accepted for the 4th International Conference on Distributed Computing Systems. May 1984.
23. Ahamad, M., and A. J. Bernstein. "The Application of Name Based Addressing to Low Level Distributed Algorithms." Technical Report #83/050, State University of New York at Stony Brook, August 1983.
24. Curtis, R., and L. D. Wittie. "BugNet: A Debugging System for Parallel Programming Environments." *Proceedings of the 3rd International Conference on Distributed Computing Systems,* 1982, pp. 394–399.
25. Van Tilborg, A., and L. D. Wittie. "High-Level Operating System Formation in Network Computers." *Proceedings of the 1980 International Conference on Parallel Processing,* Piscataway, N. J.: IEEE, 1980, pp. 131–132.
26. Van Tilborg, A., and L. D. Wittie. "Wave Scheduling: Distributed Allocation of Task Forces in Network Computers." *Proceedings of the 2nd International Conference on Distributed Computing Systems.* Piscataway, N. J.: IEEE, 1981, pp. 337–347.
27. Van Tilborg, A., and L. D. Wittie. "Distributed Task Force Scheduling in Multi-Microcomputer Networks." *AFIPS, Proceedings of the National Computer Conference* (Vol. 50), 1981, pp. 283–289.
28. Reed, D. A. "Performance Based Design and Analysis of Multimicrocomputer Networks." Ph.D. thesis, Purdue University, 1983.

Giving away the data processing store, or Does the data processing department as we know it today have a future?

by LOIS ZELLS
Yourdon, Inc.
New York, New York

ABSTRACT

Data processing's position in the organization, as we know it today, does not work! There is an ongoing communication gap between data processing groups and the rest of the world—the users. This never-ending adversity between users and data processing continues to reinforce polarization. The situation hampers productivity and drains important energy—energy that could be rechanneled and made to work for the organization.

The first step in solving any difficulty is to establish ownership of the problem. In this case, we are faced with a clear case of sibling rivalry. Often, the only way to stop the squabbling is for the parent to assume the role as arbiter of peace and establish the ground rules for a harmonious family life.

Because they are in antagonistic positions, users and data processing cannot solve problems themselves. It is executive management's responsibility to provide the framework for harmony and to continuously and visibly demonstrate the commitment to a new approach. Otherwise the whole process will just be another empty exercise in futility—better left untried.

In our attempts to remold the organizational personality we may address

1. Long-range planning
2. Managing organizational expectations
3. Training issues
4. Public relations

Then if management recognizes that we cannot continue as we are today, if management truly can envision a time in the future when the current trend will be reversed, and if management is willing to consciously choose to redirect the flow, harmony can and will be realized.

INTRODUCTION

A new management information system (MIS) director recently told me that his department had achieved such poor credibility under his predecessor that he was going to run the department by keeping the users in the dark as much as possible and not committing to anything. That way, there would be no disappointments. In another instance, a chief executive told me that he had so little confidence in his data processing department that he would only let them maintain existing systems. All new work was being handled directly in the CEO's office and executed by outside consultants.

Data processing's position in the organization, as we know it today, does not work! There is an ongoing communication gap between data processing groups and the rest of the world—the users. This never-ending adversity between users and data processing continues to reinforce polarization. The situation hampers productivity and drains important energy—energy that could be rechanneled and made to work for the organization.

WE WANT TO CHANGE THE BUSINESS AND WE WANT TO CHANGE ATTITUDES

Outdated and nonfunctional, the traditional bureaucratic business philosophies need to be swept away so that fresh and unbiased approaches can be introduced. The solution to these problems lies in restructuring the environment and remolding the personality of the organization in order to inspire teamwork and new ways of viewing the function of data processing.

There is not, however, a simple and free path to achieving these goals. Most important, none of this will work without the understanding, approval, and commitment of executive management. It will happen only if we move ownership to upper management, that is, if the process is executed at the highest levels of the organization. Furthermore, it is important to realize that more than just lip service will be required. Executives need to be willing to visibly and continuously demonstrate their commitment to this new way of doing business; otherwise the whole process will be just another empty exercise in futility; better left untried. But, if management recognizes that we cannot continue as we are today, if management truly can envision a time in the future when the current trend will be reversed, and if management is willing to consciously choose to redirect the flow, then harmony can and will be realized.

We start by going back to basics and remembering that data processing is a service group to the company, and therefore should be conducted as a *business*—whose success is determined by the goodwill it establishes through its customers; and, although rarely stated formally, it is necessary to recognize that there also are certain responsibilities that users should automatically assume in this interchange.

As a matter of fact, many businesses are successful as a result of: good public relations, educating customers to understand their roles and responsibilities, as well as what is reasonable to expect from the company and its products. If the antagonistic trend is to be reversed, an effective data processing advertising campaign should be staged so users can rethink their images of data processing.

In this paper, we will crystallize what we can reasonably expect from the data processing function, as well as offer some suggestions for improvement. However, in order to change the future, we must first understand the past.

WHERE ARE WE COMING FROM?

A controversial issue that really fires the imagination comes from trying to determine what role data processing *should* play in the organization. Turned around, the question is just as meaningful if phrased as "What is the *organization's* responsibility to data processing?" Depending upon which side of the fence you are standing, you may have some definite opinions on this subject.

The Corporation

When asked about their attitudes about the data processing investment, many corporate executives voice their dissatisfaction with the low returns they perceive they are getting from data processing expenditures.

- Often, data processing is viewed as a bottomless pit into which enormous amounts of money flow, while requests for services continue to pile onto an already overloaded backlog.
- Senior management does not get all of the information *they* need for controlling current operations and planning for the future.
- Improvement drives instituted to clean up data processing rarely do more than freshen up existing systems by scrubbing questionable reports and refining remaining ones.
- The creation of new computer systems often is abdicated to technical personnel, who, in turn, become so caught up in state-of-the-art advances that they lose sight of the real business problems that need to be solved.
- Because of their anxieties regarding ownership of the information resource, data processing departments jealously guard their territory and often are reluctant, or even totally unwilling, to support the acquisition of microcomputers unless they also can maintain control of that resource. However, data processing may be unable either to effectively introduce micros into the organization or to instill corporate confidence in their ability to achieve that goal.

To staff data processing departments, companies employ so-called experts. Large amounts of time and money are spent on these employees, and expectations are high. Since these experts are only people and not infallible, they make mistakes. Systems are rejected, even when delivered on time and within budget. Most often, however, systems not only do not deliver what the user expected, but the projects themselves are usually completed late and over budget. Credibility suffers and data processing gets a black eye. The problem is enhanced when dissatisfaction occurs because reliability of already existing systems is low and maintenance budgets become very high.

Data Processing

While the above complaints may be justified from the corporate perspective, interviews from the other side of the fence bring to light facts that are just as legitimate.

- Management professes to believe in realistic planning and control, but when project teams present their schedules for time, people, and costs, management often tries to condense these figures—without reducing the scope of the project.
- Systems developers are not always given the time to do their jobs correctly. For example, although it has been repeatedly demonstrated that more reliable systems are developed by front loading the effort into analysis and design, project participants are still pressured into doing the whole project "quick-and-dirty" or at best are rushed through the early phases to where they can do some real work—like coding. The desire for quality systems is often just lip service. Given the choice between a system that is completed late with no errors and one finished on time with imperfections, the organization often chooses to meet the target date.
- Companies declare their desire to move away from crisis-reactionary mode (where workers spend long hours of overtime in exchange for little or no compensation) to a proactive, controlled environment. When the time comes to put this into practice, what we really see is a continuing request for doing it the old way—just once more.
- Organizations establish elaborate goals for training that are either not used at all or, if trained, students are not given the opportunity to use the skills they have acquired.
- Project participants are required to deliver successful projects, but have no control over the environment that affects the project development process. In turn, project leaders (managers) are required to answer for the success of the project, but rarely are given the authority to get the job done.
- Application teams often find it impossible to uncover a user, sponsor, or owner of the system who is willing or able to participate in and direct the process.

The lists of complaints from both camps are endless. Time and money are wasted, dissatisfaction filters up the corporate structure, and declining productivity invades all levels of the organization. Departmental segregation within the company propagates divisions and barriers that generate independent islands of politics, power, and miscommunication. This lack of understanding of the organization by the organization obstructs the integration of any innovations that may benefit the organization. Large amounts of energy, which could be channeled into productive and beneficial results for the company, are wasted.

EXECUTIVE MANAGEMENT AS THE "CHANGE AGENT"

It has been stated that "everybody complains about the weather, but nobody ever does anything about it." Data processing's black eye cannot be healed by griping about inefficiencies. They are obvious! What is not so apparent is how to overcome the problems.

The first step in solving any difficulty is to establish ownership. In this case, we are faced with a clear case of sibling rivalry. Often, the only way to stop the squabbling is for the parent to assume the role as arbiter of peace and establish the ground rules for a harmonious family life.

Because they are in antagonistic positions, users and data processing cannot solve problems by themselves. It is executive management's responsibility, as the parent, to provide the framework for harmony and to continuously and visibly demonstrate a commitment to a new approach.

Successful executives know they must act on their environment rather than continue to react to it! Therefore, top management should decide:

1. What kind of data processing environment they want
2. What they are willing to pay to get it

3. When they want it
4. When they are willing to start

Ownership of the problem needs to be accepted at elevated levels and conscious choices must be exercised in choosing how to restructure the environment.

One high-powered management consulting group I know of will only do work for troubled MIS departments after a firm liaison has been established with the chief executive. The CEO must sign a contract for visible and sustained support of the remolding effort. While it is legitimate for the executive to withdraw from the process, he or she in doing so recognizes that, although withdrawal may be a necessary business choice, it will likely cause the demise of the effort. Rather than allow the project to then suffer a slow, painful death, it is immediately canceled. However, the consulting group still gets full payment. This may be considered a rather extreme approach, but it certainly demonstrates an important fact: *Either corporations sincerely want to improve the situation—or they don't!* It is necessary to qualify the seriousness of their intent; and if it is not present, then the project should not even be undertaken.

Assuming senior management recognizes that there is a problem, the project will be conducted at the executive level and will involve all segments of the organization. Agreements and conflicts will be crystallized, problems will be resolved, and an action plan will be developed. This information will be disseminated to the whole organization. In our attempts to remold the organizational personality, we may address:

1. Long-range planning
2. Managing organizational expectations
3. Training issues
4. Public relations

LONG-RANGE PLANNING: DIRECTING AN EYE TO THE FUTURE

Faced with a desire to control company direction, many organizations have adapted advanced planning methodologies such as strategic business planning and strategic systems planning. Not only do managers need to be concerned on a daily basis about problems of productivity, backlogs, and changing priorities, but the solution of these problems must be compatible with long-range company goals. Each daily decision should be evaluated based on its ability to support or obstruct future objectives. However, many organizations are still confused about exactly what business planning and systems planning are, how these two processes relate, and how to integrate them with organizational theory and the behavioral sciences.

Strategic Business Planning

During the strategic business planning effort, corporate executives identify the performance factors that can improve business results. From an analysis of this information they may select the long-range goals and objectives for the organization. Strategies and tactics are then devised that should enable attainment of these targets.

Who "Drives" The Strategic Business Plan?

At the top of the organizational structure, we may find a function for corporate planning and development. It is unencumbered by traditional and inflexible divisional borders, has the visibility and support necessary for effectiveness, and possesses the high-level perspective. This group may be further divided into:

- Strategic business planners, who lead the development of the "five-year" business plan (goals, objectives, strategies, missions, and tactics).
- Management planners, who analyze the alternatives for implementing the strategic business plan. They prioritize projects, optimize resources, and maximize staff use.
- Environmental analysts, who provide economic and political intelligence necessary for evaluating new opportunities and threats.
- Venture developers, who develop new approaches for achieving strategic goals.

The problems regarding which goals and objectives should be important to the company must be elevated to include a wide perspective of issues. However, often the current approaches do not demonstrate even a minimal level of social awareness. As a matter of fact, most current business-planning efforts tend to limit their attentions to satisfying economic and political pressures, resulting in 75–95% of their emphasis being placed in the inanimate areas of technology, revenues, methodologies, and organizational structures. There is little or no concentration on integrating the humanistic views (especially the needs, requirements, and expectations of users and the data processing professionals who plan, develop, and support their systems). Nevertheless, we should search to find ways to satisfy the conflicting objectives of:

1. The public and private goals and values of the organization
2. The public and private attitudes of the organization toward their personnel
3. The public and private attitudes of the organization toward their customers

   and
4. The public and the private goals of the employees themselves

We would be wise to acknowledge, at last, that it is necessary to consciously implement mechanisms that will foster and feed a positive social environment—where users and data processing groups can focus on common targets rather than on personalities and the behavior that supports polarization.

MANAGING ORGANIZATIONAL EXPECTATIONS

Every organizational effort is infused with many undefined and assumed attitudes. Given any kind of a transaction and two to N participants, there will be two to N views of the transaction, which may not always be in agreement. There are always dozens of subtle nuances floating like puffs of smoke above every enterprise, often in conflicting directions. We should crystallize these views, resolve the disagreements, and disseminate this information to the community.

The most successful departments within a company are not necessarily the biggest or the most visible. Rather, they are those that provide what the organization expects. More departments fail because of inflated and unreasonable expectations than for any other reason. Therefore, never underestimate the importance of managing organizational expectations. In any data processing organization, effective presentation of the various agreements and decisions is a must. The users, who range from executive managers to hands-on operators of systems, need to have a clear understanding of data processing and its functions so they do not expect more than can be furnished. At the same time, data processing personnel must raise their awareness and appreciation for the conflicts the user faces when attempting to maintain existing business operations while also supporting data processing's efforts.

Furthermore, the red-flag issues should be brought immediately into the open and dealt with objectively rather than suppressed until they become emotional hot potatoes. We often try to bury obstacles with the good hope and intention that time and short-term success will overcome them; unfortunately, we know from painful experience that they don't go away. Failure often occurs when the organization cannot or will not acknowledge problems. However, even the most taciturn managers cannot refute clearly stated facts. Organizational expectations can then be realistic, approved, documented, and disseminated.

In a different context, we could say that the group will choose what games will be played and will establish the ground rules for each game before the playing starts. Any rules will be legitimate as long as all of the participants concur. With this increased knowledge, management can then assess each venture's effect, determine if the organization is committed to successful completion, and decide if the endeavor should be continued or abandoned. In other words, every enterprise should be evaluated based on its effect on the organization, the organization's ability to complete it successfully, and whether or not it supports long-range goals.

What Causes Miscommunication?

First, we should recognize that data processors are *not* the decision makers for the organization! In the past, our conscientious enthusiasm to do a good job led to the belief that data processing should drive the decision-making process. The reality is just the opposite. We would not contract to build our dream house without commitment of our sustained involvement or the expectation that our opinions will be continuously solicited and our choices incorporated. Since data processors are only the builders of systems, why shouldn't customers of data processing "constructions" be required to provide the same level of participation?

Data processing should, therefore, be recognized as a service group to the organization, responsible for providing facts about alternatives and risks. The decision-making responsibility may then be moved back to the user, where it belongs, allowing the choices to become organizational products rather than data processing projects.

Next, we recognize that conflicting objectives are often a cause of project failure. Two essentials to the success of the process are user participation for successful definition of requirements, and detailed specifications for avoiding uncertainties, omissions, ambiguities, and error. Difficulties arise when data processing prevails upon users for participation to document and validate requirements. Because of the need to maintain existing business operations, user management may be in a bind and need to reduce, or even eliminate, their level of participation. Other times, when data processing workers negotiate for the weeks and months necessary to complete detailed specifications, they are informed that there is simply not enough time, and may be advised to do a less thorough job in order to meet the target date.

Thus, we observe conflicting objectives, which are very confusing to participants. It may be that the constraints are legitimate, and if so, recognition must be given to that fact, and a concise acknowledgment of the trade-offs must be made. Then any results are due to organizational choice, and if projects are late or fail, it is because of poor choice rather than poor management. If constraints are artificial or arbitrary, is it logical or fair to impose unrealistic target dates that serve only to reduce quality and reliability of systems? Where is this direction coming from? Is it real, or imagined? Does upper management need to clarify its position?

Third, many systems people are advised that it is more important to finish a project within a prescribed amount of time than it is to worry about maintenance costs. Not only is this amazing, but it is also confusing to people who understand the high costs of maintenance. What does the organization want from its systems? What degree of accuracy is required? Is reliability important? At the bottom line, does the company know what errors cost? Is reduced maintenance a critical factor? How can we achieve our goals? Is this information being communicated to employees?

Fourth, we must help the organization understand that project planning is an iterative process. It is impossible to present a comprehensive and detailed schedule for implementation on the first day of a project. Furthermore, it is unlikely that an inclusive project plan that is precise can be provided before design is finished. Consequently, as we migrate through the development life cycle, our knowledge base of the project becomes more comprehensive, and we are able to refine the plan.

If management, on the other hand, chooses a target date and advises the project team to retrofit a project into that time frame, the options are as follows:

- Apply more resources—work overtime, assign the superworkers, add more people, and assign the experts.
- Eliminate features.
- Do a less thorough job and accept the risk.
- Agree to do the whole project in the allotted time and finish late and over budget.

- Agree to do the whole project, but only commit to a schedule so great that it will cover all contingencies.
- Agree to the date, but do not commit to any specific deliverables.
- Agree to the date, but make the specifications ambiguous and insist that any missing features were not part of the original agreement.

Most of these options are dishonest and none is really highly desirable. Does management truly understand and appreciate the planning effort? What do they expect from the process? Are their expectations realistic?

Last of all, documenting organizational expectations takes time and people. Managers who resist dedicating time and resources to this effort are deceived into believing the effort will not be expended later in reacting to undefined expectations.

Even with all the work, the effort may not be rewarded with enthusiastic response. Tom DeMarco states, "The most perfect crystal ball makes no guarantee that users will be happy when they see into the future, only that what they see will be accurate."[13] Our purpose is simply to minimize the effects of surprise and unpreparedness. As we gain experience and credibility, we may find that unwarranted endeavors—which in the past would have gone on to completion, even though they should have been canceled—will be recognized earlier and be nullified. People who want the transactions at any cost will attack the process or the team members and ignore the projections. If approval is received, implementation can proceed very rapidly and productivity levels can be raised significantly.

ARE WE ACHIEVING THE DESIRED RESULTS FROM OUR TRAINING EXPENDITURES?

A recent survey of 800 managers revealed that training in general was not considered that important to their companies. Yet, these very managers also complained that most employees had some very basic holes in their awareness of how technologies can best be exploited to serve the organization.

With the mounting demand for proficient personnel and the parallel increase in salaries, organizations are seeking ways to realize a higher return on their personnel-investment dollar. Education of the staff is clearly one avenue to that end. However, companies often cannot or do not create an environment that nurtures high yields on any educational expenditures.

Not all companies are in the training dark ages, and those that believe they are enlightened take umbrage at being described in negative tones. We are told that the classes employees do attend are meant to improve the skills of the students and are not intended as vacations, a way to break the monotony of routine, or simply an exercise to satisfy overall organizational training requirements. On the contrary, seminars are supposed to enhance the expertise of the participants and enable them to be more productive in their jobs. Yet managers often have no idea what is being taught to their employees in the classes, have no understanding about whether or not any of the ideas being conveyed even support company goals, and consequently have no plans for implementing the concepts being taught. Thus, when students return to work, they are not even given the chance to exercise the philosophies or skills they have learned.

On the other hand, there are many times that, although a new management policy dictates that the entire group learn new concepts or skills, only half-hearted attention is given to the implementation of the new approach. Actual execution is often obstructed because proper completion is not possible within the imposed target dates.

Most participants in training seminars regard the opportunity as an employment "perk," recognizing that education is one road to career advancement. As a matter of fact, many employees also are conscientious enough to want to attend only those classes that will help them in their jobs. Attendees usually are eager and optimistic and this attitude is frequently complemented by the enthusiasm and interest of the instructor. But then something goes awry. Disillusionment sets in—either during the teaching session or later on the job. Employees up and down the organization convey feelings of extreme frustration and exasperation. Students demonstrate their skepticism by asking questions such as: "Why aren't our managers here to hear this?" "Will they really do this in my company?" "Why is there never time to do it right, but always time to do it over?"

When management prevents the growth of quality by failing to train people properly or to support the use of the techniques, then talking about the desire to improve productivity becomes a sham. Productivity does not increase by osmosis. If you are sick and the doctor prescribes medicine, you do not get well by filling the prescription and putting it in the medicine cabinet. Having students learn new concepts does not benefit the organization if these people are not given the opportunity to exercise and learn the use of the new skills and then apply their new expertise.

Does the company really know what it wants from the training experience? Are there corporate objectives against which they can evaluate training strategies? Have these objectives been crystallized and clearly communicated to all of the players? Does the training function have the visibility and recognition necessary to support fulfillment of its aims? Naturally, there are no answers that will work for all companies all of the time. Each organization must choose the correct philosophy for its enterprise and this information should then be disseminated (and continuously reinforced) to all of the appropriate individuals. A continuous, voluntary, and tailored training program that is flexible enough to adapt to the technical and managerial needs of the organization should be developed. As the company acquires new pieces of equipment, implements new technologies or software, and institutes new management philosophies, training modules should be provided for employees. It is also essential that managers take the initiative to prepare themselves in the subject matter being offered to their personnel. Bosses who believe they are too busy for training or who think they are above it all will not only experience a loss of credibility but, what is worse, will doom implementation of the new approaches to failure.

An Action Plan for Improvement

Determine what you are trying to accomplish (e.g., what development and planning philosophies and techniques you want to adapt). Make sure your plan fits in with the long-range organizational goals. Write it down and get management's agreement and support (including executive management). Learn what is being taught. Evaluate all courses to determine whether they satisfy your criteria. Assure your workers that you support these ideas—and upper management must really demonstrate that support. Listen to what the people are learning. Provide follow-up support. Look for areas of confusion and clarify them. And get your money's worth from your training investment!

PUBLIC RELATIONS

In the advertising industry, the benefits of good publicity are quite naturally recognized and accepted. Why can't we borrow and integrate their techniques into the data processing business environment? Since our goal is to rethink our image of data processing, we can use advertising strategies to discover what the organization's current attitudes are, crystallize the "new opinion," and plan a public relations campaign.

Discover the Current Attitudes

Before committing to this project, the organization should be aware of two essentials: First, this is a time-consuming and labor-intensive effort. Second, the fact-finding process must be conducted in an unbiased manner and by a group with no vested interest in the outcome. It follows therefore that it may be preferable, both in terms of time and effort as well as objectivity, that this project be handled by an outside group.

All segments of the organization should be interviewed. The interviewees must be assured that their interviews will remain confidential and that they will be given an opportunity to verify and, if necessary, correct their summaries before they become public record. When the information is collated, it may then be categorized by positive and negative attitudes; these groups may then be subdivided into agreements and conflicts. It is extremely important, at this point, to give visibility to the red-flag issues that pervade every organization.

Crystallize the New Opinions

Executive and middle management must carefully weigh and consciously choose to retain or change each idea. Sometimes, a business decision dictates that we retain some less-than-desirable approach. While this is certainly legitimate, the organization should do so only when it fully understands the trade-offs. Managers must set priorities about the kind of work environment they want to create and then translate these priorities into effective human resource management policies. The outcome of this exercise should be a new business philosophy for data processing's position within the organization. This philosophy, naturally, will include the technological and economic aspects of the function, but also will address reshaping the attitudes of both data processing and users.

Plan a Public Relations Campaign

If the company were planning to introduce a new consumer product, they might stage an advertising campaign to bombard the media. Since we are aware of the success of this strategy, we may borrow some advertising ideas, shift them around, and add some new approaches of our own.

In the simplest form, strategically placed posters may introduce new ideas. For short-term results, contests and campaigns are effective. However, the real success of any project relies on two components: (1) satisfactory project completion and installation and (2) continued follow-up. The demise of the first is often the result of insufficient focus on the second. *If you want something to happen you should make someone responsible for it.* Since we want to establish an awareness function, it may be advisable to appoint the responsiblity for the implementation of this approach to the people who are ultimately responsible for elevating organizational awareness—the educational division of the company.

Making use of the state-of-the-art training technologies such as interactive video and computer-based instruction, proper implementation of the campaign may include an integration of strategically placed "message units," tailored training modules, and continuous and voluntary training programs (especially for users on reasonable expectations for data processing and for data processing on reasonable expectations for users).

IN CONCLUSION

Most of our literature concentrates on what to do about improving data processing productivity. By continuing to view this as a data processing issue, we reinforce their segregation from the mainstream of the organization. We must acknowledge that reversal of this trend will be accomplished only when we recognize that this is an organization problem. Since data processing accounts for so much of the total business budget, it behooves executive managers to take a more active interest in directing the role of data processing within the organization. Users must be educated to understand data processing and its frustrations, and data processing must be trained to appreciate users and their business.

Finally, we should recognize that a new way of doing business does not become a *fait accompli* overnight. Organizations that choose to restructure their environments should do so only if they acknowledge that these changes will take time and money. There is no such thing as a free lunch! But, do you pay now? Or do you pay later?

ACKNOWLEDGMENTS

I am indebted to Kathy Spencer who typed this manuscript in record time, so that I would not miss the deadline for submittal—by too many weeks. Dave Appleby of FORD in

London was a dear to let me have his cartoons to help lighten up a very serious subject. If I tried to name all of the colleagues who have discussed my ideas and forced me to crystallize my concepts, I'd probably take twenty more pages, so thank you, one and all!

REFERENCES

1. Yourdon, E. *Managing the Structured Techniques.* New York: Yourdon Press, 1979.
2. Yourdon, E. *Managing the System Life Cycle.* New York: Yourdon Press, 1982.
3. Metzger, P. W. *Managing a Programming Project.* New Jersey: Prentice-Hall, 1973.
4. Burrill, C., and E. Ellsworth. *Modern Project Management.* Englewood Cliffs, N.J.: Burrill-Ellsworth Associates, Inc., 1981.
5. Thomsett, R. *People and Project Management.* New York: Yourdon Press, 1980.
6. Peters, L. *Software Design: Methods and Techniques.* New York: Yourdon Press, 1981.
7. Brooks, F. P., Jr. *Mythical Man Month.* Reading, Mass.: Addison-Wesley, 1972.
8. Myers, G. J. *The Art of Software Testing.* New York: John Wiley & Sons, 1979.
9. Dickinson, B. *Developing Structured Systems.* New York: Yourdon Press, 1981.
10. Page-Jones, M. *The Practical Guide to Structured Systems Design.* New York: Yourdon Press, 1980.
11. Weist, J. D., and F. K. Levy, *A Management Guide to Pert/CPM.* New Jersey: Prentice Hall, 1977.
12. Boehm, B. W. *Software Engineering Economics.* Englewood Cliffs, N.J.: Prentice-Hall, 1981.
13. DeMarco, T. *Controlling Software Projects.* New York: Yourdon Press, 1982.
14. Block, B. *Politics of Projects.* New York: Yourdon Press, 1983.
15. Zells, L. "Strategic Systems Planning." *Yourdon Monthly Forum,* November, 1982.
16. Zells, L. "A Practical Approach To A Project Expectations Document." *COMPUTERWORLD,* 29 (1983), pp. 1–16.
17. Zells, L. "Should We Really Spend Our Money On Training?" *Yourdon Europe Forum,* August, 1983.

Are methodologies and system design techniques independent of one another?

by DENIS A. CONNOR
The Worker's Compensation Board
Toronto, Ontario, Canada

ABSTRACT

This paper discusses a common problem faced by information systems management; the need to impose management controls over the system development process through the use of project management tools such as application system development methodologies (ASDMs) and the interfacing of these controls with effective information system specification and design techniques. The paper describes a standardized ASDM and examines the effect on this ASDM of five different information system specification and design techniques in common use today.

INTRODUCTION

During the 1970s, it was recognized that large and complex systems were being built with virtually no management control, resulting in high cost overruns and late delivery of the systems, if delivered at all. Further, systems that were delivered often did not meet the users' requirements and were supported by poor or nonexistent documentation, which made system maintenance and enhancement a nightmare.

Nature abhors a vacuum and two types of solutions appeared. The first was the design and development of a variety of system specification and design techniques such as information engineering, structured analysis and design, structured requirements definition, and Jackson system development (JSD). The second was the advent of application systems development methodologies (ASDMs). The latter were project management tools that divided the entire specification, design, construction, and implementation process into a series of phases, activities, and tasks. Each phase, activity, and task had standard outputs (deliverables) defined and at specific checkpoints, user management could decide whether to proceed or not. These methodologies or project control systems were developed either by the organizations that used them or by vendors.

Management found that now they had control over system development and insisted that these standards be strictly followed. This meant that any system being planned, developed, and implemented had to follow the standard project plan and produce the standard outputs or deliverables. This proved to be both a blessing and a curse.

It was a blessing because the standards gave management tight control over the total process. The auditors and the quality control staff loved it because at last they could demand specific documentation in specific formats and containing specific information. It was a curse because the standard specifications were either in narrative form and too general to convert into a system design that effectively met the user's requirements, or too specific and directed at particular specification and design techniques, ruling out the use of other techniques.

There is no general solution to this problem because the problem itself is different in every organization. So each organization must solve its own problems. To give an appreciation for the type of situation that could be encountered, we describe here the type of information required and a generalized model of an ASDM. We then superimpose different specification and design techniques on the model and discuss their effects.

OUTPUTS FROM SYSTEM DEVELOPMENT

The outputs or deliverables (as they are often called) from system development can be classified under four basic headings. These are management decision-making information, project management information, system development and maintenance information, and system operating information.

Problems with Standard Outputs

In general, problems encountered in defining the management decision-making information, the project control information, and the operating information are a function of management policy and the computer operating environment in a particular organization. But problems encountered with system specification and design information are a function of the system specification and design techniques used. The latter is hard to understand because the argument put forward is that the requirement is for a set of design "blueprints" and accompanying documentation. If this works for airplanes, bridges, and houses, why does it not work for computer systems?

In the case of airplanes, houses, and bridges, the blueprints reflect *what* is to be delivered. In computer systems development, the specification and design documents reflect *how* the system has been specified and designed. As a result, the possibilities for differences in specification and design approaches are endless. The next question that can be asked is why *how* and not *what*? The answer is that a part of the development and maintenance documentation is "what" information. This encompasses logical and physical file structures, record and data definitions, program code, system and subsystem content, and input and output definitions. The "how" information, that is, the deliverables specified by the techniques, describes how the "what" information was obtained.

Computer systems are constantly changing entities—unlike airplanes, bridges, and houses. To keep up with this constant change, the staff that maintain and enhance these systems must have access to the "how" information to save them time and effort that could be wasted reinventing the wheel. That is why the "how" information is so critical.

A GENERALIZED MODEL OF AN ASDM

The major activities that make up an Application System Development Methodology are the feasibility study, the business specification, the system specification, the system design, the system construction and testing, the system implementation, and the system review.

The Feasibility Study

The feasibility study is done to provide management with sufficient information to decide whether to build the system or to take other action. The report that is produced defines the project scope, the user's system objectives, performance requirements, interfacing systems, a general description of the system to be developed and the alternate choices, the effect on the organization and on the computer environment, the cost of development, the cost of operating the system, the benefits to be obtained, and the risks of not developing the system. It also includes a project plan, a budget, a detailed schedule for the next phase or major activity, and an estimated schedule and budget for the total project.

When evaluating the system choices available, the feasibility study must take into account the specificaton and design techniques that will be used. The information obtained during the feasibility study becomes the foundation for the detailed specificaton and design to be done later.

The Business Specification

The business specification is a detailed definition of the user's business needs that should be met by the proposed system. This specification could include the user's operational objectives, a description of the outputs required to meet these objectives and when they are required, the flow of information between organizational entities, the logical processes required to convert input data into file data and file data into output data, and a description of the logical files.

Every author has a different definition of the business specification because his definition fits the particular specification and design technique he advocates. For example, DeMarco's business specification is based on a logical data flow diagram, and Orr's is based on an assembly line diagram and a description of the outputs. The reader at this point is entitled to become confused. Let us examine logically the content of the business specification exclusive of the design techniques.

The user needs information to carry out the functions necessary to meet specified objectives. So the most important items to be defined are the objectives and the data needed to meet these objectives. Although some organizations might have difficulty defining objectives, they can probably define their functions. If we assume that these functions involve processes to meet objectives (even if undefined), then we can define the data needed to carry out these functions.

Having defined the data, we need to store them so that we can access them when needed. This means organizing the data into logical groupings. These groupings consist of allied items of data or records. As we will be dealing with many such records, we need to define logical record files.

These data must be obtained from somewhere. So we need to define the data sources or the inputs. Similarly, the data must be formatted before they can be used. So we need to define the outputs. The user may decide that specific outputs are not needed, but instead may choose to access the files to obtain data to meet specific needs as they arise. If this is the case, we do not need to define the outputs. The outputs or the data in the files will be needed by the user at regular intervals of time, such as immediately, daily, weekly, and so on. So we need to define the response time for each output. The organization may be centralized or decentralized, requiring either centralized or decentralized files or databases. The data input may not be in the format in which it is filed and may need to be logically combined with the file data before they are stored. Similarly, the file data may need to be processed to produce data in a different format in the outputs. All this logical data processing must be defined as a set of logical procedures. The business specification, like the feasibility study, includes a detailed budget and schedule for the next phase, an updated estimate of the budget, and a schedule to the end of the project.

The System Specification

The system specification is the division of the business specification into computerized and manual processes. It also includes descriptions of how the system could function, for example, on-line update and retrieval, overnight batch update and on-line retrieval, or a centralized database with distributed-data up-date and retrieval. The effect of each choice on the organization's hardware and software environment is evaluated. Each system choice is priced and tentatively scheduled. The choices are discussed and appropriate recommendations are made to the user. The user decides which choice to implement. This choice is budgeted and scheduled in detail for the following phase and the total project cost and schedule are updated.

The System Design

This phase is probably better termed system architecture and design. The term architecture is appropriate because the physical file or database and network architectures are defined at this point. The subsystem, program, and module hierarchies are established and the program logic is defined in detail. Test plans, file conversion, hardware and software acquisition and installation plans, and implementation strategies are prepared. The project budget and schedule are updated in detail until implementation of the production system is completed.

Construction and Testing

During this phase, all modules and programs are coded and tested, and physical files or databases are established and tested with the coded modules and programs at the program, subsystem, and system levels using the new hardware and software. Forms and screens are designed, user procedures are written, and operational documentation prepared. In short, the system is built and tested by the builders, the designers, and the users.

System Implementation

System implementation involves the training of the operating staff and users, conversion of files and databases, organizational changes if necessary, the protection of production programs and modules, and the installation of security controls for access to data in the files or databases.

System Review

During a system review, the system is examined to determine whether the user's requirements are being met and to fine-tune the system to improve system processing efficiency.

THE ASDM AND THE SYSTEM SPECIFICATION AND DESIGN TECHNIQUES

We can assume that a feasibility study is necessary, regardless of the specification and design technique to be used, accepting that the cost of the specification and design technique will influence the system choices described. We can also assume that the specification and design technique will not play a major role during the coding, testing, and implementation of the system because at this time, the files and databases have been defined, and the subsystems, programs, and modules have been specified and designed in detail. This leaves three phases or activities that must be matched against each specification and design technique; the business specification, the system specification, and the system design. For the benefit of the reader, the outputs from these activities, excluding project control information, are summarized in Table I.

To determine whether ASDMs are independent of information system design techniques, let us examine four well-known approaches in use today and how they interface with the generalized ASDM described above. The four are information engineering,[1] structured analysis and design,[2,3] structured requirements definition,[4] and Jackson system development.[5] We will also discuss a fifth technique that goes under the heading of "prototyping," which may be combined with some of the other techniques. In our examination, we will only identify those activities and outputs that are relevant to this discussion. Those readers interested in examining this subject in depth should refer to References 6 and 7.

TABLE I—Feasibility, specification, and design outputs (excluding project control information)

Feasibility Study
- —Project scope
- —User's system objectives
- —Performance requirements
- —Interfacing systems
- —General description of system to be developed with alternate choices
- —Effect on the organization
- —Effect on the Computer Environment
- —Development cost
- —Operating cost
- —Benefits and risks

Business Specification
- —Definition of the business objectives or the functions
- —Definition of the data required to meet the objectives or the functions
- —Definition of the logical records and files
- —Definition of the data input
- —Definition of the outputs (if required)
- —Identification of when output or file data is required
- —Identification of the need for centralized or decentralized files or data bases
- —Definitions of the input process logic
- —Definitions of the output process logic (if required)

System Specification
- —Logical system divided into computerized and manual processes
- —Possible implementation options, such as on-line and batch update, on-line data access, etc., with their associated costs, benefits, and estimated development schedules

System Design
- —Physical file or database design
- —Network design
- —Physical architecture of subsystems and programs
- —Detailed program and module logic
- —Test plans
- —File conversion plans
- —Hardware and software acquisition and installation plans
- —Implementation strategies

Information Engineering

The information engineering activities we will examine are information analysis, procedure formation, implementation strategies, and program specification synthesis.

In information analysis, the business objectives to be met by the system are defined along with the data required to meet these objectives. The output from information analysis is a normalized data model that provides all the output data required from the system. If distributed processing is included in the objectives, the data model should reflect either a centralized data structure or a series of distributed-data models to meet the distributed file or database needs. In procedure formation, the logical input and output processes are defined along with the inputs and outputs. The output information should include when the outputs are required. Hence, the business specification can be obtained using information engineering (Table II).

In system specification, we divide the system into computerized and manual processes. We also discuss possible implementation options such as on-line and batch update, on-line data access, and so on, with their associated costs, benefits, and estimated development schedules. In information engineering, these activities are the front-end of the activity termed implementation strategies (Table III).

The system design activity or phase includes physical file or database design, network design, the physical architecture of the subsystems and programs, and detailed program and module logic. In information engineering, the file, database, and network design are covered under physical database design.

TABLE II—Information engineering—business specification

	Inf. Anal.	Proced. format	Implem. strategies	Program Spec. synth.
Business Objectives, functions	Yes			
Data required by objectives, functions	Norm. data model			
Logical records file definition	Yes			
Data input		Yes		
Output (if required)		Yes		
When output, file data required		Yes		
Central., decentral. files, databases	Yes			
Input process logic		Event diagrams, condition tables, LAMs & DADS		
Output process logic (if required)		Yes		

TABLE III—Information engineering—system specification

	Inf. anal.	Proced. format	Implem. strat.	Program spec. synth.
Logical system into computerized, manual processes			Yes	
Implementation options			Yes	

TABLE IV—Information engineering—system design

	Inf. anal.	Proced. format.	Implem. strat.	Program spec. synth.
Physical file or database design	This is a specific activity in information engineering.			
Network design			Yes	
Physical architecture of Subsystems, Programs			Yes	
Detailed program, module logic				Yes
Test plans			Yes	
File conversion plans			Yes	
Hardware, software acquisition, installation plans			Yes	
Implementation strategies			Yes	

The subsystem and program architecture, and the detailed program and module logic are part of program specification synthesis. Test plans, file conversion plans, and hardware and software acquisition and installation plans are part of the activity termed implementation strategies (Table IV).

We conclude that information engineering can be superimposed on the business specification, system specification, and the system design activities in the ASDM. But when it is superimposed, the information engineering and ASDM activities overlap. Though the ASDM's outputs can be produced, a project control plan established for the ASDM will not fit information engineering unless the information-engineering activities are subdivided and reorganized under the ASDM.

Structured Analysis and Design

Structured analysis and design are divided into three major activities: structured analysis, structured design, and implementation.

In structured analysis, though the business objectives are not defined, the system functions provide the basis for the proposed logical data flow diagram, the minispecifications, and the data dictionary. The data dictionary contains information on the inputs and the outputs from the system. The minispecifications define the process logic. In addition, a normalized logical data structure is produced. Though not mentioned in the text,[2] it can be assumed that distributed processing could affect the logical file structures and the data flow diagrams. Identification of when the outputs are required is left until the structured design activity. Hence, the new logical environment defines the business specification, excluding the "response" times required (Table V).

The structured specification includes the partition of the proposed logical data flow diagram into computerized and manual processes, and the identification of the different physical options available with estimated costs, benefits, and schedules. This is the output required from system specification (Table VI).

The outputs from structured design are the structure charts packaged into physical modules and programs, and the detailed program and module logic. Not mentioned but implied in the text,[3] is the physical design of the files or databases and the networks. Also not specifically mentioned but assumed are the test plans, file conversion plans, hardware and software acquisition and installation plans, and the implementation strategies (Table VII).

Structured analysis and design closely complement the ASDM process with minor variations and provide the required ASDM outputs. A generalized project control plan developed for the ASDM could be expanded to fit structured analysis and design.

Structured Requirements Definition

Structured requirements definition consists of two major classes of activities; logical definition and physical definition. Logical definition is subdivided into the application context

TABLE V—Structured analysis and design—business specification

	Structured Analysis	Structured Design	Implement.
Business objectives, functions	Yes		
Data required by objectives, functions	Data dictionary		
Logical records, file definition	Normalized data structure		
Data input	Data dictionary		
Output (if required)	Data dictionary		
When output, file data required		Yes	
Central., Decentrl. files, databases	Yes		
Input process logic	Proposed logical DFD, minispecs.		
Output process logic (if required)	Proposed logical DFD, minispecs.		

TABLE VI—Structured analysis and design—System specification

	Structured Analysis	Structured Design	Implement.
Logical system into computerized, manual processes	Yes		
Implementation options	Yes		

TABLE VII—Structured analysis and design—System design

	Structured Analysis	Structured Design	Implement.
Physical file, database design			Yes
Network design			Yes
Physical architecture of Subsystems, programs		Structure chart	
Detailed program, module logic		Yes	
Test plans			Yes
File conversion plans			Yes
Hardware, software acquisitions, installation plans			Yes
Implementation strategies			Yes

definition, the application functions, and the application results.

The mainline functional flow diagram, which is an assembly-line diagram for the system, along with the process descriptions and the application results or outputs, describe the logical system. This logical system is based on the system functions and the flow of data between organizational entities. *When* the output data are provided is implicit in the mainline functional flow diagrams. The logical records and files are organized into logical structures but the text does not indicate how this is done.[4] No specific mention is made of distributed processing needs, but it can be assumed that they could affect the mainline functional flow and the logical data structures. In general, completion of the logical definition phase provides the outputs for the business specification (Table VIII).

In the physical definition phase, alternative physical solutions are examined based on computerizing part or all of the logical system. This is in line with the output required from system specification (Table IX).

The system design, that is, the physical design of the system, is not discussed in the structured requirements defini-

TABLE VIII—Structured requirements definition—Business specification

	Logical Definition			
	Applic. Context Definit.	Applic. Funct.	Applic. Results	Physical Definition
Business objectives, functions	Entity diagram, objectives			
Data required by objectives, functions			Logical data output: form, content, structure	
Logical records, file definition			Logical bases files	
Data input			Principal outputs,	
Output (if required)			include inputs	
When output, file data required			Organizational cycles	
Central., Decentrl. files, databases			Yes	
Input process logic		Assembly Line diagrams		
Output process logic (if required)		Line diagrams and mainline functional flow		

TABLE IX—Structured requirements definition—System specification

	Logical Definition			
	Applic. Context Definit.	Applic. Funct.	Applic. Results	Physical Definition
Logical system into computerized, manual processes		Expansion of functional flow		
Implementation options				Alternate physical solutions

TABLE X—Structured requirements definition—System design

	Logical Definition			
	Applic. Context Definit.	Applic. Funct.	Applic. Results	Physical Definition
Physical file, database design				Yes
Network design				Yes
Physical architecture of subsystems, programs				Yes
Detailed program, module logic				Yes
Test plans				Yes
File conversion plans				Yes
Hardware, software acquisition, installation plans				Yes
Implementation strategies				Yes

tion, but it is assumed that the selected physical solution is expanded in sufficient detail to provide the outputs for this activity (Table X).

The structured requirements definition, like structured analysis and design, closely complements the ASDM with minor variations. So a project plan designed for the ASDM can be expanded to cover Structured Requirements Definition.

Jackson System Development

Jackson system development (JSD) consists of six steps. Jackson approaches system development in a unique manner where he identifies entities in step 1; maps the actions that can be taken on the entities in the real world in step 2; converts these actions and entities into initial models for computerization in Step 3; adds functions to these models to produce required outputs in step 4; adds the response or timing requirement to the model in step 5; and builds and implements the system in step 6. Moreover, until step 5, the design is based on a single processor for each entity.

This approach is completely different from the activities and the outputs described in the ASDM. Readers intending to use JSD should be prepared to develop on their own or acquire from Jackson a project plan or methodology to build JSD systems.

Prototyping

Prototyping is not a design technique by itself. Effective prototyping can only be done in conjunction with another system design technique and its use with an ASDM will vary according to the technique with which it is combined.

STANDARD ASDM OUTPUTS

We concluded earlier that standard outputs could be defined for management decision making, project management, and system operation. But system design and maintenance outputs presented problems because they were heavily influenced by the system design techniques used. The three ASDM activities affected by these problems are the business specification, the system specification and the system design.

Based on our analysis of the generalized ASDM and four system design techniques, we can conclude that standard outputs can be defined for the business specification, the system specification, and the system design. These generic outputs are listed in Table I. There could always be exceptions to these standards as we saw in JSD. Further, secondary documentation standards should be defined for the process output from each system design technique applied. Examples of process outputs are data flow diagrams (DFDs), assembly line diagrams, condition tables, event diagrams, logical access maps (LAMs) and database action diagrams (DADs). This process documentation should simplify the tasks of system enhancement and maintenance.

We can conclude further that if an ASDM specifies outputs which are confined to individual techniques such as data flow diagrams or insists on narrative descriptions of specifications, it will probably be rigid and difficult to modify.

REFERENCES

1. Martin, J., and C. Finkelstein. *Information Engineering.* Carnforth, England: Savant Research Studies, 1981.
2. deMarco, T. *Structured Analysis and System Specification.* Englewood Cliffs, N.J.: Prentice-Hall, 1979.
3. Yourdon, E., and L. Constantine. *Structured Design.* Englewood Cliffs, N.J.: Prentice-Hall, 1979.
4. Orr, K. *Structured Requirements Definition.* Topeka, Kansas: Ken Orr and Associates, 1981.
5. Jackson, M. *System Development.* London: Prentice-Hall International, 1983.
6. Connor, D. *Information System Specification and Design "Road Map."* Englewood Cliffs, N.J.: Prentice-Hall, 1984.
7. Connor, D. *Application Systems Development Methodologies: Solution or Problem.* Carnforth, England: Savant Research Studies, 1982.

Aspects of integrated software

by CLYDE W. HOLSAPPLE and ANDREW B. WHINSTON

Purdue University
West Lafayette, Indiana

ABSTRACT

Numerous microcomputer software systems claim to have a capability of integrating several different functions such as spreadsheet, word processing, data base management, and graphics. This paper considers various alternative approaches to integration and presents a classification scheme. Examples of commercial software packages that fit into the different categories are given.

INTRODUCTION

Software packages that integrate multiple functions into a single system are becoming increasingly prominent in the micro-world. Called all-in-one systems or integrated systems, these packages are generalized tools that can be used to store and process information in a wide variety of application areas. The distinct information processing functions incorporated into an integrated system can include facilities for data management, spreadsheet analysis, programming, graphics, ad hoc inquiry, text processing, forms processing, and so forth.

Although many observers tend to lump all integrated packages together into a single pigeonhole, the emerging area of integrated packages is by no means monolithic. One obvious differentiating factor is the assortment of information-processing components that are available. Even those packages with identical types of components can differ substantially from each other. For instance, the data management component of one may have extensive, well-developed capabilities, whereas another may include only a rudimentary data management function.

Although the assortment of components and the extent of each are important in assessing a given integrated software package, there is a much more fundamental basis for characterizing one package in relation to others. This is the style or philosophy of integration embodied in the system. Three distinct integration styles are examined here. Each style has unique implications for users.

STYLES OF INTEGRATION

An appreciation of the basic styles of integration is valuable for classifying integrated software packages and evaluating which are most appropriate for a prospective user's needs. Integration generally means that multiple components are unified into a systemic whole. Style of integration is the nature of that unification. It involves the way in which components are related to each other, interact with each other, and mutually cooperate within a system. This issue can be examined quite apart from a consideration of which components exist in the system, although the style can affect the extent of individual components.

Independent Integration

One basic approach to integration provides a software setting from which a user can invoke any one of several independent components. The user is able to select one component at a time and to use its information-processing capabilities. To carry out a different type of processing, the user exits from the current component and begins working with the newly selected component's facilities. To ease the switching among components, the skeletal software setting may allow results of previous work with other components to be seen while using a different component.

Significantly, the components available to a user under this style of integration are independent. That is, a user can work with one component without a knowledge of how to use others. The user may even be unaware of the existence of components whose capabilities he or she does not need. For instance, a user who is uninterested in spreadsheet analyses does not need to learn about spreadsheets in order to produce graphics or carry out file management tasks. A further implication of this component independence is that the characteristics of one component (e.g., a spreadsheet processor) do not restrict the capacities or capabilities of other components (e.g., a file manager).

The independent integration style may be likened to a Swiss army knife (Figure 1). Several tools, each appropriate for a certain set of processing tasks, are united into a single handy package. Depending on the task at hand, the user selects the appropriate tool. At any time the user can "fold" that tool away and "fold" out a different tool. To the extent that the original design of the package allows expansion, new tools can be attached to the package as they are needed or become available.

As the Swiss army knife analogy suggests, the structure of this integration style does not permit the individual tools or components to interact with each other directly or simultaneously. A user cannot perform a file management task within the confines of the spreadsheet component, define spreadsheet cells within a program, or define a spreadsheet cell in terms of a program. Nevertheless, some degree of indirect component interaction can be achieved with the independent integration style by employing a single method of data formatting for all components.

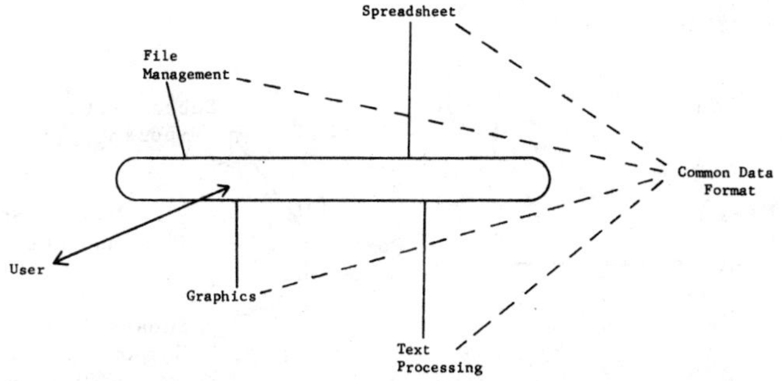

Figure 1—The independent integration style

When each component stores data according to the same format, the individual components can interact with each other, albeit indirectly through their common data storage method. When processing with one component (e.g., a file manager) concludes, the results are stored and the user can then begin processing that data with a different type of component (e.g., graphics). Without this commonality of data format, the independent integration style remains a bundling of disparate components into a handy package that makes the selection of any one of them very convenient. Leading examples of software adhering to the independent integration style include Apple's LISA software[1] and VisiCorp's VisiOn.[2]

Inclusive Integration

Inclusive integration is based on the existence of a clearly dominant component. All other components in the package are subservient to and dependent on the dominant component. A user can work with a subservient component only through or in conjunction with the dominant component, which component serves as a host environment for the use of other components. In a sense, the subservient components (text processor, graphics, etc.) are included within the dominant component (e.g., a spreadsheet processor) so that its processing capabilities are effectively extended beyond those of its stand-alone counterparts (e.g., traditional spreadsheet processors).

The user of a package that adheres to this style of integration must understand the dominant component, even if the user has no need for that component's type of processing. While subservient components may be used independently of each other, they cannot be used independently of the dominant component. A further implication of this integration style is that the capacities and capabilities of subservient components may very well be limited by the characteristics of the dominant component.

Consider, for instance, the case of a dominant spreadsheet component. It is a fairly simple matter to add a few commands that allow a user to treat designated chunks of a spreadsheet as if they were miniature files. In so doing, a file (or at least a pseudo-file) management component has been included within the dominant spreadsheet processing component. This emulation of file management is a useful advance over traditional spreadsheet processors. However, the pseudo-file manager is constrained by the dominant component's spreadsheet dimensions. Because it is actually a chunk of spreadsheet, a psuedo-file's capacity cannot exceed the number of spreadsheet rows.

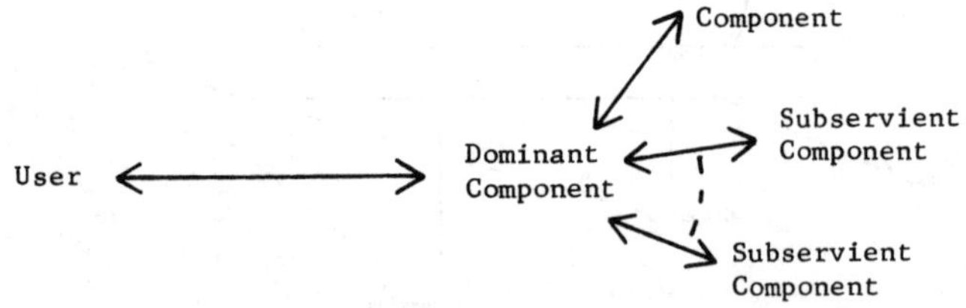

Figure 2—The inclusive integration style

Though it lacks the quality of component independence, inclusive integration has an important advantage over independent integration. There is the possibility of a much closer relationship between components. This closeness typically manifests itself in relationships between the dominant component and its subservient components; the subservient components may or may not be able to interact with each other. By "closeness" we mean that a user can rapidly alternate between the processing capabilities of functionally distinct components without being required consciously to leave (fold in) one component and enter (fold out) another. The subservient component's functions are ready for immediate use within the dominant component. Aside from the absence (or lessening) of this shuffling, "closeness" also may indicate that a user can employ several components' functions in a single command rather than a sequence of commands. Leading representatives of the inclusive integration style include the Context MBA[3] and Lotus 1-2-3[4] systems.

Synergistic Integration

A third style of integration is the one that establishes close relationships among independent components. A high degree of direct interaction among multiple components is supported, even though there is no single dominant component. Because the components are on an equal footing, any one component can be used without knowledge of how to use the others. Beyond this, a user can interweave functions of multiple components at will, without formally leaving one component and entering another.

A user may interweave these in a linear fashion, or the functions of one component may be invoked within the exercise of some other component's capabilities (perhaps in a single command). Thus, with this integration style, one component can serve another, and vice versa. However, neither is

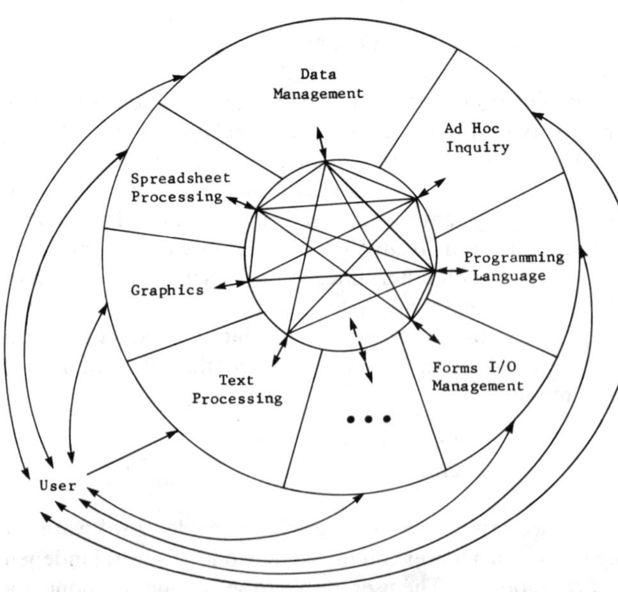

Figure 3—The synergistic integration style

subservient to the other because each can be used independently. For instance, spreadsheet processing can be invoked from within a program. Conversely, programs may be invoked within the processing of a spreadsheet. Nevertheless, the package's programming component may be used entirely independently of its spreadsheet component. This independence means that no component unduly constrains the capacity or capabilities of any other component.

An apt term for describing this style of integration is "synergy." Dictionaries define synergy as the simultaneous action of *separate* components which together have a *greater total* effect than the sum of their *individual effects*. In the synergistic integration style, separate components have individual effects, that is, effects that are uncolored and unconstrained by the existence of other components. In addition, the components can act in tandem to offer capabilities that would not exist if the components could only be used one at a time. A leading implementation of the synergistic integration style is the Knowledge Manager (KnowledgeMan) by Micro Data Base Systems Inc.[5]

ASSORTMENT OF COMPONENTS

Regardless of style, a consideration of the integrated system's assortment of components also is important. This consideration is necessarily based on a user's processing needs. For instance, the existence of a text-processing component is vital for many clerical workers, whereas it is probably of lesser value to many managerial workers. The reverse is probably true for a spreadsheet, statistical, or ad hoc inquiry component.

The intent here is not to propose prioritized rankings of components for various user classes. Instead, we identify a list of components that should be considered when assessing the suitability of a package's component assortment for a *particular* user. These components are data management, ad hoc inquiry, statistical analysis, spreadsheet analysis, programming language, graphics generation, forms management, and text processing.

For some users, a package's facilities for interfacing to external data files and external software also deserve consideration. When assessing an integrated software system's assortment of components in terms of their suitability for a given user, two points should be kept in mind. First, the user's needs may change or grow in such a way that the existence of a particular component becomes more important over time. If the user's system does not have that component, then the system can become insufficient or obsolete for this user. The results are that a different system (having the newly important component) must be learned and that data and algorithms developed under the first system may need to be converted. The obvious implication is that all else being equal, more components are preferable to fewer components. An exception is the case of an inclusive integration style in which a user may be required to deal with components that are of little immediate interest.

The second point is that within a package all components may not be uniformly extensive. Furthermore, a particular type of component may be very extensive in one package and very primitive in another package. Not only can two packages with the same kinds of components differ drastically in their integration styles, they can also differ widely in terms of the extensiveness of their individual components. Here too, the possibility of user growth should not be overlooked. A primitive data management component may suffice initially, but may become obsolete as data volume and processing requirements grow.

EXTENT OF INDIVIDUAL COMPONENTS

Just as the existence of a given component is very important to some users and of lesser importance to others, the importance of an individual component's extent depends on a particular user's needs. For each of the component types cited above, criteria for appreciating its extensiveness in a particular package can be identified. These are summarized below in a suggestive, rather than exhaustive, fashion.

As for data management, there is the basic approach to data organization. Most micro-based data management systems are file handlers: They organize data into multiple files. They also allow data to be retrieved selectively from a file, multiple files to be merged into a new file based on redundant data values, records in a file to be sorted, and so forth. In the micro-world, file handlers are often referred to as "relational database management systems." However, with few exceptions, they lack the properties normally expected of a full-fledged database management system. Nor do they begin to approach the power and sophistication of the new post-relational approach to database management.

Disregarding terminology, the crucial criteria of a data management component are its data volume capacities, the nature of its data access capabilities, and the extent of its data security features. Capacity refers to factors such as the number of fields per record type, the number of records per file, the number of files simultaneously open for processing, and the number of characters per record. Data access should be examined from the angles of data creation, modification, and extraction. For instance, can records be created interactively through user-friendly forms? Are virtual fields supported for automatic data updates? Can data be extracted by selective browsing with forms and by any of a variety of indexes? Data security can be just as important in a micro-environment as it is for mainframes. Data security for micro-data management is usually nonexistent. However, where it does exist it can range from simple password checks to field-level read–write access controls and automatic data encryption.

An ad hoc inquiry component allows a user to interrogate the system's data on a spur-of-the-moment basis without resorting to a sequence of low-level commands and the production of intermediate files. The language for specifying an inquiry ideally should resemble conversational English and should be nonprocedural. It should be capable of being used by persons who are unfamiliar with common aspects of data management. An example of a reasonably extensive facility for ad hoc inquiry is the SELECT command supported in IBM's mainframe SQL system. SQL-like query components are beginning to become available in the micro-world. Criteria for assessing the extent of an ad hoc query component include the support of multiconditioned inquiry, automatic expression–function evaluation, inquiry directed at multiple data tables in a single command, wildcard conditions, dynamic sorting of output based on multiple fields or expressions, multilevel control breaks, dynamic editing of generated data, and so forth.

A minimal component for statistical analysis can compute the basic statistics including average, variance, and standard deviation. It should be able to produce statistics not only for stored data but also for expressions based on that data. A valuable characteristic for a statistical component is the ability to generate full statistics for multiple variables from specified subsets of data held in multiple files—in response to a single command. More elaborate statistical components would have built-in facilities for performing standard types of econometric analysis.

A spreadsheet component should at least have the capabilities of traditional stand-alone spreadsheet processors such as the popular VisiCalc. Beyond these common capabilities, the extent of a spreadsheet component can be judged by such factors as the degree to which it permits a cell to be defined in terms of multiple data values that do not reside in the spreadsheet, the degree of algorithmic flexibility available when defining a cell (that is, a simple formula as opposed to a program with branching, iteration, etc.), the degree to which it supports conditional activation of special audio–visual highlighting of selected cell values, the degree of read and write security for cell definitions, and so forth.

A reasonably extensive programming component should provide the major logic control structures, such as conditional iteration, conditional branching, parameterized procedure invocation, and case testing. There should be no arbitrary limit on the depth of nesting. Nor should there be any arbitrary limit on the number of variables and arrays available for use. Both local and global declarations should be allowed. A healthy collection of built-in numeric and string manipulation functions also should be present in an extensive programming component. For application system developers, the abilities of encrypting programs and providing run-time versions of the integrated system are also highly desirable.

Graphics generation can range from low resolution to ultrahigh resolution. Given that it has a reasonably high-resolution level, a graphics component's extent can be measured in terms of the type of graphs that can be produced, the limits on data volume used to generate a graph, and the presence of various presentation conveniences. If it is intended for research, engineering, or business graphics, the component's support of the following types of graphs should be considered: bar graphs (stacked, clustered, three-dimensional), pie plots (exploded, "other" slices), scatter diagrams, high–low–close charts, area plots (cumulative, percentage), and line graphs. For some users, the ability to draw free-form pictures, logos, maps, and so forth, is important.

An extensive graphics component avoids placing low limits on the number of variables whose data can be incorporated into a single graph. Use of at least a dozen variables is desirable, and in the case of pie plots an extensive graphics component supports several dozen slices per pie. As for presentation convenience, an examination of the following factors is helpful in assessing the extent of a graphics component: simultaneous display of multiple graphs, multicolor graphs, user-controlled pattern (e.g., color, fill type, line type, point type) sequences, user-controlled legends and labels, rapid recall of previously generated graphs, long-term disk storage of graphs, graph printing, and user-controlled ranges and scaling.

A forms management component designs, maintains, and uses forms. It is capable of dealing with forms for screen input or output, as well as potentially large forms for printer output. An extensive forms management component allows a user to design or revise forms by interactively "painting" their characteristics on a console screen. This includes the drawing of various sized blocks of color at desired locations in a form, directly creating various literals (labels, titles, and prompts) wherever desired in the form, and sketching out the location of nonliteral form elements (places where data will be input or output through the form). The form designer may be able to create various special effects for each literal and nonliteral. Reverse video, half-intensity, bell sounding, and blinking are examples. The forms management component should provide high-level commands that can process, that is, display, clear, re-evaluate, and accept data input through an entire form at a time.

Text-processing components may range from simple line editors to full-scale word processors. A reasonably extensive text-processing component would have facilities that begin to approach those of elaborate stand-alone word processing software. These include flexible cursor movement, automatic vertical and horizontal scrolling, block processing, character–line–file insertion, character and line deletion, searches, and changes within user-controlled ranges and with wildcard pattern matching, and various formatting controls (wordwrap, page headers and footers, right and left justification, etc.). An extensive text component does not impose an arbitrary limit on the number of lines or characters in a piece of text.

The foregoing points are suggestive of issues to be considered when assessing the extent of an individual component. Beyond these, there also is the issue of the degree to which an individual component's innate capabilities are enhanced through synergistic relationships with other components. Although the combinatorial magnitude of such possibilities is far beyond the present scope, this difference between the total and the sum of its parts should not be overlooked in synergistically integrated packages.

USER INTERFACE

The nature of a user interface is a significant aspect of any software. It can be based on system-driven interaction (through menus), user-driven interaction (through a command language), or some compromise between the two. Each has its strengths and each is viable for integrated software packages. Combinations of these interaction protocols are also possible in an integrated software package.

System-driven interaction guides a user through a processing session by indicating permissible processing alternatives at each step of the way. At each juncture, the user can choose one of a number of predefined alternatives. Provided that the structure of alternatives can be organized hierarchically and that it is not overly massive in breadth or depth, the approach to interaction results in a user interface that can be learned quickly. It is also easy to use in certain circumstances, but can be cumbersome or very difficult to use in others.

The ease of use derives from the fixed structure that system-driven interaction imposes on a user's thought pattern. This suffices nicely as long as the user's problems conform to that predefined structure. However, system-driven interaction using moderately deep structures can become cumbersome as a user gains experience. Rather than merely saying what he or she wants, the experienced user is still required to trace through a structure of alternatives. Furthermore, as a user's needs and expertise grow, a structure of alternatives that was once sufficient may no longer be so.

User-driven interaction is predicated on the user taking the initiative in telling the system what he or she wants. The user acts rather than reacts. The crucial point here is the language that is used to tell the system what is wanted. Ideally, this language should be conversational and English-like. If it is not, it will be difficult for nontechnical persons to learn and use. There is also the issue of the language's richness: It should be sufficiently flexible to enable a user to directly express both simple and complex needs.

The assortment and individual extent of an integrated system's components influence the nature of its user interface. In the case of modest extent, system-driven interaction is quite suitable. The structure of alternatives can be kept to a manageable size. As extent increases, however, attempts to accommodate all possibilities by enumerating them tend to result in increasingly complex and cumbersome system-driven interaction. Furthermore, there are certain types of components that inherently are not well suited to system-driven interaction. An example is a programming component. User-driven interaction tends to be most appropriate in cases of very extensive components, inherently user-driven components, and highly synergistic integration where processing need not be hierarchical.

SUMMARY

Integrated packages are rapidly becoming a major force in the software world. Three significant directions in the design of integrated software packages have been identified: independent integration, inclusive integration, and synergistic integration. Along any direction the assortment of components can vary, being oriented toward certain classes of users. The extent of each individual component is another significant aspect of an integrated software system. A fourth major consideration is the nature of the system's user interface. As this type of software continues to mature, we should expect to see it incorporate new and more powerful components, data security mechanisms, the ability to support multiple, simultaneous users, user-definable interfaces, and parallel processing capabilities.

REFERENCES

1. *Lisa Owner's Guide.* Cupertino, Calif.: Apple Computer Corp., 1983.
2. *VisiOn Planning Seminar.* San Jose, Calif.: VisiCorp, 1983.
3. *MBA Reference Manual.* Torrance, Calif.: Context Management Systems, 1983.
4. *Lotus User's Manual.* Cambridge, Mass.: Lotus Development Corp., 1983.
5. *KnowledgeMan Reference Manual.* Lafayette, Ind.: Micro Data Base Systems, Inc., 1983.

The integrated software and user interface of Apple's Lisa

by EDWARD W. BIRSS
Apple Computer, Inc.
Cupertino, California

ABSTRACT

In 1979 Apple began to develop Lisa, a workstation to enhance the productivity of office workers. The hardware was built around a Motorola 68000, a bit-mapped display, and a mouse. The user interface is intuitive, using real-world concepts rather than computer concepts. It is easy to learn, and provides for both novice users still learning the system and users that have mastered the system. The user interface is modeless and consistent. The uniformity of the user interface supports transferrable learning—the ability to learn an operation once and apply it over and over again in another application in a different context.

The user interface also supports data interchange among documents of the same or different types. This interchange of data, coupled with the multitasking operating system and the multiple windows of the Lisa, permits the use of several tools to perform a task that one tool alone could not accomplish. The Lisa user interface and its applications provide an environment that allows the user to concentrate on what is to be accomplished rather than on how to accomplish it. In this way, Lisa provides tools to improve the productivity of the office worker.

INTRODUCTION

Apple Computer formed the Lisa team in 1979 to develop a personal computer that would dramatically improve the productivity of typical office workers (professionals, managers, and their assistants). To accomplish this goal, a hardware and software solution radically different from current personal computer offerings was required. At that time, personal computers had the functionality but lacked the capacity, speed, and ease of use necessary to reach a market of users who did not want to learn the details of how a computer worked.

Inspired by SMALLTALK[1] the Lisa team developed a system that has the functionality and speed users require, and additionally has a common user interface that supports gradual learning and promotes interchange of data among the same or different applications. The combination of multiple tools with a consistent user interface and data interchange among applications permits the user to work with several tools concurrently to accomplish a particular task.

LISA HARDWARE

The Lisa is a Motorola 68000-based personal computer with 512 or 1024 Kbytes of main memory, a memory management unit, a bit-mapped display, a detachable keyboard, a mouse, a built-in 400-Kbyte floppy disk drive, and a 5- or 10-megabyte Winchester disk (see Figure 1). This hardware provides the functionality, speed, and ease of use required to support the Lisa user interface.

The 68000 microprocessor was not the first choice. Development began on a home-grown bit-sliced system to provide the computing power. When the 68000 became available in sample quantities, we evaluated it and found it had good performance and was more economical.

The memory management unit (MMU) provides different logical address space contexts for processes and protection. The protection ensures that an individual application fault does not damage the rest of the system and therefore improves system reliability. The MMU also provides for code segment faulting and automatic stack expansion.

The bit-mapped display provides graphics and text support needed for the user interface. The display is 720 by 364 pixels and supports quality graphics and text fonts of different sizes and faces. This permits the word processing applications to use black on white images, proportional-spaced fonts, and different type styles including boldface, underline, and italic.

To complement the graphics output, Apple wanted to use a mouse for a graphics input device, but existing ones were unreliable and had precision bearings that made them expensive and difficult to manufacture. Apple developed a mouse that is precise, tracks on almost any surface, and is easy to manufacture. The original prototypes had three buttons, but we found users spent too much time looking away from the screen to determine which button to push; consequently we changed to a two-button mouse. Once we found alternative ways to implement the functions of the second button, we changed to a one-button mouse.

LISA SOFTWARE

Lisa's Desktop Model

The office system software provides the user with a desktop that mirrors the function of a desk in the office. On the Lisa desktop, icons (small pictures) depict the office world. In Figure 2 we see a variety of icons, a menu bar at the very top of the screen, and two windows. One of the windows contains the contents of a LisaWrite document, and the other contains the catalogue of a disk.

There are several types of icons: documents, stationery pads, folders, a wastebasket, a ProFile disk, a clipboard, and one called Preferences. The types of documents are spreadsheets, business charts, lists, text documents, etc. These document icons quickly show the user not only that the object represented is a document, but also what type of document. Stationery pads permit a user to create new documents, and in addition permit a user to configure predefined forms or templates. For example, an office usually has different types of paper stock. One might be used for letters going outside the office, and another for interoffice memoranda. In the Lisa model, a user sets up a stationery pad for both types, and then each time the user needs to write a letter, he simply tears off a new piece of letter stock from the appropriate stationery pad. Since the pad is constructed from a document, the stock can be set up with the desired initial format and content. Folders provide a convenient way of grouping logically related documents together—similar to the function of file folders in the office. Thus, folders organize the contents of diskettes, disks, and the desktop.

The desktop supports two icons that represent storage devices. The ProFile icon represents the Winchester disk drive, and the diskette icon (not shown) represents a floppy diskette inserted in the built-in drive. These devices are used for document and program storage.

The wastebasket is used to throw away documents and programs. Just as the office worker can retrieve something thrown away in the wastebasket, the Lisa user can retrieve objects thrown in the wastebasket.

The clipboard is used by the editing operations. When a user edits a document, pieces of information are placed on the

Figure 1—The Lisa

clipboard. This information can be copied into a different place in that document or into a different document altogether. Thus the clipboard acts as temporary storage for these scraps of information (more on this later).

The Preferences tool permits the user to customize the Lisa to suit his tastes. The user can set the screen brightness, the tone generator volume, the key repeat rate, the mouse click delay time, etc. Using Preferences, the user also can configure printers and disks.

The menu bar, located at the top of the screen, shows the titles of the available pull-down menus. The menus are called pull-down because when a user depresses the mouse button over a menu title, a rectangular area under the menu title pulls down like a roller blind. The rectangular area is called a menu and contains a number of labels, which are called menu items. The user moves the mouse down through the menu items and selects the desired operation. The menus, in conjunction with the current selection, give the user the ability to specify actions. For example, one changes a word in a document to italic type by selecting the word and then choosing the italic item from the Type Style pull-down menu.

The example desktop also shows two windows. Windows in Lisa show the contents of disks, documents, wastebasket, etc. Lisa displays up to 20 windows at a time, and windows can overlap or completely obscure other windows. The user has full control over the size and position of the windows.

The User Interface Philosophy

The Lisa user interface is much more than just a mouse, bit-map graphics, a desktop with icons, and overlapping windows. The Lisa user interface is designed to be intuitive. It uses real-world concepts, not computer concepts, and provides familiar office objects and ideas. The natural model enables a user to try things out that would make sense in the real world. In general they directly transfer to Lisa's desktop world.

The user interface is designed to work the way you would expect it to work. In the office, users open documents, move them around, edit them, file them, etc. With Lisa, the mouse is used to manipulate objects directly. This is one of the key features of the Lisa user interface and is in stark contrast to traditional "computerese" of command languages and tex-

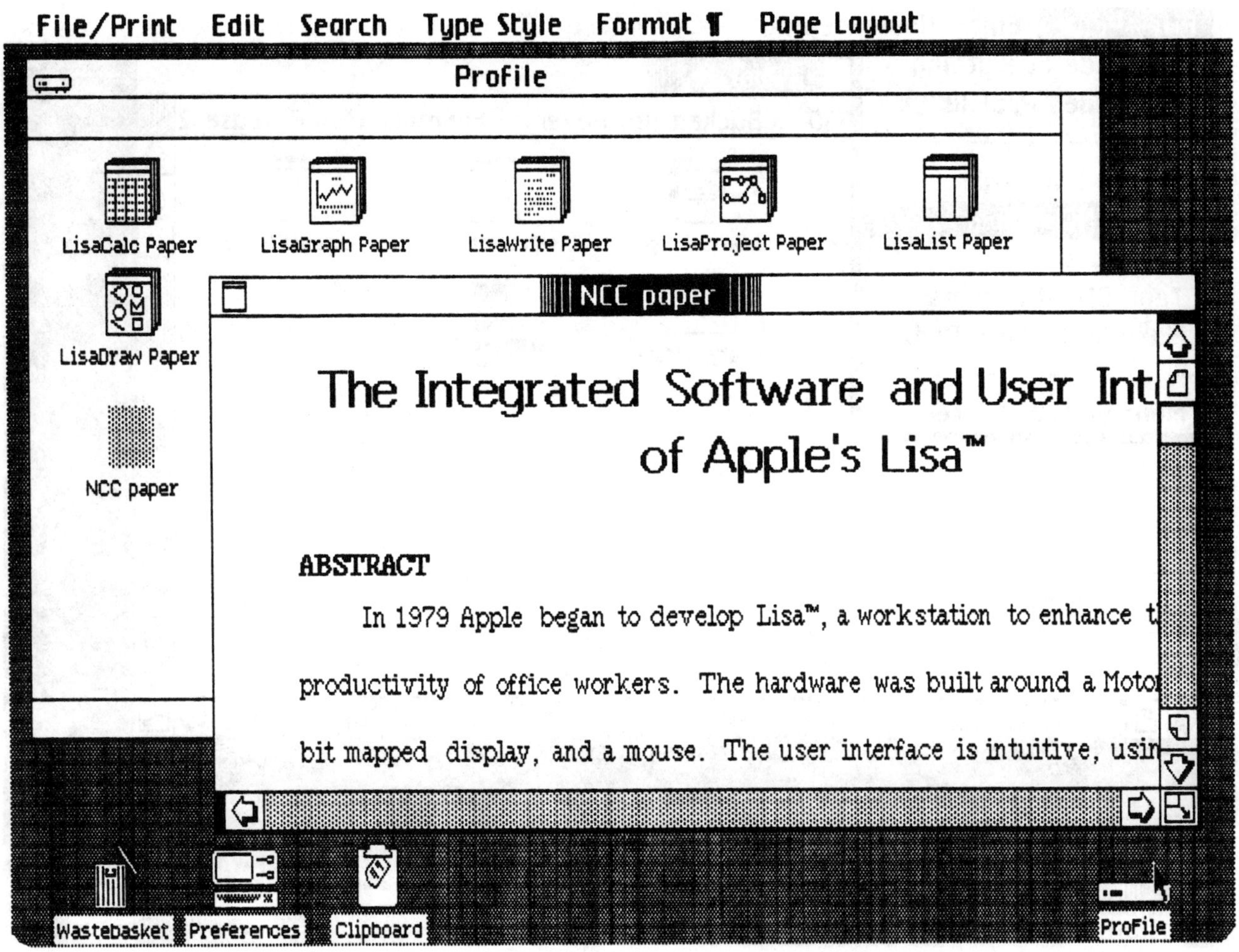

Figure 2—A Lisa screen showing the menu bar, two windows, and several icons

tual, mode-driven menus. Because there is no command language, very little typing is required to perform operations.

To ensure that Lisa is easy to use and learn, Apple developed LisaGuide, an interactive guide that teaches novices how to use the mouse as well as the basic principles of selection and menus. Once they have been through LisaGuide, they pick an application and start learning through actual use. This seems to be fairly successful; very few users will actually consult the manual.

The use of a common and consistent user interface provides for transferrable learning. The user interacts with the desktop and all applications in the same way. For example, titles of documents on the desktop are edited the same way as text within memos or numbers in LisaCalc. In addition to the editing model, the filing and printing models are the same across all applications. The time a user invests in learning the editing, filing, and printing operations immediately transfers over to the next application. Consequently, the second application is easier to learn than the first.

One of the features of the user interface is that it addresses those users learning the system and those that have mastered it. The novice can learn a few operations, just enough to accomplish his task. As the user becomes more proficient with the system, he can graduate to the more advanced uses of Lisa including shortcuts to make his interactions even more effective. In contrast to other systems, Lisa does not burden the expert user with features intended for beginners.

Using Lisa

Wherever possible in Lisa, the user moves the mouse to manipulate objects directly. For example, to move a document from one diskette to another, the user moves the mouse over the icon representing the document, depresses the mouse button, moves the mouse (and the document icon) over the appropriate container, and releases the mouse button. The mouse moves windows around, sizes them, scrolls the contents of a window, and uses the elevator to jump to a position in the document. The elevator is a rectangular white icon in the scroll bar found at the bottom and right of the active window.

Another aspect of direct operation is the modeless nature of the user interface. A modeless system is a flat, nonhierarchical model, permitting virtually any operation at any time. Thus the user need not remember what mode to enter

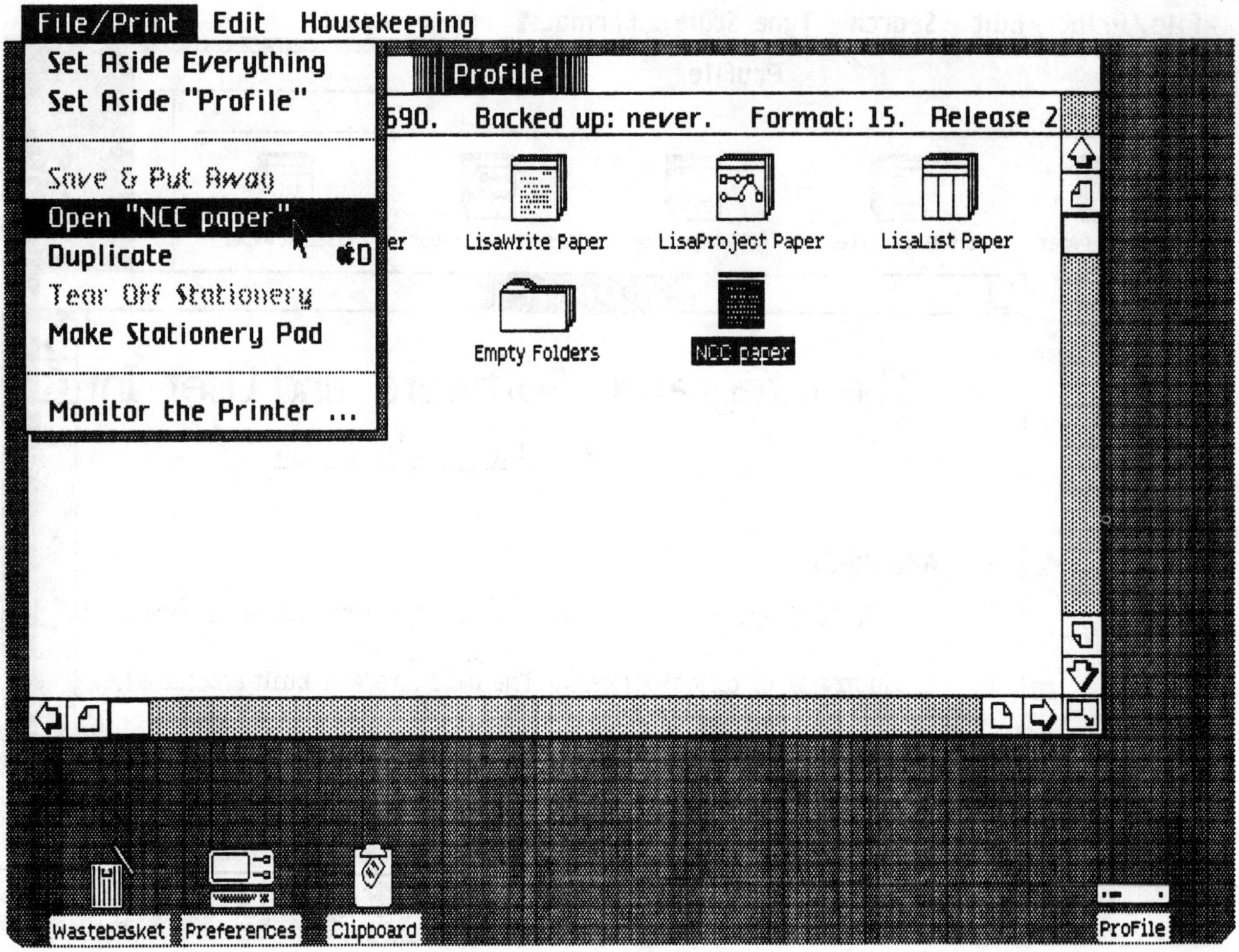

Figure 3—A Lisa screen showing a pull-down menu

to perform a function, nor what command to use to exit the mode. This flat command structure also permits the user to peruse the menus to find the most suitable operation.

When the user wants to operate on objects in the Lisa environment, the model we use is to select the objects and then operate on them with an action selected from a menu. We call this the noun–verb model, and it permeates all the applications as well as the Desktop Manager. For example, to open a document, the user moves the mouse over the icon of the document (named NCC paper in Figure 3), and clicks the button once to select the document. Then the user moves the mouse up to the menu bar and depresses the mouse button over File/Print, which causes the menu to pull down (see Figure 3). The user moves the mouse (with the mouse button down) over the "Open NCC paper" menu item, and then releases the mouse button.

In addition to a single click to select an object, several objects can be selected with single-click drag. This operation proceeds as follows: First the user positions the mouse to one side of the object, then the user depresses the mouse button and moves (drags) the mouse through the objects. When the selection includes all the objects, the user releases the mouse button. The selection of objects with single click and single-click drag, combined with menu commands can be used to perform every operation.

Two types of shortcuts are provided for the expert user—multiple clicks of the mouse button (in quick succession) and Apple keys. Double- and triple-click operations substitute for selecting an object and operating on the object with a specific frequently used command. For example, a double click on a document icon opens the document. For less frequently used operations some menu commands have Apple key sequences. For example, text-editing menu commands like cut, copy, and paste have Apple key sequences that cause the command to be invoked. Apple key sequences involve holding down the Apple key along with an alphabetic character. Thus, multiple click shortcuts are used for the most frequently used operations on the selection, and the Apple key shortcuts are used for frequently used menu commands.

Error Handling

A good user interface has good error handling. There are three aspects of error handling in Lisa: error prevention, error notification, and error recovery.

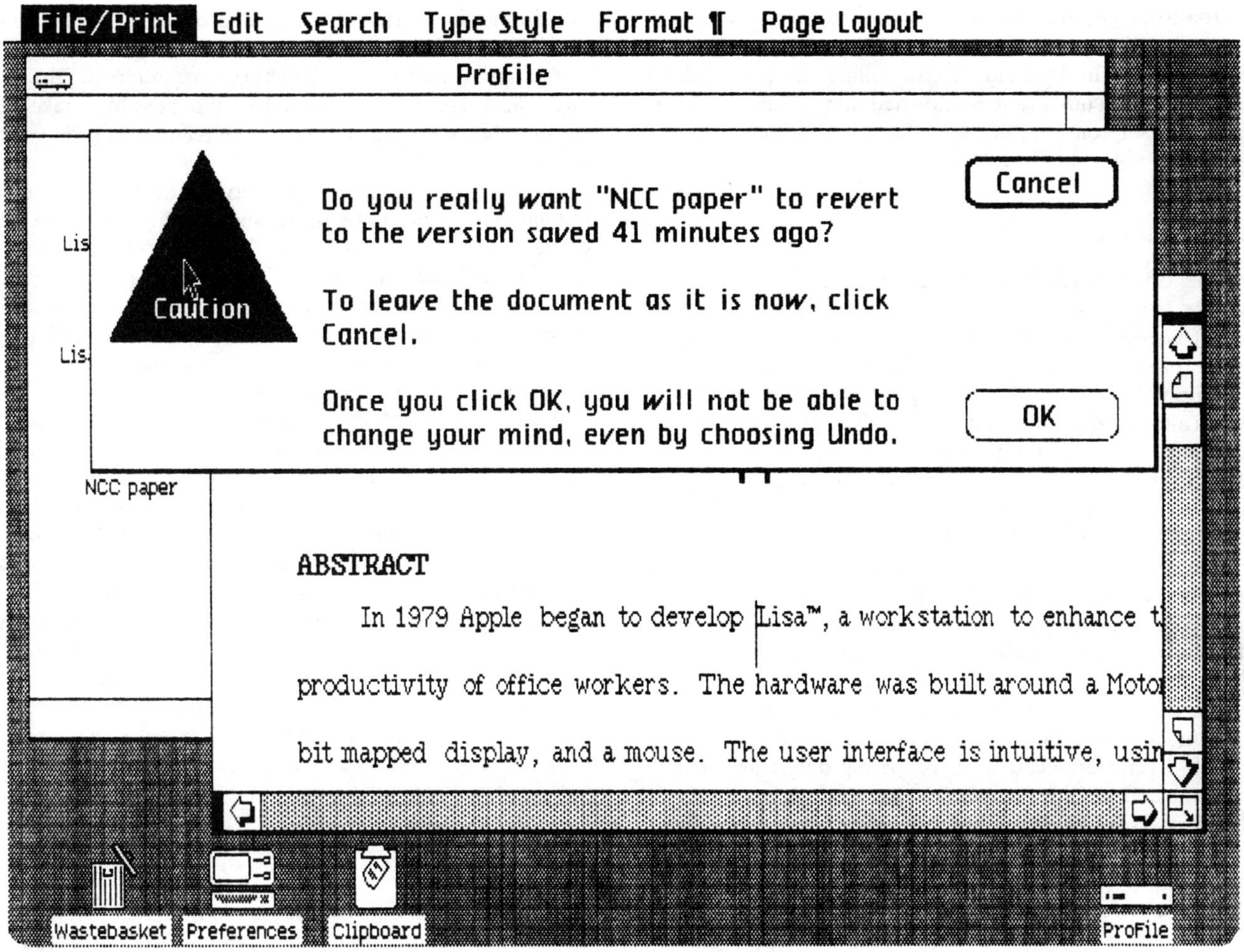

Figure 4—A Lisa screen showing an alert

With many personal computers the contents of diskettes can be damaged by ejecting a diskette or turning off the machine at an inopportune moment. To protect against such errors, Lisa has software-controlled mechanisms for the diskette eject and on–off button. To eject a diskette, the user selects the eject menu item, the software then suspends the processing of all the documents that reside on that diskette and writes out those suspended documents to the diskette. Once all the I/O has been completed, the diskette is ejected. Pushing the on–off button causes suspension of all documents, the ejection of all diskettes, and finally the power down of the Lisa. These controls help to ensure the integrity of the user's data.

Error notification in Lisa is handled with a special window called an alert (see Figure 4). An alert appears whenever the user must be notified that an error has occurred, a requested operation cannot be performed, or an explanation must be given. There are several kinds of alerts: stop, caution, note, ask, and wait. Stop alerts are used when the requested operation cannot be performed. Caution alerts inform the user that an operation has ramifications, and gives the user the opportunity to change his mind. Note alerts notify the user of something, ask alerts solicit input from the user, and wait alerts tell the user to wait until a lengthy operation completes. Alert messages that inform the user that an error has occurred have three parts. First, the user is told the nature of the problem; second, the user is told how to work around the problem; and finally, the user is told where to refer in the manual for more help.

Another level of recovery is provided by the Revert to Previous Version menu command. Sometimes a user makes several changes to a document and then changes his mind. In this event, the user can invoke the Revert to Previous Version command to return the document to the state when the document was last saved.

In the event of a program failure in Lisa, an alert message appears informing the user that the tool failed. The user is given the option to redisplay the document and if he chooses to do so, the document is shown, usually with the last changes intact.

The final area of error recovery is recovery from external errors such as power failures. If power goes off while using a computer, the disk is likely to be inconsistent; some of the current data are in memory but not on the disk. To protect against failures of this kind, the Lisa file system has redundant information permitting reconstruction of files on disk. The

Desktop Manager and the LisaList tool also detect such failures and repair and reconstruct their information. When the user powers up the Lisa after such a failure or opens a damaged LisaList document, he is informed that repair is needed. When the user confirms that the repair operation should be started, the repair begins.

Lisa Applications

Apple offers seven Lisa applications (also called tools): LisaCalc (spreadsheet), LisaWrite (word processing), LisaGraph (business graphics), LisaDraw (graphics editing), LisaProject (project scheduling), LisaList (list management), and LisaTerminal (terminal emulation). Lisa is an open system that permits third parties to develop Lisa applications, hence additional Lisa applications also are available.

The Lisa tools have effective user interfaces for their applications. LisaCalc and LisaGraph use the spreadsheet user interface developed by VisiCalc, further improved by the addition of the mouse. LisaList builds upon the user interface techniques developed in QBE.[2] LisaWrite uses techniques found in several word processors.

The unique Lisa applications are LisaDraw and LisaProject. LisaDraw is a structured graphics editor that permits the user to draw lines, circles, ovals, rectangles (both square and rounded), polygons, freehand curves, and text. It is used for such diverse applications as preparing diagrams for presentations and architectural drawings.

LisaProject is a PERT/CPM project-scheduling tool. It uses a graphical PERT chart representation to enter a project schedule. The user draws the schedule using rectangles for tasks and circles for milestones. The user specifies the task, the resources needed to accomplish it, the duration of the task, and its relation to other tasks. As tasks are added, durations changed, or scheduled dates specified, the schedule is recalculated.

The user interfaces of LisaDraw and LisaProject have opened up these tools to a much greater audience. Just as VisiCalc and QBE opened up spreadsheets and databases to those who were unable to use other offerings, LisaDraw and LisaProject have done the same in their application areas. Both these tools magnify the capabilities of the user. For example, people like myself who are totally inept at drawing are assisted by LisaDraw to the extent that very respectable results are easy to achieve. A similar result occurs with LisaProject. Administrative assistants unable to use conventional project-scheduling tools are now using LisaProject to make very large schedules.

During the development of the Lisa applications and the application libraries, we found that application development was not as easy as we would like it to be. The library structure was very hierarchical and was hard to use. Consequently we were determined to make it easier for third parties to develop Lisa applications. This led to two ways to develop Lisa applications, QuickPort and ToolKit.

QuickPort permits a third-party software developer to run standard PASCAL programs (ones that use standard PASCAL I/O) in a window in the Lisa office system. In addition, QuickPort permits cutting, copying, and pasting of information from the QuickPort window to other Lisa desktop windows. The modifications the third-party developer must make to the application to use QuickPort are minimal. The developer must use a few new units, and possibly make name conflict changes. This process can be accomplished in an afternoon.

QuickPort is the easiest way to get an application operational in the office system, but such a program cannot use all of the capabilities of the Lisa. ToolKit is used to write an application that fully uses the features of the Lisa. ToolKit is essentially a generic application that calls application-specific code to implement application-specific functions. This permits the sharing of common control structure code across several different ToolKit applications.

Because different applications have different needs, the ToolKit generic application had to be extremely flexible. The flexibility required, along with the need to call application-specific code, led to the use of classes similar to those in SMALLTALK.[1] The classes provide the ability to call the application-specific code while also permitting the developer to override or subclass a class to modify its behavior.

Both QuickPort and ToolKit promote the development of Lisa applications. This open nature of the Lisa office system permits third-party developers to develop a specific application, yet leverage off other Lisa applications. These third parties can develop applications that target specific markets while relying on the standard tools such as LisaWrite and LisaDraw for presentation of the results.

Integration in Lisa

Several components of integration in the Lisa system have already been mentioned. There is a consistent user interface that is common across all applications and the Desktop Manager. If the user wants to enter text and makes a mistake entering it, he can fix it using the standard text-editing model. The user does not have to remember which tool he is in, nor does he have to run an editor tool.

The editing model used by Lisa is the cut-and-paste model. Just as an editor might cut up a paragraph with scissors and paste-up sentences or paragraphs to improve an article, the Lisa user can cut and paste with the Clipboard. The editing model also includes the ability to copy to the Clipboard and undo the last edit operation. When a user copies or cuts an object, the object is copied onto the clipboard, a repository for scraps of information. The Paste command pastes the information from the clipboard into the active window replacing the current selection. This model is used for all objects; e.g., text within textual documents, numbers and formulas within LisaCalc, and graphics within LisaDraw. A user can cut or copy information from a paragraph and paste it into the same document or a different document. This copy and paste model is also the mechanism for data interchange between documents.

This data interchange is illustrated by the following example. Let us assume that a user has data in a LisaGraph document (a bar chart) and wishes to move them to a LisaDraw document to annotate and customize the chart for a presentation. To do this the user selects the entire graph in the Lisa-

Graph document, and then uses the Copy command in the Edit menu to copy the graph to the Clipboard. Next the user opens the LisaDraw document and selects Paste from the Edit menu. The user can then use the capabilities of the LisaDraw tool to add labels, change patterns, etc.

The direction of software integration that we see for Lisa in the future is presented in the following scenario. Lisa provides an environment where one can use LisaTerminal and gather data from a mainframe, copy the data to LisaList and subset them, copy the result to LisaCalc and perform some arithmetic manipulation to analyze the data, copy the resulting data to LisaGraph to make a chart, then copy the chart to LisaDraw to further customize it, and finally copy that customized chart to LisaWrite for inclusion in a report.

This type of integration permits the user to choose the best tools for his task. The user is free to concentrate on his task, not on the mechanics of typing the data or mastering the commands of the application. The model permits the tool's developer to concentrate more on the functionality that has to be provided, and not on extraneous features. For example, the LisaGraph tool can concentrate on drawing the best pie charts, without having to provide all the presentation flexibility (e.g., detached pie segments), since the chart can be copied to LisaDraw where the chart can be customized.

The open nature of the Lisa office system further expands the integration possibilities. The power of an open system becomes apparent when third-party tools can be used as equals in conjunction with the standard tools. This permits the Lisa to be used by a broader range of customers for a wider variety of applications. This is in contrast to closed systems, which are typically one large program, and do not permit integration of other components.

The Clipboard

The clipboard provides a common interchange form between documents. There are three distinct interchange forms—text, tables, and graphics. In most cases, the user is unaware of what type of interchange form is employed. The user merely selects the object, and copies or cuts it. The type of object determines the form of the data on the clipboard. In cases where a particular selection is ambiguous, the user is required to further specify his intent.

The cut, copy, and paste model does require that it be easy to move data from one tool's document to another. In the Lisa environment, this is provided by the multitasking operating system.[4] Lisa uses a multitasking operating system to permit the concurrent operation of processes. For example, this permits LisaGraph and LisaDraw documents to be both on the screen and in memory. When the user switches from one document to the other, the operation can complete rapidly (one or two seconds if both are in memory already).

The clipboard provides for rapid exchange of data to and from the same or different documents. It also provides the ability to undo the last cut or copy. In this way the user can undo a cut operation and then paste the previous clipboard contents. The astute reader will realize that only the last operation is undoable; undo of an undo undoes the undo.

Productivity Enhancement

Integrated software of almost any style enhances productivity.[5] Just as word processors improve productivity by minimizing retyping, integrated software has reduced the time it takes to perform tasks that require the use of several tools.

Several studies have been performed by outside groups that substantiate the assertion that Lisa enhances productivity. Seybold Publications Inc. did a comparison of Lisa, SuperCalc 3, Context MBA, and Lotus 1-2-3.[5] The task was to prepare an operating budget, which included spreadsheet calculations, making graphs, looking up information, and preparing a report. The timings did not include set-up time for the model, nor thinking time, consequently the timings do not represent the total time to complete the task, but only the time necessary to perform the four specific tests. The article reports that the total time it took was 27 minutes for a SuperCalc 3 user, 33 minutes for Context MBA, 47 minutes for Lotus 1-2-3, and 59 minutes for a Lisa user.

We couldn't understand how it took them so long to do the tasks using Lisa, so we looked into it. It turns out the users were experienced IBM PC users, and the users were inexperienced in using Lisa. We retimed the tests with an experienced Lisa user and found that it took 19 minutes. So the study should have shown it took 19 minutes for an experienced Lisa user, 27 minutes for a SuperCalc 3 user, 33 minutes for Context MBA, 47 minutes for Lotus 1-2-3, and 59 minutes for an inexperienced Lisa user. The disparity of time between the experienced Lisa user and the inexperienced Lisa user is that the inexperienced one was unaware of a mechanism for transferring data from LisaCalc to LisaGraph, and cut and pasted the data cell by cell. Another reason for the disparity was that the inexperienced user did not take advantage of background printing.

This study was chosen because it illustrates several things. The fact that an inexperienced Lisa user was in the ballpark for these tests shows that an inexperienced user can effectively get the job done (especially when the combination of set-up time and thinking time dominates). The other important point that this study illustrates is that a simple user interface leads people to some incorrect conclusions. People wrongly conclude that simple user interfaces are good only for simple things, and that features are not implemented. In the case of this study, the simple user interface led the users to believe that they had mastered the system, so they failed to look up functions in the manual.

SUMMARY

Lisa achieves integration in a variety of ways. It uses an intuitive model using familiar objects that permit direct interaction as opposed to indirect interaction with a command language. In contrast to some systems that always prompt for individual steps, Lisa's user interface supports users at every point on the learning curve. The uniform user interface also provides for transferrable learning; the user needs to learn how to edit, print, and file only once, and then can apply that knowledge throughout all applicaions. The combination of gradual and transferrable learning results in a system that is many times easier to use. This ease of use has made it possible for individuals to use tools to accomplish tasks that they could not before.

The editing model provides not only for editing information within a document, but also promotes the interchange of data among documents of similar or different types. This interchange is fostered by the ability to have several windows displayed concurrently. The ability to use documents concurrently and interchange data among them makes it possible to use several tools in a cooperative manner to perform a task that one tool alone could not accomplish. Since one of these windows can be connected to a remote computer, this permits exchange of data between mainframes and Lisa documents. In contrast to some systems, Lisa is an open system, permitting third parties to develop additional applications. Third-party-developed applications function in a manner that is similar to other Lisa applications with the uniform user interface, and are able to interchange data as well.

The combination of the uniform user interface coupled with multiple tools that operate concurrently, each of which can interchange data with others, provides an environment that increases office worker productivity. Workers are free to concentrate on their tasks, not on how to accomplish them.

REFERENCES

1. Goldberg, A., and D. Robson. *SMALLTALK-80 The Language and its Implementation.* Reading, Mass.: Addison-Wesley, 1983.
2. Zloof, M. "Query by Example." *AFIPS, Proceedings of the National Computer Conference* (Vol. 44), 1975, pp. 431–437.
3. Smith, D. C., C. Irby, R. Kimball, and E. Harslem. "The STAR User Interface." *AFIPS, Proceedings of the National Computer Conference* (Vol. 51), 1982, pp. 515–528.
4. Daniels, B. "Lisa's Alternative Operating System." *Computer Design,* 22 (1983), pp. 159–166.
5. Uttal, B. "The Best Software for Executives." *Fortune,* December 26, 1983, pp. 136–142.

FlowGuide—A programmer's work station

by PHIL J. GROUSE
University of New South Wales
Kensington, New South Wales, Australia

ABSTRACT

FlowGuide is a programmer's work station developed to assist in the writing and maintenance of programming projects. Each project is treated as a tree structure, with each node corresponding to a program module. For each module there are three documentary members: a requirements specification, a data specification, and a structured program. The last of these is expressed in flow-block notation, an orthogonal form of the Nassi–Shneiderman diagram. FlowGuide supports the design and maintenance of all three members. The integral program editor is designed to support modules expressed as flow blocks. A post-processor translates the project tree into the corresponding source code, which may be ported to a separate host if desired.

The system has been written for microcomputers that support CP/M-86, PCDOS, or both, although the layered design minimizes the effort in porting the work station to other environments. The help facility can be tailored to suit levels of skill ranging from beginning students to professional programmers.

INTRODUCTION

FlowGuide is a programmer's interactive work station. It is oriented to the preparation and maintenance of tree-structured programs in which the nodes correspond to documented source code modules. Its program editor is unique in that it is based on the structured graphical notation of the flow block,[1,2] an orthogonal form of the Nassi–Shneiderman (NS) diagram[3] more suited to representation on common display screens.

Flow blocks, like program flow charts, allow the programmer to design and document program logic. While both techniques are suited to pencil and paper methods, the flow block is designed specifically for line-oriented devices such as display screens and printers. Like the NS diagram, the flow block has the advantage of enforcing structured specifications. Both methods delimit blocks by enclosing the block text in a rectangle. A summary of the graphical syntax for flow blocks is given in the Appendix.

Without supporting software, the maintenance of flow blocks can be as difficult as if one were working with logic flow charts or NS diagrams. For example, a minor change to an inner nested block may result in the redrafting of all surrounding block structures. By delegating the drafting details to an appropriate text editor, the programmer is freed to create and change text at will, with the block delimiters being automatically redrawn by the editor.

FlowGuide's program editor does more than manage the drafting of flow blocks. The editor is sensitive to a selected set of keywords (such as IF, WHILE, and UNTIL) or their corresponding function keys. Accordingly, the appropriate block structures can be drawn in anticipation and the cursor positioned to force the programmer's attention to the next logically required step. This also requires that text be entered in a sequence corresponding to the equivalent high-level language source program, making the production of that source file a simple parallel operation.

Students in the Department of Information Systems at the University of New South Wales have been using the flow block as a design tool and for the in-line documentation of program logic. FlowGuide is geared to directing and automating as much of this process as possible.

A prototype has been developed for the IBM PC (and "workalikes"). The bit-mapped screen graphics of that machine are well suited to FlowGuide's displays; however, the system is structured for ease of porting to other hardware environments.

Although a microcomputer-based system, the work station is capable of creating source text and associated documentation for mainframe installations.

TWO-DIMENSIONAL LOGIC SPECIFICATIONS

Flow blocks or NS diagrams are not simply "boxed" alternatives to logic specifications written in high-level structured languages. By viewing alternative actions side-by-side, the programmer is more readily able to perceive the flow of control. By contrast, a program written in a pseudo-code, such as PDL[4], requires the reader to skip blocks of sequential text since alternatives are in vertical juxtaposition. If the alternatives also are nested, such specifications increasingly obscure the flow of control, in spite of the use of indention. The same is true of any of the more common high-level procedure-oriented languages. The two-dimensional nature of the flow block makes it more suited to the development and maintenance of program logic.

The author's experience with the specification of a system involving about 10,000 lines of source code suggests that the use of the flow block as a logic design tool materially assists productivity. In particular, it was found that their use naturally enforces a top-down modular structure, and aids logic walk-throughs. Almost all of that system's logical errors were located in this manner before being committed to code.

AN OVERVIEW OF FLOWGUIDE

The main motivation for the FlowGuide project was the need for a coherent and extensive support environment for programmers at all levels of ability. As a teaching tool it has a place in the classroom, yet it can also be used by competent professional programmers in the course of their normal activities. It automates the formal drafting aspects of the programming process and provides active prompting and guidance at each stage of the activity.

For each logical module (node) in a program prepared by FlowGuide, the system's editor requires (and assists) the preparation of three *members:*

1. An English language requirements document
2. A structured data specification
3. A target (or operational) language flow block

Following the completion of a project tree, FlowGuide optionally translates the related nodes into source text acceptable to the intended compiler. The output text fully reflects the prescribed scope and nesting of its component modules.

Although the design is intended to support a range of high-level languages, the initial version supports only the G-level of PL/I. Languages intended for later support include Pascal, C, and Microsoft Basic.

Projects and Productions

In FlowGuide nomenclature, the term *project* carries the familiar meaning of a self-contained programming project. During development, the project is represented and maintained as a tree structure, which links together a set of nodes. Each node consists of the three members described above unless that node is simply an *alias,* or alternative name, for another module. The use of aliases permits the normal tree structure to represent the most complex of calling sequences. A separate project index associates each node with its position in the tree, the name of the containing module, and a possible alias name. In the PL/I version, *module* and *node* are synonymous with *procedure.*

One example of the use of the alias is in the representation of recursive calls. If module A calls itself and another module "B," then we could use an alias, "C," for A, so that the call to A becomes a call to C. There would then be two branches from A—one to B and one to C. The branch to C replaces the recursive branch back to A. Since the project index identifies C as an alias for A, there would be no actual members corresponding to C. The hierarchical tree structure is therefore preserved.

A *production* is a project subtree. Thus the programmer will normally be working with a particular production at any time. A production may be *abstracted* to become a separate project. The node replacing the abstracted production is marked in the project index as an external reference. After the project is compiled, a separate linking operation restores the separately compiled abstracted production to the object program. A production may be abstracted only if it contains no aliases or containment requirements that would result in undefined references either in the resultant abstracted project or in the remaining project.

Hardware Considerations

Recently developed microcomputer-based word processor packages highlight the value of a well-designed human interface. Cognizance has been taken of object-oriented systems that use high-resolution bit-mapped screens. Such systems shift the attention from the keyboard to a cursor manipulated by a mouse, trackball, or similar device. In particular, the ability to roll down a text window partially obscuring the current display is applied both to help screens and to specifications of related modules.

Given the variety of potential supporting hardware, and the need for portability, the system is layered in the spirit of the ISO model for open systems interconnection.[5] The FlowGuide layers consist of an input layer, a display layer, a project management layer (PML), an on-line storage management layer (SML), and the logical control layer (LCL). Both the input layer and the display layer are hardware-dependent. The SML is operating-system-dependent.

Operational Language

The *operational language* is the language selected for the resulting source code file to be generated by FlowGuide. Since languages differ in the selection and syntax of their control keywords and block delimiters, FlowGuide uses an internal standard for their representation within each code member. Similarly, the program text editor assumes a standard relationship between those keywords and certain function or control keys. The user is free to revise that relationship as needed.

Many of the currently available desktop machines provide a variety of function keys generally labeled "F1," "F2," etc. The input layer is required to translate these keys into standard keystrokes for the LCL. For example, within the program editor, certain function keys map into control constructs such as WHILE, UNTIL, IF–THEN, IF–THEN–ELSE, CASE, and CASE with default. An END key is also useful for requesting the closure of the current controlled block. Other keys fulfill the role of cursor movement and general screen editing.

Provided that code members have been prepared with valid statements (excluding control statements), a post-processor for the selected operational language may be used to expand the embedded internal codes into their corresponding forms, then copy the remainder of the member in order to generate the required source file. Certain operational languages require that the post-processor include a macro translation facility. In particular, the absence of a SELECT statement in G-level PL/I requires that the PL/I post-processor create an appropriate label array together with a "computed" GOTO.

Support for languages such as PL/I, Pascal, and C is an almost trivial exercise since there is a one-to-one correspondence between most flow block control structures and the equivalent language elements. Various dialects of BASIC also will be supported, but the post-processor will need to provide for blocks by adding appropriate GOTO statements in the output text.

The provision of alternative operational languages does not mean that the code editor is required to perform syntax checking during the editing of modules, although such an enhancement is a possibility. That facility also could support the parallel development of a data dictionary as the program develops.

Help Facilities

The provision of context-sensitive help and tutorial facilities is straightforward, however, it can become expensive in terms of disk storage requirements. FlowGuide includes an extensive help facility, although the help file developed for the prototype is limited to allow the system to function effectively on systems with only 600Kb of disk storage. Additions to the help file may be made with FlowGuide's text editor. Text compression for the help file is planned for later release.

The help facility assists the user with prompts to aid in the formulation of answers to questions such as "What am I doing now?" "What did I just do?" "What should I be doing next?" "What matters are still outstanding?" "How do I do such-and-such?" and "Explain the. . .facility." The presentation of help screens is the responsibility of the display layer, since the format depends on available graphics facilities.

The help file also includes all the normal system screens. Accordingly, FlowGuide itself is user-language-independent. In other words, to redesign FlowGuide for a French-speaking user, it would be necessary to rewrite only the help file.

FLOWGUIDE LAYERS

The Logic Control Layer (LCL)

This layer (or kernel) is the "application layer" (in OSI terminology). It takes the user through the processes of creating and maintaining projects, allows projects to be reviewed, and supplies a set of housekeeping utilities. The LCL ensures that a project is developed in a top-down sequence. As each new node is reached, the LCL requires that its documentation member be completed before the data specifications and program members are commenced. Further, as each call to another module is detected, the system tests whether the called node exists. If it does not exist, the user is requested to supply the documentation member before being allowed to return to the point of invocation. When a node is coded (i.e., all three members have been prepared), the system allows the user to select an unfinished node and displays the appropriate requirements specification to assist in its completion.

The full-screen text editor in the LCL adapts to the type of member being prepared. The documentation member requires a conventional text-editing facility. The data specification member, however, requires a structure that requires the user to supply named data items, attributes, and related comments. Data structures also may be defined in a hierarchical manner for languages such as COBOL and PL/I.

The text editor for the program logic member is a program editor tailored to the particular operational language. Although this editor is geared to the preparation of flow blocks containing operational language statements, it also allows for the inclusion of comments. Since comments can consume inordinate amounts of text (and as this should not be discouraged), the editor allows comments to be included as "invisible" components attached to individual lines of text through links. The user may view individual comments one at a time by placing the cursor on the required line and pressing an appropriate function key. All the comments are included in the final operational language source file created by the postprocessor.

As text is entered within a block, it folds to the next line on reaching the current right margin (without justification or hyphenation). The end of each "real" line is indicated by the carriage return or enter key (which shows as a special character on the screen). A separate control or function key may be used to continue a logical line to the next physical line (without effect on resulting source code text). The screen window scrolls horizontally or vertically as required should a block shift off the screen.

The Display Layer

This is responsible for presenting information to the user. The normal medium is the computer's display screen (for text and graphics). The display layer also handles all output peripherals, such as printers, plotters, or audio systems. The LCL–display layer interface definition is independent of peripherals or operating systems. The display layer shares an internal device parameter block (DPB) with the input layer. The DPB defines the input–output environment. The PML also has access to the DPB.

The Input Layer

The function of this layer is to communicate "keystroke equivalents" from the user to the LCL. Although the standard keyboard remains the normal means for the entry of text and indication of special functions, the input layer may make use of additional input devices. Examples of "keystroke equivalents" include normal text-entry keys, function or control keys corresponding to keywords or special actions, and signals received from special devices.

The Project Management Layer (PML)

The PML allows the logic layer to view on-line storage as a collection of projects rather than files. This layer depends on the storage management layer (SML) to supply a set of utilities that are independent of the operating system and hardware. In particular, each project is maintained as a single partitioned data set (PDS) rather than as a set of member files. At the SML level, the PDS is a single file with a number of internal named members. An index in the PDS allows access to the members as if they were normal files. The PML adds a tree structure protocol to each PDS. The first member of each project PDS is a tree directory containing the names of the component nodes in tree-walk order. Each entry in the directory provides details concerning alias names, containing modules, and position in the tree (nodal reference). The directory structure allows for node names that are generally longer than those supported through the normal operating system.

Each project storage volume includes a project index file, PROJECT.IDX, which supplies details about each of the projects on that volume. Details recorded include a short project title, the author's name, date and time of origination, date and time of last revision, the operational language, and intended target machine. The PML maintains this index through SML utilities.

The Storage Management Layer (SML)

This layer acts as an interface between the PML and the operating system. Its role is to present a standard operating system environment to the PML. All transfers between memory and external storage are performed by the SML.

Directory space (at the operating system level) is conserved by the use of partitioned data sets accessed via the SML. The operating system views each PDS as a normal sequential file. The name of this file is the project name with an appended file type of .PRJ. The SML maintains individual projects using a minimum of storage since each PDS is packed and backed up when it is reopened.

CONCLUSION

The prototype FlowGuide is a practical attempt to meet the needs of programmers with a broad range of skills. By linking the program editor component to the flow-block notation, the programmer's attention is guided in establishing well-structured source code. The flow of control is rendered highly visible through the flow block's side-by-side juxtaposition of alternative actions. The program editor is an integral part of an overall management function, which supports the programmer in the development and maintenance of projects, and attends to the need for a structured nexus between source code, data structures, and associated documentation.

Although implemented for microcomputers, FlowGuide is well suited to the production of source code in a variety of high-level languages that may be ported to hardware ranging from microcomputers to mainframes. It is planned to test the system as an educational aid at selected secondary and tertiary teaching institutions. Tests also will be conducted shortly at selected commercial sites.

APPENDIX

Flow Block Syntax

The syntax of flow-block notation is roughly equivalent to that of Nassi–Shneiderman (NS) diagrams. But unlike NS diagrams, flow blocks do not use diagonal lines (since these are difficult to represent on a VDU screen). The number of graphical structures has been reduced to three, corresponding to the basic control forms of sequence, repetition, and selection—as shown in Figure 1. The CASE statement, in particular, is treated as a special form of the selection structure.

The contents of a sequential block may be one or more sequential operations, including selective and repetitive blocks. Blocks are stacked vertically to show execution sequence (top-to-bottom).

Repetitive blocks begin with an opening *looping clause.* Looping clauses define the conditions for the repeated execution of the *loop body* (a sequential block). Commonly used looping clauses are WHILE and UNTIL statements. Figure 2 illustrates three representative repetitive blocks.

Certain high-level languages may support other repetitive constructs, such as PL/I's qualified DO-loop. Unless the behavior of an unusual language construct is well understood by the user, it may be prudent to restrict the range to WHILE and UNTIL.

Selective blocks are marked by an opening selective clause. Selective clauses specify the rules for selection from among the electives indicated in the inner controlled section. Examples include the IF and CASE statements detailed below. The controlled section of a selective block may be a simple sequential block (such as a *then-unit* in an IF–THEN construct), or two sequential blocks placed side-by-side, where the right-hand block indicates the default action (e.g., the *else-unit* in an IF–THEN–ELSE construct, or the default action in a CASE statement).

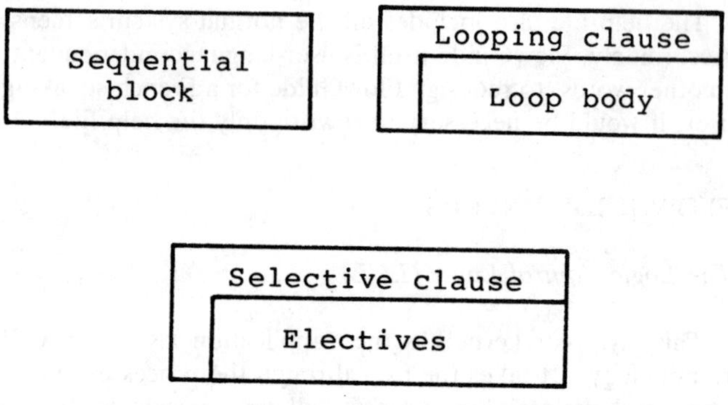

Figure 1—The basic flow block graphics corresponding to the three fundamental control forms of sequence, repetition, and selection

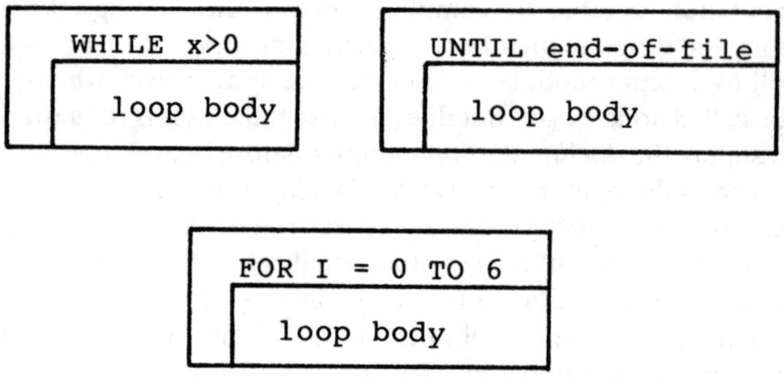

Figure 2—Some illustrative repetitive blocks

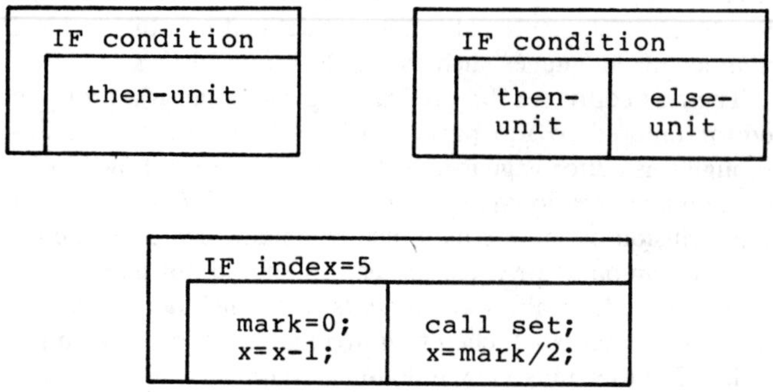

Figure 3—The two alternative forms of the IF construct and an illustrative example

The two preferred selective constructs are IF and CASE. Unlike the NS equivalent of the IF block, which heads each alternative with YES or NO, we adopt the convention that the left-hand block is the TRUE option, the right-hand block (if present) being the FALSE option. A lone elective block is considered to be a TRUE option. The IF selective clause consists of the keyword IF followed by a conditional expression. Figure 3 shows the two alternative forms of the IF block together with an example of the IF–THEN–ELSE construct.

The NS form of the CASE block requires the writer to set all alternatives side-by-side, resulting in severe restrictions in

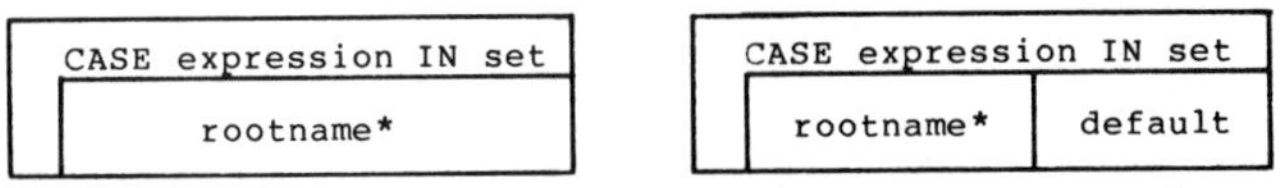

Figure 4—The CASE graphics; the second form is used where there is an explicit default block

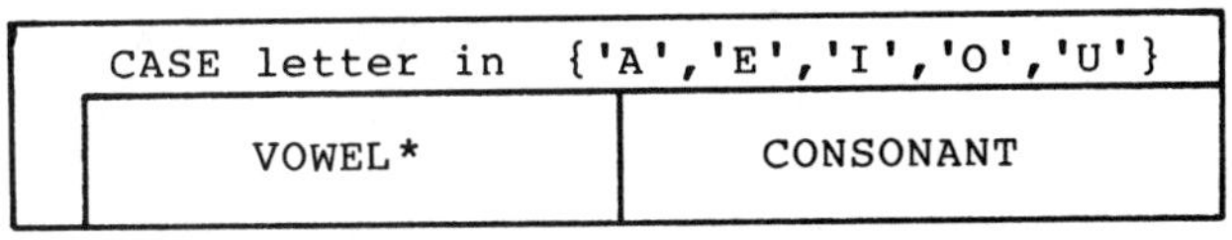

Figure 5—Example of a CASE block with an explicit default action

drafting CASE blocks with more than a few options. The flow block equivalent has, at most, two such alternatives. Far from limiting the choice to two options, there is no practical limit to the number of options. Its format is shown in Figure 4.

The contents of the left-hand (or only) block are shown as *rootname** where *rootname* is a partial module name to be completed by replacing the asterisk with the expression value if found in the set. The second form nominates an explicit default block.

In the CASE clause, the "expression" is a simple expression, resulting in a digit or short character string, which should be found within the "set." The set may be explicit (as in PASCAL), or it may be the name of a set that has been defined previously. Explicit sets consist of a list of elements (with possible ellipsis) enclosed in "curly braces." If the expression value is found in the set, it is treated as a string, which is used to complete the partial module name, "rootname." The module with the resulting name is then invoked. If the expression value is not found within the set, the default block is executed (in the second format), or no action is performed (in the first format).

In the example shown in Figure 5, one of the modules—VOWELA, VOWELE, VOWELI, VOWELO, or VOWELU—is executed if "letter" is the corresponding vowel. If "letter" is not a vowel, then the module CONSONANT is performed. Clearly the programmer must specify each of the referenced modules separately.

In some cases, it may be convenient for individual modules to be identified by more than one module name. For example, if the same actions are to be performed by modules VOWELA and VOWELE, both names may be regarded as aliases for the one module. By convention, the name of a module is written above the top left corner. If there is more than one name, the aliases are stacked vertically.

REFERENCES

1. Grouse, P. J. "Implementation and Testing." In C.H.P.B. Brookes, P. J. Grouse, D. R. Jeffery, and M. L. Lawrence (eds.), *Information Systems Design* (1st ed.). Sydney: Prentice-Hall (Australia), 1982.
2. Grouse P. J. "Flowblocks—A Technique for Structured Programming." *ACM SIGPLAN Notices,* 13 (1978), pp. 46–56.
3. Nassi, I., and B. Shneiderman. "Flowchart Techniques for Structured Programming." *ACM SIGPLAN Notices,* 8 (1973), p. 12.
4. Caine, S. H., and E. K. Gordon. "PDL—A Tool for Software Design." In *Software Design Techniques Tutorial,* New York: IEEE, 1976.
5. Zimmermann, H. "OSI Reference Model—The ISO Model of Architecture for Open Systems Interconnection." *IEEE Transactions on Communications,* COM-28 (1980), pp. 425–432.

Information resource planning and management methodologies

by KEITH GREYSTOKE
Database Consultants Europe B.V.
Amsterdam, The Netherlands

ABSTRACT

During the last ten years it has become fashionable to create structured methodologies which, in theory, are totally removed from current state-of-the-art technology. This however, is a contradiction in terms since analytical methods are only created in the computer world to solve state-of-the-art shortcomings. Thus before any analytical methodology is selected first question is knowing where your company lies with regard to the state-of-the-art technology. This paper attempts to show the evolution through the previous stages. It would be erroneous to think that the methods are driving the technology, as opposed to the other way around. This would be the case if the premise of producing methodologies in blind ignorance of the state-of-the-art were true.

This paper discusses the evaluation of analytical methods and the reasons for their development—dating from the early concept of database technology, where this technology is seen as the recognition for a shared data environment.

To understand the entire analytical process that is necessary in order to make information systems work, we must consider together three factors, which in theory we would like to separate, but which in practice are so closely linked that it is of no real use to consider them in total isolation. These three factors are

1. The problem of defining the exact requirements of the information-handling systems to be installed and reconciling those requirements among the various users of data
2. The state-of-the-art software and hardware that is available
3. The analytical tools and methods that can be used as tools to achieve specific solutions to problems within any given company

To understand our current thinking one must examine the historical evolution that has led us to where we now stand. In the 1960s we built computer systems, application-by-application, by including both the logic and the handling of the data into the programs themselves and as a consequence, converted the raw elements of data into information. Since the words "data" and "information" have distinct meanings, let us examine the difference. Data are raw elements. For example, a number—12709—in itself not very meaningful, particularly since it would be necessary to determine what that number actually meant. Let us suppose that this number were an order number. We may still consider it to be raw data, and on its own, not particularly useful. When combined with other data and presented to the user it becomes information. Thus, a combination of the order number, plus a product number, plus a quantity asked for, plus a price, would provide information possibly to a salesman. All users within a company combine different elements of data to create information as they see it.

If we consider the original systems of the sixties, we can see that programs were written based on users' requirements, piecing together various elements of data to provide information to the user. Each program would have the responsibility of manipulating, changing, updating, and generally caring for the requirements that the user had. The data were turned into records and kept inside the machine in the same form that one would keep information in a filing cabinet. As a consequence, "filing cabinets" sprung up all over the machine. These were kept on disks or tapes, since the core of the machine was not large enough to store all of this information.

Originally, it was necessary for each program to code its own access methods to get hold of the information that it had put on the disks. However, it was quickly recognized that it would be much easier if the hardware manufacturers were to provide the access methods required themselves, as a service to programmers, since this was a complex procedure requiring intimate knowledge of the hardware, channel commands, and the like. Nevertheless, the control over the information itself lay entirely within the program. As situations arose within the company where the structuring of the data needed to be changed, e.g., an element such as a delivery number might be added, each program using information made up of data from the order, which now contained a delivery number, had to be changed. Needless to say, this was a long and laborious process requiring a great deal of work. The tools available for analytical purposes as a consequence of our above-stated working methods were limited to the processing requirement—tools such as flow charts.

In the sixties certain common problems began to appear throughout companies using these conventional methods of working. These problems were clearly identifiable and the reasons behind their occurrences were also identifiable. The first problem was that duplication of data was paramount. This was obviously occurring since many users' requirements for information used common elements of the data and some users even created, or had created for them, systems that used exactly the same elements of data but in different sequences using different keys.

For example, a salesman might keep a file of information concerning clients using the client name as the key for entry into the data, and an entirely separate file by the name of the contact he had as the key within the company he was dealing with, and yet a third file with exactly the same data elements using the address as the key. As a result of the duplication, which in itself cost both time and manpower resources to keep updated, incompatibility started to creep in. For example, a file may change because a certain client changed his address and had informed the salesman, but the salesman had not informed the accounts department. Thus the files of the accounts department continued to contain the old address, although the salesman's data were correct. The next problem was that control became dissipated and virtually impossible since each user of the data was a law unto himself. Likewise, the problem of security. It is clear that it is far more difficult to protect secrets within the company when there are 50 or 100 copies of the same data, rather than the existence of only one copy.

The next problem was that the effort required to maintain systems using changing data, where those data were being used by many and being handled by the program itself, meant excessive maintenance when changes occurred. This problem was exacerbated by the fact that programmers and analysts were all left to work in their own manner with no common standards being applied from one to the other. Thus, not only was the maintenance excessive but more complex once the analyst or the author of the program had left the company.

The next problem concerns the data dictionary facilities—at that time hand-driven—representing an encyclopedia of information about the programs and the data. Each separate company clearly had such a system, even if it were only in the form of listings (which it usually was) spread around the company. Thus, there was no easy way for people to derive common terminology, find the basis of the work produced by others, or find where the data elements were being used to derive the required information.

Another problem lay in the fact that the data were structured solely for the applications that used them; in general this was unsatisfactory for other users. Even if an attempt were made to structure data over a greater variety of applications, the software facilities for achieving such desires were not available. The result of these problems was a general mixture of unprofessional implementations that proved difficult to use.

In the late sixties all the factors mentioned above caused industry to turn its attention to viewing data in a totally different manner—to removing control and structuring capabilities away from the programmer and to creating a records department on the machine itself. With respect to the analytical tools, great changes took place. Because the desire to achieve the results required a clearer view of the data—separate from the processes—in order to solve not so much the technical problems but the inherent business problems of attempting to share this data among a wider variety of users, questions needed to be answered: Who owns the data? Who can see the data? Whose data are correct when inconsistencies are found? Whose coding systems are acceptable where several exist for the same items? How would controls be implemented in terms of availability, of security, of privacy, of ease of access, of reliability, of back-up, of recovery?

Thus the industry turned its attention to analyzing the data in their own right, pulling out the elements that became known as entities, which were chunks of data representing real-world items that existed within the company, such as employee, building, order, car, invoice, etc., and attempting to view the inherent business relationships that existed between these various pieces of data. In theory, we need have looked no further, since the overall picture of the data was that which we wished to incorporate on the machine. Unfortunately the manufacturers imposed structuring rules upon us from the software, which was provided to handle the data. Not all of these relationships could be made optimal.

It was necessary to question which relationships were more important than others, which were used more frequently. The only way to gain these answers was to question the actual usage of the data in terms of the information that was required by the applications that used the data. How frequently were activities carried out? Within those activities, which data were required? Which activities took priority over others? Thus the analytical methods broke into two distinct parts—the first attempting to view the entities and their inherent relationships that existed through the eyes of the business, and the second the processes that acted on those data.

The clear view was to take a picture of the entire company's data so that the database, or records department, would provide information for the entire company—a logical argument based on the assumption that the sharing of data and information was a good thing and could be argued strenuously. It is clear that this argument was good for the following reasons. First, the data were the only resources available within a corporation that clearly could not be replaced. There were banks to meet shortfalls of cash. There were other buildings if the current ones proved unsatisfactory. There were production lines to add stock if that were necessary. There was new equipment available if the old equipment wore out. There were job-seekers to replace those who left.

But what would a company do if all its information was suddenly lost? Clearly it would have to close the doors, it could no longer function. And yet if one were to ask any question about the other resources; about such things as how much money is available; what buildings are ours; or how much stock is available, one could get answers to the very last detail. In the case of data and information, however, if one were to ask the average company how much it cost to collect the information they now have; how much they spend on maintaining the information they have obtained; or where one would find replacements; no satisfactory answer would emerge. This is an interesting factor considering that information is the only resource that is irreplaceable. Nevertheless it turned out that both the analytical methods and the software provided were incapable of coping with the entirety of a major corporation's data resources. This rendered incorrect the first assumption that we should share the data throughout entire companies.

The second assumption that was made, and for which traditional databases were produced, was that data would be centrally handled on very large mainframe machines. This was a logical assumption in the late sixties and early seventies because that was precisely the direction of the hardware manufacturers. However, as in the first case, this assumption proved to be incorrect. From the manufacturers' viewpoint, machines became smaller and smaller and more and more powerful, while the manpower investments in programming became greater and greater. This happened so much that in today's world every major department within a given company can afford to acquire its own very powerful microcomputer costing no more than $7,000 or $10,000. Thus, these departments declined to use the central service and started to build their own systems using their own data.

The third assumption made by the software manufacturers was that the relationships that existed between data were in practice, static, whereas the data themselves were volatile. For example, if there was a relationship existing between an employee and an address, when the employee moved, the data—the address—changed. If we consider an exact example, supposing Mr. Vemer currently lives in Amsterdam and then moves to Utrecht, we cross out Amsterdam and change the data to read Utrecht. This is a subtle misconception. Just because Mr. Vemer leaves Amsterdam, does not mean that Amsterdam disappears. What really happened was that the relationship that existed between Mr. Vemer and Amsterdam changed and the relationship now became between Mr. Vemer and Utrecht. Because the assumption that data, as opposed to the relationships, were volatile, it was concluded by the majority of software manufacturers that it was not a problem to incorporate physical pointers within the data; a subtle error that rendered most packages very inflexible. Of course, they were flexible in their ability to change the data by adding records, adding fields, and changing fields, because the assumption was that the data were volatile; but they proved very inflexible when it was required to change the relationships. So much so that several such changes would often imply a complete redesign.

The next assumption was that the encyclopedia-type requirement of meta-data provided by the data dictionary would require only passive assistance. This means that it would be used as a "look-up" mechanism in much the same way as a telephone directory would be used for people wishing to find information about telephone numbers. This assumption also proved to be incorrect because the majority of users of the data had difficulty in predetermining the relationships that they would use and the pieces of data that would be required to view their information. Thus, in our telephone book example, we may not know the name of the company but only its address—an impossible situation if you wish to look up a telephone number. In reality, it is necessary to be able to go to the dictionary, ask the question, and receive the answer—at the time you wish to pose the question. Would it not be easier if we had a telephone book or a service we could call and only decide at the time of the call which pieces and relationships we wished to use—and still be able to acquire our view of the information as we wished it to be determined?

The next assumption was that each user of the data must have his own language in order to communicate with the database management system. Thus different languages were invented—a data manipulation language for the programmers, a data definition language for the designers, and a query language for the users. Once again, if we were all talking about the same data, this is a totally incorrect assumption because if we are to share things, we must all communicate in the same language.

We can therefore conclude that almost all predetermined assumptions made by the industry for its requirements in the use of database management systems were wrong. This has an impressive consistency—five assumptions and a 100% record of failure. As a result of these assumptions being incorrect, certain problems began to appear generally throughout all companies. Rather than go into them in detail, I shall simply list them.

1. Duplication of data
2. Inconsistent data
3. Loss of central control
4. Excessive maintenance
5. Lack of standards
6. Unprofessional implementation
7. Duplication of effort

Ironically enough, these are exactly the same problems that we had set out to solve initially. Clearly, the analytical tools would not on their own solve these problems, although a recognition began to emerge. It was obvious that the data must be viewed quite separately from the processes that acted on them. In theory, data-modeling techniques were enough to build a database, but the state of the art did not permit us to optimize every relationship that existed between the elements of data. Thus the input from the analytical tool on examining the activities separately was required in order for us to produce a physical design. This single factor backs up the argument that the analytical tools cannot, in practice, be separated from the state-of-the-art technology that exists. Further, tools were required to bring together the modeling techniques with the activities that acted on and used the data to create information. It also became clear that there was another requirement—a clear statement as to why the analysis was being performed in the first instance, since analysis on its own will solve no problems if it turns out that the problem is not one of computer inefficiency or misuse of data. For example, suppose a company were to decide that because its bills were not being paid quickly enough, a new computer system was necessary. Upon further examination it was determined that the bills must first be presented to the accounts department, then sent to the heads of departments incurring the bills, then sent for approval to the persons who incurred them, then sent back to the heads of departments, then returned to the accounts department, and then sent to the payables department. If this cycle took 40 days, no computer system in the world would improve the situation. Consequently, it was recognized that a clear statement must be made as to the intention and purpose of the new system and for the data and analytical tools to be used.

IRP/IRM methodologies

by MICHAEL R. WOOD
Helix Corporation
Westlake Village, California

ABSTRACT

Within the next 10 years, the social, psychological, behavioral, and managerial disciplines necessary to develop and support information resource planning (IRP) and its subsequent management (IRM) will be integrated into most corporations. The assimilation, and therefore, impact of these nontechnical disciplines will completely reshape the way organizations evaluate, acquire, and use technologies available to them.

More specifically—although the EDP industry has traditionally been the primary provider of information processing technologies—the most crucial challenge facing EDP professionals today is to broaden their exclusively technical focus to include the new disciplines and methodologies that support organizational requirements as a whole.

This paper will focus on defining what information resource planning is, who should be involved in the process, and the implied impact of IRP and IRM on organizations.

WHAT IS INFORMATION RESOURCE PLANNING

Information resource planning is the process of identifying the fundamental structure of data available to an organization from both internal and external sources. The process encompasses an evaluation of how that identified data must be accessed, formulated, and manipulated in order to support the operational requirements, tactical needs, and strategic goals of the organization. IRP seeks to discover the true structure and behavior of data within an organization. At a minimum, any IRP effort must result in a definitive assessment of how the data available to an organization can be organized to support its current operational information processing requirements. Any IRP effort falling short of this goal will result in a plan that does not support the most basic organizational needs.

Prerequisites of a Successful IRP Effort

For any IRP/planning effort to be successful, an organization must commit to performance of the following activities:

1. Defining the organization's reason and purpose for being
2. Defining the organization's industry and business environment
3. Defining the organization's short- and long-term goals and expectations
4. Identifying and analyzing existing organizational activities
5. Assessing the technological, social, and organizational impact of goals and expectations against the existing business practices and activities
6. Formulating detailed tactical plans to change existing business practices and activities to bring them into alignment with the organization's short- and long-term goals and expectations

Completion of all of these tasks implies a cohesive and highly goal-directed effort by an entire organization (not just DP or management).

IRP as a Methodology and Discipline

IRP's primary responsibility is to take the goals, expectations, and dreams formulated in the boardroom and turn them into operational reality. This planning cycle cannot be accomplished on a casual basis. A discipline that incorporates pragmatic, goal-directed, profit-oriented techniques must be adopted and integrated into an organization. The discipline/methodology used and defined for the organization must be understandable and applicable by everyone from the boardroom to the assembly line. The tools and techniques must promote the effective and efficient use of the human resource while allowing the exploitation of technological resources. The methodology must maintain employee focus on the organization's goals and expectations without sacrificing the individual need for self-actualization and positive personal experiences.

Relationship between IRP, Systems Development, and IRM Methodologies

Any systems development effort must presuppose that a certain level of commitment, interest, and involvement exists on the part of the organization requesting it. That presupposition also implies that the requesting organization understands what it expects from the new system and how the new system will affect the human and technological resources available to it. Unfortunately, systems development efforts seldom begin with such suppositions and implied understandings.

Furthermore, most development efforts are clouded with miscommunications, misdirection, poor documentation, confusion, and poor attitudes. The goal of the individuals within the organization, therefore, becomes self-preservation, and the momentum of the organization and its individuals is greatly reduced.

Although the data processing group in an organization cannot issue an ultimatum to management to adopt the organizational disciplines required to make all development efforts successful, it can incorporate certain disciplines into its suborganization that can slowly influence and encourage others in the organization to follow suit. Since DP has traditionally been charged with the task of successfully and efficiently servicing and managing the organization's information requirements, and because its area of influence transcends organizational boundaries, DP is perfectly positioned to assume the role of a change agent in an organization if DP is willing.

The Role of DP in the IRP and IRM Process

Traditionally, DP has been charged with the specification, design, implementation, and maintenance of the information processing requirements of an organization. Unfortunately,

DP has traditionally been ill-equipped to effectively execute the specification phase of the charter because data processing people's background and training has been primarily technical in focus. During the 1950s and 1960s, this focus was acceptable and adequate. However, by the early 1970s the grace period of innovation was over and organizations had begun to realize that the data processing function was not keeping pace with the business requirements. Organizational management had also begun to realize that data processing cannot be a separate entity from the rest of the organization or have an unintelligible language. Data processing must be held at least as accountable to standard business practice as the rest of the organization.

The true problem is not technically related but rather people-related. Since DP has never been required to acquire and maintain any skills in interpersonal relationships, business administration, and business management, the ability of the MIS organization to communicate with the business and operational counterparts of the organization fell far short of management's expectations. Since there was no common ground for communication, management seldom got what it wanted from data processing. While management lost confidence in DP's skills and in DP's ability to perform its responsibilities, DP regarded management as unreasonable and incompetent to discuss or decide information issues. Neither management nor DP has recognized that the problem is a behavioral one. Instead, more money and human resources have been spent in an attempt to improve the technological foundation of DP. The result has been a critical decline in processing productivity, as well as a decline in the productive use of the human resource. The electronic and technical revolutions of the 1980s have increased the awareness on the part of operational and business management personnel that to solve the information backlog, a shift must take place in how the human and technological resources are employed.

The concept that information is a resource, a tool, has emerged. Terms like *decision support, corporate database,* and *fourth-generation environments* dominate the literature. Even though organizations have begun to realize that resolving the information resource requirements of an organization requires more than just technological advances, the focus is still on more productive tools and products. Organizations are spending their capital and human resources on microcomputers, local area networks, information centers, fourth-generation languages, database management systems, and design methodologies, all in the hope of resolving problems that have taken 30 years to create. The sad fact is that all the tools in the world will not resolve a single organizational information resource problem if that problem is not quantitatively defined in terms of its value to and impact on the organization as a whole. To accomplish this quantitative definition, pragmatic and humanistic planning techniques must be employed. DP is most likely to be charged by operational management with the responsibility for acquiring the skills necessary to develop IRPs and to administer IRMs. This charter, however, has a time limit. If data processing does not adopt and become proficient in these planning techniques, the charter will be reissued to an emerging group in an organization.

Information Administration Group

The new organization will be known as the information administration group (IAG) and will report directly to the executive branch of the organization. The individuals involved in the information administration function will have a strong foundation in (1) behavior psychology, (2) organizational behavior, (3) management science, and (4) systems theory.

The information administration group will employ pragmatic planning and management methods, which require participation by both the staff and line personnel of the organization, to identify and define information resource management requirements. Their charter will be to implement the strategic plans of an organization through tactical and operational levels in a proactive manner. The IAG's tools will include the following: (1) information resource planning methodology, (2) prototyping methodology, and (3) fourth-generation application development tools.

There is no doubt that this group of individuals will be firmly in place in most major organizations during the 1990s. The information center concept is evidence of the shift toward the IAG. The only questions are where this group will reside in the organization and to whom it will report. DP has until 1987 to provide leadership by implementing a plan to accomplish the information resource planning and management function, or, by default, have its role reduced to equipment operations and applications maintenance functions. Unfortunately, because it lacks the disciplines and attitude necessary to make the change, projections are that all new development and related maintenance will probably be removed from DP's jurisdiction and control. In short, if DP does not shift its technological, self-preservation focus, its focus will become its negative legacy and therefore its downfall.

Information Resource Planning Methodologies and Benefits

For DP individuals and professionals to maintain control over their destiny, they must learn to assume the role of information resource planner and manager. In order to be successful, the DP industry must reassess the manner in which systems are currently developed. Traditionally, less than 7% of the development cycle is spent on planning of user's expectations and needs. Approximately 70% of the development effort is spent in programming and testing. The remaining 23% is usually spent in some sort of design effort. As a result of the limited planning, definitive and quantifiable project scopes are never set in place. Since user organizational needs and expectations are poorly defined, the products developed meet with a less than favorable response from the organization. This in turn results in the deployment of tremendous effort and resources in maintenance, which is the remodeling, rebuilding, and reprogramming of systems that were inadequately specified to begin with.

Poor planning typically results in on-going system maintenance costs that often exceed the development costs by as much as 500% within the first five years of use. This standard scenario could easily be avoided by reallocating the development dollar as follows: (1) 30%—information resource planning, (2) 50%—prototyping, and (3) 20%—packaging and fine-tuning.

By focusing 30% of the project effort on IRP, the following benefits accrue to the following:

The human resource: (1) users learn to take responsibility for their needs, (2) communication barriers are eliminated between management, users, and DP, and (3) definitive project scopes are set in place.

The financial resource: (1) project management costs are reduced by 50% or more and (2) overall project costs are reduced approximately 20%.

The technological resource: (1) focus of project shifts from individual applications to an overall organizational processing environment and (2) data relationships and behavior replace programming as primary system foundation.

As a direct result of performing the IRP phase, the documentation required for full support of a prototyping effort is produced. This documentation includes (1) measurable statements which define the impact of the new system on the existing environment, (2) quantitative statements as to why the existing environment requires change and what changes are required, (3) definitive models of how each activity included in the project is and will be performed, (4) a definitive model depicting the structural relationship or the data required to support the activities being changed, (5) a complete data dictionary, (6) a definitive model of what source documents and data, updates, and outputs are needed to successfully complete each activity, and (7) a complete understanding of the impact of any process on the environment and what preventive or monitoring processes must be included to ensure system integrity.

IRP Implementation—Prototyping

By using IRP documentation in conjunction with the fourth-generation application development tools available today, the following additional benefits are experienced: (1) 30% reduction in overall project cost and time (50% total), (2) 70% reduction in training costs, (3) 70% reduction in user and technical manual preparation costs, (4) ongoing maintenance costs of approximately 20% of original development cost over first 5 years of use, and (5) users whose expectations are aligned with the deliverables of the system installed.

The following example illustrates the dramatic cost savings available through the combined use of IRP and prototyping techniques, as opposed to more traditional development efforts:

Traditional Project Budgeted at $250,000	
Planning costs	$ 17,500.00
Requirements and design costs	57,500.00
Programming and testing	175,000.00
TOTAL	$ 250,000.00
Subsequent maintenance cost over next 5 years	1,000,000.00
True System Cost	$ 1,250,000.00
IRP and Prototyping Equivalent	
Planning (IRP)	$ 37,500.00
Prototyping	62,500.00
Packaging and finetuning	25,000.00
TOTAL	$ 125,000.00
Subsequent maintenance cost over next 5 years	25,000.00
True System Cost	150,000.00
OVERALL COST SAVINGS	$ 1,100,000.00

Although the savings appear to be extraordinary, they are indeed attainable. However, even factoring the IRP/prototyping cost example by 100% (i.e., development costs equal to traditional development costs), the reduction in ongoing maintenance costs is still substantial ($500,000).

IRP/IRM—The Human Factor

The above example offers a great deal of encouragement to organizations currently buried underneath the proverbial applications backlog. Most DP organizations, however, are emphatically opposed to any change in the approaches or the tools currently being used. On reflection, the reason for DP opposition becomes clear—fear of the unknown and fear of change. After all, the DP and MIS professionals employed by organizations are only human, like the users they serve. Why shouldn't they react to change, especially radical change, in the same manner as anyone else? In short, technological change had a shocking impact on user organizations in the past; and now the shock of behavioral science, technology management theory, IRP/IRM methodologies, and technological changes is evidencing itself in DP. Management must commit itself to rebuilding organizational communication and productivity.

Pilot projects must be funded to build internal performance and achievement statistics (i.e., rebuild mutual credibilities). Mutual commitments must be secured from both DP and management to institutionalize IRP and prototyping methodologies. Programmers must be trained in systems and business analysis techniques. Strategies must be formulated so that they can be transferred from the labor environment and the cost-intensive procedural language environment to the high-productivity and human-resource-efficient information resource management environments.

CONCLUSION

This paper began by stating that the disciplines related to IRP and IRM will be actively in place in large organizations during the 1990s. This prediction is not motivated by desire but by the need for survival. The inertia of the productivity tools being developed today, along with the fast-increasing price of technology, will make painfully obvious the gross inadequacy of the traditional practices and approaches used to develop and manage effective information-resource environments.

The only question is who within an organization will be given the charter and responsibility for achieving such information-resource environments. Although DP departments will be given the first chance, their inability to cope with the demands of this newly emerging environment may result in a total demise of the DP organization and the emergence of a more humanistic and organizationally oriented group. There is no doubt that the waves of change are lashing at the breakwalls of the nation's organizations. Our success will lie in our ability to become adaptable and pliable enough to profit from it all.

Simulation as an aid to software transferability

by AARON H. KONSTAM
Trinity University
San Antonio, Texas
and
RONALD G. REINHARD
The Woman's Shop
San Antonio, Texas

ABSTRACT

Transferring software to a new host environment is one of the major problems facing installations wishing to upgrade their computer systems. This study investigates the effectiveness of simulation of an old host environment on a new host machine as a partial solution to the software transferability problem. A simulated environment of a Singer System Ten minicomputer was developed to run on an Alpha Micro microcomputer. The results of the project demonstrate that a simulated environment can be effectively used as an aid in transferring computer operations to a new host machine. It was also found that this technique is particularly suitable when software on the host machine is so dependent on features of the hardware that automated software translation is not feasible. The current generation of microcomputers is shown to be more than adequate to support the simulated environment of a minicomputer-based system.

INTRODUCTION

At present, computing systems are becoming cheaper and smaller, but at the same time faster and more powerful. As older computer systems are rapidly becoming obsolete, many companies have begun to explore ways to transfer their current computing tasks to these newer microcomputer systems.

The major problem in making such a transfer is the difficulty and cost of software conversion.[1,2,3] Another problem arises from the testing involved to determine whether the software runs correctly after conversion.[4] As for cost, hardware may be getting cheaper, but the labor costs of software generation are steadily rising. One solution to these problems is found in the process of simulation or emulation of the old machine on the new machine. Once the simulation or emulation software is produced, the old software can run on the new machine. If the machines have very different architectures, the old software will probably run more slowly and less efficiently in the simulated environment; so in most cases the simulation provides only an interim solution while new software accomplishing the same tasks can be written for the new machine.

The use of simulated environments to aid software conversion to a new machine is not a new idea. It has been used successfully for at least two decades.[1] What is new, however, is the use of microcomputer systems to support such an environment. This paper discusses the process of generating an environment simulating the operation of a Singer System Ten on an Alpha Micro computer system.

The Singer System Ten and the Alpha Micro represent two radically different approaches to hardware structure. Constructing the simulated environment, therefore, was a major task in software design. It was necessary to simulate not only the processor but also the rather peculiar environment in which the System Ten controls its peripherals.

Although the simulation software described in this paper specifically applies only to the two computing systems mentioned above, the problems encountered in simulating one computer system on another computer system are of general interest.

OVERVIEW OF THE SYSTEM TEN COMPUTER

The System Ten is a multitasking, multiprogramming computer capable of executing up to 20 independent programs concurrently. The computer hardware is in total control of the allocation of CPU time and system resources to each program. Each of these 20 jobs is executed in a memory partition of fixed size. Each job can transfer information in and out of the System Ten through a variety of Input/Output Controllers, can store and retrieve information from data files through a File Access Channel, and can access a common memory shared by all the jobs running in the system at that time.

All characters used by the System Ten for both data and instructions are represented by a six-bit subset of the ASCII character set. Character strings of up to 100 bytes can be manipulated by the processor in one instruction.

Numbers on the System Ten are stored in main memory in their ASCII representation. Numeric fields of one to 10 bytes can be manipulated by the processor in one instruction. When the processor is instructed to perform an arithmetic operation, it performs binary coded decimal (BCD) arithmetic on the numeric parts of the characters in each operand and leaves the result as a string of ASCII characters. The System Ten performs integer arithmetic, leaving scaling operations to the programmer.

Address fields are four bytes long. The numeric parts of the four bytes represent the addresses 0000 through 9999 in BCD. A 10,000-byte page address is formed by ASCII bit five in three of the four bytes, and ASCII bit seven in the rightmost character determines whether the address is in common or partition memory.

The instruction word is a fixed-length field 10 characters long and must always be located at a memory address that is divisible by 10. (See Figure 1.)

Main memory on the System Ten is divided into partitions that are byte-addressable. The number of partitions is determined by the number of Input/Output Controllers (IOC) physically resident in the system. Partitions from 1,000 to 80,000 bytes can be allocated by use of a hardware jumper in the IOC of each partition. At least 1,000 bytes of main memory are dedicated to a common memory that can be accessed by programs running in a partition. The first 300 positions of common memory are protected from general memory writes and are used by the hardware operating system to store status and program counters for each of the 20 partitions. Each partition contains three index registers at fixed memory locations; therefore, no special instructions exist for manipulating index registers. Memory addressing within a partition is relative to the beginning of that partition's memory; that is, the first memory position for each partition is location 0000.

The Input/Output Controllers handle all peripherals except disk and tape drives. Each device on the IOC is assigned a unique one-digit identifier. Device zero is normally a CRT used for program loading and execution. A device can only be accessed by a program residing in the partition associated with the IOC controlling that device.

The System Ten contains one File Access Channel (FAC) that can control up to four magnetic tape drives and up to 16

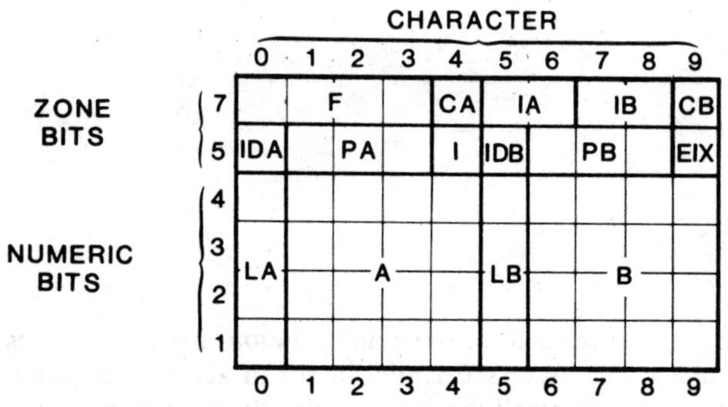

CHARACTERS OF INSTRUCTION

- F — Operation code
- IDA — A operand address is in indirect mode
- LA — A operand length
- CA — A operand address is in common or partition memory
- IA — A operand address is indexed by one of three index registers
- PA — Three bit page address for the A operand
- A — Four digit A operand address (relative to start of partition or common memory page)
- IDB — B operand address is in indirect mode
- LB — B operand length
- CB — B operand address is in common or partition memory
- IB — B operand address is indexed by one of three index registers
- PB — Three bit page address for the B operand
- B — Four digit B operand address (relative to start of partition or common memory page)
- EIX — Operand indexing indicator : Full memory indexing or page memory indexing

Figure 1—System Ten instruction word format

logical ten megabyte disk drives through associated magnetic device controllers. The FAC is a shared facility available to all partitions.

OVERVIEW OF THE ALPHA MICRO SYSTEM

The Alpha Micro System is a multitasking, multiprogramming system based on the Motorola MC68000 microprocessor. The largest model will concurrently handle up to 60 users.

The multitasking, multiprogramming features are implemented through a software executive. This software executive is part of the Alpha Micro Operating System (AMOS).[5] AMOS is made up of several components: Command Processor, Job Scheduling and Control System, Memory Control System, File Service System, Terminal Service System, and Utility Routines.

Although the Alpha Micro software and System Ten hardware approaches to multiprogramming differ considerably, they are conceptually similar. Both employ a fixed memory structure, set by system initialization on the Alpha Micro and set by hardware jumpers on the System Ten. Both the System Memory on the Alpha Micro and the Common Memory on the System Ten are usable by all jobs running in the system as a means of sharing programs, data, and communication between jobs. The Alpha Micro and System Ten both service their jobs in a round-robin fashion, sharing the CPU time among jobs.

The project described in this paper utilizes an Alpha Micro AM-1042 to support the simulated environment. This system consists of the Alpha Micro 100/L processor, 512 kilobytes of main memory, one 32-megabyte Winchester-type disk drive, one videotape recorder/player for backup, two Ampex D81 CRTs, one Texas Instruments 810 printer, and the AMOS/L version of the Alpha Micro Operating System.

SIMULATION OF THE SYSTEM TEN INSTRUCTION SET

The System Ten has five addressing modes: Absolute, Indexed, Indirect, Indirect/Indexed, and Immediate (ADD ADDRESS Instruction only).

Five instructions are used for the manipulation of numeric fields. These five—ADD, SUBTRACT, MULTIPLY, DIVIDE, and FORM NUMERIC FIELD—compose what are known as the two-length instructions. In this form the A and B operand may each be from one to 10 digits long and may use any addressing mode except Immediate. The algebraic sign of the operands and results of these operations is indicated by bit seven of the rightmost digit of the operand or result. If the bit is on, the number is negative; otherwise the number is positive. These instructions perform their functions from right to left in the operand fields. The simulator performs these operations in a manner similar to the System Ten, with one exception. The System Ten executes on the operands in place, whereas the simulator copies the operands into a work area, performs the operation, and copies the result back into the target operand field. The instructions perform the following operations:

1. ADD—Algebraically adds the numeric contents of the A operand to the numeric contents of the B operand.
2. SUBTRACT—Algebraically subtracts the numeric contents of the A operand from the numeric contents of the B operand.
3. MULTIPLY—Calculates the algebraic product of the A and B operands and develops the result in the B operand.
4. DIVIDE—Calculates the algebraic quotient of the A and B operands and develops the quotient in the rightmost positions of the B operand and the remainder in the leftmost positions of the B operand.
5. FORM NUMERIC FIELD—Moves the numeric portions of the A operand to the B operand, leaving the B operand to contain the numeric value in the form used by the arithmetic instructions.

The System Ten supports five instructions used for the manipulation of character fields. These instructions—MOVE CHARACTER, MOVE NUMERIC, EXCHANGE, COMPARE, and EDIT—make up the System Ten one-length instructions. In this form, the A and B operands are of the same length, from one to 100 characters long, and may be any addressing mode except Immediate. These instructions perform their functions from left to right in the operand fields.

The simulator performs these operations in the same manner as the System Ten:

1. MOVE CHARACTER—Transfers the characters in the A operand to the corresponding characters of the B operand.
2. MOVE NUMERIC—Transfers the numeric bits of the characters in the A operand to the numeric bits of the characters in the B operand.
3. EXCHANGE—Interchanges the characters in the A operand with the corresponding characters in the B operand.
4. COMPARE—Compares the character in the A operand with the corresponding characters in the B operand and sets the condition code register to reflect the relationship between the operands.
5. EDIT—Moves numeric parts in the A operand to the B operand. The B operand identifies a control field, which contains characters to control the suppression of leading zeros; insertion of check protection characters; and insertion of punctuation characters such as commas, hyphens, decimal points, and a sign indicator.

The System Ten has two instructions that are used for manipulating the four-byte memory address fields. These instructions are simulated in the same manner as performed on the System Ten:

1. ADD ADDRESS—Adds the address bits of the A operand to the address bits of the B operand.
2. MOVE ADDRESS—Moves the address bits of the A operand to the address bits of the B operand.

The System Ten BRANCH instruction allows the program to change the path of execution. The BRANCH may be unconditional, dependent on the result of a previous instruction, dependent on a request for service from an input device, or a link to a subroutine.

The System Ten has one instruction, SET MODE, which may be used to inhibit partition switching, to perform a system reset, and to allow changes to the protected area of common. This permits partition zero to change the program counters and status of other partitions, thus forcing another partition to load and begin execution of a program.

Two instructions are used by the System Ten to transfer data between memory and peripherals or storage devices: the READ and WRITE instructions. The System Ten supports two types of input and output devices: Terminal devices (CRTs and Printers) and File devices (Disk and Tape drives).

DESIGN OF THE SIMULATOR

Prior to developing the simulation of the System Ten on the Alpha Micro, other System Ten replacement alternatives were explored. The replacements generally entailed redesign of System Ten to employ state-of-the-art technology. These approaches allow the user to continue using the current software with conversion efforts ranging from no conversion at all to a moderate conversion that uses a totally different disk management facility. By maintaining the System Ten operating environment, a user would not be able to use the extensive software base existing on other machines, such as comprehensive word processing, spreadsheet programs, program development aids, and application packages.

Consideration was also given to developing a software translation program at the source program level. The only common language ever successfully developed on the System Ten was RPGII, and its use was relatively small. Therefore, most System Ten software, both system and application, has been developed in System Ten assembly language. Given the System Ten method for handling arithmetic operations and the programming tricks often required to write working software, the possibility of writing an effective software translation program was practically nil.

Obviously, the primary goal in any simulation project of this nature is to imitate the operations of the source computer on the target computer as efficiently as possible. To accomplish this goal, the System Ten simulator was designed to follow closely the original System Ten hardware implementation. A secondary goal was to allow the concurrent operation of simulation and native modes on the Alpha Micro. This is an important consideration when the simulation process is approached as a conversion aid rather than as a permanent solution to the problems of changing computer hardware. This goal was attained by designing the simulator to observe AMOS/L system conventions and therefore to maintain the integrity of the AMOS/L operating environment.

Although the System Ten approach to processing information and performing multitasking is radically different from most of the current computers available, it still has several of the same hardware functions, which must be simulated: Memory Access, Fetch and Instruction Decode, and Instruction Execution.

Memory Access is normally the easiest one of these hardware functions to simulate. Within the simulator program, memory exists as a large variable, and access to memory is accomplished by indexing from the beginning of the variable. It is important to maintain starting and ending memory addresses to trap memory access violations (e.g., attempts to access beyond the end of memory). In simulating the System Ten, memory access also involves converting the four-byte BCD memory address to a binary address for accessing the memory variable.

The simulated Fetch and Instruction Decode routine performs the same functions as the equivalent hardware operation: retrieving the next instruction and maintaining the program counter. As an instruction is fetched, parts of the instruction are decoded and placed into registers and variables for use during instruction execution. Subsequent to retrieving the entire instruction, the remaining functions of the decode routine are performed, including operation code validation, address modification (e.g., indexing, indirect addressing), conversion of instruction address to actual simulated memory address, memory address violation checks, operand length validations, and passing program control to the proper instruction execution routine. Since the System Ten has a fixed instruction word of 10 bytes for its 16 instructions, the Fetch cycle was relatively easy to simulate. In attempting to simulate other computers, which may have variable-length instruction words, it would be necessary to fetch the operand code, determine operand length by using an operation table or operation length algorithm, and fetch the remaining portion of the instruction. On the other hand, the Decode cycle was more complex to simulate because it performs the memory accessing verifications and conversions described above for both instruction operands. In the case of indirect and indexed operand modes, as many as five address conversions may be required for a single operand. When simulating computers using binary memory addressing, the time spent in address conversion would be significantly reduced.

For Instruction Execution, with the exception of the ADD and SUBTRACT instructions, each simulated System Ten instruction has its own routine to perform the desired operation. Since the ADD and SUBTRACT executions are so similar, there is only one routine to perform these operations. Each routine has the effective Alpha Micro address passed to it from the Decode function and is responsible for manipulating the data as required and for setting the proper condition code on the basis of the result of the operation. Upon completion, each Instruction Execution routine returns to the Fetch routine.

In addition to the three hardware functions described above, other aspects of the source computer design will influence the simulator design. The System Ten hardware, for example, is in control of partition management and time allocation and therefore requires a partition Switch Cycle. This cycle is generally not present in the operation of other CPUs, but in this case it must be simulated so that the multitasking feature of the System Ten can be faithfully modeled. In addition to its other functions, the Fetch routine is responsible for maintaining simulated instruction times and determining when a partition switch is required. When a switch is required, the Fetch routine releases control to the Switch routine, which is responsible for updating certain portions of System Ten status, finding the next partition in sequence to receive control, retrieving that partition program counter, and releasing control back to the Fetch routine to begin program execution for the new partition.

The System Ten instructions that manipulate data work strictly with memory resident operands. There are no registers and therefore no register instructions. It should be noted that the System Ten allows indexing and therefore does have index registers; however, the index registers reside at fixed locations in partition memory and are treated as memory operands. In designing simulators for computers that have true index registers and data registers, the simulation of registers and register operations would have to be addressed.

Perhaps the most difficult task of simulator development resides in imitating input and output, especially terminal input and output. Although it is possible to attach a variety of terminal devices to the System Ten, the simulator developed in this project allowed only CRT input and output and printer output. The System Ten interfaces very intimately with its peripherals and creates situations very difficult to simulate without totally simulating the peripheral in software. In effect, the latter was necessary to ensure CRT input and output compatibility with existing System Ten application software.

Since the simulation mode in this project was designed to coexist with native operations on the new system, it was important to prevent collisions in accessing system resources. Since the Alpha Micro uses a print spooler for almost all printing tasks, the simulator was designed to channel all printer output to a spool file and to recognize a special (unused) form of the System Ten WRITE instruction to allow the print file to be closed and submitted to the spooler for actual printing. This also allows a printer to be available for each simulated partition, whereas on the System Ten a manually operated peripheral switch is required to attach a printer to a partition. It is also important to note that the simulator has the responsibility for assigning the print file names. By using a combination of partition number, date, and time, unique names are assigned to avoid name collisions between partitions or the same partition at different times.

The coexistence of simulation and native modes was also taken into consideration when designing the simulated disk drive interface. The simulator was written to use the random file facility of AMOS/L. The System Ten uses a fixed-disk sector of 100 bytes. The Alpha Micro uses a fixed-disk sector of 512 bytes. The simulator maps five System Ten sectors into one Alpha Micro sector, thereby wasting 12 bytes per sector. After the six-byte BCD System Ten disk address is converted to a binary number, a simple calculation determines the record number and displacement within the Alpha Micro file. To increase efficiency, the simulated disk read checks the last block read against the block to be read to prevent extra disk seeks. The simulated disk write, however, always peforms a disk write to maintain the integrity of the data.

PROBLEMS ENCOUNTERED IN SIMULATOR DEVELOPMENT

It should be relatively easy to design and develop a simulation of one computer in another, providing that the target computer has at least the capacities and capabilities of the source computer. There are, however, three major areas in which problems may be encountered: deviations in simulated and actual hardware operations necessitated by differences in the source and target computers; interfacing input and output; and idiosyncrasies of the source computer.

Part of the design considerations in planning a simulator involve determining the most efficient method to perform the simulation on the target machine. Though it may be possible to follow the original hardware design exactly, the extra instructions required may produce an inefficient simulation. It therefore becomes necessary to deviate from the original hardware design, but it is extremely important to ensure that the proper results are generated. One example of this phenomenon in the System Ten simulator involves performing the arithmetic functions. Although the MC68000 processor has BCD add and subtract instructions, they address one byte as two BCD digits rather than as an ASCII character. The System Ten design also allows the two operands to be of different lengths, from one to 10 bytes. To accommodate these conditions, the simulator copies the operands for the lengths specified in the instruction into work areas, performs 10-digit BCD arithmetic, and copies the proper result to the target operand for the proper length.

As mentioned above, interfacing input and output is probably the most difficult part of implementing a simulator. As an example of the type of input and output problems encountered in the System Ten simulation, an output operation to a CRT that causes the screen to scroll places a 3 in the condition code register of the processor. This condition code can be used to determine whether the terminal is a hard-copy work station (which will not set the condition, since there is no screen to scroll) or a CRT. If the device is a CRT, this condition can also be used to determine if the CRT has 20 or 24 lines on the screen. Since most terminals currently available do not provide this type of feedback, it becomes necessary to perform terminal simulation as well as a processor simulation.

Another difficulty of implementing a simulator involves duplicating the idiosyncrasies of the hardware, which will often by used by operating and application systems. The CRT test just described is an example of one System Ten idiosyncrasy. Another example involves the use of overlapping operand fields, which provide consistent and predictable results but are often used by programmers to perform data transformations whose purpose is difficult to understand. The EDIT instruction, normally used for inserting punctuation characters into numeric fields to provide a formatted output, has been cleverly used to produce the absolute value of a field by overlapping the source and target operands. Still another example uses an obscure feature of the System Ten partition switching operation whereby a shared subroutine can safely execute self-modifying code in lieu of longer reentrant code. For the simulator to allow this, it was necessary to duplicate the relative execution time of each instruction, accumulate the simulated elapsed time, and allow a partition switch to occur at the exact place that the System Ten would have switched partions.

To assist in solving these problems it is extremely helpful to have debugging aids on both the source and target machines. These aids will normally take the form of trace programs, which allow single-step and continuous tracing. It is also in valuable to build a trace function into the initial version of the simulator that can produce a display of each instruction as it is executed. When this trace is compared to the trace displays from the source computer, it should be easy to spot discrepancies, although in some cases the comparison will be very time-consuming.

RESULTS

Following extensive research into the design and structure of the System Ten and the Alpha Micro, approximately two person-months were required to bring the software simulation from initial design to installation of the first production version. The simulator, written in AMOS/L MC68000 assembly language, requires approximately 18Kb of memory plus the memory required to simulate System Ten partition and common memory.

During the initial design phase of the System Ten simulator program, it was determined that the simulated environment would be considerably slower than native System Ten operation. This was due to the inordinate amount of time that would be spent encoding and decoding the unique System Ten memory addressing scheme and to the significant programming involved in simulating the System Ten arithmetic and partition switching functions. In reality, the overall simulator throughput is twice as slow as the native System Ten used for the comparison. Certain arithmetic intensive applications proved to be even slower, whereas the difference in the data entry type of task appeared to be nominal. It was also determined that adding more than three or four simulated partitions began to cause a noticeable degradation in both the simulated and native system operations. This degradation proved to be the result of the terminal simulation required to support the System Ten environment rather than overhead in the processing simulator. The area of terminal simulation appears to be the only area of the simulation that can be targeted for additional development to improve efficiency.

In the particular installation where the simulated environment is in use, the software transfer plan consists of (1) rewriting the three major applications that consume approximately 80% of the processing load into the native Alpha Micro environment and (2) using the simulation to perform the remaining 12 applications until they can be scheduled to be rewritten. This allows all production work to continue, while essential new application development can also be accomplished.

CONCLUSIONS

Simulated environments can be used effectively as aids in transferring computer operations to a new host machine. At best, this approach may offer only an interim solution to the software transferability problem. But it does allow the data processing installation to continue uninterrupted while software for the new host system is generated.

This is especially true in the case of the System Ten, where software is so dependent on features of the hardware that automated or semiautomated software translation is not feasible.

It is also evident that current generation microcomputers are more than adequate to support a computer environment that simulates that of a minicomputer-based system.

REFERENCES

1. Snyders, J. "Conversion: Trauma or Tea Party." *Computer Decisions, 14* (1982), pp. 35–50.
2. Lemoine M., and J. Mullor. "Software Transferability: A Practical Approach." *Software—Practice and Experience, 11* (1981), pp. 425–433.
3. Casey, W. "Hard Facts about Software Transferability." *Government Data Systems, 6* (1977), pp. 44–47.
4. Walker, M. G. "Program Portability." *Datamation, 28* (1982), pp. 140–149.
5. Alpha Microsystems. "Introduction to AMOS." Prepared by Alpha Microsystems, Irvine, California.

Software manufacturing techniques and maintenance

by PAUL BASSETT
Netron Incorporated
Toronto, Ontario, Canada

ABSTRACT

"As ye sow, so shall ye reap."

A good solution to the reusable code problem turns out also to provide a solid technical basis from which to understand and deal with the production, quality, and maintenance issues of the software industry. To this end, a software manufacturing methodology has been developed called Computer-Aided Programming. CAP is based on a functional programming concept called a frame. Frames were originally developed as a means of resolving the maintenance problems associated with reusable code.

The introduction explains the necessary background ideas about frames and the types of maintenance that they address. Section two presents the design principles for software that uses frames as subassemblies for program assembly purposes. The components of an existing CAP system are described in section three, and section four discusses the use of CAP as a manufacturing technique. Statistics from a case study are presented to indicate that: (1) production-quality commercial software can be manufactured at rates exceeding 2000 lines of debugged COBOL per man-day (including systems design time), and (2) less than 10% of this code needs to be hand-written or maintained.

INTRODUCTION: THE MAINTENANCE PROBLEM

Software has had a precocious, turbulent childhood, as is typical of newly emerging disciplines. In spite of many important advances, software still remains a hand-made commodity designed in an ad hoc manner with few standards; a product that is almost always late, poorly documented, and difficult to maintain.

Maintenance, more than any other factor, holds the software industry captive, strangling productivity and tying up vital programming resources. The half-life of a typical program is approximately 14 months. The maintenance statistic now approaches 70% and is still climbing.

The central thesis of this paper is that a substantial portion of the maintenance effort stems from the reusable code problem. A good solution to this problem turns out also to provide a solid technical basis to understand and deal with both the production and quality of software and the maintenance issues currently besieging the software industry.

The Reusable Code Problem

In the software industry's current cottage industry style, it is common practice to build new programs by cutting and splicing pieces of old programs together. This approach demonstrates that there is great deal of potentially reusable code available, and that it is worth the effort to adapt it rather than starting from scratch. Reference 16 shows that unfortunately

1. The programmer does not have any systematic way of isolating just what portions of programs are relevant
2. The customization process is time consuming, tedious, and prone to error
3. Once the process is finished, both old and new programs must be maintained as if each were completely unique, despite the considerable common functionality. Maintenance effort should be proportional to the novelty in the system, not the number of source statements.[4]

External Subroutines

It is still widely believed that external subroutines form a satisfactory repository of reusable code. Separately compiled and linked subroutines are obviously useful, but they are limited because there is no graceful or systematic means of effecting local customization of an external subroutine to fit each calling program's particular context of use, or of effecting global evolution of a subroutine when it must change to benefit all future callers of that subroutine without victimizing current callers.

The subtle and often frustrating side effects introduced when common components undergo maintenance directly contributes to the severity of the maintenance problem.

The root cause is that a subroutine is a representation for a single function that is not adaptable at source-program (function) construction or maintenance time. It may have considerable run-time flexibility, but at the time of actually molding the subroutine into the program that must use it, an external subroutine (by its very nature) has no flexibility at all.

Code Generators

Code generators have been around for years (e.g., RPG). Although they offer a potential to drastically simplify the maintenance of large portions of a program, their potential goes unrealized.[2,10]

The simplest kind of code generators are those that generate "raw" source code. The problem with such generators is that they are basically "one-shot" tools. Because each generator is expert at only a part of the overall problem,[3,17] programmers must supplement and modify the generated source code to suit their own needs. Having adapted the code, they have no means of reusing the generator without destroying all of their manual modifications. This forces the programmer to support the life-cycle maintenance of the program at the more difficult and error-prone level of generated source code, rather than the succinct, declarative level of the original input to the generator.

To be more useful, a code generator must allow some follow-on mechanism that can adapt the generated source code automatically, thus allowing reuse of the generator without the loss of the customizations.

More sophisticated code generators typically supply "user exits" for handling this problem. These provide linkage to separately compiled, external suroutines that usually can be written in a variety of general purpose languages. The trouble is that this is always an additive technique; there is no way to change or remove generated functionality. Also, predefined interfaces often omit information that is essential in the customization (the "black box" effect). In addition, all non-procedural parts of the generated code, such as data declarations, are simply unavailable for refinement. A proper solution requires generators to provide for automatic customization of generated code (not just run-time communication with generated modules).

The Frame Methodology

A frame methodology,[13,14] has been developed to address the reusable code problem from the perspective both of programmers and of code generators.[3] A frame is a machine-processable representation of an abstract data type,[9] with "abstract" meaning functional.[1,3] Because the data operators are functionals, not functions, frames can accommodate both local customization into an individual program and global evolution to benefit all future embedding programs. Frames are implemented as files containing a mixture of source code (e.g., COBOL) and preprocessor macro commands, but are quite unlike the proposals of Backus[1] or Evans.[8] This mixture is called frame text.

There are just four macro commands whose essential role is to automate the cutting and splicing of programs:

1. COPY-INSERT allows a frame hierarchy to be copied into a program (by naming the frame at the root of the hierarchy), and causes customizing frame text to be INSERTed anywhere into that hierarchy.
2. BREAK-DEFAULT defines a named "breakpoint." Breakpoints mark arbitrary places in a frame where custom frame text can be INSERTed to supplement or replace DEFAULT frame functionality.
3. REPLACE systematically substitutes a specific code string for a generic one (throughout a frame hierarchy). For example, field names and picture clause elements are generic if they tend to vary from program to program.
4. SELECT incorporates into a program one text module from a set of modules in the frame. SELECTs are like CASE statements (with arbitrary nesting), which operate at text construction time. An important use of SELECT is to automate version control (global evolution).

Frames are written both by analysts and by generators. Having code generators produce frames solves the problem of destroying subsequent refinements by automating the cutting and splicing of the customizing frame text into the generated frame text.

All customizing frame text for one program is localized for maintenance purposes into a SPECIFICATION, or SPC, frame. Typically, the size of this file will be less than 10% of the generated source code. An SPC governs the entire process of building the compilable source program from its frame components. As will be seen, a methodology incorporating frames at its heart offers a potential for

1. Fill-in-the-blank program specifications (rapid prototyping)
2. Automation of the process of reusing previously built, high-quality software (both human- and machine-written)
3. Automatic customization in context
4. Maintenance of only what is unique in a program
5. Evolution of reusable components without obsolescence (elimination of unnecessary retrofits)
6. Painless enforcement of good programming techniques (standards)

THE DESIGN OF SOFTWARE MANUFACTURING TOOLS

In order to realize the potential of frames, especially with regard to maintenance, a software development environment has been created, called Computer Aided Programming. CAP is fundamentally a manufacturing paradigm, in which standard frames are the standard subassemblies, various frame generation steps are the processing operations on basic components (raw materials) to produce fabricated parts, and the CAP processor operating on the SPC frame is the process of final assembly with any custom options.

The Role of Languages

Our industry continues to proliferate languages unabated, and this is both necessary and desirable.[17] The creation of each language is motivated by a desire to reduce the effort of solving, in computer executable form, some class of problems. But does this mean we can eliminate the programming?

In Reference 5 the following definitions were developed: Problem solving is fundamentally a process of finding or composing a suitable function (1) whose domain is the problem's input information, (2) whose range is the goal of the problem (i.e., the desired output), and (3) whose function is consistent with other problem constraints.

Playing chess is an example of problem solving. The domain of a chess function is the set of legal board positions. The range is the set of legal moves associated with each position. The constraints include the time available to select a move, the need to find a "good" legal move, any memory of what moves were "good" in past games and so on.

Programming is a form of problem solving by function composition, in which one must deal with either the order of composition, or the interfacing of component functions, or both. At one extreme, selecting from a menu is an effective way for nonprogrammers to solve their problems. At the other extreme, selecting assembly language instructions will solve an interesting problem only with a great deal of programming effort.

By distinguishing problem solving from programming, it becomes possible, with respect to a given class of problems, to group language expressions into three levels: underspecified, optimally specified, and overspecified.

Optimal specification languages

A language is said to optimally specify a function space (and hence an associated problem class) if and only if:[5]

1. The language is isomorphic to the function space; that is, each distinct function is denoted by only one distinct expression, and only the functions in the space are expressible.
2. The degrees of freedom (constraints) are independent, optimally specified subspaces (of constants, variables, or functions).

3. The language's well-formed expressions are the "most compact" with respect to all languages satisfying (1) and (2).

In practice, this definition is weakened. Part (1) is approximated by first designing the language to be virtually one-to-one, then assuming the function space (implied by the language's semantics) to be what was "really meant" by the solutions of the original, unformalized problem class. Part (2) is approximated first by striving for as much independence as possible, then by applying as many context-sensitive error tests as are practical to any remaining dependent degrees of freedom. Finally, Part (3) is ignored as long as the language users are happy.

It turns out that such "weak optimal-specification" languages are a realistic approach to problem solving without programming. Functions usually can be defined simply by grouping the names of some subfunctions under a new function name, without regard to the order in which these subfunctions are performed and without regard to how these subfunctions must communicate with each other. Their compilers are called code generators because each generator plays the role of a programmer, converting a declarative, optimal specification into procedural, overspecified code, which itself must be compiled. Examples of this type of language as used in CAP are described in this paper. As has been noted, CAP design principles require the generated code to be in the form of frames.

It should be clear that the properties of optimal languages permit maintenance efforts to be minimized, provided that the resulting programs can be produced automatically.

Underspecification

An underspecification language is like an optimal-specification one except that the relationship of well-formed expressions in the language to the possible solution functions is one-to-many. There may be many degrees of freedom that play secondary roles in the structure of the overall function space. There may be several functions, each expressible in a different language, which must be combined, but whose degrees of freedom intersect or are interdependent. In these situations, an underspecification language can be used to quickly "broad brush" the major functional features of the solution. The code generator then employs heuristics to specify one solution function at the optimal level that is reasonable and consistent with any overlapping degrees of freedom.

Thus, the underspecified level is the prototyping level, feeding the optimal level where the life-cycle maintenance efforts are performed. Again, the key requirement is that the software manufacturing tools automate the flow of specifications between levels.

Overspecification language

In an overspecification language, the relationship of well-formed expressions to functions is many-to-one, and properties (2) and (3) of an optimal language do not hold even weakly. Overspecification languages are ubiquitous. For example, every computer's binary or assembly language lacks the syntax to express directly the right degrees of freedom for most of the problem classes to which the machine is applied. So programming, which is often done by a compiler, is inevitable at this final stage of problem solving.

To date, virtually all software maintenance has been performed at the overspecified level (for reasons discussed earlier). This is a significant factor in increasing the maintenance effort required. Provided that the software environment is one where a homomorphic map from the optimal to the overspecified levels exists, an order-of-magnitude reduction in life-cycle maintenance effort can be expected based simply on the reduction of code to be maintained.

To sum up the role of languages, whenever a useful function space can be defined by an optimal specification language, programming can be relegated to the computer. To further enhance problem-solving leverage, multiple underspecification, front-end editor–generator pairs can be built that create optimal specifications. These expressions are processed in turn by editor–generator pairs and create programs at the overspecified level, but maintain them at the optimal level. Any special-purpose, custom functionality is kept in the SPC frame, which directs the CAP processor in its final assembly tasks of building or rebuilding the complete source program, then compiling and linking it into executable form.

The Role of Frames

Frames are used to formalize the common intermediate stage in the program construction process, prior to the frames being combined and customized into a single program (function). There are two reasons for having this stage. First, recognizing the open-ended nature of problem solving, an extensible library of standard frames and templates, together with generated frames, can support custom programming for any problem. Second, the ability to mechanize the assembly of a program, given the diversity of its components, depends on bringing them to a common notation.

Standard frames

As problems are discovered to be related, a standard frame can be *evolved* to span the implicit function space. Each frame represents a functional, whose domain defines (using the COPY and REPLACE commands) the degrees of freedom appropriate to the class of related problems, and whose range (all possible instantiations of the frame text) is the corresponding function space. By fixing those degrees of freedom in various ways, various problems in the class can be solved without programming.

This is not to say that programming has been eliminated. Usually real problems refuse to confine themselves to neat, predefined classes. Accordingly, a frame's breakpoints and SELECT clauses constitute open-ended degrees of freedom, where solutions can be arbitrarily extended, if necessary.[5]

Standard frames are used whenever the function space is too limited in scope or usage to warrant a new optimal specification language. This approach to problem solving is implemented by using templates. A template is an uncustomized SPC frame, and usually spans a hierarchy of frames. It collects in one linear list (a file) all degrees of freedom appropriate for a useful class of problems. The replacement strings, subfunction selection choices, and insertion points for the frames in the hierarchy constitute a fill-in-the-blank method of customizing the program. Thus, templates and frames together permit problems to be solved in a manner that progressively reduces traditional programming to a minimum, given the open-ended nature of real problems.

To the degree that system design expertise can be stored inside the system, the SPC frame can itself be created by designer tools working at the underspecified level.

Generated frames

Certain function spaces have degrees of freedom too dynamic to be represented by fixed, standard frames. Well-known examples are screen and keyboard interfaces and report definitions. For these cases, optimal languages can be developed in association with frame-writing generators.

By generating frames instead of raw source code, open-ended (programming) degrees of freedom become available. Such degrees of freedom are required in the overall problem class, but should be suppressed in the various optimal specification languages. Further customizing can be specified via an SPC without the hand editing or restrictive user exits associated with conventional generators. Basically what has happened is that the editing that would otherwise be necessary to properly customize the generated code has been mechanized. In so doing, we gain both an assembly line style of constructing programs and an ability to maintain the program using its optimally defined pieces (rather than its overspecified code).

Anatomy of a CAPtool

Figure 1 depicts the flow of specifications from the underspecified or designer level, through the optimally specified or customizer level, down to the overspecified or source and object levels. Life-cycle maintenance is performed with the customizer (special purpose) editors. Please note that where

Specific screen & report specifications
Fill-in-the-blank report & screen customizers
Fill-in-the blank designer
Specific Needs
Generate Custom Frames
Splice Compile Link
Custom Executable Program
Specific frame specifications
Fill-in-the-blank SPC frame customizer
Model
Solution
Frames

Figure 1—CAP flow specifications

reference is made to screen and report specifications, these are examples of optimal-specification languages with respect to the problems of commercial data processing. A CAP tool may use either, both, or neither of these languages, as well as other notations, if the problems warrant.

AN ACTUAL CAP SYSTEM

At Netron Inc., a CAP system has been developed for use on WANG VS computer systems applied to commercial data processing using COBOL. The following reflects current functionality and some soon to be released tools.

Underspecified Level Tools

1. CAPinput—for building interactive file maintenance and data entry programs
2. CAPoutput—for building report programs based on general data selection criteria
3. CAPfile—for building general file-to-file transforms and interfaces

These three tools are each structured as shown in Figure 1. Specification of a complete program requires that an analyst answer a small number of questions (most of which have defaults).

Optimal-Specification-Level Tools

1. CAPscreen—for designing and maintaining interactive screen and keyboard functionality
2. CAPreport–for designing and maintaining report functionality
3. CAPframes—a library of standard frames

The (weakly) optimal notations are used by designer tools and by analysts, either in conjunction with underspecified-level tools or independently.

A complete description of these languages is beyond the scope of this paper.[5] Very briefly, independence of degrees of freedom is typified by having screen (report) layout facilities completely independent of the attributes of each screen (report) variable. On the other hand, some degrees of freedom are not completely independent. For example, if a variable on a screen is declared as having run-time error checks, and is declared as not being assigned to an internal variable after the operator enters it at run-time, then these two degrees of freedom are in conflict (and the conflict must be resolved).

The tools themselves generate frames from the optimal specification. These frames in turn make extensive use of the hierarchy of available CAP frames. Because the frames are written using general-purpose (but overspecified) COBOL, the programmer has exact control over the "fine tuning" his particular application may need in order to convert a functional into the required function.

The CAPframes are the heart of the CAP system. Each frame implements a useful function space whose patterns have been recognized by their appearance in several programs. The frames are organized into a taxonomy that guides the problem solver to the relevant functionality.

DISCUSSION OF TOOL USAGE

Types of Users

The consistent application of the under–optimal–over design principle offers access potential to the industry's three major user groups: end-users, analysts, and programmers. In CAP's current implementation, it is an analyst-oriented software manufacturing system. The focus has been to provide tools that aid in the manufacture of larger, more complex systems.

CAP could be designed for nonprogrammers, but few are inclined to cope with the open-ended applications to building and maintenance that are CAP's main strengths. Most people like driving cars and some even enjoy fixing or rebuilding them. But who wants to design and manufacture them?

Because CAP is a manufacturing paradigm, most of the benefits stemming from the organization of a conventional manufacturing enterprise become available to data processing shops. In particular, the frame-engineering department is quite analogous to a conventional engineering department. A useful division of labor is created. Those responsible for designing and maintaining the organization's inventory of standard software components (frames) can work independently from those charged with getting the application software products out the door. The benefit of having centralized standards control is obvious.

Rapid Prototyping

While not part of maintenance as such, rapid prototyping is a very desirable feature of any software development system. Moreover, it is important to ensure that rapid prototypes do not lead to maintenance nightmares.

Conventional wisdom, stemming from the software disasters of the sixties and early seventies, has firmly entrenched the hedging policies of preparing exhaustive feasibility studies, formal requirements definitions, structured walkthroughs, and the like. Often, the time and costs to plan a system are greater than the costs of building it. In turn, the specifications are usually out of date by the time they are finally approved, and the end-users still don't really know what they are getting, or if what they get is what they need. Another danger is that it is so easy to specify features that turn out to be much more difficult to implement than they are worth to the user. In short, the institutionalized policies of large data processing groups are no small contributor to the enormous applications backlog.

Conventional wisdom can now be made wiser.[6,7,11,12,15] CAP tools can write formal specifications that are understood both by people and by computers, and then convert the specifications to equivalent programs. We can now adopt the attitude of "what you see is what you get," and even let small prototypes constitute part of the design specification.

End-users can "kick its tires" and iteratively guide the specifications. The implementation team can provide specific, detailed arguments as to why certain features should or should not be in the system, and can more accurately estimate the cost of a system's implementation based on deviations from the organization's current frame inventory.

Productivity and Quality

Using a tool such as CAPinput typically requires that the user spend a few minutes at the underspecified level. Without further customization, an executable program is available shortly thereafter. The following is the summary from a detailed case study that analyzes the actual use of CAP.

Case study: The manufacture of the Canadiana requisition system

Canadiana Garden Products Inc., is a subsidiary of NOMA Industries Ltd. In March 1983 Canadiana employed Netron Inc., to create a computerized system to replace Canadiana's manual requisition system. The system was created using CAP and is run on a WANG VS computer using interactive terminals. The system allows requisitions to be created, maintained, displayed, searched, authorized, ordered, recorded, and reported upon.

After the first week, enough of the system had been prototyped that the client recognized serious design problems. The system was subsequently redesigned and put into production by the end of the third week.

Sixteen programs were written using CAP tools to create and control the interaction of the 22 screens and three reports through which the requisition system is operated. CAP tools enabled the author to create the requisition system by writing less than 10% of the total COBOL lines needed.

One method of judging the effect on maintenance with and without CAP tools is to compare the total number of lines of submitted source code in the entire requisition system with the number of hand-written lines. Purely comment lines were discarded.

The results show a more than 10:1 reduction in lines of COBOL to be maintained. Of the 34,000 lines of submitted code contained in the 16 programs of the requisition system, only 3,000 lines were written by hand.

The following table shows, for each of the 16 programs forming the requisition system, the number of lines hand written in the SPC frame, in the generated frames, in standard frames, and in the total submitted to the COBOL compiler.

Quality

Of course, the issue here is not merely to show that there is much less code to maintain. Further analysis of the manufactured programs show that they are more consistent with respect to user-interface and structured program style, more reliable, more functionally complete, and no less efficient than conventional, hand-written programs.

TABLE I—Number of code liens

Program Name	Main CAPTool	Total Source	SPC Frame	Generated Frames	Standard Frames
PREQ1	CAPinput	2979	56	1731	1192
PREQ2	CAPinput	2130	71	1264	795
PREQ3	CAPinput	2318	78	1013	1227
PREQ4	CAPinput	1721	62	869	790
PREQ5	CAPinput	3440	421	1904	1115
PREQ6	CAPinput	2776	157	1766	853
PREQ7	CAPinput	1510	40	673	797
PREQ8	CAPinput	3018	206	1806	1006
PREQ9	CAPinput	3238	281	1910	1047
PREQA	CAPinput	3659	436	2223	1000
PREQI	CAPinput	3399	436	1916	1047
PREQF	Frame Lib.	274	187	0	87
PREQG	Frame Lib.	223	136	0	87
PREQR	CAPreport	954	140	198	616
PREQS	CAPreport	1086	226	216	644
PREQT	CAPreport	1152	179	290	683

The reason is that the standard frames and frame generators are highly seasoned components in the course of whose evolution many improvements and optimizations have been made. The cumulative effects are capital assets (no pun intended) that yield a return on investment in every incorporating program. Programs hand-written from scratch have no chance to acquire the quality and thoroughness that is the hallmark of a good frame.[15]

Life-cycle Support

As previously indicated, by storing all source code customizations in one spot, factored away from both standard and generated frames, typical program maintenance is collapsed from 50–60 pages of source listing to two or three pages. By having the code generators emit frame code that can be customized automatically, the declarative specifications also support the life cycle maintenance of the programs in a very convenient manner.

Frame maintenance

As with software, frames change through time. Standard frames tend to be relatively stable since they rapidly become seasoned through frequent reuse. But because they are functionals, they are able to absorb arbitrary amounts of change (including complete rewrites) without risking any previously written program. It is easy to arrange that the range (function space) of a new version of a functional be a superset of the previous version's range simply by providing a version control parameter governing a SELECT clause.

This still allows the improved functional to recreate all old functional versions. An old program's SPC, unaware of subsequent changes, references the frame hierarchy with its old version symbol (if any), and gets exactly the same code it has always gotten, even though new programs may get something quite different (the template always contains the latest version symbol).

This does not mean that frames and libraries become more cluttered than in conventional shops. Conventionally, complete copies are kept of all versions (using distinct names), even though only small changes might have been made. Frames keep an automatic audit trail of the version *differences,* with only occasional rewrites done to eliminate clutter. The obsolete (but still active) versions are placed in a separate library, again to eliminate clutter. Internal version references automate the retrieval of the correct version. Thus, a single external name is common to all versions and less space overall is actually required.

CONCLUSION

It is important to realize that programs are models: deliberate approximations to an elusive and ever-changing external reality. Models are useful because they exploit a simplified representation. We know that Newtonian physics is wrong, yet we never use Einstinian physics when programming everyday calculations. A payroll system has an extremely skimpy model of the human beings on file, but it is quite appropriate for the intended purpose.

From this perspective, development and maintenance are two sides of the same coin. Converging a software model to a useful approximation is called development. But the model also must be updated periodically in light of changing circumstances, and this is called maintenance. The payroll system must quickly incorporate each change to the income tax laws to the extent that its model of those laws becomes invalid.

The recent development of a software manufacturing paradigm has set the stage for changing our cottage industry into a mature technology. By unifying the techniques for program construction and maintenance, each productivity gain can simultaneously benefit both.

REFERENCES

1. Backus, J. "Can Programming Be Liberated from the von Neumann Style? A Functional Style and its Algebra of Programs." *Communications of the ACM,* 21, 8 (1978), 196–206.
2. Balzer, R. "An alternative approach to software automation." *In P. Wegner (ed.), Research Directions in Software Technology.* Cambridge, Mass.: MIT Press, 1979, pp. 851–856.
3. Bassett, P. B., and J. Giblon. "Computer Aided Programming (Part I)." In *Proceedings of IEEE Conference on Software Tools and Techniques.* (Soft Fair), Washington D.C., July 1983.
4. Bassett, P. B., and S. Rankine. "The Maintenance Challenge." *Computerworld In Depth,* May 16, 1983.
5. Bassett, P. B. *"Design Principles for Software Manufacturing Tools."* Presented at Symposium on Application and Assessment of Automated Tools for Software Development, Nov. 1–3, 1983, San Francisco, IEEE, (unpublished).
6. Bianchi, M. H., and J. R. Mashey. "Rapid Prototyping on UNIX. In *Proceedings of the Software Engineering Symposium: Rapid Prototyping.* (IEEE) Columbia, April 19–21, 1982.
7. Blattner, M., and R. Frobose. "Prototyping and the Life Cycle of Software." In *Proceedings of the Software Engineering Symposium: Rapid Prototyping.* (IEEE) Columbia, April 19–21, 1982.
8. Evans, M. "Software Engineering for the Cobol Environment." *Communications of the ACM,* 25, 12 (1982), pp. 874–882.
9. Goguen, J. A., J. W. Thatcher, and E. G. Wagner. "An Initial Algebra Approach to the Specification, Correctness and Implementation of Abstract Data Types." In R. Yeh (ed.), *Current Trends In Programming Methodology.* Vol. 4, Englewood Cliffs, N.J.: Prentice-Hall, 1979, pp. 80–149.
10. Hammer, M., and G. Rugh. "Automating the Software Development Process." In P. Wegner (ed.), *Research Directions in Software Technology.* Cambridge, Mass.: MIT Press, 1979, pp. 767–790.
11. Houghton, R. C., Jr. "Rapid Prototyping Tools: What Can We Learn from the MIS World?" In *Proceedings of the Software Engineering Symposium: Rapid Prototyping,* (IEEE) Columbia, Md. April 19–21, 1982.
12. Mason, R.E.A., and T. T. Carey, "Prototyping Interactive Information Systems." *Communications of the ACM,* 26, 5 p. 347.
13. Minsky, M. "A Framework for Representing Knowledge." In P. Winston (ed.), *The Psychology of Computer Vision.* New York: McGraw-Hill, 1975, pp. 211–277.
14. Rich, J. "Inspection Methods in Programming." Ph.D. Thesis MIT Technical Report AI-TR-604, June 1981
15. Taylor, T., and T. A. Standish. "Initial Thoughts on Rapid Prototyping Techniques." In *Proceedings of the Software Engineering Symposium: Rapid Prototyping,* (IEEE) Columbia, Md., April 19–21, 1982.
16. Wasserman, A. I., and S. Gutz, "The Future of Programming." *Communications of the ACM,* 25, 3 (1982), 196–206.
17. Wulf, W.A. "Some Thoughts on the Next Generation of Programming Languages." *In Perspectives on Computer Science.* New York: Academic Press, 1977, pp. 217–234.

A prototyping environment for real-time graphics

by NOLA DONATO
Four Phase
Cupertino, California
and
ROBERT ROCCHETTI and JANET TOM
Mattel Electronics
Chicago, Illinois

ABSTRACT

As technology advances, graphics displays are becoming more powerful and less expensive, making interactive graphics increasingly popular as a method of man–machine communication. Often, nonprogrammers play a principal role in the design and implementation of applications involving graphics. Because interactive graphics require such a high level of feedback with both human and hardware, traditional programming languages are not well suited for the graphics environment.

This paper describes CGRASS, a portable, general-purpose programming language, and how it is used for prototyping videogames. The design rationale for a game-prototyping system is given, followed by an overview of the CGRASS language with emphasis placed on features particularly helpful for user interface design and modeling. We show examples of tools implemented for different hardware architectures and targeted for users of varying backgrounds.

INTRODUCTION

Programming a production videogame requires a lot of time and an experienced assembly language programmer. Hardware for both arcade and home videogames is very inexpensive compared to other types of graphics hardware. Correspondingly, resources such as CPU time and memory are quite limited, making the use of high-level languages seldom feasible. A significant part of game development involves modifying a program to fit in the small amount of memory allocated for the game. Time is also spent optimizing certain areas of code to make the game-play fast enough. A programmer frequently has to take advantage of quirks in the game hardware to produce graphic effects.

Usually, software tools to assist in the creation of a game run almost entirely on the game unit. They are programmed in assembly language (usually by game programmers) and are subject to the same speed and memory constraints as the game programs. As a result, tools are limited in functionality and do not tend to be very user-friendly; nonprogrammers often find them difficult to use. Typically, tools exist to create data structures, such as pictures and sounds, and to manipulate them in simple ways. However, to do anything more complex, one must resort to assembly language.

As the relative costs of human professional time and computer time shift, the interface between man and machine becomes increasingly important. Many researchers are investigating methods of improving user interfaces for a variety of applications.[1–4] Powerful, user-friendly software tools are especially important in the videogame environment where nonprogrammers, such as artists, educators, game designers, and marketing experts make major contributions to the application.

One way to improve the game design process is to provide a way to make a working model of a game in a short amount of time. The decision about whether or not to manufacture a game can be made much earlier in the game's development cycle. Shortening the development loop allows more ideas to be tried, improving the quality of the game. Parts of the prototype (such as graphics, sound, and algorithms) can be applied to the final product. Finally, a good user interface can take input from novices as well as experts.[5]

DESIGN APPROACH

We had several objectives for the design of our graphics-prototyping environment.

1. The system should be easy to learn and usable both by nonprogrammers and programmers
2. It should be interactive and provide immediate feedback
3. The system should have the ability to interface with vastly different hardware architectures
4. The user interface should be consistent across satellite and host systems wherever possible.

We divided the prototyping task into two parts. User interaction is delegated to a host processor, allowing applications to be written in a high-level language. Machine-specific functions are programmed on the game unit (or, more generally, the *satellite processor*). By using a reasonably powerful computer as our host, we are freed from many of the limitations imposed by the smaller game units. Therefore, game development tools can be more comprehensive, user-friendly, and so on. Satellite graphics systems have been used successfully in both commercial and research environments.[6]

The type of host and satellite vary, as does the method of communication. For example, one configuration uses a large host, the VAX/11-780, connected to various types of satellites via serial ports. We have also been successful with a 16-bit microprocessor-based host linked through a parallel port to a graphics display.

From the host, one can invoke a variety of tools to create pictures and sounds, animate objects, and so forth. One can also write game prototypes and new applications directly. In addition, tools for translating from one target system format to another are available. For example, videocamera input from a bit-mapped display can be converted into a form usable with some character-mapped devices.

The Host System

As the basis of our system we chose CGRASS, an interpretive programming language written by the authors. The CGRASS language is implemented in C and has been successfully ported to many different machines and operating systems. This choice allows the environment for both program development and production applications to be consistent across all hosts.

In addition to being portable, the CGRASS language is very extensible. New commands may be implemented in either CGRASS or C and are easily added to the system. Programmers may create their own data types and define how the system operators and commands will interact with them. These capabilities make the language good for communicating with different satellite processors and for designing human interfaces.[7]

Because it is interactive and dynamic, CGRASS is easy to learn and use. Control structures and data types are high-level and the system does much housekeeping automatically. Automatic type conversion, dynamic allocation, succinct expressive constructs, and data abstraction mechanisms make CGRASS ideal for implementing user interfaces as well as for general programming tasks. The system has on-line helps and source level debugging facilities, which shorten program development time.

The Target Systems

Because videogame hardware is by nature idiosyncratic, we decided to implement most of the real-time graphics capabilities on the satellites. Each satellite processor has its own small, special-purpose, real-time executive that handles the coordination of graphic and audio events. This approach allows us to isolate the machine dependencies and standardize the user interface as much as possible. It also makes efficient use of the limited memory and speed resources.

LANGUAGE OVERVIEW

CGRASS borrows heavily from its predecessors GRASS3 (which ran on the PDP-11)[8] and ZGRASS (a subset of GRASS3 for the Bally Arcade).[9] Many of the ideas for graphics tools in the prototyping system are derived from work done with GRASS3.[10] Similarly, ZGRASS provided a model for development of machine specific capabilities for low resolution bitmap displays.

CGRASS is a higher level language than GRASS3, with more powerful data abstraction capabilities. It has the runtime flexibility of languages such as SNOBOL4,[11] while maintaining a structured nature similar to C.[12] Data types in the language include variable-length strings and lists as well as traditional numbers and arrays. Like C, CGRASS is operator-rich and expression-oriented. The global, local, and static identifier scoping found in C is also present in CGRASS. In addition to the C-like control structures, CGRASS provides backtracking and goal-directed evaluation similar to ICON.[13]

CGRASS has no storage declarations, explicit allocation, or deallocation. Variables may be assigned any value during execution. Storage management and type conversion are handled automatically by the system. Strings and lists may be arbitrarily long, limited only by physical resources. Like GRASS3, the number and type of arguments to procedures is determined at run time.

Execution Environment

CGRASS is a conversational system; any statement that may be included in a program can also be typed at the terminal. In this way, CGRASS functions as a command language as well as a programming language (similar to the UNIX shell[14]). LISP-based programming environments have shown this approach to be successful for numerous applications, including interactive graphics.[15]

The CGRASS program development environment allows code to be written entirely from within the system or imported from the outside. The system has a resident editor and the ability to invoke any other editor on the host operating system. Programs are debugged interactively at the source level, with assistance from the system in the form of on-line helps and descriptive error messages.

To simplify the user interface with the language, many data types are identical at the source level; the differences between types are embedded in the implementation. For example, files, strings, arrays, and lists may all be printed using the same syntax. This holds true for other operations in the language such as comparison, subscripting, etc. For the most part, disk files and strings behave identically; the use of the disk is hidden in the implementation.

Built-in DataTypes

CGRASS contains numbers, strings, and arrays, and provides ways to compare, subscript and do arithmetic operations. Strings are scalars in CGRASS, not arrays of characters as in conventional languages. They may be compared, concatenated, indexed, or executed. Another built-in data type is the variable-length list. Like strings, lists can be concatenated, indexed, or extended. CGRASS uses the same syntax for list manipulation as it does for the corresponding string or array operations.

Files are a special data type in CGRASS because they act like strings but may also be treated as programs. Any operation allowed on strings also works for files. In addition, they may be interactively debugged with the source level debugger. Files also have their own set of low-level input–output directives, making it possible to access individual lines or characters in an operating-system-dependent fashion.

Control Structures

Parameter passing in CGRASS is derived from the method used by its predecessor, GRASS3. A function does not have explicit parameters, argument input is done at run time, and the language provides a mechanism for automatically prompting the user when a required argument is omitted.

```
prompt 'What is your name'
input name NAME
prompt 'How old are you'
input integer AGE
```

In the example above, the *prompt* command will only be executed if there are no more arguments left to be parsed. The *input* command will fetch the next argument from the list passed to the function. If there are no more arguments left in the list, the program prompts the user at the terminal. This feature is especially useful for writing user interfaces.

In addition to the traditional *if, while,* and *switch* constructs, CGRASS supports goal-directed evaluation and generators.[16] Generators allow a single expression to produce different values until a computationally useful one is found. Other languages like CLU,[17] database systems, and command languages,[18,19] have similar constructs, but in a more limited setting.

```
for THING[count(size(THING))] >
                              X print THING[_count]
for each(THING) > X print this(THING)
```

Both of the above statements print all elements of the group *THING* (which may be a list, string, array, etc.) that are greater than the value of *X*. In the first statement, *count* is a generator that returns the values of 1 through its argument each time it is invoked. The current value of the counter is left in global variable *_count*. In the second statement, the *each* generator produces as its alternatives the elements of its aggregate argument. The *for* construct forces every alternative of the *each* or *count* generator to be produced and compared with *X*. Note that this comparison may require type conversion depending on the types of *X* and *this(THING)*. The body of the loop will only be executed for successful values of the *for* expression. A user can write functions that behave like generators. This facility has been used to implement a set of string manipulation primitives in CGRASS.[20]

Basic Primitives

Numerous built-in commands are provided to assist with input, output, type conversion, calculation, and debugging. Almost any data type can be printed on the terminal with the *print* command or input from the terminal with the *input* command. Output from a command or function may be redirected into a string or file using the > operator. Similarly, input can be redirected with < (like the UNIX shell). Functions exist to open and close files, and to read and write lines or characters. These functions provide a low-level communication path to serial ports as well as disk files.

CGRASS has a set of list- and string-processing functions that assist in scanning the aggregate types. Each indexable data type keeps track of the last element accessed. In the case of strings, an element is considered to be a line (not a character). At any time, one can refer to the first, last, current, previous, or next element of an aggregate.

```
function bubble {
input value V
for V[count(count(size(V) -1, 2, -1))] < next(V)
   this(V) = >prev(V)
return V
}
```

The function above performs a bubble sort on its argument, which must be indexable. Two nested *count* generators are used; the inner *count* generates subscripts starting at the back of the vector toward the first element and the outer count iterates from the first item to the inner index. Consecutive elements are compared and exchanged, with the operator, if they are out of order. Note that combined use of the scanning functions and goal-directed evaluation allows the body of the sort to be written in a single CGRASS statement without the use of temporary variables. This example illustrates how CGRASS can make a programming job easier by reducing the amount of information the programmer must handle.

Data Abstraction

In modern languages, abstract data types provide an important means by which the programmer may extend the language to include new data types not present in the base language.[21,22] CGRASS is no exception to this. Users may create their own data types and define how existing operators and functions apply to them. Operators may also be defined for built-in data types.

To illustrate how one goes about defining a new data type in CGRASS, let's define a table along the lines of SNOBOL4. For our purposes, a table will be a heterogeneous vector indexed by strings rather than integers. To keep the example simple, a linear search is used to look up each element; in reality, one would use a more efficient hashed-access method. The example below illustrates a class capable of instantiating and indexing a table.

```
class table {
if _class ==c_MAKE return table(list())
input list TABLE
if _class == c_INDEX
  {
  input string S
  for each(V)[1] == S return this(V)[2]
  V = $ list(list(S, null))
  return last(V)[2]
  }
```

The *class* declaration defines a function that will be invoked automatically whenever an operation is performed on an object of the class. The system sets the global variable *_class* to indicate which operation to perform. CGRASS then invokes the user-defined class function; this function uses *_class* to dispatch to the appropriate section and returns the result of the operation.

Internally, our table is maintained as a list of index and value pairs. Each individual table element is a list whose first element is the index string and whose second element is the value of the element. To make a table we would do the following:

```
abc = table()          : instantiate table
abc['first'] = 1       : give it elements
abc['second'] = 2
```

When the first statement above is executed, the code associated with the class *table* is invoked with *_class* equal to *c_MAKE* indicating that we are instantiating a table. When the table is indexed, as in the last two statements, the class code is again called, this time with *_class* set to *c_INDEX*. In this case, the arguments to the class function are the *table* object and the index value. The code then searches the existing table elements, comparing their index strings to the one passed. If a match is found, this element is returned. If not, a new table entry is made and appended to the end of the list. Similarly, we could define other built-in operations such as print, each, this, etc., for our new data type.

APPLICATIONS

CGRASS was used in the development of many graphics applications. Some of these were prototypes which were later recoded in assembler and became part of the satellite processor repertoire. We developed tools to create and modify pictures, to define moving objects, and to animate them in various ways. Mechanisms were also provided for color animation[23] and audio processing. For some satellites, one is given direct control over machine-dependent hardware features.

There are two kinds of display hardware in the game environment—vector (analog) and raster (digital). Digital systems can be further subdivided into character-mapped[24] and bit-mapped[25] architectures. CGRASS has been used to design tools for several different digital video displays of both types.

The remainder of this section demonstrates how CGRASS was applied in the case of a character-mapped architecture. We discuss the distribution of work between satellite and host and give examples of specific data abstractions.

Character-Mapped Architecture

Character mapping is widely used in CRT terminals and consumer electronics. It is simple, inexpensive, and supports dynamic motion in a somewhat limited framework. The screen is broken up into M-by-N pixel rectangles, each of which is assigned a pointer. The pointer for a given rectangle (cell) refers to the particular member of the character set that will be displayed in that position. In addition to a pointer to a character, an individual screen cell may have other attributes such as color, orientation, and so on. Some systems have programmable character generators with which users can define their own characters.

For the purposes of this example, we now describe a hypothetical, simplified character-mapped display. Each screen cell can have two attributes—a character number and a color. The background color of each character is fixed across the entire screen; the foreground color is variable. User-defined characters are not considered in this discussion.

The following class permits the programmer to view the screen as a two-dimensional array. Each element of the array has two attributes: the number of the character that occupies the cell, and the color of the foreground.

```
class screen {
if _class == c_MAKE return screen(null)
input value SCREEN
if _class ==  c_ASSN        : clear whole screen?
  {
  gput O_CLR, input(int); ggo     : clear to color
  return screen(SCREEN)     : return the class
  }
if _class == c_INDEX        : access cell?
  return Cell(input(int), input(int), input(int))
freturn
}
```

There are only two operations defined for the class *screen* in the declaration above. No data are associated with members of this class because they are all maintained by the satellite processor.

Assignment into an object of type *screen* clears the entire screen to the given color. In order to produce any visible change, we must tell the game unit to clear the screen by calling the *gput* and *ggo* functions, which send the appropriate information to the satellite. In this case, we send a predefined opcode *(O_CLR)* to clear the screen, followed by the color we wish to clear it to. The *gput* function stores each of its arguments in an output buffer. Invoking *ggo* causes the accumulated contents of the output buffer to be sent to the satellite processor.

Although references to individual screen cells are trapped in class *screen,* the actual work is done by class *Cell,* described below.

```
class Cell {
if _class == c_MAKE
  return Cell(list(input(int), input(int)))
input list CELL                 : get cell list
X = CELL[1], Y = CELL[2]        : get coordinates
switch _class
  {
  case c_REF                    : read cell
  gput O_CGET,X,Y;ggo           : get cell contents
  return list(gget(), gget())
  case c_ASSN                   : write cell
  input list L                  : cell contents
  gput O_CPUT,X,Y,L[1], L[2]
  ggo                           : put card number, color
  return Cell(CELL)
  }
}
```

The *Cell* class allows one to read or write the contents of an individual screen cell—that is, the character number and the color. The satellite has opcodes *O_CGET* and *O_CPUT* defined to read and write attributes of a particular cell. The *gget* function fetches the next input byte from the satellite processor, in this case the character number and then the color.

A scheme such as the one above buries a lot of the machine-dependent details inside the satellite processor. For example, the dimensions of the screen need not be known to the host; limit checks are made on the satellite. The communication mechanism used by *gput, ggo,* and *gget* is also transparent to the application.

One of our satellite processors has two serial ports and connects the terminal to the host. A single serial line transmitting ASCII hex format data handles all communication. On another system we use two serial lines. One line is used for host–satellite communications and uses a binary protocol; the other handles a terminal. Still another system uses a parallel port. The same low-level set of functions is used in all three cases. Whenever possible, we have tried to make the same opcodes accepted by different satellite processors.

Given a general view of a character-mapped architecture machine, we can go on to implement an outer layer of software tools using the abstract data type *screen.* The following is an excerpt from a picture creation utility. It uses the numeric keypad on a standard terminal to move a cursor on the screen. The space bar controls whether or not the cursor leaves a trail as it moves.

```
OLD = screen[_x, _y]                  : old screen cell
screen[_x, _y] = list(0, _col)        : draw cursor
if DRAW == 0                          : do we draw?
   screen[_x, _y] = OLD               : no, restore cell
C = getch(0)                          : get keypress
switch C                              : dispatch
  {
  case 0C8 -- _y                      : up
  case 0C2 ++ _y                      : down
  case 0C4 -- _x                      : right
  case 0C6 ++ _x                      : left
  case 0C DRAW = xor(DRAW, 1)         : toggle draw
}
```

Three global variables are maintained; *_x* and *_y* contain the coordinates of the current screen cell and *_col* is the current foreground color. *OLD* and *DRAW* are local variables that contain the displaced contents of the screen cell and a flag determining whether or not the cursor should leave a trail.

The paint program from which these lines were taken has many other features. The color *(I_col)* can be chosen from a palette. An area of the screen can be reduced and made into a character. The cursor is selectable from the list of possible characters.

Using what we learned by implementing the character manipulation tools on our prototyping system, we were able to determine quickly what capabilities were needed and what view we wished to present to the user. Once the graphics interface is defined, performance enhancements that do not affect functionality can be made without rewriting applications.

For example, on one system we recoded part of the paint program, embedding cursor movement in the satellite. For the most part, the change was transparent to the rest of the software; the body of the cursor movement function is replaced with a small sequence of code, which asks the satellite for the cursor position. Thus, response is still quite good for simple functions even when the host is heavily loaded.

FUTURE WORK

The next step in designing a game-prototyping system is to completely remove the restrictions placed by the target system hardware. Making the number and size of moving objects variable, for example, would allow a game designer to concentrate more on the game and less on the limitations of the hardware.

The communications port is also somewhat of a bottleneck. Our prototyping efforts to date indicate that the host and satellite systems must be tightly coupled for efficient simulation.

We are currently working on a system that uses a high-speed, microcodable frame buffer as a satellite. By defining very powerful real-time graphics primitives we hope to have the satellite processor handle the bulk of the simulation with directions given by the host. We will be able to plug in various analog devices, such as tablets, joysticks, dials, etc., and use them to manipulate aspects of a simulation in real time. For example, one could control the position of a moving object with a joystick and its size or color with a dial. It is our belief that capabilities such as these will elevate the level of game design, making it possible to produce a playable game prototype in a very short amount of time.

REFERENCES

1. Anson, E. "The Device Model of Interaction." *ACM Computer Graphics 16,* 3 (1982), pp. 107–114.
2. Buxton, W., S. Patel, W. Reeves, and R. Baecker. "OBJED and the Design of Timbral Resources." *Proceedings of International Conference on Computers and Music.* 1980, pp. 1–12.
3. Hayes, P. J. "Cooperative Command Interaction Through the Cousin System." *Proceedings of the International Conference on Man/Machine System.* London, July 1982.
4. Wong, P., and E. Reid. "Flair—User Interface Dialogue Design Tool." *ACM Computer Graphics 16,* 3 (1982), pp. 87–98.
5. Wasserman, A. I. "User Software Engineering and the Design of Interactive Systems." *Proceedings of the Fifth International Conference on Software Engineering,* March 1981, pp. 387–393.
6. Foley, J. D. "A Tutorial on Satellite Graphics Systems." *Computer,* August, 1976.
7. Shaw, "The Impact of Abstraction Concerns on Modern Programming Languages." *Proceedings of the IEEE 68,* 9 (1980), pp. 1119–1130.
8. Donato, N. "GRASS3—A Language for Interactive Graphics." *AFIPS, Proceedings of the National Computer Conference* (Vol. 50), 1981.
9. Defanti, T., N. Donato, and J. Fenton. "Basic Zgrass—A Sophisticated Graphics Language for the Bally Home Computer." *Computer Graphics 12,* 3 (1978), pp. 33–37.
10. Rocchetti, R. "VISION II—A Dynamic Raster Scan Display." *AFIPS, Proceedings of the National Computer Conference* (Vol. 50), 1981.
11. Griswold, R. E., J. F. Poage, and I. P. Polonsky. *The SNOBOL4 Programming Language.* Englewood Cliffs, N.J.: Prentice Hall, 1971.
12. Kernighan, B. W., and D. M. Ritchie. *The C Programming Language.* Englewood Cliffs, N.J.: Prentice Hall, 1978.
13. Griswold, R. E., and M. T. Griswold. *The Icon Programming Language.* Englewood Cliffs, N.J.: Prentice Hall, 1983.
14. Mashey, J. R. "Using a Command Language as a High-Level Programming Language." *Proceedings of the 2nd International Conference on Software Engineering,* San Francisco, October 1976, pp. 169–176.
15. Levine, J. "Why a LISP-Based Command Language?" *SIGPLAN Notices 15,* 5 (1980), pp. 49–53.
16. Griswold, R. E., D. R. Hanson, and J. T. Korb. "Generators in Icon." *ACM Transactions on Programming Languages and Systems 3,* 2 (1981), pp. 144–161.
17. B. Liskov, et al. *CLU Reference Manual,* New York: Springer-Verlag, 1981.
18. W. N. Joy. "An Introduction to the C Shell." *Technical Report, Computer Science Division,* Dept.of Electrical Engineering and Computer Science, University of California, Berkeley, Calif., 1980.
19. S. R. Bourne. "The UNIX Shell." *Bell System Technical Journal 57,* 6 (1978), pp. 1971–1990.
20. Griswold, R. E., and D. R. Hansen. "An Alternative to the Use of Patterns in String Processing." *ACM Transactions on Programming Languages and Systems 2,* 2 (1980), pp. 153–171.
21. Goldberg, A., D. Robson, and D.H.H. Ingalls. *Smalltalk-80: The Language and Its Implementation,* Reading, Mass.: Addison Wesley, 1983.
22. B. Liskov, et. al. "Abstraction Mechanisms in CLU." *Communications of the ACM 20,* 8 (1977), pp. 564–576.
23. Shoup, R. G. "Color Table Animation." *SIGGRAPH 79 Proceedings,* August, 1979.
24. Baecker, R. "Digital Video Display Systems and Dynamic Graphics." *SIGGRAPH 79 Proceedings,* 1979.
25. Blinn, J. F. "Raster Graphics." In *Tutorial: Computer Graphics,* Los Angeles: IEEE Computer Society Press, 1982.

A publisher's view of writing successful software

by GARY SWANSON
Portland, Oregon*

ABSTRACT

This paper gives dilithium Press's viewpoint of what is required to write successful software today. A discussion of the concepts behind the developmental process should be are covered as well as how that process relates to a publishing company. The basic function of an editorial department is described and the distinction between editorial and marketing in publishing is outlined. The importance of editorial philosophy is talked about and the philosophy of dilithium Press is explained in detail. After describing the editorial philosophy, I give an overview of the type of products dilithium Press is looking for. Finally, the editorial process of submissions, evaluation and development is covered.

* This paper was written while Gary Swanson was at dilithium Press, Beaverton, Oregon.

So you want to write software that sells? Well, first let's talk about the meaning of *write* and *software.* When I use the word *write,* I'm not talking about the actual coding of the program. That is one of the last steps you should perform. A more appropriate word, or first step, is design. In the development of software, there are many decisions to be made on the road to success—all before the coding ever begins. As an author you must view your program, whether it is finished or nearly finished, as changeable, not as fixed. The editorial process, which will be discussed later, necessitates that at least some minor changes be made; and in many instances major changes are needed to market your program successfully. These suggestions for the changes can be frustrating to you as an author if you are unwilling to respond to them. If, on the other hand, you view your software as a changeable product, the process of revising your program is mentally much easier. However, before we delve into the editorial process let me first give you an overview of what an editorial department does; what our software editorial philosophy is at dilithium Press; and, in general terms, what type of programs we are looking for.

The editorial function in publishing serves the same purpose as research and development in manufacturing, with one exception. Besides defining the markets, anticipating what will sell, and developing the ideas to satisfy those markets, editors work with authors who have submitted a proposal. However, knowing what will sell and why is not enough to insure sales. The development of the defined markets is just as important as the defining of those markets. This is where an aggressive marketing department comes into play. Marketing must know where and how to sell the software.

If knowing what will sell and why is the first step on the journey toward a successful software product, then editorial philosophy is the road map. At dilithium Press, we realize that there hasn't been any serious attempt to make software a true consumer product. We also understand that most people would prefer to try a product before they buy it. This is as true for software as it is for any other consumer product. Our approach to the development and marketing of software is unique in the way we permit this try-before-you-buy concept. Our software package includes both the program itself and a well-structured book that explains how to use the program. The book is also a marketing tool that can be purchased without the program, allowing the consumer to see how the program operates and what it can do. After consumers see the software's capabilities with real-life examples, they can purchase the program separately.

We also know that to be successful we must deliver good-quality products that are strongly supported and fill a variety of needs. With these facts in mind, we've developed our Software Cycle Concept, the core of our software editorial philosophy. The software cycle has four elements. Each of the four elements of the cycle is related to every other element, yet each can stand alone.

Using an application program as an example, we first develop an introductory book that stimulates a demand for the software package. This book introduces a solution to a problem that will either help the individual increase productivity or help the businessperson increase profits. The methods described in the book are related to the use of microcomputers and a specific software product, but the emphasis is on how to solve a particular problem.

Once we have stimulated a demand for the product, the next step in the cycle is to educate and instruct in the use of the software product. This is done by publishing a nontechnical but well-written book that can be either sold separately or packaged with the program. The book begins with an introduction to the concept behind the software program and is followed by a tutorial with numerous screen displays and real-life examples. Next in the book is a comprehensive reference section listing all the program functions, with an explanation of how and when to use each one. Finally, the last part of the book contains a comprehensive glossary and an index.

The third element in our software cycle is to support the sale. We do this by providing a toll-free number and a knowledgeable customer support staff that communicates with the customer on a nontechnical level. We also send product news updates to registered owners, to let them know about enhancements, and product newsletters, offering tips on how to get the most out of the program.

As the product becomes established in the marketplace, the final element is to augment or enhance the product. The enhancements either are add-on products for the original application program or are standalone, yet complementary, products.

Our software cycle is an innovative approach in stimulating and then meeting a demand and in providing a versatile, complementary system of software programs for retailers and consumers alike. The strength of this approach is twofold. First, it gives the retailer a family of products that sell themselves. Second, the consumer has different product levels from which to choose, from a basic book all the way through to a more advanced and sophisticated software product.

Some products, depending on their scope and complexity, do not require or cannot use this full cycle; but the software cycle does serve as a model to define the scope of the research and development that goes into a particular concept. A complex program, say a database management program, will include all the elements of the cycle. A less complex program, such as a recreational program, will at least have a book to instruct in the use of the program. At dilithium Press, we are interested in both programs that are large in scope and those that are less complex. In our current catalogue and in programs under development, the mix between the two is approximately equal.

With an understanding of what our editorial philosophy is, we can go on to what sort of products we are interested in. But first, let me give a summary of our editorial philosophy by emphasizing that dilithium Press is focusing on the consumer market. This means we are looking for products that have a large, mass-market appeal. We believe that we are not just publishers of software, but rather that we are publishers of information. With that thought in mind, the kind of software, or information, that we are considering is applications that focus on personal productivity, home management, education, recreation, and the "new crop." Each of these markets if further expanded briefly below.

Personal productivity software consists of spreadsheets, database management, file management, project management, business graphics, word processing, and communications. These are all functions that are necessary to increase productivity and improve the decision-making ability of the individual. Beyond the individual applications of the current crop of personal productivity software is what has been called work station productivity software. Work station software combines all these applications into one system that is networked with other computers.

Home management software consists of programs that can perform much the same function as productivity software. In many instances, the only difference is the complexity of the program. The basic goal of being more productive is much the same. The programs in this category must be creative tools and either truly save time or allow for more informed decision making.

Educational software consists of two categories, the institutional market and the home market. The first category, institutional education, is for the kindergarten through college levels. This type of software needs to be designed with a specific curriculum in mind and must be entertaining as well as educational. The second category is the home education market, the market with by far the most potential. The home products must be family-oriented, entertaining, and educational. These programs need not conform to a particular curriculum, yet they must have a sound educational basis. Also included in the educational category are tutorial programs, which either educate in the use of a particular product or instruct in a particular field of interest.

In the near future, the recreational category promises to deliver some of the most exciting and innovative concepts of the software industry. Future recreational products will not be based on the current arcade style of entertainment software, but rather on the interactive simulations that are now being developed and brought to market. These future products will incorporate a blending of sound, graphics, strategy, and education.

The new crop of software is composed of unique concepts that are just now being imagined by both authors and publishers. Areas such as home and educational robotics, the simple creation of sophisticated art and music by computers, the evolution of the home computer into an extensive resource center of information, and the use of computers for day-to-day, personal communication are just a few of the innovations that will change the way we live, work, play, and think. The foundations for this category of software are being laid today, just as the foundations of the microcomputer revolution were being laid back in 1974.

These are the general markets we are focusing on. However, just because a concept will not fit neatly into any one of the above markets doesn't mean we're not interested. If a concept can be developed into a software product with mass-market appeal, we are interested, whether or not the idea can use all of the elements of our software cycle. Besides having mass-market potential, software published by our company must also be easy and intuitive to use, provide a creative solution to a problem, be entertaining and challenging, or allow the innovative use of a computer.

With an understanding of the purpose of an editorial department and of our editorial philosophy, let's see what the editorial process is. The software editorial process consists of three phases: the submission phase, the evaluation phase, and the development phase. The submission phase consists of two rather different approaches, either the unsolicited proposal or the managed project. The first approach is used when I receive a proposal in the mail. This can be either a design idea or a program. The proposal is carefully examined and reviewed to determine its suitability for our editorial philosophy and marketing plans.

To aid in our examination and review, the proposal needs to contain a description of the major functions and features of the software, emphasizing those that are unique as well as a description of the computer system and language requirements. Next, an analysis of the intended market for the program, with a review of any competitive products currently on the market, is needed, along with a brief description of who will purchase the program and why. Finally, an outline for the book to accompany the program and a biographical sketch of the author should be included, emphasizing any expertise relating to the intended market. Our *Authors' Guide* presents this information in more detail.

Another means of developing a product is based on what I will call a *managed project:* The editorial department at dilithium Press originates the idea. We determine the functions and features, define the targeted market, and create the design specifications. We then work with one or more authors to develop both the book and the software. When the managed-project approach is used to develop a software program, the evaluation process is an integral part of the design and development of the concept.

However, if a submitted proposal fits within our editorial philosophy and has mass-market potential, the next step is the evaluation process. The proposal is carefully evaluated by both dilithium Press editors and our external editors, who review particular projects in their area of expertise for content and then recommend any enhancements. A marketing and sales analysis is performed. This analysis considers different marketing strategies and sales levels to determine the financial considerations of the proposal. If the program is included, we look at the completeness of the program as well as the reliability and the functionality of the software.

Once the evaluation process is completed and a contract is signed, the development process begins. The contract outlines a description of the items to be delivered as well as a delivery schedule. Agreed-upon enhancements, both minor and major, are incorporated into the design as defined by the contract. Now the first coding (or recoding, as the case may be) begins. The first version of the program will need to be thoroughly tested and the book will need to be edited. The suggestions from testing and copy editing are then incorporated into the final product. This process of coding, testing, and revising may take some time, so the schedule as outlined in the contract must be adhered to.

To test the programs, we go through a two-level review process. The first review, which is done in house, occurs when the manuscript for the book is compared with the program to find any inaccuracies. Then we test the program itself to find any errors or the need for any improvements. After this first level is completed, the program is given back to the author for recoding and revision. Once the in-house testing is completed and the program is almost in final form, the second review takes place. For this second level, the program and the manuscript are sent to people outside the company for a thorough testing in real-life situations. If corrections or improvements are required after this level of testing, the program is given back to the author for the final recoding. Once the program is tested and found to be reliabile and accurate and the book is complete, the software package is sent to production. The editorial process is now complete.

Admittedly, the definition of what an editorial department is, what it does, and how that relates to our editiorial process is simplified here. What really matters to us is our sound and successful editorial philosophy. As I stated before, editorial philosophy is the road map on the journey to success, and that success is determined by both the publisher who uses that philosophy as a guide and by the efforts of authors who believe in that philosophy and are willing to work hard. If you are one of those authors, *welcome!*

Versatile packaging: Software for all retail environments

by ELWIN E. LAGES
Ingram Book Company
Nashville, Tennessee

ABSTRACT

With 40,000 programs already, and the potential for expansion of possible retail outlets, the software publisher must package his product in such a way that the retailer can exercise any number of options for shelving and display. The package must be versatile, attractive, and must display enough information to be able to sell itself. In addition, the package has to be able to assist the retailer in terms of security.

INTRODUCTION

> Retail shelves cannot accommodate all the available programs, and salesmen cannot learn how to use and demonstrate even a significant number of them.[1]
>
> *New York Times*
> 10/16/83

According to P.C. Telemart, of Fairfax, Va., there are more than 15,500 titles and 40,000 software products. In addition, this title base, according to P.C. Telemart, is increasing by the hundreds each month. What this means is that the competition for space is all retail environments is intense.

As a buyer for a distributor, and a former retailer of software, I am familiar with many of the problems that beset all concerned with how to improve software sales. Being in the middle I hear of all the problems from both sides of the retailing fence. There is one problem, though, that seems to be talked about more than any other. That problem is packaging. It seems so obvious. Packaging is a natural facet of product development in all other aspects of retailing, from automobiles to books. It seems odd that software developers, all looking to make big bucks in the burgeoning software market, forget packaging in the rush to get their products out.

In the rest of this paper, one word stands out from all others: versatility. This is the ability of the package in which a piece of software is presented to serve various functions in different retail environments. Today a store owner is inundated with hundreds of products monthly, each claiming to be the premier program of its type available, each claiming to be able to sell itself. Sadly enough, no program is currently that unique that it can afford any negatives if it hopes to be placed on enough retail shelves to be noticed by the buying public.

The first person that must be impressed by a product is not the user, but the distributor or the retailer. Tough choices have to be made since no store can stock 40,000-plus titles and the package, not the program, is the first thing seen. The other sections of this paper will touch upon the new retail environments in which software will be sold in the near future, and the packaging needs of these new and old retailers.

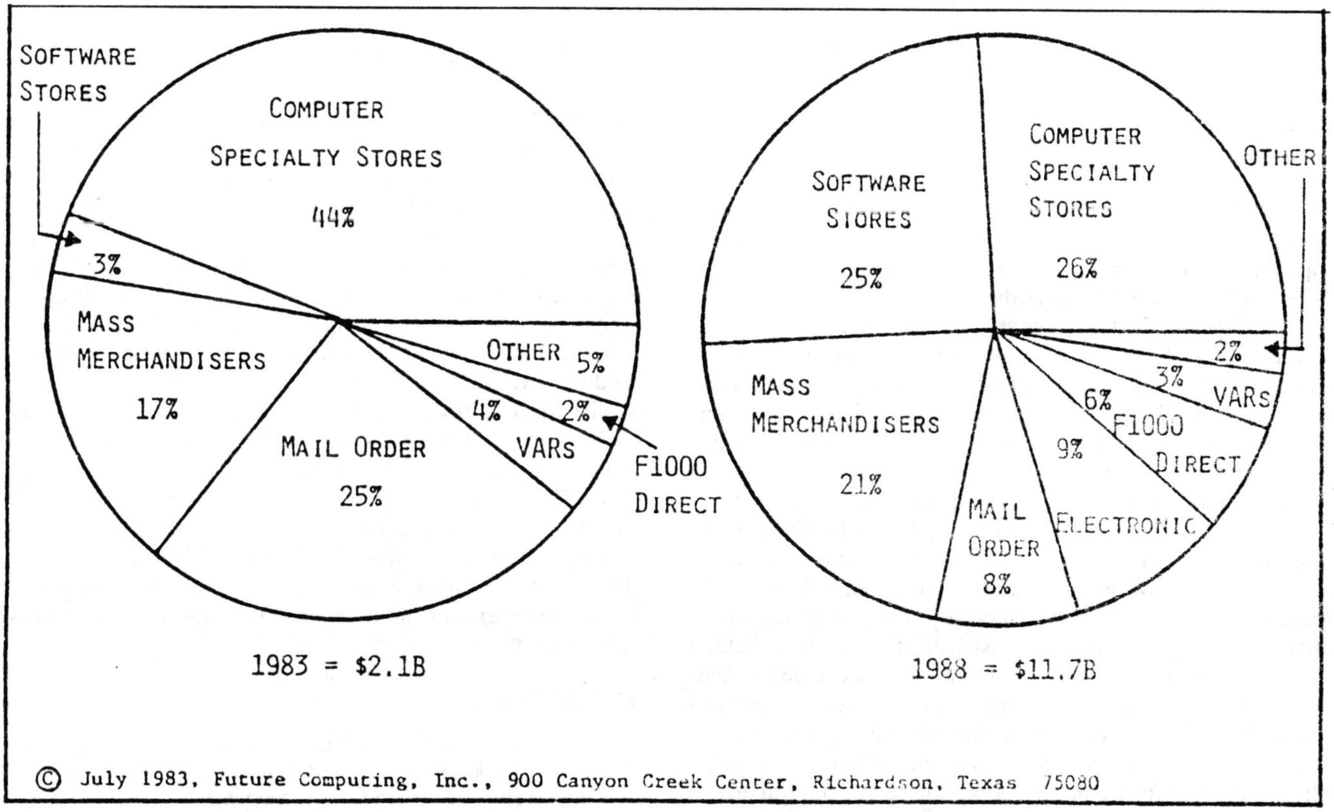

Figure 1—U.S. personal computer software distribution channels (retail value)

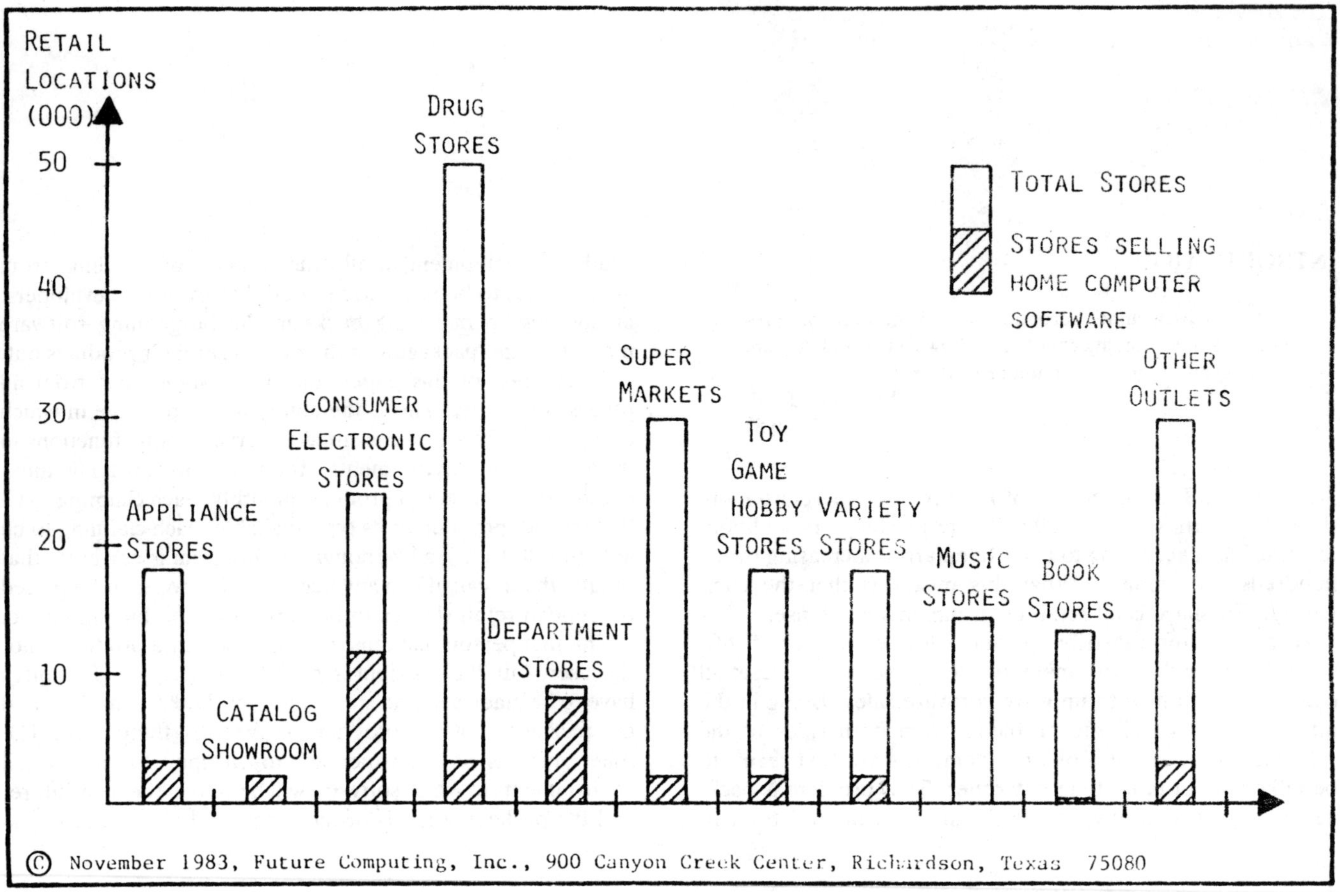

Figure 2—Potential home computer software retail outlets

RETAIL ENVIRONMENTS

Just a few short years ago there were comparatively few software packages, and these were largely sold in hardware-oriented computer stores. These stores carried software as supplements to the hardware they carried, and most of the sales efforts were with the hardware.

Today, the retail environments for software are expanding continuously. There are large software-only franchises; bookstores, both chains and independents; such mass merchandisers as Sears, Target, etc.; record stores; video stores; even a recent experiment where software was carried on some newsstands in New York City.

Future Computing, a marketing research organization based in Dallas, Tex., estimated (Figure 1) that in 1983 almost half of all software sales would be in computer specialty stores, but that by 1988 that share would shrink to approximately one quarter. Software specialty stores and mass merchandisers will account for almost half of all software sales.

In the differing markets for home computers and office computers, the potential distribution channels are staggering. Figure 2 shows that potential growth in home computer software. In such outlets as bookstores, the growth potential is phenomenal. Software in correct packaging is a natural product to be distributed in an outlet that is perceived by its customer base as the purveyor of information and entertainment.

Figure 3 shows the potential market for business software. Although not as varied as the home market, the potential growth is many times that of the potential growth of computer stores. Fully one-third of all software sales are going to be in outlets not specializing in computers or their programs. These are outlets where the personnel will not be as fully trained and where self-service is the key. That requires the publisher to prepare a product that has the potential of selling itself.

In computer and software stores the staggering number of products available from an almost inexhaustible number of publishers requires again that the program in large part sell itself. Here, the package is the key. Not demonstrations, brochures, etc., all of which are indeed useful, but the package itself. The package is a retailer's and a potential customer's introduction to the program.

If any publisher is willing to forego selling his product to almost 75% of the potential market, then he is willing to see his competitors enter the market and grab that share uncontested.

THE PACKAGE

> . . .consumer-oriented products that make learning fun, appealing packages, good advertising—are the software vendor's cost of admission into . . . the market.[1]
>
> C. David Suess, President
> Spinnaker Software Corp.

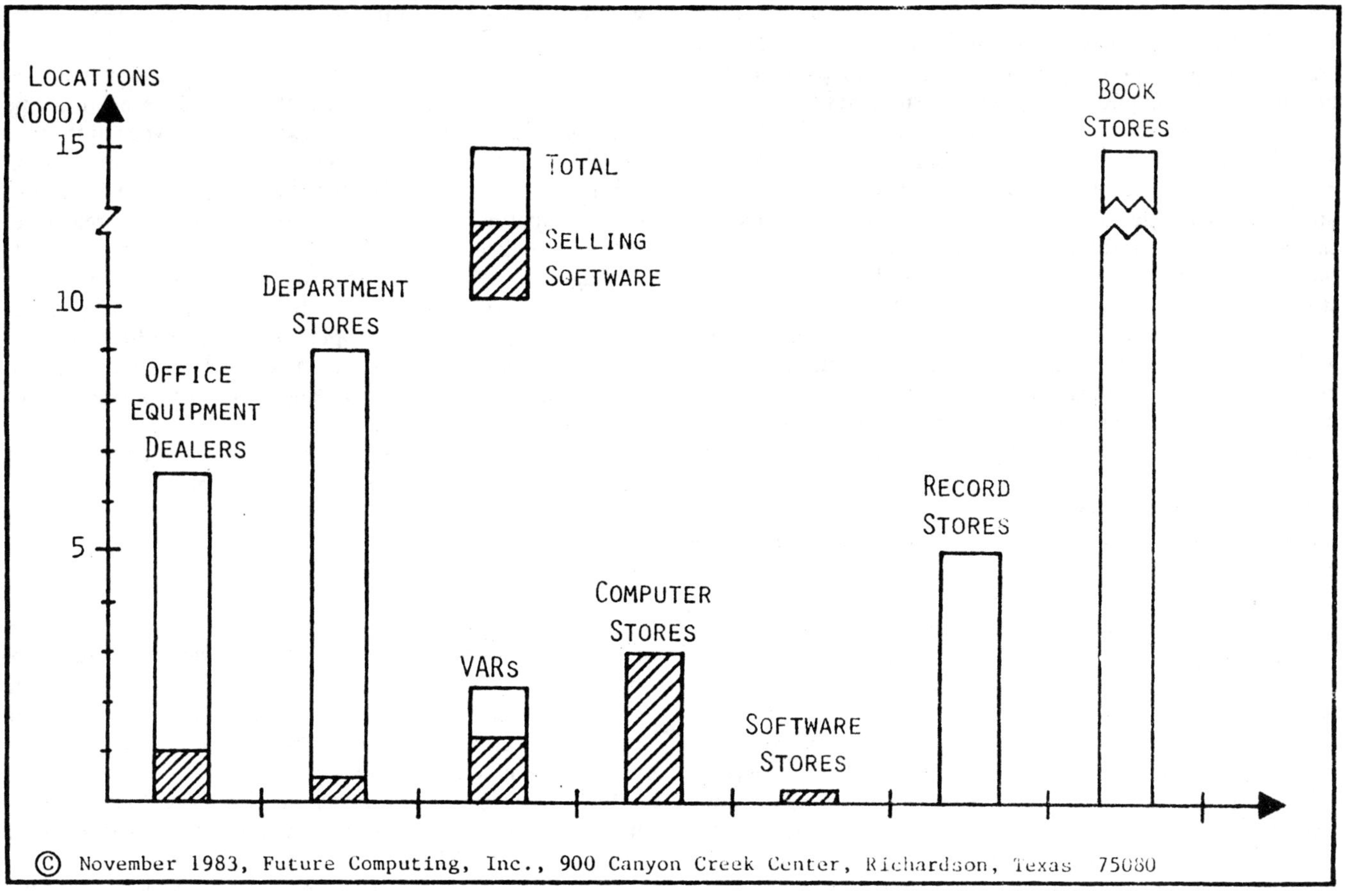

Figure 3—Potential office personal computer software distribution channels

With hundreds of software packages finding their way into the hands of distributers and retailers alike, how does anyone decide what to stock? For that matter, with such a proliferation of products, how does anyone even decide what to look at? No one has the time, the personnel, or the ambition to examine every product from every manufacturer. This is especially true of the products of new entries into the list of companies trying to get their products into the network. A retailer or distributor will go out of his way to look at the products of an established vendor, and worry about details like packaging later, but the new entry will be placed on the bottom of any pile, anywhere. If the package looks like nothing, the program might never see the light of day.

Too many vendors concentrate on what they see as the "musts" of establishing their products in the minds of the public. So millions are spent on advertising to make retailers and consumers aware of a product and the company name, then this super program is shoved into a baggie or plain brown box, and left to fend for itself. The package is the best advertising currently available. It is the package that anyone sees first, and it is the perceived value as shown by the package that prompts anyone, the distributer, the retailer, or the consumer to go farther and spend more time to find out if the program is all it is advertised to be.

Packaging must be considered as part of the whole. Each facet of the network chain, from manufacturer to consumer, has specific needs. As a distributor, I am required to see every one, but especially those of the retailer. We all have a common purpose: to sell products.

As described earlier, the retail distribution of software is no longer limited to the hardware-oriented computer store, or even the software-only store. At the lower end "consumer" market, the potential retail shelf space is in many environments. Does the manufacturer have to do a package for each environment? The obvious answer is no. Costs would escalate, and the time problem would raise its ugly head. A package, though, does have to be versatile enough to operate adequately in all environments. The package should never be the limiting factor in distribution. A package should never disqualify a product from being sold anywhere.

All retailers have one thing in common; the desire to sell merchandise quickly and with the least amount of problems. With this in mind a package must have four facets: flexibility, appearance, information, and security. The first three help to sell the product, the last helps keep enough of the product in the store to sell.

FLEXIBILITY

Two years ago there were so few programs available at retail, that the retailer, usually a hardware dealer, had trouble finding enough programs to fill available space. Today that is far from the truth. Two years ago, almost all software could be faced out or placed on pegboards with room to spare. Today that luxury is long past. The computer store has to dedicate more room to hardware, which, like software, also has proliferated over the past few years, and cannot afford to have as much space dedicated to relatively low-priced software. The nontraditional outlets (if any outlet only a few years old itself can be considered traditional) cannot or will not give 100% of their shelf space to software. And obviously, there is not a store large enough in any case to stock 40,000 titles.

Forcing any retailer to display a product in only one way is asking too much. Entertainment software is a prime example. Not very long ago, almost all games came in zip-lock plastic bags. They had little holes on the top for display on a pegboard and a store either gave over a large area to games or carried fewer than optimal sales would allow. Why? You can only shelve these bags one way, face out. Placed edge-on, and not only do they all look alike, but you cannot see them in any case.

Today's environment requires a package with more than just a face. In addition, a spine is needed that displays such simple information as title, manufacturer, and compatible hardware. In related retail ventures, books, records, video, etc., you might note that virtually all packages have spines.

In the new retail environments, especially bookstores, packages must have the flexibility to be shelved and displayed in any way the retailer wants. No outlets that traditionally have dealt in other products are going to renovate their stores to carry products that they are unsure of to begin with. Unless the manufacturers of the programs are willing to forego selling in one or more environments they must offer the retailer the ability to sell the product in any way he sees fit. And the retailer is the one who knows his customers better than any distributor or manufacturer.

APPEARANCE

This is so obvious that one wonders why it should be brought up at all. But if it is so obvious, why are so many programs brought out in such mediocre, if not downright ugly, packages? Each level of software has a different packaging requirement, but not one of them need be placed in an ugly or plain container. No line of software need be so uniform as to sow confusion.

The perceptions of the retailer and his customer are the most important aspects to be considered in package design. In the mass market, the package that stands out from the pack has the best chance of selling. This works for cars, for books, and so on. Software, on any level, is no different.

The perception of the world is that a game should look like a game, and that business software should look like business software. Distributors, retailers, and customers all have one fault in common; the tendency to judge books, as well as software, by their covers. If the cover does not look like much, it is assumed that the program is not worth buying. That initial negative view will be almost impossible to overcome.

Game programs can be packaged in as bright or original way as possible, within the framework mentioned in this paper. Other packages have to be done to fit the level for which they are intended. Professional software should look that way. But again it must be stressed that the package need not be plain or ugly. Visicorp has had two package types in its existence. At first, when VISICALC was the major program on the market, it came in a plain, brown loose-leaf binder. Looks did not matter; it was the only one. As other spreadsheet programs began to enter the market, Visicorp upgraded its packaging to reflect its position at the time as the preeminent professional software package. It created the software package equivalent to the grey pinstripe suit (in three pieces). Why? Because with previously unheard of competition it had to protect its image by presenting an outward appearance of professionalism and quality.

The appearance of the package is the first thing seen and is too important to ignore. It cannot be compromised.

INFORMATION

Somewhere out there in the computer world, a rumor has been spread that software cannot sell itself, that only by extensive demonstration could any customer hope to know what to buy. It was great for computer stores, they seemed like the gods of the new technology.

But then came 40,000 programs. No store could possibly hire a staff large enough to know them all. No store could afford the time to demonstrate a $20 game and risk losing the sale of a major software package. Then software left the computer store and entered the world of the mass market and the bookstore.

Software at all levels must either be able to sell itself or must provide enough information on itself to help guide the customer in narrowing down his choices before he goes and seeks help.

How does a book sell itself? It supplies the potential reader with enough information on what is contained within. This is called a dustcover. After the potential customer is enticed by the dustcover, he then has free access to the documentation; the book.

Should software be any different? Software, like books, should make the attempt to sell itself without any help from overworked, unknowledgeable, or uncaring salespeople. At the least, let the customer think about what he is buying, let him be able to ask intelligent questions if needed.

There are two things all people—especially those who are about to spend money—hate: feeling pressured and appearing stupid. Computer phobia exists even among those who own computers. They are using this new contraption for one reason or another, but often they do not feel competent to understand the computer or its programs. They know how books are written, in English, a language they understand, more or less. But a program! PASCAL? What is that!

There is no reason to have a package with large blank areas on it. Why? Why abandon the customer? Why not help the retailer? Why not try to make sales quickly by supplying basic information about the program at the outset?

SECURITY

This might be the last package requirement considered here, but it is not the least important, particularly to the retailer. Theft is as much of a problem with software, if not more so, as with any other product. "Shrinkage," as it is called in retail, is a special concern in nontraditional outlets. Because of its size and the fact that a program is often more costly than any of the other products the outlet might sell, retailers worry about theft.

Again, the retailer wants versatility to be inherent to the package without compromising his need for security. Some retailers are willing to display software behind glass counters or through plexiglass panels with holes in them, though for aesthetic reasons these are few. Most merchandisers want to leave the product out for self-service. They are willing to accept certain losses, but have no desire to make it overly easy for anyone to "shrink" a product out of the store.

Security in packaging is part of the manufacturer's responsibility. A 5¼-inch disk is very thin and relatively small. No package should give free access to the disk itself. A loose disk will either be stolen, lost, or trampled on, costing the retailer the price of the program. Yet with the exception of most games, the customer should have access to the documentation. In that case the program disk should be sealed as part of the binding, the box, or the folder. While theft will not disappear and no package can be made theft-proof, there is no need to make it easy. After the purchase let the customer work a little to get the disk out.

In all other programs, the packagae simply need be of such a size that the program cannot be slipped into the pages of a newspaper and disappear.

CONCLUSION

It cannot be too strongly stressed that a program's package is often as important as that program's documentation. It is the package that brings the retailer or the customer to examine the program more closely. It is the package that presents the image of the program to all who view it. It is that same package that presents its perceived value to any who might consider using it.

With this in mind, the package should be as well designed as any other facet of the program. We all judge books by their covers. Software is no different. No program in today's competitive market needs a negative staring any potential user in the face. Conversely, perfect packaging will not make a perfect program out of a bad one. The product must be seen as a whole and it is the publisher's responsibility to his distributors and retailers to supply the best product available, on time, at a reasonable price, and in a package that will sell.

REFERENCES

1. Suess, C. David. "The War for Retail Shelf Space." *Computer Retailing,* November 1983.

Commercial and military software documentation: Different steps to a common goal

by FAYE C. BUDLONG
Wang Laboratories, Incorporated
Burlington, Massachusetts

ABSTRACT

Talking about creativity in software documentation may seem like a paradox, but it exists. Even a functional specification for a new product has an element of creativity: It outlines a product that will require the creative endeavors of several developers over a period of time. Further, user manuals require ingenuity to reduce many complex functions to a series of simple, identifiable steps that the user can understand and follow. Training documents require creativity to develop examples that new users can understand and to reinforce a learning curve that allows the reader to become proficient using a new product. And reference manuals require perseverence to ensure that all functions of the product are defined and explained clearly and concisely.

This paper is an overview of the development process for software documentation from concept to initial release. It lists much of the documentation required for each major software development step and compares documentation for commercial projects with that required to meet military project standards.

INTRODUCTION

The documentation required for different kinds of users in different environments, for example military documentation vs. user documentation in a commercial environment, may vary considerably, and these differences often are difficult for development personnel and technical writers and editors to understand. This paper is arranged logically in the order of the development cycle to help define and compare the steps required in the military and commercial environments to complete the documentation process successfully and on time.

IDENTIFYING A NEW PRODUCT: THE FIRST STEP

In the commercial environment, market research personnel maintain records of what types of computer systems and applications users demand and what trends appear to be unfolding. From this information, the market research personnel identify products that should be profitable for the company to develop and outline the functions the products should possess. They give this information to the research department where a team uses it to perform a feasibility study, which will examine the possibility of creating the software and obtaining the manpower required to complete the project in a timely manner. The research team refines and builds upon the outline until all functions the software should contain have been identified. This team also determines how difficult and time consuming the project is likely to be. At this point, the research group (sometimes with the help of technical writers) produces a functional specification that details their plans.

Members from the market research group meet with members from the development group to discuss how the project should proceed. When an agreement is reached, the functional specification is made final and a project time line with identifiable milestones is established.

The main questions that arise during this early phase in the commercial development cycle are:

1. How well will the product fill an identifiable user need?
2. Will it be ready for release at a time that will ensure its market acceptance?
3. Can it be developed using manpower and materials that will help guarantee its profitability?
4. Will the new product support the existing product line?

If the product will fulfill these requirements, the functional specification becomes the product baseline and the development effort proceeds. The appropriate representatives meet regularly to track the project's progress, identify problem areas, outline necessary changes, and identify the groups the project will use to market and support the new product.

At this point, the company's technical writers may become involved in planning the documentation necessary to accompany the product at release. Nonetheless, all written documentation is still informal and subject to major revisions before it is ready for the marketplace.

Military projects develop differently. The earliest stages in product definition generally result from a need defined by the Department of Defense or through research on a new system or weapon. An example could be the need for a fault-tolerant, real-time control system for fighter aircraft.

The military describes an overall program goal and issues a request for proposal (RFP) that defines the project—and the time allowed to present a proposal—to firms interested in obtaining a military contract. Then the military contracts a company to define the requirements and phases of the project and, perhaps, to produce the end product. The contract is usually awarded on the basis of a competitive bid that responds to the RFP. Since contracts are awarded on the basis of proposals, professional documentation personnel begin their project involvement while the proposal is being developed—long before detailed specifications or product documentation are considered. (For clarity, the military organization that awards the contract is referred to as the "contracting organization" and the company that holds the contract is referred to as the "contractor" throughout this paper.)

Generally, a company must produce substantially more documentation to win a federal contract based on an RFP than it requires to launch its own new product. This documentation is required because the military needs to compare different companies' proposals for the project outlined in the RFP without having the ease of direct communication that commercial developers and market research personnel enjoy.

Military projects require development documentation that often is much more complex, and more standardized, than that needed for purely commercial applications for a variety of reasons, including the following:

1. The military contracting officer on any contract may have to administer several contracts simultaneously.
2. The contracting officer is remote from the contractor and must have some form of formal documentation to track the contract's progress.
3. When the project is complete, the contracting organization *owns* the software developed under the contract. This means that the contracting organization must have enough documentation to maintain and modify the product with minimal support from the contractor.

The main questions a military contract officer resolves when awarding a contract are as follows:

1. Are the contractor's proposed funding requirements competitive?
2. Does the proposal cover all areas of the RFP?
3. Does the company that produced the proposal have a proven record for completing projects on time and within the budget allowed?
4. Do the proposed subcontractors, if any, have a record of completing their project phases successfully?

When these questions have been answered and the contract is awarded, the contractor has its research team complete a preliminary functional specification. Writers and editors usually are involved this early in the developmental phase because the documentation standards most military contracts require are complex and sometimes difficult to understand. One example of complex standards is MIL-STD-490, *Military Standard Specification Practices,* which defines the contents of each paragraph of a product specification and how certain words, like "will" and "shall," are used in each specification.

When the preliminary functional specification is complete, members of the military contracting organization meet with the contractor's representatives to review the functional specification and contract time line. This meeting, often called a preliminary design review (PDR), determines areas of agreement between the contractor and military. The considerations of the PDR include the changes the functional specification must undergo to be acceptable to the contracting organization. The PDR also determines what changes, if any, are necessary in the project time line to complete the project in a timely manner.

Upon completing the PDR, the research team and technical writers revise the preliminary functional specification to meet the new or revised requirements determined during the PDR. They produce a detailed design specification, which is the design submitted to the contracting organization for review. Then representatives from the contracting organization and the contractor meet for a critical design review (CDR), which is similar to but more formal than the PDR.

The revisions required as a result of the CDR are incorporated into the detailed design specification, which then becomes the formal baseline from which the product is developed.

At this early phase of development, documentation for military contracts is more complex, detailed, and formal than that required for a commercial project. It also demands more pure attention to detail than commercial documentation. Generally, commercial companies can maintain informal contacts and documentation longer than is possible in the military because the individuals responsible for product development are more available in the commercial environment. Also, the company developing the product creates its own procedures for reporting progress.

PRODUCT DEVELOPMENT: THE SECOND STEP

As a product develops in the commercial environment, it evolves from the original functional specification into a marketable commodity. Any fundamental changes are outlined in memos from the research team to representatives of the market research and marketing groups. The market research group decides what basic documentation will accompany the software at release. They also meet with technical documentation managers to determine the time and manpower required to fulfill product requirements. The documentation that exists at this point usually consists of:

1. The functional specification
2. Any memos that define fundamental changes to the product
3. A market and audience analysis
4. Marketing plans and support policies

A technical documentation team, which at Wang Laboratories, Inc., consists of writers, editors, and artists, is assigned to the project. The team members work with their managers to determine the documentation milestones necessary to meet the product release date. The company has guidelines for the documentation team, but they are usually somewhat flexible to allow for creativity in manual design and presentation.

Often, the language used in reference manuals and training guides differs substantially. Even the language used in training guides will differ depending on the audience addressed. For example, the tone of a user's manual written for a computer programmer will be different from the tone of a training manual written for a first-time user of applications software. Thus, in many instances, the documentation team has the freedom, and the responsibility, to determine the scope, tone, and presentation of the materials they produce.

Technical writers meet with members of the research team to learn about the new product and how it works. The writers also learn to use the new product so they can define it accurately for customers. Then they outline the required documentation and work with editors to determine the most logical presentation. When the writing process is complete, the document is sent to the research team (and any other appropriate reviewers) to determine if it is technically correct and meets all corporate requirements.

After the revisions generated by the technical review have been incorporated into the document, an editor reviews and revises it. The editor and writer work together to prepare it for graphic arts and production.

The software documentation cycle is different in the military environment. From the time the detailed design specification is accepted as the product baseline, the military usually requires the project to be placed under configuration control by the contractor.

The role of configuration control is to identify all changes to the product formally—and in great detail. In other words, any deviations from the detailed design specification that occur during software design or coding must be reported using a discrepancy report (DR). Then, if a change to the software appears to be necessary, a software change request (SCR) is begun.

A software design review board (SDRB) meets regularly to review all SCRs, and if they are significant, submits them to a software change control board (SCCB) for final disposition.

When the SCCB decides that the software change is necessary, all relevant documentation is changed or revised formally (even changes and revisions are defined separately in some military standards), and all changes are noted on the change and revision pages in the document's front matter. Compared to the commercial configuration management some companies use, military configuration control is both extremely detailed and rigid.

Technical writers and editors working on a military contract spend much of their time during the software development cycle tracking changes to the product baseline. The changes and revisions require detailed attention to maintain the accuracy of the documentation and conformance to the applicable standards.

The formality of military documentation requires more time and attention during the development cycle than that required by commercial projects. Some military contracts even mandate a certain level of reading skill to be used for any user documentation and have reading specialists check the documents submitted under the contract to ensure that those requirements are met. Further, most military contracts require that members from the contractor's development team meet with members from the contracting organization, on a regular basis, to present their findings and review the project's progress compared to the scheduled project milestones.

This added formality allows contract officers to maintain more control over each project than they would have with fewer requirements, and it allows them to stay up to date with each project with less effort than would be needed if less formal requirements were enforced.

PRODUCT RELEASE: THE FINAL STEP

When a commercial software product is ready for release, the support documentation must be ready as well. Sometimes, the task of producing timely documentation becomes very complex during the last stages of product development because of the flexibility allowed in the commercial environment.

Writers and editors must ensure that the documentation accurately reflects the *final* software product, and the designers must present the information in a form that will be acceptable to the target audience.

This is the period that requires the most effort by commercial technical documentation personnel because they must have whatever manuals or specifications required ready for distribution at the same time the product is ready for release. Now, the documentation team must complete any appropriate revisions, produce mechanicals for printing, and make sure that the printing cycle proceeds on schedule under very tight deadlines.

The final product represents the company to customers and prospects, and the documentation is part of that final product. Commercial firms often want to maintain a particular image within their documentation. Writers and editors are responsible for assuring that the corporate image is maintained as well as making sure the documentation is complete, accurate, and presented appropriately.

Since military specifications are updated often and conform to military standards, specifications that accurately reflect the software product exist during most phases of product development. Thus, most manuals (even training manuals) can be outlined and written early in the development cycle and updated as the product matures.

Many military requirements outline *exactly* what the documents they specify will look like upon delivery. Consequently, there is limited or no flexibility in the visual presentation or in what will be covered in any given document. In the military contract environment, artists create illustrations for the documentation required. The artists are mainly responsible for ensuring that mechanicals are prepared correctly for the printing process the contractor will use. They have little input about how the final product will look because usually the design of the documents created is outlined in the military standards that apply to any given project.

Deadlines are tight because development personnel sometimes fall behind the contract schedule. However, much of the documentation needed to complete the contract and release the product already has been through numerous revisions and often is near completion before the software product is ready for release.

The job in this case is to complete whatever is necessary to comply with contract requirements by the time the contract expires. This is especially important because the military could use an overdue completion date as a reason to use a different contractor when it issues a new RFP or take other punitive action against the contractor for failure to comply with the terms of the contract.

Often, even printing is simplified because the government specifies the grade and size of paper to be used. Also, some military agencies request only mechanicals and a few photocopies of the required documentation to produce the printed versions in government print shops.

CONCLUSIONS

The main differences between the documentation process in the military and commercial environments are how decisions are made about the required documentation and how the companies involved produce that documentation.

In the commercial environment, producing a software product and documentation that will be accepted in a competitive atmosphere is the main concern. Thus, commercial companies try to tailor both the content and appearance of their documentation to the particular audiences they are trying to attract. This takes flexibility and creativity to achieve. Also, commercial companies are more flexible in early product documentation because the people responsible for a project are on-site and the product may be altered to reflect changing market needs.

The documentation required to fulfill a military contract, on the other hand, is specified in the contract. Contractors must produce accurate documentation that reflects the changing state of the software being produced from the time the detailed design specification is accepted as the product baseline until the final product is released. Thus, contractors respond to given documentation requirements rather than create their own requirements from any felt market need.

The differences between the military and commercial documentation environments appear in every phase of a development project, from inception to final release. The different requirements imposed in each atmosphere require skilled professionals to maintain the quality of the final documentation products. The challenge to produce quality documentation in a timely manner crosses all technical documentation environments. However, the steps used to meet that challenge often require different skills to achieve the goals defined within the requirements specified.

ACKNOWLEDGMENT

The author thanks her co-workers at Wang Laboratories, Inc., for their help and support during the development of this paper. Special thanks go to all those who reviewed the paper and suggested revisions to make it more effective.

SUGGESTED READING

1. MIL-STD-483(USAF). *Configuration Management Practices for Systems, Equipment, Munitions, and Computer Programs.*
2. MIL-STD-490, *Military Standard Specifications Practices,* 30 October, 1968.
3. MIL-STD-847A. *Military Standard Format Requirements for Scientific and Technical Reports Prepared by or for the Department of Defense,* January 1973.
4. OD 45748, *Ordnance Data Documentation Guidelines for TRIDENT I, MARK 5,* USN.
5. SECNAVINST 3560.1, *Tactical Digital Systems Documentation Standards,* USN, August 1974.

One person's perception of military documentation

by DON MATHER
Sanders Associates
Hudson, New Hampshire

ABSTRACT

Culture shock is perhaps the best way to describe what one experiences in moving from the world of commercial documentation into the world of military documentation. This paper uses software documentation to describe the world of military documentation. After presenting some similarities and differences between the two worlds, it describes the military's software development process in a way that highlights documentation. In so doing, it also describes the military's software documents and points out the relationships between them.

INTRODUCTION

Culture shock is perhaps the best way to describe what one experiences in moving from the world of commercial documentation into the world of military documentation. On entering the world of defense work, one quickly (1) encounters a flurry of new acronyms—CDRL, DID, PPS, B5, PDR, CM, PDS, DBDD, PDD, C5, CDR, IDS, and so on; (2) hears reference to CDRL items, military standards, data item descriptions, data items, binding requirements, configuration management, and so forth; (3) learns that plans, specifications and even end-user documents must be written "in accordance with" standardized annotated outlines; (4) learns that some information in some documents is classified and must be marked and handled according to set procedures; and (5) learns that the money funding documentation projects comes from a contract with a military customer who has a good deal of influence over documentation.

The main purpose of this paper is to describe one person's perception of the world of military documentation. A secondary purpose of this paper is to show that there are some similarities between writing documents in the two worlds of military and commercial documentation. Since the author's experience has been mostly with software engineering and writing, this paper will use software documentation to describe the world of military documentation. The intended audience of this paper is mainly technical writers, editors, and managers of editors and writers who have had little or no experience in the world of military documentation (especially military software documentation).

This paper presents the following topics: (1) The contract, CDRL, military standards, DIDs, and binding requirements, (2) a summary of similarities and differences between the worlds of military and commercial documentation, (3) the military's software development process and its documents.

THE CONTRACT, CDRL, MILITARY STANDARDS, DIDs AND BINDING REQUIREMENTS

When the Department of Defense selects a company (or team of companies) to perform some service for it, it awards that company a contract. That company is referred to as a "contractor." The contractor refers to that part of the military, which awarded it a contract, as the "customer."

The contract contains a list of documents to be written and delivered to the government. The list is called a "Contract Data Requirements List," or CDRL. Normally, CDRLs are written on standard government forms called DD-1423s (See Figure 1). Any item on the CDRL list is referred to as a "CDRL item," "data item," or simply a "deliverable."

A military standard is simply a document that specifies how something shall be done. A standard is stronger than a guideline—a standard must be complied with. There are many military standards and the subject of a standard varies from standard to standard.

The most widely used military standards for software development are MIL-STD-1679(NAVY), MIL-STD-483(USAF), and MIL-STD-490(USAF). MIL-STD-1679(NAVY) covers nearly all aspects of software development; it does not cover the style and format of software documents much beyond stating that the word "shall" is reserved for identifying binding requirements. MIL-STD-483(USAF) is used to control software development. MIL-STD-490(USAF) was intended to be a universal standard. It can be used to cover the development of software, hardware, a building, a desk, a train car, etc. MIL-STD-490 does have a section pertaining to the style and format of documents. Military standards also specify the data item descriptions that are intended to be used with them. This paper uses the names of documents given in MIL-STD-1679 to discuss software documents. Both the Air Force and the Navy have guidebooks that provide a good deal of information about how those services manage their software acquisition.

A data item description, or DID for short, is an annotated outline of one kind of document, e.g., a QA plan or a design specification. A CDRL list will specify that a certain document must be written in accordance with a particular military standard and data item description. With a DID in hand, all the contributors to a document know the title of the document, the outline of the document, have an idea of what kind of information goes in each section, and who needs the document and why.

A binding requirement is a requirement that a contractor must meet. It is a legally binding requirement. The word *shall* identifies a binding requirement. For example, if a sentence is worded "The operator interface module enables the operator to set the time of day," then the software does not necessarily have to provide the operator with that capability. On the other hand, if the sentence is worded "The operator interface module shall enable the operator to set the time of day," then the contractor can be held accountable in a court of law for supplying to the government an operator interface module which fulfills that requirement. This style device enables the contributors to a document to distinguish between explanatory information and what they believe they are required to do in order to satisfy the contract. This mechanism also enables the customer to perceive that distinction.

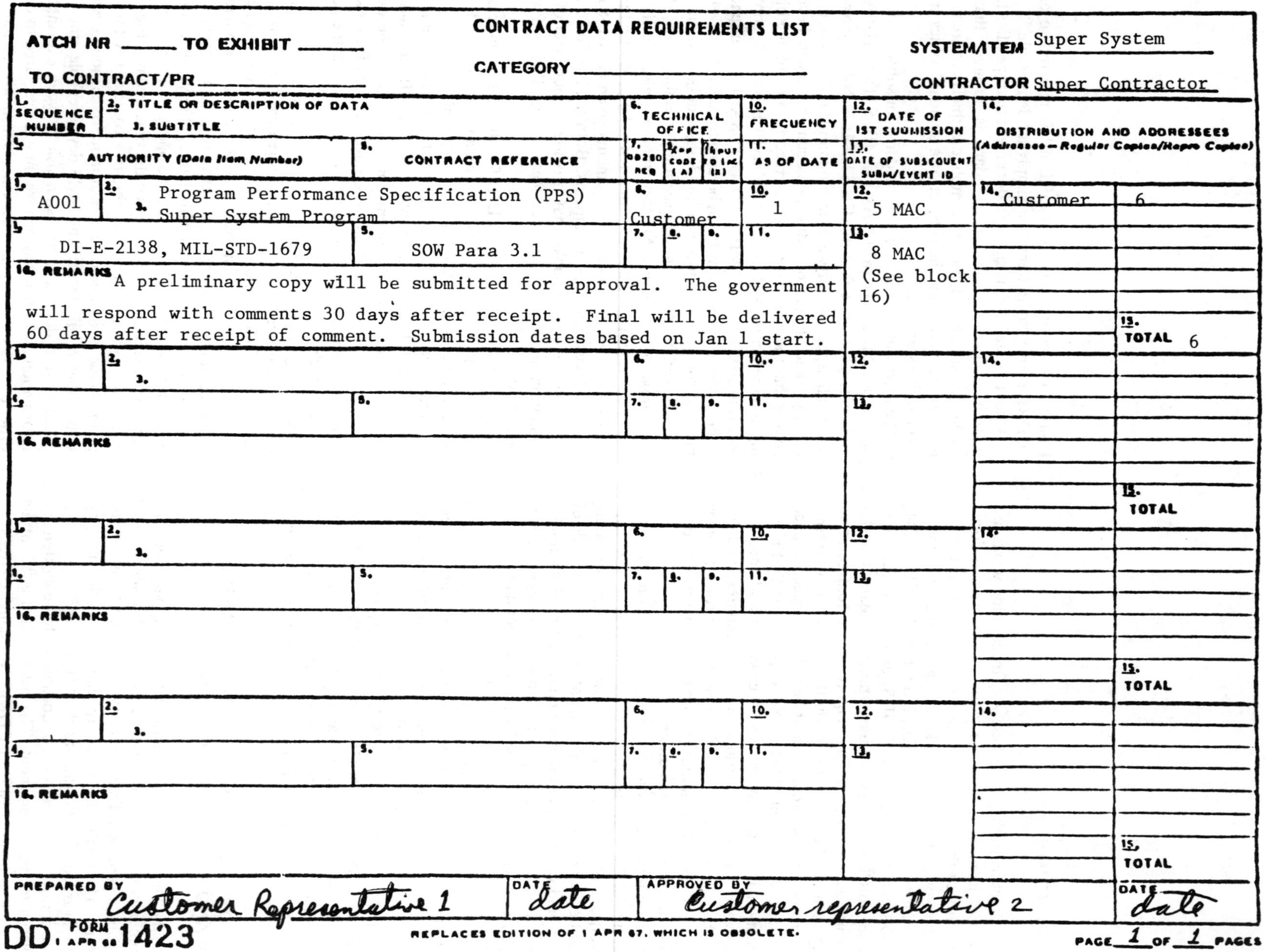

CONTRACT DATA REQUIREMENTS LIST

ATCH NR ______ TO EXHIBIT ______

TO CONTRACT/PR ______

CATEGORY ______

SYSTEM/ITEM Super System

CONTRACTOR Super Contractor

1. SEQUENCE NUMBER	2. TITLE OR DESCRIPTION OF DATA / 3. SUBTITLE		6. TECHNICAL OFFICE			10. FREQUENCY	12. DATE OF 1ST SUBMISSION	14. DISTRIBUTION AND ADDRESSEES (Addressee—Regular Copies/Repro Copies)	
4. AUTHORITY (Data Item Number)		5. CONTRACT REFERENCE	7. DD250 REQ	8. APP CODE (A)	9. INPUT TO IAC (B)	11. AS OF DATE	13. DATE OF SUBSEQUENT SUBM/EVENT ID		
1. A001	2. Program Performance Specification (PPS) 3. Super System Program		6. Customer			10. 1	12. 5 MAC	14. Customer	6
4. DI-E-2138, MIL-STD-1679		5. SOW Para 3.1	7.	8.	9.	11.	13. 8 MAC (See block 16)		
16. REMARKS A preliminary copy will be submitted for approval. The government will respond with comments 30 days after receipt. Final will be delivered 60 days after receipt of comment. Submission dates based on Jan 1 start.									15. TOTAL 6
1.	2. 3.		6.			10.	12.	14.	
4.		5.	7.	8.	9.	11.	13.		
16. REMARKS									15. TOTAL
1.	2. 3.		6.			10.	12.	14.	
4.		5.	7.	8.	9.	11.	13.		
16. REMARKS									15. TOTAL
1.	2. 3.		6.			10.	12.	14.	
4.		5.	7.	8.	9.	11.	13.		
16. REMARKS									15. TOTAL

PREPARED BY Customer Representative 1 DATE date APPROVED BY Customer representative 2 DATE date

DD FORM 1 APR 68 1423 REPLACES EDITION OF 1 APR 67, WHICH IS OBSOLETE. PAGE 1 OF 1 PAGES

Figure 1—A sample contract data requirements list (CDRL)

A SUMMARY OF SIMILARITIES AND DIFFERENCES BETWEEN THE WORLDS OF MILITARY AND COMMERCIAL DOCUMENTATION

Perhaps one of the most obvious differences between the two worlds is the presence of the customer in the development of military documentation. In the military world, the customer (1) defines what documents will be written and when they are due, (2) requires that the documents comply with standard outlines, (3) sets some style and format conventions, (4) imposes policies and procedures for marking and handling classified information when documents contain classified information, (5) has the right to approve or reject documents, (6) may include in the contract the right to award the contract money in parts paying a portion every time a document is approved. Thus, in the world of military documentation, one's freedom to develop a document as one sees fit is much more restricted than in the world of commercial documentation. On the other hand, those commercial companies which offer their services to other companies may notice a resemblance between their situation and a defense contractor's.

Technical writers and editors in the two worlds probably work on different kinds of documents most of the time. In the world of military software documentation, writers and editors work mostly on development documents rather than end-user documents. Just the opposite seems to be true in the commercial world.

Companies that are practicing a methodical software development process which emphasizes documentation may perceive a similarity between their process and the military's. The names of the documents and the emphasis given topics may be different. Generally, however, those companies will probably write the same kinds of documents, produce them in the same order and in the same software development phases, and cover the same topics.

The planning of documentation projects is probably similar. In both worlds, planning must answer the questions: (1) Who needs documentation and why? (2) What documents will be written and what are the objectives of each one? (3) How will those objectives be met? (4) How will it be determined which purposes were achieved and the degree to which the others were met? (5) What are the required sources, schedule, and costs?

In the world of military documentation, the CDRL list answers the question "What documents will be written?" and specifies when they will be due and how many copies will be delivered. Furthermore, the data item descriptions (1) identify who needs documentation and indicates why, (2) state the objectives of each document, (3) provide a partial answer to the question "How will those objectives be met?" in providing an annotated outline. The applicable military standard will shed more light on the question "How will those objectives be met?" to the extent that it specifies style and format.

Perhaps the most obvious and greatest similarity between the world of military documentation and the world of commercial documentation is the existence of a need for documentation. The fundamental goal of every document, whether it is a military or commercial document, is to communicate with someone with this need.

THE MILITARY'S SOFTWARE DEVELOPMENT PROCESS AND ITS DOCUMENTS

It is convenient to regard software documentation projects in the world of military documentation as falling into three classes:

1. Proposal
2. Development
3. Postdevelopment

The bulk of the work performed by technical writers and editors is in the area of development projects. Proposal projects tend to be short and writers perform mostly editing and production functions. Postdevelopment projects are predominantly software engineering projects and usually require little, if any, writer involvement. Writers do some actual writing as well as editing and production in the development of software documents and end-user documents. Consequently, the focus of this paper is on software development documentation.

The government has been moving toward a standardized software development process. The process emphasizes

1. A methodical development process
2. Documentation
3. Structured programming

The development process is the heart of software management. A "good" development process plus "good" scheduling and cost control result in a high percentage of successful software projects. A "good" development process is nearly always methodical, i.e., development occurs as a sequence of refinements, each of which is produced in a methodical way. This paper briefly describes the military's software development process in a way that brings out the role of documentation.

Software documentation expresses plans and software specifications. The government has developed standard sets of software documents and each document has a standard annotated outline. There are a variety of reasons for moving toward a standardized approach to documentation. This approach, for instance, is one way to deal with the complexity of working with multiple contractors and to aid end users—everyone interested in the same information can find it in the same place regardless of the contractor.

Software documentation is useful to contractors, the government, and the end-users alike. Software development documentation increases the likelihood of an orderly development process, establishes well-defined baselines, provides a vehicle for change control, provides for personnel changes during the entire life of development and maintenance, and facilitates maintenance. The end-user documentation provides the ultimate users of the developed system with the information they need to perform their jobs well. Ideally, the attributes of software documentation are completeness, accuracy, appropriateness, and clarity. These attributes result in specifications that are internally consistent, explicit, designable and/or testable, traceable between documents, and assignable to programming personnel.

Structured programming is a discipline for producing code that can significantly improve software reliability and maintainability. The main attributes of structured programming are that the code is modular, top-down, sequential, indented to bring out the structure of the logic, has one entry and one exit, and uses a restricted set of control and data structures. These attributes lead to code that is simpler, clearer, and easier to test than unstructured code.

Software is developed in phases. There are many ways to identify those phases. For the purposes of this paper, those phases are designated as

1. Initial Planning
2. Requirements Analysis
3. Preliminary Design
4. Detailed Design
5. Code, Debug, and Unit Test
6. Contractor Testing
7. Acceptance Testing

Documentation is developed or used in each of these phases. The remainder of this paper describes each of these phases and the role of documentation in each phase. It also points out the relationships between the software documents.

Initial Planning Software Development Phase

The documents produced during the Initial Planning Phase convey the contractor's plans for fulfilling the contract. Four types of software planning documents can be written during this phase:

1. Software development plan (SDP)
2. Software quality assurance plan (SQA or, simply, QA plan)
3. Software configuration management plan (SCM or, simply, CM plan)
4. Software standards and conventions

The software development plan is software management's plan for developing the program performance specification and producing software, which satisfies the requirements specified in the program performance specification, within budget and on time.

The software quality assurance plan is the quality assurance group's plan for verifying that all the requirements stated in the contract are met. Important parts of a QA plan are the plans for verifying that the software group and the configuration management group (whose function is explained below) are complying with the SDP and CM plan, respectively.

A software configuration management plan is the configuration managment group's plan for managing changes in the software's configuration during software development. (The word *configuration* may require some explanation. Suppose a contractor is developing a not-so-plain, everyday, homely desk for the government. By the *configuration* of the desk is meant all the information needed to completely describe the desk. For instance, if the current configuration of the desk calls for a 24-inch drawer and someone wants to make it a 30-inch drawer, then that is a change in the desk's configuration. In the defense industry, a defense contractor has a group of people who establish policies and procedures for controlling, or rather, managing changes in a product's configuration and who verify compliance with those procedures.)

Software standards and conventions can be covered in either a section of the software development plan or in a separate document. They specify programming standards and how some aspects of software development will be conducted.

Requirements Analysis Software Development Phase

The documentation produced during the Requirements Analysis Phase conveys the contractor's understanding of the functional performance requirements to the customer. Two kinds of documents can be written during this phase:

1. Program performance specification (PPS)
2. Interface design specification (IDS)

The program performance specification is a functional specification. This kind of document describes *what* functions the software will perform, not *how* the software will perform them. If a function should be tested at the system level, then it belongs in the PPS and, otherwise, it does not. A PPS addresses

1. System-level functions that have been delegated to software and some implied functions
2. Interfaces external to the product being developed and between the major software functions
3. Hardware environment in which the software will perform
4. Kinds of tests required to verify that the software does indeed comply with the requirements described in the PPS

The PPS is a necessary preliminary to setting up test requirements and beginning the software design. Some software projects are sufficiently large or complicated to warrant developing more than one PPS on a project. The CDRL list specifies what PPSs must be developed and then delivered to the government.

A program performance specification is referred to by several names. MIL-STD-1679(NAVY) refers to it as a program performance specification. MIL-STD-490 calls it a B5 Specification. MIL-STD-483 calls it a Part I Specification. This kind of document can also be called a data processing system requirements specification (DPSR).

The program performance specification and the software development plan are the two most important software engineering documents. A software project can be defined as a project to produce software, which has agreed-upon functions, within budget, on time, and in a manner that has an amount of risk that is acceptable to the software development manager. The PPS is software management's written vehicle for gaining and communicating agreement as to what functions the software is supposed to perform. The SDP is software management's written plan for producing the software within budget and on time. Furthermore, any significant error in either of these two documents can lead to a situation that is singularly challenging (and expensive) to correct.

The interface design specification describes the software interfaces and the data flowing between two digital processors. By "software interfaces" is meant those interfaces which send data to the software under development, which the software hands off data to, or which the software controls. The interface design specification was mainly intended to cover the interaction of the software being developed with software in another system.

The interface specification has another use when more than one company is developing the software. Specifically, it can be used to specify the interfaces between the software being developed by two of the companies. This is one way the two companies can know what to expect in the way of input from the other company and what they are expected to hand off to the other company. The interface design specification then becomes one basis for managing the interface between the two companies.

The chief importance of an interface specification to a software development manager is in its potential for shortening the Contractor's Testing Phase. This potential can be realized when the software engineers know precisely what requirements they are to implement and their manager exercises rigid control over the interfaces between the software developed by different programmers and programming teams. An interface document increases the likelihood of software developed by different programmers or teams of programmers interacting correctly. This single improvement can dramatically reduce integration time.

Preliminary Design Software Development Phase

The documents produced during the preliminary design phase describe the top-level design and planning of the contractor's approach to fulfilling and verifying the requirements specified in the program performance specification. Three kinds of documents can be written during this phase:

1. Program design specification (PDS)
2. Data base design document (DBDD)
3. Test plan

Once again, the CDRL list will define which of these documents must be written and delivered to the government as a contract requirement, but the main purpose of a PDS is to describe the design approach. It describes the architecture and organization of program modules. It provides the programmers with a logical description of the internal design of the software. A PDS is not a detailed design document, but rather, it communicates the design idea.

Program design specification is the name MIL-STD-1679(NAVY) uses to designate this kind of document. MIL-STD-490(USAF) and MIL-STD-483(USAF) do not have an exact equivalent to a PDS. Their design documents come out of the total design effort; only parts of them are developed during the preliminary design phase.

Typically, a data base design document appears on a CDRL list when there is a large data base or the data base is critical in some way. A DBDD describes all the data used by two or more software components and shows the file organization.

The test plan is a management document. It identifies the major functional areas to be tested, describes the testing methodology, and identifies the resources (people, equipment, and time) needed for testing.

These documents are often reviewed at a preliminary design review (PDR). A PDR is a formal review conducted during the preliminary design phase. The purposes of a PDR are to

(1) review the top-level design, (2) evaluate progress, (3) verify the technical adequacy of the selected design and test approach, and (4) verify compatibility between the PDS and the PPS, i.e., verify that the design covers all the requirements in the PPS and covers no more than that. More than one PDR may be conducted if the PDS and DBDD are being developed in stages. (Note: The Air Force often conducts a PDR during the Requirements Analysis Phase rather than during the design phases.)

Detailed Design Software Development Phase

This is the last phase of software design. During this phase, the programming team converts the design approach expressed in the PDS and the DBDD into detailed processing steps. The results of the conversion are expressed in the program design description (PDD) document.

The PDD describes the design details of each software component to be coded. It includes functions performed, design structure, operating constraints, inputs and outputs, diagrammatic/narrative flows, and data base organization. The PDD serves as the primary document that development and maintenance personnel use for developing software, diagnosing trouble, and modifying software.

In addition to the PDD, several other documents are produced or updated during this phase:

1. The PDS is revised with comments from the PDR and possibly with improvements identified by the contractor since the PDR
2. The DBDD is revised with comments from the PDR and possibly with improvements identified by the contractor since the PDR
3. Test plans are updated with comments from the PDR and possibly with improvements identified by the contractor since PDR
4. Test specifications, which describe how the requirements will be tested, are produced by the test team using the test plans

The C5 Specification of MIL-STD-490(USAF) and the Part II Specification of MIL-STD-483(USAF) are equivalent to the combination of a PDS and PDD.

All the documents produced or updated during the detailed design phase are often reviewed at a critical design review (CDR). A CDR is a formal review at the completion of the detailed design phase and before code development begins.

The main purpose of a CDR is to review the detailed program design. There can be more than one CDR when the detailed design is evolving in stages.

It is at the end of the detailed design phase that the information needed for writing the first draft of the maintenance and operator manuals is known. The definition of menus, prompts, error messages, what conditions cause the error messages to be issued, and how to respond to error messages, initialization and recovery procedures, and so on are all defined by the end of the detailed design phase. Thus, if this information is written down by the software engineers as soon as they know it, then work on the maintenance and operator manuals can begin in the next phase. Typically, however, these documents are not started until the contractor testing phase.

Code, Debug, and Unit Test Software Development Phase

This software development phase is when individual programmers will code and debug their software. After a pro-

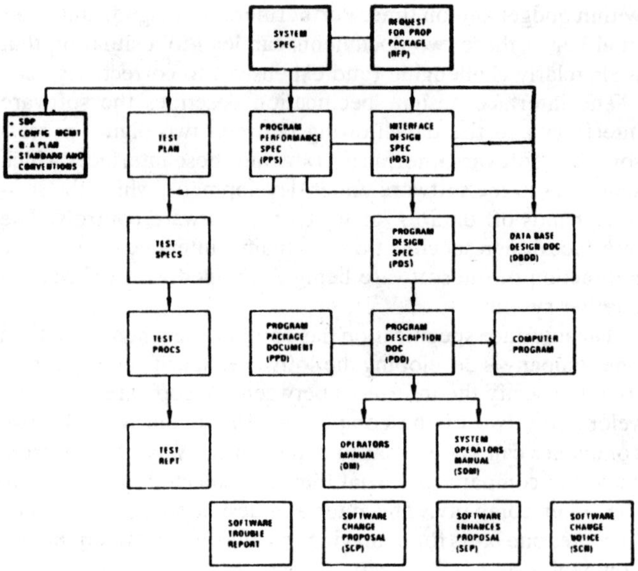

Figure 2—Document tree of the MIL-STD-1679 documents

PRELIMINARY DESIGN REVIEW (PDR) ↓ (between Preliminary Design Phase and Detailed Design Phase)
CRITICAL DESIGN REVIEW (CDR) ↓ (between Detailed Design Phase and Code, Debug and Unit Test Phase)
END-PRODUCT ACCEPTANCE ↓ (end of Acceptance Testing Phase)

SOFTWARE DOCUMENTS	INITIAL PLANNING PHASE	REQUIREMENTS ANALYSIS PHASE	PRELIMINARY DESIGN PHASE	DETAILED DESIGN PHASE	CODE, DEBUG AND UNIT TEST PHASE	PROGRAMMING TEAM TESTING PHASE	TEST TEAM TESTING PHASE	ACCEPTANCE TESTING PHASE
SOFTWARE DEVELOPMENT PLAN (SDP)	p, f							
SOFTWARE CONFIGURATION MANAGEMENT PLAN (CM PLAN)	p, f							
SOFTWARE QUALITY ASSURANCE PLAN (QA PLAN)	p, f							
SOFTWARE STANDARDS AND CONVENTIONS		p						
PROGRAM PERFORMANCE SPECIFICATION (PPS)		p, f	u	u			u	
PRELIMINARY DESIGN SPECIFICATION (PDS)			p, f	u			u	
PROGRAM DESCRIPTION DOCUMENT (PDD)				p, f			u	
DATA BASE DESIGN DOCUMENT (DBDD)				p, f			u	
TEST PLAN		p, f						
TEST SPECIFICATION(S)			p, f			u	u	
TEST PROCEDURES				p, f		u	u	
ACCEPTANCE TEST PLAN								
OPERATOR'S MANUAL					d		p, f	
SYSTEM OPERATOR'S MANUAL					d		p, f	

LEGEND
p PRELIMINARY
f FINAL
u UPDATED
d DRAFT

AM-019-036

Figure 3—Relationships between software documents and software phases grammer has written some code, he or she will unit test it until satisfied that the software performs properly. At this point, the software is ready to enter the next phase of software development. During this phase

1. Programmers use the PDD to produce code
2. Test personnel use the test specifications to write the test procedures, which are detailed procedural descriptions of how they will perform the tests described in the test specifications
3. Technical writers can begin writing the first drafts of the maintenance and operator manuals (though usually work on these documents does not begin until the next phase)

Contractor Testing Software Development Phase

During this phase, the contractor's software development team (as opposed to an individual programmer) tests software until it is ready for acceptance testing. The programming team may do some testing of its own on the software before turning it over to the test team. The test team will perform the tests described in the test procedures document (and possibly use the operator manuals if they are available) and any other tests they deem needed. If errors are detected, then the test team writes test reports and returns the software with the test results to the programming team for correction. When the programming team is satisfied the problems have been resolved, they submit the corrected software to the test team for retesting. This continues until the test team (and QA personnel) are satisfied that the software is ready for acceptance testing.

The final versions of the maintenance manuals and end-user documentation can be produced during this or the next phase. By the end of this phase, all the documentation should be revised to reflect the as-built configuration of the software. The CDRL will specify whether this will in fact be done.

Acceptance Testing Software Development Phase

During Acceptance Testing Phase, the software is tested either by the customer or in the presence of the customer. The people performing the tests can use the test procedures and the user's manuals. When the software passes this test, the customer has accepted the software and the software development process ends.

SUMMARY

The following figures summarize the software documents. Figure 2 presents the document tree, which relates the documents to each other, and Figure 3 shows relationships between software documents and software development phases.

SUGGESTED READINGS

1. MIL-STD-483(USAF), Configuration Management Practices for Systems, Equipment, Munitions, and Computer Programs.
2. MIL-STD-490(USAF), Specification Practices.
3. MIL-STD-1521A(USAF), Technical Reviews and Audits for Systems, Equipments, and Computer Programs.
4. MIL-STD-1679(NAVY), Weapon System Software Development.
5. MIL-S-83490, Specifications, Types and Forms.
6. Software Acquisition Management (SAM) Guidebooks, Electronic Systems Division (ESD), Air Force Systems Command, Hanscom Air Force Base, Massachusetts.
7. Software Acquisition Engineering (SAE) Guidebooks, Aeronautical Systems Command (ASD), Air Force Systems Command, Wright-Patterson Air Force Base, Ohio.
8. Computer Software Life Cycle Management Guide, Naval Electronic Systems Command (NAVELEX), Washington, D.C.

Note: Readings 1–5 are available from the Naval Publications and Forms Center, 5801 Tabor Ave., Philadelphia, PA 19120.

Simple dynamic assertions for interactive program validation

by CHRISTER HULTEN
Syslab, University of Stockholm
Stockholm, Sweden

ABSTRACT

It is well known that more than 50% of software life cycle costs are caused by maintenance activities: testing, debugging, modification, regression testing, and documentation updating. Therefore the importance of the validation and verification process in software development cannot be overstated. An interesting technique introduced by Stucki[9] is to instrument a program with dynamic assertions. The assertions, which are logical expressions regarding program variables, are entered into the program as comments, after which a preprocessor generates and inserts the code for dynamically checking the validity of these assertions. A number of papers describe more or less sophisticated and complicated ways of using dynamic assertions in test systems.[2,5,6,8,9] The aim of this paper is not to analyze and compare these approaches with each other or with our proposal, but rather to convey the advantages of a simple, user-friendly system based on dynamic assertions for expressing constraints, transactions, and transition constraints.

INTRODUCTION

It is well known that over 50% of the software life cycle costs are caused by maintenance activities: testing, debugging, modification, regression testing, and documentation updating. Therefore the importance of the validation and verification process in software development cannot be overstated. A survey of validation, verification, and testing techniques for computer software can be found in the work by Adrion and colleagues.[1]

Program test methods can be classified into static and dynamic methods. A static program test method does not involve executing the target program, but rather executing an analysis program that examines the source level program and tries to find errors or anomalies in the target program. Typical static methods are data flow and control flow analysis, compiler syntax and type checking, and symbolic execution and formal verification (proof techniques). Dynamic program test methods, on the other hand, do involve execution of the target program, albeit sometimes in a modified form. Typical dynamic methods are "traditional" program test methods with various test data generation techniques,[7] instrumentation and measurement techniques, and finally dynamic assertion techniques. This paper is concerned with a system for simple use of dynamic assertions.

DYNAMIC ASSERTIONS

An interesting technique introduced by Stucki[9] is to instrument a program with dynamic assertions. The assertions, which are logical expressions regarding program variables, are entered into the program as comments, after which a preprocessor generates and inserts the code for dynamically checking the validity of these assertions. A number of papers describe more or less sophisticated and complicated ways of using dynamic assertions in test systems.[2,5,6,8,9] The aim of this paper is not to analyze and compare these approaches with each other or with our proposal, but rather to convey the advantages of a simple, user-friendly system based on dynamic assertions.

There are several important benefits in using dynamic assertions:

1. The assertions should be invented at program design time, because it means that the programmer is encouraged to think in detail about what assertion is valid at a particular time in the execution of a program as well as about what invariants are valid throughout the execution of the program. This in itself will catch a substantial amount of errors that would otherwise turn up much later in the software life cycle, with corresponding higher costs for error detection and correction.[3]
2. A program in a conventional programming language is a procedural description of how to achieve some state of affairs. If it is possible to describe this state of affairs in a declarative way, which is a complementary way of looking at the problem, then many algorithmic errors may be detected not only at run time but also at design time, since the programmer will think about the problem in two complementary ways. Of course there is a probability of introducing errors when making the assertions; but at least this does not introduce errors into the program proper (and of course it is hoped that these errors will be discovered). Since the procedural and the declarative descriptions are very different, I believe it unlikely that the same errors would be made in both descriptions—that a program error would be undetected because of a corresponding assertion error. Moreover, if an error is made in an assertion, it may well reflect the fact that the problem is not well understood. A discrepancy between the declarative and procedural representations should be thought of as if the error were equally likely to be in either of the representations.
3. If appropriate dynamic assertions are inserted in a program in strategic places, debugging is greatly facilitated, and errors can be pinpointed more quickly. However, it requires that software for assertion facilities either be integrated with the compiler or be structured into a preprocessor and a postprocessor. The reason for this is the need to transform the regular error messages from the compiler and run-time system into messages regarding the true source program—i.e., the source code, including the assertions. In a more sophisticated system, integration is carried further, so that other items of software (e.g., screen editors and debuggers) are given intelligence in terms of the assertion subsystem. An assertion subsystem can be made rather independently of a compiler in a good programming environment and fits in nicely with a good interactive system.
4. One of the most important activities in most program testing methods is the construction of test case results: For every test case—sets of input data to the program—a set of output conditions must be described, and must be described in advance, so that at least a manual check of a test case can be made.[7] It is well known that programmers frequently resent and fail to describe test case result construction. I believe that one reason for this is that the test case result descriptions are not part of the final product (the production program) but only a tedious component of the "destructive"[7] testing process. In this context we advocate the use of assertions as a natural

programming activity done at program design time, since including assertions on output conditions is another (but positive) way of making test case result descriptions. What is more important is that the checking of test results is done automatically.

5. Since the dynamic assertion technique requires that (1) declarative logical assertions be made in strategic places in programs and that (2) there be a support system for managing dynamic assertions, it is tempting to try to apply other techniques. At this stage there are several types of static program test methods that can be included in a preprocessor of the kind intended for assertion management—e.g., data and control flow techniques and some simple proof techniques. As formal proof techniques develop, the preprocessor can be enhanced to include such techniques in order to advance the quality of software further.
6. Normally, after the initial test period and perhaps a trial production period, the assertions in a program would be deactivated because of performance reasons. However, as program use changes over time, assertions can once in a while be activated to discover inconsistencies between the original specifications of the programs and actual usage. We believe that this change in use of programs is a very common cause of software failure.
7. It is common that regression testing, i.e., testing a piece of software after modification, is done poorly, and often not at all. If dynamic assertions are present in a program, chances are better that the modification itself will be correct, and furthermore that regression testing will be better done, because the amount of tedious programmer work is reduced. For efficiency, it is important that it be easy to switch the assertion monitoring on and off.
8. Using dynamic assertions is one of the few ways of catching time-dependent (nonreproducible) errors.

A SIMPLE SYSTEM FOR DYNAMIC ASSERTIONS

I will now outline an assertion system that I believe is simple enough to be accepted and used by programmers and yet powerful enough to achieve the advantages mentioned above. For presentation purposes the examples will be in PASCAL. The environment in which we place an assertion system is a Berkeley Unix/C system, an environment that highly facilitates implementation of such systems. It is assumed that there exists a symbolic debug system that can be interfaced to the assertion system.

Constraints

Since it is very important to keep the number of concepts low, only two are used here: constraints and assertions. A constraint expression is a Boolean expression (it can be evaluated to True or False) in the regular programming language style. It may contain Boolean function calls, which in turn may contain other function or procedure calls. This, of course, allows complex evaluations to be made. No assumption may be made with regard to the order of evaluation of the constraint expression. This means that if any assignments are made to program variables due to function or procedure calls executed when evaluating a constraint expression, care must be taken to ensure that the constraint expression evaluation order is insignificant. The reason for allowing assignment operations at all in constraint expressions (indirectly) is that it may be necessary to set up some conditions before performing the evaluation. An example of this occurs when a constraint is concerned with the consistency between an external database and program variables.

A constraint has the following structure:

E:C:V with the types boolexp1:boolexp2:statement;

boolexp1 and *boolexp2* are Boolean expressions, and *statement* is any legal statement in the host programming language.

E denotes Enforcement condition
C denotes Constraint expression
V denotes Violation action

The constraint semantics are as follows: If E is evaluated to True, then C (the actual constraint condition) is evaluated. If C is evaluated to False—i.e., the constraint condition is violated—then the statement V, which of course can be a compound statement, is executed. The assertion system additionally reports the violation and, when appropriate, passes control to the debug system. The condition E is used for controlling the individual evaluation of a constraint expression. A constraint does not have to have all these three components. The other valid combinations are as follows:

C—this is probably the most common variation. It means that only a constraint condition is specified, and if it is found to be False, the violation is reported and the execution aborted.

E:C—this means: If E evaluate C. If C is False, report violation and abort.

C:V—this means: Always evaluate C. If C is False, execute V, report violation, and abort conditionally.

A constraint declaration has the form:

```
CONSTRAINTS E1:C1:V1;
            E2:C2:V2;
              .
              .
            En:Cn:Vn;
ENDCONSTRAINTS;
```

A CONSTRAINTS declaration can be placed anywhere in the program where a variable declaration is legal and where the scope of the constraint evaluation is the same as the scope of variables declared in that block or other entity. Furthermore, the enforcement of constraints will be in effect on that block level as well as on inner block levels.

The constraints in a CONSTRAINTS declaration are monitored; i.e., the variables referred to in a constraint expression are checked after each explicit or implicit assignment operation. Note that, since functions and procedures can be used in constraint expressions, it is not permitted to have side effects in functions/procedures on any level in a constraint expression—i.e., assignments to variables on the same level as, or global to, the CONSTRAINTS declaration. The reason for this is, of course, that when such a variable is updated and checked, the side effect will cause successive checks and consequently result in infinite recursion. This restriction, however, is not very limiting, since virtually all checking procedures will only read global variables, if any. Again, as in many cases in programming, side effects and global variables turn out to be harmful.

A CONSTRAINTS declaration is intended to represent conditions that are relatively independent of the individual statements in the program. The system therefore monitors every assignment operation where a variable involved in a constraint expression is changed. In many cases the program variables will be in an inconsistent state for a short while over several assignment operations—e.g., while transferring money between two bank accounts. There is then a need for a primitive to define transactions within which checking of the constraints is not meaningful.

Furthermore, since the monitoring of many assignment operations is very demanding from a performance point of view, it should be possible to turn off constraint checking in certain parts of the program. There is also a need for transforming a program with constraints into an efficient version without any constraint system overhead at all. There are two pairs of primitives for turning the assignment monitoring off and on. The first pair is concerned with excluding certain parts of the program from dynamic assignment checking, the second with eliminating constraints completely from the object program.

The first primitive is NOCONSTRAIN, which, when executed in the program, turns off all constraint checking until a CONSTRAIN primitive is encountered. The executing program is either in the NOCONSTRAIN mode or the CONSTRAIN mode. The default is the CONSTRAIN mode. Transactions are formed between NOCONSTRAIN-CONSTRAIN pairs. The third primitive is #NOCONSTRAIN, a preprocessor command, which statically turns off the preprocessor generation of constraint-checking code. #CONSTRAIN turns it on again. The #-commands are performed as the preprocessor scans the source program lexically from start to end.

Assertions

As seen, constraints are suitable for monitoring updates of variables throughout a program. If particular conditions must hold at a particular point in the execution of the program, it is useful to have another type of primitive to assert that these conditions hold. Typical conditions of this are (1) entry/exit conditions in procedures and functions and (2) assertions about a database state or loop invariants. The primitive for this purpose is the ASSERTION statement. An ASSERTION statement has the following structure:

```
ASSERT E1:C1:V1;
       E2:C2:V2;
       E3:C3:V3;
         .
         .
ENDASSERT;
```

Each Ei:Ci:Vi (i = 1, 2, 3, ...) is a constraint with the same semantics as before, but evaluation is performed only when the ASSERT statement is executed. As with CONSTRAINTS, there are primitives for disabling assertion statements and removing assertion statements. They are: NOASSERT, ASSERT, #NOASSERT, and #ASSERT.

Transition Constraints

In database literature it is commonly considered desirable to be able to describe a type of constraint called transition constraints.[4] A transition constraint is a constraint involving the values of a variable, before and after an update; e.g., a salary must not be increased by more than 10%.

From an assertion system point of view, there are two ways of achieving this. The first way is simple to program the recording of the preconditions manually, e.g.,

```
.
.
VAR x:INTEGER;
FUNCTION rec_precond:INTEGER;...................;
FUNCTION dyn_check (i:INTEGER) :BOOLEAN; .....;
.
BEGIN
    .
    .
    x: = rec_precond;
        S1;
        S2;
        S3;
    dyn_check (x)
END;
```

where S1,S2, and S3 are PASCAL statements.

Another way of handling transition constraints is by the use of a system-defined function OLD(x). The difference is here that the system takes care of the administration of the prior value of a variable. The resulting type of OLD(x) is the same as that of x. The value of OLD(x) is the next latest value assigned to x. Using OLD(x), however, may be very costly, since code will be generated for saving the previous value of the variable and distributed all over the program.

An example: Assume that x may not increase by more than 10%:

```
PROGRAM maxten;
VAR x,y,z:INTEGER;
    b:BOOLEAN;
.
.
BEGIN
    .
    .
    IF b THEN x: = x + y ELSE x: = x + z
    .
    .
    ASSERT x < OLD(x)*1.1;
    .
    .
END.
```

The manual method is more appropriate for complex transition constraints, whereas the OLD(x) function is possible only in simple cases.

SOME IMPLEMENTATION ASPECTS

An assertion system like the one proposed must consist of a preprocessor and a postprocessor. The main function of the postprocessor is to be a bridge between the high-level source program (the source program with assertions and constraints) and the conventional source program (the program generated by the preprocessor). The main problem, of course, is that when the compiler, the run-time system, and the operating system detect error conditions or exceptions, they return information about the generated program, not about the high-level source program. This means that it should be possible to trap run-time errors—e.g., divide by zero—so that the preprocessor can generate code for interrupt routines and communicate to the postprocessor. Further, when an error is detected, the high-level source code should be loaded into an editor that pinpoints the error, if possible.

If the restriction that no global variables may be used indirectly within constraint expressions is enforced, it enables a much less complicated preprocessor to be implemented (with a corresponding reduction in preprocessing costs). At the same time, the required run-time resources can be reduced. However, since I want to encourage usage of dynamic assertions, I feel that this restriction is too limiting.

SUMMARY AND CONCLUSIONS

This paper has attempted to point out some benefits of using a simple dynamic assertion system for typical industrial program production. I strongly believe that an approach like the one suggested has a high potential for cutting software development and maintenance costs. However, a study of the effects of using such a system in a commercial environment is necessary for assessing the approach in a quantitative way.

A drawback of dynamic checking techniques is that the run-time cost (in terms of time and space) of a program is increased, sometimes to an unacceptable degree. An advantage in this approach is that you can, to a large extent, control the amount of run-time checking and not pay for more run-time checking than you want.

It is advisable to have different levels of run-time checking in different phases of a program's life cycle. During the initial program testing you would preferably have maximum constraint and assertion checking. In preliminary production runs perhaps some of the checking would be reduced, and in heavy production runs probably only the main assertions would be activated. In time/space critical applications perhaps the run-time checking would be eliminated altogether. After program modification it is advantageous to turn on all checking again.

As mentioned, it is easy to incorporate new and advanced static program analysis methods like program control flow analysis and formal proof methods. Increased use of such methods should of course be matched by a corresponding reduction in run-time checking.

If the target language is not strongly typed, a pre- and postprocessor system for dynamic assertions can help achieve the reliability that characterizes strongly typed languages. Of course, using an assertion system well results in reliability far beyond type checking, but at the expense of more run-time checking.

Finally, I believe that an assertion system must be very simple to be used at all by industrial programmers. This paper has attempted to show what a simple system with controllable overhead can look like and to point out some of its properties.

REFERENCES

1. Adrion, W. Richards, Martha A. Branstad, and John C. Cherniavsky. "Validation, Verification, and Testing of Computer Software." *ACM Computing Surveys,* 14 (1982), pp. 159–192.
2. Andrews, Dorothy M., and Jeoffrey P. Benson. "An Automated Program Testing Methodology and its Implementation." In *Proceedings of the 5th International Conference on Software Engineering,* March 9–12, 1981, San Diego.
3. Boehm, B. W. "Seven Basic Principles of Software Engineering." In *Software Engineering Techniques,* Infotech State of the Art Report. L London: Infotech, 1977.
4. Date, C. J. *An Introduction to Database Systems (Vol. II),* Reading, Mass.: Addison-Wesley, 1983.
5. Gannon, John, Paul McMullin, and Richard Hamlet. "Data-Abstraction Implementation, Specification, and Testing. *ACM Transactions on Programming Languages and Systems,* 3 (1981), pp. 211–223.
6. McMullin, Paul R., John D. Gannon, and Mark D. Weiser. "Implementing a Compiler-Based Test Tool." In *Software—Practice and Experience,* 12 (1982), pp. 971–979.
7. Myers, Glenford J. *The Art of Software Testing,* New York: Wiley-Interscience, 1979.
8. Osterweil, L. J. "A Strategy for Effective Implementation of Verification and Testing Techniques." Technical Report CU-CS-181-80, Computer Science Department, University of Colorado, Boulder, Colorado, 1980.
9. Stucki, Leon G. "New Directions in Automated Tools for Improving Software Quality." in Yeh [ed.], *Current Trends in Programming Methodology* (Vol. II). Englewood Cliffs, N.J.: Prentice-Hall, 1977.

A tool-based approach for software testing and validation

by J.C. HUANG, PETER VALDES, and RAYMOND T. YEH
International Software Systems, Inc.
College Park, Maryland

ABSTRACT

This paper describes a methodology for software testing and validation. By recognizing that there are several major error types, this methodology uses different test strategies to expose a particular type of error. To facilitate these strategies, specific tools are needed. This paper not only identifies the desired tools, but also discusses the design concepts behind various tools as they have been built at International Software Systems, Inc. (ISSI).

INTRODUCTION

A number of software tool systems (e.g., RXVP80[2], TOOLPACK[4], and MAP[5]) have been developed recently; however, none provides an effective testing methodology that facilitates exposure of software errors during testing and maintenance. These tool systems implicitly assume that traditional methods for software testing (e.g., coverage-based testing,[1,7,10] functional testing,[1,8] boundary value testing,[14] mutation testing,[3] and domain testing[18]) are used in the actual process of exposing errors in programs. It is well recognized that none of these traditional testing strategies is powerful enough to expose all the possible errors in a program.[1,6] The best that can be hoped for is to use a specific test strategy to expose a specific error.

We have recognized the limitations of existing test strategies and testing tools and have attempted to address these problems in our SEQUEL (Software Quality Evaluation Laboratory) tool system. SEQUEL is a testing tool system whose basic objective is to increase the quality of software and productivity of software engineers during the software development process by providing a methodology for software testing plus the tools to support the said methodology. We are currently implementing SEQUEL to accept ISO (International Standards Organization) PASCAL under VAX/VMS.

The testing methodology of SEQUEL will be discussed in the next section. In the remaining sections, design concepts behind various tools will be discussed and their use illustrated with examples.

TESTING METHODOLOGY IN SEQUEL

The main purpose of testing in the software development life cycle is to verify conformance of the software with respect to its intended requirements. The intended requirements include the following:

1. System requirements developed prior to software design.
2. Functional requirements developed during software design. This category may very well include error condition requirements as well as boundary condition requirements.
3. Programming requirements developed after software design. This include syntax, semantic, compiler, and hardware restriction requirements.

Even if the policy is to always do things right the first time (e.g., the cleanroom idea), testing can never be eliminated from the software development life cycle. As long as software is developed by human beings, there is always a need to demonstrate that the software conforms with its requirements.

Any nonconformance of a given software with its intended requirements is known as a *software error*. An important prerequisite, therefore, in exposing software errors is a clear statement of software requirements (possible written in a requirements specification language). Testing to verify conformance with software requirements is really equivalent to testing a hypothesis that a given software error does/does not, in fact, exist in the software. A testing methodology that hypothesizes and tests on all possible errors in a software addresses the original objective of software testing.

Selecting an appropriate testing strategy for a given software error is still an art. Researchers have yet to collect data on software errors that frequently occur in a given environment and map these errors with the appropriate test strategies. However, it has been well recognized in the field that implementation of a testing strategy is greatly facilitated if it is supported by *software tools*. A very good example is the compiler, which is effective in exposing syntax errors and sometimes a few semantic errors. Another example is a debugger, which facilitates detection of software faults. The use of software tools not only enhances the error detecting capability of a testing strategy, but it can also be cost effective. The savings in using tools is due to (1) reducing the amount of time (and therefore cost) to expose any embedded software error and (2) reducing the amount of time needed to find the cause of the exposed error. SEQUEL addresses the need for a tool-based testing methodology.

Methodology

The methodology can be formulated in the following way:

Let

$[SR_1, SR_2, \ldots, SR_j, \ldots, SR_N]$:	Set of software requirements collected at various phases of the software development life cycle.
$e[SR_j]$:	Error associated with software that does not conform to SR_j.
E:	Set of all errors (initially unknown) that actually exist in the software. $E = \bigcup_{j=1}^{N} e(SR_j)$

Basic Method

Test of Error Hypothesis (for each SR_j)
Null Hypothesis H0: $e[SR_j]$ in E
Alternative Hypothesis is H1: $e[SR_j]$ Not in E

In software testing, we hypothesize the existence of specific software errors (nonconformance with requirements) embedded in the software. The error hypothesis is then tested by a strategy appropriate for the given error. The test result may lead to acceptance of H0 and rejection of H1 or vice versa. Not all testing strategies can be recommended for a given $e[SR_j]$. Some are imperfect relative to $e[SR_j]$ (for example, using path testing to expose boundary errors); others are nearly perfect with respect to $e[SR_j]$. It is imperative, therefore, that an appropriate testing strategy be properly selected to minimize the error of rejecting H0 when, in fact, it is true.

Nonconformance with software requirements can take many forms. The following are the more frequently occurring errors:

1. Nonconformance with compiler rules/restrictions = syntax/semantic errors
2. Nonconformance with intended functions = logic/computation errors
3. Nonconformance with erroneous input = error handling errors
4. Nonconformance with proper program boundaries = boundary condition errors
5. Nonconformance with proper data flow = data flow anomalies

An important assumption of the methodology is that the software requirements are clearly stated.

An obvious example using this hypothesize-and-test approach is the detection of syntax and some semantic errors in programs.

Error Hypothesis

H0: Syntax or semantic error in E
H1: Syntax or semantic error not in E

Strategy

1. Compile and check for syntax/semantic error. Quit if none. Tool: Compiler
2. Fix compiler-detected errors. Goto 1.

The creative energy of a programmer should not be wasted in manually exposing syntax/semantic errors (as, for example, in a code walkthrough). Compilers are very good at this, and they should do the job.

The more interesting types of software errors that one would like to expose are those that remain after successful compilation. Following the basic methodology discussed above, we hypothesize on the existence of each of these error types in a program (being tested) and specify a specific strategy to test each hypothesis. SEQUEL specifies (in its current form) test strategies for logic/computation, data flow and boundary/error condition errors. These strategies (see the next two sections) are supported by the following basic tools:

1. Program Attribute Generator
2. Static Reports Generator
3. Program Instrumenter
4. Branch Coverage Counter
5. Symbolic Trace Generator
6. Symbolic Trace Data Flow Analyzer
7. Symbolic Trace Slicer
8. Symbolic Trace Analyzer

It is not claimed that these are the only tools one would need to fully support any testing strategy. There are certainly a lot more tools one would desire to have (especially for integration testing and concurrent program testing). Some of these tools, it is hoped, will be included in future versions of SEQUEL. The role of SEQUEL tools should be emphasized:

1. These tools only support the overall testing methodology. They indirectly aid the programmer in detecting and removing software errors.
2. These tools should complement other existing tools—e.g., compilers and debuggers—and should not compete with them.

Test Strategy for Logic/Computation Errors

A computation error occurs when the set of computational statements (usually assignment statements) directly affecting a program output variable does not conform to requirements. On the other hand, a logic error occurs when the set of control statements and all other statements affecting the control statements cause traversal of an incorrect path in the program.

Error Hypothesis

H0: Logic/computation error in E
H1: Logic/computation error not in E

Strategy I

1. Generate a test case to exercise the intended software subfunctional requirement. A subfunctional requirement maps to a single program path. A set of subfunctional requirements may be contained in a specified functional requirement; hence, a corresponding set of test cases should be generated:
   a. Get the input conditions that invoke the functional requirement. This should be found from the specified software requirements.
   b. Pick an interior element that satisfies the intended function's input conditions.
   c. Check untraversed branches as (possible) guides in generating the next test case.
      Tool: Branch coverage counter
2. Produce a compile clean program (if program has previously been changed).
   Tool: Compiler

3. Generate the program's attributes and sequenced program listing.
   Tool: Static Analyzer
4. Instrument the sequenced program.
   Tool: Program Instrumenter tool of Dynamic Analyzer
5. Generate a symbolic trace of the path traversed by running the test case generated in Step 1.
   Tool: Symbolic Trace Generator of Dynamic Analyzer
6. Check for data flow anomalies on the generated symbolic trace (if desired)
   Tool: Data Flow Analyzer of Dynamic Analyzer
   Data Flow Anomaly = [Referencing an undefined variable; Not referencing a defined variable; Defining a currently defined variable]

   Note: This step can be done separately if the sole intention is to find symbolic trace data flow errors.
7. Conditional on the complexity of the symbolic trace, slice the trace to focus attention of the sublogic/subcomputational part corresponding to a suspected erroneous variable in the trace.
   Tool: Symbolic Trace Slicer
8. (Optional depending on specific situation)
   Generate the backward-substituted predicates of the slice/trace.
   Tool: Symbolic Trace Analyzer
   There are situations where the set of backward-substituted predicates are easier to compare with the specified functional requirements. A sample situation occurs when the symbolic trace is mostly composed of logic statements (control statements and other statements affecting control).
9. Compare the slices or the trace with the specified functional requirements. The specified functional requirements may be in mathematical/symbolic form or in English-prose form. The programmer/tester detects any logical discrepancies in the slice/trace and in the specified functional requirements.
10. Fix any detected logic/computation errors detected in Steps 6 and 9. Quit if none. Goto 2.
11. Proceed to the next software functional requirement. Goto 1.

It should be emphasized that the role of the test cases in Step 1 was simply to generate a symbolic trace and not to expose a logic/computation error directly. Any exposed error from the test case is only coincidental. The logic errors are detected after comparing the slice/trace with the software functional requirement. Exposing logic/computation errors directly from test cases can be difficult and time-consuming. Exposing logic errors by comparing slice/trace with functional requirements minimizes the difficult task of generating a lot of test cases and the task of comparing the test results with the expected software result. It has to be pointed out that in comparing a slice/trace with functional requirements when debugging a program, we may need information on certain attributes of the program to verify, for example, mixed mode computations or calling sequence errors. This information may be queried from the program database or by invoking any of the following tools of the static analyzer: the Variable/Statement Cross Reference Table Generator, the Sub-Program Calling Sequence Table Generator, and the Sub-Program Cross Reference Table Generator.

Test Strategy for Boundary/Error Condition Errors

The declared range of input variables in a program plus its various predicates to control logic define the boundaries of the program. A boundary condition error occurs when an input point in the boundary yields results that do not conform with intended requirements. An error condition error occurs when an input point outside the legal boundary of the program is not handled properly or causes the program to crash.

Error Hypothesis

H0: Boundary/error condition error in E
H1: Boundary/error condition error not in E

Strategy II

1. Start from a previously generated trace/slice. This may require doing Steps 1 to 6 of testing strategy recommended for logic/computation errors.
   Tools needed:
   a. Compiler
   b. Static Analyzer
   c. Program Instrumenter
   d. Symbolic Trace Generator
   e. Symbolic Trace Slicer
   f. Data Flow Analyzer
2. Generate equivalence class conditions for the selected trace/slice. Quit if no more trace/slice.
   The equivalence class conditions are generated by performing backward substitution on the predicates of the trace/slice. The backward-substituted predicates are expressed purely in terms of constants and input variables. The predicates essentially define the boundaries of the subfunction being implemented by the trace/slice.
3. Compare the generated (possibly erroneous) equivalence class conditions with the specified boundary/error requirements. Any observed discrepancy (due to incorrect or missing boundary) is a boundary condition error.
4. An alternative or complementary step is to generate a test case to test the boundary/error conditions of the selected trace/slice. The equivalence class conditions expressed purely in terms of constants and input variables greatly facilitate generating these test cases. The equivalence class conditions may be simplified symbolically using a text editor. Simplification may be necessary to further facilitate test case generation.
   Guideline:
   For each suspected erroneous boundary, generate test cases near the predicate's boundary. Test cases should be immediately inside and outside the boundary. Test inputs immediately outside the boundary should be

properly handled by the program. Test cases in the interior of the equivalence class do not really yield additional useful information. They only duplicate what the previous test case did. In a way, the set of backward-substituted predicates serves to filter out redundant test cases.

5. Execute the generated test cases and observe any erroneous program output. Test cases outside the boundary that are also illegal/invalid program inputs should not cause the program to crash. They should be properly handled by appropriate error condition routines. Test cases that are outside the boundary but that are valid program inputs should be processed by the appropriate program path. Finally, the test output should be compared with expected program output.
6. Remove any detected boundary/error condition errors. Go back to 1.

Notice that executing a test case outside the boundary of a predicate (hence, outside the boundaries of the equivalence class) traverses a different path in the program. A new path implies a new symbolic trace/slice. This new trace/slice can be compared with specified requirements for purposes of error detection and may serve as the next trace/slice to be analyzed. We can, in fact, systematically traverse all the basic paths of the program from this process.

Command Processor in SEQUEL

The command processor in SEQUEL will integrate all the testing strategies described into one overall testing strategy. It has the following basic form:

1. User invokes strategy to remove syntax/semantic errors from the program. Correct any detected errors.
2. Hypothesize an error embedded in the software. Quit if no more errors to hypothesize.
3. CASES
   Logic/Computation Error: Invoke Strategy I
   Boundary/Error Condition Error: Invoke Strategy II
4. Goto 2.
   The basic flow of the testing methodology has the following features:
   a. It is easy to integrate new test strategies and tools in the future.
   b. The user has flexibility to hypothesize the more important errors in the program first. This may be critical when testing time/resources are limited.
   c. The program to be tested may be a single module, a set of modules, or the whole program. Testing single modules or a set of modules in a bottom-up or top-down fashion may require a driver and a set of stubs. Drivers and stubs are necessary to make the module separately executable. We thus have a uniform approach for unit, integration, and system testing.

We recognize that additional features should be integrated in the command processor for it to be user-friendly. The following features are being implemented:

1. Menu-driven user interface.
2. HELP routines to
   a. Guide the user on how to use the package.
   b. Recommend the appropriate tool to use at a given point in the testing process.
3. Ability to invoke system tools (e.g., compiler or text editor) inside the processor.
4. Ability to save and recall input/output files. This can be useful, for example, in these situations:
   a. Ability to save and timestamp test cases run on the program being tested.
   b. Ability to recall previous slices/traces for further analysis.
5. Ability to gather and document error statistics on program being tested.

SYMBOLIC TRACE SLICER

Why a Symbolic Trace Should Be Sliced

The traditional approach to program slicing is to extract the smallest possible independently executable subprogram from a given program and slice criterion, which behaves equivalently with the given program as far as the variables in the slice criterion are concerned. There are, however, difficulties in following this traditional approach:

1. Treatment of array and record elements during the slicing process. Current slicing algorithms[17] treat the whole array or record as a scalar. This assumption would obviously collect more statements in the slice than necessary.
2. Treatment of functions and procedures (subprograms) in the slicing process.

We used a different approach for SEQUEL to solve these difficulties. The approach is to slice the symbolic trace generated by the Dynamic Analyzer instead of slicing the original program. The advantages of the approach are as follows:

1. There is a need to deal only with a single path (trace) in the program. This facilitates treatment of functions and procedures.
2. The specific array or record elements are known as a result of dynamically generating a trace from a test input. Thus, array and records need no longer be treated as scalars.

This approach does not in any way diminish the error-detecting capability of SEQUEL. SEQUEL's testing methodology always deals with a trace/slice in exposing program errors. Therefore, there is really no difference between slicing the program first, and then generating a symbolic trace from the slice; and generating a symbolic trace first, and then slicing the symbolic trace.

The main purpose, of course, in extracting a slice is to focus attention on the variables (possibly erroneous) in the slice criterion. This enhances error detection and facilitates finding causes of exposed errors. An example would best illustrate our point.

Example/Results Interpretation

Given

PASCAL program which finds the maximum and minimum value in an array. (Figure 1 gives a sample program.)

Test Case #1

N = 5
Array A: 4,3,1,2,5

Figure 2 is the symbolic trace generated by Test Case #1.

Note: Column 1 gives the Symbolic Trace Sequence Numbers (ST#); Column 2 gives the Sequenced Program listing sequence numbers (SPL#). generated by the Static Analyzer.

Suppose we wish to focus our attention on whether the program, in fact, correctly computes the maximum of the array given Test Case #1. We have to note that one of the properties of Test Case #1 is that the maximum element lies at the end of the array. Thus this particular test case is exploring the correctness of the program in the case when the maximum lies at the end of the array with an odd number of elements. It does not test the correctness of the program when the maximum element is inside or at the beginning of the array, or at the end of an array with an even number of elements

Slicing Criterion:

Symbolic Trace Sequence #: 19
Variable(s): MAX

Symbolic Trace Slice (Option 1):

The I/O statements were excluded to make the example short. The STS #'s also started (in this example) after the I/O statements.

STS #	*SPL #*	*Statements*
3	16	I:=2
9	33	I:=I+2
13	29	MAX:=A[I+1]
19	41	WRITELN (MAX, MIN)

Remember that Slice Option 1 extracts only computational statements directly affecting the variable(s) in the criterion (MAX in this case), which contributed to the final value of MAX. If the output value of MAX is incorrect, then the cause can easily be detected by looking at the statements in the slice. The debugging process is thus facilitated. Two major causes are possible if MAX is incorrect:

1. At least one of the statements in the outputted slice is erroneous (e.g., wrong arithmetic statement, mixed-mode computation, referencing an undefined variable, etc.)
2. One or more statement in the slice is *missing*.

In Figure 3, MAX is correctly computed.

Code:

```
1          Program xminmax (input, output);
2
3          Var     i, n, min, max : integer;
4                  a : array[1..10] of integer:
5          Begin
6                  writeln( " no. of elements in the array = ');
7                  read(n);
8                  For i: = 1 to n DO
9                     Begin
10                        read (a[i]);
11                        write (a[i]);
12                        writeln;
13                    End;
14                 min : = a[1];
15                 max : = min;
16                 i := 2:
17                 While i < n DO
18                   Begin
19                        If a[i] > a[i+1] Then
20                           Begin
21                                If a[i] > max Then
22                                       max  := a[i] ;
23                                If a[i + 1] < min Then
24                                         min  := a[i + 1] ;
25                           End
26                        Else
27                           Begin
28                                If a[i + 1] > max Then
29                                       max  := a[i + 1] ;
30                                If a[i] < min Then
31                                       min := a[i]
32                           End;
33                        i := i + 2
34                 End
35                 If i = n Then
36                        If a[n] > max Then
37                                max := a[i + 1] :
38                           Else
39                                If a[n] < min Then
40                                     min := a[n];
41                 writeln(max,min)
42                 End
```

Figure 1

```
Symbolic Trace (produced by Dynamic Analyzer)
          (Path traversed by TestCase #1 in the program)

                       .
                       .
                       .
                                                     Specific Array Elements
1         14           min := a[i];
2         15           max := min;
3         16           I := 2;
4         17           ( I < N )
5         19           ( A[I]> A[I+1] )                A[2], A[3]
6         21           NOT (A[I] > MAX )               A[2]
7         23           ( A[I + 1] < MIN)               A[3]
8         24           MIN := a[i + 1] ;               A[3]
9         33           I := I + 2;
10        17           I < N
11        19           NOT ( A[I] > A[I+1] )           A[4], A[5]
12        28           ( A[I=1] > MAX )                A[5]
13        29           MAX := A[I+1]                   A[5]
14        30           NOT ( A[I] < MIN )              A[4]
15        33           I := I + 2;
16        17           NOT (I < N)
17        35           NOT (I = N)
18        36           NOT (A[N] > MAX)                A[5]
19        41           WRITELN ( MAX, MIN )
```

Figure 2

Symbolic Trace Slice (Option 2):

STS#	SPL#	Statements	Specific Array Statements
1	14	MIN:=A[1]	
2	15	MAX:=MIN	
3	16	I:=2	
4	17	(I < N)	
5	19	(A[I] > A[I+1]	; A[2], A[3]
6	21	NOT(A[I] > MAX)	; A[2]
9	33	I:=I+2	
10	17	(I < N)	
11	19	NOT (A[I] > A[I+1])	; A[4], A[5]
12	28	(A[I+1] > MAX)	; A[5]
13	29	MAX:=A[I+1]	; A[5]
15	33	I:=I+2	
16	17	NOT (I < N)	
17	35	NOT (I = N)	
18	36	NOT (A[N] > MAX)	; A[5]
19	41	WRITELN (MAX,MIN)	

Figure 3

Option 2 generates, in addition to the computational statements directly affecting MAX, the logic ingredient that went into the traversal of this particular program path. The logic tells us that

1. MAX is initialized to A[1]
2. A[2] > A[3]
3. A[2] ≤ MAX (its current value which is A[1])
4. A[4] ≤ A[5]
5. A[5] > MAX (current value of which is A[1])
6. Terminates when I > N
7. A[5] ≤ MAX (current value is A[5])

The logic looks reasonable (based on our requirements), and we can infer that given an input with the same properties of test case #1, the program is logically correct. An incorrect logic would easily show in the slice. It may be an incorrect predicate, a missing statement, or a statement that should be removed. The location of the fault is facilitated by referring to the sequence program listing numbers.

SYMBOLIC TRACE ANALYZER

Purpose

The main function of the Symbolic Trace Analyzer tool is to perform backward substitution on the predicates of a trace or slice. The end result of this process is the same set of predicates of the given slice/trace, with the difference that all are now *expressed purely in terms of input variables and program constants.* The conjunction of all the predicates defines the program logic that caused the path traversal and the equivalence class associated with the given program path. A program input belongs to a given equivalence class if it satisfies (evaluates to TRUE) all the predicates in the equivalence class. Program inputs belonging to the same equivalence class are all treated the same by the program; i.e., all are subjected to the same logic and computational statements. This suggests that it is sufficient to pick an interior element in an equivalence class to generate the logic and computational statements that all other inputs in the equivalence class share. The generated logic and computational statements are essentially the symbolic trace.

A program input belongs to the boundary of a given equivalence class if at least one of the predicates in the equivalence class was satisfied at its boundary. For example, the predicate (A ≤ B) is satisfied at its boundary if the program input caused actual value of A to be equal to B.

A basic problem of software testing is to verify the correctness of a given equivalence class. An equivalence class is correct if (1) all its boundaries are correct, and (2) there is no missing boundary in the class. A correct equivalence class implies correct logic and computation. Testing the correctness of an equivalence class (hence, absence of boundary errors) is difficult to do (especially for missing boundary errors) if done by pure test case generation and execution. In practice, it may be very difficult to design test cases that belong to the boundaries of an equivalence class. We can avoid this difficult traditional approach by simply generating a symbolic form of the equivalence class, and then comparing the symbolic form with the intended requirements to detect any discrepancies (errors). The symbolic trace analyzer tool supports this alternative test approach. In addition, it highlights the boundaries (expressed in terms of program inputs and constants) of the equivalence class.

Example

Let us use the Symbolic Trace Slice (Option 2) given in the section entitled "Example/Results Interpretation."

1. The predicate statements are located in STS #'s 4, 5, 6, 11, 12, 16, 17, and 18.
2. Start Backward substitution with predicate #4, getting (2 < N). We then continue with predicate #5 and so on, until we finish predicate #18.
3. Figure 4 shows the generated set of backward-substituted predicates:

Predicate STS#	Backward Substituted Predicate
4	(2<N)
5	(A[2] > A[2+1])
6	NOT (A[2] > A[1])
10	((2+2) < N)
11	NOT (A[2+2] > A[2+2+1])
12	(A[2+2+1] > A[1])
16	NOT (((2+2)+2) < N)
17	NOT (((2+2)+2) = N)
18	NOT (A[N] > A[(2+2)+1])

Figure 4

Predicates 4, 10, 16, and 17 imply that N (an integer) should be equal to 5. Any other value of N will violate one or more of these predicates, causing a program boundary error. We may opt to use a text editor and simplify the predicates in the following form:

```
4     (2<N)
5     (A[2] > A[3])
6     NOT (A[2] > A[1])
10    (4<N)
11    NOT(A[4] > A[5])
12    (A[5] > A[1])
16    NOT (6<N)
17    NOT (6=N)
18    NOT (A[N] > A[5])
```

Figure 5

Predicates 5, 6, 11, 12, and 18 collectively show the logic that caused the extraction of MAX. A total of five comparisons were used. At this point we can design test cases that explore the boundaries of the path. These test cases would have one or more of the following properties:

1. A[2] = A[3] or A[2] < A[3]
2. A[2] = A[1] or A[2] > A[1]
3. A[4] = A[5] or A[4] > A[5]
4. A[5] = A[1] or A[5] < A[1]
5. A[N] = A[5] or A[N] > A[5]

This information guides us in designating further test cases that we hope will explore more logic and boundary errors in the program.

STATIC ANALYSIS

The main objective of static analysis (as well as dynamic analysis, discussed in the following section) is to determine that a given computer program has certain properties. To determine whether the program has a certain property, we need first to identify attributes that reflect the quality in question and then to devise an effective method for computing the values of the attributes. Generally speaking, there are two main types of program attributes. The first type consists of those associated with components of a program, whereas the second type consists of those associated with points in the control flow. To be more specific, let us consider the fragment of a flowchart depicted in Figure 6. In this figure, s represents a statement or a program segment, and i and j identify points in the control flow. A[i] and A[j] denote the sets of attributes associated with the corresponding points; B[s] denotes the set of attributes associated with program component s. In general, the value of B[s] (i.e., the attribute of the first type) will not be affected by an execution of s. However, an execution of s may cause a change in the value of A[j] (i.e., the attribute of the second type). Furthermore, a'[j], the new value of A[j] upon an execution of s, can be computed on the basis of A[i], B[s], and the old value of A[j]. To put it formally,

$$A'[j] = f(A[i], B[s], A[j])$$

where f is some function.

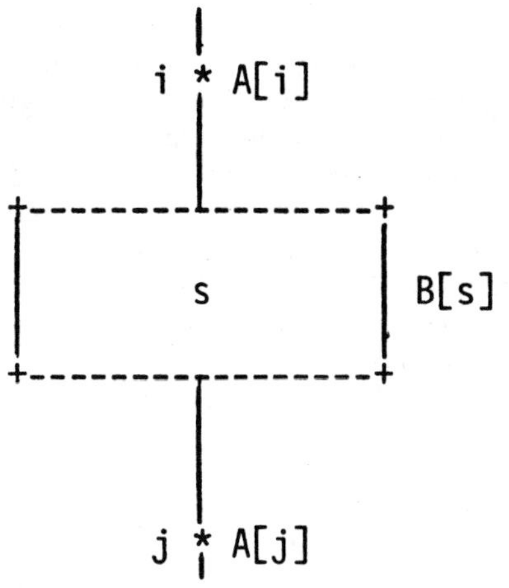

Figure 6

For convenience we shall refer to the attributes associated with program components as B-attributes and the attributes associated with points in control flow as A-attributes. A B-attribute is a local and static attribute whose value can be obtained from the associated program component. The value of a B-attribute will not be altered by an execution. An A-attribute is a global and dynamic attribute whose value can be computed on the basis of local attributes and the attributes associated with other points in control flow. The values of A-attributes may be altered in an execution. In most cases it is the values of A-attributes that reflect on the quality in question.

The above concept clearly suggests a unified approach to the problems of program analysis and validation as outlined below:

1. Identify the A-attributes that directly or indirectly reflect the quality in question and the B-attributes that are required in computing the values of the A-attributes.
2. Identify the relations among the attributes.
3. Use the result of Step 2 to devise an effective algorithm for computing the values of the A-attributes.

The values of the B-attributes and the initial values of the A-attributes are obtained by systematically parsing the program text. These extracted values are then stored in a program database. This generated program database forms the central part of the system and allows implementation of various error type specific test strategies in a single software testing tool system. Thus, the program database allows the user to query program attribute information relevant at any point in the testing process and allows building of other SEQUEL tools without reparsing the program.

DYNAMIC ANALYSIS

SEQUEL performs dynamic analysis on a program through instrumentation.[11] Program instrumentation is the process of inserting additional code statements at proper locations in the program to compute the values of program attributes. The objectives of dynamic analysis are as follows:

1. To generate symbolic trace of the program path traversed by the submitted input
2. To update branch coverage counters (i.e., number of times each program branch is traversed)
3. To detect data flow anomalies in the path traversed

Detection of data flow anomaly by means of instrumentation,[10] a unique feature of this tool system, can be briefly explained as follows.

It is observed that, in program execution, a statement may act on a variable (datum) in three different ways: define, reference, and undefine. A variable is defined in a statement if an execution of the statement assigns a value to the variable. A variable is referenced in a statement if an execution of the statement requires that the value of that variable be obtained from memory. Thus in the assignment statement

$$x := x + y - z$$

y and z are referenced, while x is first referenced and then defined. A variable may become undefined in many circumstances. For example, in a FORTRAN program, the index variable of a DO statement becomes undefined when the RETURN statement is executed. Also, if a program is written in a language that allows block structure, the local variables of a block may become undefined when control exits from the block.

A sequence of actions may be taken on a variable in a program being executed. A reference to a variable constitutes a programming error unless the value of the variable is defined previously. Furthermore, there is no need to define a variable unless it is to be referenced (i.e., its value to be used) later. Therefore, if we find that a variable in a program is (1) undefined and then referenced, (2) defined and then undefined (not referenced), or (3) defined and then defined again, then we may reasonably conclude that a programming error might have been committed. This idea has been used by Fosdick and Osterweil[20] to detect programming errors.

The three types of data flow anomalies mentioned above can be detected by means of static analysis, as suggested by Fosdick and Osterweil.[20] However, the method has some inherent limitations.[12]

The following presents a new method for detecting data flow anomalies by means of program instrumentation. For this purpose, it is useful to regard a variable as being in one of the four possible states during program execution. The four possible states are state U: undefined, state D: defined but not referenced, state R: defined and referenced, and state A: abnormal state. For error detection purposes it is proper to assume that a variable is in the state of being undefined when it is declared implicitly or explicitly. Now if the action taken on this variable is "define," then it will enter the state of being defined but not referenced. Then, depending on the next action taken on this variable, it will assume a different state, as shown in the state transition table (Figure 7).

Note that in Figure 7 d, r, and u stand for "define," "reference," and "undefine," respectively. The three types of data flow anomalies mentioned previously can thus be denoted by ur, du, and dd in this shorthand notation. It is easy to verify

present	next state		
state	action=d	action=r	action=u
U	D	A	U
D	A	R	A
R	D	R	U
A	A	A	A

Figure 7

that, if a sequence of actions taken on the variable contains either ur, du, or dd as a subsequence, the variable will enter state A, which indicated the presence of a data flow anomaly in the execution path. We let the variable remain in state A once that state is entered. Its implication and possible alternatives will be discussed later.

It is obvious from the above discussion that there is no need to compute the sequence of actions taken on a variable along the entire execution path. Instead, we need only to know if the sequence will contain ur, du, or dd as a subsequence. Since such a subsequence will invariably cause the variable to enter state A, all we need to do is to monitor the states assumed by the variable during execution. This can be readily accomplished by means of program instrumentation.

To see how this can be done, let us consider a fragment of a flowchart, shown in Figure 8. Suppose we wish to detect data flow anomalies with respect to variable, say, x. If s is in state q before statement S is executed, and if a is the sequence of actions that will be taken on x by S, then an execution of S will cause x to enter state q′ as depicted above. Given q and a, q′ can be determined on the basis of the state table given previously. However, for the discussions that follow, it is convenient to write

$$q' = f(q, a)$$

where f is called the state transition function and is completely defined by the state table given above. Thus, for example, f(U, d) = D, f(D, u) = A. For the cases where a is a sequence

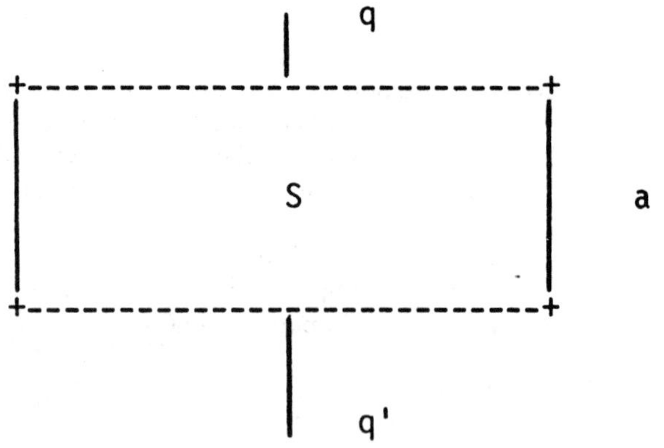

Figure 8

or more than one action, the definition of f can be naturally extended. For example, f(U, dur) = f (f(U, d), ur) = f(D, ur) = f(f)D, u), r) = f(A, r) = A.

Note that in this case a is the B-attribute associated with S, and q and q′ are the A-attributes associated with the respective control points.

Next, we observe that the computation specified by q′ = f(q, a) can be carried out by using a program statement of the form:

q :=f(q, a).

Now if we insert the above statement next to statement S as shown below, then the new state assumed by x will be automatically computed upon an execution. The augmented program

```
                 |
+----------------+----------------+
|                                 |
|                                 |
|      S; q := f(q,  a)           |
|                                 |
|                                 |
+----------------+----------------+
                 |
                 |
```

Figure 9

depicted here is said to have been instrumented with the statement q := f(q, a). This statement should be constructed in such a way that there will be no interference between this inserted statement and the original program. A simple way to accomplish this is to use variables other than those appearing in the program to construct the inserted statement.

In practice, it is more appropriate to instrument the program with procedure calls instead of assignment statements. The use of a procedure allows us to save the identification of an instrument as well as the state assumed by the variable in question. Thus the programmer will be able to tell the exact location as well as the type of data flow anomaly detected. This greatly facilitates anomaly analysis.

CONCLUSION

A tool-based approach for testing and validating software has been described in this paper. The approach specifies error-specific test strategies for path logic/computation and boundary errors. These are the two major error types that remain after the successful compilation of a program. For the application of the approach to be cost effective, the specified test strategies are supported by software tools. This paper also describes the concepts behind the design of these software tools.

The testing methodology and supporting software tools provide a number of unique features:

1. The methodology allows the user to focus attention on exposing software errors in a specific program path belonging to a specific error type.
2. The user can further focus on the sublogic of a generated symbolic path through program path *slicing*. Slicing is a powerful approach for testing and validating the correctness of a program with respect to logic/computation errors.
3. The user can generate the boundary conditions of a given path through predicate backward substitution. This facilitates design of boundary value test cases for exposing path boundary errors.
4. Path data flow analysis is done through program instrumentation.

ISSI has implemented this approach in its SEQUEL project for testing and validating ISO PASCAL programs.

REFERENCES

1. Adrion, W. R., M. A. Brandstad, and J. C. Cherniavsky. "Validation, Verification, and Testing of Computer Software." *ACM Computing Surveys,* 14, (1982), pp. 159–192.
2. Andrews, C. L., and W. R. DeHaan. "RXVP80, The Verification and Validation System for FORTRAN and COBOL." *Proc. SOFTFAIR,* Silver Spring, Md.: IEEE CS Press, 1983, pp. 38–47.
3. Budd, T., R. A. DeMillo, R. A. Lipton, and F. G. Sayward. "The Design of a Prototype Mutation System for Program Testing." *AFIPS, Proceedings of the National Computer Conference,* (Vol. 47), 1978, pp. 623–627.
4. Coweil, W. R., and L. J. Osterweil. "The Toolpack/IST Programming Environment. *Proc. SOFTFAIR,* Silver Spring, Md.: IEEE CS Press, 1983, pp. 326–333.
5. Elmendorf, W. R. "Cause-Effect Graphs in Functional Testing." TR-00.2487, IBM Systems Development Division, Poughkeepsie, N.Y., 1973.
6. Goodenough, J. B., and S. L. Gerhart. "Toward a Theory of Test Data Selection." *IEEE Transactions on Software Engineering,* SE-1 (1975), pp. 156–173.
7. Howden, W. E. "Reliability of the Path Analysis Testing Strategy." *IEEE Transactions on Software Engineering,* SE-2 (1976), pp. 208–215.
8. Howden, W. E. "Functional Program Testing." *IEEE Transactions on Software Engineering,* SE-7 (1980), pp. 162–169.
9. Howden, W. E. "Validation of Scientific Programs." *ACM Computing Surveys,* 14 (1982), pp. 193–228.
10. Huang, J. C. "An Approach to Program Testing." *ACM Computing Surveys,* 7 (1975), pp. 46–58.
11. Huang, J. C. "Program Instrumentation and Software Testing. *Computer,* 11 (1978), pp. 25–32.
12. Huang, J. C. "Detection of Data Flow Anomaly through Program Instrumentation." *IEEE Transactions on Software Engineering,* SE-5 (1979), pp. 226–236.
13. Huang, J. C. "Instrumenting Programs for Symbolic-Trace Generation." *Computer,* 13 (1980), pp. ??
14. Myers, G. J., *The Art of Software Testing.* New York: Wiley-Interscience, 1979.
15. Tischler, R., R. Schaufler, and C. Payne. "Static Analysis of Programs as an Aid to Debugging." *ACM Software Engineering Notes,* 8 (1983), pp. 155–158.
16. Waters, R. C. "A Method for Analyzing Loop Programs." *IEEE Transactions on Software Engineering,* SE-5 (1979), pp. 237–247.
17. Weiser, M. "Program Slicing." *Proceedings of the 5th International Conference on Software Engineering,* March 1981, pp. 439–449.
18. White, L. J., and E. I. Cohen. "A Domain Strategy for Computer Program Testing." *IEEE Transactions on Software Engineering,* SE-6 (1980), pp. 247–257.
19. Yeh, R. T. (ed.). *Current Trends in Programming Methodology. Vol. II: Program Validation.* Englewood Cliffs, N.J.: Prentice-Hall, 1977, pp. 16–43.
20. Fosdick, L. D., and L. J. Osterweil. "Data Floor Analysis in Software Reliability." *ACM Computing Surveys,* 8 (1976), pp. 305–330.

Guidance for test selection based on the cost of errors

by DAVID A. GUSTAFSON
Kansas State University
Manhattan, Kansas

ABSTRACT

A continual problem in the area of software testing is deciding if and where in a program additional testing should be done. Recent work by Cheung has indicated that the relative reliability of the individual nodes in a software flow graph, or modules in a software structure, can be used to guide the testing.[1] This paper attempts to aid this process by suggesting a method for assigning a cost factor to the individual nodes in the software flow graph. This cost can be used to guide selection of additional tests.

INTRODUCTION

A problem in software testing is deciding how much testing is to be done and what tests should be used. Approaches to software testing are many and varied.[2,3] Work in the area of reliability is giving guidance on how many tests should be done.[4] Test coverage measures give guidance on both how many tests to run and on what to test.[5] Functional testing proposes that test cases are to be selected for each function in the software specification.[6–8] Some methodologies combine all of these approaches.[9] However, these approaches are all based on the idea that for the chosen criterion, all the instances should be tested equally, whether the criterion is the testing of statements, decisions, branches, paths, functions, and so forth. That is, these approaches consider all errors, decisions, functions, etc. to be equally serious and important.

This equality is not always a reasonable assumption. Some errors are more probable than others because the necessary input conditions are more likely to occur. Some errors are more serious because their effects are more serious. The testing effort should concentrate on the more serious and more common errors.

As an example, consider a system designed to train people in recognizing equilateral triangles from triangles that are close to being equilateral. A set of triangles could be presented on a visual display, the trainee could be instructed to pick which one is equilateral, and the system could respond with the type of triangle that was picked. Part of the software could be a simple routine to determine the type of the triangle that was picked. The critical errors for this routine are (1) the triangle being incorrectly classified as equilateral and (2) the triangle being incorrectly classified as not equilateral. The most frequent data will probably be equilateral triangles. Those cases that are not triangles may be very rare or nonexistent. Intuitively, more emphasis should be placed on verifying that triangles are classified correctly than on whether they are equilateral or not.

Work by Cheung has indicated that some nodes in the flow graph are more critical than others to correct behavior of the program.[1] His analysis is based on the user profile of transitions between the nodes or modules. Using this empirically derived profile and a Markov model of the transitions between the nodes, he identifies which nodes are more critical. However, he does not include any parameters for the criticality of the possible errors.

There are many times that certain errors (e.g., incorrectly identifying a triangle as equilateral) are much more serious than other errors (e.g., incorrectly identifying a scalene triangle as isosceles). The model proposed in this article is based on the estimated criticality of possible errors and the estimated frequency of occurrence of cases. An estimate is calculated for the criticality of the decisions and computations made at each node in the flow graph.

ASSIGNING COSTS

The errors that occur in programs can be classified as domain errors or computational errors.[7] Domain errors are those where an incorrect decision causes a particular datapoint to be treated as a different type. That is, the inputs are considered to be from the wrong domain. The other type of error is called a computational error. That is, the computation in a particular domain is incorrect. For example, the square root may be incorrectly calculated.

All errors can be considered as one of these two types. For any datapoint (i.e., a point in the domain) a certain path through the program is executed and computations unrelated to control decisions may be done. A datapoint either follows the correct execution path or it does not (a *domain error* may occur). The noncontrol computations done on the actual execution path are either correct or incorrect (a *computation error* may occur). Although these two error categories are large, they seem to be inclusive. Other error classification schemes are valuable for other uses, but these two categories are of interest for this model. Therefore, we will consider them to be either domain or computational errors.

A number of complex situations can arise. First, both types of errors can occur for one datapoint. Second, an incorrect computation may seem to be correct (e.g., $x + 2$ instead of $2*x$ for the value $x = 2$). Finally, a datapoint may execute an incorrect path but later rejoin the correct execution path. All of these situations are considered errors and the differences are not significant in the estimations done in this paper.

Expected costs can be assigned to these two kinds of errors. The expected cost of a potential domain error is the cost of a domain error multiplied by the probability of that input case occurring. The expected cost of a potential computation error is the cost of a computation error multiplied by the probability of that computation being done.

In the triangle example, we may be able to estimate the costs of actual errors. Let us assume that two of the errors have costs associated with them. These costs may be based on the estimate of the amount of additional training necessary for the trainee to develop the necessary skill level after being misled by an incorrect answer. Assume that incorrect identification of a nonequilateral triangle as equilateral might require $200 of additional training and an incorrect typing of an equilateral triangle as nonequilateral might cost $100.

If we also knew the probability of actual errors occurring, we could calculate the expected cost of the errors. In our example, if we knew an actual frequency of these two errors (e.g., one/day and two/week), we could calculate the actual costs of these errors ($1000/week and $200/week, respectively). However, without knowledge of the actual error frequency, we can only calculate the relative expected costs of potential errors and the criticality of individual nodes.

The relative expected cost of a potential error is the estimated cost of that particular error multiplied by the relative frequency of datapoints in which that error is possible. A potential error in a commonly occurring type of data would have a higher expected cost than an error in a rarely occurring type of data. The relative expected cost is the estimated cost of a particular type of error times the relative frequency of occurrence of that type of data. In our example, the trainees might select equilateral triangles 80% of the time and other triangles 18% of the time (2% might be nontriangles). Thus, the relative expected costs would be $36 for the nonequilateral and $80 for the equilateral. These costs are relative since the frequencies are relative.

We will assume that the user can assign costs such as these to the domain errors. That is, the user must give a cost for an outcome of type i when the correct outcome is type j. Denote these costs by Cij. Cij represents the cost of an incorrect answer of type i when the correct answer was type j. For our example, Cqe = Cqi = Cqr = Cqa = Cqo = $200, and Ceq = Ciq = Crq = Caq = Coq = $100, and every other Cij is zero. Note that q stands for equilateral, i for isosceles, r for right scalene, o for obtuse scalene, a for acute scalene, and e for error (nontriangle).

The user also must estimate the cost of computation errors. That is, the cost of an incorrect calculation must be specified. Cii will denote the computation error for type i. In the triangle example, there are no nondecision computations and so Caa = Cqq = Crr = Cee = Cii = Coo = 0.

In addition, the user must be able to assign the relative frequencies of the datapoints. In the triangle example, 80% were equilateral (i.e., fq = .8), 18% were nonequilateral (assume fi = fa = fo = fr = .045), and 2% were not triangles (i.e., fe = .02).

These values will be used to analyze the criticality of the parts of the program. The analysis will be done on the standard flow graph of the program. In the flow graph, nodes stand for branch-free sections of code. The arcs stand for possible execution paths between these branch-free sections of code. Each type can be assigned to at least one node in the flow-graph. This node is where the datapoint is identified as belonging to that type. In the triangle example, each terminal node is associated with a particular type of triangle. In these nodes, the name of the particular type of triangle is returned to the calling program. Additionally, any node that does nondecision computations has particular types of datapoints associated with that node.

> Fundamental Rule: The criticality of errors in a node is related to the sum of the expected cost of potential errors in the computations done in that node plus the increase in successor nodes of the expected cost of potential domain errors due to decisions in that node.

The fundamental rule states the criticality of a node or the potential cost of errors in a node is related to two types of errors: errors in the computations done in that node and errors in the decisions made in that node. The expected cost of potential computation errors is directly related to the activities of a node. The expected cost of potential domain errors in a node is the result of decisions made in predecessor nodes. Thus, the increase in this expected cost is related to the criticality of the node. The fundamental rule, besides being intuitively correct, allows for the consistent and logical propagation of the relative expected costs throughout the flow graph.

ASSIGNING DOMAIN COSTS TO NODES

The relative expected cost of the potential domain errors can be assigned to the nodes in the flow graph. This cost is interpreted as the expected cost of incorrectly executing that node.

> Rule 1: The expected cost of potential domain errors in a terminal node is the expected cost of incorrectly being in that node.

The expected cost of incorrectly being in a terminal node that has type i datapoints assigned to it is the summation for all j of Cij*fj (i<>j). Thus, these Cij*fj will be put in the cost set of that node. The expected cost is the sum of the terms in the cost set. Thus, every terminal node in the flow graph can be given an expected cost of potential domain error.

> Rule 2: The expected cost of potential domain errors in a nonterminal node is the sum of the expected costs of potential domain errors of the successor nodes minus the terms related to the decisions made in the node.

The cost of a nonterminal node can be calculated as follows:

1. Add the cost set of each successor node
2. Subtract any pairs of terms Cij*fj and Cji*fi where both are in the cost set

Note that the criticality of errors is related to the increase in the expected cost of domain errors.

> Rule 2a: The expected cost of the potential domain errors of the nodes in a cycle is the sum of the expected costs of potential domain error of the successor nodes for all nodes in the cycle minus the terms related to all decisions made in the cycle.

This rule means that all nodes in a cycle (loop) have the same expected cost of potential domain error. This expected cost is the same because all nodes in the loop are potentially executed on each iteration. The criticality of the nodes in a loop may not be the same because of the expected costs of the successor nodes of each node in the loop.

The cost of a nonterminal node in a cycle can be calculated as follows:

1. Add all terms Cij*fj from the cost sets of the successor nodes of nodes in the cycle.
2. Subtract all pairs of terms Cij*fj where both are in the cost set

ASSIGNING COSTS OF COMPUTATION ERRORS

The expected cost of a computation error in a terminal node is the product Cii*fi for types i assigned to the node. The expected cost of a potential computation error in a non-terminal node that is involved in computations is the product of Cii and fi for all types i that are related to that node.

ASSIGNING CRITICALITY TO NODES

The criticality of a node is the sum of the increase in the expected cost of domain errors and the expected cost of computation error for all computations done in the node.

AN EXAMPLE

Figure 1 is the flow graph of the triangle problem. The task is to identify the type of triangle given the lengths of the three sides. The nodes are labeled by number to the left of each node. There are no computations involved in this problem. The only possible errors are domain errors. Table I gives the expressions for the expected costs of potential domain errors for each of the nodes. The cases are referred to by letter instead of by number. For example, Coe is the cost of identifying the triangle as obtuse when it should have been an error case. The frequency of occurrence of the cases is denoted by fi. For example, fa is the expected frequency of acute triangles. Table I shows the values of the criticality if all of the Cij are 1 and all frequencies are equal. Also indicated are the values of the expected costs and criticalities if the Cij and frequencies had the values from the example. Using the sample expected costs and relative frequencies gives a different ranking for the criticality of the nodes. Although nodes 3 and 1 are still ranked number one and two, node 4 is now ranked three and at almost the same ranking as node 1. This would indicate that much more extensive testing should be done on nodes 3, 1, and 4.

Looking at the original flow graph, this recommendation can be converted to a description of the important types of test data. The most critical node is node 3, which involves a decision about whether two of the lengths are equal. Thus, the most important type of test case involves two of the lengths being equal or close to equal.

The second most critical node is node 1. This node tests whether or not the three lengths are properly ordered. Thus the second most important type of test case involves three sides being improperly ordered. Finally, the third most critical node involves a decision about whether all three of the sides are equal or close to equal.

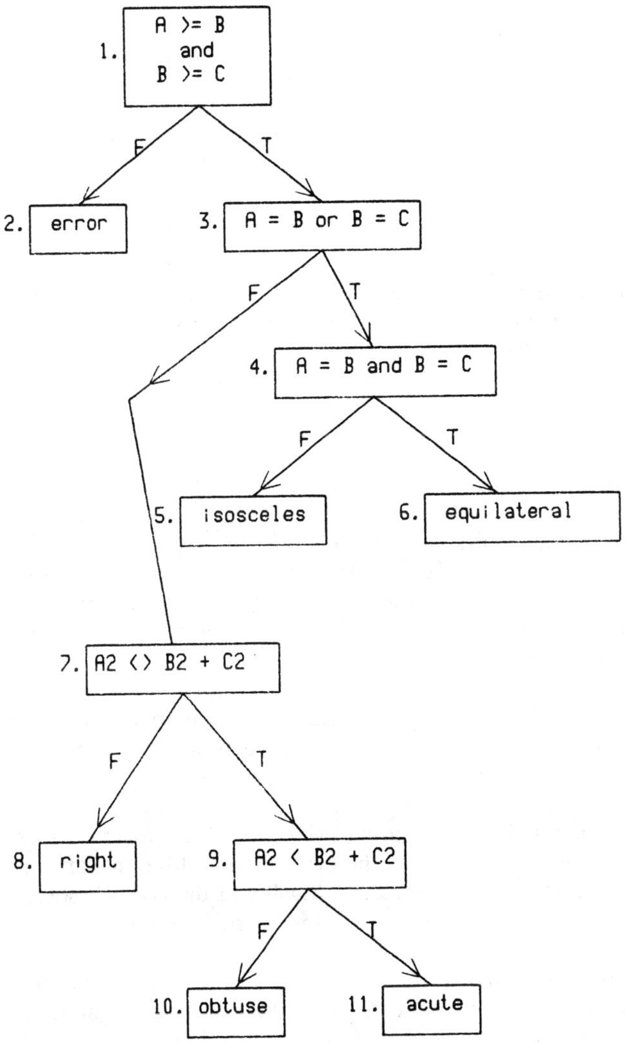

Figure 1—The triangle example

Table I—The triangle example

Expected Costs of Potential Domain Errors

Node 10 : Coe*fe + Coi*fi + Coq*fq + Cor*fr + Coa*fa

Node 11 : Cae*fe + Cai*fi + Caq*fq + Car*fr + Cao*fo

Node 9 : (Coe + Cae)*fe + (Cai + Coi)*fi +(Coq + Caq)*fq + (Cor + Car)*fr

Node 8 : Cre*fe + Cri*fi + Crq*fq + Cro*fo + Cra*fa

Node 7 : (Coe + Cae + Cre)*fe + (Cai + Coi + Cri)*fi + (Coq + Caq + Crq)*fq

Node 6 : Cqe*fe + Cqi*fi + Cqr*fr + Cqo*fo + Cqa*fa

Node 5 : Cie*fe + Ciq*fq + Cir*fr + Cio*fo + Cia*fa

Node 4 : (Cqe + Cie)*fe + (Cqr + Cir)*fr + (Cqo +Cio)*fo + (Cqa+Cia)*fa

Node 3 : (Cqe + Cie + Coe + Cae + Cre)*fe

Node 2 : Ceo*fo + Cei*fi + Ceq*fq + Cer*fr + Cea*fa

Node 1 : none

	all Cij = 1		Cij different	
Node	Expected	Criticality	Expected	Criticality
1	0	10	0	89
2	5	0	80	0
3	5	12	9	267
4	8	2	36	84
5	5	0	80	0
6	5	0	40	0
7	9	4	240	0
8	5	0	80	0
9	8	2	160	0
10	5	0	80	0
11	5	0	80	0

A possible testing approach would be to select cases of these three critical types in proportion to the criticality of those nodes, for example, three times as many cases of type one (two sides equal or almost equal) as of type two (sides ordered wrong) or type three (all sides equal or almost equal). Additional tests would be used to achieve C1 coverage of the program.[5] This approach would emphasize testing for the errors that would be more costly.

ANOTHER EXAMPLE

Figure 1 has the flow graph of a program with a loop. The terminal nodes contain a letter that represents the proper case for that node. The terminal nodes also have potential computation errors. The cost of a potential computation error is represented by Cii for case i. The expressions for expected cost of potential domain errors are shown in Table II. Note that the expressions for the three nodes in the cycle are the same. The second part of Table II shows the numeric values for the expected cost of potential domain errors, the expected cost of potential computation errors, and the potential cost for each node. These were calculated with the Cij all equal to one. Note that the potential cost of the three nodes (2, 4, and 6) in the cycle is not identical.

IMPLEMENTATION

An implementation of this algorithm was written in PASCAL. The implementation is approximately 300 lines long. A two-dimensional array is used to represent the expression for the expected cost at a node. The combining and reduction operations involve logical and transform operations on the arrays. Documentation on the implementation is available from the author.

Table II—Example with looping

Expected Costs of Potential Domain Errors

```
Node 11 : Cea*fa + Ceb*fb + Cec*fc + Ced*fd + Cef*ff

Node 12 : Cfa*fa + Cfb*fb + Cfc*fc + Cfd*fd + Cfe*fe

Node 10 : (Cea+Cfa)*fa + (Ceb+Cfb)*fb + (Cec+Cfc)*fc
      + (Ced+Cfd)*fd

Node 8 : Cca*fa + Ccb*fb + Ccd*fd + Cce*fe + Ccf*ff

Node 9 : Cda*fa + Cdb*fb + Cdc*fc + Cde*fe + Cdf*ff

Node 7 : Cba*fa + Cbc*fc + Cbd*fd + Cbe*fe + Cbf*ff

Node 5 : (Cca+Cda)*fa + (Ccb+Cdb)*fb + (Cce+Cde)*fe
      + (Ccf+Cdf)*ff

Node 6 = Node 4 = Node 2 :(Cba + Cca + Cda + Cea + Cfa)*fa

Node 3 : Cab*fb + Cac*fc + Cad*fd + Cae*fe + Cef*ff

Node 1 : none
```

Values when all the Cij are equal to one

Nodes	Expected Domain	Expected Computation	Criticality
1	0	0	10
2	5	0	14
3	5	1	1
4	11	0	5
5	8	0	2
6	11	0	2
7	5	1	1
8	5	1	1
9	5	1	1
10	8	0	2
11	5	1	1
12	5	1	1

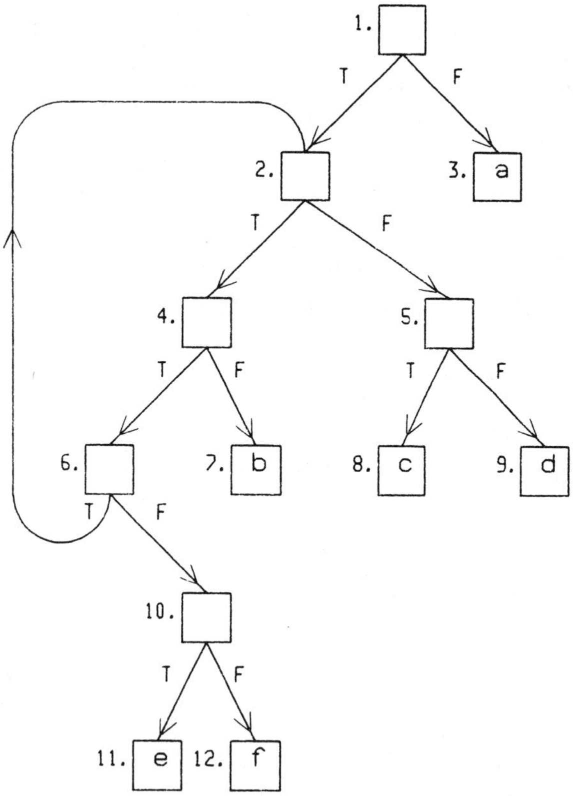

Figure 2—Example with looping

CONCLUSION

This model shows that the individual nodes in a flow graph can be analyzed for criticality using estimated costs of errors and estimated distribution of input cases. This analysis will be useful in deciding which nodes should be tested more thoroughly.

Once the criticality of each of the nodes in a flow graph is established, the testing effort can be distributed in proportion to the criticality of each node. For each node, the activities and decisions in that node will suggest what tests should be done for that node. The resulting sets of tests should evaluate the program in relation to the criticality of the possible errors.

This model also allows the evaluation of different software structures based on how the criticality of the nodes is spread throughout the flow graph. A flow graph in which the potential cost of individual nodes is minimized would seem to be preferable. Any node that has a very high potential cost should be suspect and a structure that causes a few nodes to have a high potential cost should be avoided.

This model is an initial attempt at approaching the problem

of associating input distributions and knowledge of differences in the seriousness of errors with the criticality of nodes and the evaluation of software structures. Future research will attempt to refine this model.

REFERENCES

1. Cheung, R. C. "A User-Oriented Software Reliability Model." *IEEE Transactions on Software Engineering,* 6 (1980), pp. 118–125.
2. Adrion, W. R., M. A. Branstad, and J. C. Cherniavsky. "Validation, Verification, and Testing of Computer Software." *Computing Surveys,* 14 (1982), pp. 159–192.
3. Schindler, M. "Software Testing—A Scarce Art Struggles to Become a Science." *Electronic Design,* 30 (1982), pp. 85–102.
4. Thompson, W. E., and P. O. Chelson. "Software Reliability Testing for Embedded Computer Systems." *Workshop on Quantitative Software Models* (1979). New York: IEEE, 1979, pp. 201–208.
5. Software Research Associates. Summary of Software Testing Measures, Technical Note TN-843/2, May 1981. San Francisco: Software Research Associates, 1981.
6. Goodenough, J. B., and S. L. Gerhart. "Toward a Theory of Test Data Selections." *IEEE Transactions on Software Engineering,* 2 (1976), pp. 156–173.
7. Howden, W. E. "Reliability of the Path Analysis Strategy." *IEEE Transactions on Software Engineering,* 2 (1976), pp. 38–45.
8. Howden, W. E. "Functional Testing and Design Abstractions." *Journal of Systems and Software,* 1 (1980), pp. 307–313.
9. Geiger, W., L. Gmeiner, H. Trauboth, and U. Voges. "Program Testing Techniques for Nuclear Reactor Protection Systems." *Computer,* 12 (1979), pp. 10–18.

Computer graphics—Coming of age

Alan Paller, Track Chair

During 1983 and 1984, computer graphics emerged from the shadows and became omnipresent. More than 80% of the personal computers being purchased in 1984 include some form of graphics capability. A similar percentage of the information centers at large corporations are installing new graphics software tools. Hardly any office automation system without a graphics component is being announced. Thousands of graphics designers are switching from manual to automated methods. Engineers in ever larger numbers are using computer graphics work stations for design and drafting. Even word processors are gaining computer graphics capability.

On the entertainment front, computer animation is playing an increasingly large role in successes such as the film "Star Wars." Simultaneously, video games have brought entertainment-oriented computer graphics into more than three million homes in America. Two of the NCC sessions cover state-of-the-art technology and applications in the very visible entertainment and animation areas. The remainder of the NCC '84 graphics track focuses on the fastest-growing segment and the one that directly affects the most computer users: management and business graphics. It offers a state-of-the-art overview of the hardware and software and looks ahead at the coming year.

Four major classes of graphics products are covered in the sessions: displays, work stations, hard copy output devices, and software. The computer graphics display of 1984 can best be thought of as a traditional alphanumeric display in which every dot (or pixel) on the screen is addressable. Pictures with high levels of detail require much more memory than do pictures with less. Until 1982, terminals that could display more than 1 million pixels (1000-by-1000 resolution) cost more than $25,000. However, by 1984, those terminals had dropped in price to under $10,000; and for slightly more a buyer could have a terminal with extraordinary local intelligence for panning and zooming. Simultaneously, graphics terminals with lower resolutions—e.g., those with 300-by-400 addressable pixels—were dropping radically in price. Today it is common to find black-and-white graphics terminals at less than $1,000, and color graphics terminals at less than $3,000. During this year, even higher resolution terminals (up to 2000 by 2000) will begin to appear, first in black and white and later in color.

The session entitled "Graphics on Microcomputers" discusses the stand-alone graphics work stations that are a new phenomenon created by the low-cost microprocessor. These work stations come in two varieties: the personal computer variety and the high-performance professional work stations. Graphics on personal computers are generally low resolution. They appear to be better than they are when the screens are very small. The professional work stations, on the other hand, have higher resolution and more computer power than the PCs and are used in high-payoff applications, such as slide production and scientific data analysis. Today there is a larger price premium on the professional work stations, but during this year more powerful personal computers will begin to erode the difference between professional work stations and personal computer graphics systems.

The session entitled "Experts Look at the Future" is concerned in part with new developments in hard-copy paper charts, overhead transparencies, and 35-mm slides. New technology is revolutionizing all three. The digital plotter has been the workhorse of today's management graphics systems; but it is being challenged by inkjet printers, which provide more color more quickly on both paper and transparency. At the same time, new laser printers are cutting production time for charts from 10 minutes to 10 seconds. On personal computers, low-cost plotters and inkjet printers are adding color output, while higher-resolution matrix printers (200 dots per inch) are making black-and-white output more presentable.

The 35-mm slide production market is a fast-growing application of computer graphics because computers cut the cost of slides from $35 to $7 each. New digital film recorders have brought the price of high-quality slidemaking equipment to $25,000. Later this year, even newer systems promise price reductions to $10,000 with quality similar to the output of equipment that cost $200,000 only two years ago. The same type of price erosion is occurring in laser printers: prices are expected to be in the $5,000-to-$10,000 range by 1985.

Nearly every session will have a software component, because no computer graphics can be produced without it. The graphics software industry has blossomed into a $100 million business, primarily for mainframes and minicomputers. Personal computer graphics software is also becoming important, but the vast majority is imbedded in integrated systems.

The largest vendors of graphics software have made major advances in the past year, including the following:

—New software for integrating text and graphics to produce technical documentation.
—A new standard for user friendliness.
—New database linkages.
—Predesigned chartbooks.
—Layout intelligence that automatically designs the best-looking chart for the target audience.

Application graphics software is another growth area, with both project management graphics and executive chartbook systems gaining broad acceptance.

Graphics software standards have finally arrived after seven years of effort. One session, entitled "Emerging Standards," will focus on these new developments.

During the coming year, personal computer graphics packages will continue to evolve into more powerful tools. And at the same time, the much larger development budgets of the mainframe graphics vendors will increase the distance between personal computer graphics amd mainframe graphics software capabilities. Late in the year, however, the gulf between mainframes and micros will close as new desktop computers are announced that will run the software that works only on mainframes today.

New management techniques for computer graphics in large corporations will be the focus of the session called "Graphics in the Information Center." The principal keys to effective management that pioneering users of computer graphics have found are as follows:

1. Give all computer users access to computer graphics through shared plotters, laser printers, and film recorders.
2. Provide links to databases and to old application programs.
3. Offer chartbooks as the principal user interface.
4. Offffer project management software.
5. Offer both microcomputer graphics and mainframe graphics.
6. Provide software that offers user friendliness, extreme quality and flexibility, and device independence.
7. Start with high-payoff applications for senior management.

The explosive growth being experienced by the computer graphics industry can be attributed in part to the price performance improvements of hardware and software. But equally important to this growth is the new realization that graphics work, that they are cost effective, and that the people who bring computer graphics into organizations are making computers more useful to management and therefore more valuable to the organization as a whole.

Personal computers

Jean Yates, Track Chair

More than three million personal computers will be sold in 1984 to an increasingly segmented market. There are handheld, laptop, desktop, stand-alone, networked, and supermicro personal computers. You can buy personal computers for office workers, lab technicians, data processing managers, financial planners, and people with myriad other job descriptions. Applications software for personal computers runs the gamut of agricultural to zoological. The Personal Computing track attempts to cover this multifaceted market, its key issues, and new product innovations.

1984 may go down as a year of the multiuser computer, with AT&T introducing computers from micro to mainframe; but the greatest interest is still at the personal computer level. UNIX has not achieved much acceptance on personal computers in the past, but AT&T's involvement may change things. UNIX provides a vital micro-to-mainframe link for companies connecting their personal computers to corporate mainframe equipment. The session entitled "Multi-User and Networked Personal Computers" explores this subject in depth.

The portable market has fragmented into several submarkets, including the laptop, the handheld, and the original portable: the "luggable." Apple and IBM's announcements of portables may be reducing "luggable" to an industry requirement for personal computers, not an option. More truly portable products like the Tandy 100 are gaining from new software developed for their special markets. The session "Portable Computers and their Software" reviews the latest in portables and the software being developed especially for them.

"Frontiers in Personal Computing: The User Interface" focuses on a number of recent innovations in user interfaces. The user interface continues to be a major industry issue as frustrated users try to master the intricacies of operating systems and applications, all of which use different commands. Along with menus and multiple windows, innovative devices for easing the user interface problem include the "mouse," touch-sensitive screens, softkeys, voice, and touch pads.

What will the next generation of personal computers look like? Networking and friendly user interfaces are a part of the picture. IBM's rumored "Popcorn" is said to use a 286 microprocessor. Apple's MAC is certainly a pioneer in the 32-bit, easy-to-use personal computer sweepstakes. AT&T's entry is sure to stir interest. Voice/data can't be far behind AT&T's current computer offerings. "Next Generation PCs" reviews the latest developments and presents the views of industry experts on what's coming next.

Software distribution and marketing continue to evolve, but constrained distribution channels have limited the mass appeal of some software products. New approaches to software distribution and design are described in various sessions of the Personal Computing track, with various iconoclasts describing their ideas. A particularly important issue is the prospect of a universal standard, a topic to which a session by this name has been devoted.

Integrated operating environments are packages in which all applications use the same data formats and are designed to work with each other. This is one of the most exciting trends in the standardization arena. The session "Data Management in Integrated Operating Environments" explores the key issues here and presents the reactions of those with experience in using these environments.

As the market becomes more complicated, forecast data and industry analysis become more important for those who want to stay well informed. Key industry analysts share their sometimes controversial, always interesting ideas in "The Personal Computer Industry: The Experts Forecast the Future."

The Personal Computing track gives computer users, data processing professionals, computer industry members, and educators an overview of the state of the personal computer and in-depth analyses of areas of special interest.

Will notebook computers revolutionize computer usage?

by DAVID H. AHL
Creative Computing Magazine
Morris Plains, New Jersey

ABSTRACT

Will notebook computers change patterns of computer usage? Depending on your point of view, you might give an answer of yes, no, or maybe. Some have concluded that most executives won't compute, now or ever, and for some good reasons. On the other hand, current users and manufacturers of computers are firmly convinced that every business person in the world will use a computer eventually.

The notebook computer, a natural development in the continual downsizing of computers, is more than just the next step in the evolutionary chain. For the first time, a computer is available that can truly be used anywhere. Hence, the effect of the notebook computer or the way people use computers is likely to be great.

Will notebook computers revolutionize computer usage? Depending on your point of view, you might give an answer of yes, no, or maybe. In an article in *Fortune* titled, "Why Executives Don't Compute," Walter Kiechel concludes that most executives won't compute, now or ever, and for some good reasons. On the other hand, many computer manufacturers, and many users too, are firmly convinced that every business person in the world will eventually use a computer.

The notebook computer, a natural development in the continual downsizing of computers, is more than just the next step in the evolutionary chain. Why? Because, for the first time, a computer is available that can truly be used anywhere. It is no more obtrusive than a pad of paper or a portable dictation unit. Hence, the effect of the notebook computer on the way people use computers is likely to be much greater than was originally expected.

Before looking at the likely effect of notebook computers, it is important to understand the notebook computer itself and existing patterns of computer usage among business users.

NOTEBOOK COMPUTERS

In a sense there are three, or possibly four, categories of portable computer. There is the group that first took the name portable—the Osborne, Kaypro, or Compaq type of machine. These sewing-machine-sized machines are perhaps more aptly termed transportables because they are not truly portable. Most weigh more than 20 pounds and you would not want one resting on your lap for an extended period of time. Their appeal for most users is something other than portability.

At the other end of the spectrum are pocket computers such as the Sharp PC-1500, Casio FX-700P, and Radio Shack PC-1, 2, and 3. These are capable little units for computational applications, but are rather limited for general-purpose computing.

Between these two extremes lie the notebook computers. Most of them have a keyboard that is full size, or nearly so. Their displays range from 1 to 16 lines, and are usually LCD. They are truly portable and are powered by batteries.

THE SAME AND DIFFERENT

All of the notebook computers available as of this writing—19 in total—are similar in some ways, but quite different in others. All are portable, although 1½ pounds (HP 75C) are a great deal more portable than 11 pounds (Sharp PC-5000). The majority of the machines weigh between 3 and 6 pounds and are about the size of a thick three-ring binder. In general, size and weight are proportional to capability and features, but this is not universally true.

All but one notebook computer use a liquid crystal display (LCD), and several have the ability to drive a CRT monitor as well. The size of the displays ranges from one line of 31 characters (impossible for text editing) to 16 lines of 80 characters (nearly as many characters as a typical monitor). Some have limited graphics capabilities as well.

Most notebook computers use an 8-bit mpu and have performance on a par with their 8-bit desktop counterparts. The 16-bit machines are the speed demons, with computational speeds about six times faster than the 8-bit ones.

The majority of notebook computers come with 16K or more of memory, and two come with 128K. The experience of early users indicates that extra memory, both internal and external, is a good investment. External memory takes many forms. A tape cassette is most common and least versatile. External memory cartridges (CMOS or bubble) are much handier and faster. Other approaches, each used by one manufacturer, are a 3″ micro floppy, external wafertape, and magnetic card.

Most notebook computers use a proprietary operating system, although in most cases it is not an operating system at all but just a traffic cop for directing information flow. Several of the full-function systems use a standard operating system such as CP/M or MS-DOS. All but one of the machines speak Basic, mostly Microsoft; many have communications capabilities; and several have word-processing and spreadsheet packages available.

On the machines with standard operating systems, some off-the-shelf software packages can often be loaded through the RS-232 port and will run with minor modifications. Many of the manufacturers are encouraging development of software by third-party vendors, while others, taking a rather shortsighted view, are not. Nevertheless, it appears that the big three (Basic, word processing, and communications) will be available for most machines, with spreadsheets and database packages not far behind.

As with any kind of computer, manufacturers make many different tradeoffs. Size versus extra features is an obvious tradeoff—one just can't fit a large display, modem, and printer in a package the size of a paperback novel. Price is a tradeoff against nearly everything—speed, memory capacity, features, and technical sophistication.

So, that is the hardware. Now let us take a look at computer usage before the notebook computer era.

WHY EXECUTIVES DON'T COMPUTE

Who are the users of personal computers in the business world? They are certainly not the cadre of data processing professionals, most of whom have their hands full tending their data-gobbling mainframes. The typical user is a middle manager in a job requiring a great deal of calculating (finance, engineering, research). Although the computer is a marvelous word-processing tool, the typical manager still leaves that function to a secretary. Except among professional writers, word processing is vastly underutilized.

In the ranks of top management, the use of computers is even less widespread. A few trendy executives have purchased their own machines, but for the most part, computers are rarely found in executive suites. Those executives who use them have motivation similar to many middle-management users: their jobs require a great deal of calculating and analyzing. Some other executives, in the words of Prof. John Kotter of the Harvard Business School, "get off on technology." And a third group are into the quantitative school of management and want to keep their hands on the numbers, both at the office and at home.

For the most part, companies are enthusiastic about the use of personal computers. John Bennett, director of data processing at United Technologies, says of executives who use computers at home, "I think we're getting an extra hour from them at night after dinner."

Despite this enthusiasm, the use of the computer, particularly at the top ranks, is very low. The reasons for this are many. First is simply the fear of technology—the fear of typing, the fear of loading a disk wrong, the fear of losing something, the fear of not being able to get something out when you need it, and the fear of not being able to understand the machine.

There are other related fears—the fear of not being able to use effectively the information produced by the computer, and conversely, the fear that the computer will somehow diminish the need for the skills of the executive.

Although Walter Kiechel thinks these fears are overblown, he nevertheless admits to their existence. Kiechel says, "The most important factor keeping the computer out of most executive offices is the realization, sometimes barely conscious, on the part of managers that this technological wonder has, as yet, little to offer them. The nature of their work—in a word, unstructured—is such that it's not particularly susceptible to computerization."

Kotter's observations seem to confirm this view: "Much of the information that executives deal with is a form of power. Executives know that it is written down somewhere, they can't restrict access to it."

The amount of training time needed to use a computer effectively is discouraging to some. Estimates in excess of 100 hours are not uncommon; the typical executive frequently judges, rightly so, that he just doesn't have a block of time available to devote to something of possibly marginal benefit.

It is easy to become awed by the enormous sales gains posted by the personal computer industry and to believe that every business person in the world must have one. Today, this situation is far from reality, but there is good reason to believe that the situation will change dramatically in the next few years.

A REVOLUTION IN THE MAKING

The reasons that executives are not using computers are certainly valid—at least if we consider a desktop personal computer or terminal hooked into the company mainframe. But let us weigh the use of a notebook computer against these same objections.

Since the computer is small enough to take home easily, it is much easier to devote the hours of learning necessary to make effective use of it. And as learning takes place, confidence builds and technophobia evaporates. The user can prove to himself that the fears—of typing, of doing things wrong, of not being able to get needed data out, of privacy—are groundless once he is familiar with the machine.

Moreover, the likelihood is high that the notebook computer user will discover for himself what has propelled the computer into such a position of importance today: that computer applications are limited only by the imagination of the user. The importance of this cannot be overstressed.

Frequently, the computer is likened to a tool such as a hammer or a lathe. If you wish to make the point that a computer is a tool and not an end in itself, the hammer analogy is a good one—but it doesn't go far enough. Alan Kay, originator of the Smalltalk language, goes one step further by saying that the computer is the medium and the software makes it into a tool—any tool, with the proper software. That is a better analogy, but it still does not convey the most important idea of all—that the computer is a mind-extending tool, the first that man has ever had.

The jobs that the computer has been called upon to do are related to who was doing the calling. The first computers were developed for the army to calculate projectile trajectories. This was expanded to other mathematically related applications. Later, as they were merged with tab card machines, computers started to perform tab card functions—census counting and low-level financial calculations.

Word processing didn't come until much later. Indeed the first widespread word-processing package on a microcomputer, Electric Pencil, was written by a Hollywood screen editor because he needed it. Likewise, the first spreadsheet, VisiCalc, was written by a Harvard Business School student because he needed it.

Perhaps today the compter has little to offer an executive, but after a few thousand are in the hands of executives, it seems likely that some of these executives are going to "need" something and find the computer can provide it.

Beyond being able to go home with an executive, notebook computers have many other unique advantages. They can truly go anywhere—to the library with a student, to the client with a salesman, or to the story with a reporter. A notebook computer is more useful than a notebook or pocket tape recorder because it not only encourages one to jot down ideas, but allows ideas to be immediately integrated with previous ones, i.e., filed in the right place. There is no delay while a note is typed by a secretary and the appropriate file dug out.

Notebook computers are full-function machines with enough memory to work on real-world problems and with enough external storage to enable many programs to be carried around simultaneously. The internal memory is nonvolatile so it is difficult to make a fatal error. Notebook computers communicate easily—some have built-in modems—with other personal computers, with company mainframes, and with public data bases.

Certainly the continuing avalanche of technological innovations will increase the use of computers in all parts of society. Networks will make communication with others much easier, and the use of artificial intelligence techniques will make communication with the machine itself easier. Voice recognition and speech synthesis are on the way. But important as these developments are, it was the notebook computer itself that bridged the gap of widespread accessibility.

The stories of the effects of notebook computers verge on folk legends. *Newsday,* a Long Island newspaper, ordered a small number of machines for some of its reporters. Within a few weeks the clamoring of the others became a roar, and the paper had to equip every reporter and editor with one. An article about notebook computers in the January 1984 issue of *Creative Computing* tied up the incoming phone lines at one manufacturer so that they had to put extra people on to handle the calls. These are not isolated incidents. In fact, they seem more the rule than the exception.

Do you have a notebook computer yet? You should.

Educational and societal issues

Alfred Riccomi, Track Chair

The headline reads "Do we realize that all the elements for an Orwellian Society are in place?" and we know it is 1984.[6] But except for this being "the" year, little has changed. Technology in general has often been accused of dehumanizing society.[1] We should not expect computing to be an exception. As many of us know, computers can in fact free us to spend more time with each other,[1] to be more human. In any case, all of us are involved in and affected by computing, and the young among us will very probably use computers much as previous generations used pencils; they will be eveywhere and be used by all.[1] Not that everyone will solve partial differential equations and create payroll programs with these computers, but then again not everyone wrote great poetry with pencils.[5] But today it is not clear to all how this can come to be. What are the issues, and are there any answers?

The computer takes on different perspectives when viewed by people from different backgrounds:

—To the computer manufacturer the computer is a divine gift, a source of (potentially) increasing profits.
—To the user it is all too often a source of trouble.
—The general public views the computer as a thing of magic which can do it all, but at the same time that public views it as the source of credit card and bank billing errors—and as a machine that invades their privacy.
—To many social scientists it is a device dedicated to the invasion of privacy; and they know (or at least fear) that sooner or later is sure to be used to bring about an Orwellian society.
—Some educators see computers as a major opportunity to improve the quality of education, but others see them as another imposition on their already overloaded schedules; some even see computers as a threat to their careers.
—The courts understand neither computers nor the problems surrounding them; therefore the resulting cases are often simply thrown out of court.
—Then there is the thief who sees the computer as an electronic safe just waiting to be cracked for valuable information, for money, or just for fun.
—The entrepreneur and the venture capitalist view it as a golden opportunity to get rich.

All of these viewpoints are at least in some ways correct, and all are in other ways incorrect. There is not, and perhaps cannot be, one common understanding of what the computer is.

Erik Sandberg-Diment of the New York Times leads a panel discussion titled "Media Micro Mania," which provides one or more of these views. On this panel, representatives from the news media enlighten us about how the computer industry looks to them. Are we seen as saviors of the human race, or only as hucksters promoting a shell game? Will our children really return from college as dejected dropouts? Is $49 finally the right price to pay for a home computer? Or should we deem no price too high for the gift of knowledge? Of one thing we can be certain—we will learn of these non-computing-industry views in no uncertain terms.

The next session presents an enlightening view of a few new ways that technology can free us to spend more time doing what we want to do. Thomas Cross chairs a panel, "Tele/Conferencing: the Future of Business Meetings." If all goes as planned, this session will in fact be conducted by tele/conferencing, with some of the participants being spared the need to travel to beautiful downtown Las Vegas in July in order to participate. Is this in fact the introduction of professional conferencing without travel?

Next is a session chaired by Glenn Rifkin, titled "Working

Remotely," which addresses the question: Where will the office of the future be? We experience a taste of how business meetings can be conducted without the need for traveling to distant sites; but is it even necessary to leave home in order to work? History tells us that before the Industrial Revolution, working in or near one's home was the norm. Now many believe it cannot be done: people cannot be trusted to work alone, and people need the socializing that goes with working together; it is just not natural to work remotely. Or will mass commuting between home and central work sites be just a short (two-century) aberration from the norm when viewed over the millennia by future historians?

The educational application of computers has often been viewed as a world in itself. However, here we choose to see education as just another part of the world. The impact of technology in general and computing in particular should have no more and no less impact on education than on anything else. We tend to ignore the rather significant impact upon education brought about by the electric light, central heating, and air conditioning. The printing press must have led to fears that children taught to read printed text would not learn to read or write handwritten script (and don't we all know that to a great extent those fears have proved valid!). At an earlier date the pencil and writing in general must have been viewed as a crutch used to avoid developing the memory.

Next, LaRuth Morrow brings together a panel of experts from the computer industry in a session titled "Enchancing Creativity in Education." They give us a different view of the possible roles that can be played by computers and other technologies in education. Although the fears and concerns of people involved daily with the problems confronting our schools should not and cannot be ignored, we know that major changes in the way we educate people have always taken place. There is no reason to believe that the future will not continue this pattern. Is it not reasonable to expect that TV screens and home computers (TV screens that this generation can program the way they want it to be) will change education? Some believe it already has. This panel tries to shed some light upon this future. If meeting and working remotely may be the future way of doing business, why not studying and learning remotely?[4]

All this speculation is fine. But what about the very real problem of distributing this month's Top Ten Video Game hits to the many millions of people with video game players at home? Retail store distribution channels cannot get the hits to the players fast enough. For that matter, what about distribution of software in general to the millions, soon to be tens of millions, of personal computer owners? Marvin Talbot has gathered a panel of experts on the topic "Tele-Software Delivery." They explore how the existing telephone industry and emerging videotex industry can solve problems of distributing specialty software to the masses (that's us). If the distribution problem is solved, however, what can easily be viewed as new problems can arise. Think about "mailing" lists containing information in machine-readable form identifying all the software/video games you have acquired, the databases you have accessed, the telesoftware advertising to which you will have been exposed, and that which you cut off; plus dates when all these events took place. Invasion of privacy can take on a new meaning.

Next, Henry Dreifus gathers a panel to discuss a technological development already making rapid inroads into people's lives without their knowing nor caring. "Smart Cards—the Ultimate Consumer Computer" first made inroads into the consumer world in Europe, but they are quickly finding their way into the U.S. What exactly is a "smart credit card," and do I want such a thing? There was a time most of us can easily remember when we were not sure what ordinary credit cards were, and many of us absolutely did not want anything to do with them. How many people can say they do not want credit cards today? Tomorrow, will they feel the same about smart cards? Will smart cards help eliminate all those credit card billing errors? If they do, then will everyone want them, even if such cards increase the invasion of privacy?

So the technology is here, if not already at work, either to free us or to enslave us. We have legal protections against the latter—don't we? Yes, but it is more complex than that. Richard Stern brings us a gathering of experts to address a topic that affects us all: "Legal Roadblocks to Exploitation of Technology." We know patents, copyrights, trade secrets, contract law were intended to protect us, not hinder us. What has gone wrong? Are software pirates just a fine example of free enterprise? The prospects for consistent interpretation and for changes of U.S. laws will be addressed, along with the issues listed. This is the opportunity to learn what we can do, what we can't do, and what we may soon be free to do.

So the promised age is upon us. We will use computers to work and study remotely. Others tell us that computers will diagnose our illnesses. They already manage our bank accounts, process our paychecks, defend our shores from without, and schedule our flights and hotels. Absolutely nothing can go wrong.nothing can go wrong.nothing can go wrong. But if it does who is responsible—who pays? Steven Brower brings a panel of legal experts to discuss something none of us wants to hear, something we have pretended would never come up: "Programmer Malpractice." Pretending that this issue will go unvoiced will not make it go away. Others will think of it, if they have not done so already. It is best that we address the issue; forewarned is forearmed. Furthermore, the computing industry is not alone in facing this issue. How have other industries fared? Have they all experienced the same fate as the medical profession? What can we learn from others' experience? Now is the time to study, learn, and act on this issue.

Where is all of this leading? What will the technology be like when we get there (if the law allows us to get there)? "The Fifth Generation—What, Why, and So What" presents four papers addressing this "hot" topic on the significance of the newest technology to our society. Professor Shaw has some interesting views of the fifth generation as the next stage of a new medium. "Reading" an author's work will take on a new meaning both when first acquired and for all time. Professor Gaines' paper addresses the topic of the framework for the fifth generation—how it will fit into our society. Doctor Rahimi's paper is on the computer and the future of human creativity. And the final paper, by Dr. Matley, studies how the federal government can create a national computer policy, just as it has created transportation and other policies to aid technologies important to the nation's future.

Finally, all good things must come to an end. All this study of educational and societal issues must give way to a more immediate need: making a living. How about making a better living, and making it from computing? There is still time for the would-be entrepreneur to make a go of it. No, it is probably too late to invent the apple; twice in one eternity is probably it. But there are other ways. Mary Sommerset has organized a panel to discuss "An Operational Approach to Penetrating Vertical Markets." Society is full of small segments with special needs that have yet to be served; many segments are larger than the half-million potential computer hackers served by the early personal computer vendors. These segments can be served successfully with easily defended market boundaries. But how do you identify, define, and reach these vertical markets? What distribution channels should you seek; or can you create new channels yourself? And finally, is serving these markets truly useful to society? Would doing so be in the spirit of saving the human race, or would it be nothing more than huckstering?

Have we come full circle? Probably! We started with an outside view of ourselves, and in so doing we have gained (we hope) a better understanding of what is important and what is not. We should not take ourselves nor our critics too seriously. But it is good to take time occasionally to get a glimpse of the forest surrounding us. Now it is time to get back to cutting down those trees. Perhaps if we clear out enough trees we'll see more of the forest next year at NCC '85.

REFERENCES

1. ACM notes on 35mm slide set on computers, author unknown.
2. Frates, Jeffrey, and William Moldrup. *Introduction to the Computer: An Integrated Approach.* Englewood Cliffs, N.J.: Prentice-Hall, 1980.
3. Gelfand, M. Howard. "Dealing With Computer Hard-Sell." *The Wall Street Journal,* January 24, 1984.
4. Mitgang, Lee. " 'University' lets students attend class via computer", *The Dallas Morning News,* March 11, 1984.
5. Papert, Seymour. *Mindstorms—Children, Computers, and Powerful Ideas,* New York: Basic Books, 1980.
6. Smith, Robert Ellis. "Do We Realize That All the Elements for an Orwellian Society Are in Place?" *Datamation.* (Date unknown, but 1983 or early 1984.)

Fifth-generation computing as the next stage of a new medium

by MILDRED L. G. SHAW
York University
Toronto, Ontario, Canada
and
BRIAN R. GAINES
University of Toronto
Toronto, Ontario, Canada

ABSTRACT

Computer systems provide a new technology that is very significant to human society and culture. However, computer science operates primarily within the technology and does not aid an understanding of the sociocultural impact of the computer as a mind-tool. This paper proposes to regard computers as providing a new medium for communication that can encode expertise and reproduce it through conversation. This model may be used to analyse the potential long-term effects of computer systems by analogy with the effects of past media developments on our sociocultural system. In particular, the Japanese fifth-generation computer development program may be seen as completing just those aspects of computer technology necessary to enable it to compete with other media.

INTRODUCTION

It has become common to speak of *conversational* interaction with a personal computer since the term was first used in the early days of interactive systems.[1] In recent years computing has been regarded as being part of a range of *electronic media.*[2] However, the analogy between people-people conversation and computer-people conversation has not been systematically developed. The analogy has not been explored between the use of computers to present information and experience and the use of other media such as books and television.

This paper presents a discussion of computing as providing a new medium.[3] The conversational and media analogies are shown to have formal foundations. Computing is identified as providing a two-way interactive medium for providing experience of worlds through simulation. This simulation can include that of other people and hence provide access to their encoded expertise.

What is particularly significant about this viewpoint is the light it throws on the objectives of current fifth-generation computer developments.[4] Computing provides a new medium with the unique property of being *two-way* and *interactive* with an encoded message, but the technology is currently limited. The logic behind the fifth generation may be seen as that of overcoming precisely those limitations of computers through which they lag behind other media.

CONVERSATION IN OUR SOCIETY AND CULTURE

From an early age people speak to one another. Conversation is a natural activity in every person's daily life. What is it? Not just communication because that may be in one direction only. Conversation is interactive communication that is two-way or many-way. In this sense all animals have some form of conversation. Some, such as territorial and courtship rites, can be very elaborate. However, the human species has developed the art of conversation to its highest level, employing a range of symbols and forms of expression to pass feelings, information, knowledge, and skills between people. Many tools and technology have been developed solely to enhance the capabilities to carry on conversations.

Human beings are already remarkable for their immense capability to learn from experience. They are able to adapt to a range of climates, environments, and societies as no other animal species can. However, the advantages of the human species' learning capabilities are amplified immensely by their ability to receive and impart information through conversation. The child in the jungle need not feel the injury of being mauled by a tiger in order to learn to fear the animal. Instead he can be told that the animal is dangerous and he should take care to avoid it. He can also be told how to look out for the signs of new dangers.

This capability of learning indirectly from conversations rather than direct experience, and of learning how to learn by discussing learning itself, has been crucial in the development of civilization. To take advantage of it, mechanisms have been developed that enable us to communicate over time and over distance, such as the letter, the newspaper, the book, the radio, the telephone, the television, the record, the tape. The remarkable nature of books can be seen from their ability to allow those long dead to impart their feelings and knowledge to those alive now and in the future. The remarkable nature of television can be seen from its ability to bring those far away into personal contact with events as they happen. Videotapes extend that ability across time as well as space. Transcending time and space adds new dimensions to the already dramatic powers of the human capability of learning from experience and from conversation. New media provide new extensions to everyone and radically affect our and our societies' modes of existence.[5,6,7]

PROGRAMS ARE TWO-WAY CONVERSATIONS

Books and television are one-way media. They are not able to support two-way conversations. They do not allow an interaction with the author of the book or with the events being portrayed. Correspondence through letters may be regarded as being a conversational form of a book. Discussion on a telephone or videophone may be regarded as being a conversational form of radio or television. Some computers have been added to this range of mechanisms for extending human conversations. They are remarkable in enabling the interaction with a program similar to the interaction with a person.

Computer programs are a way to extend interaction through time and space. When listening to a gramophone record one can imagine being at a live concert hearing the artist perform. When reading a book one can imagine the words spoken by the original author. If the book is a narrative, one can imagine the author playing the part of the character telling the story. Similarly, in a dialog with a computer program one can imagine interaction with the programmer who wrote it. Unlike the performer or the author, the programmer is able to provide responses to interventions, in some way to interact although he or she may be far distant or dead.

Computers enable the recording and dissemination of not only passive information but active processes with which the recipient can interact. For example, a model can be programmed of a chemical system so that persons without access to the materials and equipment required to create it can still experiment with that system. They are not told about it through a description of the experience, but rather it is made available to them in such a way that they can generate their own experience. They make their own decisions about what to do with the equipment and materials, and the model replicates what would have happened had they done this with the actual process.

Whether simulation is adequate to replace actual experience is not an absolute question but depends on the quality of the simulation and the function of the experience. Whether the interaction with a computer program is a realistic experience of interaction with another person or a simulated world depends on the technology and our capability to use it. Both of these are subject to continuing improvement.

ADVENTURE GAMES

Simulation of an interesting and exciting real-world or fantasy environment is the basis of many of the games now played on computer systems in the home. The player is a fighter pilot in a world of enemy aircraft who must fight aerial battles using skill in control of craft and weapons. The player has free access to an elaborate pinball machine with a wide range of exotic features of varying difficulty. The player is an athlete attempting various feats of skill and endurance. The player is a coach for a football team who must define its strategy; if the same winning strategy is used too long then the opponents will acquire a defense against it. The player is a businessman setting up a company in a world with certain raw materials, manufacturing processes and a population with defined, but unknown, consumption patterns.

During recent years such games have become increasingly elaborate, involving whole worlds of activity on land, sea, and air. They have also made more and more use of the rapidly improving color graphics and sound effects now available on low-cost computers. Some later games take into account moral concepts such as *good* people becoming less cooperative if *bad* actions are undertaken. This could be significant to the teaching impact of the games since the early ones incorporated a simple model of life in which everything in sight was taken or killed and most other entities in the game were enemies. This is similar in its morality to the western film genre that has been a natural foundation for the early popular games.

There are less apparent social consequences of playing with computers. It has been found that children learn to play games more readily with computers than with other children, probably because of the lack of significant social consequences. In an ordinary game if I win then you lose. You may not like losing so much that I suffer in consequence. Most computer games do not have such overtones, and this makes them easier to learn and to play. However, they also do not teach children how to cope with social interaction as does the game playing experience of real life. There is much to be learned about the social consequences of computer systems as a new medium.

THE INTERACTIVE NOVEL

On the basis of such games we can envision a novel of the future in which the author has precisely portrayed a group of characters and a situation but in which the way the situation is played out is affected by the behavior of the reader. For example, the reader may adopt the role of one of the characters and interact with the others as part of the plot. What then happens is not determined in advance but varies according to the reader's actions and the other characters' reactions to them. This interaction with the plot is not normally found even in the theatre but has been the subject of a number of unconventional experimental productions encouraging audience participation.

Much of the writer's task is the same for the book, the play, and the computer program, and he or she may well be able to generate a script that can cope with varying behavior on the part of some or all of the characters. However, the complexities possible with an interactive novel are clearly very much greater than those with a static book. The problems of the novelist with a participant reader are not as severe as those of the chemist programming the simulation of a chemical system for there is no absolute reality against which to judge the results. The participant reader may find that even his or her most outlandish behavior is somehow absorbed and accepted by the others without a marked deviation from the plot, or that the character played meets his or her demise through an unfortunate accident!

If the personalities and behavior of characters in a novel are simulated then we can also think of simulating ourselves, making access to us available through a computer program. The active process that the computer simulates may be not just a physical system but instead yourself in some guise, as teacher, friend, game player, or expert on some subject. When I write a book I present knowledge, opinions, or skills and some of the background material, experience, arguments, and results supporting them. However, I cannot possibly put together in the linear sequence of a book all the answers to the questions the reader may ask, all the alternative ways of presenting the material, all the forms of additional development that might occur if we were talking together. With an active model of at least part of me recorded in a computer program, I can provide some of these variations to be generated through a later conversation between the user and my computer model.

EXPERT SYSTEMS

The simulation of people in the roles of experts on some topic as a computer program has become an important application of computers. It has generated a new industry based on creating expert systems[8] to make the practical working knowledge of a human expert in a specific subject area such as medicine or geology widely available to those without direct access to the original expert. Programs now exist that have made practical achievements in medical diagnosis, interpretation of mass spectrometry results, analysis of geological survey data, and other problems where one would normally go to a human expert for advice.

MYCIN,[9] one of the best known expert systems, was designed to make a diagnosis and suggest therapy for patients with microbial infections. The expertise embedded in MYCIN is encoded as a set of rules of this form:

RULE 50
If 1. the infection is primary-bacteremia, and
2. the site of the culture is one of the sterile sites, and
3. the suspected portal of entry of the organism is the gastro-intestinal tract,
Then there is suggestive evidence (.7) that the identity of the organism is bacteroides.

Such rules involving fuzzy reasoning are obtained from specialists in microbial infections, and their application to particular data is fairly simple data processing. The rules are validated through their application to many cases and revised when they fail to give the correct diagnosis. A very interesting later development is TEIRESIAS,[10] a system designed to help clinicians develop MYCIN's rules. This uses metalevel reasoning about the operation of MYCIN and the likelihood of rule structures to guide the clinician.

The ultimate metalevel expert system currently is AM,[10] a program that searches for *interesting* conjectures in mathematics using rules of this form:

19.
If concept C possesses some very interesting property lacked by one of its specializations S,
Then both C and S become slightly more interesting.

38.
If there are no known examples for the interesting concept X,
Then consider spending some time looking for such examples.

AM seems to embody the highest level of scientific creation, looking for the patterns underlying knowledge. What is remarkable about AM is the very notion of what it is doing. The concept of something being interesting seems peculiarly human and certainly too vague to form the basis of a computer program. However, AM is able to exhibit not only meaningful conjectures in mathematics but also meaningful ways of arriving at them. AM uses a few hundred such rules most of which are sufficiently general to apply to other situations. Rule 19, for example, indicates that a committee with decision-making powers that do not apply to its subcommittees below a certain size has an interesting property, that of requiring a quorum. Its subcommittees also have an interesting property, that of being quorate. AM's rules form a good *code of curiosity* that might form the basis of a religion; perhaps it already exists, called science.

What is remarkable about developments such as MYCIN and AM is that they are concerned with recording what had previously been regarded as very high level human expertise, difficult to explain to another person, let alone program for a computer. However, from our previous discussion it seems reasonable to regard such programs only as one further advance in recording human expertise and simulating the human expert at work. An accountancy program for a business that keeps track of purchases and sales and prepares invoices, purchase and sales ledgers, and so on may be seen as the recording of the expertise of an accountant for use by an

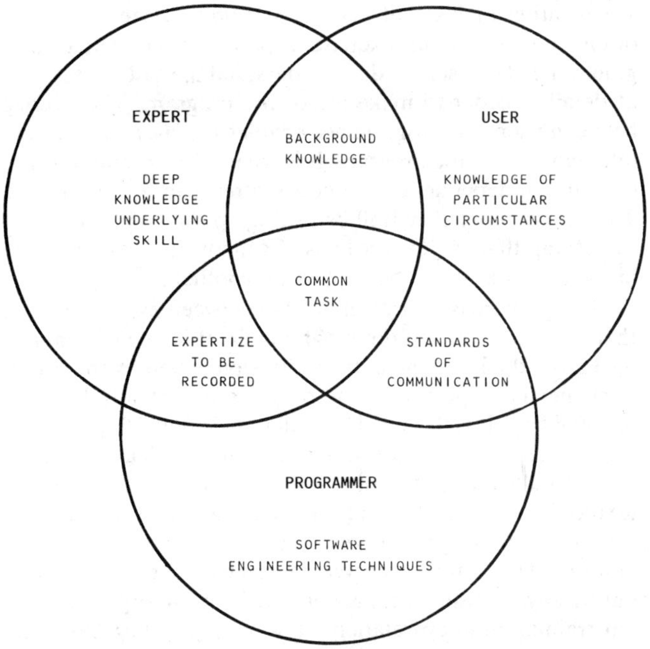

Figure 1—Relations between expert, programmer and user.

ordinary businessman. An auditor evaluating such a program may expect to be able to ask it exactly the questions he or she would ask the accountant; for example, from what original information did you calculate this figure? If the program does not have built into it audit trail facilities that enable it to answer such questions, then it is inadequate in exactly the same way an accountant would be who could not answer that question; it is a simulation of a poor accountant.

EXPERT, PROGRAMMER, AND USER

One of the peculiarities of computer systems is the role of the programmer. We can now see his/her task as being that of encoding expertise in such a way that it is accessible to another person through a computer. The diagram of Figure 1 shows how the interaction between expert, programmer, and user in using the computer to carry expertise divides into various areas of overlap. First consider the three areas where there is no overlap. These are where the individuals involved do not need shared knowledge to carry out their tasks. The expert, for example a lawyer, will have deep knowledge of the principles underlying his skill, on which it is based, but which is irrelevant to its application. The programmer does not need access to this knowledge to encode the skill, and neither does the user in replicating the skill. Similarly the programmer will have deep knowledge of software engineering techniques that are necessary to his task but irrelevant to either expert or user. The user also will have knowledge of the particular circumstances in which he or she is using the program that will modulate the use of it but will be unknown to either expert or programmer.

The overlap between expert and programmer is necessary to enable the programmer to obtain from the expert a specification of his skill. This is a form of system analysis, often treated as an exercise separate from actual programming. The user need not understand the skill at this level of detail in order to make use of the program. The overlap between user and programmer enables the user to carry out interaction with the program. It is where the programming of dialogue, independent of subject matter, can be considered. The programmer may well be setting up the computer to do something that the expert himself cannot do—communicate his skill so that it can be applied by another.

Finally, there is an area of overlap between expert and user that need not concern the programmer. It is one of common background knowledge in the profession, whereby the user is applying the expertise in the program not blindly but in a sensible way. It is this need for skill in the application of a tool that makes some professions reluctant to release their recorded skills for general use. A medical, legal, or accounting textbook in the hands of a lay person may suggest courses of action that are inappropriate because of more general considerations. The results of a psychological test that can be carried out by anyone using a computer may be misinterpreted without training in interpretation. However, encoding more and more of this background knowledge is the major challenge in developing a next generation of widely applicable computer systems.

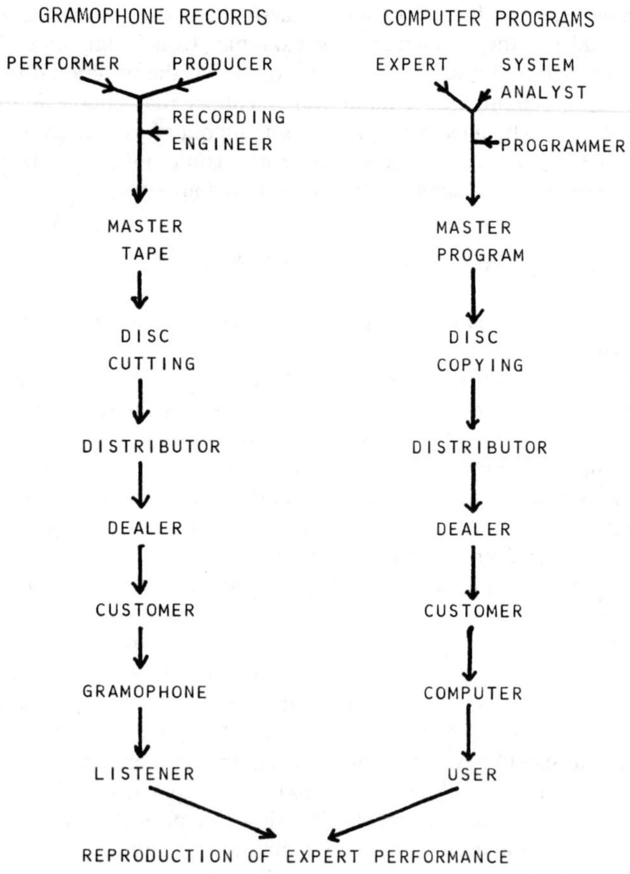

Figure 2—The recording chains for gramophone records and computer programs.

Figure 2 shows how the close analogy between computing and another medium, the gramophone, appears when this discussion is extended to include the remaining processes whereby programs for personal computers reach their users. The recording chain for computer programs and that for gramophone records are in one to one correspondence. This analogy underlies the growth of the personal computing industry, in which specialist software stores mimic record stores and in which computers and programs have taken their place alongside record players and disks in department stores. New media are marketed by analogy with the old.

CURRENT LIMITATIONS ON COMPUTER MEDIA

The computer as a new medium for conversation is still very much in its infancy. Today's personal computers have neither the picture and sound generation capabilities nor the data storage to emulate the presentation possible with television. However, the personal computer today has greater speed, processing power, and storage than the vast research machines of ten years ago and has become small enough, cheap enough, and reliable enough to take its place in the home. The giant computer technologies of today are at the heart of the movie industry, producing sounds and images that are as realistic as those of everyday life. It is not unreasonable to suppose that those capabilities will become available in personal computers during the next ten years.

A more severe limitation on the use of the computer to record models of active processes is our lack of understanding of them. I may know enough about a chemical system to write a program that faithfully reproduces all of its behavior that I have observed. However, will my program produce behavior that I have never observed when interaction is made in ways that I have never contemplated?

All new media have had initial limitations and gone through phases of improvement and development. The wax cylinder gramophone could not sustain the record industry of today, and neither could Baird's spinning disk support television as it is now known. The personal computers of today already provide an impressive new conversational medium for entertainment, education, and business. However, they cannot yet compete with television in their audio and video facilities. We mainly converse with them by typing at keyboards, not through speech. They can give access to vast stores of information, but they are not able to process it as knowledge. These limitations severely restrict the scope of the new medium as it is now, and it is precisely these limitations that the Japanese fifth-generation computer development program addresses.[3] Fifth-generation computers, if the objectives of the program are met, may be characterized as providing a two-way, interactive medium with the audiovisual facilities and knowledge processing to replicate all capabilities of the most advanced current one-way media.

CONCLUSIONS

The media of communication for mankind are at the heart of our culture. Each new medium is assimilated into society and used for some of the applications of previous media. It also provides different facilities that allow for new applications that change the fabric of society itself. Unless there is an awareness of these two processes going on as computers enter this culture, there will be no understanding of what is happening to individuals and to society. Computers provide a new medium for communication that will be used in part to mimic those already existing but will also change profoundly our society and modes of thinking in ways that we are not able to predict.

The emphasis of the computing industry has tended to be, not unnaturally, upon computers themselves. There is talk of computer science without noticing how curious this is; if the computer is a tool analogous to other tools, this is like talking of *pencil science* or *typewriter science*. In recent years the emphasis has begun to swing from the computer itself to its programs, software engineering, and data manipulation—information science. In fact there has been an uncertainty about how to regard computer technology; this is not surprising, since the use and understanding of it are still at an early stage. Everyone is a computer primitive. The development of expert systems and the realization that this is what we have all along been attempting to achieve, and achieving, points to one possible resolution of our dilemma. We can now see the computer as a new medium for carrying encoded expertise and making it available through conversation. Fifth-generation developments will enhance the facilities of that medium to equal and then exceed those of our previous media.

REFERENCES

1. Orr, W. D. (ed.). *Conversational Computers.* New York: Wiley, 1968.
2. Schwartz, B. N. (ed.). *Human Connection and the New Media.* Englewood Cliffs, N.J.: Prentice-Hall, 1973.
3. Moto-Oka, T. (ed.). *Fifth Generation Computer Systems.* Amsterdam: North-Holland, 1982.
4. Gaines, B. R., and M. L. G. Shaw. *The Art of Computer Conversation.* Englewood Cliffs, N.J.: Prentice-Hall, 1984.
5. Innis, H. A. *Empire and Communications.* Toronto, University of Toronto Press, 1971.
6. Hahn, M. E., and E. C. Simmel, *Communicative Behavior and Evolution.* New York: Academic Press, 1976.
7. Ong, W. J. "The history and the future of verbal media." In Silverstein, A. (ed.). *Human Communication: Theoretical Explorations.* New York: John Wiley, 1974.
8. Michie, D. (ed.). *Expert Systems in the Micro Electronic Age.* Edinburgh: Edinburgh University Press, 1979.
9. Shortliffe, E. H. *Computer-Based Medical Consultations: MYCIN.* New York: Elsevier, 1976.
10. Davis, R., and D. B. Lenat. *Knowledge-Based Systems in Artificial Intelligence.* New York: McGraw-Hill, 1982.

A framework for the fifth generation

by BRIAN R. GAINES
University of Toronto
Toronto, Ontario, Canada

ABSTRACT

The Japanese initiative in scheduling a development program for a fifth generation of computers has shocked a drowsy West into realizing that computer technology has reached a new maturity. We are ready to take a step forward and integrate into systems the advances in very-large-scale integration, artificial intelligence, database management systems, and the human–computer interface of the last decade. Suddenly, work on the fringes of the computer industry, particularly that in artificial intelligence, is perceived as central and of commercial and military strategic importance. This paper examines the economic, historic, social, and technical logic behind the fifth-generation program from several perspectives. It gives a basis for evaluating the program, responses to it, and its effect on our industry and society.

INTRODUCTION

The Japanese initiative in scheduling a development program for a fifth generation of computers[1,2] has shocked a drowsy West into realizing that computer technology has reached a new maturity. We are ready to take a step forward and integrate into systems the advances in very-large-scale integration (VLSI), artificial intelligence (AI), database management systems (DBMS), and the human–computer interface (HCI) of the last decade. Suddenly, work on the fringes of the computer industry, particularly that in AI, is perceived as central and of commercial and military strategic importance.

This recognition, and the accompanying prestige and funding, is clearly welcome to many, and Western research has been quickly redirected to match the Japanese program.[3,4] Wry remarks may be made that prophets have no honor in their own country. However, it is accepted that the Japanese track record of competition in the auto and semiconductor industries[5,6] does give this nation the right to credibility for its high-technology planning. This credibility is now gratefully accepted as legitimizing much related research in the West.

The activity triggered by the Japanese initiative is not a good environment in which to examine the current status of computing technology and our long-range objectives. The objectives have been set. The paradigm has become accepted, and a new value system has been widely adopted. Such shifts are common in science and technology[7] and the very fact that one has occurred will soon be forgotten.

However, there are many reasons why it is appropriate to look now at some of the deeper factors underlying the fifth-generation programs. AI was oversold in the 1960s and there was a backlash in the 1970s. Is fifth generation being oversold now and, if so, what might be the consequences? The Japanese program looks like system integration of every frontier technology in computer science. What will we have at the end and why should we want it? The program has been justified in terms of economics, market requirements, and leadership in technology. Are there other rationales for it? In the computer industry there has always been an interplay between technology-led and market-led developments. What are the technology and market forces on fifth-generation developments? The pioneers of computing technology raised questions about its long-term impact on the structure of our society. What are the implications of achieving the fifth-generation program goals?

These are not just broad questions of general interest. They also have key relevance to the planning of the fifth generation and responses to it. In establishing such activities we are engaged in both predictive and normative technological forecasting. Past forecasts for the computer industry have proved notoriously wrong. Some promising technologies have not matured; some have advanced much more rapidly than expected. In addition, new and unexpected technologies have emerged. In general, overall trends have occurred well before their predicted arrival dates. Can we learn any lessons from this history in planning current programs? If we cannot predict, how do we manage the change, the unexpected failures, and the unexpected opportunities? Will spinoffs outside the program be more important than the goals achieved within it?

This paper provides a framework for discussing these questions by examining fifth-generation computing from several perspectives: historical, social, economic, and technical. It suggests that we are in a time of fundamental change in the effect of computing on society, and society on computing, and that unusual perspectives from outside the industry can help us to focus on the key issues within it.

SURPLUS CHIPS AND THE PULL OF THE CONSUMER MARKET

Much of the publicity attending the Japanese proposals has emphasized the massive computing power envisioned for next-generation machines. It is true that MIPS abound and that MLIPS have been introduced[1] (one LIP is one logical inference per second), but this does not mean that the overall focus is on giant machines. The dominant objective of the fifth-generation proposals is *ease of use of computers by people*, and it is possible to see this as having come out of the inexorable logic of VLSI chip manufacturing. We are moving toward a surplus of chips that can be absorbed only by the worldwide consumer market.

Many of those attempting to buy certain processor and memory chips today will find the concept of a surplus ludicrous. However, scarcity of the latest devices is brought about by the current extreme price competition in small computer systems. Simplistically, all micros have much the same hardware and are differentiated primarily by cost. Sixty-four kilobyte rams and processors with inbuilt dma and communications make a big difference in board size and manufacturing cost. The newest devices will always be in great demand and short supply. For the previous generation of devices history suggests there will always be a price war between suppliers because of oversupply.

This oversupply problem will worsen with the increasing power of the coming generation of chips. The increasing number of gates in modern VLSI is achieved through decreasing element size that increases speed. Increases in complexity and in speed are positively correlated rather than subject to trade-off. Hence the potential power of modern ic's has already become extremely high. The problem is to know what to do with this power. Processor, memory, and support chips account for the bulk of high-volume demand, with communications and graphics forming a second tier.[8] The $12 billion turnover of the semiconductor industry corresponds to some 25 chips a year for every person in the world—about 1 million transistor equivalents a person a year!

We are manufacturing more and more of a product whose power is already great and increasing. The professional markets absorb much of this capacity now, but only the consumer markets can support it in the long term. However, computer technology plays as yet only a major role in these markets—one limited by the technical skills required of computer users. The key thrust of the fifth-generation program is to overcome this limitation and make computers accessible to all by moving from information processing to knowledge processing, from a machine-like interface with the user to a human-like interface through speech, writing, and vision.

Figure 1 shows the economic logic behind the fifth generation and shows the way this leads to the specified technical program. The chip surplus problem is resolved by aiming for consumer markets, and this requires that anyone be able to use a computer and have the motivation to do so in a domestic context. This in turn requires improvements to the human–computer interface, realistic simulation of real and fantasy worlds, and the capability to encode expertise for use by others. These requirements then lead to projects for speech recognition, high-resolution graphics, languages for knowledge-processing, and so on. The customizing of computers is an important capability that must not be lost and yet the volumes involved are too large for professional programming. Hence automatic programming in some form or another is also necessary. Thus the logic of the marketplace leads to the projects that form the fifth-generation program.

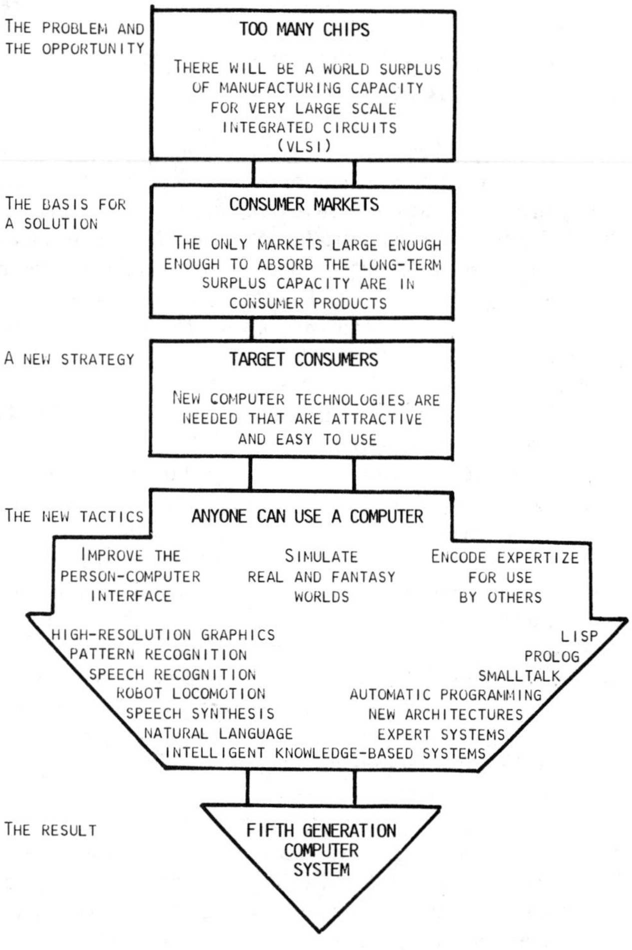

Figure 1—The logic behind the development of fifth-generation computer systems

This is not to say that a new generation of giant machines will not also come out of the program. They are probably necessary in any event as design tools for the advanced technologies underlying the consumer market machines. Yesterday we needed the large machines to help us in designing chips. Tomorrow we will need them to help us in designing knowledge structures. However, the dramatic swing of computer technology into the consumer market through the advent of the personal computer[10] will go much further as the fifth-generation objectives are achieved.

THE CHANGING GOALS OF AI RESEARCH

Perhaps the greatest element of surprise in Japanese program was its dependence on advances in AI research. This has always been an important part of frontier research in computer science but has not had major commercial significance. However, the argument of the previous section leads to a basic requirement for computing technologies that are part of AI, notably knowledge processing, natural language communication, and speech recognition. The commercial requirement that AI be routinely available marks the beginning of a new era for this field of research. The cycle of AI research shown in Figure 2, from overoptimism in the 1960s through disenchantment in the 1970s to commercial success in the 1980s, is a significant historic framework for fifth-generation developments.

The accepted starting period for Era 1 of research on AI is the late 1950s, with work by Newell and Simons on the General Problem Solver; McCarthy on programs with common sense; Selfridge on Pandemonium; Rosenblatt on the Perceptron; Widrow on Adalines; Solomonoff on mechanized induction; and McCulloch, Farley, von Foerster, Greene, and others on neural nets. Minsky's 1961 survey[11] (citing all these researchers) gives a fairly comprehensive feeling for this era worldwide. The logic behind much of the work is that new computer forms, organized as aggregates of simple, self-organizing elements, could be induced to perform a task by means of learning mechanisms, such as mimicking, reward, and punishment, similar to those of animal learning.

These objectives and this type of work characterized the worldwide goals and approaches at that time. They should be placed in the context of the early development of digital computers, where slow, expensive, unreliable machines with mercury-delay line memories were still in use, programmed in various forms of assembler or autocode. The JOSS, Culler Fried, PLATO, and Project MAC experiments on time-

ERA 1 - GENERALITY AND SIMPLICITY - THE OVER-SELL

1955-1965 GPS, PANDEMONIUM, PERCEPTRON, ADALINE, NEURAL NETS.

ERA 2 - PERFORMANCE BY ANY MEANS - THE REACTION

1965-1975 NOT BRAIN-LIKE MACHINES. EMULATE HUMAN PERFORMANCE ON GENERAL-PURPOSE COMPUTERS

- DISENCHANTMENT - THE OVER-REACTION

DREYFUS, BAR-HILLEL, LIGHTHILL, WEIZENBAUM

ERA 3 - ENCODED EXPERTIZE - ACHIEVEMENT AND EXTENSION

1975-1985 DEMONSTRATIONS OF EXPERT SYSTEMS. MORE OPEN FORUM - SIMULATION OF PERSON, ACQUISITION OF KNOWLEDGE, NEW ARCHITECTURES FOR AI.

ERA 4 - THE FIFTH GENERATION - COMMERCIALIZATION

1985-1995 A NATIONAL PRIORITY - COMMERCIAL AND MILITARY. CONVERSATIONAL INTERACTION THROUGH SPEECH AND WRITING WITH AN INTELLIGENT KNOWLEDGE-BASED SYSTEM.

Figure 2—Changing goals in the different eras of AI research

sharing were part of the same era.[12] The atmosphere was one of immense excitement over the potential for computer systems to lead to the "augmentation of human reasoning" and "man-machine symbiosis," to use the terms of books and papers of that era.[13]

The excitement and the funding died down in the 1960s as a result of two main factors. First, the work did not fulfill the promises made on its behalf: neural nets did not self-organize into brains; learning machines did not learn; perceptron-like elements did not recognize patterns. Second, the conventional digital computer became more reliable, smaller, faster, and cheaper, and the advantages of its sheer generality became widely realized. Effort switched from designing brain-like machines to emulating human-like activities on general-purpose computers. The focus of attention also became human *performance,* not human learning or human simulation. The initial rationale for this shift was that if we could not program a computer to perform a task then it was unlikely that we could program it to learn to perform that task; and if we could not program it somehow then we certainly could not in a way that simulated a person. This became the aim of legitimate artificial intelligence research in the late 1960s and early 1970s: the performance of tasks that required intelligence when performed by people.

While the AI community regrouped around the revised goals in Era 2, many outside took the opportunity to express disenchantment with the whole endeavor. Dreyfus in his 1972 book,[14] *What Computers Can't Do,* detailed many of the over-optimistic claims for AI research and the ensuing underachievement. He pointed to weaknesses in the philosophical and methodological foundations of work in Era 1. His 1979 revised edition reported some of the intervening debate resulting from his book and the changing priorities in AI research. It was a well-balanced report that can be criticized primarily because it was out of date by the time it was published. Those in the AI community felt they had already learned the lessons of Era 1 and changed their strategy.

Lighthill's negative report[15] in 1973 on behalf of the SRC on the status of AI research and the appropriate level of its funding in the U.K. reflected the disenchantment at the end of Era 1 with its oversell and lack of achievement. However, there was another motive behind the commissioning of that report, which was the fear of some of those responsible for developing computer science departments in the U.K. that AI research would be funded most strongly outside those departments. At a mundane level the misgivings came from the realization that the expensive and powerful computers then necessary for AI research might not be used to improve the research facilities of recently formed computer science departments. More fundamentally it was sensed that developments in AI might prove a major part of the future foundations of computer science. Whatever the motivation, the outcome of the report was very negative for AI research in the U.K.[16] during Era 2.

Weizenbaum's 1976 book,[17] *Computer Power and Human Reason,* was a far more personal statement than Dreyfus's by someone who had been responsible for one of the early achievements of AI research. His ELIZA program was widely acclaimed in the late 1960s as the first successful attempt at passing the Turing test for AI. It could carry out "cocktail party" conversation with a person at a terminal that was remarkably human-like. However, the acclaim became embarrassment when it was realized the simple mechanisms of ELIZA illustrated the weakness of the Turing test rather than a major advance in AI. People were all too ready to discern intelligence in machines and men, and commonsense human judgment in the matter was not an adequate criterion. The AI community was forced to reconsider what was meant by "intelligence."

AI work in Era 2 shifted from requirements for power and generality, consideration of computer architecture, and the simulation of human operation. Instead, it emphasized requirements to encode human expert knowledge and performance, by whatever means, for emulation by the computer. These targets resulted in practical achievements in the development of systems that could perform diagnostic inference tasks just as well as human experts, and the late 1970s and early 1980s became the era of *expert system* research.[18]

The strength of this paradigm shift cannot be overemphasized. It defined the boundaries of an AI community that established parameters for funding and publication. Focusing efforts on performance led to achievements recognized outside this community and hence established the legitimacy of AI research. In recent years the community has become strong enough to begin to reabsorb some of the earlier objectives and concepts. Human simulation rather than just emulation is an objective of cognitive science. Certain aspects of knowledge acquisition processes subsumed under learning are

			HARDWARE	SOFTWARE	EFFECTS
I	1953 -58	GEE WHIZ !	VACUUM TUBES & DELAY LINES	NONE	TECHNICIANS & FEARS OF AUTOMATION
II	1958 -66	PAPER PUSHERS	TRANSISTORS & MAGNETIC CORES	COMPILERS & I/O CONTROL	PROLIFERATION OF EDP GROUPS & RIGIDITY
III	1966 -74	COMMUN-ICATORS	LARGE-SCALE INTEGRATED CIRCUITS & INTERACTIVE TERMINALS	OPERATING SYSTEMS & COMMUN-ICATIONS	CENTRALIZATION OF EDP AS NEW FUNCTION
IV	1974 -82	INFORM-ATION CUSTOD-IANS	VERY LARGE FILE STORES & SATELLITE COMPUTERS	VIRTUAL MACHINES	REDISTRIBUTION OF MANAGEMENT FUNCTIONS
V	1982 -	ACTION AIDS	MAGNETIC BUBBLE, & LASER HOLO-GRAPHIC & DISTRIBUTED	INTERACTIVE LANGUAGES & CONVENIENT SIMULATION	SEMI-AUTOMATIC OPERATING DECISIONS

Figure 3—Characteristics of the five generations as seen in 1974

proving significant. The first steps are being taken toward new computer architectures aimed at AI requirements.

It would be foolish to pretend that the academic debates and funding struggles of the 1970s culminated in a clear realization of the significance of the three eras described. The oversell of Era 1 remained in many people's minds. Regrouping under siege and bitter struggle was the perception of Era 2 for many others. A nation of the East drew the attention of the West to the achievements of its AI research in Era 3 and the significance of this for the world economy.

We are now in Era 4, with the understanding and development of fifth-generation computers being treated as a national priority by many countries. The defense and commercial implications of achieving even some of the Japanese objectives are a more compelling argument than any the AI community have been able to muster. The sociocultural implications might also be overwhelming. The AI community of Eras 2 and 3 no longer exists. The financial pull of industry has fragmented effort, and it will be some time before new patterns of activity are clarified.

THE PREVIOUS GENERATIONS

In analyzing and forecasting the effects of fifth-generation developments it is useful to look at past definitions and projections. Some 10 years ago Withington[19] analyzed the 30 years of computer history to 1974 in terms of three generations of machines and projected these forward to two further generations. Figure 3 presents his main arguments in tabular form.

Withington's retrospective of the first three generations shows that they may be distinguished by hardware, software, or use, since all three are correlated. His description of the fourth generation then coming into use emphasizes large file stores and satellite computers, which came about as database and distributed systems technology. Virtual machine software also came about but did not have as much effect as expected. Other articles of the mid-1970s emphasize "universal emulators" and the need for each generation of hardware to be able to run the software of all previous generations. Many manufacturers experimented with such emulation of competitors' machines but it has not become widely adopted, possibly because of software copyright and licensing problems. This was also the era of hardware/software unbundling.

Withington's projections of the fifth generation, like all at that time, fell far short of target. Magnetic bubble technology lost out to advances in semiconductors. Interactive languages and convenient simulation were a major part of the fourth generation thrust. We can now see that VLSI goes into the hardware column and AI into the software column for the fifth generation. What we cannot see is what the sixth-generation extension of this table should be! It seems likely, however, that the often-quoted results will be continued, that each generation of about six years leads to a 10 times increase in speed, 20 times increase in memory, 10 times in reliability, and 1/10 in component cost.[20]

Withington's titles for each generation are evocative. The 1950s were an era of "gee whiz computers can do anything." This was necessary to support the belief of their users that one day they might become cost-effective. It took at least one more generation for this to happen. His name for the fifth generation is surprisingly apt; expert systems are certainly "action aids." However, it is a matter of faith today that they, and other developments coming out of AI, will become cost-effective in a wide range of applications. At least one more generation will be required, but the Japanese have already triggered this faith. We are at the beginning of a new cycle of events.

CONCLUSIONS

The Japanese fifth-generation program may have come as a surprise but it can be seen in retrospect as the logical culmination of developments in VLSI and AI technologies. The availability of VLSI in power and in quantity provides a technology that requires the consumer markets to be fully exploited. The availability of AI technology is a prerequisite for the human-like characteristics necessary in systems that can be interacted with easily by users untrained in computing.

That VLSI and AI can be developed over the next six years to provide cost-effective products is a dream. However, it requires no greater faith than that which set off this industry in the 1950s when the first generation of computers promoted the "gee whiz" reaction. During the intervening period the economic basis of our society has changed, and we can now see the knowledge economy[20] forming a new environment for the development of mankind. The fifth generation of computers is a natural product of the ecology[21] of the knowledge environment. By analogy with past predictions of computer development the fifth generation will be with us sooner than anyone might reasonably expect.

REFERENCES

1. Moto-Oka, T. (ed.) *Fifth Generation Computer Systems.* Amsterdam: North-Holland, 1982.
2. Simons, G. L. *Towards Fifth-Generation Computers.* Manchester: National Computing Centre, 1983.
3. Steier, R. "Cooperation is the Key: An Interview with B. R. Inman." *Communications of the ACM,* 26 (1983), pp. 642–645.
4. *A Programme for Advanced Information Technology: The Report of the Alvey Committee.* London: HMSO, 1982.
5. Kahn, H., and Pepper, T. *The Japanese Challenge.* New York: William Morrow, 1980.
6. Servan-Schreiber, J.-J. *The World Challenge.* New York: Simon & Schuster, 1980.
7. Kuhn, T. S. *The Structure of Scientific Revolutions.* University of Chicago Press, 1962.
8. "Technology update." *Electronics,* 56 (1983), pp. 122–235.
9. Gaines, B. R., and Shaw, M. L. G. *The Art of Computer Conversation.* New Jersey: Prentice Hall, 1984.
10. Weil, U. *Information Systems in the 80's.* New Jersey: Prentice Hall, 1982.
11. Minsky, M. "A Selected Descriptor-Indexed Bibliography to the Literature on Artificial Intelligence." *IRE Transactions on Human Factors in Electronics,* 2 (1961), pp. 39–55.
12. Orr, W. D. (ed.) *Conversational Computers.* New York: Wiley, 1968.
13. Sass, M. A., and Wilkinson, W. D. (eds.) *Computer Augmentation of Human Reasoning.* Washington: Spartan Books, 1965.
14. Dreyfus, H. L. *What Computers Can't Do: The Limits of Artificial Intelligence.* New York: Harper, 1972.
15. Lighthill, J. "Artificial Intelligence: A General Survey." In *Artificial Intelligence: a Paper Symposium.* London: Science Research Council, 1973.
16. Fleck, J. "Development and Establishment in Artificial Intelligence." In Elias, N., Martins, H., and Whitley, R. (eds.) *Scientific Establishments and Hierarchies,* Holland: Reidel, 1982, pp. 169–217.
17. Weizenbaum, J. *Computer Power and Human Reason.* San Francisco: Freeman, 1976.
18. Michie, D. (ed.) *Expert Systems in the Micro Electronic Age.* Edinburgh University Press, 1979.
19. Withington, F. G. "Five Generations of Computers." *Harvard Business Review,* July-August (1974), pp. 99–108.
20. Turn, R. *Computers in the 1980s.* New York: Columbia University Press, 1974.
21. Machlup, F. *Knowledge and Knowledge Production.* Princeton University Press, 1980.
22. Wojciechowski, J. "The Impact of Knowledge on Man: The Ecology of Knowledge." In *Hommage a Francois Meyer.* Marseille: Laffitte, 1983, pp. 161–175.

Computers and the future of human creativity

by MICHAEL CONRAD and M. A. RAHIMI
Wayne State University
Detroit, Michigan

ABSTRACT

The effects of computer science on human society can be usefully viewed within the framework of scale change. A number of examples of scale change are considered: in design, mathematics, social organization, medicine, and most especially, in the modeling and perception of the complex biological and social world in which we live. The common feature in these examples is the computer's ability to allow humans to return to modes of thought that are crucial to both the psychological and historical origins of scientific and engineering activities, but that were deemphasized in the classical scientific paradigm because of limitations on information processing. The explicit appreciation of the scale-changing power of the computer has important implications for computer science education and for its role in fully releasing the creative possibilities in the human–computer relationship.

INTRODUCTION

How can computer science education be organized so that human beings can most creatively use the power the computer makes available to them? This question is continually being addressed by educators and administrators in universities and other institutions responsible for supporting and benefiting from computer science activities.

Such a complex question could hardly be expected to have a simple answer. The immense computational power of modern computers has a social power that bears on this issue in a way that is insufficiently appreciated; the power to create changes in scale in areas as diverse as scientific investigation, artistic expression, and social interaction. By scale change, we mean sufficient change in the relative amount of effort expended on the different components of an activity to fundamentally alter its character or its relation to other human activities. While it is not difficult to recognize that changes in scale created by the computer produce dramatic transformations in many features of human society, it is difficult to appreciate the changes that must occur in human beings in order for them to adapt to and benefit from the new world of possibilities offered them by computers.

These scale changes are forcing paradigm changes on human beings. By paradigm change, we mean a change in a scheme or framework used as a reference point for evaluating experience. The framework may be determined by a set of examples shared by the community. This definition is one of several used by the historian Kuhn in his studies of scientific revolutions such as the Copernican revolution or the change from the Newtonian conception of space and time to the relativistic one.[1]

There has always been a natural human tendency to resist changes of a fundamental nature, whether they involve the developments considered by historians of science or the development currently being instituted by the computer. Since this resistance may lead to the neglect of those uses of the computer that have the greatest potential value to human beings, it is necessary to carefully examine the nature of the paradigm changes that are occurring, taking appropriate steps to ensure that our educational practices facilitate rather than resist them.

The phrase "paradigm change" is in one respect misleading. The computer creates an indefinitely large and varied number of new ways of perceiving both the world and ourselves. While instituting many new paradigms, it is destroying the traditional methodological paradigms with which scholars, scientists, engineers, and artists have worked for hundreds of years, but which inhibit the creative use of the computer.

The best way to examine the phenomenon of scale change is through examples. We consider several: in design, mathematics, social organization, medicine, and most especially, in the modeling and perception of the complex world in which we live. We shall argue that scale changes created by the computer enable man to return to modes of thinking that in both a psychological and historical sense are "primitive," but which have been discarded, in some cases thousands of years ago, because of scale changes in human activities that could not at the time be matched by scale changes in information processing.

FOUR EXAMPLES OF SCALE CHANGE

The Process of Design

For several hundred years, man has relied on lines when designing structures and devices he wished to build. Architects make line drawings of the buildings they wish to build, machine designers make two-dimensional blueprints, as do carpenters, gardeners, and city planners. If one desires to work with three-dimensional models and the problem involves the design of a small building or an uncomplicated device, it is possible to model it with clay, experimenting with different versions of it in three dimensions. If, however, the design involves a complicated machine, such as an automobile engine, or a large building, like a hospital, it is basically impossible to experiment in three dimensions. Although possible to build a model, it is necessary to design it with lines, using illusory devices such as perspective to explore its three-dimensional structure. In order to experiment with it, one has to expend too much effort demolishing and rebuilding it.

With the advent of computers, it has become possible to return to a more primitive and intuitive mode of thinking. Using the computer, it is possible to model solid objects with combinations of a few primitive solids (such as cubes, spheres, cylinders, and cones), then to experiment with different configurations and proportions of the models.[2] Such real-space design techniques are now used in architecture and in the design of machinery.

Thousands of years ago, advances in technology separated man from a direct use of space in design, inaugurating an age of designing with abstraction. Today, a further advance of technology enables man to separate himself from the use of abstraction for design, reinaugurating an age of design through experiment with perceived three-dimensional models.

The Practice of Mathematics

For a thousand years, the major mathematical activities of human beings have been routine. Although history recounts the work of great creative mathematicians such as Archimedes, Newton, Gauss, and Alkhwarizmi (for whom the word *algorithm* is named), most of the effort expended on mathematical activities has involved routine computations. Even Gauss expended years of labor calculating the motions of the planets. The possibilities for experimenting with mathematical structures have been limited to those that could be done by hand.

The most obvious capability of the computer is its ability to perform routine computations, leaving the mathematical practitioner free to concentrate on understanding the mathematical process rather than the execution of its technique. More important, by sharpening the border between the creative and routine components of mathematics, the computer is redefining what can be considered *bona fide* mathematical work. What was previously considered work for mathematicians—for example, difficult integrations or simplifications of complex algebraic expressions—is now work for computer programs. Writing the programs is creative; executing them is routine.

The paradigm change in mathematics is, however, much greater. The great mathematician Poincaré thought that induction was the basis of mathematics, and one can reasonably assume that he meant experimentation with cases. The earliest mathematicians discovered the basic features of geometry and arithmetic through experimentation. Problems then became too difficult for experiment. With Euclid began the axiomatic method that eventually became the guiding paradigm.

As in the case of design, the computer plays the role of the great scale changer. The possibility of experimenting on mathematical structures with computers has opened problems for investigation previously uncontemplated from an axiomatic point of view, thereby fundamentally altering the balance of power between investigation through experiment and investigation through formal analysis and proof. Yet the computer program used for such experimental exploration of the abstract world is the ultimate of formal prescription and constructive proof.

It is worth illustrating this point with another historical example. Leibniz, coinventor of the calculus, was perhaps the earliest writer to conceive of a symbolic language that could be used as a deductive calculus.[3] At the same time, he distinguished the process of generating the elements of a set from the process of determining whether an element is a member of that set. In modern parlance, this distinction corresponds to the distinction between recursive enumerability and recursiveness. Leibniz had the quaint idea that it would take about five years to solve all problems by deductive means using his logical symbolism. Although he had recognized the importance of questions that could only be answered through a generative process, he understandably failed to recognize that the power of computing as a means of exploring mathematical structures is greater than its power to prove theorems about these structures.

We now know that even problems that are unsolvable in principle may be answered with a degree of confidence, depending on the amount of computation invested in them.[4] It is clear that the idea of proof confidence radically alters the concept of mathematical truth, eroding the traditionally sharp distinction between deductive and inductive methodologies. These concepts and distinctions are even more radically altered when the enumerative power of the computer as a means of mathematical experimentation is recognized. This previous lack of computational power had forced Leibniz and other mathematicians to discard the experimental conception of mathematics in favor of a completely axiomatic and deductive one. The scale-changing power of the computer again returns us to a historically more primitive conception that was dominant in the time of Babylon and old Egypt and that is radically different from our present ideas. Leibniz's process of enumeration has been so amplified by the computer that it has fundamentally undermined the deductive paradigm it was originally conceived of as supporting.

The Size of Society

Human beings originally lived in small societies in which all members of a group had personal awareness of one another. As time passed and the population increased, the potential decreased for knowing all members of one's social group or even for knowing all individuals with whom one had important interactions. For some writers and social scientists, the alienation of individuals from those on whom they depend and from those who depend on them is the most pronounced feature of human society.

The usual view is that the computer increases human alienation. Although computers can increase the specialization of society, invade the privacy of the individual at will, and erect barriers between individual and institution, they need not. Properly understood, the computer can be used to decrease the effective size of society by increasing the number and value of interpersonal contacts. If properly used, it can allow individuals a greater awareness of each other's needs and a greater access to available resources. For example, an instructor in a large, diverse institution can recognize and respond to the needs of his individual students. As a researcher, he can use the computer to identify other individuals with relevant interests or skills. Computers can make large libraries essentially smaller with the use of more effective searching techniques. Computers can provide selective and effective channels of communication among individuals with common interests. In short, properly used the computer can change the scale of social interaction, recapturing some of the personal features valued in simpler societies, while avoiding the constraints and parochialisms that undoubtedly gave many the impetus, or at least the desire, to escape from these societies.

The Practice of Medicine

Prior to this century, there were no life support systems to maintain catastrophically injured and critically impaired individuals. With the development of industrial society, the number of catastrophic injuries from which an individual could survive, albeit in an impaired state, has increased. In effect, the first consequence of scientific medicine and technology has been an increase in the number of handicapped individuals in society.

With the development of intelligent microprocessor-based prosthetic devices, it is now possible and even economical for a paralyzed individual to use myoelectric signals to control effector devices or voice synthesizers to manipulate objects or create artificial speech.[5] The scale-changing power of the computer is reversing the by-products of scientific medicine and technology, returning us to a more primitive situation in which all members of society were capable of full participation.

There was previously a sharp distinction between man and the machine he created. As machines became more intelligent, this distinction became less clear. Perhaps this scale change allows a return to a time when man viewed himself as a part of nature and adapted to it.

MODELING THE EXTERNAL WORLD AND EXPERIMENTING WITH INTUITIONS

Very early in human history, thinking about the world in which we live was informal. Formal tools such as classical mathematics had not been developed. Only natural, human languages such as Greek, Hebrew, or Persian were available. Scholars and scientists used these powerful but informal languages as tools to describe the natural universe and social world and to explore the mental images they had created.

As time passed, scholars created certain specialized instruments of analysis, such as geometry, algebra, and calculus. Not everything that can be described or contemplated with natural language can be contemplated conveniently with these formal tools. What can be described may be explored by precise means that go well beyond our intuitive, informal capability. As a consequence, premathematical thinking about the world with the powerful tool of natural language gave rise to mathematical thinking about models of the world that could be formulated in tractable mathematical frameworks. Although intuition did not cease being the source of these models, scientists attempted to the greatest possible extent to couple intuition and abstraction. The ability of the human being to perform many types of computations is so weak that an enormous amount of abstraction is necessary if one is to arrive at a humanly computable model.

Not all sciences went in this direction. In some cases, notably the historical disciplines, the required degree of abstraction simplified the reality too much to be useful. In those cases, the advantages of the ability to compute were outweighed by the losses inherent in the initial abstractions. As a consequence, science has split into two parts. One part has practitioners who recognize only those phenomena that can be formulated in mathematical frameworks. The second part deals with different phenomena, and still is formulated in natural language. There are of course disciplines that use both descriptions. One example is economics, a part of which is mathematical and rigorously deductive, but unable to describe economic phenomena adequately. The very description of these refractory phenomena requires informal modes of thinking that rely on ordinary language.

The computer can again create a profound change of scale, altering the balance of power between intuitive and formal thought and introducing a potentially greater unity into the bifurcated structure of science. By enormously amplifying man's power to compute, the computer has reduced the degree to which he must abstract the world around him in order to compute. Our symbiosis with the computer has so enhanced our formal capabilities that we are now free to use our natural powers of problem formulation more fully. The mathematically oriented sciences can enlarge the sphere of problems they treat and the sphere of phenomena they are willing to contemplate. They can experiment with ideas previously rejected on the grounds of incompatibility with formal analysis. The nonmathematical, natural-language-based sciences can use the medium of formal computer languages to express and compute with models previously outside the range of formal investigation.

In fact, computers are not being used as creatively as they could be for this purpose. Although all natural and social sciences now use computers, in nearly all cases it is as a prosthetic to traditional precomputer methodology. Many examples could be given. One is from ecosystem biology: Over fifty years ago, the mathematician Volterra formulated a simple differential equations model to describe the interaction of predator and prey in an ecosystem.[6] Today the computer is used by many investigators to find numerical solutions to these equations. The studies use the computer as a prosthetic to a traditional model formulated to be analyzable, at least to some extent, without the computer. Although a legitimate use of the computer, it is not a powerful one. We can formulate our understanding of the complex interactions in an ecosystem more completely and accurately by direct use of the formal instrument of a computer language. That is, instead of mapping the reality into the formalisms of traditional mathematics, then using the computer to compute this map, we can map the reality directly, using the language instruments of computer science.[7]

Contemplate for a moment the immense complexity of the genetic and physiological processes within organisms, the spatial and temporal dynamics of the environment, the interactions among organisms and between each organism and the environment, and the flow of mass between organisms and environment. Contemplate the statistical process of variation, the problem-solving behavior of organisms and the selective action of the environment. The investigator who refuses to admit the validity of computer languages as primary instruments of analysis foregoes any possibility of giving a holistic but formal description of such a system, or, more precisely, of formally expressing a holistic theory of it. Accepting such instruments of language, we can use them to give formal expression to theories about reality that previously could be formulated only by using the instrument of natural language. We can use the computer to calculate these rigorously formulated theories as easily and automatically as we use natural language to describe them. The problem reduces to one of translating from the natural language description to the computer language description.

The difference between these computer models and precomputer mathematical models is not that one is mathematical and the other is not. The difference is that the computer has redefined the term "tractable." Traditionally, a tractable model is an analytically solvable one. Significant simplifying assumptions are necessary about the complex interactions in the real world in order to make models that are analytically manageable. For dynamic models, the indispensable assumption is that they are analytic, that is, that their local behavior can be used to derive all relevant information about their global behavior. One cannot reasonably call a model mathematical unless it is solvable—otherwise it is just symbology. The crucial point is that our scientific thinking need no longer be guided by the precomputer criteria of tractability. What was previously symbology is now *bona fide* mathematics. As in the examples of design, mathematics as such, and social organization, the computer has introduced a change in scale that returns us to modes of thought that played important roles in the early stages of human history, but that were quenched by the advance of technology; in this case, by the advance of the analytical technology of classical mathematics.

In modeling the world, we argue that the most valuable role of the computer is as a prosthetic to the human thought process itself, not as a prosthetic to precomputer methodologies. Yet most natural and social science modeling is guided by precomputer criteria. Some of it, especially in the biological and social sciences, is completely conceptual and informal. The reason, we believe, is that there are two ways of judging models and theories. One is aesthetic, the other is practical.

For the computer scientist, computer models may be aesthetically pleasing even if they have no utility. Exploring such models experimentally, using methods usually associated with experimental science, seems like a legitimate activity. For the precomputer scientist, models formulated directly in terms of computer languages and the experimental models used to study them may seem aesthetically unpleasing and dubious even if they have enormous utility. The question involves the criteria to which we have become habituated over hundreds of years. The criteria that had to be fulfilled by a model to make it useful in the precomputer stage of science have, after hundreds of years, become transformed into aesthetic criteria. These have been useful in guiding scientists in the direction of utilitarian models and theories. Now new classes of models are possible that are unaesthetic according to traditional perception, but clearly are useful. With these models, we can investigate the consistency and implications of informal theories that guide our intuitions about ecological systems, business firms, whole economies, and the thought process itself. It is the change in aesthetic criteria that is the painful but fruitful methodological paradigm shift that the computer is introducing into natural and social science.

Man's new power to formulate algorithmic models in the languages of the computer and to use the computer to explore these models has an interesting epistemological implication. Our knowledge and procedure bases are limited by biological evolution. There is a tendency, in some cases even an urge, to perceive and analyze the world in terms of one, two, or three categories. Thus, there are monistic philosophies—which view all observable phenomena as a manifestation of a single underlying reality; dualistic philosophies—such as Zoroastrianism—which attempt to perceive the world in terms of two competing forces; and triadic philosophies, such as Hegel's dialectic. The computer is not inherently subject to these limitations. We can program it to perceive and analyze in terms of many more categories than any human being could. It is possible that with the computer we will reach a point of communicating useful models without understanding how these models work. It is conceivable that man's biologically and historically developed tastes are completely arbitrary as far as his understanding of the world is concerned. Alternatively, it is conceivable that there is a fortuitous and marvelous match between the structure of reality and the structure of his thought processes. More likely, there is a good match for some aspects of reality, a poor one for others. One new possibility created by the computer is that of obtaining a deeper appreciation of the relationship between the human mind and the external world; a problem of immense philosophical interest that until now could never have been the object of serious experimentation.

EDUCATION OF THE COMPUTER SCIENTIST

How do the possibilities created by the computer bear on the education of the computer scientist and, equally important, on the computer-education of the public at large? The chief problem with the computer remains communication *with* it. At first, communication involved the arduous formulation of algorithms in primitive codes that could be used to control the state of the machine. As time passed, higher-level languages were developed in which the ideas of the programmer could be expressed more easily. The problems of compiling these languages into machine code become prominent. As more people began to use the computer, the problem of program management—essentially of operating systems—became prominent. As programs became more complex and computation less costly, the problem of writing readable, modifiable programs and of establishing the correctness of programs assumed greater importance. A great deal of emphasis in computer science education is rightfully placed on these and related issues; that is, on the issues involving the structure and use of formal languages to abstract reality for the machine.

The view we have suggested of the computer as a scale changer points to another issue that should enter computer science education more conspicuously than it does. The development of the computer has shifted the balance of effort involved in the formulation and solution of problems. The computer is a formal instrument, and our symbiosis with it has extended the formal side of our linguistic capabilities. We argue that by so doing it should free our intuitive, creative capabilities, not only because it reduces routine work, but also because it opens new possibilities for the creative formalization and exploration of intuition. For classical scientists, the problem of calculating a solution was enormously time consuming, so formulation had to be very careful. Only the very best scientists could successfully concern themselves with problem formulation. With the advent of modern computer systems, the problem of solving formulated problems has become much easier. Once a problem is posed in a computer language, the computer automatically solves it, and the problem of modeling is reduced to one of problem formulation. The computer as a scale changer has effected a major shift in the faculties of thought that a scientist can most fruitfully cultivate. As computer languages and computer systems have developed to become more powerful and usable, they have shifted the return on the investment of scientific effort from the problem-solving faculty to the faculty of problem formulation.

There is an interesting analogy to the structure of the brain itself. It is now believed that the right and left hemispheres of the brain specialize for different functions, just as left and right hands do. Evidence indicates that one hemisphere is specialized for linguistic and analytical tasks; the other for intuitive, geometric, and Gestalt thinking. These specializations are not sharp, just as the different tasks performed by the left and right hands are not sharply delineated into two classes of functions. It appears that the brain of a single individual is a symbiosis of two kinds of computing. The development of traditional mathematical techniques placed constraints on the intuitive modes of thinking that were the source of this technology. The development of computers provided such an enormous amplification of power of the linguistic–analytical side of the brain that it has created previously unknown opportunities for the intuitive–creative side.

One problem in computer education is to train the linguistic side in the proper use of formal computer languages, a difficult task even for individuals gifted in analytical capabilities. The mastery of formal skills is necessary for communication with the computer even though it seems counterproductive to concentrate solely on their cultivation when the computer is so much more effective than any human in executing formal processes. Once mastered, the formal skills should be used creatively; that is, the student's intuitive, ideational capabilities to communicate useful things to the computer should be cultivated. Arriving at an algorithm or proof idea and formulating it in a computer program involve different, though interacting modes of thought. In our teaching of computer science, we have emphasized the linguistic side. Now, as we step into the age of the new possibilities opened by the computer, it is time to emphasize the use of the formal tools to express ideas and formulate problems.

This educational goal should be consciously incorporated into our computer science curricula at the earliest levels. It is, of course, already implicitly present. For example, the field of artificial intelligence has as its main problem the communication of a world-conception to the computer. Nevertheless, in all but the most advanced areas of our computer science education, we place so much emphasis on the formal, linguistic side that the intuitive capabilities that guide program construction atrophy in many students before they reach the point where they can recultivate them. This situation can be altered. The two modes of thinking required to work effectively with the computer can be cultivated simultaneously, just as learning an artistic technique can be pursued simultaneously with the cultivation of artistic ideation by the student of creative arts. In this respect, the computer is a new medium, and computer science has an aspect of the creative arts that should be explicitly recognized at the beginning of our educational practice.

Viewed as a device forcing the programmer into inhumanly formal modes of thinking, the computer is alien, and provokes hostility in those forced to deal with it. Viewed as a new medium of expression and as a way of harnessing our most personal human potential, it should evoke pleasure in those dealing with it. Viewed merely as a prosthetic to classical scientific methodology, the use of the computer will always be seen as an admission of failure to be sufficiently clever to preclude its need. Viewed as a prosthetic to the human thought process itself, the computer can be viewed as one of the most effective means of thought. Accepted as a paradigm changer, the computer can serve to reveal new views of the world as meaningful for the evolution of human thought as those that arose during any period of scientific revolution.

ACKNOWLEDGMENT

M. Conrad acknowledges support from the National Science Foundation (Grant MCS-82-05423).

REFERENCES

1. Kuhn, Thomas S. *The Structure of Scientific Revolutions* (2nd ed.). Chicago: University of Chicago Press, 1970.
2. Boyse, John W. *Data Structures for a Solid Modeller.* G. M. Laboratories, GMR-2933, 1979.
3. Leibniz, G. W. *Leibniz Selections* P. Weiner (ed.). New York: Charles Scribner's Sons, 1951.
4. Rabin, M. O. "Probabilistic Algorithms." In J. F. Traub (ed.), *Algorithms and Complexity: New Directions and Recent Results.* New York: Academic Press, 1976.
5. Rahimi, M. A. and C. B. Friedlander. "Linguistic Significance of Myoelectric Activities of Lip Musculature." *IEEE 1980 Frontiers of Engineering in Health Care* (1980).
6. Volterra, V. *Lecons sur la Theorie Mathematique de la Lutte pour la Vie.* Paris: Gauthier-Villars, 1931.
7. Conrad, M. "Algorithmic Specification as a Technique for Computing with Informal Biological Models." *BioSystems,* 13 (1981), pp. 303–320.

A national computer policy: forging the final synergy of computers and society

by BEN G. MATLEY
Ventura College
Ventura, California
West Coast University
Los Angeles, California

ABSTRACT

National computer policies (NCPs) developed by certain nations have established those nations in such strong competitive positions in computer technology that they now challenge the U.S., which once held a near monopoly position. Japan's national computer policy, published in 1972, called for a $65 billion investment in eight computer developments between 1972 and 1985 and set the stage for development of a domestic chip industry. Thus, a national computer policy can be dramatically effective. Other nations have developed national computer policies as well.

Many of the challenges and problems facing the U.S. computer industry might be resolved if a national computer policy study were begun immediately. Such a study could help us to understand the manner in which the computer industry has changed from dominance by actions of entrepreneurships to direction by actions of sovereignties. The AFIPS member societies are called upon to provide the forum from which a national computer policy study may begin.

INTRODUCTION

Our conference theme: the synergy of technology and society. Nowhere do technology and society come closer together than through government technology policies. That was true of steam-boiler technology in the nineteenth century.[1] It became true of communications, transportation, and certain other select technologies in the twentieth century when each became recognized as crucially important to the society at large. Coincident with that recognition came the acknowledgement within each expanding technical industry that certain challenges and problems were beyond the ability of single firms to solve individually. At that point, the small technical community, which had nurtured each new technical industry, arrived at a willingness to share with the greater society some key decisions about the future direction of the industry. In turn, the greater society participated by setting some national technology policies for each industry. It also complemented private investments with public funding of selected projects. The net effect of those national technology policies and those public investments was to propel each of those young industries onto a new growth curve based upon broad societal participation.

Aviation may be used as one example of a new technological industry that progressed through the maturation process described above. That industry reached a point at which certain challenges and problems could no longer be resolved by single firms working alone. Single firms could not build airports and navigation aids, nor could single firms set traffic routes and flight rules. The small technical community that had nurtured the budding aviation industry was ready to share control of the industry's future with the greater society. The society then set some policies for the industry and invested public funds in the industry (e.g., airports and traffic control systems) because it was acknowledged as being crucially important to the society at large. With broad societal participation, the industry was propelled onto a new and rapidly rising growth curve. I hasten to note here that national technology policies are not to be confused with regulation of day-to-day operations. As illustrated in the case of aviation, the industry can be deregulated, but its importance remains. Airports, traffic control systems, navigation aids, are all maintained as ongoing public investments in a technological industry of crucial importance to the society at large.

The computer industry is now the most recent of those select technical industries to elicit a national technology policy—specifically, a national computer policy (NCP).

THE COMPUTER IN TURN

Certainly there is no doubt that the computer industry is crucially important to the society at large. Neither is there a doubt that the U.S. computer industry faces some challenges and problems that cannot be resolved by single firms working alone. For instance, some industry leaders have already acknowledged that computer R&D has become too expensive to be wastefully replicated by single firms competing individually.[2] Modification of antitrust laws is called for so that firms may pool their R&D efforts and the results may then be made available to all. Still others suggest a nationally coordinated effort to develop the next round of supercomputers, such effort said to be "crucial to economic and national security."[3] We can also acknowledge that American commercial computer supremacy, a near monopoly just 20 years ago, is under effective challenge for leadership in the 1980s. We cannot expect that each single firm will overcome that challenge individually. Nor can individual firms solve the problem of industrial espionage. On the level of international trade in computers, we sometimes find American firms competing with sovereign nations. The close industry-government partnerships in the computer industries of some nations is well known. Additional national computer policies of those nations set American competitors at a further disadvantage. In one case, an American computer firm under investigation overseas sought the help of the U.S. government in resolving the matter.[4] Other firms operating overseas complain that there is no one organization in the U.S. government to which a firm may appeal in trying to resolve matters of duties and tariffs on the companies' business data and programs.[5] The manner in which American computer firms are beset with such challenges and problems is worthy of study. That becomes a study of national computer policies—those of other nations, not of the U.S. As examples, there are two national computer policies of particular note illustrating that national computer policies can be dramatically effective in a very short time.

SELECTED NCP STUDIES

In 1972, the Japan Computer Usage Development Institute (JCUDI) presented to that nation the results of a national computer policy study, titled "The Plan for an Information Society—A National Goal Toward the Year 2000."[6] The JCUDI Plan called for an initial national investment of $65 billion in computer developments to be made between 1972 and 1985. Eight computer developments were specified, three of which were as follows: a Computopolis model city to serve as a living laboratory of an information society; a national think-tank center to provide computer databases with simulation and modeling facilities available to both private and government researchers; a Computer Peace Corps to transfer computer technology to Third World trading partners. Given such bold national computer policy plans it is understandable that an early $250 million investment in chip technology was justified in support of those policies. Similarly, an ongoing priority effort in fifth generation R&D would support ongoing efforts in all eight areas of computer development during the 1980s.

By 1980, Japan had reported significant progress in seven of her eight areas for computer development. Japan's national computer policy had helped her achieve a leadership position in computers in a very few years.

In 1978, France followed Japan's lead and published a national computer policy study of her own.[7] The French study equated sovereign control of computers and communications—that is, telematics networks—with sovereign survival. The study stated that it was imperative that France develop a domestic computer industry free of foreign ownership. Given such national computer policies, we can better understand why that government moved into Honeywell-Bull. We can also better understand why France felt it necessary to impose non-IBM communications protocol standards nationwide, and why France sought Common Market acceptance of similar protocol standards. France, like Japan, then promoted international trade in computers and communications for its domestic firms while protecting those same firms from foreign competition. Both nations also saw the need to begin immediately the reeducation of the people in preparation for the twenty-first century information society—a society of synergism rather than individualism, with an economy based on information rather than energy or consumable goods. All of these actions came in support of a national computer policy methodically developed.

OTHER BENEFITS OF NCP STUDIES

Now the mere fact that two or more nations have implemented national computer policies with notable success does not mandate that the U.S. do likewise. Neither does it follow that the computer policies adopted by those nations are the preferred ones. But the two examples cited above do help us to understand, in part, why the U.S. computer industry has found itself so quickly in a state of challenges and problems that are beyond resolution by single firms working alone. It is not that U.S. computer firms can no longer compete—they can. It is that recently the nature of competition is changing from actions solely by entrepreneurships to actions and policies of sovereign nations. Such changes deserve study on their own merit. Still, there is another reason for performing a national computer policy study at this time: National computer policy studies sometimes lead to uniquely different perceptions of the future for computerized societies. For example, the Japanese national computer policy plan led to a perception that in the twenty-first century information society there would occur what was termed a "Copernican turn in privacy," meaning that personal-data privacy as we know it today would cease to exist. The French study arrived at a similar perception, referring to "the new privacy of openness" and a "new right to access" to national and personal data through nationwide telematics networks. Yet another perception was expressed in a Swedish report, likening the impact of telecommunications to that of transportation:

> a different kind of transport philosophy could have led from the beginning to the introduction of a technique that did not segregate. . . .There could have been no need for us to get into the present-day situation if the transport system had been regarded right from the beginning as a system, and not merely as the sum of the choices of individual households through private purchases.[8]

Again, we do not suggest that these perceptions—certainly different than our own—are the preferred ones, nor policies the ideal ones. We do suggest that a national computer policy study by the U.S. might well lead us to some additional insights and understandings—maybe even a different national view—about our relative position in computer technology, as well as our desired future directions. As an added dividend, we might discover that certain present-day computer uses could eventually mitigate against other, previously established national policies.

COMPUTER POLICIES AFFECT OTHER POLICIES

The earlier quotation from the Swedish report, for example, provokes thought. A present-day transport system was said to promote segregation. Given the future for telecommunications networks, there will surely be considerable in-home work and in-home study.[9] Would not a nationwide network of teleconference schools and cable colleges mitigate against our previously established national policy of physical integration in the schools? Might a national computer policy study conclude that in-home schooling be restricted, (say, for argument, to the upper grades) so that our prior national policy of school integration may proceed?

There are other examples of computer usage in potential conflict with our stated national policies. Massive microprocessor automation efforts work against our prior policy for full employment as represented in legislation. Our experience in the auto industry from 1978 to 1982 is said to demonstrate that Norbert Wiener's concerns of the 1950s were correct in their nature, if not in their extent.[10] It has been estimated that some 200,000 of those auto workers laid off during the 1978–1982 changeover period would never be rehired even with increased production.[11] Reports from the Bureau of Labor Statistics, Office of Technology Assessment, and other agencies refer to millions of jobs lost to automation in fabrication, packaging, and production during the 1980s and the 1990s. Even so, the call has already been sounded for increased participation by government in encouraging automation in manufacturing.[12] Might a national computer policy study conclude that a certain number of those jobs not be automated in order to ease structural unemployment and to provide at least some entry level jobs for inexperienced workers? Alternatively, a national computer policy study might redirect our thoughts toward the input/output economy, wherein older, "sunset" industries are aided into orderly decline rather than being subsidized continually by taxes on the younger, "sunrise" industries. Japan has done much the same thing with her textile industry and certain other declining industries.[13]

Finally, a national computer policy study could address the

manner in which certain present-day uses of computers in government offer to alter the relationships between branches and agencies of government—maybe to alter the very nature of our government.[14] In 1979, for instance, Congress defeated a bill that would have modified the 1974 Privacy Act so that the passive draft registration system could be implemented.[15] This system would have linked the computers of Social Security, Internal Revenue, motor vehicle registration, and student loan applications to compile lists of potential draftees by age group. (A byproduct would have been a means to mobilize critical labor occupations in the event of a national emergency.) Certainly all of the data needed for draft registration are in those computers; "compliance" would have far exceeded the reported 80 percent for the 1980 registration period, and the selectees would not have been bothered with completing forms. Immediately following the defeat of that 1979 bill, in 1980, data were shared on magnetic tape by Internal Revenue and Selective Service, thus achieving about the same effect. The fact that data sharing was done rather inefficiently by sending tapes does not make moot the matter of data sharing between dissimilar agencies and the use of personal data for secondary purposes. Since that time, we have seen data sharing with Internal Revenue for the purpose of collecting debts on behalf of other agencies which had nothing to do with tax collection. Now, does the 1974 Privacy Act present a desired national policy, or not? If so, then do present-day practices of interagency data sharing work against established policies on privacy and so alter the relationships between government agencies? Otherwise, might a national computer policy study lead us to a different perception of personal data privacy than now represented in legislation—a perception more in keeping with that of the Japanese and the French, who perceive an end to personal data privacy in the computerized societies of the twenty-first century? Yet a national computer policy study might reinforce our own view of the need for personal data privacy, and so might recommend passage of a uniform code of data rights and responsibilities in order to thwart the Copernican turn in privacy that was prophesied.

To this discussion of domestic computer policy concerns we could add some foreign policy concerns.[16] One is the matter of an on-again, off-again embargo of computer trade by the U.S., in contrast with the methodical transfer of computer technology overseas by Japan and France through newly established ministries.[17] These and other crucially important questions need to be addressed by a national computer policy study in the U.S. at this time.

FORUM FOR AN NCP STUDY

I propose that the AFIPS member societies take the lead in providing a forum from which a national computer policy study for the U.S. may begin. The member societies certainly have a store of knowledge and expertise equal to the task; they provide a number of publications for the exchange of ideas; and in some cases the member societies have the natural organizations in the form of special interest groups (SIGs) on computers and society.

SUMMARY

The time for a national computer policy study by the United States is now. All the ingredients are present. The computer industry is recognized as crucially important to the society at large. Certain challenges and problems are beyond resolution by single firms working alone. Many in the technical community are ready to share decisions about the industry's future with the greater society. In that process of shared decision-making, the greater society may find it advantageous to establish some sort of national computer policy agency, as industry advocate and public partner, to coordinate R&D efforts, to fund certain research of importance to society at large, and to aid in the solution of problems that are beyond the industry itself to solve because sovereign nations are involved. We can expect that the combined effects of public and private investments would propel the industry onto a new, faster-rising growth curve. Finally, we might find that certain present-day uses of computers work against other, prior national policies we may wish to preserve. A national computer policy study could thereby help us to better understand ourselves and to better understand our preferred future directions as a computerized society.

REFERENCES

1. Burke, John G. "Bursting Boilers and the Federal Power." In M. Kranzberg and W. H. Davenport (ed.), *Technology and Culture.* New York: Meridian Books, 1975.
2. Bartimo, J. "Q & A With CDC's Founder and Chairman." *Computerworld,* April 19, 1982, pp. 5.
3. Palmer, E. J. "National Supercomputer Effort Needed." *Compufax,* 10 (1983), p. 1.
4. Malik, R. "IBM Enlists Washington in European Fight." *Computerworld,* June 7, 1982, pp. 130–131.
5. "Data Could Spark a Trade War." *Business Week,* November 29, 1982, p. 100.
6. Masuda, Y. *The Information Society* (1st ed.). Tokyo: Institute for the Information Society, 1980.
7. Nora, S. and A. Minc. *The Computerization of Society* (1st ed.). Cambridge: The MIT Press, 1980.
8. ERU Expert Board for Regional Development. "Telecommunications and Regional Development in Sweden–A Progress Report." The National Swedish Board for Technical Development Report LF/ALLF 222 77 004, April 1977.
9. Nova University. "Doctor of Arts in Information Science," Announcement, Fall 1983. Fort Lauderdale, Fla. (This announces an in-home curriculum via teleconferencing and interactive computing.)
10. Weiner, N. *The Human Use of Human Beings* (1st ed.). Boston: Houghton Mifflin, 1950.
11. UAW President Frazier, "60 Minutes" television interview, October 19, 1980.
12. General Accounting Office. "Federal Efforts Regarding Automated Manufacturing Need Stronger Leadership." Department of Commerce, GAO/AFMD-83-68, May 26, 1983.
13. General Accounting Office. "Industrial Policy: Japan's Flexible Approach." Department of Commerce, GAO/ID-82-83, June 23, 1982.
14. Unpublished correspondence. William V. Roth, Jr., chairman (R-Del.), U.S. Senate Committee on Governmental Affairs, to Dr. John H. Gibbons, director, Office of Technology Assessment. August 8, 1983. (Request for study of certain uses of computers in the federal government.)
15. Kirchner, J. "File Match May Aid Draft," *Computerworld,* May 7, 1979, p.1.
16. Goodman, S. E. "U.S. Computer Export Control Policies: Value Conflicts and Policy Choices." *Communications of the ACM,* 9, (1982), pp. 613-624.
17. Shaffer, R. A. "Computer Center Seeks to Aid Poor, Jobless and Third World," *The Wall Street Journal,* July 15, 1983, p.21.

Information processing management

Eugene Smith, Track Chair

As the title indicates, this group of eight sessions focuses on issues that will primarily concern the information processing manager. Over the years, data processing management has lost some of its mystique; however, the information processing manager is beginning to move into the mainstream of corporate management. This trend adds legitimacy and stature to the entire profession.

In a conference of this size and scope there are, of course, many other sessions of interest to managers in the field. The sessions described here include human issues, productivity issues, technology issues, planning issues, and two sessions on managerial perspectives. This group of sessions presents an opportunity to hear top-level managers discuss their experiences in areas of concern to all information processing managers. Those who attend these sessions can obtain a wealth of information to use back in their own work environments.

In addition to significant technological changes taking place, the role of information management is undergoing important changes. The session entitled "Information Management in the '80s: A Managerial Perspective" provides a broad look at the issues in information management from the systems manager perspective. Our systems managers must continually deal with change and cope with new issues as new technology is introduced into the workplace.

This session focuses on issues such as the changing role of systems, the nature of continued support and education, office automation and its role, the changing life cycle, and the end user environment. The intent is to identify how systems management is changing. An issue-oriented panel discussion is presented; following the discussion, the audience has an opportunity to question the panelists, who are high-level managers, about issues raised during the session.

Managers must continually be involved in the planning process. Any information systems plan has to be based on the plans of the *parent corporation*. The information systems plan must support and complement the corporate mission and goals. There is, however, an opportunity for the information system professional to affect changes in he plans of a business by showing how new information technology can allow a corporation to expand into new markets or improve the profitability of its products.

In the session "Business Planning and Information Systems," one panelist discusses the process and critical factors involved in the development of an information systems plan. Another focuses on the need for the information processing plan to conform with the business and how best to achieve this goal.

As a new technology is introduced, the relative cost of human resources continues to increase as the relative cost of hardware decreases. The problems of appropriate compensation for work accomplished, techniques for getting a task completed, and productivity are high on a manager's list of priorities. The "Information Systems and Productivity" session will focus on issues of productivity and people in information systems.

A key to improved productivity is awareness and appropriate control of personnel issues. The need for managing technology updates as they are introduced into the organization, as well as the managing of human resources, is addressed.

Managers are confronted with a diverse set of problems in providing computing service for end users in the business environment. "Planning For and Supporting End-User Business Computing" presents actual experiences related to planning for and supporting end users. This is a practical, how-to series of presentations, and the audience should obtain many ideas that they can use in their own organizations.

One panelist focuses on how best to educate and train first-time users. Another discusses the art of "Virtual Staffing," including how you can best leverage your end-user support staff. The last panelist discusses how to align plans for business systems and information systems by highlighting the steps his company used to successfully support and link 10,000 personal computers.

A major function of most information systems managers and technical systems developers is the distribution of information. It is also a critical responsibility of effective management in any field. Recent advances in microcomputer technology and telecommunications have resulted in innovative solutions to the problem of time information flow. In "Distributing Information—A Management Perspective," the panelists discuss their experiences with these technologies. The emphasis is on the business function of distributing information to meet the needs of local and corporate management. The discussions deal with diverse business environments as well as the applicability of various tools, including the microcomputer and network applications.

As microcomputers are increasingly applied to routine business problems, information systems managers are often faced with a major choice: acquire multiuser microcomputers or use a network of individual personal computers. Criteria for making such a decision depend on the particular needs and operating environment in a given situation. Significant factors affecting such an analysis include a requirement to access or share a common local database, the types of local networks available, and the costs of networking individual personal computers. In "Multiuser Micros Vs. Networked PCs," one panelist whose analysis resulted in the acquisition of multiuser microcomputers shares his rationale for this selection, whereas another panelist discusses why he chose to install a system of networked personal computers.

"Structured Methodologies and Automating the Systems Development Process" deals with the use of structured tools and how they can be used to generate usable code. Papers are presented about various automatic diagnostic techniques used in one or more of the structured methodologies. Experiences relating to the generation of design documentation and program code are discussed. Presentations include various automatic design techniques developed in support of a new analyst workbench, experiences in the development of an automatic code generator for large applications, and the development of computer-aided design (CAD)/computer-aided programming (CAP) work stations.

Decision support systems, of necessity, are moving into a new environment that involves distributed systems. The trend has begun and will greatly expand in this decade. "Decision Support Systems and Distributed Processing" provides an opportunity to hear leaders in the field present their thoughts on decision support system design methodologies in a distributed environment.

In this panel session the topic of decision support systems focuses on providing information for decision making by managers. Applications include resource allocation, problem diagnosis, scheduling, and assignment. The application of decision support systems in a distributed environment will increase significantly both the popularity and complexity of such systems.

Decision support in a distributed environment

by DANIEL T. LEE
University of Hartford
West Hartford, Connecticut

ABSTRACT

Traditional means of data processing, management information systems, and decision support systems cannot meet a new demand ushered in with the evolution of mini-micro computers. A modern computer end-user, especially a modern decision maker, needs a single pool of information that may be geographically dispersed. Therefore, a new combination of technologies is needed for coping with this new demand. The purpose of this paper is to develop a unified methodology for distributed-system design with distributed databases. The distributed systems designed under this unified methodology can satisfy geographical data independence in addition to logical and physical data independence in the traditional sense.

PREFACE

The increasing popularity of mini-micro computers has ushered in a new era of distributed systems. The end-users and knowledge personnel are increasingly using mini-micro computers in their daily data processing and decision making. They not only need transaction data but analytical information in an integrated fashion. This new demand requires a new combination of technologies for combining the distributed systems and distributed databases into a unified whole. This new combination of technologies will no doubt have a tremendous impact on the job performance of many people.

In the past four decades, computers have evolved through the eras of electronic data processing (EDP), management information systems (MIS), and the decision support system (DSS) eras. During the EDP era, computers made great contributions toward the automation of paper work and labor saving. Computer programs, however, are segmented, therefore redundancy and inconsistency are inevitable. MIS was conceived to integrate them for producing decision-making information. Unfortunately, it largely produces standard reports, which are either irrelevant or only indirectly relevant to the decision-maker's needs. In order to fill this gap, DSS was brought forward with the main emphasis on supporting decision-making.

Currently, DSS development basically follows the same traditional, yet inadequate means, which are only fit for static and structured tasks. The problems faced by a modern decision maker, however, are usually unstructured or semi-structured. In addition, traditional database technologies are usually conceived under centralized usage. Now the emerging mini-micro computers add another dimension of complexity: Data and processing might be geographically dispersed. This dimension introduces a new challenge to system design and database development.

The purpose of this paper is to integrate distributed system development with database design into a unified methodology for decision support, because data management is crucial for distributed systems in a dynamic environment, as Donovan indicates: "the database systems lie at the heart of decision support system tools."[18]

BASIC CONCEPTS

Definition

DSS was first defined by Norton as an interactive computer-based system that can help decision makers use data and models to solve unstructured problems.[47] It was criticized as being too restrictive; few actual systems can fit it satisfactorily. Sprague and Carlson[52] indicate that distributed data systems comprise a class of information system that draws on transaction processing systems and interacts with other parts of the overall information system to support the decision-making activities of managers and other knowledge workers in the organization. The DSS aims at less-structured tasks and unspecified problems. This approach combines the use of analytical techniques and database technologies with main emphasis placed upon the ease of use, flexibility, and adaptability in order to accommodate changes in the environment. The characteristics of the DSS have been fully exemplified in References 1, 2, 9–11, and 31–33.

Geographical Data Independence

As indicated earlier, the DSS is facing a new challenge—the distributed environment. The analytical techniques and database technologies applied to DSS development in the traditional sense are inadequate. For example, traditional database technologies emphasize logical data independence and physical data independence. The former insulates the changes made in the external end-user's programs from the global conceptual schema, whereas the latter severs the changes made in the internal physical storage with the global conceptual schema. By satisfying these two data independences, the end-user and database designer can enjoy all the freedom in modifying the database without the constraints imposed by any one of the three schemas (external, conceptual, or internal). Traditionally, the databases satisfying these data-independence requirements are regarded as being very close to ideal, but under the new distributed environment, it would be necessary to satisfy one more requirement—geographical data independence. The end-users can obtain the data for their programs without having to know where it is really located. This capability requirement is very critical for an efficient and effective DSS, working in a distributed environment.

Generally, there are three basic capability requirements for a genuine DSS: data, model, and dialogue. Data means data management capability. It basically indicates database management systems (DBMS) necessary to satisfy the information needs of the end-users and decision-makers. Model means model management capability, because a modern decision maker needs not only transactional data but also analytical information. Dialogue means friendly query languages that end-users or decision-makers can use for interfacing with the computers. Now these three capabilities must be built upon a geographical transparency. The end-users and decision-makers can interact with models and data without having to know where they are located.

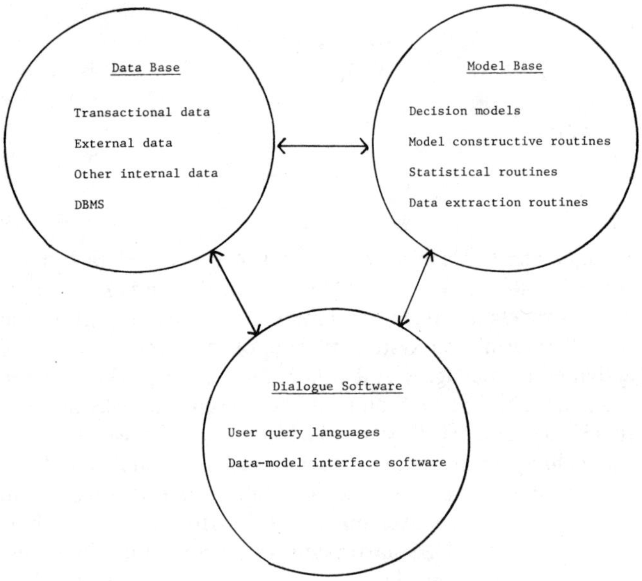

Figure 1—Components of decision support systems

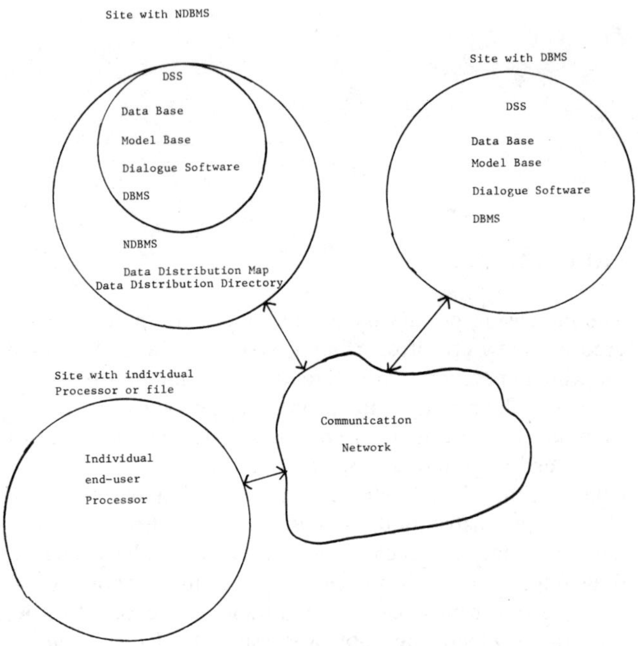

Notes: (1) NDBMS stands for network database management system. (2) The three types of site can be many in a network decision support system. For simplicity, only one of each type is shown. (3) Communication network is a network system for data communication.

Figure 2—Network decision support system diagram

Traditionally, there are usually three components in DSS, as shown in Figure 1. In order to meet geographical data independence, Figure 1 should be extended to more than one DBMS or independent files that are interlinked through communication networks, similar to Figure 2.

Three Approaches

According to Lee there are currently two approaches in DSS design methodologies, the application-specific approach (ASA) and the integrated MIS approach (IMA).[36,37] The ASA is under the notion that the knowledge personnel will try to improve their job performance by exploiting the new technologies in their specific applications. They feel that the institutionalization of DSS is very difficult, if not impossible, in terms of existing knowledge and cost–benefit justification, and that the MIS personnel are too busy producing standard reports and have no time or expertise to build up DSS for the knowledge personnel. Here the knowledge personnel are defined as the decision makers and their intermediaries, e.g., management science and OR personnel.

Unfortunately, the ASA is not general; neither is it efficient or economical. It never takes advantage of the existing information-producing mechanisms in the organization. The IMA was conceived under the notion of total system concept. The IMA tries to integrate everything in the system. It sounds great, but nobody knows "how."

Lee developed a unified approach in accordance with the contingent model. It steps down a level of abstraction by grasping the things we can manage, without losing sight of the whole. It focuses on the information flows and groups them into subsystems. The things we can clearly define are first organized into the major operational databases, and spaces are provided for data, the contents of which are not known at the present, but whose relative positions (with respect to the whole construct) are clear. When the time comes that the data do become clear, we may add them to the system. Detailed discussion of the unified approach (TUA) applied to the DSS development is presented in References 35 and 38–40.

The basics of TUA also can be applied to the design of a DSS in a distributed environment. This approach should be extended to accommodate the geographical data independence in four transaction transparencies—location, concurrency, replication, and failure. Discussion of these topics follows in the next three sections.

DISTRIBUTED SYSTEM DESIGN

The Characteristics of DS

A distributed system (DS) is defined as one in which application programs and/or data reside in separate interlinked sites and are designed in an integrated and tightly controlled fashion. This definition is somewhat biased toward an integrated approach. It should be modulated by the contingent model[36] and the unified approach for designing the DSS[35,37,38–40] that was discussed previously. After this modulation, it then can be applied to the development of a DS with DDB in a realistic and practical manner. Decision makers can then be allowed to access the data freely in an integrated fashion without being bogged down by complicated mechanisms.

The Characteristics of DDB

A distributed database is defined by Date[17] as a database that is not stored in its entirety at a single physical location, but rather is spread across a network of locations that are geographically dispersed and connected by communication links. It may best be described as the union of a set of individually centralized databases, because a distributed system is considered to be a partnership among a set of independent but cooperating centralized systems rather than some kind of monolithic and indivisible object.

The Basic Functions of DS

The centralization of strategic management and the decentralization of functional operations should be one of the most important objectives. The maximization of the autonomy of the individual units and the minimization of dependence among them also are vital to an effective distributed system. Each processing unit should be self-contained, but can be connected through database management systems and communication network protocols. In this way, foreign entanglements can be reduced to a minimum, if not completely stamped out. The DS designed under these guidelines will have autonomy of individual units and integration of the whole system. This DS design is quite complex but can be done if the design methodologies are used properly. This is the topic of the next three sections.

Design Strategies of DS

There are usually two approaches—top-down and bottom-up. In designing a decent DS, both approaches are needed. The top-down is used for macro-system design. It tries to lay down the design strategies for databases, files, and distributed data; to establish standards for database design and responsibilities of development; and finally to decide data structure, subject databases and their locations.

At the end of this process, it will become clear which data structure should reside in a given location; their subject databases, application databases, independent files, and subschema files. Production systems vs. information systems also are clearly delineated.

Design Strategies of DDB

As indicated, the above process establishes the basic strategies and guidelines for DS development. It is a macro-system design, from which we concurrently proceed to micro-system design—either during the construction of or after the completion of macro-system design. The following design guidelines follow the bottom-up approach and aim at a detailed DS design with major emphasis on DDB development. The methodologies for DDB design may use the traditional systems analysis and design methodologies. The major difference is that the complexity for DS with DDB development is much higher than that of traditional system design because the DS with DDB will have to satisfy geographical data independence. The four transaction transparencies—location, concurrency, replication, and failure—are the major concerns for an efficient and effective DS. These topics are discussed in the next two sections.

In summary, the top-down approach establishes an overall framework and a general architecture into which the end-user modules can fit into the overall architecture. The former is mainly concerned with the upper structure of the system, whereas the later is used to establish the basic modules, especially the DDB, which is the major component of DS.[46]

Design Procedures of DS

The practical steps in distributed-system development may be divided into two large phases: a subsystem delineation phase and a DDB development phase. In the subsystem delineation phase, there are five steps. First is establishing end-user sites in accordance with the processing and data requirements, such as a head office in Chicago, a warehouse in Atlanta, a warehouse in Miami, etc. Second is identifying the applications required in each end-user site for performing the functions of that site, such as credit-checking, shipping, accounts receivable, etc. Third is grouping these end-user sites with their applications into subsystems (e.g., in a manufacturing firm, there might be one head office, one or more factories, one or more branch offices, one or more laboratories). Fourth is tracing the internal and external transfers of data between internal subsystems or with the outside world, because some applications in each subsystem might share the same data or processing result. These applications should be grouped into the same subsystem, and their processing and data requirements should be closely coordinated and delineated. Fifth, separate computers for each subsystem should be identified. The interface between subsystems should also be clearly defined.

After the fifth step, a general picture of the distributed system is clearly shown, but it is still primitive and only a rough structure. A refinement is needed for its implementation. This will have to be done in the second phase.

In the DDB development phase, there are another six steps: First is establishing subject data bases and files by following the semantic data model (SDM),[26,34] or Chen's entity-relationship model (E/R),[14] because the SDM can be turned easily into an E/R model which, in turn, can be transformed straight into other database models, such as a relational data model (RDM), a network data model (NDM), or a hierarchical data model (HDM).

The subject databases are constructed in accordance with the business subjects rather than applications, such as customers, parts, vendors, accounts, etc., rather than order entry, credit checking, inventory control, accounts payable, etc.

These business subjects are selected from narrative statements. The statements are recorded from the interview of the end-users, decision makers, and application programmers, or from checking the documents of the firm, and from the personal observation of the production process along with the information flows of decision-making process. For detailed information on structured system analysis and design, please refer to References 24, 34, 54, and 55. Second is delineating the end-user sites and their applications—the same as in the first and second steps in the subsystem delineation phase. The third step is building a diagram of logical end-users, applications, and subject databases. This will clearly show that subject databases are shared by the applications, of which the applications are needed by the end-user sites. Fourth, determining the application programs needed for processing each application and the subject databases required for each application program. Fifth, classifying each application into four classes: SS, DS, SD, and DD. The classification is based on two factors: processing site and subject database. The SS class is determined in accordance with the application processed at the same location and the data required for processing is also located at the same location. The DS is decided by its being processed at different location, but the data required is located at the same location. The SD is in the reverse of DS. The DD is in the reverse of SS (Figure 3). The SS class is the most desirable. The DS is common with centralized systems. The DD class should be avoided. The transactions not in class SS must be handled by use of data replication, by data transmission, or both, to make the transaction class SS.

The sixth step is determining the traffic between end-user site and data location, showing whether the traffic is batch or on-line, and determining the volume as well as the frequency of traffic. The data distribution diagram (Figure 4) clearly shows these seven steps. Actually, the data distribution diagram could be drawn step-by-step.

The seventh step is determining the data distribution in accordance with the following factors: transaction volume, data size, frequency of data transfer, frequency of update, complexity of update, complexity of data replication, cost of transmission, and cost of data storage. For example, if the transaction volume is high, the data size is low, the data are updated infrequently, the updates are simple, and the data replication structure is simple, then the data should be replicated. In Figure 4, it is clearly shown that the products subject data base are highly shared on-line by many end-user sites. Data transmission is too expensive. It should be replicated. Following the above distribution factors, we may proceed one-by-one to the subject database to determine whether it should be replicated, partitioned, or centralized. Detailed discussion on design of distributed systems is presented in References 22 and 46.

The above eight distribution factors do not exhaust the list; there are many more other factors that should also be considered, including concurrency control, failure recovery, processing requirement, software development. Because a detailed discussion of these topics is beyond this paper, they will be briefly treated in the next two sections.

<table>
<tr><th>Application class</th><th>Processing site</th><th>Subject Data Base location</th></tr>
<tr><td>SS</td><td>Same</td><td rowspan="2">Same</td></tr>
<tr><td>DS</td><td>Different</td></tr>
<tr><td>SD</td><td>Same</td><td rowspan="2">Different</td></tr>
<tr><td>DD</td><td>Different</td></tr>
</table>

Figure 3—Application classes

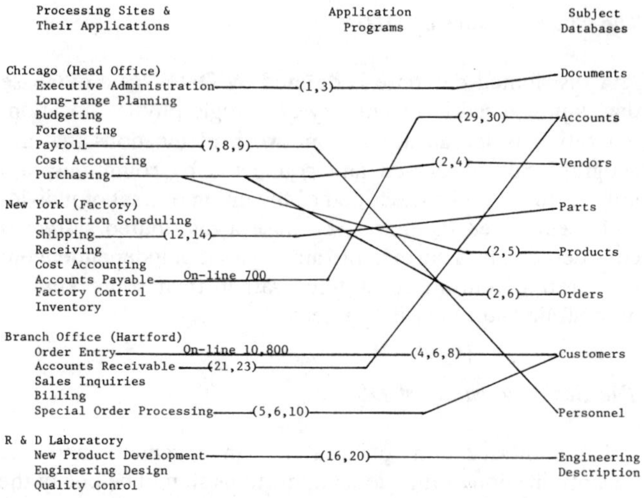

Note: In order to reduce complexity, the factory, branch office, and R&D Laboratory are listed only once. In actuality there can be many of each. In a larger firm a tabular form can be used instead of maps. The connection links among the processing sites, application programs, and databases are used for illustrative purposes only. They do not exhaust the possible connections.

Figure 4—Data description map

TRANSACTION PROCESSING

A complete distributed system is supposed to be able to process any transaction at any site and to obtain data from any location. Unfortunately, so far there is no such complete system. Rather, a task that operates at several sites must be planned and programmed to be sensitive to data location and network communication. A comprehensive discussion of communication systems and their protocols is beyond the scope of this paper. It has been fully treated and documented in many other sources.[8,17,22,25,41,44,45,49,50] This section is a discussion of transaction processing with four transparencies, and how to develop a distributed system with appropriate transparencies for decision support. Practical examples will be surveyed in the next section.

Transaction Concepts

A transaction is a unit of work. It consists of the execution of a sequence of operations. Traiger proposes a model of transactions in a distributed system with the highest levels of transparencies in location, replication, concurrency, and failure.[53] The system may consist of a geographically dispersed collection of computers, called sites, which are connected by a communication network. The system supports a set of entities that are represented by one or more segments. These segments are identified by <name, site> pairs, where name is the entity name, and site is the place in which the segment is located. At any time, a value is associated with each segment. A segment may represent an entity or a part of an entity. Several segments at a site might represent the same entity or they might represent the same entity at different sites.

If an entity is represented by multiple segments, then the entity is said to be replicated. An entity named E that is replicated at sites $S_1, \ldots, S_n$ is represented by the segments $<E, S_1>, \ldots, <E, S_n>$. A system without replicas is called partitioned because each entity is at exactly one site. If all segments reside at the same site, the system is called centralized.

A particular application may need one or more transactions. Each transaction may associate a meaning with each entity; e.g., entity E_1 represents products, entity E_2 represents accounts, and so on. The collection of entities and their relationships is called subject databases. Their representation depends on the database models used.

The Execution of Transactions

A transaction issues requests to manipulate entities. These requests are translated by the system into one or more commands on the entity. Each site provides a group of commands that manipulate entities or segments at that site. The translator at the site keeps an entity–site directory, which gives the site addresses of segments. The format for reading a record (an entity or a segment) by transaction T of segment $<E,S>$ which has value Val is represented by

[T,READ (E,S), Val]

The READ is one of the commands. If the command is WRITE, it alters the value, Val, to a new one. If the command is COMMIT, it means that the transaction is successfully executed.

Each command operates on one segment only and hence at one site only. There may be concurrency of execution in the network, but the commands at a site appear to happen in some order. All commands on segments are performed at the site of the segment. Whenever a site participates in a transaction execution, the site allocates an agent for that transaction. The agent keeps track of the local traction state and performs the commands for that transaction at that site. Whenever a transaction requests nonlocal action, the requesting site issues requests to the requested site (or the owning site) for action. The requested site follows the same procedure of execution. Thus, the transaction is executed synchronously, completing one action (request) before issuing the next, and finally issuing a COMMIT action to each site visited. Actually, transaction execution control may migrate from site to site. The control protocol of the network must be more complicated.

Data Distribution Architecture

Lo proposes a three-level distributed-database design consisting of source level, user level, and control level.[42] In the source level, the design consists of a complete set of subject (global) databases. Data in this level are fully replicated and synchronized. The user level consists of a subset of the subject databases that is derived from the source level and becomes the application databases used by the various control processing functions.

The control level consists of four components: the transaction processor, data dictionary, subject database map, and communication software. The transaction processor coordinates the data flow in the system. The data dictionary documents all facts, including update information. The subject database map is more efficient than the data dictionary in locating subject databases. The communication software handles the actual data communication in the system.

Data are globally synchronized at the control level. The distributed-database concept discussed here is applicable to the wide applications of multinational corporations. Each division of the corporation resembles the regional operation centers. The data at the branch office can be updated locally and broadcasted to the other sites for updating. The database system design proposed here allows currently available database management systems to be used in the source and user levels, but it needs to develop the communication protocols required in the control level.

User Transparencies

Friendly interface with end-users with distributed systems is highly desirable in the execution of transactions. Location transparency, replication transparency, concurrency transparency, and failure transparency are vital for a successful distribution system. With these four transparencies, an end-user can concentrate on what he wants and does not have to worry about the location of data and the question concerning whether the data are replicated, partitioned, or centralized. During the execution, he will be assured that the data will be delivered accurately and that the results of data manipulation will be consistent. Detailed discussion is presented in References 4–7, 12, 17, 19, 23, 30, 43, 46, 50, and 53. The mechanisms of these transaction transparencies will be briefly examined during our discussion of the prototypes of distributed systems in the next section.

THE PRESENT STATE OF THE ART

Examining the prototypes of distributed systems is one of the most efficient methods of understanding the underlying theory of distributed systems. It will demonstrate the architecture, design methodology, distribution application, distributed database, transaction transparency, and especially it will unveil the state of the art in distributed-system development.

Six distributed systems are selected for analysis: IMS/MSC, CICS/ISC, Distributed INGRES, R* (R Star), Tandem's Encompass Systems, and SDD-1.Most of these are experimental systems. Some are installed successfully but their software protocols in network control and database management systems still need much improvement.

IMS/MSC

IMS's Multiple System Coupling (MSC) allows two or more IMS systems to be connected. End-users or programs can invoke one program on another. The input message from a user, or the IMS DC call from a program, will be placed on the input queue. IMS will then examine a local catalogue to see whether the program to be executed for this calling program resites at which remote site. When this is accomplished, the input message will be transmitted to that site for processing. The result will be transmitted back to the original site. The transaction invocation can propagate from one remote site to another with the result being transmitted back to the original invoking site. One must remember, however, that the MSC of IMS does not really support distributed-transaction processing as in the System R or CICS. Each invoking site must complete the execution before the next one in the sequence can start. There is no parallelism among them or return of control from an invoked program to its invoking program. The system supports only transaction routing, not transaction processing. The term "transaction" is used in IMS to mean an input message rather than the execution of a program.

The end-user does not have to know where the data or programs reside, and can invoke a transaction from any site. Programs, however, can access only local data. They do need to know the precise location of remote data and this data distribution knowledge is built into the application logic. In a general sense, IMS does provide location transparency, but only in a limited form.

MSC is an IMS-only feature. IMS is also capable of participating in a different distribution scheme known as ISC (Inter Systems Communication), which is a set of protocols used for communicating with other systems, such as CICS.

Basically, the IMS/MSC provides location transparency for message handling among multiple sites. It also provides the transaction notion and failure transparency. The program isolation feature of IMS is similar to that of providing concurrency transparency for transactions within a single site. IMS has no notion of replicated or partitioned data and does not provide replication or location transparencies in a strict sense.

CICS/ISC

ISC (Inter-System Communication) is a set of protocols by which any systems conforming to those protocols can communicate with one another. Most of the ISCs are supported by Customer Information Control Systems (CICS).[22,56] CICS/ISC allows two or more CICS systems to be connected in such a way that one application program can invoke another at a different site without ceasing execution itself, or can issue a DL/1 call against a database at another site.

In the first case, in the CICS sense of the term, this is called distributed transaction processing, which allows the total application to be divided into a distributed set of programs. The end-user will initiate the transaction by invoking the first of these programs. As it executes, that program—or agent—can invoke agents at another site. The set of all agents is considered as a unit for recovery. Therefore, it does support the transaction notion. CICS does not maintain a catalogue giving the location of each program; instead, an agent A that wishes to invoke another agent B must specify the site at which the program for B resides. The data distribution knowledge is built into the application logic. Location transparency is not provided under the first case.

In the second case, it is called data request shipping. It does support location transparency at the application level. The programs can issue DL/1 database calls against a remote database and CICS/ISC will intercept the call and ship it to the appropriate remote site, using a catalogue that gives the location of each database. An agent will be assigned by that remote site to perform the necessary processing or to issue calls on behalf of the original program and to return the result to the original program. Again, all agents are considered as a unit for recovery.

In a general sense, CICS does provide the transaction notion, location transparency, and failure transparency, but not concurrency transparency because there is no lock manager. Responsibility for concurrency control is delegated to the individual subsystems, such as DL/1, TOTAL, System 2,000, etc. Similarly, CICS has no notion of replicated data.

Distributed INGRES

The distributed version of INGRES does not provide a notion of transaction, but does provide location and replication transparency. In INGRES, a single QUEL statement is a transaction. This implies that it does not have either failure or concurrency transparencies for transactions that are groups of QUEL statements.[17,20,21,27,51,53]

*R**

R* (R Star) is a distributed version of System R currently under development at the IBM San Jose Research Laboratory. The basic difference between SDD-1 and R* is that SDD-1 starts by choosing a workable strategy and then tries to improve on it, whereas the R* attempts to generate a whole set of workable strategies and then selects the cheapest one. The SDD-1 is characterized as somewhat "greedy," as Data puts it,[17] in that it always looks for immediate improvements; it will find a solution that is locally optimal, but not necessarily the one that is globally optimal.[3,56]

Tandem's Encompass Systems

The distributed EMPACT is an application of DS with DDB for business organizations. The design of distributed EMPACT illustrates the techniques used in DDB development, and the actual implementation of distributed systems.

The elements of the database are divided into two major categories, global data and local data. Private data do not enter the picture because they are used only by the individual site and are not visible to the other sites. Global data are shared by all sites, such as the list of parts that determine the TANDEM parts catalog (item master file). The local data consist of information that is uniquely important to the individual site using it but accessible by all sites, such as stock status and work-in-process data. Global data are necessarily replicated at all sites, whereas local data are single-site resident. There may be, however, a fourth kind of data called partial replication data, which permit requests by one site for material from another to be placed and processed. But these data are only known and resident at both sites, and not necessarily to the third party. Such data may be classified as semi-global.

The database consistency solution must satisfy two important objectives: continuous availability and site autonomy. Since global data are replicated at every site, query access to the database is guaranteed regardless of the status of other sites in the network. The problem is to find a way to maintain all copies in the network updated and consistent at all times.

One way is to broadcast the updates to all the sites in the network as a single transaction, but keep in mind that global files can be updated only when all sites are available. It usually requires a long wait and sacrifices site autonomy.

The solution chosen was to sacrifice the absolute consistency of the replicated files in exchange for site autonomy and short terminal response by using a suspense mechanism to maintain database consistency. Instead of immediately broadcasting the updates to all sites in the network, the server at the site where an update is initiated first updates that copy of the global data and then posts the update message to a suspense, or queue, file. A suspense monitor asynchronously polls the suspense file for transactions and, on an as-soon-as-possible basis, sends the transaction message to appropriate servers at remote sites, one at a time, as a separate transaction for updating.

The requirement of site autonomy is satisfied because updates to the global files can be initiated regardless of the status of other sites in the network. The propagation of the update to remote sites is performed asychronously by the suspense monitor.

Because the suspense mechanism introduces a delay in the propagation of updates to remote sites, the possibility of conflicting adds and updates among the sites becomes a problem. To prevent conflicting updates from occurring when two or more sites update their copies of the same data simultaneously, ownership (by site) is assigned to global records and the initiation of updates is restricted to the owning site only.

Another problem introduced by the suspense mechanism is stale data. The data are out of date because an update to the file has been posted at a remote site but has not yet been propagated to the local site. However, because the propagation time for suspense updates is considered less than the time the user community takes to act on the update, temporary staleness is not a problem. Besides, a two-step protocol of check and update is used for updating transactions. Serialization of executing transactions is maintained by a counter at the site initiating global updates. The suspense file is key-sequenced, and the value obtained by incrementing the counter determines the relative position of the record in the suspense file.

This is an example of distributed system with DDB application. The organization of the database and software closely parallel the structure and organization of the business environment. Generally, Tandem's Encompass Systems do support location, concurrency, and failure transparencies, but not replication transparency. Detailed discussion of the Tandem's Encompass Systems is presented in References 12 and 48.

SDD-1

SDD-1 (a system for distributed databases by Computer Corporation of America) is the first working DDB designed for naval command and control applications. It is also appropriate for general applications that require an integrated database and geographically distributed data. Multiple users need to access a single pool of information that is geographically distributed. It is highly desirable to have a system that can exercise decentralized processing and centralized control. The DDB poses a new technical challenge because its inherent requirements are for data communication and parallel processing. Overall architecture and basic techniques of SDD-1 will be briefly discussed. Detailed discussions are presented in References 5–7, 16, 25, 46, and 50.

SDD-1 supports a relational model.[15] Users interact with SDD-1 through a higher level language called DATACOMPUTER.[16] A single data-language command is called a transaction; this is the basic unit of interaction between SDD-1 and the users. This concept of transaction is similar to that of INGRES[27] and System R.[3,17]

An SDD-1 database consists of logical relations, which are partitioned into subrelations called logical fragments. These fragments are the units of data distribution. They are defined by horizontally and vertically subsetting relations. The assignment of fragments to sites is made when the database is designed. The end-users are unaware of data distribution or replication. They reference only relations, not fragments. The SDD-1 will translate from relations to fragments, and then select the stored fragments.

SDD-1 consists of three virtual machines: Transaction Modules (TMs), Data Modules (DMs), and a Reliable Network (RelNet). All data are stored in DMs under the supervision of TMs. DMs respond to four types of command: read, move, manipulate, and write to perform fragmentation, concurrency control, access planning, and distributed-query processing. The RelNet connects DMs and TMs and provides four services: guaranteed delivery, transaction control, site monitoring, and network clock.

Concurrency control

When multiple users access a shared database, two conflicts can occur. First, if T_1 is reading a database while T_2 is updating it, T_1 might read inconsistent data. Second, if both T_1 and T_2 are updating the database, race conditions can produce erroneous results. Traditionally, this is solved by database locking, but this solution might cause long delay and affect site autonomy.

SDD-1 adopts serializability for concurrency correctness because serial execution maintains consistency. SDD-1 uses two synchronization mechanisms that are different from locking. The first is called conflict analysis for detecting potential conflicts. Two transactions are in conflict if the read-set or write-set of one intersects the write-set of the other. The read-set of a transaction is defined as the portion of the database the transaction reads, and the write-set of a transaction is the portion of the database the transaction updates. The database administrator defines transaction classes, which are named groups of commonly executed transactions. Each class is defined by its name, a read-set, a write-set, and the TM at which it runs. A transaction is a member of a class if the transaction's read-set and write-set are contained in the class's read-set and write-set, respectively. Conflict analysis is performed on these transaction classes, but not on individual transactions, because transactions from different classes can conflict only if their classes conflict. The output of the analysis is a table that indicates for each class which other classes it conflicts with, and for each such conflict, what protocols are needed to ensure serializability.

Each TM might only be allowed to supervise transactions from one class. When a transaction issues a request, the system determines which TM should be sent in accordance with the transaction class to which it belongs. The TM synchronizes all transactions by global timestamping and pipeline rule.

The second synchronization mechanism is the global timestamp and the pipeline rule. In traditional locking, the execution order is determined by the order in which the transactions request locks. In SDD-1, the order is determined by a total ordering of transactions induced by timestamps. Each transaction submitted to SDD-1 is assigned a globally unique timestamp by its TM and is sent to the DMs. When a DM receives a READ command, it defers the command until it has processed all earlier WRITE commands. The pipeline rule requires that each TM send its WRITE commands to DMs in timestamp order.

The access planning minimizes intersite communication. Two-phase commit guarantees delivery. SDD-1 treats directories of data as ordinary user data, but the data directories also can be fragmented, distributed, and updated. A copy of the directory locator is stored at every DM. SDD-1 maintains directories that contain relation, fragment definitions, fragment locations, and usage statistics. TMs will use them for every transaction manipulation.

SDD-1 is the first working DDB and employs ARPANET's communication network and able to use the world's X.25 packet-switching networks. The work was supported by the Defense Advanced Research Project Agency. SDD-1 was designed for Naval command and control applications. The techniques can be used for DS with DDB in general. The development team analyzed the problems of directory, conflict, and efficiency of the system, which was implemented successfully.

In summary, the SDD-1 does provide both location and replication transparencies, allowing the user to think in terms of entities (files) rather than segments. It does not support the notion of transaction; so, strictly speaking, it does not provide failure or concurrency transparencies. In SDD-1, a single data-language statement is a transaction. An application usually requires several data-language statements to perform an operation.

Summary Notes on Prototypes

We have surveyed some, but by no means all, of the major DDB prototypes. Most of them surveyed are experimental systems. Some are implemented successfully, such as SDD-1 and Tandem's Encompass Systems. The IMS/MSC, CICS/ISC, and distributed version of INGRES also have been used as the basis for much of the discussion. In Figure 5, five prototypes of distributed systems with DDB are listed for comparison in terms of four transparencies and the notion of transaction. This is used only to show the general character of each prototype.

SDD-1 is atypical prototype distributed system designed and implemented in an integrated fashion to provide the user with a single, consistent view of a complete database. The system also is designed to support databases that can be physically distributed with arbitrary redundancy over a network of potential worldwide distribution. The control is completely distributed. The system will continue to function even if any one of the sites fails. New sites can be added freely. This will increase the survivability of the system. Furthermore, these distribution features can be applied to business applications. It will naturally lead the EDP, MIS, and especially the DSS into a new era of distributed systems.

CONCLUSIONS

The fundamentals of DSS have been discussed; basic characteristics of DSS, current design methodologies, and capability requirements of DSS have been covered briefly. Distributed system development and distributed database design have been discussed intensively. A step-by-step method has been used for illustrating the design process of DS and DDB. A three-level distribution architecture of DS has been shown. The notion of transaction and the four transaction transparencies are important concepts in DS and have been briefly treated.

Typical prototypes of DS with DDB have been closely scrutinized to peep into the mysteries of DS. Six types of current DS have been used for investigation. Some are installed successfully and are commercially available, such as SDD-1, but

Prototypes of DS	Location	Replication	Concurrency	Failure	Notice of Transaction
SDD-1	*	*			
Tandem's Encompass	*		*	*	
INGRES	*	*			
IMS/MSC	*		*	*	*
CICS/ISC	*			*	*

Figure 5—Survey of prototypes

most of them are experimental in nature. This prototype investigation may provide valuable information for DS designers in the selection process; when the situation arises, they may use this information as a guideline to DS development or for choosing the appropriate DS.

Currently, there are no perfect distribution systems on the market; the major bottlenecks are in the software development of communication systems and network database management protocols. Technology is progressing at a rapid pace, but it will gradually ease off in the near future. We can predict that the next decade will be the era of distributed systems, especially since the use of mini-microcomputers has become widespread. Distributed systems with distributed databases will become the major carrier for data management in the decade to come.

REFERENCES

1. Alter, S. "A Taxonomy of Decision Support Systems." *Sloan Management Review,* 19 (1977).
2. Alter, Steven L. *Decision Support Systems: Current Practice and Continuing Changes.* Reading, Mass.: Addison-Wesley, 1980.
3. Astrahan, M. M. et al. "System R: Relational Approach to Database Management." *ACM TODS,* 1 (1976).
4. Bernstein, P. A. and Goodman, N. "Multivision Concurrency Control—Theory and Algorithms," ACM Transactions on Database Systems, Vol. 8, No. 4, December 1983.
5. Bernstein, P. A., and D. W. Shipman. "The Correctness of Concurrency Control Mechanisms in a System for Distributed Database (SDD-1)." *ACM TODS,* 5 (1980).
6. Bernstein, P. A., D. W. Shipman, and J. B. Rothnie, Jr. "Concurrency Control in a System for Distributed Databases (SDD-1)." *ACM TODS,* 5 (1980).
7. Bernstein, P. A., N. Goodman, E. Wong, C. L. Reeve, and J. B. Rothnie, Jr. "Query Processing in a System for Distributed Databases (SDD-1)." *ACM TODS,* 6 (1981).
8. Bernstein, P. A., and N. Goodman. "Concurrency Control in Distributed Database Systems," *ACM Comp. Surv.,* 13 (1981).
9. Bonczek, Robert H. et al. "Aiding Decision Makers with a Generalized Data Base Management System: An Application to Inventory Management," *Decision Sciences,* 9 (1978).
10. Bonczek, R. H., C. W. Holsapple, and A. B. Whinston. *Foundation of Decision Support Systems.* New York; Academic Press, 1981.
11. Bonczek, R. H., C. W. Holsapple, and A. B. Whinston. "The Evolving Roles of Models in Decision Support Systems," *Decision Sciences,* 11 (1980).
12. Boor, A. "Transaction Monitoring in Encompass-Reliable Distributed Transaction Processing." In *Proceedings of the 7th International Conference on Very Large Databases,* New York: IEEE, 1981.
13. Ceri, S. and Pelagatti, G. "Correctness of Query Execution Strategies in Distributed Databases," ACM Transaction on Database Systems, Vol. 8, No. 4, December 1983.
14. Chen, P. "The Entity-Relationship Model: Toward a Unified View of Data," *ACM Transactions on Database Systems,* 1 (1976).
15. Codd, E. F. "A Relational Model of Data for Large Shared Data Banks," *Communications of the ACM,* 13 (1970).
16. Computer Corporation of America, "Datacomputer Version 5 User Manual," Cambridge, Mass., July 1978.
17. Date, C. J. *An Introduction to Database Systems,* Vol. II, Reading, Mass.: Addison-Wesley, 1983.
18. Donovan, J. J. "Database Approach to Management Decision Support." *ACM Transactions on Database Systems,* 1 (1976).
19. Eager, D. L. and Sevick, K. C. "Achieving Robustness in Distributed Database Systems," ACM Transactions on Database Systems, Vol. 8, No. 3, September 1983.
20. Epstein, R., and M. R. Stonebraker, "Distributed Query Processing in a Relational Data Base System." In *Proceedings of the 1978 ACM SIGMOD International Conference on Management of Data,* June 1978.
21. Stonebraker, M. R., "Analysis of Distributed Data Base Processing Strategies." In *Proceedings of the 6th International Conference on Very Large Data Bases,* October 1980.
22. Fitzgerald, J. *Business Data Communications,* John Wiley & Sons, New Jersey, 1984.
23. Garcia-Molina, H. "Using Semantic Knowledge for Transaction Processing in a Distributed Database System," ACM Transactions on Database Systems, Vol. 8, No. 2, June 1983.
24. Gane, C., and T. Sarson. *Structured System Analysis: Tools and Techniques.* John Wiley and Sons, 1973.
25. Hammer, M., and D. Shipman. "Reliability Mechanisms for SDD-1: A System for Distributed Databases." *ACM TODS,* 5 (1980).
26. Hammer, M., and D. McLeod. "Database Description with SDM: A Semantic Database Model." *ACM Transactions on Database Systems,* 6 (1981).
27. Held, G., M. Stonebraker, and E. Wong. "INGRES: A Relational Data Base System." *AFIPS, Proceedings of the National Computer Conference* (Vol 44), 1975.
28. IBM Corporation, CICS/VS System/Application Design Guide, IBM Form No. SC33-0068.
29. Kamilo, F. *Digital Communications,* Prentice-Hall, Inc., Englewood Cliffs, New Jersey, 1983.
30. Katz, R. H. and Wong, E. "Resolving Conflicts in Global Storage Through Replication," ACM Transactions on Database Systems, Vol. 8, No. 1, March 1983.
31. Keen, Peter G. W., and M. S.S. Mortton. *Decision Support Systems: An Organizational Perspective.* Reading, Mass.: Addison-Wesley, 1978.
32. Keen, P. G. W. et al. "Building a Decision Support System: The Mythical Man-Month Revisited." In J. F. Bennett (ed.), *Building Decision Support Systems.* Addison-Wesley Series on Decision Support. Reading, Mass.: Addison-Wesley, 1980.
33. Keen, P. G. W. "Decision Support Systems: Translating Analytic Techniques in Useful Tools." *Sloan Management Review,* 21 (1980).
34. Kroenke, D. "Database Processing" (2nd ed.). SRA, 1983.
35. Lee, Daniel T. "Unified Database for Decision Support." *International Journal of Policy Analysis and Information Systems,* 6 (1982).
36. Lee, D. T. "The Contingent Model of Decision Support Systems." In *Proceedings of Wesern AIDS,* 1982.
37. Lee, D. T. "The Unified Approach for Designing Decision Support Systems." *DSS-82 Transactions,* 1982.
38. Lee, D. T. "Decision Support Systems and Distributed Data Processing," *Proceedings of TIMS/ORSA,* 1983.
39. Lee, D. T. "Database-Oriented Decision Support Systems." *AFIPS, Proceedings of the National Computer Conference* (Vol. 52), 1983.
40. Lee, D. T. "Data Base Design for Decision Support Systems," In *Management and Office Information Systems* Vol. 1. Plenum, 1983.
41. Lindsay, B. G., P. G. Selinger. "Site Autonomy Issues in R*: A Distributed Database Management System." IBM Research Report RJ2927, September 1980.
42. Lo, S. C., S. L. Kota, and M. H. Aronson. "A Distributed Database Design for a Communication Network Control System." *AFIPS, Proceedings of the National Computer Conference* (Vol. 52), 1983.
43. Lynch, N. A. "Multilevel Atomicity—A New Correctness for Database Concurrency Control," ACM Transactions on Database Systems, Vol. 8, No. 4, December 1983.
44. Martin, J. *Communication Satellite Systems.* Englewood Cliffs, N.J.: Prentice-Hall, 1978.
45. Martin, J. *Computer Networks and Distributed Processing.* Englewood Cliffs, N.J.: Prentice-Hall, 1981.
46. Martin, J. *Design and Strategy for Distributed Data Processing.* Englewood Cliffs, N.J.: Prentice-Hall, 1981.
47. Morton, S. M. S. "Management Decision Systems: Computer Based Support for Decision Making." Division of Research, Harvard University, Cambridge, Mass., 1971.
48. Norman, A., and M. Anderton. "EMPACT: A Distributed Database Application." *AFIPS, Proceedings of the National Computer Conference* (Vol. 52), 1983.
49. Puzman, J. and Porizek, R. *Communication Control in Computer Networks,* John Wiley & Sons, New York, 1980.
50. Rothnie Jr., J. B., Bernstein, P. A., Fox, S., Goodman, N., Hammer, M., Landers, T. A., Reeve, C., Shipman, D. W., and Wong, E. "Introduction to a System for Distributed Databases (SDD-1)," ACM TODS, Vol. 5, No. 1, March 1980.

51. Stonebraker, M. R., and E. J. Neuhold. "A Distributed Data Base Version of INGRES," In *Proceedings of the Second Berkeley Conference on Distributed Data Management and Computer Networks*. Berkeley, Calif.: Lawrence Berkeley Laboratory, May 1977.
52. Sprague, R. H., Jr., and R. D. Carlson, *Building Effective Decision Support Systems*. Englewood Cliffs, N.J.: Prentice-Hall, 1982.
53. Traiger, I. L., J. Gray, C. A. Galtieri, and B. G. Lindsay. "Transactions and Consistency in Distributed Database Systems." *ACM TODS,* 7 (1982).
54. Tsichntzis, D. C., and F. H. Lochovsky. *Data Model.* Englewood Cliffs, N.J.: Prentice-Hall, 1982.
55. Vetter, M., and R. N. Maddison. *Database Design Methodology*. Englewood Cliffs, N.J.: Prentice-Hall, 1981.
56. Williams, R. et al. "R*: An Overview of the Architecture," IBM Research Report RJ 3225, December 1981.

Issues in the design of expert systems for management

by ROBERT W. BLANNING
Vanderbilt University
Nashville, Tennessee

ABSTRACT

The development during the past twenty years of knowledge-based systems for recognized specialists and professionals has given rise to suggestions that systems of this type might be useful to managers as well. This paper examines (1) what managers do, (2) how they differ from the other professionals for whom expert systems have been designed, and (3) the implication of these findings for the design and implementation of expert systems for management.

INTRODUCTION

The development during the past twenty years of expert systems for recognized specialists and professionals (such as physicians diagnosing and treating infectious diseases, geologists prospecting for mineral deposits, and so forth[1,2]) has given rise to the suggestion that systems of this type might be useful to managers as well.[3–5] The purpose of expert systems for managers (ESMs) would be similar to that of existing expert systems: They would contain certain judgmental assumptions and rules that a knowledgeable and experienced manager uses in arriving at a recommendation or decision and would analyze this information in a way that would be useful to a practicing manager. For example, ESMs might interrogate a manager about changes in market demand or inventory levels and offer advice about possible causes and appropriate responses, or they might be given information about proposed financial or operating decisions (e.g., capital investments or production schedules) and make recommendations.

There are three types of managerial tasks for which ESMs have already been developed and for which future ESMs might be designed. They are:

1. *Resource allocation.* ESMs have been developed for portfolio management[6] and capital budgeting,[7] and they might also be developed for R&D budgeting, the preparation of government budgets, and the like.
2. *Problem diagnosis.* There are ESMs for analyzing financial statements[8] and auditing accounts receivable.[9] Other possible tasks include the analysis of periodic control reports, such as budget variance reports (reports that compare budgeted and actual revenues and expenses), to identify potential problems.
3. *Scheduling and assignment.* ESMs have been developed for office scheduling[10,11] and personnel assignment.[12] Other scheduling and assignment problems that require more complex analyses than are found in operations research models might be analyzed with an ESM.

Although there are many ESMs that might be useful, it is not clear that the variety of judgmental tasks performed by managers can be made explicit and rendered into programmable form. Fortunately, there is a substantial body of documented research on managerial and organizational behavior, and it should be possible for the designers of ESMs to draw on this research and possibly contribute to it. In order to understand more fully the potential viability of ESMs as a field of research and practice, we will examine the following three issues:

1. What is a manager? What do managers do? How do they spend their time and what functions do they perform?
2. Can a manager reasonably be considered an expert? If so, how do managers differ from the other professionals for whom expert systems have been developed? What are the implications for ESMs?
3. What are the most important research and implementation issues, such as knowledge acquisition and technology transfer, that are likely to arise in the development of ESMs? How might these issues be addressed?

WHAT DO MANAGERS DO?

We attempt in this section to answer two questions: (1) What is a manager—that is, who is to be included in this category and who is to be excluded? (2) What do the included people do?

What Is a Manager?

The term "manager" denotes a person in an organization who is responsible for the well-being of the organization or of some part of it. This includes senior managers, such as presidents of companies or directors of government agencies; middle managers, such as branch managers in consumer products companies or project managers in government; and first-line supervisors, such as shop foreman or police sergeants. We also include staff analysts, such as financial analysts and cost accountants, who may not supervise people but who perform analyses and prepare recommendations for decisions to be made by line managers or by management committees.

We exclude members of established professions and scholarly traditions, except when they assume responsibility for the performance of other such people. Thus, we include vice-presidents for research and development and directors of engineering design, but exclude research scientists and design engineers. Finally, we note that the people we have described make long-term commitments (including capital investment) or allocate scarce resources (such as money, people, laboratory equipment, or warehouse space), which affects the performance of their organization; or they provide staff support to those who make such commitments or allocations.

What Do Managers Do?

There are two general conclusions that can be drawn about what managers do and a third about the environment in which they do it. These conclusions are based on general observations by managers and academics,[13–15] "diary studies" in which managers record how they spend their time,[16–18] and detailed direct observations not unlike the "time and motion" studies that have been performed with industrial factory workers.[19,20] Although the authors of these studies are not in complete agreement (e.g., with regard to the amount of discretion managers have in their jobs), a reasonably consistent picture of managerial behavior emerges from these and similar studies.

The first conclusion is that managers perform certain identifiable tasks, primarily decision making (making, or at least approving or influencing, commitments and allocations of the type described above), implementing and controlling (checking to see that the decisions are being implemented, making or approving changes as necessary, and reacting to opportunities and crises), and organizing and communicating (supervising and motivating subordinates and acquiring and disseminating information—both inside and outside their organizations or suborganizations). Higher-level managers devote more time to planning and less to supervising subordinates than do lower-level managers, but higher-level managers spend a substantial amount of their time dealing with people other than subordinates.

The second conclusion is that managers seldom accomplish these tasks directly, but rather work through a network of people, including subordinates, superiors, other managers in their organizations, and a variety of outsiders. They seldom appear to give direct orders, but rather exchange information and attempt to influence what others do. As a result, few managers spend much time alone, and most have an aversion to written communication (they don't like to read their mail, much less formal reports or computer printouts). They work long hours, most of them in the company of others or on the telephone.

The third conclusion concerns the work environment of managers: They work for long hours at a rapid pace on fragmented and often unpredictable activities, dealing with a variety of unstructured situations for brief periods of time. These situations seldom involve abstract long-term problems, but rather immediate problems, many of which, even in the case of high-level managers, appear to contribute only marginally to the long-term well-being of their organizations. This type of behavior, which is sometimes described as "putting out fires" or "crisis management," has given rise to speculation concerning: (1) the degree to which the allocation of a manager's time is controllable by the manager or is determined by events beyond his control, (2) whether managers focus on immediate problems because they enjoy it or because they feel that it is their proper responsibility, or both, (3) whether it is possible to infer what managers do by observing this type of behavior and whether diaries maintained by a manager are more or less revealing than direct observation by an independent researcher, and (4) the extent to which any type of computer-based system can be of assistance to people who work in such an environment.

THE MANAGER AS EXPERT

Managers clearly are experts in the sense that they have an acquired ability to perform certain tasks requiring specialized knowledge and judgment. Knowledge and judgment are needed to schedule production, price products, evaluate investment proposals, respond to cost overruns, and so on. The question is whether enough of their knowledge and judgment can be programmed to provide useful support for decision making. The research that has been done during the past forty years on managerial and organizational behavior has uncovered four characteristics of managerial decision making that are not prominent in the existing literature on expert systems, and these characteristics may affect the design of ESMs. These four characteristics and a fifth one, concerning the application of computer science and management science to decision making, are examined below.

Open-ended and Ill-defined Problems

This means that in many cases the parameters of the problem (the environment of the decision and the available alternatives) are not completely known or that it is not possible to state in advance the critieria for an acceptable solution (e.g., a "good" allocation of a research and development budget to projects). On the other hand, limited empirical research suggests that to some extent decision processes of this type can be made explicit. For example, a detailed study of 25 management decisions—including investment decisions (acquiring a subsidiary, building a plant, purchasing equipment), personnel decisions (changing a retirement policy, firing an employee), and new product and service development decisions (a new deodorant, a new brand of beer, a new treatment in a hospital)—showed that these decisions can be flow-charted, and that there are many similarities among the flow-charts.[21]

Bounded Rationality and the Allocation of Attention

Because of the open-ended nature of managerial problems and the hectic pace of managerial activities, managers find that they cannot always make economically rational decisions but must allocate their time and attention to solving problems as best they can.[22,23] This is true of all professionals, but the research on managerial decision making and organization behavior places a major emphasis on cognitive limits to economically rational behavior and the attendant need for managers to recognize that they are often forced to satisfice (that is, to make satisfactory decisions that meet a psychologically determined level of aspiration), rather than to optimize (to make decisions that best accomplish their objectives).

This suggests that an important purpose of an ESM may be to reduce the time needed to perform certain tasks and possibly to help managers allocate their time more effectively. Limited experience with the use of computer-based decision models by high-level managers suggests that the reduction in time needed to evaluate alternatives[24] and to coordinate interdivisional efforts[25] is considered a major benefit of these models. This may be true of ESMs as well.

Varied Styles and Individual Differences

A substantial part of the research on the use of information systems by managers suggests that an important consideration in the design of these systems is the psychological characteristics of the people who use them. Two such characteristics have been identified: The first concerns imperfections in the way in which people process information to arrive at subjective judgments.[26] For example, people often combine multiple cues in a far less sophisticated way than is warranted by the complexity of the problems they face. In addition, people frequently do a poor job of making subjective probability estimates, often egregiously violating the laws of probability theory.

The second characteristic concerns individual personality differences.[27] One such difference is in cognitive style, which describes the way in which people acquire and process information. Laboratory studies suggest that cognitive style may affect the usefulness of computer-based decision aids.[28] Since different managers have quite different cognitive styles,[29] one might conclude that such decision aids should be adapted to the cognitive style—or other personality characteristics, such as risk aversion or ambiguity tolerance—of their users, although arguments have been made against this suggestion.[30]

Teamwork and Networks

Managers interact closely with other managers and professionals both in formal groups, such as committees and task forces, and informally through networks of people in various organizations who exchange information on an ad-hoc basis. Because of this, some of the literature on information systems suggests that these systems may be more productive if they are used by groups of people both to provide information to them and to facilitate communication between them.[31] The purpose of the communication is to encourage more active participation by all group members (e.g., by anonymous electronic voting) and thus, to prevent a few high-status or aggressive members from dominating the group.

Limited real world experience suggests that this purpose is realized by properly designed multiuser systems,[32] and laboratory experiments are being conducted to examine this phenomenon in more detail.[33] In both cases users have access to computer-based decision models with which they can evaluate scenarios (e.g., proposed corporate debt structures). They can also communicate their results and suggestions to others through the system. It is possible that some ESMs will be similarly designed.

The Availability of Computer-based Decision Aids

The work environment of managers—especially staff analysts, such as financial analysts and market research analysts—has changed substantially during the past thirty years. These managers have available to them a variety of computer-based decision aids that allow them to retrieve and analyze data (e.g., to perform statistical analyses of sales data) and to execute decision models (such as models of production or distrubution systems or of the financial structures of a firm) in order to perform "what if" analyses of proposed decisions and of possible changes in the environment (e.g., the economic environment) of their organizations. These decision aids have been given several names, the most recent of which is decision support systems (DSSs).[34–39]

There are four areas of DSS research relevant to the design of ESMs. The first is the development of planning languages.[40] These are programming languages based on existing scientific languages, usually FORTRAN, augmented to include user interface procedures, the principal ones being sensitivity analysis commands and report writers. The second is the research being done on model management systems, which insulate their users from the physical details of model bank organization and processing, just as database management systems insulate their users from the physical details of database organization and processing.[41–44] The third is the application of artificial intelligence (AI) techniques to the integration of models when more than one model is used to respond to a specific user query. A description of the model bank is viewed as a set of premises from which a conclusion (the responses to the query) is to be deduced, and the techniques suggested for this purpose are AND/OR graphs,[45] resolution programming,[46] semantic nets,[47] connection graphs,[48] and frames.[49] The fourth is the development of natural language query processors for model management systems,[50,51] similar to those that have been developed for database management systems.[52]

The relevance of this research to ESM design stems from the fact that many ESMs probably will not be stand-alone systems but will be integrated with conventional databases and with causal models of an organization and its environment. In addition, AI languages and inference engines may have to be modified, for example, with sensitivity analysis procedures and report writers, so that they assume some of the character of a DSS.[53] The issues in this area have not yet been resolved, but it is clear that the designers of ESMs will have to take into account not only the research conducted during the past few decades on managerial and organizational behavior, but also the research, past and current, on DSSs.

ISSUES IN ESM DESIGN AND IMPLEMENTATION

In the previous section we examined five characteristics that may affect the design and implementation of ESMs: (1) many management problems are open-ended, (2) management time and attention are limited resources, (3) different managers have different problem-solving styles, (4) managers often work in groups, and (5) most managers now have access to a variety of computer-based decision aids. We now briefly examine seven issues in ESM design and implementation from these perspectives.

1. *Knowledge acquisition*. Acquiring expert knowledge from managers may be quite difficult, because many management problems are open-ended and managers employ a variety of strategies in solving them. A reasonable approach is to begin with partially structured but interesting problems (such as budget variance analyses) and move to less structured problems (e.g., those related to corporate strategy) as experience accumulates.
2. *Technology transfer between management domains*. It is

likely that ESMs performing the three functions identified in the introduction (resource allocation, problem diagnosis, and scheduling and assignment) will differ substantially, as will those implemented in different types of organizations (e.g., heavy industry, consumer products, service, defense and nondefense government) and those used at different levels of an organization (strategic, tactical, operational). It is likely that transfer of ESM technology will first take place within these groups and then will be expanded where similarities exist.

3. *Use of existing AI software*. Designers of ESMs will be able to draw on a large body of experience gained by the designers of other types of expert systems. Tangible forms of this experience are the programming languages (both list-processing and logic-programming), inference engines, and knowledge acquisition software that have been developed during the past thirty years. However, as suggested in the previous section, some of this software may have to be enhanced to incorporate certain DSS features, including sensitivity analysis commands and report writers.
4. *Possible codification of management knowledge.* The successful implementation of ESMs may contribute not only to the practice of management and to the ongoing AI subdiscipline of expert systems, but also to the substantial literature on managerial and organizational behavior. It is important for ESM designers to recognize that business schools and other academic departments concerned with managerial issues (e.g., some sociology and political science departments) contain people who have studied in detail human behavior in organizations, and ESM designers have an unusual opportunity to draw on and contribute to this body of research and experience.
5. *Explanations offered by ESMs.* Managers, like other professionals, are reluctant to implement policies whose rationales they do not understand. Therefore, ESMs, like many other expert systems, will have to justify—on demand—their findings, recommendations, and requests for input.

   There are two issues here: First, the types of explanations that managers consider acceptable may depend on certain personality characteristics or problem-solving styles. Second, most DSSs do not offer explanations of their outputs. Since DSSs may interact with or be a part of an ESM, an important issue in the design of ESMs may be the degree to which they should "tap into" DSSs in order to retrieve the outcomes of intermediate calculations to prepare their explanations.
6. *Validation of ESMs.* The principal validation method for ESMs will probably be the one used for other types of expert systems. This is the "modified Turing test," in which managers are shown two solutions to a problem—one of them the result of human judgement and the other the result of an ESM (without knowing which is which)—and are asked to compare them. There are two problems with this approach. The first is that the open-endedness of many management problems may make it difficult to describe them to an independent evaluator. Many case studies of complex management problems have been written for business school pedagogy, and even experienced managers disagree on the proper interpretation of and solutions to these cases. Second, ESMs used by teams of managers will have to be evaluated by teams of managers and hence may be more difficult to evaluate. On the other hand, the fact that an ESM might be useful if it reduces only the time needed to perform existing tasks with no reduction in quality may provide a good starting point for ESM evaluation.
7. *Metaknowledge.* Metaknowledge is understanding the type of information available and how it should be used. As stated in the previous section, an important type of metaknowledge is that of available DSSs, and certain AI techniques might be useful in deciding how to integrate them in order to perform a specific task. Viewing an ESM as an integrated system of modules (some of them DSSs) may also facilitate ESM development; the development could proceed incrementally, with new modules being developed and integrated as queries are formed for which their existence would be useful.

The acceptance of ESMs by managers will depend not only on how these and other currently unanticipated issues are resolved, but also on how well the solutions are communicated to the designers and users of ESMs. Limited empirical research on the managerial acceptance of DSS suggests that managers decide to initiate the development of a DSS or to use a DSS previously developed not by performing a cost-benefit analysis of the type appropriate to the evaluation of commercial data processing systems, but by observing (or hearing about) the successful implementation of a DSS in a similar organization and then attempting to determine how useful such a system might be in their own organizations.[54] This will probably be the case with ESMs. Therefore, it is important that the development of individual ESMs be communicated as widely as possible so as to foster a climate of acceptability for ESMs among the people who will design and use them.

CONCLUSION

The past forty years have witnessed an explosion in the scientific investigation of management problems. Economists, mathematicians, behavioral scientists, management scientists, and computer scientists have been offered an unprecedented opportunity to identify and solve interesting problems, and this has resulted in the widespread implementation of data processing systems, management information systems, decision models, and decision support systems, along with several new academic disciplines. The potential application of AI to management suggests that we are on the threshold of yet another revolution, and the development of ESMs will be an important part of this revolution.

ACKNOWLEDGMENT

This work was supported by the Dean's Fund for Faculty Research of the Owen Graduate School of Management at Vanderbilt University.

REFERENCES

1. Barr, A., and E. A. Feigenbaum (eds.). *The Handbook of Artificial Intelligence*. Los Altos, Calif.: William Kaufman, 1982 (*Applications Oriented AI Research,* Vol. 2, pp. 77–294).
2. Hayes-Roth, F., D. A. Waterman, and D. B. Lenat (eds.). *Building Expert Systems*. Reading, Mass.: Addison-Wesley, 1983.
3. Fox, M. S. "The Intelligent Management System: An Overview." In H. G. Sol (ed.), *Processes and Tools for Decision Support.* Amsterdam: North-Holland, 1983, pp. 125–130.
4. Gorry, G. A., and R. B. Krumland. "Artificial Intelligence in Decision Support Systems." In J. L. Barnett (ed.), *Building Decision Support Systems.* Reading, Mass.: Addison-Wesley, 1983, pp. 205–219.
5. Reitman, W. "Applying Artificial Intelligence to Decision Support: Where Do Good Alternatives Come From?" In M. J. Ginsberg, W. Reitman, and E. A. Stohr (eds.), *Decision Support Systems.* Amsterdam: North-Holland, 1982, pp. 155–174.
6. Clarkson, G. P. E. "A Model of the Trust Investment Process." In E. A. Feigenbaum and H. Feldman (eds.), *Computers and Thought.* New York: McGraw-Hill, 1963, pp. 347–371.
7. Bohanek, M., I. Bratko, and V. Rajkovic. "An Expert System for Decision Making." In H. G. Sol (ed.), *Processes and Tools for Decision Support*. Amsterdam: North-Holland, 1983, pp. 235–248.
8. Bouwman, M. J. "Human Diagnostic Reasoning by Computer: An Illustration from Financial Analysis." *Management Science,* 29 (1983), pp. 653–672.
9. Dungan, C. W. "A Model of Audit Judgement in the Form of an Expert System." Ph.D. Dissertation, University of Illinois, 1983.
10. Fikes, R. E. "Odyssey: A Knowledge-Based Assistant." *Artificial Intelligence,* 16 (1981), pp. 331–361.
11. Goldstein, I. P., and B. Roberts. "Using Frames in Scheduling." In P. H. Whinston and R. H. Brown (eds.), *Artificial Intelligence: An MIT Perspective.* Cambridge, Mass.: The MIT Press, 1982, pp. 253–284.
12. Barber, G. "Supporting Organizational Problem Solving with a Work Station." *ACM Transactions on Office Information Systems,* 1 (1983) pp. 45–67.
13. Barnard, C. I. *The Functions of the Executive.* Cambridge, Mass.: Harvard University Press, 1938.
14. Drucker, P. *The Effective Executive.* New York: Harper & Row, 1966.
15. Simon, H. A. *Administrative Behavior* (2nd ed.). New York: Macmillan, 1957.
16. Carlson, S. *Executive Behavior.* Stockholm: C.A. Stromberg Aktieborg, 1951.
17. Mahoney, T. A., T. H. Jerdee, and S. J. Carroll. "The Job(s) of Management." *Industrial Relations,* 4 (1965), pp. 97–110.
18. Stewart, R. *Managers and Their Jobs.* London: Pan, 1967.
19. Kotter, J. P. "What Effective General Managers Really Do." *Harvard Business Review,* 60 (1982), pp. 156–167.
20. Mintzberg, H. *The Nature of Managerial Work.* New York: Harper & Row, 1973.
21. Mintzberg, H. D. Raisinghani, and A. Theoret. "The Structure of 'Unstructured' Decision Processes." *Administrative Science Quarterly,* 21 (1970), pp. 246–275.
22. Simon, H. A. "Theories of Bounded Rationality." In C. B. McGuire and R. Radner (eds.), *Decision and Organization.* Amsterdam: North-Holland, 1972, pp. 161–176.
23. Taylor, R. N. "Psychological Determination of Bounded Rationality: Implications for Decision-Making Strategies." *Decision Sciences* 6 (1975), pp. 409–429.
24. Naylor, T. H., and H. Schauland. "A Survey of Users of Corporate Planning Models." *Management Science,* 22 (1976), pp. 927–937.
25. Scott Morton, M. S. *Management Decision Systems: Computer-Based Support for Organizational Decision Making.* Boston: Harvard University, Graduate School of Business Administration, Division of Research, 1971.
26. Bensabat, I., and R. N. Taylor. "Behavioral Aspects of Information Processing for the Design of Management Information Systems." *IEEE Transactions on Systems, Man, and Cybernetics,* SMC-12 (1982), pp. 439–450.
27. Zmud, R. W. "Individual Differences and MIS Success: A Review of the Empirical Literature." *Management Science,* 25 (1979), pp. 966–979.
28. Benbasat, I., and A. S. Dexter. "Individual Differences in the Use of Decision Support Aids." *Journal of Accounting Research,* 20 (1982), pp. 1–11.
29. McKenney, J. L., and P. G. W. Keen. "How Managers' Minds Work." *Harvard Business Review,* 52 (1974), pp. 77–90.
30. Huber, G. P. "Cognitive Style as a Basis for MIS and DSS Designs: Much Ado About Nothing?" *Management Science,* 29 (1983), pp. 567–579.
31. Huber, G. P. "Group Decision Support Systems as Aids in the Use of Structured Group Management Techniques." *DSS-82 Transactions,* 1982, pp. 96–108.
32. Wagner, G. R. "DSS: Dealing with Executive Assumptions in the Office of the Future." *DSS-81 Transactions,* 1981, pp. 113–121.
33. Gray, P., N. W. Berry, J. S. Aronofsky, O. Helmer, G. R. Kane, and T. E. Perkins. "The SMU Decision Room Project." *DSS-81 Transactions,* 1981, pp. 122–129.
34. Keen, P. G. W., and M. Scott Morton. *Decision Support Systems: An Organizational Perspective.* Reading, Mass.: Addison-Wesley, 1978.
35. Blanning, R. W. "The Functions of a Decision Support System." *Information and Management,* 2 (1979), pp. 87–93.
36. Keen, P. G., and G. R. Wagner. "DSS: An Executive Mind-Support System." *Datamation,* 25 (1979), pp. 117–122.
37. Alter, S. *Decision Support Systems: Current Practice and Continuing Challenges.* Reading, Mass.: Addison-Wesley, 1980.
38. Blanning, R. W. "Model Structure and User Interface in Decision Support Systems." *DSS-81 Transactions,* 1981, pp. 1–7.
39. Sprague, R. H., Jr., and E. D. Carlson. *Building Effective Decision Support Systems.* Englewood Cliffs, N.J.: Prentice-Hall, 1982.
40. Naylor, T. H., and M. Mann. *Computer Based Planning Systems.* Oxford: Planning Executives Institute, 1982.
41. Will, H. J. "Model Management Systems." In E. Grochla and N. Szyperski (eds.), *Information Systems and Organization Structure.* Berlin: Walter de Gruyter, 1975, pp. 468–482.
42. Blanning, R. W. "A Relational Framework for Model Management in Decision Support Systems." *DSS-82 Transactions,* 1982, pp. 16–28.
43. Blanning, R. W. "Issues in the Decision of Relational Model Management Systems." *AFIPS, Proceedings of the National Computer Conference,* (Vol. 52), 1983, pp. 395–401.
44. Konsynski, B. R. "Model Management in Decision Support Systems." In C. W. Holsapple and A. B. Whinston (eds.), *Data Base Management: Theory and Applications.* Dordrecht: D. Reidel, 1983, pp. 131–154.
45. Bonczek, R. A., C. W. Holsapple, and A. B. Whinston. *Foundations of Decision Support Systems.* New York: Academic Press, 1981.
46. Schell, G. P. "Knowledge Representation and Knowledge Manipulation in Decision Support Systems." Ph.D. Thesis, Purdue University, 1983.
47. Elam, J. J., J. C. Henderson, and L. W. Miller. "Model Management Systems: An Approach to Decision Support in Complex Organizations." *Proceedings of the First International Conference on Information Systems,* 1980, pp. 98–110.
48. Chen, M. C., J. E. Fedorowicz, and L. J. Henschen. "Deductive Processes in Databases and Decision Support Systems." *Proceedings of the North Central ACM 82 Conference,* 1982, pp. 81–100.
49. Dolk, D. R., and B. R. Konsynski. "Knowledge Representation for Model Management Systems." Available from Naval Postgraduate School, Monterey, Calif., 1982.
50. Heidorn, G. E. "Simulation Programming through Natural Language Dialogue." In M. A. Geisler (ed.), *Logistics.* Amsterdam: North-Holland, 1975, pp. 71–83.
51. Blanning, R. W. "Natural Language Query Processing for Model Management." To appear in *Proceedings of the Fourth Annual Conference on Information Systems,* 1983.
52. Tennant, H. *Natural Language Processing.* New York: Petrocelli, 1981.
53. Blanning, R. W. "Management Applications of Logic Programming." Available from author, Owen Graduate School of Management, Vanderbilt University, Nashville, Tenn., 1983.
54. Blanning, R. W. "How Managers Decide to Use Planning Models." *Long Range Planning,* 13 (1980), pp. 32–35.

An investigation of task team structure and its impact on productivity

by KATHY BRITTAIN WHITE
University of North Carolina
Greensboro, North Carolina

ABSTRACT

Productivity in the information age is widely perceived to be a major problem facing many organizations. One strategy to enhance organizational productivity has been the use of task teams. Assignment to task teams usually reflects individual technical expertise, individual availability, and/or positional politics rather than a focus on the effectiveness of the team members in the specific organizational situation. This paper investigates characteristics of team members and then examines the effect on team effectiveness of these characteristics and of the requirements of the organizational activity.

Two organizational situations were investigated. The first was a true unstructured organizational situation. A field study was used to investigate two project teams in this situation. The second organizational situation was structured and administered in a controlled setting; members of a programming class constituted the participants in the second situation. The Myers-Briggs Type Indicator was used to determine the perceptual characteristics of team members and thus determine the heterogeneity or the homogeneity of the teams.

The findings indicate that the situational structure determines the overall effectiveness of the team composition. They also offer evidence that heterogeneity in group composition is best for solving complex problems, whereas homogeneity is best for solving structured, less complex problems. It also suggests that one team might not be appropriate for all stages of a project. As the nature of the tasks involved in the project change, it could be that the optimum team composition would also change. Much further research must be aimed at strategically assembling the most productive team for any number of organizational situations.

INTRODUCTION

Productivity in the information age is widely perceived to be a major problem facing many organizations. In fact, strategies to enhance human productivity have been the focus of many research studies.[2,5,6,9,24,28,29] An idea resulting from current studies aimed at increasing organizational productivity and dealing with complex, multidimensional information systems has been that of task teams. These teams are used in such diverse organizational activities as systems development and implementation, strategic planning, and office automation. Such teams are formed and interact for the primary purpose of vitalizing decision making, innovative thinking, and productivity.[4,14,20,30,31,34,35–37] Assignment to task teams usually reflects individual technical expertise, individual availability, and/or positional politics rather than a focus on the effectiveness of the team members in the specific organizational situation.

Evidence is mounting that an optimum team composition in one situation, regardless of technical skills, is not necessarily the optimum team composition in another.[1,8,10,36] In fact, a major effect on the productivity and effectiveness of the team seems to be situational.[1,36] Little work has been done to determine the situational components that determine team effectiveness. This paper investigates characteristics of team members and then examines (1) the effects of these characteristics and (2) the requirements of the organizational activity on team effectiveness.

CHARACTERISTICS OF TEAM MEMBERS

Behavioral research theories have added credibility to the process of explaining individual perceptual differences. One of the primary contributors to such theories has been the Swiss pyschologist Carl Jung.[13] The merit of Jung's theory is that it accounts for many human differences which other theoretical frameworks leave to random variation; yet the theory has the merit of unusual simplicity. Briefly, Jung's theory is based on the assumption that much apparently random variation in human behavior is actually quite orderly and consistent, directed at the differences with which individuals prefer to gather and evaluate information in their environment. Jung combines these differences into four basic types that are summarized as follows:

1. The Intuition-Thinking (NT) type is the one who observes and inputs data from a holistic or system type of framework. He/she sees things perhaps not as they are but as they can be—as possibilities. The Output or evaluation of these possibilities is judged in accordance with some formal rules, and the NT type tends to be impersonal in judgment.
2. The Intuition-Feeling (NF) type will observe input data in the same way as the NT; but the information will be judged in a personal or value-laden manner, such as good or bad, pleasant or unpleasant. This personality does not follow formal rules of logic.
3. The Sensation-Thinking (ST) type is one who sees information as concrete facts. He/she will then turn the specific facts into a formal solution according to some well-defined set of rules. The ST type is desirous of working on specific, clear problems and will probably be characterized by a low tolerance for ambiguity.
4. The Sensation-Feeling (SF) type also prefers to observe concrete facts apart from their totality, but is less formal in his evaluation of the data. The SF type does not apply the facts to a formal solution or model but instead uses a subjective, value-laden assessment.[12] Jung's typology emphasizes only each type's major strengths and weaknesses without considering any one better than another.[17]

Mason and Mitroff[21] relate the Jungian scales specifically to information systems and discuss the heterogeneity of each type:

> Each of these types has a different concept of information and this is important for MIS design. If one is a pure thinking type, information will be entirely symbolic, e.g., some abstract system, model, or string of symbols devoid of almost any theoretical content. Thus, Sensation types speak of "raw data," "hard facts," and "numbers." For Intuition types, information will be in the form of sketches of future possibilities. Information for feeling types emphasizes a strong moral component. What is information for one type is definitely not information for another. [p. 476]

TEAM COMPOSITION

Each individual team member has a perceptual style that influences the information perceived and the behavior exhibited in problem solving and task completion. Research has shown that the more similar the perceptual styles of individuals, the more harmonious the group relationships.[8] Since much of any team's early activities are devoted to establishing group relationships, it would indicate that the more homogeneous the individual group members, the less time this early effort would require. Research has also indicated that homogeneous groups are characterized by cohesiveness and freedom from conflict.[3] Although these studies indicate that harmonious relationships are a byproduct of homogeneous teams, other researchers have important reservations about the central theme of homogeneity. Mitroff and Kilmann[22] discuss the impact of team homogeneity on task solutions:

> If the extreme homogeneity of each group is a blessing in that it reinforces the natural strengths and similar tendencies of each individual in the group, then the extreme homogeneity is also a danger in that it magnifies the weaknesses (i.e. the one-sidedness) of perceptions of the individuals. [p. 19]

Myers[25] also discusses the composition of teams and indicates that homogeneity can deter productivity. She states,

> If the group is composed of very different types, agreement will be harder to reach than if the group was homogeneous but the decision will be more broadly based and thoroughly considered, and thus in less danger of turning out badly for some unperceived reason. [p. 17]

Such findings indicate that homogeneous teams are characterized by freedom from conflict but that heterogeneous teams may be more productive. Another body of research examines the nature of the organizational problems faced by such teams.

ORGANIZATIONAL PROBLEMS

An organization faces a tremendous variety of problems, which vary considerably in degree of complexity. A framework identifying the differing complexities is that used by decision theorists, in which they refer to a problem as structured or unstructured.[23] Briefly, a structured problem is one that can be well defined in the sense that the key variables, such as the various states of nature, possible actions, possible outcomes, and utility of outcomes are known. The unstructured, or wicked, problem is one that cannot be clearly defined.[16,33] That is, one or more of the variables discussed either is unknown or cannot be determined with any degree of confidence. So decision making in organizations must deal with problems that run the gamut from the simple to the complex and beyond that to the ambiguous.[17] Specifically, it is expected that for problems characterized by a high degree of structure, the information will be processed by the team in a logical sequence. This notion is supported by a number of research studies.[7,11,27] For tasks characterized by a low degree of structure, it is exceedingly difficult for the group to evaluate information.[17] In these tasks the team structure must be able to manage not only this complexity but also large volumes of information. Very little research has been directed at determining how these variances in problem requirements affect team composition. This study investigates the effect of team composition (heterogeneous or homogeneous) on the structured and unstructured organizational problem.

RESEARCH

Setting and Method

Two organizational situations were investigated. The first was an unstructured organizational situation. A field study was used to investigate two project teams in a true unstructured organizational situation. Kilmann says that, assuming that a researcher can obtain access to such organizations, field studies can monitor the dynamics of the design process, and external validity will be moderately high. He also writes that such studies can suggest characteristics and outcomes that are otherwise unavailable.[17] The second organizational situation was structured and administered in a controlled setting. Members of a programming class constituted the participants in the second situation.

The Myers-Briggs Type Indicator (MBTI) was used to determine the perceptual characteristics of team members and thus determine heterogeneity or homogeneity. The Myers-Briggs Type Indicator has been used repeatedly to measure Jung's typology and has established reliability.[26] Although the MBTI is not the only instrument available to determine perceptual differences, it was chosen in this study because of the number of business studies utilizing this instrument.[14,15,19,21–23,35–37]

TABLE I—Perceptual styles of Project Team 1 and Project Team 2

Perceptual Styles	Project Team 1[a]	Project Team 2[a]
ST	7 (70)[b]	4 (40)
NT	3 (30)	2 (20)
SF	0 (0)	2 (20)
NF	0 (0)	2 (20)

[a] 10 individuals included on Project Teams 1 and 2.
[b] The numbers in parentheses indicate the percentage of the project team with the perceptual style.

Unstructured Situation

The two project teams that were observed had ten team members each and were charged with systems development activities. Members of the two project teams were already assigned at the time of the investigation, and thus team composition was not manipulated by this researcher. The team compositions, as identified by the MBTI, are shown in Table I. The results of the interviews with key users, team members, and MIS management are summarized as follows:

Project Team 1	Project Team 2
A. Failed system	A. Successful system
B. A technical orientation	B. Technical and people orientation
C. Inadequate documentation	C. Comprehensive documentation
D. Rated as unsuccessful	D. Rated as highly successful

An in-depth account of the interview information has previously been written.[37] Project Team 1, with a void of Feeler types (SF or NF), was classified as homogeneous. Project Team 2, with all four MBTI types represented, was classified as heterogeneous. It would seem that in such an unstructured situation as the systems development activities assigned these two project teams, it is exceedingly difficult to have all relevant information evaluated. When the group is homogeneous in its information-evaluation orientation (as in the case of Project Team 1), performance suffers. Project Team 1 exemplified a narrower perceptual viewpoint, as indicated by team members interviewed; this is attributed to their one-sided perceptual nature. Project Team 2 exemplified a broad organizational perspective, from interviews of team members; this is attributed to their diverse perceptual orientations. These findings also support research conducted by Kaiser and Bostrom that a project team with all four MBTI types represented was successful while a project team void of feelers was unsuccessful.[14]

Although many factors cannot be controlled in a field study such as the one conducted, evidence is offered that indicates that heterogeneous teams are more successful than homogeneous teams in unstructured organizational situations. Specifically, the conclusion is that the heterogeneity achieved by combining all four perceptual types on a project team is optimum in an unstructured organization situation. This conclusion is pictorially illustrated in Figure 1.

Structured Situation

To further clarify the situational variables that affect team performance, both heterogeneous and homogeneous teams were examined in a structured situation. Members of a programming class were assigned to either homogeneous or heterogeneous team combinations. A timed programming task that met the definition of a structured problem was assigned. The problem was composed of materials that had been previously taught, and all students had successfully solved similar problems. The time factor made it essential that problem definition be determined quickly to enable a team to complete the task. Solutions were considered on two dimensions: completeness and correctness. Three heterogeneous and three homogeneous teams were structured as shown in Table II. No attention was given to individual personalities; rather, groups were assembled solely on the basis of MBTI types. All MBTI types were included in heterogeneous teams. The information-gathering orientation (Sensing) was the same for

TABLE II—Perceptual styles of heterogeneous and homogeneous teams

Heterogeneous Perceptual Teams	Homogeneous Perceptual Teams
Team 1: NT, NF, ST, SF	Team 4: ST, SF, ST, SF
Team 2: NT, NT, SF, ST	Team 5: ST, ST, ST, SF
Team 3: ST, ST, NT, NF	Team 6: ST, ST, SF, SF

homogeneous teams. The results of the task by team are as follows.

Heterogeneous Teams	Homogeneous Teams
Team 1. Did not complete	Team 4: Completed, successfully
Team 2: Did not complete	Team 5: Completed, successfully
Team 3: Did not complete	Team 6: Completed, unsuccessfully

The surprising results were that the heterogeneous teams were unable to complete the task within the given time, although individual team members had previously completed similar tasks in the given time successfully. The group evaluations completed by each team member upon completion of the experiment were particularly enlightening. Individuals on heterogeneous teams said that a consensus between team members about the problem definition was not reached in time to complete the assigned task. The group evaluations completed for the homogeneous groups indicated that consensus was reached quickly and work finished quickly. In regard to group composition, the homogeneous groups had the information-gathering orientation (Sensing) in common; the heterogeneous teams did not. In this structured task, the heterogeneity of information-gathering styles seemed to hinder group process and undermine the overall effectiveness of the team. Further evidence of these findings is offered in unpublished research conducted by Aamodt and Kimbrough.[38] They found that heterogeneous teams were not as

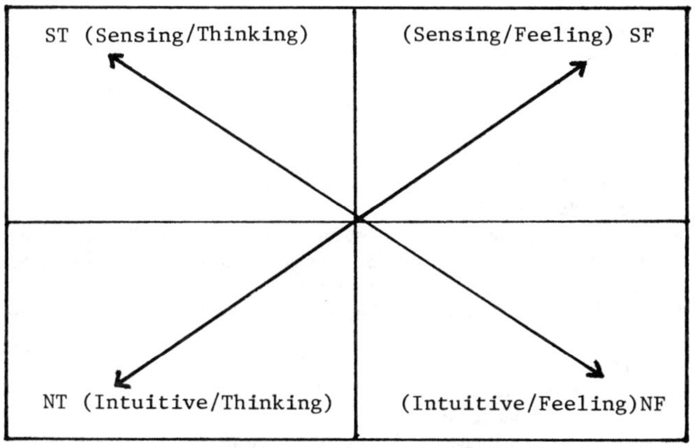

Figure 1—Unstructured decision environment

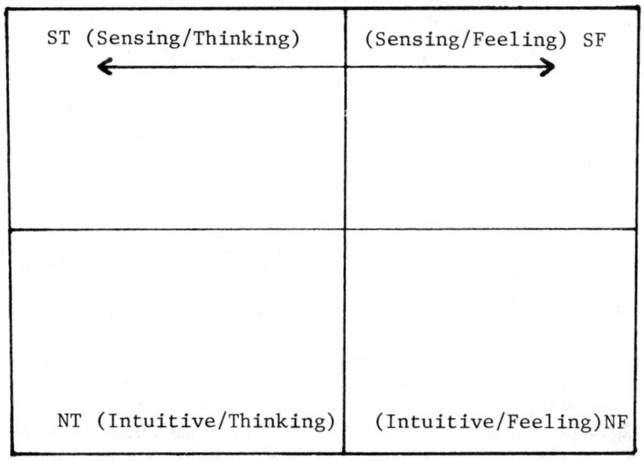

Figure 2—Structured decision environment

successful as homogeneous teams in completing a structured debugging task. In such structured situations, it could be that homogeneous groups are able to work together to complete the task quickly. Heterogeneous groups, however, may have to deal with the tension created by their diverse group composition and be unable to overcome the tension in time to complete the task.

The finding that heterogeneous groups were unable to complete the task was serendipitous; therefore many controls were not used that would have made these findings more conclusive. However, this study, together with the study by Aamodt and Kimbrough, lends evidence that in an organizational situation where the information is finite and limited, homogeneous team compositions may be the most productive. This conclusion is pictorially illustrated in Figure 2.

DISCUSSION

This study offers preliminary evidence that the situational structure determines the overall effectiveness of the team composition. It also offers evidence that heterogeneity of group composition is best for solving complex problems, whereas homogeneity is best for solving structured, less complex problems. This research points to the need for critical delineation of the nature of the problem to be solved when assembling teams. It also suggests that one team might not be appropriate for all stages of a project. As the nature of the tasks involved in the project changes, it could be that the optimum team composition would also change. The optimum team composition in the initial stages of problem definition could be counterproductive in stages of the project that were action-oriented and required quick concurrence among team members to proceed. It also suggests the need to define these stages of the project and possibly form subunits of the project team to complete various aspects of the project. It offers an explanation of the failure of many task teams. A team that worked well and productively in one stage of a project can dissolve into conflict, dissent, and inertia at another stage simply because the team composition is not compatible with the current situational variables.

Although these findings are preliminary, they do present evidence that optimum team compositions vary and depend on situational variables. Only a narrow scope of situational variables were investigated in this study. Much further research must be aimed at strategically assembling the right team for any number of organizational situations. Productivity in the information age may well hinge on task team experimentation as a method of tapping one of the crucial resources available to the organization—the human resource.

REFERENCES

1. Aamodt, M.G. and Kimbrough, W.W. "Effect of Group Heterogeneity on Quality of Task Solutions," *Psychological Reports,* 1982, Vol. 50, pp. 171–174.
2. Bariff, M.L. and Lusk, E.J. "Cognitive and Personality Tests for the Design of Management Information Systems," *Management Science,* Volume 23, Number 8, April 1977, pp. 820–829.
3. Bass, B.M. and Ryterband, E.C. *Organizational Psychology,* Boston: Allyn and Bacon, 1979.
4. Beckhard, L. "Optimizing Team-Building Efforts," *Journal of Contemporary Business,* Summer 1972, pp. 23–32.
5. Biggs, S.F. "Group Participation in MIS Project Team? Let's Look at the Contingencies First!" *MIS Quarterly,* March 1978, pp. 19–26.
6. Carroll, A.B. "Behavioral Aspects of Developing Computer-Based Information Systems, *Business Horizons,* Volume 25, Number 1, January–February 1982, pp. 42–52.
7. Collins, B.E. and Guetztew, H.S. *1964—A Social Psychology of Group Processes for Decision Making,* New York: Wiley, 1964.
8. Heider, F. "Attitudes and Cognitive Organization" *Journal of Psychology,* 1946, Vol. 21, pp. 107–112.
9. Hellriegel, D. and Slocum, J.W., Jr. "Preferred Organizational Designs and Problem-Solving Styles: Interesting Companions," *Human Systems* Management, Volume 2, Number 2, September 1980, pp. 24–35.
10. Hoffman, R.L. and Maier, N.F. "Quality and Acceptance of Problem Solutions by Members of Homogeneous and Heterogeneous Groups" in Vinacke, W.E., Wilson, W. and Mereidty, G., *Dimensions of Social Psychology,* 1961, pp. 425–431.
11. Julian, J.W. and Pevey, E.A. "Cooperation Contrasted with Intra-Group and Inter-Group Competition," *Sociometry,* 1967, Vol. 30, pp. 79–90.
12. Jung, C.G. *The Structure and Dynamics of the Psyche,* New York: Pantheon, 1960.
13. Jung, C.D. *Psychological Types,* New York: Pantheon Books, 1923.
14. Kaiser, K.M. and Bostrom, R.P. "Personality Characteristics of MIS Project Teams: An Empirical Study and Action-Research Design," *MIS Quarterly,* Volume 6, Number 4, December 1982, pp. 43–60.
15. Keen, P.G.W. and Bronseman, G. "Cognitive Style Research: A Perspective for Integration," Center for Information Systems Research, Massachusetts Institute of Technology, Report CISR-82, 1981.
16. Keen, P.G. and Morton, M. *Decision Support Systems: An Organizational Perspective,* Reading, MA: Addison-Wesley, 1978.
17. Kilmann, R.H. *Social Systems Design: Normative Theory and the Maps Design Technology,* New York: North-Holland, 1977, pp. 36.
18. Kilmann, R.H., Pendy, L.R. and Slevin, D.P. *The Management of Organization Design: Volume I and II,* New York: Elseview North-Holland, 1976.
19. Kroenke, D.M. "Currency Forum Corner," *Interface,* Volume 2, Number 6, Summer 1980, p.3.
20. Locander, W.B., Napier, H.A. and Scamell, R.W. "A Team Approach to Managing the Development of a Decision Support System," *MIS Quarterly,* Volume 3, Number 1, March 1970, p. 53.
21. Mason, R.O. and Mitroff, I.I. "A Program for Research on Management Information Systems," *Management Science,* Volume 19, 1973, pp. 475–487.
22. Mitroff, I.I. and Kilmann, R.H. "Qualitative versus Quantitative Analysis for Management Science: Different Forms for Different Psychological Types," *Intefaces,* Volume 6, Number 2, February 1976, pp. 17–27.
23. Mitroff, I.I. and Sagasti, F. "Existemology as General Systems Theory: An Approach to the Design of Complex Decision-Making Experiments," *Philosophy of Social Science,* Volume 3, 1973, pp. 117–134.
24. Moosbruker, J.M. and Loflin, R.D. "Organizational Development Methods in the Management of the Information Systems Function," *MIS Quarterly,* Volume 6, Number 3, September 1982, pp. 15–20.
25. Myers, I.B. *Introduction to Type,* Palo Alto, California: Consulting Psychological Press, 1976.
26. Myers, I.B. *The Myer-Briggs Type Indicator,* Palo Alto, California: Consulting Psychological Press, 1962.
27. Raven, G.H. and Eachus, H.T. "Cooperation and Competition in Means-Interdependent Trials," *Journal of Abnormal and Social Psyhology,* Volume 67, 1963, pp. 307–316.
28. Robey, D. and Taggart, W. "Measuring Manager's Minds: The Assessment of Style in Human Information Processing," *Academy of Management Review,* Volume 6, Number 3, July 1981, pp. 375–383.
29. Robey, D. and Taggart, W. "Human Information Processing in Information and Decision Support Systems," *MIS Quarterly,* Volume 6, Number 2, June 1982, p. 61.
30. Rogers, L.A. "Guidelines for Project Management Teams," *Industrial Engineering,* Volume 6, Number 12, 1973, pp. 12–19.
31. Scamell, R. and Baugh, E. "Team Approach to Systems Management," *Journal of Systems Management,* April 1975, pp. 32–35.

32. Shaw, M.E. *Group Dynamics: The Pscyhology of Small Group Behavior,* New York: McGraw-Hill, 1976.
33. Simon, H.A. *The New Science of Management Decision: Models of Man,* New York: Wiley, 1960, pp. 241–246.
34. Slaughter, G. "TAP: Team Approach to Productivity," *Computerworld,* Volume 16, Number 28, July 1982, p. 47.
35. White, K.B. "MIS Project Teams: A Training Program," *Data Management,* publication forthcoming, January, 1984.
36. White, K.B. "Decision Support Teams: A Model for Structuring the Human Component," Working Paper #DE 830801, School of Business and Economics, University of North Carolina, Greensboro, North Carolina, 1983.
37. White, K.B. "MIS Project Teams: A Theoretical Model Based on Empirical Research," Proceedings of IFIP WG 8.2 Working Conference on *Beyond Productivity: Information Systems Development for Organizational Effectiveness,* North-Holland Publishing Company, 1983.
38. Aamodt, M.G., and W.W. Kimbrough. "Effect of Group Heterogeneity on Group Ability to Debug Computer Programs." *Journal of Data Education, 24* (Winter 1983–84), pp. 29–30.

Incentive compensation for information systems departments

by HOWARD A. RUBIN
Hunter College, City University of New York
New York, New York
and
D. L. VON KLEECK
*Equitable Life Assurance Society**
New York, New York

ABSTRACT

The search for productivity improvement has reached new levels in the information systems world. Organizations are stockpiling tools such as application generators, program analyzers, test data generators, and workbenches in the frenzied quest for productivity. Many organizations that have taken this tool acquisition route are beginning to realize that tools alone are not enough. What is needed is an approach that motivates the use of productivity technology. In this vein, incentive compensation strategies can be applied to the information systems world in a way that focuses on productivity improvement and couples it with quality considerations. From a management viewpoint, this forces more precise definition of productivity metrics and quality quantification.

* Currently at Management and Computer Services, Great Valley Corporate Center, Valley Forge, Pennsylvania 19482.

The Senior Officer had declared war!

The arsenal was filled with some of the most fearsome weapons known to mankind, and they were now trained on the enemy position.

The molecular program degenerator was aimed at the Source Library.

The program analyzer algorithm was ready to decode the innermost secrets of the Maintenance Conspiracy.

Automated workbenches and regenerators were poised to rebuild the ruins.

A negotiations committee fluent in a new user-friendly language was prepared to discuss peace with Userland.

The Senior Officer called for the attack.

Nothing happened!

The troops had vanished!

An investigation revealed that some of the troops had been lured away by a tribe of headhunters, while others were simply out to lunch.

This story, though an exaggeration, typifies what many information systems organizations are experiencing today. An attack is being mounted on traditional development and maintenance techniques to increase productivity. The chosen weapons are tools that accelerate the powers of the individual to perform critical tasks. The organization arsenals are filling up fast, but the projected benefits are far from being realized. Why?

THE PRODUCTIVITY IMPROVEMENT TRAP

A common thread of reasoning pervades most attempts to improve information systems department productivity. The typical attack plan is formulated as follows:

The first step is to know the enemy. In the realm of information systems, this translates into understanding the nature of systems and the resources necessary to carry them from conception to implementation to maintenance to obsolescence. From such an analysis, areas of greatest potential productivity improvements can be identified.

Life cycle modeling is the cornerstone of this process and results in a view of a system's life that looks like the following:

Life Cycle Phase	Percentage of Effort
Development	
Plans & requirements	2.0
Design	6.0
Detail design	9.0
Code & unit test	8.0
Testing	15.0
Maintenance	
Fixes	13.0
Adaptation	14.0
Enhancements	27.0
Redocumentation	4.0
Efficiency recoding	2.0

Sorting this chart by percentage of effort lays the groundwork for developing attack priorities. The areas with the greatest potential payoff become evident.

Rank	Area	Percent
1.	Enhancement	27
2.	Testing	15
3.	Adaptation	14
4.	Fixes	13
5.	Detail design	9
6.	Code	8
7.	Conceptual design	6
8.	Redocumentation	4
9.	Plans and requirements	2
10.	Efficiency recoding	2

Assuming that all areas can reap the same potential productivity improvement by use of the appropriate tools, this view suggests working on selected maintenance aspects and testing first.

(As a brief disgression, it must be noted that there are numerous linkages between the various areas. A testing improvement—use of a test data generator, for example—should decrease the repair or Fixes effort required in maintenance. Likewise, uniform coding practices via a program generator might decrease the maintenance burden by minimizing the effort required to understand an existing system. In fact, productivity improvement in one area can be amplified across others. This implies that the long-range focus should be on the development side of the process.)

The next step in planning the attack involves the assessment of organizational strengths and weaknesses to adjust the previously determined priorities. Coupled with the knowledge of which areas might yield the highest benefits, a plan can be formulated.

At this point, a scouting team is usually sent in to survey the terrain, select and test weapons, and make a final choice.

The final step is to train the troops and mount the attack—this is the TRAP.

First, tools alone are not enough! The information systems staff must be motivated to learn to use them effectively and efficently.

Second, the greatest area of potential productivity improvement in the information systems environment lies with the staff itself and not with the technology they use. Barry Boehm has characterized the cost drivers associated with systems projects. Whereas tools (or the lack of them) may drive costs up by a factor of 250%, staff capability may account for cost swings up to 400%.

The message is clear: Information systems organizations must create an environment that contains the proper tools AND the motivation to apply them. In addition, a mechanism to monitor the success of the whole operation must be in place.

Many organizations believe that they are in the process of creating this total environment. They have been lulled into a false sense of security because tools acquisition is relatively easy when compared with implementing organizational and work habit change. In many instances motivational aspects have not been ignored but are being addressed by productivity measures that are fed back to the staff. Again, this is not enough. Measurement by itself does not supply the motivation for productivity improvement. (By analogy, an overweight person may weigh himself/herself every day, but not take any action).

In this vein, there have been a number of significant corporate examples in which information system development productivity measures have been implemented and later abandoned. The prime reason is that they were being applied in a vacuum—they imposed an additional administrative burden, and they had no perceived value directed toward the staff being monitored by the measurements.

Herein lies the productivity trap. Tools and measurement do not constitute the total productive environment. The way out of the trap is to add and integrate a single missing piece: *incentive.*

Additionally, the view of information systems organizations as solely development/maintenance shops is not robust enough. With the advent of the information center concept, personal computing, office automation, and data-base administration, a broader view of productivity improvement is needed.

AN INCENTIVE COMPENSATION (IC) PLAN FOR INFORMATION SYSTEMS ORGANIZATIONS

A traditional industrial method for staff motivation (behavior modification) is incentive compensation with the underlying philosophy of rewarding on-the-job performance. Let's see how this can be applied in the system's world.

The philosophy of the program is that meeting customer-based performance standards while increasing productivity will be rewarded. In addition, the program itself must meet certain design criteria: auditability, clear cause and effect, minimal overhead, and meaningfulness.

Assume for the moment that a method can be devised to measure the productivity of the many activities of an information systems organization. If the goal of the IC program is improved performance, it seems that staff bonuses should be based on productivity increases. Unfortunately, such a reward scheme is not broad enough to satisfy both the needs of the information systems organization and the business requirement of its customers.

Productivity measurement allows management to answer only the single, but important, question "Are we improving?" with regard to some unit measure of department output. It does not directly address quality and potentially can be gamed so that productivity improves while overall quality goes down. It therefore seems to make more sense to make the performance of the department the focus of our improvement efforts. By *performance* we mean customer accountability in cost, time, and quality.

To be of true business value the IC program must address the customer's concerns: Are my products being delivered on time, on cost, and at an acceptable quality level? Obviously productivity measures alone do not address any of these critical success factors. Therefore, the IC program must reward behavior that yields improvement on all fronts. It is on this basis that we must confront the key IC issues: funding, structure, and metrics.

FUNDING

Where does the money come from?

One alternative is to have the staff contribute a percentage of their salaries to an escrow pool and have it matched by the organization. The bonus, if achieved, allows them to retrieve their contribution plus additional funds from the pool. This approach probably would not readily gain acceptance in today's inflationary world.

A second more palatable alternative is possible. Funding can be based on savings to the organization based on productivity improvements. To size the pool, the organization has to answer the question "How much more money would this year's work cost us at last year's level of productivity?" (adjusted for inflation of course). This funding scheme has the advantage that the pool materializes only if productivity has improved and real dollars have been saved. This pool is then allocated to both the staff and the organization itself—they both share in the benefits.

In summary: Funding from direct dollar savings generated by productivity improvement savings will be shared between the company and the department.

STRUCTURE

As pointed out before, productivity alone is not enough to satisfy all the criteria for rating the information systems organization. The basic structural components of the program are performance (which includes accountability and quality) and productivity. They are defined as follows (see Figures 1 and 2):

Figure 1

Performance is oriented toward getting deliverables to the customer on time, on cost, and with acceptable quality.

Productivity is oriented toward lowering the unit cost of producing products and services while maintaining quality at an acceptable level.

While the primary focus is on performance level, productivity improvement is required as well. The following equation, used for departmentwide calculation, summarizes the nature of the program:

$$\text{Bonus percent} = \underset{\text{(external view)}}{\text{performance rating}} \times \underset{\text{(internal view)}}{\text{productivity improvement}}$$

The performance rating can range between 0 and 1. This implies that performance is only rewarded if the customer criteria are satisfied too.

As noted, this equation is applied on a departmentwide basis. Rewards are not based on what any individual does, but the behavior of the group. Later we will see exactly how this works.

An interesting aspect of this equation is the one to one nature of bonus percent and productivity improvement. Basically, what this means is that a one percent productivity improvement can be rewarded by up to a one percent salary bonus. Operationally it may be wise to impose a ceiling (such as 10%). This approach gives us a clear cause and effect relationship—one of the design criteria.

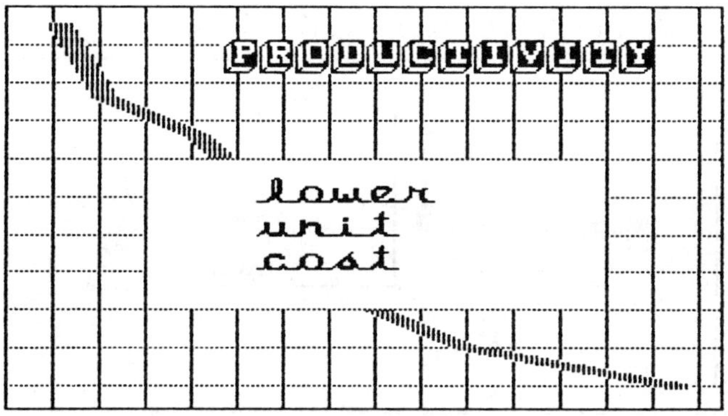

Figure 2

We will now take a top-down view of the program. Each of the structural components will first be examined in concept and then in detail.

PRODUCTIVITY

The basic productivity improvement computation is summarized below:

$$\text{Productivity improvement} = \frac{\text{last year's unit cost}^*}{\text{this year's unit cost}} - 1$$

*in today's dollars

Notice the focus of the productivity measure is "unit cost." what we are comparing is the cost of production (be it a system or a service) this year and last. If after adjusting for inflation, our unit cost has gone down, we are improving and in fact have saved the organization money. Productivity in this model is viewed based on the previous year—we always want to be improving.

PERFORMANCE

Performance is based on three components: cost, time, and quality, scored by percentage of projects falling within + or − 10% of standards.

For all three we apply the 90/10 rule: 90% of products and services should be delivered within 10% of the established estimate (for time and cost) or acceptance standard (quality). The equation computes the percentage of products and services so delivered.

The cost, time, and quality results are matched against a set of success criteria, discussed later, to arrive at the score, which can range from 0 to 1. The meaning of this is simple. To reap the full productivity bonus, these criteria must be met too.

The Computation Algorithm:

STEP 1. Compute performance.
STEP 2. Compute productivity increase.
STEP 3. Compute total organization savings.
STEP 4. Compute bonus percentage.
STEP 5. Multiply bonus percentage by salary base for total bonus.
STEP 6. Subtract total bonus from saving to get organization share.
STEP 7. Distribute bonus to each employee.

THE METRICS

The measures needed to support the IC program constitute a set of management metrics for information systems organizations. If properly chosen, they should be meaningful, easy to obtain, auditable, and evolutionary.

To understand the application of the metrics it is first necessary to look at an operational model of a contemporary information systems organization.

For purposes of this analysis we will characterize four basic functional groups of products and/or services applied:

A *staff* (STF) function, which is the management and administration of the organization as a whole. It does not deliver products or services to the customer community.
An *advanced technology support* (ATS) function, which supplies personal computing, office automtion, information center, and database products and consulting support.
A *business application products* (BAPS) function, which houses the traditional development and maintenance shop.
A *system development services* (SDS) organization, which supplies interactive computing services, staffing, and training to the information systems areas.

Although these groups may not fit your organization exactly, in total they represent a wide range of potential products and services (with the exception of the raw-data-processing plant itself).

Metrics in our two structural areas are applied to the organization as shown in Figure 3.

The interpretation of this figure is as follows:

1. Performance measures will be uniform for the areas of ATS, BAPS, and SDS. The STF group has been purposely omitted because it does not supply external products or services.
2. Productivity measurement will be unique for each functional area. As we go deeper into the model, we will find that this is applied on a lower level function basis. The uniqueness of the measures for each function is necessary to ensure that the criteria of clear cause and effect and meaningfulness are met.
3. The STF budget will be allocated across the department for computational purposes.

ATS PRODUCTIVITY

The following table describes the general types of measures used within ATS to measure the productivity of personal computing (PC), office automation (OA), data base (DB), and information center specialists (ICS).

PC: $\frac{\text{measurement}}{\text{penetration/\$}}$
OA: penetration/$
DB: service/$
ICS: service/$

The productivity measures are of two major types: penetration/$ and service/$. They clearly need explanation as both concepts are new.

First consider penetration. Suppose for the moment that the corporate mission of services such as PC and OA is to penetrate the organization with the appropriate technologies. Peak pnetration will be reached when all staff performing all applicable business functions will be using the technology for all applicable work. The job of a PC or OA group then is to fill up this penetration space in the most effective and efficient way. The space and the penetration can be visualized as shown in Figure 4.

A simplistic measure for the penetration productivity of a PC might be

$$\frac{\#\ \text{PC delivered} \times \#\ \text{packages delivered} \times \#\ \text{users}}{\text{Real cost}}$$

This measure supplies the unit cost or volume delivered per dollar.

It does seem that this can be "gamed" by perhaps just installing a lot of underused PCs. However, such manipulation can be counteracted in two ways. First, the equation can be changed so that the numerator is the sum of the products of packages and users for each PC delivered. Second, on the quality side, the customer's view of the business utility of the delivered system can be rated. A "useless" or "not used" systed would score a 0. Productivity would be pushed downward.

The scheme could be made more sophisticated if, for example, the PC group mission were to penetrate first with specific equipment types and particular packages. A multiplying weight could be applied in the equation. For example, if large VISICALC usage were desired by management while word processing on personal computers were not, a weight of 2 might be used to multiply each VISICALC installation; a word processing acquisition would rate a 0 or some small number.

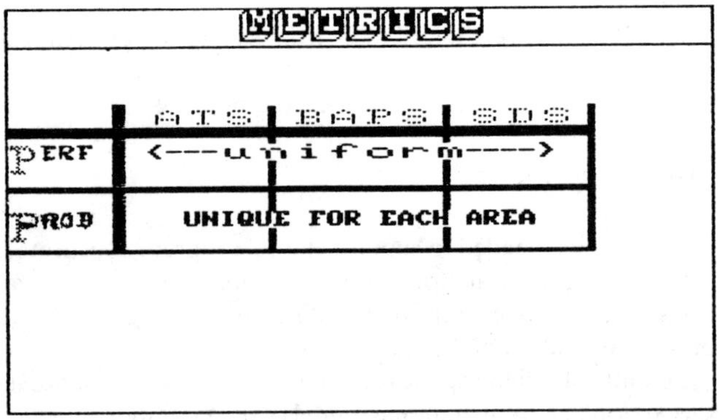

Figure 3

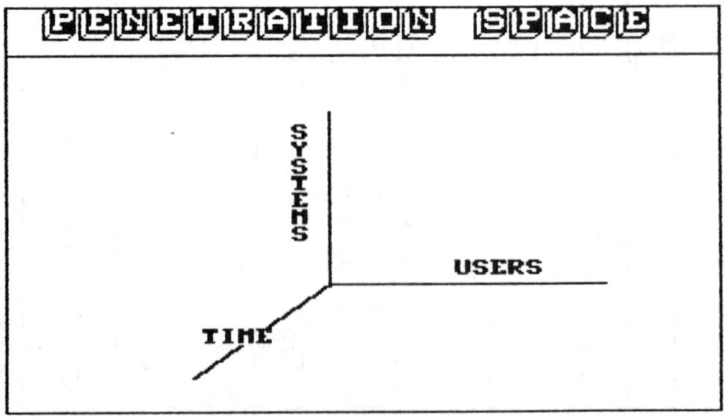

Figure 4

A similar structure for productivity measurement is also applied to OA. Again there is a potential use space; and each work station-user-package combination represents penetration into the space. Weighting could be applied to move the organization in the direction of encouraging electronic mail versus spread sheet work on the OA equipment.

In both DB and ICS, SERVICE/$ is the chosen metric for productivity. When we use this metric, we are looking at the output of each of the groups in business terms.

For example, the ICS group functions to supply reports to the business community and also builds the spinoff databases to derive them. Simply counting the reports produced and databases built, and perhaps weighting them by desired types or complexity, allows measurement of total output. Dividing this by dollars spent again yields the unit cost. The same technique can be extended to the DB group.

The quality aspect of performance measurement for ATS may seem elusive. The prime concern is that quality remain at an acceptable level or exceed it. As a management practice, delivery of a product or service to a customer should include a postdelivery review. In the outside world, even buying a toaster supplies the customer with a feedback form—why not the same in the information systems world? The key questions involve rating the quality level and business utility of the product or service provided. Remember that performance is a function of both productivity and is only rewarded if quality is there.

The productivity–quality linkage is critical. However, most organizations seem to believe that it will always remain an intangible. Quality measurement, in the context of the IC program, gives new meaning and strength to the quality assurance function, and atrophying arm of most information systems organizations.

BAPS PRODUCTIVITY

Productivity measurement in the development/maintenance environment has been the subject of almost frantic activity in the past three years. A number of measures have been discussed in recent conferences and publications: function points/labor period, lines of code/labor period, % of chargeable expenses, and $ benefit/$cost.

BAPS by our definition is the developer and maintainer of information systems. If BAPS is viewed as a production plant, its inputs are customer requirements or repair requests, and its outputs are new systems, modified systems, or repaired systems. Parsing out the repair aspect of BAPS, we are left with measuring the output of a plant producing or recycling information systems.

Contemporary trends indicate the end of the monolingual shop. Hence lines of code measures decrease in meaningfulness. Some argue that the advent of program generators and fourth-generation languages, conversions can be applied to generate equivalent lines of code measures. Unfortunately, this technique has not been accepted as credible by most system developers. What is needed is a productivity metric that in some way reflects the content of an information system in a manner independent of implementation language and technique. Both Albrecht's function points and Halstead's software science measures seem to meet this requirement. Function points are a score of the inputs, outputs, files, interfaces, and inquiry options offered by an information system; they are weighted by their complexities. This score is considered a raw score, which is further adjusted up or down by some operational design factors.

The software science measure of program volume attempts to quantify the contents of an information system on the basis of the total number of bits it would take to represent all the operators and operands required to implement the system. Although this concept seems abstract, it has been demonstrated to have greater power as a predictor of both development and repair effort than does function points. In fact, software science allows the computation of an ideal program volume, which can be used as a base for measuring the quality of a program.

With these two alternatives in mind, a method can be formulated for productivity measurement. Function points and software science are related in that they both use the basic parameters of information systems in their scoring schemes—inputs, outputs, files, etc. Although both treat these parameters differently and consider other aspects of the information system, their common base offers a good starting point on which to build. At the simplest level, an information system content unit (ISCU) can be defined as a score of the basic features of a system—inputs, outputs, files, inquiry types, interfaces, and number of business functions being realized. In this way the ISCU count for any new system can be computed as follows:

$$
\text{ISCU} = \begin{array}{lll}
\# & \text{Inputs} & *3 \\
+\# & \text{Outputs} & *5 \\
+\# & \text{Inquiry} & *4 \\
+\# & \text{Function} & *10 \\
+\# & \text{Interface} & *8 \\
+\# & \text{Databases} & *9
\end{array}
$$

The weights have been chosen on the basis of the relative complexity of each entity class being considered instead of the complexity of a specific one. For maintenance ISCU computation, an additional weight is needed as a multiplier to prorate the percentage of the entity being modified or reused in some form.

This scheme is evolutionary in that it is expandable in either the function point or software science direction as they become more refined. It also overcomes many of the subjective features of the function point approach, as well as aspects of this approach that negate its utility as a basis for estimation and projection.

The productivity of BAPS can be looked at as follows:

$$
\begin{array}{c} \text{new development} \\ \text{maintenance} \end{array} \quad \frac{\text{ISCU*}}{\$}
$$

*Information system content units

ISCUs per dollar are used to score both new development and maintenance (with the exception of corrective maintenance).

Again, renewed emphasis is placed on the quality assurance group, whose job it is to monitor the measures and audit scores.

SDS PRODUCTIVITY

The measures used here follow the mold of the ATS group. Interactive computing services (ICS) are defined as being the support services for the development staff. Penetration is again the key. Customer satisfaction and system availability offer a clear base for assessing quality. Two additional functions have been included to demonstrate the completeness of the suggested approach, recruiting (REC) and in-house training (TRN). Both can be viewed on a unit cost basis with regard to productivity.

The equation is as follows:

$$\text{ICS: } \frac{\text{MEASUREMENT}}{\text{PENETRATION/\$}}$$

REC: HIRES/$

TRN: STUDENT HRS/$

PERFORMANCE

Performance scoring is based on a set of standards derived from 90/10 rule:

	Base	STD.	Excp.
Score	75%	85%	95%
Rating	0	.5	1.0

The interpretation of this equation is that if only 75% of products and services are delivered within the 10% bandwidth a score of 0 is applied, at the 85% level .5, and at the exceptional level of getting 95% of the products and services within the bandwidth 1.0. Any value in between these is prorated. The baseline for establishing the bandwidth for a given product or service will be specified as part of the project or service initiation request process. All products and/or service supplied to a customer will be estimated at this time. In addition, acceptability criteria relating to quality will also be specified. It will be the function of the quality assurance group to set both long-term overall quality criteria relating to such things as future rate, time to repair, expected cost of operation versus actual cost, etc., and specific requirements for a given product or service.

LOOPHOLES?

At first review some questions arise:

What happens if a planned project is canceled?

What happens if an unplanned project is initiated?

What happens if there is a hiring freeze?

How can work not completed within a calendar year be treated?

The first three situations are handled in a similar manner. The IC plan is designed to be flexible. Corrections to targets are possible at any time, although they must be audited. The situation of multiyear projects can be managed by either prorating completed work by the life cycle phase percentages or scoring projects only at their completion.

Gaming in the face of the IC plan is natural. But again, revitalizing the quality assurance (QA) group and supplying upper management support should furnish the needed controls.

INSTALLING THE IC PLAN

The following tasks need to be carried out prior to installation:

1. Form quality assurance group.
2. Develop performance tracking procedures.
3. Define/refine measures: productivity measure definition, integration, and data flow, and quality baselines.
4. Develop standards for integration and data flow.
5. Sell to management and to department.

The scope of these tasks should not be underestimated. Changes in internal reporting of all facets of the organization may be required. However, if the changes implied by the plan are implemented, a stronger organization should result, driven by a set of management metrics that are both meaningful and complete.

A possible scenario for the first year is as follows: End of first quarter, form QA group. End of second quarter, QA implements measures on data collection. End of fourth quarter, QA publishes baseline findings. The goal for the first year is to install the plan. With this in mind, incentive compensation should be awarded at the end of this period simply for getting the IC plan itself defined and in place. Full operation should begin in the second year.

CONCLUSION

A recent *Harvard Business Review* article reached the conclusion that most managers rate the current flurry of productivity improvement programs as ineffective. The emphasis has been on the quick fix. Nowhere has this been more evident than in information systems departments, who by now should have learned the lesson that tools and technology are not a sole solution to business problems. Capital investment in facilities, equipment, and tools are the simplest aspect of productivity improvement. A number of more crucial elements exist:

1. Management commitment, support, and involvement
2. Employee relations, support, and participation
3. Effective training

The proposed IC plan offers a comprehensive structure for addressing all of these within the information systems environment and provides a coherent framework for managing and motivating this critical business resource.

Gaining competitive advantage, or how to succeed as the vice-president of information systems

by M. VICTOR JANULAITIS
Positive Support Review, Inc.
Los Angeles, California

ABSTRACT

Most vice-presidents of informations systems do not succeed or fail because of technical factors. Rather, their careers rise or fall according to how they meet the organization's overall business objectives.

This paper discusses in detail a methodology that can be applied to any business and/or industry. The approach has helped organizations, and their information executives in particular, to focus on the factors that must go right for information systems to be a critical component of the overall business strategies.

The paper discusses competitive strategies and the five forces that give them impetus: the relative bargaining power of buyers/consumers, the relative bargaining power of suppliers, the rivalry among existing firms, the threat of new entrants, and the threat of substitute products and/or services. The challenge of the information systems executive is to apply technology to help the organization gain a competitive advantage in these areas.

The methodology goes through five steps, including assessment of the industry's information systems technology component, how to measure and plot the risk/change relationship for the organization, how to develop a probability-of-success factor for the organization, how to measure the organization's specific risks, and last, how to develop organizational action steps.

BACKGROUND

An executive of a large western bank described his dilemma to us recently: "Every time I turn around our Vice-President of Information Systems is coming into my office with another proposal—a million dollars for some *new* word processing and computer equipment, $85,000 for an *updated* software package, or as I have sitting on my desk now, a multi-million-dollar proposal for installing an advanced worldwide telecommunications network. I am inclined to look favorably on these proposals, since our past ventures into information services have generally been successful. Interestingly, however, virtually every department in the bank also has some complaint about our current systems. What bothers me is that my intuition is not as sharp in computers and communications as it is in lending, borrowing, site location, and other traditional banking areas.

"Today electronics is a necessary part of our business. The fine line between products and services has disappeared as our bank has become more computer based. In this age of deregulation and advancing technology, I can not imagine running our bank without office automation, computers, and communication networks. In addition, we must continue to advance in these areas if we want to stay even with or get ahead of our competitors. It is dammed if you do–dammed if you don't."

RECENT HISTORY

Integrating information services technology involves risk. Many managers today feel that risk is something to be avoided. They are satisfied with the low rates of return they receive because they assume minimal risk. The questions the business executive wants answered are: (1)–Why should our organization take the risks associated with integrating information services? and (2)–What is an acceptable level of risk? The answer is that you do it to gain a competitive advantage consistent with the level of risk you can successfully manage. The challenge, then, is to develop a strategic plan for achieving this objective. Competitive strategy rests on five forces:

1. The relative bargaining power of buyers/customers
2. The relative bargaining power of suppliers
3. The rivalry among existing firms
4. The threat of new entrants
5. The threat of substitute products or services

Information services technology has helped some organizations to gain competitive advantage in each of these five dimensions. The Wizard System, for example, helped Avis improve the product and service they delivered to their customer; and it provided them with knowledge about the location, cost, and performance of its fleet. This helped Avis to bargain more effectively with its suppliers by giving them an advantage over Hertz, National, and the other car rental firms. The national network and the service levels it established *upped the ante* for getting into the business and served as a barrier to entry. Additionally, the Wizard improved the cost/performance ratios and forestalled the development of substitutes. On the other hand, AM International failed by several of these criteria—especially the inability to forestall substitution.

To expand on this topic, there are several distinct categories of information services organizations, which can be grouped into three generic sets. Each organization typically has some characteristics of each set, but for the most part it favors only one. They are:

1. *Strategic technology directed*—Information services are an integral part of the organization's unique strategy. This type of organization has an experience base allowing it to be involved with most leading-edge technology and spend significantly more than its non-strategic-technology-directed competitors on data processing. One of its interesting characteristics is the long tenure of the senior management team, including the information services organization. Some industries are technology directed (airlines in the 1960's, national hotel and car rental industries in the 1970's, and the retail and financial services industries in the 1980's).
2. *Business directed*—Information services are used to provide the necessary information support for its key strategic business units. This type of organization has an experience base that will allow it to be involved with one new technology (such as Database) at a time. The senior management team does not push its information services group to be first in the application of technology. Rather, they want to be sure the organization can do anything their competition can do within a reasonable period of time. This organization typically goes through the standard sets of confrontations within its structure in establishing priorities. In addition, multiple centers of power and expertise compete for authority in establishing, implementing, and controlling technological direction in the organization.
3. *Manager Directed*—Information services are used to provide information for basic management functions such as production, accounting, finance, and marketing. This type of organization has a very limited experience base and only takes on new technology when it is forced to. Typically there is one key decision maker who is not

in favor of computer or communication technology. In this type of organization, if a manager can justify an application of computer technology, he is the one who goes to bat for it. The typical application portfolio of this type focuses on operational control and moves towards the implementation of management control applications. We estimate that between 15% to 20% of corporations fall into this category.

METHODOLOGY

How can an organization gain a competitive advantage through information services? The following five steps help:

1. Assess the technological absorption rate and status of the industry
2. Measure and plot the risk/change relationship for the organization
3. Develop the organizational probability of success ratio (PSR) profile factors and measurements
4. Measure and plot the organizational risk/probability of success ratio
5. Develop the organizational risk management action steps

Assess the Technological Absorption Rate and Status of the Industry

One of the factors that many information system managers tend to overlook is the current level of and dependence on information services technology in their industry. This industry absorption rate dictates the overall risk the organization faces from changes caused by information services technology. The absorption rate is based on two factors: (1) *dependence*—the depth to which technology is an essential component of the industry, and (2) *maturity*—the extent and sophistication with which the industry has adopted the technology.

The combined effect of these two factors reveals the breath and depth of technology absorption in the industry. A high absorption rate generally implies that the information services in the industry are strategic technology directed (see Figure 1).

The steps to develop such a chart are (1) identify the industry's major information and communication functions, (2) rate them on maturity and dependence, (3) plot the organization's position relative to the industry. Then pose the following questions:

1. What are the applications of computers and communication in the industry today and in the future?
2. What is the combined absorption rate for the industry?
3. What is the direction, pace, and momentum of technological change within the industry and the organization?
4. Is the organization behind or ahead of the industry in its application of technology?
5. Are there opportunities to gain a meaningful competitive advantage by leading the industry in information services applications? and
6. Can we employ the technology to support a unique strategic thrust of the organization?

The result is a list of potential technological directions which will provide the organization a leadership position or enable it to gain parity within the industry. Either of these results will entail *changes* in the organization and increase its exposure to risk. To assist in managing this process the next action step is executed.

Measure and Plot the Risk/Change Ratio for the Organization

A successful strategy must achieve a proper balance between growth, control, and technological innovation. Executives need to know: "What is the potential bottom line impact of the application of information services technology?" The following questions are useful in this regard:

1. What is the current strategy for information services?
2. Have the technologies we are using paid off?
3. Do they support the business or drain its resources?
4. How do we compare with our competition?
5. Are we spending the right amount (too much or too little)?

Many factors effect the answers to these questions. Included are the technological dependence and maturity (absorption rate) of the industry and the organization; the focus of the organization's application systems—operational control, management control, strategic planning, or decision support systems; the organizational maturity of the computer, communications, user, and management team; the internal performance measurement systems of the organization; and the existing direction, pace, and momentum of implementation.

Figure 2 shows the plot of a Fortune 500 company at the point when a new information systems (IS) management team was put in place (time x) and the same organization 24 months later (time y). In that twenty four month period the organization went through significant change. The Vice President of information systems started to implement a new communications systems within his company's field operations, converted from an early 1970's based computer operation to a 1980's approach, revised the major business and information reporting systems, and developed a new charter and role direction for the information services groups within the organization.

Develop the Organizational PSR Profile Factors and Measures

An initial analysis, utilizing the Critical Success Factors approach, can identify four to eight items which have to go right for the organization to be successful. Let us review a case.

CONTROL SYSTEMS

COMPETITIVE ANALYSIS—SELECTED CHAINS

Company	MIS application areas POS	DDP	DBMS	OFFICE	SA/PGM	Type computer	MIS $	% Revenue	Comments
Bob's Big Boy	No	No	No	No	5	Sys 34	$100,000		MIS plays minor role in company
Burger Chef	Yes	No	IMS	No		370/138 4331		0.54%	
Church's	Yes	Yes	S2000	No		4341 Sys 34		0.45%	
Commonwealth Holiday Inns	Yes	No	No	Yes		370 115		0.75%	
Denny's	Yes	No	IMS	Yes		3031 370/148		0.45%	Major development effort under way
Dunkin Donuts	Yes	No	No	Yes		Wang 2000		1.00%	
Greyhound Food Mgt.	No	No	No	No		3033		0.5%	
Hardee's Food Systems	Yes	Yes	No	No		3031		0.26%	
Howard Johnsons	Yes 5 yrs	Yes 11	Total	No	35 to 60	370/158 4341 11-GA Series 1	$3.5 mil		Going to major implementation of POS over next 5 years
IHOP	No	No	No	No	6	Univ90/30	$600,000		
Jerrico	Yes	Yes	Yes	Yes		370		0.40%	
KFC	Yes	Yes	No	Yes		3031			
Krystal	No	No	No	No		370/138		0.58%	
Mannings	No	Yes	No	No		4331		0.70%	
McDonald's	Yes	Yes	Yes	Yes	40	370			
Pizza Hut	Yes	Yes	Yes	Yes		370/168			
Ponderosa	Yes	Yes	IMS	Yes	19	370/3031	$2.7 mil		Expanding role
Poppin' Fresh Pies	Yes	No	No	No		H6080		1.80%	
Shoney	Yes	Yes	No	Yes	4	NCR	$450,000		

Source: Positive Support Review Inc

LEGEND: MIS Application areas—areas of focus of the MIS organization. POS—Point of Sale. DDP—Distributed Data Processing. DBMS—Data Base Management Systems. OFFICE—Office of the future and personal computers.
SA/PGM —Number of systems analysts and programmers doing development work for new MIS applications.
Type computer —Type of Computer.
MIS $ —MIS budget in absolute dollars.
% Revenue —MIS budget as a percentage of total revenue.

This chart was prepared for *Nation's Restaurant News* by M. Victor Janulaitis, president of Positive Support Review Inc. of Malibu, Calif. Janulaitis manages and participates in management consulting engagements relating to critical success factor analysis and definition, strategic planning, operational reviews and audits, positive support reviews, MIS (management information systems) planning, and the design, development and implementation of management information systems and educational programs for senior management.

Figure 1—Absorption rate of 3 industries

A billion-dollar organization had undergone a number of significant organization changes. A new chief executive officer was installed and several new strategic decisions were made. Among these was the decision to utilize information services technology to provide the corporation with a meaningful competitive advantage. The successful IS executive immediately started to change the way the organization related to the information services group and the MIS budget increased by over 45%. However new concerns were identified by the IS executive, including:

- Senior management did not understand nor support the MIS plans for computer hardware, operating systems, data bases, communications network and facilities
- The status of four major development projects, which accounted for over 35% of the salaries in the current budget, was not known

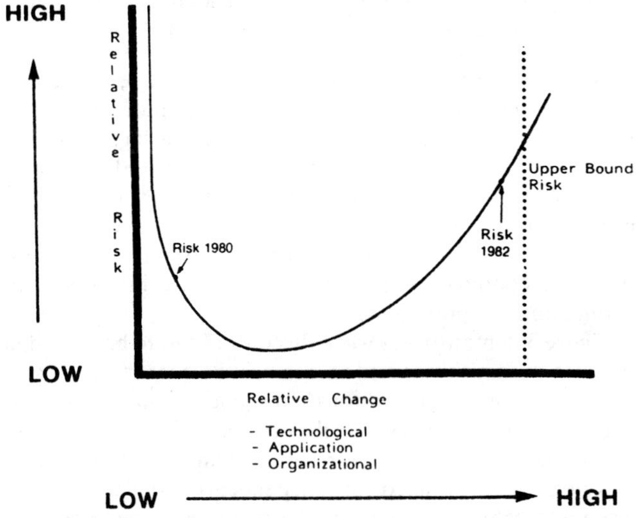

Figure 2—Risk/change relationship

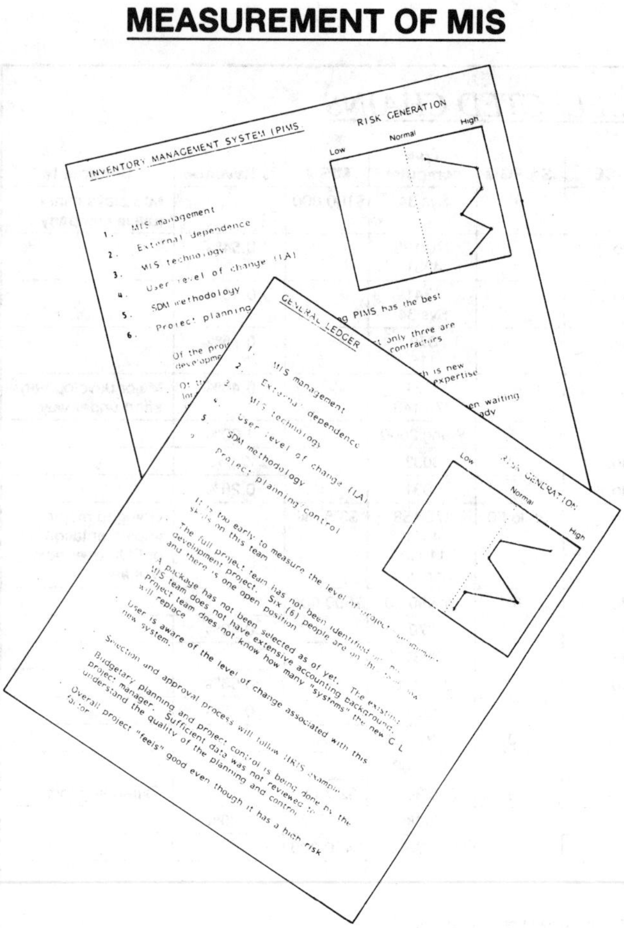

Figure 3—Summary organizational PSR profile

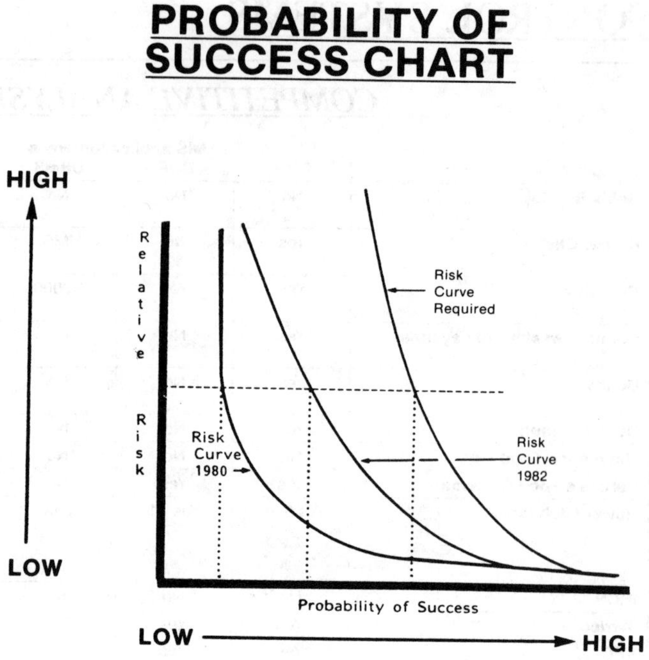

Figure 4—Probability of success

- The decision to utilize outside contractors, to modify existing software, resulted in a substantial expense during the prior four months

- Several key weaknesses of the MIS organization and key user organizations were revealed. The main concern was the high turn-over rate of key specialists

With this information the IS executive was able to identify six profile factors. They were (1), a strong information services management and delivery team, (2), a high independence from external contractors, (3), a measured growth of MIS technology, (4), a successful modification of the user organizations operational characteristics, (5), a well implemented system development, implementation, and operational methodology, and (6), a new capital prioritization, budgeting, and monitoring system.

Figure 3 demonstrates where his efforts had to be placed in order to minimize risk and to increase the probability of success. For example, the information services team, though experienced, had not been with the organization long enough to absorb its culture fully. This resulted in an overall rating that was negative. The need for independence from the outside was the greatest problem. On the other hand, technological growth was normal and the rate of change was within the overall optimal band (see Measure and Plot the Risk/Change Relationship discussion). Overall change management was low risk for the organization because a number of positive action steps had been taken. The development methodology was at a normal level of risk, as was the capital budgeting because of the control systems which had been put in place by the new IS Executive. These factors were then measured across all of the activities involved with the organization.

Measure and Plot the Organizational Risk/Probability of Success Ratio

The IS executive can develop a probability of success profile for his organization. Looking at the risk curve in Figure 4 for time x (manager directed) the relative risk (horizonal line) at point A is the same as the risk a point B (business directed) and point C (strategic technology directed). The area of difference is the probability of success. For the same level of risk the probability of success is greater for the strategic directed organization than for the manager directed one.

In Figure 4 the organization was initially manager directed. You can see the direction that this organization took. With its previous management team (manager directed), the information services group did not acquire the experience base needed to accomplish the company's objectives. For example, they had three failures in two years trying to implement a relatively simple distribution inventory control system. They improved their position by adopting a business directed strategy to help them relate inventory control problems more closely to strategic business units. The difficulty they currently face is that their corporate objectives require them to become a strategic technology directed organization and to use information technology to gain customer service advantage over their competitors. This shift in organization strategy should also improve their probability of success.

Develop the Organizational Risk Management Action Steps

With all these factors considered, it is a reasonable task for an IS executive to define the set of action steps required to gain competitive advantage for his organization. First, the IS executive needs to look at the absorption rate and review the systems that are the focus of the "future leading competitors". This data can identify the new services that a financial services organization is going to provide, or the new products that an office automation company is going to implement, or the new directions that a manufacturing or distribution organization can take to improve productivity. From these new services, a plan for the information services function can be created. Second, the IS executive can identify his organization's Risk/Change function and identify the direction, pace and momentum necessary to achieve its plan. Third, by reviewing the individual activities of the information services function, the IS executive can identify specific action steps required to change its PSR profile and to meet its objectives.

CONCLUSION

Vice Presidents of Information Systems can succeed and help their organizations achieve a meaningful competitive advantage by developing a business strategy that is based on information services technology. This advantage can be translated into new market opportunities as well as the traditional cost reduction systems. For example, any IS executive who looks only at a "simple" application of office automation and does not see potential new ways for linking this to the business strategy or his basic business units functions, may be missing an opportunity. Companies that have prospered in these difficult times, for the most part, have been innovators. Many of them have innovated a competitive advantage in the information services area.

The process presented here is straight-forward. The ideas are little more than a new application of good management practices. If you are to succeed in the next decade, you will need to manage risk, reward, and probability of success more carefully. Five steps to accomplish this are; (1) assess the technological absorption rate and status of the industry, (2) measure and plot the risk/change relationship for the organization, (3) develop the organizational probability of success ratio (PSR) profiles, (4) measure and plot the organizational risk/probability of success ratio, and (5) develop the organizational risk management action steps.

REFERENCES

1. Bullen, C. V., and J. F., Rockart. "A Primer On Critical Success Factors." Cambridge, Mass.: CISR No 69 Sloan WP NO 1220–81, Massachusetts Institute of Technology, 1981.
2. Janulaitis, M. Victor, and Richard O. Mason. "Gaining Competitive Advantage—A CEO's Perspective." Positive Support Review, Inc., Malibu, California, September 1982.
3. Janulaitis M. Victor. "The Best of Both Worlds." *Production and Inventory Management Journal,* Third Quarter 1978, p. 1.

Nolan, Richard L., and Cyrus F. Gibson "Managing The Four Stages Of EDP Growth." Harvard Bus. Rev. (January–February 1974). p. 76.

4. Keen, Peter, and Michael Scott-Morton. *Dicision Support Systems: An Organizational Perspective.* Reading, Mass.: Addison-Wesley, 1978.
5. McFarlan F. Warren. "Portfolio Approach To Information Systems." Harvard Bus. Rev. (September–October 1981). p. 142.
6. McKenney, James L., and F. Warren McFarlan. "The Information Archipelago—Maps and Bridges." Harvard Bus. Rev. (September–October 1982). p. 109.
7. McLean, Ephraim R., and John V. Soden. *Strategic Planning for MIS.* New York: John Wiley & Sons, 1977.
8. Porter, Michael. *Competitive Strategy.* New York: Free Press, 1980.
9. Rockart, John F. "Chief Executives Define Their Own Data Needs." Harvard Bus. Rev. (March–April 1979). p. 81.

Database management

Darrell Ward, Track Chair

The database track is exciting and timely for the 1984 NCC. We are pleased to present database panels and papers that are current and practical as well as indicative of new developments in the database area.

Two sessions are devoted to relational databases, which are fast becoming the standard in modern database technology. "Current Status of the Relational Database Model" develops the current status of the relational database approach and should prove invaluable for those who use a relational database or contemplate its use. The session entitled "SQL Database Language" inspects this important language and evaluates its impact on the end user community. Additionally, the session addresses the notation of a standard language for the relational model.

For the microcomputer enthusiast, "Fourth-Generation Languages (4 GL) and Personal Computers" is devoted to these application tools and their use in the ever expanding area of personal computer applications. This session provides valuable insight into future databases and application development systems for the microcomputer environment.

The "Entity Relationship Approach to Database Design" session focuses on the initial modeling of the database environment and the database design process. The need for guidelines and specifications for database design and implementation is quite apparent to experts who are required to develop such database applications. This session is clearly timely and pertinent for database developers.

Finally, the track features two refereed paper sessions. One of these, "Database Workstations," will address the general area of database environments, including the database workbench and the end user interface. The other paper session, "Database Applications and Interfaces," is intended for specialists who are interested in detailed technical aspects of current database systems.

We feel that the sessions in the database track provide a stimulating environment for continued productivity in the database world.

An interface for novice and infrequent database management system users

by JAMES A. LARSON and JENNIFER B. WALLICK
Honeywell, Inc.
Bloomington, Minnesota

ABSTRACT

Special interfaces are needed for novice and infrequent users of database management systems. Such interfaces must remind users of the structure and names of database objects as they guide users in formulating syntactically valid database commands. A prototype system developed at the Honeywell Corporate Technology Center provides such an interface by integrating schema displays depicting the contents and structure of the database and syntax diagrams representing the valid syntactic options of a database query language. By traversing these graphs, novice and infrequent database management system users can easily formulate syntactically valid database management system commands while learning the formal syntax of the database management system command language.

INTRODUCTION

The database management system (DBMS) presents formidable problems to users. New users of a DBMS must be trained to formulate commands acceptable to the DBMS. New users must also learn the structure of the database, the names and relationships of database objects, and which commands to use to access the various objects. Infrequent DBMS users may need to refresh their memories about both what data are in the database and how to formulate commands to access those data objects. An interface to the DBMS is needed for these users that will aid them in learning and relearning how to use the DBMS.

At the Honeywell Corporate Computer Sciences Center we have been investigating approaches to make DBMSs more friendly to novice users. The remainder of this paper describes one such interface under investigation. We first describe the requirements of an interface for novice and infrequent DBMS users and then give an overview of our system.

INTERFACE REQUIREMENTS FOR NOVICE AND INFREQUENT DBMS USERS

Novice and infrequent DBMS users need an interface to a DBMS that guides them in formulating database requests. Requirements of such an interface include the following:

1. Display valid options. When formulating database requests, users should not be required to know or remember the contents of the database, the structure of the database, or the formal syntax of a query language. A system for novice and infrequent users should be designed so that users formulate requests by choosing from a set of syntactically and semantically valid options.
2. Break the problem into subproblems. Novice and infrequent users need assistance in knowing how in tell the computer what information they want from the database. A system for these users should allow piecemeal formulation of database requests so that a user may concentrate on one subproblem at a time.
3. Display current status. Novice and infrequent users should be reminded of what they have accomplished. The system should display what portions of a database request the user has formulated so that the user can decide what options to choose next.
4. Allow users to change their minds. Users should be able to back up to any previous state of command formulation and resume entering options from the state to which they backed up.
5. Permit only syntactically valid commands. A system should be designed so that it minimizes command input errors and permits the user to enter only syntactically valid commands.
6. Provide online help facilities. The system should aid users with additional instructions when users are not sure about a particular option of the system. These instructions should be designed to communicate the meaning of an option with respect to what users have previously accomplished, thereby aiding them in deciding what option to choose next.
7. Move novice users to more advanced interfaces. A system for novice users should provide mechanisms to move users to more advanced and expedient interfaces. In particular, the system should help users learn the syntax of a database language as well as the contents and structure of the database.
8. Control access to a database. Database interfaces should have a mechanism whereby the database administrator can prohibit classes of users from performing various types of operations on selected database objects.

Forms and menus are two database interfaces often used for novice and infrequent users. Unlike forms and menus, the interface developed at Honeywell is an easy-to-use graphical facility for building database commands that trains users to learn the linear keyword form of the language.

SYSTEM OVERVIEW

Syntax diagrams have been used successfully in programming language manuals to illustrate visually the structure of programming languages. A syntax diagram (Figure 1) is a directed graph representing the syntactic structure of a formal language. Any path from the start node to a finish node constitutes a valid statement in the language. Our system uses syntax diagrams to guide users through DBMS commands as well as to teach the more frequent user the syntax of the DBMS language.

A syntax diagram of a query language is a directed graph that contains six types of nodes: (1) start nodes, (2) literal nodes, (3) value nodes, (4) database item nodes, (5) subgraph nodes, and (6) finish nodes.

For implementation purposes these nodes can be distinguished by color and shape; but novice users need not visually distinguish the nodes, because they will be prompted with appropriate instructions and information as each node is selected. Visual distinction of the nodes might be useful for helping users learn the command language.

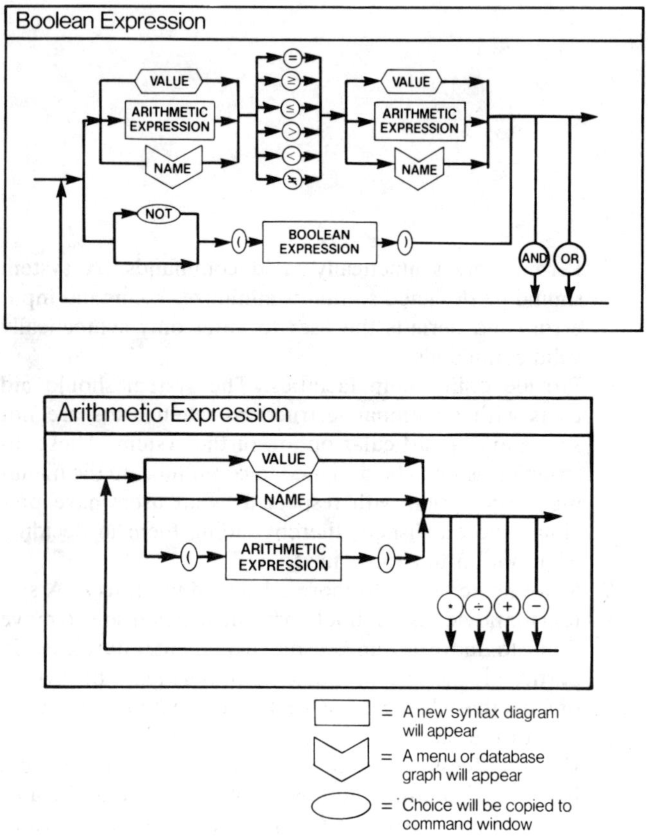

Figure 1—Syntax diagrams

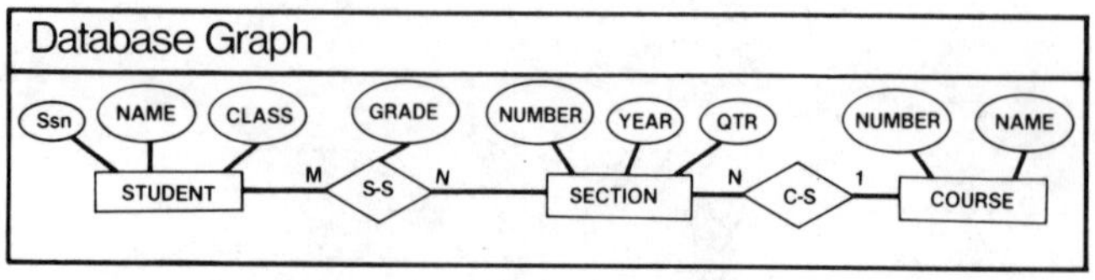

Figure 2—E-R graph representation of a database schema

Start Nodes

Beginning with this node, the user selects nodes, one at a time, along a path in the graph. A complete path specifies a valid request.

Literal Nodes

The names of these nodes correspond to the keywords of the query language. Each time the user selects a literal node, its name is appended to the request being formulated.

Value Nodes

When the user selects a value node, the user is prompted to enter an integer or character string from the keyboard. Value nodes in a query language are used for specifying conditions on attributes of records to be retrieved. The value specified is appended to the request being formulated.

Database Item Nodes

When the user selects a database item node from the syntax graph, the database schema is displayed and the user is asked to select a database object name from the schema. The selected database object name is appended to the request being formulated.

Subgraph Nodes

When the user selects this node, the current syntax graph is placed on a stack, and a syntax graph corresponding to the name of the subgraph node is displayed. This is useful for languages with complex syntax graphs, because it allows syntax graphs to be broken down into a series of subgraph displays.

Finish Nodes

This node indicates that the user has completely specified a path through the currently displayed graph. If the graph is a subgraph, then the parent graph is redisplayed and the user may continue to select nodes from that graph. If the graph was the original starting graph, then the command has been completely specified and is passed to a DBMS for processing.

When a database item node is selected from the syntax graph, a schema describing the classes of objects in the database is displayed on the screen. The schema objects may be displayed as a menu or alternatively as a graph of data objects such as that illustrated in Figure 2. The rectangles in the graph represent classes of entities, and the diamonds represent classes of relationships between entity classes. The ovals represent attributes of entity or relationship classes. This is a graphical representation of Peter Chen's Entity Relationship (ER) data model,[1] a popular style for modeling data to be maintained by a DBMS. The user selects a class of objects from the database schema by positioning the cursor in the appropriate position on the screen or by typing in the name of the desired object at the keyboard.

As the user selects nodes from the syntax diagrams, a linear-keyword-oriented version of the command is constructed in a command window at the bottom of the screen. The user is able to view partially constructed commands as they are being formulated. The user may append keywords, database objects, or values to partially constructed commands either by typing in the keyword, database object name, or value at the keyboard or by positioning the cursor to the desired node on the syntax diagram or database schema display. It is expected that some users will prefer using the cursor and others will prefer entering options at the keyboard. More advanced users will eventually abandon this interface in favor of the more traditional keyboard-only interface.

Novice and infrequent users can be expected to make mistakes. At any point the user may position the cursor to a

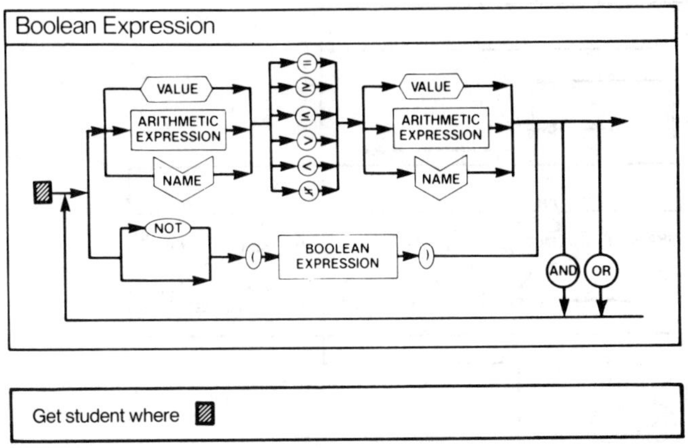

Figure 3—Terminal screen showing a partially formulated command; the user is about to formulate a Boolean expression

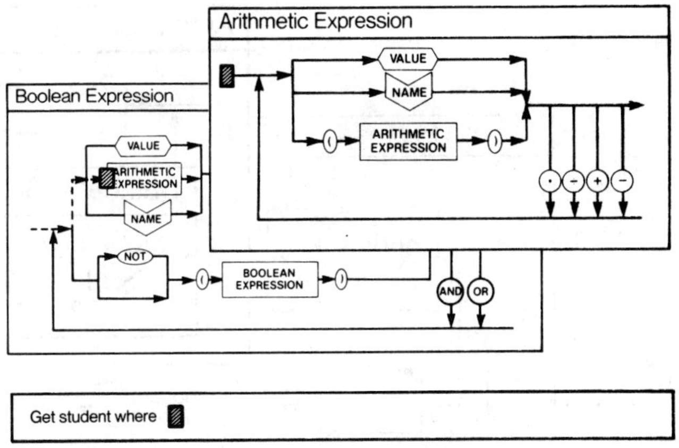

Figure 4—User selects "arithmetic expression" option, and the arithmetic expression syntax diagram is displayed

previously selected node in the syntax diagram (or backspace to a database object name, keyword, or value in the partially formulated command in the command window) and all database object names, keywords, or values following it will be erased from the command window. Thus a user can undo decisions and back up to any previous state, including the start state. The user may then continue formulating the command, possibly choosing options different from the ones previously entered.

If the user does not understand the meaning of any node or cannot decide which path to take on the graph, the user may move the cursor to the node or edge and press the HELP button. Additional information and messages to help the user will be displayed on the screen.

EXAMPLE

Suppose that the user wishes to formulate the database command "GET STUDENT WHERE SECTION.NUMBER 1 = 2 's 3 AND COURSE.Number 1 = 2 's 177". Further suppose that the user has already formulated the first part of the request, "GET STUDENT WHERE." The syntax diagrams of Figure 1 and the ER graph of Figure 2 are used to aid the user to complete the query formulation. This is illustrated in Figures 3–11. The user may move the cursor only in the "top" (most recently displayed) syntax diagram or database schema. Alternatively, the user may move the cursor in the command window and enter database object names, keywords, and values via the keyboard.

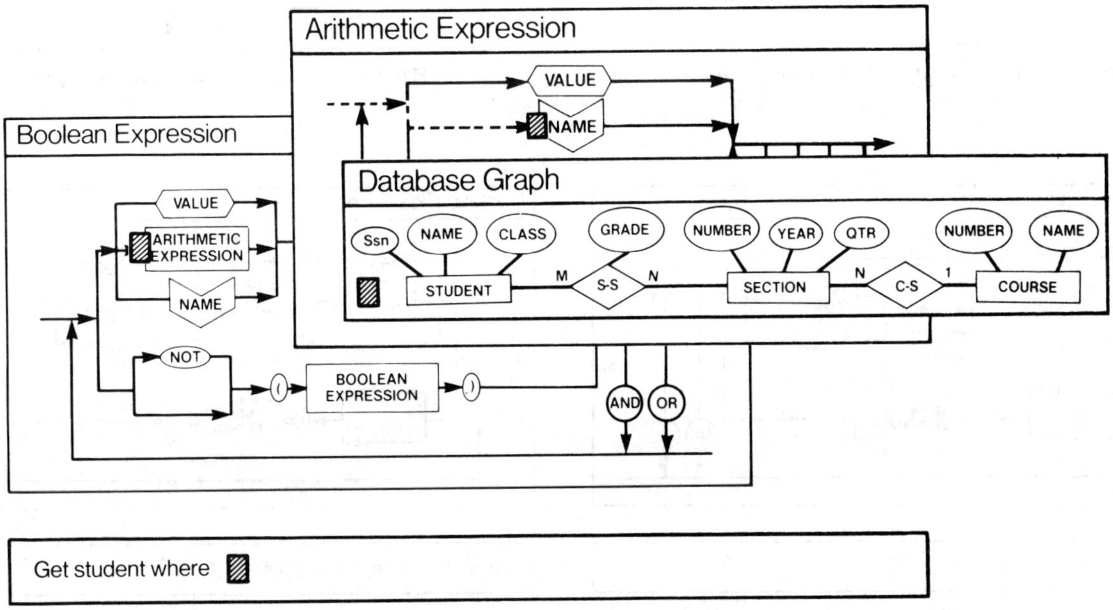

Figure 5—User selects "name" option, and the E-R graph is displayed

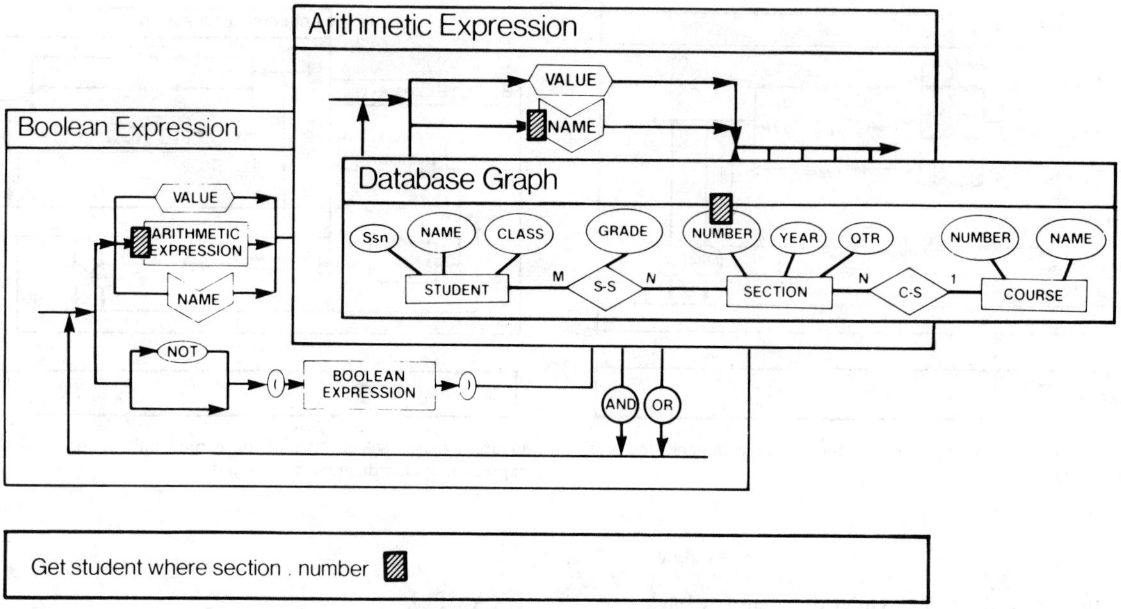

Figure 6—User selects "section.number" option from database graph

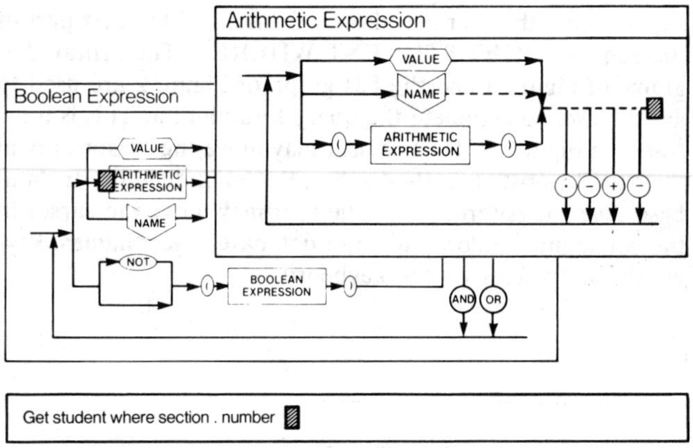

Figure 7—User selects no more options from arithmetic expression syntax diagram

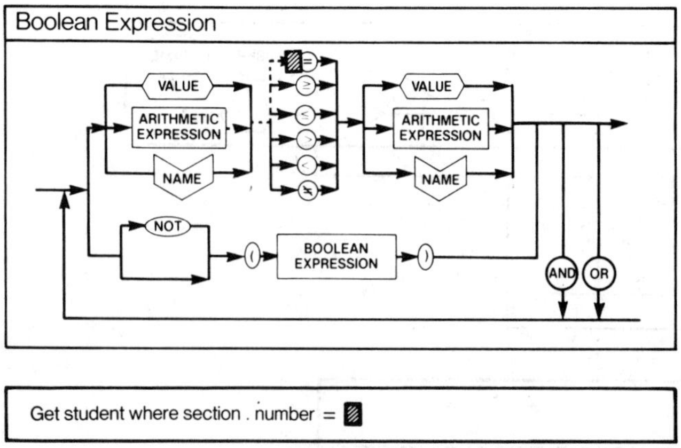

Figure 8—User selects " = " option

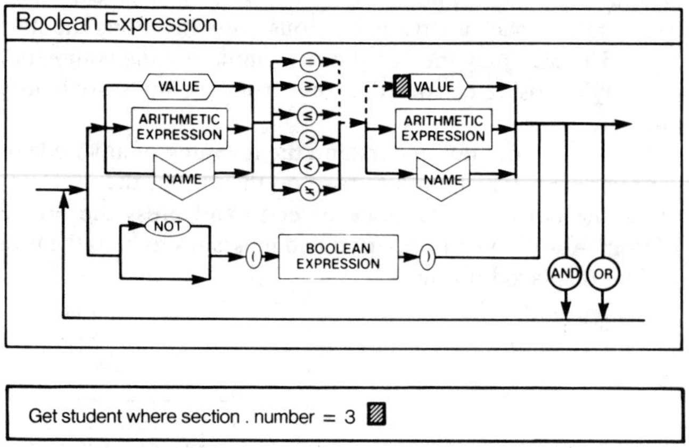

Figure 9—User selects "value" option and types "3"

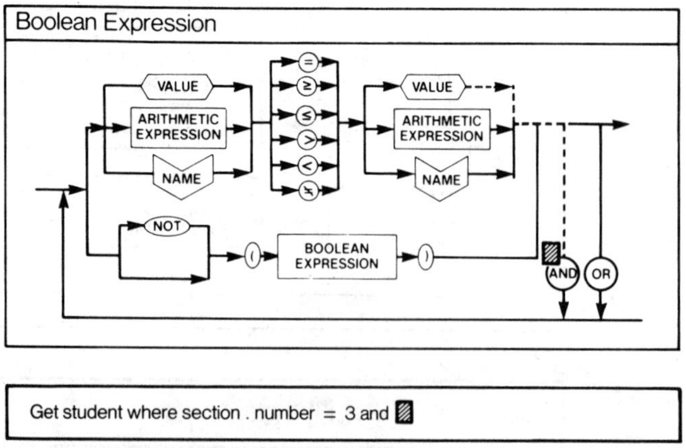

Figure 10—User selects "and" option

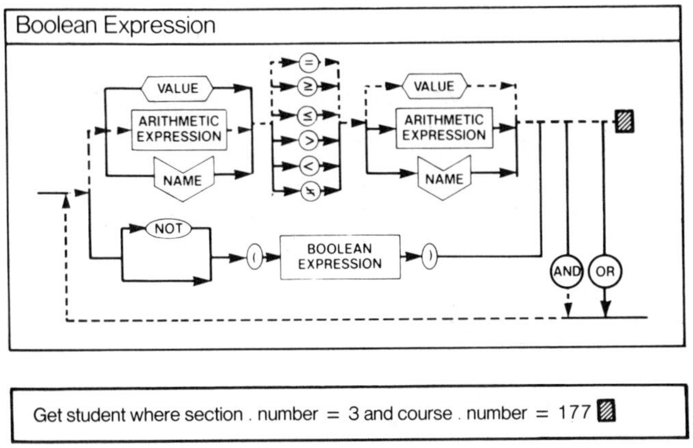

Figure 11—After repeating steps similar to those of Figures 3 through 10, user selects no more options

IMPLEMENTATION

A prototype of this system has been implemented at the Honeywell Corporate Computer Sciences Center in FORTRAN on a Honeywell Level 6 minicomputer interfaced with a Megatek Graphics Terminal. The system supports an interactive mode for building and storing arbitrary syntax diagrams as well as a mode for traversing syntax diagrams with a joystick to construct commands. Nodes can be varying sizes, with a separate color for each type of node.

FURTHER RESEARCH

In this section we investigate ways this system could be used to control access, issues in displaying ER graphs of database schemas, and the automatic creation of syntax diagrams.

Controlling Access

This system could be used to control access to a database by (1) displaying only the part of the schema that describes data the user is allowed to access and (2) modifying the syntax diagrams so that the user is prohibited from executing certain operations (such as delete or modify). We have not investigated a *dynamic syntax graph,* which would prohibit users from specifying certain selected operations on one part of the schema and other selected operations on another part of the schema.

Displaying ER Graphs

Scrolling both up-down and left-right can partially solve the problem of displaying a schema with a large number of entities in the form of an ER graph. Several other approaches to displaying portions of an ER graph should be evaluated:

1. Optionally turning off the visibility of attributes so that the entity sets and relationships sets can be displayed more densely.
2. Positioning the ER graph nodes so that the graph can be displayed in little space while minimizing the number of arcs that cross each other.[2]
3. Partitioning the ER graph into subgraphs such that the objects in each subgraph are related. This clustering can be based on semantics[3] or on statistical clustering methods.

Automatic Creation of Syntax Diagrams

The syntax diagrams and the Bachus-Naur form (BNF) of the command language are closely related. We feel that it is possible to build software that would convert BNF into equivalent syntax diagrams. However, we feel that such software needs human guidance so that (1) the resulting syntax diagrams are not too large to fit on a screen and not as small as a three-choice menu, (2) each syntax diagram corresponds to a single language concept, and (3) the nodes of the syntax diagram are positioned in an aesthetically pleasing layout.

REFERENCES

1. Chen, P. "The Entity Relationship Model: Toward a Unified View of Data." *ACM Transactions on Data Base Systems,* 1 (1976), pp. 9–36.
2. Tamissia, R., C. Batini, and M. Talamo. "An Algorithm for Automatic Layout of Entity Relationship Diagrams." In C. Davis, S. Jajodia, P. Ng, and R. Yeh (eds.), *Entity-Relationship Approach to Software Engineering.* Amsterdam: Elsevier Science Publishers B.V., pp. 421–439.
3. Vermier, Dirk. "Semantic Hierarchies and Abstractions in Conceptual Schema." *Information Systems,* 8 (1983), pp. 117–124.

REQUEST: A testbed relational database management system for instructional and research purposes

by BOGDAN CZEJDO and MAREK RUSINKIEWICZ
University of Houston
Houston, Texas

ABSTRACT

A database management system designed for instructional use should offer facilities usually not required in a commercial environment. In particular, it should support a wide range of user interfaces, access methods, and internal organizations in a modular and flexible way, so that the effect on the system performance of choosing one of them may be illustrated.

REQUEST is a relational database management system that, in addition to the usual data definition and data manipulation functions, offers facilities for use in an instructional environment. Various nonprocedural query languages are supported within a single system, using unified database dictionaries. Cross-translation between various query languages is allowed. The results of every important phase of the query transformation during its execution are available to the user.

Preliminary experience with the system has shown that it can significantly facilitate teaching important concepts of the database system organization. At the same time the system has been used as a testbed in many research and development projects.

INTRODUCTION

With the changing emphasis in data processing from algorithms to data, courses in database management are assuming a central position in undergraduate and graduate computer science curricula. When teaching a database-related course, the instructor usually faces the following alternatives[1]: either to use a commercial type DBMS (if available) or to let the students design and implement procedures functionally equivalent to some parts of the DBMS. Both approaches have significant drawbacks.

Commercial DBMSs are (very expensive) software products for the business or scientific, production-type environment. They are, naturally, concerned with problems of reliability, high performance, backup and recovery, data integrity, etc. Such systems are not suitable for use on usually limited and overloaded campus computer installations. The more serious disadvantage of their use for teaching purposes is that, however sophisticated they may be, they are usually used as "black boxes." Not only are the users not allowed to modify the source programs but they cannot even read and analyze them (even if the source code is available the details of performance and security obscure and distract from the basic concepts that support the instructional standpoint). As a result, students get limited experience in writing simple application programs in a database environment and are never exposed to the internal organization of the DBMS. This situation is, of course, highly undesirable.

Letting the students design and implement their own routines to perform some DBMS-flavored data definition and data-manipulation functions seems to be preferred. The great danger of this solution is that the necessary scope limitations and simplifications as well as the small size of such "databases" tend to underemphasize the fundamental differences (at least within current technology) between accessing objects in main memory and secondary storage. As a result, students accustomed to Pascal programming and algorithm complexity analysis tend to develop intuitions that are pathetically inappropriate in a database environment, particularly as far as the suitability of data structures and search algorithms are concerned.

A Relational Query System (REQUEST) was designed at the University of Houston to alleviate the above problems. To facilitate its use in an instructional environment the following general design objectives were adopted.

1. The system should support a wide variety of user interfaces, access methods, internal data organizations, query optimization, and concurrency control techniques in a modular and flexible way, so that the effect of choosing one of them on the user's interactions and system performance can be illustrated.
2. To facilitate the learning of nonprocedural query languages it should allow the student to analyze expressions based on the relational algebra or the relational calculus (queries, integrity constraints, and predicate locks), translate them, and investigate their equivalence or intersections.
3. As a learning tool the system should support an interactive mode in which a user may trace the execution of a query.
4. The reliability and peformance aspects should be assigned secondary importance. Rather, assuming the large number of relatively small databases, we should concentrate on keeping the size of the system manageable so it may be used in an instructional environment with minimal effect on the computer installation.

REQUEST SYSTEM STRUCTURE

The general structure of the system with its main modules and the interactions between them is illustrated in Figure 1. As can be seen from the schema the system supports the usual range of functions expected in a relational DBMS, including parsing, optimization, and interpretation of query language expressions. However, in addition to the above the system includes a number of facilities for instructional use that are not available in commercial DBMSs.

1. Various nonprocedural query languages including user-defined languages are supported within a single system. They are decomposed into a standardized parse tree based on the unified database dictionary system.
2. Cross-translation between various query languages is allowed.
3. A facility to convert query trees back into query expressions in supported languages is provided.
4. The results of every important phase of the query transformation during its execution are available to the user. A facility is provided to examine a query, its equivalent algebraic structure, corresponding parse tree before and after optimization, the access paths selected by a low-level optimizer, and the intermediate pseudocode used by the interpreter.
5. As a query in interpreted, not only the final resulting relation but also the created temporary relations are available to the user; that is, single step tracing is supported.

REQUEST was designed as a relational DBMS running under VAX/VMS. It is intended to support many users concur-

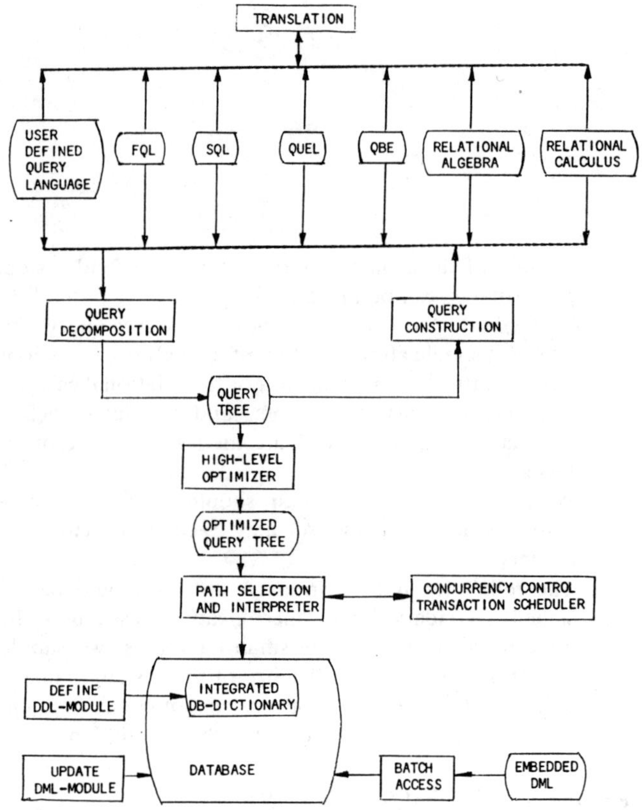

Figure 1—The general structure of the system

rently in both interactive and batch modes. The main modules of the system are discussed briefly below.

Data Definition

The main functions of the DEFINE module are to describe the intension of a databasse and to create and update an integrated data dictionary system. The dictionary is a collection of related files containing the information about database objects stored under the control of the DBMS. The dictionaries are not, however, stored as relations accessible through the system's query facility (as, for example, in SQL/DMS).[2] The reasons for this design decision are pedagogical: it was found that, for beginners, introducing a clear distinction between dictionary relations and data relations is desirable. This enables users to intuitively identify the dictionaries as containing "meta-information" about the data structure. The data dictionaries describe the following:

1. Database relations, both "real" (base tables) and "virtual" (views).
2. Attributes of every relation. For each attribute the corresponding domain together with the "null" value and attribute's location are recorded.
3. Primary and secondary keys for every relation.
4. Integrity constraints.
5. Security constraints such as security clearance required for every type of operation, passwords, etc.
6. Authorized system users with the information about passwords, access grants received, user's security clearances, etc.

The data definition operations can be performed on line, dynamically, in a multiuser environment. Proper synchronization is enforced, if necessary, by the concurrency control module. Relations can be added or dropped; attributes can be added, dropped, modified, or designated as indexes at any time.

Data Update

The update operations (INSERT, DELETE, MODIFY) are performed a record at a time. This was found to be an acceptable solution, because the volume of volatile data manipulated under REQUEST's control is usually small. In addition it allows the concurrency control to be much simplified and a higher degree of concurrency between conflicting transactions to be achieved.

The updates are performed in a user's working space and installed in the database in accordance with the "two-phase-commit" policy.[9] An automatic roll back is performed in case of system malfunction.

Query Decomposition

REQUEST is intended to support a multilanguage environment: a database described by a uniform dictionary system can be queried by any of the query modules corresponding to the different languages. Queries specified directly as sequences of operations of relational algebra and relational calculus or expressed in a user-defined language are also supported. Query decomposition is performed by a parser whose functions include validating relations and attributes names, checking the domains of attributes and constants used in comparisons, and generating an (unoptimized) parse tree.

Query Optimization

While constructing a parse tree the parser does not consider the efficiency of evaluating the tree. The problem of query tree optimization has been substantially researched.[3,10,11] The query optimizer uses several heuristic rules to convert the tree into an equivalent one that could be evaluated faster. Some of these are as follows[12]:

1. selections should be performed as early as possible; that is, select operators should be pushed toward the leaves of the expression tree,
2. selections and projections involving one file should be combined, when possible, so that only one scan of the file is required.
3. joins should be combined with the following projections,
4. if the query involves a common subexpression such as a view it is often beneficial to evaluate it once and then use the resulting relation in subsequent computations.

The optimization rules used here are based on commutative and associative algebraic laws for projections, selections, joins, and Cartesian products and allow one to convert an expression into an equivalent one. These rules can be applied independently of the information about the internal organization of files used to store the relations.

Path Selection and Query Interpretation

Before a join or a selection is performed, the file(s) should be preprocessed; in particular we should take advantage of existing secondary indices and ordering of the files (if applicable to the operation).[4] For every basic operation a decision is made on how it should be implemented, taking into account the cardinality of the relation, the number of distinct values occurring in each attribute's domain, the expected reduction of a table as a result of select operation, the existing secondary indices, etc. If a temporary table has to be created and used as an input argument for a subsequent join or selection operation, the relevant secondary indices should be created while constructing the table.

Access Method

REQUEST uses its own access method implemented on top of the VAX/VMS Record Management Services (RMS). Access method routines that could be invoked from a high-level programming language perform basic file and record manipulation functions. The decision to provide an interface to the RMS rather than implement a totally independent file system was made to achieve an acceptable speed of operation. The file organizations include index sequential, hashing, and extendible hashing.[13]

REQUEST Batch

Both data definition and data manipulation facilities discussed so far are available to the user in an interactive mode from a terminal. In many applications an access to a database from a general-purpose host programming language is required. In REQUEST, access to a database can be achieved in the embedded mode through one of the two available interfaces:

1. a Pascal preprocessor for SQL that produces relatively small executable modules by performing the syntax error checking, name validation, and access path selection at the preprocessing stage so that only selected relevant modules of the DBMS need to be linked with the host-language program
2. a general call facility that allows the DML statements to be executed from any programming language obeying VMS calling and parameter-passing conventions

Concurrency Control

To support a multiuser environment it is necessary to schedule conflicting transactions using some concurrency control mechanism. The well-known concept of serializability is employed to assure that both read-write and write-write conflicts are scheduled according to some serialization order.[9] A wide variety of concurrency control algorithms proposed in the literature can be classified into three main groups:

1. locking-based methods (exclusive and shared locks, predicate locks, intent locks)
2. timestamp-ordering-based methods (basic T/O, conservative T/O, multiversion T/O)
3. circulating-permit-based algorithms

A transaction scheduler is a program module that performs the following functions: it keeps track of the status of each data item in the database; it receives transaction's requests to access a data item; it either allows the transaction to proceed (updating the status indicators) or rejects it if the requested operation is in conflict with other transactions in progress. Depending on the concurrency control algorithm used, the rejected transaction will be queued, or under some algorithms it will be rolled back and restarted. Communication between transactions and the scheduler is implemented through mailboxes and event flags.

It was found that an intent locking scheme capable of supporting different granularities of locks seems to be particularly appropriate in a system that like REQUEST, supports both record-at-a-time and set-at-a-time operations.[8]

Query Translation

Translation of queries is an important facility that enables the user of an instructional system to see the equivalence of expressions specified in different languages.[7] Some transformations such as reduction of relational algebra to tuple-relational calculus are well described in the literature.[12] Others, such as the direct transformation from SQL to QUEL need to be investigated. The approach adopted in REQUEST is based on formulating translation rules and employing them to perform symbol and tree manipulation.[5,6]

Query Construction

Query construction is a unique feature of the instructional DBMS. This module accepts the parse tree based on relational algebra as an input. It produces as an output query expressions in any of the supported languages including a user-defined language. This feature is not necessary in commercial DBMSs but very useful for student training. In addition, this facility provides an alternate way of translating queries, by first decomposing a query into a parse tree and then constructing a query expression in a different language.

CONCLUSIONS

The development of the system started in 1980 as a research project of the authors at the Department of Computer Science of the University of Houston. The first version, which constitutes a functional subset of the system, was completed in 1981. Since then it has been used successfully both as a teaching tool in database courses and as a testbed system for research. Currently available modules include, among others, integrated data dictionary system, parsers, optimizers and an interpreter for SQL, locking and T/O based transaction schedulers, etc. An important implemented part of the system is a friendly query interface that guides an inexperienced user through the database definition process and allows him to formulate queries based on the relational algebra in a menu-driven mode. Other parts of the system including the query translation and query construction modules are currently being designed and developed.

The preliminary experiences with the system have shown that it can significantly facilitate teaching of the important concepts related to the database system organization. At the same time, REQUEST has been used in many research and development projects including the design of an integrated text and graphics database system.[14] Although the initial results are quite satisfactory, a number of important research issues will have to be resolved before the system can achieve its full functional scope.

REFERENCES

1. Bradley, J. *File and Data Base Techniques*. Holt, Rinehart and Winston, 1981.
2. Astrahan, M. M., et al. "System R: Relational Approach to Database Management." *ACM TODS,* 1 (1976).
3. Smith, J. M., and Yang, Y. T. "Optimizing the Performance of a Relational Algebra Database Interface." *Comm. ACM,* 18 (1975), pp.
4. Grifiths, P. P., et al. "Access Path Selection in a Relational Database Management System." R. J. 2479, IBM San José, 1970.
5. Czejdo, B. "Transformation of Universal Algebraic Expressions in PASCAL," ACM Computer Science Conference, Kansas City, February 12–14, 1980.
6. Czejdo, B. "ALGEBRA—Language for Automatic Transformation of Universal Algebraic Expressions," ACM Computer Science Conference, St. Louis, February 24–26, 1981.
7. Czejdo, B., and M. Rusinkiewicz. "Query Transformation in an Institutional Database System." *ACM SIGCSE Bulletin,* 1 (1984), pp. 217–223.
8. Gray, J. N., et al. "Granularity of Locks in a Large Shared Database." *Proc. 1st Int. Conf. on VLDB,* September 1975.
9. Bernstein, P. A., and Goodman, N. "Concurrency Control in Distributed Database Systems." *Computing Surveys,* 13 (1981), pp.
10. Yao, S. B. "Optimization of Query Evaluation Algorithms," *ACM TODS,* 4 (1979), pp.
11. Aho, A. V., et al. "Equivalence of Relational Expressions." *SIAM J. Computing,* 8 (1979), pp.
12. Ullman, J. D. *Principles of Database Systems.* Computer Science Press, 1983.
13. Fagin, R., et al. "Extendable Hashing—A Fast Access Method for Dynamic Files", *ACM TODS,* 4 (1979), pp. 315–344.
14. Rusinkiewicz, M., and Li, Y. Y. "Textual and Graphics Database for SAL Geophysical Models." University of Houston, *SAL Review,* 10 (1982), pp. 417–423.

Sibyl: A relational database system with remote-access capabilities

by MANFRED RUSCHITZKA,
ANDREW CHOI,
and JOHN L. CLEVENGER
University of California
Davis, California

ABSTRACT

The proliferation of inexpensive microprocessor systems and communications equipment has provided the general public with the ability to access remote database systems. It also makes off-loading of some of the query-processing load of such remote systems to microprocessor systems an attractive possibility, but problems concerning data portability and adequate software support need to be resolved. To demonstrate the feasibility of such a loose coupling of a microprocessor system with different brands of remote database systems, a relational database system capable of exchanging data with heterogeneous remote systems was designed and implemented. We describe the functionality of this operational system as well as the design and implementation of its major components.

INTRODUCTION

The maturing of database technology manifests itself in increasing numbers of very large databases that specialize—often nationwide—in specific areas of knowledge. The holdings of major libraries, weather data, news services, corporate information, and stock market reports represent examples of such domains. At the same time, the proliferation of inexpensive microprocessor systems and communications equipment increasingly provides the general public with the means to query such remote, specialized database systems. While some of these systems are capable of handling several thousand queries per minute (for example, high-performance airline reservation systems), such a rate cannot readily be exceeded with today's technology. Thus, increased access by the general public may severely saturate such remote databases. There are two approaches being taken to resolve this saturation problem: increasing the computational power and reducing the load of these systems. The former approach focuses on novel architectures for data storage devices, improved processing algorithms, and increased speed of devices. The latter approach deals with a spectrum of off-loading techniques ranging from tightly coupled distribution of the database functions over several systems to the delegation of individual subtasks to other systems.

Our approach at the Computer Systems Research Laboratory at the University of California at Davis is of the off-loading type. Specifically, we were interested in demonstrating that a microprocessor system that functions as a remote terminal of an interactive database system can itself be employed to handle a part of the generated load. Since microprocessors typically run in standalone mode and consequently tend to be lightly loaded, off-loading remote databases to them appears particularly attractive in terms of cost-effectiveness.

Over the past several years, a number of organizations have placed several thousand communicating microprocessor systems in the homes of employees. These systems provide additional computing power without requiring additional capacity from the central corporate facilities, but there is no unanimity yet on the effectiveness or desirability of such arrangements. Part of the reason is that contemporary microprocessor systems lack the sophisticated processing capabilities of the central facilities; data can be shipped, but processing is limited by the capabilities and the compatibility of the available software. In providing these software functions, however, special care must be taken to ensure the continuing uniformity, reliability, and integrity of the data.

To demonstrate the feasibility of our approach, we designed and implemented a self-contained, microprocessor-based relational database system, called Sibyl. An essential component of Sibyl is its transformer module, which allows it to exchange data with remote database systems of different brands. We describe the system's functional capabilities and characteristics in the next section and discuss design and implementation issues of its major components in the remainder of this article.

OVERVIEW OF SIBYL

Sibyl is a relational database system. The database consists of a collection of names relations (or tables) each of which consists of an arbitrary number of tuples. (or rows).[1] A tuple consists of an arbitrary number of attributes of varying types. The corresponding attributes in the rows of a table form a column. With this in mind, a user may specify operations on the data in the database in a tuple-relational calculus language. This query language is a subset of QUEL, the query language of INGRES.[2] (Its syntax, which will be discussed later, is summarized in Figure 4.) In this language, selection, projection, and joining are provided for without any implementation restrictions. In Codd's terminology,[3] Sibyl thus qualifies as a *relationally complete* system.

Sibyl is the product of continuing research effort, and its design and implementation are subject to constant change and enhancement. With minor exceptions, this article describes Version 1.0 as it existed in January 1983. This version runs on an IBM Personal Computer[4] with 192 Kbytes of primary memory and uses the DOS operating sytem.[5] An RS232 port, connected to a dial-up modem, serves as the communications link to remote database systems. The configuration also contains 320 Kbytes of diskette storage, and a 10-Mbyte Winchester disk. This capacity limits the size of the database that can be operated on at any one time. While DOS was enhanced by an interrupt-driven RS232 package[6] written in assembly language, all other modules are written in Pascal.[7] Sibyl consists of about 5000 lines of source code and its load module occupies 100 Kbytes of primary memory. Version 1.0 supported communications with only one brand of remote database system, INGRES, and an installation at the University of California at Berkeley was used for testing and demonstrations. The development effort amounted to one person-year.

The overall structure of Sibyl is shown in Figure 1. The command intepreter is invoked from the DOS command processor. It distinguishes between two types of commands: query and communications commands. A query command is passed to the query parser, which translates it into an intermediate representation, a query tree, which is then passed to the query processor. The processor executes the query, relying on the relation manager for the maintenance and accesses

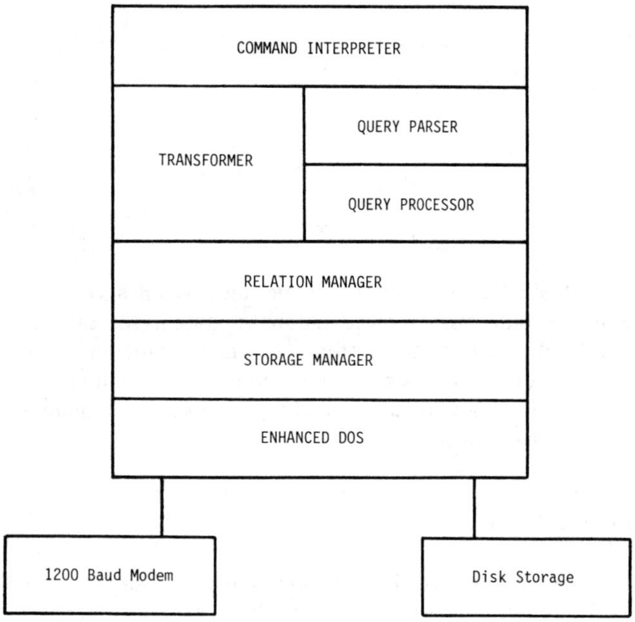

Figure 1—The structure of the components of Sibyl

to relations. The relation manager, in turn, depends on the storage manager for the physical representation of relations and their accesses. The storage manager makes use of DOS files. There are three communications commands: terminal emulation, transfer from INGRES, and transfer to INGRES. For each of these, the command interpreter invokes the transformer. Terminal emulation turns the IBM Personal Computer into a terminal, and can be used to connect to a remote INGRES installation via the RS232 port. If invoked for a transfer, the transformer transfers a relation to or from INGRES, transforming the relation to the format of the destination system in the process.

A Sibyl user typically will operate in local mode and occasionally ship a few relations to or from the remote INGRES system. In local mode, the query language provides the user with complete relational processing capabilities. In remote mode, up-to-date copies of relations at the remote system may be acquired and updated or new relations may be shipped back. The control over the remote database remains with its database manager; the Sibyl user has the same privileges as the interactive user has regarding the remote system.

STORAGE MANAGER

The storage manager[8] is responsible for the allocation and deallocation of the physical storage of all relations. Between sessions, all relations are stored in DOS files. When being accessed, however, a relation may be stored in its entirety in primary memory or it may be stored in a DOS file. In the latter case, the relation is accessed through the buffer that the DOS file system maintains for that file. When a relation is accessed, an attempt is made to move the entire relation to primary memory to speed up the most typical accessing task, query processing. Users of the storage manager are not aware of the physical storage medium of a relation; the storage manager moves relations internally between primary and secondary storage to optimize performance, and selects the appropriate routines when it is invoked for an operation.

The allocation unit both in primary (or "core") memory and on secondary (or disk) storage is a page of 512 bytes. The ordered sequence of pages of a single relation is called a heap. The storage manager maintains its own buffer pool for the allocation of core heaps, but relies on the DOS file system for the allocation of disk heaps. A heap control block (HCB) serves to locate a heap. For core heaps the HCB contains a sequence of pointers into the buffer pool. Since a disk heap it implemented as a DOS file the DOS file control block is used as the corresponding HCB. In either case, HCBs are referred to by a heap name and initialized when the named heap is activated.

A relation is encoded as a sequence of tuples. The physical counterpart of a tuple is a record, and the heap of a relation may be viewed as a sequence of records identified by number. Since records are stored contiguously, individual records may cross page boundaries. Given a record number, the HCB, which contains the size of its records, can be used to determine the page (or pages) containing the specified record, and locate its offset within that page for an access.

The interface of the storage manager, which includes the following six routines, summarizes its externally invocable functions.

- initialization and termination of the storage manager
- activation and deactivation of a heap
- reading and writing of a record

Note that the storage manager does not support accesses to the physical representation of attributes. The notion of attributes is provided by the relation manager, which stores them as fields within records and relies on the storage manager for accessing the latter.

RELATION MANAGER

The relation manager maintains and operates on relations, their tuples, and their attributes. It depends on the storage manager for allocating and accessing the physical representations of relations (heaps) and their tuples (records).

The basic building block of a relation is an attribute. It is characterized by a type (integer, string [length], etc.). A type machine[k] is also provided as a type escape mechanism: It denotes a raw block of k bytes. Note that the type implicitly specifies the size of an attribute in bytes. When an attribute is part of a relation, it is stored in some tuple and the offset within this tuple must be known in order to access the attribute. An attribute index, which consists of both the type and the tuple offset (in bytes) of an attribute, has been provided for this purpose; it is a characteristic of a column of a relation.

A tuple is a collection of attributes of possibly different types. The physical representation of a tuple is a record, and the type of the latter is machine[s] where s is the sum of the attribute sizes. Records are read and written by routines in the storage manager. A tuple identifier (TID) serves for referencing a specific tuple within a relation. It may be thought of as an imaginary attribute (column) of every relation. The TIDs of a given relation are unique.

A relation is a set of tuples. A user views it as a table where the rows correspond to tuples and the columns represent the attributes of the relation. Sibyl maintains a system catalogue of its relations. This catalogue is contained in two files: one for the relation descriptors and one for the mapping of relation names into indices of the relation descriptor file. The left half of Figure 2, to be discussed later, shows the contents of a relation descriptor. Its function is analogous to that of any file directory entry in a contemporary file system. Most of its entries are self-explanatory, but the validity map requires explanation. For reasons of efficiency, the deletion of a tuple from a relation does not result in the deletion of the corresponding record. Instead, a valid-bit can be reset for the same effect. There is one valid-bit per record in the relation, and the sequence of valid-bits is called the validity map. Since the size of the validity map is proportional to the number of records (which may be quite large), the map is actually contained in a separate map–catalogue file.

When a relation is opened, the relation manager initializes a relation control block (RCB) for accessing it. The RCB format is illustrated in Figure 2. Its relation descriptor part has been described above, but the validity map field now contains a pointer to a data structure that has been initialized from the map–catalogue file. The RCB also contains an access control block for information that is relevant only while the relation

```
   +----------------------+----------------------+
   |                      |                      |
< ===== > previous RCB    |     Next RCB   < ===== >
   |                      |                      |
   +======================+======================+
   |                      |                      |
   |  relation name       |  active              |
   +----------------------+----------------------+
   |                      |                      |
   |  tuple size [bytes]  |  modified            |
   +----------------------+----------------------+
   |                      |                      |
   |  number of rows      |  current tuple       |
   +----------------------+  identifier          |
   |                      +----------------------+
   |  number of columns   |                      |
   +----------------------|  current tuple       |
   |                      |  buffer              |
   |  number of records   |                      |
   +----------------------|                      |
   |                      |                      |
   |  format descriptor   +----------------------+
   |  (name and attribute |                      |
   |  index of each       |  heap name           |
   |  attribute)          |                      |
   +----------------------+----------------------+
   |                      |                      |
   |  validity map        |  master              |
   |                      +----------------------+
   |  +--------------+    |                      |
   |  | 1 1 1 0 1 ...|    |  heap control block  |
   |  |              |    |  pointer             |
   |  +--------------+    |                      |
   +----------------------+----------------------+

<-relation descriptor-> <-access control block->
```

Figure 2—A relation control block consists of a relation descriptor and an access control block

is open. Heap name and HCB pointer refer to the heap that contains the relation. The current tuple identifier provides for random and sequential accessing of tuples, and the current tuple buffer contains the current (or most recent) tuple accessed. The master flag will be discussed below (see subrelations). When a relation is closed, its RCB is not automatically discarded. Instead, the RCBs active-flag is reset. This design permits the reopening of a relation without the overhead of accessing the system catalogue. At the end of a session, the status of all remaining inactive relations is updated in the catalogue and the modified-flag determines whether the relation must be written out. Sibyl also supports auxiliary relations, which never enter the system catalogue; they are created and opened like any other relation, but are destroyed prior to the termination of a session.

The high frequency of selection operations during query processing demands high performance of their executions (c.f. the marking operation in ZETA/TORUS[9]). For this reason, Sibyl supports objects of the subrelation type. A subrelation consists of a subset of the tuples of another relation (the master relation) and requires no additional physical representation. A subrelation is defined by an RCB and thus has all of the characteristics of a relation. Its heap, however, is that of the master relation, and its validity map identifies its tuples as a subset of the master relation. The result of a selection can therefore be represented by a subrelation, thus avoiding the storage and copying costs otherwise affiliated with the creation of a new relation for the selected tuples. Figure 3 depicts the linkage of two subrelations to the heap of their master relation. (Version 1.0 supports only auxiliary subrelations.)

The storage manager can be invoked for a variety of operations on relations, tuples, and attributes after it is initialized. The termination procedure saves all inactive relations in the system catalogue. Relations are referred to by name. Operations on relations include creation and destruction in the system catalogue, opening and closing (including subrelations), and printing and displaying. For reasons of integrity, tuples are operated on in the current tuple buffers of the RCBs; they can be referenced by matching or sequential accessing, but cannot be passed in their entirety to and from the relation manager. Instead, attributes are the units of exchange to and

```
RCB(M)                     RCB(S1)                    RCB(S2)
+------------------------+ +-----------------------+ +-----------------------+
|                        | |                       | |                       |
|                        | |                       | |                       |
------------+-----------+ ------------+----------+ ------------+-----------+
| validity  | master    | | validity  | sub-     | | validity  | sub-      |
| map       | relation  | | map       | relation | | map       | relation  |
|           +-----------+ |           +----------+ |           +-----------+
| 11101 ... | HCB       | | 10101 ... | HCB      | | 11000 ... | HCB       |
|           | pointer   | |           | pointer  | |           | pointer   |
+-----------------|-----+ +-------------|--------+ +----------------|------+
                  |                     |                           |
                  +-------------+       |       +-------------------+
                                |       |       |
                      HCB(M)    v       v       v
                      +-----------------------------+
                      |                             |
                      |                             |
                      +-----------------------------+
```

Figure 3—Linkage of subrelations S1 and S2 to the heap of their master relation M from current tuple buffers. Attributes are referred to by attribute indices; they can be inserted, extracted, compared, operated on, inspected (for types and sizes), and displayed. A complete specification of the interface of the relation manager is contained in Reference 8.

QUERY LANGUAGE AND PARSER

Sibyl's query language is a subset of QUEL,[2] the query language of INGRES. It is complete in the sense that its expressive power is equivalent to that of relational algebra. Figure 4 describes the syntax of Sibyl's query language. The "help" command lists all Sibyl relations or, if a relation is named, the names, types, and sizes of its attributes. The "range" command is a declarative command; it associates a relation variable with a named relation. The "create" command creates an empty, named relation whose attributes are specified by the format list. "Destroy" destroys the named relation and "print" displays the named relation on the console.

The remaining four commands take as input all relations named in the qualification part and in the target to produce one output relation, the target relation. The qualification part specifies a conjunctive list of clauses, which define the set of tuples in the target relation. Version 1.0 lacks union and complementing of clauses, but since the supported comparison operators include their individual complements, this represents a loss in convenience, but not in the scope of representable queries. The name of a target relation is specified by a relation name or a relation variable (if it is omitted in a retrieve command, the target relation is displayed on the console), and its attributes are specified by the target list. The "append" and "retrieve" commands append all qualifying tuples to an existing and new target relation, respectively. The "delete" command deletes all qualifying tuples in the target relation and the "replace" command replaces them with attributes specified in the target list.

The query parser[10] receives a lexicographical query from the command buffer, checks its syntactical correctness, and translates it into an intermediate form, a query tree, to be interpreted by the query processor. The parsing technique is essentially one of recursive descent, but operator precedence is used for arithmetic expressions. Different types of linked-tree nodes are used for commands, target list items, clauses, and arithmetic expressions. Clauses are characterized by the number of relation variables they contain: zero-variable clauses (0VCs), one-variable clauses (1VCs), and multiple-variable clauses (MVCs). Owing to the importance of this distinction to query processing, the query tree contains three separate lists for them.

For illustration purposes, consider the sample query

```
append to match (NNR = nut.NUM, BCD = bolt.CODE)
where
   5 < 4+2 and
   bolt.WT < 4 and
   bolt.COLOR = nut.COLOR and
```

which searches through the two relations *nut*(NUM, WT, COLOR) and *bolt*(CODE, WT, COLOR) and adds to the relation *match*(NNR, BCD) those pairs of nut numbers and bolt codes that satisfy the four clauses. Assume that the type of the attributes NUM, WT, CODE, NNR, and BCD was specified as integer and the type of COLOR was specified as string[8] when their respective relations were created. The query tree of this sample query is illustrated in Figure 5. The command node contains the command, the target relation name, and four lists: the target list and one list each for 0VCs, 1VCs, and MVCs. To improve query-processing performance, the query tree also contains several enhancements[11] that are not shown in Figure 5.

```
<COMMAND> ::=       help <REL-NAME> |
                    help |
                    range of <REL-VAR> is <REL-NAME> |
                    create <REL-NAME> ( <FORMAT-LIST> ) |
                    destroy <REL-NAME> |
                    print <REL-NAME> |
                    append <REL-NAME> ( <TARGET-LIST> ) <QUAL-PART> |
                    append to <REL-NAME> ( <TARGET-LIST> ) <QUAL-PART> |
                    retrieve ( <TARGET-LIST> ) <QUAL-PART> |
                    retrieve <REL-NAME> ( <TARGET-LIST> ) <QUAL-PART> |
                    retrieve into <REL-NAME> ( <TARGET-LIST> ) <QUAL-PART> |
                    delete <REL-VAR> <QUAL-PART> |
                    replace <REL-VAR> ( <TARGET-LIST> ) <QUAL-PART>
<TARGET-LIST> ::= <TARGET-ITEM> | <TARGET-ITEM> , <TARGET-LIST>
<TARGET-ITEM> ::= <DOMAIN> = <EXPR> | <ATTRIB>
<QUAL-PART> ::=     where <QUAL> | { null }
<QUAL> ::=          <CLAUSE> | <CLAUSE> AND <QUAL>
<CLAUSE> ::=        <EXPR> <COMPARE-OP> <EXPR>
<COMPARE-OP> ::=    < | <= | > | >= | = | != | <>
<EXPR> ::=          <TERM> + <EXPR> | <TERM> - <EXPR> | <TERM>
<TERM> ::=          <FACTOR> * <TERM> | <FACTOR> / <TERM> | <FACTOR>
<FACTOR> ::=        abs <FACTOR> | - <FACTOR> | ( <EXPR> ) | <ATTRIB> | <CONST>
<ATTRIB> ::=        <REL-VAR> . <DOMAIN>
<DOMAIN> ::=        Pascal identifier of at most 12 characters
<REL-VAR> ::=       Pascal identifier of at most 12 characters
<REL-NAME> ::=      Pascal identifier of at most 8 characters
<CONST> ::=         valid integer or string
<FORMAT-LIST> ::= <FORMAT-ITEM> | <FORMAT-ITEM> , <FORMAT-LIST>
<FORMAT-ITEM> ::= <DOMAIN> = <FORMAT>
<FORMAT> ::=        i2 | c<ALPHA-LEN>
<ALPHA-LEN> ::=     1 | 2 | ... | 255
```

Figure 4—The syntax of the query language

THE QUERY PROCESSOR

The query processor interprets query commands that are passed to it in the form of query trees by the query parser. The utility commands "help," "create," "destroy," and "print" are interpreted by invoking the corresponding procedures in the relation manager. The commands "append," "retrieve," "delete," and "replace" constitute the actual query-processing commands; each scans all relations referenced in its qualification part and target list, and compiles a result relation. This common task is implemented by one shared procedure, the query processing nucleus.

The nucleus is a generalized framework for query-processing primitives whose invocation sequences may be altered to effect alternate heuristic strategies. Invoked with a query tree, the nucleus operates on it, and generates tuples in a result-relation whose format corresponds to the target list in

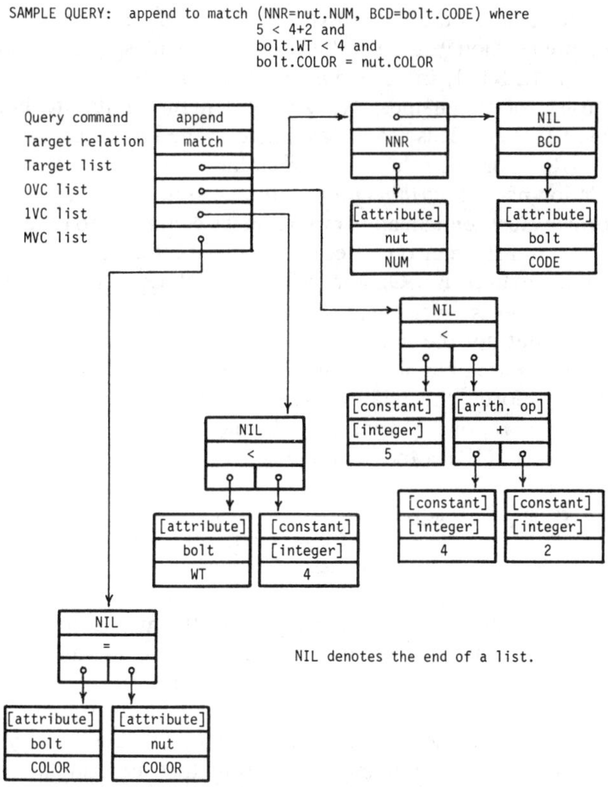

Figure 5—The query tree of the sample query

the query tree. It may invoke itself recursively with a modified query tree, but the result-relation does not change (i.e., every invocation appends tuples to the same result-relation). The initial Sibyl nucleus makes use of four primitives for evaluating 0VCs, selection, subtree generation for dissection,[12] and result generation, respectively. Before discussing the nucleus in more detail, we briefly describe these four primitives:

- function *eval0VC*(0VC): boolean; *eval0VC* evaluates the passed 0VC and returns its value (true or false)
- procedure *select*(1VC, subrelation); *select* is being passed a 1VC and the name of an empty subrelation of the relation referenced in the 1VC; it selects, from the relation referenced in the 1VC, the tuples satisfying the 1VC and returns them in into the subrelation
- function *treegen*(relation, tuple); query tree; *treegen* returns a newly created query tree, which is a copy of the query tree of the current invocation of the nucleus, except that all references to attributes of the passed relation are replaced by the corresponding attribute values of the passed tuple
- procedure *resgen; resgen* appends tuples to the result relation as specified by the target list in the query tree. When *resgen* is invoked, any attribute in the target list *either* references a relation in which all tuples qualify (this may have been assured by a prior selection and relation name substitution) *or* represents a value that has been substituted in a preceding dissection. In general, *resgen* appends the target list projection of the cross product of the relations referenced in target list attributes. If all target list attributes have been substituted by their values, the cross product projection degenerates into a single tuple consisting of these target list values.

The nucleus framework lends itself to experimentation with different query-processing heuristics and their performance evaluation. A skeleton version that is structured according to clause types is shown in Figure 6. Its algorithm is similar to INGRES's decomposition,[13] but reduction is not implemented. The nucleus is invoked with a query tree and generates a result relation which is global to all recursive invocations. It first evaluates all 0VCs; if any one is false, it implies that the result relation should be empty, and the nucleus returns. (On recursive invocations, this step will always be skipped, since all 0VCs have been dealt with.) If the query tree contains 1VCs, the appropriate selections are performed, the affected relations are substituted in the query tree by their respective subrelations, and the 1VCs are discarded from the query tree. A selection resulting in an empty subrelation indicates that no tuples qualify at this level, and the nucleus returns in such a case.

When MVCs are present, any one referenced relation may be chosen for dissection. The Version 1.0 strategy chooses the smallest. For every tuple of the chosed relation, the dissection step calls the nucleus recursively with a modified query tree returned by *treegen.* Thereafter, it returns; the final step, generating result tuples, cannot be performed until all MVCs in the query tree (if there are any) have been reduced to 1VCs and these 1VCs have been processed. Then, qualifying tuples

```
procedure nucleus(query tree);
{evaluate 0VC's}
for each 0VC var0 in the query tree:
    if not eval0VC(var0) then return,
    otherwise, remove the clause var0 from the query tree;
{evaluate 1VC's}
for each 1VC var1 in the query tree:
    select(var1, sub1);
    if sub1 is empty, return,
    otherwise, substitute in the query tree sub1 for the relation
        referenced in var1 and remove the 1VC var1 from the query
        tree;
{evaluate MVC's}
if the query tree contains any MVC's:
    choose a relation varR that is referenced in any of the MVC's;
    for each tuple varT of varR:
        nucleus(treegen(varR, varT));
    return;
{append to result relation}
resgen;
return;
end {nucleus};
```

Figure 6—Skeleton version of the query-processing nucleus

are appended to the result relation. It follows that the final step is only executed when the nucleus operates on a deepest recursive level; that is, when the MVC step, which calls the nucleus recursively and returns, is skipped.

The commands "append," "retrieve," "delete," and "replace" are implemented using the query processing nucleus. The "append" command is implemented by invoking the nucleus directly with the query tree and the command's target relation as the result relation. For the "retrieve" command, the query processor first creates the specified target relation and then passes it to the nucleus as its result relation. For the "delete" command, the nucleus is invoked with an auxiliary result-relation with only one attribute, TID, and a corresponding target list in the query tree. Upon return, the result relation contains the TIDs of the tuples to be deleted in the target relation, and the query processor uses it to perform the actual deletions. For the "replace" command, the nucleus is invoked to generate an auxiliary result-relation of replacement tuples concatenated with the TIDs of the tuples to be replaced in the target relation. The query processor subsequently uses the TIDs to locate and replace the corresponding tuples in the target relation.

THE TRANSFORMER

The transformer[14] provides for Sibyl's capability of transferring relations to and from remote database systems of a different brand, INGRES. It makes use of a communications package that includes interrupt-driven input–outout routines for the RS232 port and interactive dial-up and remote-command procedures for invoking INGRES with a specific database at the remote system. To the remote system Sibyl appears to be a terminal; the transformer sends and receives the same type of information and interactive user of the remote INGRES system would type and have displayed.

The transformer can be invoked for three functions: terminal emulation, relation transfer from INGRES to Sibyl, and relation transfer from Sibyl to INGRES. The terminal emulator turns the IBM Personal Computer into a terminal, and can be used to dial-up and log into a remote INGRES system. (It is also used to log out.) After being connected, the user may invoke either of the two transfer functions. The transformer then prompts the Sibyl user for the names of the Sibyl and the INGRES relations. When it terminates, a transformed copy of the source relation has been created at the destination system. The transformation is reversible if the attribute types of the attributes of the shipped relation are supported by the destination system. (In Sibyl Version 1.0, shipments were therefore restricted to integer and string attributes.

The transformer's function may be viewed as a generalized transformation or translation of data from a source to a destination format.[15] For such a translation, the *description* of these formats (the source and destination schemata) must be available; it may be built into the translation algorithm or it may be specified independently (e.g., in schema files). The generalization of the transformer in Sibyl stems from the fact that the schema of a remote relation must be acquired from the remote system. To do so, it requires a description of the format (the meta-schema) of requesting the schema of the remote relation (e.g., a certain command with specific parameters). In Sibyl, the schema of a relation R(A1,A2,. . .An) consists of the names, types, and lengths of its attributes A1,A2,. . .An. It is readily available in the system catalogue. INGRES, on the other hand, maintains this information in a relation named *attribute* on the remote system, and the transformer must send an appropriate query command to obtain it.

The transformer operates in two phases: the schema phase and the data phase. On a transfer from INGRES to Sibyl, the transformer is given the name of the requested INGRES relation, but not the names, types, or lengths of its attributes. The latter are obtained during the schema phase, and the data phase peforms the relation transfer. Figure 7 illustrates the major operations. During the schema phase, the transformer sends to INGRES the commands

```
range of a is attribute
retrieve (a.attname, a.attfrmt, a.attfrml) where
  a.attrelid = "<requested relation name>"
```

which searches the relation *attribute* for the names, the types, and the lengths of all attributes of the requested relation, and sends this schema information in tabular form. The transformer receives it, transforms it into Sibyl objects, stores them for subsequent use, and creates a compatible Sibyl relation by calling the storage manager. During the subsequent data phase, the transformer sends INGRES commands for displaying the requested relation. Upon its arrival in tabular form, it is first copied into a DOS file. After the complete transfer of the requested relation, each of its tuples is read back from this file, transformed into Sibyl attributes by making use of the previously stored schema information, and appended to the destination relation by calling the storage manager. When the last tuple has been processed, the Sibyl copy of the remote

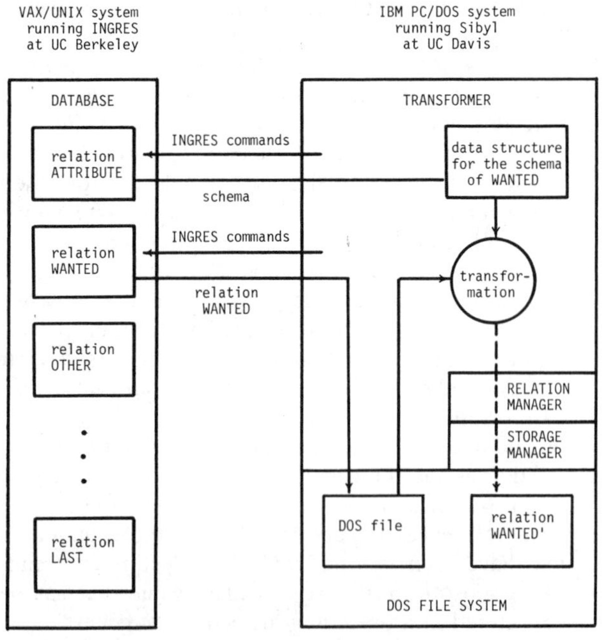

Figure 7—Transformer operations during a transfer from INGRES to Sibyl

relation is complete, and the transformer invocation terminates.

Relation transfers from Sibyl to INGRES are handled by the transformer in a similar fashion. The schema information is now obtained from the relation manager, transformed, and sent to INGRES as part of a "create" command. Subsequently, individual tuples are processed by obtaining their individual attributes from the relation manager, transforming them into ASCII representation, and embedding them into "append" commands that are shipped to INGRES.

CONCLUSION

To demonstrate the feasibility of loosely coupling a microprocessor system with heterogeneous remote database systems, a relational database system, called Sibyl, was designed and implemented at the Computer Systems Research Laboratory at the University of California at Davis. This relationally complete system runs on an IBM Personal Computer with a 10-Mbyte Winchester disk. In addition to its function as a self-contained database system with its own interactive query language, Sibyl provides the capability of transforming relations to and from the data format of a remote system and transmitting the transformed data over a dial-up line. In this paper, we described Version 1.0 of Sibyl essentially as it existed in January 1983. An INGRES system running on a VAX/UNIX configuration at the Berkeley campus served as the remote database system for this version.

The paper provides an overview of the major Sibyl components: the storage manager, the relation manager, the query parser, the query processor, and the transformer. We emphasized those features that have a substantial effect on the performance or capabilities of the system. The concept of subrelations, as provided by the relation manager, permits drastic cuts both in memory requirement and execution time for nontrivial queries. The nucleus of the query-processing algorithm permits experimentation with different heuristics. The loose coupling with the remote INGRES system is a consequence of the data transformation capability of the transformer. Control over the INGRES database remains with its manager; Sibyl has no more privileges than an interactive INGRES user.

Sibyl is the product of continuing research effort and thus is subject to continuous enhancement. We have added FRAMIS[16] to the repertoire of supported remote database systems; connected our IBM Personal Computers with an Ethernet cable, which we use to access relations; and modified the DOS file system to support Sibyl more efficiently. As for current and future research, we are addressing the design of a unified, syntax-driven transformer to deal with an open-ended set of remote systems. (Currently, two separate transformers are used for INGRES and FRAMIS interactions.) Using data translation techniques,[15] the syntax-driven transformer will make use of one syntax file for each remote system. This file contains the syntactic description of the remote data format as well as the syntax for connection commands and relation accesses. A second area concerns measurements of the performance of different query-processing heuristics. In particular, we are investigating the use of selectivity factors in the heuristics. We are focusing on verifying the conjecture that selectivity factors of relations measured during recently executed queries are a good indicator of the selectivity factors that will result from future queries involving those relations.

In any event, the operational first version of Sibyl demonstrates that microprocessors can be used cost effectively to provide a complete relational processing capability that permits the acquisition of data from and the integration of results in a remote, large-scale database system without qualitatively introducing additional problems regarding the integrity, the reliability, and the uniformity of its data.

ACKNOWLEDGMENT

Research sponsored by IBM Corporation and by Program MICRO of the State of California.

REFERENCES

1. Date, C. J. *An Introduction to Database Systems,* Reading, Mass.: Addison-Wesley, 1975.
2. Stonebraker, M., E. Wong, and P. Kreps. "The Design and Implementation of INGRES." ACM *Transactions on Database Systems*, 1, 3 (1976), pp. 189–222.
3. Codd, E. F. "Relational Database: A Practical Foundation for Productivity." *Communications of the ACM,* 25, 2 (1983), pp. 109–117.
4. Technical Reference, IBM Personal Computer, Hardware Reference Library, (1st ed.), Boca Raton, Fla.: IBM Corp., 1981.
5. Disk Operating System, Version 1.10, IBM Personal Computer, Computer Language Series, (2nd ed.), Boca Raton, Fla.: IBM Corp., 1982.
6. Clevenger, J. L. "A Pascal-Compatible Communications Package and Terminal Emulator for the IMB Personal Computer." Technical Report CSRL-83-2, University of California at Davis, Department of Electrical and Computer Engineering, 1983.
7. Pascal Compiler, IBM Personal Computer, Computer Language Series, (1st ed.), Boca Raton, Fla.: IBM Corp., 1981.
8. Choi, A. "The Storage and Relation Managers in Sibyl." Technical Report CSRL-83-5, University of California at Davis, Department of Electrical and Computer Engineering, 1983.
9. Mylopoulos, J., S. Schuster, and D. Tsichritzis. "A Multilevel Relational System." *AFIPS, Proceedings of the National Computer Conference* (Vol. 44), 1975, pp. 403–408.
10. Fernandez-Baca, D., and A. Choi. "The Query Parser in Sibyl." Technical Report CSRL-83-7, University of California at Davis, Department of Electrical and Computer Engineering, 1983.
11. Choi, A.. "Documentation of the Query Processor in Sibyl," Technical Report CSRL-83-6, University of California at Davis, Department of Electrical and Computer Engineering, 1983.
12. Ullman, J. D. *Principles of Database Systems.* Rockville, Md.: Computer Sciene Press, 1980.
13. Wong, E. and K. Youseffi. "Decomposition — A Strategy for Query Processing." *ACM Transactions on Database Systems,* 1, 3 (1976), pp. 223–241.
14. Clevenger, J. L. "A Transformer for Remote INGRES Relations." Technical Report CSRL-83-3, University of California at Davis, Department of Electrical and Computer Engineering, 1983.
15. Fry, J. P. et al. "An Assessment of the Technology for Data- and Program-Related Conversion." *AFIPS, Proceedings of the National Computer Conference* (Vol. 47), 1978, pp. 887–907.
16. Jones, S. E., D. R. Ries, L. Lyles, A. L. Dittli, and K. W. Johnson. "FRAMIS Reference Manual." Livermore Computing Systems Document LCSD-554, University of California, Lawrence Livermore National Laboratory, 1981.

Functions of the database workbench

by YAHIKO KAMBAYASHI*
Kyushu University
Fukuoka, Japan

ABSTRACT

A powerful database system can be developed by a combination of a central relational database system and intelligent terminals. In such an organization a typical function of a terminal is to offer high-level user interfaces. In this paper the concept of the database workbench is introduced and shown to be suitable for development by such terminals. As design problems usually require a large amount of interaction, typical functions of the workbench are (1) the design of database schemas, (2) the design of conversion procedures between real-world data and data in the system, and (3) the design of queries. For the first function we focus on the relational database design under the assumption that set values are permitted. Problems of set values, especially conversion problems of dependencies, are discussed. Various facilities for design conversion procedures and the design of queries are also discussed.

*This paper was written when the author was at Kyoto University.

INTRODUCTION

As a result of the recent availability of large-scale commercial relational database systems and powerful microprocessor-based systems, a user-oriented database system can be economically created by a combination of a central large relational database system and an intelligent microprocessor-based terminal (Figure 1). High-level user interfaces are provided at the terminal, including graphics, very-high-level languages, and so on. In this paper the concept of a database workbench is introduced and shown to be very suitable for development by such terminals. The major functions of the workbench are the design of database schemas, the design of the conversion procedure between real-world data and data in the system, and the design of queries. Since such design processes involve a large amount of person–machine communication, to realize these functions at terminals saves communication cost as well as shortening response time. Although the motivation of the database workbench is similar to the programmer's workbench concepts,[1] functions are completely different because of the difference between programs and databases. Since some problems appearing in these processes have already been published by various authors, we will emphasize new problems in this paper.

Among other topics, facilities for database schema design will be discussed. Instead of reviewing high-level models for design, we will focus on problems of schema design for the relational model. As set values are very often used in the real world, we permit set values for database design.[2] When we permit set values, we need to distinguish ordered sets from unordered sets and one-to-one correspondence of sets from direct products of sets. Another problem is the conversion of values to attribute names.

As checking of constraints satisfied by a schema is very important in database schema design, a procedure for schema checking will be discussed also. A database schema is defined by (1) a set of relation schemas, each of which corresponds to an attribute set; (2) constraints on attributes; and (3) constraints on sets of attributes. Each attribute is defined according to whether it corresponds to atomic values, unordered set values, ordered set values, or relation names. Attributes that will be used by selection and join operations should be distinguished. An example of constraints defined on a set of attributes is a dependency. One interesting problem discussed is the relationship among dependencies defined on attributes corresponding to atomic values as well as set values. An efficient procedure to check the existence of a join dependency is also given.

Next facilities for query design are discussed, including (1) query design using sample data; (2) query analysis facilities; and (3) a query database. We will show a practical method for obtaining a proper set of sample data as an alternative to the Armstrong relation approach,[3] which usually produces relations with too many tuples. There are two approaches for query analysis: syntactic analysis and run-time analysis. Using a query database, a user can compose a query by a Boolean combination of retrieved queries as well as a user-specified query.

We have been developing a database workbench on a Z-80-based microprocessor system.

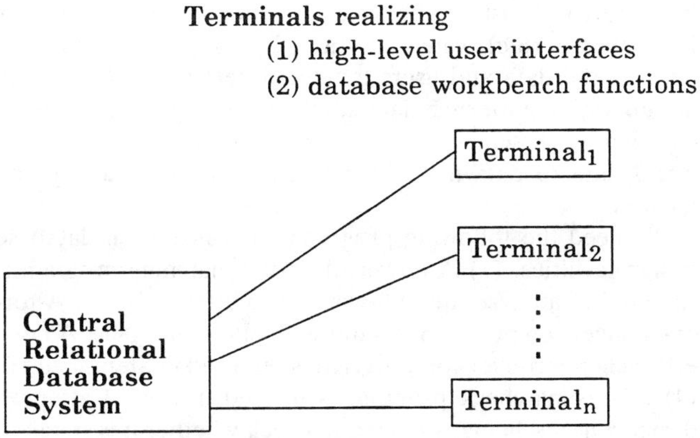

Figure 1—Organization of a database system

DATABASE SCHEMA DESIGN FACILITIES

The design of a database schema suitable for data to be stored is very important. The problem can be handled by the following steps: (1) By analyzing the real-world data, obtain a preliminary design for the database schema. (2) Using the preliminary design, convert the real-world data to relations in unnormalized form. (3) Find functional and join dependencies in the relations. (4) Design database schemas that are a collection of relation schemas. In the design, new attributes can be added, a set of values can be combined, data value can be converted to attribute names, and so on. (5) Find a suitable database schema among candidates designed in Step 4. (6) Design a procedure to convert real-world data to data represented by the database schema designed in Step 5. In Step 1 we need to find the correspondences between attributes and their values. For example, if we have the following data,

H. C. Lai and S. Muroga, "Logic Networks of Carry-Save Adders", IEEE Transaction on Computers, Sept. 1982,
Carry-save adder, multiplier

we can determine the correspondences between subsequences in the above text and attribute AUTHOR, TITLE, PUBLI-

AUTHOR	TITLE	PUBLICATION	DATE	KEYWORD
Lai, H.C. / Muroga, S.	Logic Networks of Carry-Save Adders	IEEE Trans. Computers	8209	carry-save adder / multiplier

(a)

AUTHOR	AFFILIATION		KEYWORD
Lai, H.C.	STC Computer Research		carry-save adder
Muroga, S.	University of Illinois		multiplier

(b)

AUTHOR	AUTHOR-O	TITLE
Lai, H.C.	1	Logic Networks of Carry-Save Adders
Muroga, S.	2	Logic Networks of Carry-Save Adders

(c)

Figure 2—Relations

CATION, DATE, and KEYWORD. In step 2 the data can be expressed by a relation shown in Figure 2(a).

For example, we can assume that TITLE represents the entity; i.e., TITLE is the key for the relation. In Step 3 dependencies are examined. If there are papers with the same title (published as reports and also as journals), then we have to change the key as a combination of TITLE and PUBLICATION. For sets we have to distinguish direct product and one-to-one correspondence. In Figure 2(b), there exists a one-to-one correspondence between elements in AUTHOR and AFFILIATION, and there exists a direct product property between elements in AUTHOR and KEYWORD. Whether there exist values with direct product property or not can be checked by the existence of join dependencies.

In Step 4, various schemas can be designed with dependencies and property-of-set values. Dependencies are used to determine how to decompose relations. We will define two typical properties of sets as follows: (4-a) unordered set and ordered set; and (4-b) Set to be decomposed into values.

In our example, AUTHOR is an ordered set, but KEYWORD is not. To normalize the relation we need to introduce a new attribute, AUTHOR-O, which shows the ordering. Figure 2(c) shows a normalized form for the AUTHOR, TITLE part of Figure 2(a).

There are two elementary cases in which attribute corresponds to sets. First is (4-b-1), a set of values corresponding to the same attribute. AUTHOR and KEYWORD in FIGURE 2(a) are examples of this case. Second is (4-b-2), a set that consists of values of more than one attribute. DATE in Figure 2(a) is an example of this case. The value 8209 can be decomposed into two values, YEAR = 82 and MONTH = 09.

In the case of (4-b-2), we need to introduce new attributes to decompose the set. Whether or not we have to decompose a set is determined by the usage of values. There are cases in which both (4-b-1) and (4-b-2) are mixed.

Another problem of designing a database schema is that we have to determine whether a value should be an attribute value, an attribute name, or a relation name. Figure 3 shows a timetable represented by three views. In Figure 3(a) MON-

TIME TABLE

DAY OF THE WEEK	PERIOD	CLASS
MONDAY	1	MATH
MONDAY	2	ENGLISH
MONDAY	3	HISTORY
...	.	....
...	.	....

(a)

TIME TABLE

PERIOD	COURSES ON MONDAY	COURSES ON TUESDAY	.....
1	MATH	ART	....
2	ENGLISH	PHYSICS	....
3	HISTORY	ENGLISH	....

(b)

COURSES ON MONDAY

PERIOD	CLASS
1	MATH
2	ENGLISH
3	HISTORY

COURSES ON TUESDAY

PERIOD	CLASS
1	ART
2	PHYSICS
3	ENGLISH

(c)

Figure 3—Three views of the same relation

DAY is an attribute value, and in Figure 3(b) it is regarded as attribute name, COURSES ON MONDAY. It also can be a relation name, as shown in Figure 3(c).

In Step 6, a procedure must be designed that will convert the real-world data to the data for the database schema we have designed. The procedure must handle the following problems: First (6-a), is a format conversion. In Figure 1(a) the following conversions are required:

H. C. Lai → Lai, H. C., Sept. 1982 → 8209, etc.

Second is (6-b), error checking. Typing errors and simple logical errors must be checked. For example, pp. i-j satisfies $j > i$. Next is (6-c), value addition. If keywords are not supplied in the data and users must add keywords, we need to design a system for such data addition. Finally (6-d) is schema conversion. A schema conversion procedure from the real-world data to data in the target database schema must be created.

We need the following programs to realize such database design facilities: (1) A powerful partial matching program is required to analyze the real-world data efficiently. (2) A format conversion program is required by Problem (6-a). A powerful schema conversion program is required in Steps 4 and 6. (4) A schema-check program is needed in Step 4 after we design a new schema, we need to check whether it is suitable. The program can produce sample outputs and statistical data such as number of tuples. (5) A dependency check program is needed at Step 3 to check whether a functional dependency or a join dependency is satisfied. (6) An error-checking program. By preparing a domain-value dictionary for each attribute, error checking as well as word control is realized. For example, to put keywords to papers, control of words to be used is required. Finally, (7) a flexible data preparation program is required in Step 6 for the purpose of solving Problem (6-c).

Since procedures for some programs are obvious or discussed elsewhere, we will discuss Programs 4 and 5 in the next section. For Programs 6 and 7, see the reference by Kambayashi and others.[4]

SCHEMA-CHECKING PROCEDURE

A database schema is defined by a set of relation schemas, a set of constraints on attributes, and a set of constraints defined on attribute sets. The schema-checking procedure consists of a syntactic check and a check by examining data.

A relation schema is given by a set of attributes. There are the following constraints on attributes: (1) Attributes corresponding to atomic values (atomic-value attribute for short) and attributes corresponding to sets and relations must be distinguished. (2) Attributes corresponding to set values (set-value attributes, for short) are characterized as ordered or unordered, as sets corresponding to values of the same attribute, or as sets corresponding to more than one attribute. (3) Attributes that are not used in selection, join, and division are distinguished, since such attributes can have set and relation values.

We can use attributes corresponding to set and relation values if atomic values of each set and relation value are not required to be handled separately by database operations. For example, if the relation in Figure 2 has the attribute COMMENT, we can permit sets for its values, since we are not interested in retrieving papers by specifying COMMENT values or by joining an attribute COMMENT. Values of COMMENT are only used in the result of queries.

Constraints defined on attribute sets are as follows: (1) For set-value attributes, one-to-one correspondence and direct product correspondence must be distinguished. (2) Dependencies such as functional and join dependencies exist. (3) Existence constraints are constraints such that if a value of Attribute A is not null, then a value of Attribute B is not null in every tuple. (4) Value-dependent dependencies. When a relation can be regarded as a union of subrelations and each subrelation is identified by values of some attribute set, we can permit different constraints on each subrelation. (5) There must be a set of attributes that is not handled separately by database operations.

A functional dependency $X \rightarrow Y$ is said to be satisfied if a set of values corresponding to attribute set X uniquely determines a set of values corresponding to attribute set Y. A join dependency $*[X_1,X_2, \ldots, X_n]$ is said to be satisfied in relation R if R is always expressed by a join of $R[X_1]$, $R[X_2]$, ..., $R[X_n]$. Existence constraints can be expressed by a set of objects such that for any tuple there exists an object that is an attribute set corresponding to non-null values of the tuple.[5]

If MONTH and YEAR are not separately handled, we can use a combined attribute, DATE, to replace them. If YEAR and the combination of MONTH/YEAR are required but MONTH is not handled separately, we can use YEAR and DATE, although this representation is redundant.

The syntactic check compares sets of constraints satisfied by two given database schemas. There are the following major cases: First, if sets of attributes and constraints on the attributes are the same in both schemas, we can use dependency theory to check the equivalence.[6,7] Next, if sets of attributes in both schemas are the same and there are attributes that correspond to sets in one schema and atomic values in the other schema, we need to develop a procedure to compare constraints satisfied by both schemas. Finally, when the sets of attributes are different, comparison of constraints can be realized by dividing into basic steps.

The following theorem can be used for the second case.

Theorem 1: If each subrelation of R obtained by setting values in attribute set X be constant, satisfies JD$*[Y_1,Y_2, \ldots, Y_n]$, and R satisfies JD $*[XY_1,XY_2, \ldots, XY_n]$, where XY_i means the union of X and Y_i.

This theorem is obvious, but we have the following useful corollary, which establishes the correspondence of dependencies on attributes defined on atomic values and on set values.

Corollary 1: If the relation has attributes XY where each attribute in X is an atomic-value attribute and each attribute A_i in Y is a set-value attribute ($i = 1, \ldots, n$), then the equivalent relation on XY, where all atomic-value attributes satisfy the following join dependency is as follows: $*[XA_1, XA_2, \ldots, XA_n]$

Theorem 2: If X is a set of atomic-value attributes, A is a set-value attribute and there is functional dependency $X \rightarrow A$, then the equivalent relation defined on the same attribute set except that A is an atomic-value attribute satisfies the following join dependency (multivalued dependency[8]), where U is the set of attributes of the relation schema: $*[XA, U - A]$

Since functional dependency $X \rightarrow A_1,A_2, \ldots, A_n$ can be decomposed as $X \rightarrow A_1, X \rightarrow A_2, X \rightarrow A_n$, the above theorem can be applied to the case $X \rightarrow Y$.

In Case 2, we can apply Corollary 1 and Theorem 2 to both schemas and compare the dependency set on the schema defined on the same set of attributes where all attributes correspond to atomic values.

Case 3 can be handled by the following cases:

(3-1) Conversion of attribute sets.
(3-2) Conversion among attribute values, attribute names, and relation names.
(3-3) Conversion of case 2.

For (3-1) we have the following cases:

(3-1-a) A new attribute is introduced that corresponds to a set of attributes.
(3-1-b) An attribute is decomposed into a set of attributes.
(3-1-c) A new attribute is introduced for an ordered set in order to store the order explicitly (see Figure 2(c)).

(3-1-d) A new attribute is introduced as a set identifier.
(3-1-e) A new attribute is introduced to handle the problem caused by the dependency set.

For Cases (3-1-a), (3-1-b), and (3-1-c), we can handle the dependency conversion very easily. An example of Case (3-1-d) is as follows: If: (i) A is an attribute corresponding to a set, (ii) we need to change A to be an attribute corresponding to atomic values, and (iii) there is a requirement that we need to see the original set, then we can add a new attribute B, which is a set identifier. An example is shown is Figure 4.

This kind of conversion is required when we need to introduce an attribute corresponding to an entity or we need to keep the structure of attribute values—for example, a set of set values.[9]

Corollary 2: The attributes A and B satisfy the following dependency, where A is originally a set-value attribute and B is introduced as a set identifier in order to make A be an atomic-value attribute: $*[AB, U-A]$

It is obvious from Theorem 2, since in the original relation $B \leftrightarrow A$ is satisfied.

Some conditions for conversion of attribute values and attribute names (3-2) are shown in Reference 10.

Checking by examining data is also important. There are the following problems: (1) Checking of a functional dependency, and, if it is not satisfied, finding a set of data that violate it. (2) Checking of a join dependency, and, if it is not satisfied, finding a set of data that violate it. (3) For finding constraints we need a facility to handle small sets of example data. (4) To evaluate a database schema we need to get statistical data such as the number of tuples satisfying the given condition.

Checking of a functional dependency $X \rightarrow Y$ can be done by sorting tuples by values of X. The following theorem can be used for efficient checking of a join dependency.

Theorem 3:[10] When JD $*[X_1, X_2, \ldots, X_n]$ is satisfied in R, then each subrelation of R obtained by setting values in attribute set X as a constant satisfies JD $*[X_1-X, X_2-X, \ldots, X_n-X]$.

A
a_1, a_2
a_2, a_3

A	B
a_1	1
a_2	2
a_2	1
a_3	2

Figure 4—Set identifiers

For checking of the existence of JD $*[X_1, X_2, \ldots, X_n]$ we select X as a set of attributes contained in at least two components of the JD: (1) Sort the tuples by the values of X. (2) For each subrelation having the same values for X, examine whether the JD $*[X_1-X, X_2-X, \ldots, X_n-X]$ is satisfied.

Since $X_1, X_2, \ldots$ are disjoint, we can easily check the existence of the JD as follows:

(2-1) Let p be the number of tuples in the subrelation.
(2-2) Let $q_1, q_2, \ldots, q_n$ be the number of different tuples in $R[X_1-X]$, $R[X_2-X]$, $\ldots$, $R[X_n-X]$, respectively.
(2-3) If $p = q_1 x q_2 x \ldots x q_n$, then the JD is satisfied at this subrelation. Tuples violating the join dependencies can be checked at each subrelation.

For (3) we need a schema conversion program. For the schema evaluation, one possible method is to evaluate it by the number of data contained in the schema under various conditions. We select a database schema that requires less space.

QUERY DESIGN FACILITIES

There are the following facilities for query design: (1) Query design using sample data, (2) query analysis facility, and (3) query database.

For (1) we need a procedure to design a proper set of sample data. There are two kinds of query analysis facilities, (2-a), syntactic analysis; and (2-b), run-time analysis. Query database can be used to design a query using queries already used.

In Reference 3, Armstrong relations are used for sample data. An Armstrong relation for a set of dependencies is defined as a relation satisfying exactly the dependency set, in which any dependency not derivable from the set is not satisfied by the relation. The problems with Armstrong relations are that the number of tuples in a relation tends to be very large and an actual snapshot of the relation usually satisfies dependencies not derivable from the set. We propose a practical method for selecting sample data using Theorem 3. We assume that the dependency set satisfies the following condition, since it is regarded as a practical assumption.[11]

We assume that the dependency set is equivalent to a set consisting of at most one join dependency and functional dependencies, where the left-side set of each functional dependency is contained in at least one component of the join dependency.

Let $*[X_1, \ldots, X_n]$ be the join dependency and F be the set of functional dependencies. Sample relations are designed as follows.

(1-a) Modification of the join dependency, so that every functional dependency is contained in one component of the resulting join dependency. If there exists a functional dependency $Y \rightarrow A$ such that Y is contained in X_i and A is not, replace X_i by X_iA. This conversion corresponds to a join without loss of information by $Y \rightarrow A$.

(1-b) Let Y be the set of attributes each of which is contained in at least two components of the join dependency. Let X be the set obtained by adding all possible A to Y such that

$Y \rightarrow A$ is satisfied. As shown in Theorem 3, in each subrelation defined by one combination of values of X, the join dependency $*[X_1 - X, \ldots, X_n - X]$ is satisfied and has the direct product property. Using this property, sample relations are designed as follows:

(1-c) In the following, values for each attribute are selected randomly from its domain (the set of values actually appearing in relations). For the given attribute set Y and a set F of functional dependencies satisfied in Y, we will design a sample relation on Y satisfying F as follows. For each functional dependency $X \rightarrow Y$ such that X is minimal, there are at least two tuples whose XY values are identical and others are different.

(1-d) Let F be the set of functional dependencies satisfied in X. Design a relation on X satisfying F under the condition of (1−c).

(1-e) For each tuple of the relation designed in (1-d), we can design n relations $R_1, \ldots, R_n$, where R_i is defined on the set $X_i - X$. The tuple is selected from the relation on X.

(1-f) Repeat (1-e) for every tuple of the relation designed at (1-d); the union of the tuples forms the set of sample data. For a different tuple at (1-e) we should try to design different R_i, although we can use the same R_i's for all tuples.

The method for creating a set of sample data is much simpler than preparing Armstrong relations. For the purpose of checking queries by sample data, our method seems to be adequate.

There are the following facilities for query analysis:

(2-a) Syntactic query analysis. As relational language offers wide freedom to users, sometimes semantically incorrect queries cannot be detected by conventional syntactic analysis. A proper warning message is printed in the following three cases: (1) The given query consists of two or more separated queries. (2) there exists a join of attributes that seems to be unnatural. For example, SALARY = YEAR is permitted in relational expressions, but usually queries containing such a join are wrong. For this purpose we can prepare a matrix showing the properness of joining two attributes for all possible combinations. (3) There may be an error in the value of the attribute used for a selection operation; it can be detected by checking the domain of the attribute.

(2-b) Run-time query analysis. Sometimes a user wants to get information during the execution of a query in order to improve the query. For example, if a query gives a null result, a user wants to know the number of tuples at each step of query processing. As the optimization process of the database system usually does not keep the order of the execution, the given query must be divided into subqueries corresponding to each step at the workbench and then transmitted to the main database system for stepwise execution.

The query database contains the following: (3-a) Meaning of the query. (3-b) Statistical data (number of uses, cost of processing, number of the result, etc.). (3-c) Information for optimization, to avoid recalculation of access path selection.

A query is identified by specifying a set of relations to be used in the query. A user can design a query by a Boolean combination of retrieved queries as well as a user-defined query. Conversion of such a query into a simpler form should be done at the database workbench.

ACKNOWLEDGMENT

The author is grateful to Professor Shuzo Yajima of Kyoto University for helpful discussions.

REFERENCES

1. Dolotta, T. A., and J. R. Moshey. "An Introduction to the Programmers Workbench." *Proceedings of the 2nd International Conference on Software Engineering*. October 1976, pp. 164–168.
2. Makinouchi, A. "A Consideration on Normalized Form of Not-Necessarily-Normalized Relation in the Relational Data Model." *Proceedings of the 3rd International Conference on Very Large Data Bases*. October 1977, pp. 447–453.
3. Silva, A. M., and M. A. Melkanoff. "A Method for Helping Discover the Dependencies." In *Advances in Database Theory* (Vol. 1), 1981, pp. 115–133.
4. Kambayashi, Y., C. Le Viet, S. Tokuda, and S. Yajima. "A Database Preparation System." *IEEE Computer Society, 5th International Computer Software and Applications Conference*. November 1981, pp. 335–350.
5. Goldstein, B. S. "Constraints on Null Values in Relational Databases." *Proceedings of the 6th International Conference on Very Large Data Bases*. September 1981, pp. 101–110.
6. Maier, D., A. O. Mendelzon, and U. Sagiv. "Testing Implications of Data Dependencies." *ACM TODS*, 4 (1979), pp. 455–469.
7. Sadri, F., and J. D. Ullman. "The Interaction between Functional Dependencies and Template Dependencies." *ACM SIGMOD*, May (1980), pp. 45–51.
8. Fagin, R. "Multivalued Dependencies and a New Normal Form for Relational Databases." *ACM TODS 2*, September (1977), pp. 262–278.
9. Kambayashi, Y., K. Tanaka, and S. Yajima. "A Relational Data Language with Simplified Binary Relation Handling Capacity." *Proceedings 3rd International Conference on Very Large Data Bases*, October 1977, pp. 338–350.
10. Kambayashi, Y., K. Tanaka, K. Takeda, and S. Yajima. "Representation of Relations for Database Output Utilizing Data Dependencies." *Proceedings of the 15th Hawaii International Conference on System Science*, January 1982, pp. 69–78.
11. Beeri, C., R. Fagin, D. Maier, A. Mendelzon, J. Ullman, and M. Yannakakis. "Properties of Acyclic Database Schemas." *ACM SIGACT Symposium on Theory of Computing*. May 1981, pp. 355–362.
12. Codd, E. F. "A Relational Model of Data for Large Shared Data Banks." *Comm. ACM*, 13 (1970), pp. 377–387.
13. Kambayashi, Y., K., Tanaka, and S. Yajima. "Semantic Aspects of Data Dependencies and Their Application to Relational Database Design." *COMPSAC*, November 1979, pp. 398–403.
14. Yajima, S., Y. Kambayashi, O. Konishi, K. Tanaka, C. Le Viet, and T. Kato. "Bibliographic Information Processing Facilities for Relational Database System ARIS." *Proceeding of the 13th Hawaii International Conference on System Science*. (Vol. 2), January 1980, pp. 198–207.

Fourth-generation languages (4GLs) and personal computers

by BOULTON B. MILLER
Southern Illinois University
Edwardsville, Illinois

ABSTRACT

This paper describes how fourth generation languages (4GLs) evolved from enhanced query languages and report generators into applications development tools. Pioneers, such as MAPPER, NOMAD, RAMIS, SQL, and FOCUS are example nonprocedural 4GLs with excellent records. Another area that offers the promise of 4GLs in the next generation of development are the relational databases designed for microcomputers. The third origin of 4GLs is in languages like PRO-IV, SALVO, and REVELATION, which were developed originally as application development tools.

The increases in numbers and capabilities of personal computers demonstrate the need for greater understanding of 4GLs since most of them fit on these small machines. Of special note is the upgrade of the IBM Personal Computer XT to an IBM XT/370 and the software becoming available to use on this equipment. This is but one of the many examples where less expensive hardware is changing the entire concept of corporate computing and applications development by users.

INTRODUCTION

One of the primary reasons why corporations, government agencies, and other organizations have so readily accepted personal computers has been their use in generating electronic spreadsheets. Even so, many did not realize the increasing use of personal computers until Portia Isaacson's panel discussions at NCC 1983.[1] Even her forecast was exceeded by International Data Corporation's statement that the "U.S. personal computer market will surpass mainframes by 1984."[2]

James Martin has enabled the computer industry to recognize the benefits of fourth-generation languages (4GLs) through his seminars and his book *Applications Development Without Programmers.*[3] I have used this text in four graduate courses that are part of an M.S. degree in management information systems (MIS). Each time I point out to my students that the title can be misleading because a large volume of programming is necessary, although most of it is transparent to users. For example, the software for a database package with its own 4GL for my IBM Personal Computer XT requires nine double-sided, double-density floppy diskettes to hold the two million bytes of the PC/FOCUS package.

DEVELOPMENT OF 4GLs

As yet there are no standards for 4GLs. Martin and McClure[4] point out that these languages were created to enable nonprogrammers to obtain results from computers and to greatly speed up programming. Most 4GLs link into a database, either one created by the user using the 4GL or one created by other software like IMS, IDMS, or ADABAS. Higher-level third-generation languages like ALGOL, FORTRAN, COBOL, PL/1, and now Ada are procedural languages. 4GLs are described as nonprocedural because they specify what is to be accomplished but not how it is to be done. Many professional programmers do not consider the use of 4GLs to be programming. However, a user can obtain fast results from a computer by using some brief 4GL statements that would take many lines of third-generation language code to duplicate. On the other hand, these 4GLs are not yet intended to be used for all computer applications, and it may be a long time before they are.[4]

We use the term *user-friendly* to describe the language we know. However, this term is used by almost all 4GL sales personnel, whether or not it is applicable. Martin applies the two-day training course to test user-friendliness. If a user can learn to become comfortable with a 4GL product and carry out useful work with it in two days without the need to return to class after a break of a week or two, the term *user-friendly* can be applied.[5]

Professor Daniel Teichroew has been recognized for a number of years as a leading pioneer in systems analysis automation with his Information System Design and Optimization (ISDOS) Project at the University of Michigan.[6] Professor Teichroew's project was extended (under the direction of Professors Benn R. Konsynski and Jay F. Nunamaker at the University of Arizona) and PLEXSYS, designed as an analyst's and user's workbench to facilitate the development of information systems.[7] These projects have provided much background, from which 4GLs have emerged.

About a decade ago the information center concept originated at IBM Canada.[8] The objective was to encourage computer users to learn to help themselves rather than relying entirely on computer professionals, systems analysts, and programmers to develop all their applications. Forms of the information center concept have been used by many organizations for many objectives. Special groups have been assigned to help users learn to use report generators, screen generators, query languages, statistical packages, graphics, spreadsheets, and decision support system applications. Some organizations use the information center to give users advice on which microprocessor to buy and the best software for their use. Martin, however, began stressing the use of 4GLs in the information center environment. Even though many organizations have been using a form of the information center concept to help users help themselves in a number of ways, it took IBM to formalize the concept and to educate us in its acceptance.

A 30-month backlog in applications design seemed to be agreeable to most discussants at the ACM (Association for Computing Machinery) 1982 conference in Dallas. This backlog did not begin to include the *invisible backlog,* identified by Martin as the requests users do not submit because they know the new requests will merely be added to the existing backlog.[9]

Instead of information centers' reducing applications development backlogs, they began to be used to "rob Peter to pay Paul," as pointed out in a very sobering *Computerworld* editorial.[10] As users become more familiar with what computers can do, they request more and more computer support. Although this situation can defeat the initial primary purpose, in the long run the information center staff will be accomplishing what should have been done for many years—getting users involved in helping themselves by greatly reducing their reliance on computer professionals. The concept has been implemented in the St. Louis area, where more than three dozen organizations belong to SLICE, the St. Louis Information Center Exchange.

MAPPER, accepted for many years as an application development tool, is now commonly referred to as a 4GL. For example, MAPPER was being used by the Santa Fe Railway to develop major applications in 1976. Similar examples, some even earlier, can be given for APL, NOMAD, RAMIS, and FOCUS. However, it took James Martin to identify these as fourth-generation languages. Care must be used when describing 4GLs, since the term is accepted for MAPPER, NOMAD, RAMIS, and FOCUS; however, in the case of ADABAS, the 4GL is NATURAL. On the other hand, Applied Data Research calls its DATACOM/DB a fourth-generation database and its ADR/IDEAL an application development system rather than a 4GL.

STATE OF THE ART

Organizations that use database management systems like IBM's IMS or Cullinet's IDMS also use a software package such as FOCUS to organize extracts of the database, making this separate database available to users. When a personal computer is used in an IBM 3270 environment (it looks like a 3270 to the mainframe), the user has all the benefits of the FOCUS package, including the use of the 4GL to manipulate the data with few instructions. This 3270 environment reduces costs of telecommunications and the cost of the computing load on the mainframe. Of course there are some problems of data redundancy, data updates, recovery, and security (to name a few); but in most cases the advantages outweigh the problems by merely requiring that users not eliminate, update, or add to the main corporate database. On the other hand, the data organized as a FOCUS database can be manipulated in any manner desired by the user without damage to the corporate data.

FOCUS was the first software package of its type with its own 4GL to make a personal computer version, PC/FOCUS, for use in a standalone environment. My first release arrived in the summer of 1983. This is the package referred to previously that amounted to two million bytes. This package provides most of the capabilities of the package designed for mainframes and should not be considered a subset of the older package. The obvious limitation is in the amount of data that can be handled on the smaller computer.

During the summer of 1983 numerous articles and advertisements began comparing database management systems for micro/personal computers. One such article by Robert Bowerman in *Datamation* analyzed 24 relational database systems. It seemed that the relational packages with the least to offer had the biggest promotion budgets. Bowerman did not describe one of these packages as having a 4GL.[11] On the other hand, Professional Information Systems, Ltd., describes a number of packages as fourth-generation software packages that operate on personal computers: dBase II, Dataflex, Pearl, Quick & Easi, Condor, Knowledge Man (for Management), and Data Fax.[12] However, none of these appear to have a 4GL as defined in the context of this article. MDBS III is a similar software package that earned special mention because it is a network/hierarchical database management system that can be described as IBM's IMS on a PC. Spreadsheet, database, and graphic functions are combined in Lotus 1-2-3 in an early attempt to integrate software packages; but a 4GL is not yet available. No doubt the next generation of these micro/personal computer software packages will contain 4GLs. They will be suitable for inclusion in a similar discussion at NCC 1985! What really eliminates a more detailed discussion of them now is that the user interface takes more time to design and program than could ever be tolerated with a 4GL.

Brown University's NSF-sponsored Instructional Computing Laboratory is organized around professional work stations in a network concept using Apollo hardware and its Apollo Domain System. This concept introduces students to the desirability and viability of personal computing on powerful work stations connected in a high-speed resource-sharing network rather than on standalone hobby microcomputers.[13] At Brown the language PROLOG is considered to be a 4GL rather than the 4GLs identified by this discussion.

PRO-IV is an example of a 4GL designed from the start as a development tool for use by both users and computer professionals. My personal observations of its development began in 1981 when the software was undergoing testing for implementation on microcomputers from four different vendors. By NCC 1982 many people saw the PRO-IV display at the CIE Systems booth. By NCC 1983 PRO-IV was being demonstrated on Microdata equipment under the trade name ALL and was announced for use on DEC equipment and the IBM Personal Computer XT.[14] Two competitors with similar products are SALVO from Software Automation and REVELATION by COSMOS, Inc.

As this is being written, the computer industry is beginning to realize the impact of IBM's announcement of October 18, 1983, that its IBM Personal Computer XT can be upgraded to the XT/370 status, or the upgrade purchased as a separate unit.[15] I have made the comparison that my own XT looks like an IBM system/360 Model 40 or 50 sitting on the desk. Now it can be said that when it is upgraded to the XT/370 the PC will resemble an IBM System/370 mainframe. As pointed out by Wendy B. Rauch-Hindin during the SIGBDP breakfast at the ACM 1983 conference in New York, this means that the software and programs written to run under the VM/CMS and other 370 operating systems will run on the XT/370. Of major importance to organizations with large mainframes is their interface with micros.[16]

Numerous FOCUS competitors are announcing their software for use, like PC/FOCUS, directly on personal computers. These announcements, such as those about NOMAD 2 from D & B Computing Services (formerly NCSS), System W from COMSHARE, IDMS/R from Cullinet Software, Inc., and ADR's IDEAL, demonstrate that the vendors are taking advantage of the IBM Personal Computer XT and the enhanced XT/370. Others have made similar announcements or are sure to make them, including IBM for its Data Base 2. These systems will find many users in plants, sales offices, divisions, branches, subsidiaries, and small organizations.

In summary, 4GLs suitable for users as well as computer professionals are emerging from three primary sources: (1) database management systems designed for mainframes that include a language (a 4GL) capable of doing joins, for report generation, for query, and for prototyping administrative and business computer applications; (2) relational database management packages designed initially for personal computers with integrated spreadsheets and other functions, including a

4GL, for an applications development tool; and (3) 4GLs designed originally as applications development tools.

With the emergence of 4GLs there are some new problems. One concern is for the expense involved when large numbers of personal computers are purchased. Of major concern is the protection of organizational data. IDMS/R from Cullinet Software, Inc., provides for a separate but interconnected information database for data extracted from the production database for downloading to the IBM Personal Computer XTs.[17]

According to Harold Uhrbach, over 800 organizations have written software in anticipation of their corporate and organizational database protection problems. This software is in the form of database input/output (I/O) controllers, or data I/O controllers where there are multiple databases.[18]

Organizations using software with 4GLs need to provide data administrators with the capability of involving users in modeling database structures. Users can be taught how to work with database administrators to obtain inputs from the administrators' vast knowledge of user experience. On the other hand, database administrators must be expected to realize the importance of data normalization and teach users to understand the concept.[19]

All current software packages with 4GLs have limitations and are not capable of generating all applications desired. These software packages are not all designed with an escape feature that permits modules written in a procedural language to be added to increase their use.[20] In other cases it is necessary to make the proper choice among the software items available. For instance, if there is a heavy requirement for use of mathematical techniques for optimization—common in DSS applications—the choice could be either EXPRESS or COMSHARE'S System W. Information center managers need to realize these capabilities and limitations and encourage their superiors to provide their centers with more than one software tool when the requirements so indicate.

REFERENCES

1. Isaacson, Portia, and Benjamin M. Rosen. "Personal Computing Industry: The Experts Forecast the Future." Paper presented at National Computer Conference 1983, May 16, 1983, Anaheim, California.
2. *EDP Industry Report.* The International Data Corporation, July 8, 1983, p. 1.
3. Martin, James. *Applications Development Without Programmers.* Englewood Cliffs, N.J.: Prentice-Hall, 1982.
4. Martin, James, and Carma McClure. *Software Maintenance.* Englewood Cliffs, N.J.: Prentice-Hall, 1983, pp. 238–241.
5. Martin, James. *Applications Development Without Programmers.* Englewood Cliffs, N.J.: Prentice-Hall, 1982, p. 108.
6. Teichroew, Daniel, and Hasan Sayani. "Automation of Systems Building." *Datamation,* August 15, 1971, pp. 25–30.
7. Konsynski, Benn R., and Jay F. Nunamaker. "PLEXSYS: A System Development System." *Advanced System Development/Feasibility Techniques,* May 1982, pp. 399–423.
8. Hammond, L. W. "Management Considerations for an Information Center." *IBM Systems Journal* 21 (1982), pp. 131–161.
9. Martin, James. *Applications Development Without Programmers.* Englewood Cliffs, N.J.: Prentice-Hall, 1982, p. 4.
10. *Computerworld,* April 18, 1983, p. 36.
11. Bowerman, Robert. "Relational Database Systems for Micros." *Datamation,* July 1983, pp. 128–134.
12. *Technology Transfer News,* 1 (1983), pp. S4–S8.
13. Brown, Marc, Norman Meyrowitz, and Andries van Dam. "Personal Computer Networks and Graphical Animation: Rationale and Practice for Education." *AEDS Monitor,* May/June 1983, pp. 15–24.
14. Miller, Boulton B. *Computers and Data Processing.* Edwardsville, IL: Bainbridge, 1982, p. 224.
15. *Wall Street Journal,* Midwest Edition, 19 October 1983, p. 3.
16. Rauch-Hindin, Wendy B. "Mainframes and Micros." *Systems and Software,* June 1983, pp. 68–89.
17. IDMS/R Seminar conducted by Cullinet Software, Inc., September 6, 1983, St. Louis.
18. Uhrbach, Harold. "Trends in Distributed Data Architecture. "Presentation at SIGBDP Breakfast Meeting, ACM 1983, October 25, 1983, New York.
19. Martin, James, and Carma McClure. *Software Maintenance.* Englewood Cliffs, N.J.: Prentice-Hall, 1983, p. 166.
20. Martin, James. *Applications Development Without Programmers.* Englewood Cliffs, N.J.: Prentice-Hall, 1982, p. 18.

SALVO—a fourth-generation language for personal computers

by MARVIN ELDER
Software Automation, Inc.
Dallas, Texas

ABSTRACT

Personal computer users are generally nontechnical people. Fourth-generation products can be of great assistance to these users, especially to those who have no access to database administrators or other computer professionals.

SALVO is a fourth-generation language for personal computers. This product was developed over a three-year period. Since the first working prototype (August 1982), this product has evolved into areas of artificial intelligence (AI), particularly natural-language processing and expert systems. The addition of AI functions to a fourth-generation language represents a departure from most fourth-generation products written for mainframe computers (except INTELLECT).

The synergism of this new area of AI research, coupled with relational database management, has proved to be extremely beneficial in assisting end users: they can extract information and generate applications in a much more nonprocedural manner than with more conventional fourth-generation approaches.

INTRODUCTION

SALVO is a fourth-generation language that runs on a wide variety of personal computers, both in a standalone mode and in an office automation environment.

The product combines several advanced software technologies, most notably relational database management and artificial intelligence. Its principal target is the end user who wants to manage and retrieve information without attending to the underlying technical details of data processing. At the same time, it will appeal to professional programmers who want to improve their productivity. Contrary to many "friendly" packages, SALVO's ease of use has not been purchased at the expense of power and functionality.

To achieve its intended purpose, SALVO's developers have automated most of the how-to functions, allowing the end user to concentrate on what information is required. This design philosophy has resulted in a product that differs in many respects from fourth-generation products designed for the mainframe environment, where database administrators and other data processing professionals can provide technical support for corporate end users.

The technical features of SALVO are arranged and described in the following categories:

1. Relational database management features
2. Application generator features
3. Artificial intelligence features
   a. Natural language processing
   b. Expert systems
4. Graphic automated information management

Before each set of features is described in detail, an overall perspective of SALVO will be presented by briefly stating the designers' working notion concerning the difference between *information* and *data*.

Information is entered into a computer in discrete pieces of datum elements. These data are best stored and managed by a relational database management system (for reasons explained below). Processing these pieces of data requires a "procedural language" (even fourth-generation languages must have procedural capabilities). Retrieving information from a system, on the other hand, is possible through a nonprocedural language.

Most end users who want to get information from a computer do not want to perform any detailed data processing functions. A system that automates all of the details of data processing would understand natural language at the level of a human being. Of course, there are some jobs that even human beings have to perform in a procedural, algorithmic fashion (e.g., compute the payroll).

A major hypothesis according to which SALVO is designed is this: If data are organized and managed by a relational database management system—one that is truly relational, according to Codd's definition[1]—then an expert system (having the expertise of a database administrator and programmer) can automate many of the detailed how-to functions involved in data processing and can retrieve and manage information for the user. SALVO's designers call this "software automation."

This approach of combining relational database theory and artificial intelligence theory actually surpasses the notion of fourth-generation languages and approaches the fifth-generation ideas now being formulated and researched in some areas.

The first two categories of features in SALVO discussed below—relational database management and application generation—concern themselves with the data management and data processing functions (i.e., the procedural aspects) required of a fourth-generation product.

The third and fourth categories, artificial intelligence and user interface features, are concerned with the nonprocedural information management functions—of particular importance to personal computer users.

RELATIONAL DATABASE MANAGEMENT FEATURES

There are many so-called relational database management software packages that run on personal computers. Most of these are not true relational systems. According to E. F. Codd's definition, a true relational system has the following components:

1. A relational data structure (i.e., flat files, relations, tables)
2. A collection of relational algebraic functions, or rules of inference
3. A collection of relational integrity rules

In light of the criteria stated above, the majority of "relational" software packages for personal computers can be broadly characterized by noting that many of them do keep data in relations (although normalization is usually not enforced); some of them provide most of the relational algebraic operators; and few (perhaps none) of them enforce the relational integrity rules.

An important objective of the relational data model, according to Codd, was to make the model structurally simple so that users and programmers could communicate with one another about the database (Codd calls this the "communicability objective").

Without going into detailed discussion about the merits (and drawbacks) of the relational model, the most important reasons for using it in SALVO are the following:

1. If data are kept in normalized relational form, with their integrity enforced by the relational integrity checks, then a set of inference rules (the relational algebra functions) can be installed as an expert system that can find and manipulate related pieces of data in the database.
2. Therefore users can more easily understand the structure and relationship of their database and can formulate requests for information that may be accurately inferred by SALVO'S expert system and processed through its concept of software automation.

Despite the many advantages of the relational model over other database models, critics often point out that relational database systems are inherently slow in execution. SALVO has three aspects of relational database management designed to overcome certain inherent disadvantages of the relational data model.

Virtual Join

The relational algebraic operation called join compares the values of a data field common to two tables (files) and produces a third *result table,* which may be much larger than either of the two tables being joined. In some cases a result table may be too large to fit on a floppy disk on a personal computer. To avoid this common problem, SALVO employs a Virtual Join, in which the result of a join is not a physical table but the output device itself (CRT screen or printer).

In conventional systems, join operations over several tables or files must be performed sequentially. SALVO's virtual join operation can simultaneously join up to 16 tables in a single pass, resulting in dramatic timesaving compared with other systems.

Automatic ISAM Indexing

Before attempting a virtual join operation, SALVO automatically builds ISAM indexes (if they are not already built) that speed up the execution of the join operation.

Automatic Normalization

In a large company using a mainframe relational system, a highly paid database administrator usually sets up and maintains the database structure. This individual uses and enforces an integral part of database design called normalization. Relational databases should be maintained in third normal form (or higher) to avoid storage anomalies that can result in lost or redundant data in conventional, unnormalized databases.

SALVO employs a sophisticated automatic normalization concept, since the average user of a personal computer does not have a database administrator to consult. This unique feature hides the complexities of normalization from the user; in fact, the user is not even aware of this operation at all.

To summarize its relational database features, SALVO is thought to be one of the first true relational database management systems running on personal computers. This rigid enforcement of the relational model provides a basis for SALVO's automatic navigation, expert system, and other advanced information management concepts. SALVO also employs sophisticated database methods not generally found on mainframe computers, much less on personal computers with only 64 Kbytes of memory!

Application Generator Features

A fourth-generation language that is entirely nonprocedural will allow users to retrieve information without detailed programming but will be limited to queries only. To develop applications that involve any logical decisions and/or the processing of data (e.g., storing, adding), a language must have procedural aspects. Since personal computer users want to be able to do many of their own computer applications without the assistance of professional programmers, a simple but effective procedural capability is a requirement of a fourth-generation language.

The difference between a procedural fourth-generation language and the third-generation languages (such as COBOL and BASIC) is the number of procedural instructions necessary to write an application.

James Martin, in his book *Application Development Without Programmers,*[2] defined a fourth-generation procedural language as one that requires fewer than one-tenth as many instructions as present-generation languages.

SALVO does much better than Martin's minimum requirements. Many benchmark programs have been written that compare SALVO with other languages. For the type of applications needed for personal computers, SALVO has been often found to be 30 to 40 times more powerful than BASIC or COBOL. Even when compared with "database languages" that run on personal computers, SALVO is often found to be 3 to 10 times as powerful.

Much of SALVO's power as an application generator is derived from its automatic navigation feature. Whereas other languages require many lines of instruction just to open a file, read a record, and test some data element to match up related records with a "foreign" file, SALVO does this type of job automatically. Especially when several files are to be related in a report, SALVO's automatic navigation (combined with its virtual join feature) can save hundreds of lines of code compared with other languages.

Professional programmers are of course interested in fourth-generation procedural languages for the same reason—fewer lines of code do the same job. On a personal computer, a fairly simple application written in COBOL (say a payroll) could easily cost more to program than the computer itself! SALVO has very powerful commands for the professional programmer. Many users will never use some of these advanced features. Other reasons than simply fewer lines of code are also important to software developers: no need for specification documents and less need for documentation, for example.

ARTIFICIAL INTELLIGENCE FEATURES

The field of artificial intelligence (AI) comprises many diverse areas. Two particular areas of AI are important to the development of user languages: natural language processing and expert systems.

SALVO contains elements of both of these AI concepts; however, SALVO does not purport to be a sophisticated AI product. In fact, AI concepts are used in SALVO only to the extent that the user interface portions of the package are made simpler, as will be explained below.

Natural Language Processing

Computer programming languages are notoriously insistent upon a rigid syntax: The commands in the language have to be stated in a precise order of words. Human language is much richer and diverse in the *way* that an idea may be expressed.

SALVO has a Request facility, which allows users to ask for information (i.e., make a query) in natural language. This facility is not intended to allow purely "conversational" queries—as if one were talking to another human being. The major benefit of the Request facility is to state a query in a straightforward way, using declarative natural language commands, without having to obey the syntax rules of a computer language.

Using Request, a user can state a query that can be run immediately and never see the underlying procedural language, which is actually translated from the natural language request. Alternatively, the user can view (and then modify) the SALVO procedural template program, which the natural language processor built from his or her request.

SALVO's natural language processor employs a frame-and-slot approach to decompose the user's request into a format appropriate for an internal expert system (explained in the next section).

This AI method allows the user a considerable amount of freedom in the way his or her request is stated. As an example, if the user does not include a verb in a command, a default verb (list) is supplied automatically. In SALVO the following three requests are identical: "List the accounts for salesman Smith," "For salesman Smith, list his accounts," and "Salesman Smith accounts." These examples illustrate the degree of syntactical freedom allowed in SALVO's natural language processor.

Expert Systems

An expert system emulates the decision making and the knowledge of a human expert in a particular field. Two major components of an expert system are (1) a means of making inferences based on a set of rules (formal and/or intuitive) that the expert uses to make decisions and (2) a knowledge base that models the knowledge accumulated by the expert pertaining to his or her field of expertise.

SALVO contains an expert system with the following components:

1. A set of inference rules that a database administrator would use
2. A knowledge base consisting of the data dictionary of the user's particular database

SALVO's expert system is utilized in three different areas of the software:

1. Translating a user request from natural language to a SALVO procedural template program
2. Assisting a user or programmer in setting up his or her database (i.e., automatic normalization)
3. Compiling a SALVO procedural program into executable form—specifically, deciding internally how to handle most of the details of conventional programming.

GRAPHIC "AUTOMATIC INFORMATION MANAGEMENT"

The research and development of SALVO, over a three-year period, evolved in ways that were unanticipated at the outset. One discovery that evolved out of the project is a new working model of information processing, not previously published (to our knowledge) in the literature.

This new working model of information processing is roughly stated as follows: Given a relational database, given a perspective of looking at that database from a particular user's viewpoint, and given an expert system that "knows" the rules of relational database navigation, it is possible to determine what information can be derived for just this particular view.

SALVO's developers have named this new approach "automatic information management" and have provided a graphics user interface to implement this approach.

This facility in SALVO is accessed through a function called "view." First the user selects a particular file that serves as the focus point of his or her intended request for information. A graphic representation of the user's view of the primary file and its related files is then displayed. A natural language request is started for the user, first of all to simply list the primary file selected. The user can then include information from other related files in the request by simply selecting from the graphic display of the files.

As each related file is selected, the user's request is built automatically in natural language, just as if the user had typed the query through the request function.

The view function of SALVO allows people with no programming experience, and with no desire to see or manipulate even a fourth-generation language, to request and generate information from their personal computers.

OPERATING ENVIRONMENTS

SALVO incorporates several state-of-the-art features into a software package that runs in a 64-Kbyte environment on a personal computer. Written in FORTH, this new fourth-generation language is transportable to many popular types of microcomputers and/or operating systems.

The first version of SALVO is designed for a single user personal computer system. SALVO-II, a version available in the first quarter of 1984, has features desirable in distributed database processing environments (i.e., the office automation environment).

SUMMARY

Personal computers need a particular type of fourth-generation language—one that end users can use without any help from programmers, database administrators, or other computer professionals.

The combination of two advanced software technologies, relational database management and artificial intelligence, provides a synergistic approach to information management that is perhaps more powerful than either of these technologies by itself has been able to achieve. SALVO may be the first of this type of fourth-generation product to run on a personal computer.

REFERENCES

1. Codd, E. F. "Relational Database: A Practical Foundation for Productivity." *Communications of the ACM,* 25 (1982), p. 111.
2. Martin, J. *Application Development Without Programmers.* Englewood Cliffs, N.J.: Prentice-Hall, 1982.

Uniform organization of inverted files

by DALIA MOTZKIN and KENNETH WILLIAMS
Western Michigan University
Kalamazoo, Michigan
and
KARL CHANG
University of Nebraska
Omaha, Nebraska

ABSTRACT

A range attribute is defined as an attribute that may assume a range of values. Examples might be Age = (1–10, 11–14, 15–16, . . .) or Salary = (0–1000, 1001–1500, . . .). This paper is concerned with the selection of ranges that will produce reasonably uniform numbers of records in each range. A set of algorithms has been developed to enable the file designer to obtain a set of ranges such that records are distributed uniformly between the ranges. Although in a given case perfect uniformity may not be achievable, the algorithms can find ranges such that for a set of X records in a range, bounds a and b may be given so that $a \le X \le b$ for all ranges. The algorithms have been tested with a PASCAL program.

INTRODUCTION

Applications such as database management systems have made widespread use of inverted file directories for many years. General descriptions of inverted files can be found in Knuth,[10] Horowitz and Sahni,[5] and others. This wide usage of inverted files stems from their suitability for retrieval of data associated with dense attributes. As Knuth[10] points out, they are extremely efficient in the processing of Boolean queries. Efficient use of inverted files in query optimization has been shown by Lie[11] and Putkanen.[14,15]

Many recent publications have described systems using inverted files. Harding and Willet[3] show how inverted files provide an efficient tool for automatic document classification. Schultheisz et al.[18] use inverted files in a chemical dictionary. Schultheisz[19] uses inverted files to retrieve data from TOXLINE, a bibliographic database on toxicology composed of 11 different files from different sources. He found inverted files to be an efficient tool in handling data from differently structured files, with many replications of bibliographic records. Conrad et al.[2] used inverted files in a statistical package with a cancer database at Boston University hospital. This includes only a small sample of the uses of inverted files.

A number of improvements and modifications for inverted files have been developed. Such modifications address some of the drawbacks of large inverted files, such as excessive space requirements or long access times. Compression techniques that improve the use of space in inverted files have been developed by Schuegraf,[17] Jakobsson,[6,8] and Jakobsson and Nevalainen.[7] Combinations of clustering of records together with compression techniques have been suggested by Nevalainen, Jakobsson, and Berg.[13] This technique improves space utilization and at the same time reduces access time. Motzkin[12] incorporated inverted files into normal multiplication table directories. In normal multiplication tables the attribute values as well as the address lists are organized in clusters. Several attributes can be stored in the same "Table." This technique provides for very rapid access to single as well as multiple attributes, while it is economical in space utilization. Hoffer[4] concentrates on the process of selecting the attributes to be inverted and makes some recommendations. Cardenas[1] provides ways to measure the performance of inverted files and suggests that the attribute values may be kept in a separate, hierarchical structure with pointers to the address lists. Johnson and Webster[9] propose an efficient way to update an inverted file. Additional references, especially regarding earlier development, can be found in the extensive bibliography compiled by Schkolnick.[16]

In most cases, designers of inverted file directories use ranges of values for attributes that are selected in an arbitrary manner. The problem of optimization of the lengths of address lists has not been adequately addressed. Arbitrary selections may produce ranges with widely disparate numbers of records within each range. This paper provides some algorithms that may be used to produce ranges with more uniform numbers of associated records. The algorithms are in a form excerpted from the original PASCAL program.

To illustrate these concepts we start with a master file consisting of a set of records numbered 1–N. Each record will contain certain attributes. From the master file, one may construct an Initial Directory involving one of the attribute fields of each record. For this discussion we are interested in an attribute field whose values may assume a large number (possibly infinite) of values. This Initial Directory will consist of a set of ordered pairs containing (attribute value, record number). We also may refer to record numbers as addresses or keys. As an example, suppose N = 6, the record numbers are integers 1–6, and the attribute of interest is Monthly Salary. The Initial Directory might then contain the following:

Monthly Salary	*Record Number*
600	1
1100	2
800	3
700	4
600	5
1000	6

One then sorts the initial directory on attribute value (this is necessary in order to use the algorithms developed here), which, for this example, would produce the following:

600	1
600	5
700	4
800	3
1000	6
1100	2

Although this small example does not completely illustrate the problem, it is easy to see that if arbitrary ranges for monthly salary, such 0–500, 501–1000, 1001–1500, 1501–2000, 2001–100,000, are chosen for the construction of an inverted file, the number of records in each range may exhibit no uniformity of size. If the above ranges are selected, for this example, the following Master Directory will be produced:

0–500
No entries

501–1000
1, 5, 4, 3, 6

1001–1500
2

1501–2000
No entries

2001–100,000
No entries

Note that the Master Directory consists of two parts, the attribute ranges and the associated file addresses.

The algorithms presented here rely on first producing the Sorted Directory. This is a normal step in the production of most inverted file directories. The next step is to determine a desirable number of records per interval as appropriate ranges for the Master Directory are considered. This number should be chosen in such a way that when the user requests all records in a range, not too many records for the application are returned. The ranges, however, should not be chosen too small, or a very large number of such ranges may be required, which will cause a correspondingly large amount of time to be devoted to searching for the proper range entries in the Master Directory. In this case the Master Directory will occupy a great deal of space, and Master File updates will often involve updating the Master Directory.

Consider a file consisting of 1,000,000 records with a Monthly Salary range from $15.00 (for some part-time employee) to $700,000.00 (for the company president). If only a few ranges are chosen, the number of records in each range is very large. On the other hand, if salary ranges of $100.00 are chosen, say 0–99, 100–199, etc., the Master Directory will consist of 7,000 range entries.

OPTIMIZATION OPTIONS

The algorithms presented here provide the designer of the inverted file structure with four options to optimize with different criteria. We assume the master file contains N records.

Option 1

The user specifies the range for each interval.

This represents the typical nonoptimized approach. The algorithm simply finds pointers to the records within each interval as it constructs the Master Directory. This is done by a single sequential pass through the Sorted Directory.

This option may also be used to obtain uniform distributions manually. After the file designer requests a given range, the algorithm informs the designer how many records the range will contain and allows for a possible redefinition of the range.

A range can also be completely omitted from the inverted file. This may be desirable when a specific attribute value corresponds to a large number of the records in the file. For example, the salary of $1,000 in a file of 1,000,000 records might occur 100,000 times.

Option 2

The file designer specifies the total number of interval ranges.

If M ranges are specified, the program then finds the proper ranges so that $\lceil N/M \rceil$ items will be placed in each range. This is done by constructing appropriate range sizes as it makes a single sequential pass through records in the Sorted Directory. No backtracking is necessary. The same range may be included in more than one interval; e.g., if we have 60 records per interval and if there are 180 records with the value 1000, then we will have at least 3 intervals corresponding to the value 1000.

The advantage of Option 2 is that fixed-size address lists are provided. One may choose the size to exactly fill one physical block.

Option 3

The file designer specifies the desired number of records per interval.

If K records per interval are specified, the program will construct approximately N/K ranges. The designer may specify a lower bound, a, and an upper bound, b, on the permissible number of records per range. Otherwise, the algorithm will use a = .5K and b = 2K. In this option the algorithm does not allow a specific attribute value to belong to more than one range. This organization requires a certain amount of latitude in the number of records per interval. Consider a sorted file as follows:

500, 4
600, 2
600, 3
600, 1
700, 6
1400, 5
1800, 7

Ranges cannot be chosen to provide exactly three records per range without having the value 600 belong to two intervals.

The (a, b) range will not be violated without specific permission from the designer; but if permission is not granted, some ranges may be omitted from the Master Directory. It may be desirable to omit ranges. For example, if an attribute value occurs in 1/5 of the records, then it is more efficient simply to look for records with such an attribute value with a sequential search of the file. The maintenance and the space allocation of such a large list of addresses cannot be justified.

A user or an application program requesting records with a very frequent attribute value that has not been included in the directory will first be notified as to the number of corresponding records; and if the records are still requested, they may be obtained with a direct search.

If one regards a single pass through the Sorted Directory as involving a read and write for each entry, Option 3 may involve 1.5 passes, since certain entries may be read twice but only written once.

Option 4

The algorithm selectes the number of ranges, M, and the desired number of records per range, K.

In this case, with the goal of minimizing future search time, M = N**(½) and K = N**(½) are chosen. The user may then specify permissible upper and lower bounds on the number of records per range. Otherwise, the program will select .5K and 2K, as in Option 3. Also as in Option 3, these will not be violated without specific directions from the designer. Again, at most 1.5 passes through the Sorted Directory are required.

ALGORITHM OVERVIEW OF OPTIONS 3 AND 4

We start by trying to allocate the first K entries to the first range, the second K entries to the second range, etc. Problems may arise. Suppose the first K-2 records are in the first range but entries K − 1, K, K + 1, . . ., K + W all have equal attribute values. In practice such situations may occur frequently. In an inverted file for the Monthly Salary attribute with 1,000,000 records, one may want 1000 records in each interval; but there may be 5000 people earning, say, the exact salary of $1500.

The general approach to these problems is to allow the number of records to vary. Lower and upper bounds, a and b, must be either specified by the user or selected by default by the program. The algorithm then chooses the value between a and b that is closest to K. Consider the example in the sorted-file list with K = 3 and bounds 2 and 4. The ranges chosen will be 500–600 with 4 records and 700–1,800 with 3 records. If no value between a and b will work, the file designer is provided with the choice of violating these size boundaries or of simply not including the offending attribute value with many occurences in the final Master Directory. Consider a military employment file with 50,000 soldiers receiving a salary of $606 per month, thus producing the range 606–606 with 50,000 entries.

When an attribute value of a very high frequency occurs with more than the allowed number of records, it is either removed or kept in a separate interval. Then the previous distribution between the two previous intervals is optimized. (See procedure COMBINE_OR_REDISTRIBUTE_TWO_INTERVALS in Appendix A.) Consider the following:

100, 3
200, 7
200, 4
300, 8
400, 2
400, 1
400, 6
400, 9
400, 5
.
.
.

If we have a Sorted Directory as in the list immediately above, with K = 3, a = 2, and b = 4, then initially the first range will be 100–200; but after determining that the value 400 cannot be included in the interval, the first range is modified to be 100–300. In other situations the ranges of the two previous intervals may be reassigned to provide both intervals with a better distribution of records than a single combined one.

ADDITIONAL NOTES

No matter how intervals are chosen, it may become necessary to obtain a set of records for a range not originally specifically included. Suppose the ranges are 0–999, 100–1499, 1500–2000, . . ., and a system user specifies the range 1200–1600. The query language program should have a module to find the union of 100–1499 and 1500–2000, then to check each record to determine whether it is in the desired range. This is part of handling general logical queries. The uniform approach developed here will yield more efficient results for this in most cases, since the union of small intervals normally involves a desirable smaller number of records.

Note that the algorithms may occasionally find a range having fewer records than the lower bound specifies. This can only occur when there are two attribute values with high frequency and a very few values between these two. (In practice this case will probably occur infrequently.)

The concept of inverted files using ranges of values is not limited to those with numeric attributes. It can also be used for fields such as names or bibliographic keywords. Alphabetic ranges may be used. In the case of an attribute such as a bibliographic keyword a given attribute value may fill a complete range or (in the case of Option 2) several ranges.

ALGORITHM EFFICIENCY

Most methods of creating a Master Directory for inverted files will involve an initial sort by attribute value. This 0(N log N) process then may be considered as the initial fixed portion of the time required. From this point at most 1.5 passes (Options 3 and 4) through the Sorted Directory are required. Options 1 and 2 require only a single pass. The extra time over a single pass is required in Options 3 and 4 when equal values are found at what should be interval range boundaries. The worst case is when the whole file has the same attribute value and it is kept in the directory. After sorting, all algorithms are of Order N.

In terms of space for the Master Directory, clearly no additional space (more than other methods) is necessary. In fact, less space than normal will be required if the file designer elects to not include certain items whose attribute values have numerous occurences. Therefore, the space requirement is less than or equal to that required for arbitrary selection of ranges.

UPDATING

Updating may be done in a manner similar to that for any inverted files. There are two basic approaches:

1. All deleted addresses are flagged and all additions are maintained in a separate file. Periodically the whole directory is reorganized. Reorganization will require at most 2.5 passes, 1 pass to merge the address lists and obtain a new Sorted Directory and 1.5 passes to reconstruct the new uniform inverted file.
2. Flag the addresses to be deleted. Insert each new address immediately and remove deleted records at this time also. After some period of time the bounds $a \leq X \leq b$ for the size of ranges may no longer hold, and the whole directory will need to be reorganized.

Further work on efficient updating procedures and work to develop more optimal organization methods for discrete attributes may hold value.

CONCLUDING REMARKS

Methods have been developed to enable a file designer to produce Master Directories of attribute values with ranges that provide for uniform numbers of records in each. Algorithms have been developed and programmed in PASCAL to implement these processes. The algorithms are flexible and efficient. The method may be applied to attributes with non-numeric values by choosing some ordering—e.g., alphabetical order.

Listings of the algorithms, a sample data file, and the results of computer runs are included in the appendices.

REFERENCES

1. Cardenas, A.F. "Analysis and Performance of Inverted Database Structures." *Communications of the ACM,* 18 (1975), pp. 253–263.
2. Conrad, L., S. Bloom, C. Cooper, T. Cannon, R.H. Friedman, J. Horowitz, J. Krikorian, and J. Lopez. "The Cancer Data Management System Statistics Package," *Proceedings of the Fourth Annual Symposium on Computer Applications in Medical Care.* New York:IEEE, 1980, pp. 1281–1285.
3. Hardings, A.F., and P.W. Willet. "Matrices." *Journal of the American Society of Information Science,* 31 (1980), pp. 298–300.
4. Hoffer, J.A. "Database Design Practices for Inverted Files." *Information and Management,* 3 (1980), pp. 149–161.
5. Horowitz, E., and S. Sahni. *Fundamentals of Data Structures.* Potomac, Md.: Computer Science Press, 1976 pp. 531–532.
6. Jakobsson, M. "Reducing Block Accesses in Inverted Files by Partial Clustering." *Information Systems,* 5 (1980), pp. 1–5.
7. Jakobsson, M., and D. Nevalaines. "On the Organization of Hybrid Indexes." *Proceedings of the International Conference on Databases,* 1980, pp. 250–259.
8. Jakobsson, M. "Evaluation of a Hierarchical Bit Vector Compression Technique." *Information Processing Letters,* 14 (1982), pp. 147–149.
9. Johnson, J.S., and D.B. Webster. "Updating an Inverted File Index—A Performance Comparison of Two Techniques." *Computer Journal,* 25 (1982), pp. 169–175.
10. Knuth, D.E., *The Art of Computer Programming,* Volume 3. Reading, Mass.: Addison-Wesley, 1973.
11. Lie, J.W. "Algorithms for Parsing Search Queries in Systems with Inverted Files." *ACM Transactions on Database Systems,* 1 (1976), pp. 299–316.
12. Motzkin, D. "The Use of Normal Multiplication Tables for Information Storage and Retrieval." *Communications of the ACM,* 22, (1979), pp. 193–207.
13. Nevalainen, O., M. Jakobsson, and R. Berg. "Compression of Clustered Inverted Files." *Mathematical Foundations of Computer Science.* Berlin:Springer-Verlag, 1978, pp. 393–402.
14. Putkanen, A. "On the Selection of Access Paths in Inverted Database Organization." *Information Systems,* 4, (1979), pp. 219–225.
15. Putkanen, A. "The Order of Merging Operations for Queries in Inverted File Systems." *International Journal of Computer and Information Sciences,* 9 (1980).
16. Schkolnick. "A Survey of Physical Database Design Methodology and Technique." *Proceedings of Fourth International Conference on Very Large Databases.* New York:IEEE, 1978, pp. 474–487.
17. Schuegraf, E.J., D.F. Walker, and K.L. Kahnan. "Design and Implementation of an On-Line Chemical Dictionary." *Journal of the American Society of Information Science,* 29, (1978), pp. 173–179.
18. Schultheisz, R.J.; D.F. Walker; and K.L. Kanaan. "Design and Implementation of an On-Line Chemical Dictionary." *Journal of the American Society of Information Science,* 29, (1978), pp. 173–179.
19. Schultheisz, R.J. "Toxline Evolution of an On-Line Interactive Bibliographic Database." *Journal of the American Society of Information Science,* 32, (1981), pp. 421–429.

APPENDIX A (The Algorithms)

```
(****************************************************************************
 *       SUBJECT: AN OPTIMAL DESIGN OF INVERTED FILE                       *
 ****************************************************************************)

PROGRAM OPTIMAL_INVERTED_FILE(INPUT*,OUTPUT);

VAR        SORTED_ATR_LIST : ARRAY[0..1000,1..2] OF INTEGER;    (* THE TABLE CONTAINS  SORTED  LIST OF RECORD NO. & ITS
                                                                   CORRESPONDING ATTRIBUTE VALUE PAIRS *)
           ORIGIN_ATR_LIST : ARRAY[0..1000,1..2] OF INTEGER;    (* THE TABLE CONTAINS ORIGINAL LIST OF RECORD NO. & ITS
                                                                   CORRESPONDING ATTRIBUTE VALUE PAIRS *)
                    MASDIR : ARRAY[1..50,1..100] OF INTEGER;    (* THE MASTER DIRECTORY OF INVERTED FILE WHICH CONTAINS
                                                                  NUMBER OF INTERVALS, EACH INTERVAL CONTAINS LOW & HIGH
                                                                   ATTRIBUTE VALUES & LIST OF RECORDS WHOSEATTRIBUTE VALUE
                                                                   BETWEEN THEM *)

      TOTAL_ATR_OF_INTVAL : ARRAY[1..50] OF INTEGER;            (* TOTAL NUMBER OF RECORDS CORRESPONDING TO EACH INTERVAL *)
                       HV : INTEGER;                            (* THE HIGHEST ATTRIBUTE VALUE ON EACH INTERVAL *)
                       LV : INTEGER;                            (* THE LOWEST  ATTRIBUTE VALUE ON EACH INTERVAL *)
                       NI : INTEGER;                            (* THE TOTAL   NUMBER OF INTERVALS *)
                       NR : INTEGER;                            (* THE TOTAL   NUMBER OF RECORDS IN PILE FILE *)
                      NRI : INTEGER;                            (* THE DESIRED NUMBER OF RECORDS PER INTERVAL *)
                  MAX_NRI : INTEGER;                            (* THE MAXIMUM NUMBER OF RECORDS PER INTERVAL *)
                  MIN_NRI : INTEGER;                            (* THE MINIMUM NUMBER OF RECORDS PER INTERVAL *)
              USER_OPTION : INTEGER;                            (* THE CHOICE USER CAN HAVE IN ORDER TO DETERMINE THE
                                                                   INTERVAL DISTRIBUTION *)
```

```
                ATRVAL : INTEGER;                   (* A SPECIFIC ATTRIBUTE VALUE *)
       DELETED_INTVAL : INTEGER;                    (* AN INTERVAL HAS BEEN EXHAUSTED *)
POS_OF_1ST_ATR_CUR_INTVAL : INTEGER;                (* POINT TO 1ST ATTRIBUTE POSITION OF CURRENT INTERVAL *)
POS_OF_LST_ATR_LST_INTVAL : INTEGER;                (* POINT TO LAST ATTRIBUTE POSITION OF PREVIOUS INTERVAL *)
           CUR_INTVAL : INTEGER;                    (* THE CURRENT INTERVAL NUMBER *)
               EXPAND : INTEGER;                    (* COUNT HOW MANY ATTRIBUTE VALUES IN A SPECIFIC INTERVAL *)
   NO_OF_EQUAL_ATRVALS : INTEGER;                   (* COUNT PARTICULAR EQUAL ATTRIBUTE VALUES IN AN INTERVAL *)
          I,J,K,L,M,N : INTEGER;                    (* THE INDICES OF LOOPS *)
                 DONE : BOOLEAN;                    (* THE SWITCH STATES TRUE OR FALSE TO CONTROL THE LOOPS *)
        USER_RESPONES : CHAR;                       (* THE USER RESPONES EITHER YES OR NO *)

(*************************************************************************************************************)

PROCEDURE USER_CHOOSE_INTERVALS;   // OPTION 1  //

// THIS PROCEDURE IS TO LET USER SELECT THE RANGE OF EACH INTERVAL FOR MASTER DIRECTORY //

 N <-- 0;                    // INITIALIZE COUNTER FOR INTERVAL NUMBER //
 I <-- 0;                    // INITIALIZE COUNTER FOR NUMBER OF INTERVALS //
 J <-- 1;                    // INITIALIZE POINTER WHICH POINT TO A SPECIFIC RECORD NUMBER & ATTRIBUTE VALUE //

 REPEAT
  N <-- N + 1;
  READ(LV,HV);
  IF (LV <> 0) OR (HV <> 0)  THEN

      I <-- I + 1;
      MASDIR[I,1] <-- LV;
      MASDIR[I,2] <-- HV;
      K <-- 0;
      WHILE (SORTED_ATR_LIST[J,2] <= HV) AND (J <= NR)
          K <-- K + 1;
          MASDIR[I,K+2] <-- SORTED_ATR_LIST[J,1];
          PRINT (MASDIR[I,K+2]);
          J <-- J + 1;
      PRINT ('NUMBER OF RECORDS = ',K);
      TOTAL ATR OF INTVAL[N] <-- K;
      READ(USER_RESPONES);
      IF USER_RESPONES = 'N' THEN
          TOTAL_ATR OF INTVAL[I] <-- 0;
          MASDIR[I,1] <-- 0;
          MASDIR[I,2] <-- 0;
 UNTIL(LV = 0) AND (HV = 0);
 NI <-- N;

END USER_CHOOSE_INTERVALS;

//***********************************************************************************************************//

PROCEDURE PROGRAM_EQUALLY_DISTRIBUTE_INTERVALS;  //  OPTION 2  //

  PRINT('ENTER THE TOTAL NUMBER OF INTERVALS YOU WANT >> '); BREAK(); RESET();
  READ(NI);

  NRI <-- NR DIV NI;
  IF NR MOD NI <> 0
    THEN NRI <-- NRI + 1;
  POS_OF_LST_ATR_LST_INTVAL <-- 0;
  FOR I <-- 1 TO NI-1
      TOTAL_ATR_OF_INTVAL[I] <-- NRI;
      MASDIR[I,1] <-- SORTED_ATR_LIST[POS_OF_LST_ATR_LST_INTVAL+1,2];
      MASDIR[I,2] <-- SORTED_ATR_LIST[POS_OF_LST_ATR_LST_INTVAL+NRI,2];
      J <-- 2;
      FOR K <-- POS_OF_LST_ATR_LST_INTVAL+1 TO POS_OF_LST_ATR_LST_INTVAL+NRI
          J <-- J + 1;
          MASDIR[I,J] <-- SORTED_ATR_LIST[K,1];
      POS_OF_LST_ATR_LST_INTVAL <-- POS_OF_LST_ATR_LST_INTVAL + NRI;

  MASDIR[NI,1] <-- SORTED_ATR_LIST[POS_OF_LST_ATR_LST_INTVAL+1,2];
  MASDIR[NI,2] <-- SORTED_ATR_LIST[NR,2];
  J <-- 2;
  FOR K <-- POS_OF_LST_ATR_LST_INTVAL+1 TO NR
      J <-- J + 1;
      MASDIR[I,J] <-- SORTED_ATR_LIST[K,1];
  TOTAL_ATR_OF_INTVAL[NI] <-- J - 2;

END PROGRAM_EQUALLY_DISTRIBUTE_INTERVALS;

//***********************************************************************************************************//
```

```
PROCEDURE COMBINE_OR_REDISTRIBUTE_TWO_INTERVALS;

// THIS PROCEDURE CHECKS PREVIOUS 2 INTERVALS TO SEE IF THEY CAN COMBINE /REDISTRIBUTE IN ORDER TO HAVE UNIFORM INTERVALS //

// CHECK IF THERE EXISTS TWO INTERVALS OR IF TWO INTERVALS SHOULD COMBINE OR REDISTRIBUTE //

IF (CUR_INTVAL > 2) AND (CUR_INTVAL - 1 <> DELETED_INTVAL) THEN
  FIRST <-- CUR_INTVAL - 2;
  SECOND <-- CUR_INTVAL - 1;
  SUM <-- TOTAL_ATR_OF_INTVAL[FIRST] + TOTAL_ATR_OF_INTVAL[SECOND];

  // CHECK IF THESE TWO INTERVALS CAN COMBINE SO THAT BOTH INTERVALS HAVE UNIFORM FREQUENCIES //

  IF (SUM <= MAX_NRI) AND (SUM DIV 2 < NRI)
   THEN
        MASDIR[FIRST,2] <-- MASDIR[SECOND,2];
        MASDIR[SECOND,1] <-- 0;
        MASDIR[SECOND,2] <-- 0;
        EXPAND <-- 2;
        FOR N <-- TOTAL_ATR_OF_INTVAL[FIRST]+3 TO SUM+2
            EXPAND <-- EXPAND + 1;
            MASDIR[FIRST,N] <-- MASDIR[SECOND,EXPAND];
        TOTAL_ATR_OF_INTVAL[SECOND] <-- 0;

        TOTAL_ATR_OF_INTVAL[FIRST] <-- SUM
        CUR_INTVAL <-- CUR_INTVAL - 1;
   ELSE
        // CHECK IF THESE TWO INTERVALS CAN REDISTRIBUTE, SO BOTH INTERVALS CAN HAVE UNIFORM FREQUENCIES //

        IF TOTAL_ATR_OF_INTVAL[SECOND] <= SUM DIV 2
          THEN
            REPEAT
              NO_OF_EQUAL_ATRVALS <-- 1;
              EXPAND <-- TOTAL_ATR_OF_INTVAL[FIRST] + 2;
              ATRVAL <-- ORIGIN_ATR_LIST[MASDIR[FIRST,EXPAND],2];
              NE <-- FALSE;
              EXPAND <-- EXPAND - 1;
              WHILE (EXPAND > 2) AND (NE = FALSE)
              IF ORIGIN_ATR_LIST[MASDIR[FIRST,EXPAND],2] = ATRVAL
                THEN
                    NO_OF_EQUAL_ATRVALS <-- NO_OF_EQUAL_ATRVALS + 1;
                    EXPAND <-- EXPAND - 1;
                ELSE NE <-- TRUE;

              OLD_DIFFER <-- TOTAL_ATR_OF_INTVAL[FIRST] - TOTAL_ATR_OF_INTVAL[SECOND];
              FIRST_INTVAL_NEW_TOTAL_ATR <-- TOTAL_ATR_OF_INTVAL[FIRST] - NO_OF_EQUAL_ATRVALS;
              SECOND_INTVAL_NEW_TOTAL_ATR <-- TOTAL_ATR_OF_INTVAL[SECOND] + NO_OF_EQUAL_ATRVALS;
              NEW_DIFFER <-- ABS(FIRST_INTVAL_NEW_TOTAL_ATR - SECOND_INTVAL_NEW_TOTAL_ATR);

              IF OLD_DIFFER - NEW_DIFFER > 0
                THEN
                    MASDIR[FIRST,2]  <-- ORIGIN_ATR_LIST[MASDIR[FIRST,EXPAND],2];
                    MASDIR[SECOND,1] <-- ORIGIN_ATR_LIST[MASDIR[FIRST,EXPAND+1],2];

                    TOTAL_ATR_OF_INTVAL[FIRST] <-- FIRST_INTVAL_NEW_TOTAL_ATR;
                    TOTAL_ATR_OF_INTVAL[SECOND] <-- SECOND_INTVAL_NEW_TOTAL_ATR;

                    EXPAND <-- 2;
                    FOR N <-- NO_OF_EQUAL_ATRVALS+3 TO SECOND_INTVAL_NEW_TOTAL_ATR+2
                        EXPAND <-- EXPAND + 1;
                        MASDIR[SECOND,N] <-- MASDIR[SECOND,EXPAND];

                    EXPAND <-- FIRST_INTVAL_NEW_TOTAL_ATR + 2;
                    FOR N <-- 3 TO NO_OF_EQUAL_ATRVALS+2
                        EXPAND <-- EXPAND + 1;
                        MASDIR[SECOND,N] <-- MASDIR[FIRST,EXPAND];

                    FOR N <-- FIRST_INTVAL_NEW_TOTAL_ATR+3 TO FIRST_INTVAL_NEW_TOTAL_ATR+NO_OF_EQUAL_ATRVALS+2
                      MASDIR[FIRST,N] <-- 0;
            UNTIL OLD_DIFFER - NEW_DIFFER < 0;

END COMBINE_OR_REDISTRIBUTE_TWO_INTERVALS;

//*****************************************************************************************************************//

PROCEDURE FIT_ATTRIBUTES_INTO_CURENT_INTERVALS;

// THIS PROCEDURE IS TO FIT 'PROPER' NUMBER OF ATTRIBUTE VALUES INTO THE CURRENT INTERVAL OF MASTER DIRECTORY //

  POS_OF_1ST_ATR_CUR_INTVAL <-- POS_OF_LST_ATR_LST_INTVAL + 1;
  POS_OF_LST_ATR_CUR_INTVAL <-- POS_OF_LST_ATR_LST_INTVAL + EXPAND;
```

```
  IF POS_OF_LST_ATR_CUR_INTVAL > NR
    THEN POS_OF_LST_ATR_CUR_INTVAL <-- NR;

  MASDIR[CUR_INTVAL,1] <-- SORTED_ATR_LIST[POS_OF_1ST_ATR_CUR_INTVAL,2];
  MASDIR[CUR_INTVAL,2] <-- SORTED_ATR_LIST[POS_OF_LST_ATR_CUR_INTVAL,2];
  M <-- 2;
  FOR L <-- POS_OF_1ST_ATR_CUR_INTVAL TO POS_OF_LST_ATR_CUR_INTVAL
      M <-- M + 1;
      MASDIR[CUR_INTVAL,M] <-- SORTED_ATR_LIST[L,1];
  TOTAL_ATR_OF_INTVAL[CUR_INTVAL] <-- M - 2;
  CUR_INTVAL <-- CUR_INTVAL + 1;
END FIT_ATTRIBUTES_INTO_CURENT_INTERVALS;

//*************************************************************************************************************//

PROCEDURE SPLIT_ATTRIBUTES_INTO_TWO_INTERVALS;

// THIS PROCEDURE IS TO CHECK HOW MANY ATTRIBUTE VALUES CAN PUT IN CURRENT INTERVAL,
   LEAVE REST EQUAL VALUES AT BEGINNING OF NEXT INTERVAL *)

  DONE <-- FALSE;
  EXPAND <-- EXPAND - 1;
  TOTAL_ATR_OF_INTVAL[CUR_INTVAL] <-- TOTAL_ATR_OF_INTVAL[CUR_INTVAL] - 1;
  NO_OF_EQUAL_ATRVALS <-- 1;

  WHILE (SORTED_ATR_LIST[POS_OF_LST_ATR_LST_INTVAL+EXPAND,2] = SORTED_ATR_LIST[POS_OF_LST_ATR_LST_INTVAL+EXPAND+1,2])
    AND (DONE = FALSE)
      NO_OF_EQUAL_ATRVALS <-- NO_OF_EQUAL_ATRVALS + 1;
      TOTAL_ATR_OF_INTVAL[CUR_INTVAL] <-- TOTAL_ATR_OF_INTVAL[CUR_INTVAL] - 1;
      EXPAND <-- EXPAND - 1;
      IF EXPAND = 0
         THEN DONE <-- TRUE;     // CURRENT INTERVAL HAS TOO MANY ATTRIBUTE VALUES
                                    IF USER DOESN'T WANT PUT IN DIRECTORY, IT WILL BE EXHAUSTED //

  IF DONE = FALSE
    THEN  CALL FIT_ATTRIBUTES_INTO_CURENT_INTERVAL;
  CALL COMBINE_OR_REDISTRIBUTE_TWO_INTERVALS;

  IF NO_OF_EQUAL_ATRVALS > MAX_NRI  THEN
        PRINTLN('THE ATTRIBUTE VALUE ',HV:5,' OCCURS ',NO_OF_EQUAL_ATRVALS:3,' TIMES');
        PRINT(' YOU WANT THIS VALUE INCLUDED IN THE DIRECTORY (ENTER Y OR N) ? '); BREAK(); RESET();
        READ(USER_RESPONES);
        IF USER_RESPONES = 'Y'
          THEN
              EXPAND <-- NO_OF_EQUAL_ATRVALS;
              CALL FIT_ATTRIBUTES_INTO_CURENT_INTERVAL;
          ELSE
              POS_OF_LST_ATR_LST_INTVAL <-- NO_OF_EQUAL_ATRVALS + POS_OF_LST_ATR_LST_INTVAL;
              DELETED_INTVAL <-- CUR_INTVAL;
END SPLIT ATTRIBUTES_INTO_CURRENT_INTERVAL;

//*************************************************************************************************************//

PROCEDURE PROGRAM_MAKES_UNIFORM_INTERVALS;   //  OPTIONS 3 AND 4  //

// THIS PROCEDURE MAKES THE INTERVAL UNIFORM //

  // INTERACT WITH USER PROCESS, EITHER USER ENTER AVERAGE, MINIMUM OR MAXIMUM NUMBER OF RECORDS PER INTERVAL
     OR PROGRAM GENERATE THESE VALUES //

  PRINT('ENTER THE AVERAGE NUMBER OF RECORDS PER INTERVAL ?');
  READ(NRI);
  IF NRI <> 0
    THEN NI <-- NR DIV NRI
    ELSE
        NI <-- ROUND(SQRT(NR));
        NRI <-- NI;

  PRINT('ENTER THE MINIMUM NUMBER OF RECORDS PER INTERVAL ?');
  READ(MIN_NRI);
  IF MIN_NRI = 0 THEN
      MIN_NRI <-- NRI DIV 2;
      PRINTLN('THE PROGRAM GENERATES MINIMUM NUMBER OF RECORDS PER INTERVAL IS '.MIN NRI:4);
  PRINT('ENTER THE MAXIMUM NUMBER OF RECORDS PER INTERVAL ?');
  READ(MAX_NRI);
  IF (MAX_NRI = 0) OR (MAX_NRI < 2 * MIN_NRI) THEN
      IF MAX_NRI = 0
        THEN MAX_NRI <-- 2 * NRI
        ELSE MAX_NRI <-- 2 * MIN_NRI;
```

```
    PRINTLN('THE PROGRAM GENERATES MAXIMUM NUMBER OF RECORDS PER INTERVAL IS ',MAX_NRI:4);

  // INITIALIZE THE DESIRED NUMBER OF ATTRIBUTE VALUES PER INTERVAL //

  FOR I <-- 1 TO NI
    TOTAL_ATR_OF_INTVAL[I] <-- NRI;

  // INITIALIZE THE POSITION OF LAST ATTRIBUTE VALUE OF PREVIOUS INTERVAL TO ZERO TO START WITH //

  POS_OF_LST_ATR_LST_INTVAL <-- 0;
  CUR_INTVAL <-- 1;

  // THE PROCESS TO COMBINE THE ATTRIBUTE VALUES INTO INTERVALS WITH UNIFORM FREQUENCIES //

  WHILE POS_OF_LST_ATR_LST_INTVAL < NR
      EXPAND <-- NRI;

      // CHECK IF THE LAST ATTRIBUTE VALUE OF CURRENT INTERVAL IS EQUAL TO THE FIRST ATTRIBUTE VALUE OF NEXT INTERVAL //

      IF (SORTED_ATR_LIST[POS_OF_LST_ATR_LST_INTVAL+EXPAND,2] <> SORTED_ATR_LIST[POS_OF_LST_ATR_LST_INTVAL+EXPAND+1,2])
        OR (POS_OF_LST_ATR_LST_INTVAL + EXPAND > NR)
        THEN CALL FIT_ATTRIBUTES_INTO_CURENT_INTERVAL
        ELSE
          // COUNT HOW MANY EQUAL ATTIBUTE VALUES AT END OF CURRENT INTERVAL TOGETHER WITH BEGIN OF NEXT INTERVAL //

          WHILE SORTED_ATR_LIST[POS_OF_LST_ATR_LST_INTVAL+EXPAND,2] = SORTED_ATR_LIST[POS_OF_LST_ATR_LST_INTVAL+EXPAND+1,2]
              EXPAND <-- EXPAND + 1;
              TOTAL_ATR_OF_INTVAL[CUR_INTVAL] <-- TOTAL_ATR_OF_INTVAL[CUR_INTVAL] + 1;
          END WHILE LOOP
          HV <-- SORTED_ATR_LIST[POS_OF_LST_ATR_LST_INTVAL+EXPAND,2];

          // CHECK IF THE DESIRED NUMBER OF ATTRIBUTE VALUES PLUS THESE EQUAL VALUES CAN FIT IN THE CURRENT INTERVAL //

          IF TOTAL_ATR_OF_INTVAL[CUR_INTVAL] <= MAX_NRI
            THEN CALL FIT_ATTRIBUTES_INTO_CURENT_INTERVAL
            ELSE CALL SPLIT_ATTRIBUTES_INTO_TWO_INTERVALS;
  END WHILE LOOP

  // CHECK IF THE LAST INTERVAL NEEDS TO BE COMBINED OR REDISTRIBUTED WITH THE PREVIOUS INTERVAL //

  CALL COMBINE_OR_REDISTRIBUTE_TWO_INTERVALS;

END PROGRAM_MAKES_UNIFORM_INTERVALS

//************************************************************ MAIN  PROGRAM  **************************************************//

PROGRAM OPTIMAL_INVERTED_FILE;

  CALL GET_INPUT_FROM_PILE;    // GET INITIAL DIRECTORY //

  CALL SORT_ATTRIBUTE_VALUE;    // SORT INITIAL DIRECTORY //

  // THE PROCESS TO SELECT THE INTERVALS OF MASTER DIRECTORY FOR INVERTED FILE //

  WHILE USER_OPTION <> 5

      IF (USER_OPTION > 0) AND (USER_OPTION < 5)  THEN
          CASE  USER_OPTION  OF
            1 : CALL USER_CHOOSE_INTERVALS;
            2 : CALL PROGRAM_EQUALLY_DISTRIBUTE_INTERVALS;
            3 : CALL PROGRAM_MAKES_UNIFORM_INTERVALS;
            4 : CALL PROGRAM_MAKES_UNIFORM_INTERVALS;
          END CASE

          CALL PRINT_MASTER_DIRECTORY_TABLE;
  END WHILE LOOP
END OPTIMAL_INVERTED_FILE.
```

APPENDIX B

SORTED INITIAL FILE

Attribute	Record(s)	Number of Occurrences
100	204, 223, 325, 448, 457, 505	6
200	50, 202, 233, 358	4
300	131, 339, 360, 491, 583	5
400	47, 61	2
410	54, 69	2
430	157	1
450	442, 561	2
500	70, 159, 198, 234, 266, 371, 418, 558	8
700	10	1
900	41, 113	2
1000	4, 13, 15, 17, 40, 52, 53, 57, 71, 82, 87, 98, 119, 130, 141, 147, 152, 155, 165, 177, 180, 184, 189, 195, 210, 218, 228, 240, 257, 263, 268, 272, 282, 288, 314, 328, 333, 335, 361, 391, 397, 430, 431, 466, 471, 476, 521, 524, 527, 531, 535, 550, 559, 565, 567, 591	56
1200	43, 60, 64, 75, 83, 89, 185, 213, 269, 277, 286, 332, 345, 363, 383, 386, 409, 436, 462, 465, 467, 526, 537, 598, 599	25
1400	85, 410, 489, 563, 594	5
1500	169, 190, 246, 316, 367, 486, 584	7
1600	9, 27, 56, 68, 136, 256, 271, 299, 529	9
1700	162, 273, 308, 445, 447, 452, 556	7
1800	44, 395, 480, 500	4
1900	8, 32, 133, 137, 247, 279, 439, 483	8
2000	511, 597	2
2100	166, 377	2
2400	1, 29, 37, 42, 48, 51, 149, 158, 200, 248, 280, 283, 305, 311, 318, 366, 385, 388, 390, 449, 470, 473, 485, 503, 520, 533, 571, 582	28
2700	49, 146, 167, 217, 243, 276, 354, 424, 463, 546, 579, 592	12
2800	58, 203, 216, 502, 509	5
2900	3, 26, 65, 66, 81, 84, 91, 97, 116, 118, 123, 124, 140, 153, 173, 175, 258, 262, 275, 285, 289, 292, 293, 324, 344, 370, 380, 405, 429, 443, 446, 469, 479, 490, 493, 499, 501, 514, 515, 539, 555, 564, 577, 586, 590	45
3600	156, 249, 284, 290, 421, 435, 478, 487, 566	9
3700	73, 411, 516, 568	4
3800	115, 239, 310, 474, 519, 532, 585	7
3900	106, 201, 456, 562	4

Attribute	Record(s)	Number of Occurrences
4000	5, 23, 36, 55, 72, 100, 103, 120, 121, 139, 148, 163, 168, 183, 187, 188, 191, 205, 207, 208, 209, 211, 214, 220, 224, 229, 244, 250, 261, 287, 301, 302, 312, 326, 330, 341, 350, 353, 374, 376, 378, 382, 387, 392, 406, 408, 413, 420, 423, 426, 428, 441, 453, 458, 475, 518, 525, 554, 569, 572	60
4100	77, 227, 313, 315, 425, 507, 574	7
5000	35, 172, 178, 327, 337, 477, 570	7
5100	129, 151, 225, 232, 253, 551	6
5300	33, 76, 144, 221, 274, 359, 384, 536, 557	9
5500	86, 320, 407, 444, 450, 488, 549	7
5700	59, 296, 396, 495, 508, 512	6
5800	2, 18, 22, 24, 25, 63, 79, 88, 90, 92, 93, 99, 109, 114, 132, 142, 145, 150, 154, 160, 170, 186, 199, 245, 254, 260, 264, 267, 303, 306, 338, 348, 355, 356, 362, 369, 379, 381, 398, 401, 414, 419, 461, 468, 472, 484, 494, 506, 517, 575, 578, 589	52
6200	19, 28, 181, 193, 226, 304, 347, 399, 497, 553	10
6300	112, 194, 196, 230, 307, 547, 552	7
6500	12, 94, 111, 143, 176, 237, 281, 322, 329, 342, 389	11
6800	39, 122, 126, 174, 192, 206, 241, 278, 298, 346, 394, 417, 437	13
7100	30, 297, 403, 438, 451, 454, 455, 498	8
7400	20, 108, 127, 134, 219, 251, 522	7
7500	38, 62, 164, 309, 336, 523, 581, 600	8
7700	6, 161, 197, 492, 542	5
8400	45, 125, 135, 179, 182, 291, 295, 368, 400, 415, 432, 510, 543	13
8500	78, 265, 294, 340, 352, 530, 534, 548, 573	9
8600	7, 11, 14, 16, 46, 67, 80, 96, 102, 104, 105, 110, 128, 138, 171, 212, 215, 236, 238, 242, 252, 259, 300, 317, 319, 321, 331, 334, 343, 349, 364, 372, 393, 402, 404, 412, 427, 433, 434, 460, 482, 496, 504, 538, 540, 545, 560, 580, 587, 595	50
8700	34, 95, 107, 235, 373, 416, 440, 464, 596	9
8800	31, 117, 231, 357, 422, 459, 481	7
8900	21, 74, 222, 375, 513, 544, 588, 593	8
9600	101, 255, 270, 323, 351, 365, 528, 541, 576	9

```
APPENDIX C SAMPLE RUN USING OPTION 1

INVERTED FILE --- INTERVAL SELECTION PROCESS :
=============================================================
ENTER 1 --- YOU SPECIFY THE RANGE FOR EACH INTERVAL
ENTER 2 --- YOU SPECIFY THE TOTAL NUMBER OF EQUAL INTERVAL RANGES
ENTER 3 --- YOU SPECIFY THE DESIRED NUMBER OF RECORDS PER INTERVAL
ENTER 4 --- PROGRAM SELECT INTERVALS
ENTER 5 --- EXIT THE PROGRAM

ENTER OPTION HERE >>> 1

USER CHOOSE INTERVALS PROCESS :
###############################

INTERVAL NO.   1
================
ENTER THE  LOW ATTRIBUTE VALUE FOR THIS INTERVAL >> 100

ENTER THE HIGH ATTRIBUTE VALUE FOR THIS INTERVAL >> 1000

INTERVAL VALUES
LOW   -  HIGH      POINTERS TO PILE FILE                                                             # OF RECORDS
=====================================================================================================================
 100       1000
                    204  223  325  448  457  505   50  202  233  358  131  339  360  491  583   47   61   54   69  157
                    442  561   70  159  198  234  266  371  418  558   10   41  113    4   13   15   17   40   52   53
                     57   71   82   87   98  119  130  141  147  152  155  165  177  180  184  189  195  210  218  228
                    240  257  263  268  272  282  288  314  328  333  335  361  391  397  430  431  466  471  476  521
                    524  527  531  535  550  559  565  567  591
                                                                                                                   89
=====================================================================================================================
DO YOU WANT TO KEEP THIS INTERVAL IN MASTER DIRECTORY(ENTER Y OR N) ? Y

USER CHOOSE INTERVALS PROCESS :
###############################

INTERVAL NO.   2
================
ENTER THE  LOW ATTRIBUTE VALUE FOR THIS INTERVAL >> 1100

ENTER THE HIGH ATTRIBUTE VALUE FOR THIS INTERVAL >> 2000

INTERVAL VALUES
LOW   -  HIGH      POINTERS TO PILE FILE                                                             # OF RECORDS
=====================================================================================================================
 1100      2000
                     43   60   64   75   83   89  185  213  269  277  286  332  345  363  383  386  409  436  462  465
                    467  526  537  598  599   85  410  489  563  594  169  190  246  316  367  486  584    9   27   56
                     68  136  256  271  299  529  162  273  308  445  447  452  556   44  395  480  500    8   32  133
                    137  247  279  439  483  511  597
                                                                                                                   67
=====================================================================================================================
DO YOU WANT TO KEEP THIS INTERVAL IN MASTER DIRECTORY(ENTER Y OR N) ? Y

USER CHOOSE INTERVALS PROCESS :
###############################

INTERVAL NO.   3
================
ENTER THE  LOW ATTRIBUTE VALUE FOR THIS INTERVAL >> 2100

ENTER THE HIGH ATTRIBUTE VALUE FOR THIS INTERVAL >> 3500

INTERVAL VALUES
LOW   -  HIGH      POINTERS TO PILE FILE                                                             # OF RECORDS
=====================================================================================================================
 2100      3500
                    166  377    1   29   37   42   48   51  149  158  200  248  280  283  305  311  318  366  385  388
                    390  449  470  473  485  503  520  533  571  582   49  146  167  217  243  276  354  424  463  546
                    579  592   58  203  216  502  509    3   26   65   66   81   84   91   97  116  118  123  124  140
                    153  173  175  258  262  275  285  289  292  293  324  344  370  380  405  429  443  446  469  479
                    490  493  499  501  514  515  539  555  564  577  586  590
                                                                                                                   92
=====================================================================================================================
DO YOU WANT TO KEEP THIS INTERVAL IN MASTER DIRECTORY(ENTER Y OR N) ? Y
```

```
USER CHOOSE INTERVALS PROCESS :
#################################

INTERVAL NO.    4
=================
ENTER THE  LOW ATTRIBUTE VALUE FOR THIS INTERVAL >> 3600

ENTER THE HIGH ATTRIBUTE VALUE FOR THIS INTERVAL >> 5000

INTERVAL VALUES
LOW    -   HIGH      POINTERS TO PILE FILE                                                                   # OF RECORDS
==========================================================================================================================
 3600      5000
                     156  249  284  290  421  435  478  487  566   73  411  516  568  115  239  310  474  519  532  585
                     106  201  456  562    5   23   36   55   72  100  103  120  121  139  148  163  168  183  187  188
                     191  205  207  208  209  211  214  220  224  229  244  250  261  287  301  302  312  326  330  341
                     350  353  374  376  378  382  387  392  406  408  413  420  423  426  428  441  453  458  475  518
                     525  554  569  572   77  227  313  315  425  507  574   35  172  178  327  337  477  570
                                                                                                                    98
==========================================================================================================================
DO YOU WANT TO KEEP THIS INTERVAL IN MASTER DIRECTORY(ENTER Y OR N) ? Y

USER CHOOSE INTERVALS PROCESS :
#################################

INTERVAL NO.    5
=================
ENTER THE  LOW ATTRIBUTE VALUE FOR THIS INTERVAL >> 5100

ENTER THE HIGH ATTRIBUTE VALUE FOR THIS INTERVAL >> 6000

INTERVAL VALUES
LOW    -   HIGH      POINTERS TO PILE FILE                                                                   # OF RECORDS
==========================================================================================================================
 5100      6000
                     129  151  225  232  253  551   33   76  144  221  274  359  384  536  557   86  320  407  444  450
                     488  549   59  296  396  495  508  512    2   18   22   24   25   63   79   88   90   92   93   99
                     109  114  132  142  145  150  154  160  170  186  199  245  254  260  264  267  303  306  338  348
                     355  356  362  369  379  381  398  401  414  419  461  468  472  484  494  506  517  575  578  589
                                                                                                                    80
==========================================================================================================================

DO YOU WANT TO KEEP THIS INTERVAL IN MASTER DIRECTORY(ENTER Y OR N) ? Y

USER CHOOSE INTERVALS PROCESS :
#################################

INTERVAL NO.    6
=================
ENTER THE  LOW ATTRIBUTE VALUE FOR THIS INTERVAL >> 0

ENTER THE HIGH ATTRIBUTE VALUE FOR THIS INTERVAL >> 0
```

```
APPENDIX D Sample run using Option 2

INVERTED FILE --- INTERVAL SELECTION PROCESS :
=============================================================

ENTER 1 --- YOU SPECIFY THE RANGE FOR EACH INTERVAL
ENTER 2 --- YOU SPECIFY THE TOTAL NUMBER OF EQUAL INTERVAL RANGES
ENTER 3 --- YOU SPECIFY THE DESIRED NUMBER OF RECORDS PER INTERVAL
ENTER 4 --- PROGRAM SELECT INTERVALS
ENTER 5 --- EXIT THE PROGRAM

ENTER OPTION HERE >>> 2


PROGRAM EQUALLY DISTRIBUTE INTERVALS PROCESS :
###############################################

ENTER THE TOTAL NUMBER OF INTERVALS YOU WANT >> 10


                                   ***********************************************
                                   *     INVERTED FILE --- MASTER DIRECTORY      *
                                   ***********************************************

INTERVAL VALUES
LOW   -   HIGH     POINTERS TO PILE FILE                                                                              # OF RECORDS
==================================================================================================================================
  100     1000
                    204 223 325 448 457 505  50 202 233 358 131 339 360 491 583  47  61  54  69 157
                    442 561  70 159 198 234 266 371 418 558  10  41 113   4  13  15  17  40  52  53
                     57  71  82  87  98 119 130 141 147 152 155 165 177 180 184 189 195 210 218 228
                                                                                                                           60
----------------------------------------------------------------------------------------------------------------------------------
 1000     1500
                    240 257 263 268 272 282 288 314 328 333 335 361 391 397 430 431 466 471 476 521
                    524 527 531 535 550 559 565 567 591  43  60  64  75  83  89 185 213 269 277 286
                    332 345 363 383 386 409 436 462 465 467 526 537 598 599  85 410 489 563 594 169
                                                                                                                           60
----------------------------------------------------------------------------------------------------------------------------------
 1500     2400
                    190 246 316 367 486 584   9  27  56  68 136 256 271 299 529 162 273 308 445 447
                    452 556  44 395 480 500   8  32 133 137 247 279 439 483 511 597 166 377   1  29
                     37  42  48  51 149 158 200 248 280 283 305 311 318 366 385 388 390 449 470 473
                                                                                                                           60
----------------------------------------------------------------------------------------------------------------------------------
 2400     2900
                    485 503 520 533 571 582  49 146 167 217 243 276 354 424 463 546 579 592  58 203
                    216 502 509   3  26  65  66  81  84  91  97 116 118 123 124 140 153 173 175 258
                    262 275 285 289 292 293 324 344 370 380 405 429 443 446 469 479 490 493 499 501
                                                                                                                           60
----------------------------------------------------------------------------------------------------------------------------------
 2900     4000
                    514 515 539 555 564 577 586 590 156 249 284 290 421 435 478 487 566  73 411 516
                    568 115 239 310 474 519 532 585 106 201 456 562   5  23  36  55  72 100 103 120
                    121 139 148 163 168 183 187 188 191 205 207 208 209 211 214 220 224 229 244 250
                                                                                                                           60
----------------------------------------------------------------------------------------------------------------------------------
 4000     5300
                    261 287 301 302 312 326 330 341 350 353 374 376 378 382 387 392 406 408 413 420
                    423 426 428 441 453 458 475 518 525 554 569 572  77 227 313 315 425 507 574  35
                    172 178 327 337 477 570 129 151 225 232 253 551  33  76 144 221 274 359 384 536
                                                                                                                           60
----------------------------------------------------------------------------------------------------------------------------------
 5300     5800
                    557  86 320 407 444 450 488 549  59 296 396 495 508 512   2  18  22  24  25  63
                     79  88  90  92  93  99 109 114 132 142 145 150 154 160 170 186 199 245 254 260
                    264 267 303 306 338 348 355 356 362 369 379 381 398 401 414 419 461 468 472 484
                                                                                                                           60
----------------------------------------------------------------------------------------------------------------------------------
 5800     7400
                    494 506 517 575 578 589  19  28 181 193 226 304 347 399 497 553 112 194 196 230
                    307 547 552  12  94 111 143 176 237 281 322 329 342 389  39 122 126 174 192 206
                    241 278 298 346 394 417 437  30 297 403 438 451 454 455 498  20 108 127 134 219
                                                                                                                           60
----------------------------------------------------------------------------------------------------------------------------------
 7400     8600
                    251 522  38  62 164 309 336 523 581 600   6 161 197 492 542  45 125 135 179 182
                    291 295 368 400 415 432 510 543  78 265 294 340 352 530 534 548 573   7  11  14
                     16  46  67  80  96 102 104 105 110 128 138 171 212 215 236 238 242 252 259 300
                                                                                                                           60
----------------------------------------------------------------------------------------------------------------------------------
 8600     9600
                    317 319 321 331 334 343 349 364 372 393 402 404 412 427 433 434 460 482 496 504
                    538 540 545 560 580 587 595  34  95 107 235 373 416 440 464 596  31 117 231 357
                    422 459 481  21  74 222 375 513 544 588 593 101 255 270 323 351 365 528 541 576
                                                                                                                           60
----------------------------------------------------------------------------------------------------------------------------------
```

APPENDIX E Sample run using Option 3

```
INVERTED FILE --- INTERVAL SELECTION PROCESS :
=================================================================
ENTER 1 --- YOU SPECIFY THE RANGE FOR EACH INTERVAL
ENTER 2 --- YOU SPECIFY THE TOTAL NUMBER OF EQUAL INTERVAL RANGES
ENTER 3 --- YOU SPECIFY THE DESIRED NUMBER OF RECORDS PER INTERVAL
ENTER 4 --- PROGRAM SELECT INTERVALS
ENTER 5 --- EXIT THE PROGRAM

ENTER OPTION HERE >>> 3


PROGRAM MAKES UNIFORM INTERVALS PROCESS :
##########################################

ENTER THE AVERAGE NUMBER OF RECORDS PER INTERVAL ?ENTER 0, PROGRAM WILL USE THE SQUARE ROOT OF TOTAL NUMBER OF RECORDS  AS ITS VALUE

ENTER VALUE HERE >>> 20

------------------------------------------------------------------------------------------------------------------------------------

ENTER THE MINIMUM NUMBER OF RECORDS PER INTERVAL ?ENTER 0, PROGRAM WILL USE (0.5 * AVERAGE INTERVAL SIZE) THAT IS >> 10 AS ITS VALUE

ENTER VALUE HERE >>> 0

THE PROGRAM GENERATES MINIMUM NUMBER OF RECORDS PER INTERVAL IS   10
------------------------------------------------------------------------------------------------------------------------------------

ENTER THE MAXIMUM NUMBER OF RECORDS PER INTERVAL ?ENTER 0, PROGRAM WILL USE ( 2  * AVERAGE INTERVAL SIZE) THAT IS >> 40 AS ITS VALUE
ENTER VALUE NO LESS THAN (2 * MINIMUM INTERVAL SIZE), ELSE PROGRAM WILL USE ( 2  * MINIMUM INTERVAL SIZE) THAT IS >> 20 AS ITS VALUE

ENTER VALUE HERE >>> 0

THE PROGRAM GENERATES MAXIMUM NUMBER OF RECORDS PER INTERVAL IS   40
------------------------------------------------------------------------------------------------------------------------------------

THE ATTRIBUTE VALUE  1000 OCCURS  56 TIMES
DO YOU WANT THIS VALUE INCLUDED IN THE DIRECTORY (ENTER Y OR N) ? N

THE ATTRIBUTE VALUE  2900 OCCURS  45 TIMES
DO YOU WANT THIS VALUE INCLUDED IN THE DIRECTORY (ENTER Y OR N) ? Y

THE ATTRIBUTE VALUE  4000 OCCURS  60 TIMES
DO YOU WANT THIS VALUE INCLUDED IN THE DIRECTORY (ENTER Y OR N) ? N

THE ATTRIBUTE VALUE  5800 OCCURS  52 TIMES
DO YOU WANT THIS VALUE INCLUDED IN THE DIRECTORY (ENTER Y OR N) ? Y

THE ATTRIBUTE VALUE  8600 OCCURS  50 TIMES
DO YOU WANT THIS VALUE INCLUDED IN THE DIRECTORY (ENTER Y OR N) ? Y


                                              ************************************************
                                              *     INVERTED FILE --- MASTER DIRECTORY       *
                                              ************************************************

INTERVAL VALUES
LOW    -   HIGH     POINTERS TO PILE FILE                                                                             # OF RECORDS
====================================================================================================================================
  100        900
                      204  223  325  448  457  505   50  202  233  358  131  339  360  491  583   47   61   54   69  157
                      442  561   70  159  198  234  266  371  418  558   10   41  113
                                                                                                                                 33
------------------------------------------------------------------------------------------------------------------------------------
 1200       1200
                       43   60   64   75   83   89  185  213  269  277  286  332  345  363  383  386  409  436  462  465
                      467  526  537  598  599
                                                                                                                                 25
------------------------------------------------------------------------------------------------------------------------------------
 1400       1600
                       85  410  489  563  594  169  190  246  316  367  486  584    9   27   56   68  136  256  271  299
                      529
                                                                                                                                 21
------------------------------------------------------------------------------------------------------------------------------------
 1700       2000
                      162  273  308  445  447  452  556   44  395  480  500    8   32  133  137  247  279  439  483  511
                      597
                                                                                                                                 21
------------------------------------------------------------------------------------------------------------------------------------
 2100       2400
                      166  377    1   29   37   42   48   51  149  158  200  248  280  283  305  311  318  366  385  388
                      390  449  470  473  485  503  520  533  571  582
                                                                                                                                 30
```

2700	2800	49 146 167 217 243 276 354 424 463 546 579 592 58 203 216 502 509	17
2900	2900	3 26 65 66 81 84 91 97 116 118 123 124 140 153 173 175 258 262 275 285 289 292 293 324 344 370 380 405 429 443 446 469 479 490 493 499 501 514 515 539 555 564 577 586 590	45
3600	3900	156 249 284 290 421 435 478 487 566 73 411 516 568 115 239 310 474 519 532 585 106 201 456 562	24
4100	5100	77 227 313 315 425 507 574 35 172 178 327 337 477 570 129 151 225 232 253 551	20
5300	5700	33 76 144 221 274 359 384 536 557 86 320 407 444 450 488 549 59 296 396 495 508 512	22
5800	5800	2 18 22 24 25 63 79 88 90 92 93 99 109 114 132 142 145 150 154 160 170 186 199 245 254 260 264 267 303 306 338 348 355 356 362 369 379 381 398 401 414 419 461 468 472 484 494 506 517 575 578 589	52
6200	6500	19 28 181 193 226 304 347 399 497 553 112 194 196 230 307 547 552 12 94 111 143 176 237 281 322 329 342 389	28
6800	7100	39 122 126 174 192 206 241 278 298 346 394 417 437 30 297 403 438 451 454 455 498	21
7400	7700	20 108 127 134 219 251 522 38 62 164 309 336 523 581 600 6 161 197 492 542	20
8400	8500	45 125 135 179 182 291 295 368 400 415 432 510 543 78 265 294 340 352 530 534 548 573	22
8600	8600	7 11 14 16 46 67 80 96 102 104 105 110 128 138 171 212 215 236 238 242 252 259 300 317 319 321 331 334 343 349 364 372 393 402 404 412 427 433 434 460 482 496 504 538 540 545 560 580 587 595	50
8700	9600	34 95 107 235 373 416 440 464 596 31 117 231 357 422 459 481 21 74 222 375 513 544 588 593 101 255 270 323 351 365 528 541 576	33

APPENDIX F Sample run using Option 4

```
INVERTED FILE --- INTERVAL SELECTION PROCESS :
==================================================================
ENTER 1 --- YOU SPECIFY THE RANGE FOR EACH INTERVAL
ENTER 2 --- YOU SPECIFY THE TOTAL NUMBER OF EQUAL INTERVAL RANGES
ENTER 3 --- YOU SPECIFY THE DESIRED NUMBER OF RECORDS PER INTERVAL
ENTER 4 --- PROGRAM SELECT INTERVALS
ENTER 5 --- EXIT THE PROGRAM

ENTER OPTION HERE >>> 4


PROGRAM MAKES UNIFORM INTERVALS PROCESS :
##########################################

ENTER THE AVERAGE NUMBER OF RECORDS PER INTERVAL ?ENTER 0, PROGRAM WILL USE THE SQUARE ROOT OF TOTAL NUMBER OF RECORDS  AS ITS VALUE

ENTER VALUE HERE >>> 0

THE PROGRAM GENERATES AVERAGE NUMBER OF RECORDS PER INTERVAL IS   24
------------------------------------------------------------------------------------------------------------------------------------

ENTER THE MINIMUM NUMBER OF RECORDS PER INTERVAL ?ENTER 0, PROGRAM WILL USE (0.5 * AVERAGE INTERVAL SIZE) THAT IS >> 12 AS ITS VALUE

ENTER VALUE HERE >>> 0

THE PROGRAM GENERATES MINIMUM NUMBER OF RECORDS PER INTERVAL IS   12
------------------------------------------------------------------------------------------------------------------------------------

ENTER THE MAXIMUM NUMBER OF RECORDS PER INTERVAL ?ENTER 0, PROGRAM WILL USE ( 2  * AVERAGE INTERVAL SIZE) THAT IS >> 48 AS ITS VALUE
ENTER VALUE NO LESS THAN (2 * MINIMUM INTERVAL SIZE), ELSE PROGRAM WILL USE ( 2  * MINIMUM INTERVAL SIZE) THAT IS >> 24 AS ITS VALUE

ENTER VALUE HERE >>> 0

THE PROGRAM GENERATES MAXIMUM NUMBER OF RECORDS PER INTERVAL IS   48
------------------------------------------------------------------------------------------------------------------------------------

THE ATTRIBUTE VALUE  1000 OCCURS  56 TIMES
DO YOU WANT THIS VALUE INCLUDED IN THE DIRECTORY (ENTER Y OR N) ? Y

THE ATTRIBUTE VALUE  4000 OCCURS  60 TIMES
DO YOU WANT THIS VALUE INCLUDED IN THE DIRECTORY (ENTER Y OR N) ? N

THE ATTRIBUTE VALUE  5800 OCCURS  52 TIMES
DO YOU WANT THIS VALUE INCLUDED IN THE DIRECTORY (ENTER Y OR N) ? Y

THE ATTRIBUTE VALUE  8600 OCCURS  50 TIMES
DO YOU WANT THIS VALUE INCLUDED IN THE DIRECTORY (ENTER Y OR N) ? Y


                                    ***********************************************
                                    *     INVERTED FILE --- MASTER DIRECTORY     *
                                    ***********************************************

INTERVAL VALUES
LOW    -    HIGH     POINTERS TO PILE FILE                                                                            # OF RECORDS
====================================================================================================================================
  100      900
                     204  223  325  448  457  505   50  202  233  358  131  339  360  491  583   47   61   54   69  157
                     442  561   70  159  198  234  266  371  418  558   10   41  113
                                                                                                                               33
------------------------------------------------------------------------------------------------------------------------------------
 1000     1000
                       4   13   15   17   40   52   53   57   71   82   87   98  119  130  141  147  152  155  165  177
                     180  184  189  195  210  218  228  240  257  263  268  272  282  288  314  328  333  335  361  391
                     397  430  431  466  471  476  521  524  527  531  535  550  559  565  567  591
                                                                                                                               56
------------------------------------------------------------------------------------------------------------------------------------
 1200     1200
                      43   60   64   75   83   89  185  213  269  277  286  332  345  363  383  386  409  436  462  465
                     467  526  537  598  599
                                                                                                                               25
------------------------------------------------------------------------------------------------------------------------------------
 1400     1700
                      85  410  489  563  594  169  190  246  316  367  486  584    9   27   56   68  136  256  271  299
                     529  162  273  308  445  447  452  556
                                                                                                                               28
------------------------------------------------------------------------------------------------------------------------------------
 1800     2400
                      44  395  480  500    8   32  133  137  247  279  439  483  511  597  166  377    1   29   37   42
                      48   51  149  158  200  248  280  283  305  311  318  366  385  388  390  449  470  473  485  503
                     520  533  571  582
                                                                                                                               44
```

2700	2800	49 146 167 217 243 276 354 424 463 546 579 592 58 203 216 502 509	17
2900	2900	3 26 65 66 81 84 91 97 116 118 123 124 140 153 173 175 258 262 275 285 289 292 293 324 344 370 380 405 429 443 446 469 479 490 493 499 501 514 515 539 555 564 577 586 590	45
3600	3900	156 249 284 290 421 435 478 487 566 73 411 516 568 115 239 310 474 519 532 585 106 201 456 562	24
4100	5700	77 227 313 315 425 507 574 35 172 178 327 337 477 570 129 151 225 232 253 551 33 76 144 221 274 359 384 536 557 86 320 407 444 450 488 549 59 296 396 495 508 512	42
5800	5800	2 18 22 24 25 63 79 88 90 92 93 99 109 114 132 142 145 150 154 160 170 186 199 245 254 260 264 267 303 306 338 348 355 356 362 369 379 381 398 401 414 419 461 468 472 484 494 506 517 575 578 589	52
6200	6500	19 28 181 193 226 304 347 399 497 553 112 194 196 230 307 547 552 12 94 111 143 176 237 281 322 329 342 389	28
6800	7400	39 122 126 174 192 206 241 278 298 346 394 417 437 30 297 403 438 451 454 455 498 20 108 127 134 219 251 522	28
7500	8500	38 62 164 309 336 523 581 600 6 161 197 492 542 45 125 135 179 182 291 295 368 400 415 432 510 543 78 265 294 340 352 530 534 548 573	35
8600	8600	7 11 14 16 46 67 80 96 102 104 105 110 128 138 171 212 215 236 238 242 252 259 300 317 319 321 331 334 343 349 364 372 393 402 404 412 427 433 434 460 482 496 504 538 540 545 560 580 587 595	50
8700	9600	34 95 107 235 373 416 440 464 596 31 117 231 357 422 459 481 21 74 222 375 513 544 588 593 101 255 270 323 351 365 528 541 576	33

A generalized method for maintaining views

by KATHRYN C. KINSLEY
Datawise, Inc.
Orlando, Florida
and
JAMES R. DRISCOLL
University of Central Florida
Orlando, Florida

ABSTRACT

A generalized method for maintaining views, which takes into account each view's pattern of usage, is described. This method involves storing views in both actual and potential forms. When views exist in actual form (concrete views), updates are deferred until the view is queried. Differential files are formed from tuples inserted and deleted from the defining relations. These differential files are then used in conjunction with specified update schemes to update the view. Views alternate between actual and potential form based on their usage and the storage replacement algorithm.

INTRODUCTION

In 1971 the CODASYL Data Base Task Group defined derived data as data derived procedurally from related data items instead of being explicitly stored and directly retrieved.[1] The relational model, introduced by Codd,[2] extended this concept by introducing views. A view is defined from existing relations and reflects updates made to its defining relations. In other words, it is a "dynamic window" of the database in that when an update is made to any one of its defining relations, the derived relation is automatically updated in accordance with its definition. Views have been used to support users' views, integrity constraints,[3–5] and access control.[6]

There are two basic approaches to the support of views—the potential-form and the actual-form methods. Implementation using potential form involves describing the view so that it can be generated when needed. This description could use access paths or a formula of the view. The view is constructed each time it is involved in a query. Implementation using the actual-form approach involves physically storing each view. Therefore, the relation "actually" exists. Any updates made to the defining relation must be explicitly reflected in the view. Such views are called concrete views.

Although Kim[7] states that the potential method supporting views is better for most applications, performance analysis of both methods using an analytical model has shown that neither method is consistently superior. Instead, performance is highly dependent on patterns of usage.[8] It was found that the potential method is particularly vulnerable when the view is accessed often and if the calculation involves a large number of tuples. The actual-form method performed poorly when it was expected to maintain in actual form a large number of views that were seldom accessed.

The purpose of this paper is to describe a generalized method for supporting views. This method involves storing views in both actual and potential form according to patterns of usage. Specific update schemes are presented for maintaining views in their concrete state. This method controls use of storage by maintaining only those views accessed often in actual form. We will discuss the algorithm for maintaining views in actual form, and a generalized implementation technique, which supports views in both actual and potential form. Finally, we will examine some advantages of the implementation technique.

SUPPORTING VIEWS IN ACTUAL FORM

An implementation technique using actual results has been presented that makes use of set operations in developing update schemes.[9,10] These schemes are shown in Figure 1 and indicate that, in all but one case, relational operations can be used to update a concrete view whenever a defining relation is updated. The exception to this is reflecting a deletion update to a defining relation into a concrete view formed by a projection. It is implicit that checkpoints within each scheme abort the update process if the update to the defining relation will not affect the concrete view. The principle upon which these update schemes were developed is as follows.

The procedure for inserting a tuple into a relation involves one relation and one tuple; however, inserting a tuple into a relation can be represented as the union of the relation to be updated and the relation formed from the tuple to be inserted.[11] For instance, if relation B were to be updated by inserting a tuple contained in relation I, the update could be represented as BUI, where the relation formed by BUI would be the updated B and would replace the "old" B.

Now assume X is a view formed by A ∩ B. If relation B were updated by the insertion tuple that forms relation I, then X can be updated implicitly by creating A ∩ (BUI), where BUI is the updated B, and A ∩ (BUI) is the updated X. However, the expression A ∩ (BUI) is equivalent to (A ∩ B)U(A ∩ I). Therefore, XU(A ∩ I) is the updated X. Using this approach, a scheme has been developed for insertion of a tuple into a view under each operation. These

	Definition of X	Operation	Insertion Update
1.	AUB	union	XUI
2.	A ∩ B	intersection	XU(A ∩ I)
3.	B–A	difference	XU(I–A)
4.	A–B	difference	X–I
5.	B(list)	projection	XUI(list)
6.	B(qual)	selection	XUI(qual)
7.	A*B	join	XU(A*I)

(a) Insertion Updates for Views

	Definition of X	Operation	Deletion Update
1.	AUB	union	X–(D–A)
2.	A ∩ B	intersection	X–D
3.	B–A	difference	X–D
4.	A–B	difference	XU(A ∩ D)
5.	B(list)	projection	X = (B–D) (list)
6.	B(qual)	selection	X–D
7.	A*B	join	X–(A*D)

(b) Deletion Updates for Views

Figure 1—Updates schemes for views using actual results method. View X is defined by relation B (and, if needed, A). Relation B has been updated. Relation I holds the tuple inserted in relation B. Relation D holds the tuple deleted from relation B. Join refers to natural join on a key.

insertion schemes are shown in Figure 1a. Each scheme takes advantage of the fact that X physically exists in its actual form.

The operation of deleting a tuple from a relation can be represented as the relative complement of the relation to be updated and a relation formed from the tuple to be deleted. For instance, if relation B were to be updated by deleting the tuple contained in relation D, the update could be represented as $B - D$, where the relation formed by $B - D$ would be the updated B.

Now assume X is a view formed by $A \cup B$. If relation B were updated by the deletion tuple that forms relation D, then X can be updated by creating $A \cup (B - D)$ where $B - D$ is the updated B and $A \cup (B - D)$ is the updated X. However, the expression $A \cup (B - D)$ is equivalent to $(A \cup B) - (D - A)$. Therefore, $X - (D - A)$ is the updated X. Using this approach, a scheme has been developed for deletion of a tuple from a view under every operation, except projection. As before, each deletion scheme takes advantage of the fact that X physically exists in its actual form.

Modifying an existing tuple can be implemented as a deletion followed by an insertion. Therefore, all tuple update operations—insertion, deletion, and modification—can be represented by using the insertion and deletion update methods just mentioned. An insertion update table (I) and a deletion update table (D) must exist for each relation used to define a view.

The algorithm presented in Figure 2 defers updates until the specific view is queried. Updates are collected in differential files[12] according to the algorithm and the update schemes of Figure 1 are used to update the view. In this case, differential files I and D may hold more than one tuple. Also, the algorithm may reduce the total number of tuples involved in the actual update due to a culling process, which is carried out when update tuples are added to the differential files. The same tuple used in more than one update is reduced to only the last update before the database is accessed. Proof of the algorithm can be found in a more detailed document.

A summary of the procedure is as follows: As updates occur to defining relations, those updates are placed in the relations' differential files with an indication as to the update type. When a concrete view is queried, the following occurs:

1. One of the defining relations' differential files is referenced.
2. Consecutive tuples of the same update type are pulled off the differential file in the order they were placed on it, put into the corresponding update table I or D, and the appropriate update scheme of Figure 1 is invoked for each group.
3. When the end of the differential file is reached, the pointer to this differential file is changed to reference the end of the file. The next defining relation's differential file is then referenced and the process is repeated. If no other defining relation is used to define the view, the concrete view is now in updated form and the query can be answered.

As an example, suppose that X is defined as AUB and appears as below.

A NO	A LT	B NO	B LT	X NO	X LT
1	a	2	b	1	a
2	b	3	c	2	b
3	c	5	e	3	c
4	d	6	f	4	d
				5	e
				6	f

Now assume that entries have been made into the database transaction file as shown in Figure 3. Note that the two entries

INPUT. A concrete view

OUTPUT. A concrete view in updated form

METHOD. This procedure updates the view whenever the view is retrieved. Until that time, update tuples are collected in a differential file. A check is made if the tuple has been previously entered into the defining relation's update tables. If it has, and the transaction types are the same (i.e., insertion or deletion), no action occurs. If the transaction types do not match, the tuple is deleted from that update table and inserted into the update table that matches its transaction type. If the type is not in the defining relation's update tables, it is inserted into the corresponding update table. When all tuples have been checked, the update schemes of Figure 1 are invoked, using the I and D tables.

```
PROCEDURE MAINTAIN-ACTUAL (concrete view)
BEGIN
  FOR all tuples used to update the defining relation DO
    IF tuple already a member of defining relation's update file
       THEN
    IF update file type is same as tuple type THEN no action
    ELSE
       BEGIN
         delete tuple from update file;
         insert tuple into update file with its type
       END
    ELSE (*TUPLE IS NOT IN UPDATE FILES*)
       insert tuple into update file with its type
  END; (* END OF BUILDING I AND D TABLES *)
  apply update schemes of Figure 1 to concrete view
  END; (*MAINTAIN-ACTUAL*)
```

Figure 2—Algorithm for maintaining views in actual form

TUPLE	RELATION	UPDATE TYPE	TIME	USER
<2 b>	A	deleted	1000	1111
<3 c>	A	deleted	1001	1111
<3 h>	A	inserted	1001	1111
.	.	.	.	.
<3 c>	B	inserted	1005	1112
.	.	.	.	.
.	.	.	.	.
<5 e>	A	inserted	1010	1111
.	.	.	.	.
.	.	.	.	.
<5 e>	B	deleted	1015	1112
.	.	.	.	.
.	.	.	.	.
<1 a>	B	deleted	1020	1111
<3 c>	B	deleted	1021	1111
<6 f>	B	deleted	1022	1111

Figure 3—An example transaction file for relations A and B

IA

NO	LT
3	h
5	e

DA

NO	LT
2	b
3	c

DB

NO	LT
5	e
1	a
3	c
6	f

A

NO	LT
1	a
3	h
4	d
5	e

B

NO	LT
2	b

X

NO	LT
1	a
2	b
3	h
4	d
5	e

Figure 4—Relations A and B, their associated differential files, and the updated X, resulting from applying the Actual Update Algorithm of Figure 2

at time 1001 constitute a tuple modification. A tuple modification is implemented by a deletion followed by an insertion. The reader should note that tuple <3 c> is inserted into B at time 1005; however, <3 c> already exists in relation B. In actual situations, this can occur and thus is handled with this method. The resulting deletion and insertion tables are shown in Figure 4.

GENERALIZED METHOD

The use of differential files as discussed in the previous section supports concrete views. In the introduction, it was pointed out that both potential results and actual results have advantageous features. This section describes a generalized implementation method that uses both potential and actual results.

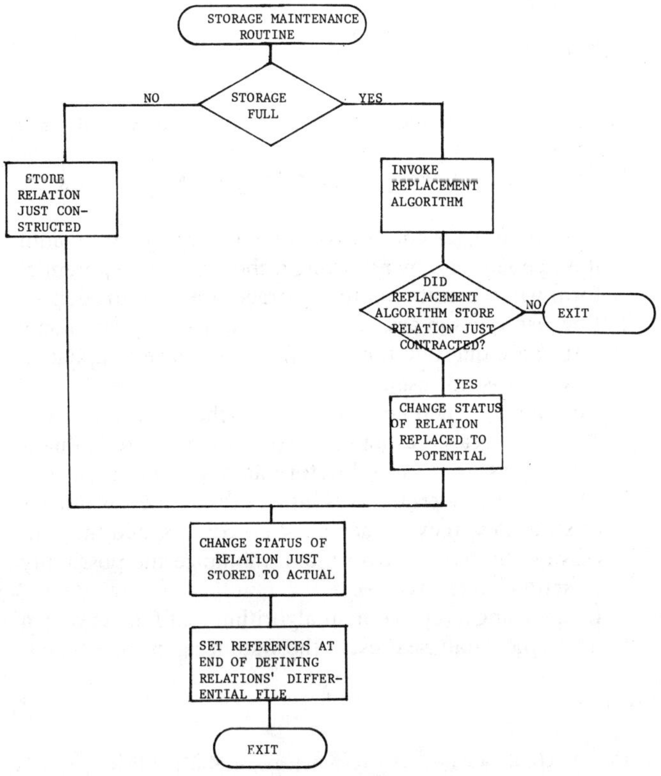

Figure 5—General flow for maintaining use of storage

In this method, each defining relation has a differential file, into which go all tuples inserted and deleted. When a view is first defined, it exists in potential form; i.e., the formula is stored, but the relation itself is not. The view exists in potential form until it is first queried. Until that time, updates to its defining relations need no other action involving the view. These updates will be automatically reflected when the view is calculated.

When a query is issued concerning a view in potential form, the relation is formed according to its formula, presented to the user, and actually stored—if storage space permits. Its status is then changed to actual. If no storage space exists, a replacement algorithm is invoked. If the replacement algorithm does not store the newly constructed relation, the relation remains in potential form and its construction is lost. If the replacement algorithm stores the newly constructed relation, the relation is now in actual form and the view it replaced returns to potential form. Both of these status changes must be recorded.

When a view is stored, a reference to each of its defining relations' differential files must be stored. This reference points to the end of the differential file. This is because update tuples entered prior to the creation of the concrete view were already reflected into the relation when it was created. The general flow of this storage maintenance is illustrated in Figure 5. Once a view actually exists, all tuples inserted or deleted from the defining relation must be explicitly reflected into the concrete view. It is maintained according to the algorithm in Figure 2 and the update schemes of Figure 1.

To illustrate, we will trace a view through the technique. Let X be a view formed by AUB. When the definition of X is entered, the formula AUB is stored and X has a status of "potential form." As long as X remains in potential form, updates to A or B need not be reflected into X. This will be done automatically when X is constructed. As updates occur to A or B, the tuples and their update types are entered into the respective relation's differential file. This is done to support other concrete views defined by A or B.

Now assume X is queried. Because it currently exists in potential form, it is constructed from its formula. The query is completed and storage space is checked. We will assume that storage space exists and X is stored. The status of relation

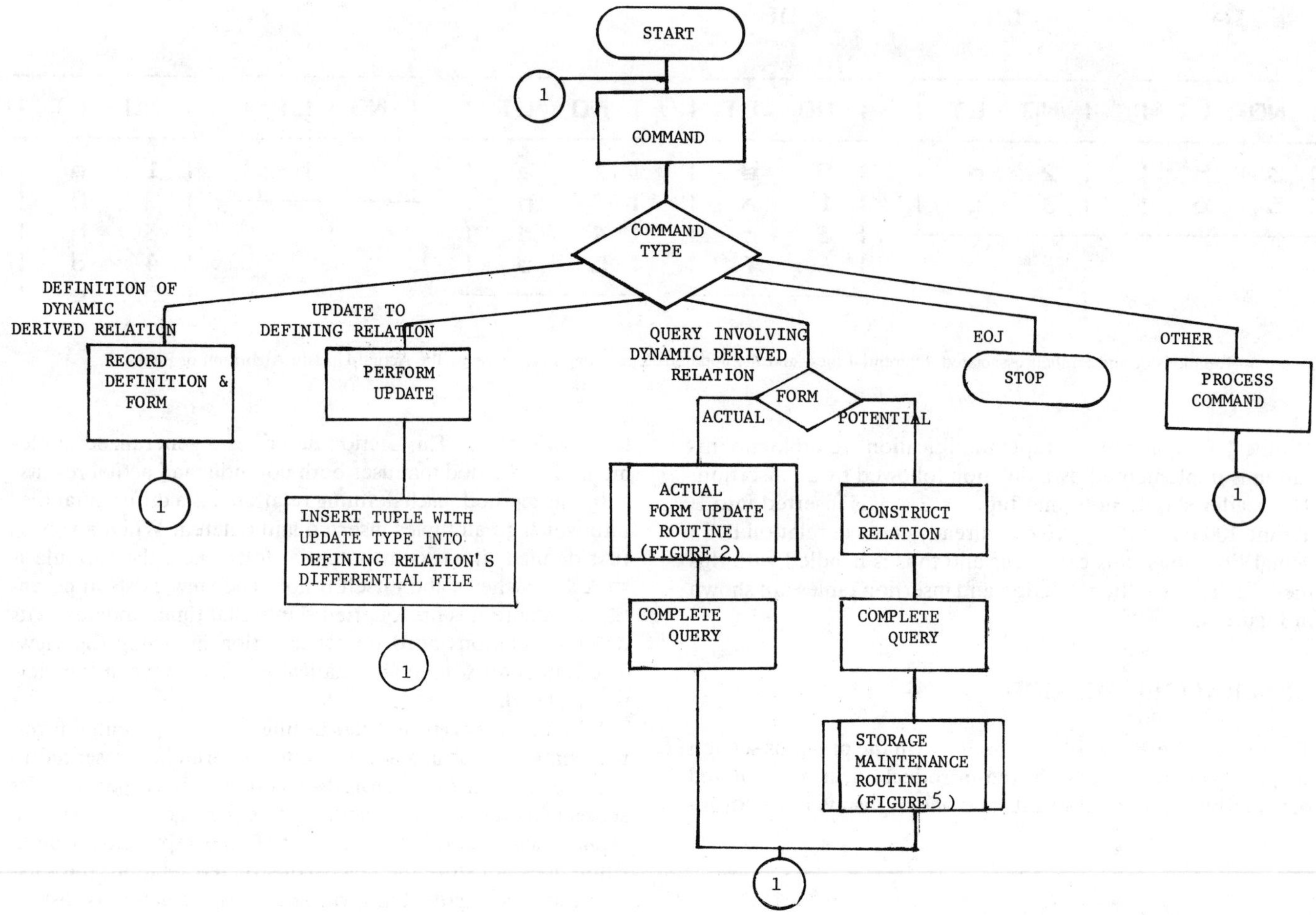

Figure 6—Flowchart of the generalized method

X is changed to actual and references are set to the end of each of X's defining relations' differential files.

When X is again queried, because it currently exists in actual form, all updates made to relations A and B after X was constructed must be reflected into X. This is done by the algorithm presented in Figure 2. As long as X exists in actual form, this method must be repeated whenever X is queried.

View X may return to potential form if it is deleted by the replacement algorithm. When this occurs, the status of X is changed to potential and X again is defined only in terms of its formula. A flowchart of this generalized method is shown in Figure 6.

CONCLUSION

A generalized method for implementing views has been described. This method involves storing dynamic derived relations in both actual and potential form. A view exists in potential form when it is defined and until it is queried. Once a query involving a view is issued by the user, it is constructed and actually stored if room exists in storage. When a view exists in actual form, updates to its defining relations are reflected immediately using the update schemes in Figure 1. The view may, at any time, return to its potential form according to storage needs, thus system requirements are accommodated.

The major advantages of this technique are as follows:

1. Storage usage is controlled. By not forming a view until it is needed, and by returning a chosen view to potential form when memory is full, storage use is controlled.
2. Because views in actual form are explicitly updated only if they are queried, the system will not have to update a view that is not used.
3. The number of times the update schemes are invoked can be decreased using the algorithm in Figure 2; duplicate tuples are reduced before accessing the database.
4. The use of differential files introduces all the advantages of such files; they reduce back-up costs, speed the process of database recovery, and minimize the possibility of serious data loss.
5. By choosing a replacement algorithm that fits the way in which the database is used, the system can be fine-tuned.

REFERENCES

1. CODASYL. Data Base Task Group Report, ACM, April 1971.
2. Codd, E. F. "A Relational Model of Data for Large Shared Data Banks." *Communications of the ACM,* 13 (1970), pp. 377–387.

3. Stonebraker, M. "Implementation of Integrity Constraints and Views—Query Modification." *Proceedings of 1975 SIGMOD Conference.* New York: ACM, 1975, pp. 65–78.
4. Bernstein, P. A., and B. T. Blaustein. "A Simplification Algorithm for Integrity Assertions and Concrete Views." *Proceedings of 5th Computer Software and Applications Conference.* New York: ACM, 1981, pp. 90–99.
5. Bernstein, P. A., and B. T. Blaustein. "Fast Methods for Testing Quantified Relational Calculus Assertions." *Proceedings, International Conference on Management of Data.* New York: ACM, 1982, pp. 39–50.
6. Eswaran, K. P., and D. D. Chamberlin. "Functional Specification of a Subsystem for Database Integrity." *Proceedings, Very Large Data Bases.* New York: ACM, 1975, pp. 624–633.
7. Kim, W. "Relational Database Systems." *ACM Computing Surveys,* 11 (1979), pp. 185–210.
8. Kinsley, K. Ph.D. dissertation, University of Central Florida, Orlando, Fla., 1983.
9. Kinsley, K., and J. Driscoll. "Dynamic Derived Relations Within the RAQUEL II DBMS." *Proceedings of ACM '79.* New York: ACM, 1979, pp. 69–80.
10. Kinsley, K. and J. Driscoll. "Efficiently Maintaining Dynamic Derived Relations in Actual Form." Technical Report CS-TR-48, Department of Computer Science, University of Central Florida, Orlando, Fla., 1980.
11. Date, C. J. *An Introduction to Database Systems,* (3rd ed.). Reading, Mass.: Addison-Wesley, 1979.
12. Severance, D. G. "Differential Files: Their Application to the Maintenance of Large Databases." *ACM Transactions on Database Systems* 1 (1976), pp. 256–267.

The representation of debate as a basis for information storage and retrieval

by DAVID LOWE
Stanford University
Stanford, California

ABSTRACT

Interactive computer networks offer the potential for creating a body of information on any given topic that combines the best available contributions from a large number of users. This paper describes a system for cooperatively structuring and evaluating information through well-specified interactions by many users with a common database. At the heart of the system is a structured representation for debate, in which conclusions are explicitly justified or negated by individual items of evidence. Through debates on the accuracy of information and on aspects of the structures themselves, a large number of users can rank cooperatively all available items of information in terms of significance and relevance to each topic. Individual users can then choose the depth to which they wish to examine these structures for the purposes at hand. The function of the debate is not to arrive at specific conclusions, but rather to collect and order the best available evidence on each topic. This use of an interactive system for structuring information offers many further opportunities for improving the accuracy, currency, and accessibility of information.

INTRODUCTION

There are currently more than 60,000 scientific journals being published regularly, as well as numerous conference proceedings, books, and technical reports. Frequently cited problems with these current methods of distribution include literature scatter, publication delays, rising costs, and inaccessibility. It would probably even now be economically advantageous to replace this paper-based distribution of scientific literature with electronic distribution through computer networks,[1,2] and the economic advantage will continue to improve with rapidly falling computer and telecommunications costs. Electronic distribution also would provide important advantages in speed, flexibility, and retrieval capabilities.[3–5] In particular, this paper will present new methods for structuring and retrieving information in interactive computer networks that could not be implemented within a paper-based medium.

Except for narrow specialties, within which a research can continuously monitor all the relevant journals and conferences, the sheer volume of the literature makes it very difficult to locate the most useful references on a given topic. There are a number of large bibliographic retrieval systems in operation that allow a user to search for references with combinations of subject keywords,[6,7] but there are inadequacies in the use of keywords that make these systems unreliable or difficult to use. For example, many English words have ambiguous or multiple meanings and therefore may not precisely specify a subject topic. In addition, these systems make no attempt to evaluate documents on the basis of accuracy, clarity, or other subjective criteria, although these criteria are of major importance in selecting documents for use. The use of keywords to index documents is historically an outgrowth of the use of subject headings in library card catalogues, but there have been a number of more recent attempts to design new indexing facilities that make greater use of the computer's capabilities. In particular, there has been considerable interest in generalized methods for linking and referring to sections of text, as in the Xanadu system.[8] However, the basis for these linked-text systems is still the individually authored document —a restriction that the system described in this paper attempts to overcome.

Computers offer capabilities that would be almost impossible to provide through the traditional use of the printing press and the distribution of paper documents. Computers allow large numbers of people to interactively examine and modify a common body of information, and they allow information to be structured far more flexibly than is possible within the linear order imposed by paper. These capabilities will be exploited in this paper to describe the design of a form of scientific communication very different from those currently available. Rather than creating independent, individually authored documents which are then indexed and filed by editors and librarians, this new information resource would be created and rearranged interactively by the users themselves and would allow their many contributions and opinions to be examined as one unified structure.

At a first level, a goal of this new medium is to allow many users to create a structured description for each field of study, within which documents can be referenced and evaluated according to the roles they play in that field. In this way the system would act as an up-to-date, extremely detailed textbook or survey article, evaluating and ranking documents according to their relationship to each topic within a field of study. However, another more radical goal of this medium is to combine the *content* of many contributions on any given topic into a single structure. Each item of information would be broken down into individual concepts, and a well-specified set of user interactions with the system would select the best ordering and relationships between these concepts. By removing the redundancy of many individual contributions and representing each concept only once, the sheer quantity of information can be greatly reduced. By allowing many researchers to examine and suggest modifications to each structure, the accuracy, currency, and clarity of each presentation is likely to be much better than is possible with documents written by single authors.

The key development allowing many individuals to combine their thoughts and opinions on a topic is a representation for debate and for the multiple viewpoints that can arise about any issue. The representation for debate described below requires each person to indicate explicit reasons for a given opinion, so that argument over a conclusion is transferred as much as possible to argument over the various sources of evidence. The purpose of debate is not to choose one answer to the exclusion of others, but rather to collect and order the presentation of evidence and summarize concisely the range of opinion. Although a voting procedure is used to select the best candidates for initial presentation on any given topic, all contributions are retained and can be accessed if a topic is examined in sufficient depth. The explicit representation of debate allows many subjective matters—such as the significance of a topic or contribution—to be addressed, whereas it might not be politically acceptable to make these judgements in an information system created by a few individuals.

THE SYSTEM IN OPERATION

A version of this proposed information system has been implemented as a computer program and used for a number of experiments. The system has been named SYNVIEW to indicate its goal of combining multiple viewpoints into a single

```
{A}  Overview:  Information retrieval methods for access to document
       collections
{B}      Keyword-based methods                                     [3,3]
{C}          Use of Boolean combinations of keywords for retrieval    [3,1]
               specification
{D}          Evaluation of keyword-based retrieval systems currently  [2,2]
               in operation
{E}          Keyword-based systems require a controlled vocabulary    [1,2]
               for accurate recall
{F}          Automatic generation of subject keywords from documents  [1,1]
{G}      Methods based on structural descriptions of document      [2,4]
           contents
{H}          Synstructuring of subject areas                          [6,4]
{I}          Hierarchical representations of subject areas            [3,2]
{J}      Methods based on natural language understanding           [1,3]
{K}          Current capabilities of natural language understanding   [5,1]
               systems
{L}          Research on the use of natural language understanding    [2,2]
               for information retrieval
{M}          Predictions of future natural language capabilities of   [2,1]
               computers
{N}      More...                                                   [1,1]
{O} Alternates [2,1]; {P} Search index; {Q} Back up; {R} Modify
```

Figure 1—The above display is shown to the user after a request for information on a specific topic such as "information retrieval." It presents an overview of the topic in familiar outline form. By typing the letters shown in braces (e.g., {B}), a user can examine any part of the structure in more detail or suggest modifications. For example, typing the letter "E" results in the display shown in Figure 2

structure. Several examples of its use will be presented to give the reader a feel for the representation before we embark on more theoretical issues.

Figure 1 gives an example of the first display shown when a user asks for information on "information retrieval" (we will describe later how this request is made). This display presents an overview of the topic in familiar outline form—the subtopics and sub-subtopics correspond roughly to what might be chapter and section headings in a textbook on the lead topic. However, the topics are ranked strictly in order of decreasing "importance," in the sense of which topics are the most important to know for a general understanding of the lead topic, rather than by any of the other criteria that are often used in writing. The first number in brackets to the right of each subtopic gives its rated importance with respect to the next highest level, and the second number is an indication of the range of disagreement in assigning the first number. The letters in braces at the begining of each line (e.g., {A}) are menu-selection terms—by typing a given letter the user can descend in the hierarchy of topics to examine any subtopic in more detail. SYNVIEW does not display all topics at one level before displaying any topics at the next level; rather, the display is balanced so that the cutoff in importance is at a constant value with respect to the head topic. In order to see more of the top-level topics, the user can select the line labeled "More . . ."

The creation and modification of these information structures is based on the input of many individuals. Given the display shown in Figure 1, a user can suggest modifications or additions along any of a number of dimensions. At the simplest level, a user can give an opinion on the importance of a subtopic; all votes will be averaged in determining the ordering of the subtopics. If the user disagrees with the wording used for some topic, a different wording may be suggested. The choice between alternative wordings then becomes a topic for debate (as described below), with different users entering and voting on reasons as to why one wording is superior to another. Any user can also add new subtopics below any topic, although they may be ranked far down on the list if others judge them to be unimportant or irrelevant. When suggesting a new wording for a topic, it is possible to create an entirely new set of subtopics and thereby completely redesign the organization of a presentation. The choice between these alternative organizations also becomes a topic for debate.

The overview shown in Figure 1 is useful for listing all the

```
{A} Keyword-based information retrieval systems require a        [5,3]
      controlled vocabulary for accurate retrieval
{B}      Most English words have imprecise or multiple            [6,2] ↑[4,2]
           meanings
{C}      A controlled vocabulary is needed for precoordination    [6,4] ↑[4,3]
           of index terms
{D}      There are usually many approximately synonymous words    [8,2] ↑[1,2]
           for any given topic
{E}      However: Within small specialized technical domains      [2,2] ↑[-1,2]
           the natural vocabulary may have adequate precision
{F}      All large commercial bibliographic retrieval systems     [4,1] ↑[1,1]
           have chosen to use a controlled vocabulary
{G}      Can accurate retrieval be achieved through               [-1,4] ↑[4,3]
           statistical operations on ambiguous keywords?
{H}      More...                                                  [0,1]
{I} Alternates [3,2]; {J} Search index; {K} Back up; {L} Modify
```

Figure 2—This display is an example of the top-level structure of debate. The line labeled {A} is the assertion or question for which the following lines are items of evidence in decreasing order of importance. Each item of evidence can be individually selected to examine its own support or to debate the relationship between the evidence and the assertion. For example, selecting {B} produces the display shown in Figure 5. Selecting the top line (i.e., {A}) produces introductory information on the topic as shown in Figure 6

relevant subtopics for some field of study. However, a type of structure much more central to this medium of communication is the representation of debate. Most of the items shown in Figure 1 are noun phrases naming general topics of discussion. However, the line labeled {E} is a declarative sentence, signaling the start of a structured debate. In such a debate, all subtopics are further statements giving specific items of evidence in support of or against the topic of the debate. Figure 2 shows the display that is presented when the user selects the item {E}. Each item of evidence can be questioned in two different ways: The evidene itself may be judged true or false to varying degrees, and the implication of the original assertion may or may not follow from the truth of the evidence (the two sets of numbers to the right of each line of evidence refer respectively to these judgements). Of course, each item of evidence is itself an assertion that can be examined in the same way as the original one. In addition to representing much of the material of any scientific discipline, these debate structures are used within SYNVIEW to resolve various areas of disagreement during the creation of structures. The next section of this paper will examine the representation and use of debate in greater detail.

THE REPRESENTATION OF DEBATE

The explicit representation of the evidence and reasoning involved in reaching conclusions is the most important requirement for the development of this system. Without a representation of the reasons for reaching a conclusion, many aspects of the structure would amount to little more than opinion polls on the accuracy of some statement. By representing the evidence and forcing users to specify which evidence they are using for their conclusions—and their reasons for discounting contrary evidence—the user will be able to compare his or her own judgements on individual items of evidence to those of the other users of the system. It should be emphasized again that the purpose of representing debate is not to reach absolute conclusions, but rather to collect and order the best available sources of evidence for each significant issue.

Fortunately, there has already been an extensive amount of research into the representation of human reasoning. Philosophers, for example, have debated the structure of reasoning and inference since the time of Aristotle. Unfortunately, the model of deductive inference studied by most philosophers treats highly idealized cases ("all men are mortal") and fails to capture the form of most human debates, which are not subject to absolute proof. However, there has been some more practical work, in particular the work of the philosopher Stephen Toulmin on the layout of arguments. In his book, *The Uses of Argument,*[9] Toulmin questions the usefulness of traditional work on logic and deductive inference, and proposes a practical form of structuring argument as shown in Figures 3 and 4. Figure 3 shows an argument resembling the traditional Aristotelian syllogism, which is used in most work on deductive inference. However, very few human arguments can be fully cast within this framework because of the indefinite number of exceptions and counterclaims that typically can be brought to bear on any argument. For this reason Toulmin introduced a number of other components to the layout of an argument, including the qualifier, rebuttal, and backing, as shown in Figure 4.

The representation of arguments in SYNVIEW follows Toulmin's general structure and terminology, but also makes

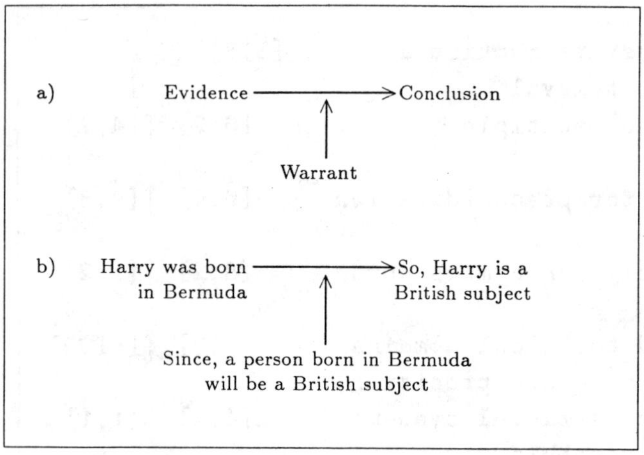

Figure 3—This example from Toulmin shows the most basic form of argument, in which evidence is presented for a conclusion based on an (often unstated) warrant. This is similar to the syllogistic form of argument typically studied by logicians. The diagram in (a) is the general form, and (b) shows a specific example

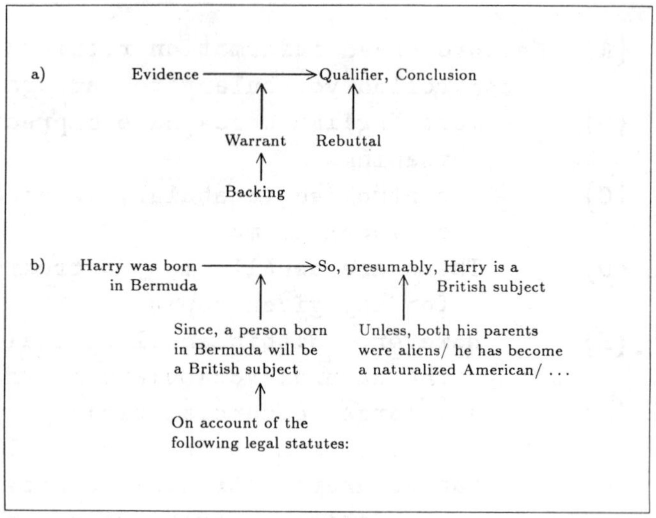

Figure 4—Human reasoning is seldom based on absolute proof, and there are typically an indefinite number of exceptions to any rule. Toulmin introduced the concepts of a qualifier (which indicates the universality of an argument), a rebuttal (which gives conditions of exception to the warrant), and backing (which gives evidence for the warrant). Once again, (a) is the general form and (b) is an example

a number of simplifications. In Figure 2 we saw how an argument is represented at the first level by a ranked list of items of evidence for and against a particular conclusion. However, that list contained no explicit consideration of the warrant linking each item of evidence to the conclusion. When one of the items of evidence is selected from a display, such as that in Figure 2, a new type of display is created, as shown in Figure 5, in which the original conclusion is introduced with the word "Context" and the warrant is shown explicitly and justified with its own evidence. In this way, the warrant becomes just another conclusion for which items of evidence can be presented. These items of evidence for and against the warrant combine Toulmin's backing and rebuttal categories, and the use of numbers for evaluation correspond to his qualifier. The example in Figure 5 has been made somewhat more complicated than the typical case for the purposes of demonstration. It is usually more straightforward to reason with steps that place most of the debate under the conclusions rather than the warrant, since it can be tedious to debate the strength of an implication rather than the truth of a more concrete assertion. Toulmin himself said that in normal debate evidence usually is appealed to explicitly; warrants implicitly.

THE ASSIGNMENT OF VALUES

Given an understanding of warrants, it is possible to explain in more detail the function of the bracketed numbers at the end of each line. Within each pair (e.g., [3,2]) the first number is the average of the votes cast on the degree of truth or correctness of some statement, and the second number is an indication of the divergence of opinion in calculating the first number (currently the spread at two standard deviations). The votes on truth are given on a scale ranging from -10 (for false with no possible doubt), through 0 (for no idea whether true or false), to 10 (for true with no possible doubt). At the moment, the intermediate point of five has been pegged as the point at which there is only a one-percent chance that the statement is false. In order to assure the maximum agreement and repeatability among different users, a full scale should be prepared to give more accurate guidelines for assigning these numbers. The first pair of numbers following any assertion refers to the truth of that item. The second pair of numbers following an item of evidence is preceded by an upward arrow (e.g., ↑[3,2]) and refers to the truth of the warrant linking that item of evidence to the stated conclusion. In other words, if the evidence was definitely true then this is the strength with which it would imply the truth of the conclusion. For an item of evidence to be significant, both its own strength and the strength of its warrant must be high. Therefore, items of evidence are automatically ranked in decreasing order of the minimum of these two values.

INTERFACE WITH TUTORIAL MATERIAL AND DOCUMENTS

A basic function of information retrieval is to not only answer specific questions but also to teach the user what he or she must know in order to understand material in some subject area. As mentioned earlier, the outline form of presentation seems less useful for tutorial purposes than for those who already have some understanding of the material. For this reason, a standard interface is provided between the outline structures and the best available introductory material on any given topic. When the first line (the {A}) of a display such as those in Figures 1 or 2 is selected, the system has already displayed the subtopics for that line and therefore switches to an "Introduction" display as shown in Figure 6. This display contains definitions for any words or ideas not dealt with in higher-level displays and gives references to the most useful

```
{A}  Context:  Keyword-based information retrieval systems
       require a controlled vocabulary for accurate retrieval
{B}      Most English words have imprecise or multiple            [6,2]
           meanings
{C}          From 60 to 80% of English words have more than         [6,3] ↑[7,2]
               one currently used meaning
{D}          At least 10% of English word definitions vary          [4,2] ↑[3,1]
               substantially according to subject area,
               geographical region, or educational level
{E}          Experiments show large individual differences in       [6,1] ↑[1,1]
               the categorization of some objects according
               to common nouns
{F}      ↑Warrant:  The ambiguity of English words implies that   [4,2]
           the choice of keywords must be controlled
{G}          If a keyword has meanings other than the intended      [7,2] ↑[5,4]
               one, it could result in the incorrect retrieval
               of items specified by the other meanings
{H}          However:  Technical words and compound words are       [7,2] ↑[-2,1]
               less ambiguous than English words in general
{I}          However:  The retrieval system could engage in a       [3,2] ↑[-2,4]
               dialogue with the user to select the appropriate
               meaning for an ambiguous keyword
{J} Alternates [3,2]; {K} Search index; {L} Back up; {M} Modify
```

Figure 5—This display examines in greater detail the reasoning from an item of evidence to a conclusion. The conclusion is given with the heading "Context" in line {A}, the evidence is given in line {B}, and a paraphrase of the warrant linking the evidence to the conclusion is given in line {F}. The evidence and warrant are then justified by their own items in evidence in the remaining lines

tutorial documents on the topic (evaluated according to their tutorial value). This section could be expanded in numerous ways: there could be interfaces to computer-aided instruction programs, lists of examples or problems to solve, names of experts in the field who would be willing to answer questions, access to courses on the topic, and so on.

Of course, references to individually authored documents can appear in many parts of the information structure other than just the tutorial sections. The evidence for any conclusion can consist of experiments, statements, or eyewitness testimony reported in traditional documents. The documents and the claims they make would become further topics for overview and debate structures. In this way, documents can be integrated and indexed in a natural way. Ideally, the documents would be available on-line for immediate access. In addition to textual documents, there would be considerable value in similarly integrating graphics, tables, pictures, and multimedia material as the technology allows.

INDEX FOR INITIAL ACCESS

The examples above illustrate how retrieval is accomplished by traversing the structures describing the relevant area of knowledge. As the user becomes familiar with the representation of the subject area, it should become continuously easier to find some desired item of information. However, this still leaves the question of how a search is initiated at the most relevant starting point in a potentially very large base of knowledge. There would probably be some use in having a hierarchical description of the entire knowledge base for the purpose of browsing to see what is available, but there also must be much more direct methods for accessing any particular structure.

SYNVIEW's indexing method uses keywords and modifying phrases as illustrated in Figure 7. The display is much like that typically used for a book index, but with a few differences. One difference is that the modifying phrases under any indexing phrase are not in alphabetical order. In general, there is never a need to put things in alphabetical order in a computer, since the purpose of alphabetical order is to allow easy searching for a specific item, which is a task that the computer can perform directly. More important the computer can keep track of how often the various modifying phrases are selected and rank them in decreasing order by frequency of selection. This minimizes the average distance that a person must search to find the phrase of interest, and allows the list

```
{A}  Introduction:  Keyword-based information retrieval systems
       require a controlled vocabulary for accurate retrieval
{B}        Definitions
{C}            A controlled vocabulary is a list of allowable         [4,3]
                 words with a single definition specified for
                 each word
{D}            Recall is considered accurate if all relevant          [3,3]
                 items and only relevant items are recalled by
                 a knowledgeable request
{E}        Introductory references
{F}            [Controlled vocabularies for information               [6,2]
                 retrieval (350 words)] {G}
{H}            [Salton and McGill, 1983, Chapter 4 (4000 words)]      [1,1]
{I}            [Lancaster, 1976, Chapter 2 (2000 words)]              [1,2]
{J} Search index; {K} Back up; {L} Modify
```

Figure 6—This display provides tutorial material to introduce a user to an unfamiliar topic. Short definitions of new words or concepts are given, and a number of introductory references are suggested. The first reference is written expressly for use in this retrieval system, and is available on-line by selecting {G}. Of course, further information and discussion on any definition or reference can be obtained by selecting the line on which it appears

to be of indefinite length without increasing the average search time.

As with all other aspects of the system, the index is constructed interactively by all the users of the system. Not only can users suggest indexing terms when they create a specific structure, but they can suggest new terms whenever they use the index and find that some necessary term is not present. If there is disagreement as to which structure is the most relevant for some index term, this too can become a topic for debate.

```
        Information retrieval {A}
{B}         Computer access to documents {C}
{D}         Computer access to databases {E}
{F}         Traditional library methods for {G}
{H}         Future of {I}
{J}         Economic justification of {K}
{L}         Current systems for {M}
{N}         Keyword-based methods for {O}
{P}         Computer use of natural language for {Q}
{R}         History of {S}
{T}         More...
```

Figure 7—This section of the index is displayed when the user enters an index request for "information retrieval." The menu items on the left search the index to a greater depth, while those on the right move to the appropriate location in the information structure dealing with that topic. Items are ranked by decreasing frequency of access

SOCIAL CONSIDERATIONS

It is probably inevitable that the results of voting on the correctness and importance of statements will carry more significance for the user than just ordering evidence for personal evaluation. In many cases a user is likely to base his or her decisions on what is presumably the carefully considered expert opinion of people who have examined and voted earlier on the strength of statements and implications. This brings up the difficult question of whether only "experts" in some field should be allowed to contribute opinions or whether every user should be given equal status. Rather than trying to come up with a single answer to this question, it would be more useful to keep track of the results of a number of voting groups for each topic and allow the user to choose and compare among them. In order to maintain the credibility of the system, it is important that any certification process for assigning users to voting groups should be based on degree of knowledge rather than viewpoint-based criteria. An important benefit of this type of information system is that it can comfortably incorporate a wider range of viewpoints than do the current methods of information distribution.

A related issue is whether the identities of users and their votes on specific topics should be accessible. This is the case with most current distribution methods, since almost all current academic writing is publicly identified with a particular author. Having identities available allows people to examine and comment on important issues, such as conflict of interest, which may influence voting behavior. On the other hand, there are some opinions that people would avoid expressing if their names were attached publicly. Once again, the best answer is probably to allow users to choose anonymity in those cases in which they consider it useful. Of course, the system itself must still maintain some sort of record of identities in order to prevent double voting. Given a record of this information, other capabilities such as tracing the areas of agreement and disagreement leading to a conflict in opinion and examining correlations in opinions usually can be done without revealing the identities of individual contributors.

One case in which users definitely want their names to be public is when they seek credit as the originator of some idea. In fact, a major function of current academic literature is to establish claims and credit for research results. The system can of course maintain a record of the original contributor of each idea, and this record can be debated by other users as to which contributions were the most important for the development of some new result.

One of the potentially most significant social effects of a system like SYNVIEW is also one of the most difficult to measure. This is the potential for aiding in conflict resolution. Many strong conflicts in opinion can be traced to a reliance on different sources of information which are themselves written from the viewpoints of their readers. There is therefore some reason to believe that conflict would be lessened by exposing users to all available evidence and by making the user justify his or her evaluations of a conclusion in terms of each item of evidence. The use of a range of values provides ample middle ground for consensus where evidence is lacking or contradictory. Only extended experience with a working system will tell how strong these effects are.

SUMMARY

There have been previous attempts to collect information from many contributors into a common resource (e.g., collections of papers, peer commentary,[10] electronic bulletin boards), but these have been limited in scope and usefulness by the amount of time that it takes readers to wade through the accumulation of material. In contrast, this paper has outlined methods for synthesis and selection that can operate on indefinitely large quantities of information and yet present them in manageable structures that can be examined to whatever depth the user desires. These methods operate by structuring and ranking information so that each structure starts with the most important and reliable items of information on that topic. Perhaps of even greater importance, these methods leave an explicit trail of the collective reasoning that went into arriving at each conclusion. This feature allows any new user to compare his or her use of the available evidence with that of those who have provided previous input to the system. The use of these facilities could result in a major improvement in the availability of accurate, clear, concise, clear, and up-to-date information.

A working version of SYNVIEW produced the various examples shown in this paper. Experience with the working system was a major factor in many design decisions, and no doubt more extensive use would suggest further modification. This paper has not gone into detail about some aspects of the interaction between multiple users, and there are planned modifications to the current system that would improve this interaction. For example, the current system does an inadequate job of displaying conflicts in the choice of wording: The examples in this paper displayed only the single highest-ranked wording for each concept, whereas the system should do a better job of alerting the reader to the cases in which there is strong disagreement regarding the presentation of some topic. However, even direct use of the current system should provide most of the potential benefits.

Of course, use of an information system of this type need not be confined to the sciences or even to academic discussion. Examples of other applications include providing consumer information in which products or services are evaluated, evaluating and predicting the effects of legislative or other proposals before they are implemented, and distributing updates on current events as a component of the news media.

Possibly more significant than the actual system which has been described is the idea of having many people cooperatively build a common structure containing the best of their many contributions. If nothing else, I hope this paper is persuasive of the importance and potential of this topic.

REFERENCES

1. Lancaster, F. W. *Toward Paperless Information Systems,* New York: Academic Press, 1978.
2. Senders, J. "The Scientific Journal of the Future." *The American Sociologist,* 11 (1976), pp. 160–164.
3. Englebart, D. C. "NLS Teleconferencing Features: The Journal, and Shared-screen Telephoning." *Proc. IEEE Compcon,* (1975), pp. 173–176.
4. Shackel, B. "Plans and Initial Progress with BLEND—An Electronic Network Communication Experiment." *International Journal Man Machine Studies,* 17 (1982), pp. 225–233.
5. Turoff, M., and S. Hiltz. "The Electronic Journal: A Progress Report." *Journal of the American Society for Information Science,* (1982), pp. 195–202.
6. McCarn, D. B. "MEDLINE: An introduction to on-line searching." *Journal of the American Society for Information Science,* (1980), pp. 181–192.
7. Salton, G., and M. J. McGill. *Introduction to Modern Information Retrieval,* New York: McGraw-Hill, 1983.
8. Nelson, T. H. *Literary Machines.* (1983, Available from Ted Nelson, Box 128, Swarthmore, Pa. 19081).
9. Toulmin, S. E. *The Uses of Argument.* London: Cambridge University Press, 1958.
10. Harnad, S. (ed.). "Peer Commentary on Peer Review." *The Behavioral and Brain Sciences,* 5 (1982), pp. 185–255,
11. Cox, J. R., and C. A. Willard (eds.). *Advances in Argumentation Theory and Research.* Southern Illinois University Press, 1982.

KSAM: A B^+-tree-based keyed sequential-access method

by KEMAL KOYMEN
University of Petroleum and Minerals
Dhahran, Saudi Arabia

ABSTRACT

This paper reports research undertaken to design and implement a B^+-tree-based keyed sequential-access method (KSAM). KSAM provides primary and secondary access, which can be based on direct or sequential processing. Primary access to a data file requires three levels of indexes: super, master, and primary indexes. Secondary access requires an additional index level: secondary indexes. The super-index and master indexes are transparent to the user and are used solely by the system.

The primary index is organized as a B^+-tree containing proper linkages to the respective data files. In the implementation of secondary indexes a file is used to store accession lists of the secondary indexes, and each secondary index is in turn organized as a B^+-tree containing proper linkages to accession list files. Thus, linkage from the B^+-tree of a secondary index to the respective data files is provided via the accession list file. Finally, another file is used to represent all the B^+-trees associated with a data file. Thus, three files suffice for the implementation of a KSAM data file and its associated indexes. The implementation schema organizes each of the three files as a direct-access file. Thus the high popularity of direct-access files makes the implementation possible in almost any programming language.

INTRODUCTION

Run-time performance of a database (or file) system is drastically influenced by the types of techniques used by the software to organize and subsequently access the requested data. This is a significant factor that should be considered when selecting a software package for an environment where timeliness of information is highly critical. Examples are found in airline reservation systems, military applications, banking systems, and other inventory types of applications. A design or processing requirement for such a system is that it give suitably fast responses to inquiry and update requests originating at terminals. How fast the response should be depends on the nature of the access request and the application. Many interactive systems need a response time of about 3 seconds—not much longer than the response time required in human conversation.[1] The response time includes delays introduced by both database and teleprocessing systems.

An access request involves (1) the specification of data records of interest via logical conditions containing primary or secondary keys and (2) the specification of operations to be performed on those records. Fast-access methods can generally be designed[2] when all logical conditions are expressed in terms of primary keys alone—that is, all access requests are to single records via their primary keys. It is much more difficult to design fast-access methods when logical conditions contain secondary keys—that is, when access requests are to sets of records. The design of an access method is influenced not only by the types of access requests but also by the type of data environment. Two types of data environment can be distinguished: static and volatile. In a volatile data environment, new records are inserted, and possibly the old ones are deleted, at a high rate (e.g., an airline environment). In a static data environment, the rate of insertion and deletion is very low (e.g., a banking environment).

A comprehensive discussion of access methods that tend to be faster is provided in two references;[2,3] one of these access methods is the so-called inverted file organization. In this technique a secondary index is maintained for each nonprimary key field used as a secondary key in specifying access requests to data records. A secondary index is defined in relation to a secondary key (say, SK_i) specified over a single or composite field in a data file, and this index relates each SK_i value to a set of data records. Figure 1 depicts an inverted file organization, where each of the m secondary indexes is represented as a logical file of variable-length records. The records in a secondary index contain lists of pointers used in accessing the data records; hence the term *accession list* is applied to such a list. The pointers can be absolute or symbolic pointers. The use of symbolic pointers allows the data file to be reorganized, if required, without the need to update the secondary indexes. Since primary key values uniquely identify the data records, they are used as symbolic pointers in accession lists; of course, this requires the existence of a primary index for the data file. The primary index is defined in relation to the primary key (say, PK) for the data file and relates each PK value to a single data record. Figure 2 depicts the inverted file organization using primary and secondary indexes.

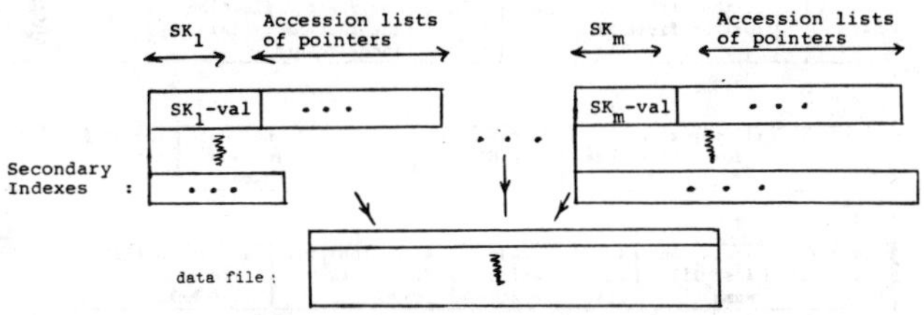

Figure 1—Inverted file organization

The objective of the research, partly reported here, is to develop a fast keyed sequential-access method (KSAM). KSAM is based on B+-trees[3,7] and provides both primary and secondary direct as well as sequential access. Access via a primary key is termed a primary access, whereas access via a secondary key is termed a secondary access. Primary and secondary keys are allowed to be of varying length. Access methods based other types of data structures have been described elsewhere.[4,5,6]

This paper describes data structures (in levels of abstraction) used by KSAM. The appendix contains a partial description of the KSAM user interface. A comprehensive description of KSAM interfaces will be reported in a future paper.[8] Implementation of a KSAM data file (of variable-length records) and its associated primary and secondary indexes is achieved by using three direct-access files. One of the files is

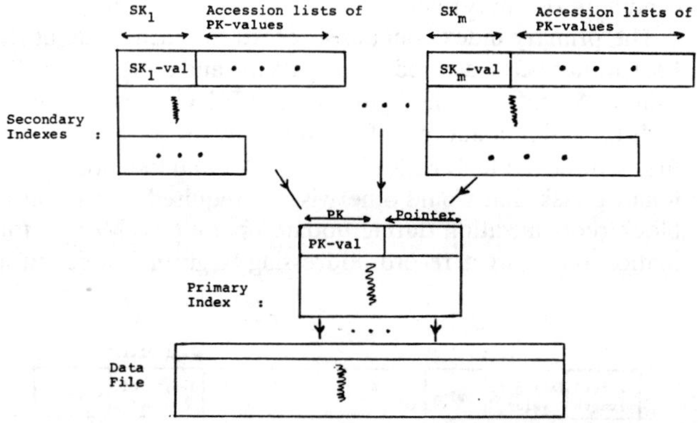

Figure 2—Inverted file organization using primary and secondary indexes

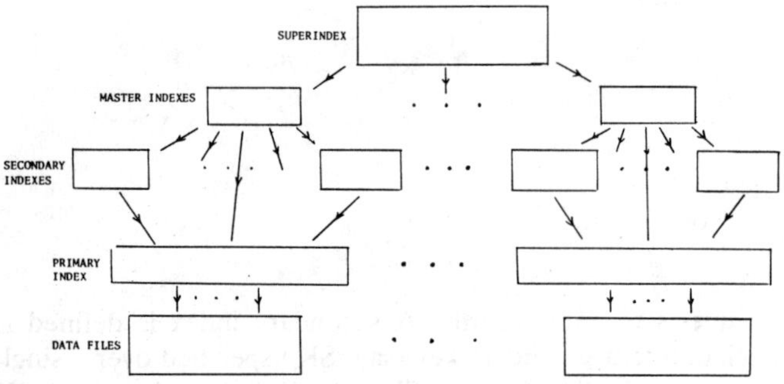

Figure 3—Logical organization of KSAM files and indexes

used to represent the data file, and the other two are used to represent the primary and secondary indexes. Use of direct-access files makes the implementation of KSAM possible in any high-level language supporting direct access files (e.g., FORTRAN, PL/I).

KSAM FILE AND INDEX STRUCTURE

Figure 3 illustrates the logical organization of KSAM files and indexes. KSAM provides access to a data file via indexes organized in four levels. Primary access requires three levels of indexes—super, master, and primary indexes—whereas secondary access requires indexing at all levels.

A KSAM (data) file is viewed as an unordered (i.e., random) file of variable-length records, where maximum record length and other parameters defining the logical record structure are specified by the user at file definition time (see create-KSAM-file statement in Section 4). Figure 4 depicts the logical structure for a KSAM file record.

The master index contains a record for each secondary key and the primary key defined for data file and is ordered by key names. Figure 5 describes the logical record structure. The first field contains an internal code for the key name specified by the user. Internal codes are used to enhance the run-time performance of the system. The second and third fields are used to save two pointers to the index file comprising the primary and secondary indexes (see Section 3). KSAM uses the first and second pointers in managing direct and sequential access to the data file, respectively. The last field contains a flag and indicates whether the (secondary) key is a candidate (primary) key.[9]

The primary index contains a record for each value of the PK (primary key) defined in the data file and is ordered by PK values. As indicated in Figure 6, each PK value is associated with the indirect address of the respective record in the data file. Indirect addressing is used to get around the index maintenance task that would otherwise be required as a result of block reorganization during update operations. More information on indirect record addressing is given in Section 4.

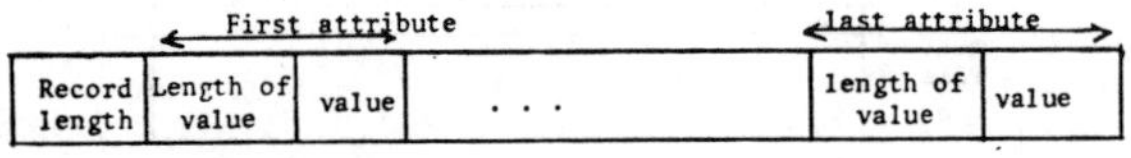

Figure 4—KSAM file record structure

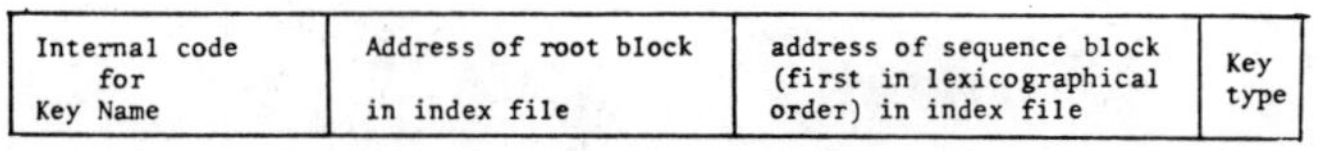

Figure 5—Master index record structure

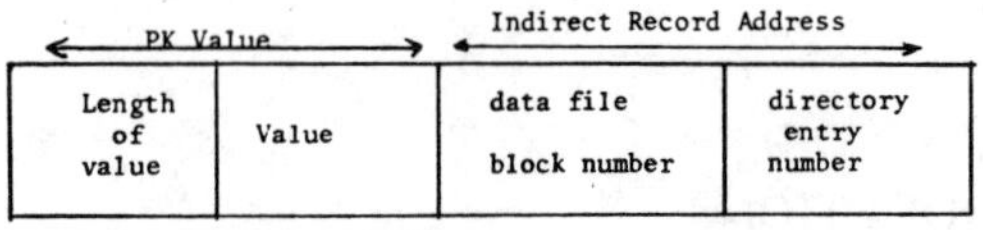

Figure 6—Primary index record structure

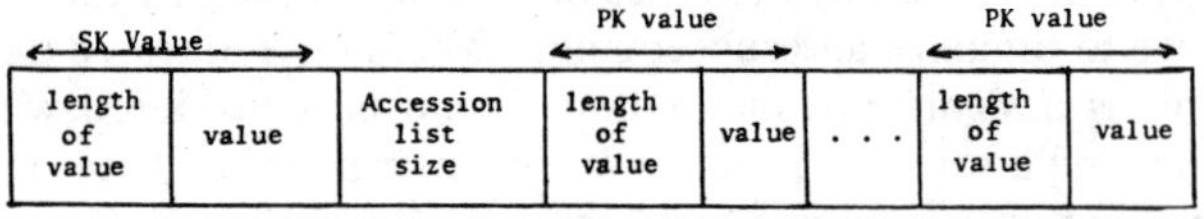

Figure 7—Secondary index (variable-length) record structure

A secondary index contains a record for each distinct value of the respective secondary key (SK) and is ordered by SK values. As Figure 7 indicates, a secondary-index record is actually a variable-length record, and the varying portion of information is termed an accession list. The accession list associated with an SK value consists of a set of PK values, each denoting a data file record with the given SK value.

The superindex contains a record for each data file defined by the user and also contains a record for itself. The superindex is ordered by file names. Figure 8 shows the logical record structure for a superindex.

IMPLEMENTATION

This section describes implementation of data files as well as primary and secondary indexes. Super- and master index implementation will be discussed elsewhere.[8]

Figure 9 illustrates implementation of a KSAM file and its

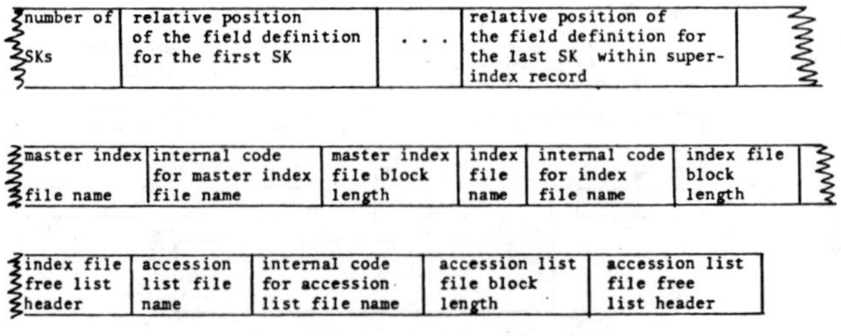

Figure 8—Superindex record structure

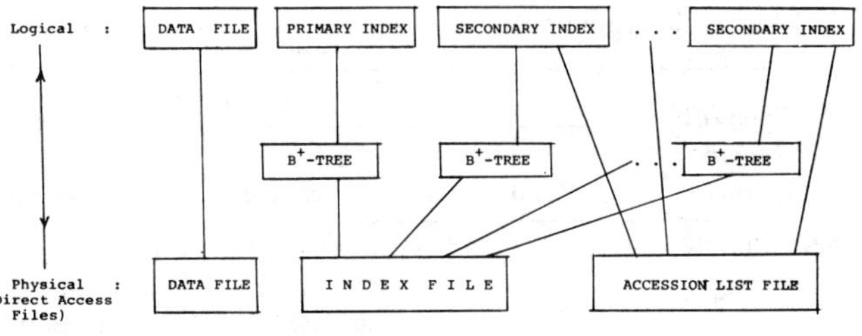

Figure 9—Implementation of a KSAM file and its associated indexes

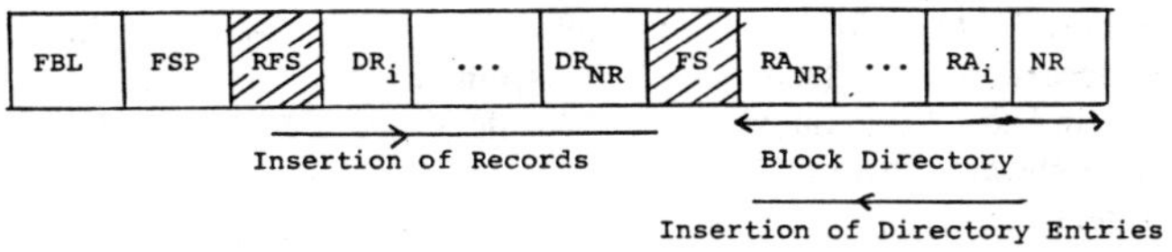

Note: FBL: free block link; FSP: free space pointer; RFS: reserved free space; DR_i: ith record in the block (see Figure 2); FS: free space; RA_i: relative address of the ith record in the block; NR: number of records in the block.

Figure 10—Block structure for data file

associated indexes in terms of data structures in levels of abstraction. Data files are implemented by means of direct-access files with blocked records. Figure 10 shows the block structure for the direct-access data file. The right portion of the block is used as a directory to the records in the block.

Directory growth is from right to left. Space is allocated to the directory from FS as new records are stored in the block. The FBL field is used to maintain a list of free blocks (as well as partially filled blocks) for dynamic (space) management of blocks. Initially, all blocks of the file are placed on the list by initializing the FBL fields accordingly. Furthermore, the list header is set to the first block of the list and saved in the superindex. A freed block is always added to the beginning of the list. Block allocation process always starts from the beginning of the list and traverses the list until a block with enough free space is encountered.

The user-specified parameter, RFS, indicates how much free space will be reserved in the block to satisfy the requirements of future update operations. The second parameter, FSP, initially points to the area following the reserved free space. A new KSAM data record (DR_i) is always written at the location pointed to by FSP, and the relative address (RA_i) of the record is saved in the ith entry of the directory. Thus, the record address defined by two parameters (block number and directory entry number) functions as an indirect address. Indirect addressing greatly reduces index maintenance overhead due to update operations on data records. More specifically, if an update operation causes the record to be moved to a different location in the block, the address of the record is updated only in the directory, not in the indexes.

As Figure 9 indicates, the primary index is logically organized as a B^+-tree.[3,7] The sequence nodes, that is, nodes in the sequence set of the tree, contain primary index records, which have been described in the preceding section (see Figure 6). On the other hand, the index nodes, that is, nodes in the index set of the tree, contain records that have the same structure as primary-index records but carry different information. In the latter case, the last field (directory entry number) is defined to be null, and the third field contains the (node) number of the (child) node pointed to by the record in the node. The first two fields are used in the same way. Furthermore, the first record in each index node contains a null value as its key; that is, it contains the quadruple: (O, $\wedge$, node number, $\wedge$).

Since secondary-index records contain accession lists of varying length (see Figure 7), the lists are brought together into a direct-access file (called an accession list file), and each secondary index is in turn logically organized into a B^+-tree. The records in the index nodes have the same structure and information as those of the B^+-tree for the primary index. However, although the sequence node records have the same structure, they carry different information: namely, the third field in the record contains the (block) number of the block in the accession list file, containing the first element of the accession list associated with the SK value in the record. Naturally, in this case, the value in the first field is interpreted as a SK value.

B^+-trees associated with the primary and secondary indexes for a KSAM (data) file are represented in a direct access file, referred to as the *index file*. Tree representations in the index file are independent of each other. In the representation of a B^+-tree, nodes are implemented by different blocks in the file. Figure 11 describes the block structure for the index file.

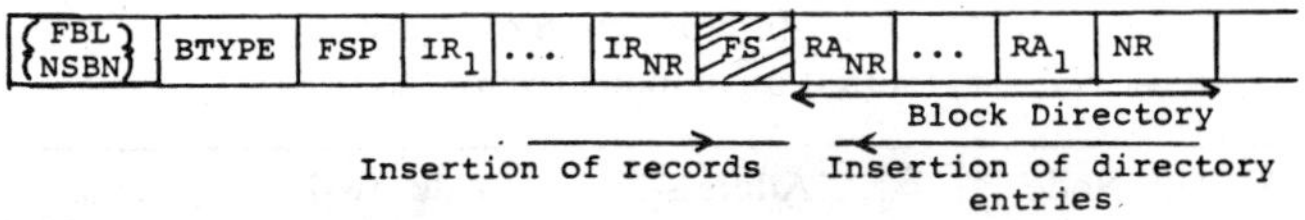

Note: FBL: free block link; NSBN: number of sequence block next (in order); BTYPE: block type; FSP: free space pointer; IR_i: ith index record; FS: free space; RA_i: relative address of IR_i; NR: number of records in the block.

Figure 11—Block structure for index file

The first field (FBL) in a block is used to maintain a list of free blocks for dynamic (space) management of blocks. Initially, all blocks of the file are placed on the list by initializing the FBL fields accordingly. Moreover, the list header is also set to the first block of the list and saved in the superindex. Subsequently, block allocation from the list or addition of a freed block to the list takes place at the beginning of the list. Once a block is allocated to the running process, the same field is used for a different purpose if it happens to be a sequence block: It is used to store the (block) number of the sequence block next in lexicographical order. If the block is of index type, the field is not used any longer. The second field, BTYPE, indicates the type of the block (node): index or sequence. Figure 12 describes the structure of index records (IR) in a block. Index records contain different information, based on the type of index for which they stand (primary or secondary) and on the type of block (node) in which they are contained (index or sequence). Table I shows possible types of information that may be contained in index records. Other

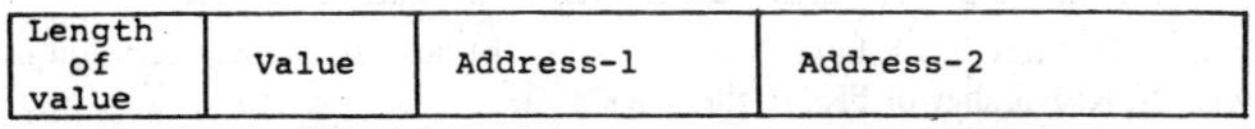

Figure 12—Logical structure of an index record (IR)

TABLE I—Interpretation of information stored in an index record (IR)

IR and Node	Address-1	Address-2	Value
Primary IR			
Index node	Index file block no.	Λ	
Sequence node	Data file block no.	Directory entry no. in a data file block	PK
Secondary IR			
Index node	Index file block no.	Λ	
Sequence node	Accesion list file block no.	Λ	SK

fields in the block are interpreted as those which have been described in the context of data file block structure (see Figure 10).

Each B^+-tree in the index file is identified by its root block (node), and the root block numbers are stored in the master index. As mentioned in the preceding section, a master index exists for each KSAM data file, and there is an entry in the master index for each secondary key and the primary key defined for the data file. Part of the information in the master index entry, for some keys, consists of two pointers to the index file. One of the pointers is the address of the respective root block in the index file. The other is the address of the respective sequence block, first in lexicographical order, in the index file. Thus, given a key, KSAM can easily locate the corresponding B^+-tree in the index file for subsequent direct or sequential access.

Figure 13 shows the block structure for an accession list file. An accession list is implemented by linking as many blocks as required through the accession list link (ALL) fields. The total number of PKs (i.e., ALSIZE) in an accession list is stored in the first block of the list. The current number of PKs in a block is also indicated in a field (NPK) of the block. The FBL field is used to maintain a list of free blocks for dynamic (space) management of blocks. Initially, all blocks of the file are placed on the list by initializing the FBL fields accordingly. Moreover, the list header is also set to the first block of the list and saved in the superindex. Subsequently, block allocation from the list or addition of a freed block to the list takes place at the beginning of the list.

The PK entries in a block can be organized in different ways to enhance run-time performance of KSAM. Table II shows three types of organization, which are compared on the basis of macro-operations that can be performed on PKs. Each table entry indicates the micro-operations required to implement the respective macro-operations within the respective organization. The decision about which type of organization is best depends on the type of application and the nature of data (i.e., static or volatile).

FBL	ALL	ALSIZE	NPK	PK	. . .

Note: FBL: free block link; ALL: accession list link; ALSIZE: accession list size; NPK: Number of PKs in the block.

Figure 13—Block structure for accession list file

TABLE II—Three different organizations for PKs in a block

Type of Macro Operation	Type of Organization: Random	Binary Search Tree	Sorted Array
INSERTION of an entry into accession list	*Write*	*Search* (to determine the father node) *Write*	*Search* *Shift* (required if located entry is not logically deleted) *Write*
RETRIEVAL of accession list (in lexicographical order)[a]	*Read* (sequentially) *Sort*	*Read* (in symmetric order)[b]	*Read* (sequentially)
DELETION of an entry from accession list	*Search* (logical deletion)	*Search* *Shift* (if located entry is not a leaf node) (Physical deletion)	*Search* (logical deletion)

[a] Retrieval in lexicographical order is necessary for the sake of effective secondary access.
[b] In case of threaded repr. symmetric-order traversal is more efficient.

CONCLUSION

Data structures used by KSAM have been described in levels of abstraction. A KSAM data file, with a primary index and any number of secondary indexes, has been implemented by using three direct-access files. The high popularity of direct-access files makes the implementation task feasible in almost any programming language. Implementation details of KSAM will be reported in a future paper.[8]

ACKNOWLEDGMENTS

The author would like to express his thanks to the University of Petroleum and Minerals for its support for the research reported here.

APPENDIX: USER INTERFACE

Figure A1 describes interfaces for a KSAM user that can be an application program or an end user. A variety of KSAM utility and maintenance routines are provided to the user via user interface. Algorithms used in these routines for index maintenance are based on original B-tree index maintenance algorithms by Bayer.[6] This appendix lists the routines provided by the user interface and provides brief descriptions of functions performed by these routines.

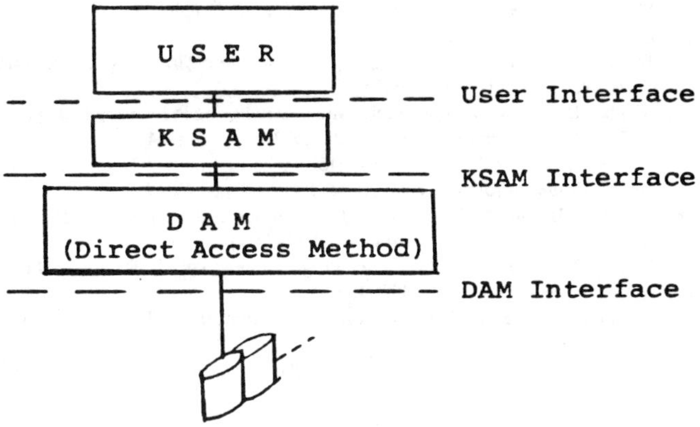

Figure A1—Interfaces for a KSAM user

Detailed description of these routines and other interfaces will be provided elsewhere.[8]

1. CREATE-SUPER-INDEX
   This routine is invoked only once by the system administrator to create and initialize a superindex.
2. CREATE-KSAM-FILE
   This routine creates a KSAM data file. In addition, it also creates a KSAM master index and a KSAM index file. The index file is created for representation of a primary index and possible future secondary indexes. The routine performs suitable initialization in super- and master indexes, as well as in index and data files based on user-specified parameters, such as data file name, number of attributes in a data file record, definition and order of attributes within a record, PK definition, block lengths for index and data files.
3. CREATE-SECONDARY-INDEX
   This routine is invoked to create one or more secondary indexes for an existing KSAM file. Upon the first invocation, it creates and initializes a KSAM accession list file. On each invocation it enters a new entry in the master index and updates the respective entry in the superindex.
4. DELETE-KSAM-FILE
   This routine deletes the specified KSAM data file. In addition, it deletes the respective master index file and accession-list file (if it exists). It also deletes the respective entry from the superindex.
5. DELETE-SECONDARY-INDEX
   This routine is used to delete a secondary index. The routine frees the blocks of the index file allocated to the secondary index and links them to the free list on index file. It in turn deletes the respective entry from the master index. It also frees the respective blocks from the accession list file and places them on the free list in the accession list file.
6. OPEN-KSAM-FILE
   This routine is invoked to activate a KSAM file in dynamic-access node (i.e., sequential and/or direct) and to inform the system about the type of I/O to be performed on file (i.e., input, output, or input-output). The routine establishes an access path[9] for each index, and the system sequence[9] and all access paths are initially positioned at the first entries in the respective file or index. As a result of activation, an entry is created in the AFT (active file table) for the data file, and an entry is created in the AIT (active index table) for each index. The AFT and AIT are initialized from information in the super- and master indexes and are maintained by KSAM. Finally, the routine might also read the root block for primary index into a buffer for subsequent references.
7. CLOSE-KSAM-FILE
   This routine is used to deactivate an opened KSAM file. It updates the super- and master indexes and deletes the respective entries from AFT and AIT.
8. READ-RECORD-BY-PK
   The routine reads the record specified by its PK from the KSAM data file into a user-specified buffer.
9. READ-RECORD-BY-SK
   This routine reads the record specified by three parameters (SK name, SK value, and occurrence number) from the KSAM data file into a user-specified buffer. An occurrence number, associated with each SK value, indicates the position of the PK of the desired record in the accession list for the SK value.
10. READ-RECORD-BY-SS
    The routine reads the record specified by its indirect address (block number, directory entry number) from the KSAM data file into a user-specified buffer.
11. POSITION-ACCESS-PATH
    This routine is used to position an access path in accordance with parameters specified by the user. The parameters indicate the access path (i.e., primary, secondary, or system sequence) as well as the new current position. The new current position is reflected in the AIT.
12. READ-CURRENT-INDEX-ENTRY
    The routine is used to read the index entry defined by the current position of the specified (index) access path. The routine updates the respective entry in the AIT to reflect the new current position. A primary-index entry consists of PK value, whereas a secondary-index entry consists of SK value and ALSIZE for the respective accession list.
13. READ-CURRENT-RECORD
    This routine reads the record defined by the current position of the specified access path from the KSAM file into a user-specified buffer. The new current position is reflected in the AIT.
14. WRITE-RECORD
    This routine is used to write a record from a specified buffer into the KSAM data file. The indexes are updated accordingly. The current positions on access paths remain unchanged.
15. The following deletion operations are similar to corresponding READ operations. However, in this case, indexes are also updated accordingly.
    a. DELETE-RECORD-BY-PK
       Same as (8), but deletion is performed.
    b. DELETE-RECORD-BY-SK
       Same as (9), but deletion is performed.

c. DELETE-RECORD-BY-SS
Same as (10), but deletion is performed.

d. DELETE-CURRENT-RECORD
Same as (13), but deletion is performed.

16. REWRITE-RECORD
This routine is used to rewrite the (updated) record from a specified buffer into the KSAM file. Indexes are updated accordingly.

REFERENCES

1. Martin, J. *Design of Man-Computer Dialogues.* Englewood Cliffs, N.J.: Prentice-Hall, 1977, Chapter 18.
2. Martin, J. *Computer Data-Base Organization.* Englewood Cliffs, N.J.: Prentice-Hall, 1977, Chapter 35.
3. Teorey, T. J., and J. P. Fry. *Design of Database Structures.* Englewood Cliffs, N.J.: Prentice-Hall, 1982.
4. Nicklas, B. M. and G. Schlayeter. "Index Structuring in Inverted Data bases by Tries," *The Computer Journal,* 20 (1977), pp. 321–324.
5. Cardenas, A. F. "Analysis and Performance of Inverted Database Structures," *Communications of the ACM,* 5 (1975), pp. 253–263.
6. Bayer, R. B., and E. McCreight. "Organization and Maintenance of Large Ordered Indexes." *Acta Informatica,* 1 (1972), pp. 173–189.
7. Knuth, D. E. *The Art of Computer Programming* (Vol. 3), Reading, Mass.: Addison-Wesley, 1972, pp. 473–489.
8. Koymen, K. "KSAM Interfaces." In preparation: Technical Report AR05143.
9. Date, C. J. *An Introduction to Database Systems."* Reading, Mass.: Addison-Wesley, 1981.

A database machine based on the data distribution approach

by YAHIKO KAMBAYASHI
*Kyushu University**
Fukuoka, Japan

ABSTRACT

Various VLSI circuits, each of which realizes a specific database operation, have been studied; and a VLSI database machine can be created by a collection of these circuits. Such a method is called the function distribution approach. The problems of this approach are that (1) the data transmission cost is very high and (2) some circuits become very slow when the data size exceeds the maximum size handled by the circuits. Since database systems handle a large number of data, we need to develop another approach that costs less for data transmission and has expandability. Because most database operations can be divided into operations on subsets of data, this paper proposes the data distribution approach. In this approach a subset of data is stored in a functional storage circuit, and each circuit can realize most database operations. The whole system can be viewed as a file system having functions for database operations. Compared with conventional file systems, the system has the following advantages: (1) frequent rebalancing is not required, and (2) parallel processing of database operations is realized. Three methods to realize functional storage circuits are described. Selection is made by cost, performance, and available VLSI technology. An organization of such circuits with efficient database processing is discussed in detail; it will be realized by technology in the near future.

*This paper was written when the author was at Kyoto University.

MOTIVATION FOR THE RESEARCH

Pipeline processing is very effective in computers as well as factories (A).

Pipeline Processing

(A)

In order to handle a large amount of data, it is economical to move processors instead of data (B).

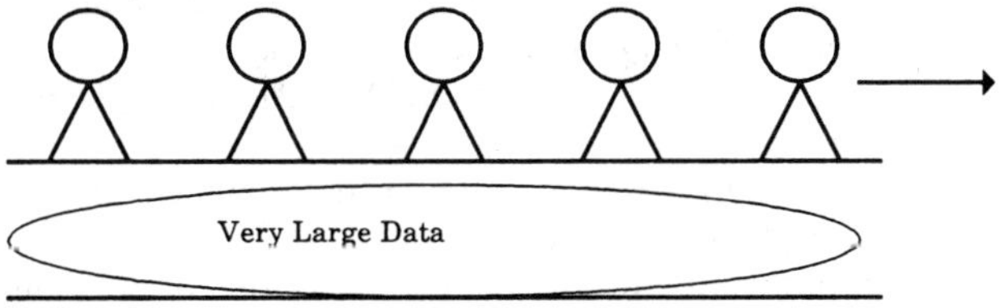

(B)

Instead of moving processors, (B) can be equivalently realized by changing the functions of processors. This method seems to be suitable for databases, since basic operations are rather simple (C).

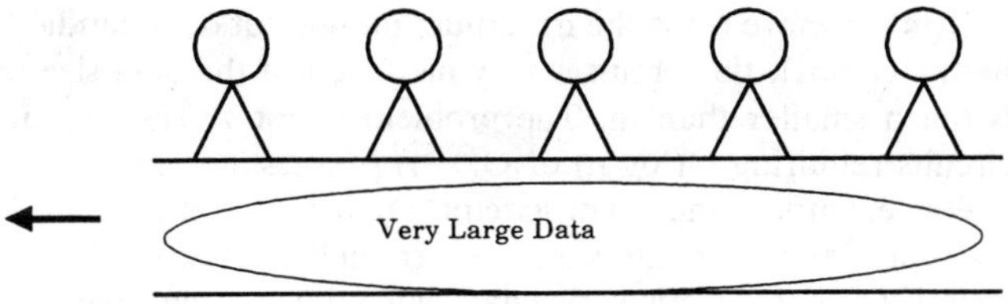

Data Distribution Approach

(C)

BACKGROUND

As a result of the recent development of VLSI technology, hardware realization of various functions has been studied by many authors. Such research is especially important in the areas of databases, picture processing, inference systems, and similar areas, where current computer systems do not offer enough efficiency. A typical system organization is as follows: A system consists of a number of hardware components, each of which can perform one or more specific operations efficiently. To perform an operation on data, the data are transmitted to the component that can perform the required operation. This method will be termed the function distribution approach. In this approach, the computation time is determined mainly by the communication cost. This paper will introduce the concept of the data distribution approach, which is especially suitable for database systems. Organization of the system in this approach is also discussed.

Database machines using associative disk devices and bubble devices have been studied by many authors.[1,11,12,18,22] In the near future there will be a VLSI-based database machine. For this purpose various circuits for database operations, such as sort, search, select, and join are separately discussed. A VLSI database machine can be created through a collection of these circuits by taking the function distribution approach. The approach has the following problems.

To realize a required operation, data must be transmitted to the circuit that can perform the operation, and the result has to be transmitted to some circuit or storage. If the operation is binary, usually three units of data transmission (two for input and one for output) are required. Because the number of pins of each VLSI chip is limited, the cost of data transmission is O(n) for transmitting n data. The problem can be summarized as follows: (1) the data transmission cost is very high, and (2) there is a control problem in data transmission. There are two possible approaches to handle (1): (a) operations can be performed during the data transmission so that the effective time for the transmission is reduced; (b) a suitable approach can be found at less communication cost. There are many circuits taking the first approach, such as the up-down sorter[10] and the parallel enumeration sorter,[25] which produce serial sorted data immediately after the end of the serial input operation. The data distribution approach is an example of (b).

In the data distribution approach, the data are partitioned into small sets, each of which can be handled by one circuit. Each circuit can perform most of required operations as well as the storage function. Data transmission among components can be reduced. Such an approach is suitable for operations having the following two properties: (1) each operation can be divided into a set of operations each of which requires a subset of the whole data, and (2) each operation is simple.

Database operations satisfy the above properties. Restriction and projection operations can be realized by collecting the result of these operations to the subsets of data. For sorting and searching, the bucket sort can be used. For each bucket the upper and lower bounds of data to be sorted are determined (usually the intervals for buckets are disjoint), and buckets are numbered in increasing order. Then sort and search of the whole data can be realized by sort and search for each bucket that corresponds to one component circuit.

The next section compares the function distribution approach with the data distribution approach introduced in this paper for realizing database machines. In the following section, definitions of relational operations are given. The next section discusses the organization of component circuits for database machines designed under the data distribution approach. The final section discusses one possible circuit configuration for realizing component circuits by using VLSI chips. A good database machine should be realized by a proper combination of the function distribution approach and the data distribution approach.

APPROACHES TO REALIZING DATABASE MACHINES

First we will summarize the approaches and the problems for database machine realization. In the function distribution approach,

1. Each component is designed to perform one function or a set of related functions
2. The system consists of a storage and component circuits discussed above.
3. Data usually reside in the storage. When a specific operation is required, the data to be processed are transmitted to the component circuit that can perform the operation. The result and the data are transmitted to the storage or to other components for further processing.

In the data distribution approach,

1. Each component circuit can store data, and it realizes most required operations.
2. All data are divided into each component circuit so that there is a simple procedure for realizing an operation on all the data by performing corresponding operations at each component circuit separately. Figure 1 shows the organization of systems by these two approaches.

The properties of database operations are as follows:

1. Each operation is rather simple.
2. Each operation can be realized by operations applied to subsets of data.
3. The number of data to be handled by each operation varies from very small to very large.
4. Even if the volume of data is very large, usually, a query or a modification operation needs only a portion of the data, selected by some specified criteria.

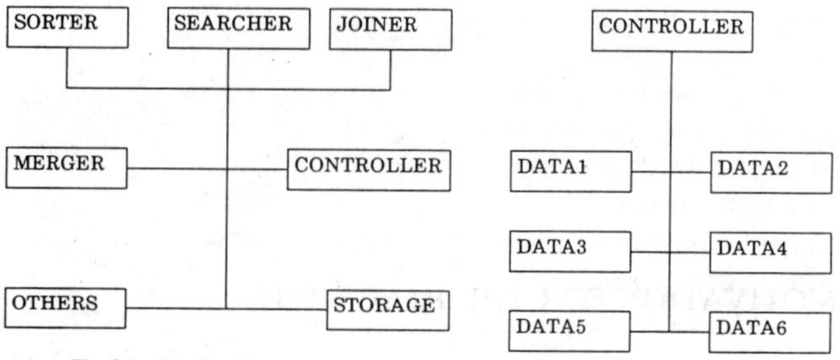

(a) The function distribution approach (b) The data distribution approach

Figure 1—Approaches to developing database machines

5. There are operations like join, sort, and search, which are time-consuming.

If the data distribution approach is taken most operations can be realized at a reduced transmission cost. As shown above, database operations are suitable for this approach. Previously known approaches are as follows: (1) a system consisting of components each of which can store at least one relation and in each of which database operations are performed; (2) the function distribution approach.

The first approach is usually used by intelligent disk-based systems. The data distribution approach can handle cases in which the number of data is large or component size is small, which occurs when VLSI circuits are used to realize each component.

Requirements for each component circuits are as follows:

1. Since the hardware approach is better than the software approach for a large number, n, of data, a circuit must be designed that can handle as many data as possible. A circuit requiring an area of $O(n^P)(p>2)$ does not seem to be practical for replacing software.
2. The computation time should be determined by the volume of data, not by the circuit size.
3. A proper and efficient method must exist for handling a set of data whose number exceeds the maximum limit of the circuit capability.

There are hardware methods whose computation time is determined by the maximum number of data processed by the circuit. For example, the time required by a high-speed 64-bit multiplier is usually almost fixed, even if the inputs are 5-bit numbers. For arithmetic operations this problem is not serious, since the ratio of the most frequently used data volume to the maximum volume handled by the circuit is usually not high. As in database systems, when the volume of data varies very widely, the problem is serious. When the processing time is O(m) or more (m is the maximum number of data handled by the circuit), the circuit is very inefficient if the data size n is much smaller than m. The problem is not so serious for circuits requiring O(log n) or $O(\sqrt{n})$ processing time.

For example, the joint circuit realized by the systolic approach[9] always requires time determined by the circuit size, even if the data size is very small. For joining large relations a large circuit is needed, since if the relation size exceeds the bound determined by the hardware size, efficiency decreases very much. If we use a large circuit, however, we need a fixed amount of time to process relations, even if it is a small amount. Pipeline processing is very important in order to improve efficiency when the same operations are used repeatedly. The approach, however, increases the complexity of the data transmission control. In this approach an attempt will be made to increase efficiency by simultaneous processing of each component circuit, i.e., parallel processing.

BASIC OPERATIONS OF RELATIONAL DATABASES

A relation R is defined as a finite set of tuples, each of which is a combination of domain values for the attribute set R, called a database schema. Figure 2(a) shows a relation STUDENT. NAME and DEPT are attributes, and $\underline{\text{STUDENT}}$={NAME, DEPT}. There are three tuples in $\underline{\text{STUDENT}}$. The first tuple (Anderson, Computer Science) shows that Anderson studies at the computer science department.

For a tuple t in R, $t[X]$ denotes the part of t containing only values of attributes in $X (X \subseteq R)$. The following notations are used for basic relational operations.

STUDENT

NAME	DEPT
Anderson	Computer Science
Baker	Physics
Clark	Electronics

(a)

LOCATION

DEPT	BUILDING
Chemistry	B
Computer Science	A
Electronics	A

(b)

R_1

NAME	DEPT	BUILDING
Anderson	Computer Science	A
Clark	Electronics	A

(c)

R_2

DEPT	BUILDING
Computer Science	A
Electronics	A

(d)

Figure 2—Examples of relations

Projection: $R[X] = \{t[X] \mid t \in R\}$
Restriction: $R[X\theta C] = \{t \mid t[X]\theta C,\ t \in R\}$
θ–Join: $R_1[X_1\theta X_2]R_2 = \{t_1t_2 \mid t_1[X_1]\theta t_2[X_2],\ t_1 \in R_1,\ t_2 \in R_2\}$

Here, $X \subseteq R$, $X_1 \subseteq R_1$, $X_2 \subseteq R_2$, C is a vector of constants and θ is a comparison operator (= , <, >, etc.).

Projection of R on X is obtained by removing all attributes not in X. R_2 in Figure 2(d) is obtained by a projection from R_1 in Figure 2(c).

$$R_2 = R_1\ [\text{DEPT, BLDG}]$$

The restriction $R[X\theta C]$ shows the subrelation of R consisting of tuples satisfying $X\theta C$. LOCATION and R_2 in Figures 2(b) and 2(d) have the following relationship:

$$R_2 = \text{LOCATION [BLDG = A]}$$

R_1 in Figure 2(c) is obtained by joining the two relations STUDENT and LOCATION in Figures 2(a) and 2(b).

$$R_1 = \text{STUDENT[DEPT = DEPT] LOCATION}$$

Since the result of the join contains two identical columns, one of them is omitted. Such a join is called a natural join.

For two relations R_1 and R_2 defined on the same attribute set ($R_1 = R_2$), set operations can be defined. $R_1 \cup R_2$ is a relation consisting of all tuples in R_1 and R_2. $R_1 \cap R_2$ and $R_1 - R_2$ are also defined similarly.

Division is also known as a relational operator, which can be expressed by a combination of other operations.

There are aggregate functions, such as count, sum, and ave (average). The result of count is the number of different values. For example, COUNT(LOCATION[BUILDING]) = COUNT({B, A}) = 2. Sum takes the summation of values, and ave calculates average values.

Since contents in a relation can change, update operations, such as add, delete, and modify, are needed. In these operations, tuples are added, deleted, and modified (i.e., a part of a tuple is changed).

For efficient processing of some of the above operations, operations such as sort and search are needed. These operations are summarized in Figure 3, which includes operations not discussed above. This paper will discuss VLSI circuits to perform these operations effectively.

Basic relational operations
- Projection, Selection, Join, Division

Set operations
- Union, Intersection, Difference, Direct product

Aggregate functions
- Count, Sum, Average

Update operations
- Add, Delete, Modify

Sort and search
- Sort, Direct search, Sequential search

Figure 3—Major operations of databases

DESIGN OF A DATABASE MACHINE BY THE DATA DISTRIBUTION APPROACH

This section will discuss the organization of database machines based on the data distribution approach. Since the system will be realized by VLSI circuits, we assume that there are relations that cannot be contained in one component. Such a relation is divided into sets of tuples, so that each set can be stored in one component circuit called a functional storage circuit.

Before the organization of each functional storage circuit is discussed, methods to realize database operations will be discussed. They are classified as follows:

1. Operations that can be realized by local processing only: projection, selection, search, update.
2. Operations that can be realized by local processing and simple global processing: count, sum, average.
3. Operations that require data transmission among functional storage circuits: join, intersection, difference.
4. Operations that require reloading of the whole data: sort, division.

It is obvious that the projection, selection, search, and update operations can be realized at functional storage circuits. For aggregate functions, simple arithmetic operations on the results obtained by functional storage circuits are needed. To perform a join (or intersection, difference) operation on two relations stored in two sets of component circuits, joins must be realized on all possible combinations of the contents of two functional storage circuits (one from each relation). For sorted data the number of possible combinations will be reduced. To reduce the cost of operations in 3 and 4 above, we will use the bucket sort.

For each functional storage circuit the upper and lower bounds of sort key values are determined. For example, the first functional storage circuit stores tuples whose key values are contained in the intervals [A,B], and the second functional storage circuit stores tuples in the interval [C,D]. In this case the tuple whose key value starts from D should be stored in the second functional storage circuit. We assume that a unique order number and a key interval are assigned to each functional storage circuit. These values are stored in the index circuit as shown in Figure 4. The following condition is satisfied by order o(s) and interval i(s) for functional storage circuit s.

For any functional storages s and t,

$$j \leq k \text{ if } o(s) < o(t),\ j \in i(s),\ k \in i(t).$$

Since tuples are sorted in each functional storage circuit, all the tuples in the relation are sorted by retrieving functional storage circuits according to the ascending order of o(s).

Sorting of n data can be realized by O(n) steps by the above system. As shown below, overflow of a bucket will usually not increase the number of steps. Division can also be realized by sorting. For example, R(A,B) ÷ S(B) can be realized by sorting by A.

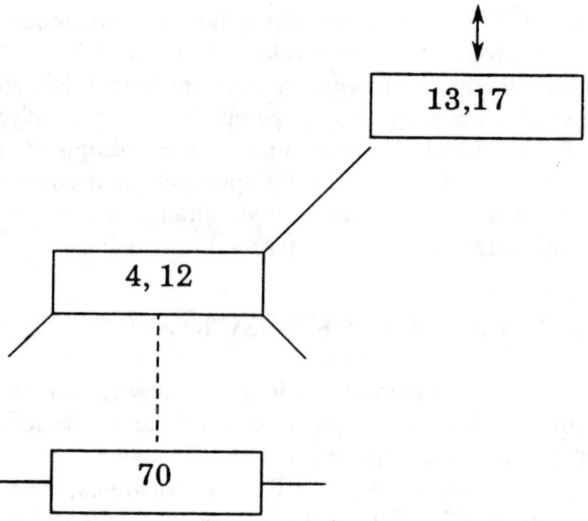

Figure 4—An index circuit

The system consisting of the index circuits and component circuits is called a hardware file system.

Compared with conventional file systems, a hardware file system has the following advantages: (1) frequent rebalancing operations are not required, (2) parallel processing is possible, and (3) various operations can be realized. The next subsections discuss these advantages.

Balancing

In B trees dynamic balancing of a tree is required. Since the index is realized by hardware, balancing of the tree is not important. When there are two functional storage circuits with the consecutive o(s) values and the contents of the two can be fitted into one functional storage circuit, they can be merged by the merging operation. If one functional storage circuit becomes full, we need only to prepare another functional storage circuit with the same o(s) and i(s) values. New tuples can be added to either one having empty cell space. If a sorted output of the two functional storage circuits is required, we can use the merging hardware, to be discussed below (see Figure 5). Thus we can use more than one functional storage circuit with identical o(s) and i(s) values. If the number of functional storages with identical o(s) exceeds some predetermined threshold value, we actually need to split these functional storage circuits into storages with consecutive

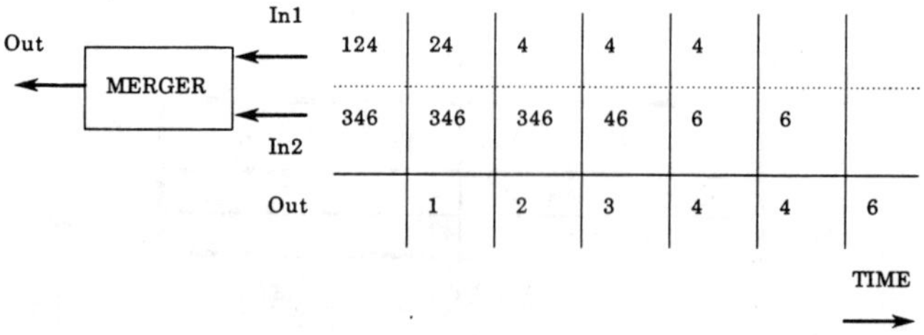

Figure 5—Merger

o(s) and i(s) values. Reorganization of the contents of the index circuit is not required as frequently as conventional file systems, since overflow tuples can usually be handled without reorganization (as discussed above).

Parallel processing

The index circuit can be duplicated in order to increase efficiency. If there are k indices, the expected sorting time becomes at most k times faster than one index case. Versions of such parallel bucket sorts are discussed by several authors.[13,14,17,24] Most of the other operations can also be done at each functional storage circuit in parallel. For example, searching tuples satisfying some condition determined by values of each tuple can be realized at each functional storage circuit independently.

Operations

Various functions discussed in the previous section can be realized. In some cases a combination of operations can be realized by the maximum processing time required by each of these operations.

A merger is used to generate one sorted sequence from a set of sorted subsequences. When these subsequences are given in ascending order, the merger always takes the tuple with the smallest key value among tuples at the top of subsequences. Figure 5 shows an example of the merging of two subsequences. One application of the merger is discussed above. Another application is to sort by values different from the key. When such sorting is required, sort is first performed at each functional storage circuit, and then merging of these results is performed.

Join of two relations sorted in functional storages can be realized by the method discussed by Merrett et al.[16]

For functional storage circuits, the structure shown in Figure 7 will be used. It consists of a tree part and a linear part, for the following reasons:

1. To store n data, we need 2n memory cells, since the original data in the functional storage circuit should be kept during an operation and an intermediate result must be also stored.
2. Since we need 2n memory cells, we will use a tree consisting of n cells and a linear arrangement of n cells, since most operations are suitable for one of the two structures.

This structure is also suitable to realize index circuits.

The following methods realize index circuits and function storage circuits (Figure 6): (a) use of a microprocessor system, (b) use of a tree realized by assigning one processor to each level, and (c) use of storage cells integrated with processors.

Methods (a) and (b) can be realized by current technology. To realize a tree having n nodes, Method (a) requires only one processor, Method (b) requires O(log n) processors, and Method (c) requires O(n) processing elements. Realization of a tree by log n processors is used for sorting circuits.[19,20] The Method (a) is the most economical, and Method (c) realizes the fastest operations. The selection is determined by cost, performance, and available technology.

Method (a), shown in Figure 6(a), is simple; but the amount of communication between the processor and memory is large, which reduces the speed. In sorting of data, only one of the cells in each level is active at a time. Method (b) uses one processor to each level, which improves performance remarkably compared with method (a). Method (b), however, has the following problems:

1. Each processor has a different number of memory cells. This fact makes the embedding on the VLSI chip difficult. The processing time required for a processor with a larger number of memory cells is longer because of the address decoding time. It may cause a problem to synchronize all the processors.
2. There are still data communications between a processor and its memory, and it will make the system not so fast as Method (c).

Figure 7 shows the organization by the Method (c), where each rectangle corresponds to a storage with some processing capability.

Although by current technology Method (b) is the best choice, we will discuss the organization of the circuits by Method (c) in the next section. The author believes that such circuits can be realized in the near future.

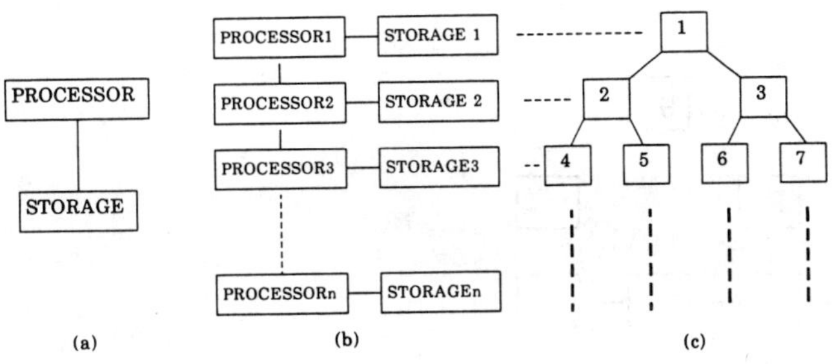

Figure 6—Three methods of realizing index circuits and function storage circuits: (a), microprocessor system; (b), a tree realized by assigning one processor to each level; (c), storage cells integrated with processors

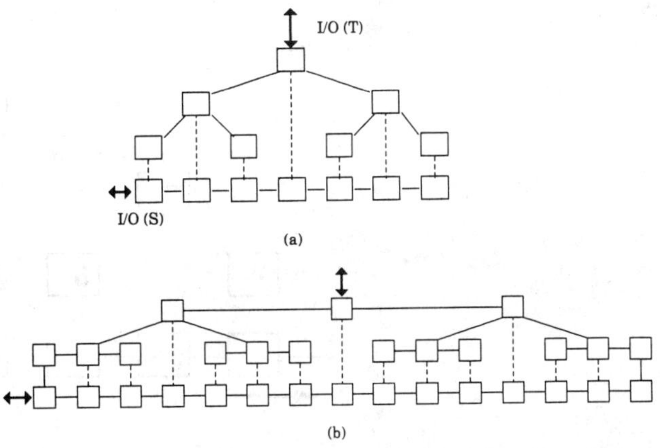

Figure 7—Functional storage for n = 7 and n = 15

ORGANIZATION OF A VLSI FUNCTIONAL STORAGE CIRCUITS

In this section the VLSI functional storage organized by Method (c) of the previous section is called a functional storage for short.

Fig. 7(a) shows a basic organization for a functional storage proposed in this paper for data size n = 7. We assume that each cell can store one tuple. If the given relation has more than n tuples, it is distributed to more than one functional storage. It consists of a tree part and a shift register part. To handle n tuples there are 2n storage cells and O(n) connections; thus the circuit consists of O(n) elements. Since the height of the tree is O(log n), the area required for the circuit is O(nlog n), although the coefficient part can be minimized by a proper embedding of the circuit (see Figure 7(b)).

We will show how database operations are realized by a functional storage using very simple examples (n = 7). In the following, T and S stand for a tree and a shift register, respectively, which show the part mainly used by the operation. There are two input/output terminals for the circuit. The terminal for the shift register part is denoted by I/O(S), and the terminal for the tree part is denoted by I/O(T). To use the tree part for fast access of data, data should be arranged in ascending or descending order. In the following examples, the ascending order is used for simplicity.

Initial data loading (S): A sequence of data is supplied from I/O(S). The sequence starts from L (loading) and ends at E (end of data). The data sequence can contain B (blank). Figure 8 shows an example when 9B7531 is supplied. The first L sets the operation of each shift register cell so that only shift operation is realized. After six steps we have the situation shown in Fig. 8(b). Here E is supplied from the input terminal. In this case, instead of the data's being shifted, the con-

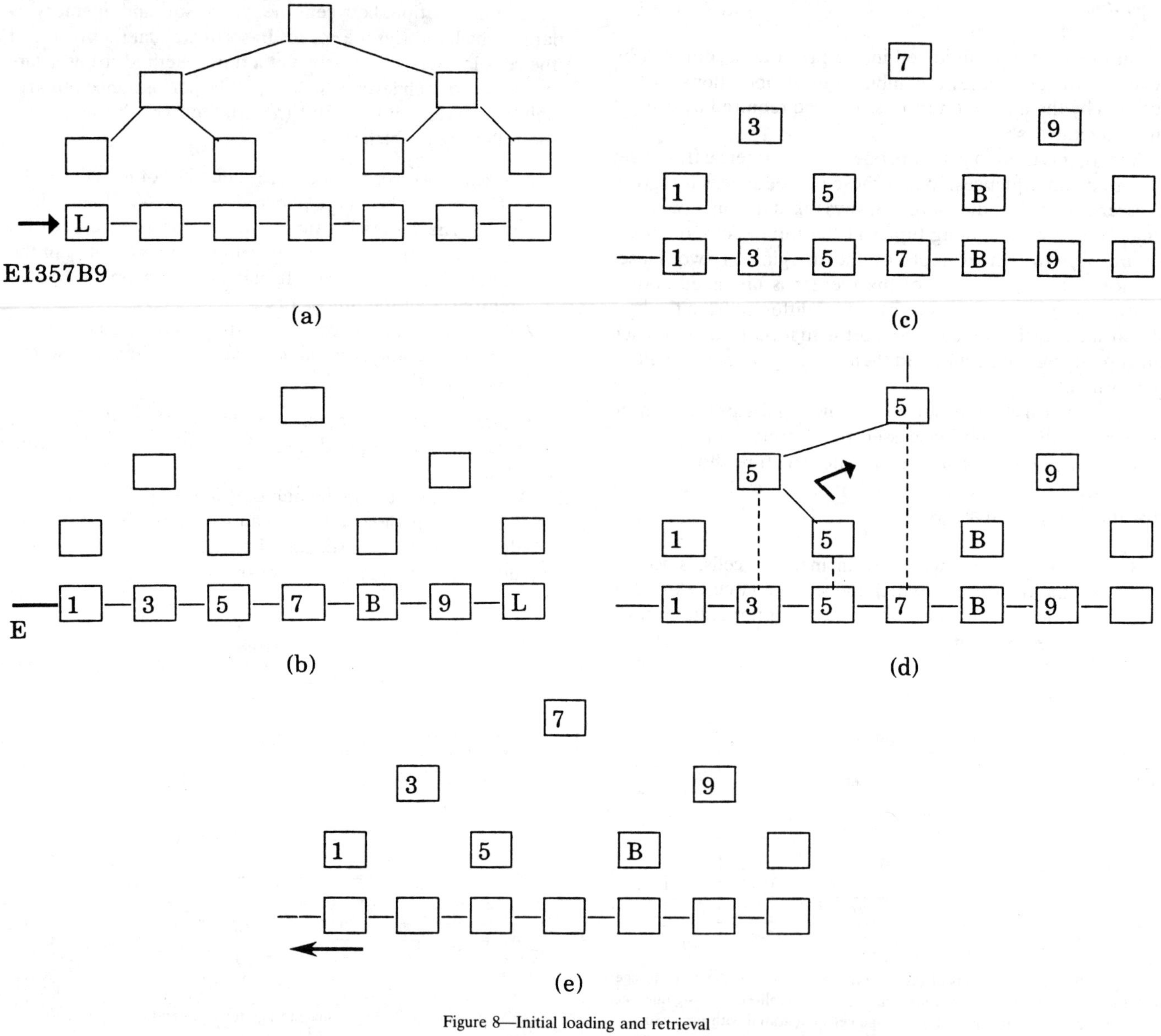

Figure 8—Initial loading and retrieval

tents of the shift register part are copied by corresponding tree nodes and L is replaced by B. The result is shown in Figure 8(c). If the data size is 7, L is shifted out; and if the data size is over 7, a proper warning signal is created. The initial loading can be used instead of the sort in the following cases:

1. Put blanks in the sequence of data in order to handle the increase of data easily.
2. The data are required not to be sorted. For unsorted data we cannot usually use the tree part for an efficient search. It can be used when the data are clustered by related key values, etc.

Single tuple retrieval (T): If we want to retrieve the data whose key value is 5 in Figure 8(c), we put 5 from I/O(T). This value is compared with the contents of the node. Since 5 is smaller than 7, the left son, the node containing 3, is examined; 5 is larger than 3, and the right son is examined, which contains a tuple whose key value is 5. The tuple is retrieved by traversing the path in the opposite direction (see Figure 8(d)). The changed data on the path are recovered by copying data from the corresponding shift register cells.

Multiple data retrieval (S): If all the tuples are required, the output terminal for the shift register is used. After shifting out (Figure 8(e)), all shift register cells become empty. The data are recovered by copying values contained in the tree nodes.

Replacement of blanks (T,S): If a blank node is a parent of a nonblank node in the tree part, the search mechanism of the tree will not work. Such a tree is called improper. An improper tree may be produced by addition or deletion of a tuple. In a proper tree every subtree must satisfy the condition that every node of the subtree is blank if the root of the subtree is blank. There are two methods of handling the problem:

1. Exchange of blank and nonblank values at the tree part: By a proper exchange of values, an improper tree is converted into a proper tree. Figure 9(c) shows an exam-

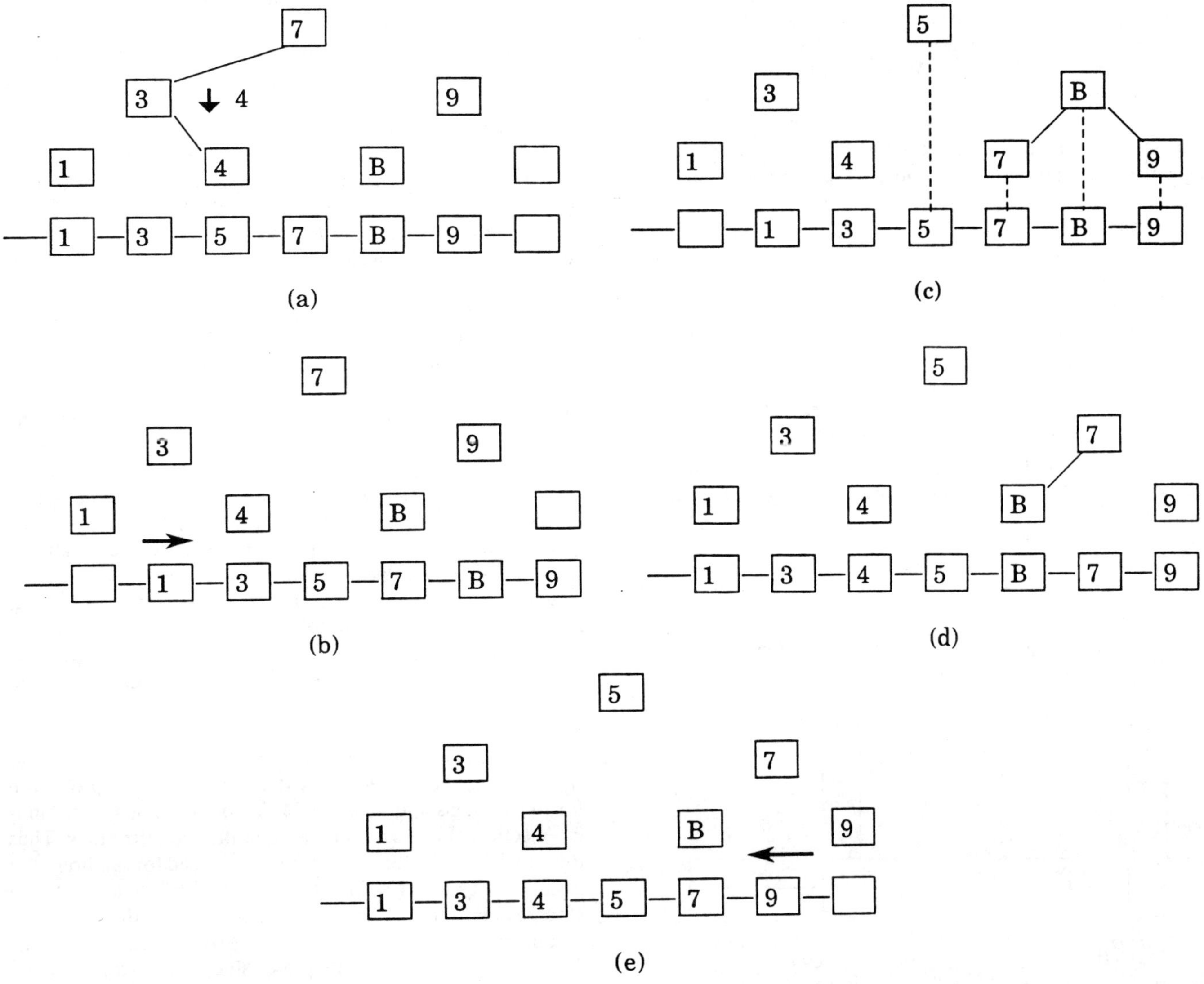

Figure 9—Addition of one tuple and handling of blanks

ple of an improper tree. In this case exchange of data between the blank node and one of its sons generates a proper tree (Figure 9(d)).

2. Blank suppression (S): The shift register part can be used to remove all blanks contained in the sequence by shifting nonblank values to fill blank values. For the circuit shown in Figure 9(a), the situation shown in Fig. 9(e) is obtained. By copying values in shift register cells, blanks in the trees are erased except blanks at the right side end.

Addition of one tuple (T,S): When a tuple whose key is 8 must be inserted in the circuit in Figure 8(c), just apply the same operation as single-tuple retrieval; since the left son of 9 is B, the tuple is stored here. When there is no blank cell, we must use the shift register part, as shown in Figure 9(a), (b), (c), and (d).

Deletion of a tuple (S): Deletion of a tuple is very easy, since we need only replace it by blank symbol B, then remove B by using the shift register cells.

Sort (S,T): Sorting is realized by a hardware version of the bubble sort. Tuples are given from the I/O(S), and larger values are shifted to the right. In order to perform sort, the sequence starts from S (Sort). When S passes in the cell, cell operation becomes as shown in Figure 10. If the key value sorted in a shift register cell is a and the corresponding tree node stores b, the new values for the tree node and the shift register cell to the right are c and d, respectively, where

$$c=\min(a,b)$$
$$d=\max(a,b)$$

for descending order.

S is considered to be larger than blank, and blank is considered to be larger than any value.

Figure 11 shows an example when 63714 is an input. Shift register cells are initialized by S, which contains (1) the definition of the key and (2) the definition of the ordering, ascending or descending. In Figure 11(g), S is shifted out. In Figure 11(k) all the tuples are sorted at the tree part. In Figure 11(l) values in tree nodes are duplicated, and the whole result can be sequentially retrieved from I/O(S). Other operations can be also applied to the result.

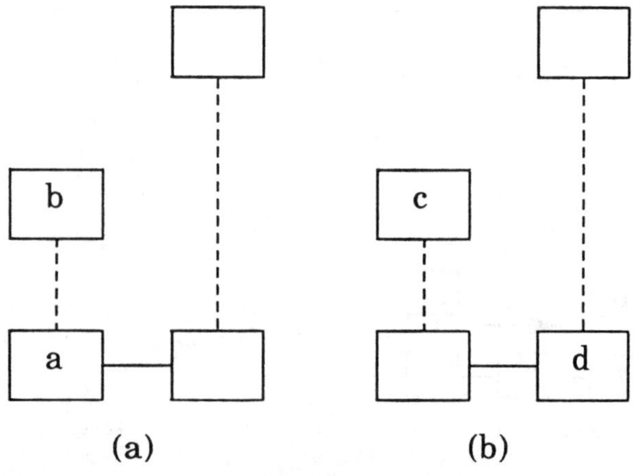

Figure 10—A basic step for sorting

The circuit can simulate the operation of the up-down counter developed by Lee et al.[10] and Kikuno et al. The advantage of the counter is that after the input is finished we can start to get the sorted result, although the result does not remain in the circuit. Any time after Figure 11(f) we can start to get the output. Figure 12 shows the case in which the retrieval operation starts from Figure 11(g). First, values in tree cells and shift register cells are exchanged. Figure 13 shows a basic operation, where c and d satisfy the same condition as Figure 10. Details of the operation are omitted here.

Addition of tuples, merge (S,T): By using the sorting function, a set of tuples can be added very easily. This operation is the merge operation for sorted tuples.

Deletion of tuples, set subtraction (S): A sequence of tuples to be deleted is given from I/O(S). The top of the sequence is D (delete) in order to set the cell operation, and the last symbol is E. These tuples are shifted to the right, and the sequence is examined to determine whether the values at a shift register cell and the corresponding tree cell are equivalent. If they are, the value in the tree node is replaced by B (blank). The blank removal operation is applied after the deletion.

Intersection (S): Intersection is almost the same as deletion, except that tuples replaced by Bs are the results of intersection. Each storage cell contains a tuple and a binary value to indicate the result. The binary values of all cells are initially 0. Let S_1 be the set stored in the functional storage and S_2 be the set given from the outside. The input is given from I/O(S). The sequence of tuples in S_2 starts from I (intersection) and ends at E. I contains the information on which part of the tuples is to be compared. Tuples in S_2 are shifted to the right; and at each step, values at each tree cell and the corresponding shift register cells are examined. If these are equivalent, the binary values at both cells are set to 1. After E passes the cell corresponding to the rightmost tree cell containing a tuple, the results is obtained as binary values. The binary value for a tuple in $S_1 \cap S_2$ is 1. By the above method we require that $n > |S_1| + |S_2|$. Another method requiring $n \geq \max\{|S_1|,|S_2|\}$ is as follows. After all values in S_2 are given to the functional storage, tree cell values and shift register cell values are exchanged. Then values in shift registers are shifted to the left. At the terminal I/O(S) the binary values are examined, and tuples whose binary values are 0 are erased. In this case the result is shifted out from I/O(S). This method can be also used for deletion. In this case tuples in S_2 that are not in $S_1 \cap S_2$ can be detected.

Join (S): It is known that any query can be converted into tree queries.[6] For a tree query there is an efficient procedure for joins using semijoins. The basic operation of a semijoin is intersection of two sets contained in the join attributes. Thus the above intersection procedure can be used for semijoin. We assume that S_1 and S_2 are stored in two different functional storages and the intersection is performed by the functional storage containing S_1. The result must be transmitted to the functional storage containing S_2. Since S_2 is stored in the functional storage, we need only transmit the binary values for

Figure 11—An example of sorting

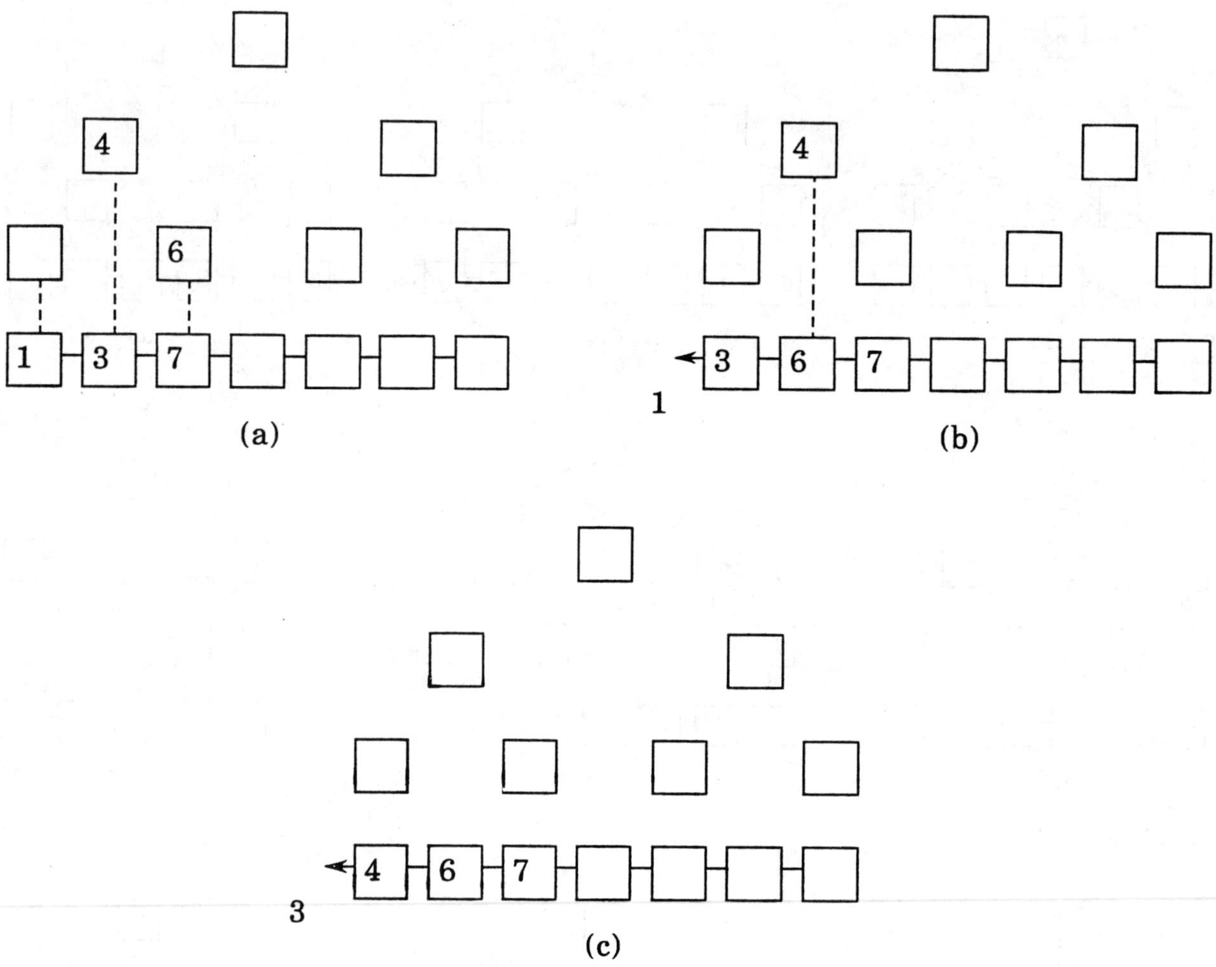

Figure 12—Simulation of the up-down sorter

S_2 that indicate the result. In this way the cost of data transmission can be reduced.

Pseudo-operations and composite operations (T,S): By using binary values we can indicate tuples satisfying some conditions. More than one condition can be indicated by permitting more than one binary value for each cell. Operations that do not change tuples are called pseudo-operations. Binary values can be used to realize more than one operation. For example, sorting and intersection can be realized by modifying the sorting operation.

There are two modes in the functional storage. The first mode keeps tuples with the same key values, and the second mode erases duplicated keys. We can also specify the first key, second key, etc., for sorting tuples.

In Section 2 we discussed the facts that (1) if the computation time is O(log n), it is not serious, even if n is the circuit size; and (2) if the computation time is O(n), n should be the data volume and not the circuit size. Functional storage satisfies these conditions. For operations using the tree part, the computation is O(log m) where m is the circuit size. For operations using the shift register part, the computation time is O(n) where n is the data size. Functional storage can be also used as an index circuit, as discussed in the previous section.

We can further generalize functional storage in order to improve efficiency by adding (1) a bus line for the shift register part, (2) a calculation capability to the tree part (aggregate functions can be realized) and (3) fast internal sort capability.

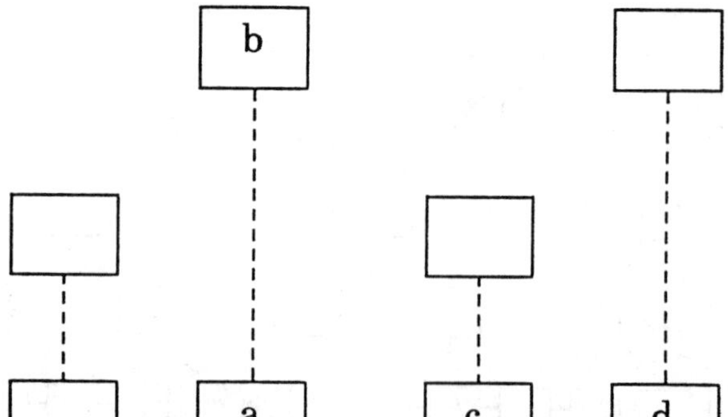

Figure 13—A basic step for the up-down sorter

ACKNOWLEDGMENT

The author is grateful to Professor Shuzo Yajima, Mr. Hiroto Yasuura, and Mr. Naofumi Takagi for their discussion. The work is supported in part by a grant from the Ministry of Education of Japan.

REFERENCES

1. Babb, E. "Implementing a Relational Database by Means of Specialized Hardware." *ACM Transactions on Database Systems,* 4 (1979), pp. 1–29.
2. Dobosiewicz, W. "Sorting by Distributive Partitioning." *Information Processing Letters* 7 (1978), pp. 1–6.
3. Estein, R., and P. Hawthorn. "Design Decision for the Intelligent Database Machine." *AFIPS, Proceedings of the National Computer Conference* (Vol. 49), 1980, pp. 237–241.
4. Goodman, N., and O. Schmueli. "Transforming Cyclic Schemes into Trees." *Proceedings of the ACM PODS,* 1982, pp. 49–54.
5. B. Hsiao, D.K. "Data Base Computers." In *Advances in Computers, Vol. 19.* New York: Academic Press, 1980.
6. Kambayashi, Y., M. Yoshikawa, and S. Yajima. "Query Processing for Distributed Databases Using Generalized Semi-Joins." *Proceedings of ACM SIGMOD,* (1982), pp. 151–160.
7. Kim, W., D.J. Kuck, and D. Gajski. "A Bit Serial/Tuple-Parallel Relational Query Processor." Report, 1981.
8. Kung. H.T. "Why Systolic Architecture?" *IEEE Transactions on Computers,* 15, (1982), pp. 37–46.
9. Kung, H.T., and P.L. Lehman. "Systolic (VLSI) Arrays for Relational Database Operations." *Proceedings of the ACM SIGMOD,* (1980), pp. 105–116.
10. Lee, D.T., H. Chang, and C.K. Wong. "An On-Chip Compare/Steer Bubble Sorter." *IEEE Transactions on Computers,* C-30, (1981), pp. 398–405.
11. Lin, C.S., D. Smith, and J. Smith. "The Design of a Rotating Associative Memory for Relational Database Applications." *ACM Transactions on Database Systems,* 1 (1976), pp. 53–65.
12. Lipovski, G.J. "Architectural Features of CASSM: A Context Addressed Segment Sequential Memory." *Proceedings of the Annual Symposium on Computer Architecture,* (1978), pp. 31–38.
13. Maekawa, M. "Quick Parallel Join and Sorting Algorithms." *Proceedings of the 14th IBM Japan Computer Science Symposium,* 133, (1979), pp. .
14. Maekawa, M. "Parallel Sort and Join for High Speed Database Machine Operations." *Proceedings of the National Computer Conference,* (Vol. 50), 1981, pp. 515–520.
15. Merrett, T.H. "Practical Hardware for Linear Execution of Relational Database Operations," Technical Report SOCS-81-30, School of Computer Science, McGill University, September 1981.
16. Merrett, T.H., Y. Kambayashi, and H. Yasuura. "Scheduling of Page-Fetches in Join Operations," *Proceedings on Very Large Data Bases,* (1981), pp. 488–498.
17. Orenstein, J.A., and T.H. Merrett. "Linear Sorting Methods Using Log n Processors," Technical Report SOCS-81-24, School of Computer Science, McGill University, October 1981.
18. Ozkarahan, E.A., S.A. Schuster, and K.C. Sevcik. "Performance Evaluation of a Relational Associative Processor." *ACM Transactions on Database Systems,* 2, (1977), pp. 175–195.
19. Tanaka, Y., Y. Nozaka, and A. Masuyama. "Pipeline Searching and Sorting Modules as Components of a Data Flow Database Computer," *Proceedings of IFIP 80,* (1980), pp.
20. Todd, S. "Algorithm and Hardware for a Merge Sort Using Multiple Processors," *IBM Journal of Research and Development,* 22 (1978).
21. Tong, F., and S.B. Yao. "Performance Analysis of Database Join Processors." *AFIPS, Proceedings of the National Computer Conference.* (Vol. 51), 1982, pp. 627–637.
22. Uemura, T., T. Yuba, A. Kokubu, R. Ooomote and Y. Sugawara. "Implementation of a Magnetic Bubble Database Machine." *Proceedings of IFIP 80,* (1980), pp. 433–438.
23. Wah, B. W., and S.B. Yao. "DIALOG—A Distributed Processor Organization for Database Machines." *AFIPS Proceedings of the National Computer Conference* (Vol. 49), 1980, pp. 243–253.
24. Winslow, L.E., and Y.C. Chow. "Parallel Sorting Machines: Their Speed and Efficiency," *AFIPS, Proceedings of the National Computer Conference* (Vol. 50), 1981, pp. 163–165.
25. Yasuura, H., N. Takagi, and S. Yajima. "The Parallel Enumeration Sorting Scheme for VLSI." *IEEE Transactions on Computers,* (1982).

Artificial intelligence

James R. Miller, Track Chair

The 1980s have seen artificial intelligence (AI) moving out of the laboratory and into the marketplace. This movement has been especially clear in 1984: Practical systems are in use daily on a wide range of hardware and in such diverse domains as database retrieval, VLSI chip design, geological exploration, and computer system configuration. At the same time, the topics under exploration in research laboratories are building a better understanding of what would be required to build increasingly powerful and intelligent computer systems. The six sessions in this track bring a survey of all these areas to NCC.

AI and the computer industry—The purpose of two sessions in this track is to consider how AI is changing the computer industry itself. Part of this focus is addressed in the session "Expert Systems in the Computing Industry," which examines how expert system technology—the development of computer systems that capture some significant part of human expertise in a complex technical domain—is being applied to problems central to the computer science community. To provide a balanced perspective on this topic, the presentations in this session discuss these systems from the perspective of both the system builder and the end user.

The last few years have also seen the growth of companies developing tools for building AI systems. The session on "Tools for Commercial AI Systems" describes tools under development in two areas: computers and programming environments that are especially well-suited for AI system development; and high-level software tools designed to relieve system developers from much of the effort of building the basic architecture of the AI system, allowing them to focus on the problem at hand. As in the previous session, the presentations will discuss these tools from the perspectives of system builders as well as users.

AI application areas—Two sessions have been designed to take a careful look at application areas that have been studied increasingly by the AI community. These sessions are intended to show how artificial intelligence workers approach a problem, what aspects of problems are easy and hard, and what results might be expected in the short term and in the long term. One of these, "Knowledge-Based Training Systems," examines a number of systems that are applying AI techniques to problems in training and education—what a system must know about the domain being taught, about the educational process, and about the student in order to truly help the student acquire a body of knowledge. The second, "AI Techniques for Signal Interpretation," considers how AI techniques are being applied to problems that have traditionally been attacked by complex numerical methods, such as seismic exploration and speech signals. This approach requires transforming the basic signals under analysis to a symbolic representation of the phenomena responsible for those signals. While constructing this representation is not a simple task, its richness allows much more powerful analyses to take place and provides a depth of analysis not possible before.

AI and natural language—A final pair of sessions focuses on one of the oldest dreams of human-computer interaction—being able to communicate with a computer in natural language. While most natural-language understanding systems to date have been designed to provide a convenient interface to a structured database system, the presentations in the session "Natural-Language Interfaces to Software Systems" consider the use of natural language for a wide range of purposes. The second session, "Intelligent Aids to Document Preparation," discusses the use of computer systems in one of the most time-consuming parts of any job—the generation of documents. Both general-purpose and domain-specific systems are being developed to this end, and the presentations focus on the underlying structure of these systems, how they are used, and what they can achieve.

Menu-based natural language understanding

by HARRY TENNANT
Texas Instruments
Dallas, Texas

ABSTRACT

Menu-Based Natural Language Understanding is a new approach to building natural language interfaces. It retains the main goals of natural language systems: flexibility, expressive power, learnability and mnemonicity. However, it solves most of the problems inherent to conventional natural language systems. All queries are understood by the system, interface generation is much simpler, and less computing power is required. Many interfaces have been built using the menu-based natural language technology.

INTRODUCTION

We at Texas Instruments have developed a new approach to building natural language interfaces. We call it Menu-Based Natural Language Understanding (NLMenu).

NLMenu grew out of research on building conventional natural language interfaces—the kind where users are invited to ask whatever questions they have and the natural language understanding system will do its best to decipher what the user means. We were attempting to build a natural language interface to a help system. We had run simulations of the help system where users were to perform an editing task. When they ran into difficulties, they were to type questions, in English, into the help system. But instead of a help system, we routed the questions to a person. He would then send answers back to the user. The glich was that users had great problems expressing their difficulties. If they were having difficulties with the editing task, they seemed to have even more difficulty expressing the problems, in English, to the simulated help system. Now, add to this the problems that we knew the users would have in making a natural language system (instead of a person) understand what they were trying to express. We reluctantly concluded that the users would have more trouble trying to use a help system with a natural language front-end than they were likely to have with the original application for which they required help.

From this experiment, coupled with other problems of natural language interfaces, it was concluded that a new approach was needed. We wanted to keep the advantages of natural language: It is highly expressive, requires no learning time, and it will not be forgotten over a period of disuse. However, we wanted to eliminate some of the many problems of conventional natural language systems. The result was NLMenu. It retains the advantages of conventional natural language systems, but it solves most of their problems. It also provides some new opportunities that are not possible with conventional natural language systems.

We have accumulated a considerable amount of experience with NLMenu systems. A number of prototype interfaces have been built on LISP machines (approximately 15 such interfaces have been built by our research team). A large natural language system incorporating graphic input and output has been prototyped and is being implemented as part of a large defense contract. The teohnology also has been applied to the Texas Instruments Professional Computer (TIPC) and there are natural language interface products on the market today, including NaturalLink. NLMenu interfaces on the TI-PC also have been interfaced to speech recognition technology.

PROBLEMS WITH CONVENTIONAL NATURAL LANGUAGE SYSTEMS

Research has been conducted on natural language systems as interactive user interfaces for more than 20 years.[1] Although progress has been made, there are some problems inherent to the technology and the existing implementations. I will cover these for background in discussing the advantages of NLMenu. For the sake of brevity, I will restrict my comments to natural language interfaces to database systems, the most common application for natural language systems.

A conventional natural language system is one in which the user is presented with a blinking cursor and the opportunity to type in whatever question he has. It is then the natural language system's problem to understand what the user wants and return data to him. A number of problems with this have been described, and the discussion below is based primarily on the work on evaluation of natural language interfaces.[2] In this study, users were given problems to solve (data that they were to extract from a database). Their protocols were recorded and analyzed.

First, there were mechanical problems. Most of the users did not know how to type, or at least they could not type well. They all managed to peck out their queries with greater or less facility, but for some, typing was a major obstacle in itself. Users also had considerable difficulties with spelling. The natural language system under test had a spelling corrector, but misspellings still got by, which caused difficulty. Finally, users had a lot of trouble getting started. They seemed to find it difficult to articulate what they wanted to say, in spite of the fact that they had very explicit problems to solve.

Next, there were problems with understanding language itself. It was not uncommon to ask a question in a way that the system could not understand. If properly rephrased, these questions could be understood, but in their present form, they were not. This is called exceeding the linguistic coverage of the system.[3] With lots of hard work, system developers can anticipate every possible synonym, paraphrase, or point of view and prepare the natural language system for them all. So, with enough hard work, the problem of linguistic coverage could be effectively eliminated. Notice, however, that this could be difficult—imagine providing all possible synonyms for all the database values and keeping them current with a dynamically changing database.

A problem related to exceeding the linguistic coverage is exceeding the conceptual coverage of the system. If I were to ask "How many trucks did we ship in January?" I might be told that the system did not understand my query. I would assume that I had exceeded the linguistic coverage and rephrase, "How many January truck shipments did we have?" I might again be told to rephrase, and this could go on until I ran out of patience. The problem could be that the system does not know about truck shipments. If so, my questions have exceeded the conceptual coverage of the system.

The limits of coverage, both linguistic and conceptual, are difficult for users to infer. They tend not to learn quickly what is acceptable and what is not. Part of the problem is that natural language systems fail in very different ways from human understanding. If I ask you a question that you do not understand, one likely strategy is to ask again in simpler terms. This tends to have disastrous effects on natural language systems: They tend to be able to accept jargon but not simplified paraphrases.

We find that users tend to retreat to asking simple questions. They tend to use sentence templates that have been found to work through trial and error ("You want to ask for averages? You have to ask it this way . . ."). They also tend not to learn or use the full capabilities that the system has to offer. If they don't happen to stumble on a capability (such as making graphs of data), they may just assume that no such capability exists. Of course, they could read the documentation and find the limits of conceptual coverage and what all the capabilities are, but the whole motivation of natural language systems is to provide an interface to inexperienced users who will not need or have time for reading documentation.

The last major set of problems relates to the implementation of natural language systems. Conventional natural language systems tend to be quite large. Indeed, they must anticipate every likely synonym and paraphrase of questions from users. If they interface to large databases, they must at least be large enough to accept the database values and synonyms for those values. Generally, the dictionaries, grammars, and meaning translations are largely hand-coded. The range of likely synonyms and paraphrases must be determined, at least in part, empirically by observing how users express themselves. The large natural language systems require computers with large memories. Simple systems can be developed very quickly, but for significant applications that make the probability of entering an unacceptable question very small, considerable hand-tuning is generally required.

MENU-BASED NATURAL LANGUAGE INTERFACES

NLMenu solves the problems with conventional natural language systems outlined in the last section. In this section. NLMenu will be illustrated. In the next section, the solutions to the various problems of natural language systems will be covered, and then additional advantages of NLMenu will be discussed.

An example will illustrate the operation of menu-based natural language understanding. The user constructs a natural language query (in this case in English) in window number 1 (see Figure 1) from constituents that he selects from the active menus above. In these figures, the menus with heavy borders are active. The other menus are temporarily inactive.

Choices can be made from the active menus in a variety of ways. These examples come from an implementation on LISP machines and choices are made with a mouse. On the TI-PC, selections are made through the keyboard using arrow keys for positioning; alternatively, selections can be made in sev-

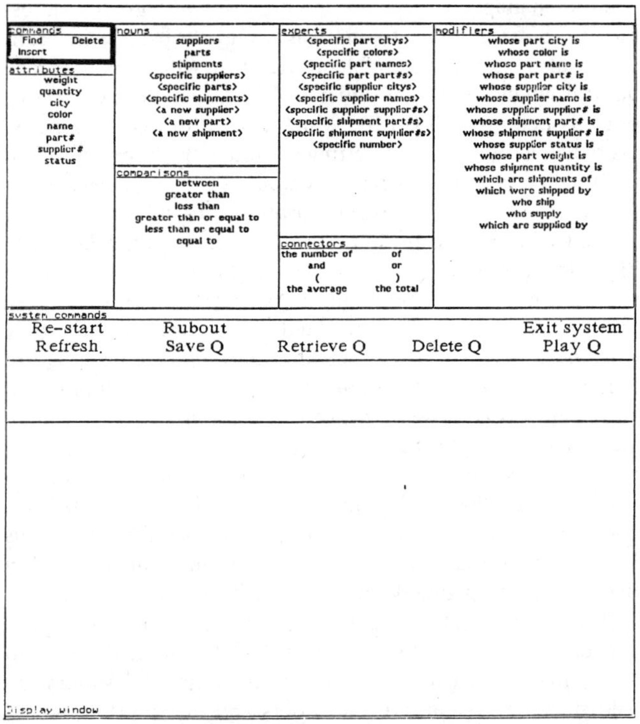

Figure 1—Building an NL menu query

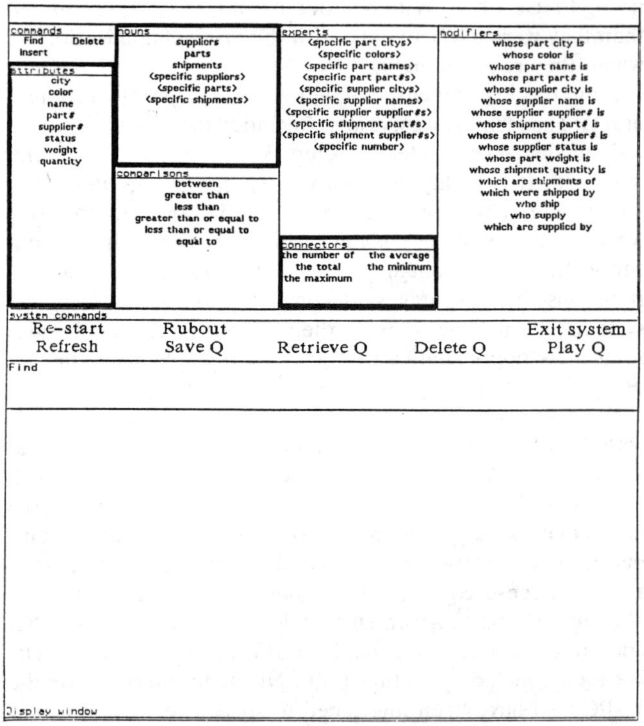

Figure 2—Building an NL menu query

eral other ways, such as dynamic text searching or selection with a mouse or other pointing device.

The user selects "Find" from the active menu in Figure 1. "Find" appears in the query window in Figure 2. He then selects "color," "and," "name," "of," "parts," and "whose color is" from a succession of active menus (Figures 2, 3, and 4, some selections are not illustrated). He then selects "<specific colors>" to specify actual database values. A special window pops up (Figure 5) with specific colors in it. The user selects "green" and "blue."

These special windows, called experts, are for specific database values. There are several ways to deal with these, depending on the application. One may select from a menu, type in a database value, or use another means. One application that we have implemented pops up a map. The user can input latitude and longitude values by pointing at the area of interest on the map.

The sentence now reads "Find color and name of parts whose color is green or blue." This is a complete sentence, understandable to the system, so the system presents the "Execute" option in the window just above the query window. The user may execute the query as it stands or continue to qualify it. He elects to execute it and the result is shown in Figure 6.

This system will understand any query that the user composes. As the user selects constituents to build his sentence, the system parses the sentence fragment. It then looks ahead in the grammar and presents the user with only those options that make sense given the current context. For example, in Figure 3, the user selected the noun "parts." The modifiers menu has become active. Phrases that did not make sense, such as "who supply" have been eliminated from the modifiers menu. Once "parts" is selected and the modifiers menu becomes active, it is limited to only those constituents that make sense; "who supply" and several others do not appear as options for the user. In this way, the user is prevented from saying anything that will not be understood. However, since the system is built on the same technology as conventional natural language systems (context-free parser, lambda-composition semantics),[5,6] it has the same expressive power as conventional natural language understanding systems.

THE PERFORMANCE OF NLMenu

NLMenu interfaces provide the same expressive power as conventional natural language systems, but the problems of conventional systems are largely eliminated. First, the mechanical problems: typing, spelling, and articulating questions. With an NLMenu interface, there is no typing. Our version on LISP runs completely from mouse selection (a mouse is a pointing device with buttons for selection). The TI-PC version works from positioning the cursor with cursor keys. In either case, the problems of typing and spelling are eliminated.

With conventional natural language systems, users often find it difficult to phrase queries, or to know how to start. With conventional systems they are confronted with nothing more than a blinking cursor, so they must compose their queries entirely by themselves. With an NLMenu interface, on the other hand, the user is presented with words and phrases from which he sees what sorts of questions can be asked.

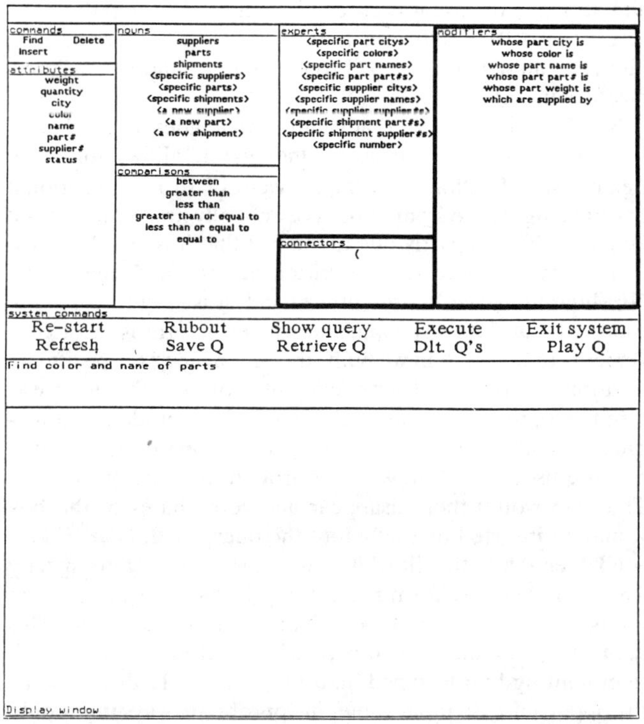

Figure 3—Building an NL menu query

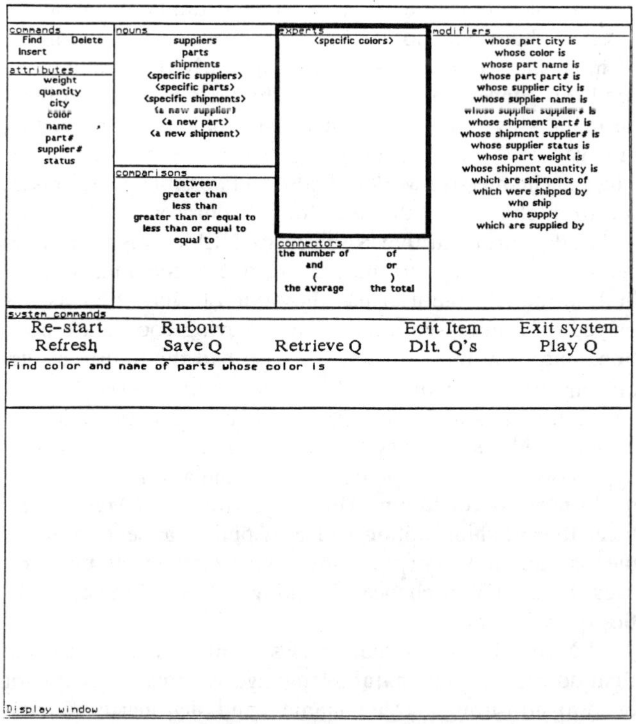

Figure 4—Building an NL menu query

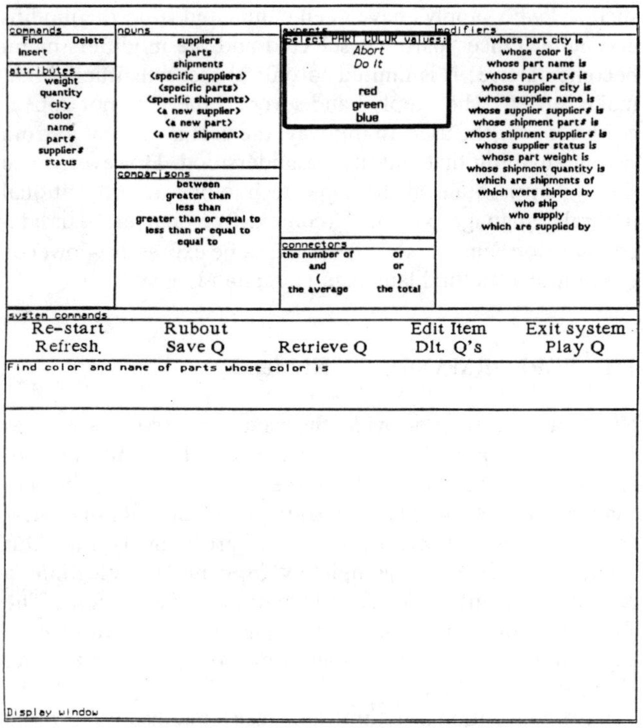

Figure 5—Building an NL menu query

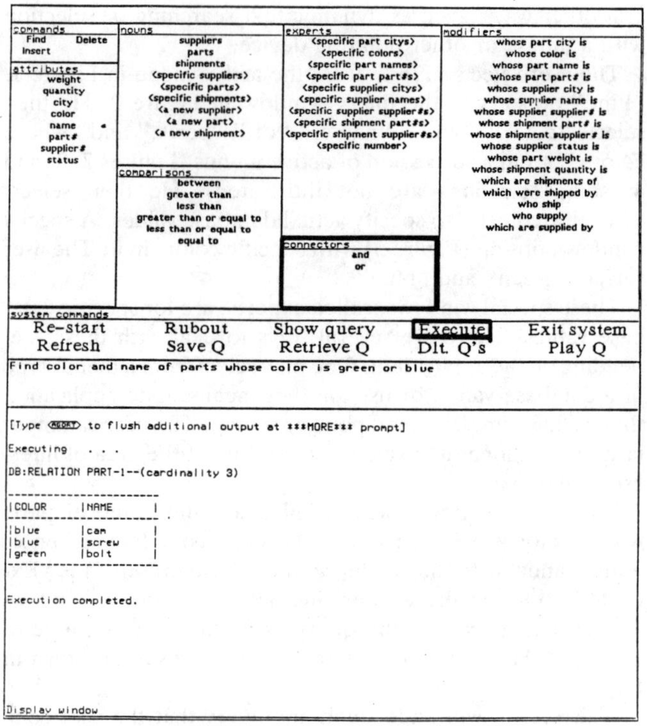

Figure 6—Building an NL menu query

Instead of composing a question, one can think of it as recognizing his question—an easier task—one phrase at a time.

The most dramatic advantage of the NLMenu interface is with language understanding itself. As was noted at the end of the last section, all queries input through the NLMenu interface are accepted—the user gets no opportunity to compose a question that would not be accepted. As a result, the problem of linguistic coverage disappears. Similarly, one cannot exceed the conceptual coverage of the system—that problem disappears as well. Notice that the problems of exceeding linguistic and conceptual coverage have disappeared not because of the massive work of finding all possible paraphrases, but from eliminating the need for paraphrases.

Another problem that is solved by NLMenu is that of revealing the coverage to the user. In one of the interfaces we built in the lab, the user had the option to have objects displayed on a map—an alternative to having coordinate positions output in tabular form. He also had the option of displaying the map with latitude and longitude grid lines. In a conventional natural language system, it is quite possible that a user could query the system for some time, and never happen to discover the graphing option or the grid line option. It might never occur to him. However, with an NLMenu interface, the graphing option and grid option appear in active menus when the context is appropriate for them. In this way, users have a better chance of making full use of the capabilities of the system.

NLMenu interfaces require less memory and processing than do conventional natural language systems. They do not need to sift through large grammars and dictionaries to analyze sentences. We also have found ways of expressing database queries in such a way that the interfaces can largely be generated automatically from a description of the database. In fact, the interface for the sample dialogue was generated from a description of the database.[6] The generation process requires a description of the names of the relations (in this case a relational database was used), their attributes, and the characteristics of the values of the attributes (whether they are numeric, alphabetic, etc.). From this information, an interface is generated.

NLMenu has another advantage that goes beyond conventional natural language technology: It allows for more flexible specification of database values.[7] In a conventional natural language system, input is essentially limited to natural language. This is partly due to the fact that it is not clear how to mix input modes in typewritten natural language. In an NLMenu interface, on the other hand, it is easy to allow the user to input database values in whatever form is most convenient. In one system we built, the user needed to specify the location (latitude and longitude) of airports. The user was given an option: He could either enter the latitude and longitude textually, or he could ask for a map. A map would appear and the user would draw a box around the area of interest. The map would then disappear and coordinates of the box would be inserted textually into the query.

NLMenu has the flexibility to allow the user to specify values in whatever form is most appropriate: graphics, form filling, menu selection, typed input, or any other mode. This seems to allow the user to express himself more "naturally" than limiting him to typed natural language. It also presents the opportunity to input values in appropriate ways that would tend to reduce gross input errors.

CONCLUSIONS

As we have discussed above, NLMenu has many advantages over conventional natural language systems.[8–10] It has the same expressive power as conventional systems, but solves the biggest problems that natural language systems have.

One question that is frequently asked is whether NLMenu understands language. I think there are two answers.

If conventional natural language systems understand language, then NLMenu must also. It uses the same technology as they do, represents and translates questions in the same way that they do. Behind the menus, one cannot tell the difference between these systems. Assuming that one says that conventional systems understand language, the answer is "yes."

The other answer to the question is "Who cares?" This is a technology, and the appropriate forum for evaluating technology is in solving problems. If it provides a flexible, mnemonic, and powerful interface, what difference does it make if we declare that it does or does not understand language?

REFERENCES

1. Tennant, H. R. *Natural Language Processing, An Introduction to An Emerging Technology*. Princeton, N.J.: Petrocelli Books, 1981.
2. Tennant, H. R. Ph.D. Dissertation, Department of Computer Science, University of Illinois, 1980.
3. Tennant, H. R. "Experience with the Evaluation of Natural Language Question Answerers." In *Proceedings of the 6th International Joint Conference on Artificial Intelligence,* Tokyo, 1979, pp. 874–876.
4. Tennant, H. R. et al. "Menu-based Natural Language Understanding." In *Proceedings of the Conference of the Association for Computational Linguistics,* Cambridge, Mass., 1983, pp. 151–158.
5. Tennant, H. R., K. M. Ross, and C. W. Thompson. "Usable Natural Language Interfaces through Menu-based Natural Language Understanding." In *Proceedings of the Conference on Human Factors in Computing Systems,* Cambridge, Mass., 1983.
6. Thompson, C. W. et al. "Building Usable Menu-based Natural Language Interfaces to Databases." In *Proceedings of the 9th International Conference on Very Large Databases,* Florence, Italy, 1983, pp. 43–45.
7. Thompson, C. W. Ph.D. Dissertation, Department of Computer Science, University of Texas at Austin, 1984.
8. Grosz, B. et al. "TEAM: A Transportable Natural Language System." Technical Note 263, Menlo Park, Calif.: SRI International, April, 1982.
9. Harris, L. "Experience with ROBOT in 12 Commercial Natural Language Database Query Applications." In *Proceedings of the 6th International Joint Conference on Artificial Intelligence,* Tokyo, 1979, pp. 365–368.
10. Hendrix, G. and W. Lewis. "Transportable Natural Language Interfaces to Databases." In *Proceedings of the 19th Annual Meeting of the ACL,* Stanford, Calif., 1981, 159–166.

An analysis of scripts generated in writing between users and computer consultants

by DAVID CHIN
University of California at Berkeley
Berkeley, California

ABSTRACT

The scripts generated in written interactive communications between users and a computer consultant program were investigated in a controlled experiment. The program was a simulation of UC, the UNIX Consultant, which users believed to be the actual program. An analysis of the scripts generated while solving a predefined set of problems showed the heavy use of context in forms such as ellipsis, anaphora, indirect speech acts, and grammatically incomplete sentences in over one-quarter of input clauses. Also present were grammatically ill-formed constructions and spelling errors. A comparison with a control group of users solving the same problem set with human consultants showed that the control group relied on context about twice as much as the simulation group. This suggests that people naturally use context in language and that the simulation group tried to rely less on context because they believed that they were speaking to a computer. Even so, contextual information is essential to understanding a large part of the simulation group's input.

INTRODUCTION

UC, the UNIX Consultant, is a large natural language interface under development at the University of California, Berkeley. The main goal of UC is to provide a natural help facility for naive users of the UNIX operating system. The user can converse with UC in English in the domain of UNIX and obtain advice on problems much as one would with a human consultant. The UC system is described at length in Wilensky, Arens, and Chin,[1] and a brief overview can be found in Wilensky.[2] Other aspects of UC are described in Arens,[3] Chin,[4] Jacobs,[5] and Faletti.[6]

During the development of UC, it was decided that it was necessary to test UC in a real setting to obtain actual performance requirements data for a system like UC. Although transcripts of user interactions with human consultants had been collected and used as models for UC, there was still a question of whether or not users would behave differently with a computer consultant. As with many large software projects, UC was not yet at the stage where field testing was possible, mostly because UC did not have sufficient knowledge to ensure a high enough hit ratio when users queried UC. Therefore, the usual solution of running a simulation of UC was tried, in this case, with actual human consultants who simulated UC in a controlled experiment.

In order to keep the scope of the experiment manageable, it was decided to focus on a single topic of interest, although the general procedure described in this paper is applicable to other areas. This experiment was designed mainly to evaluate how much users relied on contextual information in interactive written communications with a computer consultant. Currently UC is capable of handling a simple question/answer dialogue in the domain of the UNIX operating system. UC has some capabilities for handling contextual references, including anaphora, some elliptical constructs, and simple speech act analysis. There is a large effort underway to expand the capabilities of UC in these areas, with the ultimate aim of creating a version that will be able to carry on a coherent conversation with the user. Before embarking on such a large project, it was deemed advisable to determine if such additional capabilities would be useful.

THE EXPERIMENT

This experiment was designed to test for differences in language usage when users communicate with a computer consultant program and when users communicate with human consultants. Because only the actual communications were of interest, only transcripts of experiment sessions were collected. However, similar procedures can be used to collect mental protocols, as defined by Lindsay and Norman,[7] perhaps by having the subjects think aloud and using videotaping equipment as Lewis and Mack did.[8] Also neglected in this experiment were timing information, task level analyses, and other human factors issues. A general introduction to such issues can be found in Card, Moran, and Newell.[9]

Volunteer students from an introductory data structures course were enlisted to participate in an evaluation of UC. Six students were put through simulated UC sessions following a predefined problem set. Six additional students provided a control group and were told that they were writing to actual people. The instructions were in a written format to ensure uniformity and to avoid unplanned verbal biases. A sample of the instructions and problem set can be found in the Appendix.

The Simulation Group

In order to distract attention from the true aims of the experiment, participants were told when they were enlisted that they were there to test and evaluate the performance of the actual UC program. This perception was further corroborated by the instructions and the problem set, which asks for evaluations of ease of use for each problem and for an overall evaluation at the end of the session.

The Problem Set

The participants were expected to be at about an intermediate experience level in UNIX; therefore, the problems selected were for an intermediate to expert level. The aim was to design problems that most of the students had never encountered or that were obscure enough that the participants would be unsure of the solutions. Because the influence the problem types and degree of difficulty might have on the scripts was unknown, the problems were designed to be new to the students so that they would not tailor their questions to what they considered the proper answers. In addition, the problems were worded in a format using the least possible information. This was done in order to approximate actual problems that users might encounter and to avoid biasing the scripts that the participants might use to communicate with UC. Finally, the problem set was designed to be a series of interrelated problems; it was felt that a cohesive set would be more typical of an actual session than a set of unrelated problems (there is no evidence for this "neglected" conjecture) and, more important that such a cohesive set would provide opportunities for participants to use conversational context in their dialogue with UC.

Running the Simulation

The simulators were the expert implementors of UC. In order better to simulate UC, which sends the entire response at one time and which provides a prompt, a small program was written to simulate the interface. This program utilizes an emacs editor buffer to allow the simulators to edit the entire response before transmission. The actual transmission was done by the UNIX write utility. Simulators were also provided with a small number of frequent UC responses, including UC's query about misspelled or unknown words, UC's response to undecipherable input, and UC's typical response to questions about what UC knows. These responses were automated and bound to function keys for convenience and speed and to ensure uniformity of response within a session. The send key also automatically added UC's "#" prompt to the end of the transmission.

The Control Group

The second half of the experiment was a control. Six additional students were told that they were writing to actual people and that they were a part of the control for the previous experiment. These students were also given the same problem set as the simulation group and proceeded in much the same fashion as the simulation group. The only difference was that the control group were told that they were communicating with people. In several cases, the consultants to whom they were writing were in the same room.

Running the Control

The control group was run using the UNIX write command, which allows line at a time communications between two terminals. Using write, a line is not sent to the receiving terminal until the return is hit. This allows users to correct mistakes on the same line before transmission. The sessions were recorded using the UNIX script command, which keeps a file copy of input/output for a terminal.

RESULTS

Of the six simulation participants, four considered themselves intermediates in UNIX experience, one was a beginner, and another was an advanced intermediate. The control group included four intermediates, one beginner, and two experts; however, the beginner and one of the experts combined to run one control session due to a shortage of terminals and time.

In the evaluations, the users consistently rated UC as a program they would use in learning UNIX and would recommend to friends who were starting out on UNIX. How much of this was biased by the participants' relationship to the experimenters or by the fact that these students volunteered is uncertain; however, it is encouraging to see the very positive reception to UC as a possible utility for UNIX. A consistent complaint was that UC as simulated by humans was much too slow. This means that UC will have to be much faster than its human equivalent to be acceptable.

Perusal of the transcripts from the simulation group shows about 7 cases of elliptical constructs used by the students, 12 cases of anaphora, 4 cases of words or sentences used only to maintain conversational coherence, 3 cases of grammatically ill-formed input, and 6 misspellings.

One of the control students did not believe that he was writing to a human, so that session was dropped from the statistical analysis. The other 5 sessions showed 18 cases of ellipsis, 19 cases of anaphoric references, 8 cases of conversational coherence constructs, 6 cases of grammatically ill-formed input, and 3 misspellings.

Normalizing the statistics from the simulation and the control groups to counts per 100 clauses (or counts per 1000 words) shows that the control group used context about twice as often as the simulation group. A summary of the results is presented in [Table I.]

Table I—Comparison of context usage.

Construction	Simulation	Control
	counts per 100 clauses	
ellipsis	8	21
anaphora	13	22
conversational	4	9
ill-formed	3	7
total clauses	91	85
total words	668	615

CONCLUSIONS

The doubled frequency of usage of contextual information when participants believed themselves to be talking to actual human beings rather than a computer program seems to indicate that the simulation group was consciously or unconsciously trying to rely less on context than the control group did. This was most likely because of preconceived notions about what computers can and cannot understand. One student remarked with surprise in his evaluation that "UC" was able to remember the previous query and use that to understand the next question.

Although the students may have tried to avoid dependence on contextual information in their queries, the data shows that the attempts were certainly not very successful. More than one-fourth of all clauses used by the simulation group still required some knowledge of the context for a program like UC to be able to understand the clause. This means that any natural language program like UC would need to have such capabilities in order to be acceptable to the general public. Moreover, as the control group shows, "natural" conversation would require contextual understanding in over half the clauses.

APPENDIX

Evaluation Form and Problem Set

1. Introduction

UC is an experimental AI project that is supposed to behave like an expert UNIX Consultant. The idea is that since UNIX (and other operating systems) are very cryptic to the beginning user, it would be useful to have a computer utility that could take the place of a human consultant. This program like its human counterpart should be able to answer questions and provide advice about Unix *in English*. The UC system is at a point in development where we (the implementors—about 8 grad students in the Berkeley Artificial Intelligence Research group) desperately need experience with real use of the system and evaluations of its utility. This is where you come in.

2. Your Background

Just a few questions to help us establish your background.

How many years/months have you used Unix? ____years and ____months.

How would you describe yourself as a Unix user? (circle one)
beginner intermediate expert

Please describe in words how often you have used Unix: For example: Only for courses cs153 and cs3. Worked for one summer as a C programmer. Have written various game programs and done extensive hacking.

3. Instructions

This is your session with UC. Do not look at what your neighbor is doing. If you have used/played with UC before, please let us know so that we can take that into account in analyzing your session. Pretend that you are a beginning Unix user. You have encountered the following problems and would like to get the answers from UC:

(a) You have an account on ucbcory and you have just gotten a new account on another machine (ucbkim) on the ethernet (a high speed interconnection among different machines much like the old berknet). You would like to move some of your files from ucbcory to your new account on ucbkim. A friend has told you that there is a very easy way to do this, but you can't remember what the command(s) were. Since it is late at night and no one else is around, you decide to ask UC.
ease of use (circle one): 1 2 3 4 5
(1 is very hard, 5 is very easy)
(space for notes on your interaction)

(b) Now that you have the solution for the above problem, you realize that what you really want to do is to copy whole directories over to your new account and maybe there is an easy way to do this.
ease of use (circle one): 1 2 3 4 5
(1 is very hard, 5 is very easy)

(c) One of the things you tried to do was to make a link to one of your friend's files. However, new machine, ucbkim gave you the error message "/na/friend/foo: Cross-device link." Pretend that you have never seen that error before and ask UC about this problem.
ease of use (circle one): 1 2 3 4 5
(1 is very hard, 5 is very easy)

(d) You now go off to another terminal and try the command suggested by UC for copying files from one machine to another via the ethernet, but find out that it doesn't work. You get the error message "Login incorrect." So now you come back to this terminal and want to know why it didn't work.
ease of use (circle one): 1 2 3 4 5
(1 is very hard, 5 is very easy)

(e) This space is left for you to be creative and ask your own questions.
ease of use (circle one): 1 2 3 4 5
(1 is very hard, 5 is very easy)

4. Evaluation

If you were a new Unix user, would you use UC?

yes no

If UC were available, would you recommend it to your friends who are getting started on Unix?

yes no

If you had a home computer and a similar system were available for the operating system of your micro, would you buy it, and what price (in % of the computer system price) would you be willing to pay? (Note that this does not mean that UC-like systems are even close to commercial availability, for one thing, UC is much too big to fit on almost any home computer—this question is just to estimate the value of such a facility).

yes no if yes, then price____%.

This space is left for you to make general comments/suggestions/criticisms. All your comments will be seriously considered and are very much appreciated.

REFERENCES

1. Wilensky, R., Y. Arens, and D. N. Chin. "Talking to UNIX in English: An Overview of UC." To appear in the *Communications of the ACM,* June 1984.
2. Wilensky, R. "Talking to UNIX in English: An Overview of UC." In the *Proceedings of the National Conference on Artificial Intelligence.* 1982.

3. Arens, Y. "The Context Model: Language Understanding in Context." In the *Proceedings of the Fourth Annual Conference of the Cognitive Science Society*. 1982.
4. Chin, D. N. "Knowledge Structures in UC, the UNIX Consultant." In the *Proceedings of the 21st Annual Meeting of the Association for Computational Linguistics*. 1983.
5. Jacobs, P. "Generation in a Natural Language Interface." In the *Proceedings of the Eighth International Joint Conference on Artificial Intelligence*. 1983.
6. Faletti, J. "PANDORA—A Program for Doing Commonsense Planning in Complex Situations." In the *Proceedings of the Second Annual National Artificial Intelligence Conference*. 1982.
7. Lindsay, P., and D. Norman. *Human Information Processing: An Introduction to Psychology*. New York: Academic Press, 1972.
8. Lewis, C., and R. Mack. "Learning to Use a Text Processing System: Evidence from 'Thinking Aloud' Protocols." In the *Proceedings of the Human Factors in Computer Systems Conference*. 1982.
9. Card, S. K., T. P. Moran, and A. Newell. *The Psychology of Human-Computer Interaction* (1st ed.). Hillsdale, N. J.: Lawrence Erlbaum Associates, Publishers, 1983.

Transportable English-language processing for office environments

by BRUCE W. BALLARD, JOHN C. LUSTH, and NANCY L. TINKHAM
Duke University
Durham, North Carolina

ABSTRACT

This article describes the Layered Domain Class system (LDC), a state-of-the-art natural language processor whose major goals are (1) to provide English-language retrieval capabilities for medium-sized office domains that have been stored on the computer as text-edited files, rather than more restrictive database structures and (2) to eliminate the need to call in the system designer when extensions into new domains are desired, without sacrificing the depth or reliability of the interface. Early developments in the design of portions of LDC were presented at NCC-83, and the entire system became operational in July 1983. The article gives an overview of the construction of the system, gives examples of the English structures provided for, briefly describes the most recently completed portions of the system, and mentions current directions the project is taking.

INTRODUCTION

During the 1970s, a number of experimental systems providing limited natural language processing capabilities were developed to permit computer access by casual or untrained users. The most frequent application was for database query, and other application areas have included automatic programming, computer-aided instruction, office automation, and medical information retrieval. Several prototype systems have been tested with prospective users, and at least one system (INTELLECT) has been used in several dozen commercial database environments and is currently being marketed by IBM.

Our interest is in adapting and extending techniques developed for previous natural language (NL) systems, especially those used in database query systems and in our own natural language programming system NLC[1,2,3] for use in office environments. This article gives a brief overview of the Layered Domain Class system (LDC), a state-of-the-art natural language processor whose primary goals are (1) to provide English-language retrieval capabilities for medium-sized office domains that have been stored on the computer as text files, that is, files produced with a standard text editor, rather than more restrictive database structures, and (2) to eliminate the need to call in the system designer when extensions into new domains are desired, without sacrificing the depth or reliability of the inteface. Depth of an English-language processor refers to the degree to which the system supports the natural syntax and semantics of the language. That is, we distinguish a natural language system from English-like languages that make use of English vocabulary in what otherwise operates as a formal language interface.

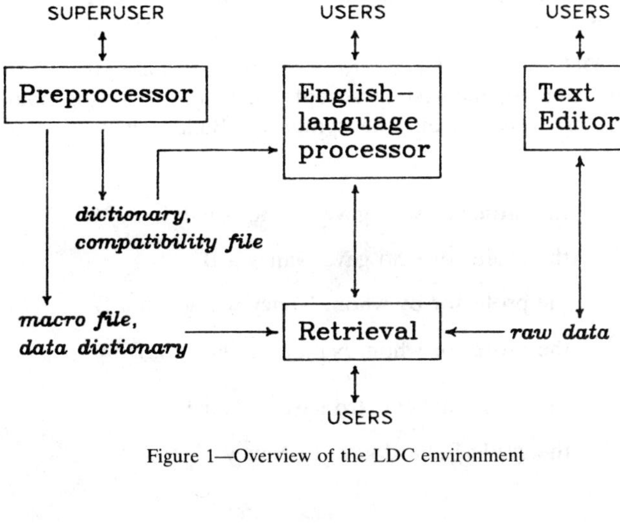

Figure 1—Overview of the LDC environment

In designing LDC, we have sought to identify a broad class of domains that have similar structure but contain entirely different sorts of data. For the prototype LDC system, we have chosen to consider domains with semantics similar to those of our previous NLC matrix-domain system. Some of the more abstract properties we have incorporated are hierarchical decomposition, uniform breakdown of entities, and implicit orderings of domain elements. Thus, LDC provides capabilities to learn about domains where decomposition serves as the primary structuring relation. We refer to these as layered domains. Previous papers discuss some of the mathematical and psychological properties of these domains[4] and give partial descriptions of pre-prototype system components.[5] A discussion of the internal processing that takes place during the processing of inputs by LDC can also be found elsewhere.[6]

OVERVIEW OF LDC

An overview of the environment in which LDC operates is suggested in Figure 1. As shown in Figure 1, our system is designed to take as input preexisting data files that will have been created using a standard text editor, and LDC is composed of three major modules. The first of these is the preprocessor, through which an experienced user, or "super-user," customizes the system to operate in a new domain. As a result of preprocessing, various files are created that provide domain-specific information for later processing. The next module is the English-language processor, which receives English inputs, currently in typed mode, and by a series of steps to be described later produces an appropriate formal query for the third module of LDC, the retrieval module. As shown in Figure 1, our retrieval module has been designed to be usable in stand-alone mode, independent of the English processing portion of LDC, somewhat like a conventional database retrieval module. We will occasionally refer to the English-language processor and retrieval module collectively as the User-Phase processor.

KNOWLEDGE ACQUISITION

The initial interaction between a user and LDC, which involves telling the system about a new domain, consists of a dialogue with the preprocessor, which we call "Prep." Prep operates by acquiring information about the names of each type of entity of the domain; the nature of the relationships among them; the English words that will be used as nouns, verbs, and modifiers; morphological and semantic properties of these new words; and the relation between the conceptual domain structure and the physical objects of the raw data file.

For example, in describing a data file that contains information about building locations, the user might say the following:

1. A "room" is an independent domain object.
2. A given room is found on exactly one "floor."
3. An "office" and a "conference room" are types of rooms, and rooms may be spoken of as "large," "vacant," and "small."
4. A floor is said to be "restricted" if it contains one or more offices.
5. Information about the location of a room is found in the Loc column of some particular text file.

In addition to its primary role of asking for information, Prep also allows the user to probe its knowledge and make corrections or updates as desired.

THE ENGLISH-LANGUAGE PROCESSOR

In this section, we seek to convey a feeling for the types of English inputs LDC is able to process. Our initial interest in developing LDC was to study the specification by users of complex semantics; therefore, we chose for our system to expect noun phrases rather than full question forms. We note that the power of the system is only minimally reduced by restricting users to noun phrases because there is a corresponding equivalent noun phrase for most questions. For example, the answer to the question

What grade did Mary get from Biermann?

is precisely the referent of the noun phrase

the grade that Mary got from Biermann

We first discuss accepted forms, then give examples of presently unaccepted forms.

English Structures Processed by LDC

Noun phrases in LDC consist of two types: (1) proper-noun phrases, such as "Jack," "CPS201," and "a B+," and (2) descriptive phrases, such as "the best student Ballard taught in CPS201." Because the syntax of proper-noun phrases is trivial, the following presentation deals with descriptive phrases. It is important to note that the presence of prepositional phrases, comparative phrases, and relative clauses leads to nesting of one or more noun phrases within another.

Descriptive noun phrases are composed of a head noun preceded by zero or more premodifiers, usually single words, and followed by zero or more postmodifiers, usually multiple-word phrases. Permissible premodifiers in the current LDC grammar are the articles the, a, and an; ordinal numbers; superlatives; adjectives; noun modifiers; and single-word possessives. Some examples are:

article: *the* offices

ordinal: the *third* floor

superlative: the *largest* room

adjective: the *vacant* offices

noun modifier: the *conference* rooms

possessive: *Biermann's* lab

Cardinal numbers may occur in a noun phrase if they appear together with ordinals or superlatives:

the *first two* floors

Premodifiers may be used freely in combination with one another:

the largest vacant office

However, there are restrictions in English regarding the usage of premodifiers with one another, the ordering of premodifiers, and the choice of modifiers for nouns. These restrictions are upheld in the LDC grammar so that constructions such as the following are disallowed:

the smallest last room

largest Ballard's office

the lastly person

It is important that such spurious constructions be disallowed in order to help reduce potential ambiguities of nested structures, problems caused by typing errors, or problems of the noise present in spoken input.

The simplest form of postmodifier provided for in LDC is the predicative specification of an ordinal:

section 3 of CPS51

The simplest multiple-word postmodifier is the prepositional phrase, which consists of a preposition followed by an arbitrarily complex noun pharase:

the undergraduates in the course Joe failed

the student with the lowest grade in EE291

LDC also provides a variety of relative clause structures. For example, the system accepts all of the following noun phrases derived from the sentence "Ballard gave a B to Nancy."

the professor who gave a B to Nancy

the professor who gave Nancy a B

the professor by whom Nancy was given a B

the professor whom Nancy was given a B by

the grade that Ballard gave to Nancy

the grade Ballard gave to Nancy

the grade that Ballard gave Nancy

the grade Ballard gave Nancy

the grade which was given to Nancy by Ballard

the grade which was given Nancy by Ballard

the grade given to Nancy by Ballard

the grade given Nancy by Ballard

the student to whom Ballard gave a B

the student Ballard gave a B to

the student who was given a B by Ballard

the student given a B by Ballard

For simplicity we have shown these 16 forms with only proper-noun embedded phrases, but in general arbitrary noun phrases may occur, as in

instructors who gave an F to a student who made a passing grade in a course taught by Ballard

The words *which* and *that* may be substituted for each other in the sentences shown. A relative clause will occasionally contain a verb with a particle, such as *add up* or *give up,* and the LDC grammar allows the particle to occur either before or after the object of the verb:

the students who made up a graduate course

the students who made EE157 up

Finally, LDC accepts certain comparative structures. One such type of construction is a relative clause containing the comparative form of an adjective and optionally containing a form of the verb to be:

the courses that were smaller than CPS152 (was)

the grades lower than B

the courses smaller than Ballard's smallest course

A second type of comparative construction in LDC is somewhat different in that it functions as a noun phrase. This particular form also extends to superlatives:

the larger of CPS200 and CPS51

the largest of CPS200, CPS51, CPS224, and EE157

the largest of CPS215, Carroll's courses, and EE209

the largest of the courses Anne took

English Forms Not Presently Accepted

To give an idea of the limits of LDC, we will list some of the constructions that cannot be processed at this time. First, LDC does not allow the use of cardinal numbers without an ordinal or superlative, as in

the professor who failed six students

Second, LDC is not able to derive the meaning of a participial adjective (for example, passing) automatically from the meaning of the verb that is its root (for example, pass); at present, "-ing" forms of verbs must be included separately in the dictionary and labeled as adjectives. This is a limitation of the parser and is transparent to the user. Third, LDC is not yet able to parse "discontinuous constituents," constructions such as

add *the positive entries* up *in row 3*

a *higher* grade *than John made*

in which components of a single phrase or clause have been separated by another sentence element. Fourth, LDC does not currently allow arbitrary nouns to be used as modifiers, as in "the B students," due to the difficulty in determining the intended meaning. Fifth, for similar reasons, the system does not yet handle possessive phrases such as "the best EE157 student's instructor," consisting of a possessive noun with premodifiers that function as premodifiers for another noun. Finally, LDC is not yet able to handle pronoun references—personal pronouns, demonstrative pronouns and determiners, and words such as each and all when used as pronouns—because it is not yet able to use context to determine the referents of pronouns.

THE RETRIEVAL MODULE

The retrieval module of LDC has been designed to meet several criteria:

1. To be able to access loosely structured text files of the kind typically maintained in office environments rather more formal database structures
2. To provide a rich repertoire of primitive operations
3. To provide a macro facility for user customizations so that frequent compositions of primitives can be made in abbreviated form
4. To be able to deal with many user domains without intervention on the part of the system designers
5. To render query syntax independent of the specific physical structure of the data file being accessed

In addition to these criteria, the retrieval component is expected to be useful both in stand-alone mode and as a convenient retrieval component for LDC.

The query language supported by our retrieval module is very much like formal query languages for database query, but there are some important differences. For example, our provision for macros has no counterpart in most conventional systems. Furthermore, like many modern programming languages, our query structures make no distinction among levels of operations, and any sequence of commands can occur as an embedded query inside any of the others, wherever a single primitive value is required. We also provide an ordinal retrieval function and a percentage informational function that are nonstandard.

DATA FILES PROVIDED FOR

It is convenient to regard LDC as viewing its text-edited input file as a sequentially accessed file in which each line corresponds to a separate record. As a familiar example, which we will use for much of the remainder of the article, consider a final grades domain, with text lines such as:

CPS51.2	Ballard	Young, Charles	A −
CPS241.1	Starmer	Smith, John	B +
CPS241.1	Starmer	Taylor, Sue	A −

Although a certain degree of time and space overhead may result from some of the text-edited files LDC allows, most of the domains for which our interface has been designed are on the order of hundreds of records, not hundreds of thousands of records, so time and space concerns are less critical than for large conventional databases. Finally, we note that LDC makes a clear distinction between the conceptual and the physical organization of its data file, thereby allowing text-edited files to be more loosely structured than most formal database structures.

FUTURE WORK

We have described a fully operational NL processor that reached the prototype stage in May 1983. Some of the features currently being worked on are negation, limited conjunction, more elaborate verb forms, and capabilities for multiple files. Several additional capabilities we would like to provide for were mentioned earlier, and several of these are also being worked on. In the case of pronouns, we expect to adapt the domain-independent strategies developed for NLC based on a "focus list" concept similar to that being used in the related NL efforts at Duke.[7] We are also engaged in restructuring Prep, the knowledge acquisition component of LDC, to permit more English-like, as opposed to formal, specifications. Another important direction we are considering is the incorporation of the voice processing techniques being used in Biermann's VNLC and VIPS systems.[7,8]

The implementation of negation is virtually complete; therefore, we shall briefly mention how it is being handled. First of all, postnominal modifiers may be negated by using the word "not," as in:

students *not* in CPS241

CPS215 students who made a grade *not* higher than a B

courses that Steve *did not take*

instructors who did not give an F to Bill

It is instructive to note the inherent ambiguity of English phrases such as "students not failed by Ballard," which might or might not be intended to include students not taught by Ballard. Our system in fact returns this broader interpretation, as the user can obtain the narrower meaning by asking for "Ballard's students not failed by Ballard." Certain prenominal modifiers may also be negated by using "non," as in:

a *non passing* grade

the *non graduate* students in Starmer's course

Clearly, these facilities for negation are somewhat awkward when compared to the rest of the English structures of LDC, but the feature is a semantically important one. When the intended generality of negative semantics has been achieved, attention will be given to making the feature more natural.

RELATED WORK

The experimental LDC system is closest in its present form to database interface systems, because of its question-answering behavior. However, our overall research program involves the development of methods whereby complex semantics may be specified by users of an office system, regardless of whether the application of the system is for answering questions, carrying out commands (as in our previous NLC system), or performing some other task. It is therefore appropriate that we mention related efforts to customize NL systems.

The first serious attention to large-scale customizations by users was made by the REL system.[9] Recent work by these researchers at Caltech is represented by the ASK[10] and POL[11] systems, which seek to provide users with access to various software services in addition to providing simple question-answering facilities. Their emphasis is on providing for broad kinds of capabilities, whereas our effort has been to allow very complex specifications for a restricted class of domains.

A major effort seeking to allow for transportability at the database-administrator level is the TEAM project at SRI.[12,13] The TEAM approach is to carry out an interactive dialogue with database administators; the system asks questions that enable it to acquire a lexicon relating to the language to be used, a conceptual schema telling about the conceptual relations among objects, and a database schema telling about the underlying database format. A system similar to TEAM, also being developed at SRI but more loosely related to conventional database systems than TEAM, is KLAUS.[14]

Other current work in transportable NL system design includes a system being designed at Bell Labs,[15] the IRUS system[16] at BBN, and the CONSUL system[17,18] at ISI. The last of these has special potential value for office environments because it is directed toward software services at personal workstations.

ACKNOWLEDGMENTS

The authors wish to thank Alan Biermann, Martha Evens, Gary Hendrix, George Heidorn, Martha Palmer, Frank Starmer, Sharon Salveter, and Bozena and Fred Thompson for valuable discussions on our work.

This research has been supported in part by the National Science Foundation, Grant Numbers MCS-81-16607 and IST-83-01994, and in part by the National Library of Medicine, Grant Number LM-07003.

REFERENCES

1. Ballard, B., and A. Biermann. "Programming in Natural Language: NLC As a Prototype." *Proceedings of the 1979 National Conference.* Detroit, Michigan: ACM, 1979, pp. 228–237.
2. Biermann, A., and B. Ballard, "Toward Natural Language Computation." *American Journal of Computational Linguistics,* 6 (1980), pp. 71–86.
3. Biermann, A., B. Ballard, and A. Sigmon, "An Experimental Study of Natural Language Programming." *International Journal of Man-Machine Studies,* 18 (1983), pp. 71–87.
4. Ballard, B. "A Domain Class Approach to Transportable Natural Language Processing." *Cognition and Brain Theory,* 5 (1982), pp. 269–287.
5. Ballard, B., and J. Lusth, "An English-Language Processing System That 'Learns' about New Domains." *AFIPS, Proceedings of the National Computer Conference* (Vol. 52), 1983, pp. 39–46.
6. Ballard, B., J. Lusth, and N. Tinkham, "LDC-1: A Transportable, Knowledge-Based Natural Language Processor for Office Domains," Technical Report CS-1983-15, Dept. of Computer Science, Duke University, August 1983.
7. Biermann, A. "A Natural Language Processor for Office Automation." *Proceedings of the 1982 Office Automation Conference,* 1982, San Francisco.
8. Biermann, A., R. Rodman, B. Ballard, T. Betancourt, G. Bilbro, H. Deas, L. Fineman, P. Fink, K. Gilbert, and F. Heidlage, "Interactive Natural Language Processing: a Pragmatic Approach." *Conference on Applied Natural Language Processing.* Santa Monica, Ca.: Association for Computational Linguistics, 1983, pp. 180–191.
9. Thompson, F., and B. Thompson, "Practical Natural Language Processing: The REL System as Prototype." In M. Rubinoff and M. Yovits (eds.), *Advances in Computers, Vol. 3.* New York: Academic Press, 1975.
10. Thompson, B., and F. Thompson, "Introducing ASK, a Simple Knowledgeable System," *Conference on Applied Natural Language Processing.* Santa Monica, Ca.: Association for Computational Linguistics, 1983, pp. 17–24.
11. Thompson, F., and B. Thomspon, "Shifting to a Higher Gear in a Natural Language System." *AFIPS, Proceedings of the National Computer Conference* (Vol. 50), 1981, pp. 657–662.
12. Grosz, B. "TEAM: a Transportable Natural Language Interface System." *Conference on Applied Natural Language Processing.* Santa Monica, Ca.: Association for Computational Linguistics, 1983, pp. 39–45.
13. Hendrix, G., and W. Lewis, "Transportable Natural-Language Interfaces to Databases." *Proceedings of the Ninteenth Annual Meeting of the ACL.* Palo Alto, Ca.: Association for Computational Linguistics, 1981, pp. 159–165.
14. Haas, N., and G. Hendrix, "An Approach to Acquiring and Applying Knowledge." *First National Conference on Artificial Intelligence.* Palo Alto, Ca.: American Association for Artificial Intelligence, 1980, pp. 235–239.
15. Ginsparg, J. "A Robust Portable Natural Language Data Base Interface." *Conference on Applied Natural Language Processing.* Santa Monica, Ca.: Association for Computational Linguistics, 1983, pp. 25–30.
16. Bates, M., and R. Bobrow, "A Transportable Natural Language Interface for Information Retrieval." Working paper, Bolt, Beranek and Newman, Cambridge, Mass., 1983.
17. Mark, W. "Representation and Inference in the Consul System." *International Joint Conference on Artificial Intelligence,* 1981.
18. Wilczynski, D. "Knowledge Acquisition in the Consul System." *International Joint Conference on Artificial Intelligence,* 1981.

Really arguing with your computer in natural language

by MARGOT FLOWERS and MICHAEL G. DYER
University of California at Los Angeles
Los Angeles, California

ABSTRACT

Recently, the computer science community has been hearing a lot about "fifth generation" computers and the Japanese large-scale project to build intelligent software that can "think," "reason," and "understand human languages."[1] It is in the field of artificial intelligence (AI) where such intelligence machines and programs are being designed and created. How far along is the field of AI? How close are AI programs to being able to "reason" or "understand" as humans do? This paper is intended to give scientists outside the field of AI some insight about the problems, issues, and current status of computational models of human argumentation.

INTRODUCTION

As researchers in one subarea of artificial intelligence (AI), called cognitive modeling, we are particularly interested in building models of human cognitive abilities. This paper is intended to give scientists outside of the field of AI some insight about the problems, issues, and current status of one specific area of AI research. In this paper we examine briefly what issues are involved in building a computer capable of engaging in an argument, and then review some past and recent computer programs that have addressed these issues.

MOTIVATION

Before embarking on such an effort, we might first ask why anyone would want to argue with one's own (or anyone else's) computer. First of all, people are always arguing. People argue, for instance, over the U.S. role in Central America, whether the U.S. should restrict Japanese imports, whether God exists, about the importance of the Equal Rights Amendment, and about numerous other topics concerning sex, religion, law, and politics. If we are ever going to have truly intelligent machines, they should, at minimum, be able to understand what's going on in an argument and participate in an argument by defending or justifying a given viewpoint.

Second, as expert systems[2] become more sophisticated, it becomes essential that such systems be able to explain their decision-making processes.[3] In medical expert systems,[4] for example, this involves printing a trace of the rules the system used for arriving at diagnoses. There are many complex domains, however, where the rules are not so clear, and where argumentation and debate are essential to understanding and formulating plans and strategies. Consider a military general, for example: Who would trust the decisions of a general who can not defend his views in the give and take of a debate?

Finally, understanding or engaging in arguments requires both fundamental reasoning and language comprehension skills. Argumentation turns out to be an ideal task domain for scientifically exploring these basic human capabilities.

A TYPICAL ARGUMENT

Before we can design and implement computational arguers, we must know what problems typically arise in everyday arguments. Consider the following argument fragment, based on the recent destruction by a Soviet military jet of a Korean airliner that strayed into Soviet air space.

[a] Korean: The USSR should be punished for downing the Korean jet.
[b] Soviet: It was a spy plane.
[c] Korean: With 269 people on board?
[d] Soviet: They were being used as a cover to protect the U.S. spies hidden on board.
[e] Korean: The U.S. has no need to use a commercial jetliner. Their satellite system is more than adequate.
[f] Soviet: Well, the USSR has a right to protect its borders.
[g] Korean: That may be true, but the USSR has no right to use force against nonmilitary aircraft. Other countries do not shoot down Soviet commercial jets when they stray across national borders.

There is nothing exceptional about this argument fragment. After the Korean jetliner incident, numerous debates arose, many of them similar to this one. We can begin to appreciate the inferential capabilities involved in processing the argument fragment above simply by replacing the 'obvious' responses above with alternative responses.

[a] Korean: The USSR should be punished for downing the Korean jet.
[b] Soviet: It was a spy plane.

Alternative responses to [a]:

[b1] Soviet: Why thank you.
[b2] Soviet: It was a white plane.
[b3] Soviet: It was a big plane.

Why is [b] reasonable and not [b1–3]? To avoid generating [b1] for instance, the Soviet must realize that [a] is not a compliment, but an attack. In addition, both the Soviet and Korean must understand the world of international espionage, national borders, and justifications for military force in order to both generate and appreciate the significance of the word "spy" in [b].

[b] Soviet: It was a spy plane.
[c] Korean: With 269 people on board?

Alternative responses to [b]:

[c1] Korean: With 300 windows on board?
[c2] Korean: With 4 bathrooms on board?

[c] is phrased on the surface as a question. However, both argument participants know that [c] does not expect a "yes" or "no" answer. In fact, the Korean is actually saying: "I disagree that it was a spy plane, since 269 spies on board a single plane would be ridiculous. It was therefore a passenger plane; not a spy plane."

[f] Soviet: The USSR has a right to protect its borders.
[g] Korean: . . .Other countries do not shoot down Soviet commercial jets when they stray across national borders.

Alternative responses to [f]:

[g1] Korean: . . .Other countries do not shoot down Soviet sea gulls when they stray across national borders.
[g2] Korean: . . .Other countries do not shoot down American planes when they stray across national borders.

[g1] is perfectly correct, but a totally unreasonable statement. Why? [g2] is also a perfectly true statement, but totally irrelevant to the argument at hand. But how do we know this? Clearly, the Korean is *reasoning by analogy* in [g] to rebut his opponent's justification. But how is the correct analogy found?

For a computer to hold up its end in an argument, it must first understand what's been said. Most arguments are in a natural language; in this case, English. It is doubtful that anyone will find arguments stated in a formal language, such as a mathematical notation or programming language. One can argue about whether a mathematical proof or computer program is correct, but the argument itself most assuredly will be in a natural language.

In addition to understanding the meaning of each natural language statement, the computer must also be able to comprehend the intention[5] or significance of what is being said, as it relates to the argument at hand. For instance, understanding the significance of "with 269 people on board" requires not only understanding the meanings of the words "on board" (refers to people inside a plane, and not on top of a flat wooden object) but also that the Korean has just given *evidence* to refute the claim that it was a spy plane.

Clearly, an argument involves claims or beliefs about facts or appropriate behavior. These claims often have a moral element: that someone was wrong to do something or responsible for a wrongful deed. Our argument starts out with just such a claim, that is, that the Soviets were wrong to shoot down the Korean airliner.

Even if the computer understands that the opponent has attacked it, it must still figure out what kind of attack it is, and then decide how to defend itself against such an attack.

Simply recognizing an attack as being a member of a given class of attacks is nontrivial. "It was a spy plane" is a justification for shooting down the Korean plane. But why? Here we see that comprehension requires specific world knowledge. This is a truism in AI. It is hard to argue without arguing about something. That something, in this case, involves knowing how spying relates to defense of borders through the use of military force. The computer must already know which situations allow military force and which do not. Without this knowledge comprehension of the significance of an attack or a rebuttal becomes impossible.

ISSUES IN ARGUMENTATION

To build such a computational arguer, we must address the following problems:

1. How do we represent the meaning of each participant's statements?
2. How do we encode the world knowledge to which our arguer's statements are implicitly referring?
3. How do we access these meanings and apply world knowledge in order to go from sentences in the language to these representations of meaning?
4. How do we organize this knowledge so that only the relevant knowledge is applied and the "right" inferences are made at the right time?
5. How do we keep track of the argument as it unfolds, and how do we represent and apply the argument-so-far as a context for statements yet to follow?
6. How do we represent the beliefs of the argument participants?
7. What are the strategies used by argument participants, and how do we represent them?
8. What does the resulting memory of an argument look like?
9. How do factors, such as world knowledge, reasoning ability, memory search, knowledge of language, and argument strategies interact?

There is not enough space here to go into all of these issues in detail, but we will address several of them briefly.

Understanding Language

In the past decade a good deal of progress has been made in text comprehension. Much of this work in natural language understanding has concentrated on the memory structures, inference mechanisms, knowledge representations, and parsing schemes for handling narrative texts. For example, the SAM program[6] used the notion of scripts[7] to read stories concerning stereotypic action sequences, such as going to a restaurant. PAM[8] read stories that dealt with goal and plan relationships between narrative characters. OPUS[9] answered questions about stories involving the use of physical objects. These earlier language-understanding programs were limited to the extent that each dealt only with the application of a single knowledge construct. The next research step involved exploring the adequacy and limitations of these knowledge constructs in the context of more complicated narratives. An important part of this research also involved exploring the way in which multiple sources of knowledge interact during narrative comprehension.

One result of this research effort was a story-understanding program named BORIS.[10] Below is a story fragment read by BORIS:

Divorce—1

Richard hadn't heard from his college roommate Paul for years.... When a letter finally arrived from San Francisco, Richard was anxious to find out how Paul was.

Unfortunately, the news was not good. Paul's wife Sarah wanted a divorce. She also wanted the car, the house, the children, and alimony. Paul. . .didn't want to see Sarah walk off with everything he had. His salary from the state school system was very small. Not knowing who to turn to, he was hoping for a favor from the only lawyer he knew. . . .

Richard eagerly picked up the phone and dialed. After a brief conversation, Paul agreed to have lunch with him the next day. He sounded extremely relieved and grateful.

The next day, as Richard was driving to the restaurant he barely avoided hitting an old man on the street. He felt extremely upset by the incident, and had three drinks at the restaurant. When Paul arrived Richard was fairly drunk. After the food came, Richard spilled a cup of coffee on Paul. Paul seemed very annoyed by this so Richard offered to drive him home for a change of clothes.

When Paul walked into the bedroom and found Sarah with another man he nearly had a heart attack. Then he realized what a blessing it was. With Richard there as a witness, Sarah's divorce case was shot. . . .

To understand this story, BORIS must have access to multiple sources of knowledge, including those listed in Figure 1. BORIS coordinates and applies these different knowledge constructs to build an episodic memory of causally connected actions, motivations, settings, interpersonal relationships, and so on. The program then demonstrates its understanding through answering questions.[11] Below are some of the verbatim questions presented to BORIS and the verbatim answers generated:

What happened to Richard at home?
Richard got a letter from Paul.
Why was Paul upset about the divorce?
Paul and Sarah were fighting over the family possessions.
What did Paul do for a living?
Paul was a teacher.
Why did Paul write to Richard?
Paul wanted Richard to be his lawyer.
What happened to Richard on the way to the restaurant?
Richard almost ran over an old man.
Why did Richard spill the coffee?
Richard was drunk.
How did Paul feel?
Paul was mad at Richard.
What happened to Paul at home?
Paul caught Sarah committing adultery.

Knowledge	Examples
scripts	restaurant, phoning, driving
plans	deciding to go home, deciding to meet for lunch
goals	wanting to win the case, wanting help from a friend
relationships	friend, roommate, wife
social roles	lawyer, waitress, teacher
settings	home, restaurant, road, bedroom
physical objects	phone, liquor, money, food, letter
physical actions	eating, talking, walking
emotions	gratitude, anger, surprise, worry
empathy	congratulations
abstract scripts	favors, service contracts
themes	adulterous spouse caught cheating

Figure 1—Multiple sources of knowledge used in BORIS

In BORIS, all processes of language analysis, knowledge application, and knowledge interactions are implemented as *demons*. Demons fall within the class of production systems.[12,13] Demons implement a form of delayed processing and wait until their test conditions are satisfied, at which point they fire and execute their actions. Each live (active) demon is in charge of its own life cycle, deciding how long to stay alive and when to die.

BORIS reads each narrative sentence in a left-to-right order. Entries in the lexicon may be words, phrases, roots, or suffixes. Associated with each lexical item are conceptualizations and attached demons. When a lexical item is recognized, the associated conceptualization is placed into a working memory and its attached demons are spawned.

When demons "fire," they bind together conceptual structures in working memory and instantiate long-term conceptual structures in episodic memory. These conceptual structures are then accessed by other demons. Thus, both episodic and working memory serve as contexts for parsing. Consider the phrase "picked up the phone and dialed" in "Divorce—1." In the lexicon, "pick up" is defined in terms of the conceptual dependency[14] conceptualization of GRASP. Associated with this conceptualization are demons that fill in cases associated with GRASP, as in Figure 2. Associated with each unambiguous lexical entry is a single conceptualization. Each unfilled role is followed by an asterisk (*), which acts as a place-holder for a binding. Demons whose task it is to fill these roles appear after the arrow (⇐). Each arrow indicates where to bind the return values of the demons. Demons that take parameters are enclosed within parentheses, followed by the arguments passed to them.

When BORIS reads "picked up," the GRASP conceptualization is placed in working memory and the associated demons are spawned. Immediately one of the demons fires and binds George as the ACTOR of the GRASP. When "phone" is encountered, another instantiation of the same EXPECT

```
Lexical Entry

pick up         (GRASP ACTOR * <==(EXPECT 'HUMAN 'BEFORE)
                       OBJECT * <==(EXPECT 'PHYS-OBJ 'AFTER)
                       INSTAN * <==(APPLY-KS))

phone           (PHYS-OBJ TYPE (PHONE))


Associated demons:

EXPECT [Pattern, Direction]
  Search Working Memory for Pattern in the Direction
  specified When found, bind to role

APPLY-KS [ACT]
  If a primitive CD ACT is encountered
  Then examine the OBJECT of the ACT
    and If the OBJECT has an associated script or MOP
        Then apply that script of MOP to the ACT
           If MOP found which is uninstantiated,
           Then create an instance in episodic memory
```

Figure 2—Demons associated with "GRASP"

demon fires and binds PHONE as the OBJECT of the GRASP. At this point, APPLY-KS fires. It is the task of this demon to reinterpret the GRASP in terms of a larger knowledge structure. APPLY-KS contains several heuristics. One heuristic is to search BORIS's object-primitive knowledge of whatever is bound in the OBJECT slot. Through the physical object of PHONE, BORIS accesses the knowledge structure M-PHONE, which holds information about how to answer and make calls. APPLY-KS then applies M-PHONE to the GRASP conceptualization. Since GRASP(phone) is an act in M-PHONE, the match succeeds. Since this is the first instance of a phone call with Richard as the caller, BORIS creates an instantiation of this event in episodic memory with Richard as CALLER. When "dialed" is read, the demon associated with dialing will immediately find M-PHONE instantiated in working memory with a pointer to a corresponding event in episodic memory. As a result, the dialing action will simply update this instance of M-PHONE. Meanwhile, demons associated with M-PHONE have been spawned. These demons look for the recipient of the call, the message being conveyed, and whatever goal Richard plans to achieve by making this call.

Thus, the process of comprehension may be abstractly characterized as a cycle of processes that build new knowledge structures, where both demons and knowledge structures arise from lexical input.

The research described here is based on the premise that natural language comprehension is a process of intelligent inference, memory access, and knowledge application. Comprehension requires a great deal of prior world knowledge. The key to understanding lies in computational insight about human knowledge and memory constructs: their representation, application, instantiation, interaction, control, coordination, indexing, access, search, and retrieval. For each class of knowledge there are associated different processes of memory search, inference, and language analysis. Knowledge constructs also interact with one another in different ways. For example, knowledge of emotions[15] will interact with goal and plan situations, for example, the failure of a plan or goal may cause frustration or anger.

The knowledge constructs used by current story-understanding and question-answering systems serve as a necessary but insufficient foundation for dealing with arguments. Although argument participation requires knowledge of goals, plans, scripts, themes, and so on, additional knowledge and processing constructs are required.

Representing Beliefs About the World

In an argument, the arguer defends his own beliefs while attacking those of his opponents. Understanding the conceptual content of an argument, therefore, requires the computer to possess a representation of opposing ideologies.

Two researchers who have worked on computational models of political beliefs are Abelson[16] and Carbonell.[17] Abelson developed a model of conservative political ideology called the "Cold Warrior," which was intended to capture Sen. Barry Goldwater's belief system. The most important notion

```
                  Fuzzy                          Communist
             liberal thinking                     schemes
                    |                                |
                    |            Use of              |
                    |       Free World power         |
Our call    --------+--------------------------------+------  Free World
to action           |                                |          victory
                    |                                |
                    v                                v
               Free World                        Communist
               paralysis                          victory

                                              (Abelson 1973, p. 291)
```

Figure 3—Conservative Cold War ideology

in Abelson's work was the *master script,* which modeled relationships among various themes in a conservative Cold War ideology, as depicted in Figure 3. Sequences of interactions and conflicts among themes were organized by *answer frames.* For example, one ideologically conservative answer frame contained the sequence given in Figure 4.

The master script notion was very useful for capturing the relationships among several of Goldwater's beliefs. Using this master script, Abelson's "Cold Warrior" could express its conservative point of view. Carbonell has pointed out that the Cold Warrior lacked a knowledge of mundane reality.[17] In addition, while capable of expressing a point of view, the Cold Warrior model was incapable of defending it. In contrast, the real senator can support his own beliefs and can refute the attacks and criticisms of his opponents, using counterexamples and various forms of reasoning and argumentation.

In his program, POLITICS, Carbonell modeled political ideologies in terms of *goal trees.* Goal trees both organized a set of goals according to subgoal relationships and ranked them in terms of their relative importance. For example, the goal tree fragments in Figure 5 represent a portion of a U.S. conservative ideology in Carbonell's model. In addition to their own set of goals, the liberal and conservative each maintain goal trees representing perceived Soviet ideologies. For example, the conservative believes that the Soviet's most important goal is Western domination, while the liberal does not.

Carbonell used goal trees combined with counterplanning strategies in POLITICS to model subjective understanding of political events. The POLITICS program could predict events and answer questions by accessing the goals and counterplans of the characters involved. For example, if asked the question: "Should character X do act Y?" POLITICS then checked the consequences of the act to see if it might achieve one of the character's goals. If asked a question of the form: "What should character1 do if character2 does act X?" the program

```
when:            Communist Schemes,
then:            Communist Victory,
unless:          Use of Free World Power,
in which case:   Free World Victory.
```

Figure 4—Conservative answer frame

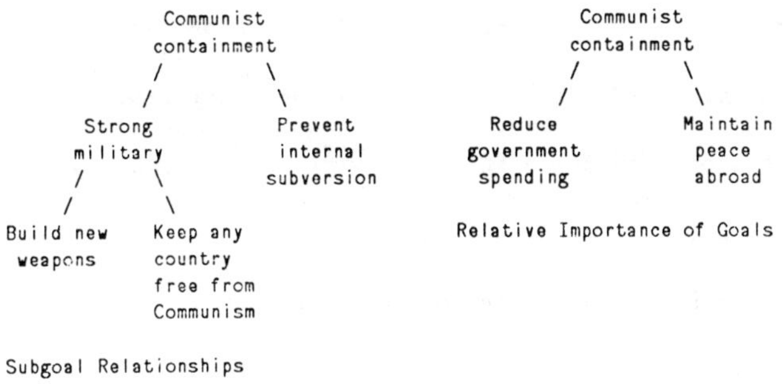

Figure 5—Conservative's goal tree fragments

checked whether the act blocked character1's goals, and if so, it accessed an appropriate counterplan to formulate an answer to the question. Below is a fragment of POLITICS' question-answering behavior after being told a single political fact:

> INPUT STORY: The U.S. Congress is expected to approve the Panama Canal treaty.
> (INTERPRET U.S.—CONSERVATIVE)
> Q: *Should the U.S. approve the treaty?*
> A: No, the treaty is bad for the United States.
> Q: *Why is the treaty bad for the U.S.?*
> A: The United States would lose the canal to Panama and the United States will be weaker.
> Q: *Why should the U.S. worry about Russia taking over the canal?*
> A: Because Russia wants to control the world.
>
> (INTERPRET U.S.—LIBERAL)
> Q: *Should the U.S. approve the treaty?*
> A: Yes. The Panama Canal Treaty is good for the United States.
> Q: *What if Russia tries to take over the Canal?*
> A: Russia does not want conflict with the U.S. . . .

Applying Argument Strategies

Recently, research has been done in building process models of argumentation. One computer program, ABDUL/ILANA[18,19,20] can model either side of an argument between an Arab (ABDUL) and Israeli (ILANA) over who was responsible for the 1967 Arab-Israeli war. This argument dialogue appears below:

[a] Arab: Who started the 1967 War?
[b] Israeli: The Arabs did, by blockading the Straits of Tiran.
[c] Arab: But Israel attacked first.
[d] Israeli: According to international law, blockades are acts of war.
[e] Arab: Were we supposed to let you import American arms through the Straits?
[f] Israeli: Israel was not importing arms through the Straits. The reason for the blockade was to keep Israel from importing oil from Iran.
[g] Arab: But Israel was importing arms, and that's because Israel is trying to take over the Middle East.
[h] Israeli: If Israel were trying to take over the Middle East, then why didn't Israel take Cairo in 1973?

Major issues addressed in ABDUL/ILANA were (1) How does X even recognize that X's opponent Y has attacked a belief of X, or has supported one of Y's beliefs? (2) Given an attack by Y, how does X choose a defense? and (3) How is an argument represented in memory? We will briefly discuss these issues using the argument dialogue above.

We can see that each participant here is accusing the other participant's nation of starting a war. To recognize that [b] is an accusation, ABDUL must know that wars are "bad," that parties responsible for causing bad events to occur are also bad, that accusations involve attributing responsibility for a morally reprehensible event, that any accusation should receive a rebuttal if possible. To counter the accusation in [b], ABDUL searches its memory of historical events and notices that Israel fired first. This fact forms a useful rebuttal, but why? There are other events in historical memory, such as resolutions before the United Nations, results of Israeli elections, and so on, yet none of these constitute a useful rebuttal. ABDUL must know general facts, such as: (1) a war contains a sequence of events and (2) the initiator of the first event in certain sequences of events can be viewed as responsible for the entire sequence.

In [e], the Arab asked the Israeli a question that ostensibly requires an answer of "yes" or "no." However, ILANA must realize that neither answer is appropriate; that the question is actually rhetorical, and that it contains an indirect accusation. In [f], the Israeli directly denies the accusation made in [e] and counters with another accusation. Notice that in [f] and [g] the argument revolves around whether oil or arms were being imported into Israel. As readers we realize that this distinction is highly relevant, but how? To recognize the relevance of this distinction, ABDUL/ILANA must possess knowledge about the world of foreign trade and of armaments. Furthermore, ABDUL/ILANA also must possess more abstract knowledge of how goals and plans interact with argument strategies. This knowledge includes rules, such as:

> IF X believes that Y is executing action A to enable X to violate a goal G of Y
> THEN Y may block A and use the fact of X's intention as a justification for Y's action

In [g], the Arab accuses the Israeli of "trying to take over the Middle East." The Israeli's rebuttal in [h] is very effective, but how did ILANA come up with this, especially since the event of taking Cairo never happened? Clearly, there are an infinite number of nonevents, so storing them all in memory is simply impossible. In this case, ABDUL/ILANA contains a theory of *expectation failures,*[21] which organize memory around predicted and unpredicted events. Since the take-over of Cairo was predicted but unfulfilled, it is stored explicitly in memory as an expectation failure. Such failures are then used in arguments as one source of counterexamples.[22]

```
                          a
Israel responsible <----------> Egypt responsible
for '67 war                     for '67 war
        ↑                               ↑
        |                               |
        | s  attacks are                | s  blockades are
        |    acts of war                |    acts of war
        |                               |
Israel fired on Egypt           Egypt blockaded Israel
```

Figure 6—A-graph fragment

As the argument progresses, ABDUL/ILANA builds up a conceptual, language-independent representation of the argument, called an *argument graph* (or a-graph).[18,23] The a-graph is composed of beliefs connected by relationships of *attack* (a) and *support* (s). Figure 6 is a simplified fragment of the a-graph for part of the argument over the Six-Day War. Whenever ABDUL/ILANA received an opponent's input, it searched the argument graph to determine what belief was being supported or attacked. For example, a belief could be attacked by a direct contradiction, such as:

Israeli: The Arabs are responsible for the war.
Arab: No. The Israelis are responsible for the war.

However, direct attacks are not very effective. Furthermore, use of direct contradiction by both opponents leads to the "Did!" "Didn't!" "Did!" "Didn't!" argument "loop" that children's arguments often exhibit. A more effective approach is to attack one's opponent by finding support for a claim that contradicts a claim of the opponent. By using this strategy, ABDUL determines that the following response is more suitable:

Israeli: The Arabs are responsible for the war.
Abdul: But Israel fired first.

Reasoning During Argumentation

People support their beliefs with chains of reasoning. The HARRY program[24] explores the role of reasoning during arguing. A fundamental notion in HARRY is that human reasoning frequently makes use of previous examples, prior chains of reasoning formed from previous arguments, and adaptations of situations related to the current problem. Human reasoning rarely relies on the application of general-purpose rules. Thus, reasoning in HARRY is viewed as a memory-based process. In general, turning what was a rule-based task into a memory-based task makes the process of comprehension easier.

HARRY has been used to model various forms of reasoning in economic and political domains. Consider the following transcript, taken from an interview with the economist, Seymour Melman, on the "MacNeil/Lehrer Report":

"*Economist:* The increased funding of DOD [the Department of Defense] has lead to today's higher rate of inflation in the U.S."

```
Machinery producers customers of the government
                |
Cost maximizing became a part of machinery producers
                |
Costs of production and administration increased
                |
Prices of new machinery rose
                |
New machinery purchase no longer desirable
                |
New machinery purchases no longer made
                |
Productivity growth rate falls
               ...
                |
Inflation increases
```

Figure 7—Melman's reasoning

"*Interviewer:* Why do you believe that?"

"*Economist:* Well, DOD is publicly funded. As a result, they tend to cost maximize. That is, they do not carefully monitor their costs. Starting in the fifties, DOD became a major customer of machinery-producing industries. Thus, the heavy machinery industry began to cost maximize as well, causing the prices for new heavy machinery to increase. As the purchase of heavy machinery decreased, the mechanization per worker decreased, causing the productivity growth rate to decrease as well. As a result, inflation has increased."

The reasoning chain produced by Melman is rather complicated and includes the components depicted in Figure 7. How might Melman have produced this chain of reasoning? Producing this particular chain through the application of very general rules is possible but would be very costly. Clearly, Melman had already produced identical, or at least related, chains of reasoning before appearing on "MacNeil/Lehrer." Instead of applying general reasoning rules, experts such as Melman more likely retain previous reasoning chains in memory. These chains are generalized, chunked, indexed in various ways in memory, and then subsequently retrieved, adapted, and applied.

The first time HARRY produced the above chain of reasoning, it was done laboriously through the application of general rules. The resulting chain was then abstracted to form *reasoning scripts* (e.g., $R–GOV–SPEND→INFLATION). These reasoning scripts are then applied to similar reasoning problems. Thus, HARRY's reasoning becomes more memory-based and less rule-based as HARRY goes through successive reasoning experiences.

CONCLUSIONS

Traditionally, reasoning has been characterized as a process of logic. This is not surprising since some of the first people to address reasoning were logicians. Also, a common tactic in arguments and editorials is to accuse one's opponent of being "illogical." However, protocols indicate that people do not reason by syllogism, nor do they employ carefully constructed proof-style chains of deductive reasoning.

Whether an arguing system is implemented in a logic-programming language, such as PROLOG,[25] or a functional programming language, such as LISP,[26] the choice made is actually neutral toward the problems raised in modeling human argumentation. The most interesting issues that arise during everyday arguments are not logical as such, but rather involve problems in representing, organizing, and applying human knowledge constructs. The limitations of our programs reflect our limited theoretical understanding in these areas. Meanwhile, it will be some time before our home computers start arguing with us or requiring us to possess Socratic debating skills just to talk them into executing our home income tax programs.

ACKNOWLEDGMENTS

At UCLA, the work of both authors has been supported in part by the National Science Foundation. Part of the work described here was performed while the authors were at Yale University, supported in part by the Office of Naval Research, in conjunction with Larry Birnbaum, Pete Johnson, Rod McGuire, and Tom Wolf.

REFERENCES

1. Feigenbaum, E., and P. McCorduck. *The Fifth Generation: Artificial Intelligence and Japan's Computer Challenge to the World.* Menlo Park, Calif.: Addison-Wesley, 1983.
2. Davis, R., and D. Lenat. *Knowledge-Based Systems in Artificial Intelligence.* New York: McGraw-Hill, 1980.
3. Hayes-Roth, F., D. A. Waterman, and D. B. Lenat (eds.). *Building Expert Systems,* Reading, Mass.: Addison-Wesley, 1983.
4. Shortliffe, E. *Computer-Based Medical Consultations: MYCIN.* New York: American Elsevier, 1976.
5. Allen, J., and C. Perrault. "Analyzing Intention in Utterances." *Artificial Intelligence,* 15 (1980), pp. 143–178.
6. Cullingford, R. C. "Script Application: Computer Understanding of Newspaper Stories." Technical Report 116, Yale University Department of Computer Science, 1978.
7. Schank, R. C., and R. Abelson. *Scripts, Plans, Goals, and Understanding.* Hillsdale, N.J.: Lawrence Erlbaum Associates, 1977.
8. Wilensky, R. "Understanding Goal-Based Stories." Technical Report 140, Yale University Department of Computer Science, 1978.
9. Lehnert, W. G. "Representing Physical Objects in Memory." Technical Report 131, Yale University Department of Computer Science, 1978.
10. Dyer, M. G. *Understanding: A Computer Model of Integrated Processing for Narrative Comprehension.* Cambridge, Mass.: MIT Press, 1983.
11. Lehnert, W. G. *The Process of Question Answering.* Hillsdale, N.J.: Lawrence Erlbaum, 1978.
12. Davis, R., and J. King. "An Overview of Production Systems." In *Machine Intelligence,* 1977.
13. Newell, A. "Production Systems: Models of Control Structures." In P. Winston (ed.), *Visual Information Processing.* New York: Academic Press, 1973.
14. Schank, R. C., and K. Colby (eds.). *Computer Models of Thought and Language.* San Francisco: W. H. Freeman, 1973.
15. Dyer, M. G. "The Role of Affect in Narratives." *Cognitive Science,* 3 (1983).
16. Abelson, R. P. "The Structure of Belief Systems." In R. C. Schank and K. Colby (eds.), *Computer Models of Thought and Language.* San Francisco: W. H. Freeman, 1973.
17. Carbonell, J. *Subjective Understanding: Computer Models of Belief Systems.* Ann Arbor, Mich.: UMI Research Press, 1981.
18. Flowers, M., R. McGuire, and L. Birnbaum. "Adversary Arguments and the Logic of Personal Attacks." In W. G. Lehnert and Ringle (eds.), *Strategies for Natural Language Processing.* Hillsdale, N. J.: Lawrence Erlbaum Associates, 1982.
19. Birnbaum, L., M. Flowers, and R. McGuire. "Toward an AI Model of Argumentation." *Proceedings of the First Annual National Conference on Artificial Intelligence.* The American Association for Artificial Intelligence, August 1980.
20. McGuire, R., L. Birnbaum, and M. Flowers. "Opportunistic Processing in Arguments." *Proceedings of the Seventh International Joint Conference on Artificial Intelligence,* IJCAI, Vancouver, British Columbia, August 1981.
21. Schank, R. C. *Dynamic Memory: A Theory of Learning in Computers and People.* Cambridge: Cambridge University Press, 1982.
22. Flowers, M. "On Being Contradictory," *Proceedings of the Second National Conference on Artrificial Intelligence.* The American Association for Artificial Intelligence, Pittsburgh, Pa., August 1982.
23. Birnbaum, L. Ph.D. Dissertation, Yale University, forthcoming.
24. Flowers, M. *Memory-Based Reasoning: A Computer Model of Human Reasoning.* Ph.D. Dissertation, Yale University, forthcoming.
25. Clocksin, W., and C. Mellish. *Programming in Prolog.* New York: Springer-Verlag, 1981.
26. Winston, P., and B. Horn. *LISP.* Menlo Park, Calif.: Addison-Wesley, 1980.

Introducing VIPS: A voice-interactive processing system for document management

by ALAN W. BIERMANN, KERMIT C. GILBERT, and LINDA S. FINEMAN
Duke University
Durham, North Carolina

ABSTRACT

The voice-interactive processing system enables a user to display office-related data on a screen and manipulate it through a combination of voice and touch commands. The system responds immediately to each request, updating the screen so that the correctness of each action can be verified. If an undesired result is achieved, the user may back up and restate the command in more exacting language.

The processor is a general system interface designed to handle various domains including text manipulation, file handling, calendar management, message passing, and desk calculation. Examples of its behavior in the text manipulation domain are given.

BACKGROUND

The voice-interactive processing system (VIPS) is a voice-driven natural-language processor designed to perform in several areas of application within the general framework of office automation. VIPS is aimed at the naive or casual computer user, such as an upper level manager, and its major goal is to improve the accessibility of office automation systems for such individuals.

The architecture of VIPS embodies our second thoughts on natural-language processing. It benefits from our earlier experience in building a natural language system for matrix calculations.[1,2] A major design goal has been to concentrate the domain-dependent aspects of the system as much as possible, so that transitions from one application area to the next will not necessitate major changes to the code. The agenda for bringing office systems tasks within the scope of VIPS begins with text manipulation, continues to file management, and may eventually cover calendar management, message passing, and desk calculation. The text manipulation function is operative and is being tested currently. The modifications necessary to refit that system for managing a tree-structured file system are understood. Calendar management seems to pose no new problems, but that application and the remaining ones have not yet been examined closely.

SYSTEM FEATURES

In the text domain, VIPS allows the user to retrieve from a file a preexisting document, to enter a new document from a keyboard, to edit the document, and to store all or any part of it in a file. Commands take the form of English imperative sentences, optionally augmented by typed input or by touch input to a display screen. Spoken input is recognized by a commercial connected or discrete speech recognition machine. Recently we have obtained the most reliable performance from a Votan V-5000 discrete recognizer. Touch input is captured by a Carroll Touch Technology touch screen mounted on a large-screen color monitor.

Commands are uttered as a sequence of discrete words, using a vocabulary of about 100 words. The speech recognizer produces best and second best guesses for each word spoken and these are passed to the error-correcting parser, which attempts to identify an acceptable command utterance. Audio feedback indicates to the user those occasions when the recognizer is unable to make any guesses about the input. An utterance ends with the token, "over," as in "delete this word over." Other control words in the vocabulary are "correction," which indicates that the user wants to alter the current unfinished command, and "goodbye," which is the graceful way out of VIPS.

The touch input capability permits the use of very succinct commands, such as "put this sentence after that sentence," where "this" and "that" are instantiated by temporally appropriate touches to the display.

Keyboard input is used to instantiate string variables mentioned in a spoken command. These string variables allow the user to identify to the system proper names, such as names of files or segments of the document, which could not otherwise be referenced with the limited voice vocabulary. For example, the command, "insert xl after each x2 in paragraph two," would require typed input for x1 and x2, where x1 is a string to be inserted and x2 is a string to be searched for in paragraph two. The user is prompted for this input.

The user brings a document into VIPS by issuing the command, "retrieve x1" and typing the name of the file (i.e., instantiating x1) containing the text of interest. Alternatively, a user may say, "enter x1" and respond to the prompt by typing a document directly to VIPS. A document is written back to a given file by the command, "store the document in x1," where x1 is the name of some (possibly new) file. Selected parts of a document can be written to a file. For example, "store the title of each section in x1" could be used to create a table of contents.

When a file is retrieved, a screenful of formatted text is displayed, starting at the beginning of the document. Each subsequent command that alters the document causes the updating of the display. To step through the document, the user says "goto paragraph two" or "goto the first subsection," etc.

Editing commands insert or delete text, move it from one place to another, or cause one string to replace another string. The system can be focused on a text object or a class of objects by the "consider" command. If VIPS fails to execute the user's intent, that fact becomes apparent when the display is updated. The previous state of the text, in that case, can be restored by issuing the "backup" command.

SYSTEM COMPONENTS

VIPS consists of four PASCAL modules and is designed to run on an IBM Personal Computer interfacing with an IBM 5520 office automation system. The four modules are composed of an ATN-style parser, which time-stamps and merges touch and voice input, prompts for and captures typed input (if necessary), and produces a parse tree that identifies all the constituents of the command utterance. Second is a translator, which accepts a parse tree, an array of touch coordinates (if any), and a package of typed input (if any). It produces a "bubble structure," described in detail later, which guides the execution of the semantics module. Next is the semantics module, which receives the bubble structure and any typed input, maintains the text–data world and the context of the user–VIPS dialogue, and effects the user's command by interpreting the bubble structure. The fourth module is the formatter, which receives the text–data world (or a portion of it) and formats it for display and printing after the execution of each command utterance, then returns to the semantics module a map of the updated display for the purpose of resolving subsequent touch inputs.

DESIGN CONSIDERATIONS

Text–Data World

The objects of discourse in our text domain form a logical containment hierarchy of characters, words, sentences, paragraphs, subsections, sections, and documents. Titles and other such entities are defined. A left- and right-bracket character pair is defined for each object class in the domain. When a document is first brought into the VIPS text–data world, a transducer identifies the objects in it according to a few, simple rules. This identification is preserved by enclosing the object in the appropriate left and right brackets and entering this marked-up object into a linear array. Single text characters are not bracketed as a matter of course, to conserve memory, but can be under certain circumstances.

In the text domain it is necessary to transduce a document once to establish the containment hierarchy. Violations of the hierarchy are possible and can handled by the system. For example, it might be reasonable to put a paragraph, perhaps some quoted material, inside a sentence. VIPS allows this, but it is the user's responsibility to decide whether or not such an act makes sense. Our goal has been to exclude knowledge about text from VIPS as much as possible, relying on the user's knowledge, the immediate updating of the display, and the back-up capability to keep the text–data world well formed.

Context Mechanism

The context for interpreting commands in VIPS is developed and preserved by a stack of "focus" lists. Each list consists of a set of pointers to a set of objects of some class, for example, pointers to some words or paragraphs. All the objects pointed to by a given list are actually contained by the objects pointed to by the list immediately below in the stack. The focus stack determines the order in which objects are searched for in the text–data world during the execution of a command.

An example will clarify the context mechanism. The command "retrieve x1," will cause a pointer to the retrieved document to be pushed onto the stack. A subsequent command to "consider the last two sentences" will cause the search for sentences within the object pointed to by the focus list at the top of the stack. In this case, the system looks for the "last two sentences" in the document. If two or more sentences are found, a pointer to each of the last two of them will be entered into a list and the list will be pushed onto the focus stack. The stack would then become as shown.

2. sent(last-1), sent(last)
1. document

If acceptable objects are not found, the focus stack is removed (or popped) and another search for appropriate objects ensues based on the list now at the top of the stack. In this example, after being popped once, the stack would be empty, and, thus, the search would terminate unsuccessfully.

Assuming that "the last two sentences" were found, if the next command is "capitalize the first character in those sentences," then a search of the focus stack will be made for a list of pointers to sentences. In this case, a list referencing two sentences will be found at the top of the stack and the first character of each of the sentences will be capitalized. Pointers to those two characters will then be added to the stack to yield

3. char, char
2. sen(last—1), sent(last)
1. document

If a command is given referencing objects not found on the top of the stack, the stack is popped until appropriate objects are found.

If touch inputs have been associated with the command utterance, then "those sentences" will be searched for in that part of the text–data world described by the display map generated at the end of the execution of the previous command. This is equivalent to searching the display itself. This type of search takes precedence over any use of the focus stack. When a successful search of this type is completed, the focus stack will have at its top a list of pointers to the touched sentences. Directly below that list will be a list pointing to objects that actually contain the sentences that were touched. The list below the touched sentences list frequently would point only to the document. However, if the touched sentences were in a paragraph, say, that was represented by a list already on the stack, then the pointer to that paragraph would remain on the stack immediately below the list pointing to "those sentences." Thus, touch processing wipes out only as much preexisting focus as necessary to maintain the principle that an actual (narrowing) containment hierarchy is represented by the focus stack.

Before leaving this topic, it should be noted that no effort is made to develop a complete path of narrowing containment relationships on the focus stack. Only an actual path is desired. A stack with a pointer to single character at the top and a pointer to the entire document just below is often a sufficient representation of context in our scheme.

EXECUTION OF A COMMAND

Semantics execution will be illustrated for the utterance "print the title of each subsection in section two." The parse of the sentence will indicate that the verb, "print," has one operand, "title," and that the operand has one postnominal modifier, "of each subsection," and that the modifier is postnominally modified by "in section two." The roles of the quantifier, "each," and the ordinal, "two" (i.e. "the second"), are also identified in the parse. The parse is translated into a network of nodes we have named the "bubble structure." By interpreting this structure, the semantics module achieves the intended result of the user's spoken command.

In the case of the example utterance, the following bubble structure guides semantic processing:

```
VERB(print)
  CONTAINEROF(section)
  TYPEGEN(section)
  APPLY(second)
  APPLY(the)
  TYPEGEN(subsection)
  APPLY(each)
  TYPEGEN(title)
  APPLY(the)
  COLLECT
EXECUTE
```

The initial command notes the imperative verb, "print," and sets it aside for later execution. The indented sequence of instructions (CONTAINEROF to COLLECT) finds the set of objects referenced by the noun phrase, "the title of each subsection in section two." A list of pointers to this set of objects is handed to the imperative verb for dereferencing in the final EXECUTE bubble. Noun group resolution involves finding, passing, testing, and collecting objects from the text–data world. In fact, it is always the pointer to an object that moves through the bubble process, not the object itself. For brevity, object pointers will be referred to below as objects.

The interpretation of the indented sequence of bubbles follows a data-driven control flow with objects precipitating down through the bubbles and collecting at the final COLLECT instruction. Two of the instructions, CONTAINEROF and TYPEGEN, are object generators. The APPLY instructions are filters that either delete objects or pass them along as they arrive.

The task of "CONTAINEROF(x)" is to find some object that has recently been mentioned in the dialogue (possibly implicitly) and which can contain an x. For example, a person might say "consider the title of the paper," and then say, "capitalize each word." In interpreting the second utterance CONTAINEROF(word) appears in the bubble structure. The CONTAINEROF function uses the focus stack, described previously, to help find the meaning of "word." Since the title has just been mentioned, and is on the focus stack, and since it does, in fact, contain words, we have (conceptually):

CONTAINEROF(word) = title of the paper.

The command, then, results in only the words in the title being capitalized even though there may be many other words in the environment.

Continuing with the earlier example, the bubble, CONTAINEROF(section), will find an object that does contain at least one section, say, the document. This object, the document, is passed to the second bubble, TYPEGEN(section). This bubble has the task of generating all possible objects of the type, section, from the object it received, that is, from the document. The first section is passed down through the lower bubbles in the structure, then the second section, and so forth. This continues until either all sections in the container have been generated or until the TYPEGEN bubble is turned off.

The APPLY bubbles filter objects passed to them. APPLY(second) will absorb the first object that arrives and pass the second one, and then turn off the generator above it. APPLY(the) is largely a clear passage for all objects except that it does check that the correct number are passed; exactly one for a singular definite noun group, for example.

When a section arrives at the TYPEGEN(subsection) bubble, processing similar to that described above, finds subsections and passes them down to the APPLY(each) bubble, which in turn, passes each one down to the TYPEGEN(title) bubble. Here titles within subsections are generated and passed through the APPLY(the) bubble to the COLLECT bubble where the set of titles is accumulated. Finally, the EXECUTE bubble is handed the imperative, "print," and the set of titles and prints the items in the set.

This model of semantics is broadly applicable to office automation domains such as file manipulation, calendar management, and desk calculations that have hierarchical organization similar to the text example given here. For example, in the calendar domain, the sentence "list the first appointment in each day of the second week" would be processed identically to the preceding example.

HUMAN FACTORS

At the time of writing, the VIPS system is not ready for human-factors testing, but we expect it to outperform its predecessor, VNLC,[3] on most dimensions. In problem-solving sessions, users speak to VNLC at the rate of about one word per second, and they utter several sentences per minute. Error rates from the speech equipment have been high—on the order of 10%—but system error correction has reduced this rate significantly. The VNLC system executes about 75% of user commands immediately and correctly with most errors caused by voice misrecognition.

RELATED WORK

A number of projects have developed natural language database interfaces,[4–16] but few have built task-oriented processors of the kind we describe here. There also have been many projects over the past two decades in speech technology, where the goal has been to learn how to build voice recognition equipment.[17–21] Our project seeks not to develop a voice recognizer but to use existing recognizers efficiently with a well-designed error-correcting natural-language processor.

ACKNOWLEDGMENT

This work has been supported by the IBM Corporation GSD Agreement No. 260880.

REFERENCES

1. Biermann, A. H., and B. W. Ballard. "Towards Natural Language Computation." *American Journal of Computational Linguistics,* 6 (1980), pp. 71–86.
2. Biermann, A. W., B. W. Ballard, and A. H. Sigmon. "An Experimental Study of Natural Language Programming." *International Journal of Man ≈ Machine Studies,* 18 (1983), pp. 71–87.
3. Biermann, A. W., R. Rodman, B. Ballard, T. Betancourt, G. Bilbro, H. Deas, L. Finemann, P. Fink, K. Gilbert, D. Gregory, and F. Heidlage. "Interactive Natural Language Problem Solving: A Pragmatic Approach." *Proceedings of Conference on Applied Natural Language Processing,* Santa Monica, Calif., February 1983, pp. 180–191.
4. Bronnenberg, W., S. Landsbergen, R. Scha, and W. Schoenmaker. "PHLIQA-1, A Question-Answering System for Data-Base Consultation in Natural English." *Philips Technology Review,* 38 (1978; 1979), pp. 229–239; 269–284.
5. Damerau, F. J. "Operating Statistics for the Transformational Question Answering System." *American Journal of Computational Linguistics,* 7 (1981), pp. 30–42.
6. Egly, D., and K. Westcourt. "Cognitive Style, Categorizations, and Vocational Effects on Performance of REL Database Users." Paper presented at Joint Conference on Easier and More Productive Use of Computing Systems. Ann Arbor, Mich., May 1981.
7. Haas, N., and G. Hendrix. "An Approach to Acquiring and Applying Knowledge." Paper presented at First National Conference on Artificial Intelligence, Stanford, Calif., August 1980.
8. Harris, L. "User Oriented Data Base Query with the ROBOT Natural Language Query System." *International Journal of Man—Machine Studies.* September 1977, pp. 697–713.
9. Hendrix, G. G., E. D. Sacerdoti, D. Sagalowicz, and J. Slocum. "Developing a Natural Language Interface to Complex Data." *ACM Transaction on Database Systems.* 3 (1978), pp. 105–147.
10. Hendrix, G. G. "Human Engineering for Applied Natural Language Processing." *Proceedings of the Fifth International Conference on Artificial Intelligence,* Cambridge, Mass., August 22–25, 1977, pp. 183–191.
11. Mylopoulos, J., A. Bourgida, P. Cohen, N. Roussopoulos, J. Tsotsos, and H. Wong. "TORUS—A Natural Language Understanding System for Data Management." *Proceedings of the Fourth International Conference on Artificial Intelligence,* Tbilisi, Georgia, USSR, September 3–8, 1975.
12. Petrick, S. R. "On Natural Language Based Computer Systems." *IBM Journal of Research and Development.* 20 (1976), pp. 314–325.
13. Plath, W. J. "REQUEST: A Natural Language Question Answering System." *IBM Journal of Research and Development.* 20 (1976), pp. 326–335.
14. Thompson, F. B., and B. H. Thompson. "Practical Natural Language Processing: The REL System as Prototype." In M. Rubinoff and M. C. Yovits (eds.), *Advances in Computers,* (Vol. 13), New York: Academic Press, 1975.
15. Waltz, D. L. "An English Language Question Answering System for a Large Relational Database." *Communications of the ACM.* 21 (1978), pp. 526–539.
16. Woods, W. A., R. M. Kaplan, and B. Nash-Webber. "The Lunar Sciences Natural Language Information System: Final Report." Report 2378. Cambridge, Mass.: Bolt, Beranek, and Newman, 1972
17. Haton, J. P., and J. M. Pierrel. "Data Structures and Organization of the MYRTILLE II System." *Fourth T.I.C.P.R.,* Kyoto, Japan, 1978.
18. Lea, W. A. (ed.), *Trends in Speech Recognition.* Englewood Cliffs, N.J.: Prentice-Hall, 1982.
19. Reddy, D. R. "Speech Recognition by Machine: A Review." *Proceedings of the IEEE.* 64 (1976), pp. 501–531.
20. Walker, D. E. (ed.), *Understanding Spoken Language.* New York: Elsevier North-Holland, 1978.
21. Woods, W. A. "Motivation and Overview of SPEECHLIS: An Experimental Prototype for Speech Understanding Research." *IEEE Transactions on Acoustics, Speech, and Signal Processing.* ASSP-23 (1976), pp. 2–10.

An expert system for drafting legal documents

by JAMES SPROWL
IIT/Chicago Kent College of Law
Chicago, Illinois
and
PERIYASAMY BALASUBRAMANIAN, TAIZOON CHINWALLA, MARTHA EVENS, *and* HENRIETTE KLAWANS
Illinois Institute of Technology
Chicago, Illinois

ABSTRACT

ABF is an expert system that assists attorneys in designing legal documents. The system starts by extracting from a library of legal forms a skeleton template that has embedded within it programming constructs such as conditionals and loops, references to other texts, and variables, which are later replaced by client-specific information in the course of a legal interview. Alternative passages are included or excluded dynamically as the interpreter encounters loops and conditionals. As the system analyzes the document, when it discovers that information is missing, it first looks in the client data file, then it tries to compute it, calling a subprogram if necessary. If all else fails, it generates an English question asking the user for the missing data. The user can stop the interpreter at any time, edit the draft, and reinitiate processing at any point. ABF has been implemented in PASCAL and runs on an IBM PC.

INTRODUCTION

For the past nine years, the American Bar Foundation (ABF) has been conducting research into automating some of the more routine aspects of practicing law, such as client interviewing and automated document assembly. The goal of this research has been the development of a computer sytem that can be set up by an attorney expert to assist other attorneys and their assistants in will, trust, and complaint drafting, tax return preparation, and other such tasks. A prototype system, called the ABF system, was developed on a large CDC computer at Northwestern University and was tested in the law student practice clinic at Illinois Institute of Technology's Chicago-Kent College of Law. The clinic staff attorneys developed a number of useful document libraries for generating wills, trusts, divorce petitions and decrees, guardianship petitions, and real estate closing agreements. The will and trust libraries developed by Robert Seibel (now at the University of Maine Law School) were the most successful. More than 500 wills were generated by the clinic for senior citizens living in Chicago. Later, the ABF system prototype was converted to an all-FORTRAN system by Professor Charles Saxon at Eastern Michigan University and was installed on an Amdahl computer at the University of Michigan, where it is used by students of law professor Layman Allen. The FORTRAN ABF system was also installed at the Newcastle (upon Tyne) Polytechnic School of Law, where it is used by students of law professor Michael Heather.

The recent emergence of powerful microcomputers has now made it possible to make this prototype system available to many law schools and law offices. After due consideration, we have decided to reimplement the prototype in PASCAL, using the UCSD P-System because of its well-known portability and widespread current availability in law schools and law offices. IBM and SAGE microcomputers have been used for the development work.

The microcomputer ABF prototype will be the first fully integrated prototype. It will include its own document library system and full-screen text editor and will be entirely self-sufficient.

In this paper we describe the new prototype and the ABF programming language it implements.

THE ABF LANGUAGE

Since attorneys are accustomed to working with form legal documents and statutes, the ABF system is designed to accept document descriptions that resemble closely the documents that can be found in an attorney's book of legal forms. The computational procedures that control document assembly are drafted in a language that causes these procedures to resemble statutes. The attorney is thus given the feeling that he or she is feeding form documents and statutes into a computer, which then writes its own client interviews and document drafts. But in reality the document and procedure drafting languages are simply subsets of a new general-purpose programming language, which we have named the ABF language.

Drafting Documents

In a typical legal document, variable information must be inserted in the text at many different points. For example, a typical divorce document might begin: "This matter was heard upon the verified petition of. . ." followed by the name of the petitioner, which naturally varies from client to client. When such a document is drafted in the ABF language, variable names are enclosed in square brackets and inserted at such points. Accordingly, an ABF model divorce document might begin as follows:

> This matter was heard upon the verified petition of [the name of the petitioner] for dissolution of marriage. . . .

When assembling this document for a specific client, the ABF system later scans the model document, finds this bracketed variable, and transforms the variable name into a question by putting "What is" in front of it and "?" after it. So the system (unless it already knows the name of the petitioner) will generate the question:

> What is the name of the petitioner?

The name supplied by the user is then inserted into the document in place of the variable name enclosed in square brackets wherever that variable name appears. It is also placed in a client data file. In this manner a unique client data file is created for each client and may be used to control the assembly of other documents without having to ask the same questions over again.

The name of the petitioner appears in a number of different places within the divorce library. To save typing, the author of the document may define a short abbreviation for the variable name and use the abbreviation instead of the full variable name. If the document designer chooses the abbreviation "petname" for "the name of the petitioner," that fact can be communicated to the system by simply slipping it into the document like this:

> This matter was heard upon the verified petition of [petname: the name of the petitioner] for. . . .

Thereafter, the short form [petname] may be used. The system expands all such short names into full variable names automatically.

For logical (true-false) variables, the "What is" question is inappropriate. If the user capitalizes a helper verb in such a variable's name, the system forms a question beginning with that helper verb. Thus, the variable name "stp fld: a stipulation HAS been filed" is converted into the question: "Has a stipulation been filed?"

Sometimes the document designer wishes to insert not just the value of a simple variable but an entire document. A document name is actually a variable name; the value associated with this new kind of variable name is the text of the document itself. To insert the text of one document into the middle of another document, the author simply inserts the name of the one document, enclosed in square brackets, into the other document.

The insertion of optional passages is controlled using an IF. . .END IF construction, and the insertion of repetitive passages is controlled using a REPEAT. . .END REPEAT construction. Both of these constructions are explained below.

Optional and Alternative Passages

The ABF language includes a full IF statement that permits optional and alternative passages to be selected. The full IF statement has the form

```
IF Boolean expression INSERT
    document 1
OTHERWISE
    document 2
END IF
```

The Boolean expression is a logical proposition or expression that the processor evaluates to get a value of TRUE or FALSE. The following are examples of such propositions and expressions:

the client's income IS GREATER THAN $10,000
the testator IS NOT married

If the proposition or expression is true, then Document 1 is processed and Document 2 is skipped. If it is false, then Document 1 is skipped. If the optional "OTHERWISE Document 2" part of the IF statement is omitted, Document 1 is processed if the Boolean expression is true and is skipped if the Boolean expression is false.

There is also an expanded IF statement that may be used to select one of several alternatives based upon the evaluation of several conditions:

```
IF Boolean expression 1 INSERT
    document 1
OR IF Boolean expression 2 INSERT
    document 2
OR IF Boolean expression 3 INSERT
    document 3
END IF
```

A Boolean expression is made up of simple conditions connected by ANDs and ORs. The NOT operation is used within one or more of the simple conditions. There are two kinds of simple conditions: logical expressions and propositions. A logical expression is similar to the logical or relational expressions found in many well-known programming languages: two algebraic expressions of the same type separated by a relational operator such as GREATER THAN, EQUAL, or IS NOT GREATER THAN. The proposition is a construction not usually found in programming languages, so it requires more explanation. A proposition, like a logical expression, has a value of TRUE or FALSE, but its value is determined directly from a user response rather than from a calculation. For example, the proposition "the color of the sky IS blue" is evaluated by asking the question, "Is the color of the sky blue?" to which the user must respond either "yes" or "no." A proposition may also be stated negatively, e.g., "the color of the sky IS NOT blue." In this case, the system also asks "Is the color of the sky blue?" but now the value of the proposition is set TRUE for the "no" response rather than the "yes" response.

The proposition "the color of the sky IS blue" could be replaced by the logical expression "the color of the sky EQUALS <blue>." This expression is evaluated by comparing the value of the variable "the color of the sky" to the string constant "blue." If the variable is undefined, the system asks "What is the color of the sky?" to which the user may respond "blue" or "red" or any other legal value.

Repetitive passages—that is, passages that are to be duplicated and inserted into a document repeatedly—are bracketed by the commands REPEAT and END REPEAT. Within such passages, array variables are simply marked by a number-sign prefix to distinguish them from non-array variables, and the indexing of array variables is automatic. An embedded WHILE. . ., UNTIL. . ., or EXIT statement controls termination of the repetitive insertion process, as in most standard programming languages. For example:

```
This contract covers the following states:

    REPEAT

        [the name of a state]
      UNTIL     that IS the last state
    END REPEAT
```

This simple example, when processed, causes the questions

What is the name of a state?
Is that the last state?

to be asked repeatedly until the latter question is answered "no." In this manner any number of state names may be added to the list.

Much more complicated examples are possible, since REPEAT. . .END REPEAT passages may be nested to any desired depth.

Drafting Computational Procedures

There are times when it is possible to calculate the value of a variable from the values of other variables. The document designer may then decide to write an ABF procedure to perform this calculation. In our divorce example, the system can calculate the personal pronoun *he or she* for the respondent once the user has supplied the personal pronoun *he or she* for the petitioner, since the petitioner and respondent are of the opposite sex. The procedure to calculate the value of *respron: the personal pronoun of the respondent* might look like this:

```
IF petpron: the personal pronoun of the petitioner
  EQUALS <she>
    LET respron: the personal pronoun of the respondent
      = <he>
OTHERWISE
    LET respron = <she>
```

The syntax for procedures was deliberately chosen to make it possible to write procedures that resemble statutes very closely.

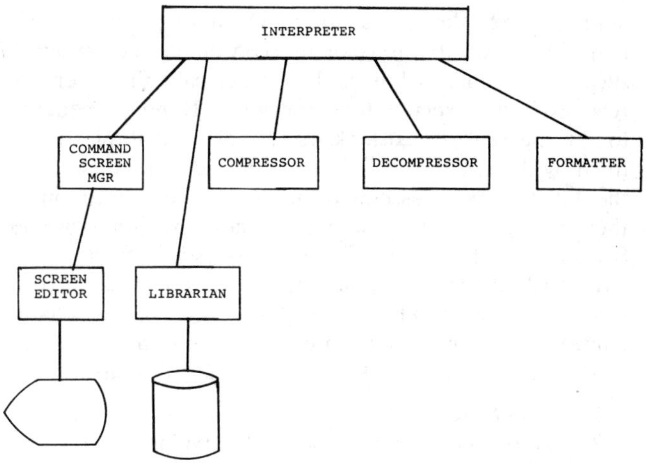

Figure 1—Components of The ABF system.

INTERNAL OPERATIONS OF THE ABF SYSTEM

To simplify the task of building a complex information-gathering and document assembly system, the ABF system permits one to begin by simply drafting form documents that define the system output. By extracting variable names from these documents and converting them into questions, the ABF system is able to ask for the data it needs to assemble the documents. Whenever the system asks for data, the system designer may alter the way the question is asked or supply the system with a procedure containing instructions on how the data are to be computed from other data values. In this manner, the system is actually redesigned from the top down while it is running.

The articulation of the main components of the ABF system necessary to give the user this freedom can be seen in Figure 1. The user of the ABF system starts out looking at the command screen provided by the command screen manager. The command screen is split three ways. The top of the screen contains a list of the commands available in the current context. A window of text may appear next. Below the text is a snapshot of the top of a historical command list containing the names of the most recently executed commands. Prompts for new commands and questions formulated by the system appear at the bottom of the screen, where the user types in new commands and the answers to questions.

When the user is ready for a client interview, he/she signals the system by a command such as "PROCESS draft will OF John Smith." In response, the Librarian (the ABF file handler) locates the model document called "will"; and if necessary, the Compressor is called to put the document into compressed internal form. When the Compressor finds a new variable name, it inserts this name into the Variable Name Table and the System Identifier Table and replaces it in the document by a number indicating its offset in the System Identifier Table. Much of the document is just straight text—boilerplate text, as lawyers call it. This text is inserted in string form into the Boilerplate Table and is represented in the compressed document by a pair of integers indicating the table offsets of the first and the last characters. Operators are replaced by the special operator tokens encoding operator type and precedence. The compressed version of the document is typically much shorter than the raw version. It contains only operator tokens, system identifier table offsets, and boilerplate offsets. This compressed document serves as input to the Interpreter.

When the Interpreter processes a document, it must execute the operators in turn; but before it can execute an operator, it needs to know the values of the arguments. It calls the Seeker to find these values, as will be explained below.

Once the Interpreter has finished with a document, it calls the Decompressor to reassemble it into text form. If the Decompressor finds that some part of the document could not be finished because of missing data, it calls upon a Decompiler to pick up the pieces and put them together.

When the draft document is in satisfactory shape, the user calls the Formatter to put it into final form. The user can then display or print this final form or even edit it further.

The user can also edit an existing document or create a new one. The system sets up the document for editing on the full screen and calls the Screen Editor. This same Screen Editor is also used on a partial screen whenever the user enters input, whether it is a command or the answer to a question.

The ABF System recognizes four elementary data types: numbers, dollar amounts, text strings, and logical values. Array variables are also permitted. The system also recognizes three complex data structures: documents, procedures, and replacement questions.

Finding Values for Variables

When the Seeker is asked by the Interpreter to find the value of a variable, it first checks to see if the variable has already been defined. If so, the value of the variable is retrieved from the client data file. If the variable has not been defined, the Seeker checks to see whether a procedure exists that can be executed to compute the value of the variable. If such a procedure is found, the Seeker calls the Interpreter recursively to execute the procedure. If no procedure is found, the Seeker next looks for a replacement question defined by the document designer. If it finds one, it calls upon the Interpreter to assemble the replacement question and then prompts the user with that question. Otherwise, the Seeker must build-form a default question by appending "What is" or "Is it true that" to the variable's name (or by shifting a capitalized helper verb to the start of the variable's name) and then prompt the user with the question so formed.

The user has three different options at this point:

1. Answer the question.
2. Refuse to answer the question by typing "!"
3. Replace the question with a new replacement question.
4. Replace the question with a new procedure that computes the variable.

If the user answers the question, the system accepts the answer and replaces all occurrences of that variable with the value supplied as long as the data type is correct. The ABF system decides the type of a variable, not from a formal declaration, but by remembering the type of the value associated with a variable the first time a document is processed.

If the user refuses to answer a question, the Seeker marks the variable as never-to-be-defined. This causes the system to leave the bracketed variable name in the document and to refrain from bothering the user with questions about it again during the processing of the draft.

The user may also supply a Replacement Question to the system. The Replacement Question is stored in the system library, and any subsequent reference to this same variable when it is undefined involves the Replacement Question. Replacement Questions may contain bracketed variables and optional passages.

If the user feels that the necessary information can be computed from facts already known to the system, then he or she may decide to supply the system with a procedure to compute its value. (The code given above to calculate the personal pronoun for the respondent is a trivial example of such a procedure.) Unlike procedures in conventional programming languages, an ABF procedure is not given a name. Instead, it is referenced by the names of the variables it computes.

From the user's point of view, there is no program. The user sees only a library containing a collection of documents, procedures, replacement questions, and client data files arranged by the system in neat document form to suit the user's convenience. The statute-like procedures appear to govern the automated assembly of the legal documents.

DESIGNING A SYSTEM TO OPERATE WITHOUT CRUCIAL ITEMS OF DATA

One cannot design an automated law office system to anticipate all possible client circumstances. Not only is the range of possible client circumstances entirely open-ended, but a system that even attempts to anticipate all possible circumstances produces an unbearably long interview. Such a system will frequently ask questions that are irrelevant or inappropriate to the needs of any particular client. Sometimes questions cannot be answered because answers are simply not available. It is essential that legal practice systems be capable of generating usable documents, even when data are not supplied to the system (either because the data are not available or because the questions asked are irrelevant or inappropriate).

After much thought and discussion, we decided to design the system so that an exclamation mark typed in answer to any question signals to the system that the user does not wish to answer the question. In response, the system sets the corresponding variable into a special never-to-be-defined state. The system then proceeds to execute procedures and assemble documents as best it can without the values of the variables the user has elected not to supply.

The system proceeds as follows: If the variable is one that is simply inserted into the text of the document at various points, the system leaves the bracketed name of the variable in the document text and does not replace it with a value. The finished document is thus partly finished—it still contains bracketed variables corresponding to the unanswered questions. These may be edited out manually, or the document may be reprocessed at a later time.

If the variable is one that appears in the preamble of an IF. . .END IF optional passage, the system normally cannot determine whether to insert or exclude the passage. Accordingly, the optional passage is simply left in the document preceded by the IF command and followed by the END IF command. Insofar as values of variables are available, they are plugged into the optional passage; but no questions are generated from the text of the optional passage. Repetitive passages may also have to be left in a document if the user refuses to answer a question essential to determining how many copies of such a passage are to be inserted into a document.

From the viewpoint of the computer scientist, the system effectively decompiles all passages that cannot be processed because the user refuses to supply the necessary answers to questions. The decompiled versions of documents and procedures may be simplified in comparison to the originals to the extent that data were available to enable mathematical and logical expressions to be partially evaluated and simplified. For example, by supplying some answers and withholding others, one can cause the system to simplify a complex set of tax code provisions into a much simpler set of provisions that illustrate what legal effect the answers withheld will have upon a particular client. Thus, the expression

```
LET txblinc: the taxable income = ginc: the gross income
  − adj: the adjustments to gross income − ded: the deductions from gross income
```

Might produce the interview

```
What is the gross income?
$10,000
What is the adjustments to gross income?
$3,750
What is the deductions from gross income?
!
```

Since the user did not answer the final question, the expression could not be fully evaluated but was simplified to:

LET txblinc: the taxable income = $6,250 − ded: the deductions from gross income

Some very interesting and not fully explored problems arise when one attempts to execute programs with less than a complete set of data in this manner. Of particular interest is the case where a passage in a document that could not be fully processed contains a command to alter a variable that has already been assigned a value. For example, consider the following document:

```
    (text)
    [the name of the contractor]
    (more text)
IF a second contract with a different contractor is desired
  INSERT
    (text)
LET the name of the contractor = the new contractor's
name
    (text)
    [the name of the contractor]
    (more text)
END IF
```

When this document is processed, the following interview might be generated:

What is the name of the contractor?
George L. Burroughs

Is a second contract with a different contractor desired?
!

Here, the user does not yet know whether a second contract is desired, so the user refuses to answer the question. Accordingly, the language IF. . .INSERT. . .END IF is left in the document. But the system must scan this text and discover that a new value will be assigned to the variable "the name of the contractor" if this optional passage is ever selected. The system must therefore set the variable "the name of the contractor" into an undefined state and refrain from inserting its value into the remainder of the document.

The above example illustrates why the system must scan all document portions, procedures, and new questions that cannot be fully processed because the user has refused to answer one or more questions. The scanning must cover every possible algorithmic path. For example, if an IF. . .INSERT. . . OTHERWISE INSERT. . .END IF clause cannot be processed, the system must scan both the IF part and the OTHERWISE part, searching for commands that redefine variables. Had the same clause been processed fully, the system would have processed only one of these two parts, discarding the other. Any defined variable that is redefined must be set into a never-to-be-defined state to avoid the possibility of the wrong value being inserted into a document or used in a computation.

This whole field of processing without a complete set of data, decompiling, and scanning unprocessed portions for commands that redefine variables is a field that needs to be much more fully explored by the computer science community to ensure that this kind of processing is given a sound theoretical basis.

SUMMARY

The conversion of the ABF System to run in PASCAL in the UCSD P-System on an IBM Personal Computer has involved redesign of the language to take advantage of full-screen editing and recursion. The result integrates word processing and artificial-intelligence techniques to provide a novel system for writing legal documents. ABF forms English questions when it cannot find values for variables. It provides a rich collection of conditional operators to control the insertion of alternative passages in the text, and it enables repetitive passages to be created without explicit subscripts for the variables. The ABF System is unique in its ability to function without crucial items of data, decompiling expressions where they cannot be fully processed. It is also unique in its ability to generate a client data file that may be used to control the assembly of other documents. The System encourages both top-down and bottom-up design by causing any portion of a system to be fully operative without dummy subroutines and by permitting new procedures and questions to be defined at run time. And by generating questions directly from variable names, the system gives the programmer positive incentives to provide long, meaningful variable names.

REFERENCES

1. Sprowl, James A. "Automating the Legal Reasoning Process: A Computer That Uses Regulations and Statutes to Draft Legal Documents." *American Bar Foundation Research Journal,* Vol. 1979, pp. 1–8.
2. Sprowl, James A., and Ronald W. Staudt. "Computerizing Client Services In The Law School Teaching Clinic: An Experiment In Law Office Automation." *American Bar Foundation Research Journal,* Vol. 1981, pp. 699–751.
3. Cook, Sandra, Carole D. Hafner, L. Thorne McCarty, Jeffrey A. Meldman, Mark Peterson, James A. Sprowl, N. S. Sridharan, and D. A. Waterman. "The Applications of Artificial Intelligence to Law: A Survey of Six Current Projects." *AFIPS, Proceedings of the National Computer Conference* (Vol. 50), 1981, pp. 689–696.
4. Saxon, Charles S. "Computer-aided Drafting of Legal Documents." *American Bar Foundation Research Journal,* Vol. 1982, pp. 685–754.

Computer communications

Neal Laurance, Track Chair

The Computer Communications track, NCC '84, is composed of six sessions covering a range of communications issues from satellite links to downloading programmable controllers in manufacturing plants. In addition to the sessions specifically on communications, the track includes a session on the use of computers in manufacturing. Besides this track, one can find elements of computer communications developments in the tracks entitled The Automated Office, Information Processing Management, Personal Computers, Educational and Societal Issues, Software, and Database Management. Indeed, as distributed processing becomes the norm, the problems and promises of computer communication systems become an issue that pervades the whole field of computing today.

The past year has been one of enormous advances. In the area of local area networks, the IEEE 802 committee has completed work on two standards, and it now seems possible to connect many different vendors' products to the same local area network. But at the same time the divestiture of AT&T from the regional Bell Operating Companies has opened up whole new areas of communications possibilities. The question now is whether the advent of digital telephones and computer communication technology wil make local area networks obsolete before they really get started.

The two "Multi-Vendor Networks" sessions on Tuesday morning deal with the results of some pilot programs on an implementation of the draft ISO protocols for Levels 3 and 4 of the OSI reference model. During the past year the National Bureau of Standards (NBS) has been conducting workshops on this implementation with participants from both the computer industry and communications users. The workshops have resulted in two pilot implementations, each involving several computer vendors. The first pilot program, carried out at the NBS in Gaithersburg, uses for its communication medium an IEEE 802.3 CSMA/CD coaxial cable. It has the office environment as a general background assumption. The second pilot program was led by General Motors Corporation as part of their Manufacturing Automation Project (MAP). It uses the same ISO transport layer for its demonstration, but it is based on the IEEE 802.4 token bus system. It assumes a manufacturing plant floor as an environment and includes as one of its elements communications to and from programmable controllers. Each pilot program has about six active computer equipment vendors as participants, and NBS and GM are demonstrating the multivendor method in the conference exhibit area. The two sessions consist of panel discussions by participants in each pilot, outlining the progress in this area to date and anticipating the future developements in an ISO communication network.

The session titled "Videotex" brings together a panel of experts to discuss the latest developments in this very interesting technology. Last year we heard reports of highly successful field trials of videotex and teletext in limited geographical areas. This was to be the year of the first commercial offerings in what promises to be the next mass communication market. What have been the experiences in this area? Is videotex on track with its promise of two-way video communication in the nation's homes, or have the effects of the recent economic recession delayed the timetable?

Despite the successful efforts of IEEE 802 committee to bring a degree of standardization to the local area network arena, the number of different offerings in the local area network field continues to grow. In part this growth is fueled by the ubiquitous personal computer and its need to communicate at a cost commensurate with the low cost of the computer itself. The session entitled "Update on Local Area Networks" will bring together a panel to discuss the latest developments in this area and help chart a path to the future.

Of special interest will be the outlook for the yet-to-be-announced IBM entry into the local area network field. And how will AT&T's participation in this market change the course of future developments?

Of special interest these days is the linking of manufacturing plant floor information to the corporate data structure. Traditionally, manufacturing plants used computers for their operations independently from the computer systems used in corporate reporting and analysis. That situation is slowly changing, with the result that office-level systems are finding their way into manufacturing environments. The "Computer Integrated Automation" session focuses on several examples of the use of personal computers in manufacturing plants and explores the effect of automation and computer systems on manufacturing productivity.

"Computer Systems and Devices" brings together four papers on communication. One paper explores the concept of a work station tied to remote computer facilities via satellite links, as might be used in the travel industry. A second discusses a very low-cost implementation of a shared medium network, using only RS 232 hardware and twisted pair. The fundamental problem of relating the design of a telecommunications system to a corporate business strategy is discussed in the third. The last treats a different kind of communication: conveying to the driver of an automobile information about the route to be followed to his/her destination.

The next session in this track assembles a panel to discuss one of the fascinating events of the past year, the divestiture of AT&T. Far from being a smooth transition, the repercussions of the breakup are still being felt. Understandably, news accounts have focused on effects on the general public. The effects on business communications have been at least as significant, and the biggest effect of all may prove to be the changes in data communication. Certainly, at this point, the communications market does not look the way the experts predicted as recently as 12 months ago. What are the continued long-term effects likely to be? Will the imposition of usage fees signal a large scale move to digital PBXs? What effect will that have on the development of local area networks? This session will attempt to answer these and other questions.

The final session of this track, "Integrated Networks," assembles a panel of experts to discuss the issues and potential benefits of tying diverse networks together. Communications gateways now make possible the connection of local area networks, wide area networks, and data processing networks into an integrated communications system. These gateways offer exciting possibilities for information processing and transmission.

LCNET: Ethernet concepts+ubiquitous RS232C ports=Low Cost NETwork

by JAY B. JORDAN
and VICTOR P. HOLMES
New Mexico State University
Las Cruces, New Mexico

ABSTRACT

The LCNET is a very low cost local-area network consisting of single-board microcomputers. The network hardware adapts standard RS232C input–output ports to drive a common contention bus. The network software supports an Ethernet-like protocol that has been tailored to experimental distributed operating systems. A unique variable-length-packet management scheme provides efficient handling of large data objects throughout the network.

INTRODUCTION

There is a proliferation of small, very low cost, single-board computers on the market today. Many of these units have a substantial amount of computing power. Thus, it would seem that a network of these computers, together with general-purpose network software, would make an excellent test bed for studying loosely coupled networks and for running distributed operating system experiments.

When an attempt is made to assemble a number of different single board computers (SBCs) into a usable network, several problems immediately arise. First, it is often tedious and difficult to download programs from a software development system unless the SBC and the software development system are manufactured by the same company. Even when SBCs and development systems are from the same manufacturer, there seldom is provision for a network of any sort, and certainly no provision for downloading via that network. Second, the cost of purchasing and interfacing an Ethernet controller or Cambridge Ring controller is usually more than twice the cost of the SBC with which it is to be used. This destroys the whole idea of a low-cost network (LCNET). The desire to develop a network of SBCs with minimal financial commitment and the desire to download substantial programs into the computer in the network quickly and conveniently have motivated the development of the LCNET presented here. Low cost is the fundamental consideration in this system. System performance is, of course, a consideration, but it is not the primary one.

The garden variety SBC has at least one and usually two RS232C serial communications input—output ports. One for connection to a standard CRT or TTY terminal and one, supposedly, for downloading and uploading programs. The typical SBC also has a timer circuit that can provide interrupts at programmable intervals. These items, standard equipment on most SBCs, are the only hardware required for an SBC to be usable in the LCNET.

The LCNET is composed of simple hardware and software subsystems and is based on some of the fundamental concepts of Ethernet.[1] The hardware subsystem adapts standard RS232C channels to drive a common contention bus. Low-cost circuits provide protection and buffering so that two or more stations can attempt to access the bus at the same time without physical damage to their RS232C drivers. Simultaneous access of the bus results in nothing more than a harmless "collision," which is detectable by each station. The software subsystem is a collection of device driver routines and other primitives, which control message passing and bus arbitration. Utilities also are included for downloading programs from a software development system into the network processors. This report is an overview of the LCNET—both hardware and software—as it is currently implemented, we also give comments on related experiments and plans for the future.

LCNET HARDWARE

The hardware portion of the LCNET, as presently implemented, consists of a Hewlett-Packard Model 64000 Microprocessor Software Development System and four Motorola MC68000 Single Board Design Modules connected with a single modified RS232C-type asynchronous serial bus (Figure 1). Each unit has the capability of detecting bus conflicts and sensing when the bus is in use.

LCNET Physical Layer

The physical layer of the network is a twisted pair wire bus and processor interfacing circuits. It is very similar to an RS232C serial communications system in that the voltage levels are compatible with standard RS232C line receivers (such as National Semiconductor DS1489). The voltage range of −3 to −25 volts is defined as a "mark," logical "1," or "line idle and connected" state. The voltage range from +3 to +25 volts is the "space," logical "0," or "line open" (break) state. The transition region between the logical states is −3 to +3v. The output from each line driver in this system is buffered with an open collector driver transistor so that simultaneous access by two or more line drivers is not harmful. The line driver buffer also serves to lower the driving impedance of the bus, allowing the twisted pair cable to be terminated in its characteristic impedance (about 200 ohms). With the terminated bus and the low impedance drivers, a 1000-foot-long system operating at 9600 baud can typically accommodate more than 50 stations. Figure 2 shows the transition from standard RS232C to the LNCET bus. Note that the modifications to the RS232C ports are external to each unit and are implemented as part of the bus cable and connectors. The bus bias voltages (+12v and −12v) are provided by a small power supply located at one of

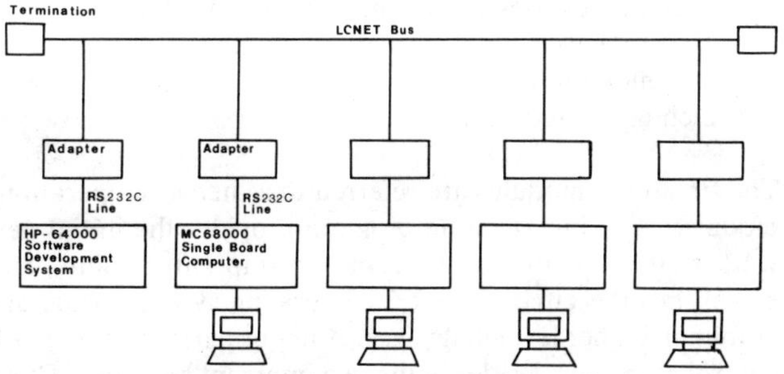

Figure 1—Present LCNET configuration

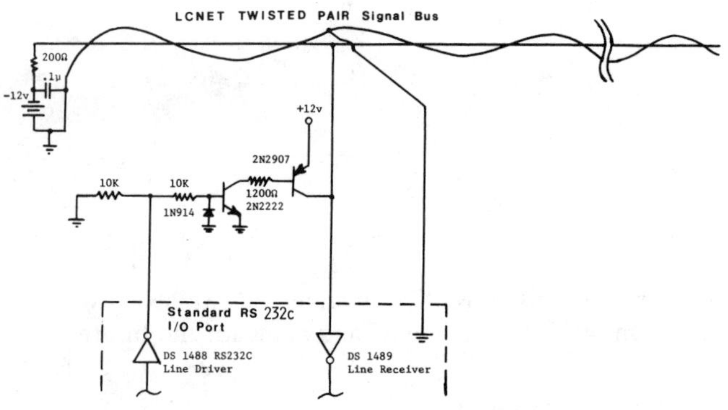

Figure 2—RS232C to LCNET adapter

the terminating ends. The bias voltages are supplied to the adapters and terminators by a second twisted pair cable. From Figure 2 it is also seen that each unit receives its own transmissions. This is the fundamental mechanism by which a unit detects that a bus conflict or collision has occurred.

LCNET Data Link Layer

The data link layer is RS232C 9600 baud, asynchronous with eight data bits, one stop bit, and odd parity. The data are transferred asynchronously, one byte at a time. The data link protocol is handled by serial hardware communications devices. (Motorola MC6850 Asynchronous Communications Adapters [ACIAs] for the MC68000 SBCs and an Intel 8251 Programmable Universal Asynchronous Receiver Transmitter [UART] for the HP 64000 system.) This protocol is a widely used standard and is compatible with many other commercially available devices. The remaining higher levels of network protocol are handled by the LCNET software.

LCNET SOFTWARE

The software portion of the LCNET consists of five modules residing in read only memory in each of the SBCs in the network. These modules define the network layer protocol[2] and provide utilities and functions specifically aimed at supporting experimental distributed operating systems, particularly COSMOS,[3] a distributed operating system for a personal work station. The LCNET software modules are:

1. System initialization program
2. Communications device interrupt handler
3. Timer device interrupt handler
4. Download utility
5. Debugging monitor

The first three modules are referred to as network operations modules. The initialization program provides the initial network state, sets up the interrupt and trap entry points, and establishes the environment for operating systems programs written in higher level languages. A major part of the network control algorithm resides in the two interrupt handlers. These three modules provide a well-defined interface to user-developed programs. The hardware and network control details are effectively handled at this level, leaving the operating system designer free to concentrate on operating systems research rather than troubleshooting interrupt service routines. The remaining utilities—the download module and the debugging monitor—are provided to load the operating system nucleus and to develop network software.

LCNET Operations Software Implementation

The basic network control philosophy is that each unit in the LCNET receives its own transmissions and determines whether or not the bytes sent have been corrupted. The sending unit compares each received byte with the one sent; if they do not match or if there is a parity error, the network control routine assumes a collision has occurred and releases the bus by ceasing to transmit. The routine then waits a short but random amount of time before attempting to resend. The randomness in the waiting time before trying to reaccess the bus ensures that any repeated collision deadlock betwen two senders will be broken eventually.

Most Ethernet-like systems have a hardware "carrier-sense" circuit, which indicates whether or not the bus is in use. Carrier sense circuits are not used in this system. Instead, the determination of an idle channel is based on the time between characters transmitted. The interrupt service routine and the message-passing philosophy are designed to operate the bus at its maximum possible speed. This ensures that once a transmission is in progress, the time between characters will be a fixed constant. The network control routine in each unit either loads or reloads a communications timer as each character is received. The timer is loaded with the time required to transmit two characters. Consequently, the timer never times out until a transmission is either complete or aborted. Each unit reloads its timer on receipt of a character even if it is not the sender or the addressee of the current message. By observing whether or not the timer is active, each unit "knows" the status of the bus at all times. When a unit with traffic to send detects an idle bus, it does not immediately attempt to send, but rather waits a short, random amount of time. This prevents initial access collisions when the network is heavily loaded. This scheme has proven to be very reliable and effective. It has the further advantage that no additional carrier sense hardware is required. The LCNET communications receive–interrupt device is the highest priority in the system to guarantee the operation of this mechanism. From this overview, it can be seen that the timer and communications device interrupt service routines are very closely coupled. Part of the network control algorithm must necessarily be contained in each routine.

LCNET Network Layer

The network layer protocol is common to all units in the network. It is a hardware independent, packet-based protocol. In this system there are two basic kinds of packets: control and data. Every packet consists of an eight-byte header terminated in a checksum. A data packet includes, in addition to the header, a variable-length data segment terminated in a checksum. The structure of the header is shown in Figure 3. The "destination" and "source" fields identify the units involved. The "sequence number" is raised by increments of one each time a new message is sent from a processor. The "applies to" field is used if the message is being sent in response to another message. This field is particularly important for coordinating the high-speed transmission and reception of large data packets. The "type" field indicates the message type. At the network layer level only the most significant bit of the "type" byte is noted. If set, this bit indicates that a variable-length data segment is attached to the header and that the "applies to" and the following byte "count" fields are to be used by software at this level to position the data correctly in memory without the use of any intermediate buffering. For control packets, the "count/optional" and "optional" fields are used by the upper levels of the network to pass further information related to the "type" of control message.

Allowing variable-length messages to be sent over a network usually presents several problems. One of the most severe of these is allocation and management of buffer space in the message receiver. Many solutions to this problem have evolved, the two most common of which are segmentating the message into several fixed-length packets as in X.25,[2] and allowing variable-length packets, but placing a relatively small maximum length restriction on the packet size, as in Ethernet.[4] Each of these solutions keeps the size of the receiver buffer manageable. In the first, the buffer is a multiple of the packet size. Packets with little information require the same transmission time and occupy the same amount of buffer space as full packets. This is particularly wasteful for short control messages. The second approach, using variable-length packets, is much more efficient for handling control traffic, but requires a potentially larger receiver buffer and a much more complex buffer management scheme.

The LCNET protocol taks a slightly different approach to handling variable-length traffic. Since the LNCET evolved out of a message-based operating systems research project,

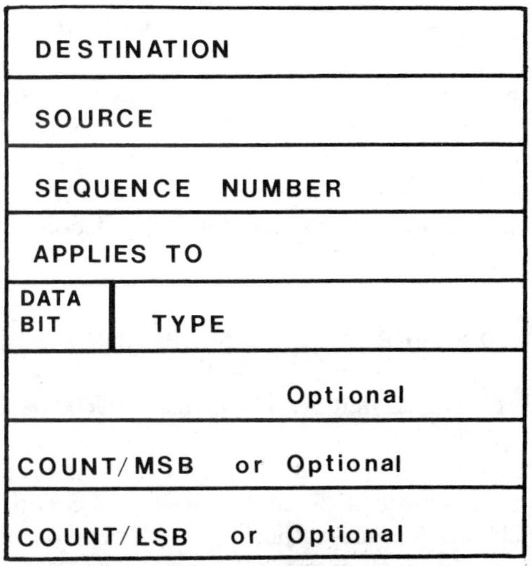

Figure 3—LCNET to message header structure

the message-passing philosophy has been tailored to support such distributed operating systems. In the early phases of the project, both of the message-handling schemes described above were implemented. Both schemes exhibited the same deficiency: The data portion of a message always had to be moved from a buffer area to its final intended destination. This process always proved inefficient, not only because of internal data movement, but also because upper-level operating systems policy decisions had to be made to determine whether or not the data could be accepted and where they should go. The problem was finally resolved when it was determined that, at the operating system level, there need never be an unsolicited data message. Once this observation was made, the present scheme was implemented and it proved to be far superior to either of the two solutions described above. Each varible-length data message is always preceded by a short (header only) control message. This establishes the length and memory destination for the data. When the data message is finally sent, it is expected by the receiver and is stored in its final position as it is received. This is handled rapidly at the network layer level by the LCNET operations software. No operating system buffer is required and a data object can be as large as desired within the limits of user memory.

The detailed operation of this scheme is best shown by an example. Suppose a file is to be transferred from a file server to another unit over the network. The requester initiates activity by sending a control message of the type "request file service." This message consists of only a header with a count value in the "count" fields, indicating the size of a variable-length data portion (a file name), which will follow in another message. The file server now knows the requester of file service and the length of the associated file name. Several policy decisions can now be made to determine whether or not to grant the file request and whether or not there is a place to store the file name.

Assuming that there is a place for the file name and that the server desires to grant file service, a "file service granted" control message is assembled. The "applies to" field of this message is loaded with the sequence number of the original message. This "applies to" response is needed because in general a requester will have several outstanding requests for other services. The sequence number for this reply message is created and is actually an index into a transaction table containing the memory address for positioning the file name when it arrives. The requester, upon receipt of "file service granted," responds with an "open file" message, with the file name contained in a variable-length data segment. The "applies to" field of this data message contains the sequence number of the "file service granted" message. When the data message arrives, it is expected and the data portion is positioned directly at its proper memory location via the transaction table entry. The file server then makes several more policy decisions determining the availability of the file and whether or not to open it. Assuming that file opening is allowed, a "file opened" control message is returned to the requester. The "file opened" message contains (1) the length of the file in the header count field, (2) an "applies to" corresponding to the "open file" message, and (3) a short integer file descriptor. The requester now knows the length of the file and has a file descriptor for future references.

A policy decision can then be made as to whether or not there is room for all or only part of the file and where it is to be placed. After these decisions have been made, a pointer to the desired starting location of the file is placed in the requester's transaction table at the first available position. This index will be used on later requests. A control message to use the file, say a "read file" message, is later issued from the requester. This "read file" message includes (1) the number of bytes desired specified in the count field, (2) the index of the local transaction table entry in the "applies to" field, and (3) the file descriptor assigned by the file server in the count/optional fields. The file server replies with a "data" message, with all or part of the requested amount contained in a variable-length data segment. The size of this segment also is contained in the count field. As the file is received, it is positioned correctly and a checksum is accumulated during the process. If the data segment is received intact, the message header associated with the data is enqueued for the upper levels. The fact that a "data" header is in the received-header queue is the indication that the data associated with it have already been received, checked, and stored in the desired position. The final data transfer takes place at maximum bus speed and the data segment is placed directly into its desired position in memory.

At first, it may appear that the several short messages used to coordinate the transfer of the file add unnecessary overhead to the activity, but when the communication is studied at the operating system level, each step in the transaction sequence is normally required. When a process requires a file, a file must be requested. The server must verify the privileges of the requester and the state of the file (it may already be in use). The requester must then get some idea of the size of the file in order to determine whether all of part of it can be accepted. Also, the requester, at some point, must make a decision about where to put the file. From the operating system's point of view, therefore, unsolicited data messages are neither needed nor desired.

From this example, it is also seen that messages are not acknowledged explicitly; rather, the operation requested, when performed by the remote station, is itself an implicit acknowledgment of both the message and the action requested. This important concept follows directly from the work of Spector.[5] Policy decisions concerning how long to wait for a response, whether or not to make a repeat request, and how to detect and process duplicate messages are not made at the network level but are handled at the operating system level and above. This philosophy, similar to that used in some datagram systems,[2] not only makes the network more efficient, but also makes it more versatile for operating systems research.

LCNET—User Interface

The user interface consists of two queues of headers. There are 16 headers (maximum) in each queue. One queue is the receive-queue, containing headers of messages received from other stations. The other is the send-queue, which contains headers of messages to be sent to other units in the network. The queues are in a globally accessible data area established by the LCNET initialization software module. Each queue is managed by two pointers, one indicating the next empty position and one indicating the oldest entry in the queue. These pointers are also located in the global data area. The queue is considered full when the pointers are exactly one queue position apart and empty when they point to the same position. Headers are only enqueued whenever all aspects of the associated message, including checksums and data if any, are received correctly. The network user level discovers waiting packets by checking header queue pointers.

There is another data structure associated with the "applies to" or "transaction number" previously mentioned. This data structure, called the transaction table, is used to control the positioning and transmission of data segments from one processor to another. As presently implemented, the transaction table holds up to 16 data transaction addresses. Each data transaction address indicates the area in memory from which data are to be taken for a send, or the area in which data are to be placed for a receive. A data transaction address of zero indicates that there is no data segment associated with the transaction number. These are the only data structures concerned with the sending and receiving of messages.

The LCNET send routine, driven by a timer interrupt, checks the send-queue periodically to determine whether or not the user level program has enqueued a message (or messages) to be sent. Headers and their associated data segments, if any, are sent whenever the network becomes idle. The send-queue pointer is updated only after an entire message is sent without collision.

All receiving stations in the network examine the first byte (destination byte) of each message. Whenever this byte contains a station's address, that station starts accumulating the remainder of the header and verifies the checksum. The data portion, if any, is received and positioned starting at the address found in the transaction table. The received header of a message containing a data segment is enqueued only when there is a valid transaction address and the data have been completely received with the checksum verified. The presence of a header in the queue indicates that a message is complete and ready for processing by the user level. If the receive-queue is full because the user level has failed to remove enqueued headers, the header is not enqueued. Although received activity continues even with a full queue, all further messages are lost because they cannot be enqueued. The operation of the network level software is not affected by a full receive-queue, nor are flow control policy decisions made at this level.

RELATED EXPERIMENTS AND PLANS

The LCNET is operated asynchronously at 9600 baud to provide compatibility with many of the single-board computers on the market. The basic hardware, however, is not restricted to this operating speed. Recent experiments conducted with Zilog Z80 serial input–output (SIO) devices have demonstrated asynchronous network rates of 62K baud. With an additional LCNET bus configured as a clock contention bus, synchronous data rates in excess of 250K baud have been demonstrated using a modified network control program. In this experiment, the SIO device is used in the synchronous data link control (SDLC) protocol mode and provides some of the network management functions. Network data rate is limited by the central processing unit and not by the SIO device. These experiments suggest that low-cost front-end communications processors can greatly improve network performance. This appears to be a promising area for future investigations. Present efforts, however, involve extending the existing network to other single-board computers and developing distributed operating systems concepts. Specifically, a parallel contention bus based on the LCNET concepts presented here has been proposed to support the COSMOS system.[3]

SUMMARY

The LCNET allows a designer to connect low-cost, yet powerful single-board microcomputers with a common contention bus to from a network. The bus medium is twisted pair wire and is interfaced to the SBCs through modified RS232C adapters. The network supports a modified Ethernet-like protocol with listening capability and collision detection. The network software is small (less than 8K bytes) and may reside in EPROM on the SBC. The system is tailored to message passing and provides a unique mechanism for passing variable-length data packets. The system has proven very useful in building and studying experimental distributed operating systems and loosely coupled networks, in general.

ACKNOWLEDGEMENT

This research was funded in part by the Army Research Office under grant DAAG29-79-C-0100.

REFERENCES

1. Metcalfe, M. M. and D. R. Boggs, "Ethernet: Distributed Packet Switching for Local Computer Networks." *Communications of the ACM,* 19 (1976), pp. 395–404.
2. Tanenbaum, A. S. *Computer Networks,* Englewood Cliffs, N. J.: pp. 288–320; pp. 187–196.
3. Holmes, V. P., J. B. Jordan, and T. H. Little, "Mercury: A Message-Based Nucleus for Distributed System." *Proceedings of the 17th Hawaii International Conference for System Services,* 1984, in press.
4. *The Ethernet, A Local Area Network: Data Link Layer and Physical Layer Specifications,* Version 1.0, published by Digital Equipment Corporation, Intel, and Xerox, Stamford, Conn., 1980.
5. Spector, A. Z. "Performing Remote Operations Efficiently on a Local Computer Network." *Communications of the ACM,* 25 (1982), pp. 246–259.

Direct work station to remote computer communications via satellite

by MICHAEL H. ARONSON
Ford Aerospace & Communications Corporation
Palo Alto, California

ABSTRACT

This paper addresses communications between office CRT/keyboard intelligent work stations and a remote computer installation using a satellite. The travel industry is used as an example of an industry that could employ direct satellite communications. The office will have a small, inexpensive earth terminal on the premises to support several work stations at that location. A commercial communications satellite with high-gain antenna beams supports the small office terminals. Performance of several channel-sharing protocols is described, and an optimum protocol for this application is discussed. For the example studied, a reservation assignment protocol with slotted Aloha orderwire was selected for its high efficiency. This protocol will support 130 office earth terminals (approximately 390 work stations) in a single satellite channel. The system provides highly responsive service time ($1\frac{1}{2}$ seconds average). The cost of digital communications via satellite channels and terrestrial links is compared, and the advantages of satellite communications are discussed.

INTRODUCTION

Advances in communications technology will soon permit business offices to communicate from point to point through satellite links instead of terrestrial telephone connections. The office of the future will not only employ computers and word processing systems but will also have a small earth terminal on the customer premises to support the office's business communications requirements (see Figure 1). Typically, the need exists for interactive work stations (CRT/keyboards) in the office to interface with a large computer at another location. An exchange of messages will occur frequently between an employee at the work station and the database in the remote computer. For businesses such as a travel agency, a customer is usually in the office or on the telephone waiting for a response from the computer. Thus the response time of the system, including the communications delay, must be very short. Rapid response time usually implies high-rate, high-cost communications capacity. Approaches to minimizing this cost by using satellite communications resources are discussed.

BUSINESS ENVIRONMENT

Many businessess require an interactive dialogue between a user at a work station and a central computer system. Examples of such businesses are the travel industry, for airline and hotel reservations, and the banking industry, for checking and savings transactions. Frequently a large number of interactive work stations will be concentrated in a few major metropolitan areas and an additional large number of work stations will be dispersed over a much wider geographic region (such as the areas of a state outside the large cities). Larger business offices may have 7 to 10 work stations all performing similar functions and, therefore, communicating with the same remote computer or computers. Such offices will be served by a larger earth terminal on the premises supporting all of the terminals. Medium size offices (four to six terminals) and small offices (one to three terminals) would be served by a smaller earth terminal; the medium-size offices would use more powerful transmitters.

The terminals are used on a low- to medium-duty cycle, where a series of message transmissions and receptions occurs for each transaction initiated by the operator. In the travel industry a client may ask about choices of flights to a particular location, then have a reservation placed on a particular flight. In addition, a hotel and rental car reservation may be made. Certain clients with extensive itineraries will have multiple reservations placed. Thus, a complete business transaction consists of an exchange of relatively short messages. For purposes of this discussion, it is assumed that the typical reservation transaction involves transmissions to the computer and transmissions to the office, as shown in Table I. The exchange consists of relatively short messages (approximately 65 characters each), with equal traffic in both directions. The

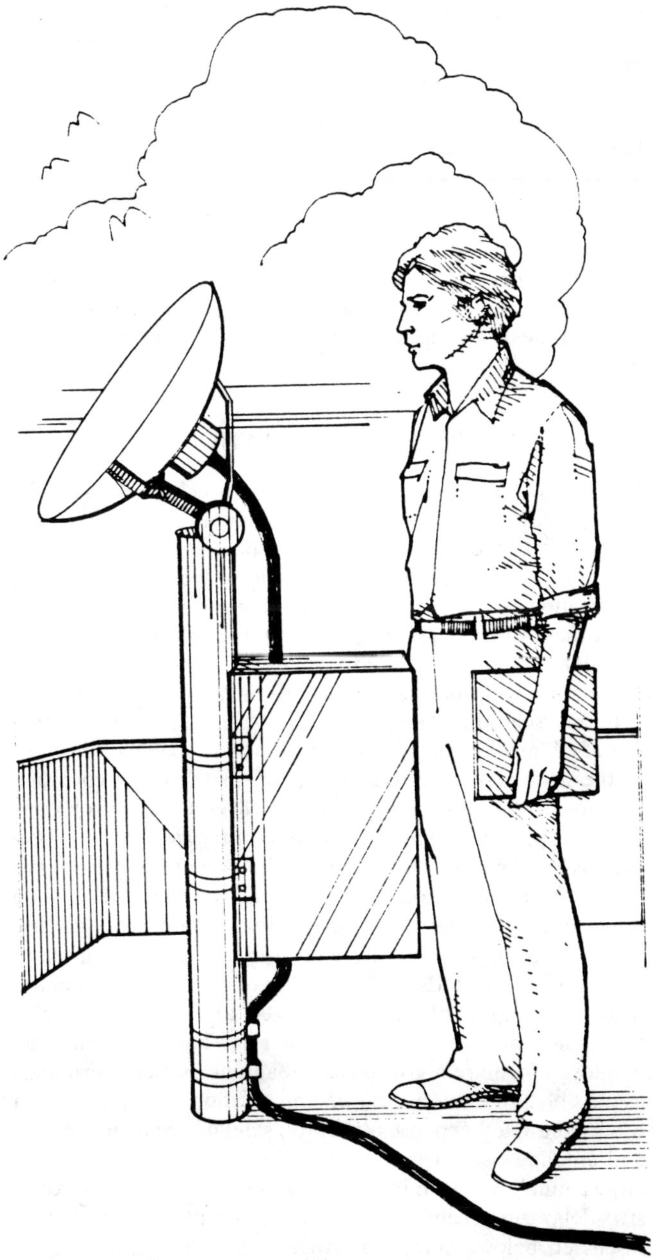

Figure 1—Small earth terminals support office communications

TABLE I—Typical transaction for flight reservation

Message	From	To	Size → Characters	Bits	From	To	Size → Characters	Bits
Flight Inquiry	Office	Remote Computer	60	480				
Inquiry Response					Remote Computer	Office	60	480
Flight Reservation	Office	Remote Computer	65	520				
Flight Confirmation					Remote Computer	Office	65	520
Rental Car Reservation	Office	Remote Computer	60	480				
Rental Car Confirmation					Remote Computer	Office	70	560
			185	1480			195	1560

per-terminal reservation (transaction) rate will vary from 4 transactions per hour to as many as 10 per hour during the peak business hour at larger offices serving major corporate customers.

COMMUNICATIONS CONSIDERATIONS

Figure 2 shows the approximate distribution of travel agencies within California. The major metropolitan areas of Los Angeles, San Diego, and San Francisco have such high densities of agencies that high-gain, spot beam service from the communications satellite would be feasible to support the traffic from these offices. The rest of the state could be served by a broader spot beam with lower gain. The remote computer installation will operate in the state beam.

In the communications satellites of the near future, leasing a spot beam will still be relatively expensive compared to use of the general-service antennas (such as the earth coverage antenna or the statewide spot beam). Therefore, consortiums of users, perhaps organized by an industrywide organization such as the American Society of Travel Agents, will share the expenses in proportion to the call rate of each office. The organization of users will also lease a number of satellite channels to support the offered traffic. The number of channels required depends on the number of earth terminals in the beam, the amount of traffic (messages) to and from the office terminals, the traffic transmission rate, and the technique employed to share a given channel among as many terminals as possible. To minimize the communication costs billed to an office, the fixed expenses (i.e., the satellite channel capacity and antenna beam rental charges) must be spread across as large a number of terminals as possible without causing excessive delays in receiving responses. Each of these factors is discussed below. Since Los Angeles has the densest population of travel agencies, it will be used as a specific example.

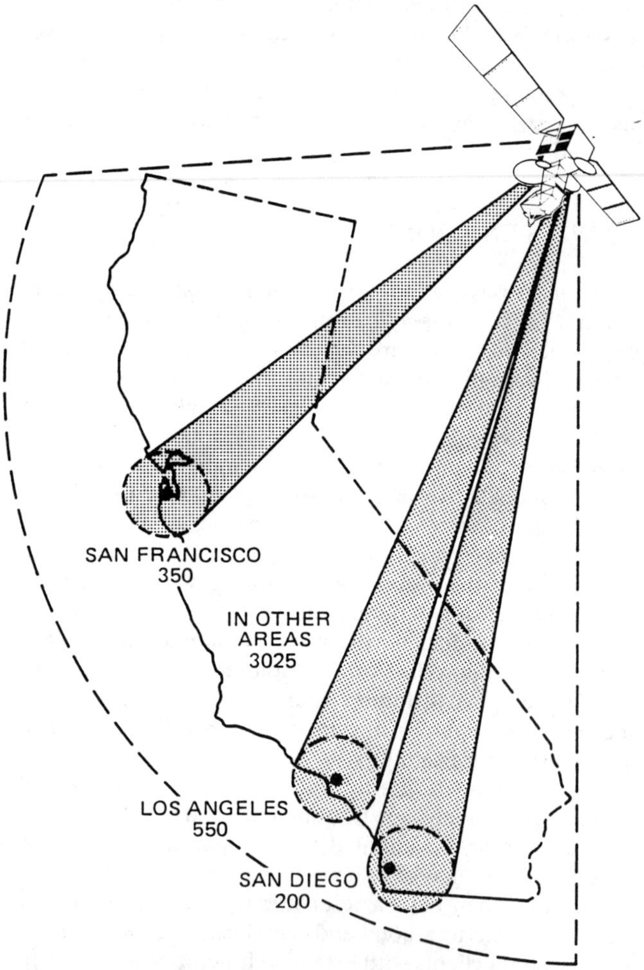

Figure 2—Travel agencies are distributed in major metropolitan areas and throughout California

Number of Terminals

Figure 2 (shown previously) indicated the number of travel agencies that will be served by spot beams and by the statewide spacecraft beam for this application of future communications satellites. We will assume an average of three work stations per office; therefore, the total number of work stations that participate in reservation message generation and reception is 3 × 550 = 1650 in the Los Angeles spot beam, assuming all offices participate (a worst-case assumption).

Amount of Traffic

The reservation rate per work station will vary with the size and clientele of the office. Assuming 4 reservations (transactions) per hour per work station, and 3 work stations per office, the number of transactions in the Los Angeles area during the peak hour is estimated to be 3 work stations/office × 550 offices × 4 transactions/hour = 6,600 transactions/hour. As shown previously in Table I, each transaction involves an exchange of 3 message transmissions and 3 message receptions, each of which contains approximately 65 characters (520 bits). At this point, we state the above information in terms of a traffic model.

The total traffic transmitted in the spot beam by the travel agency terminals is measured in erlangs, a dimensionless quantity. erlangs (E) are defined as

$$E = \frac{(N\lambda'\bar{l}\bar{m})}{3600\,r} \qquad (1)$$

where:

N = Number of work stations offering traffic (dimensionless)
λ' = average work station call rate, transactions/hour
$\bar{l}$ = average message length, bits
$\bar{m}$ = transaction component rate, messages/transaction
r = traffic transmission rate, bits/second

The following values are assumed:

Number of work stations (N): 1650 in Los Angeles
Call rate per work station (λ'): 4 transactions/hour
Transaction component rate ($\bar{m}$): 3 messages/transaction each direction
Average message length ($\bar{l}$): 65 characters (520 bits)

Therefore, the total traffic load during the peak hour that must be supported is:

$$E = \frac{(1650 \times 4 \times 520 \times 3)}{3600\,r} = \frac{2860}{r} \qquad (2)$$

The rate of traffic transmission, r, will be discussed next.

Transmission Rate

The transmission rate to and from the office depends on the capabilities of the office's small earth terminal. The terminal must have enough effective radiated power to transmit messages to the satellite (and then on to the reservation computer) with a minimum of errors. Effective radiated power is a combination of transmitter power and gain from the terminal antenna. The higher the message transmission rate, the greater the power required to maintain a low error rate. To keep the size of the terminal antenna small, a data transmission rate of 9600 bits/s will be assumed. Such a rate wold be relatively expensive to lease using terrestrial communication facilities. With r = 9600 bits/, the traffic load = 2860/9600 = 0.3 erlangs from the offices to the remote reservation computer.

Channel-Sharing Protocols

A number of papers have been written on channel-sharing protocols. The protocols have been analyzed with queueing models to determine comparative performance.[1,2,3] The models use the assumptions of exponentially distributed message lengths and message interarrival rates. The key factors in assessing the performance of a channel-sharing protocol are

1. Wait time: The time between reception at the earth terminal of a message from the user work station to the completion of transmission of the message over the channel.
2. Efficiency: The ratio of information bits transmitted per second to the channel transmission rate (bit/s).

A number of different protocols are available. These are classified as fixed assigned access to the traffic channel, random access, or on-demand access based on a "reservation." The reservation is a message that indicates that the terminal has traffic available for transmission and is waiting for access to the traffic channel. Thus, only the terminals with traffic are considered for access to the traffic channel. This method avoids the inefficiency of fixed-assignment protocols where stations without traffic (and there may be many at any given time) are offered the channel whether or not they need it. The reservations mentioned above may be offered in the traffic channel itself or may use a separate frequency (channel) called an orderwire, which operates in parallel with the traffic channel. The orderwire is usually operated at a lower transmission rate than is the traffic channel. It permits one terminal to be transmitting traffic while, in parallel, other terminals are sending reservation messages.

In order to share a satellite communications channel effectively, the access protocol must be automated and must use a microprocessor in the earth terminal. This microprocessor has the following functions:

1. Generate orderwire messages (if used by the access-sharing protocol) and output them to the terminal transmitter.

2. Receive and decode messages to the terminal from the orderwire channel.
3. Make possible the flow of traffic from the user's work station (which contains the traffic message) to the terminal when the terminal has been given the use of the traffic channel.
4. Disable the terminal transmitter when the user work station completes sending its traffic message to the terminal.
5. Enable/disable transmission in synchronization with specific time markers required by certain channel-sharing protocols.

With this background, the operation of several important channel-sharing protocols is discussed. They are grouped into the following categories:

1. Fixed-assignment protocols
   a. Polled
   b. Time division multiple access (TDMA)
2. Random-assignment protocols
   a. Slotted Aloha traffic channel
3. Reservation assignment protocols
   a. Time division multiple access (TDMA) orderwire
   b. Slotted Aloha orderwire

   The following discussion provides an overview of each protocol.

1a. Polled

In the polled protocol, one terminal is given the duty of acting as controller for the traffic channel. An orderwire channel is used to coordinate the transmissions in the traffic channel. As mentioned above, the orderwire may be on a separate frequency and can operate in parallel with transmissions in the traffic channel. However, it is possible to timeshare the traffic channel between traffic transmissions and orderwire transmissions. If the transmission rate is high enough, the orderwire appears to achieve parallel operation.

In the polled protocol, a list of terminals that are potential users of the traffic channel is entered into the control terminal's database. This terminal (the channel access controller) mediates the use of the traffic channel by sending an orderwire message to the first terminal in the list: "You Have the Traffic Channel." The terminal receives the message and, if it happens to have a user message available, outputs the entire message over the traffic channel. The terminal then sends an orderwire message back to the controller terminal: "I'm Finished with the Traffic Channel." The controller terminal then sends the "You Have the Traffic Channel" orderwire message to the next terminal on the list. After all terminals in the polling list have been offered an opportunity to use the traffic channel, the cycle repeats, polling the first station in the list again. Thus a fixed-access sequence is implemented, and all terminals are offered a chance to transmit. The polled protocol can be optimized by polling high-call-rate stations more than once in the polling sequence.

The polled protocol has several disadvantages. Terminals that have no traffic at their user work stations are polled. During the polling process, an orderwire message is sent to the terminal ("You Have the Traffic Channel") and the terminal sends back an orderwire message ("I'm Finished with the Traffic Channel"). This exchange takes a small, but finite, amount of time (two round-trip propagation delays plus computer processing time at each terminal). During this time the traffic channel is unused, and an inefficiency is introduced. For a round-trip signal propagation time of 0.265 seconds to a synchronous satellite, the dead time due to each poll is $2 \times 0.265 +$ terminal computer processing time $= 0.6$ seconds (typical). When many terminals are in the polling list, a large number of unnecessary polls occurs if the call rate of individual terminals is low (as is the case here). Since the traffic channel is idle during the exchange of orderwire polling messages, the traffic channel efficiency suffers.

Another disadvantage of the polled protocol is that a terminal with traffic must wait until all other terminals ahead of it are polled and, if they have traffic, complete their traffic transmissions. To keep the average wait time short, fewer terminals are permitted to share the channel. This implies a higher per-terminal (i.e., per-office) share of the satellite communications service costs. Another disadvantage is that control of access to the traffic channel is centralized at the control terminal. A backup control terminal must be provided to protect against failure of the control terminal. Further, if terminals are added to or deleted from the polling sequence, the control terminal must always be notified.

1b. Time division multiple access (TDMA)

In a TDMA protocol, the traffic channel is sliced into discrete, prespecified time slots (see Figure 3). Each terminal is assigned one or more time slots; and when the beginning of the appropriate slot occurs, the terminal transmits traffic in the slot. After all slots assigned to terminals have occurred (τ seconds), the pattern of slots repeats in a fixed sequence. The period between repetitions of a specific slot (every τ seconds) is called the frame duration.

TDMA is suitable for message communications systems where the message lengths are relatively short or where the message can be segmented into *packets.* A packet is a fixed-length piece of the message than can be independently transmitted in one slot transmission time (the receiving terminal collects the message packets on the basis of an address field and reassembles the entire message). If the terminal call rate

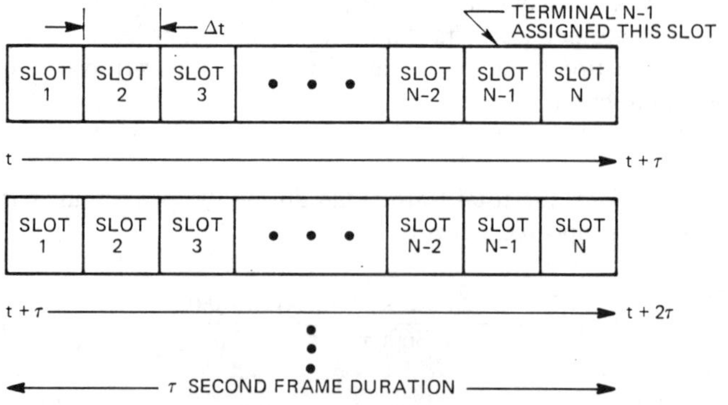

Figure 3—Time division multiple access sharing of the traffic channel

is high, then the terminal will almost always have a message to transmit when its slot occurs, and the traffic channel will experience a high efficiency. The advantage of TDMA is that no orderwire is used for control of access to the traffic channel; i.e., the responsibility for access control is fully distributed among all member terminals. Each is responsible for keeping track of time in order to count slots and begin transmission at the proper time. Note that the time we are talking about is the time at which the satellite receives the message for retransmission. All terminal transmissions must be synchronized to cause the timesharing of the channel (as shown in Figure 3) to occur at the satellite communications transponder input. This means that each terminal must know how long it takes for its signals to reach the satellite, since the distance from terminal to satellite varies slightly, depending on terminal location. To avoid overlapping traffic transmissions, some dead time in each slot must be included, since each individual terminal does not know time exactly, nor does it know its exact propagation delay to the satellite exactly.

In the application described in this paper, TDMA has several disadvantages:

1. The terminal call rate is low. As a result, many terminals have no traffic to offer when their time slot occurs. During these slot times, the traffic channel is unused.
2. The messages exchanged between terminal and remote computer in the example of this paper are too small to packetize. In addition, they have variable lengths. As a result, it is possible for a specific message to be too long to transmit in one time slot. When this occurs, a very long delay occurs in receiving the entire message (i.e., all of the pieces).
3. It is difficult to add or delete terminals. If traffic time slots are left vacant to accommodate future added terminals, time on the traffic channel is wasted. If an additional terminal must be accommodated and no spare slots are available, all participating terminals must be notified administratively of an extension in the frame duration (there is no orderwire to permit dissemination of frame change information). Likewise, if a large number of terminals drop out of the network and give up their traffic time slots, then the traffic channel has unnecessary dead time.

2a. Slotted Aloha traffic channel

The slotted Aloha random-assignment protocol has been studied by Roberts.[4] In this protocol, the traffic channel is divided into discrete time slots as in TDMA (see Figure 4). Also, like TDMA, the duration of a time slot is chosen to accommodate an optimum amount of information in a packetized system. Unlike TDMA, *any* terminal may transmit in

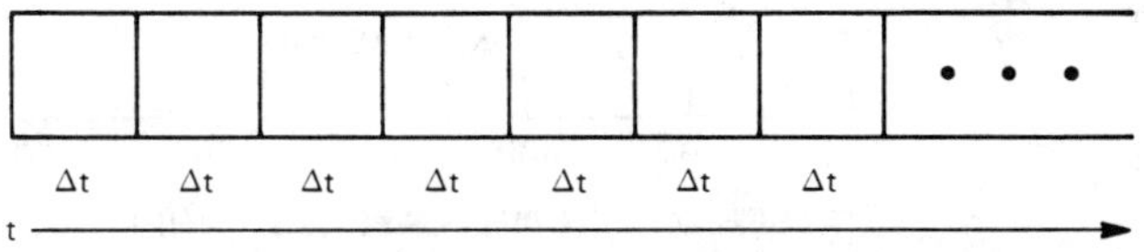

Figure 4—Slotted Aloha sharing of the traffic channel

the current traffic channel time slot; the only restriction is that the transmission must start at the beginning of the slot. Whereas TDMA is most efficient when the terminal call rate is high, slotted Aloha sharing of the traffic channel is efficient when the terminal call rate is low. This is due to the small likelihood of a "collision" (two terminals transmitting simultaneously) at lower call rates. Note that every terminal transmitting traffic must listen to the satellite transmissions to determine whether a collision has occurred. If it detects an error in the just-transmitted message (or packet), it must retransmit the message after a random number of slots have gone by. Since the random delay (typically uniformly distributed between 1 and 15 slots) occurs at both terminals that need to transmit traffic, usually the retransmission attempt occurs in different time slots and there is no repeated collision.

Control of access to the traffic channel is distributed among the terminals using the communications channel; thus an orderwire is not required (this is also the case with TDMA). However, in slotted Aloha, any terminal may transmit traffic in the current traffic channel time slot. This decreases the average message delay relative to TDMA. Since time slot assignments are not fixed, terminals can be added to (or deleted) from the network without affecting the control of access to the traffic channel. The disadvantages of slotted Aloha in the traffic channel are that when terminal call rates are high, collisions are frequent. Retransmissions cause further collisions, and the effective throughput (successful message transmissions per second) becomes limited. Stated another way, the wait time to transmit the message approaches infinity. It has been found that the maximum efficiency possible with a slotted Aloha traffic channel is less than $1/e = 0.368$.

3a. Reservation assignment with TDMA orderwire

In this protocol a time-division orderwire is provided for terminals to request use of the traffic channel (i.e., place a reservation). The reservation is a short message that includes the requesting terminals' identification number and in some systems also includes a message priority. The orderwire is sliced into assigned slots (similar to Figure 3, shown previously) for a TDMA traffic channel. Each terminal is assigned one or more orderwire time slots (depending on the call rate). In the example described in this paper, very large travel agencies with large numbers of work stations would be assigned several orderwire slots spread through the orderwire frame. Small offices with only a few work stations would be assigned one slot per frame for reservation requests.

All terminals monitor the orderwire and keep track of the reservation requests. Reservations are accepted on a first-come, first-served basis. When a reservation is honored, the terminal obtains exclusive use of the traffic channel to transmit its message. When a terminal finishes transmission on the traffic channel, it examines its copy of the reservation queue list and sends an orderwire message to the terminal at the head of the queue: "You Have the Traffic Channel." Since all terminals monitor the orderwire, they update their reservation queue list by deleting the reservation (now honored) from the new user of the traffic channel.

The use of reservations for the traffic channel permits the channel to be used fully (up to 100% efficiency). Since any terminal can receive the channel as needed, message delays are shorter than with TDMA. The control of access to the traffic channel is decentralized in that all terminals maintain a copy of the reservation queue list and issue reservations as a message is received from the work station. The current user of the traffic channel hands the channel directly to the next terminal that will use the channel. Adding to or deleting terminals from the network requires management of orderwire time slot assignments, the same as in the TDMA traffic channel protocol. The orderwire itself, however, can be used to disseminate the slot assignments.

3b. Reservation assignment with Slotted Aloha orderwire
This protocol also uses an orderwire for the placement of reservation requests for the traffic channel. The orderwire is partitioned into time slices. As in the slotted Aloha traffic channel protocol (Figure 4), any terminal may use the current time slot to issue a reservation request. The terminal monitors its satellite orderwire transmission to determine whether the message has collided with a reservation request from another terminal. If it has, the terminal waits a random number of time slots and then retries to place the reservation. As in Reservation Assignment with a TDMA orderwire, when the current user passes the traffic channel to the terminal with the reservation at the head of the queue, the next terminal uses the traffic channel on an exclusive basis until message transmission is complete.

The advantage of a slotted Aloha orderwire is that access control of the traffic channel is completely distributed. Orderwire slot assignments do not have to be managed, since any terminal can use the current orderwire time slot to place a reservation. Terminals may join or drop out of the network (due to new offices' receiving earth terminals or maintenance of hardware at existing earth terminals) without changing the orderwire operation. An additional restriction exists with this protocol, however. In all the previous protocols, the number of terminals that may share a traffic channel is based on not exceeding the specified average message transmission wait time. Further, the orderwire channel (if used by that protocol) can have a throughput of no more than 100%. With a slotted Aloha orderwire, an additional constraint is that the throughput of the orderwire is limited to 36.8%. Therefore this protocol is most useful when the terminal call rate is low.

COMPARISON OF PROTOCOLS

The selection of the best channel-sharing protocol for a particular system depends on several parameters. The key parameters are as follows:

1. Product of the number of terminals in the network and the terminal call rate ($N\lambda'$): When $N\lambda'$ is large, fixed-assignment protocols such as TDMA are suitable. When $N\lambda'$ is small, the polled and slotted Aloha protocols are useful.
2. Average message length ($\bar{l}$): The longer the message length, the longer a terminal must use the traffic channel each time it transmits a message. Fewer terminals are able to share a given channel.
3. Data transmission rate (r): The higher the traffic transmission rate, the shorter the time that a given terminal uses the traffic channel for transmission of a message. This increases the number of terminals that may share the channel.

Figures 5 and 6 show the performance of the system for the protocols and traffic load discussed previously. The figures were calculated with a traffic transmission rate of 9600 b/s and

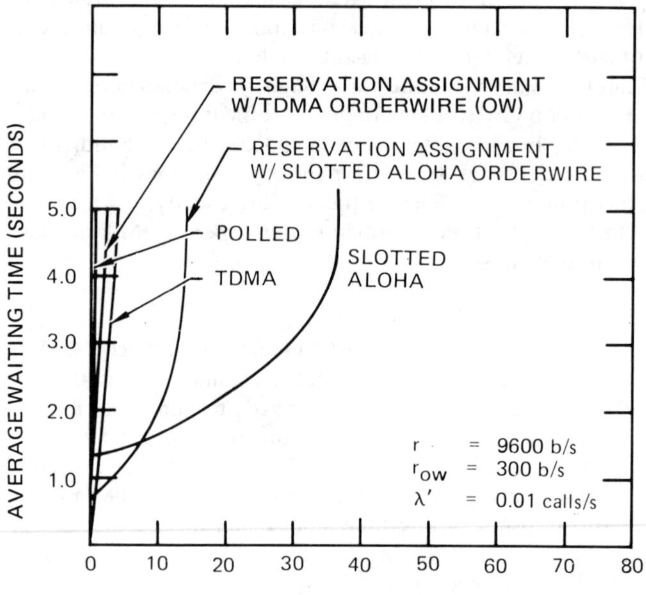

Figure 5—Efficiency of channel sharing protocols at low call rate

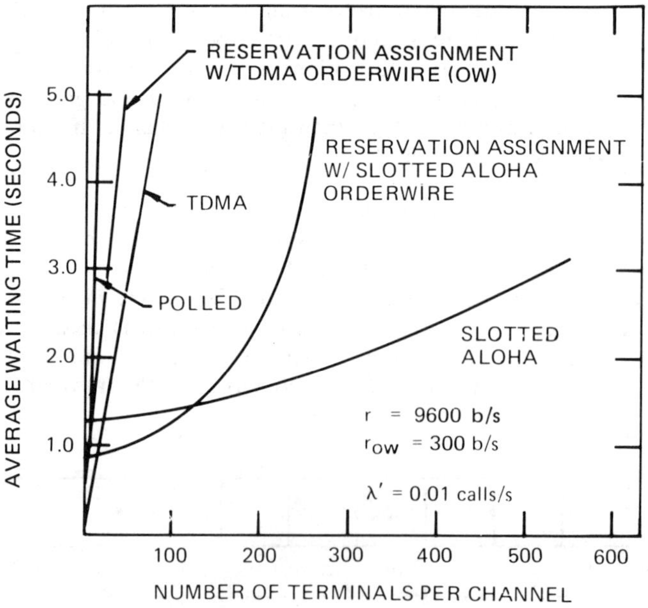

Figure 6—Terminals per channel at low call rate

an orderwire transmission rate (when used) of 300 b/s. An acceptable average wait time of 1.5 s has been assumed. The per-terminal call is rate 0.01 calls/s (3 work stations per office, 4 transactions per hour, 3 messages per transaction).

Figure 5 shows that for the type of small-business application discussed here—with large numbers of terminals, low call rates, relatively short message lengths, and small permitted wait times—the slotted Aloha or reservation assignment with slotted Aloha orderwire protocols are both suitable at 1.5 s average wait times. The advantage of the reservation assignment protocol is that the traffic does not have to be packetized. Once an orderwire reservation is honored, that earth terminal is given exclusive use of the satellite channel and transmits the entire traffic message.

Figure 6 shows the number of terminals that can be accommodated in each leased traffic channel. The reservation assignment protocol with slotted Aloha orderwire will support 130 office earth terminals per satellite channel. Therefore, five channels and one city spot beam will accommodate all of the communications requirements of the travel agencies in the Los Angeles area.

Figure 7 compares the channel efficiency versus wait time when the per-terminal call rate is increased by a factor of 100. For such applications where the call rate is high, other protocols (such as TDMA) become quite efficient.

CONCLUSIONS

Kleinrock has projected digital data transmission cost for satellite communications versus land line communications.[1] Figure 8 is based on his projections. Although the slope of the land line costs may change with the breakup of the AT&T system, the relative cost advantage of satellite communications is expected to continue. The costs are minimized by sharing a channel among terminals as needed, maintaining the channel continuously to minimize access time. Several protocols for channel sharing are available. For applications such as the travel agency industry, the reservation assignment protocol with slotted Aloha orderwire is suitable. This protocol premits a large number of earth terminals to share a channel while maintaining small transmission wait times. Work stations in the business offices will be connected to low-cost earth terminals on the customer premises, providing direct satellite communications to the central reservation computer. Commercial communications satellites will in the near future provide high-gain spot beams to permit the customer premises terminals to use small antennas (2-ft diameter) and low-power solid-state transmitters (under 20 watts).

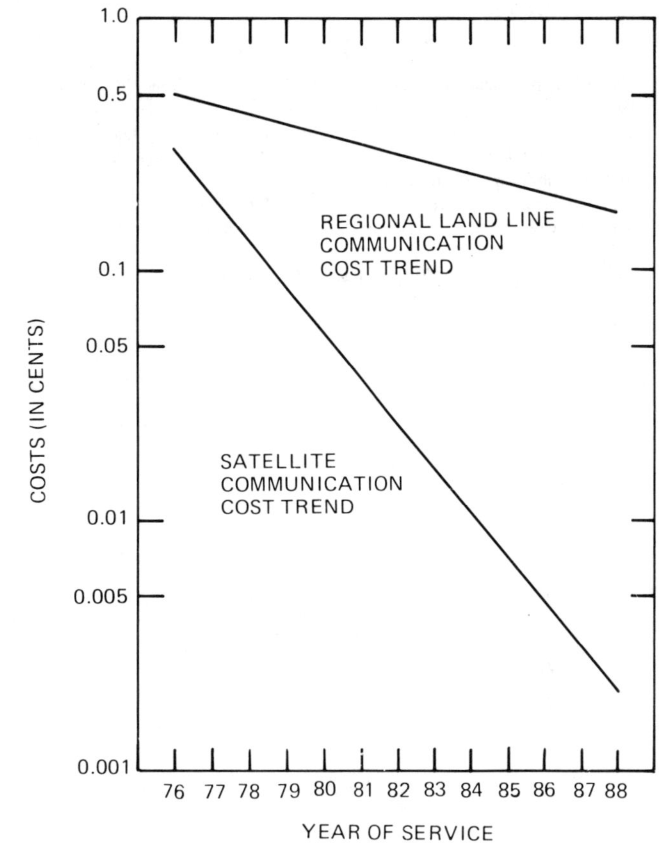

Figure 8—Incremental cost for sending 1 megabit through nationwide network

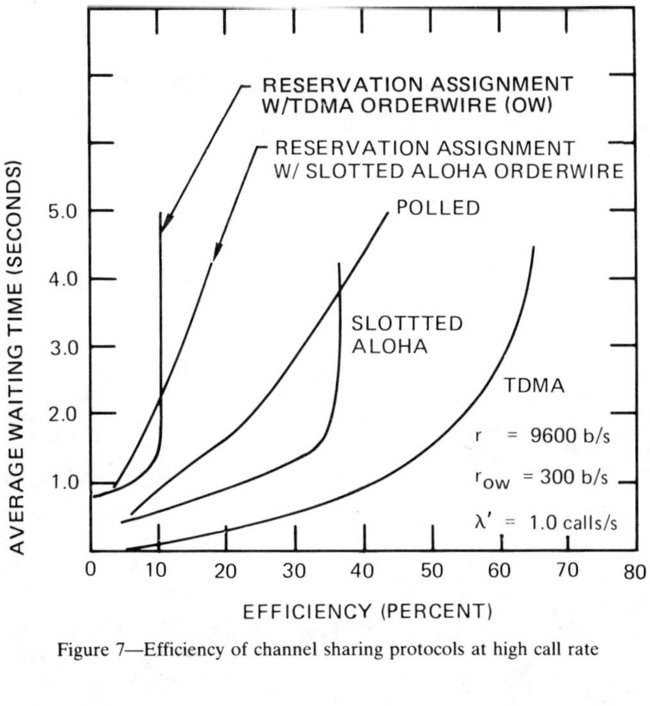

Figure 7—Efficiency of channel sharing protocols at high call rate

ACKNOWLEDGMENTS

The author would like to thank several associates at Ford Aerospace for assisting in the preparation of this paper. Thanks are due to Chaw-Chi Yu and Art Reisman for programming the protocol-queueing equations, Cindy Whyte for preparing the performance curves, Vijaya Korwar for calculating the communications link parameters, and Shaaron Wright for preparing the pictorial artwork.

REFERENCES

1. Kleinrock, L. *Queueing Systems* (Vol. II). New York: John Wiley & Sons, 1975.
2. Capetanakis, J. "Capacity Allocation Techniques in a Multi-User Satellite System." MIT Lincoln Laboratory Technical Note 34, Massachusetts Institute of Technology, Cambridge, July 18, 1979.
3. Collins Corporation "Demand Assignment Techniques Study for Military Satellite Communication Applications." Technical Report 523-076775-00221M, June 25, 1977.
4. Roberts, L. G. "Extensions of Packet Communication Technology to a Hand-Held Terminal." *AFIPS, Proceedings of the Spring Joint Computer Conference* (Vol. 44), 1972, pp. 295–298.
5. Chu, W., and Konheim, A. "On the Analysis and Modeling of a Class of Computer Communications Systems." *IEEE Transactions on Communications* COM-20, No. 3, June 1972.
6. Abramson, N., and Kuo, F. *Computer-Communication Networks*. Englewood Cliffs, N. J.: Prentice-Hall, 1973.
7. Binder, R., N. Abramson, F. Kuo, A. Okinaka, and D. Wax. "ALOHA Packet Broadcasting—A Retrospect." *AFIPS, Proceedings of the National Computer Conference* (Vol. 44), 1975, pp. 203–215.
8. Abramson, N. "Packet Switching with Satellites." *AFIPS, Proceedings of the National Computer Conference* (Vol. 42), 1973, pp. 695–702.

CARGuide—on-board computer for automobile route guidance

by M. SUGIE,* O. MENZILCIOGLU, and H. T. KUNG
Carnegie-Mellon University
Pittsburgh, Pennsylvania

ABSTRACT

This paper describes the Computer for Automobile Route Guidance (CARGuide), a prototype system designed and built at Carnegie-Mellon University. CARGuide is a portable, microcomputer-based system to aid drivers in route finding and navigation in city streets. Given starting and destination intersections, CARGuide calculates an optimum route to the destination, displays portions of the street map containing the route, and highlights the streets on the route by flashing them on a display. It provides automatic or manual zooming into the map picture and speaks driving directions along the route. Both hardware and software design is explained in the paper. The hardware consists of a 68000 processor on a Multibus, bubble memories for secondary storage, a 128 × 128 dot matrix fluorescent display, a speech synthesizer, RAM, control and interface logic for the components, and a keyboard. A total of six circuit boards are used, four of them designed at CMU. A compact street map database is constructed from a regular street map and is stored in CARGuide's half megabyte secondary storage. An efficient optimum route-finding scheme was implemented, which uses a divide and conquer method and precomputed routes to improve the performance of a shortest-path algorithm. For optimum route calculations, streets are given weights estimating the travel time, and penalties are introduced for turns and crossing intersections. CARGuide has been tested by implementing a portion of the Pittsburgh street map.

*M. Sugie was a visiting researcher at CMU on leave from Hitachi Ltd. when this paper was written.

INTRODUCTION

Route finding in street maps is a practical problem, especially for those driving in an unfamiliar city and for vehicles that must find the route with the shortest driving time between two points—emergency vehicles, utility service vehicles, and taxis. Given starting and destination locations, the first part of the problem is to find these locations on the street map. This usually involves an exhaustive search over a region and reading some fine print. The second part of the problem is to determine an optimum route between the source and the destination. A study on human subjects[1] shows that humans approach this problem by using heuristics. In general, people first identify the important roads going roughly in the direction of the destination and then try to connect the source and the destination to the important roads using a local depth first search. The study also shows that, when asked to find a route between two given points on a map, people vary significantly in the routes they find and the time they take to find a route. In most cases, the routes people find are not the shortest possible.

A street map can be considered a graph, in which streets are the edges and intersections are the vertices. In graph theory, the route-finding problem is known as the shortest-path problem. It is covered substantially in the literature and a number of shortest-path algorithms are known.[2,3,4,5,6,7,8] A representative of the complexities of single-source shortest-path algorithms is $O(n^2)$, where n is the number of vertices.[9] The average city street map has on the order of 10^4 intersections, therefore, the complexity of the algorithm that will be used for route finding is important. (Within Pittsburgh city limits, approximately a 60-square mile area, there are 8400 vertices and 11300 edges. These numbers would more than double for the Pittsburgh metropolitan area (140 square miles). See reference 1 for some other cities.) Since shortest-path algorithms deal with graphs in general (i.e., graphs with no geometrical properties) direct application of these algorithms for route finding in street maps is not efficient. For more efficient solutions, algorithms taking advantage of the planarity and directionality of the street map, divide and conquer methods, precomputed routes, heuristics, or a combination of these may be used. Another problem is that the optimum route is not necessarily the one with the shortest distance. People consider several factors in addition to the distance: number of turns, size of the road, number of traffic lights, etc.[10] Somehow, these factors must also be incorporated into the algorithm.

Navigation along a chosen route may be a more difficult problem for the driver than finding the route on the map. The driver has to know where the vehicle is at the time and know which road or direction to take next. To find out which way to go next, one need only look at the map. However, this may be a problem while driving. This problem can be helped if a device that can speak out the directions and show the route is installed in the vehicle. Knowing where the vehicle is, whether it is off course or not, is a more demanding problem. Besides looking at the map, one has to look for street names or road signs. This is difficult, especially at night. A navigation device that can point the position of the vehicle on a map display would solve this problem. Several navigational systems have been proposed to determine the position of land vehicles. The proposed methods include using inputs from the vehicle's steering system and speedometer,[11] using inertial devices (gyros),[12,13] or using signals broadcasted from three or more fixed stations (this method is more suitable for nonurban areas).[14] However, building the navigation device to pinpoint the position of the vehicle is much different than building the rest of the route guidance system. This paper deals with the computer systems aspect of the problem and not with a position-fixing navigation system.

Using computers for route guidance is a promising idea. However, implementing a practical and cost-effective system remains a problem. Two directions can be taken toward the implementation of a route guidance system, centralized or independent. In the centralized approach, there is a central system where people can call and ask for directions. If the vehicle is equipped with a transceiver, communication with the central facility can be kept during travel. The central system can also be used to guide the vehicles depending on traffic conditions.[15]

The problems with this approach are the lack of real-time navigational help and limitations brought by the transmission bandwidth of the central facility—response time and availability. (A centralized route guidance system would be feasible for emergency vehicles, which can be incorporated into a computerized dispatching facility.[16]) The other approach is to have a small system installed in the vehicle. This has the advantages of being self-contained and providing fast real-time interaction. The on-board system can also be used to provide navigational aid. This paper describes a prototype route guidance system based on this idea that has been built at CMU. Several commercial devices have also been announced with different implementation approaches.[12,17]

The problems involved in implementing an on-board map/route guidance system are the following. The hardware must be compact and insensitive to mechanical disturbance. The map and route data must be stored in a permanent storage medium that is interchangeable or writable in order to allow changing maps or making updates. Both visual and voice outputs are necessary assuming that the person is driving alone. The map database must be detailed and accurate enough to

Figure 1—CARGuide

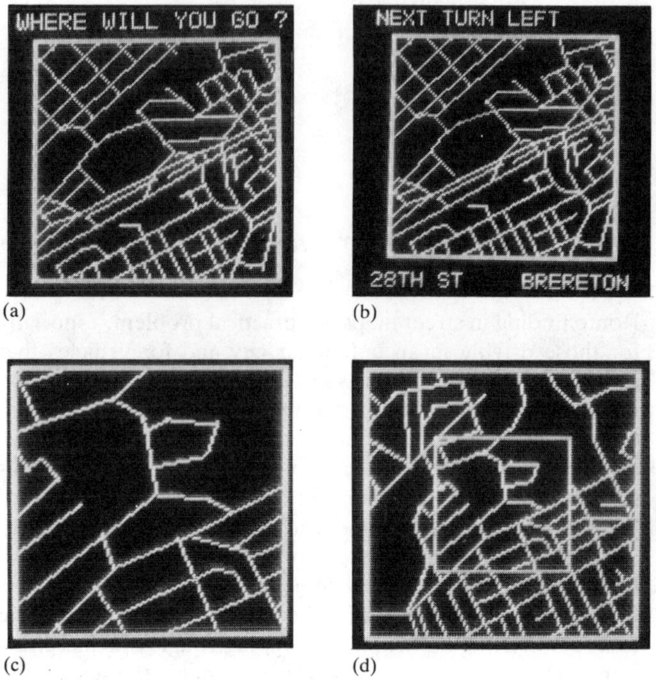

Figure 2—Street map display

avoid misinterpretation but should be compact to fit in a portable storage. An efficient route finding algorithm must be used to provide quick response using a microcomputer. In the following sections, the Computer for Automobile Route Guidance, CARGuide, is described and the solutions used for the above problems are explained.

The next section describes the overview and operation of CARGuide from the user's point of view. The hardware section explains CARGuide's hardware configuration, components, and interesting aspects of operation. In the database section, the organization of the street map database is shown and manipulation of the database is explained. The last section explains the route-finding method used by CARGuide.

OVERVIEW AND OPERATION

On the outside, CARGuide consists of four pieces of equipment: a card cage containing circuit boards, a speech synthesizer box with a speaker, a keyboard, and a 128×128 bit map fluorescent display (Figure 1). Being a prototype for research, the system has been kept modular and an effort was not made to compact it into a single unit. CARGuide can also be connected to a host, in this case a VAX, for the development of software. At the time of this writing, the functionality of the system had been tested by implementing a portion of the Pittsburgh street map, but it has not been installed in an automobile.

The operation of CARGuide is as follows. The user communicates with CARGuide using the keyboard, and CARGuide responds using speech and display. The user inputs have been kept to a minimum, and inputs can be entered using as few key strokes as possible. CARGuide speaks messages in full sentences and displays them in writing at the same time, but with fewer words. The idea is to require as little use of the driver's hands and eyes as possible. From the user's point of view, CARGuide can be in three modes: entry mode, view mode, and trip mode. After start-up, CARGuide is in *entry* mode when the user enters the starting and destination locations interactively. CARGuide is in *view* mode any time a map picture is displayed. In this mode, the user can manipulate the picture by zooming into parts of it with the use of a cursor. When the vehicle starts traveling along the route determined by CARGuide, it enters the *trip* mode. In trip mode, as intersections are approached, CARGuide displays the names of the street being traveled on and the street to be crossed next, shows them on the map, and speaks which way to go at the intersection.

In entry mode, CARGuide first asks for a starting location. The starting and destination locations are to be entered as intersections—using two street names to enter an intersection. After the first street name is entered, CARGuide repeats the name in speech and writing, and if it is correct, asks for the second street name. If the street name is spelled wrong or if the street does not exist in the map database, the user is notified by an error message and is asked to enter again. Entering only the name of the street is sufficient in most cases—i.e., without specifying whether it is an AVE., ST., DR., etc.—unless it is a numbered street, in which case the appropriate abbreviation must be used. In any case, if there is an ambiguity caused by more than one street having the same name, it can be resolved by the user entering the full name of the street or by entering the second street name, which almost always defines a unique intersection. (A few exceptions to this rule exist in Pittsburgh where the same streets intersect each other more than once. In that case, one of the intersections is chosen and a caution message is output to the user.) After two street names have been entered, if their intersection can not be found, the user is notified and asked to enter again.

After an intersection has been entered, CARGuide finds the intersection in the map and displays the block of the street map containing the intersection (Figure 2(a)). The map is divided into square blocks. A block corresponds to an area 0.7 mile on each side and it is displayed as a 100×100 dot matrix image. The intersection point is highlighted by flashing it on and off. In general, after displaying a picture, CARGuide enters the view mode. In view mode, if the image resolution is not satisfactory, the user can zoom in a part of the image, using a square cursor (Figure 2(c)(d)). The size and position of the cursor can be manipulated incrementally using single key strokes (corresponding to Center, Up, Down, Left, Right, Smaller, Larger, Fullview). The magnification ratio can be increased with successive zoomings, and different parts of the image can be inspected by zooming in and out of the picture and by moving the cursor.

The optimum route between the starting and the destination intersections is computed after the user indicates that he is finished viewing the destination picture. The computed route is highlighted in the map picture by flashing it periodically. If starting and destination intersections are in the same block, the route is flashed in its entirety. If they are in different blocks, the route is displayed in portions, one block at a time. In either case, CARGuide enters the view mode after a block is displayed so that the user may inspect the route.

CARGuide enters the trip mode when the user indicates that he is ready to travel. In trip mode, the route to be followed is shown incrementally as the car travels through intersections. Before the trip, CARGuide asks which view mode option will be used during the trip. The user has two options for the view mode: manual zoom or auto zoom. In the manual zoom mode, the block is displayed in full scale. The user may zoom in to a part of the picture using the adjustable cursor described earlier. However, since manual zooming requires driver time and attention, an auto zoom mode is provided that requires no user inputs. In this mode, a constant magnification ratio of 4 × (over the full scale view) is used and a fixed section of the block through which the car is traveling is displayed. The block is divided into five sections, as shown in Figure 3. A full-scale view gives a better perspective of the distance traveled and requires fewer picture changes, while a zoomed picture gives better resolution.

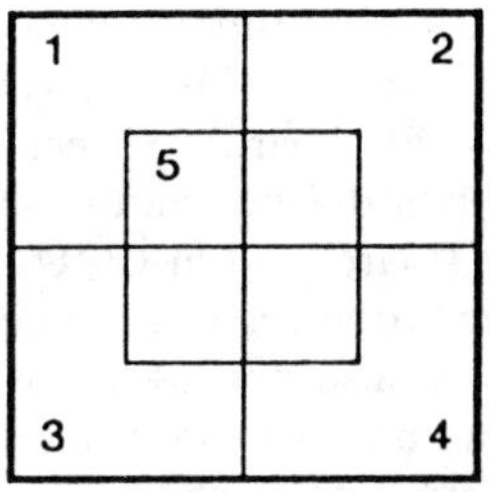

Figure 3—Block sections for autozoom

During the trip, CARGuide flashes the portion of the route between the intersection the car has just passed and the next two intersections it should be going through. The name of the street currently being traveled on is displayed at the lower left of the display, and the street to be crossed next is displayed at the lower right (Figure 2(b)). If the car should be taking the crossing street at the next intersection, the street's name is flashed. Before each intersection, CARGuide speaks which direction to go—straight, left, or right—and the name of the street to take. Currently, CARGuide does not have the ability to actually track the motion of the vehicle. (The position of the vehicle can be pinpointed in the map and flashed continuously as a moving point in the display, assuming accurate inputs of the vehicle's speed and direction exist. However, implementing the navigational device to provide those inputs was beyond the scope of this project.) It is assumed that the driver never gets off course. In the current scheme, the driver has to hit a key after passing each intersection so as to invoke CARGuide for information about the next portion of the route.

HARDWARE

Figure 4 shows a block diagram of CARGuide's hardware organization. The hardware consists of six boards—68000/

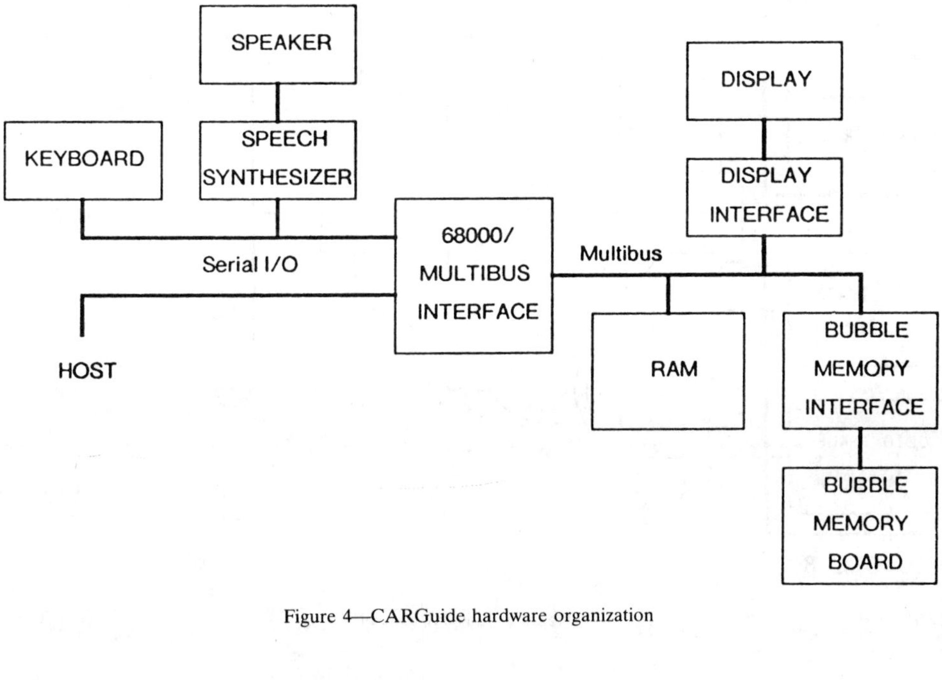

Figure 4—CARGuide hardware organization

Multibus Interface, RAM, Bubble Memory, Bubble Memory Interface, Display Interface, Display (the display device is also mounted on a PC board), Speech Synthesizer with a speaker, and a keyboard. The heart of the system is a 68000 Multibus Interface Board built at CMU. The board contains a Motorola 68000 microprocessor and interfaces it to the Intel Multibus. The board also houses 8 Kbytes of ROM and 4 Kbytes of RAM and has two independent serial I/O lines. A resident monitor program is stored in ROM, which starts executing after a power up. It initializes the system and enables commüнications with the outside. The resident monitor provides functions to download programs and data from a host, which were used during software development, and to run programs. CARGuide software requires less than 50 Kbytes of RAM to execute; therefore, a 64 Kbyte RAM is sufficient. However, a 500 Kbyte RAM board was used as the main memory because of its availability.

Bubble Memory Board contains four 1 Mbit bubble memories by Hitachi (a total of 500 Kbytes), and a bubble memory controller. Bubble memories were chosen for secondary storage for the following reasons. They provide a writable mass storage that allows changing map databases or making updates. The bubble memory chips being used on the board are stationary; however, plug-in type cassettes are also available. Compared with other magnetic storage devices—tape cassettes or floppies—bubble memories are more suitable for use in an automobile because of their nonvolatility, compactness, and nonmechanical operation. The average access time is 15 msec and transfer rate is 100 Kbits/second. Bubble Memory Interface Board, which was designed and built at CMU, interfaces the bubble memory controller to Multibus. It contains a DMA Controller and other control logic for bubble memory I/O. The I/O can be done in DMA mode or Processor I/O (PIO) mode, which uses a busy-wait scheme. DMA mode is used for transferring entire files and saves processor time especially when the processor is busy generating map pictures. PIO mode is used when bubble memory is accessed in a RAM-like fashion where only a single page of a file is accessed as in a directory or table look up. Since bubble memories provide fast access and small page size (32 Bytes/page), this kind of operation is feasible and helps to save RAM space by not having to keep the entire file in RAM for quick access.

The Display Board houses a 128×128 dot matrix fluorescent display device (by Noritake), and driver circuitry, and was designed at CMU. The Display Interface Board, also designed at CMU, contains four 16 Kbit static RAM display buffers, control logic, and the interface to Multibus. Figure 5 shows a simple logic diagram of display control. In general, the processor generates 128×128 bit map images (16 Kbits/image) and writes them into one of the display buffers. At one time, the Display Interface can store two pictures, shown as PICTURE A and PICTURE B in Figure 5. A picture consists of two images—a solid image and a flash image—as will be explained later. Although only one picture is displayed at a time, the reason for storing two pictures is the following. It takes 15 msec to display an image already stored in a display buffer, whereas it takes a few seconds, depending on the number of splines in the image, to generate it. Hence, in changing pictures, the new picture is written into the unused buffer while the other buffer is being displayed. When the generation of the new picture is finished, the buffer select signal is switched and the change is sudden. Also, a full-scale

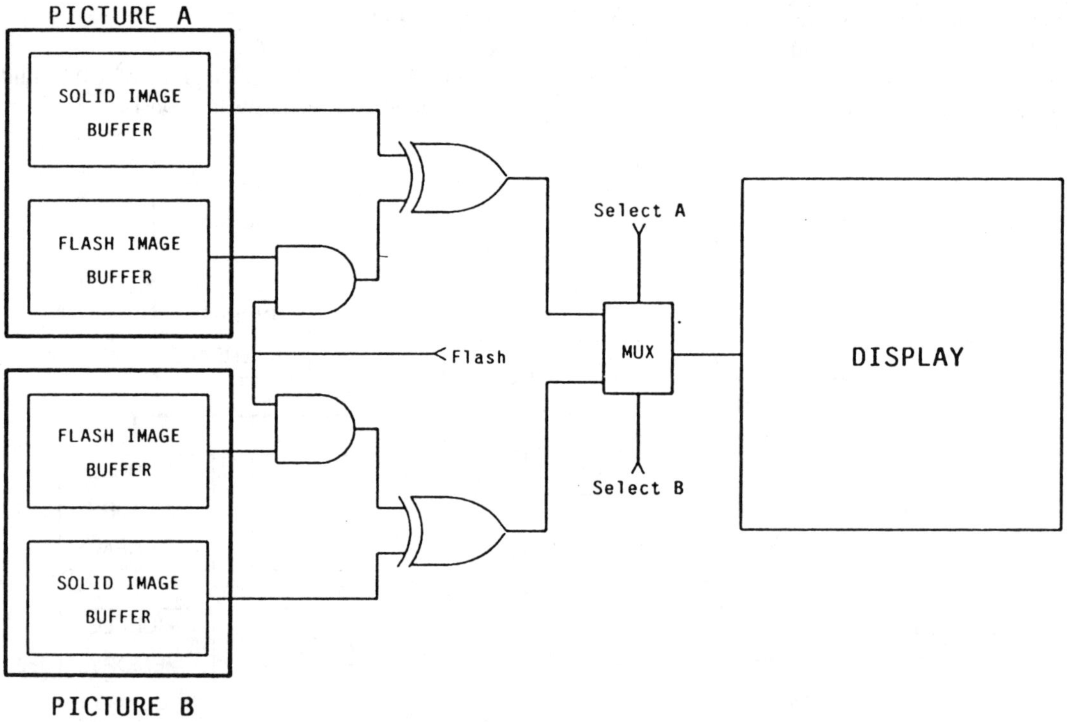

Figure 5—Display control

picture of a block is kept in one buffer while the other is used for a zoomed part during a zooming process. Since the full-scale picture has to be restored frequently to zoom into different parts of it, time is saved by not having to regenerate it every time.

The flashing effect is realized by using two images per picture, and by periodically taking the exclusive OR of the flash image and the solid image buffers. The flashing period is 1 second, 0.5 second each for on and off. The approach considered first was to store the image in two buffers, where one image would be complete and the parts to be flashed would be missing in the other. The flashing could be achieved by periodically switching between the two buffers. However, since the parts to be flashed are much smaller than the parts that stay solid, it would save processor time if only the parts to be flashed are written into the flash image buffer instead of the parts that stay solid. In this case, flashing is achieved by taking the exclusive OR of the two buffers periodically.

For speech generation, a TSI PROSE 2000 speech synthesizer is used, which converts text to speech algorithmicly. The Speech Synthesizer Board is mounted in a box together with a speaker that is separate from the rest of the system. For connection, one of the serial lines from 68000 is used. The same serial line is also connected to the keyboard; however, this does not constitute a problem since they do not operate in parallel. (The speech board can also be activated and deactivated by using control characters.) The other serial line is used for connection to a host for downloading data to change or update the database when needed. In an actual implementation the host can be a remote databank. The same serial line can also be used for receiving inputs from a navigation device when installed in a car.

STREET MAP DATABASE

Organization

The street map is divided into square blocks, each corresponding to one grid in Figure 6, covering a 0.5 square mile area. The block organization is reflected in the majority of the database. The street map database contains three types of information: *identification* information relating street names to intersections, *graph and route* information about connections between the intersections, and *pictorial* information for picture generation. Figure 7 shows a sequence of block diagrams representing the manipulation of the database and the use of each information type. Steps 1 and 2 represent the identification operations; where an intersection (given street names) or street names (given an intersection) are determined. Steps 3, 4, and 5 represent the operations on pictorial data. Given a block, step 3 determines the list of splines constituting the block picture. Step 4 is the incremental picture generation step, where a spline expression is converted to

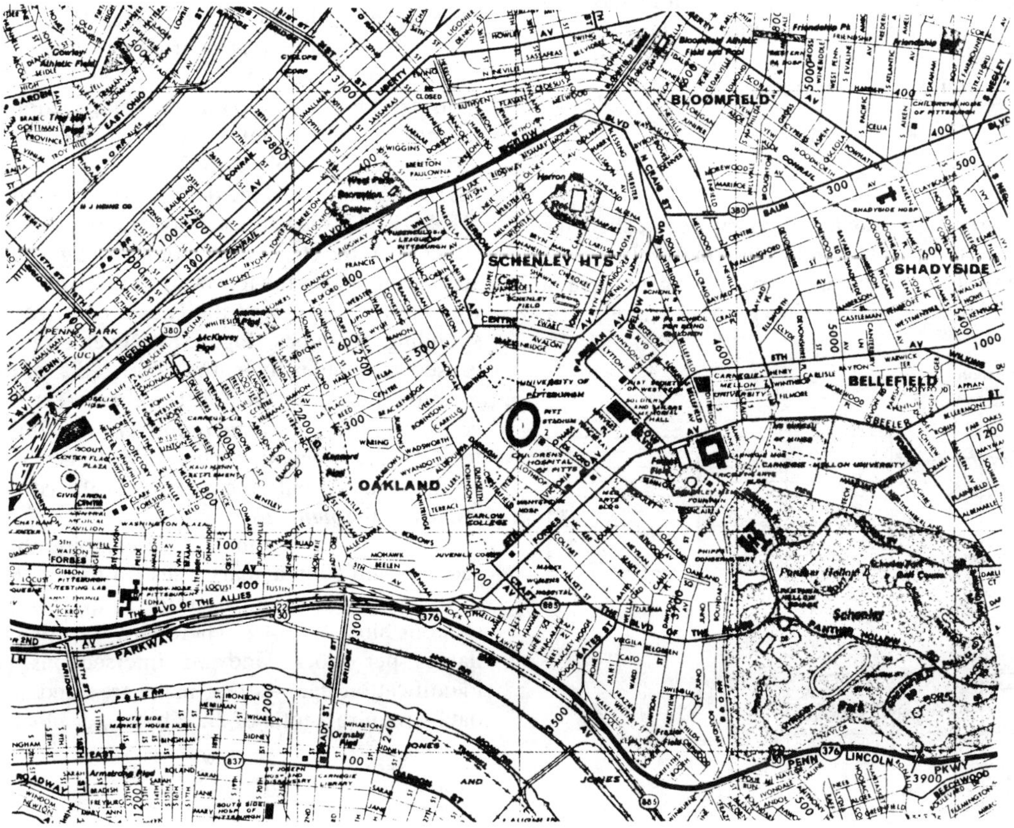

Figure 6—Portion of Pittsburgh street map

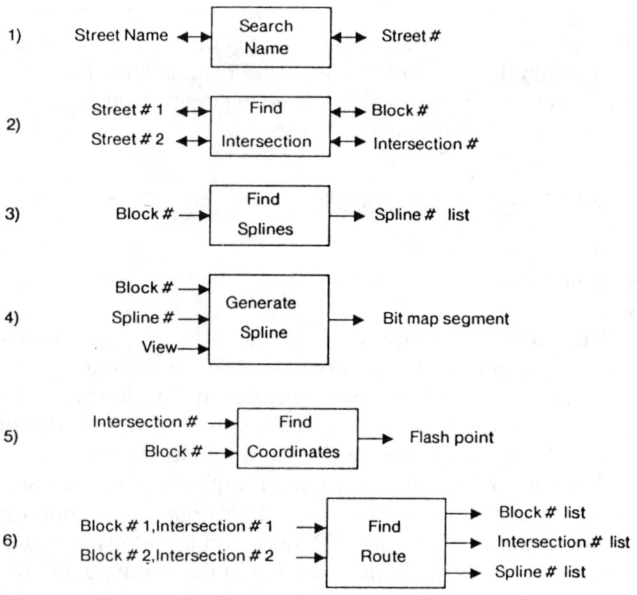

Figure 7—Database manipulation

a segment of the bit map picture—depending on the current view boundaries and magnification of the picture, which vary during zooming. Step 5 is used to flash an intersection point in the picture. Step 6 represents the route-finding process where graph and route information is used. Given two intersections, an optimum route is found and a list of blocks containing the route, a sequence of intersections to be visited in each block, and a list of splines representing the street segments forming the route are determined.

Identification Information

Street names are organized as an n-ary tree, called the *name tree,* where n is equal to five. Each node of the tree is stored in one page of the bubble memory. During a search of the tree, bubble memory is accessed in a RAM-like mode, one node (page) per access. Therefore, larger n means fewer accesses and a shorter search time since access time is the dominating factor. Each node of the tree contains four street names. A street name consists of 10 characters for the name and an encoded type affix for ST., AVE., RD., HWY., etc. Although 8 characters are enough to identify a street name, 10 characters were used in order to fully generate the names for speech. Four street names are packed into a 32 byte page using the following scheme. The alphabet is restricted to capital letters and numerals; hence, a 6 bit ASCII code is used for each character. For each name, 4 bits are used to encode the type affix, requiring a total of 8 bytes per street name. There is a mapping between the nodes of the tree and the corresponding page addresses of the bubble memory, which minimizes the average access time to a node during a search. 3000 names can be searched in 5 accesses ($\log_5 3000$) in 20 msec.

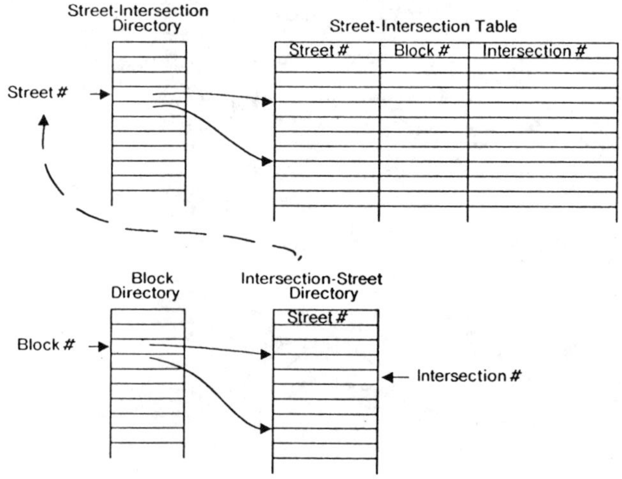

Figure 8—Street intersection data

Figure 8 shows the portion of the database containing the information about intersections. Each street is given a number (street#) corresponding to the index of the street name in the alphabetical ordering. Given the level, node, and box a street name occupies in the name tree, the street# can be computed directly if the total number of streets in the name tree is known. Similarly, given a street#, the location of the street name in the name tree is directly computed. Two street#s define a unique intersection. Given two street#s, S_1 and S_2, S_1 is used to index a pointer array called the *street-intersection directory*. The pointer points to the beginning of the list of intersections on S_1 which are stored in the *street-intersection table* (the end of the list is determined by the next pointer). A search over the list for S_2 determines the intersection of S_1 and S_2. An intersection is represented by a block# and an intersection# within that block. The block# specifies the geometrical block containing the intersection. At the block boundaries, virtual intersections are defined with imaginary streets called BTOP, BBOTTOM, BLEFT, and BRIGHT. Also, in order to include dead-end streets, an imaginary street DEADEND was defined whose intersection with a dead-end street gives the street's end point. Going from intersections to street names uses the following path. A *block directory* is used to point to a portion of the *intersection-street directory* corresponding to a block (Figure 8). Given an intersection# I_x, I_x is used as an index to get the street#, S_1, for one of the streets forming I_x. The street# for the other street, S_2, is obtained by consulting the *street-intersection directory* for S_1 and searching for I_x in the *street-intersection table* to get S_2. Then S_1 and S_2 are used to compute the location of the corresponding street names in the *name tree.*

The average street map block contains about 80 real intersections and 30 imaginary ones. In the implemented portion of the map, central Pittsburgh, the average number of intersections/block is 145. There are approximately 60 street names per block, and 2.5 intersections per street. The identification data—street name tree and street-intersection data—require a total of 2.2 Kbytes per block on the average.

Graph and Route Information

The information on the connectivity of the intersections in a block is stored using the data structure shown in Figure 9. A

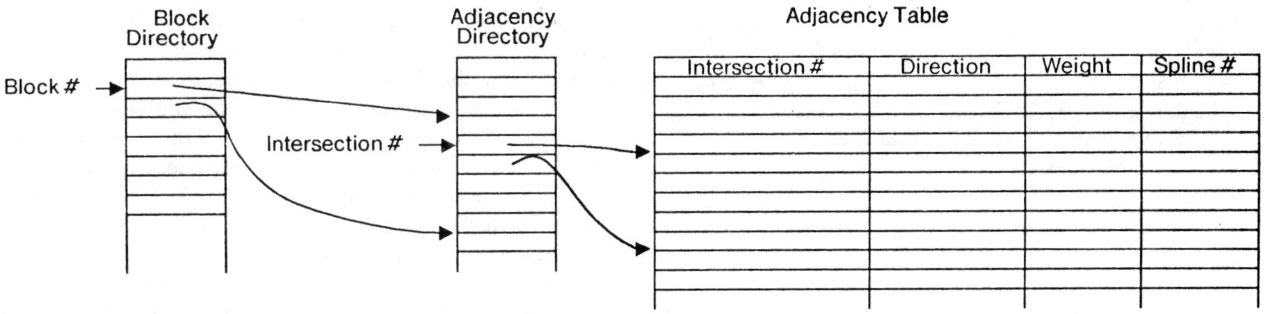

Figure 9—Intersection adjacency data

block directory is used to identify the portion of data belonging to each block. Given an intersection# I_s, I_s is used to index an *adjacency directory* that points to the beginning of the list of intersections adjacent to I_s. The list is a part of the *adjacency table* that also stores information about the connecting *edges* from I_s to the adjacent intersections. The term *edge* is used to indicate the graph nature of the street map. A street segment connecting two intersections may have different weights for each direction (as in one-way streets). Therefore, edge implies a directed street segment. For each intersection in the list, *direction* indicates whether the adjacent intersection lies to the north, south, etc. of I_s. Eight directions can be encoded, including intermediate ones. Each edge is given a *weight* which is *a measure of the time to travel that edge.* The weighting scheme is the foundation of the optimum route-finding operation. Currently, the weights are determined by dividing the physical distance of the road segment by the maximum allowable speed in that road, and normalizing to a 12-bit integer. A more accurate measure would be to use the average speed instead of the allowable speed, but such figures were not available. A *spline #* is assigned to each edge, which is used to access spline data in the pictorial database to construct the shape of the edge. In general, two edges based on the same street segment have the same spline#. A spline# consists of a one-bit *type* tag that indicates whether the segment has linear or nonlinear shape, and an *index* to a segment table in the pictorial database. There are 350 edges/block (2.4 edges/intersection), and the adjacency data require a total of 1.7 Kbytes/block on the average.

Connectivity among blocks is represented using two types of information: a list of intersections connecting the graphs of two adjacent blocks, and a sequence of blocks connecting two nonadjacent blocks. Between two adjacent blocks, virtual intersections at the shared boundary constitute the list of intersections connecting the two blocks. Since those intersections may have different intersection#s in each block, correspondence between intersection#s at the two sides of the boundary must be established. Using the numbering scheme shown in Figure 10, the correspondence can be established by storing minimal information. Within each block, intersections at a boundary are numbered sequentially and a convention is used to increase the numbers along a boundary in the same direction for all blocks (left to right and bottom to top in Figure 10). The correspondence on intersection numbers between two adjacent blocks (Block 1 and 2 in the figure) is established by storing the range of intersection numbers at the shared boundary in one block (4–6 in Block 1), and an offset from one block to the other (+2 from Block 1 to Block 2).

Between nonadjacent blocks, connectivity can be determined based on the connectivities between adjacent blocks. However, to avoid a long search in route-finding operations, block sequences based on predetermined routes are used to connect nonadjacent blocks. The block sequence represents the blocks to be traveled through, going from one block to the other. Figure 11 shows the data structures used to store that information. Given source and destination blocks B_s and B_d, the pointer matrix called the *Interblock Route Directory* is used to point to a list of blocks connecting B_s to B_d. For each block in the list, an *entry* and an *exit* point are stored, which are virtual intersections on the block boundary and are used to determine the actual route in the block. Since interblock routes mostly correspond to major routes in the map, usually more than one B_s–B_d pair share the same route. Thus, those block pairs point to different parts of the same interblock route in the Interblock Route Table. For a 100-block area, the interblock route data would require 1.8 Kbytes/block.

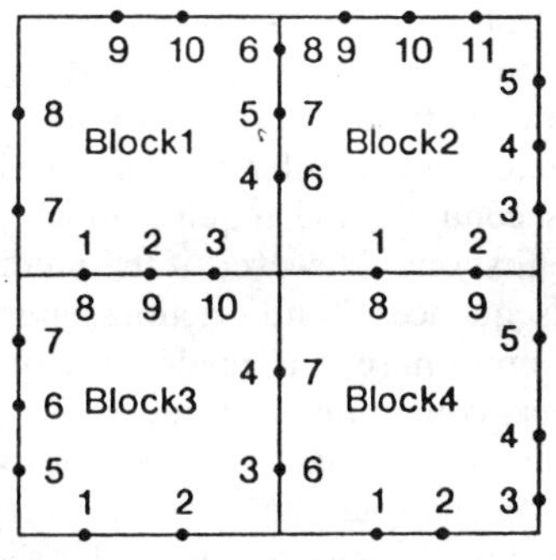

Figure 10—Adjacent block boundaries

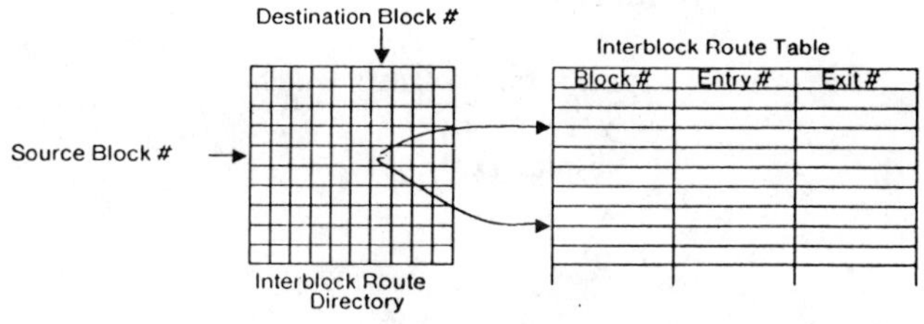

Figure 11—Interblock connectivity data

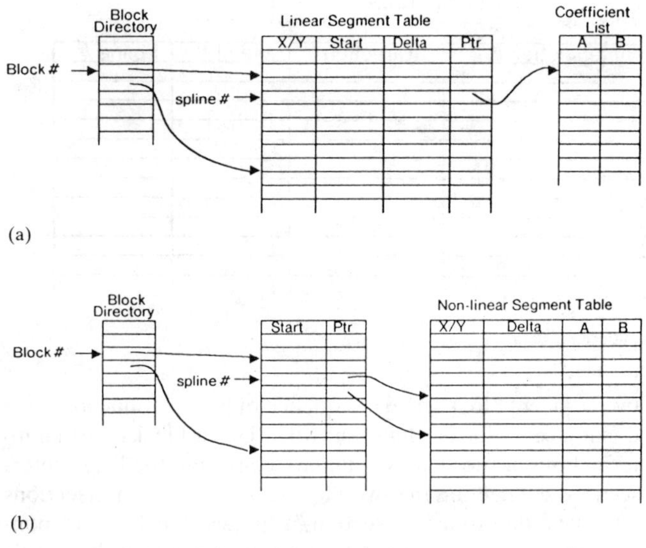

Figure 12—Picture database: (a) linear segments; (b) nonlinear segments

Pictorial Information

The pictorial data were obtained digitizing a regular street map and using an image-processing system to extract the line data representing the streets. Since the picture consists of only lineal features, the data was organized in vector format rather than in raster format. If the purpose were only to generate a street map picture on the display, 100 × 100 bit map representation for each block would be more efficient. It would require 10Kbits/block (somewhat wasteful of storage since the average block picture consists of 1200 bits) and no computation, compared with 7.4 Kbits/block and 1.8 sec/block computation time of the current vector scheme. However, it was necessary to associate each street segment with a geometric entity in order to flash selected routes against a solid picture. Furthermore, vector representation is more convenient for the zooming process. Figure 12 shows the structure of the picture database. The database is based on the geometric entity called *segment,* which represents the shape of a street segment connecting two intersections. The database consists of two parts: a linear segment part (Figure 12(a)), and a nonlinear segment part (Figure 12(b)). A tag bit in the spline# is used to determine which part to access.

The linear segments represent street segments that have either a straight line shape or can be closely approximated by one, 85% of the segments fall into this category. Using coordinates in the range 0–100, a linear segment is constructed using the straightforward algorithm

```
for x = start to start + delta{
  y = Ax + B;
  display (x,y);
  x = x + 1;
}
```

where x and y are interchangeable. The entry *X*/*Y* in the linear segment table indicates whether x or y is the independent variable. To construct the line smoothly, without any missing dots, A has to be smaller than or equal to one. Thus, in constructing the database, the independent coordinate in the line equation is chosen depending on the slope of the line segment. Since, on the average, two to three linear segments are part of the same street, they use the same coefficients. Hence, some storage is saved by having a separate coefficient table which the segments point to.

Nonlinear segments constitute approximately 15% of the segments and were initially planned to be represented by cubic splines. However, an initial testing was done to compare the effectiveness of cubic splines with piecewise linear approximation. It was discovered that the extra effort used in fitting the cubic splines and the computation overhead in construction did not bring an appreciable improvement in the final picture over a piecewise linear approximation. If the picture size were greater than 100 × 100, the result would probably have been different. Figure 12(b) shows the data structure used for representing nonlinear segments. On the average, 2.2 line segments were used to construct a nonlinear segment.

ROUTE FINDING

For route finding, a divide and conquer method (dividing the map into blocks), precomputed routes (interblock routes), and a shortest-path algorithm (Dijkstra's algorithm[6]) are used. Directly using a general shortest-path algorithm is not efficient for street maps. Since street maps have Euclidian properties, short streets between distant intersections do not exist. Therefore, it is reasonable to partition the graph into local subgraphs, using a divide and conquer method. It is assumed that subgraphs do not overlap but that two subgraphs are connected along a boundary. If two vertices belong to the same subgraph, it is assumed that the shortest path between the two vertices is contained within the subgraph. The block partitioning of the street map is based on this divide and conquer idea. For now, it can be assumed that each block consists of one connected subgraph; exceptions will be explained later. The term "shortest route" must be interpreted as the route with shortest estimated driving time. Within a block, the shortest route is determined using the shortest-path algorithm. From one block to an adjacent block, the shortest-path algorithm is used successively for each block with connections across the boundary. From one block to a nonadjacent block, the problem is more difficult. One method could start with the source block and carry a directed search through adjacent blocks toward the destination block, using the directionality in the street map. Another method might be to store predetermined routes from each block to all other blocks. The second method requires much less computation than does the first one. However, if the predetermined routes are stored as sequences of intersections, much storage will be needed. A compromise was made by storing only the sequence of blocks containing the route and storing an entry and an exit point on the boundaries for each block in the sequence (see Figure 13). The route between the entry and exit points within each block is computed using the shortest-path algorithm. If there are *b* blocks in the map, b^2 routes need to be

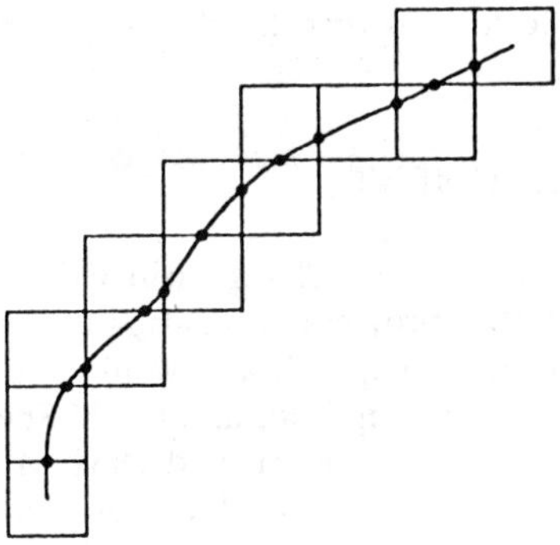

Figure 13—An interblock route

stored. By using pointers to eliminate duplicate storage of shared routes, for 100 blocks approximately 200 Kbytes is required in secondary storage.

Given source and destination intersections I_S and I_d, three different schemes may be used to determine the optimum route from I_s to I_d depending on the relationship of blocks containing I_s and I_d. If I_s and I_d are in the same block, the route is determined using Dijkstra's algorithm. Starting with I_s, the set of intersections closest to I_s is expanded until I_d is included in the set. In general, the algorithm requires $O(n^2)$ computations where n is the number of intersections. One block has 145 intersections on the average, but usually the destination is reached in less than 10K computations. To determine a realistic optimum route, the edges between intersections are given weights that correspond to the time to travel that edge rather than to the edge's physical length. To include some of the human factors in determining an optimum route, right turns are given a one-point (equivalent to one minute) penalty, while left turns are given a two-point penalty. Also, each intersection crossed along the route adds a half-point penalty. The weights estimating the travel time and the penalties can be made more realistic in an actual implementation if statistical data are available.

If I_s and I_d are in adjacent blocks, the route calculation is carried as follows. Figure 14 shows eight blocks that are considered to be adjacent to Block 0, Blocks 1–4 are strictly adjacent, and Blocks 5–8 are semiadjacent. If I_s is in Block 0 and I_d is in Block 3, first, shortest routes from I_s to intersections 1 and 2 on the Block 0–3 boundary are calculated using Dijkstra's algorithm. Using the total travel times to 1 and 2 as base values for the equivalent intersections 7 and 8 in Block 3, Dijkstra's algorithm is repeated for Block 3 until I_d is reached. If I_d is in Block 8, one route is found by going from Block 0 to Block 3 to Block 8, another route is found by going from Block 0 to Block 4 to Block 8. Comparison of the two routes determines the shorter one. Using this scheme, the route to a strictly adjacent block (Block 3) is determined in $2N$ computations, where N is the number of computations to execute Dijkstra's algorithm in one block. The shortest route to a semiadjacent block (Block 8) is determined in $4N$ computations. If the same graph area were not divided into 9 blocks, the calculations would take $9^2\,N$ computations since N is $O(n^2)$.

If I_s and I_d are in distant blocks, the route is found using the scheme of carrying the optimum route calculation from one block to a strictly adjacent block (Figure 13) along a predetermined block sequence, as explained earlier in the section. If the route passes through m blocks, mN computations are required.

So far, it has been assumed that each block consisted of one connected subgraph and thus that every intersection can be reached from another intersection within the block. However, in a strictly square grid partitioning of the map, a block may have intersections that are disjoint from the rest of the intersections in the block. Usually those intersections are near the boundaries, on extensions of streets from a neighboring block (fortunately, such intersections account for less than 5% of the intersections). Another case is when the block is physically divided into two sections with no connections in between (as a block with a river passing through). If I_s and I_d are in the same block, but after executing Dijkstra's algorithm, it is found that I_d cannot be reached, then I_s and I_d are not connected within the block (Figure 15). In that case, connections from I_s and I_d to the block boundaries are determined (to boundaries 1, 2, 3, 4 from I_s, and to boundaries 3 and 4 from I_d in Figure 15). Identifying a block boundary that can be reached from both I_s and I_d (boundaries 3 and 4), the route-finding algorithm is carried to the block adjacent to that boundary. If there is more than one boundary that can be reached from I_s and I_d, the one with the shortest total travel time to I_s and I_d is given priority (boundary 4).

The divide and conquer method and using predetermined routes bring considerable improvement in performance over a direct application of a shortest-path algorithm in route find-

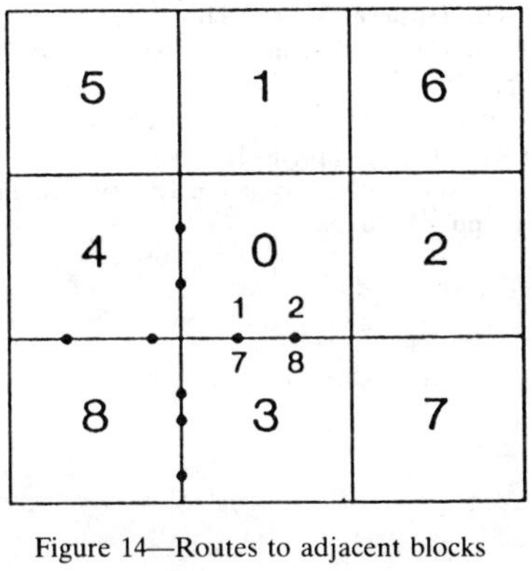

Figure 14—Routes to adjacent blocks

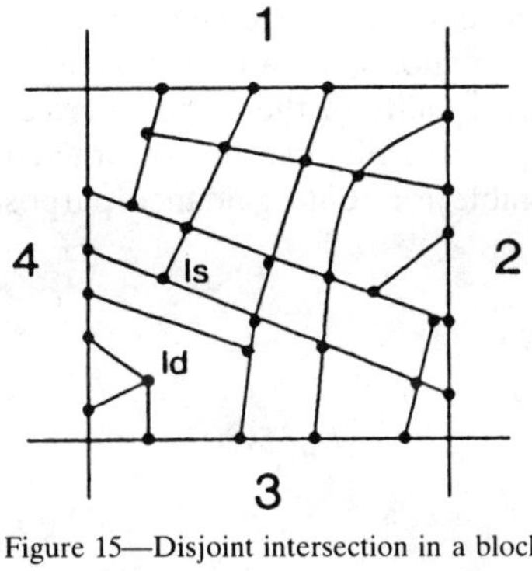

Figure 15—Disjoint intersection in a block

ing. By partitioning the map into blocks, the route-finding problem is restricted to local subgraphs around the source, the destination, and along the predetermined routes. However, the storage required for the predetermined routes increases squarely with the number of blocks. For a large number of blocks, a higher-level partitioning of the map can be made where blocks are grouped into regions. A hierarchical partitioning of the street map seems a viable approach for route finding in street maps.

CONCLUSION

The basic objective for this project was to demonstrate the feasibility of building a sophisticated on-board route guidance system using current technology. There were two other motivations for this work. In building customized systems, it is conceivable that all levels of the system be well integrated and tailored for the application. Hence, one motivation was to build a complete system for a specific application to evaluate the idea. Designing CARGuide involved an integrated effort at all levels of the system—from secondary storage up to the user interface—with the purpose of building an on-board route guidance system. It was observed that CARGuide is especially efficient because the hardware and software were designed hand in hand. The other motivation was to test the feasibility of actually building customized systems in a research environment so as to assess capabilities for building larger systems. It took less than a year to design and implement CARGuide. The CAD tools, and software and hardware development facilities at CMU were instrumental in realization of the project.

As a route guidance system, CARGuide demonstrates that an on-board computer for route guidance is realizable using current technology. An on-board computer is a practical alternative to centralized route guidance because an on-board system is self contained and not affected by transmission limitations. CARGuide provides sufficient functionality and ease of use to be an effective system. Two major components of CARGuide—the secondary storage and the display device—determine the capacity and sophistication of the system. More than 1 Mbyte of secondary storage is needed to implement the entire Pittsburgh street map. Bubble memories are a good candidate for secondary storage because they provide high-density, nonvolatile, and compact storage. The current 500 Kbyte capacity of CARGuide can be upgraded to 2 Mbyte by using 4 Mbit bubble memory chips. Extra secondary storage can be used to enhance the functionality of the system by storing an information database such as on points of interest in the city. The quality of the display device determines the type of map pictures that can be constructed. A dot matrix display is suitable for route guidance purposes. A portable CRT is needed to construct detailed map pictures similar to regular maps.

ACKNOWLEDGMENT

We would like to thank Chang Hsin Chang for his major contribution to this project in preparing the pictorial data for the Pittsburgh street map. We also would like to thank Andy Gruss of CS Engineering Lab, and CMU Speech Group for providing us hardware support, and Dave McKeown for the use of CMU image-processing facilities. This research was supported in part by Defense Advanced Research Projects Agency (DOD), ARPA Order No. 3597, monitored by the Air Force Avionics Laboratory under Contract F33615-81-K-1539.

REFERENCES

1. Elliott, R. J. and Lesk M. E. "Route Finding in Street Maps by Computers and People." *Proc. AAAI,* 1(1982), pp. 258–261.
2. Pierce, A. R. "Bibliography on Algorithms for Shortest Path, Shortest Spanning Tree, and Related Circuit Routing Problems." *Networks* (6). 1975.
3. Floyd, R. W. "Algorithm 97: Shortest Path," *Commun. ACM* (5), 1962, p. 345.
4. Dial, R. B. "Algorithm 360: Shortest-Path Forest With Topological Ordering," *Commun. ACM* (12), 1969, pp. 632–633.
5. Pape, U. "Implementation and Efficiency of Moore Algorithms for the Shortest-Path Problem." *Math. Progr.* (7), 1974, pp. 212–222.
6. Dijkstra, E. W. "Note on Two Problems in Connection With Graphs." *Numer. Math,* 1(1959), pp. 269–271.
7. Caldwell, T. "On Finding Minimum Routes in a Network with Turn Penalties." *Commun. ACM* (4), 1961, pp. 107–108.
8. Tarjan, R. E. "Fast Algorithms for Solving Path Problems." *J. Assoc. Comp. Mach.* (28), 1981, pp. 594–614.
9. Aho, A. V., Hopcroft, E. J., and Ullman J. D. *The Design and Analysis of Computer Algorithms.* Addison-Wesley, 1974.
10. Vaziri, M., and Lam, T. N. "Perceived Factors Affecting Driver Route Decisions." *J. Transp. Eng.,* 109, (1983), pp. 297–311.
11. Tsumura, T., Fujiwara, N., Shirakawa, T., and Hashimoto, M. "Automatic Vehicle Guidance—Commanded Map Routing." *Proc. IEEE Vehicular Technology Conf.,* IEEE, 1982., pp. 49–54.
12. Tagami, K., Takahashi, K., and Takahashi, F. "Electronic "Gyro-Cator" New Inertial Navigation System for Use in Automobiles." *Proc. Int. Symp. on Automotive Technology and Automation* (Vol. 2), ISATA, 1982, pp. 145–161.
13. Feng, P. D., and Hung, J. C. "Gyrocompassing on a Moving Land Vehicle." *Proc. 15th Southeastern Symp. on System Theory. Reading, Mass.:* Addison-Wesley, 1983, pp. 254–257.
14. Carter, D. A. "Using Loran-C for Automatic Vehicle Monitoring" *Navigation* (29), 1982, pp.43–46.
15. Nakamura, O., Tsuzawa, M. and Hiraoka, S. "On Automobile Traffic Information and Control System." *IEE Int. Conf. Road Traffic Signaling,* IEE, 1982, pp. 165–167.
16. "Mobile Graphics—State of the Art in Phoenix," Mobile Radio Technology, No. 1, Jan. 1983, pp. 18–22.
17. Goodman, D. "Automotive Navigation Systems." *Radio—Electronics,* No. 54, July 1983, pp. 43–46.

Telecommunications and business strategy: Basic variables for design

by ERIC K. CLEMONS
University of Pennsylvania
Philadelphia, Pennsylvania
and
PETER G. W. KEEN
Nolan, Norton & Company
Lexington, Massachusetts
and
STEVEN O. KIMBROUGH
University of Pennsylvania
Philadelphia, Pennsylvania

ABSTRACT

The problems of telecommunications planning and management are rapidly becoming more complex and more pressing: Significant advances in technology have greatly increased the capabilities of communications networks, costs are declining, and simultaneously deregulation and the AT&T divestiture have introduced a confusing array of new options. And yet the strategic opportunities for application of telecommunications—the opportunities to use telecommunications and information systems to alter in some fundamental way a firm, its position in its marketplace, or its relationships with customers and competitors—have never been greater.

This paper presents a preliminary framework for TC systems planning. It is not concerned with detailed network design, either local or long-haul. Rather, it progresses from determination of the network's purpose and essential functionality, through general policy, financial considerations, and analysis of uncontrollable factors, to conclude with determination of design targets that must then be met by the detailed network design.

This paper was written while Steven O. Kimbrough was at the Massachusetts Institute of Technology, Cambridge, Massachusetts.

INTRODUCTION

It is commonly accepted that communications systems have strategic importance.[1,2] This is not only true for a large number of firms (and other organizations), but it is particularly significant for firms representing a large percentage of the world's economic activity. Knowledge, at more than a superficial level, of how and why communications are strategically important is only beginning to emerge. There is some literature and there is some oral tradition.[3–5] What we call the strategic network design problem—understanding how strategic opportunities, presented or augmented by communications technology, can be recognized and translated into tactics and operations—lies almost entirely within the oral tradition and is not well developed. The purpose of this paper is to contribute to, if not initiate, the literature on the problem of strategic network design (SND). This problem covers both design of new networks and design of changes to existing networks.

Our approach to the SND problem is to begin with a framework. The framework—which is the main subject of discussion in this paper—is essentially a structured list of what needs to be considered in solving (or merely handling intelligently) the strategic network design problem. Our aim in developing the framework has been to be complete, clear, and concise. Moreover, we hope the various elements in the list are "conceptually orthogonal," that is, pretty much entirely distinct.

The name of our framework is the Communications Network Design Template (or merely "the template"). Implicit in the template are two assumptions. The first is that a top-down and decomposition approach is appropriate and will prove useful. For problems as difficult and complex as the SND problem, we can hardly imagine a plausible alternative to this assumption. The second assumption is that the common tripartite framework (distinguishing strategic, tactical, and operational decisions in the firm) is roughly applicable in the present case. Table I illustrates how we interpret the framework in terms of the strategic network design problem.

TABLE I—Framework in terms of strategic network design

Level of Decision Making	Example Problems for Design of Communications Networks
Strategic	Where and how can we use communications for business advantage?
Tactical	What should our network do? How much should we invest in it?
Operational or Implementation	How reliable should a given network service be?

Our aim is to provide a method that can be used linking the strategic business objectives of the firm with the choices among options presented by communications technology. The framework is, in part, a communication device, meant to serve various parts of an organization (e.g., strategic planning, telecommunications, data processing, user groups, etc.) involved in the SND problem. Also, we intend the framework to facilitate and clarify the many tradeoffs that are made, explicitly or implicitly, when firms handle the strategic network design problem.

Work on the Communications Network Design Template is hardly complete. While we believe from direct and indirect experience that the framework has significant face validity, we assume that considerable effort needs to be made in validating (and amending) the template. In addition, there is enormous room for extending the framework and for investigating the nature of interactions among the elements in the template. Our hope is that the response to this paper will further this work of validating and extending the template.

THE FRAMEWORK: A COMMUNICATIONS NETWORK DESIGN TEMPLATE

Our SND framework is a tree, expressing decomposition as it branches downward. At the most general level, the framework is a list of strategic communications factors, which we divide into five kinds: application opportunities, general policy, uncontrollable factors, pricing and costing, and network design variables (NDVs). Figure 1 displays the beginning of the template.

Each of the Level 1 factors can be broken down and analyzed. This decomposition is the subject of the next five sections of this paper. In this section we confine ourselves mainly to discussion of Level 1.

We mean Level 1 to be read left to right. Our suggestion is that in dealing with the strategic network design problem, one begins by taking a look at application opportunities. If these seem favorable, one then develops some general policies for the system, examines uncontrollable factors, and so on. Of course, we intend this as only an approximation to a good

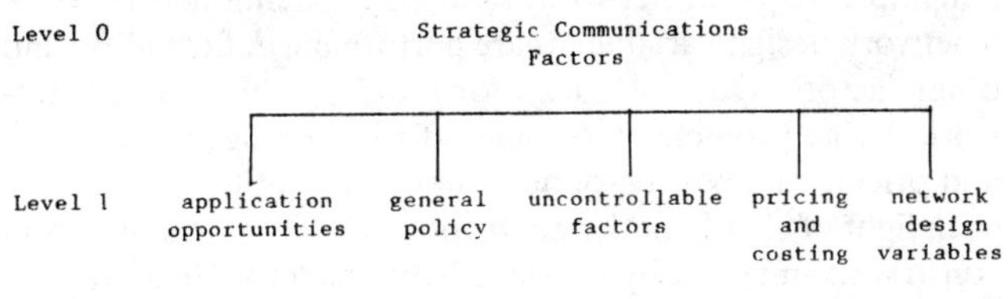

Figure 1—SND template

procedure. Even if one proceeds left to right, there will inevitably be much thinking ahead, thinking behind, and integrating.

By "application opportunities" we mean that the first step, in the process of dealing with the strategic network design problem, is to take a good, high-level look at what an investment in communications might do for the firm. Even beyond that, initially ignoring the costs of this investment, we seek to determine where enhanced communication capability would be of significant benefit.

General policies, the second Level 1 entry in Figure 1, are general, high-level rules that serve to determine what will and will not be considered when designing a network or a network improvement. The purpose of general policies is to delimit the decision space for the strategic network design problem by ignoring alternatives that the organization will not accept for other than straightforward telecommunications (TC) reasons, and thereby to save time and money when attempting to solve the TC design problem. By their nature, general policies are basic assumptions that can be made early on and probably will not have to be challenged later. Risk is an example of an area in which it may be advisable to make general policy. There are different sorts of risks associated with network design and operation. We believe that general guidelines on acceptable levels of risk, informed by an awareness of the application opportunities, will usually be valuable to those making technical design decisions relating to the handling of errors and system failures, for example.

Uncontrollable factors are things that may affect the value of a proposed network improvement, or that may limit the options and opportunities available to the TC designer, without at the same time being under the control of the decision maker or firm in question. For example, statutes and government regulations are (usually, at least within the time horizon of the network design effort) beyond the control of the firm. On the other hand, reliability is not an uncontrollable factor because it is possible to make design decisions that influence reliability.

"Pricing and costing" refers to the financial aspects of a proposed network improvement. Although the cost of network components is largely determined outside the firm and cannot be controlled, the level of investment can be controlled and it can be traded off against other aspects of a network, such as performance. Thus, network costs are major design variables. Pricing refers to the various methods and schemes for recovering the cost of a network, and must be addressed both within and outside of the firm.

Network design variables are those factors that acutally determine the design and the functionality of a network. Of course, they also carry or influence the value and the cost of a network largely under the control of the firm when it designs and implements the network. Reliability, mentioned above, is a network design variable, as are performance, flexibility, and other factors. Our basic idea for handling the strategic network design problem is to trade off network design variables and pricing and costing options among each other, but to do so in light of clearly understood application opportunities and constraints imposed by uncontrollable factors. General policies are heuristics for making the problem a bit easier.

We shall now discuss each of these Level 1 factors in greater detail.

APPLICATION OPPORTUNITIES

Identifying application opportunities—identifying those areas where developing or enhancing communication capabilities can fundamentally change the nature of a business or a firm's competitive position—is certainly the most difficult part of communications systems design. Likewise, it is certainly the most important. Before building a network, or before having the technical design people begin work on a network, it is necessary to determine its purpose. What precisely do we want to do with it? Purpose and use imply functionality, which then provides an essential starting point for detailed design. But this does not convey the essentially ad hoc nature of sensing a business opportunity and the communications strategy needed for it to succeed. On occasion, sensing the opportunity, through insight, vision, or chance, offers a brilliant corporate strategy. While it is not accurate to say that everything that follows is merely engineering, it is fair to say that if technology or engineering are to produce enormous strategic influence, they must be applied in support of significant corporate goals.

Unfortunately, we don't really know how to characterize the process of identifying these rewarding areas that represent opportunities for application of telecommunications. This is not surprising. It will never be possible to provide simple guidelines or a checklist for providing brilliant strategic insights about this or any other area. Moreover, we don't know how to characterize the vision, creativity, and foresight to see an opportunity and then design the organizational, communications, and software systems to exploit it.

We have, however, examined a number of communications-based business innovations and can, therefore, begin to characterize innovations that were creative, well-matched to significant opportunities, and very successful. We draw on work by Peter G. W. Keen on network "exemplars." We study these examplars as surrogates for studying principles and guidelines for finding opportunities; thus, we seek to improve our foresight by improving our hindsight.

Beginning a Classification: Strategic Applications of Communications

The following classification is based on our analyses of successful strategic application of telecommunications. This classification is preliminary and incomplete, but we believe that even in its current form it is useful. We classify, as follows,

1. By *function,* to trade bandwidth for some other scarce or more expensive resource.
2. By desired *result,* adding value, creating a product or service, decreasing or transferring costs.
3. By *innovation,* to create a connection, add another connection, or extend a connection.

Strategic applications, by function

This, in essence, involves trading bandwidth for another scarce or more expensive resource. Moving corporate data processing out of Midtown Manhattan is an example of *trading bandwidth for rent.* Sending briefings to sales force via videotext, or using full video teleconferencing in place of monthly meetings are examples of moving bits in place of people, or *trading bandwidth for travel.* And gaining tighter control over a manufacturing process, reducing extra machine stations and work in process inventory, can be viewed as *trading bandwidth for slack.*

Strategic applications, by result

The previous paragraph dealt with the function of the telecommunications project—what direct, observable process was being supported or replaced by moving bits. Here we treat intent—why we are moving bits—and what result we hope to achieve. We suggest the following three-way classification: cost-avoidance; value-added, internal; and value-added, external.

Cost avoidance occurs whenever telecommunications offers a less expensive way of running the business in much the same way as at present, such as the previous example of trading bandwidth for rent. *Internal value-added* applications generally involve running the business better, but usually are not directly visible to clients and customers. An example of this might be using videotext to keep a field sales force in close contact with the head office.

It is the *external value-added* applications—the applications directly visible to clients and customers—that offer most of the opportunities for new products, new services, improved market position, and generally strategic potential. Airlines have long recognized that an airline seat on a particular flight is a perishable good, in the sense that it has no value if it is not sold at takeoff. Tour operators in the U.S. and the U.K. are just recently coming to realize that the same is true of a vacation, and that a customer who cannot get through the phone queue, or is placed too long on hold, will turn to another tour operator; at least one major operator is using videotext to permit the customer to book directly, even if no agent is available.

Opportunities for preemptive strike are particularly attractive. Although the Merrill Lynch Cash Management Account appeared only a few months before Shearson/American Express responded, and although years have passed, Merrill Lynch still has six times Shearson's CMA customer base. Particularly attractive targets for preemptive strikes are those opportunities where the customer is unlikely to accept a second terminal; whoever gets the first terminal in will probably have exclusive occupancy for a considerable period.

Of course, we look for opportunities to piggyback on existing strengths. Sears Financial Services piggybacks on its existing client or customer base, while Merrill Lynch exploits its existing financial and investment experience and Shearson exploits American Express's network. Sometimes the exploited resource is TC- or technology-driven, as is the case with the new and extremely successful Reuters financial data services, which of course depends entirely on the network developed initially for Reuters wire service.

Strategic application, by communications innovation

Sometimes the ability to exploit telecommunications will require seeing the opportunity to eliminate a manual data hand-off and place a new application, and a customer, directly on our information system network. An example of this might entail replacing a funds transfer operation, initiated by customer financial representative telephoning his contact bank officer, with an operation where the customer at his own terminal or work station directly enters the transfer request into the bank's network. There are many advantages, not least of which are the customer's feeling of speed, control, and accuracy, and the bank's off-loading responsibility to the customer for keying errors and resulting delay of funds transfer. This kind of innovation requires *running a new wire.* We offer the following four-part classification of communications network innovation:

1. Run a new wire—e.g., customer-initiated funds transfer.
2. Run a longer wire—e.g., move the computing center.
3. Run a better wire—e.g., upgrade the network.
4. Run the first wire (like running a new wire, but relies on exclusive occupancy)—e.g., put in a terminal that allows the customer to order directly from your warehouse, and to rely on you to manage his inventory.

Concluding Remarks on Application Opportunities

We believe that developing classification based on the three axes introduced above will be useful in a first effort at producing a theory of telecommunications for business advantage. It requires a general understanding of many factors, of which technology is the last:

1. What is happening in our business?
2. What business are we really in, and what opportunities are we missing? (e.g., are we a news service? or *any* information wire service?)
3. Who is, and who will be, our real competition? (e.g., another brokerage house? Citibank? Shearson/American Express? Sears?)
4. Where can we run the business better?
5. How can we get, or who can get us, from the business strategy to the technological solution?

GENERAL POLICY

General policy reflects decisions made before the TC design commences, which reflect decisions more general in scope than TC design, and which frequently are outside the scope or charter of the TC design. These include questions about whether there must be a backup network, whether a system must remain IBM-compatible, or whether one should take any box with less than a three-digit serial number. The determination of what is a general policy consideration, rather than a network design variable, is extremely context-specific and will change not only with advances in TC technology, but with changes in the firm, its management, and its environment. It is probably not possible to offer general policy guidelines; instead, we offer several areas that should be of interest when considering policy for strategic network design. The template for general policy variables is shown in Figure 2.

VENDORS

Multiplicity of Vendors

A variety of possible policies exist, including single vendors (or a single vendor as much as possible); multiple vendors with the architecture and protocols of a single vendor (e.g., they comply with IBM's SNA, but use plug-compatible equipment or incompatible equipment with protocol conversion); multiple vendors and multiple architectures (e.g., because you need to protect an installed base). At the opposite extreme of the last-mentioned policy is the single-vendor-we-are-an-IBM-(or whatever)-shop policy. It is worth noting that a policy on vendor multiplicity will likely interact strongly with system integration, a network design variable.

Quality of Vendors

It may be useful to set a standard or cut-off level (distinguished from an aspiration level) for vendor quality. This may be especially germane for hardware selection. There are many ways of specifying acceptable vendors: listing them, listing a reference group of vendors by quality (excellent, ok, poor), or specifying a measure of vendor quality (e.g., price-to-earnings ratio of stock, quality of reports by market analysts). All of this can be done on any or all of several dimensions, including management quality, financial stability of the firm, extent and quality of servicing arrangements, and so forth.

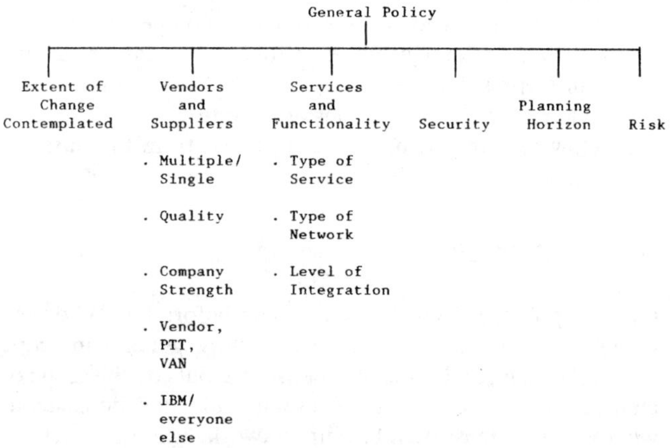

Figure 2—Template for general policy variables

Services and Functionality

Without prejudicing detailed tradeoffs to be made later, it may often be possible to promote general policies on what functionality should be made available. We distinguish four broad categories: voice (analog, digital, voice messaging, etc.), data (transactions, inquiries, updates, file transfers, etc.), image ("still pictures," mainly fax), and video (moving images, including full-motion, full-color television, slow scan, freeze-frame, etc.).[6,7] We would put videotext under data.

Security

This is almost certainly an area in which general, high-level policies need to be considered. There may be, of course, circumstances in which security is not an issue, but we think it likely that nearly always it will be worthwhile to consider whether and how security matters. At the level of general policy, it is common to distinguish three sorts of security problems:

1. *Leakage.* Can the system be passively monitored and information captured? Can this be detected?
2. *Intrusion.* Can, for example, an intruder change transactions or even initiate them? Can this be detected?
3. *Destruction.* Is the system safe from vandalism? from malicious destruction of data or hardware?

A possible general policy on security would be a statement of absolute requirements for security levels for various aspects of the network and the services provided by it.

Planning Horizon

This is an important subject for general policy, if only because the assumed planning horizon affects the level of uncertainty to be accommodated (the further the horizon, the greater the uncertainty) and because it serves to limit the use of advanced technologies (the nearer the horizon, the less that anticipated technological, regulatory, or other developments can be brought into the planning process).

Risk

Once more, this is a factor that should almost always be the subject of a general policy. The question is what level of risk should be undertaken. The issue of risk interacts with the security issue, but involves much more. We divide risk into four kinds:

1. *Technical.* Possible policy: Do not use equipment or software that has not been on the market for at least one year.
2. *Financial.* Possible policy: Design a network in which costs are fairly insensitive to traffic levels, or design a network in which cost trends are quickly monitored and brought to the attention of management.

3. *Operational.* Possible policy: Invest heavily to get state-of-the-art functionality in network management and fault diagnosis.
4. *Management.* Possible policy: Stick with hardware and software familiar to present employees.

There are other areas that have potential for general policies. In fact, any of the factors falling under the other Level 1 headings might be the subject for general policies. Much work remains to be done by way of finding and clarifying the subjects of general policy in the SND problem.

UNCONTROLLABLE FACTORS

These are the things that one can do little or nothing about, but that may significantly affect the value of an implemented (or attempted) communications system. The uncontrollable factors may on occasion be the subject of general policies; they will more often be the result of someone else's policies or of the policies of some other organization. The phone companies in the U.S., post, telephone, and telegraph (PTTs) abroad, and industrial or trade organizations are all bodies whose policies may result in our uncontrollable factors. Like policy factors, they also limit the decision space in and of themselves, and they may affect the tradeoffs made among the network design variables.

As in the case of general policies, context often will determine what the uncontrollable factors are and which are important. So, following the strategy outlined in the section on general policy, we have identified several types and sources of uncontrollable factors. The template for uncontrollable factors is shown in Figure 3.

Laws and Regulations

From the point of view of a firm using telecommunications (rather than acting as a primary supplier of communications), laws and regulations may perhaps be more significant factors for operations outside the U.S. than for operations within the country. This is the inevitable effect of regulation. Nevertheless, the move towards deregulation of long-distance communications in the U.S. still has significant regulatory consequences (especially at the local level) and, by greatly affecting the telecommunications industry, deregulation will importantly affect the options, and the economics of the options, presented to users.

Industry Practices

There are numerous industry standards, emerging trends, industry practices, and so on, that merit attention. Some examples include IEEE standards; ISO OSI developments, such as file transfer protocols and virtual terminal protocols; large vendor standards, e.g., Ethernet, SNA, and other local area network standards; and special practices, such as SWIFT and CHIPS in U.S. banking.

Organizational Capability

Communications systems need to be developed and delivered, then maintained. This requires management, coordination, and control of people and other resources. The capabilities of one's organization in this regard often may have to be taken more as given than as determined by management's decisions. In any case, the extent to which organizational capability in communications may be changed by education, training, hiring, or other practices is something to be discovered and taken as an uncontrollable factor.

There are other categories of uncontrollable factors that need to be identified and examined. What the critical uncontrollable factors are, and in what circumstances they appear, is largely unknown.

FINANCIAL CONSIDERATIONS

Financial considerations in TC planning can be divided into components of cost and pricing mechanisms. These are summarized in Figure 4, which shows the template for financial variables. Cost considerations are as in any other large project. Components of costs are similar to those in a data processing project.

Pricing mechanisms are similar to those employed in pricing any other service. We may use incentive pricing—less-than-full-recovery pricing—to encourage use, particularly when we want communications system use to displace current use of

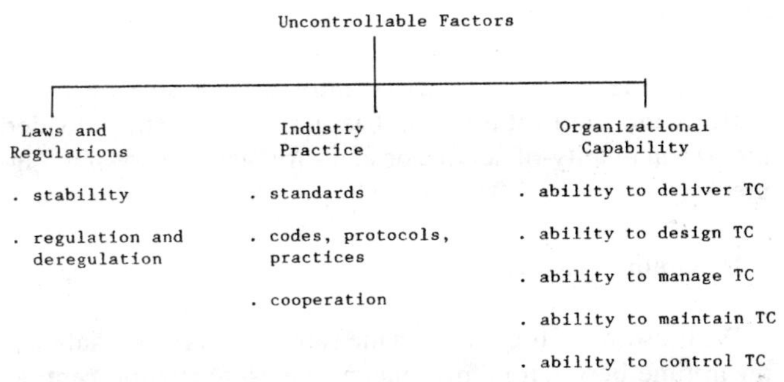

Figure 3—Template for variables corresponding to uncontrollable factors

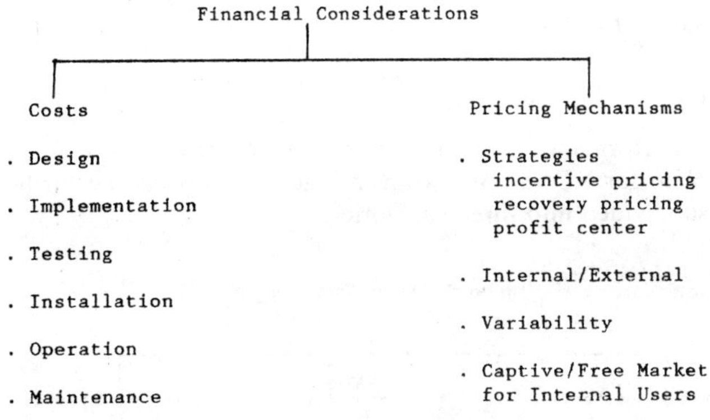

Figure 4—Financial considerations

other resources. This will be especially important when we want users to get over initial resistance and the effort required to learn the new system. The most extreme form of incentive pricing is to make communications a free resource, as most users view their local telephone calls; when learning and sufficient user acceptance are accomplished, a less extreme form of incentive pricing will usually be offered. As usage begins to approach capacity, recovery pricing often ensues. Finally, in a mature environment, the communications service may become a profit center, much as often happens with corporate data processing.

This relatively simple state of affairs may be made more complex by making distinctions between internal corporate and outside users, or even among users by division, function, or reason for system use. Rates may be guaranteed or variable, fixed, or sensitive to traffic, usage, and time of day. Internal users may be captive customers or free to use competing outside services.

NETWORK DESIGN VARIABLES

Introduction to the Network Design Variables

Earlier sections of this paper deal with major strategic considerations, general policy, external or uncontrollable factors, and financial and economic factors that influence or constrain communications system design. Generally, these factors impose design restrictions that must be observed, and thus place restrictions on designs that must be evaluated. This serves to delimit the solution space that must be examined.

In this section we address those aspects of TC service—performance, flexibility, functionality, and quality of service—that are subject to control by the communications network designer. That is, we consider here what might be called the controllable or discretionary network design decisions. We do not consider long-term optimization through algorithms for backbone network design, or local premises optimization through local-area networks; in fact, in this paper we do not even discuss the processes by which these designs might be developed. Rather, we discuss setting objectives—targets and ranges—within which the design can operate. We also treat, at least implicitly, tradeoffs: performance vs. cost, quality of service vs. complexity of maintenance, etc. Subsequent papers will cover these tradeoffs more explicitly and apply them to the network design process. Network design variables are summarized in Figure 5.

Nature of Service

Performance is the first factor to be considered in the template for NDVs. As shown in Figure 6, this can be further subdivided into three categories:

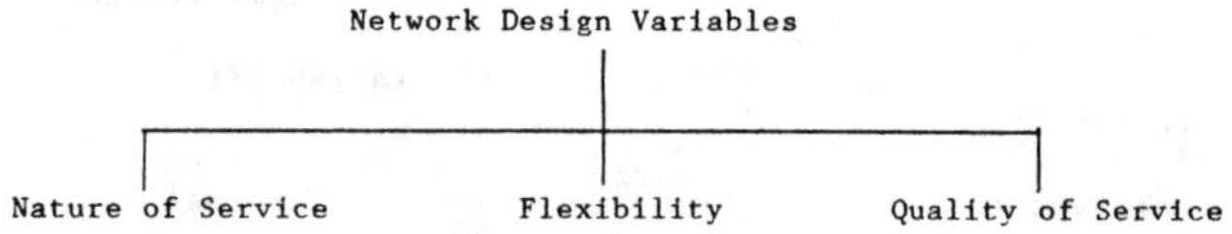

Figure 5—Overview of network design variables

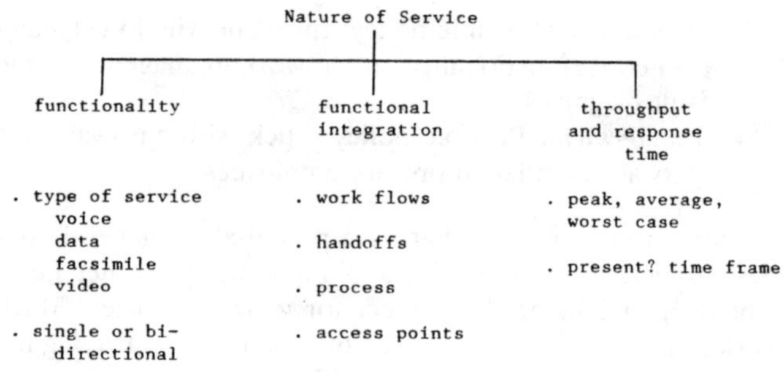

Figure 6—Performance variable template

1. *Functionality*. What types or classes of communication service are provided?
2. *Functional integration*. Are system-to-system hand-offs and application-to-application hand-offs automated? Or does the word processing operator type out the message, tear it off, and hand it to the telex operator for rekeying?
3. *Throughput, delay, and response time*. How long to get a line? to get a message out? to get acknowledgment of receipt?

Functional integration is particularly important. To the extent that we can avoid the rekeying of information on system-to-system or application-to-application handoffs, we can begin to receive the full benefits of our applications and communications systems.

Throughput and response time are treated more fully in the section on quality of service. Below certain levels, however, they represent changes not just in degree but in kind. Five-minute response time, for example, precludes interactive computing.

Flexibility

Of course, the only network that will not be outgrown is one that is not used. Networks, like all other data processing systems, will require extension, modification, and repair. We are, of course, concerned with the ability to make needed changes. We are especially interested in the sensitivity of network cost to changes in traffic: If traffic increases by 15% can we add capacity? Or will we find that our switches block, in which case we can only add capacity by replacing components. Figure 7 shows the flexibility template.

Quality of Service

We divide quality of service into two coarse categories: performance and robustness. These are then further divided into seven quality-of-service design variables, as shown in Figure 8.

Reliability of service

We list some of the standard measures for system reliability: mean time between failure; mean time to repair; percentage of time operational; failure mode—degradation of service

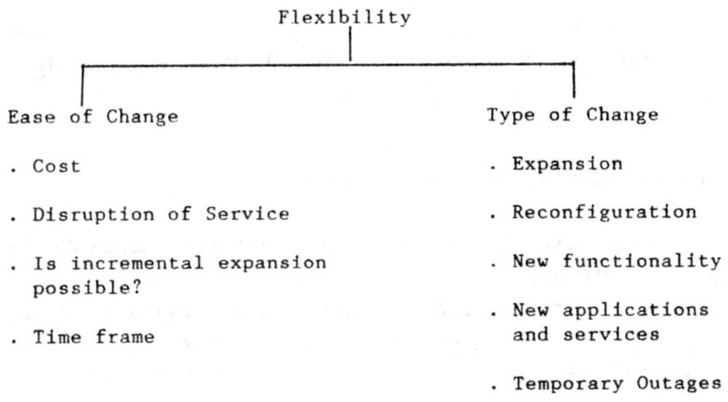

Figure 7—Flexibility variable template

(fail-soft) or hard crash; and undetected error rate. We also note that the significance of reliability measures is extremely dependent on the nature of applications being supported. A single bit error in video conferencing produces snow; in process control it's an outlying reading corrected in a fraction of a second; and in funds transfer it may be quite expensive. Depending on the needs of applications, the organization may take defensive action, including redundant arcs and extra switches to prevent loss of a portion of the network.

Accessibility

Accessibility is related to reliability. It asks not whether the network is up, but whether can we get on it now. Can we get on it from here? Likewise, this is related to response time. Not, whether our message is in queue for transmission, but whether we are still waiting for log-on.

Security

Some form of security, of course, is essential. We can make a first, crude distinction between unauthorized receipt of messages directed at another party and unauthorized initiation of transactions. Log-on procedures with authentication are a necessary first step at restricting unauthorized initiation of transactions. Physical security, to protect lines, premises, and passwords also is important. Public key encryption and data encryption standard (DES) offer some protection against eavesdropping. Threat monitoring and risk and threat analyses are certainly advisable.

Response time

Response time is the first of our four NDVs related to performance. Significance of response time depends very heavily on the nature of the application. When exploiting a momentary imbalance in foreign exchange rates—which exists only for several seconds—response must be virtually immediate. The designer should seek to identify targets or acceptable ranges for response time, and should seek to make clear costs and application tradeoffs implied by different targets.

Throughput

We first need to identify our measures. What are our traffic volumes and how will they be measured?

1. Telex messages per day
2. CCS/handset (hundred call seconds per telephone)
3. Conversations per day
4. Inquiries per salesman per day

We need to know the accuracy of these volume estimates (e.g., ± 20%) and we need to know how they will change over time. We need to know where our key bottlenecks are, e.g., availability of telex operators; when London market is still open, availability of (outside) trunk lines.

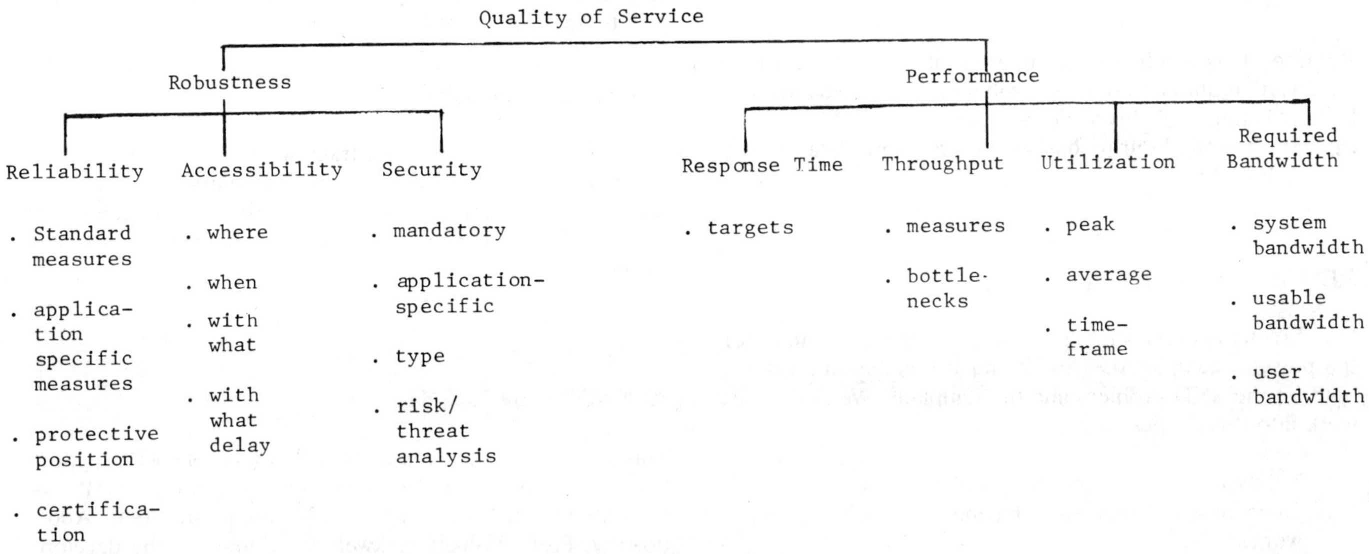

Figure 8—Quality of service

Network use

Unfortunately, high network use, which appears good, is incompatible with low queueing delay, which also would be good. Phrased another way, a network in which expensive TC systems are seldom idle is also one that often will be congested, with lengthy queueing delays and other expensive systems or personnel idle instead. How should capacity, use, and queueing delay be traded off? Do we build for average, peak, or irreducible minimum demands?

Some very crude guidelines are possible. When building a local network, communications are cheap and we may wish them to be perceived as essentially free. If the network is to displace physically transporting a memo or physically retrieving a colleague's diskette, queueing delay must be low and limited network use may be acceptable. In a long-haul environment, the network is more expensive, physically walking the memo from Philadelphia to Boston or using the U.S. mail for same-day delivery is not an option, and we may be willing to design for greater use rather than for greater speed.

Required bandwidth

Bandwidth is a rough measure of communications channel capacity. Bandwidth in a communications network is not really a decision variable; it is determined as a by-product of evaluating functionality, traffic, delay time, availability, and reliability. It still seems useful to make some distinctions among different terms:

1. Bandwidth is the full frequency range that can be carried by the medium.
2. Effective bandwidth is that portion of the bandwidth available after network control. In CSMA/CD, for example, effective bandwidth may be reduced by about two thirds.
3. User bandwidth is the portion of effective bandwidth actually used for user data rather than error control and retransmission.

Required bandwidth is some multiple of the minimum user bandwidth required for message volume. Required bandwidth by application probably varies with time of day. More voice capacity is needed during business hours; more data may be moved at night.

REMAINING WORK

Our discussion of the strategic network design template is, for the present, completed. Clearly, much remains to be done, both on the SND problem and the template. We divide this work into three types:

1. Validating and refining the template.
2. Deepening the discussion and analysis within the framework.
3. Extending the framework.

Our purpose in this concluding section is to discuss briefly each of these three ways of extending the work reported upon here.

Validating and Refining the Template

To move beyond face validity, the framework needs validation by more rigorous empirical methods. We see two ways to do this: The first is to use interviews, surveys, and small group discussions to gain information about the validity of the SND template. This is a legitimate and entirely conventional way to proceed. The main disadvantage of this first way is the great effort required in terms of time and expense. The second way of gaining empirical validation of the framework is to perform a series of content analysis studies on pertinent literature.[8–12] These include published telecommunications literature, requests for proposals (RFPs), requests for bids (RFBs), corporate annual reports, government budget documentation, trade journals, reports and other documents produced by consulting firms in communications, and so on. We believe that both the first way (person-directed) and the second way (document-directed) can lead to important findings for validating the template, and that the two ways complement each other. We plan to pursue both.

Deepening the Discussion and Analysis within the Framework

Our template is intended to be descriptively valid, not in the sense that it lists what people always do consider when designing a network in light of the firm's strategic goals, but in the sense that it lists the things intelligent and informed managers would like to consider had they the time and resources to do so. To this end, our discussion of the items in the framework can be greatly deepened in every instance. Not only should more detail be given, but attention should be directed to the interactions among the various items in the framework and to ways of measuring and scaling the items. Again, all this will be the subject of future work.

Extending the Framework

Finally, the tree that is our framework needs to grow downward. That is, we believe that further decomposition would be most useful. This requires additional field study, and is not entirely divorced from efforts to validate material already developed.

ACKNOWLEDGMENTS

This paper is an extension of work that was done with support from Nolan, Norton & Company, in Lexington, Mass. It was presented to the clients of Nolan, Norton in June 1983. Additionally, Prof. William Maxwell contributed to the development of our classification for application opportunities.

REFERENCES

1. "Telecommunications: The Global Battle." *Business Week,* No. 2183, Oct. 24, 1983, pp. 126–148.
2. Jonscher, C. "Information Resources and Economic Productivity." *Information Economics and Policy,* 1 (1983), pp. 13–35.
3. Cypser, R. J. *Communications Architecture for Distributed Systems.* Reading, Mass.: Addison-Wesley, 1968.
4. Doll, D. R. *Data Communications.* New York: John Wiley & Sons, 1978.
5. Martin, J. *Computer Networks and Distributed Processing.* Englewood Cliffs, N. J.: Prentice-Hall, 1981.
6. Johansen, R. *Electronic Meetings.* Reading, Mass.: Addison-Wesley, 1982.
7. Rossner, R. D. *Distributed Telecommunications Networks.* Belmont, Calif.: Lifetime Learning Publications, 1982, p. 167.
8. Bowman, E. H. "Risk Seeking by Troubled Firms." *Sloan Management Review,* 23 (1982), pp. 33–42.
9. Holsti, O. R. *Content Analysis for the Social Sciences and Humanities.* Reading, Mass.: Addison-Wesley, 1969.
10. Holsti, O. R. "Content Analysis." In G. Lindzey, and E. Aronson, (eds.), *The Handbook of Social Psychology* (2nd ed.), Vol 2. Reading, Mass.: Addison-Wesley, 1968, pp. 596—692.
11. Krippendorff, K. *Content Analysis.* Beverly Hills, Calif.: Sage Publications, 1980.
12. Pool, I. de Sola (ed.). *Trends in Content Analysis.* Urbana, Ill.: University of Illinois Press, 1959.

1984 NATIONAL COMPUTER CONFERENCE COMMITTEES

PROGRAM COMMITTEE

Chairman
Dennis J. Frailey
Texas Instruments
Austin, TX

Members

Michael R. Alsup
Arthur Andersen & Co.
Houston, TX

Fayé A. Briggs
Rice University
Houston, TX

A. Winsor Brown
Volition Systems
Del Mar, CA

Harry Kepner
Electronic Data Systems
Richardson, TX

Neal Laurance
Ford Motor Company
Dearborn, MI

James R. Miller
Computer* Thought Corporation
Plano, TX

Alan Paller
AUI Data Graphics/ISSCO
Washington, DC

Alfred Riccomi
Texas Instruments
Lewisville, TX

Eugene B. Smith
Texas A&M University
College Station, TX

Darrell L. Ward
HyperGraphics Corporation
Denton, TX

Jean Yates
Yates Ventures
Los Altos, CA

Special Consultant

Robert Stirling
IBM Corporation
Hartford, CT

CONFERENCE STEERING COMMITTEE

General Chairman
Russell K. Brown
The Benchmark Group
Houston, TX

Vice-Chairman
William J. Carlisle
AT&T/CSO
Piscataway, NJ

Program Chairman
Dennis J. Frailey
Texas Instruments
Austin, TX

Professional Development Seminars Chairman
Lowry McKee
Singer-Link Flight Simulation
Houston, TX

Film Forum Chairman
Joe Van Hook
Occidental Petroleum Services
Houston, TX

Operations Chairman
Mary Rich
PFS, Inc.
El Segundo, CA

Pioneer Day Chairman
Sidney Fernbach
Consultant
Alamo, CA

Protocol Chairman
Albert K. Hawkes
Sargent & Lundy Engineers
Chicago, IL

Special Activities Chairman
Stephen Gill
City of Las Vegas MIS Department
Las Vegas, NV

Promotions Chairman
Herbert B. Safford
GTE Data Services, Inc.
Marina del Rey, CA

NCC Liaison
William H. Sitter
Tenneco, Inc.
Houston, TX

AFIPS Representative
John Gilbert
AFIPS
Reston, VA

Secretary
Jan Brown
Brown & Associates
Houston, TX

FILM FORUM COMMITTEE

Chairman
Joe Van Hook
Ford Aerospace & Communications, Inc.
Colorado Springs, CO

Members

Sandra Carkin
Occidental Petroleum Services, Inc.
Houston, TX

Linda Nash
Tenneco Systems Center
Houston, TX

Eddie Truncellito
Schlumberger Well Services, Inc.
Houston, TX

Vickie Van Hook
Spring Branch ISD Televised Instruction
Houston, TX

OPERATIONS COMMITTEE

Chair

Mary L. Rich
PFS, Inc.
El Segundo, CA

Members

Joanne Barringer
American Express
Phoenix, AZ

Virginia S. Lashley
Glendale Community College
Glendale, CA

Don A. Carlos
Claremont Computing Center
Claremont, CA

Steve Groves
Personnel Resource Corp.
Phoenix, AZ

Don B. Medley
California State Polytechnic Univ.
Pomona, CA

Patricia Wade
Total Information Systems
Phoenix, AZ

Jerry Wagner
California State Polytechnic Univ.
Pomona, CA

Larry Doyle
U.S. Public Health Service
Rockville, MD

Barbara McNurlin
Canning Publications
Torrance, CA

Roberta Phin
Garrett Turbine Engine Co.
Phoenix, AZ

Charles Sherbow
Business Pro
Phoenix, AZ

Gilbert R. Hedger
Laventhol & Horwath
Phoenix, AZ

Robert L. Tellef
Salt River Project
Phoenix, AZ

Doug Caddell
Ernst & Whinney
Phoenix, AZ

Terry S. Dorsett
Central Arizona College
Coolidge, AZ

Evelyn Teed
Specialized Professionals
Phoenix, AZ

Ann Goodine
Electronic Conventions
Los Angeles, CA

Miriam K. Weimer
MKW Associates
Phoenix, AZ

Robert L. White
Office of the Director
Bureau of the Census
Washington, DC

Rex Farley
Phoenix, AZ

Steve Herold
Ford Aerospace
Newport Beach, CA

Robert Hopson
North American College
Mesa, AZ

Richard B. Blue, Jr.
City of Las Vegas
Las Vegas, NV

PIONEER DAY COMMITTEE

Chairman
Sidney Fernbach
Consultant
Alamo, CA

Members

Terry Contreras
Lawrence Livermore National Laboratory
Livermore, CA

Barbara Costello
Lawrence Livermore National Laboratory
Livermore, CA

John Fletcher
Lawrence Livermore National Laboratory
Livermore, CA

Carl Hammer
Consultant
Washington, DC

Raymond Jaeger
Lawrence Livermore National Laboratory
Livermore, CA

Tadashi Kishi
Lawrence Livermore National Laboratory
Livermore, CA

Sam Mendicino
Lawrence Livermore National Laboratory
Livermore, CA

Alice Pitts
Lawrence Livermore National Laboratory
Livermore, CA

Marcey Skinnell
Lawrence Livermore National Laboratory
Livermore, CA

Henry Tropp
Humboldt State University
Arcata, CA

Edward LaFranchi
Lawrence Livermore National Laboratory
Livermore, CA

PROFESSIONAL DEVELOPMENT SEMINARS COMMITTEE

Chairman
Lowry McKee
Singer—Link Flight Simulation Division
Houston, TX

Members

Joe Campisi
Aetna Life & Casualty
Hartford, CT

Mary Jo Hernandez
Singer—Link Flight Simulation Division
Houston, TX

Charles McKay
University of Houston—Clear Lake
Houston, TX

Richard Rosborough
University of Nevada—Las Vegas
Las Vegas, NV

Pete Sivillo
Singer–Link Flight Simulation Division
Houston, TX

PROMOTIONS COMMITTEE

Chairman Emeritus

Ted E. Lorber
Printronix
Cypress, CA

Chairman

Herbert B. Safford
GTE Data Services, Inc.
Marina del Rey, CA

PROTOCOL COMMITTEE

Chairman
Albert K. Hawkes
Sargent & Lundy Engineers
Chicago, IL

Members

Mary Charles Blakeborough
IBM Data Systems Division
Poughkeepsie, NY

Ocie M. Gamble
Sun Gas Company
Dallas, TX

JoAnne Lockett
Xerox Corporation
El Segundo, CA

Alfred Ritchie
Bell Communications Research
Piscataway, NJ

Susan Rosenbaum
AT&T Information Systems
Parsippany, NJ

David K. Oppenheim
Abacus Programming Corporation
Van Nuys, CA

SPECIAL ACTIVITIES COMMITTEE

Chairman
Stephen D. Gill
City of Las Vegas
Las Vegas, NV

Subcommittees

Guest Services Committee
Bonnie Milliken
Instructor
Las Vegas, NV

Disabled Persons Committee
Beverly A. Ewing
Dimension Cable Television
Las Vegas, NV

International Visitors Committee
Dave Thornton
Nevada Power Company
Las Vegas, NV

VIPs & Entertainment Committee
Katy Bryan
City of Las Vegas
Las Vegas, NV

NCC '84 SESSION LEADERS

Dave Ackmann
Monsanto Company
St. Louis, MO

Dharma P. Agrawal
North Carolina State University
Raleigh, NC

Gary Arlen
Arlen Communications, Inc.
Bethesda, MD

Michael Azzara
Computer Systems News
San Jose, CA

Bruce W. Ballard
Duke University
Durham, NC

Robert Blanc
National Bureau of Standards
Washington, DC

Mike Blasgen
IBM Research
Yorktown Heights, NY

Dick Bonzagni
Management Decision Systems
Waltham, MA

Bob Brazile
North Texas State University
Denton, TX

Fayé A. Briggs
Rice University
Department of Electrical Engineering
Houston, TX

David Brodwin
Arthur D. Little, Inc.
San Francisco, CA

Steven Brower
Wood, Lucksinger & Epstein
Los Angeles, CA

William S. Brown
North American Consultancy
Corrales, NM

Peter Chen
Louisiana State University
Baton Rouge, LA

George F. Colony
Forrester Research Inc.
Cambridge, MA

Denis Connor
Ontario Worker's Compensation
Toronto, Ontario, Canada

Thomas B. Cross
Cross Information Company
Boulder, CO

Byron Davies
Texas Instruments Incorporated
Dallas, TX

Richard DeMillo
Georgia Institute of Technology
Atlanta, GA

Shaun Devlin
Ford Motor Company
Dearborn, MI

Henry Dreifus
Corpra Research, Inc.
Rosemont, PA

Martha Evens
Illinois Institute of Technology
Chicago, IL

David J. Farber
University of Delaware
Newark, DE

Sidney Fernbach
Consultant
Alamo, CA

Michael Flitterman
Digital Equipment Corporation
Burlington, MA

George C. Fowler
Texas A&M University
College Station, TX

Peter Freeman
University of California at Irvine
Irvine, CA

Peter Friedland
Stanford University
Palo Alto, CA

Jerome Garfunkel
Jerome Garfunkel Associates, Inc.
Litchfield, CT

Philip J. Gill
Tech Valley Publishing, Inc.
UNIX/World Magazine
Los Altos, CA

Stacy Goff
Hudson Henry and Associates, Inc.
Portland, OR

Michael Hammer
Hammer & Co., Inc.
Cambridge, MA

Deborah Hastings
dilithium Press
Beaverton, OR

Paul Heckel
QuickView Systems
Los Altos, CA

Gordon C. Howell
Georgia State University
Atlanta, GA

Kai Hwang
Purdue University
West Lafayette, IN

Portia Isaacson
Future Computing Incorporated
Richardson, TX

J. R. Jump
Rice University
Houston, TX

Michael A. Kaminski
General Motors Corporation APMES
Warren, MI

Thomas P. Kehler
IntelliCorp
Palo Alto, CA

Franklin F. Kuo
SRI International
Menlo Park, CA

Dale Kutnick
The Yankee Group
Boston, MA

Edward Lafranchi
Lawrence Livermore National Laboratory
Livermore, CA

Daniel T. Lee
University of Hartford
West Hartford, CT

Heinz Lycklama
INTERACTIVE Systems Corporation
Santa Monica, CA

Robert J. Lydon
Personal Computing and *Personal Software* Magazines
Cupertino, CA

Rita Gail MacAuslan
Sanders Associates, Inc.
Nashua, NH

Mel Mandell
Computer Decisions Magazine
Hasbrouck Heights, NJ

Jody Martin
Pacific Institute
Westlake Village, CA

Richard Mateosian
National Semiconductor
Berkeley, CA

Addie Mattox
The Mattox Group
South Laguna, CA

Joel McCormack
Volition Systems
Del Mar, CA

Ned McDaniel
InfoSci, Inc.
Menlo Park, CA

Janet Millenson
Sperry Corporation
Blue Bell, PA

Boulton B. Miller
Southern Illinois University
Edwardsville, IL

Phillip S. Mittelman
MAGI-SynthaVision
Elmsford, NY

Howard Morgan
Advanced Office Concepts
Bala Cynwyd, PA

LaRuth Morrow
Stellar Solutions
Richardson, TX

Richard Morrow
HyperGraphics Corporation
Denton, TX

Mike Murray
Apple Computer
Cupertino, CA

Ken Orr
Ken Orr and Associates
Topeka, KS

Alan Paller
AUI Data Graphics/ISSCO
Washington, DC

Maria Penedo
TRW-DSG
Redondo Beach, CA

Alfred Riccomi
Texas Instruments Inc.
Lewisville, TX

Glenn Rifkin
CW Communications—
Computerworld OA
Framington, MA

John Riganati
National Bureau of Standards
Washington, DC

Arnold Romberg
Romberg and Romberg
Dallas, TX

Jean Sammet
IBM Federal Systems Division
Bethesda, MD

Erik Sandberg-Diment
The New York Times
Hampton, CT

Omri Serlin
ITOM International Company
Los Altos, CA

Patricia B. Seybold
The Seybold Report
Boston, MA

Lynne C. Shaw
Warner Communications Inc.
New York, NY

Allen N. Smith
Atlantic Richfield Co.
Los Angeles, CA

Elliot Soloway
Yale University
New Haven, CT

Mary Sommerset
Symposia Marketing Corporation
San Mateo, CA

John Squilla
Eastman Kodak Company
Rochester, NY

Einar Stefferud
Network Management Associates, Inc.
Huntington Beach, CA

Richard H. Stern
Law Office of Richard H. Stern
Washington, DC

Marvin Talbott
Texas Instruments Inc.
Dallas, TX

Walter Ulrich
Walter E. Ulrich Consulting
Houston, TX

Mark Ursino
Technology Services Corporation
Bellevue, WA

Benjamin W. Wah
Purdue University
West Lafayette, IN

Joe Wetherington
Independent Consultant
Green Village, NJ

Andrew Whinston
Purdue University
West Lafayette, IN

Turner Whitted
Numerical Design Ltd.
University of North Carolina
Chapel Hill, NC

Evelyn S. Wilk
Arthur Andersen & Co.
Chicago, IL

Ron Willis
Hughes Aircraft
Fullerton, CA

Amy Wohl
Advanced Office Concepts
Bala Cynwyd, PA

Tom Wright
ISSCO Graphics
San Diego, CA

Jean Yates
Yates Ventures
Los Altos, CA

Raymond Yeh
University of Maryland
College Park, MD

William Zachmann
International Data Corporation
Framingham, MA

Nicholas Zvegintzov
Independent Consultant
Staten Island, NY

NCC '84 REFEREES

Ackerman, Frank A.
Ackmann, David A.
Agrawal, Dharma P.
Alden, John
Alexander, Winser E.
Archibald, Julius A., Jr.
Arendt, M. L.
Aurbach, Richard L.
Awad, Elias M.
Azzara, Michael

Ballew, Lowell N.
Barnard, H. Jack
Barnes, Ben B.
Barr, John R.
Bates, Jane
Bauman, Ben M.
Beidler, John
Belford, Geneva
Bhavsar, V. C.
Black, John B.
Blue, Richard
Bocast, Alexander K.
Borko, Harold
Bowen, John B.
Bretz, Robert W.
Brunner, Richard
Buckley, Gael N.
Bui, Tung
Burke, Ed
Byrne, Wes

Chapin, Ned
Charp, Sylvia
Chen, Chi H.
Chen, Pin-Yee
Choy, Steven J.
Claybrook, Billy G.
Cohen, Shimon
Colucci, Michael
Cormier, Robert W.
Cross, Thomas B.
Cross, F.

Dalphin, John F.
Damodaran, Meledath
Dankel, Douglas D., II
Davidson, Edward
Davis, James
De, Prabuddha
DeKock, Arlan R.
Denbaum, Carol
Deogun, Jitender S.
Dordick, H. S.
Dreifus, Henry N.
Dubenezic, Charles
Dyment, Doug

Edrington, Jimmie
Eliot, Lance B.
Elmaghraby, Adel S.
Ernst, Dennis
Esbin, Jack
Evens, Martha
Evert, Carl F.

Fendrich, John
Field, George
Fischer, Herman
Fleisch, Brett D.
Flynn, William G.
Foster, Mark J.
Frederick, Terry J.
Friedman, Frank

Gabrieli, H.
Gabrielsen, Larry L.
Gajski, Daniel D.
Gessford, John F.
Gildersleeve, James L.
Gill, Philip J.
Gintz, Christopher J.
Glaseman, Steven
Goel, Amrit L.
Goldberg, Marty
Goodwin, David L.
Gorsline, G. W.
Graham, Marshall A.
Graham, Marc H.
Gray, Robert

Hac, Anna
Hamilton, William E., Jr.
Harris, Michael C.
Hawthorne, G. B., Jr.
Heafner, John
Hedges, Harry G.
Heimbigner, Dennis
Henry, Hudson H.
Higginbotham, T. F.
Hill, Thomas L.
Hill, Gregory P.
Hirst, Graeme
Hofkin, Bob
Holmes, William M., Jr.
Hooten, Anthony D.
Horch, John W.
Horvath, Edward E.
Hussau, K. M.

Jackson, Durward P.
Jacobs, Steven M.
Jagannathan, V.
Jain, Hemant K.
Jakobson, Gabriel E.
James, Philip N.
Jehn, Lawrence A.
Johnson, James Lee
Jones, Douglas W.
Juell, Paul

Kamel, Khaled
Kearns, Phil
Kenett, Ron
Kocher, Bryan
Kolstad, Rob
Koory, Jerry
Kuklin, Scott A.
Kundu, S.
Kuzdas, Adrian C.

LaFrance, Jacques
Lake, Robin B.
Lakshmi, Seetha
Larson, Arvid G.
Lawrence, Robert
Lee, K. P.
Lee, Daniel T.
Leinius, Ronald P.
Lewis, Paul J.
Lillevik, Sigurd L.
Lissner, L. Scott
Little, Rainey
Liu, Hsun K.
Lively, Mac
Loach, K. W.
Look, Harry W.
Loomis, Mary E.
Love, Hubert H., Jr.
Luke, Tim

MacAuslan, Joel
MacAuslan, Rita Gail
Marriott, Philip C.
Mateosian, Richard
McClure, Carma
McCullough, Tim
McFarland, Clay
Meads, Jon
Medley, Don B.
Metzner, John R.
Miller, Raymond E.
Miller, Thomas K., III
Milutinovic, Velco
Mitchell, Don B.
Mok, Al K.
Molloy, Michael K.
Motzkin, Dalia
Mucchetti, Stephen A.
Mullens, David G.
Murray, Dale N.

Naifeh, Kim L.
Navathe, Sham
Neblock, Charles E.
Nelles, Alan
Norton, Sue

Olavesen, Ole Bernt
Oursler, Gerald W.
Overgaard, Mark

Partridge, Derek
Penedo, M. H.
Perkins, Sharon
Perkins, Michael T.
Peterson, Emery G.
Peterson, Robert W.
Phillips, Jim
Potter, Marshall R.
Pyron, Howard D.

Rabinowitz, Irving N.
Ramakrishna, K.
Ransom, M. N.
Reed, Daniel A.
Riccardi, Gregory A.
Ridgley, Jay
Riganati, John P.
Rine, David C.
Roberts, Philip
Rocchetti, Bob
Rollwitz, Bill
Romanowsky, Helen E.
Rosen, Robert
Rosenthal, Paul H.
Rosinski, Richard R.
Rubin, Howard A.
Ruchinskas, John E.
Ruh, Lawrence A.
Ruschitzka, Manfred

Safford, Herbert B.
Sagues, Paul
Sander, Bernard T., Jr.
Savage, T. R.
Schell, Roger R.
Scheuermann, L. E.
Schiebe, Lowell H.
Schlesinger, Richard
Schmookler, Martin
Schneider, Edward A.
Schneidewind, N. F.
Schroeder, Charles
Schutzer, Daniel
Sellers, A. Martin
Serlin, Omri
Shaffron, Nancy
Sheaffer, Marilyn
Shetler, Toni
Shoquist, Marc
Siefert, David M.
Siep, Thomas M.
Simmons, Dick B.
Simon, Horst D.
Smartt, Melissa
Smith, Lyle B.
Smith, J. W.
Smoliar, Stephen W.
Soffa, Mary Lou
Soloway, Elliot
Souder, H. Ray
Spaniol, Roland
Stafford, Ronald E.
Stavely, Allan M.
Stearns, Daniel J.
Stehling, Al
Stern, Richard H.
Stevens, Dave
Stockman, George
Sutter, Gordon F.
Swigger, Kathleen M.
Talbott, Marvin
Tanik, Murat M.
Tanniru, Mohan R.
Taylor, Javin M.
Taylor, Linda T.
Thakkar, S. S.
Thebaut, S. M.
Tucker, Allen
Tulk, Jon

Uckan, Yuksel
Ulicny, Susan W.
Ulrich, Walter E.
Umbaugh, L. David

VanTilbury, R. L.

Wallace, Dolores R.
Wang, R. S.
Ware, Joel
Wexelblat, R. L.
Whinston, Andrew B.
Whitesell, James T.
Willard, Leigh B.
Williams, Donald S.
Williams, Kenneth
Wolf, Thomas E.
Woodfill, Marvin C.
Wortz, Charles

Yost, Robert

Zachmann, William F.
Zells, Lois
Zunde, Pranas

NCC '84 SPEAKERS AND PANELISTS

Abbott, Bob
Abrahams, Paul
Ahl, David H.
Angus, Robert
Anselmo, Don
Arlen, Gary
Aronson, Michael
Avizienis, Algirdas
Azzara, Michael

Bass, Charles
Bassett, Paul
Belady, Les A.
Bell, Stuart
Bell, Florence J.
Bennett, James S.
Berkman, Samuel
Bernstein, Phil
Beshara, Gary J.
Bice, Ken
Biermann, Alan W.
Billadeau, Thomas R.
Binkowski, John
Birss, Edward W.
Black, John
Blackmarr, Brian
Blanc, Robert
Blank, Steve
Blanning, Robert W.
Blauman, Sheldon
Boehm, Barry
Boer, Garrett
Bolton, Tony
Boney, Joel
Brady, Joseph
Bramson, Robert S.
Brandin, David H.
Brice, Linda
Brodwin, David
Broome, Ken
Brown, Kathie
Brown, A. Winsor
Browne, James C.
Bruijnes, Hans
Budlong, Faye
Burton, Robert

Catmull, Edwin
Chang, S. K.
Chiang, T. C.
Chin, David N.
Chu, Chuan
Clancey, William
Claytor, C. Royce
Clemons, Eric K.
Colony, George F.
Connell, John
Connor, Denis
Cook, Charles C.
Cooper, Wilson
Cross, Thomas B.
Crume, Larry
Csuri, Charles
Cugini, John
Cullem, Ron

Davies, Byron
DeMillo, Richard
Dement, Ralph
Diehr, George
Dimancesco, Dimitri
Dietz, Larry
Drexler, Jerome
Dubrall, Mike
Dunn, Connie
Dyson, Esther

Ehlers, Bryan
Elder, Marvin
Elliott, David J.
Ellis, Ron
Elmer-DeWitt, Philip
Epstein, Robert

Fairbanks, Robert
Farber, David J.
Fernbach, Sidney
Ferreira, Joe
Fletcher, John
Flies, William
Flitterman, Michael
Flowers, Margot
Floyd, Ronald
Fly, Bill
Fong, Wendy
Foss, Dick
Fredriksson, Einar
Friedland, Peter
Fuchi, Kazuhiro

Gaffner, Haines
Gagle, Michael
Gaines, B. R.
Garfunkel, Jerome
Gehring, Bo
Georg, Denny
Giardina, E. Ric
Gilberg, Dick
Glazer, Sam
Gobel, Collin
Goff, Stacy A.
Goldberg, Aaron
Golden, Jack
Goodrich, Curtiss
Gordon, Gil E.
Greenfeld, Norton
Greystoke, Keith R.
Grouse, Phil
Gustafson, David

Haack, Marr T.
Hammer, Michael
Hardy, Norm
Harkness, Richard
Haruki, Kazuhito
Hazelton, Leslie R.
Heckel, Paul
Heidorn, George
Henderson, Lofton
Henry, Hudson
Ho, S. Frank
Hoerner, Charles C.
Holland, Joe
Holsapple, Clyde W.
Hopkins, Greg
Hoxie, Gib
Hughes, Kevin G.
Hughes, Christine
Hulten, Christer
Hurd, Cuthbert

Inselberg, Armond
Irvine, C. A.
Isaacson, Portia

Janca, Peter C.
Janulaitis, M. Victor
Johnson, Melody
Jordan, Jay B.
Joy, Bill
Jump, J. R.

Kahn, Robert E.
Kambayashi, Yahiko
Kaplan, Henry A.
Kapor, Mitchell
Kavianpour, A.
Kehler, Thomas P.
Kelly, John E.
Kenrich, Chester
Kevorkian, Douglas
Kilty, Lawrence
Kimbrough, Kerry
Kinsley, Kathryn C.
Kirchner, Michael
Kleinman, Neil
Klimek, Tom
Kline, Paul
Konsynski, Benn R.
Koymen, Kemal
Kuehler, Jack

Kuklin, Scott
Kunz, John C.
Kurtz, Tom
Kutnick, Dale

Lafranchi, E.
Lages, Elwin
Larson, James A.
Lauck, Anthony G.
Lee, Daniel
Lee, Edwin
Lee, Randall M.
Leith, Chuck
Lelevier, Robert
Levin, K. Dan
Levy, Steven
Liddle, David E.
Lillevik, Sigurd L.
Livingston, John
Loesh, Robert E.
Lombardi, Bart J.
Lomuto, Nico
Look, Harry W.
Lowe, David
Lu, Priscilla
Ludlow, Michael
Lusth, John C.
Lycklama, Heinz
Lydon, Robert J.
Lynn, Kurt

MacAuslan, Rita Gail
Mackie, Peter
Manyion, Jim
Martin, Jody
Martin, Larry
Martin, Ray
Mateosian, Richard
Mather, Don
Mathis, Robert F.
Matlack, Richard
Matley, Ben G.
Mattox, Addie
Maysonave, Steve
McCloskey, James P.
McConnell, Peter R. H.
McDaniel, Ned
McDowell, Bob
McDowell, Jerry
McKee, James R.
McPhee, William S.
Melnikoff, Richard
Mendocino, Sam
Menzilcioglu, Onat
Mertes, Louis H.
Metcalfe, Robert
Michael, George
Mikami, Yukihiro
Millenson, Janet

Miller, Boulton B.
Miller, James R.
Miller, Mark
Miller, Merl
Mittelman, Phillip S.
Miura, Kenichi
Mockapetris, Paul V.
Morgan, Howard
Mothersole, David
Muller, Roger
Murray, Michael
Myers, Daniel A.

Narrow, Bernard
Neff, Mary
Nelson, Donald F.
Neves, Kenneth W.
Nikora, Leo
Nofrey, Louis C.
Norton, James S.

Oakley, Brian W.
Orr, Ken
Osborne, Adam

Paller, Alan
Parker, Reginal O.
Patel, Anil
Pechner, Robert M.
Pehrson, Dave
Phelps, Nelson
Pehrson, Dave
Pinkston, John
Puette, Robert

Quigley, James J.

Rahimi, M. A.
Ranelletti, John
Rawlings, Terry L.
Reinhard, Ronald G.
Richardson, Gary L.
Riley, Mike
Rivera, Romel
Roberts, Roger
Rochkind, Allen B.
Rosenberg, Steven
Rubin, Howard A.
Ruschitzka, Manfred
Rusinkiewicz, Marek
Rusznak, George
Rutkowski, Chris
Ryan, Hugh

Sabil, John
Sakoman, Steve
Sammet, Jean
Sandberg-Diment, Erik
Sarna, David

Schuster, Stewart
Scott, Ed
Scullion, Joseph F.
Seelinger, William
Sekino, Akira
Selinger, Patricia
Sellers, Martin
Serlin, Omri
Sewell, Duane
Seybold, Patricia B.
Shaw, Lynne C.
Shaw, M. L. G.
Shiel, Beau
Shoch, John
Shoemaker, Harry
Shrobe, Howie
Shuey, David
Simon, Art
Smith, Allen N.
Smith, Barry
Smith, Jeffrey W.
Soloway, Elliot
Southworth, Glen
Sprowl, James
Squilla, John
Stahlman, Mark
Stansky, Eileen M.
Stefferud, Einar
Stensrud, Bill
Stern, Richard H.
Stiffler, Jack
Strigel, Wolfgang B.
Su, Stephen Y. H.
Svigals, Jerome

Tennant, Harry
Terrell, Paul
Terzopoulos, Demetri
Thorndyke, Lloyd M.
Thornton, James
Tiede, Ken
Tinnirello, Paul
Tom, Janet R.
Traiger, Irv
Treleaven, Phillip C.
Trocchoi, Robert

Upham, Dave
Ursino, Mark

Valdes, Peter
Valentine, Dennis
Von Meister, William

Wade, Larry
Wah, Benjamin W.
Wallace, Bob
Walter, Skip
Wasserman, Anthony I.

Watson, Dick
Weber, Herbert
Weiss, Chuck
Wetherington, Joe
Whinston, Andrew
White, Kathy Brittain
Whitted, Turner
Wiegler, Barry
Wilk, Evelyn S.
Williams, Kenneth
Wilson, Charles
Winner, Roger L.
Witkin, Andy
Wittie, Larry
Wong, Carla M.
Wood, Michael R.
Wright, Tom
Wu, Chuan-Lin
Wyman, Robert

Yates, Jean
Young, John W., Jr.

Zells, Lois

AMERICAN FEDERATION OF INFORMATION PROCESSING SOCIETIES, INC. (AFIPS)

OFFICERS

President
Sylvia Charp
The School District of Philadelphia
Philadelphia, PA

Vice President
Stephen S. Yau
Northwestern University
Evanston, IL

Secretary
Arthur C. Lumb
Procter & Gamble Co.
Cincinnati, OH

Treasurer
Walter A. Johnson
Consolidated Papers, Inc.
Wisconsin Rapids, WI

Executive Director
Paul J. Raisig
AFIPS
Arlington, VA

BOARD OF DIRECTORS

AFIPS Immediate Past President
J. Ralph Leatherman
Hughes Tool Company
Houston, TX

American Society for Information Science (ASIS)
James N. Cretsos
Merrell Dow Pharmaceuticals, Inc.
Cincinnati, OH

American Statistical Association (ASA)
Jack Moshman
Moshman Associates, Inc.
Bethesda, MD

Association for Computational Linguistics (ACL)
Norman K. Sondheimer
USC Information Sciences Institute
Marina del Rey, CA

Association for Computing Machinery (ACM)
David Brandin
SRI International
Menlo Park, CA

Michael A. Harrison
University of California
Berkeley, CA

David Kniefel
Deloitte, Haskins & Sells
New York, NY

Association for Educational Data Systems (AEDS)
John Hamblen
National Bureau of Standards
Washington, DC

Data Processing Management Association (DPMA)
Jerry Knierim
Pioneer Corporation
Amarillo, TX

Carroll L. Lewis
Commercial Data Corporation
Memphis, TN

Donald E. Price
Sierra College
Rocklin, CA

IEEE Computer Society
Rolland B. Arndt
Sperry Univac
Saint Paul, MN

Tse-yun Feng
Ohio State University
Columbus, OH

Martha Sloan
Michigan Technological University
Houghton, MI

Instrument Society of America
Chun H. Cho
Fisher Controls International, Inc.
Marshalltown, IA

Society for Computer Simulation (SCS)
Per Holst
The Foxboro Company
Foxboro, MA

Society for Industrial and Applied Mathematics (SIAM)
Shmuel Winograd
IBM Research Center
Yorktown Heights, NY

Society for Information Display
Howard L. Funk
IBM Corporation
White Plains, NY

NATIONAL COMPUTER CONFERENCE BOARD MEMBERS

Chairman and IEEE-CS Representative
Stanley Winkler
IBM Corporation
Armonk, NY

Vice Chairman and AFIPS Representative
Chun H. Cho
Fisher Controls International, Inc.
Marshalltown, IA

Treasurer and AFIPS Representative
Walter A. Johnson
Consolidated Papers, Inc.
Wisconsin Rapids, WI

Secretary and ACM Representative
Seymour Wolfson
Wayne State University
Detroit, MI

AFIPS Representative
Sylvia Charp
The School District of Philadelphia
Philadelphia, PA

Stephen S. Yau
Northwestern University
Evanston, IL

ACM Representative
Seymour Wolfson
Wayne State University
Detroit, MI

DPMA Representative
George Eggert
Defense Contract Administration
Chicago, IL

SCS Representative
Carl Malstrom
North Carolina State University
Raleigh, NC

ACM President—Ex Officio
David Brandin
SRI International
Menlo Park, CA

DPMA President—Ex Officio
Carroll L. Lewis
Commercial Data Corporation
Memphis, TN

IEEE-CS President—Ex Officio
Martha Sloan
Michigan Technological University
Houghton, MI

SCS President—Ex Officio
Walter J. Karplus
University of California, Los Angeles
Los Angeles, CA

NCCC Chairman—Ex Officio
Robert C. Spieker
AT&T Company
New Brunswick, NJ

IAP Chairman—Ex Officio
S. A. Lanzarotta
Xerox Corporation
El Segundo, CA

AFIPS Executive Director—Ex Officio
Paul J. Raisig
AFIPS
Arlington, VA

NATIONAL COMPUTER CONFERENCE COMMITTEE OF THE NCC BOARD

Chairman
Robert C. Spieker
AT&T Company
New Brunswick, NJ

Secretary
Arnold P. Smith
IBM Corporation
White Plains, NY

Members
Morton M. Astrahan
IBM Corporation
San Jose, CA

Harvey L. Garner
Moore School of Electrical Engineering
University of Pennsylvania
Philadelphia, PA

Floyd O. Harris
Life of Georgia
Atlanta, GA

Albert K. Hawkes
Sargent & Lundy Engineering
Chicago, IL

Jerry L. Koory
The Rand Corporation
Santa Monica, CA

Hans D. Puehse
Fireman's Fund Insurance Companies
San Rafael, CA

William H. Sitter
Tenneco, Inc.
Houston, TX

NCC '84 Chairman
Don B. Medley
California State Polytechnic University
Pomona, CA

NCC '83 Chairman
Russell K. Brown
The Benchmark Group
Houston, TX

OAC '85 Chairman
James F. Foley, Jr.
Life Office Management Association
Atlanta, GA

OAC '84 Chairman
Steven M. Abraham
Price Waterhouse
Los Angeles, CA

AFIPS HEADQUARTERS STAFF

OFFICE OF EXECUTIVE DIRECTOR

Executive Director
Paul J. Raisig

Executive Secretary
Joan Tackett

CONFERENCE DEPARTMENT

Director of Conferences
John Gilbert

Administrative Assistant
Cathy Isaacs

Budget Coordinator
John Balderson

Operations Manager
Sam Lippman

Conference Operations Coordinator
Margaret Dyer

Exhibit Operations Coordinator
Jill Newman

Conference Operations Support
Sally Gorham

Registration Manager
Dennis Smoot

Registration Support
Terry DiMurro

Exhibit Sales Manager
Richard Dobson

Exhibit Sales Coordinator
Katherine Stormont

Exhibit Sales Support
Molly Finney

Marketing Manager
Ann-Marie Bartels

Senior Marketing Coordinator
Marty Byrne

Marketing Coordinator
Trudi Riley

Marketing Secretary
Helen Mugnier

COMMUNICATIONS DEPARTMENT

Director of Communications
Dianne Edgar

Communications Coordinator
Alice-Lynne Ryssman

Editor (Acting)
Kaylee Jennings

Administrative Assistant
Mary Ford

Receptionist
Felicity White

FINANCE DEPARTMENT

Director of Finance
William R. Grubb, Jr.

Administrative Assistant/Secretary
Vacant

Accounting Manager
Hope Reynolds

Bookkeeper
Carrol Reid

Accounting Clerks
Ethel Baltimore
Reem Qubain

AFIPS PRESS

Director of AFIPS Press
Christopher N. Hoelzel

Fulfillment Administrator
Olive Shilland

Administrative Assistant
Sharon Lee Conway

NCC Proceedings Production Editor
Elizabeth G. Emanuel

AFIPS OFFICE ADMINISTRATION

Office Manager
Debra Guazzo

Office Assistant
Chris Powers

AUTHOR INDEX